NINTH EDITION

ADVANCED ACCOUNTING

NINTH EDITION

ADVANCED
ACCOUNTING

Floyd A. Beams
Virginia Polytechnic Institute
and State University

Joseph H. Anthony
Michigan State University

Robin P. Clement
University of Oregon

Suzanne H. Lowensohn
Colorado State University

Prentice Hall
Upper Saddle River, New Jersey 07458

Library of Congress Cataloging-in-Publication Data

Advanced accounting / Floyd A. Beams . . . [et al.].—9th ed.
    p. cm.
    Includes bibliographical references and index.
    ISBN 0-13-185122-5
    1. Accounting. I. Beams, Floyd A.

HF5635 .B41517 2006
  657'.046—dc22

2005045932

Acquisitions Editor: Bill Larkin
VP/Editorial Director: Jeff Shelstad
Project Manager: Sam Goffinett
Editorial Assistant: Joanna Doxey
Media Project Manager: Caroline Kasterine
Marketing Manager: John Wannemacher
Marketing Assistant: Tina Panagiotou
Managing Editor (Production): Cynthia Regan
Production Editor: Carol Samet
Permissions Supervisor: Charles Morris
Manufacturing Buyer: Michelle Klein
Design Manager: Maria Lange
Art Director: Kevin Kall
Interior Design: Darlene Vanasco/Kevin Kall
Cover Design: DePinho Graphic Design
Cover Illustration/Photo: Comstock
Manager, Print Production: Christy Mahon
Composition/Full-Service Project Management: Preparé Inc.
Printer/Binder: Courier-Westford
Typeface: 10/12 Times

Credits and acknowledgments borrowed from other sources and reproduced, with permission, in this textbook appear on appropriate page within text. The GASB Statement No. 33, *Accounting for Financial Reporting for Nonexchange Transactions*, Appendix C summary chart, "Classes and Timing of Recognition of Nonexchange Transactions," copyright by the Governmental Accounting Standards Board, 401 Merritt 7, Norwalk, CT 06856-5116, U.S.A., is reprinted with permission. Complete copies of this document are available from the GASB.

Copyright © 2006, 2003, 2000, 1996, 1992 by Pearson Education, Inc., Upper Saddle River, New Jersey, 07458. Pearson Prentice Hall. All rights reserved. Printed in the United States of America. This publication is protected by Copyright and permission should be obtained from the publisher prior to any prohibited reproduction, storage in a retrieval system, or transmission in any form or by any means, electronic, mechanical, photocopying, recording, or likewise. For information regarding permission(s), write to: Rights and Permissions Department.

Pearson Education LTD.
Pearson Education Australia PTY, Limited
Pearson Education Singapore, Pte. Ltd
Pearson Education North Asia Ltd
Pearson Education, Canada, Ltd
Pearson Educación de Mexico, S.A. de C.V.
Pearson Education–Japan
Pearson Education Malaysia, Pte. Ltd

10 9 8 7 6 5 4
ISBN 0-13-185122-5

To Madeline

JOE ANTHONY

To my father, Robert, and brother, Scott

ROBIN P. CLEMENT

To Tom, Grant, and Tara

SUZANNE LOWENSOHN

ABOUT THE
AUTHORS

FLOYD A. BEAMS, PH.D., is Professor Emeritus of Accounting at Virginia Tech. He holds B.S. and M.A. degrees in Business Administration from the University of Nebraska and a Ph.D. in Accounting from the University of Illinois. His journal articles have appeared in *The Accounting Review, Journal of Accounting, Auditing and Finance, Journal of Accountancy, The Atlantic Economic Review, Management Accounting,* and others, and have included topics on accounting theory, social accounting, financial reporting, income measurement, auditing, and cost accounting. Professor Beams has written a number of continuing professional education courses for the American Institute of Certified Public Accountants and was a frequent speaker for Virginia Tech's Accounting and Auditing Conference and Trends in the Education of Accountants seminar. He is a member of the American Accounting Association and the Institute of Management Accountants, and has served on various committees for both organizations. He received the National Association of Accountants' Lybrand Bronze Medal Award for outstanding contribution to accounting literature, a Distinguished Career in Accounting Award from the Virginia Society of CPAs, and the Virginia Outstanding Accounting Educator award from the Carman G. Blough student chapter of the Institute of Management Accountants.

JOSEPH H. ANTHONY, Associate Professor of Accounting, The Eli Broad College of Business, Michigan State University. B.A. 1971, M.S. 1974, Pennsylvania State University, Ph.D. 1984, The Ohio State University.

Professor Anthony joined the Michigan State University faculty in 1983. He is a Certified Public Accountant, a member of the American Accounting Association, American Institute of Certified Public Accountants, American Finance Association, and Canadian Academic Accounting Association. He has been recognized as a Lilly Foundation Faculty Teaching Fellow and as the MSU Accounting Department's Outstanding Teacher in 1998–99.

Professor Anthony teaches a variety of courses, including undergraduate introductory, intermediate, and advanced financial accounting. He also teaches financial accounting theory and financial statement analysis at the master's level, as well as financial accounting courses in the Executive MBA programs, and a doctoral seminar in financial accounting and capital markets research. He has previously co-authored an introductory financial accounting textbook.

Professor Anthony's research interests include financial statement analysis, corporate reporting, and the impact of accounting information in the securities markets. He has published a number of articles in leading accounting and finance journals, including *The Journal of Accounting & Economics, The Journal of Finance, Contemporary Accounting Research, The Journal of Accounting, Auditing, & Finance,* and *Accounting Horizons.*

ROBIN P. CLEMENT is an Instructor of Accounting in the Ourso College of Business Administration at Louisiana State University. She holds a bachelor's degree in Accounting from The Ohio State University, an MBA from the University of Wisconsin-Milwaukee, and a Ph.D. from Michigan State University. Dr. Clement has taught at The University of Wisconsin-Milwaukee, Michigan State University, and Tulane University. Her area of specialty is financial accounting, having taught master's level Financial Accounting theory, Intermediate Accounting, and Advanced Accounting. Dr. Clement serves as the faculty adviser for the LSU chapter of Beta Alpha Psi. Dr. Clement has published *A Study Guide for Financial Accounting: In an Economic Context* with Joseph H. Anthony, currently in its 5th edition. Dr. Clement is also a member of the American Accounting Association.

SUZANNE LOWENSOHN, PH.D., CPA, is an Assistant Professor of Accounting at Colorado State University. She earned a Ph.D. from the University of Miami and a Master of Accountancy from the University of South Florida. Suzanne's research interests include governmental accounting, governmental auditing, and managerial accounting. She has published articles in such journals as *Accounting and the Public Interest, Journal of Public Budgeting, Accounting and Financial Management, Research in Accounting Regulation, Behavioral Research In Accounting,* and *Research in Governmental and Nonprofit Accounting.*

Suzanne's professional activities include membership in the American Accounting Association, the Government Finance Officers Association, the Association of Government Accountants, and the Institute of Management Accountants.

Suzanne enjoys sports, traveling, and spending time with her husband, Tom, and two children, Grant and Tara.

BRIEF CONTENTS

CONTENTS

CHAPTER 9
Indirect and Mutual Holdings 283

 CHAPTER 10
Subsidiary Preferred Stock, Consolidated Earnings per Share, and Consolidated Income Taxation 319

 CHAPTER 11
Consolidation Theories, Push-Down Accounting, and Corporate Joint Ventures 371

 CHAPTER 12
Foreign Currency Concepts and Transactions 413

CHAPTER 18
An Introduction to Accounting for State and Local Governmental Units   643

CHAPTER 19
Accounting for State and Local Governmental Units—Governmental Funds   679

CHAPTER 20
Accounting for State and Local Governmental Units—Proprietary and Fiduciary Funds   723

CHAPTER 21
Accounting for Not-For-Profit Organizations   749

APPENDIX A
SEC Influence on Accounting   A-2

APPENDIX B
Estates and Trusts   B-1

PREFACE

The ninth edition of *Advanced Accounting* includes 21 chapters designed for financial accounting courses beyond the intermediate level. The ninth edition has been updated to reflect recent business developments and changes in accounting standards and regulatory requirements, especially the coverage of consolidated financial statements, goodwill, and other intangible assets and derivative securities.

An important feature of the book is the continued student orientation, which has been further enhanced with this edition. The ninth edition strives to maintain an interesting and readable text for the students. The focus on the complete equity method is maintained to allow students to focus on accounting concepts rather than bookkeeping techniques in learning the consolidation materials. The edition maintains the reference text quality of prior editions through the use of Electronic Supplements to chapters provided on the *Advanced Accounting* Web site.

The ninth edition maintains several student-oriented features from the last edition. The presentation of consolidation materials highlights working-paper-only entries with shading, and presents working papers on single upright pages. All chapters include excerpts from the popular business press and references to real world companies, institutions, and events. We use examples from annual reports of companies and governmental and non-profit institutions to illustrate key concepts and maintain student interest. Assignment materials include items from past CPA Examinations and have been updated and expanded to maintain close alignment with coverage of the chapter concepts. We maintain identification of names of parent and subsidiary companies beginning with P and S, allowing immediate identification. We also maintain parenthetical notation in journal entries to clearly indicate the direction and types of accounts affected by transactions. The ninth edition introduces the use of learning objectives throughout all chapters to allow students to better focus their study time on the important concepts.

NEW TO THIS EDITION

Important changes in the ninth edition of *Advanced Accounting* include:

- Coverage of ethics in financial accounting and reporting has been expanded to reflect recent accounting scandals. This includes coverage of provisions from Sarbanes-Oxley, where appropriate.
- All chapters have been updated to include coverage of international reporting standards and issues, where appropriate.
- Learning objectives for the students are numbered and identified throughout the text.
- Chapters 1 through 11 have been updated to reflect the most recent FASB statements and interpretations related to consolidated financial reporting, including accounting for variable interest entities under FIN 46(R).

- Chapters 3 and 4 now include detailed examples on how to prepare consolidation working papers using electronic spreadsheet software. Students will find this especially useful, although instructors who prefer not to use class time on these mechanics will also benefit.

- Descriptions have been added to all exercises and problems to permit easy identification.

- Chapter 12 coverage of derivative instruments and hedging activities has been revised and updated to permit easier understanding of these complex topics by the students.

- The governmental and not-for-profit chapters have been updated to include all standards through GASB 46. These chapters have also been enhanced with the addition of illustrations from the financial statements from Golden, Colorado. Coverage now includes service efforts and accomplishments, as well as post-employment benefits other than pensions.

ORGANIZATION

Chapters 1 through 11 cover business combinations, the equity and cost methods of accounting for investments in common stock, and consolidated financial statements. This emphasizes the importance of business combinations and consolidations in advanced accounting courses, as well as in financial accounting and reporting practices.

Accounting and reporting standards for purchase method business combinations are introduced in Chapter 1. The chapter also provides necessary background material on the form and economic impact of business combinations. Chapter 2 introduces the complete equity method of accounting as a one-line consolidation, and this approach is integrated throughout subsequent chapters on consolidations. This approach permits alternate computations for such key concepts as consolidated net income and consolidated retained earnings, and helps instructors to explain the objectives of consolidation procedures. The alternative computational approaches also assist students by providing a check figure for their logic on these key concepts.

The one-line consolidation is maintained as the standard for a parent company in accounting for investments in its subsidiaries. Procedures for situations in which the parent company uses the cost method or an incomplete equity method to account for investments in subsidiaries are covered in Electronic Supplements to the chapters which are available on the Web site at **www.prenhall.com/beams**. The supplements include assignment materials for these alternative methods so that students can be prepared for consolidation assignments regardless of the method used by the parent company.

New pooling of interest accounting has been eliminated as the result of *FASB Statement No. 141*. However, existing poolings are grandfathered in under SFAS 141. Coverage of pooling of interests accounting and reporting is maintained either in appendices or in Electronic Supplements on the *Advanced Accounting* Web site.

Chapter 3 introduces the preparation of consolidated financial statements. Students learn how to allocate the purchase price to the fair values of the subsidiary's identifiable net assets and to implied goodwill. Chapter 4 continues consolidations coverage, introducing working paper techniques and procedures. The text emphasizes the three-section, vertical financial statement working paper approach throughout, but Chapter 4 also offers a trial balance approach in the appendix. The standard employed throughout the consolidation chapters is working papers for a parent company that uses the complete equity method of accounting (i.e., one-line consolidations) for investments in subsidiaries.

Chapters 5 through 7 cover intercompany transactions in inventories, plant assets, and bonds. Chapter 8 discusses changes in the level of subsidiary ownership, and Chapter 9 introduces more complex affiliation structures. Chapter 10 covers several consolidation-related topics: (1) subsidiary preferred stock, (2) consolidated earnings per share, and (3) income taxation for consolidated business entities. Branch accounting is the topic covered in the Electronic Supplement to Chapter 10. Chapter 11 is a theory chapter. It discusses alternative consolidation theories, push-down accounting, leveraged buyouts, corporate joint ventures, and key concepts related to accounting and reporting by variable interest entities. The appendix presents current cost implications for consolidated financial reporting.

Chapters 9 through 11 cover specialized topics and have been written as stand-alone materials. Coverage of these chapters is not necessary for assignment of subsequent text chapters.

Business enterprises become more global in nature with each passing day. Survival of the modern business depends on access to foreign markets, suppliers, and capital. Some of the unique challenges of international business and financial reporting are covered in Chapters 12 and 13. Chapter 12 discusses accounting for derivative financial instruments and applies these concepts to foreign currency transactions. Coverage includes import and export activities and forward or similar contracts used to hedge against potential exchange losses. Chapter 13 covers translation and remeasurement of foreign-entity financial statements, one-line consolidation of equity investees, consolidation of foreign subsidiaries for financial reporting purposes, and combining foreign branch operations.

Chapter 14 introduces topics of segment reporting under FASB Statement No. 131, as well as interim financial reporting issues. Partnership accounting and reporting are covered in Chapter 15 and 16. Chapter 17 discusses accounting and reporting procedures related to corporate liquidations and reorganizations.

Chapters 18 through 20 provide an introduction to governmental accounting, and Chapter 21 (the final chapter) introduces accounting for voluntary health and welfare organizations, hospitals, and colleges and universities. These chapters are completely updated through GASB Statement No. 46, providing students with a good grasp of key concepts and procedures related to governmental and not-for-profit accounting.

As in the last edition, we maintain coverage of SEC accounting requirements and fiduciary accounting for estates and trusts in Appendices A and B, respectively, which are available on the *Advanced Accounting* Web site.

INSTRUCTOR'S RESOURCES

- Solutions Manual: Prepared by the authors. Includes updated answers to questions and solutions to exercises and problems. Solutions to assignment materials included in the Electronic Supplements are also included. Solutions are provided in electronic format, making electronic classroom display easier for instructors. All solutions have been accuracy checked to maintain a high quality of work.

- Instructor's Manual: Contains (a) comprehensive outlines of all chapters; (b) class illustrations; (c) descriptions for all exercises and problems, including estimated times for completion; (d) alternative lesson plans covering different chapters; and (e) a checklist for students of key figures in the problems.

- Test Item File: Includes more than 1,000 up-to-date test questions in True/False. Multiple Choice, Short Answer, and Problem formats. Solutions to all test items are also included.

- Companion Website: To access visit **www.prenhall.com/beams**. The faculty portion of the Web site is a one-stop resource and includes files available for download of Spreadsheet Templates.

STUDENT RESOURCES

Companion Website: To access, visit **www.prenhall.com/beams**. The student portion of the Web site includes Spreadsheet Templates, and electronic supplements for certain chapters.

ACKNOWLEDGMENTS

Many people have made valuable contributions to the ninth edition of *Advanced Accounting*, and we are pleased to recognize their contributions. We are indebted to the many users of prior editions for their helpful comments and constructive criticism. We also acknowledge the help and encouragement that we received from students at Colorado State, Louisiana State, Michigan State, Oregon, and Virginia Tech who, often unknowingly, participated in class testing of various sections of the manuscript.

We want to thank our faculty colleagues for the understanding and support that made nine editions of *Advanced Accounting* possible.

We would like to thank the Prentice Hall book team for their hard work and dedication: Jane Avery, Joanna Doxey, Sam Goffinet, Ann Koonce, Bill Larkin, Elena Picinic, Carol Samet, and Frank Weihenig.

FLOYD A. BEAMS

JOSEPH H. ANTHONY

ROBIN CLEMENT

SUZANNE LOWENSOHN

1 CHAPTER

BUSINESS COMBINATIONS

- In May 2004, *Citizens Financial Group, Inc.,* announced an agreement to acquire *Charter One Financial, Inc.,* for $10.5 billion, making Citizens one of the 10 largest U.S. commercial banks.
- In October 2001, *Chevron* and *Texaco* announced completion of their merger agreement valued in excess of $30 billion. In 1998, gasoline-producing rivals *Exxon* and *Mobil* merged to form *Exxon Mobil* Corporation in a deal valued at $80 billion. Similar combinations had occurred in the industry, including *BP Amoco's* acquisition of *Atlantic Richfield*.
- In 1999, *Citibank*, *Travelers Life*, and *Salomon Smith Barney* joined to form the *Citigroup* financial-services conglomerate.
- In 2001, *America Online (AOL)* acquired control of *Time Warner* for $147 billion.

LEARNING OBJECTIVES

1 Understand the economic motivations underlying business combinations.

2 Learn about the alternative forms of business combinations, from both the legal and accounting perspectives.

3 Introduce concepts of accounting for business combinations, emphasizing the purchase method.

4 See how firms make cost allocations in a purchase method combination.

Welcome to the world of business combinations. The 1990s witnessed a period of unparalleled growth in merger and acquisition activities in both the United States and in international markets (often referred to as merger mania), and the trend continues.

Merger activities slowed with the stock market downturn in 2001, but as the market recovered, the pace began to pick up. The following firms announced combinations in December 2004. *Symantec* (manufacturer of the Norton antivirus software) acquired *Veritas Software* for $13.5 billion. Veritas is a storage-system and backup-program manufacturer. *Oracle Corporation* acquired **PeopleSoft, Inc.**, for $10.3 billion. *Johnson & Johnson* acquired *Guidant* for $25.4 billion. Guidant produces pacemakers, defibrillators, heart stents, and other medical devices. *Sprint* announced plans to acquire rival *Nextel Communications* for approximately $35 billion, creating a new *Sprint Nextel*. Management cited estimated operating-cost savings and network upgrades of over $12 billion as a major motivation for the merger. In January 2005, *Rayovac*, a leading battery maker, announced it would acquire *United Industries* for $476 million. The combination would allow Rayovac to diversify by adding United's lawn-care products, insect repellants, and pet-supplies business.

Business firms constantly strive to produce economic value added for their shareholders. Related to this strategy, expansion has long been regarded as a proper goal of business entities. A business may choose to expand either internally (building its own facilities) or externally (acquiring control of other firms in business combinations). The focus in this chapter will be on why firms often prefer external over internal expansion options and how financial reporting reflects the outcome of these activities.

In general terms, **business combinations** unite previously separate business entities. The overriding objective of business combinations must be increasing profitability; however, many firms can become more efficient by horizontally or vertically integrating operations or by diversifying their risks through conglomerate operations.

Horizontal integration is the combination of firms in the same business lines and markets. The business combinations of Chevron and Texaco, Exxon and Mobil, Citigroup, and Citizens and Charter One are examples of horizontal integration. The past decade has witnessed significant consolidation activity in banking and other industries. *Chemical Bank* merged with *Chase Manhattan*. *Kimberly-Clark* acquired *Scott Paper*, creating a consumer paper and related products giant. Paint manufacturers *Sherwin-Williams* and *Pratt and Lambert* combined in a $400 million deal. *Delta Air Lines* took control of its rival *Western Air Lines*, at a cost of $787 million. Automakers *Daimler-Benz* and *Chrysler Corporation* were consolidated to form *Daimler-Chrysler*. Deregulation of electric and natural gas utilities is likely to generate a wave of combinations in that industry in the future.

Vertical integration is the combination of firms with operations in different, but successive, stages of production or distribution or both. In June 2004, *Briggs & Stratton Corporation* announced an agreement to acquire *Simplicity Manufacturing, Inc.,* for $227.5 million. Briggs & Stratton is the world's largest producer of small gasoline-powered engines, whereas Simplicity is a leader in design, manufacture, and marketing of premium commercial and consumer lawn-and-garden equipment. *Disney* acquired *ABC Television* during 1995 to provide ready access to mass broadcasting markets for Disney-produced films, as well as a convenient advertising outlet for other Disney products. Also during 1995, computer maker *IBM* purchased software producer *Lotus Development Corporation* at a cost of $3.2 billion. Internet portal America Online's acquisition of media giant Time Warner in 2001 provided AOL an opportunity to offer electronic access to Time Warner's vast media content. Warner's cable television holdings offered AOL an opportunity to expand its Internet presence with high-speed, broadband access through cable systems.

Conglomeration is the combination of firms with unrelated and diverse products or service functions, or both. Firms may diversify to reduce the risk associated with a particular line of business or to even out cyclical earnings, such as might occur in a utility's acquisition of a manufacturing company. Several utilities combined with telephone companies after the 1996 Telecommunications Act allowed utilities to enter the telephone business. For example, in November 1997, *Texas Utilities Company* acquired *Lufkin-Conroe Communications Company*, a local-exchange telephone company, to diversify into a communications business. The early 1990s saw tobacco maker *Phillip Morris Company* acquire food producer *Kraft* in a combination that included over $11 billion of recorded goodwill alone. Telephone giant *AT&T* acquired computer maker *NCR Corporation* for $6.4 billion in 1991. Although all of us have probably purchased a light bulb manufactured by **General Electric Company**, the scope of the firm's operations goes well beyond that household product. General Electric made a move into broadcasting when it purchased *RCA* for $6.4 billion. RCA already owned the NBC network. Exhibit 1-1 provides Note 27 from General Electric's 2003 annual report on its major operating segments.

■ ■ ■

Reasons for Business Combinations

If expansion is a proper goal of business enterprise, why would a business expand through combination rather than by building new facilities? Among the many possible reasons are the following:

Cost Advantage. It is frequently less expensive for a firm to obtain needed facilities through combination than through development. This is particularly true in periods of inflation. Reduction of total cost for research and development activities was a prime motivation in AT&T's acquisition of NCR.

Lower Risk. The purchase of established product lines and markets is usually less risky than developing new products and markets. The risk is especially low when the goal is diversification. Scientists may discover that a certain product provides an environmental or health hazard. A single-product, nondiversified firm may be forced into bankruptcy by such a discovery, while a multiproduct, diversified company is more likely to survive. For companies in industries already plagued with excess manufacturing capacity, business combinations may be the only way to grow. When *Toys 'R' Us* decided to diversify its operations to include baby furnishings and other related products, it purchased retail chain *Baby Superstore* in February 1997 for $376 million.

Fewer Operating Delays. Plant facilities acquired through a business combination are operative and already meet environmental and other governmental regulations. The time to market is critical, especially in the technology industry. Firms constructing new facilities can expect numerous

EXHIBIT 1-1

Segment Reporting at General Electric

OPERATING SEGMENTS

Revenues

For the Years Ended December 31 (In millions)	Total Revenues			Intersegment Revenues			External Revenues		
	2003	2002	2001	2003	2002	2001	2003	2002	2001
Advanced materials	$ 7,078	$ 6,963	$ 7,069	$ 31	$ 25	$ 21	$ 7,047	$ 6,938	$ 7,048
Commercial finance	20,813	19,592	17,723	195	128	99	20,618	19,464	17,624
Consumer finance	12,845	10,266	9,508	23	12	12	12,822	10,254	9,496
Consumer & industrial	12,843	12,887	13,063	290	347	212	12,553	12,540	12,851
Energy	19,082	23,633	21,030	213	287	254	18,869	23,346	20,776
Equipment & other services	4,427	5,545	7,735	(241)	(142)	(124)	4,668	5,687	7,859
Healthcare	10,198	8,955	8,409	2	2	2	10,196	8,953	8,407
Infrastructure	3,078	1,901	392	85	84	93	2,993	1,817	299
Insurance	26,194	23,296	23,890	23	2	13	26,171	23,294	23,877
NBC	6,871	7,149	5,769	—	—	—	6,871	7,149	5,769
Transportation	13,515	13,685	13,885	772	1,044	1,315	12,743	12,641	12,570
Corporate items and eliminations	(2,757)	(1,662)	(2,057)	(1,393)	(1,789)	(1,897)	(1,364)	127	(160)
Consolidated revenues	$134,187	$132,210	$126,416	$ —	$ —	$ —	$134,187	$132,210	$126,416

(In millions)	Assets At December 31			Property, Plant and Equipment Additions (Including equipment leased to others) For the Years Ended December 31			Depreciation and Amortization For the Years Ended December 31		
	2003	2002	2001	2003	2002	2001	2003	2002	2001
Advanced materials	$ 12,359	$ 11,372	$ 10,573	$ 797	$ 703	$ 814	$ 655	$ 632	$ 557
Commercial finance	214,016	202,462	178,217	7,405	8,999	12,325	3,466	3,133	2,586
Consumer finance	106,530	76,965	62,978	191	221	195	276	232	178
Consumer & industrial	7,526	8,387	8,213	318	449	519	560	516	487
Energy	17,121	16,372	13,837	514	734	779	555	517	343
Equipment & other services	64,098	28,104	28,789	1,136	2,417	2,066	1,151	1,034	1,234
Healthcare	10,816	7,573	6,625	289	170	177	278	247	177
Infrastructure	5,977	4,998	919	177	388	41	120	113	10
Insurance	169,882	182,297	155,500	35	71	37	469	432	502
NBC	11,619	10,401	5,572	121	252	64	117	109	94
Transportation	13,285	12,599	12,030	595	348	454	412	377	373
Corporate items and eliminations	14,254	13,714	11,770	179	121	141	126	165	1,413
Consolidated totals	$647,483	$575,244	$495,023	$11,757	$14,873	$17,612	$8,185	$7,507	$7,954

Source: 2003 General Electric annual report.

delays in construction, as well as in getting the necessary governmental approval to commence operations. Environmental impact studies alone can take months or even years to complete.

Avoidance of Takeovers. Many companies combine to avoid being acquired themselves. Smaller companies tend to be more vulnerable to corporate takeovers; therefore, many of them adopt aggressive buyer strategies as the best defense against takeover attempts by other companies.

Acquisition of Intangible Assets. Business combinations bring together both intangible and tangible resources. Thus, the acquisition of patents, mineral rights, research, customer databases, or management expertise may be a primary motivating factor in a particular business combination. When IBM purchased Lotus Development Corporation, $1.84 billion of the total cost of $3.2 billion was allocated to purchase research and development in process.

Other Reasons. Firms may choose a business combination over other forms of expansion for business tax advantages (for example, tax-loss carryforwards), for personal income and estate-tax advantages, and for personal reasons. One of several motivating factors in the 1998 business combination of **Wheeling-Pittsburgh Steel**, a subsidiary of **WHX**, and **Handy & Harman** was Handy & Harman's overfunded pension plan, which virtually eliminated Wheeling-Pittsburgh Steel's unfunded pension liability. The egos of company management and takeover specialists may also play an important role in some business combinations.

Antitrust Considerations

Federal antitrust laws prohibit business combinations that restrain trade or impair competition. The U.S. Department of Justice and the Federal Trade Commission (FTC) have primary responsibility for enforcing federal antitrust laws. For example, in 1997 the FTC blocked **Staples's** proposed $4.3 billion acquisition of **Office Depot**, arguing in federal court that the takeover would be anticompetitive.

On July 20, 2004, *The Wall Street Journal* (p. B6) reported that the FTC had conditionally approved **Sanofi-Synthelabo SA's** $64 billion takeover of **Aventis SA**, creating the world's third-largest drug manufacturer. Sanofi agreed to sell certain assets and royalty rights in overlapping markets in order to gain approval of the acquisition.

Business combinations in particular industries are subject to review by additional federal agencies. The Federal Reserve Board reviews bank mergers, the Department of Transportation scrutinizes mergers of companies under its jurisdiction, the Department of Energy has jurisdiction over some electric utility mergers, and the Federal Communications Commission (FCC) rules on the transfer of communication licenses. After the Justice Department cleared a $23 billion merger between **Bell Atlantic Corporation** and **Nynex Corporation**, the merger was delayed by the FCC because of its concern that consumers would be deprived of competition. The FCC later approved the merger. Such disputes are settled in federal courts.

In addition to federal antitrust laws, most states have some type of statutory takeover regulations. Some states try to prevent or delay hostile takeovers of the business enterprises incorporated within their borders. On the other hand, some states have passed antitrust exemption laws to protect hospitals from antitrust laws when they pursue cooperative projects.

Interpretations of antitrust laws vary from one administration to another, from department to department, and from state to state. Even the same department under the same administration can change its mind. A completed business combination can be reexamined by the FTC at any time. Deregulation in the banking, telecommunication, and utility industries permits business combinations that once would have been forbidden. In 1997, the Justice Department and the FTC jointly issued new guidelines for evaluating proposed business combinations that allow companies to argue that cost savings or better products could offset potential anticompetitive effects of a merger.

THE LEGAL FORM OF BUSINESS COMBINATIONS

Business combination is a general term that encompasses all forms of combining previously separate business entities. Such combinations are **acquisitions** when one corporation acquires the productive assets of another business entity and integrates those assets into its own operations. Business combinations are also acquisitions when one corporation obtains operating control over the productive facilities of another entity by acquiring a majority of its outstanding voting stock. The acquired company need not be dissolved; that is, the acquired company does not have to go out of existence.

The terms **merger** and **consolidation** are often used as synonyms for acquisitions. However, legally and in accounting there is a difference. A merger entails the dissolution of all but one of the business entities involved. A consolidation entails the dissolution of all the business entities involved and the formation of a new corporation.

A *merger* occurs when one corporation takes over all the operations of another business entity and that entity is dissolved. For example, Company A purchases the assets of Company B directly from Company B for cash, other assets, or Company A securities (stocks, bonds, or notes). This business combination is an acquisition, but it is not a merger unless Company B goes out of existence. Alternatively, Company A may purchase the stock of Company B directly from Company B's stockholders for cash, other assets, or Company A securities. This acquisition will give Company A operating control over Company B's assets. It will not give Company A legal ownership of the assets unless it acquires all the stock of Company B and elects to dissolve Company B (again, a merger).

A *consolidation* occurs when a new corporation is formed to take over the assets and operations of two or more separate business entities and dissolves the previously separate entities. For example, Company D, a newly formed corporation, may acquire the net assets of Companies E and F by issuing stock directly to Companies E and F. In this case, Companies E and F may continue to hold Company D stock for the benefit of their stockholders (an acquisition), or they may distribute the Company D stock to their stockholders and go out of existence (a consolidation). In either case, Company D acquires ownership of the assets of Companies E and F.

Alternatively, Company D could issue its stock directly to the stockholders of Companies E and F in exchange for a majority of their shares. In this case, Company D controls the assets of Company E and Company F, but it does not obtain legal title unless Companies E and F are dissolved. Company D must acquire all the stock of Companies E and F and dissolve those companies if their business combination is to be a consolidation. If Companies E and F are not dissolved, Company D will operate as a holding company, and Companies E and F will be its subsidiaries.

Future references in this chapter will use the term *merger* in the technical sense of a business combination in which all but one of the combining companies go out of existence. Similarly, the term *consolidation* will be used in its technical sense to refer to a business combination in which all the combining companies are dissolved and a new corporation is formed to take over their net assets. *Consolidation* is also used in accounting to refer to the accounting process of combining parent and subsidiary financial statements, such as in the expressions "principles of consolidation," "consolidation procedures," and "consolidated financial statements." In future chapters, the meanings of the terms will depend on the context in which they are found.

Mergers and consolidations do not present special accounting problems or issues after the initial combination, apart from those discussed in intermediate accounting texts. This is because only one legal and accounting entity survives in a merger or consolidation.

THE ACCOUNTING CONCEPT OF A BUSINESS COMBINATION

The accounting concept of a business combination was originally given in *Accounting Principles Board* (APB) *Opinion No. 16*, "Business Combinations," which became effective on November 1, 1970. According to the APB:

> *A business combination occurs when a corporation and one or more incorporated or unincorporated businesses are brought together into one accounting entity. The single entity carries on the activities of the previously separate, independent enterprises.*[1]

In June 2001, the Financial Accounting Standards Board (FASB) reaffirmed the concept, issuing *FASB Statement No. 141*. The FASB definition differs only slightly from that offered by the APB in *Opinion No. 16*:

> *For purposes of applying this Statement, a business combination occurs when an entity acquires net assets that constitute a business or acquires equity interests of one or more other entities and obtains control over that entity or entities.*[2]

---

[1] *APB Opinion No. 16*, paragraph 1.

[2] *FASB Statement No. 141*, paragraph 9.

Note that the accounting concept of a business combination emphasizes the creation of a single entity and the independence of the combining companies before their union. Although one or more of the combining companies may lose its separate legal identity, dissolution of the legal entities is not necessary within the accounting concept.

Previously separate businesses are brought together into one entity when their business resources and operations come under the control of a single management team. Such control within one business entity is established in business combinations in which:

1. One or more corporations become subsidiaries.
2. One company transfers its net assets to another, or
3. Each company transfers its net assets to a newly formed corporation.[3]

A corporation becomes a **subsidiary** when another corporation acquires a majority (more than 50%) of its outstanding voting stock.[4] Thus, one corporation need not acquire all the stock of another corporation to consummate a business combination. In business combinations in which less than 100% of the voting stock of other combining companies is acquired, the combining companies necessarily retain their separate legal identities and separate accounting records even though they have become one entity for primary reporting purposes.

Business combinations in which one company transfers its net assets to another can be consummated in a variety of ways, but the acquiring company must acquire substantially all the net assets in any case. Alternatively, each combining company can transfer its net assets to a newly formed corporation. Because the newly formed corporation has no net assets of its own, it issues its stock to the other combining companies or to their stockholders or owners.

A Brief Background on Accounting for Business Combinations

Accounting for business combinations is one of the most important and interesting topics of accounting theory and practice. At the same time, it is complex and controversial. Business combinations involve financial transactions of enormous magnitudes, business empires, success stories and personal fortunes, executive genius, and management fiascos. By their nature, they affect the fate of entire companies. Each is unique and must be evaluated in terms of its economic substance, irrespective of its legal form.

Historically, much of the controversy concerning accounting requirements for business combinations involved the **pooling of interests method**, which became generally accepted in 1950 when the Committee on Accounting Procedure issued *Accounting Research Bulletin* (ARB) *No. 40*. Although there are conceptual difficulties with the pooling method, the underlying problem that arose with *ARB No. 40* was the introduction of alternative methods of accounting for business combinations (pooling versus purchase). Numerous financial interests are involved in a business combination, and alternate accounting procedures may not be neutral with respect to different interests. That is, the individual financial interests and the final plan of combination may be affected by the method of accounting.

Until 2001, accounting requirements for business combinations were found in *APB Opinion No. 16*, which recognized both the pooling and purchase methods of accounting for business combinations. In August 1999, the FASB issued a report supporting its proposed decision to eliminate pooling. Principal reasons cited included the following:

- Pooling provides less relevant information to statement users.
- Pooling ignores economic value exchanged in the transaction and makes subsequent performance evaluation impossible.
- Comparing firms using the alternative methods is difficult for investors.

Pooling creates these problems because it uses historical book values to record combinations, rather than recognizing fair values of net assets at the transaction date. Generally accepted accounting principles (GAAP) generally require recording asset acquisitions at fair values.

---

[3] *APB Opinion No. 16,* paragraph 5.

[4] The FASB favors a consolidation policy based on control of another enterprise, rather than majority ownership.

Further, the FASB believes that the economic notion of a pooling of interests rarely exists in business combinations. More realistically, virtually all combinations are acquisitions, in which one firm gains control over another.

FASB Statement No. 141 eliminated the pooling of interests method of accounting for all transactions initiated after June 30, 2001. Combinations initiated subsequent to that date must use the purchase method. The new standard also made other changes to accounting for business combinations, which will be discussed in detail later.

Because the new standard prohibits the use of the pooling method only for combinations initiated after the issuance of the revised standard, prior combinations accounted for under the pooling of interests method will be grandfathered; that is, both the purchase and pooling methods will continue to exist as acceptable financial reporting practices for past business combinations.

Therefore, one cannot ignore the conditions for and reporting requirements under the pooling approach. On the other hand, because no new poolings will be permitted, this discussion focuses on the purchase method. More-detailed coverage of the pooling of interests method is relegated to the *Advanced Accounting* Web site.

INTERNATIONAL ACCOUNTING The FASB elimination of pooling makes U.S. GAAP more consistent with international accounting standards. Most major economies, including France, Japan, and Germany, prohibit the use of the pooling method to account for business combinations. The International Accounting Standards Board (IASB) issued *International Financial Reporting Standard 3* (IFRS 3) "Business Combinations" on March 31, 2004, requiring business combinations to be accounted for using the purchase method. IFRS 3 specifically prohibits the pooling of interests method. In introducing the new standard, IASB Chairman Sir David Tweedie noted:

> *Accounting for business combinations diverged substantially across jurisdictions. IFRS 3 marks a significant step toward high quality standards in business combination accounting, and in ultimately achieving international convergence in this area.*

The FASB continues to work on its joint standards harmonization project with the IASB, including accounting for business combinations. As this text goes to press, the FASB has made available on its Web site a proposed revision to *FASB Statement No. 141* that would bring U.S. and international standards even closer together. The FASB intends to issue an exposure draft and a revised standard by the end of 2005. You will find occasional references to the proposed standard revision throughout our discussions of business combinations and preparation of consolidated financial statements.

ACCOUNTING FOR BUSINESS COMBINATIONS UNDER THE PURCHASE METHOD

All business combinations initiated after June 30, 2001, must be accounted for as purchases under *FASB Statement No. 141*. The new standard supersedes *APB Opinion No. 16*, "Business Combinations," and supersedes or amends the numerous interpretations of the former standard. However, the FASB retains virtually all of *APB Opinion No. 16* except the pooling of interests method for business combinations.

In general, the **purchase method** follows the same generally accepted accounting principles for recording a business combination as we follow in recording other assets and liabilities.[5] We record the combination using the historical-cost principle. In other words, we measure the cost to the purchasing entity of acquiring another company in a purchase business combination by the amount of cash disbursed or by the fair value of other assets distributed or securities issued.

---

[5] Assume that "we" are the parent company accountants responsible for preparation of consolidated financial statements for the combined reporting entity. This convention appears throughout the chapters on consolidations and business combinations.

NOTE TO THE STUDENT

The topics covered in this text are sometimes complex and involve detailed exhibits and illustrative examples. Understanding the exhibits and illustrations is an integral part of the learning experience, and you should study them in conjunction with the related text. Carefully review the exhibits as they are introduced in the text. Exhibits and illustrations are designed to provide essential information and explanations for understanding the concepts presented.

Understanding the financial statement impact of complex business transactions is an important element in the study of advanced financial accounting topics. To assist you in this learning endeavor, this book depicts journal entries that include the types of accounts being affected and the directional impact of the event. Conventions used throughout the text are as follows: A parenthetical reference added to each account affected by a journal entry indicates the type of account and the effect of the entry. For example, an increase in accounts receivable, an asset account, is denoted as "Accounts receivable (+A)." A decrease in this account is denoted as "Accounts receivable (−A)." The symbol (A) stands for assets, (L) for liabilities, (SE) for stockholders' equity accounts, (R) for revenues, (E) for expenses, (Ga) for gains, and (Lo) for losses.

We also include the direct costs of combination (such as accounting, legal, consulting, and finders' fees) other than those for the registration or issuance of equity securities. We charge registration and issuance costs of equity securities issued in a purchase combination against the fair value of securities issued, usually as a reduction of additional paid-in capital. We expense indirect costs such as management salaries, depreciation, and rent under the purchase method. We also expense indirect costs incurred to close duplicate facilities.

To illustrate, assume that Poppy Corporation issues 100,000 shares of $10 par common stock for the net assets of Sunny Corporation in a purchase business combination on July 1, 2006. The market price of Poppy common stock on this date is $16 per share. Additional direct costs of the business combination consist of Securities and Exchange Commission (SEC) fees of $5,000, accountants' fees in connection with the SEC registration statement of $10,000, costs for printing and issuing the common stock certificates of $25,000, and finder's and consultants' fees of $80,000.

Poppy records the issuance of the 100,000 shares on its books as follows (in thousands):

Investment in Sunny (+A)	1,600	
Common stock, $10 par (+SE)		1,000
Additional paid-in capital (+SE)		600

To record issuance of 100,000 shares of $10 par common
    stock with a market price of $16 per share in a purchase
    business combination with Sunny Corporation.

Poppy records additional direct costs of the business combination as follows:

Investment in Sunny (+A)	80	
Additional paid-in capital (−SE)	40	
Cash (or other net assets) (−A)		120

To record additional direct costs of combining with Sunny
    Corporation: $80,000 for finder's and consultants' fees and
    $40,000 for registering and issuing equity securities.

We treat registration and issuance costs of $40,000 as a reduction of the fair value of the stock issued and charge these costs to Additional paid-in capital. We add other direct costs of the business combination ($80,000) to the cost of acquiring Sunny Corporation. The total cost to Poppy of acquiring Sunny is $1,680,000, the amount entered in the Investment in Sunny account.

We accumulate the total cost incurred in purchasing another company in a single investment account, regardless of whether the other combining company is dissolved or the combining companies continue to operate in a parent-subsidiary relationship. If we dissolve Sunny Corporation, we record its identifiable net assets on Poppy's books at their fair values, and we record any excess of investment cost over fair value as goodwill. In this case, we allocate the balance recorded in the Investment in Sunny account by means of an entry on Poppy's books. Such an entry might appear as follows:

Receivables (+A)	XXX	
Inventories (+A)	XXX	
Plant assets (+A)	XXX	
Goodwill (+A)	XXX	
Accounts payable (+L)		XXX
Notes payable (+L)		XXX
Investment in Sunny (−A)		1,680

        To record allocation of the $1,680,000 cost of acquiring
            Sunny Corporation to identifiable net assets according
            to their fair values and to goodwill.

If we dissolve Sunny Corporation, we formally retire the Sunny Corporation shares. The former Sunny shareholders are now shareholders of Poppy.

If Poppy and Sunny Corporations operate as parent company and subsidiary, Poppy will not record the entry to allocate the Investment in Sunny balance. Instead, Poppy will account for its investment in Sunny by means of the Investment in Sunny account, and we will make the allocation of the investment cost to identifiable net assets required in the consolidation process.

Because of the additional complications of accounting for parent-subsidiary operations, the remainder of this chapter is limited to business combinations in which a single acquiring entity receives the net assets of the other combining companies. Subsequent chapters cover parent-subsidiary operations and the preparation of consolidated financial statements.

Cost Allocation in a Purchase Business Combination

LEARNING OBJECTIVE **4**

The first step in allocating the cost of an acquired company is to determine the fair values of all identifiable tangible and intangible assets acquired and liabilities assumed. This can be a monumental task, but much of the work is done before and during the negotiating process of the proposed merger. Companies generally retain outside appraisers to determine fair market values. *FASB Statement No. 141*, paragraph 37, provides guidelines for assigning amounts to specific categories of assets received and liabilities assumed in the purchase, as follows:

- Marketable securities—fair values
- Merchandise inventories and finished goods—net realizable value less a reasonable profit[6]
- Work-in-process inventories—net realizable value less a reasonable profit
- Raw materials—current replacement costs
- Receivables—present values determined at current interest rates less an allowance for uncollectibility
- Plant and equipment—current replacement costs for similar capacity if the assets are to be used, and net realizable value for assets to be sold
- Other assets, including land, natural resources, and nonmarketable securities—appraisal values
- Identifiable intangible assets—estimated fair values
- Liabilities—present value determined at appropriate current interest rates

We determine fair values for all identifiable assets and liabilities regardless of whether they are recorded on the books of the acquired company. For example, an acquired company may have expensed the costs of developing patents, blueprints, formulas, and the like under the provisions of *FASB Statement No. 2*, "Accounting for Research and Development Costs." However, we assign fair values to such identifiable intangible assets of an acquired company in a business combination accounted for as a purchase.[7]

---

[6] Net realizable value of assets is the estimated selling price in the ordinary course of business less reasonably predictable costs of completion and disposal (*ARB 43*, Chapter 4, "Inventory Pricing," paragraph 8).

[7] *FASB Interpretation No. 4*, "Applicability of *FASB Statement No. 2* to Business Combinations Accounted for by the Purchase Method," February 1975, paragraph 4.

Similarly, *FASB Statement No. 87*, "Employers' Accounting for Pensions," requires that when the acquired company is an employer with a defined-benefit pension plan, the assignment of the purchase price at the date of combination should include either a liability (the amount of projected benefit obligation in excess of plan assets) or an asset (the amount of plan assets in excess of the projected benefit obligation).

We assign no value to goodwill recorded on the books of an acquired subsidiary under *FASB Statement No. 141* because such goodwill is an unidentifiable asset and because we value the goodwill resulting from the business combination directly:

> *The excess of the cost of an acquired entity over the net of the amounts assigned to assets acquired and liabilities assumed shall be recognized as an asset referred to as goodwill.*[8]

RECOGNITION AND MEASUREMENT OF INTANGIBLE ASSETS OTHER THAN GOODWILL *FASB Statement No. 141* also clarifies the recognition of intangible assets in business combinations under the purchase method. Under *APB Opinion No. 16*, firms recognized any intangibles that they could identify and name. Now firms should recognize intangibles separate from goodwill only if they fall into one of two categories. Recognizable intangibles must meet either a separability criterion or a contractual–legal criterion.

The FASB defines intangible assets as either current or noncurrent assets (excluding financial instruments) that lack physical substance. Per the FASB:

> *An intangible asset shall be recognized as an asset apart from goodwill if it arises from contractual or other legal rights (regardless of whether those rights are transferrable or separable from the acquired entity or from other rights and obligations). If an intangible asset does not arise from contractual or other legal rights, it shall be recognized as an asset apart from goodwill only if it is separable, that is, it is capable of being separated or divided from the acquired entity and sold, transferred, licensed, rented, or exchanged (regardless of whether there is an intent to do so).*[9]

Intangible assets that cannot be so identified should be included in goodwill. For example, acquired firms will have a valuable employee workforce in place, but this asset cannot be recognized as an intangible separately from goodwill. Appendix A of *Statement No. 141* (reproduced in part in Exhibit 1-2) provides more detailed discussion and an illustrative list of intangibles that firms can recognize separately from goodwill.

CONTINGENT CONSIDERATION IN A PURCHASE BUSINESS COMBINATION Some purchase business combinations provide for additional payments to the previous stockholders of the acquired company, contingent on future events or transactions. *FASB Statement No. 141* (paragraphs 25 to 27) provides guidance in accounting for contingent consideration in a purchase business combination. The contingent consideration may include the distribution of cash or other assets or the issuance of debt or equity securities.

We record contingent consideration that is determinable at the date of acquisition as part of the cost of combination. We recognize contingent consideration that is not determinable at the date of acquisition when the contingency is resolved and the consideration is issued or becomes issuable.

When the contingency involves future earnings levels, we recognize the fair market value of the consideration distributed or issued as an additional cost of the acquired company. Typically we recognize this additional cost as goodwill, which we no longer amortize.

If the contingency is based on security prices, the recorded cost of the acquired company should not change. Instead, when the contingency is resolved, we record the additional consideration that is distributed at its fair market value. We should write down securities issued and recorded at the date of acquisition proportionately. When the acquiring entity issued capital stock, the write-down is usually to other paid-in capital. A write-down of debt securities would result in recording a discount on debt, which we must then amortize from the date of settlement of the contingency.

---

[8] *FASB Statement No. 141*, paragraph 43.
[9] *FASB Statement No. 141*, paragraph 39.

The following are examples of intangible assets that meet the criteria for recognition as an asset apart from goodwill. The following illustrative list is not intended to be all-inclusive, thus, an acquired intangible asset might meet the recognition criteria of this Statement but not be included on that list. Assets designated by the symbol (†) are those that would be recognized apart from goodwill because they meet the contractual–legal criterion.* Assets designed by the symbol (▲) do not arise from contractual or other legal rights, but shall nonetheless be recognized apart from goodwill because they meet the separability criterion. The determination of whether a specific acquired intangible asset meets the criteria in this Statement for recognition apart from goodwill shall be based on the facts and circumstances of each individual business combination.

a. Marketing-related intangible assets
   (1) Trademarks, trade names†
   (2) Service marks, collective marks, certification marks†
   (3) Trade dress (unique color, shape, or package design)†
   (4) Newspaper mastheads†
   (5) Internet domain names†
   (6) Noncompetition agreements†

b. Customer-related intangible assets
   (1) Customer lists▲
   (2) Order or production backlog†
   (3) Customer contracts and related **customer relationships**†
   (4) Noncontractual customer relationships▲

c. Artistic-related intangible assets
   (1) Plays, operas, ballets†
   (2) Books, magazines, newspapers, other literary works†
   (3) Musical works such as compositions, song lyrics, advertising jingles†
   (4) Pictures, photographs†
   (5) Video and audiovisual material, including motion pictures, music videos, television programs†

d. Contract-based intangible assets
   (1) Licensing, royalty, standstill agreements†
   (2) Advertising, construction, management, service, or supply contracts†
   (3) Lease agreements†
   (4) Construction permits†
   (5) Franchise agreements†
   (6) Operating and broadcast rights†
   (7) Use rights such as drilling, water, air, mineral, timber cutting, and route authorities†
   (8) Servicing contracts such as mortgage servicing contracts†
   (9) Employment contracts†

e. Technology-based intangible assets
   (1) Patented technology†
   (2) Computer software and mask works†
   (3) Unpatented technology▲
   (4) Databases, including title plants▲
   (5) Trade secrets, such as secret formulas, processes, recipes†

*The intangible assets designated by the symbol (†) also might meet the separability criterion. However, separability is not a necessary condition for an asset to meet the contractual–legal criterion.

COST AND FAIR VALUE COMPARED After assigning fair values to all identifiable assets acquired and liabilities assumed, we compare the investment cost with the total fair value of identifiable assets less liabilities. If the investment cost exceeds net fair value, we first allocate it to identifiable net assets according to their fair values and then allocate the excess to goodwill.

In some business combinations, the total fair value of identifiable assets acquired over liabilities assumed may exceed the cost of the acquired company. Paragraph 46 of *FASB Statement No. 141* offers accounting procedures to dispose of the excess fair value in this situation.

> *That excess should be allocated as a pro rata reduction of the amounts that otherwise would have been assigned to all of the acquired assets except (a) financial assets other than investments accounted for by the equity method, (b) assets to be disposed of by sale, (c) deferred tax assets, (d) prepaid assets relating to pension or other postretirement benefit plans, and (e) any other current assets.*

If the allocation reduces these assets to zero value, we recognize the remainder of the excess over cost as an extraordinary gain as described in *APB Opinion No. 30*.

Illustration of a Purchase Combination

Pitt Corporation acquires the net assets of Seed Company in a purchase combination consummated on December 27, 2006. The assets and liabilities of Seed Company on this date, at their book values and at fair values, are as follows (in thousands):

	Book Value	Fair Value
Assets		
Cash	$ 50	$ 50
Net receivables	150	140
Inventories	200	250
Land	50	100
Buildings—net	300	500
Equipment—net	250	350
Patents	—	50
Total assets	$1,000	$1,440
Liabilities		
Accounts payable	$ 60	$ 60
Notes payable	150	135
Other liabilities	40	45
Total liabilities	$ 250	$ 240
Net assets	$ 750	$1,200

CASE 1: GOODWILL

Pitt Corporation pays $400,000 cash and issues 50,000 shares of Pitt Corporation $10 par common stock with a market value of $20 per share for the net assets of Seed Company. The following entries record the business combination on the books of Pitt Corporation on December 27, 2006:

Investment in Seed Company (+A)	1,400	
Cash (−A)		400
Common stock, $10 par (+SE)		500
Additional paid-in capital (+SE)		500

To record issuance of 50,000 shares of $10 par common
  plus $400,000 cash in a purchase business combination with
  Seed Company.

Cash (+A)	50	
Net receivables (+A)	140	
Inventories (+A)	250	
Land (+A)	100	
Buildings (+A)	500	
Equipment (+A)	350	
Patents (+A)	50	
Goodwill (+A)	200	
Accounts payable (+L)		60
Notes payable (+L)		135
Other liabilities (+L)		45
Investment in Seed Company (−A)		1,400

To assign the cost of Seed Company to identifiable assets
  acquired and liabilities assumed on the basis of their fair
  values and to goodwill.

We assign the amounts to the assets and liabilities based on fair values, except for goodwill. We determine goodwill by subtracting the $1,200,000 fair value of identifiable net assets acquired from the $1,400,000 purchase price for Seed Company's net assets.

CASE 2: FAIR VALUE EXCEEDS INVESTMENT COST (NEGATIVE GOODWILL)

Pitt Corporation issues 40,000 shares of its $10 par common stock with a market value of $20 per share, and it also gives a 10%, five-year note payable for $200,000 for the net assets of Seed Company. Pitt's books record the Pitt/Seed business combination as a purchase on December 27, 2006, with the following journal entries:

Investment in Seed Company (+A)	1,000	
Common stock, $10 par (+SE)		400
Additional paid-in capital (+SE)		400
10% Note payable (+L)		200

To record issuance of 40,000 shares of $10 par common
plus a $200,000, 10% note in a purchase business
combination with Seed Company.

Cash (+A)	50	
Net receivables (+A)	140	
Inventories (+A)	250	
Land (+A)	80	
Buildings (+A)	400	
Equipment (+A)	280	
Patents (+A)	40	
Accounts payable (+L)		60
Notes payable (+L)		135
Other liabilities (+L)		45
Investment in Seed Company (−A)		1,000

To assign the cost of Seed Company to identifiable assets
acquired and liabilities assumed on the basis of their fair
values less a proportionate share of the excess of fair value
over investment cost.

We assign the amounts to the individual asset and liability accounts in this entry in accordance with the provisions of *FASB Statement No. 141* for business combinations. The $1,200,000 fair value of the identifiable net assets acquired exceeds the $1,000,000 purchase price by $200,000, so we reduce the amounts otherwise assignable to assets by 20% ($200,000 excess/$1,000,000 fair value of noncurrent assets). The reduction in specific assets is as follows (in thousands):

	Asset Fair Values	Less 20% Reduction for the Excess of Fair Values over Cost*	Amounts Assignable to Assets
Land	$ 100	$ 20	$ 80
Buildings	500	100	400
Equipment	350	70	280
Patents	50	10	40
Total	$1,000	$200	$800

*Alternatively, we could compute the reduction in individual assets for the excess of fair value over cost as follows:

Land	$100/$1,000 × $200 =	$ 20
Buildings	$500/$1,000 × $200 =	100
Equipment	$350/$1,000 × $200 =	70
Patents	$50/$1,000 × $200 =	10
		$200

In some instances, the excess fair value over cost may be so large that a balance remains after reducing the assets to zero. We report the remaining excess in this case as an extraordinary gain.

The Goodwill Controversy

GAAP defines *goodwill* as the excess of the investment cost over the fair value of assets received. Theoretically, it is a measure of the present value of the combined company's projected future excess earnings over the normal earnings of a similar business. Estimating it requires considerable speculation. Therefore, the amount that we generally capitalize as goodwill is the portion of the purchase price left over after all other identifiable tangible and intangible assets and liabilities have been valued. Errors in the valuation of other assets will affect the amount capitalized as goodwill.

Under *FASB Statement No. 142*, goodwill is no longer amortized for financial reporting purposes. There are also income tax controversies relating to goodwill. In some cases, firms can deduct goodwill amortization for tax purposes over a 15-year period. The tax consequences of goodwill are discussed in Chapter 10.

INTERNATIONAL ACCOUNTING FOR GOODWILL U.S. companies had long complained that the accounting rule for amortizing goodwill put them at a disadvantage in competing against foreign companies for merger partners. Some countries, for example, permit the immediate write-off of goodwill to stockholders' equity. Even though the balance sheet of the combined company may show negative net worth, the company can begin showing income from the merged operations immediately. The new standard should alleviate these competitive disadvantages.

Companies in most other industrial countries historically capitalized and amortized goodwill acquired in business combinations. The amortization periods vary. For instance, the maximum amortization period in Australia and Sweden is 20 years; in Japan, it is 5 years. Some countries permit deducting goodwill amortization for tax purposes, which makes short amortization periods popular.

The North American Free Trade Agreement (NAFTA) increased trade and investments between Canada, Mexico, and the United States and also increased the need for the harmonization of accounting standards. The standard-setting bodies of the three trading partners are looking at ways to narrow the differences in accounting standards. Canadian companies no longer amortize goodwill. Canadian GAAP for goodwill is now consistent with the revised U.S. standards. Mexican companies amortize intangibles over the period benefited, not to exceed 20 years. Negative goodwill from business combinations of Mexican companies is reported as a component of stockholders' equity and is not amortized.

The IASB is successor to the IASC, a private-sector organization formed in 1973 to develop international accounting standards and promote harmonization of accounting standards worldwide. Coincident with the issuance of IFRS 3 on March 31, 2004, the IASB revised *International Accounting Standard* (IAS) *36,* "Impairment of Assets," and *IAS 38*, "Intangible Assets." Under the revised rules, goodwill and other intangible assets having indeterminate lives will no longer be amortized but will be tested for value impairment. Impairment tests will be conducted annually, or more frequently if circumstances indicate a possible impairment. Firms may not reverse previously recognized impairment losses for goodwill. These revisions make the IASB rules consistent with both U.S. and Canadian GAAP. Although accounting organizations from all over the world are members, the IASB does not have the authority to require compliance. However, this situation is changing rapidly. The European Union requires IFRS in the financial reporting of all listed firms beginning in 2005. Russia, Bulgaria, New Zealand, and many other countries are replacing, or considering replacing, their own GAAP with the IASB standards.

Both the IASB and FASB are working to eliminate differences in accounting for business combinations under IFRS and U.S. GAAP. The FASB is considering revising its standards to harmonize with *IFRS 3* requirements. For example, under U.S. GAAP, amounts assigned to purchased in-process research and development must be expensed, whereas *IFRS 3* permits capitalization of these costs as a separate and identifiable asset.

Current U.S. Accounting for Goodwill and Other Intangible Assets

The FASB dramatically changed accounting for goodwill in *FASB Statement No. 142*. They maintained the basic computation of goodwill, but the revised standards mitigate many of the previous controversies.

FASB Statement No. 141 provides clarification and more detailed guidance on when previously unrecorded intangibles should be recognized as assets, which can affect the amount of goodwill that firms recognize.

Under *FASB Statements No. 141* and *No. 142*, firms record goodwill but do *not* amortize it. Instead, the FASB requires that firms periodically assess goodwill for impairment in its value. An impairment occurs when the recorded value of goodwill is greater than its fair value. We calculate the fair value of goodwill in the same manner as in the original calculation at the date of the business combination. Should such impairment occur, firms will write down goodwill to a new estimated amount and will record an offsetting loss in calculating net income for the period.

FASB Statement No. 142 does not retroactively change treatment of goodwill, but firms will cease amortization of previously recorded goodwill. In other words, further amortization is not permitted, but firms may not write goodwill back up to reverse the impact of prior-period amortization charges.

Firms will no longer amortize goodwill or other intangible assets that have indefinite useful lives. Instead, firms will periodically review these assets (at least annually) and adjust for value impairment. The FASB provides detailed guidance for determining and measuring impairment of goodwill and other intangible assets. *FASB Statement No. 142* amends *FASB Statement No. 121*, "Accounting for the Impairment of Long-Lived Assets and for Long-Lived Assets to Be Disposed Of," to exclude goodwill and other nonamortizable intangible assets.

Firms must apply *FASB Statement No. 142* in all fiscal years beginning after December 15, 2001. The FASB permits early adoption only for those firms with fiscal years beginning after March 15, 2001, that have not previously issued interim financial statements.

Firms treat impairment losses on goodwill and other intangibles not subject to amortization, recognized for the first time under application of *FASB Statement No. 142*, as losses due to a change in accounting principle. Firms should apply immediately the amortization and nonamortization provisions of the standard to goodwill and intangibles acquired after June 30, 2001.

The standard also redefines the reporting entity in accounting for intangible assets. Under *APB Opinion No. 17*, firms treated the acquired entity as a stand-alone reporting entity. The FASB recognized that many acquired entities are integrated into the operations of the acquirer. Under *FASB Statement No. 142*, firms will treat goodwill and other intangibles as assets of the business reporting unit, as defined under *FASB Statement No. 131*, "Disclosures About Segments of an Enterprise and Related Information."

Firms will report intangible assets, other than those acquired in business combinations, based on their fair value at the acquisition date. Firms should allocate the cost of a group of assets acquired (which may include both tangible and intangible assets) to the individual assets based on relative fair values and "shall not give rise to goodwill" (paragraph 9).

FASB Statement No. 142 (paragraph 10) retains *APB Opinion No. 17*'s accounting for internally developed intangible assets.

> *Costs of internally developing, maintaining, or restoring intangible assets (including goodwill) that are not specifically identifiable, that have indeterminate lives, or that are inherent in a continuing business and related to the entity as a whole, shall be recognized as an expense when incurred.*

Similarly, the FASB retains the requirement for expensing acquired research and development costs.

RECOGNIZING AND MEASURING IMPAIRMENT LOSSES The goodwill impairment test under *FASB Statement No. 142* is a two-step process. Firms must first compare carrying values (book values) to fair values at the business-reporting-unit level. Carrying value includes the goodwill amount. If fair value is less than the carrying amount, then firms will proceed to the second step, measurement of this impairment loss.

The second step requires a comparison of the carrying amount of goodwill to its implied fair value. Firms should again make this comparison at the business-reporting-unit level. If the carrying amount exceeds the implied fair value of the goodwill, the firm must recognize an impairment loss for the difference. The loss amount cannot exceed the carrying amount of the goodwill. Firms cannot reverse previously recognized impairment losses.

Firms should determine the implied fair value of goodwill in the same manner used to originally record the goodwill at the business combination date. Firms allocate the fair value of the reporting unit to all identifiable assets and liabilities as if they purchased the unit on the measurement date. Any excess fair value is the implied fair value of goodwill.

Fair value of assets and liabilities is the value at which they could be sold, incurred, or settled in a current arm's-length transaction. The FASB considers quoted market prices as the best indicators of fair values, although these are often unavailable. When market prices are unavailable, firms may determine fair values using market prices of similar assets and liabilities or other commonly used valuation techniques. For example, firms may employ present value techniques to value estimated future cash flows or earnings. Firms may also employ techniques based on multiples of earnings or revenues.

Firms should conduct the impairment test for goodwill at least annually. *FASB Statement No. 142* (paragraph 28) requires more-frequent impairment testing if any of the following events occurs:

    a. *A significant adverse change in legal factors or in the business climate*

    b. *An adverse action or assessment by a regulator*

    c. *Unanticipated competition*

    d. *A loss of key personnel*

    e. *A more-likely-than-not expectation that a reporting unit or a significant portion of a reporting unit will be sold or otherwise disposed of*

    f. *The testing for the recoverability under Statement 121 of a significant asset group within a reporting unit*

    g. *Recognition of a goodwill impairment loss in the financial statements of a subsidiary that is a component of a reporting unit*

The goodwill impairment testing required under *FASB Statement No. 142* is complex and may have significant financial statement impact. A whole industry has sprung up to assist companies in making the goodwill valuations. For example, the Web site of **Appraisal Economics, Inc.**, offers to help: "At Appraisal Economics we have the personnel, experience and research resources required to provide the kind of goodwill impairment testing that will stand up to SEC scrutiny. A goodwill impairment opinion from Appraisal Economics is the product of a comprehensive analysis that takes into account all areas of concern to the SEC."

AMORTIZATION VERSUS NONAMORTIZATION Firms must amortize intangible assets with a finite useful life over that life. The FASB defines *useful life* as estimated useful life to the reporting entity. Firms must amortize intangible assets with an indefinite useful life over the best estimate of that life. The method of amortization should reflect the expected pattern of consumption of the economic benefits of the intangible. If firms cannot determine a pattern, then they should use straight-line amortization.

Firms will not amortize intangible assets with an indefinite useful life that cannot be estimated. If these intangibles later have a life that can be estimated, they should be amortized at that point. Firms should periodically review intangibles that are not being amortized for possible impairment loss.

DISCLOSURE REQUIREMENTS

Notes to the financial statements of the acquiring corporation must disclose that the business combination was accounted for by the purchase method. The notes also should provide the name and a brief description of the acquired company, the period for which results of operations of the acquired company are included in the income statement, the cost of the acquired company and, if applicable, the number and valuation of shares of stock issued or issuable, and a description of any contingent payments. Information relating to several minor acquisitions may be combined for disclosure purposes.

For material acquisitions, the financial statement notes for the period of combination should include supplemental information on a pro forma basis as follows: (1) the results of operations for the current period as though the companies had combined at the beginning of the period and (2) the results of operations for the immediately preceding period as though the companies had combined at the beginning of that period, if the firm presents comparative financial statements. The FASB does not require disclosure of these pro forma results for nonpublic enterprises.[10]

---

[10] *FASB Statement No. 79*, "Elimination of Certain Disclosures for Business Combinations by Nonpublic Enterprises," 1984, paragraph 4.

EXHIBIT 1-3

Intangible Assets Disclosure Requirements

Source: FASB Statement No. 142, pp. 16–17

For intangible assets acquired either individually or with a group of assets, the following information shall be disclosed in the notes to the financial statements in the period of acquisition:

a. For intangible assets subject to amortization:
   (1) The total amount assigned and the amount assigned to any major **intangible asset class**
   (2) The amount of any significant residual value, in total and by major intangible asset class
   (3) The weighted-average amortization period, in total and by major intangible asset class

b. For intangible assets *not* subject to amortization, the total amount assigned and the amount assigned to any major intangible asset class

c. The amount of research and development assets acquired and written off in the period and the line item in the income statement in which the amounts written off are aggregated.

The following information shall be disclosed in the financial statements or the notes to the financial statements for each period for which a statement of financial position is presented:

a. For intangible assets subject to amortization:
   (1) The gross carrying amount and accumulated amortization, in total and by major intangible asset class
   (2) The aggregate amortization expense for the period
   (3) The estimated aggregate amortization expense for each of the five succeeding fiscal years

b. For intangible assets *not* subject to amortization, the total carrying amount and the carrying amount for each major intangible asset class

c. The changes in the carrying amount of goodwill during the period, including:
   (1) The aggregate amount of goodwill acquired
   (2) The aggregate amount of impairment losses recognized
   (3) The amount of goodwill included in the gain or loss on disposal of all or a portion of a reporting unit.

Entities that report segment information in accordance with Statement 131 shall provide the above information about goodwill in total and for each reportable segment and shall disclose any significant changes in the allocation of goodwill by reportable segment. If any portion of goodwill has not yet been allocated to a reporting unit at the date the financial statements are issued, that unallocated amount and the reasons for not allocating that amount shall be disclosed.

For each impairment loss recognized related to an intangible asset, the following information shall be disclosed in the notes to the financial statements that include the period in which the impairment loss is recognized:

a. A description of the impaired intangible asset and the facts and circumstances leading to the impairment

b. The amount of the impairment loss and the method for determining fair value

c. The caption in the income statement or the statement of activities in which the impairment loss is aggregated

d. If applicable, the segment in which the impaired intangible asset is reported under Statement 131.

For each goodwill impairment loss recognized, the following information shall be disclosed in the notes to the financial statements that include the period in which the impairment loss is recognized:

a. A description of the facts and circumstances leading to the impairment

b. The amount of the impairment loss and the method of determining the fair value of the associated reporting unit (whether based on quoted market prices, prices of comparable businesses, a present value or other valuation technique, or a combination thereof)

c. If a recognized impairment loss is an estimate that has not yet been finalized (refer to paragraph 22), that fact and the reasons therefor and, in subsequent periods, the nature and amount of any significant adjustments made to the initial estimate of the impairment loss

FASB Statement No. 141 expands required disclosures, especially those related to recognized intangible assets. Firms must disclose the primary business reason for the combination and the allocation of the purchase price by major balance sheet categories for assets acquired and liabilities assumed.

FASB Statement No. 142 requires firms to report material aggregate amounts of goodwill as a separate balance sheet line item. Likewise, firms must show goodwill impairment losses separately in the income statement, as a component of income from continuing operations (unless the impairment relates to discontinued operations). *FASB Statement No. 142* also provides increased disclosure requirements for intangible assets *(FASB Statement No. 142,* paragraphs 45 through 47, which are reproduced in Exhibit 1-3).

EXHIBIT 1-4

Note 2—Acquisition

Source: 2002 Sears annual report.

On June 17, 2002, the Company acquired 100 percent of the outstanding common shares of Lands' End. The results of Lands' End's operations have been included in the consolidated financial statements since that date. Headquartered in Dodgeville, Wisconsin, Lands' End is a leading direct merchant of traditionally styled, casual clothing for men, women and children, accessories, footwear, home products and soft luggage.

The Company acquired Lands' End for $1.8 billion in cash. The acquisition has been accounted for using the purchase method in accordance with SFAS No. 141, "Business Combinations." Accordingly, the total purchase price has preliminarily been allocated to the assets acquired and liabilities assumed based on their estimated fair values at acquisition as follows (amounts in millions):

Merchandise inventories	$ 238
Property and equipment	185
Intangible assets (primarily indefinite-lived trade names)	704
Goodwill	834
Other assets	48
Accounts payable and other liabilities	(169)
Total	$1,840

Of the $704 million acquired intangibles, $700 million was assigned to registered trade names that are not subject to amortization, and $4 million was assigned to customer lists with an estimated useful life of three years.

The amount allocated to goodwill is reflective of the benefit the Company expects to realize from leveraging the Lands' End brand name across its retail business. The goodwill related to the Lands' End acquisition is not deductible for tax purposes.

The following unaudited pro forma information presents the results of operations of the Company as if the Lands' End acquisition had taken place at the beginning of each respective period. Pro forma adjustments have been made to reflect additional interest expense from the $1.8 billion in debt associated with the acquisition. The pro forma results of operations include $18 million of nonrecurring transaction costs incurred by Lands' End in 2002.

in millions, except per share data

	2002 (Pro forma)	2001 (Pro forma)
Revenues	$42,040	$42,524
Income before cumulative effect of accounting change	1,571	736
Net income	1,363	736
Earnings per share		
Basic		
Earnings per share	4.29	2.25
Diluted		
Earnings per share	4.25	2.24

The unaudited pro forma results have been prepared for comparative purposes only and do not purport to be indicative of the results of operations that would have occurred had the Lands' End acquisition occurred at the beginning of the respective periods.

Before completing the chapter, let's look at a summary example of required disclosures under *FASB Statements No. 141* and *142* from a real-world company. In June 2002, **Sears** acquired the catalog and online clothing and household goods merchandiser **Lands' End** for $1.8 billion. Sears planned to add Lands' End branded merchandise to its own retail offerings. Exhibit 1-4 provides Note 2 from Sears' 2002 annual report regarding the Lands' End acquisition. Notice, in particular, that the bulk of the $1.8 billion price tag relates to acquired intangible assets. Sears allocates $704 million to trademarks and another $834 million to goodwill.

The detailed disclosures under *SFAS No. 141* disappear quickly. Here is the reference to the Lands' End acquisition from Note 2 of the Sears 2003 annual report:

On June 27, 2002, the Company acquired 100 percent of the outstanding common shares of Lands' End, Inc. ("Lands' End") for $1.8 billion in cash. The allocation of the purchase price assigned $834 million to goodwill and $704 million to intangible assets. The results of Lands' End's operations have been included in the consolidated financial statements since that date. Lands' End is a leading direct merchant of traditionally styled, casual clothing, accessories and footwear for men, women and children, as well as home products and soft luggage.

Interestingly, Sears itself was acquired by rival **Kmart** during November 2004 at a price of $11 billion. You may recall that Kmart had only recently emerged from Chapter 11 bankruptcy protection and reorganization. The newly merged business will take the name **Sears Holdings** and will continue to operate both Sears and Kmart stores.

THE SARBANES-OXLEY ACT OF 2002

You have likely heard about Sarbannes-Oxley and are wondering why we haven't mentioned it yet. The financial collapse of **Enron Corporation** and **WorldCom** (among others) and the demise of public accounting firm **Arthur Andersen and Company** spurred Congress to initiate legislation intended to prevent future financial reporting and auditing abuse. The result was the *Sarbanes-Oxley Act of 2002* (SOX). For the most part, the new rules focus on corporate governance, auditing and internal-control issues, rather than the details of financial reporting and statement presentation that are the topic of this text. However, you should recognize that the law will impact all of the types of companies that we study. Here are a few of the important areas covered by SOX:

- Establishes the independent Public Company Accounting Oversight Board (PCAOB) to regulate the accounting and auditing profession
- Requires greater independence of auditors and clients, including restrictions on the types of consulting and advisory services provided by auditors to their clients
- Requires greater independence and oversight responsibilities for corporate boards of directors, especially for members of audit committees
- Requires management (CEO and CFO) certification of financial statements and internal controls
- Requires independent auditor review and attestation on management's internal-control assessments
- Increases disclosures about off–balance sheet arrangements and contractual obligations
- Increases types of items requiring disclosure on Form 8-K and shortens the filing period

Enforcement of Sarbanes-Oxley is under the jurisdiction of the Securities and Exchange Commission. The SEC treats violations of SOX or rules of the PCAOB the same as violations of the Securities Exchange Act of 1934. Congress has also increased the SEC's budget to permit improved review and enforcement activities. SEC enforcement actions and investigations have increased considerably since the Enron collapse. One recent example is **Krispy Kreme Doughnuts, Inc.** A January 4, 2005, press release on the company's Web site announced that earnings for fiscal 2004 and the last three quarters would be restated. Apparently the company did not make as much "dough" as originally reported. Pre-tax income will be reduced by between $6.2 million and $8.1 million. Another example appeared in a *Reuters Limited* story on January 6, 2005, which noted that former directors of **WorldCom** agreed to a $54 million settlement in a class-action lawsuit brought by investors. This included $18 million from personal funds, with the remainder being covered by insurance.

Exhibit 1-5 provides an example of the required management responsibilities under SOX from the 2003 annual report of ChevronTexaco Corporation (p. 45). Notice that management's statement reads much like a traditional independent auditor's report. Management takes responsibility for preparation of the financial reports, explicitly notes compliance with GAAP, and declares amounts to be fairly presented. Management also takes explicit responsibility for designing and maintaining internal controls. Finally, the statement indicates the composition and functioning of the Audit Committee, which is designed to comply with SOX requirements. The statement is signed by the CEO, CFO, and comptroller of the company.

EXHIBIT 1-5

Report of Management

Source: 2003 Chevron Texaco Corp. annual report.

To the Stockholders of ChevronTexaco Corporation:

Management of ChevronTexaco is responsible for preparing the accompanying financial statements and for ensuring their integrity and objectivity. The statements were prepared in accordance with accounting principles generally accepted in the United States of America and fairly represent the transactions and financial position of the company. The financial statements include amounts that are based on management's best estimates and judgments.

The company's statements have been audited by PricewaterhouseCoopers LLP, independent auditors selected by the Audit Committee and approved by the stockholders. Management has made available to PricewaterhouseCoopers LLP all the company's financial records and related data, as well as the minutes of stockholders' and directors' meetings.

Management of the company has established and maintains a system of internal accounting controls that is designed to provide reasonable assurance that assets are safeguarded, transactions are properly recorded and executed in accordance with management's authorization, and the books and records accurately reflect the disposition of assets. The system of internal controls includes appropriate division of responsibility. The company maintains an internal audit department that conducts an extensive program of internal audits and independently assesses the effectiveness of the internal controls.

The Audit Committee is composed of directors who are not officers or employees of the company. It meets regularly with members of management, the internal auditors and the independent auditors to discuss the adequacy of the company's internal controls, its financial statements, and the nature, extent, and results of the audit effort. Both the internal and the independent auditors have free and direct access to the Audit Committee without the presence of management.

DAVID J. O'REILLY
Chairman of the Board and
Chief Executive Officer

JOHN S. WATSON
Vice President, Finance and
Chief Financial Officer

STEPHEN J. CROWE
Vice President and Comptroller

February 25, 2004

We will note other relevant material from Sarbanes-Oxley throughout the text, as applicable. For example, transactions with related parties and variable interest entities are included in Chapter 11.

SUMMARY

A business combination occurs when two or more separate businesses join into a single accounting entity. Under *FASB Statement No. 141*, all combinations initiated after June 30, 2001, must be accounted for as purchases. Purchase accounting requires the recording of assets acquired and liabilities assumed at their fair values at the date of the combination.

The illustrations in this chapter are for business combinations in which there is only one surviving entity. Later chapters cover accounting for parent–subsidiary operations in which more than one of the combining companies continue to exist as separate legal entities.

QUESTIONS

1. Describe the accounting concept of a business combination.
2. Is dissolution of all but one of the separate legal entities necessary in order to have a business combination? Explain.
3. What are the legal distinctions between a business combination, a merger, and a consolidation?
4. When does goodwill result from a business combination? How does goodwill affect reported net income after a business combination?
5. What is negative goodwill? Describe the accounting procedures necessary to record and account for negative goodwill.

EXERCISES

E 1-1
General Questions

1. A business combination in which a new corporation is formed to take over the assets and operations of two or more separate business entities, with the previously separate entities being dissolved, is a:
   a *Consolidation*
   b *Merger*
   c *Pooling of interests*
   d *Purchase*

2. In a purchase business combination, the direct costs of registering and issuing equity securities are:

a   Added to the parent/investor company's investment account

b   Charged against other paid-in capital of the combined entity

c   Deducted from income in the period of combination

d   None of the above

3. Which of the following accounts would be adjusted to its fair market value in a merger accounted for under the purchase method, regardless of the price paid?

a   Inventories

b   Goodwill

c   Patents

d   Equipment

4. An excess of the fair value of net assets acquired in a purchase business combination over the price paid is:

a   Reported as negative goodwill and amortized over a maximum period of 40 years

b   Applied to a reduction of noncash assets before negative goodwill may be reported

c   Applied to reduce noncurrent assets other than marketable securities to zero before negative goodwill may be reported

d   Applied to reduce goodwill to zero before negative goodwill may be reported

5. Cork Corporation acquires Dart Corporation in a business combination accounted for as a purchase. Which of the following would be excluded from the process of assigning fair values for purposes of recording the purchase?

a   Patents developed by Dart, because the costs were expensed under the provisions of FASB Statement No. 2, "Accounting for Research and Development Costs"

b   Dart's mortgage payable because it is fully secured by land that has a market value far in excess of the mortgage

c   An asset or liability amount for over- or underfunding of Dart's defined-benefit pension plan

d   None of the above

E 1-2

[AICPA adapted] General Problems

1. Fast Corporation paid $50,000 cash for the net assets of Agge Company, which consisted of the following:

	Book Value	Fair Value
Current assets	$10,000	$14,000
Plant and equipment	40,000	55,000
Liabilities assumed	(10,000)	(9,000)
	$40,000	$60,000

The plant and equipment acquired in this business combination should be recorded at:

a $55,000

b $50,000

c $45,833

d $45,000

2. On April 1, Jack Company paid $800,000 for all the issued and outstanding common stock of Ann Corporation in a transaction properly accounted for as a purchase. The recorded assets and liabilities of Ann Corporation on April 1 follow:

Cash	$ 80,000	80
Inventory	240,000	190
Property and equipment (net of accumulated depreciation of $320,000)	480,000	560
Liabilities	(180,000)	(180)

On April 1, it was determined that the inventory of Ann had a fair value of $190,000 and the property and equipment (net) had a fair value of $560,000. What is the amount of goodwill resulting from the business combination?

a   0

b $50,000

c $150,000

d $180,000

E 1-3

Prepare stockholders' equity section

The stockholders' equities of Pillow Corporation and Sleep-bank Corporation at January 1 were as follows (in thousands):

	Pillow	Sleep-bank
Capital stock, $10 par	$1,500	$ 800
Other paid-in capital	200	400
Retained earnings	600	300
Stockholders' equity	$2,300	$1,500

On January 2, Pillow issued 150,000 of its shares with a market value of $20 per share for all of Sleep-bank's shares, and Sleep-bank was dissolved. On the same day, Pillow paid $5,000 to register and issue the shares and $10,000 for other direct costs of combination.

REQUIRED: Prepare the stockholders' equity section of Pillow Corporation's balance sheet immediately after the business combination on January 2.

E 1-4

Journal entries to record business combinations

IceAge Company issued 120,000 shares of $10 par common stock with a fair value of $2,550,000 for all the voting common stock of Jester Company. In addition, IceAge incurred the following costs:

Legal fees to arrange the business combination	$25,000
Cost of SEC registration, including accounting and legal fees	12,000
Cost of printing and issuing net stock certificates	3,000
Indirect costs of combining, including allocated overhead and executive salaries	20,000

Immediately before the business combination in which Jester Company was dissolved, Jester's assets and equities were as follows (in thousands):

	Book Value	Fair Value
Current assets	$1,000	$1,100
Plant assets	1,500	2,200
Liabilities	300	300
Common stock	2,000	
Retained earnings	200	

REQUIRED: Prepare all journal entries on IceAge's books to record the business combination.

E 1-5

Journal entries to record a purchase with direct costs and fair value/book value differences

On January 1, Danders Corporation pays $200,000 cash and also issues 18,000 shares of $10 par common stock with a market value of $330,000 for all the outstanding common shares of Harrison Corporation. In addition, Danders pays $30,000 for registering and issuing the 18,000 shares and $70,000 for the other direct costs of the business combination, in which Harrison Corporation is dissolved. Summary balance sheet information for the companies immediately before the merger is as follows (in thousands):

	Danders Book Value	Harrison Book Value	Harrison Fair Value
Cash	$350	$ 40	$ 40
Inventories	120	80	100
Other current assets	30	20	20
Plant assets—net	260	180	280
Total assets	$760	$320	$440
Current liabilities	$160	$ 30	$ 30
Other liabilities	80	50	40
Common stock, $10 par	420	200	
Retained earnings	100	40	
Total liabilities and owners' equity	$760	$320	

REQUIRED: Prepare all journal entries on Danders Corporation's books to account for the business combination.

P 1-1

Prepare balance sheet after purchase business combination

Comparative balance sheets for Pine and Sain Corporations at December 31, 2005, are as follows (in thousands):

	Pine	Sain
Current assets	$130	$ 60
Land	50	100
Buildings—net	300	100
Equipment—net	220	240
Total assets	$700	$500
Current liabilities	$ 50	$ 60
Capital stock, $10 par	500	200
Additional paid-in capital	50	140
Retained earnings	100	100
Total equities	$700	$500

On January 2, 2006, Pine issues 30,000 shares of its stock with a market value of $20 per share for all the outstanding shares of Sain Corporation in a purchase business combination. Sain is dissolved. The recorded book values reflect fair values, except for the buildings of Pine, which have a net realizable value of $400,000, and the current assets of Sain, which have a net realizable value of $100,000.

Pine pays the following expenses in connection with the business combination:

Costs of registering and issuing securities	$15,000
Other direct costs of combination	25,000

REQUIRED: Prepare the balance sheet of Pine Corporation immediately after the purchase business combination.

P 1-2

Prepare balance sheet after purchase business combination

On January 2, 2006, Pelican Corporation enters into a business combination with Seabird Corporation in which Seabird is dissolved. Pelican pays $825,000 for Seabird, the consideration consisting of 33,000 shares of Pelican $10 par common stock with a market value of $25 per share. In addition, Pelican pays the following expenses in cash at the time of the merger:

Finders' fee	$ 35,000
Accounting and legal fees	65,000
Registration and issuance costs of securities	40,000
	$140,000

Balance sheet and fair value information for the two companies on December 31, 2005, immediately before the merger, is as follows (in thousands):

	Pelican Book Value	Seabird Book Value	Seabird Fair Value
Cash	$ 150	$ 30	$ 30
Accounts receivable—net	230	50	40
Inventories	520	80	120
Land	400	100	150
Buildings—net	1,000	200	300
Equipment—net	500	300	250
Total assets	$2,800	$760	$890
Accounts payable	$ 300	$ 40	$ 40
Note payable	600	200	180
Capital stock, $10 par	800	300	
Other paid-in capital	600	50	
Retained earnings	500	170	
Total liabilities and owners' equity	$2,800	$760	

REQUIRED: Prepare a balance sheet for Pelican Corporation as of January 2, 2006, immediately after the merger, assuming the merger is treated as a purchase.

P 1-3

Journal entries and balance sheet for purchase business combination

On January 2, 2006, Persis Corporation issues its own $10 par common stock for all the outstanding stock of Sineco Corporation in a purchase business combination. Sineco is dissolved. In addition, Persis pays $20,000 for registering and issuing securities and $30,000 for other costs of combination. The market price of Persis's stock on January 2, 2006, is $30 per share. Relevant balance sheet information for Persis and Sineco Corporations on December 31, 2005, just before the business combination, is as follows (in thousands):

	Persis Historical Cost	Sineco Historical Cost	Sineco Fair Value
Cash	$ 120	$ 10	$ 10
Inventories	50	30	60
Other current assets	100	90	100
Land	80	20	100 –20
Plant and equipment—net	650	200	350 –70
Total assets	$1,000	$350	$620
Liabilities	$ 200	$ 50	$ 50
Capital stock, $10 par	500	100	
Additional paid-in capital	200	50	
Retained earnings	100	150	
Total liabilities and owners' equity	$1,000	$350	

REQUIRED

1. Assume that Persis issues 25,000 shares of its stock for all of Sineco's outstanding shares.
   a. Prepare journal entries to record the business combination of Persis and Sineco.
   b. Prepare a balance sheet for Persis Corporation immediately after the business combination.

2. Assume that Persis issues 15,000 shares of its stock for all of Sineco's outstanding shares.
   a. Prepare journal entries to record the business combination of Persis and Sineco.
   b. Prepare a balance sheet for Persis Corporation immediately after the business combination.

P 1-4

Allocation schedule and balance sheet

The balance sheets of Phule Corporation and Sen Corporation at December 31, 2005, are summarized together with fair value information as follows (in thousands):

	Phule Corporation		Sen Corporation	
	Book Value	Fair Value	Book Value	Fair Value
Assets				
Cash	$115	$115	$ 10	$ 10
Receivables—net	40	40	20	20
Inventories	120	150	50	30
Land	45	100	30	100 –15
Buildings—net	200	300	100	150 –22.5
Equipment—net	180	245	90	150 –22.5
Total assets	$700	$950	$300	$460
Equities				
Accounts payable	$ 90	$ 90	$ 30	$ 30
Other liabilities	100	90	60	70
Capital stock, $10 par	300		100	
Other paid-in capital	100		80	
Retained earnings	110		30	
Total equities	$700		$300	

On January 1, 2006, Phule Corporation acquired all of Sen Corporation's outstanding stock for $300,000. Phule paid $100,000 cash and issued a five-year, 12% note for the balance. Sen Corporation was dissolved.

REQUIRED

1. Prepare a schedule to show how the investment cost is allocated to identifiable assets and liabilities.

2. Prepare a balance sheet for Phule Corporation on January 1, 2006, immediately after the business combination.

P 1-5

Journal entries and balance sheet for a purchase combination

Celistia Corporation paid $2,500,000 for Dawn Corporation's voting common stock on January 2, 2006, and Dawn was dissolved. The purchase price consisted of 100,000 shares of Celistia's common stock with a market value of $2,000,000, plus $500,000 cash. In addition, Celistia paid $50,000 for registering and issuing the 100,000 shares of common stock and $100,000 for other costs of combination. Balance sheet information for the companies immediately before the business combination is summarized as follows (in thousands):

| | Celistia | Dawn | | Celistia |
	Book Value	Book Value	Fair Value	After Merger
Cash	$ 3,000	$ 240	$ 240	2,590
Accounts receivable—net	1,300	360	360	1,660
Notes receivable—net	1,500	300	300	1,800
Inventories	2,500	420	500	3,000
Other current assets	700	180	200	900
Land	2,000	100	200 − 10	2,190
Buildings—net	9,000	600	1,200 − 60	10,140
Equipment—net	10,000	800	600 − 30	10,570
Total assets	$30,000	$3,000	$3,600	32,850
Accounts payable	$ 1,000	$ 300	$ 300	1,300 A/R
Mortgage payable—10%	5,000	700	600	5,600 Mortgage
Capital stock, $10 par	10,000	1,000		11,000 Cap stock
Other paid-in capital	8,000	600		8,950 APIC
Retained earnings	6,000	400		6,000 RE
Total equities	$30,000	$3,000		32,850

REQUIRED

1. Prepare journal entries for Celistia Corporation to record its acquisition of Dawn Corporation, including all allocations to individual asset and liability accounts.

2. Prepare a balance sheet for Celistia Corporation on January 2, 2006, immediately after the acquisition and dissolution of Dawn.

INTERNET ASSIGNMENT

1. What can you learn about business combinations from the Internet? Visit the Web sites of at least three major publicly traded companies. Review their recent annual reports for evidence of significant merger and acquisition activities over the past three years. Answer the following questions for each company.

   a. What information is provided about merger activity?

   b. What was the cost of the company's most significant acquisition? How was that cost allocated? What amount of goodwill was recorded?

   c. What was the business strategy motivation underlying the merger activity?

   d How were major acquisitions financed (e.g., common stock, preferred stock, cash, debt securities, or some combination thereof)?

2. For one of your chosen firms, review the company's Form 10-K. You may find a direct link on the company Web site, or you can view the filing by visiting the SEC's EDGAR Web site. What additional information about merger activity do you find in the Form 10-K that was not available in the company's annual report?

SELECTED READINGS

Accounting Interpretations Nos. 1–39 of APB Opinion No. 16. New York: American Institute of Certified Public Accountants, 1970–73.

Accounting Principles Board Opinion No. 16. "Business Combinations." New York: American Institute of Certified Public Accountants, 1970.

Accounting Principles Board Opinion No. 17. "Intangible Assets." New York: American Institute of Certified Public Accountants, 1970.

BEIER, RAYMOND J. "Do Acquirers Have Carte Blanche to Get Rid of Goodwill?" *Mergers & Acquisitions* (November/December 1993), pp. 6–8.

BERESFORD, DENNIS R., and BRUCE J. ROSEN. "Accounting for Preacquisition Contingencies." *The CPA Journal* (March 1982), pp. 39–42.

CATLETT, GEORGE R., and NORMAN O. OLSON. "Accounting for Goodwill." *Accounting Research Study No. 10.* New York: American Institute of Certified Public Accountants, 1968.

DAVIS, MICHAEL. "Goodwill Accounting: Time for an Overhaul." *Journal of Accountancy* (June 1992), pp. 75–83.

DEMOVILLE, WIG, and GEORGE A. PETRIE. "Accounting for a Bargain Purchase in a Business Combination," *Accounting Horizons* (September 1989), pp. 38–43.

DIETER, RICHARD. "Is Now the Time to Revisit Accounting for Business Combinations?" *The CPA Journal* (July 1989), pp. 44–48.

DUVALL, LINDA, ROSS JENNINGS, JOHN ROBINSON, and ROBERT B. THOMPSON II. "Can Investors Unravel the Effects of Goodwill Accounting?" *Accounting Horizons* (June 1992), pp. 1–14.

GRINYER, J. R., A. RUSSELL, and M. WALKER. "The Rationale for Accounting for Goodwill." *The British Accounting Review* (September 1990), pp. 223–235.

JOHNSON, JEANNIE D., and MICHAEL G. TEARNEY. "Goodwill—An Eternal Controversy." *The CPA Journal* (April 1993), pp. 58–62.

JOHNSON, L. TODD, and KIMBERLY R. PETRONE. "Viewpoints—Why Not Eliminate Goodwill?" *FASB, Financial Accounting Status Report No. 139* (November 17, 1999).

MOEHRLE, STEPHEN R., and JENNIFER A. REYNOLDS-MOEHRLE. "Say Good-Bye to Pooling and Goodwill Amortization." *Journal of Accountancy* (September 2001), pp. 31–38.

MORTENSEN, ROGER. "Accounting for Business Combinations in the Global Economy: Purchase, Pooling, or _____" *Journal of Accounting Education* Vol. 12, No. 1 (1994), pp. 81–87.

NURNBERG, HUGO, and JAN SWEENEY. "The Effect of Fair Values and Historical Costs on Accounting for Business Combinations." *Issues in Accounting Education* (Fall 1989), pp. 375–395.

SIROWER, MARK. "What Acquiring Minds Need to Know." *Wall Street Journal* (February 22, 1999).

Statement of Financial Accounting Standards No. 38. "Accounting for Preacquisition Contingencies of Purchased Enterprises—An Amendment of *APB Opinion No. 16.*" Stamford, CT: Financial Accounting Standards Board, 1980.

Statement of Financial Accounting Standards No. 87. "Employers' Accounting for Pensions." Stamford, CT: Financial Accounting Standards Board, 1985.

Statement of Financial Accounting Standards No. 141. "Business Combinations." Stamford, CT: Financial Accounting Standards Board, 2001.

Statement of Financial Accounting Standards No. 142. "Goodwill and Other Intangible Assets." Stamford, CT: Financial Accounting Standards Board, 2001.

WYATT, ARTHUR R. "A Critical Study of Accounting for Business Combinations." *Accounting Research Study No. 5.* New York: American Institute of Certified Public Accountants, 1963.

2 CHAPTER

STOCK INVESTMENTS–INVESTOR ACCOUNTING AND REPORTING

LEARNING OBJECTIVES

1 Recognize investors' varying levels of influence or control, based on the level of stock ownership.

2 Anticipate how accounting adjusts to reflect the economics underlying varying levels of investor influence.

3 Apply the fair value/cost and equity methods of accounting for stock investments.

4 Identify factors beyond stock ownership that affect an investor's ability to exert influence or control.

5 Apply the equity method to purchase price allocations.

6 Learn how to test goodwill for impairment.

Chapter 1 illustrated business combinations in which one surviving entity received the net assets of other combining companies. A single legal and accounting entity, with one record-keeping system, integrated the net assets and operations of all combining companies. In Chapter 1, we recorded the business combination in an investment account and immediately eliminated the account through allocation to individual asset and liability accounts.

Chapter 2 looks at equity investments in which the investor maintains the investment account on a continuous basis. It includes accounting for investments under the fair value/cost (fair value for marketable securities and cost for nonmarketable securities) method, in which the investor company does not have the ability to influence the activities of the investee, as well as accounting under the equity method, in which the investor company can exercise significant influence over the investee's operations. Generally accepted accounting principles (GAAP) generally prescribe equity method accounting for investments that represent greater than 20% ownership but less than a controlling 50% ownership interest.

Investors also use the equity method for internal parent-company accounting for investments in subsidiaries. This situation arises when the investor controls the operating, investing, and financing decisions of the investee through ownership of more than 50% of the voting stock of the investee company as the result of a business combination in which one or more companies became subsidiaries. For financial-reporting purposes, such combinations result in the preparation of consolidated financial statements.

This chapter covers parent-company accounting for its subsidiaries under the purchase method, but it does *not* cover consolidated financial statements. Consolidated financial statements for parent and subsidiary companies appear in Chapter 3 and subsequent chapters.

ACCOUNTING FOR STOCK INVESTMENTS

LEARNING OBJECTIVE 1

GAAP for recording common stock acquisitions requires that the investor record the investment at its cost. The basic guidelines measure investment costs by including cash disbursed; the fair value of other assets given or securities issued; and additional direct costs of obtaining the investment, other than the costs of registering and issuing equity securities, which GAAP charges to additional paid-in capital.

One of the two basic methods of accounting for noncurrent, common stock investments generally applies—the **fair value (cost) method** or the **equity method**. If the fair value method is used, we account for the investment according to the provisions of *FASB Statement No. 115,* "Accounting for Certain Investments in Debt and Equity Securities." If the equity method of accounting applies, we account for the investment under the provisions of *APB Opinion No. 18,* "The Equity Method of Accounting for Investments in Common Stock," as amended by *FASB Statement No. 94,* "Consolidation of All Majority-Owned Subsidiaries."

Concepts Underlying Fair Value/Cost and Equity Methods

Under the fair value/cost method, we record investments in common stock at cost and report dividends from subsequent earnings as dividend income. There is an exception. Dividends received in excess of the investor's share of earnings after the stock is acquired are considered returns of capital (or liquidating dividends) and are recorded as reductions in the investment account.[1] We classify equity securities that have a readily determinable fair value as either trading securities (securities bought and held principally for the purpose of resale in the near term) or available-for-sale securities (investments not classified as trading securities) under the provisions of *FASB Statement No. 115*.

Both classifications are carried at fair values and report realized gains, losses, and dividends as earnings. However, we include unrealized gains and losses from the trading-securities classification in earnings. We report unrealized gains and losses from the available-for-sale securities classification at a net amount as a separate line item under other comprehensive income. *FASB Statement No. 130* allows other comprehensive income to be reported either on the income statement, as a separate statement of comprehensive income, or in a statement of changes in equity. These amounts would accumulate in the equity section of the balance sheet in the account titled *Accumulated other comprehensive income*. *FASB Statement No. 115* does not apply to investments in equity securities accounted for under the equity method or to investments in consolidated subsidiaries.

The equity method of accounting is essentially accrual accounting for equity investments that enable the investor to exercise significant influence over the investee.[2] Under the equity method, we record the investments at cost and adjust for earnings, losses, and dividends. The investor company reports its share of the investee's earnings as investment income and its share of the investee's losses as investment loss. We increase the investment account for investment income and decrease it for investment losses. Dividends received from investees are disinvestments under the equity method, and they are recorded as decreases in the investment account. Thus, investment income under the equity method reflects the investor's share of the net income of the investee, and the investment account reflects the investor's share of the investee's net assets.

We account for an investment in voting stock that gives the investor the ability to exercise significant influence over the financial and operating policies of the investee using the equity method of accounting. Paragraph 17 of *APB Opinion No. 18* explains:

> *The Board concludes that the equity method of accounting for an investment in common stock should ... be followed by an investor whose investment in voting stock gives it the ability to exercise significant influence over operating and financial policies of an investee even though the investor holds 50% or less of the voting stock.*

The APB bases the ability to exert significant influence on a 20% ownership test:

> *An investment (direct or indirect) of 20% or more of the voting stock of an investee should lead to a presumption that in the absence of evidence to the contrary an investor has the ability to exercise significant influence over an investee. Conversely, an investment of less than 20% of the voting stock of an investee should lead to a presumption that an investor does not have the ability to exercise significant influence unless such ability can be demonstrated.[3]*

An investor may be able to exert significant influence over its investee with an investment interest of less than 20%, according to *Opinion No. 18*. The following statement from *SBC Communications'* 2003 annual report (p. 47) provides an example of the exception:

> *As of December 31, 2003, our investments in equity affiliates included an 8.0% interest in Telmex, Mexico's national telecommunications company; a 7.6% interest in America Movil, primarily a wireless provider in Mexico, with telecommunications investments in the U.S. and Latin America; ...*

---

[1] *APB Opinion No. 18,* "The Equity Method of Accounting for Investments in Common Stock," paragraph 6a.

[2] Intermediate-level accounting texts provide additional detail on application of the equity method of accounting. See, for example, Chapter 16 of L. Revsine, D. W. Collins, and W. B. Johnson, *Financial Reporting & Analysis,* 2d ed. (Upper Saddle River, NJ: Prentice Hall, 2002).

[3] *APB Opinion No. 18,* paragraph 17.

The equity method should not be applied if the investor's ability to exert significant influence is temporary or if the investees are foreign companies operating under severe exchange restrictions or controls.[4] ***Ford Motor Company*** provides an example of use of the equity method (rather than consolidation) for temporarily controlled subsidiaries. Ford's note describes its accounting for equity method affiliates in its 2000 annual report (p. 55) as follows:

> *Affiliates that are 20% to 50% owned, principally Mazda Motor Corporation and AutoAlliance International, Inc., subsidiaries where control is expected to be temporary, principally investments in certain dealerships, are accounted for on an equity basis.*

FASB Interpretation No. 35 cites (1) opposition by the investee that challenges the investor's influence, (2) surrender of significant stockholder rights by agreement between investor and investee, (3) concentration of majority ownership, (4) inadequate or untimely information to apply the equity method, and (5) failure to obtain representation on the investee's board of directors as indicators of an investor's inability to exercise significant influence.[5] Application of the equity method should be discontinued when the investor's share of losses reduces the carrying amount of the investment to zero.

The equity method of accounting is important for several reasons. First, these investments represent a significant component of total assets, net income, or both for some firms. Second, corporate joint ventures and other special-purpose entities widely use the equity method. Third, the equity method is used in the discussion of the preparation of consolidated financial statements in later chapters.

Accounting Trends and Techniques (2003) reports that 304 of the 600 firms surveyed reported using the equity method for investments in other companies. ***Microsoft*** discloses equity and other investments, principally joint ventures, of $13.7 billion (17.4% of total assets) in its 2003 Annual Report. ***SBC Communications, Inc.***, a Texas-based telecommunications giant, reports investments in equity method affiliates of $6.9 billion in its 2003 Annual Report. SBC net income was $8,505 million in 2003, including $1,253 million from these equity method investments. ***Dow Chemical's*** 2003 Annual Report discloses equity method investments of $1.878 billion (4.5% of total assets) and income from those investments of $322 million (18.6% of net income). ***Disney*** records a 39% ownership interest in ***Euro Disney*** using the equity method.

THE EQUITY METHOD AND FASB STATEMENT NO. 94 A parent company may use the equity method to account for its subsidiary investments even though the financial statements of the subsidiaries are subsequently included in the consolidated financial statements for the parent company and its subsidiaries. In other words, the parent company maintains the "investment in subsidiary account" by taking up its share of the subsidiary's income and reducing the investment account for its share of subsidiary dividends declared. Under the equity method, the parent company's income and consolidated net income are equal. They reflect the income of the parent company and its subsidiaries as a single economic entity.

Before the issuance of *Statement No. 94* in 1987, parent companies were able to determine their own consolidation policies, and they had broad discretion in deciding whether to consolidate particular subsidiaries. Unconsolidated subsidiaries (in other words, subsidiaries whose assets and liabilities were not consolidated with those of the parent company) were accounted for by the equity method and *reported* both in the parent's and the consolidated financial statements as equity investments. However, the provisions of *Statement No. 94* require that all majority-owned subsidiaries be consolidated, except when control is likely to be temporary or when control does not lie with the majority interests. Examples of control of a subsidiary not resting with the parent include a subsidiary in legal reorganization or in bankruptcy, or a subsidiary operating under severe foreign-exchange restrictions or other governmentally imposed uncertainties. An investment in an unconsolidated subsidiary is reported in the financial statements by either the cost or the equity method, according to the significant-influence provisions *of APB Opinion No. 18*. Chapter 3 discusses situations in which certain subsidiaries should not be consolidated.

---

[4] Ibid., footnotes 4 and 7.

[5] *FASB Interpretation No. 35*, 1981, paragraph 3.

SBC Communications provides an example in which even majority ownership is not deemed sufficient for control related to its *Cingular Wireless* joint venture, described in Note 6 of its 2003 Annual Report:

> *We account for our 60% economic interest in Cingular under the equity method of accounting in our consolidated financial statements since we share control equally (i.e., 50/50) with our 40% economic partner in the joint venture. We have equal voting rights and representation on the board of directors that controls Cingular.*

Accounting Procedures Under the Fair Value/Cost and Equity Methods

Assume that Pilzner Company acquires 2,000 of the 10,000 outstanding shares of Sud Corporation at $50 per share on July 1, equal to the book value and fair value of Sud's net assets. Sud Corporation's net income for the entire year is $50,000, and dividends of $20,000 are paid on November 1. If there is evidence of an inability to exercise significant influence, Pilzner should apply the fair value/cost method, revaluing the investment account to fair market value at the end of the accounting period. Otherwise, the equity method is required. Accounting by Pilzner Company under the two methods is as follows:

Entry on July 1 to Record the Investment:

Fair Value/Cost Method		Equity Method	
Investment in Sud (+A) 100,000		Investment in Sud (+A) 100,000	
Cash (−A)	100,000	Cash (−A)	100,000

Entry on November 1 to Record Dividends:

Fair Value/Cost Method		Equity Method	
Cash (+A)	4,000	Cash (+A)	4,000
Dividend income (R, +SE)	4,000	Investment in Sud (−A)	4,000

Entry on December 31 to Recognize Earnings:

Fair Values/Cost Method	Equity Method	
None (Assume that the stock is either nonmarketable or has a market price = $50 per share so that no revaluing is needed.)	Investment in Sud (+A) 5,000	
	Income from Sud (−A) (R, +SE)	5,000
	($50,000 × 1/2 year × 20%)	

Under the fair value/cost method, Pilzner recognizes income of $4,000 and reports its investment in Sud at its $100,000 cost. Under the equity method, Pilzner recognizes $5,000 in income and reports the investment in Sud at $101,000 (equal to $100,000 cost plus $5,000 income less $4,000 dividends received). Here is a summary of Pilzner's equity method investment account activity:

July 1	Initial cost	$100,000
November 1	Dividends received	(4,000)
December 31	Recognize 20% of Sud's net income for 1/2 year	5,000
December 31	Ending balance	$101,000

The entries to illustrate the fair value/cost method reflect the usual situation in which the investor records dividend income equal to dividends actually received. An exception arises when dividends are received in excess of the investor's share of earnings after the investment has been acquired. From the investor's point of view, dividends in excess of the investor's share of earnings since acquisition of the investment are a return of capital, or liquidating dividends. For example, if Sud's net income for the year had been $30,000, Pilzner's share would have been $3,000 ($30,000 × 1/2 year × 20%). The $4,000 dividend received exceeds the $3,000 equity in Sud's income, so the $1,000 excess would be considered a return of capital and credited to the Investment in Sud account. Assuming that Pilzner records the $4,000 cash received on November 1 as dividend income, a year-end entry to adjust dividend income and the investment account would be needed. The investor would record such an entry as follows:

Dividend income (−R, −SE)	1,000	
Investment in Sud (−A)		1,000

To adjust dividend income and investment accounts
for dividends received in excess of earnings.

This entry reduces dividend income to Pilzner's $3,000 share of income earned after July 1 and reduces the investment in Sud to $99,000, the new fair value/cost basis for the investment. If, after the liquidating dividend, the stock had a value of $120,000, then another entry would be required to increase the investment to its fair value.

Allowance to adjust available-for-sale securities		
to market value (+A)	21,000	
Other comprehensive income (+SE)		21,000

Economic Consequences of Using the Fair Value/Cost and Equity Methods

The different methods of accounting (fair value/cost and equity) result in different investment amounts in the balance sheet of the investor corporation and different income amounts in the income statement. When the investor can significantly influence or control the operations of the investee, including dividend declarations, the fair value/cost method is unacceptable. By influencing or controlling investee dividend decisions, the investor corporation is able to manipulate its own investment income. The possibility of income manipulation does not exist when the financial statements of a parent company/investor are consolidated with the statements of a subsidiary/investee because the consolidated statements are the same, regardless of which method of accounting is used.

Although the equity method is not a substitute for consolidation, the income reported by a parent company/investor in its separate income statement under the equity method of accounting is generally the same as the income reported in consolidated financial statements for a parent company and its subsidiary.

EQUITY METHOD OF ACCOUNTING—A ONE-LINE CONSOLIDATION

LEARNING OBJECTIVE 4

The equity method of accounting is often called a **one-line consolidation**. The name comes about because the investment is reported in a single amount on one line of the investor company's balance sheet, and investment income is reported in a single amount on one line of the investor's income statement (except when the investee has extraordinary or other "below-the-line" items that require separate disclosure). "One-line consolidation" also means that a parent-company/investor's income and stockholders' equity are the same when a subsidiary company/investee is accounted for under a complete and correct application of the equity method and when the financial statements of a parent company and subsidiary are consolidated. Consolidated financial statements show the same income and the same net assets but include the details of revenues and expenses and assets and liabilities.

The equity method creates many complexities; in fact, it involves the same computational complexities encountered in preparing consolidated financial statements. For this reason, the equity method is the standard of parent-company accounting for its subsidiaries, and the one-line consolidation is integrated throughout the consolidation chapters of this book. This parallel one-line consolidation/consolidation coverage permits you to check your work just as practitioners do, by making alternative computations of such key financial statement items as consolidated net income and consolidated retained earnings.

Basic accounting procedures for applying the equity method are the same whether the investor has the ability to exercise significant influence over the investee (20% to 50% ownership) or the ability to control the investee (more than 50% ownership). This is important because investments of more than 50% are business combinations and are subjects to the provisions of *FASB Statement No. 141*. Thus, the accounting principles that apply to purchase business combinations also apply to accounting for investments of 20% to 100% under the equity method. The difference between the way combination provisions are applied in this chapter and the way they are applied in Chapter 1 arises because:

1. Both the investor and investee companies continue to exist as separate legal entities with their own accounting systems (an acquisition).
2. The equity method applies to only one of those entities—the investor company.
3. The investor's equity interest may range from 20% to 100%.

Equity Investments at Acquisition

Equity investments in voting common stock of other entities are subject to the provisions of *FASB Statement No. 141,* so we measure the investment cost by the cash disbursed or the fair value of other assets distributed or securities issued. Similarly, we charge direct costs of registering and issuing equity securities against additional paid-in capital, and we add other direct costs of acquisition to the acquisition cost. We enter the total investment cost in an investment account under the one-line consolidation concept.

Assume that Payne Company purchases 30% of Sloan Company's outstanding voting common stock on January 1 from existing stockholders for $2,000,000 cash plus 200,000 shares of Payne Company $10 par common stock with a market value of $15 per share. Additional cash costs of the equity interest consist of $50,000 for registration of the shares and $100,000 for consulting and advisory fees. Payne Company would record these events with the following journal entries (in thousands):

January 1

Investment in Sloan (+A)	5,000	
Common stock (+SE)		2,000
Additional paid-in capital (+SE)		1,000
Cash (−A)		2,000

To record acquisition of a 30% equity investment in
Sloan Company.

January 1

Investment in Sloan (+A)	100	
Additional paid-in capital (−SE)	50	
Cash (−A)		150

To record additional direct costs of purchasing a 30%
equity interest in Sloan.

Under a one-line consolidation, these entries can be made without knowledge of book value or fair value of Sloan Company's assets and liabilities.

Assignment of Excess Cost over Underlying Equity

Information regarding the individual assets and liabilities of Sloan Company at the time of the purchase is important because subsequent accounting under the equity method entails accounting for any differences between the investment cost and the underlying equity in the net assets of the investee.

Assume that the following book value and fair value information for Sloan Company at December 31 is available (in thousands):

	Book Value	Fair Value
Cash	$ 1,500	$ 1,500
Receivables—net	2,200	2,200
Inventories	3,000	4,000
Other current assets	3,300	3,100
Equipment—net	5,000	8,000
Total assets	$15,000	$18,800
Accounts payable	$ 1,000	$ 1,000
Note payable, due in five years	2,000	1,800
Common stock	10,000	
Retained earnings	2,000	
Total liabilities and stockholders' equity	$15,000	

EXHIBIT 2-1

Schedule for
Allocating the
Excess of
Investment Cost
over the Book Value
of the Interest
Acquired

PAYNE COMPANY AND ITS 30%-OWNED EQUITY INVESTEE, SLOAN COMPANY (IN THOUSANDS)

Investment in Sloan		$5,100
Book value of the interest acquired		
(30% × $12,000,000 equity of Sloan)		(3,600)
Total excess of cost over book value acquired		$1,500

Assignment to Identifiable Net Assets and Goodwill

	Fair Value	−	Book Value	×	% Interest Acquired	=	Amount Assigned
Inventories	$4,000		$3,000		30%		$ 300
Other current assets	3,100		3,300		30		(60)
Equipment	8,000		5,000		30		900
Note payable	1,800		2,000		30		60
Total assigned to identifiable net assets							1,200
Remainder assigned to goodwill							300
Total excess of cost over book value acquired							$1,500

The underlying equity in the net assets of Sloan Company is $3,600,000 (30% of the $12,000,000 book value of Sloan Company's net assets), and the difference between the investment cost and the underlying equity is $1,500,000. The investor assigns this difference to the identifiable assets and liabilities based on their fair values and allocates the remaining difference to goodwill. Exhibit 2-1 illustrates the assignment to identifiable net assets and goodwill.

Payne Company does not record separately the asset and liability information given in Exhibit 2-1. Instead, Payne records the $1,500,000 excess cost over underlying equity in its Investment in Sloan account. Under the equity method of accounting, we eliminate this difference by periodic charges (debits) and credits to income from the investment and by equal charges or credits to the investment account. Thus, the original difference between investment cost and book value acquired disappears over the remaining lives of identifiable assets and liabilities. Exceptions arise for land, goodwill, and intangible assets having an indeterminate life, which are not amortized under the provisions of *FASB Statement No. 142.*

We determined the $300,000 assigned to goodwill in Exhibit 2-1 as a remainder of the total excess over amounts assigned to identifiable assets and liabilities. However, we can also compute the amount as the excess of the investment cost of $5,100,000 over the $4,800,000 fair value of Sloan's net assets acquired (30% × $16,000,000). We consider the difference as goodwill (or negative goodwill) if it cannot be related to identifiable assets and liabilities.

Recall from our discussion in Chapter 1 that, under provisions of *FASB Statement No. 142,* firms do not amortize goodwill and other intangible assets that have an indeterminate life. Instead, we review such assets for impairment on a periodic basis. We write these assets down when impairment losses become evident.

FASB Statement No. 142 also applies to equity method accounting. However, the impairment test differs, according to paragraph 40:

> *[Equity method goodwill] shall not be amortized. However, equity method goodwill shall not be tested for impairment in accordance with this Statement. Equity method investments shall continue to be reviewed for impairment in accordance with paragraph 19(h) of Opinion 18.*

APB Opinion No. 18 (paragraph 19h) requires that "A loss in value of an investment which is other than a temporary decline should be recognized."

Accounting for Excess of Investment Cost over Book Value Acquired

Assume that Sloan Company pays dividends of $1,000,000 on July 1 and reports net income of $3,000,000 for the year. The excess cost over book value acquired is amortized as follows:

	Amortization Rates
Excess allocated to:	
Inventories—sold in the current year	100%
Other current assets—disposed of in the current year	100%
Equipment—depreciated over 20 years	5%
Note payable—due in 5 years	20%

Payne Company makes the following entries under a one-line consolidation to record its dividends and income from Sloan:

July 1

Cash (+A)	300	
Investment in Sloan (−A)		300

Dividends

To record dividends received from Sloan
($1,000,000 × 30%).

December 31

Investment in Sloan (+A)	900	
Income from Sloan (R, +SE)		900

% of Net Inc

To record equity in income of Sloan
($3,000,000 × 30%).

December 31

Income from Sloan (E, −SE)	300	
Investment in Sloan (−A)		300

To record write-off of excess allocated to inventory
items that were sold in the current year.

December 31

Investment in Sloan (+A)	60	
Income from Sloan (R, +SE)		60

Adj of excess cost over book value items

To record income credit for overvalued other current
assets disposed of in the current year.

December 31

Income from Sloan (E, −SE)	45	
Investment in Sloan (−A)		45

To record depreciation on excess allocated to
undervalued equipment with a 20-year remaining
useful life ($900,000 ÷ 20 years).

December 31

Income from Sloan (E, −SE)	12	
Investment in Sloan (−A)		12

To amortize the excess allocated to the overvalued
note payable over the remaining life of the note
($60,000 ÷ 5 years).

The last five journal entries all involve the income and investment accounts, so Payne could record its income from Sloan in a single entry at December 31, as follows:

Investment in Sloan (+A)	603	
Income from Sloan (R, +SE)		603
To record equity income from 30% investment		
in Sloan calculated as follows:		

Equity in Sloan's reported income ($3,000,000 × 30%)	$900
Amortization of excess cost over book value:	
Inventories sold in the current year ($300,000 × 100%)	(300)
Other current assets sold in the current year ($60,000 × 100%)	60
Equipment ($900,000 × 5% depreciation rate)	(45)
Note payable ($60,000 × 20% amortization rate)	(12)
Total investment income from Sloan	$603

(handwritten: 297)

Payne Company reports its investment in Sloan at December 31 on one line of its balance sheet at $5,403,000 (see the following summary), and its income from Sloan at $603,000 on one line of its income statement. Sloan's net assets (stockholders' equity) increased by $2,000,000 to $14,000,000, and Payne's share of this underlying equity is 30%, or $4,200,000. The $1,203,000 difference between the investment balance and the underlying equity at December 31 represents the unamortized excess of investment cost over book value acquired. Confirm this amount by subtracting the $297,000 net amortization from the original excess of $1,500,000.

Here is a summary of Payne's equity method investment account activity:

(handwritten:
1,500,000
− 297,000
‾‾‾‾‾‾‾‾
1,203,000
)

January 1	Initial cost	$5,000,000
January 1	Additional direct costs	100,000
July 1	Dividends received	(300,000)
December 31	Recognize 30% of Sloan's net income	900,000
December 31	Write off excess allocated to inventory	(300,000)
December 31	Record income from Sloan's overvalued current assets sold in the current year	60,000
December 31	Additional equipment depreciation	(45,000)
December 31	Amortize note payable excess	(12,000)
December 31	Ending balance	$5,403,000

If the full $1,500,000 excess has been amortized (or written off as an impairment loss in the case of goodwill), the investment balance will equal its underlying book value minus 30% of the stockholders' equity of Sloan. A summary of these observations follows (in thousands):

	Stockholders' Equity of Sloan (A)	Underlying Equity (30% of Sloan's Equity) (B)	Investment in Sloan Account Balance (C)	Unamortized Cost/ Book Value (C − B)
January 1	$12,000	$3,600	$5,100	$1,500
Dividends, July	(1,000)	(300)	(300)	—
Income	3,000	900	900	—
Amortization	—	—	(297)	(297)
December 31	$14,000	$4,200	$5,403	$1,203

Excess of Book Value Acquired over Investment Cost

The book value of the interest acquired in an investee corporation may be greater than the investment cost. This situation indicates that the identifiable net assets of the investee corporation are overvalued or that the interest was acquired at a bargain price. If the total excess relates to overvalued assets (in other words, investment cost is equal to fair value), the excess is assigned to reduce the specific assets that are overvalued. However, if identifiable net assets are recorded at their fair values, the excess of fair value (and book value) of the interest acquired over investment cost is negative goodwill. Negative goodwill is assigned to reduce noncurrent assets other than marketable securities, as explained in Chapter 1.

Amounts assigned to reduce specific assets are amortized over the assets' remaining useful lives. The income effect of such amortization under a one-line consolidation is the reverse of the goodwill situation that reduces income and investment account balances. That is, both the investment and investment income accounts of the investor corporation increase when an excess of book value over cost is amortized.

To illustrate, assume that Post Corporation purchases 50% of the outstanding voting common stock of Taylor Corporation on January 1 for $40,000. A summary of the changes in Taylor's stockholders' equity during the year appears as follows (in thousands):

Stockholders' equity January 1	$100
Add: Income	20
Deduct: Dividends paid July 1	(5)
Stockholders' equity December 31	$115

The $10,000 excess of book value acquired over investment cost ($100,000 × 50% − $40,000) was due to inventory items and equipment that were overvalued on Taylor's books. Taylor's January 1 inventory was overvalued by $2,000 and was sold in December. The remaining $18,000 overvaluation related to equipment with a 10-year remaining useful life from January 1. No goodwill or negative goodwill results because the $40,000 cost is equal to fair value acquired (50% × $80,000).

The assignment of the difference between book value acquired and investment cost is as follows (in thousands):

Cost of the investment in Taylor	$ 40
Less: Underlying book value of Post's 50% interest in Taylor ($100,000 stockholders' equity × 50%)	(50)
Excess book value over cost	$(10)
Excess assigned to:	
Inventories ($2,000 overvaluation × 50% owned)	$ (1)
Equipment ($18,000 overvaluation × 50% owned)	(9)
Excess book value over cost	$(10)

Journal entries to account for Post Corporation's investment in Taylor Corporation are as follows:

January 1

Investment in Taylor (+A)	40	
Cash (−A)		40

    To record purchase of 50% of Taylor's outstanding voting stock.

July 1

Cash (+A)	2.5	
Investment in Taylor (−A)		2.5

    To record dividends received ($5,000 × 50%).

December 31

Investment in Taylor (+A)	10	
Income from Taylor (R, +SE)		10

    To recognize equity in the income of Taylor ($20,000 × 50%).

December 31

Investment in Taylor (+A)	1.9	
Income from Taylor (R, +SE)		1.9

    To amortize excess of book value over investment cost assigned to:

Inventory ($1,000 × 100%)	$ 1
Equipment ($9,000 × 10%)	.9
Total	$ 1.9

Because assets were purchased at less than book value, Post reports investment income from Taylor of $11,900 ($10,000 + $1,900) and an Investment in Taylor balance at December 31 of $49,400. Amortization of the excess of book value over investment cost increases Post's Investment in Taylor balance by $1,900 during the year.

Here is a summary of the equity method investment account activity:

January 1	Initial cost	$40,000
July 1	Dividends received	(2,500)
December 31	Recognize 50% of Taylor's net income	10,000
December 31	Amortization of excess of book value over investment cost	1,900
December 31	Ending balance	$49,400

Negative Goodwill

Assume that Post Corporation also acquires a 25% interest in Saxon Corporation for $110,000 on January 1, at which time Saxon's net assets consist of the following (in thousands):

	Book Value	Fair Value	Excess Fair Value
Inventories	$240	$260	$20
Other current assets	100	100	
Equipment—net	50	50	
Buildings—net	140	200	60
	530	610	
Less: Liabilities	130	130	
Net assets	$400	$480	$80

Saxon's net income and dividends for the year are $60,000 and $40,000, respectively. The undervalued inventory items were sold during the year, and the buildings and equipment each had four-year remaining useful lives when Post acquired its 25% interest. Exhibit 2-2 illustrates the assignment of the excess cost over book value.

In reviewing Exhibit 2-2, notice that the excess cost over book value is first assigned to fair values of identifiable net assets, after which the negative goodwill is reassigned to reduce noncurrent assets other than marketable securities. Recall from Chapter 1 that had the negative goodwill reassignment been so large that it reduced noncurrent assets to zero, we would recognize any remaining amount as an extraordinary gain.

EXHIBIT 2-2

Schedule for Allocating Negative Goodwill

POST CORPORATION AND ITS 25%-OWNED EQUITY INVESTEE, SAXON CORPORATION (IN THOUSANDS)

Investment cost		$110
Book value acquired ($400,000 × 25%)		(100)
Excess cost over book value acquired		$ 10

	Assignment to Fair Value	Reassignment of Negative Goodwill	Final Assignment
Inventory ($20,000 × 25%)	$ 5		$ 5
Equipment—net	—	$(2)*	(2)
Buildings—net ($60,000 × 25%)	15	(8)*	7
Negative goodwill	(10)	10	
Excess cost over book value acquired	$10	0	$10

*Based on fair values: $50,000/$250,000 to equipment
$200,000/$250,000 to buildings

Journal entries for Post Corporation to account for its investment in Saxon Corporation follow:

January 1

Investment in Saxon (+A)	110	
Cash (−A)		110
To record purchase of a 25% interest in Saxon's voting stock.		

2006

Cash (+A)	10	
Investment in Saxon (−A)		10
To record dividends received ($40,000 × 25%).		

December 31

Investment in Saxon (+A)	8.75	
Income from Saxon (R, +SE)		8.75
To recognize investment income from Saxon computed as follows:		

25% of Saxon's $60,000 net income	$15,000
Excess allocated to inventories	(5,000)
Excess allocated to equipment ($2,000 ÷ 4 years)	500
Excess allocated to buildings ($7,000 ÷ 4 years)	(1,750)
	$ 8,750

Post Corporation's Investment in Saxon balance at December 31 is $108,750, and the underlying book value of the investment is $105,000 ($420,000 × 25%). The $3,750 difference consists of the $5,250 unamortized excess assigned to buildings less the $1,500 unamortized negative goodwill assigned to equipment.

INTERIM ACQUISITIONS OF AN INVESTMENT INTEREST

Accounting for equity investments becomes more specific when the firm makes acquisitions within an accounting period (interim acquisitions). Additional computations determine the underlying equity at the time of acquisition and the investment income for the year. We compute stockholders' equity of the investee company by adding income earned since the last statement date to the beginning stockholders' equity and subtracting dividends declared to the date of purchase. In accounting for interim acquisitions, we assume that income of the investee is earned proportionately throughout the year unless there is evidence to the contrary.

Assume that Petron Corporation acquires 40% of the voting common stock of Fairview Company for $80,000 on October 1. Fairview's net assets (owners' equity) at January 1 are $150,000, and it reports net income of $25,000 and declares $15,000 dividends on July 1. The book values of Fairview's assets and liabilities are equal to fair values on October 1, except for a building worth $60,000 and recorded at $40,000. The building has a 20-year remaining useful life from October 1. GAAP requires application of the equity method and assignment of any difference between investment cost and book value acquired first to identifiable assets and liabilities and then to goodwill.

The excess of Petron's investment cost over the book value of its 40% interest in Fairview is computed and assigned to identifiable assets and goodwill, as shown in Exhibit 2-3.

Journal entries on Petron's books to account for the 40% equity interest in Fairview for the current year are as follows (in thousands):

October 1

Investment in Fairview (+A)	80	
Cash (−A)		80
To record acquisition of 40% of Fairview's voting stock.		

PETRON CORPORATION AND ITS 40%-OWNED EQUITY INVESTEE, FAIRVIEW CORPORATION		
Investment cost		$80,000
Less: Share of Fairview equity on October 1		
Beginning equity	$150,000	
Add: Income to October 1	18,750	
Less: Dividends	(15,000)	
	153,750	
Times: Interest purchased	40%	(61,500)
Excess cost over book value		$18,500
Excess assigned to: Buildings [($60,000 − $40,000) × 40%]		$ 8,000
Goodwill (remainder)		10,500
Excess cost over book value		$18,500

EXHIBIT 2-3

Schedule for Allocating the Excess of Investment Cost over Book Value Acquired

December 31

Investment in Fairview (+A)	2.5	
Income from Fairview (R, +SE)		2.5
To record equity in Fairview's income		
(40% × $25,000 × 1/4 year).		

December 31

Income from Fairview (E, −SE)	.1	
Investment in Fairview (−A)		.1
To record amortization of excess of cost over book value		
allocated to the undervalued building		
($8,000 ÷ 20 years) × 1/4 year.		

At December 31, after the entries are posted, Petron's Investment in Fairview account will have a balance of $82,400 ($80,000 cost + $2,400 income). This investment account balance is $18,400 more than the $64,000 underlying book value of Petron's interest in Fairview on that date (40% × $160,000). The $18,400 consists of the original excess cost over book value acquired of $18,500 less the $100 amortized in the current year.

Here is a summary of Petron's equity method Investment in Fairview account activity:

October 1	Initial cost	$80,000
December 31	Recognize 40% of Fairview's net income for 1/4 year	2,500
December 31	Amortization of excess of cost over book value for 1/4 year	(100)
December 31	Ending balance	$82,400

Notice that we do not recognize 40% of the dividends declared and paid by Fairview in this example. The dividends were paid on July 1, prior to Petron's investment. Under the equity method, investors recognize dividends received, not their proportional share of total dividends declared and/or paid. Of course, if the investment is owned for the entire year, these amounts will be the same.

INVESTMENT IN A STEP-BY-STEP ACQUISITION

An investor may acquire the ability to exercise significant influence over the operating and financial policies of an investee corporation in a series of stock acquisitions, rather than in a single purchase. For example, the investor may acquire a 10% interest in an investee and later acquire another 10% interest. We account for the original 10% interest by the fair value/cost method until we reach a 20% interest. Then we adopt the equity method and adjust the investment and retained earnings accounts retroactively.

Assume that Hop Corporation acquires a 10% interest in Skip Corporation for $750,000 on January 2, 2006, and another 10% interest for $850,000 on January 2, 2007. The stockholders' equity of Skip Corporation on the dates of these acquisitions is as follows (in thousands):

	January 2, 2006	January 2, 2007
Capital stock	$5,000	$5,000
Retained earnings	2,000	2,500
Total stockholders' equity	$7,000	$7,500

Hop Corporation is not able to relate the excess of investment cost over book value acquired to identifiable net assets. Accordingly, the excess of cost over book value from each of the acquisitions is goodwill.

On January 2, 2007, when the second 10% is acquired, Hop Corporation adopts the equity method of accounting for its 20% interest. This requires converting the carrying value of the original 10% interest from its $750,000 cost to its correct carrying value on an equity basis. The entry to adjust the investment account of Hop Corporation is as follows (in thousands):

January 2, 2007

Investment in Skip (+A)	50	
Retained earnings (+SE)		50

To adjust the Investment in Skip account from a cost to an equity basis as follows: Share of Skip's retained earnings increase during 2006 of $50,000 [$500,000 × 10% interest held during the year] equals the retroactive adjustment from accounting change of $50,000.

Skip's $500,000 retained earnings increase for 2006 represents its income less dividends for 2006. Hop reports its share of dividends received from Skip as income under the cost method; therefore, Hop's income for 2006 under the equity method is greater by 10% of Skip's retained earnings increase for 2006.

Changes in the cost, equity, and consolidation methods of accounting for subsidiaries and investments are changes in the reporting entity that require restatement of prior-period financial statements if the effect is material.[6]

SALE OF AN EQUITY INTEREST

When an investor sells a portion of an equity investment that reduces its interest in the investee to below 20% or to less than a level necessary to exercise significant influence, the equity method of accounting is no longer appropriate for the remaining interest. We account for the investment under the fair value/cost method from this time forward, and the investment account balance after the sale becomes the new cost basis. We require no other adjustments, and the investor accounts for the investment under the fair value/cost method in the usual manner. Gain or loss from the equity interest sold is the difference between the selling price and the book value of the equity interest immediately before the sale.

---

[6] See *APB Opinion No. 20,* "Accounting Changes," paragraph 34.

To illustrate, Leighton Industries acquires 320,000 shares (a 40% interest) in Sergio Corporation on January 1, 2006, for $580,000. Sergio's stockholders' equity is $1,200,000, and the book values of its assets and liabilities equal their fair values. Leighton accounts for its investment in Sergio under the equity method during the years 2006 through 2009. At December 31, 2009, the balance of the investment account is $700,000, equal to 40% of Sergio's $1,500,000 stockholders' equity plus $100,000 goodwill.

On January 1, 2010, Leighton sells 80% of its holdings in Sergio (256,000 shares) for $600,000, reducing its interest in Sergio to 8% (40% × 20%). The book value of the interest sold is $560,000, or 80% of the $700,000 balance of the Investment in Sergio account. Leighton recognizes a gain on the sale of its interest in Sergio of $40,000 ($600,000 selling price less $560,000 book value of the interest sold). The balance of the Investment in Sergio account after the sale is $140,000 ($700,000 less $560,000 interest sold). Leighton determines that it can no longer exercise significant influence over Sergio, and accordingly, it switches to the fair value/cost method and accounts for its investment under the provisions of *FASB Statement No. 115*, with the $140,000 balance becoming the new cost basis of the investment.

STOCK PURCHASES DIRECTLY FROM THE INVESTEE

We have assumed up to now that the investor corporation purchased its shares from existing stockholders of the investee corporation. In that situation, the interest acquired was equal to the shares acquired divided by the investee's outstanding shares. If an investor purchases shares directly from the issuing corporation, however, we determine the investor's interest by the shares acquired divided by the shares outstanding after the investee issues the new shares.

Assume that Karl Corporation purchases 20,000 shares of previously unissued common stock directly from Master Corporation for $450,000 on January 1, 2007. Master's stockholders' equity at December 31, 2006, consists of $200,000 of $10 par common stock and $150,000 retained earnings.

We compute Karl's 50% interest in Master Corporation as follows:

A	Shares purchased by Karl		20,000 shares
B	Shares outstanding after new shares are issued:		
	Outstanding December 31, 2006	20,000	
	Issued to Karl	20,000	40,000 shares
	Karl's interest in Master: A/B = 50%		

The book value of the interest acquired by Karl is $400,000, which is determined by multiplying the 50% interest acquired by Master's $800,000 stockholders' equity immediately after the issuance of the additional 20,000 shares. Computations are as follows:

Master's stockholders' equity before issuance ($200,000 capital stock + $150,000 retained earnings)	$350,000
Sale of 20,000 shares to Karl	450,000
Master's stockholders' equity after issuance	800,000
Karl's percentage ownership	50%
Book value acquired by Karl	$400,000

INVESTEE CORPORATION WITH PREFERRED STOCK

The equity method applies to investments in common stock, and some adjustments in applying the equity method are necessary when an investee has preferred as well as common stock outstanding. These adjustments require the following:

1. Allocation of the investee corporation's stockholders' equity into preferred and common equity components upon acquisition in order to determine the book value of the common stock investment

2. Allocation of the investee's net income into preferred and common income components to determine the investor's share of the investee's income to common stockholders

Assume that Tech Corporation's stockholders' equity is $6,000,000 at the beginning of 2006 and $6,500,000 at the end of 2006. Its net income and dividends for 2006 are $700,000 and $200,000, respectively.

(Amounts in thousands)	January 1	December 31
10% cumulative preferred stock, $100 par	$1,000	$1,000
Common stock, $10 par	3,000	3,000
Other paid-in capital	500	500
Retained earnings	1,500	2,000
	$6,000	$6,500

If Mornet Corporation pays $2,500,000 on January 2, 2006, for 40% of Tech's outstanding common stock, the investment is evaluated as follows (in thousands):

Cost of 40% common interest in Tech		$2,500
Book value (and fair value) acquired:		
Stockholders' equity of Tech	$6,000	
Less: Preferred stockholders' equity	1,000	
Common stockholders' equity	5,000	
Percent acquired	40%	2,000
Goodwill		$ 500

The equity of preferred stockholders is equal to the par value of outstanding preferred stock, increased by the greater of any call or liquidating premium and by preferred dividends in arrears.

Mornet's income from Tech for 2006 from its 40% interest is computed as follows (in thousands):

Tech's net income for 2006	$700
Less: Preferred income ($1,000,000 × 10%)	100
Income to common	$600
Share of Tech's common income ($600,000` × 40%)	240

APB Opinion No. 18, paragraph 9k, provides that when an investee company has cumulative preferred stock outstanding, an investor in common stock computes its share of earnings or losses after deducting preferred dividends, whether or not preferred dividends are declared. Additional coverage of accounting matters related to investees with preferred stock outstanding is provided in Chapter 10.

EXTRAORDINARY ITEMS, CUMULATIVE-EFFECT-TYPE ADJUSTMENTS, AND OTHER CONSIDERATIONS

In accounting for a stock investment under the equity method, the investor corporation reports its share of the ordinary income of an investee on one line of its income statement. However, the one-line consolidation does not apply to the reporting of investment income when the investee corporation's income consists of extraordinary items or cumulative-effect-type adjustments. In this case, the investment income must be separated into its ordinary, extraordinary, and cumulative-effect components and reported accordingly.

Assume that Carl Corporation owns 40% of the outstanding stock of Homer Corporation and that Homer's income for 2006 consists of the following (in thousands):

Income from continuing operations before extraordinary item	$500
Extraordinary item—casualty loss (less applicable income taxes of $25,000)	(50)
Net income	$450

Carl records its investment income from Homer as follows:

Investment in Homer (+A)	180	
Casualty loss—Investee (E, −SE)	20	
Income from Homer (R, +SE)		200

To record investment income from Homer.

Carl reports the $200,000 income from Homer as investment income and reports the $20,000 casualty loss along with any extraordinary items that Carl may have had during the year. If Homer had a cumulative-effect-type adjustment, Carl would record it in similar fashion and report it along with Carl's cumulative-effect-type adjustments, if any. A gain or loss on an investee's disposal of a segment of a business would be treated similarly.

Other Requirements of the Equity Method

In reporting its share of earnings and losses of an investee under the equity method, an investor corporation must eliminate the effect of profits and losses on transactions between the investor and investee corporations until they are realized. This means adjusting the investment and investment income accounts as we have illustrated for identifiable net assets. Transactions of an investee that change the investor's share of the net assets of the investee corporation also require adjustments under the equity method of accounting. These and other complexities of the equity method are covered in subsequent chapters, along with related consolidation procedures. Chapter 10 covers preferred stock, earnings per share, and income tax considerations.

DISCLOSURES FOR EQUITY INVESTEES

The extent to which separate disclosure should be provided for equity investments depends on the significance (materiality) of such investments to the financial position and results of operations of the investor company. If equity investments are significant, the investor should disclose the following information, parenthetically or in financial statement notes or schedules.

1. The name of each investee and percentage of ownership in common stock
2. The accounting policies of the investor with respect to investments in common stock
3. The difference, if any, between the amount at which an investment is carried and the amount of underlying equity in net assets, including the accounting treatment of the difference

Additional disclosures for material equity investments include the aggregate value of each identified investment for which quoted market prices are available and summarized information regarding the assets, liabilities, and results of operations of the investees. Firms that have made these disclosures for nonconsolidated subsidiaries under *APB Opinion No. 18* are required to continue the disclosures under *FASB Statement No. 94,* even though the subsidiaries now are consolidated.

An excerpt from The Walt Disney Company and Subsidiaries' 2003 annual report is presented in Exhibit 2-4 to illustrate the disclosure requirements. Financial information is separately presented for Euro Disney and for all other significant equity investees as a group. Disney includes its share of the underlying net assets of these investees as "Investments" in the balance sheet and includes its share of the investees' net income in the income statement as "Equity in income of investees." The operating-activities section of Disney's consolidated statement of cash flows shows both "Equity in income of investees" and "Cash distributions from equity investees" as adjustments to net income.

Related-Party Transactions

FASB Statement No. 57, "Related Party Disclosures," explains that there is no presumption of arm's-length bargaining between related parties. The statement identifies material transactions between affiliated companies as related-party transactions requiring financial statements disclosure. Related-party transactions arise when one of the transacting parties has the ability to influence significantly the operations of the other. The required disclosures include the following:

1. The nature of the relationship
2. A description of the transaction
3. The dollar amounts of the transaction and any change from the previous period in the method used to establish the terms of the transaction for each income statement presented
4. Amounts due to or due from related parties at the balance sheet date for each balance sheet presented

EXHIBIT 2-4

Financial Statement
Disclosures for
Equity Investments

THE WALT DISNEY COMPANY AND SUBSIDIARIES 2003 ANNUAL REPORT NOTES TO CONSOLIDATED FINANCIAL STATEMENTS: NOTE 4, INVESTMENTS (PARTIAL) (IN MILLIONS OF DOLLARS)

A summary of U.S. GAAP financial information for Euro Disney as of and for the years ended September 30, 2003, is as follows:

	2003	2002	2001
Results of Operations:			
Revenues	$ 1,077	$ 909	$ 905
Costs and expenses	(1,032)	(891)	(871)
Net interest expense and other	(101)	(75)	(80)
Loss before income taxes	(56)	(57)	(46)
Income taxes	—	—	—
Net loss	$ (56)	$ (57)	$ (46)
Balance Sheet:			
Cash and cash equivalents	$ 103	$ 66	
Other current assets	191	199	
Total current assets	294	265	
Parks, resorts, and other property, net	2,951	2,687	
Other noncurrent assets	128	60	
	$ 3,373	$ 3,012	
Accounts payable and other accrued liabilities	$ 421	$ 404	
Current portion of borrowings	2,528	47	
Other current liabilities	66	81	
Total current liabilities	3,015	532	
Borrowings	—	2,126	
Other noncurrent liabilities	289	244	
Shareholders' equity	69	110	
	$ 3,373	$ 3,012	

A summary of combined financial information for the other equity investments (including Hong Kong Disneyland) is as follows:

	2003	2002	2001
Results of Operations:			
Revenues	$ 3,458	$ 3,111	$ 3,161
Net income	$ 825	$ 635	$ 763
Balance Sheet:			
Current assets	$ 1,924	$ 1,938	
Noncurrent assets	1,696	1,419	
	$ 3,620	$ 3,357	
Current liabilities	$ 907	$ 956	
Noncurrent liabilities	840	717	
Shareholders' equity	1,873	1,684	
	$ 3,373	$ 3,357	

CHEVRONTEXACO CORPORATION 2003 ANNUAL REPORT NOTE 14:
INVESTMENTS AND ADVANCES (PARTIAL) (IN MILLIONS OF DOLLARS)

Other Information. 'Sales and other operating revenues' on the Consolidated Statement of Income includes $6,308, $6,522 and $15,238 with affiliated companies for 2003, 2002 and 2001, respectively. 'Purchased crude oil and products' includes $1,740, $1,839 and $4,069 with affiliated companies for 2003, 2002 and 2001, respectively.

'Accounts and notes receivable' on the Consolidated Balance Sheet includes $827 and $615 due from affiliated companies at December 31, 2003 and 2002, respectively. 'Accounts payable' includes $118 and $161 due to affiliated companies at December 31, 2003 and 2002, respectively.

EXHIBIT 2-5

Related-Party Disclosures for Affiliates

Exhibit 2-5 illustrates related-party disclosures for affiliated companies for *ChevronTexaco Corporation*. ChevronTexaco's 2003 annual report identifies *Tengizchevroil, Equilan Enterprises LLC, Motiva Enterprises LLC, LG-Caltex Oil Corporation, Star Petroleum Refining Company Ltd., Caltex Australia Ltd., Chevron Phillips Chemical Company LLC,* and *Dynegy, Inc.*, as major equity method affiliated companies. ChevronTexaco's balance sheet lists "Investments and advances in equity method affiliates" totaling $12.319 billion (15.1% of total consolidated assets).

TESTING GOODWILL FOR IMPAIRMENT

LEARNING OBJECTIVE 6

Chapter 1 introduced the new rules for goodwill and other intangible assets under *FASB Statement of Financial Accounting Standards No. 142*. This section provides additional discussion and examples of impairment tests under the new standard.

FASB Statement No. 142 eliminates former requirements for amortization of goodwill and certain other intangible assets having an indefinite useful life. Recorded intangible assets having a definite useful life continue to be amortized over that life. If an intangible asset has a definite, but unknown, useful life, firms should amortize over the best estimate of useful life.

Those intangibles (including goodwill) having an indefinite life are not amortized, but rather are subject to annual review and testing for impairment. The focus here is impairment testing and reporting for goodwill.

The new rules can dramatically affect firms' reported earnings in one of two ways. First, some firms may adopt the new standard and recognize significant impairment losses on initial adoption. Firms may find this option appealing because FASB Statement No. 142 requires that impairment losses recorded in initial application be treated as a "cumulative effect of an accounting change." Under this approach, the loss would appear after the calculation of "income from operations." In subsequent periods, impairment losses would be included in calculating income from operations.

Second, firms will likely report higher future earnings. Firms will no longer report periodic expense charges for goodwill amortization. Further, any goodwill amounts written off upon initial adoption of the new standard cannot lead to future impairments.

Time Warner, Inc., (formerly *AOL Time Warner*) provides an example of significant goodwill and intangible asset impairment write-offs. In its 2003 annual report, the consolidated income statement includes "Impairment of goodwill and other intangible assets" of $318 million in calculating income from operations. This amount pales in comparison to the 2002 amounts. Operating income for 2002 included an impairment loss for goodwill and intangibles of $44.039 billion. Net income for 2002 included an additional cumulative effect of accounting changes of $(54.235) billion, due mostly to goodwill write-offs, and this number is net of tax. Note 2 to the financial statements, reproduced in part in Exhibit 2-6, provides additional detail on the impairments.

Add up the numbers and you discover that total goodwill impairments (including the discontinued operations) were $98.884 billlion in 2002, and an additional $1.418 billion in 2003. The note also discloses an $853 million impairment write-off for brands and trademarks at the Music segment. A review of Note 2 in Exhibit 2-6 discloses Time Warner's methods for the calculations of the impairment losses. To put this in perspective, Time Warner's total assets at December 31, 2001, were $208.5 billion; the impairment write-offs represent almost 50% of that amount. Time Warner points out, correctly, that these are noncash charges, however, this is still a lot of shareholder value wiped off the books.

Notice in the final paragraph of Exhibit 2-6 that the new rules improve Time Warner's earnings by approximately $5.7 billion in 2003. Goodwill and intangible amortization now stands at $640 million, compared with $6.366 billion in 2001. Future earnings will be similarly affected.

EXHIBIT 2-6

Write-offs of
Goodwill and
Intangible Asset
Impairments

TIME WARNER, INC., 2003 ANNUAL REPORT NOTE 2: GOODWILL AND INTANGIBLE ASSETS (PARTIAL) (IN MILLIONS OF DOLLARS)

As discussed in Note 1, in January 2002, Time Warner adopted FAS 142, which requires companies to stop amortizing goodwill and certain intangible assets with an indefinite useful life. Instead, FAS 142 requires that goodwill and intangible assets deemed to have an indefinite useful life be reviewed for impairment upon adoption of FAS 142 (January 1, 2002) and at least annually thereafter.

Upon adoption of FAS 142 in the first quarter of 2002, Time Warner recorded a non-cash charge of $49.403 billion to reduce the carrying value of goodwill. Excluded from this charge was an impairment of the former Music segment's goodwill of $4.796 billion. Such charge was non-operational in nature and was reflected as a cumulative effect of an accounting change in the accompanying consolidated statement of operations. In calculating the impairment charge, the fair value of the impaired reporting units underlying the segments was estimated using either a discounted cash flow methodology, market comparisons, recent comparable transactions, or a combination thereof. . . .

During the fourth quarter of 2002, the Company performed its annual impairment review for goodwill and recorded a non-cash charge of $44.039 billion, which was recorded as a component of operating income in the accompanying consolidated statement of operations. The $44.039 billion reflected the overall decline in market values and includes charges to reduce the carrying value of goodwill at the AOL segment ($33.489 billion) and Cable segment ($10.550 billion). . . . Excluded from this charge were impairments of the Music segment's goodwill of $646 million and brands and trademarks of $853 million, which are included in discontinued operations. The company determined during its annual impairment review for goodwill, which occurred in the fourth quarter of 2003, that no additional impairment existed.

During 2003, the Company recorded impairment losses of $318 million to reduce the carrying value of certain intangible assets of the Turner winter sports teams and certain goodwill and intangible assets of the Time Warner Book Group, which were recorded at the time of the America Online—Historic TW Merger. In addition, in December 2003, the Company recognized an impairment charge of approximately $1.1 billion to reduce the carrying value of the Music segment's intangible assets, which is included in discontinued operations. . . .

The Company recorded amortization expense of $640 million in 2003, compared to $557 million in 2002 and $6.366 billion in 2001. . . .

Time Warner is not alone in taking large goodwill and intangible asset impairment charges. *MCI, Inc.,* (formerly *WorldCom*) reported $5.7 billion in impairment charges in 2001 and an additional $400 million in 2002. *Corning's* 2002 annual report included a $294 million after-tax impairment charge for goodwill related to its telecommunications reporting unit. *E.I. Du Pont De Nemours* included a charge of $2.9 billion for the cumulative effect of adoption of the new goodwill impairment standard in its 2002 annual report. *Dillard's, Inc.,* the department store chain, reported a $530 million impairment charge in 2002. *Intel Corporation's* 2002 impairment loss was $617 million. A recent research study of 352 firms indicated that the average goodwill impairment loss upon adopting *SFAS No. 142* was $290.6 million.[7]

There is also still a lot of goodwill sitting on companies' balance sheets, which could potentially create future write-offs. *Ford Motor Company* includes $5.378 billion of goodwill for its automotive segments and another $769 million of goodwill for its financial services segment on the December 31, 2003, balance sheet. Note 7 to the financial statements discloses that goodwill impairment testing in 2003 required no adjustment; however, the firm wrote off approximately $1 billion when adopting *SFAS 142* in 2002. In its 2003 annual report, *Hewlett-Packard* discloses $14.894 billion of goodwill and another $4.356 billion of purchased intangible assets arising primarily from its acquisition of *Compaq Computer Corporation*.

Recognizing and Measuring Impairment Losses

The goodwill impairment test under *FASB Statement No. 142* is a two-step process. Firms must first compare carrying values (book values) to fair values at the business-reporting-unit level. Carrying value includes the goodwill amount. For purposes of applying the standard, the FASB defines the reporting unit as an operating segment or one level below an operating segment, as described in *FASB Statement of Financial Accounting Standards No. 131,* "Disclosures About Segments of an Enterprise and Related Information." Chapter 14 of the text covers *FASB Statement No. 131* in detail, including the definition of business reporting units.

If the reporting unit's fair value exceeds its carrying value, goodwill is deemed to be unimpaired. No further action is needed.

---

[7] Zining Li, Pervin K. Shroff, and Ramgopal Venkataraman. "Goodwill Impairment Loss: Causes and Consequences," unpublished working paper, University of Minnesota, April 2004.

If fair value is less than the carrying amount, then firms proceed to step 2, measurement and recognition of the impairment loss. Step 2 requires a comparison of the carrying amount of goodwill to its implied fair value. Firms should again make this comparison at the business-reporting-unit level. If the carrying amount exceeds the implied fair value of the goodwill, the firm must recognize an impairment loss for the difference. The loss amount cannot exceed the carrying amount of the goodwill. Firms cannot reverse previously recognized impairment losses.

Implied Fair Value of Goodwill

Firms should determine the implied fair value of goodwill in the same manner used to originally record the goodwill at the business combination date. Firms allocate the fair value of the reporting unit to all identifiable assets and liabilities, as if they had purchased the unit on the measurement date. Any excess fair value is the implied fair value of goodwill.

Assume that Paul Corporation owns 80% of Surly Corporation, which qualifies as a business reporting unit under *FASB Statement No. 142*. Paul carries goodwill of $5 million related to its investment in Surly. Paul would assess the implied fair value of goodwill as follows.

Paul first estimates that if it purchased its investment in Surly today, the total fair value of Surly would be $36.25 million, based on current market prices for Surly's shares. Paul's 80% investment would have a total fair value of $29 million. Paul allocates the total fair value to the identifiable assets and liabilities of Suny as shown (figures are in millions):

	Book Value	Fair Value
Current assets	$11.10	$12.85
Property, plant, and equipment	43.00	48.00
Patents	4.00	5.40
Current liabilities	(9.00)	(9.00)
Long-term liabilities	(26.00)	(26.00)
Net	$23.10	$31.35
80% of net fair value		$25.08

The fair value of Suny's identifiable assets and liabilities is $31.35 million. Paul's 80% interest would have a fair value of $25 million. Therefore, goodwill has an implied fair value of $4 million ($29 million less $25 million). Notice that goodwill applies only to Paul's 80% interest.

Because Paul's current carrying value for goodwill is $5 million and its implied fair value is only $4 million, Paul must record a goodwill impairment loss of $1 million. The carrying value of goodwill is adjusted to $4 million for purposes of future impairment testing. (If Paul's carrying value for goodwill had been less than $4 million, no impairment loss would have been recognized.)

Determining the Fair Value of the Reporting Unit

Fair values of assets and liabilities are the amounts at which they could be exchanged in an arm's-length transaction. Therefore, the fair value of a reporting unit is the amount for which it could be purchased or sold in a current transaction. The previous example assumed that a current quoted market price was available for Suny's shares. The FASB considers current market prices (in an active market) to be the most reliable indicator of fair value for a reporting unit.

Of course, these values will not always be available. If Paul owned 100% of Suny's common stock, there would no active market for Suny's shares. The same situation holds if Suny's shares are not publicly traded. In these cases the FASB suggests estimating fair values by using prices for similar assets and liabilities or by applying other valuation techniques. For example, Paul might estimate future cash flows from Suny's operations and apply present value techniques to estimate the value of the reporting unit. Paul might also employ earnings or revenue multiples techniques to estimate the fair value of Suny.

Firms must conduct the impairment test for goodwill at least annually. The FASB requires more-frequent impairment testing if any of the following events occurs:

- Significant adverse changes in legal factors or business climate
- Adverse regulatory actions or assessments
- New and unanticipated competition
- Loss of key personnel
- A more-likely-than-not expectation that a reporting unit or a significant portion of a reporting unit will be sold or disposed of

- Testing for the recoverability under *Statement 121* of a significant asset group within a reporting unit
- Recognition of a goodwill impairment loss of a subsidiary that is a component of the reporting unit

Reporting and Disclosures

FASB Statement No. 142 requires firms to report material aggregate amounts of goodwill as a separate line item on the balance sheet. Likewise, firms must show goodwill impairment losses separately in the income statement, as a component of income from continuing operations (unless the impairment relates to discontinued operations). Goodwill impairments from discontinued operations should be reported separately (net of income tax effects) in the discontinued operations section of the income statement.

FASB Statement No. 142 offers one additional reporting option. In the year of adoption of the new rules, firms may treat the initial application as a change in accounting principle. In other words, a large write-down in the year of adoption is excluded from income from continuing operations. The cumulative effect of a change in accounting principle is reported (net of income tax effects) after income from continuing operations under current GAAP.

Equity Method Investments

The previous discussion on goodwill impairment applies only to goodwill arising from purchase method business combinations (i.e., a parent company acquires a controlling interest in a subsidiary). *FASB Statement No. 142* also applies to goodwill reflected in investments reported under the equity method of accounting.

Once again, the new rules eliminate periodic amortization of goodwill, replacing that treatment with periodic tests for impairment. However, equity method investment impairment tests do not follow *FASB Statement No. 142*. Impairment tests for equity investments continue to follow the guidance provided in *APB Opinion No.* 18. Under those rules, impairment tests are to be performed based on fair value versus book value of the investment taken as a whole. An impairment loss may be recognized for the equity method investment, but equity method goodwill is not separately tested for impairment.

Potential Problems

The new FASB rules are straightforward in concept, but practical application may be difficult, especially in those cases in which quoted market prices are unavailable to value business reporting units. Alternative valuation methods are highly subjective.

The new rules also pose considerable problems for auditors. Fair value estimations will be very difficult to verify objectively. Auditors are also going to be faced with earnings-management issues for some clients. If a firm chooses to take a big bath by writing off large amounts of goodwill, the conservative nature of financial reporting makes it difficult to challenge managers' estimates.

SUMMARY

Exhibit 2-7 is a flow chart summary of accounting procedures for business investments. Investments in the voting common stock of an investee corporation are accounted for under the fair value/cost method if the investment does not give the investor an ability to exercise significant influence over the investee. Otherwise, investors should normally use the equity method (a one-line consolidation). In the absence of evidence to the contrary, a 20%-ownership test determines whether the investor has the ability to exercise significant influence over the investee.

The equity method is referred to as a one-line consolidation because its application produces the same net income and stockholders' equity for the investor as would result from consolidation of the financial statements of the investor and investee corporations. Under the one-line consolidation, the investment is reflected in a single amount on one line of the investor's balance sheet, and the investor reports income from the investee on one line of the investor's income statement, except when the investee's income includes extraordinary or cumulative-effect-type items.

As you can see in the flow chart in Exhibit 2-7, the equity method is equally applicable to investments accounted for under the purchase method. The flow chart also indicates that consolidated statements are generally required for investments in excess of 50% of the voting stock of the investee and that the one-line consolidation (equity method) is used in reporting investments of 20% to 50% in the investor's financial statements and in consolidated financial statements.

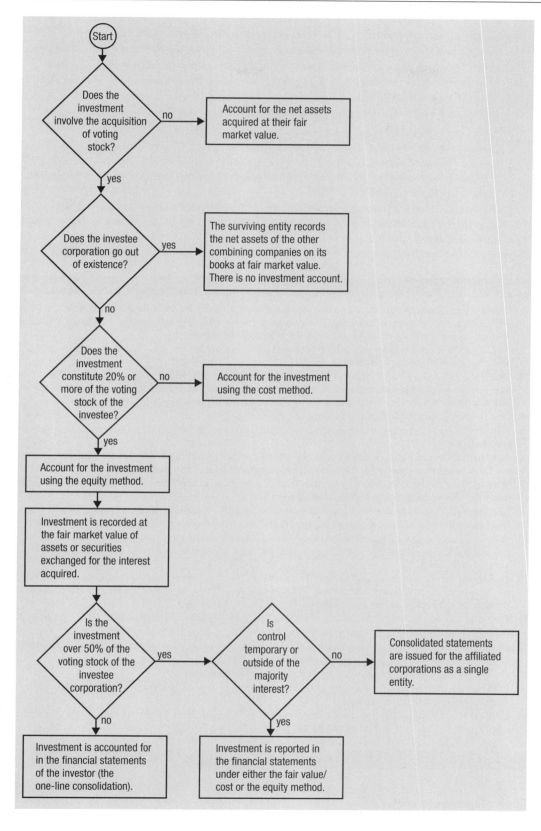

EXHIBIT 2-7

**Accounting for
Equity Investments
Generally**

NOTE TO THE STUDENT

In solving problems in the areas of business combinations, equity investments, and consolidations, we frequently must make assumptions about the nature of the difference between investment cost and book value of the net assets acquired, the timing of income earned within an accounting period, the period in which inventory items affecting intercompany investments are sold, and the source from which an equity interest is acquired. In the absence of evidence to the contrary, you should make the following assumptions:

1. *An excess of investment cost over book value of the net assets acquired is goodwill.*
2. *Goodwill is not amortized.*
3. *Income is earned evenly throughout each accounting period.*
4. *Inventory items on hand at the end of an accounting period are sold in the immediately succeeding fiscal period.*
5. *An equity interest is purchased from the stockholders of the investee company rather than directly from the investee corporation (that is, the total outstanding stock of the investee corporation does not change).*

QUESTIONS

1. How are the accounts of investor and investee companies affected when the investor acquires stock from stockholders of the investee company (for example, a New York Stock Exchange purchase)? When the investor acquires previously unissued stock directly from the investee?
2. Would goodwill arising from an equity investment of more than 20% be recorded separately on the books of the investor corporation? Explain.
3. Under the fair value/cost method of accounting for stock investments, an investor records dividends received from earnings accumulated after the investment is acquired as dividend income. How does an investor treat dividends received from earnings accumulated before an investment is acquired?
4. Describe the equity method of accounting.
5. Why is the equity method of accounting for equity investments frequently referred to as a one-line consolidation?
6. Is there a difference between the amount of a parent company's net income under the equity method and the consolidated net income for the same parent company and its subsidiaries?
7. What is the difference in reporting income from a subsidiary in the parent company's separate income statement and in consolidated financial statements?
8. Cite the conditions under which you would expect the balance of an equity investment account on a balance sheet date subsequent to acquisition to be equal to the underlying book value represented by that investment.
9. What accounting procedures or adjustments are necessary when an investor uses the cost method of accounting for an investment in common stock and later increases the investment such that the equity method is required?
10. Ordinarily, the income from an investment accounted for by the equity method is reported on one line of the investor company's income statement. When would more than one line of the income statement of the investor be required to report such income?
11. Describe the accounting adjustments needed when a 25% equity interest in an investee company is decreased to a 15% equity interest.
12. Does cumulative preferred stock in the capital structure of an investee affect the way that an investor company accounts for its 30% common stock interest? Explain.
13. Briefly outline the steps to calculate a goodwill impairment loss.
14. Is there any difference in computing goodwill impairment losses for a controlled subsidiary company versus an equity method investment?
15. Explain the reporting differences for ongoing goodwill impairment losses versus reporting an initial impairment loss upon adoption of *SFAS 142*.

EXERCISES

E 2-1

General questions

1. Indicators of an investor company's inability to exercise significant influence over an investee are provided in *FASB Interpretation No. 35*. Which of the following is *not* included among those indicators?
    a *Surrender of significant stockholder rights by agreement*
    b *Concentration of majority ownership*
    c *Failure to obtain representation on the investee's board*
    d *Inability to control the investee's operating policies*

2. A 20% common stock interest in an investee company:

  a *Must be accounted for under the equity method*

  b *Is accounted for by the cost method because over 20% is required for the application of the equity method*

  c *Is presumptive evidence of an ability to exercise significant influence over the investee*

  d *Enables the investor to apply either the cost or the equity method*

3. The cost of a 25% interest in the voting stock of an investee that is recorded in the investment account includes:

  a *Cash disbursed, the book value of other assets given or securities issued, and additional direct and indirect costs of obtaining the investment, other than the cost of registering and issuing equity securities*

  b *Cash disbursed, the book value of other assets given or securities issued, and additional direct costs of obtaining the investment and registering and issuing equity securities*

  c *Cash disbursed, the fair value of other assets given or securities issued, and additional direct costs of obtaining the investment, other than the cost of registering and issuing equity securities*

  d *Cash disbursed, the fair value of other assets given or securities issued, and additional direct costs of obtaining the investment and registering and issuing equity securities*

4. The underlying equity of an investment at acquisition:

  a *Is recorded in the investment account under the equity method*

  b *Minus the cost of the investment is assigned to goodwill or negative goodwill*

  c *Is equal to the fair value of the investee's net assets times the percentage acquired*

  d *Is equal to the book value of the investee's net assets times the percentage acquired*   ← Is this right?

5. Jarret Corporation is a 25%-owned equity investee of Marco Corporation. During the current year, Marco receives $12,000 in dividends from Jarret. How does the $12,000 dividend affect Marco's financial position and results of operations?

  a *Increases assets*

  b *Decreases investment*

  c *Increases income*

  d *Decreases income*

E 2-2

[AICPA adapted] General problems

1. Investor Company owns 40% of Alimand Corporation. During the calendar year, Alimand had net earnings of $100,000 and paid dividends of $10,000. Investor mistakenly recorded these transactions using the cost method rather than the equity method of accounting. What effect would this have on the investment account, net earnings, and retained earnings, respectively?

  a *Understate, overstate, overstate*

  b *Overstate, understate, understate*

  c *Overstate, overstate, overstate*

  d *Understate, understate, understate*

Cost Method
Cash   4,000
* DIV Inc   4,000*

Equity → Cash   4,000
*   Investment In Alimand 36,000*
*   Investment Inc   40,000*

2. The corporation exercises control over an affiliate in which it holds a 40% common stock interest. If its affiliate completed a fiscal year profitably but paid *no* dividends, how would this affect the investor corporation?

  a *Result in an increased current ratio*

  b *Result in increased earnings per share*

  c *Increase several turnover ratios*

  d *Decrease book value per share*

3. An investor uses the cost method to account for an investment in common stock. A portion of the dividends received this year were in excess of the investor's share of investee's earnings after the date of the investment. The amount of dividends revenue that should be reported in the investor's income statement for this year would be:

  a *Zero*

  b *The total amount of dividends received this year*

  c *The portion of the dividends received this year that were in excess of the investor's share of investee's earnings after the date of investment*

  d *The portion of the dividends received this year that were not in excess of the investor's share of investee's earnings after the date of investment*

4. On January 1 Grade Company paid $300,000 for 20,000 shares of Medium Company's common stock, which represents a 15% investment in Medium. Grade does not have the ability to exercise significant influence over Medium. Medium declared and paid a dividend of $1 per share to its stockholders during the year. Medium reported net income of $260,000 for the year ended December 31. The balance in Grade's balance sheet account "Investment in Medium Company" at December 31 should be

  a *$280,000*

  b *$300,000*

  c *$319,000*

  d *$339,000*

$260,000 Net Inc
*   × 15%*
$39,000 Portion of Inc

$20,000 Dividend

5. On January 2, 2006, Troquel Corporation bought 15% of Zafacon Corporation's capital stock for $30,000. Troquel accounts for this investment by the cost method. Zafacon's net income for the years ended December 31, 2006, and December 31, 2007, were $10,000 and $50,000, respectively. During 2007 Zafacon declared a dividend of $70,000. No dividends were declared in 2006. How much should Troquel show on its 2007 income statement as income from this investment?

   a $1,575

   b $7,500

   c $9,000

   d $10,500

   Net Inc $60,000 × 15% = 9,000
   Dividend $70,000 × 15% = 10,500
   Diff   1,500

6. Pare purchased 10% of Tot Company's 100,000 outstanding shares of common stock on January 2 for $50,000. On December 31, Pare purchased an additional 20,000 shares of Tot for $150,000. There was no goodwill as a result of either acquisition, and Tot had not issued any additional stock during the year. Tot reported earnings of $300,000 for the year. What amount should Pare report in its December 31 balance sheet as investment in Tot?

   a $170,000

   b $200,000

   c $230,000

   d $290,000

   10,000 shares → $50,000
   20,000 shares → $150,000
   Cost = 200,000 = 30%
   Net Inc = $300,000 × 10% = $30,000

7. On January 1, Point purchased 10% of Iona Company's common stock. Point purchased additional shares, bringing its ownership up to 40% of Iona's common stock outstanding, on August 1. During October, Iona declared and paid a cash dividend on all of its outstanding common stock. How much income from the Iona investment should Point's income statement report?

   a **10% of Iona's income for January 1 to July 31, plus 40% of Iona's income for August 1 to December 31**

   b **40% of Iona's income for August 1 to December 31 only**

   c **40% of Iona's income**

   d **Amount equal to dividends received from Iona**

8. On January 2, Kean Company purchased a 30% interest in Pod Company for $250,000. On this date, Pod's stockholders' equity was $500,000. The carrying amounts of Pod's identifiable net assets approximated their fair values, except for land, whose fair value exceeded its carrying amount by $200,000. Pod reported net income of $100,000 and paid no dividends. Kean accounts for this investment using the equity method. In its December 31 balance sheet, what amount should Kean report as investment in subsidiary?

   a $210,000

   b $220,000

   c $270,000

   d $280,000

   Equity 500,000
   Land   200,000
   Fair Value 700,000 × 30% = 210,000
   Paid   250,000
   Goodwill 40,000

   Cost $250,000
   Net Inc   30,000 (100,000 × 30%)
   *   280,000*

... and goodwill on investment acquired directly from

...'s equity at December 31 consisted of the following (in thousands):

...,000 shares issued and outstanding	$ 600
...l	150
	250
...uity	$1,000

...n purchased 20,000 previously unissued shares of Trevor stock directly

...centage ownership in Trevor.

...n's investment in Trevor.

...nvestment Carson Corporation pays $600,000 for a 30% interest in ...e book value of Medley's net assets equals fair value. Information relating

	December 31, 2006	December 31, 2007
Capital stock, $1 par	$ 600	$ 600
Retained earnings	400	500
Total stockholders' equity	$1,000	$1,100
Medley's net income earned evenly throughout 2007		$200
Medley's dividends for 2007 (paid $50,000 on March 1 and $50,000 on September 1)		$100

REQUIRED: Calculate Carson's income from Medley for 2007.

E 2-5

Calculate income and investment balance allocation of excess to undervalued assets

Dokey Company acquired a 30% interest in Oakey on January 1 for $2,000,000 cash. Dokey assigned the $500,000 cost over book value of the interest acquired to the following assets:

Inventories	$100,000 (sold in the current year)
Building	$200,000 (4-year remaining life at January 1)
Goodwill	$200,000

During the year Oakey reported net income of $800,000 and paid $200,000 dividends.

REQUIRED

1. Determine Dokey's income from Oakey.
2. Determine the December 31 balance of the Investment in Oakey account.

E 2-6

Journal entry to record income from investee with loss from discontinued operations

Martin Corporation purchased a 40% interest in Neighbors Corporation for $500,000 on January 1, 2006, at book value, when Neighbors's assets and liabilities were recorded at their fair values. During 2006, Neighbors reported net income of $300,000 as follows (in thousands):

Income from continuing operations	$350
Less: Loss from discontinued operations	50
Net income	$300

REQUIRED: Prepare the journal entry on Martin Corporation's books to recognize income from the investment in Neighbors for 2006.

E 2-7

General problems

1. On January 3, 2006, Harrison Company purchases a 15% interest in Bennett Corporation's common stock for $50,000 cash. Harrison accounts for the investment using the cost method. Bennett's net income for 2006 is $20,000, but it declares no dividends. In 2007, Bennett's net income is $80,000, and it declares dividends of $120,000. What is the correct balance of Harrison's Investment in Bennett account at December 31, 2007?

   a *$47,000*
   b *$50,000*
   c *$62,000*
   d *$65,000*

2. Screwsbury Corporation's stockholders' equity at December 31, 2006, follows (in thousands):

Capital stock, $100 par	$3,000
Additional paid-in capital	500
Retained earnings	500
Total stockholders' equity	$4,000

   On January 3, 2007, Screwsbury sells 10,000 shares of previously unissued $100 par common stock to Pannell Corporation for $1,400,000. On this date the recorded book values of Screwsbury's assets and liabilities equal their fair values. Goodwill from Pannell's investment in Screwsbury at the date of purchase is:

   a *0*
   b *$50,000*
   c *$300,000*
   d *$400,000*

3. On January 1, Leighton Company paid $300,000 for a 20% interest in Monroe Corporation's voting common stock, at which time Monroe's stockholders' equity consisted of $600,000 capital stock and $400,000 retained earnings. Leighton was not able to exercise any influence over the operations of Monroe and accounted for its investment in Monroe using the cost method. During the year, Monroe had net income of $200,000 and paid dividends of $150,000. The balance of Leighton's Investment in Monroe account at December 31 is:

   a *$330,000*
   b *$310,000*
   c *$307,500*
   d *$300,000*

4. Jollytime Corporation owns a 40% interest in Krazy Products acquired several years ago at book value. Krazy Products' income statement contains the following information (in thousands):

Income before extraordinary item	$200
Extraordinary loss	50
Net income	$150

Jollytime should report income from Krazy Products in its income from continuing operations at:

a $20,000

b $60,000

c $80,000

d $100,000

E 2-8

Calculate investment balance four years after acquisition Raython Corporation owns a 40% interest in the outstanding common stock of Treaton Corporation, having acquired its interest for $2,400,000 on **January 1, 2006,** when Treaton's stockholders' equity was $4,000,000. The cost/book value differential was allocated to inventories that were undervalued by $100,000 and sold in 2006, to equipment with a four-year remaining life that was undervalued by $200,000, and to goodwill for the remainder.

The balance of Treaton's stockholders' equity at **December 31, 2010,** is $5,500,000, and all changes therein are the result of income earned and dividends paid.

REQUIRED: Determine the balance of Raython's investment in Treaton account at December 31, 2010.

E 2-9

Calculate income and investment balance when investee capital structure includes preferred stock Runner Company had net income of $400,000 and paid dividends of $200,000 during 2007. Runner's stockholders' equity on December 31, 2006, and December 31, 2007, is summarized as follows (in thousands):

	December 31, 2006	December 31, 2007
10% cumulative preferred stock, $100 par	$ 300	$ 300
Common stock, $1 par	1,000	1,000
Additional paid-in capital	2,200	2,200
Retained earnings	500	700
Stockholders' equity	$4,000	$4,200

On January 2, 2007, Nickie Corporation purchased 300,000 common shares of Runner at $4 per share and also paid $50,000 direct costs of acquiring the investment.

REQUIRED: Determine (1) Nickie's income from Runner for 2007 and (2) the balance of the Investment in Runner account at December 31, 2007.

E 2-10

Calculate income and investment balance for midyear investment Arbor Corporation acquired 25% of Tree Corporation's outstanding common stock on October 1, for $600,000. A summary of Tree's adjusted trial balances on this date and at December 31 follows (in thousands):

	December 31	October 1
Debits		
Current assets	$ 500	$ 250
Plant assets—net	1,500	1,550
Expenses (including cost of goods sold)	800	600
Dividends (paid in July)	200	200
	$3,000	$2,600
Credits		
Current liabilities	$ 300	$ 200
Capital stock (no change during the year)	1,000	1,000
Retained earnings January 1	500	500
Sales	1,200	900
	$3,000	$2,600

Arbor uses the equity method of accounting. No information is available concerning the fair values of Tree's assets and liabilities.

REQUIRED

1. Determine Arbor's investment income from Tree Corporation for the year ended December 31.

2. Compute the correct balance of Arbor's investment in Tree account at December 31.

E 2-11

Adjust investment account and determine income when additional investment qualifies for equity method of accounting Summary balance sheet and income information for Twizzle Company for two years is as follows (in thousands):

	January 1, 2006	December 31, 2006	December 31, 2007
Current assets	$100	$120	$150
Plant assets	400	480	500
	$500	$600	$650
Liabilities	$ 80	$100	$100
Capital stock	300	300	300
Retained earnings	120	200	$250
	$500	$600	$650

	2004	2005
Net income	$200	$100
Dividends	120	50

On January 2, 2006, Ratterman Corporation purchases 10% of Twizzle Company for $50,000 cash, and it accounts for its investment in Twizzle using the fair value method. On December 31, 2006, the fair value of all of Twizzle's stock is $1,000,000. On January 2, 2007, Ratterman purchases an additional 10% interest in Twizzle stock for $100,000 and adopts the equity method to account for the investment. The fair values of Twizzle's assets and liabilities were equal to their book values as of the time of both stock purchases.

REQUIRED

1. Prepare a journal entry to adjust the Investment in Twizzle account to an equity basis on January 2, 2007.

2. Determine Ratterman's income from Twizzle for 2007.

E 2-12

Journal entries (investment in previously unissued stock) The stockholders' equity of Tall Corporation at December 31, 2006, was $380,000, consisting of the following (in thousands):

Capital stock, $10 par (24,000 shares outstanding)	$240
Additional paid-in capital	60
Retained earnings	80
Total stockholders' equity	$380

On January 1, 2007, Tall Corporation, which was in a tight working capital position, sold 12,000 shares of previously unissued stock to River Corporation for $250,000. All of Tall's identifiable assets and liabilities were recorded at their fair values on this date except for a building with a 10-year remaining useful life that was undervalued by $60,000. During 2007, Tall Corporation reported net income of $120,000 and paid dividends of $90,000.

REQUIRED: Prepare all journal entries necessary for River Corporation to account for its investment in Tall for 2007.

E 2-13

Prepare journal entries and income statement, and determine investment account balance BIP Corporation paid $195,000 for a 30% interest in Crown Corporation on December 31, 2006, when Crown's equity consisted of $500,000 capital stock and $200,000 retained earnings. The price paid by BIP reflected the fact that Crown's inventory (on a FIFO basis) was overvalued by $50,000. The overvalued inventory items were sold in 2007.

During 2006 Crown paid dividends of $100,000 and reported income as follows (in thousands):

Income before extraordinary items	$170
Extraordinary loss (net of tax effect)	20
Net income	$150

REQUIRED:

1. Prepare all journal entries necessary to account for BIP's investment in Crown for 2007.

2. Determine the correct balance of BIP's Investment in Crown account at December 31, 2007.

3. Assume that BIP's net income for 2007 consists of $1,000,000 sales, $700,000 expenses, and its investment income from Crown. Prepare an income statement for BIP Corporation for 2007.

E 2-14

Calculate income and investment account balance (investee has preferred stock) Valley Corporation paid $290,000 for 40% of the outstanding common stock of Water Corporation on January 2, 2006. During 2006, Water paid dividends of $48,000 and reported net income of $108,000. A summary of Water's stockholders' equity at December 31, 2005 and 2006, follows (in thousands):

December 31,	2005	2006
8% cumulative preferred stock, $100 par	$100	$100
Common stock, $10 par	300	300
Premium on preferred stock	10	10
Other paid-in capital	90	90
Retained earnings	100	160
Total stockholders' equity	$600	$660

REQUIRED: Calculate Valley Corporation's income from Water for 2006 and its Investment in Water account balance at December 31, 2006.

E 2-15

Goodwill impairment Park Corporation recorded goodwill in the amount of $200,000 in its acquisition of Steele Company in 2006. Park paid a total of $700,000 to acquire Steele. In preparing its 2007 financial statements, Park estimates that identifiable net assets still have a value of $500,000, but the total value of Steele is now only $640,000. Calculate the implied value of goodwill at December 31, 2007, and indicate how the change in value (if any) will affect Park's 2007 income statement.

E 2-16

Goodwill impairment Flash, Inc., has two primary business reporting units: Alfa and Beta. In preparing its 2006 financial statements, Flash conducts an annual impairment review of goodwill. Alfa has recorded goodwill of $35,000 that has an estimated fair value of $30,000. Beta has recorded goodwill of $65,000 that has an estimated fair value of $80,000. What amount of impairment loss, if any, must Flash report in its 2006 income statement? Where in the income statement should this appear?

PROBLEMS

P 2-1

Computations for a midyear purchase (investee has an extraordinary gain)

Ritter Corporation paid $343,000 for a 30% interest in Telly Corporation's outstanding voting stock on April 1, 2007. At December 31, 2006, Telly had net assets of $1,000,000 and only common stock outstanding. During 2007, Telly declared and paid dividends of $20,000 each quarter on March 15, June 15, September 15, and December 15 ($80,000 in total). Telly's 2007 income was reported as follows:

Income before extraordinary item	$120,000
Extraordinary gain, December 2007	40,000
Net income	$160,000

REQUIRED: Determine the following:

1. Goodwill from the investment in Telly

2. Income from Telly for 2007

3. Investment in Telly account balance at December 31, 2007

4. Ritter's equity in Telly's net assets at December 31, 2007

5. The amount of extraordinary gain that Ritter will show on its 2007 income statement

---

 P 2-2　　　　　　　　　Book Val = $88,000

Journal entries for midyear investment (cost and equity methods) Putter Company

paid $110,000 for an 80% interest in Siegel Company on July 1, 2006, when Siegel Company had total equity of $110,000. Siegel Company reported earnings of $10,000 for 2006 and declared dividends of $8,000 on November 1, 2006.

Dec. 31 total equity = $112,000

REQUIRED: Give the entries to record these facts on the books of Putter Company:

1. Assuming that Putter Company uses the cost method of accounting for its subsidiaries.

2. Assuming that Putter Company uses the equity method of accounting for its subsidiaries. (Any difference between investment cost and book value acquired is to be assigned to equipment and amortized over a 10-year period.)

P 2-3

Computations for investee when excess allocated to inventories, building, and goodwill Vatter Company acquired a 30% interest in the voting stock of Zelda Company for $331,000 on January 1, 2006, when Zelda's stockholders' equity consisted of capital stock of $600,000 and retained earnings of $400,000. At the time of Vatter's investment, Zelda's assets and liabilities were recorded at their fair values, except for inventories that were undervalued by $30,000 and a building with a 10-year remaining useful life that was overvalued by $60,000. Zelda has income for 2006 of $100,000 and pays dividends of $50,000.

REQUIRED

1. Compute Vatter's income from Zelda for 2006.

2. What is the balance of Vatter's Investment in Zelda account at December 31, 2006?

3. What is Vatter's share of Zelda's recorded net assets at December 31, 2006?

P 2-4

Journal entries for midyear investment (excess allocated to land, equipment, and goodwill) Diller Corporation paid $380,000 for 40% of Dormer Corporation's outstanding voting common stock on July 1, 2006. Dormer's stockholders' equity on January 1, 2006, was $500,000, consisting of $300,000 capital stock and $200,000 retained earnings.

During 2006, Dormer had net income of $100,000, and on November 1, 2006, Dormer declared dividends of $50,000.

Dormer's assets and liabilities were stated at their fair values on July 1, 2006, except for land that was undervalued by $30,000 and equipment with a five-year remaining useful life that was undervalued by $50,000.

REQUIRED: Prepare all the journal entries (other than closing entries) on the books of Diller Corporation during 2006 to account for the investment in Dormer.

P 2-5

Prepare an allocation schedule, compute income and the investment balance
Earth-Q Corporation paid $1,680,000 for a 30% interest in Tremor Corporation's outstanding voting stock on January 1, 2006. The book values and fair values of Tremor's assets and liabilities on January 1, along with amortization data, are as follows (in thousands):

	Book Value	Fair Value		30%	2006 Amort
Cash	$ 400	$ 400			
Accounts receivable—net	700	700			
Inventories (sold in 2006)	1,000	1,200	200	60	−60
Other current assets	200	200			
Land	900	1,700	800	240	−0
Buildings—net (10-year remaining life)	1,500	2,000	500	150	−15
Equipment—net (7-year remaining life)	1,200	500	(700)	(210)	+30
Total assets	$5,900	$6,700			
Accounts payable	$ 800	$ 800			
Other current liabilities	200	200			
Bonds payable (due January 1, 2013)	1,000	1,100	100	30	+6
Capital stock, $10 par	3,000				
Retained earnings	900				
Total equities	$5,900				

Tremor Corporation reported net income of $1,200,000 for 2006 and paid dividends of $600,000.

RE @ 12/31 = 900 + 1,200 − 600 = 1,500

REQUIRED

1. Prepare a schedule to allocate the investment cost/book value differentials relating to Earth-Q's investment in Tremor.
2. Calculate Earth-Q's income from Tremor for 2006.
3. Determine the balance of Earth-Q's Investment in Tremor account at December 31, 2006.

P 2-6

Computations for a midyear acquisition Pauly Corporation purchased for cash 6,000 shares of voting common stock of Stapleton Corporation at $16 per share on July 1, 2006. On this date, Stapleton's equity consisted of $100,000 of $10 par capital stock, $20,000 retained earnings from prior periods, and $10,000 current earnings (for one-half of 2006).

Stapleton's income for 2006 was $20,000, and it paid dividends of $12,000 on November 1, 2006.

All of Stapleton's assets and liabilities were stated at their fair values at July 1, 2006, and any differences between investment cost and book value acquired should be assigned to equipment and amortized over a 10-year period.

REQUIRED: Compute the correct amounts for each of the following items using the equity method of accounting for Pauly's investment:

1. Pauly Corporation's income from its investment in Stapleton for the year ended December 31, 2006.
2. The balance of Pauly's Investment in Stapleton account at December 31, 2006.

(Note: Assumptions on page 50 are needed for this problem.)

P 2-7

Partial income statement with an extraordinary item Dill Corporation acquired 30% of the voting stock of Larkspur Company at book value on July 1, 2006. During 2008, Larkspur paid dividends of $80,000 and reported income of $250,000 as follows:

Income before extraordinary item	$150,000
Extraordinary gain (tax credit from operating loss carryforward)	100,000
Net income	$250,000

REQUIRED: Show how Dill's income from Larkspur should be reported for 2008 by means of a partial income statement for Dill Corporation.

P 2-8

Step-by-step acquisition of equity interest over several years Hazel Corporation purchased a 10% interest in Brady Company on January 1, 2006, for $20,000 and an additional 20% interest for $50,000 on July 1, 2008. The fair value of Hazel's 10% interest in Brady was worth $22,000 on December 31, 2006, $25,000 on December 31, 2007, and $21,000 on December 31, 2008. The Brady stock was consistently classified as an available-for-sale security. Brady had total stockholders' equity of $150,000 when the 10% interest was acquired and $235,000 when the 20% interest was acquired. Any difference between investment cost and book value acquired is to be assigned to equipment and amortized over a 10-year period. Brady reported net income and paid dividends for the years 2006 through 2009 as follows (in thousands):

	2006	2007	2008	2009
Net income for the year	$50	$60	$70	$90
Dividends paid in November	30	30	30	40

Hazel accounts for its investment in Brady in accordance with generally accepted accounting principles.

REQUIRED

1. Determine Hazel's investment income from Brady for 2008.
2. Determine Hazel's prior-period adjustment for 2008 relating to this investment and prepare any necessary journal entries to update the investment account at the point of the purchase of additional shares.

3. Calculate the balance of Hazel's Investment in Brady account at December 31, 2009, for its 30% interest.

4. On January 1, 2010, Brady increases its outstanding shares from 10,000 to 12,000 by selling 2,000 shares to Hazel for $70,000. What adjustment should Hazel make in its Investment in Brady account on this date?

P 2-9

Computations and journal entries with excess of book value over cost Sigma Corporation became a subsidiary of Provo Corporation on July 1, 2006, when Provo paid $1,980,000 cash for 90% of Sigma's outstanding common stock. The price paid by Provo reflected the fact that Sigma's inventories were undervalued by $50,000 and its plant assets were overvalued by $500,000. Sigma sold the undervalued inventory items during 2006 but continues to hold the overvalued plant assets that had a remaining useful life of nine years from July 1, 2006.

During the years 2006 through 2008, Sigma's paid-in capital consisted of $1,500,000 capital stock and $500,000 additional paid-in capital. Sigma's retained earnings statements for 2006, 2007, and 2008 were as follows (in thousands):

	Year Ended December 31, 2006	Year Ended December 31, 2007	Year Ended December 31, 2008
Retained earnings January 1	$525	$600	$700
Add: Net income	250	300	200
Deduct: Dividends (declared in December)	(175)	(200)	(150)
Retained earnings December 31	$600	$700	$750

Provo uses the equity method in accounting for its investment in Sigma.

REQUIRED

1. Compute Provo Corporation's income from its investment in Sigma for 2006.

2. Determine the balance of Provo Corporation's Investment in Sigma account at December 31, 2007.

3. Prepare the journal entries for Provo to account for its investment in Sigma for 2008.

P 2-10

Prepare allocation schedules under different stock price assumptions (negative goodwill) Creape Corporation exchanged 40,000 previously unissued no par common shares for a 40% interest in Tantani Corporation on January 1, 2006. The assets and liabilities of Tantani on that date were as follows (in thousands):

	Book Value	**Fair Value**
Cash	$ 100	$ 100
Accounts receivable—net	200	200
Inventories	500	600
Land	100	300
Buildings—net	600	400
Equipment—net	400	500
Total assets	$1,900	$2,100
Liabilities	$ 900	$ 900
Capital stock	700	
Retained earnings	300	
Total equities	$1,900	

The direct cost of issuing the shares of stock was $10,000, and other direct costs of combination were $40,000.

REQUIRED

1. Assume that the January 1, 2006, market price for Creape's shares is $12 per share. Prepare a schedule to allocate the investment cost/book value differentials.

2. Assume that the January 1, 2006, market price for Creape's shares is $7 per share. Prepare a schedule to allocate the investment cost/book value differentials.

P 2-11

Computations for a piecemeal acquisition Prudy Corporation made three investments in Spandix during 2006 and 2007, as follows:

Date Acquired	Shares Acquired	Cost
July 1, 2006	3,000	$ 48,750
January 1, 2007	6,000	99,000
October 1, 2007	9,000	162,000

Spandix Corporation's stockholders' equity on January 1, 2006, consisted of 20,000 shares of $10 par common stock and retained earnings of $100,000. Prudy's initial intention was to buy a controlling interest in Spandix, so it never considered its investment in Spandix as a trading security. Spandix stock had a market value of $16.50 on December 31, 2006, and $19.00 on December 31, 2007.

Spandix had net income of $40,000 and $60,000 in 2006 and 2007, respectively, and paid dividends of $15,000 on May 1 and November 1, 2006 and 2007 ($60,000 total for the two years).

Prudy Corporation accounts for its investment in Spandix using the equity method of accounting. It does not amortize differences between investment cost and book value acquired.

REQUIRED: Compute the following amounts:

1. Prudy's income from its investment in Spandix for 2006
2. The balance of Prudy's Investment in Spandix account at December 31, 2006
3. Prudy's income from its investments in Spandix for 2007
4. The balance of Prudy's Investment in Spandix account at December 31, 2007

P 2-12

Computations and a correcting entry (errors) Pilot Corporation purchased 40% of the voting stock of Sassy Corporation on July 1, 2006, for $300,000. On that date, Sassy's stockholders' equity consisted of capital stock of $500,000, retained earnings of $150,000, and current earnings (just half of 2006) of $50,000. Income is earned proportionately throughout each year.

The Investment in Sassy account of Pilot Corporation and the retained earnings account of Sassy Corporation for 2006 through 2009 are summarized as follows (in thousands):

RETAINED EARNINGS (SASSY)

Dividends November 1, 2006	$40	Balance January 1, 2006	$150
Dividends November 1, 2007	40	Earnings 2006	100
Dividends November 1, 2008	50	Earnings 2007	80
Dividends November 1, 2009	50	Earnings 2008	130
		Earnings 2009	120

INVESTMENT IN SASSY (PILOT)

Investment July 1, 2006 40%	$300	Dividends 2006	$16
Income 2006	40	Dividends 2007	16
Income 2007	32	Dividends 2008	20
Income 2008	52	Dividends 2009	20
Income 2009	48		

REQUIRED

1. Determine the correct amount of the investment in Sassy that should appear in Pilot's December 31, 2009, balance sheet. Assume a 10-year period for any difference between investment cost and book value acquired.
2. Prepare any journal entry (entries) on Pilot's books to bring the Investment in Sassy account up to date on December 31, 2009, assuming that the books have not been closed at year-end 2009.

P 2-13

Allocation schedule and computations (excess cost over fair value) Publican Corporation acquired a 70% interest in Samaritan Corporation on April 1, 2006, when it purchased 14,000 of Samaritan's 20,000 outstanding shares in the open market at $13 per share. Additional costs of acquiring the shares consisted of $5,000 brokerage fees and $5,000 legal and consulting fees. Samaritan Corporation's balance sheets on January 1 and April 1, 2006, are summarized as follows (in thousands):

	January 1, 2006 (per books)	April 1, 2006 (per books)	April 1, 2006 (fair values)	
Cash	$ 40	$ 45	$ 45	
Inventories	35	60	50	*sold Sep'06*
Other current assets	25	20	20	
Land	30	30	50	
Equipment—net	100	95	135	*remaining useful life of 4yrs*
Total assets	$230	$250	$300	
Accounts payable	$ 45	$ 40	$ 40	
Other liabilities	15	20	20	
Capital stock, $5 par	100	100		
Retained earnings January 1	70	70		
Current earnings		20		
Total liabilities and equity	$230	$250		

ADDITIONAL INFORMATION

1. The overvalued inventory items were sold in September 2006.

2. The undervalued items of equipment had a remaining useful life of four years on April 1, 2006.

3. Samaritan's net income for 2006 was $80,000 ($60,000 from April to December 31, 2006).

4. On December 1, 2006, Samaritan declared dividends of $2 per share, payable on January 10, 2007.

5. Any unidentified assets of Samaritan are not amortized.

REQUIRED

1. Prepare a schedule showing how the difference between Publican's investment cost and book value acquired should be allocated to identifiable and/or unidentifiable assets.

2. Calculate Publican's investment income from Samaritan for 2006.

3. Determine the correct balance of Publican's Investment in Samaritan account at December 31, 2006.

P 2-14

Allocation schedule and computations (excess fair value over cost) Use the information in Problem 2-13, except change the per share market price to $7 per share.

REQUIRED

1. Prepare a schedule showing how the difference between Publican's investment cost and book value acquired should be allocated to identifiable and/or unidentifiable assets.

2. Calculate Publican's investment income from Samaritan for 2006.

3. Determine the correct balance of Publican's Investment in Samaritan account at December 31, 2006.

P 2-15

Goodwill impairment Cooper Corporation is adopting *SFAS 142* for the first time during the current year. Cooper reviews goodwill for impairment on January 1 and estimates that a $100,000 loss has occurred. During the fourth quarter, Cooper conducts its annual review of goodwill and estimates there has been an additional impairment of $40,000. How should these losses be reported in Cooper's income statement for the year? (You may ignore income tax considerations.)

P 2-16

Goodwill impairment Cardinal Tire Company is adopting *SFAS 142* for the first time during the current year. Cardinal reviews goodwill for impairment on January 1 and estimates that a $200,000 loss has occurred. During the fourth quarter, Cardinal conducts its annual review of goodwill and estimates there has been a recovery in the value of goodwill of $40,000 since January 1. How should these impairment calculations be reported in Cooper's income statement for the year? (You may ignore income tax considerations.)

INTERNET ASSIGNMENT

Visit the Ford Motor Company Web site and review Ford's 2003 annual report. You will note that Ford makes numerous investments in other companies. Prepare a brief summary of intercompany investments included by Ford (you will want to look at the financial statements and the notes).

    a. Does Ford report any investments carried as trading securities, available-for-sale securities, or held-to-maturity securities? If so, summarize their significance to both the balance sheet and income statement.

    b. Does Ford report any investments carried under the equity method? If so, summarize their significance to both the balance sheet and income statement. What additional disclosures, if any, are made concerning equity method investments?

    c. Did Ford realize any gains or losses from security sales during 2003?

    d. Has Ford tested for goodwill impairment during 2003? Did Ford experience an impairment during 2003?

SELECTED READINGS

Accounting Interpretations Nos. 1 and 2 of APB Opinion No. 17. New York: American Institute of Certified Public Accountants, 1971 and 1973.

Accounting Interpretation No. 1 of APB Opinion No. 18. New York: American Institute of Certified Public Accountants, 1971.

Accounting Principles Board Opinion No. 18. "The Equity Method of Accounting for Investments in Common Stock." New York: American Institute of Certified Public Accountants, 1971.

BUKICS, ROSE MARIE L., AND BENSON J. CHAPMAN. "The Big Splash: Goodbye Pooling, Hello Goodwill Impairment Testing." *The CPA Journal* (March 2002), p. 32.

FASB Interpretation No. 35. "Criteria for Applying the Equity Method of Accounting for Investments in Common Stock." An Interpretation of *APB Opinion No. 18.* Stamford, CT: Financial Accounting Standards Board, May 1981.

MEETING, DAVID T., RANDALL W. LUECKE, AND LINDA GARCEAU. "Future Cash Flow Measurements." *Journal of Accountancy* (October 2001), pp. 57–67.

MOEHRLE, STEPHEN R., JENNIFER A. REYNOLDS-MOEHRLE, AND JAMES S. WALLACE. "How Informative Are Earnings Numbers That Exclude Goodwill Amortization?" *Accounting Horizons* (September 2001), pp. 242–255.

Statement of Financial Accounting Standards No. 94. "Consolidation of All Majority-Owned Subsidiaries." Stamford, CT: Financial Accounting Standards Board, 1986.

Statement of Financial Accounting Standards No. 115. "Accounting for Certain Investments in Debt and Equity Securities." Norwalk, CT: Financial Accounting Standards Board, 1993.

Statement of Financial Accounting Standards No. 141. "Business Combinations." Stamford, CT: Financial Accounting Standards Board, 2001.

Statement of Financial Accounting Standards No. 142. "Goodwill and Other Intangible Assets." Stamford, CT: Financial Accounting Standards Board, 2001.

3 CHAPTER

AN INTRODUCTION TO CONSOLIDATED FINANCIAL STATEMENTS

This chapter contains background material necessary for understanding consolidated financial statements and provides an overview of the procedures necessary to the consolidation process. The purchase method of accounting for business combinations is applied in the chapter, and pooled subsidiaries are covered on the *Advanced Accounting* Web site. We assume the parent company/investor uses the equity method of accounting for subsidiary investments. Further discussions of business combinations in this book assume purchase accounting.

Required consolidated financial statements include a consolidated balance sheet; a consolidated income statement; a consolidated retained earnings statement, or consolidated statement of changes in stockholders' equity; and a consolidated statement of cash flows. The consolidated balance sheet and consolidated income and retained earnings statements introduced in this chapter are prepared from the separate financial statements of the parent company and its subsidiaries. We prepare the consolidated statement of cash flows from consolidated income statements and consolidated balance sheets. The consolidated statement of cash flows is introduced in Chapter 4.

• • •

BUSINESS COMBINATIONS CONSUMMATED THROUGH STOCK ACQUISITIONS

LEARNING OBJECTIVE 1

The accounting concept of a business combination, as described in *FASB Statement No. 141*, includes those combinations in which one or more companies become subsidiaries of a common parent corporation. A corporation becomes a subsidiary when another corporation acquires a controlling interest in its outstanding voting stock. Ordinarily, one company gains control of another directly by acquiring a majority (more than 50%) of its voting stock. An investor may also gain control of another corporation through indirect stock ownership. Indirect stock-ownership situations are covered in Chapter 9 of this book.[1] Until Chapter 9, assume that direct ownership of a majority of the voting stock of another corporation is required for control and in order to have a parent–subsidiary relationship.

A business combination occurs when one corporation acquires more than 50% of the voting stock of another corporation, but once a parent–subsidiary relationship has been established, the purchase of additional subsidiary shares is not a business combination. In other words, separate entities can combine only once. Increasing a controlling interest is the same as simply making an

---

[1] See *ARB No. 51*, "Consolidated Financial Statements," paragraph 2.

LEARNING OBJECTIVES

1 Recognize the benefits and limitations of consolidated financial statements.

2 Understand the requirements for inclusion of a subsidiary in consolidated financial statements.

3 Apply the consolidation concepts to parent company recording of the investment in a subsidiary company at the date of acquisition.

4 Allocate the excess of the investment cost over the book value of the subsidiary at the date of acquisition.

5 Learn the concept of noncontrolling interest when the parent company acquires less than 100% of the subsidiary's outstanding common stock.

6 Prepare consolidated balance sheets subsequent to the date of acquisition, including preparation of eliminating entries.

7 Amortize the excess of the investment cost over the book value in periods subsequent to the acquisition.

8 Apply the concepts underlying preparation of a consolidated income statement.

9 **For the Students:** Create an electronic spreadsheet to prepare a consolidated balance sheet.

additional investment. The acquisition of additional shares of a subsidiary is accounted for by the purchase method, as explained in paragraph 14 of *FASB Statement No. 141*:

> *The acquisition of some or all of the noncontrolling interests in a subsidiary—whether acquired by the parent, the subsidiary itself, or another affiliate—shall be accounted for using the purchase method.*

The Reporting Entity

A business combination brings two previously separate corporations under the control of a single management team (the officers and directors of the parent company). Although both corporations continue to exist as separate legal entities, the purchase creates a new reporting entity that encompasses all operations controlled by the management of the parent company.

When an investment in voting stock creates a parent–subsidiary relationship, the purchasing entity (parent company) and the entity acquired (subsidiary) continue to function as separate entities and to maintain their accounting records on a separate legal basis. Separate parent-company and subsidiary financial statements are converted into consolidated financial statements that reflect the financial position and the results of operations of the combined entity. The new reporting entity is responsible for reporting to the stockholders and creditors of the parent company and to other interested parties.

This chapter begins to discuss the difficulties of combining the separate accounting records of the parent and subsidiary into a more meaningful set of consolidated financial statements for the reporting entity. As you continue through the remaining chapters on business combinations, you may at times feel that companies maintain their separate legal entities and accounting systems only to make life difficult for advanced accounting students. In fact, there are sound business reasons for keeping these separate identities.

A parent company may acquire a subsidiary in a very different industry from its own as a means of diversifying its overall business risk. In such cases, the management experience and skills required in the subsidiary's line of business are already in place and are preserved within the separate entity. Further, the subsidiary may have established supply-chain and distribution systems very different from its parent's. The subsidiary also may have established customer loyalties, which are easier to maintain with a separate identity.

Brand names and trademarks associated with the subsidiary represent extremely valuable intangible assets. If **Goodyear** were to purchase the **Coca-Cola Company** or **PepsiCo**, it likely would not be a great strategic move to rename it as Goodyear Tire and Cola!

There are also compelling legal reasons for maintaining separate identities. In a typical investment, the parent company buys the common stock of the subsidiary. Under the U.S. legal system, stockholders enjoy limited legal liability. If a major lawsuit results in a significant loss (e.g., from an environmental catastrophe involving the subsidiary), the parent cannot be held accountable for more than the loss of its investment.

The Parent–Subsidiary Relationship

We presume that a corporation that owns more than 50% of the voting stock of another corporation controls that corporation through its stock ownership, and a parent–subsidiary relationship exists between the two corporations. When parent–subsidiary relationships exist, the companies are affiliated. Often the term **affiliate** is used to mean subsidiary, and the two terms are used interchangeably in this book and throughout much of the literature of accounting. The FASB exposure draft titled "Consolidated Financial Statements: Policy and Procedures" defined *affiliate* as "an entity that, directly or indirectly through one or more intermediaries, controls, is controlled by, or is under common control with another entity. A parent and its subsidiary(ies) are affiliates, and subsidiaries of a common parent are affiliates." In many annual reports, however, the term *affiliate* is used to include all investments accounted for by the equity method. The following excerpt from the **Deere & Company** 2003 annual report (p. 22) is an example of this latter usage of the term *affiliate*: "Deere & Company records its investment in each unconsolidated affiliated company (generally 20 to 50 percent ownership) at its related equity in the net assets of such affiliate."

Exhibit 3-1 illustrates an affiliation structure with two subsidiaries, with Percy Company owning 90% of the voting stock of San Del Corporation and 80% of the voting stock of Saltz

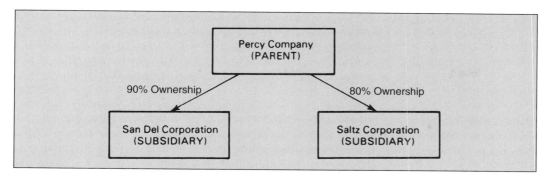

EXHIBIT 3-1

Affiliation Structure

Corporation. Percy Company owns 90% of the voting stock of San Del, and stockholders outside the affiliation structure own the other 10%. These outside stockholders are the noncontrolling stockholders, and their interest is referred to as a **noncontrolling interest**.[2] Outside stockholders have a 20% noncontrolling interest in Saltz Corporation.

Percy Company and each of its subsidiaries are separate legal entities that maintain separate accounting records. In its separate records, Percy Company uses the equity method described in Chapter 2 to account for its investments in San Del and Saltz Corporations. For reporting purposes, however, the equity method of reporting usually does not result in the most meaningful financial statements. This is so because the parent, through its stock ownership, is able to elect subsidiary directors and control subsidiary decisions, including dividend declarations. Although affiliated companies are separate legal entities, there is really only one economic entity because all resources are under control of a single management—the directors and officers of the parent company.

The opening paragraph of *ARB No. 51*, "Consolidated Financial Statements," states that:

> *The purpose of consolidated statements is to present, primarily for the benefit of stock-holders and creditors of the parent company, the results of operations and the financial position of a parent company and its subsidiaries essentially as if the group were a single company with one or more branches or divisions.*

Thus, consolidated statements are intended primarily for the parent company's investors, rather than for the noncontrolling stockholders and subsidiary creditors. (The subsidiary, as a separate legal entity, continues to report the results of its own operations to the noncontrolling shareholders.)

Consolidation Policy

Consolidated financial statements provide much information that is not included in the separate statements of the parent corporation, and they are usually required for fair presentation of the financial position and results of operations for a group of affiliated companies. The usual condition for consolidation is ownership of more than 50% of the voting stock of another company. Under the provisions of *FASB Statement No. 94*, "Consolidation of All Majority-Owned Subsidiaries," a subsidiary can be excluded from consolidation in only two situations: (1) when control is likely to be temporary or (2) when control does not rest with the majority owner. Control does not rest with the majority owner if the subsidiary is in legal reorganization or bankruptcy or is operating under severe foreign-exchange restrictions, controls, or other governmentally imposed uncertainties.

As we noted, *Ford Motor Company* excludes certain majority-owned investments in dealer-ships from consolidation, based on the temporary-control criterion. *Anheuser-Busch Companies'* 2003 annual report (p. 47) provides an example of exclusions in which the majority owner lacks the ability to control the subsidiary companies.

Note 2. International Equity Investments (Partial)

Groupo Modelo

From 1993 to 1998, Anheuser-Busch accumulated a 50.2% direct and indirect equity interest in Diblo, S.A. de C.V. (Diblo), the operating subsidiary of Groupo Modelo, S.A.

---

[2] *FASB Statement No. 141* appears to prefer the term *noncontrolling interest* to minority interest. However, the statement itself uses the two terms interchangeably. Many companies retain the more-traditional minority interest designation in their annual reports, but we use noncontrolling throughout this text.

de C.V. (Modelo), Mexico's largest brewer and producer of the Corona brand, for a total cost of $1.6 billion. The company holds 9 of 19 positions on Modelo's Board of Directors (with the Controlling Shareholders holding the other 10 positions) and also has membership on the Audit Committee. Anheuser-Busch does not have voting or other effective control of either Diblo or Modelo and consequently accounts for its investment using the equity method.

HISTORY *ARB No. 51*, issued in 1959, allowed parent-company management broad discretion in determining consolidation policy as long as the objective was to provide the most meaningful financial presentation in the circumstances. Many firms adopted a policy of excluding from consolidation those subsidiaries whose operations differed greatly from those of the parent company. Manufacturing and merchandising companies routinely excluded their finance, insurance, and real estate subsidiaries. These "nonhomogeneous" subsidiaries were included in the financial statements as unconsolidated subsidiaries and were accounted for by the equity method. As explained in Chapter 2, accounting by the equity method provides the same net income as consolidating the accounts of the parent and subsidiary corporations. However, the assets, liabilities, revenues, and expenses of the unconsolidated subsidiary are not included in the financial statements under the equity method. It was concern over the possible omission of significant amounts of debt from the balance sheet that prompted the issuance of *FASB Statement No. 94* in 1987.

The FASB is considering a consolidation policy based on control, rather than majority ownership. The FASB issued *Preliminary Views on Major Issues Related to Consolidation Policy* in 1994 and an exposure draft, "Consolidated Financial Statements: Policy and Procedures," in 1995. Both the *Preliminary Views* and the exposure draft proposed that a corporation consolidate all entities that it controls unless control is temporary at the time the business becomes a subsidiary. Control of an entity was defined as power over its assets. During the deliberations of the exposure draft, the board was asked to further define control and to clarify the presumption of control. Other questions about when a subsidiary should be consolidated arose during the redeliberations: Should the parent receive some level of benefits? Should a level of ownership be required? Eventually, the board agreed that a consolidation policy should include both control and benefits.[3]

DISCLOSURE OF CONSOLIDATION POLICIES A description of significant accounting policies is required for financial reporting under *APB Opinion No. 22*, "Disclosure of Accounting Policies," and traditionally, consolidation-policy disclosures were among the most frequent of all policy disclosures. *FASB Statement No. 94* eliminates acceptable alternative consolidation policies, so consolidation-policy disclosures under *APB Opinion No. 22* are only needed to report exceptions (temporary control or inability to control) to the *Statement 94* requirement for consolidation of all majority-owned subsidiaries. Even so, the disclosure of consolidation policies in annual reports is not likely to decline significantly because the SEC requires publicly held companies to report their consolidation policies under Regulation S-X, Rule 3A-03. Consolidation policy is usually presented under a heading such as "principles of consolidation" or "basis of consolidation." Anheuser-Busch Companies' 2003 annual report (p. 44) contains a typical "principles of consolidation" policy note:

> *The Consolidated Financial statements include the company and all its subsidiaries. The company consolidates all majority-owned and controlled subsidiaries, uses the equity method of accounting for investments in which the company is able to exercise significant influence, and uses the cost method for all other investments. All significant intercompany transactions have been eliminated. Minority interests in the company's China subsidiary are not material.*

Parent and Subsidiary with Different Fiscal Periods

When the fiscal periods of the parent company and its subsidiaries are different, we prepare consolidated statements for and as of the end of the parent's fiscal period. If the difference in fiscal periods is not in excess of three months, it usually is acceptable to use the subsidiary's statements for its fiscal year for consolidation purposes, with disclosure of "the effect of intervening events

---

[3] Financial Accounting Series, *Status Report 295*, November 26, 1997.

which materially affect the financial position or results of operations."[4] Otherwise, the statements of the subsidiary should be adjusted so that they correspond as closely as possible to the fiscal period of the parent company. ***Abbott Laboratories*** and Subsidiaries' 2003 annual report (p. 51) includes the following explanation of its fiscal year:

> *The accounts of foreign subsidiaries are consolidated as of November 30, due to the time needed to consolidate these subsidiaries. No events occurred related to these foreign subsidiaries in December 2003, 2002, and 2001 that materially affected the financial position or results of operations.*

Financing the Acquisition

There are many avenues available for financing the purchase of a subsidiary's shares. As students, you are well aware that sufficient cash isn't always available for the things you'd like to buy; companies face the same problem in making significant purchases. The investor may pay cash, sell shares of authorized but previously unissued common stock, issue preferred shares, sell debt securities (bonds), or utilize some combination of these financial instruments.

Prior to *FASB Statement No. 141* in 2001, firms often exchanged shares of common stock in order to qualify for the pooling of interests method of accounting for the combination. For example, ***America Online*** (AOL) used this approach to account for its combination with ***Time Warner***. Management of AOL made a strategic move, using the market price runup for AOL and other technology companies in the late 1990s to make this major investment possible.

The financing decision can be important strategically. Common shares are accompanied by voting rights, and an especially large acquisition may cost management its voting control. Nonvoting preferred shares or other financing alternatives are useful in cases in which keeping voting control is an important consideration.

Compaq Computer Corporation's 2000 annual report (p. 52) provides some interesting examples:

> **Note 3. Acquisitions and Divestitures (Partial)**
>
> *In August 1999, Compaq sold an 81.5 percent equity interest in AltaVista for approximately 38 million CMGI common shares, CMGI preferred shares convertible into 3.6 million CMGI common shares and a $220 million three-year note receivable. In October 1999, CMGI converted the CMGI preferred shares held by Compaq into 3.6 million CMGI common shares. The CMGI common shares acquired by Compaq in this transaction carry certain restrictions whereby Compaq may not sell more than 50 percent (20.8 million) of such shares prior to August 2001.*
>
> *In June 1998, Compaq consummated its acquisition of Digital for an aggregate purchase price of $9.1 billion. The purchase price consisted of approximately $4.5 billion in cash, the issuance of approximately 141 million shares of Compaq common stock valued at approximately $4.3 billion and the issuance of approximately 25 million options to purchase Compaq common stock valued at approximately $249 million.*

CONSOLIDATED BALANCE SHEET AT DATE OF ACQUISITION

A consolidated entity is a fictitious (conceptual) reporting entity. It is based on the assumption that the separate legal and accounting entities of a parent and its subsidiaries can be combined into a single meaningful set of financial statements for external reporting purposes. *Note that the consolidated entity does not have transactions and does not maintain a consolidated ledger of accounts.*

Parent Acquires 100% of Subsidiary at Book Value

Exhibit 3-2 shows the basic differences between separate-company and consolidated balance sheets. Penn Corporation acquires 100% of Skelly Corporation at its book value and fair value of $40,000 in a purchase business combination on January 1, 2006. Exhibit 3-2 shows the balance sheets prepared immediately after the investment. Penn's "Investment in Skelly" appears in the

---

[4] *ARB No. 51*, paragraph 5.

EXHIBIT 3-2

100% Ownership Acquired at Book Value

(in thousands)	Separate Balance Sheets		Consolidated Balance Sheet: Penn and Subsidiary
	Penn	Skelly	
Assets			
Current assets			
Cash	$ 20	$10	$ 30
Other current assets	45	15	60
Total current assets	65	25	90
Plant assets	75	45	120
Less: Accumulated depreciation	(15)	(5)	(20)
Total plant assets	60	40	100
Investment in Skelly—100%	40	—	—
Total assets	$165	$65	$190
Liabilities and Stockholders' Equity			
Current liabilities			
Accounts payable	$ 20	$15	$ 35
Other current liabilities	25	10	35
Total current liabilities	45	25	70
Stockholders' equity			
Capital stock	100	30	100
Retained earnings	20	10	20
Total stockholders' equity	120	40	120
Total liabilities and stockholders' equity	$165	$65	$190

separate balance sheet of Penn, but not in the consolidated balance sheet for Penn and Subsidiary. When preparing the balance sheet, we eliminate the Investment in Skelly account (Penn's books) and the stockholders' equity accounts (Skelly's books) because they are reciprocal—both representing the net assets of Skelly Corporation at January 1, 2006. We combine the nonreciprocal accounts of Penn and Skelly and include them in the consolidated balance sheet of Penn Corporation and Subsidiary. Note that the consolidated balance sheet is not merely a summation of account balances of the affiliated corporations. We eliminate reciprocal accounts in the process of consolidation and combine only nonreciprocal accounts. The capital stock that appears in a consolidated balance sheet is the capital stock of the parent company, and the consolidated retained earnings are the retained earnings of the parent company.

Parent Acquires 100% of Subsidiary—with Goodwill

Exhibit 3-2 presented the consolidated balance sheet prepared for a parent company that purchased all the stock of Skelly Corporation at book value. If, instead, Penn purchases all of Skelly's stock for $50,000, there will be a $10,000 excess of investment cost over book value acquired ($50,000 investment cost less $40,000 stockholders' equity of Skelly). The $10,000 appears in the consolidated balance sheet at acquisition as an asset of $10,000. In the absence of evidence that identifiable net assets are undervalued, this asset is assumed to be goodwill. Exhibit 3-3 illustrates procedures for preparing a consolidated balance sheet for Penn Corporation, assuming that Penn pays $50,000 for the outstanding stock of Skelly.

EXHIBIT 3-3

100% Ownership,
Cost $10,000 Greater
Than Book Value

PENN CORPORATION AND SUBSIDIARY
CONSOLIDATED BALANCE SHEET WORKING PAPERS
JANUARY 1, 2006 (IN THOUSANDS)

	Penn	100% Skelly	Adjustments and Eliminations		Consolidated Balance Sheet
			Debits	Credits	
Assets					
Cash	$ 10	$10			$ 20
Other current assets	45	15			60
Plant assets	75	45			120
Accumulated depreciation	(15)	(5)			(20)
Investment in Skelly	50			a 50	
Goodwill			a 10		10
Total assets	$165	$65			$190
Liabilities and Equity					
Accounts payable	$ 20	$15			$ 35
Other current liabilities	25	10			35
Capital stock—Penn	100				100
Retained earnings—Penn	20				20
Capital stock—Skelly		30	a 30		
Retained earnings—Skelly		10	a 10		
Total liabilities and stockholders' equity	$165	$65			$190

a To eliminate reciprocal investment and equity accounts and to assign the excess of investment cost over book value acquired to goodwill.

We need only one working paper entry to consolidate the balance sheets of Penn and Skelly at acquisition. Take a few minutes to review the format of the working paper in Exhibit 3-3. The first two columns provide information from the separate balance sheets of Penn and Skelly. The third column is used to record adjustments and eliminations, subdivided into debits and credits. The last column presents the totals that will appear in the consolidated balance sheet. We calculate amounts in the Consolidated Balance Sheet column by adding together amounts from the first two columns and then adding or subtracting the adjustments and eliminations, as appropriate. This basic working paper format is used throughout the discussions of business combinations and preparation of consolidated financial statements in this book. The entry is reproduced in general journal form for convenient reference:

a	Capital stock—Skelly (–SE)	30	
	Retained earnings—Skelly (–SE)	10	
	Goodwill (+A)	10	
	Investment in Skelly (–A)		50

To eliminate reciprocal investment and equity accounts and to assign the excess of investment cost over book value acquired to goodwill.

EXHIBIT 3-4

90% Ownership,
Cost $14,000 Greater
Than Book Value

PENN CORPORATION AND SUBSIDIARY
CONSOLIDATED BALANCE SHEET WORKING PAPERS
JANUARY 1, 2006 (IN THOUSANDS)

	Penn	90% Skelly	Adjustments and Eliminations Debits	Adjustments and Eliminations Credits	Consolidated Balance Sheet
Assets					
Cash	$ 10	$10			$ 20
Other current assets	45	15			60
Plant assets	75	45			120
Accumulated depreciation	(15)	(5)			(20)
Investment in Skelly	50			a 50	
Goodwill			a 14		14
Total assets	$165	$65			$194
Liabilities and Equity					
Accounts payable	$ 20	$15			$ 35
Other current liabilities	25	10			35
Capital stock—Penn	100				100
Retained earnings—Penn	20				20
Capital stock—Skelly		30	a 30		
Retained earnings—Skelly		10	a 10		
	$165	$65			
Noncontrolling interest				a 4	4
Total liabilities and stockholders' equity					$194

a To eliminate reciprocal investment and equity balances, assign the $14,000 excess of investment cost ($50,000) over book value acquired ($36,000) to goodwill, and recognize a $4,000 noncontrolling interest in the net assets of Skelly ($40,000 equity × 10% noncontrolling interest).

Entries such as those shown in Exhibit 3-3 are only working paper adjustments and eliminations and *are not recorded in the accounts of the parent or subsidiary corporations.* The entries will never be journalized or posted. Their only purpose is to facilitate completion of the working papers to consolidate a parent and subsidiary at and for the period ended on a particular date. In this book, working paper entries are shaded to avoid confusing them with actual journal entries that are recorded in the accounts of the parent and subsidiary companies.

In future periods, the difference between the investment account balance and the subsidiary equity will decline *if, and only if, goodwill is written down due to impairment.*

Parent Acquires 90% of Subsidiary—with Goodwill

Assume that instead of acquiring all of Skelly's outstanding stock, Penn acquires 90% of it for $50,000. In this case, the excess of investment cost over book value acquired is $14,000 ($50,000 cost less $36,000 book value acquired), and there is a noncontrolling interest in Skelly of $4,000 ($40,000 equity × 10% noncontrolling interest). The working papers in Exhibit 3-4 illustrate procedures for preparing the consolidated balance sheet for Penn and Skelly under the 90% ownership assumption.

Working paper entry a consolidates the balance sheets of Penn and Skelly and recognizes the noncontrolling interest in Skelly at the date of acquisition.

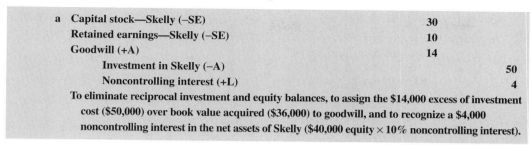

a	Capital stock—Skelly (–SE)	30	
	Retained earnings—Skelly (–SE)	10	
	Goodwill (+A)	14	
	Investment in Skelly (–A)		50
	Noncontrolling interest (+L)		4

To eliminate reciprocal investment and equity balances, to assign the $14,000 excess of investment cost ($50,000) over book value acquired ($36,000) to goodwill, and to recognize a $4,000 noncontrolling interest in the net assets of Skelly ($40,000 equity × 10% noncontrolling interest).

Noncontrolling Interest

We include all the assets and liabilities of the subsidiary in the consolidated balance sheet and make a separate deduction for the noncontrolling interest's share of subsidiary net assets based on book values.

Working papers provide the basis of preparing formal financial statements, and the question arises about how the $4,000 noncontrolling interest that appears in Exhibit 3-4 would be reported in a formal balance sheet. Although practice varies with respect to classification, the noncontrolling interest in subsidiaries is generally shown in a single amount in the liability section of the consolidated balance sheet, frequently under the heading of noncurrent liabilities.[5] Conceptually, the classification of noncontrolling stockholder interests as liabilities is inconsistent because the interests of noncontrolling stockholders represent equity investments in the consolidated net assets by stockholders outside the affiliation structure. The alternatives are to include the noncontrolling interest in consolidated stockholders' equity or to place it in a separate noncontrolling interest section. When classified as stockholders' equity, the noncontrolling interest should be separated from the equity of majority stockholders, that is, stockholders of the parent company.

The FASB, as part of its consolidations project, made the following tentative decisions in its discussions on the presentation of a noncontrolling interest:[6]

- A noncontrolling interest in a subsidiary should be displayed and labeled in the consolidated balance sheet as a separate component of equity.
- Income attributable to the noncontrolling interest is not an expense or a loss but a deduction from consolidated net income to compute income attributable to the controlling interest.
- Both components of consolidated net income (net income attributable to noncontrolling interest and net income attributable to controlling interest) should be disclosed on the face of the consolidated income statement.

CONSOLIDATED BALANCE SHEETS AFTER ACQUISITION

The account balances of both parent and subsidiary corporations change to reflect their separate operations after the parent–subsidiary relationship has been established. Subsequently, we make additional adjustments to eliminate other reciprocal balances. If a consolidated balance sheet is prepared between the time a subsidiary declares and the time it pays dividends, the parent's books will show a dividend receivable account that is the reciprocal of a dividends payable account on the books of the subsidiary. Such balances do not represent amounts receivable or payable outside the affiliated grouping; therefore, they must be reciprocals that we eliminate in preparing consolidated statements. We also eliminate other intercompany receivables and payables, such as accounts receivable and accounts payable, in preparing consolidated statements.

The balance sheets of Penn and Skelly Corporations at December 31, 2006, one year after affiliation, contain the following (in thousands):

---

[5] *Accounting Trends & Techniques—2003* shows that 160 of the 600 reporting corporations reported minority interest in the "Other Noncurrent Liabilities" section of the balance sheet (p. 301).

[6] *FASB Statement No. 141* does not address proper balance sheet classification of minority/noncontrolling interests as liabilities or equity. These issues remain on the FASB agenda, linked to both the project on consolidations and the project on establishing clear definitions of liabilities versus equities. The FASB likely will require firms to treat noncontrolling interest as equity when they issue the revision to *SFAS No. 141*.

	Penn	Skelly
Cash	$ 22.4	$15
Dividends receivable	9	—
Other current assets	41	28
Plant assets	75	45
Accumulated depreciation	(20)	(8)
Investment in Skelly (90%)	59	—
Total assets	$186.4	$80
Accounts payable	$ 30	$15
Dividends payable	—	10
Other current liabilities	20	5
Capital stock	100	30
Retained earnings	36.4	20
Total equities	$186.4	$80

Assumptions

1. Penn acquired a 90% interest in Skelly for $50,000 on January 1, 2006, when Skelly's stockholders' equity was $40,000 (see Exhibit 3-4).

2. The accounts payable of Skelly include $5,000 owed to Penn.

3. During 2006 Skelly had income of $20,000 and declared $10,000 in dividends.

Exhibit 3-5 presents consolidated balance sheet working papers reflecting this information. We determine the balance in the Investment in Skelly account at December 31, 2006, using the equity method of accounting. Calculations of the December 31, 2006, investment account balance are as follows:

Original investment January 1, 2006	$50,000
Add: 90% of Skelly's $20,000 net income for 2006	18,000
Deduct: 90% of Skelly's $10,000 dividends for 2006	(9,000)
Investment account balance December 31, 2006	$59,000

Even though the amounts involved are different, the *process* of consolidating balance sheets after acquisition is basically the same as at acquisition. In all cases, we eliminate the amount of the subsidiary investment account and the equity accounts of the subsidiary. We enter the excess of the investment account balance over the book value of the interest owned (goodwill in this illustration) in the working papers during the process of eliminating reciprocal investment and equity balances. Goodwill does not appear on the books of the parent; we add it to the asset listing when preparing the working papers. The noncontrolling interest is equal to the percentage of noncontrolling ownership times the equity of the subsidiary at the balance sheet date. Consolidated retained earnings equal the parent company's retained earnings.

The working paper entries necessary to consolidate the balance sheets of Penn and Skelly are reproduced in general journal form for convenient reference:

a	Capital stock—Skelly (−SE)	30	
	Retained earnings—Skelly (−SE)	20	
	Goodwill (+A)	14	
	Investment in Skelly (−A)		59
	Noncontrolling interest (+L)		5
	To eliminate reciprocal investment and equity balances, record goodwill, and enter the noncontrolling interest ($50,000 × 10%).		
b	Dividends payable (−L)	9	
	Dividends receivable (−A)		9
	To eliminate reciprocal dividends receivable and payable amounts (90% of $10,000 dividends payable of Skelly).		
c	Accounts payable (−L)	5	
	Accounts receivable (−A)		5
	To eliminate intercompany accounts receivable and accounts payable.		

EXHIBIT 3-5

90% Ownership,
Consolidation One
Year After
Acquisition

PENN CORPORATION AND SUBSIDIARY
CONSOLIDATED BALANCE SHEET WORKING PAPERS
DECEMBER 31, 2006 (IN THOUSANDS)

	Penn	90% Skelly	Adjustments and Eliminations Debits	Credits	Consolidated Balance Sheet
Assets					
Cash	$ 22.4	$15			$ 37.4
Dividends receivable	9			b 9	
Other current assets	41	28		c 5	64
Plant assets	75	45			120
Accumulated depreciation	(20)	(8)			(28)
Investment in Skelly	59			a 59	
Goodwill			a 14		14
Total assets	$186.4	$80			$207.4
Liabilities and Equity					
Accounts payable	$ 30	$15	c 5		$ 40
Dividends payable		10	b 9		1
Other current liabilities	20	5			25
Capital stock—Penn	100				100
Retained earnings—Penn	36.4				36.4
Capital stock—Skelly		30	a 30		
Retained earnings—Skelly		20	a 20		
	$186.4	$80			
Noncontrolling interest				a 5	5
Total liabilities and stockholders' equity					$207.4

a To eliminate reciprocal investment and equity balances, record unamortized goodwill, and enter the noncontrolling interest ($50,000 × 10%).
b To eliminate reciprocal dividends receivable and payable amounts (90% of $10,000 dividends payable of Skelly).
c To eliminate intercompany accounts receivable and accounts payable.

ALLOCATION OF EXCESS TO IDENTIFIABLE NET ASSETS AND GOODWILL

We assigned the excess of investment cost over the book value acquired in the Penn–Skelly illustration to goodwill. An underlying assumption of that assignment of the excess is that the book values and fair values of identifiable assets and liabilities are equal. When the evidence indicates that fair values exceed book values or book values exceed fair values, however, we allocate the excess accordingly.

Effect of Allocation on Consolidated Balance Sheet at Acquisition

The separate books of the affiliated companies do not record cost/book value differentials in acquisitions that create parent–subsidiary relationships. We use working paper procedures to adjust subsidiary book values to reflect the cost/book value differentials. The adjusted amounts appear in the

EXHIBIT 3-6

Preacquisition Book
and Fair Value
Balance Sheets

(in thousands)	Pilot Corporation		Sand Corporation	
	Per Books	Fair Values	Per Books	Fair Values
Assets				
Cash	$ 6,600	$ 6,600	$ 200	$ 200
Receivables—net	700	700	300	300
Inventories	900	1,200	500	600
Other current assets	600	800	400	400
Land	1,200	11,200	600	800
Buildings—net	8,000	15,000	4,000	5,000
Equipment—net	7,000	9,000	2,000	1,700
Total assets	$25,000	$44,500	$8,000	$9,000
Liabilities and Equity				
Accounts payable	$ 2,000	$ 2,000	$ 700	$ 700
Notes payable	3,700	3,500	1,400	1,300
Common stock, $10 par	10,000		4,000	
Additional paid-in capital	5,000		1,000	
Retained earnings	4,300		900	
Total liabilities and stockholders' equity	$25,000		$8,000	

consolidated balance sheet. We determine the amount of the adjustment to individual assets and liabilities using the one-line consolidation approach presented in Chapter 2.

On December 31, 2006, Pilot purchases 90% of Sand Corporation's outstanding voting common stock directly from Sand Corporation's stockholders for $5,000,000 cash plus 100,000 shares of Pilot Corporation $10 par common stock with a market value of $5,000,000. Additional costs of combination are $200,000. Pilot pays these additional costs in cash. Pilot and Sand must continue to operate as parent company and subsidiary because 10% of Sand's shares are outstanding and held by noncontrolling stockholders. We include these $200,000 costs in recording the cost of the investment.

Comparative book value and fair value information for Pilot and Sand immediately before their combination on December 31, 2006, appears in Exhibit 3-6. Pilot records the business combination on its books with the following journal entries:

Investment in Sand (+A)	10,000	
Common stock (+SE)		1,000
Additional paid-in capital (+SE)		4,000
Cash (−A)		5,000

To record acquisition of 90% of Sand Corporation's
outstanding stock for $5,000,000 in cash and 100,000
shares of Pilot common stock with a value of $5,000,000.

Investment in Sand (+A)	200	
Cash (−A)		200

To record additional costs of combining with Sand.

EXHIBIT 3-7

Schedule for
Allocating the
Excess of
Investment Cost
over the Book Value
of the Interest
Acquired

PILOT CORPORATION AND ITS 90%-OWNED SUBSIDIARY, SAND CORPORATION (IN THOUSANDS)

Investment in Sand—cost		$10,200
Book value of interest acquired		
90% × $5,900,000 equity of Sand		(5,310)
Total excess of cost over book value acquired		$ 4,890

Allocation of Identifiable Assets and Liabilities

	Fair Value	−	Book Value	×	Interest Acquired	=	Excess Allocated
Inventories	$ 600		$ 500		90%		$ 90
Land	800		600		90		180
Buildings	5,000		4,000		90		900
Equipment	1,700		2,000		90		(270)
Notes payable	1,300		1,400		90		90
Total allocated to identifiable net assets							990
Remainder allocated to goodwill							3,900
Total excess of cost over book value acquired							$4,890

These are the only entries on Pilot's books necessary to record the business combination of Pilot and Sand. Sand records no entries because Pilot acquired its 90% interest directly from Sand's stockholders. We do not use the balance sheet information given in Exhibit 3-6 in recording the business combination on Pilot's books; we use it in preparing the consolidated balance sheet for the combined entity immediately after combination.

ALLOCATING THE COST/BOOK VALUE DIFFERENTIAL   We determine the adjustments necessary to combine the balance sheets of parent and subsidiary corporations by *assigning* the difference between investment cost and book value acquired to identifiable assets and liabilities and then to goodwill for any remainder. The schedule in Exhibit 3-7 illustrates the adjustment necessary to consolidate the balance sheets of Pilot and Sand at December 31, 2006.

Although we do not use the book values of assets and liabilities in determining fair values for individual assets and liabilities (these are usually determined by management), we use book values in the mechanical process of combining the balance sheets of parent and subsidiary.

The underlying book value of the 90% interest acquired in Sand Corporation is $5,310,000 (as shown in Exhibit 3-7), and the excess of investment cost over book value acquired is $4,890,000. We allocate this excess first to the identifiable assets acquired and liabilities assumed and then assign the remainder to goodwill. The amounts assigned to identifiable assets and liabilities are for 90% of the fair value and book value difference because the price paid by Pilot Corporation is for 90% of the identifiable assets less liabilities of Sand Corporation. The other 10% in Sand's identifiable net assets relates to the interests of noncontrolling stockholders that are not adjusted to their fair values on the basis of the price paid by Pilot for its 90% interest.[7] The interest acquired by the parent/investor determines the allocation of the cost/book value differences.

WORKING PAPER PROCEDURES TO ENTER ALLOCATIONS IN CONSOLIDATED BALANCE SHEET   We incorporate the allocation of the excess cost over book value as determined in Exhibit 3-7 into a consolidated balance sheet through working paper procedures. Exhibit 3-8 illustrates these procedures for Pilot and Sand as of the date of their affiliation.

---

[7] Revaluation of all assets and liabilities of a subsidiary on the basis of the price paid by the parent for its majority interest is supported by the entity theory of consolidations. Entity theory is covered in Chapter 11.

EXHIBIT 3-8

90% Ownership, Excess Allocated to Identifiable Net Assets and Goodwill

PILOT CORPORATION AND SUBSIDIARY
CONSOLIDATED BALANCE SHEET WORKING PAPERS
AFTER COMBINATION ON DECEMBER 31, 2006 (IN THOUSANDS)

	Pilot	90% Sand	Adjustments and Eliminations Debits	Credits	Consolidated Balance Sheet
Assets					
Cash	$ 1,300	$ 200			$ 1,500
Receivables—net	700	300			1,000
Inventories	900	500	b 90		1,490
Other current assets	600	400			1,000
Land	1,200	600	b 180		1,980
Buildings—net	8,000	4,000	b 900		12,900
Equipment—net	7,000	2,000		b 270	8,730
Investment in Sand	10,200			a 10,200	
Goodwill			b 3,900		3,900
Unamortized excess			a 4,890	b 4,890	
Total assets	$29,900	$8,000			$32,500
Liabilities and Equity					
Accounts payable	$ 2,000	$ 700			$ 2,700
Notes payable	3,700	1,400	b 90		5,010
Common stock— Pilot	11,000				11,000
Other paid-in capital—Pilot	8,900				8,900
Retained earnings— Pilot	4,300				4,300
Common stock— Sand		4,000	a 4,000		
Other paid-in capital—Sand		1,000	a 1,000		
Retained earnings— Sand		900	a 900		
	$29,900	$8,000			
Noncontrolling interest				a 590	590
Total liabilities and stockholders' equity					$32,500

a To eliminate reciprocal subsidiary investment and equity balances, establish noncontrolling interest, and enter the unamortized excess.
b To allocate the unamortized excess to identifiable assets, liabilities, and goodwill.

The consolidated balance sheet working papers show two working paper entries for the consolidation. Entry a in general journal form follows.

a Unamortized excess (+A)	4,890	
Common stock, $10 par—Sand (−SE)	4,000	
Additional paid-in capital—Sand (−SE)	1,000	
Retained earnings—Sand (−SE)	900	
Investment in Sand (−A)		10,200
Noncontrolling interest—10% (+L)		590

This working paper entry eliminates reciprocal investment in Sand and stockholders' equity amounts of Sand, establishes the noncontrolling interest in Sand, and enters the total unamortized excess from Exhibit 3-7.

A second working paper entry allocates the unamortized excess to individual assets and liabilities and to goodwill.

b Inventories (+A)	90	
Land (+A)	180	
Buildings—net (+A)	900	
Goodwill (+A)	3,900	
Notes payable (−L)	90	
Equipment—net (−A)		270
Unamortized excess (−A)		4,890

We add a step and employ an unamortized excess account to simplify working paper entries when allocating the cost/book value differential to numerous asset and liability accounts. We skip this step when allocating the total excess to goodwill, as in Exhibit 3-4 and 3-5. Working paper entries a and b enter debits and credits equal to the unamortized excess, so the account has no final effect on the consolidated balance sheet.

We combine debit and credit working paper amounts with the line items shown in the separate statements of Pilot and Sand to produce the amounts shown in the Consolidated Balance Sheet column. Sand is a partially owned subsidiary, so we do not include its assets and liabilities in the consolidated balance sheet at either their fair values or book values. Instead, the consolidated assets and liabilities include Pilot's assets and liabilities at book value, plus Sand's assets and liabilities at book value, plus or minus unamortized cost/book value differentials from Pilot's investment in Sand.

Effect of Amortization on Consolidated Balance Sheet After Acquisition

The effect of amortizing the $4,890,000 excess on the December 31, 2007, consolidated balance sheet is based on the following assumptions about the operations of Pilot and Sand during 2007 and about the relevant amortization periods of the assets and liabilities to which we allocate the excess in Exhibit 3-7. These assumptions are as follows:

INCOME FOR 2007

Sand's net income	$ 800,000
Pilot's income excluding income from Sand	2,523,500

DIVIDENDS PAID IN 2007

Sand	$ 300,000
Pilot	1,500,000

AMORTIZATION OF EXCESS

Undervalued inventories—sold in 2007
Undervalued land—still held by Sand; no amortization
Undervalued buildings—useful life 45 years from January 1, 2007
Overvalued equipment—useful life 5 years from January 1, 2007
Overvalued notes payable—retired in 2007
Goodwill—no amortization

At December 31, 2007, Pilot's Investment in Sand account has a balance of $10,504,000, consisting of the original $10,200,000 cost, increased by $574,000 investment income from Sand and decreased by $270,000 dividends received from Sand. Pilot's income from Sand for 2007 is calculated under a one-line consolidation as follows:

Equity in Sand's net income ($800,000 × 90%)		$720,000
Add: Amortization of overvalued equipment ($270,000 ÷ 5 years)		54,000
Deduct: Amortization of excess allocated to:		
Inventories (sold in 2007)	$ 90,000	
Land	—	
Buildings ($900,000 ÷ 45 years)	20,000	
Notes payable (retired in 2007)	90,000	
		(200,000)
Income from Sand 2007		$ 574,000

Pilot's net income for 2007 is $3,097,500, consisting of income from its own operations of $2,523,500 plus $574,000 income from Sand. Sand's stockholders' equity increased $500,000 during 2007, from $5,900,000 to $6,400,000. Pilot's retained earnings increased $1,597,500, from $4,300,000 at December 31, 2006, to $5,897,500 at December 31, 2007. We reflect this information in consolidated balance sheet working papers for Pilot and Subsidiary at December 31, 2007, in Exhibit 3-9.

We reproduce the working paper entries as follows:

a	**Common stock—Sand (−SE)**	4,000	
	Other paid-in capital—Sand (−SE)	1,000	
	Retained earnings—Sand (−SE)	1,400	
	Unamortized excess (+A)	4,744	
	Investment in Sand (−A)		10,504
	Noncontrolling interest (+L)		640
	To eliminate reciprocal subsidiary investment and equity accounts, establish noncontrolling interest, and enter the unamortized excess.		
b	**Land (+A)**	180	
	Buildings—net (+A)	880	
	Goodwill (+A)	3,900	
	Equipment—net (−A)		216
	Unamortized excess (−A)		4,744
	To allocate the unamortized excess to identifiable assets and goodwill.		

The differences in the adjustments and eliminations in Exhibit 3-8 and 3-9 result from changes that occurred between December 31, 2006, when the investment was acquired, and December 31, 2007, when the investment had been held for one year. The following schedule provides the basis for the working paper entries that appear in Exhibit 3-9.

	Unamortized Excess December 31, 2006	Amortization 2007	Unamortized Excess December 31, 2007
Inventories	$ 90,000	$ 90,000	$ —
Land	180,000	—	180,000
Buildings—net	900,000	20,000	880,000
Equipment—net	(270,000)*	(54,000)*	(216,000)*
Notes payable	90,000	90,000	—
Goodwill	3,900,000	—	3,900,000
	$4,890,000	$146,000	$4,744,000

*Excess book value over fair value.

PILOT CORPORATION AND SUBSIDIARY
CONSOLIDATED BALANCE SHEET WORKING PAPERS
ON DECEMBER 31, 2007 (IN THOUSANDS)

EXHIBIT 3-9

90% Ownership,
Unamortized Excess
One Year After
Acquisition

	Pilot	90% Sand	Adjustments and Eliminations Debits	Adjustments and Eliminations Credits	Consolidated Balance Sheet
Assets					
Cash	$ 253.5	$ 100			$ 353.5
Receivables—net	540	200			740
Inventories	1,300	600			1,900
Other current assets	800	500			1,300
Land	1,200	600	b 180		1,980
Buildings—net	9,500	3,800	b 880		14,180
Equipment—net	8,000	1,800		b 216	9,584
Investment in Sand	10,504			a 10,504	
Goodwill			b 3,900		3,900
Unamortized excess			a 4,744	b 4,744	
Total assets	$32,097.5	$7,600			$33,937.5
Liabilities and Equity					
Accounts payable	$ 2,300	$1,200			$ 3,500
Notes payable	4,000				4,000
Common stock—Pilot	11,000				11,000
Other paid-in capital—Pilot	8,900				8,900
Retained earnings—Pilot	5,897.5				5,897.5
Common stock—Sand		4,000	a 4,000		
Other paid-in capital—Sand		1,000	a 1,000		
Retained earnings—Sand		1,400	a 1,400		
	$32,097.5	$7,600			
Noncontrolling Interest				a 640	640
Total liabilities and stockholders' equity					$33,937.5

a To eliminate reciprocal subsidiary investment and equity balances, establish noncontrolling interest, and enter the unamortized excess.
b To allocate the unamortized excess to identifiable assets and goodwill.

The following summarizes the transactions recorded by Pilot in its Investment in Sand account:

Initial cost—December 31, 2006	$10,200,000
90% of Sand's 2007 net income	720,000
90% of Sand's 2007 dividends	(270,000)
Amortization of the cost/book value differential	(146,000)
Balance—December 31, 2007	$10,504,000

The consolidated balance sheet working paper adjustments in Exhibit 3-9 show elimination of reciprocal stockholders' equity and Investment in Sand balances. This elimination, entry a, involves debits to Sand's stockholders' equity accounts of $6,400,000, a credit to the noncontrolling interest in Sand of $640,000, and a credit to the Investment in Sand account of $10,504,000. The difference between these debits and credits totals $4,744,000, representing the unamortized excess of investment over book value acquired on December 31, 2007, and we enter it in the working papers as unamortized excess.

The undervalued inventory items and the overvalued notes payable on Sand's books at December 31, 2006, were fully amortized in 2007 (the inventory was sold and the notes payable were retired); therefore, these items do not require balance sheet adjustments at December 31, 2007. We enter the remaining items—land, $180,000; buildings, $880,000; equipment, $216,000 (overvaluation); and goodwill, $3,900,000 (which account for the $4,744,000 unamortized excess)—in the consolidated balance sheet working papers through working paper entry b, which allocates the unamortized excess as of the balance sheet date. Technically, the working paper entries shown in Exhibit 3-9 are combination adjustment and elimination entries, because we eliminate the Investment in Sand and stockholders' equity accounts of Sand, reclassify the noncontrolling interest into a single amount representing 10% of Sand's stockholders' equity, and adjust the asset accounts.

CONSOLIDATED INCOME STATEMENT

Exhibit 3-10 presents comparative separate-company and consolidated income and retained earnings statements for Pilot Corporation and Subsidiary. These statements reflect the previous assumptions and amounts that were used in preparing the consolidated balance sheet working papers for Pilot and Sand. Detailed revenue and expense items have been added to illustrate the consolidated income statement, but all assumptions and amounts are completely compatible with those already introduced. Adjustments and elimination entries have not been included in the illustration. These entries are covered extensively in Chapter 4.

The difference between a consolidated income statement and an unconsolidated income statement of the parent company lies in the detail presented rather than the net income amount. You can see this in Exhibit 3-10 by comparing the separate income statement of Pilot with the consolidated income statement of Pilot and Subsidiary.

Pilot's separate income statement shows the revenues and expenses from Pilot's own operations plus its investment income from Sand.[8] By contrast, the consolidated income statement column shows the revenues and expenses of both Sand and Pilot but does not show the investment income from Sand. The $574,000 investment income is excluded because the consolidated income statement includes the detailed revenues ($2,200,000), expenses ($1,400,000), net amortization of the excess ($146,000), and the noncontrolling interest deduction ($80,000) that account for the investment income.

We reflect the net amortization in the consolidated income statement by increasing cost of goods sold for the $90,000 undervalued inventories that were sold in 2007, increasing depreciation expense on buildings for the $20,000 amortization on the excess allocated to buildings, decreasing depreciation on equipment for the $54,000 amortization of the excess allocated to overvalued equipment, and increasing interest expense for the $90,000 allocated to overvalued notes payable that were retired in 2007.

Consolidated income statements, like consolidated balance sheets, are more than summations of the income accounts of affiliated companies. A summation of all income statement items for Pilot and Sand would result in a combined income figure of $3,897,500, whereas consolidated net income is only $3,097,500. The $800,000 difference between these two amounts lies in the investment income of $574,000, the $146,000 net amortization, and the $80,000 income allocated to noncontrolling stockholders.

Note that consolidated net income represents income to the stockholders of the parent corporation. Income of noncontrolling stockholders is a deduction in the determination of consolidated net income.

If the parent company sells merchandise to its subsidiary, or vice versa, there will be intercompany purchases and sales on the separate books of the parent and its subsidiary. Intercompany purchases and sales balances are reciprocals that must be eliminated in preparing consolidated income

---

[8] A parent company's income from subsidiary investments is referred to as income from subsidiary, equity in subsidiary earnings, investment income from subsidiary, or other descriptive captions.

	Separate Company		
	Pilot	Sand	Consolidated
Sales	$ 9,523.5	$2,200	$11,723.5
Investment income from Sand	574		
Total revenue	10,097.5	2,200	11,723.5
Less: Operating expenses			
Cost of sales	4,000	700	4,790
Depreciation expense—buildings	200	80	300
Depreciation expense—equipment	700	360	1,006
Other expenses	1,800	120	1,920
Total operating expense	6,700	1,260	8,016
Operating income	3,397.5	940	3,707.5
Nonoperating item:			
Interest expense	300	140	530
Net income	**$ 3,097.5**	**$ 800**	
Subtotal			3,177.5
Less: Noncontrolling interest expense			80
Consolidated net income			**$ 3,097.5**
Retained earnings December 31, 2006	4,300	900	4,300
	7,397.5	1,700	7,397.5
Deduct: Dividends	1,500	300	1,500
Retained earnings December 31, 2007	$ 5,897.5	$1,400	$ 5,897.5

PILOT AND SAND CORPORATIONS
SEPARATE COMPANY AND CONSOLIDATED STATEMENTS
OF INCOME AND RETAINED EARNINGS
FOR THE YEAR ENDED DECEMBER 31, 2007 (IN THOUSANDS)

EXHIBIT 3-10

Separate Company and Consolidated Income and Retained Earnings Statements

statements because they do not represent purchases and sales to parties outside the consolidated entity. Intercompany inventory transactions are discussed in greater detail in Chapter 5. Adjustments for intercompany sales and purchases reduce revenue (sales) and expenses (cost of goods sold) by the same amount and therefore have no effect on consolidated net income. Reciprocal rent income and expense amounts are likewise eliminated without affecting consolidated net income.

Observe that Pilot's separate retained earnings are identical to consolidated retained earnings. As expected, the $5,897,500 ending consolidated retained earnings in Exhibit 3-10 is the same amount that appears in the consolidated balance sheet for Pilot and Subsidiary at December 31, 2007 (see Exhibit 3-9).

PUSH-DOWN ACCOUNTING

In the Pilot and Sand illustration, we recorded the investment on the books of Pilot at cost and allocated the purchase price of identifiable assets and liabilities and goodwill through working paper adjusting entries. In some instances, the allocation of the purchase price may be recorded in the subsidiary accounts—in other words, pushed down to the subsidiary records. **Push-down accounting** is the process of recording the effects of the purchase price allocation directly on the books of the subsidiary.

Push-down accounting affects the books of the subsidiary and separate subsidiary financial statements. It does not alter consolidated financial statements and, in fact, simplifies the consolidation process.

The SEC requires push-down accounting for SEC filings when a subsidiary is substantially wholly owned (approximately 90%) with no publicly held debt or preferred stock outstanding.

Pack Corporation gives 5,000 shares of Pack $10 par common stock and $100,000 cash for all the capital stock of Simm Company, a closely held company, on January 3, 2006. At this time, Pack's stock is quoted on a national exchange at $55 a share. We summarize Simm's balance sheet and fair value information on January 3 as follows (in thousands):

	Book Value	Fair Value
Cash	$ 30	$ 30
Accounts receivable—net	90	90
Inventories	130	150
Land	30	70
Buildings—net	150	130
Equipment—net	80	120
	$510	$590
Current liabilities	$100	$100
Long-term debt	150	150
Capital stock, $10 par	150	
Retained earnings	110	
	$510	

Under push-down accounting, Pack records its investment in Simm in the usual manner:

Investment in Simm (+A)	375	
Cash (−A)		100
Capital stock, $10 par (+SE)		50
Paid-in capital (+SE)		225
To record acquisition of Simm Company.		

On Parent's Books

An entry must also be made on Simm's books on January 3 to record the new asset bases, including goodwill, in its accounts. Because Simm is considered similar to a new entity, it also has to reclassify retained earnings. Simm makes the following entry to record the push-down values:

Inventories (+A)	20	
Land (+A)	40	
Equipment—net (+A)	40	
Goodwill (+A)	35	
Retained earnings (−SE)	110	
Building—net (−A)		20
Push-down capital (+SE) RE + GW + FV of Assets ↑ or ↓		225

Made on Subsidiary Books

Simm (the subsidiary) records this entry on its separate accounting records when using push-down accounting.

A separate balance sheet prepared for Simm Company immediately after the business combination on January 3 includes the following accounts and amounts (in thousands):

Cash	$ 30
Accounts receivable—net	90
Inventories	150
Land	70
Buildings—net	130
Equipment—net	120
Goodwill	35
	$625
Current liabilities	$100
Long-term debt	150
Capital stock, $10 par	150
Push-down capital	225
	$625

In consolidating the balance sheets of Pack and Simm at January 3, 2006, after the push-down entries are made on Simm's books, we eliminate the investment in Simm account on Pack's books against Simm's capital stock and push-down capital and combine the other accounts.

PREPARING A CONSOLIDATED BALANCE SHEET WORKSHEET

LEARNING OBJECTIVE 9

In this section you will learn how to set up a worksheet to prepare a consolidated balance sheet. Refer to Exhibit 3-11. We have two columns to record the balance sheet information for a parent company and (in our example) a 90%-owned subsidiary company. The numbers in these two columns are simply copied from the individual-company balance sheets. We include two columns to record the debits and credits for consolidation adjustments and eliminations. The final column provides calculations of the correct consolidated balance sheet totals.

Exhibit 3-11 shows spreadsheet formulae used in preparing the worksheet. Notice that most of these can be input using the COPY command *available in the spreadsheet software*. In the first two columns, total assets and total equities are simple summations of the relevant balances. The adjustments and eliminations columns each contain a single summation formula for the column totals. This is useful in verifying the equality of debits and credits—that in other words, you have not made any errors in posting your consolidation entries.

There are lots of formulae in the consolidated statements column, but again most of these can be entered with the COPY command. Let's look at the formula for Cash (=B7+C7+D7−E7). We

EXHIBIT 3-11

Worksheet for Consolidated Balance Sheet

PARENT CORPORATION AND SUBSIDIARY
CONSOLIDATED BALANCE SHEET WORKING PAPER
DECEMBER 31, 2006

(in thousands)	Parent	Subsidiary	Adjustments and Eliminations Debits	Credits	Consolidated Balance Sheet
Cash	420	200			=B7+C7+D7−E7
Receivables—net	500	1,300			=B8+C8+D8−E8
Inventories	4,000	500			=B9+C9+D9−E9
Land	1,500	2,000			=B10+C10+D10−E10
Equipment—net	6,000	1,000			=B11+C11+D11−E11
Investment in Subsidiary	4,090				=B12+C12+D12−E12
					=B13+C13+D13−E13
Total assets	=SUM(B7:B13)	=SUM(C7:C13)			=B14+C14+D14−E14
Accounts payable	4,100	800			=B15+C15−D15+E15
Dividends payable	600	100			=B16+C16−D16+E16
Capital stock	10,000	3,000			=B17+C17−D17+E17
Retained earnings	1,810	1,100			=B18+C18−D18+E18
Total equities	=SUM(B15:B18)	=SUM(C15:C18)			
					=SUM(F15:F21)
			=SUM(D7:D22)	=SUM(E7:E22)	

simply sum parent-company cash plus subsidiary-company cash and then make any needed adjustments and eliminations. Notice that cash has a normal debit balance, so we add the debit adjustments (+D7) and subtract credits (−E7) to arrive at the consolidated total. We can copy our formula for all accounts having normal debit balances (i.e., all assets).

Now let's review the formula for Accounts payable (=B15+C15−D15+E15). We sum parent-company payables plus subsidiary-company accounts payable and then make adjustments and eliminations. Notice that accounts payable has a normal credit balance, so we subtract debit adjustments (−D15) and add credits (+E15) to arrive at the consolidated total. We can copy our formula for all accounts having normal credit balances (i.e., all liabilities and equities).

We will discuss the completion of the worksheet by working through a sample problem. Separate company balance sheets for Parent Corporation and Subsidiary Company at December 31, 2006, are summarized as follows (in thousands):

	Parent Corporation	Subsidiary Company
Cash	$ 420	$ 200
Accounts receivable—net	500	1,300
Inventories	4,000	500
Land	1,500	2,000
Equipment—net	6,000	1,000
Investment in Subsidiary	4,090	
Total assets	$16,510	$5,000
Accounts payable	$ 4,100	$ 800
Dividends payable	600	100
Capital stock	10,000	3,000
Retained earnings	1,810	1,100
Total equities	$16,510	$5,000

Parent Corporation acquired 90% of the outstanding voting shares of Subsidiary Company for $4,000,000 on January 1, 2006, when Subsidiary's stockholders' equity was $4,000,000. All of the assets and liabilities of Subsidiary were stated at their fair values when Parent acquired its 90% interest. During 2006, Subsidiary reported net income of $200,000 and declared a dividend of $100,000. The dividend remained unpaid on December 31.

We enter the data into our worksheet in Exhibit 3-11. We record balance sheet amounts picked up from the parent and the subsidiary. Total assets and total equities are simple summation functions. Next, we will review the required consolidation adjustments and eliminations. We provide a separate Exhibit 3-12 to show the final worksheet, after posting the adjustments and eliminations. This is simply Exhibit 3-11 updated to reflect the entries that follow. Notice too, that we have added some new accounts. We create noncontrolling interest and goodwill and copy the relevant formulae. The first working paper entry in Exhibit 3-12 is the following:

a	**Capital stock (−SE)**	**3,000**	
	Retained earnings (−SE)	**1,100**	
	Goodwill (+A)	**400**	
	Investment in Subsidiary (−A)		**4,090**
	Noncontrolling interest (+L)		**410**
	To enter goodwill and the noncontrolling interest and to eliminate		
	subsidiary capital accounts and the parent-company investment account.		

Here is a journal entry for working paper entry b for Exhibit 3-12:

b	**Dividends payable (−L)**	**90**	
	Receivables—net (−A)		**90**
	To eliminate the intercompany receivable and payable for dividends.		

EXHIBIT 3-12

Final Worksheet

PARENT CORPORATION AND SUBSIDIARY
CONSOLIDATED BALANCE SHEET WORKING PAPER
DECEMBER 31, 2006

(in thousands)	Parent	Subsidiary	Adjustments and Eliminations Debits	Credits	Consolidated Balance Sheet
Cash	420	200			620
Receivables—net	500	1,300		b 90	1,710
Inventories	4,000	500			4,500
Land	1,500	2,000			3,500
Equipment—net	6,000	1,000			7,000
Investment in Subsidiary	4,090			a 4,090	0
Goodwill	_____	_____	a 400		400
Total assets	16,510	5,000			17,730
Accounts payable	4,100	800			4,900
Dividends payable	600	100	b 90		610
Capital stock	10,000	3,000	a 3,000		10,000
Retained earnings	1,810	1,100	a 1,100		1,810
Total equities	16,510	5,000			
Noncontrolling interest				a 410	410
					17,730
			4,590	4,590	

Our spreadsheet formulae compute the consolidated totals for us in the final column, completing the worksheet. Practice creating the spreadsheet for a few problems to be certain you understand the mechanics. However, you will not need to create your own spreadsheet for all problem assignments. We eliminate the drudgery, and allow you to focus on learning the concepts, by providing spreadsheet templates for many assignments on the *Advanced Accounting* Web site. An icon in the assignment material indicates the availability of a template. The templates include the data for the parent and subsidiary companies and the formulae for calculating the consolidated balances.

SUMMARY

GAAP usually requires consolidated financial statements for the fair presentation of financial position and the results of operations of a parent company and its subsidiaries. Consolidated financial statements are not merely summations of parent-company and subsidiary financial statement items. Consolidated statements eliminate reciprocal amounts and combine and include only nonreciprocal amounts. We eliminate the investment in subsidiary and the subsidiary stockholders' equity accounts in the preparation of consolidated financial statements because they are reciprocal, both representing the net assets of the subsidiary. Sales, borrowing, and leasing transactions between parent and subsidiaries also give rise to reciprocal amounts that we eliminate in the consolidating process.

The stockholders' equity amounts that appear in the consolidated balance sheet are those of the parent company, except for the equity of noncontrolling stockholders, which may be reported as a separate item within or outside of consolidated stockholders' equity. Consolidated net income is a measurement of income to the stockholders of the parent company. Any income accruing to the benefit of noncontrolling stockholders is a deduction in determination of consolidated net income. Parent-company net income and retained earnings are equal to consolidated net income and consolidated retained earnings, respectively.

QUESTIONS

1. When does a corporation become a subsidiary of another corporation?
2. In allocating the excess of investment cost over book value acquired of a subsidiary, are the amounts allocated to identifiable assets and liabilities (land and notes payable, for example) recorded separately in the accounts of the parent company? Explain.
3. If the fair value of a subsidiary corporation's land was $100,000 and its book value was $90,000 when the parent company acquired its 100% interest for cash, at what amount would the land be included in the consolidated balance sheet immediately after the acquisition? Would your answer be different if the parent company had acquired an 80% interest?
4. Define or explain the terms *parent company*, *subsidiary company*, *affiliated companies*, and *associated companies*.
5. What is a noncontrolling interest?
6. Describe the circumstances under which the accounts of a subsidiary would not be included in the consolidated financial statements.
7. Who are the primary users for which consolidated financial statements are intended?
8. What amount of capital stock is reported in a consolidated balance sheet?
9. In what general ledger would you expect to find the account "goodwill from consolidation"?
10. How should the parent company's investment in subsidiary account be classified in a consolidated balance sheet? In the parent company's separate balance sheet?
11. Name some reciprocal accounts that might be found in the separate records of a parent company and its subsidiaries.
12. Why are reciprocal amounts eliminated in the preparation of consolidated financial statements?
13. How does the stockholders' equity of the parent company that uses the equity method of accounting differ from the consolidated stockholders' equity of the parent company and its subsidiaries?
14. Is there a difference in the amounts reported in the statement of retained earnings of a parent that uses the equity method of accounting and the amounts that appear in the consolidated retained earnings statement?
15. Is noncontrolling interest expense an expense? Explain.
16. Describe how the total noncontrolling interest at the end of an accounting period is determined.
17. What special procedures are required to consolidate the statements of a parent company that reports on a calendar-year basis and a subsidiary whose fiscal year ends on October 31?
18. Does the acquisition of shares held by noncontrolling shareholders constitute a business combination?

NOTE: Don't forget the assumptions on page 50 when working exercises and problems in this chapter.

EXERCISES

E 3-1
General questions

1. A 75%-owned subsidiary should not be consolidated under the provisions of *FASB Statement No. 94*, "Consolidation of All Majority-Owned Subsidiaries," when:
   a Its operations are dissimilar from those of the parent company
   b Control of the subsidiary does not lie with the parent company
   c There is a dominant noncontrolling interest in the subsidiary
   d Management feels that consolidation would not provide the most meaningful financial statements

2. Under the provisions of *FASB Statement No. 94*, an 80% owned subsidiary that cannot be consolidated must be accounted for:
   a Under the equity method
   b Under the cost method
   c Under the equity method if the parent can exercise significant influence over the subsidiary
   d At market value if the subsidiary is in bankruptcy

3. Consolidated statements for Porter Corporation and its 60%-owned investee, Spinelli Company, will not be prepared under the provisions of *FASB Statement No. 94* if:

  a The fiscal periods of Porter and Spinelli are more than three months apart
  b Porter is a major manufacturing company and Spinelli is an insurance company
  c Spinelli is a foreign company
  d Porter will spin off all Spinelli shares to Porter stockholders within the next year

4. Armor Industries owns 7,000,000 shares of Babbitt Corporation's outstanding common stock (a 70% interest). The remaining 3,000,000 outstanding common shares of Babbitt are held by Ottman Insurance Company. On Armor Industries' consolidated financial statements, Ottman Insurance Company is considered:

  a An investee
  b An associated company
  c An affiliated company
  d A noncontrolling interest

5. Pella Corporation owns a 60% interest in Sanico Company and an 80% interest in Talbert Company. Pella consolidates its investment in Sanico, but Talbert, which is currently under protection of the bankruptcy court, is not consolidated, and Pella accounts for this investment by the equity method. Which statement is correct?

  a Consolidated retained earnings will not reflect the earnings of Talbert.
  b Consolidated net income will be the same as if both subsidiaries were consolidated.
  c The individual assets and liabilities of Sanico and Talbert are reflected in Pella's consolidated statements.
  d Noncontrolling income will be reported the same as if both subsidiaries were consolidated.

6. On January 1, 2006, Paxton Company purchased 75% of the outstanding shares of Salem Company at a cost exceeding the book value and fair value of Salem's net assets. Using the following notations, describe the amount at which the plant assets will appear in a consolidated balance sheet of Paxton Company and Subsidiary prepared immediately after the acquisition:

P_{bv} = book value of Paxton's plant assets
P_{fv} = fair value of Paxton's plant assets
S_{bv} = book value of Salem's plant assets
S_{fv} = fair value of Salem's plant assets

  a $P_{bv} + S_{bv} \pm 0.75(S_{fv} - S_{bv})$
  b $P_{bv} + 0.75(S_{bv}) \pm 0.75(S_{fv} - S_{bv})$
  c $P_{bv} + 0.75(S_{fv})$
  d $P_{fv} + S_{bv} \pm 0.75(S_{fv} - S_{bv})$

E 3-2

General questions

1. Under *FASB Statement No. 94*, "Consolidation of All Majority-Owned Subsidiaries," a parent company should exclude a subsidiary from consolidation if:

  a It measures income from the subsidiary under the equity method
  b The subsidiary is in a regulated industry
  c The subsidiary is a foreign entity whose books are recorded in a foreign currency
  d The parent expects to sell the subsidiary investment within a year

2. The FASB's primary motivation for issuing *FASB Statement No. 94*, "Consolidation of All Majority-Owned Subsidiaries," was to:

  a Ensure disclosure of all loss contingencies
  b Prevent the use of off–balance sheet financing
  c Improve comparability of the statements of cash flows
  d Establish criteria for exclusion of finance and insurance subsidiaries from consolidation

3. Parent-company and consolidated financial statement amounts would not be the same for:

  a Capital stock
  b Retained earnings
  c Investments in unconsolidated subsidiaries
  d Investments in consolidated subsidiaries

4. Noncontrolling interest, as it appears in a consolidated balance sheet, refers to:

  a Owners of less than 50% of the parent company's stock
  b Parent's interest in subsidiary companies
  c Interest expense on subsidiary's bonds payable
  d Equity in the subsidiary's net assets held by stockholders other than the parent

5. Pat Corporation acquired an 80% interest in Sal Corporation on January 1, 2007, and issued consolidated financial statements at and for the year ended December 31, 2007. Pat and Sal had issued separate-company financial statements in 2006.

a *The change in reporting entity is reported by restating the financial statements of all prior periods presented as consolidated statements.*

b *The cumulative effect of the change in reporting entity is shown in a separate category of the income statement net of tax.*

c *The income effect of the error is charged or credited directly to beginning retained earnings.*

d *The income effect of the accounting change is spread over the current and future periods.*

6. The noncontrolling interest expense that appears in the consolidated income statement is computed as follows:

a *Consolidated net income is multiplied by the noncontrolling interest percentage.*

b *The subsidiary's income less amortization of cost/book value differentials is multiplied by the noncontrolling interest percentage.*

c *Subsidiary net income is subtracted from consolidated net income.*

d *Subsidiary income determined for consolidated statement purposes is multiplied by the noncontrolling interest percentage.*

7. The retained earnings that appear on the consolidated balance sheet of a parent company and its 60%-owned subsidiary are:

a *The parent company's retained earnings plus 100% of the subsidiary's retained earnings*

b *The parent company's retained earnings plus 60% of the subsidiary's retained earnings*

c *The parent company's retained earnings*

d *Pooled retained earnings*

E 3-3

[AICPA adapted] General problems Use the following information in answering questions 1 and 2:

Apex Company acquired 70% of the outstanding stock of Nadir Corporation. The separate balance sheet of Apex immediately after the acquisition and the consolidated balance sheet are as follows:

	Apex	Consolidated	Nadir
Current assets	$106,000	$146,000	40,000
Investment in Nadir—cost	100,000	—	
Goodwill	—	8,100	
Fixed assets—net	270,000	370,000	90,000
	$476,000	$524,100	
Current liabilities	$ 15,000	$ 28,000	13,000
Capital stock	350,000	350,000	
Minority interest	—	35,100	117,000
Retained earnings	111,000	111,000	
	$476,000	$524,100	

Of the excess payment for the investment in Nadir, $10,000 was ascribed to undervaluation of its fixed assets. The balance of the excess payment was ascribed to goodwill. Current assets of Nadir included a $2,000 receivable from Apex, which arose before they became related on an ownership basis.

The following two items relate to Nadir's separate balance sheet prepared at the time Apex acquired its 70% interest in Nadir.

1. What was the total of the current assets on Nadir's separate balance sheet immediately before Apex acquired its 70% interest?

a $38,000
b $40,000
c $42,000
d $104,000

consolidated 146,000
- Apex Curr Ass -106,000
+ Receiva from Apex 2,000
42,000

2. What was the total stockholders' equity on Nadir's separate balance sheet at the time Apex acquired its 70% interest?

a $64,900
b $70,000
c $100,000
d $117,000

35,100 / 30% = 117,000

3. Cobb Company's current receivables from affiliated companies at December 31, 2006, are (1) a $75,000 cash advance to Hill Corporation (Cobb owns 30% of the voting stock of Hill and accounts for the investment by the equity method), (2) a receivable of $260,000 from Vick Corporation for administrative and selling services (Vick is 100% owned by Cobb and is included in Cobb's consolidated financial statements), and (3) a receivable of $200,000 from Ward Corporation for merchandise sales on credit (Ward is a 90%-owned, unconsolidated

subsidiary of Cobb accounted for by the equity method). In the current assets section of its December 31, 2006, consolidated balance sheet, Cobb should report accounts receivable from investees in the amount of:

a $180,000
b $255,000
c $275,000
d $535,000

75,000 Hill
200,000 Ward - unconsolidated

Use the following information in answering questions 4 and 5:

On January 1, 2006, Owen Corporation purchased all of Sharp Corporation's common stock for $1,200,000. On that date, the fair values of Sharp's assets and liabilities equaled their carrying amounts of $1,320,000 and $320,000, respectively. Owen's policy is to amortize intangibles other than goodwill over 10 years. During 2006, Sharp paid cash dividends of $20,000.

Selected information from the separate balance sheets and income statements of Owen and Sharp as of December 31, 2006, and for the year then ended follows (in thousands):

	Owen	Sharp
Balance Sheet Accounts		
Investment in subsidiary	$1,320	—
Retained earnings	1,240	$ 560
Total stockholders' equity	2,620	1,120
Income Statement Accounts		
Operating income	$ 420	$ 200
Equity in earnings of Sharp	140	—
Net income	400	140

4. In Owen's 2006 consolidated income statement, what amount should be reported for amortization of goodwill?

a 0
b $12,000
c $18,000
d $20,000

5. In Owen's December 31, 2006, consolidated balance sheet, what amount should be reported as total retained earnings?

a $1,240,000
b $1,360,000
c $1,380,000
d $1,800,000

6. Wright Corporation has several subsidiaries that are included in its consolidated financial statements. In its December 31, 2006, trial balance, Wright had the following intercompany balances before eliminations:

	Debit	Credit
Current receivable due from Main Co.	$ 32,000	
Noncurrent receivable from Main	114,000	
Cash advance from Corn Corp.	6,000	
Cash advance from King Co.		$ 15,000
Intercompany payable to King		101,000

7. In its December 31, 2006, consolidated balance sheet, what amount should Wright report as intercompany receivables?

a $152,000
b $146,000
c $36,000
d 0

All intercompany receivables and payables are eliminated.

E 3-4

Correction of consolidated net income Pina Corporation paid $900,000 for a 90% interest in Santa Maria Corporation on January 1, 2006, at a price of $30,000 in excess of underlying book value. The excess was allocated as follows: $12,000 to undervalued equipment with a three-year remaining useful life and $18,000 to goodwill. The income statements of Pina and Santa Maria for 2006 are summarized as follows (in thousands):

	Pina	Santa Maria
Sales	$2,000	$800
Income from Santa Maria	90	
Cost of sales	(1,000)	(400)
Depreciation expense	(200)	(120)
Other expenses	(400)	(180)
Net income	$ 490	$100

REQUIRED

1. Calculate the goodwill that should appear in the consolidated balance sheet of Pina and Subsidiary at December 31, 2006.

2. Calculate consolidated net income for 2006.

E 3-5

Disclosure of consolidated dividends On December 31, 2006, the separate-company financial statements for Panderman Corporation and its 70%-owned subsidiary, Sadisman Corporation, had the following account balances related to dividends (in thousands):

	Panderman	Sadisman
Dividends for 2006	$600	$400
Dividends payable at December 31, 2006	300	100

REQUIRED

1. At what amount will dividends be shown in the consolidated retained earnings statement?

2. At what amount should dividends payable be shown in the consolidated balance sheet?

E 3-6

Prepare journal entries and balance sheet under push-down accounting Book values and fair values of Slider Corporation's assets and liabilities on December 31, 2006, are as follows (in thousands):

	Book Value	Fair Value
Cash	$ 70	$ 70
Accounts receivable—net	80	80
Inventories	80	100
Land	150	200
Buildings—net	350	500
Equipment—net	220	300
	$950	$1,250
Accounts payable	$100	$ 100
Note payable	140	150
Capital stock	500	
Retained earnings	210	
	$950	

On January 1, 2007, Portal Corporation acquires all of Slider's capital stock for $1,250,000 cash. The acquisition is recorded using push-down accounting.

REQUIRED

1. Prepare the January 1 journal entry on Slider's books to record push-down values.

2. Prepare a balance sheet for Slider Corporation immediately after the business combination on January 1 under push-down accounting.

E 3-7

Prepare consolidated income statements with and without cost-book value differentials Summary income statement information for Pasture Corporation and its 70%-owned subsidiary, Situation Specialists Corporation, for the year 2007 is as follows (in thousands):

	Pasture	Situation Specialists
Sales	$1,000	$400
Income from Situation Specialists	49	—
Cost of sales	(600)	(200)
Depreciation expense	(50)	(40)
Other expenses	(199)	(90)
Net income (2007)	$ 200	$ 70

REQUIRED

1. Assume that Pasture acquired its 70% interest in Situation Specialists at book value on January 1, 2006, when Situation Specialists' assets and liabilities were equal to their recorded book values. There were no intercompany transactions during 2006 and 2007. Prepare a consolidated income statement for Pasture Corporation and Subsidiary for 2007.

2. Assume that Pasture acquired its 70% interest in Situation Specialists on January 1, 2006, at a price of $20,000 in excess of book value and that $10,000 *was allocated* to a reduction of overvalued equipment with a five-year remaining useful life and $30,000 was allocated to goodwill. There were no intercompany transactions during 2006 and 2007. Prepare a consolidated income statement for Pasture Corporation and Subsidiary for 2007.

E 3-8

Calculate consolidated balance sheet amounts with goodwill and noncontrolling interest

Poball Corporation acquired an 80% interest in Softcan Corporation on January 2, 2006, for $700,000. On this date the capital stock and retained earnings of the two companies were as follows (in thousands):

	Poball	Softcan
Capital stock	$1,800	$500
Retained earnings	800	100

The assets and liabilities of Softcan were stated at their fair values when Poball acquired its 80% interest. Poball uses the equity method to account for its investment in Softcan.

Net income and dividends for 2006 for the affiliated companies were as follows:

	Poball	Softcan
Net income	$300	$90
Dividends declared	180	50
Dividends payable December 31, 2006	90	25

REQUIRED: Calculate the amounts at which the following items should appear in the consolidated balance sheet on December 31, 2006.

1. Capital stock
2. Goodwill
3. Consolidated retained earnings
4. Noncontrolling interest
5. Dividends payable

E 3-9

Prepare stockholders' equity section of consolidated balance sheet one year after acquisition

Paskey and Salam Corporations' balance sheets at December 31, 2006, are summarized as follows (in thousands):

	Paskey	Salam
Cash	$255	$ 60
Other assets	200	175
Total assets	$455	$235
Liabilities	$ 70	$ 35
Capital stock, par $10	300	175
Additional paid-in capital	50	15
Retained earnings	35	10
Total equities	$455	$235

Paskey acquired 80% of the voting stock of Salam on January 2, 2007, at $15 per share. The fair values of Salam's net assets were equal to their book values on January 2, 2007.

During 2007, Paskey reported earnings of $55,000, including income from Salam of $16,000, and paid dividends of $25,000. Salam's earnings for 2007 were $20,000 and its dividends were $15,000.

REQUIRED: Prepare the stockholders' equity section of the December 31, 2007, consolidated balance sheet for Paskey Corporation and Subsidiary.

E 3-10

Prepare consolidated income statement 3 years after acquisition Comparative income statements of Peekos Corporation and Slogger Corporation for the year ended December 31, 2008, are as follows (in thousands):

	Peekos	Slogger
Sales	$1,600	$500
Income from Slogger	130	—
Total revenue	1,730	500
Less: Cost of goods sold	900	200
Operating expenses	400	150
Total expenses	1,300	350
Net income	$ 430	$150

ADDITIONAL INFORMATION

1. Slogger is a 90%-owned subsidiary of Peekos, acquired by Peekos for $820,000 on January 1, 2006, when Slogger's stockholders' equity was $700,000.
2. The excess of the cost of Peekos's investment in Slogger over book value acquired *was allocated* $30,000 to inventories that were sold in 2006, $20,000 to equipment with a four-year remaining useful life, and the remainder to goodwill.

REQUIRED: Prepare a consolidated income statement for Peekos Corporation and Subsidiary for the year ended December 31, 2008.

PROBLEMS

P 3-1

Prepare a consolidated balance sheet at acquisition and compute consolidated net income one year later On December 31, 2006, Pennyvale Corporation purchased 80% of the stock of Sutherland Sales Company at book value. The data reported on their separate balance sheets immediately after the acquisition follow. At December 31, 2006, Pennyvale Corporation owes Sutherland Sales $5,000 on accounts payable. (All amounts are in thousands.)

	Pennyvale Corporation	Sutherland Sales
Assets		
Cash	$ 32	$ 18
Accounts receivable	45	34
Inventories	143	56
Investment in Sutherland	200	
Equipment—net	380	175
	$800	$283
Liabilities and Stockholders' Equity		
Accounts payable	$ 40	$ 33
Common stock, $10 par	460	150
Retained earnings	300	100
	$800	$283

REQUIRED

1. Prepare a consolidated balance sheet for Pennyvale Corporation and Subsidiary at December 31, 2006.
2. Compute consolidated net income for 2007 assuming that Pennyvale Corporation reported separate income of $170,000 and Sutherland Sales Company reported net income of $90,000. (Separate incomes does *not* include income from the investment in Sutherland Sales.)

P 3-2

Allocation schedule for cost-book value differential and consolidated balance sheet at acquisition Parlor Corporation acquired 70% of the outstanding common stock of Setting Corporation on January 1, 2006, for $178,000 cash. Immediately after this acquisition the balance sheet information for the two companies was as follows (in thousands):

	Parlor Book Value	Setting Book Value	Fair Value
Assets			
Cash	$ 32	$ 20	$ 20
Receivables—net	80	30	30
Inventories	70	30	50
Land	100	50	60
Buildings—net	110	70	90
Equipment—net	80	40	30
Investment in Setting	178	—	—
Total assets	$650	$240	$280
Liabilities and Stockholders' Equity			
Accounts payable	$ 90	$ 80	$ 80
Other liabilities	10	50	40
Capital stock, $10 par	500	100	
Retained earnings	50	10	
Total equities	$650	$240	

REQUIRED

1. Prepare a schedule to allocate the difference between the cost of the investment in Setting and the book value of the interest to identifiable and unidentifiable net assets.

2. Prepare a consolidated balance sheet for Parlor Corporation and Subsidiary at January 1, 2006.

P 3-3

Prepare allocation schedule with reallocation of negative goodwill
PJ Corporation pays $2,700,000 for an 80% interest in Softback Books Corporation on January 1, 2006, at which time the book value and fair value of Softback Books' net assets are as follows (in thousands):

	Book Value	Fair Value
Current assets	$1,000	$1,500
Equipment—net	2,000	3,000
Other plant assets—net	1,000	1,000
Liabilities	(1,500)	(1,500)
Net assets	$2,500	$4,000

REQUIRED: Prepare a schedule to allocate the cost/book value differentials to Softback Books' net assets.

P 3-4

Given separate and consolidated balance sheets, reconstruct the schedule to allocate the cost-book value differential
Pharm Corporation purchased a block of Specht Company common stock for $260,000 cash on January 1, 2006. Separate-company and consolidated balance sheets prepared immediately after the acquisition are summarized as follows (in thousands):

Pharm Corporation and Subsidiary Consolidated Balance Sheet at January 1, 2006

	Pharm	Specht	Consolidated
Assets			
Current assets	$ 190	$100	$ 290
Investment in Specht	260	—	—
Plant assets—net	550	200	758
Goodwill	—	—	44
Total assets	$1,000	$300	$1,092
Equities			
Liabilities	$ 400	$ 40	$ 440
Capital stock, $10 par	500	200	500
Retained earnings	100	60	100
Noncontrolling interest	—	—	52
Total equities	$1,000	$300	$1,092

REQUIRED: Reconstruct the schedule to allocate the cost/book value differential from Pharm's investment in Specht.

P 3-5

Prepare a consolidated balance sheet one year after acquisition Adjusted trial balances for Palmer and Sorrel Corporations at December 31, 2006, are as follows (in thousands):

	Palmer	Sorrel
Debits		
Current assets	$ 240	$100
Plant assets—net	500	300
Investment in Sorrel	420	—
Cost of sales	300	300
Other expenses	100	50
Dividends	50	—
	$1,610	$750
Credits		
Liabilities	$ 450	$210
Capital stock	300	50
Retained earnings	340	90
Sales	500	400
Income from Sorrel	20	—
	$1,610	$750

Palmer purchased all the stock of Sorrel for $400,000 cash on January 1, 2006, when Sorrel's stockholders' equity consisted of $50,000 capital stock and $90,000 retained earnings. Sorrel's assets and liabilities were fairly valued except for inventory items that were undervalued by $20,000 and sold in 2006, and plant assets that were undervalued by $40,000 and had a remaining useful life of four years from the date of business combination.

REQUIRED: Prepare a consolidated balance sheet for Palmer Corporation and Subsidiary at December 31, 2006.

P 3-6

Consolidated balance sheet working papers with goodwill and dividends Perry Corporation paid $400,000 cash for 90% of Sim Corporation's common stock on January 1, 2006, when Sim had $300,000 capital stock and $100,000 retained earnings. The book values of Sim's assets and liabilities were equal to fair values. During 2006, Sim reported net income of $20,000 and declared $10,000 in dividends on December 31. Balance sheets for Perry and Sim at December 31, 2006, are as follows (in thousands):

	Perry	Sim
Assets		
Cash	$ 42	$ 20
Receivables—net	50	130
Inventories	400	50
Land	150	200
Equipment—net	600	100
Investment in Sim	409	—
	$1,651	$500
Equities		
Accounts payable	$ 410	$ 80
Dividends payable	60	10
Capital stock	1,000	300
Retained earnings	181	110
	$1,651	$500

REQUIRED: Prepare consolidated balance sheet working papers for Perry Corporation and Subsidiary for December 31, 2006.

P 3-7

Calculate items that may appear in consolidated statements two years after acquisition
Portly Corporation acquired 80% of the outstanding stock of Slender Corporation for $280,000 cash on January 3, 2006, on which date Slender's stockholders' equity consisted of capital stock of $200,000 and retained earnings of $50,000.

There were no changes in the outstanding stock of either corporation during 2006 and 2007. At December 31, 2007, the adjusted trial balances of Portly and Slender are as follows (in thousands):

At 12/31/2007	Portly	Slender
Debits		
Current assets	$ 204	$ 75
Plant assets—net	400	300
Investment in Slender—80%	340	—
Cost of goods sold	250	120
Other expenses	50	30
Dividends	60	25
	$1,304	$550
Credits		
Current liabilities	$ 162	$ 50 → include 10,000 dividends pay
Capital stock	500	200
Retained earnings	202	100
Sales	400	200
Income from Slender	40	—
	$1,304	$550

ADDITIONAL INFORMATION

1. All of Slender's assets and liabilities were recorded at their fair values on January 3, 2006.
2. The current liabilities of Slender at December 31, 2007, include dividends payable of $10,000.

REQUIRED: Determine the amounts that should appear in the consolidated statements of Portly Corporation and Subsidiary at December 31, 2007, for each of the following:

1. Noncontrolling interest expense   10,000
2. Current assets   271,000
3. Income from Slender   0
4. Capital stock   500,000
5. Investment in Slender   0
6. Excess of investment cost over book value acquired   80,000
7. Consolidated net income   140,000
8. Consolidated retained earnings, December 31, 2006 — corr answer $202,000
9. Consolidated retained earnings, December 31, 2007 — corr answer $282,000
10. Noncontrolling interest, December 31, 2007   65,000

P 3-8

[AICPA adapted] Prepare journal entries to account for investments, and compute noncontrolling interest, consolidated retained earnings, and investment balances
On January 1, 2006, Todd Corporation made the following investments:

1. Acquired for cash, 80% of the outstanding common stock of Meadow Corporation at $70 per share. The stockholders' equity of Meadow on January 1, 2006, consisted of the following:

Common stock, par value $50 (1,000 shares)	$50,000
Retained earnings	20,000

70,000 × 80% = 56,000

2. Acquired for cash, 70% of the outstanding common stock of Van Corporation at $40 per share. The stockholders' equity of Van on January 1, 2006, consisted of the following:

Common stock, par value $20 *(3,000 shares)* $60,000
Capital in excess of par value 20,000 } *120,000 × 70% = 84,000*
Retained earnings 40,000

After these investments were made, Todd was able to exercise control over the operations of both companies.

An analysis of the retained earnings of each company for 2006 is as follows:

	Todd	Meadow	Van
Balance January 1, 2006	$240,000	$20,000	$40,000
Net income (loss)	104,600	36,000	(12,000)
Cash dividends paid	(40,000)	(16,000)	(9,000)
Balance December 31, 2006	$304,600	$40,000	$19,000

REQUIRED

1. What entries should have been made on the books of Todd during 2006 to record the following?

a. Investments in subsidiaries
b. Subsidiary dividends received
c. Parent's share of subsidiary income or loss

2. Compute the amount of noncontrolling interest in each subsidiary's stockholders' equity at December 31, 2006.

3. What amount should be reported as consolidated retained earnings of Todd Corporation and subsidiaries as of December 31, 2006?

4. Compute the correct balances of Todd's Investment in Meadow and Investment in Van accounts at December 31, 2006.

P 3-9

Consolidated balance sheet working papers (excess allocated to equipment and goodwill) Pansy Corporation purchased 90% of Snowdrop Corporation's outstanding stock for $3,000,000 cash on January 1, 2006, when Snowdrop's stockholders' equity consisted of $2,000,000 capital stock and $700,000 retained earnings. The $570,000 excess was allocated $350,000 to undervalued equipment with a seven-year remaining useful life and $220,000 to goodwill. Snowdrop's net income and dividends for 2006 were $500,000 and $200,000, respectively. Comparative balance sheet data for Pansy and Snowdrop Corporations at December 31, 2006, are as follows (in thousands):

	Pansy	Snowdrop
Cash	$ 300	$ 200
Receivables—net	600	400
Dividends receivable	90	—
Inventory	700	600
Land	600	700
Buildings—net	2,000	1,000
Equipment—net	1,500	800
Investment in Snowdrop	3,220	—
	$9,010	$3,700
Accounts payable	$ 300	$ 600
Dividends payable	500	100
Capital stock	7,000	2,000
Retained earnings	1,210	1,000
	$9,010	$3,700

REQUIRED: Prepare consolidated balance sheet working papers for Pansy Corporation and Subsidiary on December 31, 2006.

P 3-10

Calculate investment cost and account balances from a consolidated balance sheet four years after acquisition The consolidated balance sheet of Pandora Corporation and its 80% subsidiary, Snaplock Corporation, contains the following items on December 31, 2010 (in thousands):

Cash	$ 20
Inventories	180
Other current assets	70
Plant assets—net	270
Patents from consolidation	60
	$600
Liabilities	$120
Capital stock	400
Retained earnings	30
Noncontrolling interests	50
	$600

Pandora Corporation uses the equity method of accounting for its investment in Snaplock. Snaplock Corporation stock was acquired by Pandora on January 1, 2006, when Snaplock's capital stock was $200,000 and its retained earnings were $20,000. The fair values of Snaplock's net assets were equal to their book values on January 1, 2006, except for Patents, which had not been recorded, and there have been no changes in outstanding stock of either Pandora or Snaplock since January 1, 2006.

Patents are being amortized over a 20-year period.

REQUIRED: Determine the following:

1. The purchase price of Pandora's investment in Snaplock stock on January 1, 2006.
2. The total of Snaplock's stockholders' equity on December 31, 2010.
3. The balance of Pandora's Investment in Snaplock account at December 31, 2010.
4. The balances of Pandora's Retained earnings and Capital stock accounts on December 31, 2010.

P 3-11

Consolidated balance sheet working papers (cost/book value differentials and noncontrolling interest) Pope Corporation acquired a 70% interest in Stubb Corporation on January 1, 2006, for $670,000, when Stubb's stockholders' equity consisted of $500,000 capital stock and $300,000 retained earnings. On this date, the book value of Stubb's assets and liabilities was equal to the fair value, except for inventories that were undervalued by $20,000 and sold in 2006, and plant assets that were undervalued by $80,000 and had a remaining useful life of eight years from January 1. Stubb's net income and dividends for 2006 were $70,000 and $10,000, respectively.

Separate-company balance sheet information for Pope and Stubb Corporations at December 31, 2006, follows (in thousands):

	Pope	Stubb	
Cash	$ 60	$ 20	80
Accounts receivable—customers	440	200	640
Accounts receivable from Pope	—	10	
Dividends receivable	7	—	
Inventories	500	320	820
Land	100	150	250
Plant assets—net	700	350	1099
Investment in Stubb	691	—	40 Goodwill
	$2,498	$1,050	2929
Accounts payable—suppliers	$ 300	$ 80	80
Accounts payable to Stubb	10	—	
Dividends payable	40	10	3
Long-term debt	600	100	700
Capital stock	1,000	500	1,000
Retained earnings	548	360	548
	$2,498	$1,050	258 Non-Controlling Int
			2589

REQUIRED: Prepare consolidated balance sheet working papers for Pope Corporation and Subsidiary at December 31, 2006.

P 3-12

Calculate separate company and consolidated statement items given investment account for three years
A summary of changes in Pendleton Corporation's Investment in Shasti account from January 1, 2006, to December 31, 2008, follows (in thousands):

INVESTMENT IN SHASTI (80%)

January 1, 2006	$ 760		
Income —2006	64	Dividends—2006	$ 32
—2007	80	—2007	40
—2008	96	—2008	48
		to balance	880
	$1,000		$1,000
December 31, 2008			
Balance forward	$ 880		

ADDITIONAL INFORMATION

1. Pendleton acquired its 80% interest in Shasti Corporation when Shasti had capital stock of $600,000 and retained earnings of $300,000.

2. Dividends declared by Shasti Corporation in each of the years 2006, 2007, and 2008 were equal to 50% of Shasti Corporation's reported net income.

3. Shasti Corporation's assets and liabilities were stated at their fair values on January 1, 2006.

REQUIRED: Compute the following amounts:

1. Shasti Corporation's dividends declared in 2007
2. Shasti Corporation's net income for 2007
3. Goodwill at December 31, 2007
4. Noncontrolling interest expense for 2008
5. Noncontrolling interest at December 31, 2008
6. Consolidated net income for 2008, assuming that Pendleton's separate income for 2008 is $280,000

P 3-13

Determine amounts on consolidated balance sheet at acquisition and one year later
Separate balance sheets for Peyton Corporation and Sidney Corporation at December 31, 2006, are as follows (in thousands):

	Peyton	Sidney
Assets		
Cash	$ 50	$ 20
Other current assets	150	80
Land	300	50
Buildings	600	200
Less: Accumulated depreciation	(200)	(50)
	$900	$300
Liabilities and Stockholders' Equity		
Current liabilities	$100	$ 50
Common stock, $10 par	600	100
Additional paid-in capital	60	75
Retained earnings	140	75
	$900	$300

Peyton issued 10,000 shares of its own common stock with a market value of $300,000 on January 2, 2007, in exchange for 80% of Sidney's outstanding stock. All of Sidney's assets and liabilities were recorded at their fair values, except for buildings that had a fair value of $170,000 and a remaining useful life of five years.

REQUIRED

1. At what amount would each of the following items appear in Peyton's consolidated balance sheet prepared on January 2, 2007, immediately after the business combination?

    a. Total current assets
    b. Total plant and equipment (land and buildings less accumulated depreciation)
    c. Common stock
    d. Additional paid-in capital
    e. Retained earnings

2. Assume that Sidney has net income of $40,000 and pays dividends of $20,000 during 2007 and that Peyton has income from its own operations (does not include investment income) of $90,000 during 2007 and pays dividends of $50,000. Determine the correct amounts for each of the following:

    a. Peyton's income from Sidney for 2007
    b. Peyton's Investment in Sidney account at December 31, 2007
    c. Consolidated net income for 2007
    d. Consolidated retained earnings at December 31, 2007
    e. Noncontrolling interest at December 31, 2007

P 3-14

Schedule to allocate cost-book value differentials and prepare a consolidated balance sheet at acquisition Portland Corporation purchased 80% of the voting common stock of Sidney Corporation for $2,760,000 cash on January 2, 2006. On this date, before combination, the book values and fair values of Portland and Sidney were as follows (in thousands):

	Portland Corporation		Sidney Corporation	
	Book Value	**Fair Value**	**Book Value**	**Fair Value**
Cash	$ 3,000	$ 3,000	$ 60	$ 60
Receivables—net	800	800	200	200
Inventories	1,100	1,200	400	500
Other current assets	900	900	150	200
Land	3,100	4,000	500	600
Buildings—net	6,000	8,000	1,000	1,800
Equipment—net	3,500	4,500	800	600
	$18,400	$22,400	$3,110	$3,960
Accounts payable	$ 400	$ 400	$ 200	$ 200
Other liabilities	1,500	1,600	610	560
Capital stock, $10 par	15,000		2,000	
Retained earnings	1,500		300	
	$18,400		$3,110	

[handwritten annotation: Alloc Neg Goodwill Based on FV]

REQUIRED

1. Prepare a schedule showing how the excess of Portland's investment cost over book value acquired should be allocated.

2. Prepare a consolidated balance sheet.

P 3-15

Calculate separate company and consolidated statement items given investment account for three years (negative goodwill) Use the information in Problem 3-14, except change the amount of cash that Portland Corporation paid for the 80% interest in Sidney Corporation to $1,660,000. [*Hint:* Portland's $3,000,000 cash less $1,660,000 paid for the 80% interest in Sidney equals $1,340,000. Portland's cash of $1,340,000 plus Sidney's cash of

$60,000 equals $1,400,000 consolidated cash, rather than the $300,000 consolidated cash ($240,000 + $60,000) in Problem 3-14.]

REQUIRED

1. Prepare a schedule to allocate the cost/book value differential.

2. Prepare a consolidated balance sheet immediately after the business combination.

INTERNET ASSIGNMENT

Visit the Web site of *Sprint-Nextel* and obtain the 2004 annual report. Summarize the disclosures made concerning the recent merger.

SELECTED READINGS

Accounting Principles Board Opinion No. 16. "Business Combinations." New York: American Institute of Certified Public Accountants, 1970.

American Accounting Association's Financial Accounting Standards Committee. "Comment Letter to the FASB Discussion Memorandum 'New Basis of Accounting.' " *Accounting Horizons* (March 1994), pp. 119–121.

American Accounting Association's Financial Accounting Standards Committee. "Response to the FASB Discussion Memorandum 'Consolidation Policy and Procedures.' " *Accounting Horizons* (June 1994) pp. 120–125.

American Accounting Association's Financial Accounting Standards Committee. "Response to the FASB Special Report, 'Issues Associated with the FASB Project on Business Combinations.' " *Accounting Horizons* (March 1998), pp. 87–89.

BOSSIO, RONALD J., and GISELE DION. "Revisiting Consolidated Financial Statements." *The CPA Journal* (February 1995), pp. 46–49.

Committee on Accounting Procedure. *Accounting Research Bulletin No. 51.* "Consolidated Financial Statements." New York: American Institute of Certified Public Accountants, 1959.

DEMOVILLE, WIG, and A. GEORGE PETRIE. "Accounting for a Bargain Purchase in a Business Combination." *Accounting Horizons* (September 1989), pp. 38–43.

Financial Accounting Standards Board. *An Analysis of Issues Related to Consolidation Policy and Procedures.* Discussion Memorandum. Norwalk, CT: Financial Accounting Standards Board, 1991.

Financial Accounting Standards Board. *Preliminary Views on Major Issues Related to Consolidation Policy.* Financial Accounting Series. Norwalk, CT: Financial Accounting Standards Board, 1994.

JOHNSON, L. TODD, and KIMBERLEY R. PETRONE. "Is Goodwill an Asset?" *Accounting Horizons* (September 1998), pp. 293–303.

PACTER, PAUL. "Revising GAAP for Consolidations: Join the Debate." *The CPA Journal* (July 1992), pp. 38–47.

Statement of Financial Accounting Standards No. 94. "Consolidation of All Majority-Owned Subsidiaries." Stamford CT: Financial Accounting Standards Board, 1987.

Statement of Financial Accounting Standards No. 141. "Business Combinations." Stamford, CT: Financial Accounting Standards Board, 2001.

Statement of Financial Accounting Standards No. 142. "Goodwill and Other Intangible Assets." Stamford, CT: Financial Accounting Standards Board, 2001.

CONSOLIDATION TECHNIQUES AND PROCEDURES

This chapter examines procedures for consolidating the financial statements of parent and subsidiary companies. Some differences in the consolidation process result from different methods of parent-company accounting for subsidiary investments. Consolidation working papers for a parent company/investor that uses the equity method of accounting are illustrated in the chapter to set the standard for good consolidation procedures. The illustrations for an incomplete equity method and the cost method of parent-company accounting are presented in the electronic supplement on the *Advanced Accounting* Web site. The chapter examines additional complexities that arise from errors and omissions in the separate-company records and detailed allocations of cost/book value differentials. The chapter also illustrates the trial balance working paper format, which is an alternative to the financial statement format used in other sections of the chapter.

Chapter 3 presented the balance sheet working papers used to organize the information needed for consolidated balance sheets. By contrast, this chapter presents working papers that develop the information needed for consolidated balance sheets and income and retained earnings statements. A consolidated statement of cash flows is illustrated in a later section of this chapter.

• • •

CONSOLIDATION UNDER THE EQUITY METHOD

The following example of a parent company that uses the equity method of accounting for its subsidiary explains basic procedures used to consolidate the financial statements of affiliated companies.

Equity Method—Year of Acquisition

LEARNING OBJECTIVE 1

Prep Corporation pays $87,000 for 80% of the outstanding voting stock of Snap Corporation on January 1, 2006, when Snap Corporation's stockholders' equity consists of $60,000 capital stock and $30,000 retained earnings. We allocate the $15,000 excess of investment cost over book value acquired [$87,000 − ($90,000 × 80%)] to previously unrecorded patents with a 10-year amortization period. Snap's net income and dividends are as follows:

	2006	2007
Net income	$25,000	$30,000
Dividends	15,000	15,000

Financial statements for Prep and Snap Corporations for 2006 are presented in the first two working paper columns of Exhibit 4-1. Prep's $18,500 income from Snap for 2006 consists of 80% of Snap's $25,000 net income for 2006 less $1,500 patent amortization. Its $93,500 Investment in Snap account at December 31, 2006, consists of $87,000 investment cost plus $18,500 income from Snap, less $12,000 dividends received from Snap during 2006.

Numerous consolidation approaches and any number of different adjustment and elimination combinations will result in correct amounts for the consolidated financial statements. The adjustment and elimination entries that appear in the working papers *do not affect the general ledger accounts of either the parent or its subsidiaries*. Adjusting or eliminating accounts or balances simply means that the amounts listed in the separate-company columns of the working papers are either (1) adjusted before inclusion in the consolidated statement column or (2) eliminated and do not appear in the consolidated statement column. A single working paper entry often adjusts some items and eliminates others. Labeling the working paper entries as either adjusting or eliminating entries is not important. It is important that you understand the consolidation process and develop your working paper skills.

Take a few minutes to review the consolidation working paper form in Exhibit 4-1. This same format is used extensively throughout the chapters on consolidated financial statements. The worksheet rows for net income and ending retained earnings are in boldface to highlight that we do not make adjustments or eliminations directly on these line items. We do this because consolidated net income consists of consolidated revenues less consolidated expenses, and if we require adjustments, they will be made to the individual revenue and expense accounts, not directly to net income.

Similarly, the consolidated balance sheet reflects consolidated retained earnings. We calculate the balance sheet amount for consolidated retained earnings as follows:

Beginning consolidated retained earnings
Plus: Consolidated net income
    (or minus a consolidated net loss)
Less: Parent-company dividends
Ending consolidated retained earnings

In our working paper format, we carry the net income line down to the *Retained Earnings* section of the worksheet without any further adjustment. We similarly carry the ending retained earnings row down to the *Balance Sheet* section, again without further adjustments or eliminations. Notice too that each row in the working paper generates the consolidated amounts by adding together the parent-company and subsidiary account balances and then adding or subtracting the adjustments and eliminations as appropriate.

Important checks

Parent-company net income and retained earnings under the complete equity method of accounting are equal to consolidated retained earnings. Because Prep Corporation (Exhibit 4-1) correctly applies the equity method, its net income of $68,500 equals consolidated net income. Its beginning and ending retained earnings balances equal the $5,000 and $43,500 consolidated retained earnings amounts, respectively.

The first working paper entry in Exhibit 4-1 is the following:

a	**Income from Snap (−R, −SE)**	**18,500**	
	Dividends (+SE)		**12,000**
	Investment in Snap (−A)		**6,500**
	To eliminate income and dividends from Snap and return the investment account to its beginning-of-the-period balance.		

Recall that throughout the consolidation coverage in this text working paper entries are shaded to avoid confusion with journal entries that are recorded by parent companies and subsidiaries. We eliminate investment income because the consolidated income statement shows the details of revenue and expense rather than the one-line consolidation reflected in the Income from Snap account. We eliminate dividends received from the subsidiary because they are mere transfers within the consolidated entity for which we prepare the consolidated statements.

The difference between income from a subsidiary recognized on the books of the parent company and the dividends received represents the change in the investment account for the period. The $6,500 credit to the Investment in Snap account reduces that account to its $87,000 beginning-

PREP CORPORATION AND SUBSIDIARY CONSOLIDATION WORKING PAPERS FOR THE YEAR ENDED DECEMBER 31, 2006 (IN THOUSANDS)			Adjustments and Eliminations		
	Prep	80% Snap	Debits	Credits	Consolidated Statements
Income Statement Revenue	$ 250	$65			$ 315
Income from Snap	18.5		a 18.5		
Expenses	(200)	(40)	d 1.5		(241.5)
Noncontrolling interest expense ($25,000 × 20%)			b 5		(5)
Net income	**$ 68.5**	**$ 25**			**$ 68.5**
Retained Earnings Retained earnings—Prep	$ 5				$ 5
Retained earnings—Snap		$ 30	c 30		
Add: Net income	**68.5**	**25**			**68.5**
Deduct: Dividends	(30)	(15)		a 12	
				b 3	(30)
Retained earnings—December 31	**$ 43.5**	**$ 40**			**$ 43.5**
Balance Sheet Cash	$ 40	$ 10			$ 50
Other current assets	90	50			140
Investment in Snap	93.5			a 6.5	
				c 87	
Plant and equipment	300	100			400
Accumulated depreciation	(50)	(30)			(80)
Patents			c 15	d 1.5	13.5
	$ 473.5	$ 130			$ 523.5
Liabilities	$ 80	$ 30			$ 110
Capital stock	350	60	c 60		350
Retained earnings	**43.5**	**40**			**43.5**
	$ 473.5	$ 130			
Noncontrolling interest January 1 ($90,000 × 20%)				c 18	
Noncontrolling interest December 31				b 2	20
					$ 523.5

EXHIBIT 4-1

Equity Method— Working Papers for Year of Acquisition

of-the-period balance and thereby establishes reciprocity between the investment in Snap and Snap's stockholders' equity at January 1, 2006.

Here is a journal entry for working paper entry b from Exhibit 4-1:

Entry made if < 100% owned

b	**Noncontrolling interest expense (E, –SE)**	5,000	
	Dividends—Snap (+SE)		3,000
	Noncontrolling interest (+L)		2,000
	To enter noncontrolling interest share of subsidiary income and dividends.		

Entry b incorporates the noncontrolling interest in a subsidiary's net income and the noncontrolling interest's share of dividends declared by the subsidiary directly into the consolidation working papers. This approach explains all noncontrolling interest components through consolidation working paper entries.

The portion of a subsidiary's net income not accruing to the parent company is referred to as *noncontrolling interest expense* throughout this text. Alternatively, GAAP permits the use of the terms *minority interest expense*, *minority interest income*, or *noncontrolling interest income*. Minority interest (income or expense) is the more-traditional term still commonly found in published financial statements.

In this book, the term *noncontrolling interest* is used to reflect the balance sheet amount. Note that often noncontrolling interest does not appear in published, consolidated balance sheets or income statements because the amounts are immaterial.

The FASB recommends noncontrolling interest as better reflecting the complexities of the modern business world. Many firms create *special purpose entities* (SPEs), not surprisingly created for a special business purpose. For example, SPEs may be created to facilitate leasing activities, loan securitizations, research and development activities, hedging transactions, or other business arrangements. SPEs gained fame (or infamy) with ***Enron Corporation***, which used these as a vehicle to set up energy futures trading and related business ventures. By excluding such ventures from consolidation, Enron was able to keep billions of dollars of debt off its balance sheet, hiding significant business risk from investors.

The FASB issued *FASB Interpretation No. 46*, "Consolidation of Variable Interest Entities" (*FIN No. 46*) in January 2003 and a revision (*FIN No. 46R*) in December 2003. *FIN No. 46R* provides an interpretation of *ARB No. 51* to clarify rules defining a *variable interest entity* as a subset of SPEs which should be included in preparing consolidated financial statements. *ARB No. 51* (Paragraph 2) states that "the usual condition for a controlling financial interest is ownership of a majority voting interest." *FIN No. 46R* (Paragraph 1) clarifies, adding: "However, application of the majority voting interest requirement in *ARB 51* to certain types of entities may not identify the party with a controlling financial interest because the controlling financial interest may be achieved through arrangements that do not involve voting interests." It is possible to achieve financial control of an entity with only a small equity voting interest, through other contractual arrangements. Chapter 11 will discuss *FIN No. 46R* in greater detail. These voting, non–majority control situations are consistent with the FASB preference for the controlling and noncontrolling, versus majority and minority interests, terminology.

Working paper entry c in journal entry form is as follows:

c	**Retained earnings—Snap (beginning) (–SE)**	30,000	
	Capital stock—Snap (–SE)	60,000	
	Patents (+A)	15,000	
	Investment in Snap (–A)		87,000
	Noncontrolling interest (+L)		18,000
	To eliminate reciprocal equity and investment balances, establish		
	beginning noncontrolling interest, and enter unamortized patents.		

This entry eliminates reciprocal investment and equity balances, enters the unamortized excess of investment cost over book value acquired as of the beginning of the year, and constructs beginning noncontrolling interest ($90,000 × 20%) as a separate item. Observe that entry c eliminates reciprocal investment and equity balances as of the beginning of the period and enters noncontrolling interest as of the same date. Therefore, the patents (cost/book value differential) portion of the entry is also a beginning-of-the-period unamortized amount.

Many accountants prefer to eliminate only the parent's percentage of the capital stock and retained earnings of the subsidiary and to transfer the amount not eliminated directly to the noncontrolling interest. Although the difference is solely a matter of preference, the approach used here emphasizes that we eliminate all the individual stockholders' equity accounts of a subsidiary in the process of consolidation.

Entry d in the working papers of Exhibit 4-1 enters the current year's patents amortization as an expense of the consolidated entity and reduces unamortized patents from its $15,000 unamortized balance at January 1 to its $13,500 unamortized balance at December 31, 2006.

d Expenses (E, –SE)	**1,500**	
Patents (–A)		**1,500**
To enter current amortization of patents.		

We need this working paper entry to adjust consolidated expenses even though Prep Corporation amortized patents on its separate books under the equity method. Prep reflects amortization of the patents in its Income from Snap account, and working paper entry a eliminated that account for consolidation purposes in order to disaggregate the revenue and expense components in reporting consolidated income.

Sequence of Working Paper Entries

The sequence of the working paper entries in Exhibit 4-1 is both logical and necessary. Entry a adjusts the investment in Snap for changes during 2006, and entry c eliminates the investment in Snap after adjustment to its beginning-of-the-period balance in entry a. Entry c also enters unamortized patents in the working papers as of the beginning of the period. Subsequently, entry d amortizes the patents for the current period and reduces the asset patents to its unamortized amount at the balance sheet date. As we encounter additional complexities of consolidation, the sequence of working paper adjustments and eliminations expands to the following:

1. Adjustments for errors and omissions in the separate parent-company and subsidiary statements

2. Adjustments to eliminate intercompany profits and losses (Inventory, Fix Assets, Bonds)

3. Adjustments to eliminate income and dividends from subsidiary and adjust the investment in subsidiary to its beginning-of-the-period balance   entry a, pg 102

4. Adjustment to record the noncontrolling interest in subsidiary's earnings and dividends   entry b, pg 104

5. Eliminations of reciprocal investment in subsidiary and subsidiary equity balances   entry c, pg 104

6. Allocation and amortization of cost/book value differentials (from step 5)   entry d, pg 105

7. Elimination of other reciprocal balances (intercompany receivables and payables, revenues and expenses, and so on)

Although other sequences of working paper entries may be adequate in a given consolidation, the sequence just presented will always work. You should learn it and apply it throughout your study of consolidation.

We compute the noncontrolling interest reflected in the consolidated balance sheet as beginning noncontrolling interest plus noncontrolling interest expense less noncontrolling interest dividends. In case the ownership in a subsidiary increases during a period, the noncontrolling interest computation will reflect the noncontrolling interest at the balance sheet date, with noncontrolling interest expense and dividends also reflecting the ending noncontrolling interest percentages.

Note that we always eliminate the investment in subsidiary balances when a subsidiary is consolidated. Although the investment in subsidiary account may be adjusted to establish reciprocity, it never appears in a consolidated balance sheet when the subsidiary accounts are consolidated.

checks *

Likewise, we always eliminate investment income from subsidiaries that are consolidated. We compute consolidated net income by deducting consolidated expenses and noncontrolling interest expense from consolidated revenues. It is *not* determined by adjusting the separate net incomes of parent and subsidiary.

Capital stock and other paid-in capital accounts appearing in a consolidated balance sheet are those of the parent company.

Equity Method—Year Subsequent to Acquisition

Prep Corporation maintains its 80% ownership interest in Snap throughout 2007, recording income from Snap of $22,500 for the year (80% of Snap's $30,000 net income less $1,500 patents amortization). At December 31, 2007, Prep's Investment in Snap account has a balance of $104,000, determined as follows:

Investment cost January 1, 2006	$ 87,000
Income from Snap—2006	18,500
Dividends from Snap—2006	−12,000
Investment in Snap December 31, 2006	93,500
Income from Snap—2007	22,500
Dividends from Snap—2007	−12,000
Investment in Snap December 31, 2007	$104,000

The only intercompany transaction between Prep and Snap during 2007 was a $10,000 non-interest-bearing loan to Snap during the third quarter of the year.

Consolidation working papers for Prep Corporation and Subsidiary for 2007 are presented in Exhibit 4-2.

There were no errors or omissions or intercompany profits relating to the consolidation, so the first working paper entry is to eliminate income and dividends from Snap as follows:

a	**Income from Snap (–R, –SE)**	**22,500**	
	Dividends (+SE)		**12,000**
	Investment in Snap (–A)		**10,500**
	To eliminate income and dividends from Snap and return the investment account to its beginning-of-the-period balance.		

This entry adjusts the Investment in Snap account to its $93,500 December 31, 2006, balance and establishes reciprocity with Snap's stockholders' equity at December 31, 2006.

Entry b incorporates the noncontrolling interest in Snap's net income and the noncontrolling share of Snap's dividends.

b	**Noncontrolling interest expense (E, –SE)**	**6,000**	
	Dividends—Snap (+SE)		**3,000**
	Noncontrolling interest (+L)		**3,000**
	To enter noncontrolling interest share of subsidiary income and dividends.		

Entry c eliminates Investment in Snap and stockholders' equity of Snap as follows:

c	**Retained earnings—Snap (–SE)**	**40,000**	
	Capital stock—Snap (–SE)	**60,000**	
	Patents (+A)	**13,500**	
	Investment in Snap (–A)		**93,500**
	Noncontrolling interest (+L)		**20,000**
	To eliminate reciprocal investment and equity balances, establish beginning noncontrolling interest, and enter unamortized patents.		

EXHIBIT 4-2

Equity Method—
Working Papers for
Year Subsequent to
Acquisition

PREP CORPORATION AND SUBSIDIARY CONSOLIDATION WORKING PAPERS FOR THE YEAR ENDED DECEMBER 31, 2007 (IN THOUSANDS)

	Prep	80% Snap	Adjustments and Eliminations		Consolidated Statements
			Debits	Credits	
Income Statement Revenue	$ 300	$ 75			$ 375
Income from Snap	22.5		a 22.5		
Expenses	(244)	(45)	d 1.5		(290.5)
Noncontrolling interest expense ($30,000 × 20%)			b 6		(6)
Net income	**$ 78.5**	**$ 30**			**$ 78.5**
Retained Earnings Retained earnings—Prep	$ 43.5				$ 43.5
Retained earnings—Snap		$ 40	c 40		
Add: Net income	**78.5**	**30**			**78.5**
Deduct: Dividends	(45)	(15)		a 12 b 3	(45)
Retained earnings—December 31	**$ 77**	**$ 55**			**$ 77**
Balance Sheet Cash	$ 46	$ 20			$ 66
Note receivable—Snap	10			e 10	
Other current assets	97	70			167
Investment in Snap	104			a 10.5 b 93.5	
Plant and equipment	300	100			400
Accumulated depreciation	(60)	(40)			(100)
Patents			c 13.5	d 1.5	12
	$ 497	$ 150			$ 545
Note payable—Prep		$ 10	e 10		
Liabilities	$ 70	25			$ 95
Capital stock	350	60	c 60		350
Retained earnings	**77**	**55**			**77**
	$ 497	$ 150			
Noncontrolling interest January 1 ($100,000 × 20%)				c 20	
Noncontrolling interest December 31				b 3	23
					$ 545

Entry c eliminates the Investment in Snap and stockholders' equity of Snap amounts at December 31, 2006, and enters the noncontrolling interest at December 31, 2006; therefore, the $13,500 investments cost/book value difference reflects unamortized patents at December 31, 2006. Thus, entry d amortizes this amount to the $12,000 balance at December 31, 2007.

d	Expenses (E, –SE)	1,500	
	Patents (–A)		1,500
	To enter current amortization.		

The final working paper entry eliminates intercompany notes payable and notes receivable balances because the amounts are not assets and liabilities of the consolidated entity.

e	Note payable—Prep (–L)	10,000	
	Note receivable—Snap (–A)		10,000
	To eliminate reciprocal receivable and payable balances.		

The intercompany loan was not interest bearing, so the note receivable and the note payable are the only reciprocal balances created by the intercompany transaction. We would need additional eliminations for reciprocal interest income and interest expense and interest receivable and interest payable balances if the intercompany loan had been interest bearing.

Compare the consolidation working papers of Exhibit 4-2 with those of Exhibit 4-1. Notice that the December 31, 2006, noncontrolling interest from Exhibit 4-1 is the beginning noncontrolling interest in Exhibit 4-2. Also note that the unamortized patents amount in the consolidated balance sheets of Exhibit 4-1 is the beginning-of-the-period unamortized patents in Exhibit 4-2.

LOCATING ERRORS

The last part of consolidation working papers to be completed is the consolidated balance sheet section. Most errors made in consolidating the financial statements will show up when the consolidated balance sheet does not balance. If the consolidated balance sheet fails to balance after recomputing totals, we should then check individual items to ensure that all items have been included. Omissions involving the noncontrolling interest expense in the consolidated income statement and noncontrolling interest equity in the consolidated balance sheet occur frequently because these items do not appear on the separate-company statements. We check the equality of debits and credits in the working paper entries by totaling the adjustment and elimination columns. Although proper coding of each working paper entry minimizes this type of error, many accountants prefer to total the adjustment and elimination columns as a regular working paper procedure.

EXCESS ALLOCATED TO IDENTIFIABLE NET ASSETS

Both *FASB Statements No. 141* and *No. 142* require firms to provide at least summary disclosures regarding the allocation of the purchase price of an acquired subsidiary, especially as related to acquired goodwill and other intangible assets. *FASB Statement No. 141* specifically requires firms to disclose, in the year of acquisition, the cost of the acquired enterprise, a condensed balance sheet showing amounts assigned to major classes of assets and liabilities, the amounts of purchased research and development in process acquired and written off, and total amounts assigned to major intangible asset categories. *FASB Statement No. 142* further requires that the amount of goodwill be shown as a separate balance sheet line item (assuming it is material).

Prior standards had similar requirements. However, many firms chose to report a combined total for goodwill and all other intangibles on the balance sheet, while others provided substantial disclosures. Firms must also disclose material noncontrolling interests on the balance sheet and report noncontrolling interests' share of subsidiary income.

For example, **Walt Disney Company's** 2003 annual report discloses goodwill of $17 billion and other intangible assets of $2.8 billion on its balance sheet. The balance sheet also itemizes minority interest of $428 million. The notes disclose that Disney allocated $5 billion of the total $2.8 billion net cost of its October 2001 acquisition of **ABC Family** to goodwill and another $47 million to identifiable intangible assets. Note that the excess of the intangibles and goodwill over the purchase price is not a misprint. Disney assumed $2.4 billion of borrowings and preferred stock as a part of the combination agreement. The separate listing of goodwill versus other intangible assets reflects new disclosure requirements for these assets under *FASB Statement No. 142*.

In 2003, **Ford Motor Company** reported $6.1 billion of goodwill and $1.1 billion of other intangible assets. The income statement revealed $314 million of minority interest expense. **Dow Chemical's** 2003 annual report discloses goodwill of over $3.2 billion and other intangible assets of $579 million. The 2002 annual report of **Hewlett-Packard Company** reports goodwill of $15.1 billion and purchased intangibles of $4.9 billion. These amounts are mostly due to their May 2002 acquisition of **Compaq Computer Corporation**. Note 3 to the financial statements tells us that the total purchase price of $24.2 billion included goodwill of $14.5 billion and various amortizable intangible assets, including: customer contracts, lists, and distribution agreements of $1.9 billion; patents of $1.5 billion; and trademarks valued at $74 million. Hewlett-Packard also purchased $735 million of in-process research and development, but that amount is charged to expense.

The discussions thus far have assumed that firms allocate any excess of investment cost over book value either to previously unrecorded patents or to goodwill. Consolidation working paper procedures for allocating an excess to specific assets and liabilities are similar to those illustrated for patents. The working paper entries are more complex, however, because they affect more accounts and require additional allocation, amortization, and depreciation schemes. We illustrate these additional working paper complexities here for Pate Corporation and its 90%-owned subsidiary, Solo Corporation.

Pate acquired its equity interest in Solo on December 31, 2006, for $365,000 cash, when Solo's stockholders' equity consisted of $200,000 capital stock and $50,000 retained earnings. On the date that Solo became a subsidiary of Pate, the following assets of Solo had book values different from their fair values (amounts in thousands):

	Fair Value	Book Value	Undervaluation (Overvaluation)
Inventories	$ 60	$ 50	$ 10
Land	60	30	30
Buildings	180	100	80
Equipment	70	90	(20)
	$370	$270	$100

Based on this information, Pate allocated the $140,000 excess cost over book value acquired [$365,000 cost − (90% × $250,000 equity of Solo)] to identifiable assets and goodwill, as shown in the following schedule:

	Undervaluation (Overvaluation)		Interest Acquired		Excess Allocation	Amortization Period
Inventories	$10	×	90%	=	$ 9	Sold in 2007
Land	30		90		27	None
Buildings—net	80		90		72	36 years
Equipment—net	(20)		90		(18)	9 years
Goodwill—remainder					50	None
					$140	

The schedule also shows the amortization periods assigned to the undervalued and overvalued assets.

Consolidation at Acquisition

Exhibit 4-3 shows consolidated balance sheet working papers for Pate Corporation and Subsidiary immediately after the business combination on December 31, 2006. The excess cost over book value allocation is reasonably complex, so we use an unamortized excess account in the working papers.

The first working paper entry eliminates reciprocal Investment in Solo and stockholders' equity accounts of Solo, enters the 10% noncontrolling interest in Solo, and debits the unamortized excess account for the $140,000 excess cost over book value acquired. A second working paper entry allocates the excess to identifiable net assets and goodwill. The amounts allocated in the second working paper entry are the original allocations because the accounts of Pate and Solo are being consolidated immediately after the business combination.

EXHIBIT 4-3

Consolidation at
Acquisition

PATE CORPORATION AND SUBSIDIARY CONSOLIDATED BALANCE SHEET WORKING PAPERS ON DECEMBER 31, 2006 (IN THOUSANDS)

	Pate	90% Solo	Adjustments and Eliminations		Consolidated Balance Sheet
Assets					
Cash	$ 20	$ 5			$ 25
Receivables—net	90	25			115
Inventories	80	50	b 9		139
Land	60	30	b 27		117
Buildings—net	200	100	b 72		372
Equipment—net	135	90		b 18	207
Investment in Solo	365			a 365	
Goodwill			b 50		50
Unamortized excess			a 140	b 140	
Totals	$950	$300			$1,025
Liabilities and Equity					
Accounts payable	$130	$ 50			$ 180
Capital stock—Pate	700				700
Retained earnings—Pate	120				120
Capital stock—Solo		200	a 200		
Retained earnings—Solo		50	a 50		
Noncontrolling interest				a 25	25
Totals	$950	$300			$1,025

Consolidation After Acquisition

Solo reports $60,000 net income for 2007 and declares dividends of $10,000 on June 1 and December 1 ($20,000 total for 2007). Solo pays the June 1 dividend on July 1, but the December 1 dividend remains unpaid at December 31, 2007. During 2007, Solo sells the undervalued inventory items, but the undervalued land and buildings and overvalued equipment are still in use by Solo at December 31, 2007. On the date of business combination, the buildings had a remaining useful life of 36 years, and the equipment, 9 years.

During 2007, Solo borrows $20,000 from Pate on a non-interest-bearing note. Solo repays the note on December 30, but the repayment check to Pate was in transit and was not reflected in Pate's separate balance sheet at December 31, 2007.

Pate made the following journal entries in 2007 to account for its investment in Solo.

July 1
Cash (+A) 9,000
    Investment in Solo (−A) 9,000
  To record dividends from Solo ($10,000 × 90%).

December 31

Investment in Solo (+A)	45,000	
Income from Solo (R, +SE)		45,000

To record investment income from Solo, determined as follows:

Share of Solo's net income ($60,000 × 90%)	$54,000
Amortization of excess allocated to:	
Inventories ($9,000 × 100% recognized)	−9,000
Buildings ($72,000 ÷ 36 years)	−2,000
Equipment ($18,000 ÷ 9 years)	+2,000
Income from Solo for 2007	$45,000

These entries show that Pate has used a one-line consolidation in accounting for its $45,000 income from Solo for 2007, but it has failed to recognize Solo's December 1 dividend declaration. Accordingly, Pate has overstated its investment in Solo at December 31, 2007, by $9,000 (90% of Solo's $10,000 December 1 dividend declaration). Consolidation working papers for Pate and Subsidiary for 2007 in Exhibit 4-4 show Pate's investment in Solo at $401,000 ($365,000 cost plus $45,000 income less $9,000 dividends received), whereas the correct amount is $392,000. The overstatement is corrected in working paper entry a of Exhibit 4-4.

a	Dividends receivable (+A)	9,000	
	Investment in Solo (−A)		9,000
	To correct investment balance for unrecorded dividends receivable.		

This entry is different from previous working paper entries because it represents a real adjustment that should also be recorded on Pate's books.

    Working paper entry b adjusts for the $20,000 cash in transit from Solo to Pate at December 31, 2007.

b	Cash (+A)	20,000	
	Note receivable—Solo (−A)		20,000
	To enter receipt of intercompany note receivable.		

Working paper entry b is also a real adjustment. Pate records this entry on its separate books, as well as in the consolidation working paper. If Pate fails to record entries a and b as correcting entries on its separate books, it will record them in the normal course of events in 2008 when Pate receives the $9,000 dividend and the $20,000 note repayment checks from Solo. It is important that we always review year-end transactions between affiliates to make sure that both parent and subsidiary records properly reflect these events.

    Entry c eliminates the income from Solo and 90% of Solo's dividends, and it adjusts the Investment in Solo account to its $365,000 beginning-of-the-period balance. Entry d incorporates the noncontrolling interest in Solo's net income and the noncontrolling share of Solo's dividends. Entry e eliminates the reciprocal Investment in Solo account and the stockholders' equity accounts of Solo, records the 10% noncontrolling interest at the beginning of the period, and enters the $140,000 excess.

c	Income from Solo (−R, −SE)	45,000	
	Dividends (+SE)		18,000
	Investment in Solo (−A)		27,000
	To eliminate income and dividends of Solo and return		
	Investment account to beginning-of-the-period balance.		

EXHIBIT 4-4

Consolidation After
Acquisition

PATE CORPORATION AND SUBSIDIARY CONSOLIDATION WORKING PAPERS FOR THE YEAR ENDED DECEMBER 31, 2007 (IN THOUSANDS)

	Pate	90% Solo	Adjustments and Eliminations Debits	Adjustments and Eliminations Credits	Consolidated Statements
Income Statement					
Sales	$900	$300			$1,200
Income from Solo	45		c 45		
Cost of goods sold	(600)	(150)	f 9		(759)
Operating expenses	(190)	(90)	g 2	h 2	(280)
Noncontrolling interest expense ($60,000 × 10%)			d 6		(6)
Net income	**$155**	**$ 60**			**$ 155**
Retained Earnings					
Retained earnings—Pate	$120				$ 120
Retained earnings—Solo		$ 50	e 50		
Net income	155	60			155
Dividends	(100)	(20)		c 18 / d 2	(100)
Retained earnings—December 31	**$175**	**$ 90**			**$ 175**
Balance Sheet					
Cash	$ 8	$ 15	b 20		$ 43
Accounts receivable—net	76	25			101
Note receivable—Solo	20			b 20	
Inventories	90	60			150
Land	60	30	f 27		117
Buildings—net	190	110	f 72	g 2	370
Equipment—net	150	120	h 2	f 18	254
Investment in Solo	401			a 9 / c 27 / e 365	
Dividends receivable			a 9	i 9	
Goodwill			f 50		50
Unamortized excess			e 140	f 140	
	$995	$360			$1,085
Accounts payable	$120	$ 60			$ 180
Dividends payable		10	i 9		1
Capital stock	700	200	e 200		700
Retained earnings	**175**	**90**			**175**
	$995	$360			
Noncontrolling interest January 1				e 25	
Noncontrolling interest December				d 4	29
					$1,085

d Noncontrolling interest expense (E, –SE)	6,000	
Dividends—Solo (+SE)		2,000
Noncontrolling interest (+L)		4,000
To enter noncontrolling interest share of subsidiary income and dividends.		
e Retained earnings—Solo (–SE)	50,000	
Capital stock—Solo (–SE)	200,000	
Unamortized excess (+A)	140,000	
Investment in Solo (–A)		365,000
Noncontrolling interest—January 1 (+L)		25,000
To eliminate reciprocal investment and equity amounts, establish beginning noncontrolling interest, and enter unamortized excess.		

We allocate the unamortized excess entered in working paper entry e to identifiable assets and goodwill as of December 31, 2006, in entry f and amortize it in entries g and h. It is convenient to prepare a schedule to support these allocations and amortizations in preparing the working paper entries and to provide documentation for subsequent consolidations.

	Unamortized Excess December 31, 2006	Amortization 2007	Unamortized Excess December 31, 2007
Inventories	$ 9,000	$9,000	$ —
Land	27,000	—	27,000
Buildings—net	72,000	2,000	70,000
Equipment—net	(18,000)	(2,000)	(16,000)
Goodwill	50,000	—	50,000
	$140,000	$9,000	$131,000

With the exception of the $9,000 excess allocated to cost of goods sold, the allocation in working paper entry f of Exhibit 4-4 is the same as the allocation in working paper entry b in the consolidated balance sheet working papers of Exhibit 4-3. We allocate the $9,000 excess assigned to inventories to cost of goods sold because the related undervalued inventories from December 31, 2006, were sold in 2007, thus increasing cost of goods sold in the 2007 consolidated income statement. We journalize working paper entry f as follows:

f Cost of goods sold (E, –SE)	9,000	
Land (+A)	27,000	
Building—net (+A)	72,000	
Goodwill (+A)	50,000	
Equipment—net (–A)		18,000
Unamortized excess (–A)		140,000
To allocate unamortized excess to identifiable assets and goodwill.		

Working paper entries g and h are necessary to increase operating expenses for depreciation on the $72,000 excess allocated to undervalued buildings and to decrease operating expenses for excessive depreciation on the $18,000 assigned to overvalued equipment. Entry g for recording depreciation on the excess allocated to buildings is procedurally the same as the adjustment for patents shown previously, except that we credit buildings—net of depreciation. We also show the credit to accumulated depreciation or to buildings—net on a net-of-depreciation basis. The $2,000 debit to equipment—net and credit to operating expenses in working paper entry h corrects for excessive depreciation on the overvalued equipment. Procedurally, this adjustment is the exact opposite of entry g, which corrects for underdepreciation on the buildings:

g	Operating expenses (E, −SE)	2,000	
	Buildings—net (−A)		2,000
	To enter current depreciation on excess allocated to buildings.		
h	Equipment—net (+A)	2,000	
	Operating expenses (E, +SE)		2,000
	To adjust current depreciation for excess allocated to reduce equipment.		

Working paper entry i eliminates reciprocal dividends payable and dividends receivable amounts:

i	Dividends payable (−L)	9,000	
	Dividends receivable (−A)		9,000
	To eliminate reciprocal receivables and payables.		

The $1,000 dividends payable of Solo that is not eliminated relates to the noncontrolling interest. We include it among consolidated liabilities because it represents an amount payable outside the consolidated entity.

CONSOLIDATED STATEMENT OF CASH FLOWS

We prepare the consolidated statement of cash flows (SCF) from consolidated income statements and consolidated balance sheets, rather than from the separate parent-company and subsidiary statements. With minor exceptions, the preparation of a consolidated SCF involves the same analysis and procedures that are used in preparing the SCF for separate entities.

Exhibit 4-5 presents consolidated balance sheets at December 31, 2006 and 2007, and the 2007 consolidated income statement for Polski Corporation and its 80%-owned subsidiary, Seed Corporation. We use consolidated balance sheets at the beginning and end of the year to calculate the year's changes, which must be explained in the SCF. Other information pertinent to the preparation of Polski's consolidated SCF is as follows:

1. During 2007, Seed sold land that cost $20,000 to outside entities for $10,000 cash.
2. Polski issued a $300,000, two-year note on January 8, 2007, for new equipment.
3. Patents amortization from the Polski-Seed business combination is $10,000 per year.
4. Polski received $10,000 in dividends from its investments in equity investees.
5. Changes in plant assets not explained above are due to provisions for depreciation.

We prepare the SCF using a single concept: cash and cash equivalents. GAAP permits two presentations for reporting net cash flows from operations. The indirect method begins with consolidated net income and includes adjustments for items not providing or using cash to arrive at net cash flows from operations. The direct method offsets cash received from customers and investment income against cash paid to suppliers, employees, governmental units, and so on to arrive at net cash flows from operations. Although the Financial Accounting Standards Board has expressed a preference for the direct method of reporting net cash flows from operations, the 2003 issue of *Accounting Trends & Techniques* reported that 7 of 600 surveyed companies presenting a statement of cash flows used the direct method, and 593 used the indirect method.[1]

---

[1] *FASB Statement No. 95*, "Statement of Cash Flows," paragraph 119.

EXHIBIT 4-5

Consolidated
Balance Sheets and
Income Statement
for Polski and
Subsidiary

POLSKI CORPORATION AND SUBSIDIARY COMPARATIVE BALANCE SHEETS AT DECEMBER 31 (IN THOUSANDS)

	2007	2006	Year's Change: Increase (Decrease)
Cash	$ 255	$ 180	$ 75
Accounts receivable—net	375	270	105
Inventories	250	205	45
Equity investments	100	95	5
Land	80	100	(20)
Buildings—net	200	220	(20)
Equipment—net	800	600	200
Patents	90	100	(10)
	$2,150	$1,770	$380
Accounts payable	$ 250	270	$ (20)
Dividends payable	20	20	—
Note payable due 2009	300	—	300
Common stock	500	500	—
Other paid-in capital	300	300	—
Retained earnings	670	600	70
Noncontrolling interest—20%	110	80	30
	$2,150	$1,770	$380

CONSOLIDATED INCOME STATEMENT FOR THE YEAR ENDED DECEMBER 31, 2007

Sales			$750
Income from equity investees			15
Total revenue			765
Less expenses:			
Cost of goods sold		$ 300	
Depreciation expense		120	
Patents amortization		10	
Wages and salaries		54	
Other operating expenses		47	
Interest expense		24	
Loss on sale of land		10	(565)
Total consolidated income			200
Less: Noncontrolling interest expense			(50)
Consolidated net income			150
Consolidated retained earnings January 1			600
Less: Cash dividends paid			(80)
Consolidated retained earnings December 31			$670

EXHIBIT 4-6

Consolidated
Statement of Cash
Flows—Indirect
Method

POLSKI CORPORATION AND SUBSIDIARY CONSOLIDATED STATEMENT OF CASH FLOWS FOR THE YEAR ENDED DECEMBER 31, 2007 (IN THOUSANDS)

Cash Flows from Operating Activities		
Consolidated net income		$150
Adjustments to reconcile net income to cash provided by operating activities:		
Noncontrolling interest expense	$ 50	
Undistributed income—equity investees	(5)	
Loss of sale of land	10	
Depreciation on equipment	100	
Depreciation on buildings	20	
Amortization of patents	10	
Increase in accounts receivable	(105)	
Increase in inventories	(45)	
Decrease in accounts payable	(20)	15
Net cash flows from operating activities		165
Cash Flows from Investing Activities		
Proceeds from sale of land	$ 10	
Net cash flows from investing activities		10
Cash Flows from Financing Activities		
Payment of cash dividends—majority	$ (80)	
Payment of cash dividends—noncontrolling	(20)	
Net cash flows from financing activities		(100)
Increase in cash for 2007		75
Cash on January 1, 2007		180
Cash on December 31, 2007		$255
Listing of Noncash Investing and Financing Activities		
Equipment purchased for $300,000 by issuing a two-year note payable		

Consolidated Statement of Cash Flows—Indirect Method

Exhibit 4-6 presents a consolidated SCF for Polski Corporation and Subsidiary under the indirect method. This statement is based on the consolidated balance sheet changes and the 2007 consolidated income statement that appears in Exhibit 4-5 for Polski Corporation and Subsidiary. Exhibit 4-7 presents a statement of cash flows worksheet that organizes the information for statement preparation using the schedule approach. We prepare the consolidated SCF directly from the Cash Flow from Operations, Cash Flow—Investing Activities, and Cash Flow—Financing Activities columns of the worksheet in Exhibit 4-7.

Noncontrolling interest expense is an increase in the cash flow from operating activities because noncontrolling interest expense increases consolidated assets and liabilities in exactly the same manner as consolidated net income. Similarly, we deduct noncontrolling interest dividends in reporting the cash flows from financing activities.

Income and Dividends from Investees Under the Indirect and Direct Methods

Income from equity investees is an item that requires special attention in the consolidated SCF when using the indirect method. Income from equity investees increases income without increasing cash because the investment account reflects the increase. Conversely, dividends received from equity investees increase cash but do not affect income because the investment account reflects the decrease.

We deduct (or add) the net amount of these items from net income in the Cash Flows from Operating Activities section of the SCF. We add an excess of dividends received over equity

EXHIBIT 4-7

Worksheet for Consolidated SCF—Indirect Method

POLSKI CORPORATION AND SUBSIDIARY WORKING PAPERS FOR THE STATEMENT OF CASH FLOWS (INDIRECT METHOD) FOR THE YEAR ENDED DECEMBER 31, 2007 (IN THOUSANDS)

	Year's Change	Reconciling Items		Cash Flow from Operations	Cash Flow— Investing Activities	Cash Flow— Financing Activities
		Debit	Credit			
Asset Changes						
Cash	75					
Accounts receivable—net	105		k 105			
Inventories	45		l 45			
Equity investments	5		e 5			
Land	(20)	f 20				
Buildings—net	(20)	i 20				
Equipment—net	200	h 100	g 300			
Patents	(10)	j 10				
Total asset changes	380					
Equity Changes						
Accounts payable	(20)		m 20			
Dividends payable	0					
Note payable due 2009*	300	g 300				
Common stock	0					
Other paid-in capital	0					
Retained earnings	70	a 150	b 80			
Noncontrolling interest	30	c 50	d 20			
Total equity changes	380					
Consolidated net income			a 150	150		
Noncontrolling interest expense			c 50	50		
Income—equity investees		e 5		(5)		
Loss of sale of land			f 10	10		
Depreciation on equipment			h 100	100		
Depreciation on buildings			i 20	20		
Amortization of patents			j 10	10		
Increase in receivables		k 105		(105)		
Increase in inventories		l 45		(45)		
Decrease in accounts payable		m 20		(20)		
Proceeds from sale of land			f 10		10	
Payment of dividends—majority		b 80				(80)
Payment of dividends—noncontrolling		d 20				(20)
		925	925	165	10	(100)
Cash flows from operations				$165		
Cash flows from investing activities				10		
Cash flows from financing activities				(100)		
Increase in cash for 2007 = cash change above				$ 75		

*Noncash investing and financing transaction: equipment purchased for $300,000 by issuing a two-year note payable.

income. We simply report dividends received from equity investees as cash inflows from operating activities when using the direct method to prepare the SCF.

Consolidated Statement of Cash Flows—Direct Method

Exhibit 4-8 presents a consolidated SCF for Polski Corporation and Subsidiary under the direct method. This statement is identical to the one presented in Exhibit 4-6, except for cash flows from operating activities. Under the direct method, we convert the consolidated income statement items that involve cash flows from the accrual to the cash basis, and we explain those items that do not

EXHIBIT 4-8	POLSKI CORPORATION AND SUBSIDIARY CONSOLIDATED STATEMENT OF CASH FLOWS FOR THE YEAR ENDED DECEMBER 31, 2007 (IN THOUSANDS)		
Consolidated Statement of Cash Flows—Direct Method	*Cash Flows from Operating Activities* Cash received from customers		$645
	Dividends received from equity investees		10
	Less: Cash paid to suppliers Cash paid to employees Paid for other operating items Cash paid for interest expense Net cash flows from operating activities	$ 365 54 47 24	(490) 165
	Cash Flows from Investing Activities Proceeds from sale of land	$ 10	
	Net cash flows from investing activities		10
	Cash Flows from Financing Activities		
	Payment of cash dividends—majority interests	$ (80)	
	Payment of cash dividends—noncontrolling interests Net cash flows from financing activities	(20)	(100)
	Increase in cash for 2007		75
	Cash on January 1, 2007		180
	Cash on December 31, 2007		$255
	Listing of Noncash Investment and Financing Activities Equipment was purchased for $300,000 through the issuance of a two-year note payable		
	Reconciliation of Consolidated Net Income to Operating Cash Flows Cash flows from operating activities		
	Consolidated net income		$150
	Adjustments to reconcile net income to cash provided by operating activities: Noncontrolling interest Undistributed income—equity investees Loss on sale of land Depreciation on equipment Depreciation on buildings Amortization of patents Increase in accounts receivable Increase in inventories Decrease in accounts payable Net cash flows from operating activities	$ 50 (5) 10 100 20 10 (105) (45) (20)	15 $165

involve cash in notes or schedules supporting the cash flow statement. Exhibit 4-9 shows a worksheet that organizes information for a consolidated statement of cash flows under the direct method. We prepare the SCF from the last three columns of the worksheet.

If you compare the cash flow statements in Exhibits 4-6 and 4-8, you should observe that the cash flows from investing and financing activities are identical. The significant differences lie in the presentation of cash flows from operating activities and the additional schedule to reconcile consolidated net income to operating cash flows under the direct method. Although the presentation in Exhibit 4-8 under the direct method may be less familiar, it is somewhat easier to interpret.

EXHIBIT 4-9

Worksheet for Consolidated SCF—Direct Method

POLSKI CORPORATION AND SUBSIDIARY WORKING PAPERS FOR THE STATEMENT OF CASH FLOWS (DIRECT METHOD) FOR THE YEAR ENDED DECEMBER 31, 2007 (IN THOUSANDS)

	Year's Change	Reconciling Items		Cash Flow from Operations	Cash Flow— Investing Activities	Cash Flow— Financing Activities
		Debit	Credit			
Asset Changes						
Cash	75					
Accounts receivable—net	105		a 105			
Inventories	45		c 45			
Equity investments	5		b 5			
Land	(20)	h 20				
Buildings—net	(20)	f 20				
Equipment—net	200	e 100	d 300			
Patents	(10)	g 10				
Total asset changes	380					
Equity Changes						
Accounts payable	(20)		c 20			
Dividends payable	0					
Note payable due 2006**	300	d 300				
Common stock	0					
Other paid-in capital	0					
Retained earnings*	70					
Noncontrolling interest	30	i 50	j 20			
Total equity changes	380					
*Retained Earnings Changes**						
Sales	750	a 105		645		
Income—equity investees	15	b 5		10		
Cost of goods sold	(300)	c 65		(365)		
Depreciation on equipment	(100)		e 100			
Depreciation on buildings	(20)		f 20			
Patents amortization	(10)		g 10			
Wages and salaries	(54)			(54)		
Other operating expenses	(47)			(47)		
Interest expense	(24)			(24)		
Loss on sale of land	(10)		h 10			
Noncontrolling interest expense	(50)		i 50			
Dividends paid by Polski	(80)		k 80			
Change in retained earnings	70					
Payment of dividends—majority		k 80				(80)
Payment of dividends—noncontrolling		j 20				(20)
Proceeds from the land sale			h 10		10	
		775	775	165	10	(100)

*Retained earnings changes replace the retained earnings account for reconciling purposes.
**Noncash investing and financing transaction: equipment purchased for $300,000 by issuing a two-year note payable.

PREPARING A CONSOLIDATION WORKSHEET

LEARNING
OBJECTIVE **7**

In this section you will learn how to set up a three-part worksheet to prepare a consolidated income statement, retained earnings statement, and balance sheet. This worksheet follows the same basic pattern as that described in Chapter 3 to prepare a consolidated balance sheet at the combination date. Refer to Exhibit 4-10. We have two columns to record trial balance information for a parent company and (in our example) a 70%-owned subsidiary company. Most of the numbers in these two columns are simply copied from the individual company trial balances. Note that we record 100% of

EXHIBIT 4-10

Preparing a Complete Consolidation Worksheet

PARENT AND SUBSIDIARY CONSOLIDATION WORKSHEET FOR THE YEAR ENDED DECEMBER 31, 2006

(in thousands)	Parent	70% Subsidiary	Adjustments & Eliminations Debits	Adjustments & Eliminations Credits	Consolidated Statements
Income Statement					
Sales					=B6+C6–D6+E6
Income from Subsidiary					=B7+C7–D7+E7
Cost of goods sold					=B8+C8–D8+E8
Operating expenses					=B9+C9–D9+E9
					=B10+C10–D10+E10
Net income	=SUM(B6:B10)	=SUM(C6:C10)			=SUM(F5:F10)
Retained Earnings					
Retained earnings—Parent					=B13+C13–D13+E13
Retained earnings—Subsidiary					=B14+C14–D14+E14
Net income	=B11	=C11			=F11
Dividends					=B16+C16–D16+E16–D17+E17
Ret earnings—ending	=SUM(B13:B16)	=SUM(C13:C16)			=SUM(F13:F17)
Balance Sheet					
Cash					=B20+C20+D20–E20
Receivables—net					=B21+C21+D21–E21
Inventories					=B22+C22+D22–E22
Plant & equipment—net					=B23+C23+D23–E23
Investment in Subsidiary					=B24+C24+D24–E24+D25–E25
					=B26+C26+D26–E26
Total assets	=SUM(B20:B26)	=SUM(C20:C26)			=SUM(F20:F26)
Accounts payable					=B28+C28–D28+E28
Other liabilities					=B29+C29–D29+E29
Capital stock, $10 par					=B30+C30–D30+E30
Other paid-in capital					=B31+C31–D31+E31
Retained earnings	=B18	=C18			=F18
Total equities	=SUM(B28:B32)	=SUM(C28:C32)			
					=B34+C34–D34+E34–D35+E35
			=SUM(D6:D33)	=SUM(E6:E33)	=SUM(F28:F34)

amounts from the subsidiary company, even though the parent company owns only 70% of the common stock. We will adjust for the 30% of the subsidiary company not controlled by the parent (the noncontrolling interest) in computing our consolidated totals. We include two columns to record the debits and credits for consolidation adjustments and eliminations. The final column provides calculations of the correct consolidated financial statement balances. Vertically, we divide the worksheet into three separate parts for the three financial statements we want to prepare. Notice the bold-faced items: **net income**, **retained earnings**, **total assets**, and **total equities**. No amounts are input for these items. They are either calculated or are carried forward from a previous part of the worksheet.

Exhibit 4-10 shows spreadsheet formulae used in preparing the worksheet. Notice that most of these can be input using the COPY command available in the spreadsheet software. In the first two columns, net income, retained earnings—ending, total assets, and total equities are simple summations of the relevant balances. Notice too that net income in the retained earnings section of the worksheet and retained earnings in the balance sheet section are simple amount carryforwards from the income statement and retained earnings sections, respectively. The adjustments and eliminations columns each contain a single summation formula for the column totals. This is useful in verifying the equality of debits and credits (in other words, that you have not made any errors in posting your consolidation entries).

There are lots of formulae in the final consolidated statements column, but again most of these can be entered with the COPY command. As in the first two columns, net income, retained earnings—ending, total assets, and total equities are simple summations of the relevant balances, and net income in the retained earnings section and retained earnings in the balance sheet section are simple amount carryforwards from the income statement and retained earnings sections, respectively. Let's look at the formula for Sales (=B6+C6–D6+E6). We simply sum parent-company sales plus subsidiary-company sales and then make any needed adjustments and eliminations. Notice that sales has a normal credit balance, so we subtract the debit adjustments (–D6) and add credits (+E6) to arrive at the consolidated total. We can simply copy our formula for all accounts having normal credit balances (i.e., revenues, liabilities, and equities).

We keep the same basic formula for cost of goods sold and any other expenses in the income statement portion of the worksheet. We do so because we enter the expenses as negative amounts.

If you look to the balance sheet section, our formula for consolidated cash (=B20+C20+D20–E20) reflects the fact that cash has a normal debit balance that is increased by debit adjustments and decreased by credits. Formulae for the remaining asset balances are entered using the COPY command. Before leaving Exhibit 4-10, pay attention to the formula for the investment in subsidiary. This is a bit longer than the cash formula, and it simply illustrates how to adjust the formula when we have multiple debit and credit adjustments to the same account.

We will discuss the completion of the worksheet by working through a sample problem. Separate-company trial balances for Parent Corporation and Subsidiary Company at December 31, 2006, are summarized as follows (in thousands):

	Parent Corporation	Subsidiary Company
Sales	$3,100	$1,000
Income from Subsidiary	105	—
Accounts payable	300	180
Other liabilities	200	120
Capital stock, $10 par	1,500	500
Other paid-in capital	200	40
Retained earnings—January 1	650	110
	$6,055	$1,950
Cash	$ 455	$ 150
Accounts receivable—net	600	300
Cost of sales	2,000	650
Dividends	300	100
Inventory	240	200
Investment in Subsidiary—70%	490	—
Operating expenses	770	200
Plant & equipment—net	1,200	350
	$6,055	$1,950

Parent Corporation acquired 70% of the outstanding voting shares of Subsidiary Company for $455,000 on January 1, 2006, when Subsidiary's stockholders' equity was $650,000. All of the assets and liabilities of Subsidiary were stated at their fair values when Parent acquired its 70% interest.

We enter the data into our worksheet in Exhibit 4-11. Exhibit 4-11 is our template worksheet from Exhibit 4-10, but we have added the example data in columns one and two. We begin with the income statement accounts. Note that we record revenues as positive amounts and expenses as negatives. Net income is then a simple summation of revenues and expenses. We carry the calculated net income down to the *Retained Earnings* section of the worksheet with no further adjustment required.

Beginning-of-the-year retained earnings amounts come from the Parent and Subsidiary trial balances. We record dividends as negative amounts because they reduce retained earnings. Ending retained earnings is now a simple summation. We carry the calculated ending retained earnings down to the *Balance Sheet* section of the worksheet with no further adjustment required.

We record balance sheet amounts picked up from the Parent and Subsidiary trial balances. Notice that we record assets, liabilities, and equities as positive amounts. Total assets and total equities are simple summation functions.

EXHIBIT 4-11

Building the Worksheet

PARENT AND SUBSIDIARY CONSOLIDATION WORKSHEET FOR THE YEAR ENDED DECEMBER 31, 2006 (IN THOUSANDS)

	Parent	70% Subsidiary	Adjustments & Eliminations Debits	Adjustments & Eliminations Credits	Consolidated Statements
Income Statement					
Sales	3,100	1,000			4,100
Income from Subsidiary	105				105
Cost of goods sold	(2,000)	(650)			(2,650)
Operating expenses	(770)	(200)			(970)
Net income	**435**	**150**			**585**
Retained Earnings					
Retained earnings—Parent	650				650
Retained earnings—Subsidiary		110			110
Net income	435	150			585
Dividends	(300)	(100)			
					(400)
Ret earnings—ending	**785**	**160**			**945**
Balance Sheet					
Cash	455	150			605
Receivables—net	600	300			900
Inventories	240	200			440
Plant & equipment—net	1,200	350			1,550
Investment in Subsidiary	490				490
					0
Total assets	**2,985**	**1,000**			**3,985**
Accounts payable	300	180			480
Other liabilities	200	120			320
Capital stock, $10 par	1,500	500			2,000
Other paid-in capital	200	40			240
Retained earnings	785	160			945
Total equities	**2,985**	**1,000**			
					3,985

Parent's $105,000 income from Subsidiary for 2006 consists of 70% of Subsidiary's $150,000 net income for 2006. Its $490,000 Investment in Subsidiary account balance at December 31, 2006, consists of the $455,000 investment cost plus $105,000 income from Subsidiary, less $70,000 dividends received from Subsidiary during 2006.

In our working paper format, we carry the net income line down to the retained earnings section of the worksheet without any further adjustment. We similarly carry the ending retained earnings row down to the balance sheet section, again without further adjustments or eliminations. Notice, too, that each row in the working paper generates the consolidated amounts by adding together the Parent company and Subsidiary account balances and then adding or subtracting the adjustments and eliminations as appropriate.

Parent Company net income and retained earnings under the complete equity method of accounting are equal to consolidated retained earnings. Because Parent Company correctly applies the equity method, its net income of $435,000 equals consolidated net income. Its beginning and ending retained earnings balances equal the $650,000 and $785,000 consolidated retained earnings amounts, respectively.

Finally, we are going to review the required consolidation adjustments and eliminations. We provide a separate Exhibit 4-12 to show the final consolidation worksheet, after posting our the adjustments and eliminations. This is simply Exhibit 4-11, updated to reflect the entries that follow. Notice, too, that we have added some new accounts. We create noncontrolling interest expense in the income statement section and noncontrolling interest in the balance sheet section

EXHIBIT 4-12

Completing the Worksheet

PARENT CORPORATION AND SUBSIDIARY CONSOLIDATION WORKSHEET FOR THE YEAR ENDED DECEMBER 31, 2006 (IN THOUSANDS)

	Parent	70% Subsidiary	Adjustments & Eliminations Debits	Adjustments & Eliminations Credits	Consolidated Statements
Income Statement					
Sales	3,100	1,000			4,100
Income from Subsidiary	105		a 105		0
Cost of goods sold	(2,000)	(650)			(2,650)
Operating expenses	(770)	(200)			(970)
Noncontrolling interest expense			b 45		(45)
Net income	435	150			435
Retained Earnings					
Retained earnings—Parent	650				650
Retained earnings—Subsidiary		110	c 110		0
Net income	435	150			435
Dividends	(300)	(100)		a 70	(300)
				b 30	
Ret earnings—ending	785	160			785
Balance Sheet					
Cash	455	150			605
Receivables—net	600	300			900
Inventories	240	200			440
Plant & equipment—net	1,200	350			1,550
Investment in Subsidiary	490			a 35	0
				c 455	
Total assets	2,985	1,000			3,495
Accounts payable	300	180			480
Other liabilities	200	120			320
Capital stock, $10 par	1,500	500	c 500		1,500
Other paid-in capital	200	40	c 40		200
Retained earnings	785	160			785
Total equities	2,985	1,000			
Noncontrolling interest				c 195	210
				b 15	
			800	800	3,495

and copy the relevant formulae for expense accounts and liabilities. The first working paper entry in Exhibit 4-12 is the following:

a	**Income from Subsidiary (−R, −SE)**	105,000	
	Dividends (+E)		70,000
	Investment in Subsidiary (−A)		35,000
	To eliminate income and dividends from Subsidiary and return the investment account to its beginning-of-the-period balance.		

The difference between income from a subsidiary recognized on the books of the parent company and the dividends received represents the change in the investment account for the period. The $35,000 credit to the investment in Subsidiary account reduces that account to its $455,000 beginning-of-the-period balance and thereby establishes reciprocity between the investment in Subsidiary and Subsidiary's stockholders' equity at January 1, 2006.

Here is a journal entry for working paper entry b for Exhibit 4-12:

b **Noncontrolling interest expense (E, –SE)**	**45,000**	
Dividends—Subsidiary (+SE)		**30,000**
Noncontrolling interest (+L)		**15,000**
To enter noncontrolling interest share of Subsidiary income and dividends.		

Entry b incorporates the noncontrolling interest in a Subsidiary's net income and the noncontrolling interest's share of dividends declared by Subsidiary directly into the consolidation working papers.

Working paper entry c in journal entry form is as follows:

c **Retained earnings—Sub. (beginning) (–SE)**	**110,000**	
Capital stock—Subsidiary (–SE)	**500,000**	
Other paid in capital—Subsidiary (–SE)	**40,000**	
Investment in Subsidiary (–A)		**455,000**
Noncontrolling interest (+L)		**195,000**
To eliminate reciprocal equity and investment balances, establish beginning noncontrolling interest, and enter unamortized patents.		

This entry eliminates reciprocal investment and equity balances, enters the unamortized excess of investment cost over book value acquired as of the beginning of the year (zero in this example), and constructs beginning noncontrolling interest ($650,000 \times 30\%$) as a separate item. Observe that entry c eliminates reciprocal investment and equity balances as of the beginning of the period and enters noncontrolling interest as of the same date.

Our spreadsheet formulae compute the final consolidated statement totals for us in the final column. The worksheet is complete. You may want to practice creating the spreadsheet for a few problems to be certain you understand the mechanics. However, you will not need to create your own spreadsheet for all problem assignments. We eliminate the mechanical drudgery, and allow you to focus on learning the advanced accounting concepts, by providing spreadsheet templates for many assignments. An icon in the assignment material indicates the availability of a template. The templates already include the data from the problem for the Parent and Subsidiary companies and the formulae for calculating the consolidated balances. You can find the templates on the *Advanced Accounting* Web site.

SUMMARY

Working papers are prepared to produce meaningful financial reports for the consolidated business entity. Preparation of meaningful consolidated financial statements is the objective. The working papers are tools for organizing and manipulating data. If you clearly understand the objective, you can determine the proper amounts for the consolidated statements without preparing the working papers.

Throughout the chapter it was assumed that the parent company uses the complete equity method to account for its investment in the subsidiary. Alternative methods of parent-company accounting and necessary revisions to the eliminations and adjustments are discussed on the *Advanced Accounting* Web site.

The consolidated statement of cash flows can be prepared from the consolidated balance sheets and income statements.

QUESTIONS

1. How are consolidated financial statements affected by the manner in which the parent company accounts for its subsidiary investments?

2. Is it ever acceptable for a parent company to use the cost method of accounting for its investments in subsidiary corporations? Explain.

3. If a parent company in accounting for its subsidiary investment amortizes patents on its separate books, why is it necessary to include an adjustment for patents amortization in the consolidation working papers?

4. How is noncontrolling interest expense entered in consolidation working papers? Is there an alternative method?

5. How are the working paper procedures for the investment in subsidiary, income from subsidiary, and subsidiary's stockholders' equity accounts alike?

6. If a parent company uses the equity method but does not amortize the difference between investment cost and book value acquired on its separate books, its net income and retained earnings will not equal consolidated net income and consolidated retained earnings. How does this affect consolidation working paper procedures?

7. Are working paper adjustments and eliminations entered on the parent-company books? The subsidiary books? Explain.

8. The financial statement and trial balance working paper approaches illustrated in the chapter generate comparable information, so why learn both approaches?

9. In what way do the adjustment and elimination entries for consolidation working papers differ for the financial statement and trial balance approaches?

10. When is it necessary to adjust the parent-company's retained earnings account in the preparation of consolidation working papers? In answering this question, explain the relationship between parent-company retained earnings and consolidated retained earnings.

11. What approach would you use to check the accuracy of the consolidated retained earnings and noncontrolling interest amounts that appear in the balance sheet section of completed consolidation working papers?

12. Explain why noncontrolling interest expense is added to consolidated net income in determining cash flows from operating activities.

13. Consolidated net income is a measurement of income to the stockholders of the parent company, but does a change in cash as reflected in a statement of cash flows also relate to other stockholders of the parent company?

EXERCISES

E 4-1
General questions

1. Working paper entries normally:
   a **Are posted to the general ledger accounts of one or more of the affiliated companies**
   b **Are posted to the general ledger accounts only when the financial statement approach is used**
   c **Are posted to the general ledger accounts only when the trial balance approach is used**
   d **Do not affect the general ledger accounts of any of the affiliated companies**

2. Working paper techniques assume nominal accounts are:
   a **Open when the financial statement approach is used**
   b **Open when the trial balance approach is used**
   c **Open in all cases**
   d **Closed**

3. Most errors made in consolidating financial statements will appear when:
   a **The consolidated balance sheet does not balance**
   b **Consolidated net income does not equal parent-company net income**
   c **The retained earnings amount on the balance sheet does not equal the amount on the retained earnings statement**
   d **Adjustment and elimination column totals do not equal**

4. Net income on consolidation working papers is:
   a **Adjusted when the parent company uses the cost method**
   b **Adjusted when the parent company uses the equity method**
   c **Adjusted in all cases**
   d **Not an account balance and not subject to adjustment**

5. On consolidation working papers, individual stockholders' equity accounts of a subsidiary are:
   a **Added to parent-company stockholders' equity accounts**
   b **Eliminated**
   c **Eliminated only to the extent of noncontrolling interest**
   d **Eliminated to the extent of the parent company's interest**

6. On consolidation working papers, investment income from a subsidiary is:
   a **Added to the investment account**
   b **Added to the parent company's beginning retained earnings**
   c **Allocated between majority and noncontrolling stockholders**
   d **Eliminated**

7. On consolidation working papers, the investment in consolidated subsidiary account balances are:
   a **Allocated between majority and noncontrolling interests**
   b **Always eliminated**
   c **Carried forward to the consolidated balance sheet**
   d **Eliminated when the financial statement approach is used**

8. On consolidation working papers, consolidated net income is determined by:
   a **Adding net income of the parent and subsidiary companies**
   b **Deducting consolidated expenses and minority interest expense from consolidated revenues**
   c **Making adjustments to the parent company's income**
   d **Subtracting noncontrolling interest expense from parent-company net income**

9. On consolidation working papers, consolidated end-of-the-period retained earnings is determined by:
   a **Adding beginning consolidated retained earnings and consolidated net income and subtracting parent-company dividends**
   b **Adding end-of-the-period retained earnings of the affiliated companies**
   c **Adjusting beginning parent-company retained earnings for subsidiary profits and dividends**
   d **Adjusting the parent company's retained earnings account balance**

10. Under the trial balance approach to consolidation working papers, which of the following is used?
    a **Unadjusted trial balances**
    b **Adjusted trial balances**
    c **Postclosing trial balances**
    d **Either a or b, depending on the circumstances**

E 4-2

Consolidated statement items with equity method Ponder Corporation purchased 80% of the outstanding voting common stock of Sally Forth Corporation on January 2, 2006, for $300,000 cash. Sally Forth's balance sheets on this date and on December 31, 2006, are as follows:

Sally Forth Corporation Balance Sheets

	January 2, 2006	December 31, 2006
Inventory	$ 50,000	$ 20,000
Other current assets	50,000	80,000
Plant assets—net	200,000	220,000
Total assets	$300,000	$320,000
Liabilities	$ 50,000	$ 60,000
Capital stock	150,000	150,000
Retained earnings	100,000	110,000
Total equities	$300,000	$320,000

ADDITIONAL INFORMATION

1. Ponder uses the equity method of accounting for its investment in Sally Forth.

2. Sally Forth's 2006 net income and dividends were $70,000 and $60,000, respectively.

3. Sally Forth's inventory, which was sold in 2006, was undervalued by $12,500 at January 2, 2006.

REQUIRED

1. What is Ponder's income from Sally Forth for 2006?

2. What is the noncontrolling interest expense for 2006?

3. What is the total noncontrolling interest at December 31, 2006?

4. What will be the balance of Ponder's Investment in Sally Forth account at December 31, 2006, if investment income from Sally Forth is $50,000? *Ignore* your answer to 1.

5. What is consolidated net income for Ponder Corporation and Subsidiary if Ponder's net income for 2006 is $180,200? (Assume income from subsidiary is $50,000.)

E 4-3

General problems

1. Peggy Corporation owns a 70% interest in Sandy Corporation, acquired several years ago at book value. On December 31, 2006, Sandy mailed a check for $10,000 to Peggy in part payment of a $20,000 account with Peggy. Peggy had not received the check when its books were closed on December 31. Peggy Corporation had accounts receivable of $150,000 (including the $20,000 from Sandy), and Sandy had accounts receivable at $220,000 at year-end. In the consolidated balance sheet of Peggy Corporation and Subsidiary at December 31, 2006, accounts receivable will be shown in the amount of:

a *$370,000*

b *$360,000*

c *$350,000*

d *$304,000*

Use the following information in answering questions 2 and 3.

Primrose Corporation purchased a 70% interest in Starman Corporation on January 1, 2006, for $15,000, when Starman's stockholders' equity consisted of $3,000 common stock, $10,000 additional paid-in capital, and $2,000 retained earnings. Income and dividend information for Starman for 2006, 2007, and 2008 is as follows:

	2006	2007	2008
Net income (or loss)	$1,000	$200	$(500)
Dividends	400	100	—

2. Primrose reported separate income of $12,000 for 2008. Consolidated net income for 2008 is:

a *$11,387*

b *$11,500*

c *$11,537*

d *$11,650*

3. Primrose's Investment in Starman balance at December 31, 2008, under the equity method is:

a *$14,800*

b *$14,802*

c *$14,960*

d *$15,137*

answer s/B 15,140

E 4-4

Equity and incomplete equity methods
The stockholder's equity accounts of Penair Corporation and Stine Corporation at December 31, 2006, were as follows (in thousands):

	Penair Corporation	Stine Corporation
Capital stock	$1,200	$500
Retained earnings	500	100 +40+60 = 200
Total	$1,700	$600

On January 1, 2007, Penair Corporation acquired an 80% interest in Stine Corporation for $580,000. The excess of cost over book value acquired was due to Stine Corporation's equipment being undervalued by $50,000 and unrecorded patents. The undervalued equipment had a 5-year remaining useful life when Penair acquired its interest. Patents are amortized over a 10-year period.

The income and dividends of Penair and Stine for 2007 and 2008 are as follows:

	Penair		Stine	
	2007	2008	2007	2008
Net income	$340	$350	$120	$150
Dividends	240	250	80	90

RE 40   60

REQUIRED

1. Assume that Penair Corporation uses the equity method of accounting for its investment in Stine.

a. Determine consolidated net income for Penair Corporation and Subsidiary for 2007.

b. Compute the balance of Penair's Investment in Stine account at December 31, 2007.

c. Compute noncontrolling interest expense for 2007.

d. Compute noncontrolling interest at December 31, 2008.

2. Compute consolidated net income for Penair Corporation and Subsidiary for 2007 assuming that Penair uses the equity method of accounting except that it does not amortize the difference between cost and book value acquired on its separate books. (*Hint:* Determine separate income of Penair Corporation as a first step in your computation.)

E 4-5

General questions on statement of cash flows

1. In preparing a statement of cash flows, the cost of acquiring a subsidiary is reported:
   a *As an operating activity under the direct method*
   b *As an operating activity under the indirect method*
   c *As an investing activity*
   d *As a financing activity*

2. In computing cash flows from operating activities under the direct method, the following item is an addition:
   a *Cash dividends from equity investees*
   b *Collection of principal on a loan made to a subsidiary*
   c *Noncontrolling interest dividends*
   d *Noncontrolling interest expense*

3. In computing cash flows from operating activities under the indirect method, the following item is an addition to consolidated net income:
   a *Noncontrolling interest dividends*
   b *Noncontrolling interest expense*
   c *Income from equity investees in excess of dividends received*
   d *Write-off of negative goodwill*

4. In computing cash flows from operating activities under the direct method, the following item is an addition:
   a *Sales*
   b *Noncontrolling interest expense*
   c *Cash received from customers*
   d *Depreciation expense*

5. Dividends paid as presented in a consolidated cash flow statement are:
   a *Parent company dividends*
   b *Subsidiary dividends*
   c *Parent and subsidiary dividends*
   d *Parent and noncontrolling interest dividends*

E 4-6

Prepare cash flows from operating activities section Information needed to prepare the Cash Flow from Operating Activities section of Party Corporation's consolidated statement of cash flows for 2006 is included in the following list:

Amortization of patents	$ 8,000
Consolidated net income	75,000
Decrease in accounts payable	10,000
Depreciation expense	60,000
Increase in accounts receivable	52,500
Increase in inventories	22,500
Loss on sale of land	50,000
Noncontrolling interest expense	25,000
Noncontrolling interest dividends	12,000
Undistributed income of equity investees	2,500

REQUIRED: Prepare the Cash Flows from Operating Activities section of Party's consolidated statement of cash flows under the indirect method.

E 4-7

Prepare cash flows from operating activities section The information needed to prepare the Cash Flow from Operating Activities section of Prolax Corporation's consolidated statement of cash flows for 2006 is included in the following list:

Cash received from customers	$322,500
Cash paid to suppliers	182,500
Cash paid to employees	27,000
Cash paid for other operating items	23,500
Cash paid for interest expense	12,000
Cash proceeds from sale of land	60,000
Noncontrolling interest dividends	10,000
Dividends received from equity investees	7,000

REQUIRED: Prepare the Cash Flows from Operating Activities section of Prolax's consolidated statement of cash flows under the direct method.

P 4-1

Calculations four years after acquisition Pearl Corporation purchased 75% of the outstanding voting stock of Seine Corporation for $2,500,000 on January 1, 2006. Steine's stockholders' equity on this date consisted of the following (in thousands):

Capital stock, $10 par	$1,000
Additional paid-in capital	600
Retained earnings December 31, 2005	800
Total stockholders' equity	$2,400

The excess of investment cost over book value of the net assets acquired was allocated 10% to undervalued inventory (sold in 2006), 40% to plant assets with a remaining useful life of eight years, and 50% to unidentifiable intangible assets.

Comparative trial balances of Pearl Corporation and Seine Corporation at December 31, 2010, are as follows:

	Pearl	Seine
Other assets—net	$3,850	$2,600
Investment in Seine—75%	2,255	—
Expenses (including cost of sales)	3,180	600
Dividends	500	200
	$9,785	$3,400
Capital stock, $10 par	$3,000	$1,000
Additional paid-in capital	850	600
Retained earnings	1,670	800
Sales	4,000	1,000
Income from Seine	265	—
	$9,785	$3,400

(handwritten: 2,400 bracketing the $1,000, 600, 800)

REQUIRED: Determine the amounts that would appear in the consolidated financial statements of Pearl Corporation and Subsidiary for each of the following items:

1. Goodwill at December 31, 2010

2. Noncontrolling interest expense for 2010

3. Consolidated retained earnings at December 31, 2009

4. Consolidated retained earnings at December 31, 2010

5. Consolidated net income for 2010

6. Noncontrolling interest at December 31, 2009

7. Noncontrolling interest at December 31, 2010

8. Dividends payable at December 31, 2010

P 4-2

Working papers and financial statements in year of acquisition Palm Corporation acquired 70% of the outstanding voting stock of Sail Corporation for $45,500 cash on January 1, 2006, when Sail's stockholders' equity was $65,000. All the assets and liabilities of Sail were stated at their fair values when Palm acquired its 70% interest.

Financial statements of the two corporations at and for the year ended December 31, 2006, are summarized as follows (in thousands):

	Palm	Sail
Combined Income and Retained Earnings Statements for the Year Ended December 31		
Sales	$310	$100
Income from Sail	10.5	—
Cost of goods sold	(200)	(65)
Operating expenses	(77)	(20)
Net income	43.5	15
Add: Retained earnings January 1	65	11
Deduct: Dividends	(30)	(10)
Retained earnings December 31	$ 78.5	$ 16
Balance Sheet at December 31		
Cash	$ 45.5	$ 15
Receivables—net	60	30
Inventories	24	20
Plant and equipment—net	120	35
Investment in Sail	49	—
Total assets	$298.5	$100
Accounts payable	$ 30	$ 18
Other liabilities	20	12
Capital stock, $10 par	150	50
Other paid-in capital	20	4
Retained earnings	78.5	16
Total equities	$298.5	$100

REQUIRED

1. Prepare consolidation working papers for Palm Corporation and Subsidiary for 2006.
2. Prepare a consolidated income statement and a consolidated balance sheet for Palm Corporation and Subsidiary.

P 4-3

Working papers in year of acquisition (goodwill and intercompany transactions)
Pan Corporation acquired a 75% interest in Saf Corporation on January 1, 2006. Financial statements of Pan and Saf Corporations for the year 2006 are as follows (in thousands):

	Pan	Saf
Combined Income and Retained Earnings Statements for the Year Ended December 31		
Sales	$400	$100
Income from Saf	17	—
Cost of sales	(250)	(50)
Other expenses	(97)	(26)
Net income	70	24
Add: Retained earnings January 1	180	34
Deduct: Dividends	(50)	(16)
Retained earnings December 31	$200	$ 42
Balance Sheet at December 31		
Cash	$ 61	$ 15
Accounts receivable—net	80	20
Dividends receivable from Saf	6	—
Inventories	95	10
Note receivable from Pan	—	5
Land	65	30
Buildings—net	170	80
Equipment—net	130	50
Investment in Saf	183	—
Total assets	$790	$210
Accounts payable	$ 85	$ 10
Note payable to Saf	5	—
Dividends payable	—	8
Capital stock, $10 par	500	150
Retained earnings	200	42
Total equities	$790	$210

REQUIRED: Prepare consolidation working papers for Pan Corporation and Subsidiary for the year ended December 31, 2006. Only the information provided in the financial statements is available; accordingly, your solution will require some standard assumptions. Saf owned unrecorded patents having a fair value of $53,300. The patents have a life of 40 years.

P 4-4

Consolidation working papers from separate financial statements Pal Corporation acquired a 75% interest in Sun Corporation on January 1, 2006. Financial statements of Pal and Sun Corporations for 2006 are as follows (in thousands):

	Pal	Sun
Combined Income and Retained Earnings Statements for the Year Ended December 31		
Sales	$400	$100
Income from Sun	18	—
Cost of sales	(250)	(50)
Other expenses	(97)	(26)
Net income	71	24
Add: Retained earnings January 1	180	34
Deduct: Dividends	(50)	(16)
Retained earnings December 31	$201	$ 42
Balance Sheet at December 31		
Cash	$ 61	$ 15
Accounts receivable—net	80	20
Dividends receivable from Sun	6	—
Inventories	95	10
Note receivable from Pal	—	5
Land	65	30
Buildings—net	170	80
Equipment—net	130	50
Investment in Sun	184	—
Total assets	$791	$210
Accounts payable	$ 85	$ 10
Note payable to Sun	5	—
Dividends payable	—	8
Capital stock, $10 par	500	150
Retained earnings	201	42
Total equities	$791	$210

REQUIRED: Prepare consolidation working papers for Pal Corporation and Subsidiary for the year ended December 31, 2006. Only the information provided in the financial statements is available; accordingly, your solution will require some standard assumptions.

P 4-5

Working papers in year of acquisition (excess allocated to inventory, building, equipment, and goodwill) Pari Corporation acquired a 70% interest in Soul Corporation's outstanding voting common stock on January 1, 2006, for $500,000 cash. The stockholders' equity of Soul on this date consisted of $500,000 capital stock and $100,000 retained earnings. The differences between the price paid by Pari and the underlying equity acquired in Soul were allocated $5,000 to Soul's undervalued inventory, $14,000 to undervalued buildings, $21,000 to undervalued equipment, and $40,000 to previously unrecorded patents.

The undervalued inventory items were sold during 2006, and the undervalued buildings and equipment had remaining useful lives of seven years and three years, respectively. The patents have a 40-year life. Depreciation is straight line.

At December 31, 2006, Soul's accounts payable include $10,000 owed to Pari. This $10,000 account payable is due on January 15, 2007. Pari sold equipment with a book value of $15,000 for $25,000 on June 1, 2006. This is not an intercompany sale transaction. Separate financial statements for Pari and Soul for 2006 are summarized as follows (in thousands):

	Pari	Soul
Combined Income and Retained Earnings		
Statements for the Year Ended December 31		
Sales	$ 800	$700
Income from Soul	55	—
Gain on equipment	10	—
Cost of sales	(300)	(400)
Depreciation expense	(155)	(60)
Other expenses	(160)	(140)
Net income	250	100
Add: Retained earnings January 1	300	100
Deduct: Dividends	(200)	(50)
Retained earnings December 31	$ 350	$150
Balance Sheet at December 31		
Cash	$ 86	$ 60
Accounts receivable—net	100	70
Dividends receivable	14	—
Inventories	150	100
Other current assets	70	30
Land	50	100
Buildings—net	140	160
Equipment—net	570	330
Investment in Soul	520	—
Total assets	$1,700	$850
Accounts payable	$ 200	$ 85
Dividends payable	100	20
Other liabilities	50	95
Capital stock, $10 par	1,000	500
Retained earnings	350	150
Total equities	$1,700	$850

REQUIRED: Prepare consolidation working papers for Pari Corporation and Subsidiary for the year ended December 31, 2006. Use an unamortized excess account.

P 4-6

Working papers (determine ownership interest, year after acquisition, excess allocated to land and goodwill) Separate company financial statements for Pen Corporation and its subsidiary, Syn Company, at and for the year ended December 31, 2007, are summarized as follows (in thousands):

	Pen	Syn
Combined Income and Retained Earnings		
Statements for the Year Ended December 31		
Sales	$400	$100
Income from Syn	17.6	—
Cost of sales	(250)	(50)
Expenses	(100.6)	(26)
Net income	67	24
Add: Retained earnings January 1	177	34
Deduct: Dividends	(50)	(16)
Retained earnings December 31	$194	$ 42
Balance Sheet at December 31		
Cash	$ 18	$ 15
Accounts receivable—net	80	20
Dividends receivable from Syn	7.2	—
Note receivable from Pen	—	5
Inventory	95	10
Investment in Syn	218.8	—
Land	65	30
Buildings—net	170	80
Equipment—net	130	50
Total assets	$784	$210

Accounts payable	$ 85	$ 10
Note payable to Syn	5	—
Dividends payable	—	8
Capital stock, $10 par	500	150
Retained earnings	194	42
Total equities	$784	$210

ADDITIONAL INFORMATION

1. Pen Corporation acquired 13,500 shares of Syn Company stock for $15 per share on January 1, 2006, when Syn's stockholders' equity consisted of $150,000 capital stock and $15,000 retained earnings.

2. Syn Company's land was undervalued when Pen acquired its interest, and accordingly, $14,000 of the cost/book value differential was allocated to land. Any remaining differential is allocated to unrecorded patents with a 10-year remaining life.

3. Syn Company owes Pen $5,000 on account, and Pen owes Syn $5,000 on a note payable.

REQUIRED: Prepare consolidated working papers for Pen Corporation and Subsidiary for the year ended December 31, 2007.

P 4-7

Working papers (year of acquisition, excess allocated to inventory, building equipment, and goodwill, intercompany balances) Par Corporation acquired a 70% interest in Sol Corporation's outstanding voting common stock on January 1, 2006, for $500,000 cash. The stockholders' equity of Sol on this date consisted of $500,000 capital stock and $100,000 retained earnings. The differences between the price paid by Par and the underlying equity acquired in Sol were allocated $5,000 to Sol's undervalued inventory, $14,000 to undervalued buildings, $21,000 to undervalued equipment, and $40,000 to goodwill.

The undervalued inventory items were sold during 2006, and the undervalued buildings and equipment had remaining useful lives of seven years and three years, respectively. Depreciation is straight line.

At December 31, 2006, Sol's accounts payable include $10,000 owed to Par. This $10,000 account payable is due on January 15, 2007. Par sold equipment with a book value of $15,000 for $25,000 on June 1, 2006. This is not an intercompany sale transaction. Separate financial statements for Par and Sol for 2006 are summarized as follows (in thousands):

	Par	Sol
Combined Income and Retained Earnings Statements for the Year Ended December 31		
Sales	$ 800	$700
Income from Sol	56	—
Gain on equipment (not inter-company)	10	—
Cost of sales	(300)	(400)
Depreciation expense	(155)	(60)
Other expenses	(160)	(140)
Net income	251	100
Add: Retained earnings January 1	300	100
Deduct: Dividends	(200)	(50)
Retained earnings December 31	$ 351	$150
Balance Sheet at December 31		
Cash	$ 86	$ 60
Accounts receivable—net	100	70
Dividends receivable	14	—
Inventories	150	100
Other current assets	70	30
Land	50	100
Buildings—net	140	160
Equipment—net	570	330
Investment in Sol	521	—
Total assets	$1,701	$850

Accounts payable	$ 200	$ 85
Dividends payable	100	20
Other liabilities	50	95
Capital stock, $10 par	1,000	500
Retained earnings	351	150
Total equities	$1,701	$850

REQUIRED: Prepare consolidation working papers for Par Corporation and Subsidiary for the year ended December 31, 2006. Use an unamortized excess account.

P 4-8

Working papers (excess allocated to land and goodwill) Separate-company financial statements for Pun Corporation and its subsidiary, Son Company, at and for the year ended December 31, 2007, are summarized as follows (in thousands):

	Pun	Son
Combined Income and Retained Earnings Statement for the Year Ended December 31		
Sales	$400	$100
Income from Son	21.6	—
Cost of sales	(250)	(50)
Expenses	(100.6)	(26)
Net income	71	24
Add: Retained earnings January 1	181	34
Deduct: Dividends	(50)	(16)
Retained earnings December 31	$202	$ 42
Balance Sheet at December 31		
Cash	$ 18	$ 15
Accounts receivable—net	80	20
Dividends receivable from Son	7.2	—
Note receivable from Pun	—	5
Inventory	95	10
Investment in Son	226.8	—
Land	65	30
Buildings—net	170	80
Equipment—net	130	50
Total assets	$792	$210
Accounts payable	$ 85	$ 10
Note payable to Son	5	—
Dividends payable	—	8
Capital stock, $10 par	500	150
Retained earnings	202	42
Total equities	$792	$210

ADDITIONAL INFORMATION

1. Pun Corporation acquired 13,500 shares of Son Company stock for $15 per share on January 1, 2006, when Son's stockholders' equity consisted of $150,000 capital stock and $15,000 retained earnings.

2. Son Company's land was undervalued when Pun acquired its interest, and accordingly, $14,000 of the cost/book value differential was allocated to land. Any remaining differential is goodwill.

3. Son Company owes Pun $5,000 on account, and Pun owes Son $5,000 on a note payable.

REQUIRED: Prepare consolidation working papers for Pun Corporation and Subsidiary for the year ended December 31, 2007.

P 4-9

Working papers (year of acquisition, excess allocated to inventory, equipment and goodwill, intercompany transactions) Pas Corporation acquired 80% of Sel Corporation's common stock on January 1, 2006, for $210,000 cash. The stockholders' equity of Sel at this time consisted of $150,000 capital stock and $50,000 retained earnings. The difference between the price paid by Pas and the underlying equity acquired in Sel was due to a $12,500 undervaluation of Sel's inventory, a $25,000 undervaluation of Sel's equipment, and unrecorded patents with a 20-year life.

The undervalued inventory items were sold by Sel during 2006, and the undervalued equipment had a remaining useful life of five years. Straight-line depreciation is used.

Sel owed Pas $4,000 on accounts payable at December 31, 2006.

The separate financial statements of Pas and Sel Corporations at and for the year ended December 31, 2006, are as follows (in thousands):

	Pas	Sel
Combined Income and Retained Earnings Statements for the Year Ended December 31		
Sales	$200	$110
Income from Sel	17	—
Cost of sales	(80)	(40)
Depreciation expense	(40)	(20)
Other expenses	(25.5)	(10)
Net income	71.5	40
Add: Retained earnings January 1	75	50
Deduct: Dividends	(40)	(20)
Retained earnings December 31	$106.5	$ 70
Balance Sheet at December 31		
Cash	$ 29.5	$ 30
Trade receivables—net	28	40
Dividends receivable	8	—
Inventories	40	30
Land	15	30
Buildings—net	65	70
Equipment—net	200	100
Investment in Sel	211	—
Total assets	$596.5	$300
Accounts payable	$ 40	$ 50
Dividends payable	100	10
Other liabilities	50	20
Capital stock, $10 par	300	150
Retained earnings	106.5	70
Total equities	$596.5	$300

REQUIRED: Prepare consolidation working papers for Pas Corporation and Subsidiary at and for the year ended December 31, 2006.

P 4-10

Working papers (year of acquisition, cost/book value differentials, intercompany balances) Plastik Corporation acquired 80% of Seldane Corporation's common stock on January 1, 2006, for $210,000 cash. The stockholders' equity of Seldane at this time consisted of $150,000 capital stock and $50,000 retained earnings. The difference between the price paid by Plastik and the underlying equity acquired in Seldane was due to a $12,500 undervaluation of Seldane's inventory, a $25,000 undervaluation of Seldane's equipment, and goodwill.

The undervalued inventory items were sold by Seldane during 2006, and the undervalued equipment had a remaining useful life of five years. Straight-line depreciation is used.

Seldane owed Plastik $4,000 on accounts payable at December 31, 2006.

The separate financial statements of Plastik and Seldane Corporations at and for the year ended December 31, 2006, are as follows (in thousands):

	Plastik	Seldane
Combined Income and Retained Earnings Statements for the Year Ended December 31		
Sales	$200	$110
Income from Seldane	18	—
Cost of sales	(80)	(40)
Depreciation expense	(40)	(20)
Other expenses	(25.5)	(10)
Net income	72.5	40
Add: Retained earnings January 1	75	50
Deduct: Dividends	(40)	(20)
Retained earnings December 31	$107.5	$ 70
Balance Sheet at December 31		
Cash	$ 29.5	$ 30
Trade receivables—net	28	40
Dividends receivable	8	—
Inventories	40	30
Land	15	30
Buildings—net	65	70
Equipment—net	200	100
Investment in Seldane	212	—
Total assets	$597.5	$300
Accounts payable	$ 40	$ 50
Dividends payable	100	10
Other liabilities	50	20
Capital stock, $10 par	300	150
Retained earnings	107.5	70
Total equities	$597.5	$300

REQUIRED: Prepare consolidation working papers for Plastik Corporation and Subsidiary at and for the year ended December 31, 2006.

P 4-11

Balance sheet (four years after acquisition, cost/book value differentials) Pill Corporation paid $170,000 for an 80% interest in Stud Corporation on December 31, 2006, when Stud's stockholders' equity consisted of $100,000 capital stock and $50,000 retained earnings. A summary of the changes in Pill's Investment in Stud account from December 31, 2006, to December 31, 2010, follows:

Investment cost December 31, 2006		$170,000
Increases		
80% of Stud's income 2007 through 2010		112,000
		282,000
Decreases		
80% of Stud's dividends 2007 through 2010	$56,000	
Amortization of excess cost over book value:		
Allocated to inventories, $7,000 (sold in 2007)	7,000	
Allocated to plant assets, $18,000 (depreciated over a nine-year period) 2007 through 2010	8,000	
Allocated to patents, $25,000 (amortized over a five-year period) 2007 through 2010	20,000	91,000
Investment balance December 31, 2010		$191,000

Financial statements for Pill and Stud at and for the year ended December 31, 2010, are summarized as follows (in thousands):

	Pill	Stud
Combined Income and Retained Earnings Statements for the Year Ended December 31		
Sales	$300	$200
Income from Stud	25	—
Cost of sales	(180)	(140)
Other expenses	(50)	(20)
Net income	95	40
Add: Retained earnings January 1	255	100
Deduct: Dividends	(50)	(20)
Retained earnings December 31	$300	$120
Balance Sheet at December 31		
Cash	$ 41	$ 35
Trade receivables—net	60	55
Dividends receivable	8	—
Advance to Stud	25	—
Inventories	125	35
Plant assets—net	300	175
Investment in Stud	191	—
Total assets	$750	$300
Accounts payable	$ 50	$ 45
Dividends payable	—	10
Advance from Pill	—	25
Capital stock	400	100
Retained earnings	300	120
Total equities	$750	$300

ADDITIONAL INFORMATION

1. The accounts payable of Stud at December 31, 2010, include $5,000 owed to Pill.

2. Pill advanced $25,000 to Stud during 2008. This advance is still outstanding.

3. Half of Stud's 2010 dividends will be paid in January 2011.

REQUIRED: Prepare working papers to consolidate the balance sheets only of Pill and Stud Corporations at December 31, 2010.

P 4-12

Working papers (two years after acquisition, cost/book differentials, adjustments) Pat Corporation acquired an 80% interest in Sci Corporation for $240,000 on January 1, 2006, when Sci's stockholders' equity consisted of $200,000 capital stock and $25,000 retained earnings. The excess cost over book value acquired was allocated to plant assets that were undervalued by $50,000 and to goodwill. The undervalued plant assets had a four-year useful life.

ADDITIONAL INFORMATION

1. Pat's account receivable includes $5,000 owed by Sci.

2. Sci mailed its check for $20,000 to Pat on December 30, 2007, in settlement of the advance.

3. A $10,000 dividend was declared by Sci on December 30, 2007, but was not recorded by Pat.

4. Financial statements for Pat and Sci Corporations for 2007 follow (in thousands):

	Pat	Sci
Statements of Income and Retained Earnings for the Year Ended December 31		
Sales	$900	$300
Income from Sci	38	—
Cost of sales	(600)	(150)
Operating expenses	(190)	(90)
Net income	148	60
Add: Retained earnings January 1	122	50
Less: Dividends	(100)	(20)
Retained earnings December 31	$170	$ 90

[handwritten: NI $48,000 / Amort −10,000 / 38,000]

Balance Sheet at December 31

Cash	$ 6	$ 15
Accounts receivable—net	26	20
Inventories	82	60
Advance to Sci	20	—
Other current assets	80	5
Land	160	30
Plant assets—net	340	230
Investment in Sci	280	—
Total assets	$994	$360
Accounts payable	$ 24	$ 15
Dividends payable	—	10
Other liabilities	100	45
Capital stock	700	200
Retained earnings	170	90
Total liabilities and stockholders' equity	$994	$360

REQUIRED: Prepare consolidation working papers for Pat Corporation and Subsidiary for 2007.

P 4-13

Given separate and consolidated statements, reconstruct adjustments and eliminations
Separate company and consolidated financial statements are presented for Powerhouse Corporation and its subsidiary, Starmark Corporation, at and for the year ended December 31, 2006.

(in thousands)	Powerhouse	Starmark	Consolidated
Income Statement			
Sales	$1,000	$400	$1,400
Income from Starmark	80	—	—
Cost of goods sold	(500)	(150)	(650)
Operating expenses	(385)	(150)	(545)
Noncontrolling interest expense	—	—	(10)
Net income	$ 195	$100	$ 195
Retained Earnings Statement			
Retained earnings January 1, 2006	$ 350	$150	$ 350
Add: Net income	195	100	195
Deduct: Dividends	(100)	(50)	(100)
Retained earnings December 31, 2006	$ 445	$200	$ 445
Balance Sheet			
Cash	$ 118	$ 25	$ 143
Accounts receivable—net	155	50	200
Dividends receivable	27	—	—
Inventories	250	175	425
Plant assets—net	500	300	815
Investment in Starmark	445	—	—
Patents	—	—	25
Total assets	$1,495	$550	$1,608
Accounts payable	$ 150	$ 70	$ 215
Dividends payable	50	30	53
Capital stock, $10 par	700	100	700
Additional paid-in capital	150	150	150
Retained earnings	445	200	445
Noncontrolling interest	—	—	45
Total equities	$1,495	$550	$1,608

REQUIRED: Reproduce in general journal form the working paper adjustments and eliminations that were made to consolidate the financial statements of Powerhouse and its subsidiary, Starmark, at December 31, 2006. Include a working paper entry for noncontrolling interest expense, dividends, and equity. Patents had a remaining useful life of six years at January 1, 2006.

P 4-14

[Appendix] Working papers for two successive years (equity method misapplied in second year) Comparative adjusted trial balances for Ply Corporation and Ski Corporation at December 31, 2005, 2006, and 2007 are given here. Ply Corporation acquired an 80% interest in Ski Corporation on January 1, 2006, for $80,000 cash. Except for inventory items that were undervalued by $1,000 and equipment that was undervalued by $4,000, all of Ski's identifiable assets and liabilities were stated at their fair values on December 31, 2005. The additional excess was assigned to previously unrecorded intangibles, which had a 40-year remaining life.

Ski Corporation sold the undervalued inventory items during 2006 but continues to own the equipment, which had a four-year remaining useful life as of December 31, 2005. (All amounts are in thousands.)

	December 31, 2005		December 31, 2006		December 31, 2007	
	Ply	**Ski**	**Ply**	**Ski**	**Ply**	**Ski**
Cash	$100	$ 30	$ 24.7	$ 15	$ 26.7	$ 20
Trade receivables—net	30	15	25	20	45	30
Dividends receivable	—	—	4	—	4	—
Inventories	50	20	40	30	40	30
Plant and equipment—net	90	60	100	55	95	60
Investment in Ski	—	—	86.3	—	94.3	—
Cost of sales	100	40	105	35	110	35
Operating expenses	20	30	35	30	30	35
Dividends	10	5	10	5	15	10
	$400	$200	$430	$190	$460	$220
Accounts payable	$ 30	$ 35	$ 20.7	$ 15	$ 17.7	$ 25
Dividends payable	10	—	9	5	6	5
Capital stock	100	40	100	40	100	40
Other paid-in capital	60	20	60	20	60	20
Retained earnings	50	25	70	30	90.3	40
Sales	150	80	160	80	170	90
Income from Ski	—	—	10.3	—	16	—
	$400	$200	$430	$190	$460	$220

REQUIRED: Prepare consolidation working papers for Ply Corporation and Subsidiary for 2006 and 2007 using the financial statement approach. (*Hint:* Ply Corporation's accountant applied the equity method correctly for 2006 but misapplied the equity method for 2007.)

P 4-15

Investment account analysis and trial balance working papers Pepper Company paid $100,000 for a 90% interest in Simple on January 5, 2006, when Simple's capital stock was $60,000 and its retained earnings $20,000. Trial balances for the companies at December 31, 2009, are as follows (in thousands):

	Pepper	**Simple**
Cash	$ 11	$ 15
Accounts receivable	15	25
Plant assets	220	180
Investment in Simple	138	—
Cost of goods sold	50	30
Operating expenses	25	40
Dividends	20	10
	$479	$300
Accumulated depreciation	$ 90	$ 50
Liabilities	80	30
Capital stock	100	60
Paid-in excess	20	—
Retained earnings	73	70
Sales	100	90
Income from Simple	16	—
	$479	$300

The excess of investment cost over book value acquired was allocated $8,000 to undervalued inventory items that were sold in 2006 and the remainder to patents having a remaining useful life of 10 years from January 1, 2006.

REQUIRED

1. Summarize the changes in Pepper Company's Investment in Simple account from January 5, 2006, through December 31, 2009.

2. Prepare consolidation working papers for Pepper Company and Subsidiary for 2009 using the trial balance approach for your working papers.

P 4-16

Trial balance working papers and financial statements in year of acquisition

Peggy Corporation owns 90% of the voting stock of Super Corporation and 25% of the voting stock of Ellen Corporation.

The 90% interest in Super was acquired for $20,000 cash on January 1, 2006, when Super's stockholders' equity was $20,000 ($18,000 capital stock and $2,000 retained earnings).

Peggy's 25% interest in Ellen was purchased for $7,000 cash on July 1, 2006, when Ellen's stockholders' equity was $24,000 ($15,000 capital stock, $6,000 retained earnings, and $3,000 current earnings—first half of 2005).

The difference between investment cost and book value acquired is due to unrecorded patents and is amortized over 10 years.

Adjusted trial balances of the three associated companies at December 31, 2006, are as follows:

	Peggy	Super	Ellen
Cash	$ 16,950	$ 4,000	$ 1,000
Other current assets	40,000	11,000	10,000
Plant assets—net	120,000	14,000	20,000
Investment in Super—90%	21,600	—	—
Investment in Ellen—25%	6,450	—	—
Cost of sales	60,000	16,000	15,000
Other expenses	25,000	7,000	9,000
Dividends (paid in November)	10,000	3,000	5,000
Total debits	$300,000	$55,000	$60,000
Current liabilities	$ 25,000	$ 7,000	$ 9,000
Capital stock	150,000	18,000	15,000
Retained earnings	20,000	2,000	6,000
Sales	100,000	28,000	30,000
Income from Super	4,300	—	—
Income from Ellen	700	—	—
Total credits	$300,000	$55,000	$60,000

REQUIRED

1. Reconstruct the journal entries that were made by Peggy Corporation during 2006 to account for its investments in Super and Ellen Corporations.

2. Prepare an income statement, a retained earnings statement, and a balance sheet for Peggy Corporation for December 31, 2006.

3. Prepare consolidation working papers (trial balance format) for Peggy and Subsidiaries for 2006.

4. Prepare consolidated financial statements other than the cash flows statement for Peggy Corporation and Subsidiaries for the year ended December 31, 2006.

P 4-17

Prepare cash flows from operating activities section (direct method) The accountant for Pillory Corporation collected the following information that he thought might be useful in the preparation of the company's consolidated statement of cash flows (in thousands):

Cash paid for purchase of equipment	$ 270
Cash paid for other expenses	450
Cash paid to suppliers	630
Cash received from customers	1,600
Cash received from sale of land	500
Cash received from treasury stock sold	400
Dividends from equity investees	40
Dividends paid to noncontrolling stockholders	20
Dividends paid to Pillory's stockholders	50
Gain on sale of land	200
Income from equity investees	80
Interest received from short-term loan	5
Noncontrolling interest expense	45

REQUIRED: Prepare the Cash Flows from Operating Activities section of the consolidated statement of cash flows for Pillory Corporation and Subsidiaries using the *direct method* of presentation.

P 4-18

Prepare consolidated statement of cash flows using the direct method or indirect method
Comparative consolidated financial statements for Pesek Corporation and its 90%-owned subsidiary, Snider Corporation, at and for the years ended December 31, 2008 and 2007, are as follows:

Pesek Corporation and Subsidiary Comparative Consolidated Financial Statements

	Year 2008	Year 2007	2008–2007
Income and Retained Earnings			
Statements for the Year			*Change*
Sales	$ 675	$600	$ 75
Cost of sales	(350)	(324.5)	(25.5)
Depreciation expense (51)	(51)	0	
Other operating expenses	(139)	(120.5)	(18.5)
Noncontrolling interest expense	(5)	(4)	(1)
Consolidated net income	130	100	30
Add: Beginning retained			
earnings	190	130	60
Less: Dividends	(40)	(40)	0
Ending retained earnings	$ 280	$190	$ 90
Balance Sheets at December 31			
Assets			
Cash	$ 55.5	$ 65	$ (9.5)
Accounts receivable—net	85	80	5
Inventories	140	120	20
Other current assets	100	81	19
Plant and equipment—net	674	600	74
Patents	19	19.5	(.5)
Total assets	$1,073.5	$965.5	$108
Equities			
Accounts payable	$ 85	$ 63	$ 22
Dividends payable	21	17	4
Long-term liabilities	35	46	(11)
Capital stock	500	500	0
Other paid-in capital	120	120	0
Retained earnings	280	190	90
Noncontrolling interest—10%	32.5	29.5	3
Total equities	$1,073.5	$965.5	$108

REQUIRED: Prepare a consolidated statement of cash flows for Pesek Corporation and Subsidiary for the year ended December 31, 2008, using either the indirect method or the direct method. All changes in plant assets are due to asset acquisitions and depreciation. Snider's net income and dividends for 2008 are $50,000 and $20,000, respectively.

P 4-19

[AICPA adapted] Prepare consolidated statement of cash flows The consolidated working paper balances of Push, Inc., and its subsidiary, Storr Corporation, as of December 31, 2006 and 2005, are as follows (in thousands):

	2006	2005	Net Change Increase (Decrease)
Assets			
Cash	$ 313	$ 195	$ 118
Marketable equity securities at cost (MES)	175	175	—
Allowance to reduce MES to market	(13)	(24)	11
Accounts receivable—net	418	440	(22)
Inventories	595	525	70
Land	385	170	215
Plant and equipment	755	690	65
Accumulated depreciation	(199)	(145)	(54)
Patents—net	57	60	(3)
Total assets	$2,486	$2,086	$ 400
Liabilities and Stockholders' Equity			
Note payable, current portion	$ 150	$ 150	$ —
Accounts and accrued payables	595	474	121
Note payable, long-term portion	300	450	(150)
Deferred income taxes	44	32	12
Noncontrolling interest in Storr	179	161	18
Common stock—$10 par	580	480	100
Additional paid-in capital	303	180	123
Retained earnings	335	195	140
Treasury stock at cost	—	(36)	36
Total equities	$2,486	$2,086	$ 400

ADDITIONAL INFORMATION

1. On January 20, 2006, Push issued 10,000 shares of its common stock for land having a fair value of $215,000.

2. On February 5, 2006, Push reissued all of its treasury stock for $44,000.

3. On May 15, 2006, Push paid a cash dividend of $58,000 on its common stock.

4. On August 8, 2006, equipment was purchased for $127,000.

5. On September 30, 2006, equipment was sold for $40,000. The equipment cost $62,000 and had a carrying amount of $34,000 on the date of sale.

6. On December 15, 2006, Storr Corporation paid a cash dividend of $15,000 on its common stock.

7. Deferred income taxes represent temporary differences relating to the use of accelerated depreciation methods for income tax reporting and the straight-line method for financial reporting.

8. Consolidated net income for 2006 was $198,000. Storr's net income was $110,000.

9. Push owns 70% of its subsidiary, Storr Corporation. There was no change in the ownership interest in Storr during 2005 and 2006. There were no intercompany transactions other than the dividend paid to Push by its subsidiary.

REQUIRED: Prepare a consolidated statement of cash flows for Push and Subsidiary for the year ended December 31, 2006. Use the *indirect method*.

P 4-20

Prepare consolidated statement of cash flows using either the direct or indirect method Comparative consolidated financial statements for Pilgrim Corporation and its 80%-owned subsidiary at and for the years ended December 31, 2007 and 2006, are summarized as follows:

**Pilgrim Corporation and Subsidiary Comparative Consolidated Financial
Statements at and for the Year Ended December 31 (in thousands)**

	Year 2007	Year 2006	Year's Change 2007–2006
Income and Retained Earnings			
Sales	$2,600	$2,400	$200
Income—equity investees	60	50	10
Cost of sales	(1,450)	(1,408)	(42)
Depreciation expense	(200)	(150)	(50)
Other operating expenses	(470)	(462)	(8)
Noncontrolling interest expense	(40)	(30)	(10)
Net income	500	400	100
Retained earnings, January 1	1,000	700	300
Dividends	(150)	(100)	(50)
Retained earnings, December 31	$1,350	$1,000	$350
Balance Sheet			
Cash	$ 430	$ 360	70
Accounts receivable—net	750	540	210
Inventories	700	700	0
Plant and equipment—net	1,800	1,500	300
Equity investments	430	400	30
Patents	190	200	(10)
Total assets	$4,300	$3,700	$600
Accounts payable	$ 492	$ 475	$ 17
Dividends payable	38	25	13
Long-term note payable	600	400	200
Capital stock	1,000	1,000	0
Other paid-in capital	600	600	0
Retained earnings	1,350	1,000	350
Noncontrolling interest—20%	220	200	20
Total equities	$4,300	$3,700	$600

REQUIRED: Prepare a consolidated statement of cash flows for Pilgrim Corporation and Subsidiary for the year ended December 31, 2007. Assume that all changes in plant assets are due to asset acquisitions and depreciation. Income and dividends from 20%- to 50%-owned investees for 2007 were $60,000 and $30,000, respectively. Pilgram's only subsidiary reported $200,000 net income for 2007 and declared $100,000 in dividends during the year. Patents amortization for 2007 is $10,000.

INTERNET ASSIGNMENT

Merck & Company has a long history of intercompany investment activity. Visit Merck's Web site and download a copy of its 2003 annual report. Review the financial statements and accompanying notes for evidence of current and past acquisition activities.

a. What amounts does Merck report for goodwill and other intangible assets at December 31, 2003?
b. Summarize Merck's intangible assets for recent acquisitions.
c. Briefly summarize Merck's amortization policies related to intangible assets. What accounting methods and lives are assigned to the assets?
d. Does Merck indicate similar assets and amortization for its joint ventures? If so, summarize.
e. Does Merck report material balance sheet or income statement amounts for non-controlling interests in 2003?

Trial Balance Working Paper Format

The main text of Chapter 4 discusses preparation of consolidated statements using a working paper format called the financial statement approach. This appendix presents an alternative working paper format using parent- and subsidiary-company trial balances.

The trial balance approach to consolidation working papers brings together the adjusted trial balances for affiliated companies. Both the financial statement approach and the trial balance approach generate the same information, so the selection is based on user preference. If completed financial statements are available, the financial statement approach is easier to use because it provides measurements of parent and subsidiary income, retained earnings, assets, and equities that are needed in the consolidating process. If the accountant is given adjusted trial balances to consolidate, the trial balance approach may be more convenient.

Working paper entries illustrated in this chapter are designed for convenient switching between the financial statement and trial balance approaches for consolidation working papers. Recall that we adjust or eliminate account balances. Net income is not an account balance, so it is not subject to adjustment. We assume all nominal accounts are open to permit adjustment. The only retained earnings amount that appears in an adjusted trial balance is the beginning retained earnings amount. Therefore, the adjustments and eliminations are exactly the same whether we use the trial balance approach or the financial statement approach. This is so because we are working with beginning retained earnings and adjusting actual account balances.

Consolidation Example—Trial Balance Format and Equity Method

Exhibit 4-13 illustrates consolidation working papers using the trial balance format for Pibb Corporation and its 90%-owned subsidiary, Shad Corporation. Pibb acquired its interest in Shad on January 1, 2006, at a price $14,000 in excess of underlying book value, and it assigned the excess to patents with a 10-year amortization period.

A summary of changes in Pibb's Investment in Shad account from the date of acquisition to December 31, 2007, the report date, is as follows:

Investment cost January 1, 2006	$50,000
Add: Income—2006 (90% of Shad's $10,000 net income less $1,400 amortization of patents)	7,600
Investment balance December 31, 2006	57,600
Add: Income—2007 (90% of Shad's $20,000 net income less $1,400 amortization of patents)	16,600
Deduct: Dividends received from Shad (90% × $10,000)	−9,000
Investment balance December 31, 2007	$65,200

The working papers presented in Exhibit 4-13 reflect the additional assumptions that Pibb sold merchandise to Shad during 2007 for $14,000, and that, as of December 31, 2007, Shad owed Pibb $5,000 from the sale. The merchandise was sold by Shad to its customers, so the consolidated entity realized all profit from the sale during 2007.

Separate adjusted trial balances are presented in the first two columns of Exhibit 4-13. As shown in the exhibit, debit-balance accounts are presented first and totaled, and credit-balance accounts are presented and totaled below the debit-balance accounts.

The working paper entries to prepare consolidated financial statements using the trial balance are the same as those for the financial statement approach. However, we classify the accounts in a trial balance according to their debit and credit balances, so the locations of the accounts vary from those found in the financial statement format. Also, the trial balance includes only beginning-of-the-period retained earnings amounts.

EXHIBIT 4-13

Trial Balance Approach for Working Papers

PIBB CORPORATION AND SUBSIDIARY CONSOLIDATION WORKING PAPERS FOR THE YEAR ENDED DECEMBER 31, 2007 (IN THOUSANDS)

	Pibb	90% Shad	Adjustments and Eliminations		Income Statement	Retained Earnings	Balance Sheet
Debits							
Cash	$ 6.8	$ 20					$ 26.8
Accounts receivable	30	15		f 5			40
Inventories	50	25					75
Plant and equipment		75	45				120
Investment in Shad	65.2			b 7.6 d 57.6			
Cost of goods sold	80	30		a 14	$(96)		
Operating expenses	19.6	20	e 1.4		(41)		
Dividends	15	10		b 9 c 1		$(15)	
Patents			d 12.6	e 1.4			11.2
	$341.6	$165					$273
Credits							
Accumulated depreciation	$ 25	$ 11					$ 36
Accounts payable	45	34	f 5				74
Common stock	100	30	d 30				100
Retained earnings	35	20	d 20			35	
Sales	120	70	a 14		176		
Income from Shad	16.6		b 16.6				
	$341.6	$165					
Noncontrolling interest January 1				d 5			
Noncontrolling interest expense ($20,000 × 10%)			c 2		(2)		
Consolidated net income						$ 37	37
Consolidated retained earnings December 31						$ 57	57
Noncontrolling interest December 31				c 1			6
							$273

Working paper entries to consolidate the trial balances of Pibb and Subsidiary at December 31, 2007, are as follows:

a	Sales (−R, −SE)	14,000	
	Cost of goods sold (−E, +SE)		14,000
	To eliminate reciprocal sales and cost of sales from intercompany purchases.		
b	Income from Shad (−R, −SE)	16,600	
	Dividends (+SE)		9,000
	Investment in Shad (−A)		7,600
	To eliminate income and dividends from Shad and adjust the investment account to its beginning-of-the-year amount.		
c	Noncontrolling interest expense (E, −SE)	2,000	
	Dividends—Shad (+SE)		1,000
	Noncontrolling interest (+L)		1,000
	To enter noncontrolling interest share of subsidiary income and dividends.		
d	Common stock—Shad (−SE)	30,000	
	Retained earnings—Shad (−SE)	20,000	
	Patents (+A)	12,600	
	Investment in Shad (−A)		57,600
	Noncontrolling interest (10%) (+L)		5,000
	To eliminate reciprocal investment in Shad and equity amounts of Shad, record beginning noncontrolling interest, and enter unamortized patents.		
e	Operating expenses (E, −SE)	1,400	
	Patents (−A)		1,400
	To record current amortization of patents as an expense.		
f	Accounts payable (−L)	5,000	
	Accounts receivable (−A)		5,000
	To eliminate reciprocal accounts payable and receivable balances.		

After entering all adjustments and eliminations in the working papers, we carry items not eliminated to the Income Statement, Retained Earnings Statement, or Balance Sheet columns. Next, we independently compute noncontrolling interest expense and include it in the Income Statement column as a deduction.

Here we can see an inconvenience of the trial balance working paper approach. We must compute Shad's $20,000 net income from the revenue and expense data before multiplying by the noncontrolling interest percentage. We computed noncontrolling interest expense directly when we used the financial statement working paper approach.

We total the Consolidated Income Statement column and carry the total to the Consolidated Retained Earnings Statement column. We next total the consolidated Retained Earnings Statement column and carry that total to the consolidated Balance Sheet column. Finally, we total the consolidated Balance Sheet debits and credits and complete the working paper. We prepare the consolidated financial statements directly from the consolidated Income Statement, consolidated Retained Earnings Statement, and consolidated Balance Sheet columns.

SELECTED READINGS

Statement of Financial Accounting Standards No. 95. "Statement of Cash Flows." Stamford, CT: Financial Accounting Standards Board, 1987.

FASB Interpretation No. 46. "Consolidation of Variable Interest Entities: An Interpretation of ARB No 51." Norwalk, CT: Financial Accounting Standards Board, January 2003.

FASB Interpretation No. 46 (Revised). "Consolidation of Variable Interest Entities: An Interpretation of ARB No 51." Norwalk, CT: Financial Accounting Standards Board, December 2003.

5 CHAPTER

INTERCOMPANY PROFIT TRANSACTIONS—INVENTORIES

We prepare consolidated statements to show the financial position and the results of operations of two or more affiliated companies as if they were one business enterprise. Therefore, we eliminate the effects of transactions between the affiliated companies (referred to as *intercompany transactions*) from consolidated financial statements.

Intercompany transactions may result in reciprocal account balances on the books of the affiliated companies. For example, intercompany sales transactions produce reciprocal sales and purchases (or cost of goods sold) balances, as well as reciprocal balances for accounts receivable and accounts payable. Intercompany loan transactions produce reciprocal notes receivable and notes payable balances, as well as reciprocal interest income and interest expense balances. These intercompany transactions are intracompany transactions from the viewpoint of the consolidated entity; therefore, we eliminate their effects in the consolidation process.

In addition to reciprocal account balances, we also eliminate gains and losses from intercompany transactions until realized through use or through sale outside of the consolidated entity. As stated in *Accounting Research Bulletin No. 51*, consolidated statements "should not include gain or loss on transactions among the companies in the group. Accordingly, any intercompany profit or loss on assets remaining within the group shall be eliminated; the concept usually applied for this purpose is gross profit or loss."[1]

ARB No. 51 also notes in paragraph 14 that the amount of intercompany profit to eliminate is not affected by the existence of a noncontrolling interest and should be eliminated in its entirety. The reason for eliminating intercompany profits and losses is that the management of the parent company controls all intercompany transactions, including authorization and pricing, without arm's-length bargaining between the affiliated companies. In eliminating the effect of intercompany profits and losses from consolidated statements, however, the issue is not whether the intercompany transactions were or were not at arm's length. *The objective is to show the income and financial position of the consolidated entity as they would have appeared if the intercompany transactions had never taken place*, irrespective of the amounts involved in such transactions. The same reasoning applies to the measurement of the investment account and investment income under a one-line consolidation. In the case of a one-line consolidation, however, evidence that intercompany transactions were not at arm's length may necessitate additional adjustments for fair presentation of the parent company's income and financial position in separate parent-company financial statements. These additional adjustments are covered in *Accounting*

LEARNING OBJECTIVES

1 Understand the impact of intercompany profit for inventories on preparation of consolidation working papers.

2 Apply the concepts of upstream versus downstream inventory transfers.

3 Defer unrealized inventory profits remaining in ending inventory of either the parent or subsidiary.

4 Recognize realized, previously deferred inventory profits in the beginning inventory of either the parent or subsidiary.

5 Adjust the calculations of noncontrolling interest amounts in the presence of intercompany inventory profits.

6 Electronic supplement: Understand differences in consolidation working paper techniques related to intercompany inventory profits when the parent company uses either an incomplete equity method or the cost method.

---

[1] *ARB No. 51*, "Consolidated Financial Statements," paragraph 6.

Interpretation No. 1 of APB Opinion No. 18, "The Equity Method of Accounting for Investments in Common Stock."

Most intercompany transactions involving gains and losses can be grouped as inventory items, plant assets, and bonds. Consolidation procedures involving inventory items are discussed in this chapter, and those involving plant assets and bonds are covered in subsequent chapters. Although the discussion and illustrations in this chapter relate to intercompany profit situations, the examples also provide a basis for analyzing and accounting for intercompany losses. Tax considerations are covered in Chapter 10.

∎∎∎

INTERCOMPANY INVENTORY TRANSACTIONS

Firms recognize revenue (record it as revenue) when it is realized, that is, when it is earned. For revenue to be earned from the viewpoint of the consolidated entity, there must be a sale to outside entities. Revenue on sales between affiliated companies cannot be recognized until merchandise is sold outside of the consolidated entity. No consolidated income results from transfers between affiliated companies. The sale of inventory items by one company to an affiliated company produces reciprocal sales and purchases accounts when the purchasing entity has a periodic inventory system, and reciprocal sales and cost of goods sold accounts when the purchasing entity uses a perpetual inventory system. We eliminate these reciprocal sales and cost of goods sold (or purchased) amounts in preparing a consolidated income statement in order to report sales and cost of goods sold for the consolidated entity; eliminating equal sales and cost of goods sold has no effect on consolidated net income.

As mentioned in Chapter 1, vertical integration of operating activities is often a prime motivation for business combinations. ***Walt Disney's*** 2003 annual report makes some related disclosures in *Note 1, Segments (p. 73)*. Here we find that the studio entertainment segment generated intersegment revenues of $52 million from sales to the consumer products segment. Disney does not offer any evidence about how they price these intersegment transfers, but they eliminate them in consolidation.

Segment information in the ***Anheuser-Busch Companies'*** 2003 annual report (p. 56) shows intersegment sales by the packaging segment of $869.2 million. That's a lot of cans and bottles, but they need some way to get that beer into the hands of consumers. Similarly, ***Chevron Corporation*** discloses intersegment sales of $6.3 billion in the United States and $8.1 billion in its international exploration and production segments (2003 annual report, p. 60).

Some companies, such as ***SBC Communications***, prepare *consolidating statements of income*, providing another source of information about intersegment revenues. SBC's 2003 annual report (p. 44) discloses adjustments in consolidation of revenues amounting to $15.5 billion, presumably due to elimination of unrealized profits on intercompany inventory transfers.

Elimination of Intercompany Purchases and Sales

We eliminate intercompany sales and purchases in the consolidation process in order to report consolidated sales and purchases (or cost of goods sold) at amounts purchased from and sold to outside entities. When a periodic inventory system is used, the working paper entry to eliminate intercompany sales and purchases is simply a debit to sales and a credit to purchases. The working paper elimination under a perpetual inventory system, used throughout this book, is a debit to sales and a credit to cost of goods sold. The reason is that a perpetual inventory system includes intercompany purchases in the separate cost of goods sold account of the purchasing affiliate. These observations are illustrated for Pint Corporation and its subsidiary, Shep Corporation.

Pint Corporation formed a subsidiary, Shep Corporation, in 2006 to retail a special line of Pint's merchandise. All Shep's purchases are made from Pint Corporation at 20% above Pint's cost. During 2006, Pint sold merchandise that cost $20,000 to Shep for $24,000, and Shep sold all the merchandise to its customers for $30,000. Both Pint and Shep record journal entries relating to the merchandise on their separate books, as follows:

PINT'S BOOKS

Inventory (+A)	20,000	
Accounts payable (+L)		20,000
To record purchases on account from other entities.		
Accounts receivable—Shep (+A)	24,000	
Sales (R, +SE)		24,000
To record intercompany sales to Shep.		
Cost of sales (E, −SE)	20,000	
Inventory (−A)		20,000
To record cost of sales to Shep.		

SHEP'S BOOKS

Inventory (+A)	24,000	
Accounts payable—Pint (+L)		24,000
To record intercompany purchases from Pint.		
Accounts receivable (+A)	30,000	
Sales (R, +SE)		30,000
To record sales to customers outside the consolidated entity.		
Cost of sales (E, −SE)	24,000	
Inventory (−A)		24,000
To record cost of sales to customers.		

At year-end 2006, Pint's sales include $24,000 sold to Shep, and its cost of sales includes the $20,000 cost of merchandise transferred to Shep. Shep's sales consist of $30,000 in merchandise sold to other entities, and its cost of sales consists of the $24,000 transfer price from Pint. Pint and Shep are considered one entity for reporting purposes, so their combined sales and cost of sales are overstated by $24,000. We eliminate that overstatement in the consolidation working papers, where measurements for consolidated sales and cost of sales are finalized. The working paper elimination is as follows:

	Pint	100% Shep	Adjustments and Eliminations		Consolidated
Sales	$24,000	$30,000	a 24,000		$30,000
Cost of sales	20,000	24,000		a 24,000	20,000
Gross profit	$ 4,000	$ 6,000			$10,000

The working paper elimination has no effect on consolidated net income because it eliminates equal sales and cost of sales amounts, and combined gross profit equals consolidated gross profit. However, the elimination is necessary to reflect merchandising activity accurately for the consolidated entity that purchased merchandise for $20,000 (Pint) and sold it for $30,000 (Shep). The fact that Pint's separate records include $4,000 gross profit on the merchandise and Shep's records show $6,000 is irrelevant in reporting the consolidated results of operations. In addition to eliminating intercompany profit items, it is necessary to eliminate intercompany receivables and payables in the consolidation process.

Elimination of Unrealized Profit in Ending Inventory

The consolidated entity realizes and recognizes the full amount of intercompany profit on sales between affiliated companies in the period in which the merchandise is resold to outside entities. Until reselling the merchandise, any profit or loss on intercompany sales is unrealized, and we must eliminate its effect in the consolidation process. The *ending inventory of the purchasing affiliate* reflects any unrealized profit or loss on intercompany sales because that inventory reflects the intercompany transfer price rather than cost to the consolidated entity. The elimination is a debit to cost of goods sold and a credit to the ending inventory for the amount of unrealized profit. The credit reduces the inventory to its cost basis to the consolidated entity; and the debit, when considered in conjunction with the elimination of intercompany purchases, reduces cost of goods sold to its cost basis. These relationships are illustrated by continuing the Pint and Shep example for 2007.

During 2007 Pint sold merchandise that cost $30,000 to Shep for $36,000, and Shep sold all but $6,000 of this merchandise to its customers for $37,500. Journal entries relating to the merchandise transferred intercompany during 2007 are as follows:

PINT'S BOOKS

Inventory (+A)	30,000	
Accounts payable (+L)		30,000
To record purchase on account from other entities.		
Accounts receivable—Shep (+A)	36,000	
Sales (R, +SE)		36,000
To record intercompany sales to Shep.		
Cost of sales (E, −SE)	30,000	
Inventory (−A)		30,000
To record cost of sales to Shep.		

SHEP'S BOOKS

Inventory (+A)	36,000	
Accounts payable—Pint (+L)		36,000
To record intercompany purchases from Pint.		
Accounts receivable (+A)	37,500	
Sales (R, +SE)		37,500
To record sales to customers outside the consolidated entity.		
Cost of sales (E, −SE)	30,000	
Inventory (−A)		30,000
To record cost of sales to outside entities.		

Pint's sales for 2007 include $36,000 sold to Shep, and its cost of sales reflects the $30,000 cost of merchandise transferred to Shep. Shep's $37,500 sales for 2007 consist of merchandise acquired from Pint, and its $30,000 cost of sales equals 5/6, or $30,000/$36,000, of the $36,000 transfer price of merchandise acquired from Pint. The remaining merchandise acquired from Pint in 2007 stays in Shep's December 31, 2007, inventory at the $6,000 transfer price, which includes $1,000 unrealized profit.

WORKING PAPER ENTRIES The consolidated entity views this as an intercompany transfer of merchandise that cost $30,000.

- $25,000 (or 5/6) of this merchandise was then sold to outside entities for $37,500.
- $5,000 (or 1/6) remains in inventory at year-end.
- The consolidated entity realizes a gross profit of $12,500.

We accomplish these consolidated results through working paper entries that eliminate the effects of the intercompany transactions from sales, cost of sales, and inventory. Although a single working paper entry can be made to reduce combined sales by $36,000, combined cost of sales by $35,000, and inventory by $1,000, two working paper entries are ordinarily used in order to separate the elimination of intercompany sales and purchases from the elimination (deferral) of unrealized profit.

The working paper eliminations follow:

	Pint	Shep	Adjustments and Eliminations		Consolidated
Income Statement					
Sales	$36,000	$37,500	a 36,000		$37,500
Cost of sales	30,000	30,000	b 1,000	a 36,000	25,000
Gross profit	$ 6,000	$ 7,500			$12,500
Balance Sheet					
Inventory		$ 6,000		b 1,000	$ 5,000

The first working paper entry eliminates intercompany sales and purchases, journalized as follows:

a	Sales (−R, −SE)	36,000	
	Cost of sales (−E, +SE)		36,000
	To eliminate intercompany sales and purchases.		

This entry is procedurally the same as the one made in 2006 to eliminate intercompany purchases and sales.

A secondary entry defers the $1,000 intercompany profit that remains unrealized ($13,500 combined gross profit − $12,500 consolidated gross profit) and reduces the ending inventory from $6,000 to its $5,000 cost to the consolidated entity.

b	Cost of sales (E, −SE)	1,000	
	Inventory (−A)		1,000
	To eliminate intercompany profit from cost of sales and inventory.		

The debit to cost of sales reduces profit by increasing consolidated cost of sales, and the credit reduces the valuation of inventory for consolidated statement purposes from the intercompany transfer price to cost. From the viewpoint of the consolidated entity, Shep overstated its ending inventory by the $1,000 unrealized profit. An overstated ending inventory understates cost of sales and overstates gross profit, so we correct the error with working paper entry b, which increases (debits) cost of sales and decreases (credits) the overstated ending inventory. This elimination entry reduces consolidated gross profit by $1,000 (income effect) and consolidated ending inventory by $1,000 (balance sheet effect).

These two working paper entries should be learned at this time because they are always the same, regardless of additional complexities to be introduced later.

EQUITY METHOD On December 31, 2007, Pint computes its investment income in the usual manner, except that Pint defers $1,000 intercompany profit. Pint's one-line consolidation entry reduces income from Shep by the $1,000 unrealized profit in the ending inventory and accordingly reduces the Investment in Shep account by $1,000.

Recognition of Unrealized Profit in Beginning Inventory

Unrealized profit in an ending inventory is realized for consolidated statement purposes when the merchandise is sold outside the consolidated entity. Ordinarily, realization occurs in the immediately succeeding fiscal period, so firms simply defer recognition for consolidated statement purposes until the following year. Recognition of the previously unrealized profit requires a working paper credit to cost of goods sold because the amount of the beginning inventory is reflected in cost of goods sold when the perpetual system is used. The direction of the sale, noncontrolling ownership percentage, and parent-company method of accounting for the subsidiary may complicate the related working paper debits. These complications do not affect consolidated gross profit, however, and we extend the previous example to reflect 2008 operations for Pint and Shep.

During 2008, Pint Corporation sold merchandise that cost $40,000 to Shep for $48,000, and Shep sold 75% of the merchandise for $45,000. Shep also sold the items in the beginning inventory with a transfer price of $6,000 to its customers for $7,500. Journal entries relating to the merchandise transferred intercompany follow:

PINT'S BOOKS

Inventory (+A)	40,000	
Accounts payable (+L)		40,000
To record purchase on account from other entities.		
Accounts receivable—Shep (+A)	48,000	
Sales (R, +SE)		48,000
To record intercompany sales to Shep.		
Cost of sales (E, −SE)	40,000	
Inventory (−A)		40,000
To record cost of sales to Shep.		

(continued)

SHEP'S BOOKS

Inventory (+A)	48,000	
Accounts payable—Pint (+L)		48,000
To record intercompany purchases from Pint.		
Accounts receivable (+A)	52,500	
Sales (R, +SE)		52,500
To record sales of $45,000 and $7,500 to outside entities.		
Cost of sales (E, −SE)	42,000	
Inventory (−A)		42,000
To record cost of sales ($48,000 transfer price × 75% sold) and $6,000 from beginning inventory.		

Shep sold 75% of the merchandise purchased from Pint, so its ending inventory in 2008 is $12,000 ($48,000 × 25%), and that inventory includes $2,000 unrealized profit [$12,000 − ($12,000/1.2 transfer price)].

WORKING PAPER ENTRIES From the viewpoint of the consolidated entity, merchandise that cost $40,000 was transferred intercompany:

- $30,000 of this merchandise, plus $5,000 beginning inventory, was sold for $52,500.
- $10,000 remained in inventory at year-end 2008.
- The consolidated entity realized a gross profit of $17,500.

The working papers that eliminate the effects of intercompany transactions from sales, cost of sales, and inventory reflect these consolidated results. Three working paper entries eliminate intercompany purchases and sales, recognize previously deferred profit from beginning inventory, and defer unrealized profit in the ending inventory, as follows:

	Pint	Shep	Adjustments and Eliminations		Consolidated
Income Statement					
Sales	$48,000	$52,500	a 48,000		$52,500
Cost of sales	40,000	42,000	c 2,000	a 48,000	
				b 1,000	35,000
Gross profit	$ 8,000	$10,500			$17,500
Balance Sheet					
Inventory		$12,000		c 2,000	$10,000
Investment in Shep	XXX			b 1,000	

Journal entries to eliminate the effects of intercompany transactions between Pint and Shep for 2008 follow:

a	**Sales (−R, −SE)**	48,000	
	Cost of sales (−E, +SE)		48,000
	To eliminate intercompany purchases and sales.		
b	**Investment in Shep (+A)**	1,000	
	Cost of sales (−E, +SE)		1,000
	To recognize previously deferred profit from beginning inventory.		
c	**Cost of sales (E, −SE)**	2,000	
	Inventory (−A)		2,000
	To defer unrealized profit in ending inventory.		

Working paper entries a and c are procedurally the same as the entries for 2007. Their purpose is to eliminate intercompany purchases and sales and defer unrealized profit in the ending inventory. From the consolidated viewpoint, the $1,000 overstated beginning inventory overstates cost of sales in 2008. Entry b recognizes previously deferred profit from 2007 by reducing consolidated cost of sales and thereby increasing consolidated gross profit. (Note, of course, that entry b is only made in those cases in which the inventory has subsequently been sold to a customer outside the consolidated entity.) The related debit to the Investment in Shep account adjusts for the one-line consolidation entry that reduced the Investment in Shep account in 2007 to defer unrealized profit in the ending inventory of that year. Although the credit side of this working paper entry is always the same, additional complexities sometimes arise with the debit side of the entry.

The Pint–Shep example illustrates the effects of intercompany inventory transactions on consolidated sales, cost of sales, and gross profit, and these effects are always the same. But the example did not cover the effects of intercompany inventory transactions on noncontrolling interest computations or on parent-company accounting under the equity method. These ramifications are discussed and illustrated next.

DOWNSTREAM AND UPSTREAM SALES

A **downstream sale** is a sale by a parent company to a subsidiary, and a sale by a subsidiary to its parent is an **upstream sale**. The upstream and downstream designations relate to the usual diagram of affiliation structures that places the parent company at the top. Thus, sales from top to bottom are downstream, and sales from bottom to top are upstream.

Consolidated statements eliminate reciprocal sales and cost of goods sold (or purchased) amounts regardless of whether the sales are upstream or downstream. We also eliminate any unrealized gross profit in inventories in its entirety for both downstream and upstream sales. However, the effect of unrealized profits on separate parent-company statements (as investor) and on consolidated financial statements (which show income to the majority stockholders) is determined by both the direction of the intercompany sales activity and the percentage ownership of subsidiary companies, except for 100%-owned subsidiaries, which have no noncontrolling ownership.

In the case of downstream sales, the parent company's separate income includes the full amount of any unrealized profit (included in its sales and cost of sales accounts), and the subsidiary's income is not affected. When sales are upstream, the subsidiary company's net income includes the full amount of any unrealized profit (included in its sales and cost of sales accounts), and the parent company's separate income is not affected. The consolidation process eliminates the full amount of intercompany sales and cost of sales, regardless of whether the sales are downstream or upstream. However, the noncontrolling interest expense *may be affected* if the subsidiary's net income includes unrealized profit (the upstream situation). It *is not affected* if the parent company's separate income includes unrealized profit (the downstream situation) because the noncontrolling shareholders have an interest only in the income of the subsidiary. When subsidiary net income is overstated (from the viewpoint of the consolidated entity) because it includes unrealized profit, the income allocated to noncontrolling interests should be based on the *realized income of the subsidiary*. A subsidiary's realized income is its reported net income adjusted for intercompany profits from upstream sales.

Noncontrolling interest expense *may be affected* by unrealized profit from upstream sales because accounting standards are not definitive with respect to the computation. *ARB No. 51*, paragraph 14, provides that "the elimination of intercompany profit or loss may be allocated proportionately between majority and minority interests" but does not require such allocation. The alternative to allocation is to eliminate intercompany profits and losses from upstream sales in the same manner as for downstream sales, charging (crediting) the full amount of unrealized gain (loss) to the parent's income.

The approach that allocates unrealized profits and losses from upstream sales proportionately between noncontrolling and majority interests is conceptually superior because it applies the viewpoint of the consolidated entity consistently to both majority and noncontrolling interests. That is, both consolidated net income and noncontrolling interest expense are computed on the basis of income that is realized from the viewpoint of the consolidated entity. In addition, material amounts of unrealized profits and losses from upstream sales may be allocated between majority and noncontrolling interests in accounting practice. *Accordingly, unrealized profits and losses from upstream sales are allocated proportionately between consolidated net income (majority interests) and noncontrolling interest expense (noncontrolling interests) throughout this book.* Using the same allocation approach in accounting for the parent company/investor's interest under the equity method accomplishes a consistent treatment between consolidation procedures and equity method accounting (the one-line consolidation).

Downstream and Upstream Effects on Income Computations

Assume that the separate incomes of a parent company and its 80%-owned subsidiary for 2006 are as follows (in thousands):

	Parent	Subsidiary
Sales	$600	$300
Cost of sales	300	180
Gross profit	300	120
Expenses	100	70
Parent's separate income	$200	
Subsidiary's net income		$ 50

Intercompany sales during the year are $100,000, and the December 31, 2006, inventory includes $20,000 unrealized profit.

Noncontrolling Interest Expense Computation If the intercompany sales are downstream, the parent company's sales and cost of sales accounts reflect the $20,000 unrealized profit, and the subsidiary's $50,000 net income is equal to its realized income. In this case the noncontrolling interest computation is unaffected by the intercompany transactions and is computed as

$50,000 net income of subsidiary × 20% = $10,000

If the intercompany sales are upstream, the subsidiary's sales and cost of sales accounts reflect the $20,000 unrealized profit, and the subsidiary's realized income is $30,000. In this case the noncontrolling interest expense computation is

($50,000 net income of subsidiary – $20,000 unrealized) × 20% = $6,000

Consolidated Net Income Computation Exhibit 5-1 shows comparative consolidated income statements for the parent and its 80%-owned subsidiary under the two assumptions. In examining the exhibit, note that the only difference in the computation of consolidated net income under the two assumptions lies in the computation of noncontrolling interest expense. This is so because the eliminations for intercompany purchases and sales and intercompany inventory profits are the same regardless of whether the sales are downstream or upstream. Parent-company net income under the equity method is equal to consolidated net income, so the approach used in computing income from subsidiary must be consistent with the approach used in determining consolidated net income. For downstream sales, the full amount of unrealized profit is charged against income from subsidiary, but for upstream sales, only the parent's proportionate share is charged against its investment income from subsidiary. Computations are as follows (in thousands):

EXHIBIT 5-1

Consolidated Income Effect of Downstream and Upstream Sales

PARENT CORPORATION AND SUBSIDIARY CONSOLIDATED INCOME STATEMENTS (IN THOUSANDS) FOR THE YEAR ENDED DECEMBER 31, 2006

	Downstream Sales	Upstream Sales
Sales ($900 – $100)	$800	$800
Cost of sales ($480 + $20 – $100)	400	400
Gross profit	400	400
Expenses ($100 + $70)	170	170
Total realized income	230	230
Less: Noncontrolling interest	10	6
Consolidated net income	$220	$224

	Downstream	Upstream
Parent's separate income	$200	$200
Add: Income from subsidiary		
Downstream		
Equity in subsidiary's reported income less unrealized profit [($50,000 × 80%) − $20,000]	20	
Upstream		
Equity in subsidiary realized income [($50,000 − $20,000) × 80%]		24
Parent (and consolidated) net income	$220	$224

Recognize that affiliated companies may engage in simultaneous upstream and downstream inventory transactions. In such cases, it is necessary to eliminate both the upstream and downstream sales/purchases. These transactions do not simply offset one another, due to the deferral of unrealized intercompany inventory profits.

For example, assume that the parent company sells $100,000 of inventory to its wholly owned subsidiary at a profit of $20,000. The entire inventory remains unsold at year-end. The subsidiary company likewise sells $100,000 of inventory to the parent, including an identical intercompany inventory profit of $20,000. This inventory also remains unsold at year-end.

We could simply assume that the two transactions appear offsetting. This would distort both the consolidated balance sheet and the consolidated income statement. The combined parent and subsidiary balance sheets include the inventory at the total intercompany transfer price of $200,000. However, $40,000 of this total is intercompany profit. The correct consolidated balance sheet inventory should be the cost of $160,000.

We would also overstate consolidated net income by $40,000. The intercompany profit must be deferred until the affiliates realize the gains through sales to parties outside the consolidated reporting entity.

We can avoid these misstatements only if we separately eliminate the effects of all upstream and downstream transactions. Notice that intercompany inventory transactions provide a convenient means of managing reported consolidated net income if the impact of simultaneous upstream and downstream sales is not properly eliminated.

UNREALIZED PROFITS FROM DOWNSTREAM SALES

Sales by a parent company to its subsidiaries increase parent-company sales, cost of goods sold, and gross profit but do not affect the income of subsidiaries until the merchandise is resold to outside parties. The full amount of gross profit on merchandise sold downstream and remaining in subsidiary inventories increases parent-company income, so the full amount must be eliminated from the parent-company income statement under the equity method of accounting. Consistent with the one-line consolidation concept, this is done by reducing investment income and the investment account. Consolidated financial statements eliminate unrealized gross profit by increasing consolidated cost of goods sold and reducing merchandise inventory to a cost basis to the consolidated entity. The overstatement of the ending inventory from the consolidated viewpoint understates consolidated cost of goods sold.

Deferral of Intercompany Profit in Period of Intercompany Sale

The following example illustrates the deferral of unrealized profits on downstream sales. Porter Corporation owns 90% of the voting stock of Sorter Corporation. Separate income statements of Porter and Sorter for 2006, before consideration of unrealized profits, are as follows (in thousands):

	Porter	Sorter
Sales	$100	$50
Cost of goods sold	60	35
Gross profit	40	15
Expenses	15	5
Operating income	25	10
Income from Sorter	9	—
Net income	$ 34	$10

Porter's sales include $15,000 to Sorter at a profit of $6,250, and Sorter's December 31, 2006, inventory includes 40% of the merchandise from the intercompany transaction. Porter's operating income reflects the $2,500 unrealized profit in Sorter's inventory ($6,000 transfer price less $3,500 cost). On its separate books, Porter takes up its share of Sorter's income and defers recognition of the unrealized profit with the following entries:

Investment in Sorter (+A)	9,000	
Income from Sorter (R, +SE)		9,000
To record share of Sorter's income.		
Income from Sorter (−R, −SE)	2,500	
Investment in Sorter (−A)		2,500
To eliminate unrealized profit on sales to Sorter.		

The second entry on Porter's books reduces Porter's income from Sorter from $9,000 to $6,500. Reciprocal sales and cost of goods sold, as well as all unrealized profit, must be eliminated in consolidated financial statements. These working paper adjustments are shown in the partial working papers in Exhibit 5-2.

Entry a deducts the full amount of intercompany sales from sales and cost of goods sold. Working paper entry b then corrects cost of goods sold for the unrealized profit at year-end and reduces the inventory to its cost basis to the consolidated entity. Note that working paper entries a and b are equivalent to a single debit to sales for $15,000, a credit to cost of goods sold for $12,500, and a credit to inventory for $2,500.

In examining Exhibit 5-2, observe that Porter's net income on an equity basis is equal to consolidated net income. This equality would not have occurred without the one-line consolidation adjustment that reduced Porter's income from $34,000 to $31,500. The $1,000 noncontrolling interest expense shown in Exhibit 5-2 is not affected by the unrealized profit on Porter's sales because noncontrolling stockholders share only in subsidiary profit and Sorter's reported income for 2006 (equal to its realized income) is unaffected by the unrealized profit in its inventory. (Sorter's goods available for sale and its ending inventory are overstated by the amount of unrealized profit, but its cost of goods sold is not affected by the unrealized profit in its ending inventory.)

EXHIBIT 5-2	PORTER AND SUBSIDIARY, SORTER, PARTIAL WORKING PAPERS FOR THE YEAR ENDED DECEMBER 31, 2006 (IN THOUSANDS)

Inventory Profit on Downstream Sales in Year of Intercompany Sales

	Porter	90% Sorter	Adjustments and Eliminations Debits	Adjustments and Eliminations Credits	Consolidated Statements
Income Statement					
Sales	$100	$50	a 15		$135
Income from Sorter	6.5		c 6.5		
Cost of goods sold	(60)	(35)	b 2.5	a 15	(82.5)
Expenses	(15)	(5)			(20)
Noncontrolling interest expense ($10,000 × 10%)					(1)
Net income	$ 31.5	$10			$ 31.5
Balance Sheet					
Inventory		$ 7.5		b 2.5	$ 5
Investment in Sorter	XXX			c 6.5	

a Eliminates reciprocal sales and cost of goods sold.
b Adjusts cost of goods sold and ending inventory to a cost basis to the consolidated entity.
c Eliminates investment income and adjusts the Investment in Sorter account to the January 1, 2006, balance.

Recognition of Intercompany Profit upon Sale to Outside Entities

Now assume that the merchandise acquired from Porter during 2006 is sold by Sorter during 2007, and there are no intercompany transactions between Porter and Sorter during 2007. Separate income statements for 2007 before consideration of the $2,500 unrealized profit in Sorter's beginning inventory are as follows (in thousands):

	Porter	Sorter
Sales	$120	$60
Cost of goods sold	80	40
Gross profit	40	20
Expenses	20	5
Operating income	20	15
Income from Sorter	13.5	—
Net income	$ 33.5	$15

Porter's operating income for 2007 is unaffected by the unrealized profit in Sorter's December 31, 2006, inventory. But Sorter's 2007 profit is affected because the $2,500 overstatement of Sorter's beginning inventory overstates cost of goods sold from a consolidated viewpoint. From Porter's viewpoint, the unrealized profit from 2006 is realized in 2007, and its investment income is recorded and adjusted as follows:

| Investment in Sorter (+A) | 13,500 | |
| Income from Sorter (R, +SE) | | 13,500 |

To record investment income from Sorter.

| Investment in Sorter (+A) | 2,500 | |
| Income from Sorter (R, +SE) | | 2,500 |

To record realization of profit from 2006 intercompany sales to Sorter.

This entry increases Porter's investment from $13,500 to $16,000 and Porter's net income from $33,500 to $36,000. The partial working papers for Porter and Sorter for 2007 reflect the adjusted amounts as shown in Exhibit 5-3.

EXHIBIT 5-3

Inventory Profit on Downstream Sales in Year After Intercompany Sales

PORTER AND SUBSIDIARY, SORTER, PARTIAL WORKING PAPERS FOR THE YEAR ENDED DECEMBER 31, 2007 (IN THOUSANDS)

	Porter	90% Sorter	Adjustments and Eliminations Debits	Adjustments and Eliminations Credits	Consolidated Statements
Income Statement					
Sales	$120	$60			$180
Income from Sorter	16		b 16		
Cost of goods sold	(80)	(40)		a 2.5	(117.5)
Expenses	(20)	(5)			(25)
Noncontrolling interest expense ($15,000 × 10%)					(1.5)
Net income	$ 36	$15			$ 36
Balance Sheet					
Investment in Sorter	XXX		a 2.5	b 16	

a Adjusts cost of goods sold to a cost basis and adjusts the Investment in Sorter account balance to reestablish reciprocity with the beginning subsidiary equity accounts.

b Eliminates investment income and adjusts the Investment in Sorter account to the January 1, 2007, balance.

In examining the partial working papers in Exhibit 5-3, note that entry a debits the Investment in Sorter account and credits cost of goods sold for $2,500. The beginning inventory of Sorter has already been closed to cost of goods sold under a perpetual inventory system, so the inventory cannot be adjusted. The adjustment to the investment account is necessary to increase the investment account at the beginning of the year to reflect realization during 2007 of the unrealized profit that was deferred at the end of 2006. *This adjustment reestablishes reciprocity between the investment balance at January 1, 2007, and the subsidiary equity account at the same date. It is important to record this adjustment before eliminating reciprocal investment and equity balances.* The computation of noncontrolling interest expense in Exhibit 5-3 is not affected because the sales are downstream.

Unrealized inventory profits in consolidated financial statements are self-correcting over any two accounting periods and are subject to the same type of analysis as inventory errors. Total consolidated net income for Porter and Sorter for 2006 and 2007 is unaffected by the $2,500 deferral in 2006 and recognition in 2007. The significance of the adjustments lies in the accurate statement of the income of the consolidated entity for each period.

UNREALIZED PROFITS FROM UPSTREAM SALES

Sales by a subsidiary to its parent company increase the sales, cost of goods sold, and gross profit of the subsidiary, but they do not affect the operating income of the parent until the merchandise is resold by the parent to other entities. The parent's net income is affected, however, because the parent recognizes its share of the subsidiary's income on an equity basis. If the selling subsidiary is a 100%-owned affiliate, the parent defers 100% of any unrealized profit in the year of intercompany sale. If the subsidiary is a partially owned affiliate, the parent company defers only its proportionate share of the unrealized subsidiary profit.

Deferral of Intercompany Profit in Period of Intercompany Sale

Assume that Salt Corporation (subsidiary) sells merchandise that it purchased for $7,500 to Park Corporation (parent) for $20,000 during 2006 and that Park Corporation sold 60% of the merchandise to outsiders during the year for $15,000. At year-end the unrealized inventory profit is $5,000 (cost $3,000, but included in Park's inventory at $8,000). If Salt reports net income of $50,000 for 2006, Park recognizes its proportionate share as shown in Exhibit 5-4. The exhibit compares parent-company accounting for a one-line consolidation of a 100%-owned subsidiary and a 75%-owned subsidiary.

EXHIBIT 5-4		
Entries for a One-Line Consolidation on the Books of Park		

Part A *If Salt Is a 100%-Owned Subsidiary*		
Investment in Salt (+A)	50,000	
Income from Salt (R, +SE)		50,000
To record 100% of Salt's reported income as income from subsidiary.		
Income from Salt (–R, –SE)	5,000	
Investment in Salt (–A)		5,000
To defer 100% of the unrealized inventory profits reported by Salt until realized.		
A single entry for $45,000 [($50,000 – $5,000) × 100%] is equally acceptable.		

Part B *If Salt Is a 75%-Owned Subsidiary*		
Investment in Salt (+A)	37,500	
Income from Salt (R, +SE)		37,500
To record 75% of Salt's reported income as income from subsidiary.		
Income from Salt (–R, –SE)	3,750	
Investment in Salt (–A)		3,750
To defer 75% of the unrealized inventory profits reported by Salt until realized.		
A single entry for $33,750 [($50,000 – $5,000) × 75%] is equally acceptable.		

As the illustration shows, if Park records 100% of Salt's income under the equity method, it must eliminate 100% of any unrealized profit included in that income. However, if Park records only 75% of Salt's income under the equity method, it must eliminate only 75% of any unrealized profit included in Salt's income. In both cases, Park eliminates all the unrealized profit from its income and investment accounts.

The elimination of unrealized inventory profits from upstream sales in consolidated financial statements results in the elimination of 100% of all unrealized inventory profits from consolidated sales and cost of goods sold accounts. However, because consolidated net income is a measurement of income to the stockholders of the parent company, noncontrolling interest expense is reduced for its proportionate share of any unrealized profit of the subsidiary. This involves deducting the noncontrolling interest's share of unrealized profits from the noncontrolling interest's share of the subsidiary's reported net income. Thus, the effect on consolidated net income of unrealized profits from upstream sales is the same as the effect on parent-company income under the equity method of accounting.

Exhibit 5-5 illustrates partial consolidation working papers for Park Corporation and its 75%-owned subsidiary, Salt Corporation. Although the amounts for sales, cost of goods sold, and expenses are presented without explanation, the data provided are consistent with previous assumptions for Park and Salt Corporations.

Part B of Exhibit 5-4 explains the $33,750 income from Salt that appears in Park's separate income statement in Exhibit 5-5. Noncontrolling interest is computed by subtracting unrealized profit from Salt's reported income and multiplying by the noncontrolling interest percentage. Failure to adjust the noncontrolling interest expense for unrealized profit will result in a lack of equality between parent-company net income on an equity basis and consolidated net income. This potential problem is, of course, absent in the case of a 100%-owned subsidiary because there is no noncontrolling interest.

Recognition of Intercompany Profit upon Sale to Outside Entities

The effect of unrealized profits in a beginning inventory on parent-company and consolidated net incomes is just the opposite of the effect of unrealized profits in an ending inventory. That is, the relationship between unrealized profits in ending inventories (year of intercompany sale) and

LEARNING OBJECTIVE **5**

EXHIBIT 5-5

Inventory Profit on Upstream Sales in Year of Intercompany Sales

PARK AND SUBSIDIARY, SALT (75% OWNED), PARTIAL WORKING PAPERS FOR THE YEAR ENDED DECEMBER 31, 2006 (IN THOUSANDS)

	Park	75% Salt	Adjustments and Eliminations Debits	Adjustments and Eliminations Credits	Consolidated Statements
Income Statement					
Sales	$250	$150	a 20		$380
Income from Salt	33.75		c 33.75		
Cost of goods sold	(100)	(80)	b 5	a 20	(165)
Expenses	(50)	(20)			(70)
Noncontrolling interest expense [($50,000 − $5,000) × 25%]					(11.25)
Net income	$133.75	$ 50			$133.75
Balance Sheet					
Inventory	$ 10			b 5	$ 5
Investment in Salt	XXX			c 33.75	

a Eliminates reciprocal sales and cost of goods sold.
b Adjusts cost of goods sold and inventory to a cost basis.
c Eliminates investment income and adjusts the Investment in Salt account to beginning-of-period balance.

consolidated net income is direct, whereas the relationship between unrealized profit in beginning inventories (year of sale to outside entities) and consolidated net income is inverse. This is illustrated by continuing the Park and Salt example to show realization during 2007 of the $5,000 unrealized profit in the December 31, 2006, inventories. Assume that there are no intercompany transactions between Park and Salt during 2007, that Salt is a 75%-owned subsidiary of Park, and that Salt reports income of $60,000 for 2007. Park records its share of Salt's income under the equity method as follows:

Investment in Salt (+A)	45,000	
Income from Salt (R, +SE)		45,000
To record 75% of Salt's reported income as income from subsidiary.		
Investment in Salt (+A)	3,750	
Income from Salt (R, +SE)		3,750
To record realization during 2007 of 75% of the $5,000 unrealized inventory profits of Salt from 2006.		

Exhibit 5-6 illustrates consolidation procedures for unrealized profits in beginning inventories from upstream sales for Park and Subsidiary. Several of the items in Exhibit 5-6 differ from those for upstream sales with unrealized profit in the ending inventory (Exhibit 5-5). In particular, cost of goods sold is overstated (because of the overstated beginning inventory) and requires a worksheet adjustment to reduce it to a cost basis. This is shown in working paper entry a, which also adjusts the investment account and beginning noncontrolling interest. *Consolidated statements require the allocation between the investment balance (75%) and the noncontrolling interest (25%) for unrealized profits in beginning inventories from upstream sales to correct for prior-year effects on the investment account and the noncontrolling interest.*

<table>
<tr><td>

EXHIBIT 5-6

Inventory Profit on Upstream Sales in Year After Intercompany Sales

</td><td>

PARK AND SUBSIDIARY, SALT (75% OWNED), PARTIAL WORKING PAPERS FOR THE YEAR ENDED DECEMBER 31, 2007 (IN THOUSANDS)

	Park	75% Salt	Adjustments and Eliminations Debits	Adjustments and Eliminations Credits	Consolidated Statements
Income Statement					
Sales	$275	$160			$435
Income from Salt	48.75		b 48.75		
Cost of goods sold	(120)	(85)		a 5	(200)
Expenses	(60)	(15)			(75)
Noncontrolling interest expense [($60,000 + $5,000) × 25%]					(16.25)
Net income	$143.75	$ 60			$143.75
Balance Sheet					
Investment in Salt	XXX		a 3.75	b 48.75	
Noncontrolling interest: January 1, 2007			a 1.25		

---

a Reduces cost of goods sold to a cost basis to the consolidated entity and adjusts the Investment in Salt account to establish reciprocity between it and subsidiary equity at January 1, 2007, and eliminates intercompany profit from beginning minority interest.
b Eliminates investment income and adjusts the Investment in Salt account to its January 1, 2007, balance.

</td></tr>
</table>

CONSOLIDATION EXAMPLE—INTERCOMPANY PROFITS FROM DOWNSTREAM SALES

Seay Corporation is a 90%-owned subsidiary of Peak Corporation, acquired for $94,500 cash on July 1, 2006, when Seay's net assets consisted of $100,000 capital stock and $5,000 retained earnings. The cost of Peak's 90% interest in Seay was equal to book value and fair value of the interest acquired ($105,000 × 90%), and accordingly, no allocation to identifiable and unidentifiable assets was necessary.

Peak sells inventory items to Seay on a regular basis, and the intercompany transaction data for 2010 are as follows:

Sales to Seay in 2010 (cost $15,000), selling price	$20,000
Unrealized profit in Seay's inventory at December 31, 2009	2,000
Unrealized profit in Seay's inventory at December 31, 2010	2,500
Seay's accounts payable to Peak December 31, 2010	10,000

Equity Method

At December 31, 2009, Peak's Investment in Seay account had a balance of $128,500. This balance consisted of Peak's 90% equity in Seay's $145,000 net assets on that date less $2,000 unrealized profit in Seay's December 31, 2009, inventory.

During 2010, Peak made the following entries on its books for its investments in Seay under the equity method:

Cash (+A)	9,000	
Investment in Seay (−A)		9,000
To record dividends from Seay ($10,000 × 90%).		
Investment in Seay (+A)	26,500	
Income from Seay (R, +SE)		26,500

To record income from Seay for 2010 computed as follows:

Equity in Seay's net income ($30,000 × 90%)	$27,000
Add: 2009 inventory profit recognized in 2010	2,000
Less: 2010 inventory profit deferred at year-end	−2,500
	$26,500

The intercompany sales that led to the unrealized inventory profits were downstream, so we recognize the full amount of profit deferred in 2009 in 2010, and the full amount of the unrealized inventory profit originating in 2010 is deferred at December 31, 2010. Peak's Investment in Seay account increased from $128,500 at January 1, 2010, to $146,000 at December 31, 2010, the entire change consisting of $26,500 income less $9,000 dividends for the year. Exhibit 5-7 shows these amounts in the separate-company columns of the consolidation working papers for Peak Corporation and Subsidiary for the year ended December 31, 2010.

The working paper entries in Exhibit 5-7 are presented in journal form as follows:

a	Sales (−R, −SE)	20,000	
	Cost of goods sold (−E, +SE)		20,000
	To eliminate intercompany sales and related cost of goods sold amounts.		
b	Investment in Seay (+A)	2,000	
	Cost of goods sold (−E, +SE)		2,000
	To adjust cost of goods sold and the beginning investment balance for unrealized profits in the beginning inventory.		
c	Cost of goods sold (E, −SE)	2,500	
	Inventory (−A)		2,500
	To eliminate unrealized profits in the ending inventory and to increase cost of goods sold to a cost basis to the consolidated entity.		

(continued)

EXHIBIT 5-7

Intercompany Profits
on Downstream
Sales—Equity
Method

PEAK CORPORATION AND SUBSIDIARY CONSOLIDATION WORKING PAPERS FOR THE YEAR ENDED DECEMBER 31, 2010 (IN THOUSANDS)

	Peak	90% Seay	Adjustments and Eliminations Debits	Adjustments and Eliminations Credits	Consolidated Statements
Income Statement Net sales	$1,000	$300	a 20		$1,280
Income from Seay	26.5		d 26.5		
Cost of goods sold	(550)	(200)	c 2.5	a 20 b 2	(730.5)
Other expenses	(350)	(70)			(420)
Noncontrolling interest expense ($30,000 × 10%)			e 3		(3)
Net income	**$ 126.5**	**$ 30**			**$ 126.5**
Retained Earnings Retained earnings—Peak	$ 194				$ 194
Retained earnings—Seay		$ 45	f 45		
Net income	**126.5**	**30**			**126.5**
Dividends	(50)	(10)		d 9 e 1	(50)
Retained earnings—December 31	**$ 270.5**	**$ 65**			**$ 270.5**
Balance Sheet Cash	$ 30	$ 5			$ 35
Accounts receivable	70	20		g 10	80
Inventories	90	45		c 2.5	132.5
Other current assets	64	10			74
Plant and equipment	800	120			920
Investment in Seay	146		b 2	d 17.5 f 130.5	
	$1,200	$200			$1,241.5
Accounts payable	$ 80	$ 15	g 10		$ 85
Other liabilities	49.5	20			69.5
Capital stock	800	100	f 100		800
Retained earnings	**270.5**	**65**			**270.5**
	$1,200	$200			
Noncontrolling interest January 1				f 14.5	
Noncontrolling interest December 31				e 2	16.5
					$1,241.5

d Income from Seay (–R, –SE)	26,500	
Dividends (+SE)		9,000
Investment in Seay (–A)		17,500

    To eliminate the investment income and 90% of the
dividends of Seay and to reduce the investment account
to its beginning-of-the-period balance, plus the $2,000
from entry b.

e Noncontrolling interest expense (E, –SE)	3,000	
Dividends—Seay (+SE)		1,000
Noncontrolling interest (+L)		2,000

    To enter noncontrolling interest share of subsidiary income
and dividends.

f Capital stock—Seay (–SE)	100,000	
Retained earnings—Seay (–SE)	45,000	
Investment in Seay (–A)		130,500
Noncontrolling interest (+L)		14,500

    To eliminate reciprocal investment and equity balances
and record beginning noncontrolling interest.

g Accounts payable (–L)	10,000	
Accounts receivable (–A)		10,000

    To eliminate reciprocal payables and receivables from
intercompany sales.

In examining the working papers of Peak Corporation and Subsidiary in Exhibit 5-7, note that Peak's net income ($126,500) is equal to consolidated net income, and Peak's retained earnings amount ($270,500) equals consolidated retained earnings. These equalities are expected from a correct application of the equity method of accounting. The sales that gave rise to the intercompany profits in Seay's inventories were downstream, so neither beginning noncontrolling interest ($14,500) nor noncontrolling interest expense ($3,000) was affected by the intercompany transactions.

CONSOLIDATION EXAMPLE—INTERCOMPANY PROFITS FROM UPSTREAM SALES

Smith Corporation is an 80%-owned subsidiary of Poch Corporation, acquired for $480,000 on January 2, 2006, when Smith's stockholders' equity consisted of $500,000 capital stock and $100,000 retained earnings. The investment cost was equal to the book value and fair value of Smith's net assets acquired, so no cost/book value differential resulted from the business combination.

Smith Corporation sells inventory items to Poch Corporation on a regular basis. The intercompany transaction data for 2007 are as follows:

Sales to Poch in 2007	$300,000
Unrealized profit in Poch's inventory, December 31, 2006	40,000
Unrealized profit in Poch's inventory, December 31, 2007	30,000
Intercompany accounts receivable and payable at December 31, 2007	50,000

Equity Method

At December 31, 2006, Poch's Investment in Smith account had a balance of $568,000, consisting of $600,000 underlying equity in Smith's net assets ($750,000 × 80%) less 80% of the $40,000 unrealized profit in Poch's December 31, 2006, inventory from upstream sales.

During 2007, Poch made the following entries to account for its investment in Smith under the equity method:

Cash (+A)	40,000	
Investment in Smith (−A)		40,000
To record dividends from Smith ($50,000 × 80%).		
Investment in Smith (+A)	88,000	
Income from Smith (R, +SE)		88,000

To record income from Smith for 2007, computed as follows:

Equity in Smith's net income ($100,000 × 80%)	$ 80,000
Add: 80% of $40,000 unrealized profit deferred in 2006	32,000
Less: 80% of $30,000 unrealized profit at December 31, 2007	−24,000
	$ 88,000

The intercompany sales that led to the unrealized inventory profits in 2006 and 2007 were upstream, and, accordingly, only 80% of the $40,000 unrealized profit from 2006 is recognized by Poch in 2007. Similarly, only 80% of the $30,000 unrealized profit from 2007 sales is deferred by Poch at December 31, 2007. Poch's Investment in Smith account was increased by the $88,000 income from Smith during 2007 and decreased by $40,000 dividends received from Smith. Thus, the $568,000 Investment in Smith account at December 31, 2006, increased to $616,000 at December 31, 2007. These amounts, combined with other compatible information to provide complete separate-company financial statements, are shown in the separate-company columns of the consolidation working papers for Poch Corporation and Subsidiary in Exhibit 5-8.

The working paper entries in Exhibit 5-8 appear below in journal form for convenient reference.

a	**Sales (−R, −SE)**	**300,000**	
	Cost of goods sold (−E, +SE)		**300,000**
	To eliminate reciprocal sales and cost of goods sold amounts.		
b	**Investment in Smith (+A)**	**32,000**	
	Noncontrolling interest (−L)	**8,000**	
	Cost of goods sold (−E, +SE)		**40,000**
	To adjust cost of goods sold for unrealized profit in beginning inventory and to allocate the unrealized profit 80% to the parent's investment account and 20% to noncontrolling interest.		
c	**Cost of goods sold (E, −SE)**	**30,000**	
	Inventory (−A)		**30,000**
	To eliminate unrealized profit from ending inventory and cost of goods sold.		
d	**Income from Smith (−R, −SE)**	**88,000**	
	Dividends (+SE)		**40,000**
	Investment in Smith (−A)		**48,000**
	To eliminate investment income and 80% of the dividends by Smith and to reduce the investment account to its beginning balance.		
e	**Noncontrolling interest expense (E, −SE)**	**22,000**	
	Dividends—Smith (+SE)		**10,000**
	Noncontrolling interest (+L)		**12,000**
	To enter noncontrolling interest share of subsidiary income and dividends.		
f	**Retained earnings—Smith (−SE)**	**250,000**	
	Capital stock—Smith (−SE)	**500,000**	
	Investment in Smith (−A)		**600,000**
	Noncontrolling interest (+L)		**150,000**
	To eliminate reciprocal investment and equity balances and to enter beginning noncontrolling interest.		

(continued)

EXHIBIT 5-8

Intercompany Profits on Upstream Sales— Equity Method

POCH CORPORATION AND SUBSIDIARY CONSOLIDATION WORKING PAPERS FOR THE YEAR ENDED DECEMBER 31, 2007 (IN THOUSANDS)

	Poch	80% Smith	Adjustments and Eliminations Debits	Adjustments and Eliminations Credits	Consolidated Statements
Income Statement Sales	$3,000	$1,500	a 300		$4,200
Income from Smith	88		d 88		
Cost of goods sold	(2,000)	(1,000)	c 30	a 300 b 40	(2,690)
Other expenses	(588)	(400)			(988)
Noncontrolling interest expense*			e 22		(22)
Net income	**$ 500**	**$ 100**			**$ 500**
Retained Earnings Retained earnings—Poch	$1,000				$1,000
Retained earnings—Smith		$ 250	f 250		
Add: Net income	**500**	**100**			**500**
Deduct: Dividends	(400)	(50)		d 40 e 10	(400)
Retained earnings—December 31	**$1,100**	**$ 300**			**$1,100**
Balance Sheet Cash	$ 200	$ 50			$ 250
Accounts receivable	700	100		g 50	750
Inventories	1,100	200		c 30	1,270
Other current assets	384	150			534
Plant and equipment—net	2,000	500			2,500
Investment in Smith	616		b 32	d 48 f 600	
	$5,000	$1,000			$5,304
Accounts payable	$ 500	150	g 50		$ 600
Other liabilities	400	50			450
Capital stock	3,000	500	f 500		3,000
Retained earnings	**1,100**	**300**			**1,100**
	$5,000	$1,000			
Noncontrolling interest January 1			b 8	f 150	
Noncontrolling interest December 31				e 12	154
					$5,304

*Noncontrolling interest expense ($100,000 + $40,000 − $30,000) × 20% = $22,000

g	Accounts payable (–L)	50,000	
	Accounts receivable (–A)		50,000
	To eliminate reciprocal accounts receivable and payable.		

The consolidation working paper entries shown in Exhibit 5-8 are similar to those in the Peak–Seay illustration. Only entry b, which allocates the unrealized profit in Poch's beginning inventory between investment in Smith (80%) and noncontrolling interest (20%), differs significantly. Allocation is necessary because the unrealized profit arises from an upstream sale and was included in Smith's reported income for 2006. Poch's share of the $40,000 unrealized profit is only 80%. The other 20% relates to noncontrolling interests, and, accordingly, the $8,000 charge is necessary to reduce beginning noncontrolling interest from $150,000 (20% of Smith's reported equity of $750,000) to $142,000—20% of Smith's realized equity of $710,000 ($750,000 – $40,000) at December 31, 2006.

NONCONTROLLING INTEREST In computing noncontrolling interest expense for 2007, it is necessary to adjust Smith's reported net income for unrealized profits before multiplying by the noncontrolling interest percentage. The computation is:

Reported net income of Smith	$ 100,000
Add: Inventory profits from 2006 realized in 2007	+40,000
Deduct: Unrealized profits at December 31, 2007	–30,000
Smith's realized income for 2007	110,000
Noncontrolling interest percentage	20%
Noncontrolling interest expense	$ 22,000

The $154,000 noncontrolling interest at December 31, 2007, is determined in the working papers by adding noncontrolling interest expense of $22,000 to beginning noncontrolling interest of $142,000 and subtracting noncontrolling interest dividends. An alternative computation that may be used as a check is to deduct unrealized profit in the December 31, 2007, inventory from Smith's equity at December 31, 2007, and multiply the resulting realized equity of Smith by the 20% noncontrolling interest [($800,000 – $30,000) × 20% = $154,000]. The advantage of this approach is that only unrealized profits at the balance sheet date need to be considered in the computation.

SUMMARY

Intercompany sales and purchases of inventory items result in reciprocal sales and cost of goods sold amounts that do not reflect merchandising activity of the consolidated entity. These intercompany transactions also give rise to unrealized intercompany profits. The consolidated entity defers recognition of these profits until they can be realized by subsequent sales to parties outside the consolidated entity.

The direction of intercompany sales is important, except for consolidated companies with only 100%-owned subsidiaries. We charge the full amount of the unrealized intercompany profit from downstream sales against parent-company and consolidated net income. In the case of upstream sales, however, we charge unrealized profits to consolidated net income and noncontrolling interest expense on the basis of majority and noncontrolling ownership. Intercompany profits that are deferred in one period are subsequently recognized in the period in which the related inventory items are sold to nonaffiliated entities. Exhibit 5-9 presents a summary illustration of the effect of intercompany profit eliminations on parent-company and consolidated net income.

Under the assumption that P sells to S, P's net income and consolidated net income are exactly the same as if the sales had never taken place. In that case, P's separate income would have been $95,000 ($100,000 + $5,000 – $10,000), and P's income from S would have been $45,000 ($50,000 × 90%), for a total of $140,000. Under the assumption that S sells to P, P's net income and consolidated net income are exactly the same as if the intercompany sales had never taken place. In that case, P's separate income would have been $100,000 (as given), and S's net income would have been $45,000 ($50,000 + $5,000 – $10,000). P's $100,000 separate income plus P's income from S of $40,500 ($45,000 × 90%) is equal to P's net income and consolidated net income.

EXHIBIT 5-9

Summary Illustration— Unrealized Inventory Profits

Assumptions

1. Parent company's income, excluding income from subsidiary, is $100,000.
2. 90%-owned subsidiary reports net income of $50,000.
3. Unrealized profit in beginning inventory is $5,000.
4. Unrealized profit in ending inventory is $10,000.

	Downstream: Assume That P Sells to S	Upstream: Assume That S Sells to P
P's Net Income—Equity Method		
P's separate income	$100,000	$100,000
P's share of S's reported net income:		
($50,000 × 90%)	45,000	45,000
Add: Unrealized profit in beginning inventory:		
($5,000 × 100%)	5,000	
($5,000 × 90%)		4,500
Deduct: Unrealized profit in ending inventory:		
($10,000 × 100%)	(10,000)	
($10,000 × 90%)		(9,000)
P's net income	$140,000	$140,500
Consolidated Net Income		
P's separate income plus S's net income	$150,000	$150,000
Adjustments for unrealized profits:		
Beginning inventory ($5,000 × 100%)	5,000	5,000
Ending inventory ($10,000 × 100%)	(10,000)	(10,000)
Total realized income	145,000	145,000
Less: Noncontrolling interest expense:		
($50,000 × 10%)	(5,000)	
($50,000 + $5,000 − $10,000) × 10%		(4,500)
Consolidated net income	$140,000	$140,500

QUESTIONS

1. The effect of unrealized profits and losses on sales between affiliated companies is eliminated in preparing consolidated financial statements. When are profits and losses on such sales realized for consolidated statement purposes?

2. In eliminating unrealized profit on intercompany sales of inventory items, should gross profit or net profit be eliminated?

3. Is the amount of intercompany profit to be eliminated from consolidated financial statements affected by the existence of a noncontrolling interest? Explain.

4. What effect does the elimination of intercompany sales and purchases (or cost of goods sold) have on consolidated net income?

5. What effect does the elimination of intercompany accounts receivable and accounts payable have on consolidated working capital?

6. Explain the designations *upstream sales* and *downstream sales*. Of what significance are these designations in computing parent-company and consolidated net income?

7. Would failure to eliminate unrealized profit in inventories at December 31, 2006, have any effect on consolidated net income in 2007? 2008?

8. Under what circumstances is noncontrolling interest expense affected by intercompany sales activity?

9. How does a parent company adjust its investment income for unrealized profit on sales it makes to its subsidiaries (a) in the year of the sale and (b) in the year in which the subsidiaries sell the related merchandise to outsiders?

10. How is the combined cost of goods sold affected by unrealized profit in (a) the beginning inventory of the subsidiary and (b) the ending inventory of the subsidiary?

11. Is the effect of unrealized profit on consolidated cost of goods sold influenced by (a) the existence of a noncontrolling interest and (b) the direction of intercompany sales?

12. Unrealized profit in the ending inventory is eliminated in consolidation working papers by increasing cost of sales and decreasing the inventory account. How is unrealized profit in the beginning inventory reflected in the consolidation working papers?

13. Describe the computation of minority interest in a year in which there is unrealized inventory profit from upstream sales in both the beginning and ending inventories of the parent company.

14. Consolidation working paper procedures are usually based on the assumption that any unrealized profit in the beginning inventory of one year is realized through sales in the following year. If the related merchandise is not sold in the succeeding period, would the assumption result in an incorrect measurement of consolidated net income?

NOTE: Don't forget the assumptions on page 50 when working exercises and problems in this chapter.

EXERCISES

E 5-1
General questions

1. Intercompany profit elimination entries in consolidation working papers are prepared in order to:
   a Nullify the effect of intercompany transactions on consolidated statements
   b Defer intercompany profit until realized
   c Allocate unrealized profits between majority and noncontrolling interests
   d Reduce consolidated income

2. The direction of intercompany sales (upstream or downstream) does not affect consolidation working paper procedures when the intercompany sales between affiliated companies are made:
   a At fair value
   b Above market value
   c At book value
   d To a 100%-owned subsidiary

3. Peterson Corporation sells inventory items for $100,000 to Steven Corporation, its 80%-owned subsidiary. The consolidated working paper entry to eliminate the effect of this intercompany sale will include a debit to sales for:
   a $100,000
   b $80,000
   c The amount remaining in Steven's ending inventory
   d 80% of the amount remaining in Steven's ending inventory

4. Sarah Corporation, a 90%-owned subsidiary of Painter Corporation, buys half of its raw materials from Painter. The transfer price is exactly the same price as Sarah pays to buy identical raw materials from outside suppliers and the same price as Painter sells the materials to unrelated customers. In preparing consolidated statements for Painter Corporation and Subsidiary:
   a The intercompany transactions can be ignored because the transfer price represents arm's-length bargaining
   b Any unrealized profit from intercompany sales remaining in Painter's ending inventory must be offset against the unrealized profit in Painter's beginning inventory
   c Any unrealized profit on the intercompany transactions in Sarah's ending inventory is eliminated in its entirety
   d Only 90% of any unrealized profit on the intercompany transactions in Sarah's ending inventory is eliminated

5. Pritchard Corporation sells an inventory item to its subsidiary, Shinault Company, to be used as a plant asset by Shinault. The working paper entry to eliminate intercompany profits in the year of sale will *not* include:
   a A debit to sales
   b A credit to cost of sales
   c A credit to inventories
   d A credit to plant assets

6. Smeltzer Corporation regularly sells inventory items to its parent, Pullano Corporation. In preparing the consolidated income statement, which of the following items would *not* be affected by the direction (upstream or downstream) of these intercompany sales?
   a Consolidated gross profit
   b Noncontrolling interest expense
   c Consolidated net income
   d Consolidated retained earnings

7. Pentacost Corporation regularly sells inventory items to its subsidiary, Schumaker Corporation. If unrealized profits in Schumaker's 2006 year-end inventory exceed the unrealized profits in its 2007 year-end inventory:

 a **Combined cost of sales will be greater than consolidated cost of sales in 2006**
 b **Combined cost of sales will be less than consolidated cost of sales in 2006** ~2007~
 c **Combined gross profit will be greater than consolidated gross profit in 2006**
 d **Combined sales will be less than consolidated sales in 2006**

8. Spartacus Corporation is a 90%-owned subsidiary of Plymouth Corporation, acquired on January 1, 2006, at a price equal to book value and fair value. Plymouth accounts for its investment in Spartacus using the equity method of accounting. The only intercompany transactions between the two affiliates in 2006 and 2007 are as follows:

2006	Plymouth sold inventory items that cost $200,000 to Spartacus for $250,000. One-fourth of this merchandise remains unsold at December 31, 2006
2007	Plymouth sold inventory items that cost $300,000 to Spartacus for $375,000. One-third of this merchandise remains unsold at December 31, 2007

+ 12,500
− 25,000
− 12,500

At December 31, 2007, Plymouth's Investment in Spartacus account:

 a **Will equal its underlying equity in Spartacus**
 b **Will be $12,500 greater than its underlying equity in Spartacus**
 c **Will be $25,000 less than its underlying equity in Spartacus**
 d **Will be $12,500 less than its underlying equity in Spartacus**

E 5-2

[AICPA adapted] General problems

1. Perez, Inc., owns 80% of Senior, Inc. During 2006, Perez sold goods with a 40% gross profit to Senior. Senior sold all of these goods in 2006. For 2006 consolidated financial statements, how should the summation of Perez and Senior income statement items be adjusted?

 a **Sales and cost of goods sold should be reduced by the intercompany sales.**
 b **Sales and cost of goods sold should be reduced by 80% of the intercompany sales.**
 c **Net income should be reduced by 80% of the gross profit on intercompany sales.**
 d **No adjustment is necessary.**

2. Clark Company had the following transactions with affiliated parties during 2006.

- Sales of $60,000 to Dean, with $20,000 gross profit. Dean had $15,000 of this inventory on hand at year-end. Clark owns a 15% interest in Dean and does not exert significant influence. *– No Adj Needed*
- Purchases of raw materials totaling $240,000 from Kent Corporation, a wholly owned subsidiary. Kent's gross profit on the sale was $48,000. Clark had $60,000 of this inventory remaining on December 31, 2006.

240,000 Sale
– 48,000 Profit
192,000 Cost
Mark-up = 1.25

Before eliminating entries, Clark had consolidated current assets of $320,000. What amount should Clark report in its December 31, 2006, consolidated balance sheet for current assets?

 a **$320,000**
 b **$317,000**
 c **$308,000**
 d **$303,000**

320,000   Sales   240,000
– 12,000   Cost of Sales   240,000
306,000   Cost of Sales   12,000
         Inventory   12,000 ← unrealized profit

3. Parker Corporation owns 80% of Smith's common stock. During 2006, Parker sold Smith $250,000 of inventory on the same terms as sales made to third parties. Smith sold all of the inventory purchased from Parker in 2006. The following information pertains to Smith's and Parker's sales for 2006:

80%

	Parker	Smith
Sales	$1,000,000	$700,000
Cost of Sales	400,000	350,000
	$ 600,000	$350,000

+   350,000 − 250,000 = 500,000

What amount should Parker report as cost of sales in its 2006 consolidated income statement?

 a **$750,000**
 b **$680,000**
 c **$500,000**
 d **$430,000**

E 5-3

Downstream sales

1. The separate incomes of Philly Corporation and Silvio Corporation, a 100%-owned subsidiary of Philly, for 2007 are $1,000,000 and $500,000, respectively. Philly sells all of its output to Silvio at 150% of Philly's cost of production. During 2006 and 2007, Philly's sales to Silvio were $4,500,000 and $3,500,000, respectively. Silvio's inventory at

December 31, 2006, included $1,500,000 of the merchandise acquired from Philly, and its December 31, 2007, inventory included $1,200,000 of such merchandise.

A consolidated income statement for Philly Corporation and Subsidiary for 2007 should show consolidated net income of:

a **$1,100,000**

b **$1,400,000**

c **$1,500,000**

d **$1,600,000**

USE THE FOLLOWING INFORMATION IN ANSWERING QUESTIONS 2 AND 3:

Pansy Corporation owns 75% of the voting common stock of Saturn Corporation, acquired at book value during 2006. Selected information from the accounts of Pansy and Saturn for 2008 are as follows:

	Pansy	**Saturn**
Sales	$900,000	$500,000
Cost of Sales	490,000	190,000

During 2008 Pansy sold merchandise to Saturn for $50,000, at a gross profit to Pansy of $20,000. Half of this merchandise remained in Saturn's inventory at December 31, 2008. Saturn's December 31, 2007, inventory included unrealized profit of $4,000 on goods acquired from Pansy.

---

2. In a consolidated income statement for Pansy Corporation and Subsidiary for the year 2008, consolidated sales should be:

a **$1,450,000**

b **$1,400,000**

c **$1,362,500**

d **$1,350,000**

3. In a consolidated income statement for Pansy Corporation and Subsidiary for the year 2008, consolidated cost of sales should be:

a **$686,000**

b **$680,000**

c **$636,000**

d **$624,000**

E 5-4

Upstream sales Pride Corporation owns an 80% interest in Sedita Corporation and at December 31, 2006, Pride's investment in Sedita on an equity basis was equal to 80% of Sedita's stockholders' equity. During 2007, Sedita sells merchandise to Pride for $100,000, at a gross profit to Sedita of $20,000. At December 31, 2007, half of this merchandise is included in Pride's inventory. Separate incomes for Pride and Sedita for 2007 are summarized as follows:

$10,000
unrealized

	Pride	**Sedita**
Sales	$500,000	$300,000
Cost of sales	(250,000)	(200,000)
Gross profit	250,000	100,000
Operating expenses	(125,000)	(40,000)
Separate incomes	$125,000	$ 60,000

1. Pride's income from Sedita for 2007 is:

a **$48,000**

b **$40,000**

c **$38,000**

d **$28,000**

2. Consolidated cost of sales for 2007 is:

a **$460,000**

b **$450,000**

c **$440,000**

d **$360,000**

3. Noncontrolling interest expense for 2007 is:

a **$12,000**

b **$10,000**

c **$4,000**

d **$2,000**

E 5-5

Upstream sales Parcon Corporation owns an 80% interest in Shelly Corporation acquired several years ago. Shelly regularly sells merchandise to its parent at 125% of Shelly's cost. Gross profit data of Parcon and Shelly for 2007 are as follows:

	Parcon	Shelly
Sales	$1,000,000	$800,000
Cost of goods sold	800,000	640,000
Gross profit	$ 200,000	$160,000

During 2007, Parcon purchased inventory items from Shelly at a transfer price of $400,000. Parcon's December 31, 2006 and 2007, inventories included goods acquired from Shelly of $100,000 and $125,000, respectively.

1. Consolidated sales of Parcon Corporation and Subsidiary for 2007 were:
   a *$1,800,000*
   b *$1,425,000*
   c *$1,400,000*
   d *$1,240,000*

2. The unrealized profits in the year-end 2006 and 2007 inventories were:
   a *$100,000 and $125,000, respectively*
   b *$80,000 and $100,000, respectively*
   c *$20,000 and $25,000, respectively*
   d *$16,000 and $20,000, respectively*

3. Consolidated cost of goods sold of Parcon Corporation and Subsidiary for 2007 was:
   a *$1,024,000*
   b *$1,045,000*
   c *$1,052,800*
   d *$1,056,000*

E 5-6

Upstream and downstream sales

1. Patti Corporation owns 70% of Susan Company's common stock, acquired January 1, 2007. Patents from the investment are being amortized at a rate of $20,000 per year. Susan regularly sells merchandise to Patti at 150% of Susan's cost. Patti's December 31, 2007, and 2008 inventories include goods purchased intercompany of $112,500 and $33,000, respectively. The separate incomes (do not include investment income) of Patti and Susan for 2008 are summarized as follows:

	Patti	Susan
Sales	$1,200,000	$800,000
Cost of sales	(600,000)	(500,000)
Other expenses	(400,000)	(100,000)
Separate incomes	$ 200,000	$200,000

Total consolidated income should be allocated to consolidated net income and noncontrolling interest expense in the amounts of:
   a *$338,550 and $67,950, respectively*
   b *$358,550 and $60,000, respectively*
   c *$346,500 and $60,000, respectively*
   d *$346,500 and $67,950, respectively*

2. Packman acquired a 60% interest in Slocum on January 1, 2006, for $360,000, when Slocum's net assets had a book value and fair value of $600,000. During 2006, Packman sold inventory items that cost $600,000 to Slocum for $800,000, and Slocum's inventory at December 31, 2006, included one-fourth of this merchandise. Packman reported separate income from its own operations (excludes investment income) of $300,000, and Slocum reported a net loss of $150,000 for 2006. Consolidated net income for Packman Corporation and Subsidiary for 2006 is:
   a *$260,000*
   b *$180,000*
   c *$160,000*
   d *$100,000*

3. Santini Corporation, a 75%-owned subsidiary of Parnell Corporation, sells inventory items to its parent at 125% of cost. Inventories of the two affiliated companies for 2006 are as follows:

	Parnell	Santini
Beginning inventory	$400,000	$250,000
Ending inventory	500,000	200,000

Parnell's beginning and ending inventories include merchandise acquired from Santini of $150,000 and $200,000, respectively. If Santini reports net income of $300,000 for 2006, Parnell's income from Santini will be:

a $255,000

b $217,500

c $215,000

d $195,000

E 5-7

Determine consolidated net income with downstream intercompany sales Pansy Corporation owns an 80% interest in the common stock of Sheridan Corporation, acquired several years ago at book value. Pansy regularly sells merchandise to Sheridan. Information relevant to the intercompany sales and profits of Pansy and Sheridan for 2007, 2008, and 2009 is as follows:

	2007	2008	2009
Sales to Sheridan	$100,000	$120,000	$200,000
Unrealized profit in Sheridan's inventory at December 31	30,000	40,000	20,000
Sheridan's separate income	500,000	550,000	475,000
Pansy's separate income (does not include investment income)	300,000	400,000	350,000

REQUIRED: Prepare a schedule showing consolidated net income for each of the three years.

E 5-8

Consolidated income statement with downstream sales The separate incomes (which do not include investment income) of Pycus Corporation and Sylvia Corporation, its 80%-owned subsidiary, for 2009 were determined as follows (in thousands):

	Pycus	Sylvia
Sales	$400	$100
Less: Cost of sales	200	60
Gross profit	200	40
Other expenses	100	30
Separate incomes	$100	$ 10

During 2009, Pycus sold merchandise that cost $20,000 to Sylvia for $40,000, and at December 31, 2009, half of these inventory items remained unsold by Sylvia.

REQUIRED: Prepare a consolidated income statement for Pycus Corporation and Subsidiary for the year ended December 31, 2009.

E 5-9

Compute noncontrolling interest and consolidated cost of sales (upstream sales) Income statement information for 2006 for Purgatory Corporation and its 60%-owned subsidiary, Seven Corporation, is as follows:

	Purgatory	Seven
Sales	$900	$350
Cost of sales	400	250
Gross profit	500	100
Operating expenses	250	50
Seven's net income		$ 50
Purgatory's separate income	$250	

Intercompany sales for 2006 are upstream (from Seven to Purgatory) and total $100,000. Purgatory's December 31, 2005, and December 31, 2006, inventories contain unrealized profits of $5,000 and $10,000, respectively.

REQUIRED

1. Compute noncontrolling interest expense for 2006.

2. Compute consolidated sales, cost of sales, and total consolidated income for 2006.

E 5-10

Consolidated income statement (upstream sales) Papillion Corporation purchased an 80% interest in Saiki Corporation for $600,000 on January 1, 2010, at which time Saiki's stockholders' equity consisted of $500,000 common stock and $200,000 retained earnings. The excess cost over book value was assigned to patents with a 10-year amortization period. Comparative income statements for the two corporations for 2011 are as follows:

	Papillion	**Saiki**
Sales	$1,000	$500
Income from Saiki	112	—
Cost of sales	(400)	(250)
Depreciation expense	(130)	(40)
Other expenses	(90)	(60)
Net income	$ 492	$150

Dividends of Papillion and Saiki for all of 2011 were $300,000 and $100,000, respectively. During 2010 Saiki sold inventory items to Papillion for $80,000. This merchandise cost Saiki $50,000, and one-third of it remained in Papillion's December 31, 2010, inventory. During 2011 Saiki's sales to Papillion amounted to $90,000. This merchandise cost Saiki $60,000, and one-half of it remained in Papillion's December 31, 2011, inventory.

REQUIRED: Prepare a consolidated income statement for Papillion Corporation and Subsidiary for the year ended December 31, 2011.

E 5-11

Consolidated income statement (downstream sales) Pill Corporation purchased an 80% interest in Sam Corporation for $600,000 on January 1, 2010, at which time Sam's stockholders' equity consisted of $500,000 common stock and $200,000 retained earnings. The excess cost over book value was assigned to goodwill, which is not amortized. Comparative income statements for the two corporations for 2011 are as follows:

	Pill	**Sam**
Sales	$1,000,000	$500,000
Income from Sam	116,000	—
Cost of sales	(400,000)	(250,000)
Depreciation expense	(130,000)	(40,000)
Other expenses	(90,000)	(60,000)
Net income	$ 496,000	$150,000

Dividends of Pill and Sam for all of 2011 were $300,000 and $100,000, respectively. During 2010 Sam sold inventory items to Pill for $80,000. This merchandise cost Sam $50,000, and one-third of it remained in Pill's December 31, 2010, inventory. During 2011, Sam's sales to Pill amounted to $90,000. This merchandise cost Sam $60,000, and one-half of it remained in Pill's December 31, 2011, inventory.

REQUIRED: Prepare a consolidated income statement for Pill Corporation and Subsidiary for the year ended December 31, 2011.

E 5-12

Upstream sales On January 1, 2004, Pres Corporation acquired 60% of the voting common shares of Suey Corporation at an excess of cost over book value of $1,000,000. This excess was attributed to plant assets with a remaining useful life of five years. For the year ended December 31, 2011, Suey prepared *condensed* financial statements as follows (in thousands):

Condensed Balance Sheet at December 31, 2011

Current assets (except inventory)	$ 600
Inventories	300
Plant assets—net	5,000
Total assets	$5,900
Liabilities	$ 400
Capital stock	3,400
Retained earnings	2,100
Total equities	$5,900

Condensed Statement of Income and Retained Earnings

Sales	$1,000
Cost of sales	(500)
Other expenses	(300)

Net income	200
Add: Retained earnings January 1, 2011	2,000
Less: Dividends	(100)
Retained earnings December 31, 2011	$2,100

Suey regularly sells inventory items to Pres at a price of 120% of cost. In 2010 and 2011, sales from Suey to Pres are as follows:

	2010	2011
Sales at selling price	$840	$960
Inventory unsold by Pres on December 31	120	360

1. Under the equity method, Pres reports investment income from Suey for 2011 of:
   a $120
   b $96
   c $80
   d $104 loss

2. Noncontrolling interest on December 31, 2011, is:
   a $2,200
   b $2,184
   c $2,176
   d $2,140

3. On the books of Pres Corporation, the investment account is properly reflected on December 31, 2011, at:
   a $3,240
   b $3,264
   c $3,276
   d Not enough information is given.

E 5-13

[AICPA adapted] General questions Selected information from the separate and consolidated balance sheets and income statements of Pard, Inc., and its subsidiary, Spin Company, as of December 31, 2009, and for the year then ended is as follows (in thousands):

	Pard	Spin	Consolidated
Balance Sheet Accounts			
Accounts receivable	$ 26	$ 19	$ 39
Inventory	30	25	52
Investment in Spin	67	—	—
Patents	—	—	30
Noncontrolling interest	—	—	10
Stockholders' equity	154	50	154
Income Statement Accounts			
Revenues	$200	$140	$308
Cost of goods sold	150	110	231
Gross profit	50	30	77
Equity in earnings of Spin	11	—	—
Amortization of patents	—	—	2
Net income	36	20	40

During 2009, Pard sold goods to Spin at the same markup on cost that Pard uses for all sales. At December 31, 2009, Spin had not paid for all of these goods and still held 37.5% of them in inventory.

Pard acquired its interest in Spin on January 2, 2006. Pard's policy is to amortize patents by the straight-line method.

1. What was the amount of intercompany sales from Pard to Spin during 2009?
   a $3
   b $6
   c $29
   d $32

2. At December 31, 2009, what was the amount of Spin's account payable to Pard for intercompany sales?
   a $3
   b $6
   c $29
   d $32

3. In Pard's consolidated balance sheet, what was the carrying amount of the inventory that Spin purchased from Pard?
  a $3
  b $6
  c $9
  d $12

4. What is the percentage of noncontrolling interest ownership in Spin?
  a 10%
  b 20%
  c 25%
  d 45%

5. Over how many years has Pard chosen to amortize?
  a 15
  b 19
  c 23
  d 40

15 years remaining

E 5-14

Consolidated income statement (intercompany sales correction) The consolidated income statement of Pullen and Swain for 2006 was as follows (in thousands):

Sales	$1,380
Cost of sales	(920)
Operating expenses	(160)
Income to 20% noncontrolling interest in Swain	(40)
Consolidated net income	$ 260

After the consolidated income statement was prepared, it was discovered that intercompany sales transactions had not been considered and that unrealized profits had not been eliminated. Information concerning these items follows (in thousands):

	Cost	Selling Price	Unsold at Year-End
2005 Sales—Pullen to Swain	$160	$180	25%
2006 Sales—Swain to Pullen	90	120	40

REQUIRED: Prepare a corrected consolidated income statement for Pullen and Swain for the year ended December 31, 2006.

PROBLEMS

P 5-1

Consolidated income and retained earnings (upstream sales, noncontrolling interest) Proctor Corporation acquired its 90% interest in Samel Corporation at its book value of $360,000 on January 1, 2007, when Samel had capital stock of $300,000 and retained earnings of $100,000.

The December 31, 2007 and 2008, inventories of Proctor included merchandise acquired from Samel of $30,000 and $40,000, respectively. Samel realizes a gross profit of 40% on all merchandise sold. During 2007 and 2008, sales by Samel to Proctor were $60,000 and $80,000, respectively.

Summary adjusted trial balances for Proctor and Samel at December 31, 2008, follow (in thousands):

	Proctor	Samel
Cash	$ 100	$ 20
Receivables—net	200	50
Inventories	240	100
Plant assets—net	250	480
Investment in Samel—90%	435.6	—
Cost of sales	800	390
Other expenses	340	160
Dividends	100	50
	$2,465.6	$1,250

	Proctor	Samel
Accounts payable	$ 150	$ 90
Other liabilities	60	60
Capital stock, $10 par	500	300
Retained earnings	369.2	150
Sales	1,300	650
Income from Samel	86.4	—
	$2,465.6	$1,250

REQUIRED: Prepare a combined consolidated income and retained earnings statement for Proctor Corporation and Subsidiary for the year ended December 31, 2008.

P 5-2

Computations (upstream sales) Putt Corporation acquired a 90% interest in Slam Corporation at book value on January 1, 2005. Intercompany purchases and sales and inventory data for 2005, 2006, and 2007 are as follows:

	Sales by Slam to Putt	Intercompany Profit in Putt's Inventory at December 31
2005	$200,000	$15,000
2006	150,000	12,000
2007	300,000	24,000

Selected data from the financial statements of Putt and Slam at and for the year ended December 31, 2007, are as follows:

	Putt	Slam
Income Statement		
Sales	$900,000	$600,000
Cost of sales	625,000	300,000
Expenses	225,000	150,000
Income from Slam	124,200	—
Balance Sheet		
Inventory	$150,000	$ 80,000
Retained earnings December 31, 2007	425,000	220,000
Capital stock	500,000	300,000

REQUIRED: Prepare well-organized schedules showing computations for each of the following:

1. Consolidated cost of sales for 2007

2. Minority interest expense for 2007

3. Consolidated net income for 2007

4. Minority interest at December 31, 2007

P 5-3

Computations (parent buys from one subsidiary and sells to the other) Potter Company owns controlling interests in Scan and Tray Corporations, having acquired an 80% interest in Scan in 2006, and a 90% interest in Tray on January 1, 2007. Potter's investments in Scan and Tray were at book value equal to fair value.

Inventories of the affiliated companies at December 31, 2007, and December 31, 2008, were as follows:

	December 31, 2007	December 31, 2008
Potter inventories	$60,000	$54,000
Scan inventories	38,750	31,250
Tray inventories	24,000	36,000

Potter sells to Scan at a 25% markup based on cost, and Tray sells to Potter at a 20% markup based on cost. Potter's beginning and ending inventories for 2008 consisted of 40% and 50%, respectively, of goods acquired from Tray. All of Scan's inventories consisted of merchandise acquired from Potter.

REQUIRED

1. Calculate the inventory that should appear in the December 31, 2007, consolidated balance sheet.

2. Calculate the inventory that should appear in the December 31, 2008, consolidated balance sheet.

P 5-4

Computations (upstream and downstream sales) Comparative income statements of Stuff Corporation for the calendar years 2007, 2008, and 2009 are as follows (in thousands):

	2007	2008	2009
Sales	$4,000	$4,250	$4,750
Cost of sales	2,100	2,200	2,500
Gross profit	1,900	2,050	2,250
Operating expenses	1,500	1,600	1,900
Net income	$ 400	$ 450	$ 350

ADDITIONAL INFORMATION

1. Stuff was a 75%-owned subsidiary of Plier Corporation throughout the 2007–2009 period. Plier's separate income (excludes income from Stuff) was $1,800,000, $1,700,000, and $2,000,000 in 2007, 2008, and 2009, respectively. Plier acquired its interest in Stuff at its underlying book value, which was equal to fair value on July 1, 2006.

2. Plier sold inventory items to Stuff during 2007 at a gross profit to Plier of $200,000. Half the merchandise remained in Stuff's inventory at December 31, 2007. Total sales by Plier to Stuff in 2007 were $500,000. The remaining merchandise was sold by Stuff in 2008.

3. Plier's inventory at December 31, 2008, included items acquired from Stuff on which Stuff made a profit of $100,000. Total sales by Stuff to Plier during 2008 were $400,000.

4. There were no unrealized profits in the December 31, 2009, inventories of either Stuff or Plier.

5. Plier uses the equity method of accounting for its investment in Stuff.

REQUIRED

1. Prepare a schedule showing Plier's income from Stuff for each of the years 2007, 2008, and 2009.

2. Compute Plier's net income for each of the years 2007, 2008, and 2009.

3. Prepare a schedule of consolidated net income for Plier Corporation and Subsidiary for each of the years 2007, 2008, and 2009, beginning with the separate incomes of the two affiliated corporations and including noncontrolling interest computations.

P 5-5

Working papers (100% owned, downstream sales, year after acquisition) Pane

Corporation acquired 100% of Seal Corporation's outstanding voting common stock on January 1, 2006, for $660,000 cash. Seal's stockholders' equity on this date consisted of $300,000 capital stock and $300,000 retained earnings. The difference between the price paid by Pane and the underlying equity acquired in Seal was allocated $30,000 to Seal's undervalued inventory and the remainder to patents with a five-year write-off period. The undervalued inventory items were sold by Seal during 2006.

Pane made sales of $100,000 to Seal at a gross profit of $40,000 during 2006; during 2007, Pane made sales of $120,000 to Seal at a gross profit of $48,000. One-half the 2006 sales were inventoried by Seal at year-end 2006, and one-fourth the 2007 sales were inventoried by Seal at year-end 2007. Seal owed Pane $17,000 on account at December 31, 2007.

The separate financial statements of Pane and Seal Corporations at and for the year ended December 31, 2007, are summarized as follows (in thousands):

	Pane	Seal
Combined Income and Retained Earnings Statements for the Year Ended December 31, 2007		
Sales	$ 800	$400
Income from Seal	102 ✓	—
Cost of sales	(400)	(200)
Depreciation expense	(110)	(40)
Other expenses	(192)	(60)
Net income	200	100
Beginning retained earnings	600	380 ✓
Less: Dividends	(100)	(50)
Retained earnings December 31, 2007	$ 700	$430
Balance Sheet at December 31, 2007		
Cash	$ 54	$ 37
Receivables—net	90	60
Inventories	100	80
Other assets	70	90
Land	50	50
Buildings—net	200	150
Equipment—net	500	400
Investment in Seal	736 ✓	—
Total assets	$1,800	$867
Accounts payable	$ 160	$ 47
Other liabilities	340	90
Common stock, $10 par	600	300 ✓
Retained earnings	700	430
Total equities	$1,800	$867

REQUIRED: Prepare working papers to consolidate the financial statements of Pane Corporation and Subsidiary at and for the year ended December 31, 2007.

P 5-6

Working papers (noncontrolling interest, downstream sales, year after acquisition) Patty Corporation acquired a 75% interest in Sue Corporation for $300,000 on January 1, 2007, when Sue's equity consisted of $150,000 capital stock and $50,000 retained earnings. The fair values of Sue's assets and liabilities were equal to their book values on this date, and any goodwill is not amortized. Patty uses the equity method of accounting for Sue.

During 2007, Patty sold inventory items to Sue for $80,000, and at December 31, 2007, Sue's inventory included items on which there were $10,000 unrealized profits. During 2008, Patty sold inventory items to Sue for $130,000, and at December 31, 2008, Sue's inventory included items on which there were $20,000 unrealized profits.

On December 31, 2008, Sue owed Patty $15,000 on account for merchandise purchases. The financial statements of Patty and Sue Corporations at and for the year ended December 31, 2008, are summarized as follows (in thousands):

	Patty	Sue
Combined Income and Retained Earnings Statements for the Year Ended December 31, 2008		
Sales	$ 600	$400
Income from Sue	102.5	—
Cost of sales	(270)	(210)
Operating expenses	(145)	(40)
Net income	287.5	150
Beginning retained earnings	182.5	90
Deduct: Dividends	(150)	(50)
Retained earnings December 31, 2008	$ 320	$190

Balance Sheet at December 31, 2008

Cash	$ 85	$ 30
Accounts receivable	165	100
Dividends receivable	15	—
Inventories	60	80
Land	80	50
Buildings—net	230	100
Equipment—net	200	140
Investment in Sue	385	—
Total assets	$1,220	$500
Accounts payable	$ 225	$100
Dividends payable	70	20
Other liabilities	155	40
Common stock, $10 par	450	150
Retained earnings	320	190
Total equities	$1,220	$500

REQUIRED: Prepare consolidation working papers for Patty Corporation and Subsidiary for the year ended December 31, 2008.

P 5-7

Consolidation working papers (upstream sales, noncontrolling interest) Poly

Corporation purchased a 90% interest in Susan Corporation on December 31, 2004, for $275,000 cash, when Susan had capital stock of $200,000 and retained earnings of $50,000. All Susan's assets and liabilities were recorded at their fair values when Poly acquired its interest. The excess of cost over book value is due to previously unrecorded patents and is being amortized over a 10-year period.

The Poly–Susan affiliation is a vertically integrated merchandising operation, with Susan selling all of its output to Poly Corporation at 140% of its cost. Poly sells the merchandise acquired from Susan at 150% of its purchase price from Susan. All of Poly's December 31, 2006, and December 31, 2007, inventories of $28,000 and $42,000, respectively, were acquired from Susan. Susan's December 31, 2006, and December 31, 2007, inventories were $80,000 each.

Poly's accounts payable at December 31, 2007, includes $10,000 owed to Susan from 2007 purchases.

Comparative financial statements for Poly Corporation and Susan Corporation at and for the year ended December 31, 2007, are as follows (in thousands):

	Poly	Susan
Combined Income and Retained Earnings Statement for the Year Ended December 31, 2007		
Sales	$819	$560
Income from Susan	81.4	—
Cost of sales	(546)	(400)
Other expenses	(154.4)	(60)
Net income	200	100
Add: Beginning retained earnings	120	70
Deduct: Dividends	(100)	(50)
Retained earnings December 31, 2007	$220	$120
Balance Sheet at December 31, 2007		
Cash	$ 75.8	$ 50
Inventory	42	80
Other current assets	60	20
Plant assets—net	300	300
Investment in Susan	312.2	—
Total assets	$790	$450
Current liabilities	$170	$130
Capital stock	400	200
Retained earnings	220	120
Total equities	$790	$450

REQUIRED: Prepare consolidation working papers for Poly Corporation and Subsidiary for the year ended December 31, 2007.

P 5-8

Correcting entries and financial statement working papers Sert is a 90%-owned subsidiary of Phil Corporation, acquired by Phil in 2004 at a price $5,000 in excess of fair value. The excess was assigned to previously unrecorded patents and amortized over a five-year period beginning with 2004. Comparative financial statements for Phil and Sert for the year ended December 31, 2011, are presented as follows (in thousands):

	Phil	Sert
Combined Income and Retained Earnings Statement for the Year Ended December 31, 2011		
Sales	$500	$100
Income from Sert	27.5	—
Cost of sales	(240)	(40)
Expenses	(174)	(30)
Net income	113.5	30
Add: Beginning retained earnings	105.5	40
Deduct: Dividends	(70)	(20)
Retained earnings December 31, 2011	$149	$ 50
Balance Sheet at December 31, 2011		
Cash	$ 63	$ 30
Accounts receivable	40	20
Inventories	60	15
Plant assets—net	220	105
Investment in Sert	113	—
Total assets	$496	$170
Accounts payable	$ 47	$ 40
Capital stock	300	80
Retained earnings	149	50
Total equities	$496	$170

During 2011, Phil sold merchandise to Sert for $10,000. This merchandise cost Phil $6,000 and was not paid for or resold by Sert until 2012. Phil's inventory at December 31, 2007, included merchandise acquired from Sert on which Sert reported a profit during 2010 of $5,000.

REQUIRED

1. Prepare correcting entries for Phil's investment in Sert. None

2. Prepare consolidation working papers for 2011 after adjusting the separate statements of Phil for prior errors and omissions.

P 5-9

Consolidated working papers (upstream sales) Pan Corporation acquired 100% of Sal Corporation's outstanding voting common stock on January 1, 2006, for $660,000 cash. Sal's stockholders' equity on this date consisted of $300,000 capital stock and $300,000 retained earnings. The difference between the price paid by Pan and the underlying equity acquired in Sal was allocated $30,000 to Sal's undervalued inventory and the remainder to goodwill (which is not amortized). The undervalued inventory items were sold by Sal during 2006.

Pan made sales of $100,000 to Sal at a gross profit of $40,000 during 2006; during 2007, Pan made sales of $120,000 to Sal at a gross profit of $48,000. One-half the 2006 sales were inventoried by Sal at year-end 2006, and one-fourth the 2007 sales were inventoried by Sal at year-end 2007. Sal owed Pan $17,000 on account at December 31, 2007.

The separate financial statements of Pan and Sal Corporations at and for the year ended December 31, 2007, are summarized as follows:

	Pan	Sal
Combined Income and Retained Earnings Statements		
for the Year Ended December 31, 2007 (in thousands)		
Sales	$ 800	$400
Income from Sal	108	—
Cost of sales	(400)	(200)
Depreciation expense	(110)	(40)
Other expenses	(192)	(60)
Net income	206	100
Beginning retained earnings	606	380
Less: Dividends	(100)	(50)
Retained earnings December 31, 2007	$ 712	$430
Balance Sheet at December 31, 2007		
Cash	$ 54	$ 37
Receivables—net	90	60
Inventories	100	80
Other assets	70	90
Land	50	50
Buildings—net	200	150
Equipment—net	500	400
Investment in Sal	748	—
Total assets	$1,812	$867
Accounts payable	$ 160	$ 47
Other liabilities	340	90
Common stock, $10 par	600	300
Retained earnings	712	430
Total equities	$1,812	$867

REQUIRED: Prepare working papers to consolidate the financial statements of Pan Corporation and Subsidiary at and for the year ended December 31, 2007.

P 5-10

Consolidated working papers (upstream sales) *downstream* Pat Corporation acquired a 75% interest in Sun Corporation for $300,000 on January 1, 2007, when Sun's equity consisted of $150,000 capital stock and $50,000 retained earnings. The fair values of Sun's assets and liabilities were equal to their book values on this date. The excess purchase price was allocated to an unrecorded patent, which had a remaining life of 15 years. Pat uses the equity method of accounting for Sun.

During 2007, Pat sold inventory items to Sun for $80,000, and at December 31, 2007, Sun's inventory included items on which there were $10,000 unrealized profits. During 2008, Pat sold inventory items to Sun for $130,000, and at December 31, 2008, Sun's inventory included items on which there were $20,000 unrealized profits.

On December 31, 2008, Sun owed Pat $15,000 on account for merchandise purchases.

The financial statements of Pat and Sun Corporations at and for the year ended December 31, 2008, are summarized as follows:

	Pat	Sun
Combined Income and Retained Earnings Statements		
for the Year Ended December 31, 2008 (in thousands)		
Sales	$ 600	$400
Income from Sun	92.5	—
Cost of sales	(270)	(210)
Operating expenses	(145)	(40)
Net income	277.5	150
Beginning retained earnings	172.5	90
Deduct: Dividends	(150)	(50)
Retained earnings December 31, 2008	$ 300	$190
Balance Sheet at December 31, 2008		
Cash	$ 85	$ 30
Accounts receivable	165	100
Dividends receivable	15	—

	Pat	Sun
Inventories	60	80
Land	80	50
Buildings—net	230	100
Equipment—net	200	140
Investment in Sun	365	—
Total assets	$1,200	$500
Accounts payable	$ 225	$100
Dividends payable	70	20
Other liabilities	155	40
Common stock, $10 par	450	150
Retained earnings	300	190
Total equities	$1,200	$500

REQUIRED: Prepare consolidation working papers for Pat Corporation and Subsidiary for the year ended December 31, 2008.

P 5-11

Consolidated working papers (noncontrolling interest, upstream sales, intercompany receivables/payables) Po Corporation purchased a 90% interest in San Corporation on December 31, 2007, for $275,000 cash, when San had capital stock of $200,000 and retained earnings of $50,000. All San's assets and liabilities were recorded at their fair values when Po acquired its interest. The excess of cost over book value is goodwill and not amortized.

The Po–San affiliation is a vertically integrated merchandising operation, with San selling all of its output to Po Corporation at 140% of its cost. Po sells the merchandise acquired from San at 150% of its purchase price from San. All of Po's December 31, 2009, and December 31, 2010, inventories of $28,000 and $42,000, respectively, were acquired from San. San's December 31, 2009, and December 31, 2010, inventories were $80,000 each.

Po's accounts payable at December 31, 2010, includes $10,000 owed to San from 2010 purchases.

Comparative financial statements for Po Corporation and San Corporation at and for the year ended December 31, 2010, are as follows:

	Po	San
Combined Income and Retained Earnings Statement for the Year Ended December 31, 2010 (in thousands)		
Sales	$819	$560
Income from San	86.4	—
Cost of sales	(546)	(400)
Other expenses	(154.4)	(60)
Net income	205	100
Add: Beginning retained earnings	130	70
Deduct: Dividends	(100)	(50)
Retained earnings December 31, 2010	$235	$120
Balance Sheet at December 31, 2010		
Cash	$ 75.8	$ 50
Inventory	42	80
Other current assets	60	20
Plant assets—net	300	300
Investment in San	327.2	—
Total assets	$805	$450
Current liabilities	$170	$130
Capital stock	400	200
Retained earnings	235	120
Total equities	$805	$450

REQUIRED: Prepare consolidation working papers for Po Corporation and Subsidiary for the year ended December 31, 2010.

INTERNET ASSIGNMENT

Visit **Ford Motor Company's** Web site and download copies of both the 2002 and 2003 annual reports. First, review the 2003 annual report and summarize any information you find concerning intercompany inventory transfers, or intersegment sales. Next, go to the 2002 annual report and look for the same information. You will notice that the reported amounts for 2002 in the 2003 annual report do not agree with those originally reported in 2002. What's going on here? Was 2002 just a misprint? Review the 2003 annual report for other events that may have caused the difference. Prepare a brief summary of your findings.

SELECTED READINGS

Accounting Interpretation No. 1 of APB Opinion No. 18. New York: American Institute of Certified Public Accountants, 1971.

Accounting Principles Board Opinion No. 18. "The Equity Method of Accounting for Investments in Common Stock." New York: American Institute of Certified Public Accountants, 1971.

Accounting Research Bulletin No. 51. "Consolidated Financial Statements." New York: American Institute of Certified Public Accountants, 1959.

Financial Accounting Standards Board. Discussion Memorandum. *An Analysis of Issues Related to Consolidation Policy and Procedures.* Financial Accounting Series. Norwalk, CT: Financial Accounting Standards Board, 1991.

INTERCOMPANY PROFIT TRANSACTIONS–PLANT ASSETS

Transactions between affiliates for sales and purchases of plant assets create unrealized profits and losses to the consolidated entity. The consolidated entity eliminates (defers) such profits and losses in reporting the results of operations and its financial position. We also eliminate these in reporting the financial position and results of operations of a parent company under the equity method of accounting. The adjustments to eliminate the effects of intercompany profits on plant assets are similar to, but not identical with, those for unrealized inventory profits. Unrealized inventory profits self-correct over any two accounting periods, but unrealized profits or losses on plant assets affect the financial statements until the related assets are sold outside the consolidated entity or are exhausted through use by the purchasing affiliate. This chapter covers concepts and procedures for eliminating the effect of unrealized profits on plant assets in one-line consolidations under the equity method of accounting and in consolidated statements.

• • •

INTERCOMPANY PROFITS ON NONDEPRECIABLE PLANT ASSETS

LEARNING OBJECTIVE 1

The transfer of nondepreciable plant assets between affiliated companies at a price other than book value gives rise to unrealized profit or loss to the consolidated entity. An intercompany gain or loss appears in the income statement of the selling affiliate in the year of sale. However, such gain or loss is unrealized and must be eliminated from investment income in a one-line consolidation by the parent company. We also eliminate its effects in preparing consolidated financial statements.

Intercompany transfers of plant assets are much less frequent than intercompany inventory transfers. They most likely occur when mergers are completed, as a part of a reorganization of the combined companies. For example, *PepsiCo* announced a reorganization of business units and integration of facilities in its 2001 acquisition of *Quaker Oats Company*.[1] Note 20 provides segment information in the 2003 annual report of *Ford Motor Company* (p. 98). If we look at total reported revenues for 2003, we see an elimination of $5.655 billion of intersegment revenues. Ford is not required to break this amount down, but presumably a large part is deferral of unrealized profits on intercompany transfers of inventory and plant assets. We can get some additional information by looking at capital expenditures for the *Hertz* segment. These total $254 million in 2003. Ford sells inventory, and Hertz buys operating assets (automobiles) for its rental fleet.

---

[1] *The Wall Street Journal*, August 9, 2001, p. B4.

LEARNING OBJECTIVES

1 Assess the impact of intercompany profit on transfers of plant assets in preparing consolidation working papers.

2 Defer unrealized profits on asset transfers by either the parent or subsidiary.

3 Recognize realized, previously deferred profits on asset transfers by either the parent or subsidiary.

4 Adjust the calculations of noncontrolling interest amounts in the presence of intercompany profits on asset transfers.

5 Electronic supplement: Understand differences in consolidation techniques for plant asset transfers when the parent company uses either an incomplete equity method or the cost method.

The direction of intercompany sales of plant assets, like intercompany sales of inventory items, is important in evaluating the effect of unrealized profit on parent-company and consolidated financial statements. Any gain or loss on sales downstream from parent to subsidiary is initially included in parent-company income and must be eliminated. The amount of elimination is 100%, regardless of the noncontrolling interest percentage. Subsidiary accounts include any profit or loss from upstream sales from subsidiary to parent. The parent company recognizes only its share of the subsidiary's income, so only the parent's proportionate share of unrealized profits should be eliminated. The effect on consolidated net income is the same as for the parent.

This section of the chapter discusses and illustrates accounting practices for intercompany sales of land, covering both downstream and upstream sales.

Downstream Sale of Land

Stan Corporation is a 90%-owned subsidiary of Park Corporation, acquired for $270,000 on January 1, 2006. Investment cost was equal to book value and fair value of the interest acquired. Stan's net income for 2006 was $70,000, and Park's income, excluding its income from Stan, was $90,000. Park's income includes a $10,000 unrealized gain on land that cost $40,000 and was sold to Stan for $50,000. Accordingly, Park makes the following entries in accounting for its investment in Stan at December 31, 2006:

Investment in Stan (+A)	63,000	
Income from Stan (R, +SE)		63,000
To record 90% of Stan's $70,000 reported income.		
Income from Stan (−R, −SE)	10,000	
Investment in Stan (−A)		10,000
To eliminate unrealized profit on land sold to Stan.		

Exhibit 6-1 presents consolidation working papers for Park and Subsidiary for 2006. Separate summary financial statements for Park and Stan appear in the first two columns of the working papers.

Gain on the sale of land should not appear in the consolidated income statement, and the land should be included in the consolidated balance sheet at its cost of $40,000. Entry a eliminates the gain on sale of land and reduces the land account to $40,000—its cost to the consolidated entity. This is the only entry that is significantly different from adjustments and eliminations illustrated in previous chapters.

a Gain on sale of land (−Ga, −SE)	10,000	
Land (−A)		10,000
To eliminate gain on intercompany sale of land and reduce land to its cost basis.		

The overvalued land will continue to appear in the separate balance sheet of Stan in subsequent years until it is sold outside of the consolidated entity, but the gain on land does not appear in the separate income statements of Park in subsequent years. Therefore, entry a as shown in Exhibit 6-1 applies only in the year of the intercompany sale.

YEARS SUBSEQUENT TO INTERCOMPANY SALE Here is the working paper adjustment to reduce land to its cost to the consolidated entity in years subsequent to the year of the intercompany downstream sale:

Investment in Stan (+A)	10,000	
Land (−A)		10,000
To reduce land to its cost basis and adjust the investment account to establish		
reciprocity with Stan's equity accounts at the beginning of the period.		

The debit to the investment account adjusts its balance to establish reciprocity with the subsidiary equity accounts at the beginning of each subsequent period in which the land is held. For example, the investment account balance at December 31, 2006, is $323,000. This is $10,000 less than Park's underlying equity in Stan of $333,000 on that date ($370,000 × 90%). The difference arises from the entry on the parent-company books to reduce investment income and the investment account for the intercompany profit in the year of sale.

EXHIBIT 6-1

Intercompany Profit from Downstream Sale of Land

PARK CORPORATION AND SUBSIDIARY CONSOLIDATION WORKING PAPERS FOR THE YEAR ENDED DECEMBER 31, 2006 (IN THOUSANDS)

	Park	90% Stan	Adjustments and Eliminations Debits	Credits	Consolidated Statements
Income Statement					
Sales	$380	$220			$600
Income from Stan	53		b 53		
Gain on sale of land	10		a 10		
Expenses (including cost of goods sold)	(300)	(150)			(450)
Noncontrolling interest expense ($70,000 × 10%)			c 7		(7)
Net income	**$143**	**$ 70**			**$143**
Retained Earnings					
Retained earnings—Park	207				$207
Retained earnings—Stan		$100	d 100		
Add: Net income	**143**	**70**			**143**
Retained earnings—December 31	**$350**	**$170**			**$350**
Balance Sheet					
Other assets	$477	$350			$827
Land		50		a 10	40
Investment in Stan	323			b 53	
				d 270	
	$800	$400			$867
Liabilities	$ 50	$ 30			$ 80
Capital stock	400	200	d 200		400
Retained earnings	**350**	**170**			**350**
	$800	$400			
Noncontrolling interest				c 7	
				d 30	37
					$867

a Eliminates gain on sale of land and reduces land to a cost basis.
b Eliminates investment income and reduces the investment account to its January 1, 2006, balance.
c Records the noncontrolling interest in earnings for the current period.
d Eliminates reciprocal equity and investment amounts and establishes beginning noncontrolling interest.

Sale in Subsequent Year to Outside Equity

Assume that Stan uses the land for three years and sells it for $65,000 in 2010. In the year of sale, Stan reports a $15,000 gain ($65,000 proceeds less $50,000 cost), but the gain to the consolidated entity is $25,000 ($65,000 proceeds less $40,000 cost to Park).

Park recognizes its gain on the land in 2010 under the equity method of accounting by adjusting its investment income in that year. The entry on Park's books is:

Investment in Stan (+A)	10,000	
Income from Stan (R, +SE)		10,000
To recognize previously deferred profit on sale of land to Stan.		

This entry on Park's separate books reestablishes equality between the investment account and 90% of the equity of Stan on the same date.

The following working paper entry adjusts the $15,000 gain to Stan to the $25,000 consolidated gain on the land:

Investment in Stan (+A)	**10,000**	
Gain on land (Ga, +SE)		**10,000**
To adjust gain on land to the $25,000 gain to the consolidated entity.		

This entry in the year of sale is almost the same as the working paper entry in each of the years 2007, 2008, and 2009 to eliminate the unrealized profit from the land account. The difference is that the credit is to gain because the land no longer appears on the separate books of Park or Stan.

Upstream Sale of Land

To illustrate the accounting for upstream sales of nondepreciable plant assets, assume that Park purchases the land referred to in the previous section during 2006 from its 90%-owned affiliate, Stan. As before, Stan's net income for 2006 is $70,000, and Park's income, excluding its income from Stan, is $90,000. However, the $10,000 unrealized profit on the intercompany sale of land is now reflected in the income of Stan, rather than Park. In accounting for its investment in Stan at year-end 2006, Park makes the following entries:

Investment in Stan (+A)	63,000	
Income from Stan (R, +SE)		63,000
To record 90% of Stan's reported net income.		
Income from Stan (−R, −SE)	9,000	
Investment in Stan (−A)		9,000
To eliminate 90% of the $10,000 unrealized profit on land purchased from Stan.		

These entries record Park's investment income for 2006 in the amount of $54,000 ($63,000 − $9,000). Note that the $54,000 investment income consists of 90% of Stan's $60,000 realized income for 2006 ($70,000 reported income less $10,000 unrealized gain on land). Park's net income for 2006 is $144,000 ($90,000 separate income plus $54,000 investment income), as compared with $143,000 in the case of the downstream sale. The difference lies in the $1,000 unrealized gain attributed to noncontrolling interest and charged against noncontrolling interest expense.

Exhibit 6-2 presents consolidation working papers for Park Corporation and Subsidiary for 2006. The working papers use the same information as the working papers in Exhibit 6-1 except for minor changes necessary to switch to the upstream sale situation.

The adjustments reflected in the consolidation working papers in Exhibit 6-2 are the same as those in Exhibit 6-1 except for the amount of entry b, which is $54,000 rather than $53,000. Entry a eliminates the full amount of the gain on the sale of land and reduces the land to its cost basis to the consolidated entity whether the intercompany sale is upstream or downstream.

NONCONTROLLING INTEREST EXPENSE Noncontrolling interest expense is $7,000 in Exhibit 6-1 but only $6,000 in Exhibit 6-2. We charge noncontrolling interest with its share of the unrealized gain on Stan's sale of land to Park. We do this in the consolidation working papers by converting Stan's reported net income into realized income and multiplying by the noncontrolling interest percentage. Thus, the $6,000 noncontrolling interest expense is 10% of Stan's $60,000 realized income.

EXHIBIT 6-2

Intercompany Profit from Upstream Sale of Land

PARK CORPORATION AND SUBSIDIARY CONSOLIDATION WORKING PAPERS FOR THE YEAR ENDED DECEMBER 31, 2006 (IN THOUSANDS)

	Park	90% Stan	Adjustments and Eliminations Debits	Credits	Consolidated Statements
Income Statement					
Sales	$390	$210			$600
Income from Stan	54		b 54		
Gain on sale of land		10	a 10		
Expenses (including cost of goods sold)	(300)	(150)			(450)
Noncontrolling interest expense [($70,000 – $10,000) × 10%]			c 6		(6)
Net income	**$144**	**$ 70**			**$144**
Retained Earnings					
Retained earnings—Park	$207				$207
Retained earnings—Stan		$100	d 100		
Add: Net income	144	70			144
Retained earnings—December 31	**$351**	**$170**			**$351**
Balance Sheet					
Other assets	$427	$400			$827
Land	50			a 10	40
Investment in Stan	324			b 54 d 270	
	$801	$400			$867
Liabilities	$ 50	$ 30			$ 80
Capital stock	400	200	d 200		400
Retained earnings	351	170			351
	$801	$400			
Noncontrolling interest				c 6 d 30	36
					$867

a Eliminates gain on sale of land and reduces land to a cost basis.
b Eliminates investment income and reduces the investment account to its January 1, 2006, balance.
c Records the noncontrolling interest in earnings for the current period.
d Eliminates reciprocal equity and investment amounts and establishes beginning noncontrolling interest.

YEAR SUBSEQUENT TO INTERCOMPANY SALE While Park continues to hold the land in subsequent years, the consolidation working papers will require an adjusting entry to reduce the land account to its cost basis to the consolidated entity. The working paper entry to eliminate unrealized profit from the land account is:

Investment in Stan (+A)	9,000	
Noncontrolling interest (−L)	1,000	
Land (−A)		10,000

To reduce land to its cost basis and adjust the investment account and beginning noncontrolling interest to establish reciprocity with Stan's equity accounts at the beginning of the period.

We enter noncontrolling interest in the working papers at the noncontrolling interest share of *reported* subsidiary equity when reciprocal investment and subsidiary equity accounts are eliminated, so we need the forgoing adjustment to reduce noncontrolling interest to its *realized* amount each time we prepare consolidation working papers. In other words, this adjustment makes the beginning noncontrolling interest in 2007 equal to ending noncontrolling interest in 2006, and so on.

Sale in Subsequent Year to Outside Entity

Assume that Park uses the land for three years and sells it for $65,000 in 2010. In the year of sale, Park will report a $15,000 gain ($65,000 proceeds less $50,000 cost), but the gain to the consolidated entity is $25,000, allocated $24,000 [$15,000 + ($10,000 × 0.9)] to majority stockholders (consolidated net income) and $1,000 to noncontrolling stockholders.

Park adjusts its investment income from Stan in 2010 with the following entry:

| Investment in Stan (+A) | 9,000 | |
| Income from Stan (R, +SE) | | 9,000 |

To recognize previously deferred intercompany profits on land.

The $15,000 gain on the sale of land plus the $9,000 increase in investment income on Park's books equals the $24,000 effect on consolidated net income in 2010.

In the consolidation working papers, the adjustment of the $15,000 gain of Park to the $25,000 consolidated gain requires the following working paper entry:

Investment in Stan (+A)	9,000	
Noncontrolling interest (−L)	1,000	
Gain on land (Ga, +SE)		10,000

To adjust gain on land to the $25,000 gain to the consolidated entity.

This entry allocates the $10,000 gain between the Investment in Stan (90%) and noncontrolling interest (10%).

INTERCOMPANY PROFITS ON DEPRECIABLE PLANT ASSETS

The accounts of the selling affiliate reflect intercompany sales of plant assets subject to depreciation, depletion, or amortization that result in unrealized gains or losses. Firms must eliminate the effects of these gains and losses from parent-company and consolidated financial statements until the consolidated entity realizes them *through sale to other entities or through use within the consolidated entity*. The adjustments to eliminate the effects of unrealized gains and losses on parent-company and consolidated financial statements are more complex than in the case of nondepreciable assets. This additional complexity stems from the depreciation (or depletion or amortization) process that affects parent-company and consolidated income in each year in which the related assets are held by affiliated companies.

The discussion of intercompany sales of plant assets in this section is limited to depreciable assets, but the analysis and procedures illustrated apply equally to assets subject to depletion or amortization. Intercompany gains and losses from downstream sales of depreciable plant assets are considered initially, and the upstream-sale situation is covered next.

Downstream Sales of Depreciable Plant Assets

The initial effect of unrealized gains and losses from downstream sales of depreciable assets is the same as for nondepreciable assets. Gains or losses appear in the parent-company accounts in the year of sale and must be eliminated by the parent company in determining its investment income under the equity method of accounting. Similarly, we eliminate such gains or losses from consolidated statements by removing each gain or loss and reducing the plant assets to their depreciated cost to the consolidated entity.

DOWNSTREAM SALE AT THE END OF A YEAR Assume that Perry Corporation sells machinery to its 80%-owned subsidiary, Soper Corporation, on December 31, 2006. The machinery has an undepreciated cost of $50,000 on this date (cost, $90,000, and accumulated depreciation, $40,000), and it is sold to Soper for $80,000. Journal entries to record the sale and purchase on Perry's and Soper's books are as follows:

PERRY'S BOOKS

Cash (+A)	80,000	
Accumulated depreciation (+A)	40,000	
Machinery (−A)		90,000
Gain on sale of machinery (Ga, +SE)		30,000

SOPER'S BOOKS

Machinery (+A)	80,000	
Cash (−A)		80,000

There is an unrealized gain on Perry's books at December 31, 2006, and, accordingly, Perry adjusts its investment income for 2006 under the equity method of accounting for the full amount of the unrealized gain:

Income from Soper (−R, −SE)	30,000	
Investment in Soper (−A)		30,000

The gain on machinery should not appear in the consolidated income statement for 2006, and Perry should include the machinery in the consolidated balance sheet at $50,000, its depreciated cost to the consolidated entity. A consolidation working paper adjustment accomplishes this effect:

Gain on sale of machinery (−Ga, −SE)	**30,000**	
Machinery (−A)		**30,000**

We could also record this effect by debiting Gain on sale of machinery for $30,000, debiting Machinery for $10,000, and crediting Accumulated depreciation—machinery for $40,000. Conceptually, this entry is superior because it results in reporting plant assets and accumulated depreciation at the amounts that would have been shown if the intercompany sale had not taken place. From a practical viewpoint, however, the additional detail is usually not justified by cost-benefit considerations, because the same net asset amounts are obtained without the additional recordkeeping costs. The examples in this book reflect the more practical approach.

No adjustment of the noncontrolling interest is necessary, because the intercompany sale does not affect Soper's income. Note that the analysis up to this point is equivalent to the one for the intercompany sale of land discussed earlier in this chapter.

DOWNSTREAM SALE AT THE BEGINNING OF A YEAR If the sale from Perry to Soper had occurred on January 1, 2006, the machinery would have been depreciated by Soper during 2006, and any depreciation on the unrealized gain would be considered a piecemeal recognition of the gain during 2006. Assume that on January 1, 2006, the date of the intercompany sale, the machinery has a five-year remaining useful life and no expected residual value at December 31, 2010. Straight-line depreciation is used. The journal entries to record the sale and purchase are the same as for the December 31 sale; however, Soper also records depreciation expense of $16,000 for 2006 ($80,000 ÷ 5 years). Of this $16,000 depreciation, $10,000 is based on cost to the consolidated entity ($50,000 cost ÷ 5 years), and $6,000 is based on the $30,000 unrealized gain ($30,000 ÷ 5 years). The $6,000 is considered a piecemeal recognition of one-fifth of the $30,000 unrealized gain on the intercompany transaction. Conceptually, this is equivalent to the sale to other entities of one-fifth of the services remaining in the machinery.[2]

In eliminating the effect of the intercompany sale from its Investment in Soper account for 2006, Perry Corporation makes the following entries:

Income from Soper (−R, −SE)	30,000	
Investment in Soper (−A)		30,000
Investment in Soper (+A)	6,000	
Income from Soper (R, +SE)		6,000

Thus, elimination of the effect of the intercompany sale reduces Perry's investment income in 2006 by $24,000 ($30,000 unrealized gain less $6,000 realized through depreciation). Although Soper's income decreases by the $6,000 excess depreciation during 2006, the $6,000 is considered realized through use, and, accordingly, no adjustment of the noncontrolling interest expense is necessary.

EFFECT OF DOWNSTREAM SALE ON CONSOLIDATION WORKING PAPERS Partial consolidation working papers illustrate the effects of the January 1 intercompany sale of machinery on the consolidated financial statements as follows (in thousands):

	Perry	80% Soper	Adjustments and Eliminations		Consolidated Statements
Income Statement					
Gain on sale of machinery	$30		a 30		
Depreciation expense		$16		b 6	$10
Balance Sheet					
Machinery		$80	a 30		$50
Accumulated depreciation		16		b 6	10

The first consolidation working paper entry eliminates the $30,000 unrealized gain on machinery and reduces machinery to its cost basis to the consolidated entity at the time of intercompany sale. The second entry reduces depreciation expense and accumulated depreciation in order to adjust these items to the depreciated cost basis to the consolidated entity at December 31, 2006. Noncontrolling interest computations are not affected by the working paper adjustments because the sale was downstream.

In each of the years 2007 through 2010, Perry Corporation adjusts its investment income for the piecemeal recognition of the previously unrecognized gain on the machinery with the following entry:

2007, 2008, 2009, and 2010		
Investment in Soper (+A)	**6,000**	
Income from Soper (R, +SE)		**6,000**

Accordingly, by December 31, 2010, the end of the useful life of the machinery, Perry will have recognized the full $30,000 gain as investment income. Its investment account balance will reflect the elimination and piecemeal recognition of the unrealized gain as follows:

Year	Elimination of Gain on Machinery	Piecemeal Recognition of Gain Through Depreciation	Effect on Investment Balance at December 31
2006	$−30,000	$+6,000	$−24,000
2007		+6,000	−18,000
2008		+6,000	−12,000
2009		+6,000	−6,000
2010		+6,000	0

In consolidation working papers, it is necessary to establish reciprocity between the investment and subsidiary equity accounts at the beginning of the period before eliminating reciprocal bal-

---

[2] We assume that the machine services have entered the cost of goods delivered to customers during the current period. If, instead, they are included in inventory, realization has not yet occurred and appropriate adjustments should be made. This additional refinement is not justified when the amounts involved are immaterial.

ances. Thus, we eliminate the effect of the unrealized gain on the December 31, 2006, investment account in 2007 consolidation working papers with the following working paper entry:

Investment in Soper (+A)	24,000	
Accumulated depreciation (+A)	6,000	
Machinery (−A)		30,000

The partial consolidation working papers shown in Exhibit 6-3 for Perry and Soper include the entry for 2007. The exhibit shows consolidation eliminations for each subsequent year (after 2006) in which the unrealized gain on machinery would require working paper adjustment.

The partial working papers in Exhibit 6-3 show two working paper adjustments for each of the years 2007 through 2010. We use two entries for each year in order to isolate the effect on beginning-of-the-period balances and current-year changes. Current-year changes only affect depreciation expense and accumulated depreciation in equal amounts, so the entries can be combined and frequently are combined in subsequent illustrations and in problem solutions.

Upstream Sales of Depreciable Plant Assets

Upstream sales of depreciable assets from subsidiary to parent company result in unrealized gains or losses in the subsidiary accounts in the year of sale (unless the assets are sold at their book values). In computing its investment income in the year of sale, the parent company adjusts its share of the reported income of the subsidiary for (1) its share of any unrealized gain on the sale and (2) its share of any piecemeal recognition of such unrealized gain through the depreciation process.

EFFECT OF UPSTREAM SALE ON THE AFFILIATED COMPANIES' SEPARATE BOOKS The effect of a gain on an upstream sale is illustrated by the following example. Pruitt Corporation purchases a truck from its 80%-owned subsidiary, Scott Corporation, on January 1, 2006. Other information is as follows:

Scott's reported net income for 2006	$50,000
Use life of the truck at January 1, 2006	3 years
Depreciation method	Straight line
Trade-in value of the truck at December 31, 2008	$ 3,000
Cost of truck to Scott	$14,000
Accumulated depreciation on truck at December 31, 2005	$ 5,000

If Scott sells the truck to Pruitt for $12,000 cash, Scott and Pruitt make the following journal entries on their separate books for 2006:

SCOTT'S BOOKS

January 1, 2006 (sale of truck)		
Cash (+A)	12,000	
Accumulated depreciation (+A)	5,000	
Trucks (−A)		14,000
Gain on sale of truck (Ga, +SE)		3,000
To record sale of truck.		

PRUITT'S BOOKS

January 1, 2006 (purchase of truck)		
Trucks (+A)	12,000	
Cash (−A)		12,000
To record purchase of truck.		

December 31, 2006 (depreciation expense)		
Depreciation expense (E, −SE)	3,000	
Accumulated depreciation (−A)		3,000
To record depreciation for one year		
[($12,000 cost − $3,000 scrap) ÷ 3 years]		*(continued)*

EXHIBIT 6-3

Downstream Sale of
Depreciable Asset—
Years Subsequent
to Sale

PERRY CORPORATION AND SUBSIDIARY PARTIAL CONSOLIDATION WORKING PAPERS FOR THE YEARS 2007, 2008, 2009, AND 2010 (IN THOUSANDS)

	Perry	80% Soper	Adjustments and Eliminations Debits	Credits	Consolidated Statements
2007					
Income Statement					
Depreciation expense		$16		b 6	$10
Balance Sheet—					
December 31					
Machinery		80		a 30	50
Accumulated depreciation		32	a 6		
			b 6		20
Investment in Soper	XXX*		a 24		
2008					
Income Statement					
Depreciation expense		$16		b 6	$10
Balance Sheet—					
December 31					
Machinery		80		a 30	50
Accumulated depreciation		48	a 12		
			b 6		30
Investment in Soper	XXX*		a 18		
2009					
Income Statement					
Depreciation expense		$16		b 6	$10
Balance Sheet—					
December 31					
Machinery		80		a 30	50
Accumulated depreciation		64	a 18		
			b 6		40
Investment in Soper	XXX*		a 12		
2010					
Income Statement					
Depreciation expense		$16		b 6	$10
Balance Sheet—					
December 31					
Machinery		80		a 30	50
Accumulated depreciation		80	a 24		
			b 6		50
Investment in Soper	XXX*		a 6		

* Whatever the balance of the investment account, it will be less than the underlying book value of the investment at the beginning of the year by the amount of the unrealized profit.
a Eliminates unrealized profit from machinery and accumulated depreciation as of the beginning of the year and adjusts the Investment in Soper account to establish reciprocity with Soper's equity accounts at the beginning of the period.
b Eliminates the current year's effect of unrealized profit from depreciation expense and accumulated depreciation.

December 31, 2006 (investment income)

Investment in Scott (+A)	38,400	
Income from Scott (R, +SE)		38,400

To record investment income for 2006 computed as follows:

Share of Scott's reported net income ($50,000 × 80%)	$40,000
Less: Unrealized gain on truck ($3,000 × 80%)	−2,400
Add: Piecemeal recognition of gain	
[($3,000 gain ÷ 3 years) × 80%]	+800
Investment income for 2006	$38,400

The deferral of the intercompany gain on the truck decreases Pruitt's investment income for 2006 by $1,600 (from $40,000 to $38,400). This is 80% of the unrealized gain at December 31, 2006 ($3,000 unrealized gain from sale − $1,000 piecemeal recognition through depreciation × 80%). Pruitt will recognize the remaining $1,600 during 2007 and 2008 at the rate of $800 per year.

EFFECT OF UPSTREAM SALE ON CONSOLIDATION WORKING PAPERS To illustrate the working paper procedures for Pruitt and Scott, we include the following investment and equity balances—and changes in them—as additional assumptions.

	Investment in Scott 80%	80% of the Equity of Scott	100% of the Equity of Scott
December 31, 2005	$400,000	$400,000	$500,000
Income—2006	+38,400	+40,000	+50,000
December 31, 2006	438,400	440,000	550,000
Income—2007	+40,800	+40,000	+50,000
December 31, 2007	479,200	480,000	600,000
Income—2008	+40,800	+40,000	+50,000
December 31, 2008	$520,000	$520,000	$650,000

Pruitt's Investment in Scott account at December 31, 2006, is $1,600 below its underlying book value ($438,400, compared with $440,000), and at December 31, 2007, it is $800 below its underlying book value ($479,200, compared with $480,000). By December 31, 2008, the $3,000 gain on the truck has been realized through depreciation. Pruitt's share of that gain ($2,400) has been recognized at the rate of $800 per year in 2006, 2007, and 2008. Thus, reciprocity between Pruitt's investment account and its underlying book value is reestablished at the end of 2008.

Partial consolidation working papers for 2006, the year of sale, appear next, followed by the working paper entries in journal form.

2006: YEAR OF SALE (IN THOUSANDS)

	Pruitt	80% Scott	Adjustments and Eliminations Debits	Adjustments and Eliminations Credits	Consolidated Statements
Income Statement					
Income from Scott	$ 38.4		c 38.4		
Gain on sale of truck		$ 3	b 3		
Depreciation expense	3			a 1	$ 2
Noncontrolling interest expense			d 9.6		9.6
Balance Sheet					
Trucks	$ 12			b 3	$ 9
Accumulated depreciation	3		a 1		2
Investment in Scott	438.4			c 38.4	
				e 400	
Equity of Scott—January 1		$500	e 500		
Noncontrolling interest				d 9.6	
				e 100	109.6

a Accumulated depreciation (+A)	1,000	
Depreciation expense (−E, +SE)		1,000

To eliminate the current year's effect of unrealized gain
from depreciation accounts.

b Gain on sale of truck (−Ga, −SE)	3,000	
Trucks (−A)		3,000

To eliminate unrealized gain and to reduce trucks to a cost basis.

c Income from Scott (−R, −SE)	38,400	
Investment in Scott (−A)		38,400

To eliminate investment income and to adjust the investment
account to its beginning-of-the-period balance.

d Noncontrolling interest expense (E, −SE)	9,600	
Noncontrolling interest (+L)		9,600

To enter noncontrolling interest share of subsidiary income and dividends.

e Equity of Scott January 1, 2006 (−SE)	500,000	
Investment in Scott (−A)		400,000
Noncontrolling interest January 1, 2006 (+L)		100,000

To eliminate reciprocal investment and equity accounts and
to establish beginning noncontrolling interest.

Note that we compute noncontrolling interest expense of $9,600 for 2006 as 20% of Scott's realized income of $48,000 [($50,000 − $3,000 + $1,000) × 20%].

Partial consolidation working papers and the working paper entries in journal form for 2007, the first subsequent year after the upstream sale, are as follows:

2007: FIRST SUBSEQUENT YEAR (IN THOUSANDS)

	Pruitt	80% Scott	Adjustments and Eliminations Debits	Adjustments and Eliminations Credits	Consolidated Statements
Income Statement					
Income from Scott	$ 40.8		c 40.8		
Depreciation expense	3			a 1	$ 2
Noncontrolling interest expense			d 10.2		10.2
Balance Sheet					
Trucks	$ 12			b 3	$ 9
Accumulated depreciation	6		a 1		
			b 1		4
Investment in Scott	479.2		b 1.6	c 40.8	
				e 440	
Equity of Scott—January 1		$550	e 550		
Noncontrolling interest			b .4	d 10.2	
				e 110	119.8

a Accumulated depreciation (+A)	1,000	
Depreciation expense (−E, +SE)		1,000

To eliminate the effect of the 2006 unrealized gain from
current depreciation accounts.

b Accumulated depreciation (+A)	1,000	
Investment in Scott (+A)	1,600	
Noncontrolling interest January 1, 2007 (−L)	400	
Trucks (−A)		3,000

To eliminate the effect of 2006 unrealized gain from accumulated depreciation and truck accounts and to charge the unrealized gain of $2,000 at January 1 to the investment account (80%) and noncontrolling interest (20%).		
c Income from Scott (−R, −SE)	40,800	
Investment in Scott (−A)		40,800
To eliminate investment income and to adjust the investment account to its beginning-of-the-period balance.		
d Noncontrolling interest expense (E, −SE)	10,200	
Noncontrolling interest (+L)		10,200
To enter noncontrolling interest share of subsidiary income and dividends.		
e Equity of Scott January 1, 2007 (−SE)	550,000	
Investment in Scott (−A)		440,000
Noncontrolling interest January 1, 2007 (+L)		110,000
To eliminate reciprocal investment and equity accounts and to establish beginning noncontrolling interest.		

Noncontrolling interest expense of $10,200 for 2007 consists of 20% of Scott's reported net income of $50,000 plus 20% of the $1,000 gain realized through depreciation in 2007. In 2008 the computation of noncontrolling interest is the same as in 2007.

To explain further, noncontrolling interest expense in 2006 (the year of sale) is decreased by $400, the noncontrolling interest's share of the $2,000 gain not realized through depreciation in 2006. The beginning equity of Scott is not affected by the intercompany sale in 2006, so beginning noncontrolling interest is unaffected and does not require adjustment. Depreciation expense for each of the years 2006, 2007, and 2008 of $3,000 is reduced to $2,000 by a working paper adjustment of $1,000. The $2,000 depreciation expense that appears in the consolidated income statement is simply one-third of the book value less residual value of the truck at the time of intercompany sale [($9,000 − $3,000) ÷ 3 years].

EFFECT OF UPSTREAM SALE ON SUBSEQUENT YEARS In 2007, the first subsequent year after the intercompany sale, the unrealized gain affects both the beginning investment account and the beginning noncontrolling interest. Working paper entry b allocates the $2,000 unrealized gain 80% to the Investment in Scott account and 20% to beginning noncontrolling interest. The debit to the Investment in Scott account adjusts for the $1,600 difference between the investment account and 80% of Scott's equity at December 31, 2006. The $400 debit to noncontrolling interest is necessary to adjust beginning minority interest in 2007 to $109,600, equal to the ending noncontrolling interest in 2006.

In the partial consolidation working papers for 2006, the second subsequent year after the upstream sale, the amounts allocated are $800 to the investment account and $200 to noncontrolling interest because only $1,000 of the initial $3,000 unrealized gain is unrealized at January 1, 2008. No further adjustments are necessary in 2009 because the full amount of the unrealized gain has been realized through depreciation. Observe that the truck account less accumulated depreciation at December 31, 2008, is equal to the $3,000 residual value of the truck on that date (trucks, $9,000, less accumulated depreciation, $6,000).

2008: SECOND SUBSEQUENT YEAR (IN THOUSANDS)

	Pruitt	80% Scott	Adjustments and Eliminations Debits	Credits	Consolidated Statements
Income Statement					
Income from Scott	$ 40.8		c 40.8		
Depreciation expense	3			a 1	$ 2
Noncontrolling interest expense			d 10.2		10.2

(continued)

2008: SECOND SUBSEQUENT YEAR (IN THOUSANDS)

	Pruitt	80% Scott	Adjustments and Eliminations		Consolidated Statements
			Debits	Credits	
Balance Sheet					
Trucks	$ 12			b 3	$ 9
Accumulated depreciation	9		a 1		6
			b 2		
Investment in Scott	520		b .8	c 40.8	
				e 480	
Equity of Scott—January 1		$600	e 600		
Noncontrolling interest			b .2	d 10.2	
				e 120	130

a	**Accumulated depreciation (+A)**	1,000	
	Depreciation expense (−E, +SE)		1,000
	To eliminate the effect of the 2006 unrealized gain from current depreciation accounts.		
b	**Accumulated depreciation (+A)**	2,000	
	Investment in Scott (+A)	800	
	Noncontrolling interest January 1, 2007 (−L)	200	
	Trucks (−A)		3,000
	To eliminate the effect of 2006 unrealized gain from accumulated depreciation and truck accounts and to charge the unrealized gain of $1,000 at January 1 to the investment account (80%) and noncontrolling interest (20%).		
c	**Income from Scott (−R, −SE)**	40,800	
	Investment in Scott (−A)		40,800
	To eliminate investment income and to adjust the investment account to its beginning-of-the-period balance.		
d	**Noncontrolling interest expense (E, −SE)**	10,200	
	Noncontrolling interest (+L)		10,200
	To enter noncontrolling interest share of subsidiary income and dividends.		
e	**Equity of Scott January 1, 2007 (−SE)**	600,000	
	Investment in Scott (−A)		480,000
	Noncontrolling interest January 1, 2007 (+L)		120,000
	To eliminate reciprocal investment and equity accounts and to establish beginning noncontrolling interest.		

PLANT ASSETS SOLD AT OTHER THAN FAIR VALUE

An intercompany sale of plant assets at a loss requires special evaluation to make sure that the loss is not one that the selling affiliate should have recognized on its separate books prior to the intercompany sale (or in the absence of an intercompany sale). For example, if a parent company sells a machine with a book value of $30,000 to its 90%-owned subsidiary for $20,000 on January 1, 2006, a question should arise as to the fair value of the asset at the time of sale. If the fair value is in fact $20,000, then the parent company should have written the asset down to its $20,000 fair value before the sale and recognized the actual loss on its separate company books. If the fair value is $30,000, then the propriety of the parent company's action is suspect because the majority stockholders lose and the noncontrolling stockholders gain on the exchange. Parent company officers and directors may be charged with improper stewardship.

Similar suspicions arise if a subsidiary sells an asset to the parent at less than its fair value, because the transaction would have been approved by parent-company officials who also serve as directors of the subsidiary.

Intercompany sales at prices above fair value also create inequities. The Federal Trade Commission charged **Nynex Corporation** with overcharging its own telephone subsidiaries for equipment, supplies, and services. The telephone companies were fined $1.4 million for passing the costs of the overpayments along to their customers.[3]

Consolidation with Loss on Intercompany Sale

Consolidation procedures to recognize intercompany losses are essentially the same as those to eliminate unrealized gains. Assume that the machine referred to earlier had a remaining useful life of five years when it was sold to the 90%-owned subsidiary for $20,000. The parent company has a $10,000 unrealized loss that is recognized on a piecemeal basis over five years. If the subsidiary's net income for 2006 is $200,000 and there are no other intercompany transactions, the parent records its income from subsidiary as follows:

Investment in subsidiary (+A)	188,000	
Income from subsidiary (R, +SE)		188,000

To record income for 2006 determined as follows:

Equity in subsidiary's income ($200,000 × 90%)	$180,000
Add: Unrealized loss on machine	10,000
Less: Piecemeal recognition of loss ($10,000 ÷ 5 years)	(2,000)
	$188,000

Consolidation working paper entries relating to the intercompany loss for 2006 would be as follows:

Machinery (+A)	**10,000**	
Loss on sale on machinery (–Lo, +SE)		**10,000**
To eliminate unrealized intercompany loss on downstream sale.		
Depreciation expense (E, –SE)	**2,000**	
Accumulated depreciation (–A)		**2,000**
To increase depreciation expense to reflect depreciation on a cost basis.		

In the years 2007 through 2010, the parent company's income from subsidiary will be reduced by $2,000 each year under the equity method of accounting. Consolidated net income is also reduced by $2,000 each year through working paper entries to eliminate the effect of the intercompany loss. The elimination reduces consolidated income by increasing depreciation expense to a cost basis for consolidated statement purposes. In 2007 the working paper entry would be as follows:

Machinery (+A)	**10,000**	
Depreciation expense (E, –SE)	**2,000**	
Accumulated depreciation (–A)		**4,000**
Investment in subsidiary (–A)		**8,000**
To eliminate the effects of intercompany sale at a loss.		

An upstream sale of plant assets at a loss would be accounted for in similar fashion, except that the intercompany loss and its piecemeal recognition would be allocated proportionately to majority stockholders (investment income and consolidated net income) and noncontrolling interests.

---

[3] *The Wall Street Journal*, February 21, 1990, p. B8.

CONSOLIDATION EXAMPLE—UPSTREAM AND DOWNSTREAM SALES OF PLANT ASSETS

Plank Corporation acquired a 90% interest in Sharp Corporation at its underlying book value of $450,000 on January 3, 2006. Since Plank Corporation acquired its interest in Sharp, the two corporations have participated in the following transactions involving plant assets:

1. On July 1, 2006, Plank sold land to Sharp at a gain of $5,000. Sharp resold the land to outside entities during 2008 at a loss to Sharp of $1,000.

2. On January 2, 2007, Sharp sold equipment with a five-year remaining useful life to Plank at a gain of $20,000. This equipment was still in use by Plank at December 31, 2008.

3. On January 5, 2008, Plank sold a building to Sharp at a gain of $32,000. The remaining useful life of the building on this date was eight years, and Sharp still owned the building at December 31, 2008.

Exhibit 6-4 shows comparative financial statements for Plank and Sharp Corporations for 2008 in the separate-company columns of the consolidation working papers.

Equity Method

An examination of the consolidation working papers in Exhibit 6-4 shows that Plank Corporation uses the equity method of accounting. The fact that Plank's net income of $300,000 is equal to consolidated net income, as well as the equality of Plank's retained earnings and consolidated retained earnings are evidence of the use of the equity method. A reconciliation of Plank's Investment in Sharp account at December 31, 2007, and December 31, 2008, follows:

Underlying equity in Sharp December 31, 2007	
($600,000 equity of Sharp × 90%)	$540,000
Less: Unrealized profit on land	(5,000)
Less: 90% of unrealized profit on equipment ($16,000 × 90%)	(14,400)
Investment in Sharp December 31, 2007	520,600
Add: Income from Sharp 2008 (90% of Sharp's $80,000 net income + $5,000 gain on land + $3,600 piecemeal recognition of gain on equipment − $28,000 unrealized profit on building)	52,600
Less: Dividends received 2008	(27,000)
Investment in Sharp December 31, 2008	$546,200

Plank Corporation sold land to Sharp in 2006 at a gain of $5,000. This gain was realized in 2008 when Sharp sold the land to another entity. However, Sharp sold the land at a $1,000 loss based on the transfer price, and the net result is a $4,000 gain for the consolidated entity during 2008. Working paper entry a converts the $1,000 loss included in Sharp's separate income to a $4,000 consolidated gain.

a	Investment in Sharp (+A)	5,000	
	Gain on land (Ga, +SE)		5,000
	To recognize previously deferred gain on land.		

Entry b relates to the $20,000 intercompany profit on Sharp's sale of equipment to Plank at the beginning of 2007. The working paper adjustment is:

b	Investment in Sharp (+A)	14,400	
	Noncontrolling interest January 1, (−L)	1,600	
	Accumulated depreciation—equipment (+A)	8,000	
	Depreciation expense (−E, +SE)		4,000
	Equipment (−A)		20,000
	To eliminate unrealized profit on upstream sale of equipment.		

Depreciation on the unrealized gain is $4,000 per year ($20,000 ÷ 5 years), and the portion unrealized at the beginning of 2008 was $16,000, the original gain less piecemeal recognition of $4,000 through depreciation in 2007. The sale was upstream, so the $16,000 unrealized profit is allocated

EXHIBIT 6-4

Intercompany Sales of Plant Assets— Equity Method

PLANK CORPORATION AND SUBSIDIARY CONSOLIDATION WORKING PAPERS FOR THE YEAR ENDED DECEMBER 31, 2008 (IN THOUSANDS)

	Plank	90% Sharp	Adjustments and Eliminations		Consolidated Statements
Income Statement					
Sales	$2,000	$700			$2,700
Gain on building	32		c 32		
Loss (or gain) on land		(1)		a 5	4
Income from Sharp	52.6		d 52.6		
Cost of goods sold	(1,000)	(320)			(1,320)
Depreciation expense	(108)	(50)		b 4	
				c 4	(150)
Other expenses	(676.6)	(249)			(925.6)
Noncontrolling interest expense			e 8.4		(8.4)
Net income	**$ 300**	**$ 80**			**$ 300**
Retained Earnings					
Retained earnings—Plank	$ 400				$ 400
Retained earnings—Sharp		$200	f 200		
Net income	**300**	**80**			**300**
Dividends	(200)	(30)		d 27	
				e 3	(200)
Retained earnings—December 31, 2008	**$ 500**	**$250**			**$ 500**
Balance Sheet					
Cash	$ 131.8	$ 32			$ 163.8
Other current assets	200	150			350
Land	160	40			200
Buildings	500	232		c 32	700
Accumulated depreciation—buildings	(200)	(54)	c 4		(250)
Equipment	620	400		b 20	1,000
Accumulated depreciation—equipment	(258)	(100)	b 8		(350)
Investment in Sharp	546.2		a 5 d 25.6		
			b 14.4 f 540		
	$1,700	$700			$1,813.8
Current liabilities	$ 200	$ 50			$ 250
Capital stock	1,000	400	f 400		1,000
Retained earnings	**500**	**250**			**500**
	$1,700	$700			
Noncontrolling interest			b 1.6 e 5.4		
			f 60		63.8
					$1,813.8

90% and 10% on investment in Sharp ($14,400) and beginning noncontrolling interest ($1,600), respectively. The $14,400 is debited to the Investment in Sharp account because Plank used the equity method of accounting.

Working paper entry c eliminates intercompany profit on the buildings that Plank sold to Sharp in 2008 at a gain of $32,000:

c	Gain on buildings (–Ga, –SE)	32,000	
	Accumulated depreciation—buildings (+A)	4,000	
	Buildings (–A)		32,000
	Depreciation expense (–E, +SE)		4,000
	To eliminate unrealized gain on the downstream sale of buildings.		

The transaction occurred at the beginning of the current year, so the sale did not affect prior-period balances. We eliminate the $32,000 gain in the adjustment and reduce buildings to reflect their cost to the consolidated entity. We also eliminate depreciation expense and accumulated depreciation amounts relating to the unrealized gain.

Entry d in the consolidation working papers eliminates income from Sharp and 90% of Sharp's dividends, and it credits Investment in Sharp for the $25,600 difference in order to establish reciprocity between investment and equity accounts at the beginning of the year. Entry f eliminates reciprocal investment and equity accounts and establishes the noncontrolling interest at the beginning of the year.

d	Income from Sharp (–R, –SE)	52,600	
	Dividends (+SE)		27,000
	Investment in Sharp (–A)		25,600
	To eliminate income and dividends from subsidiary.		
e	Noncontrolling interest expense (E, –SE)	8,400	
	Dividends—Sharp (+SE)		3,000
	Noncontrolling interest (+L)		5,400
	To enter noncontrolling interest share of subsidiary income and dividends.		
f	Retained earnings—Sharp (–SE)	200,000	
	Capital stock—Sharp (–SE)	400,000	
	Investment in Sharp (–A)		540,000
	Noncontrolling interest—beginning (+L)		60,000
	To eliminate reciprocal investment and equity balances.		

The $8,400 deduction for noncontrolling interest in the consolidated income statement of Exhibit 6-4 is equal to 10% of Sharp's reported income for 2008 plus the piecemeal recognition of the gain in 2008 from Sharp's sale of equipment to Plank [(80,000 + $4,000) × 10%]. At December 31, 2008, the noncontrolling interest's share of the unrealized gain on the equipment is $1,200. This $1,200 is reflected in the $63,800 noncontrolling interest that is shown in the consolidated balance sheet. If the effect of the unrealized gain applicable to noncontrolling interest had not been eliminated, noncontrolling interest in the consolidated balance sheet would be $65,000, 10% of Sharp's reported equity at December 31, 2008.

INVENTORY ITEMS PURCHASED FOR USE AS OPERATING ASSETS

Intercompany asset transactions do not always fall neatly into the categories of inventory items or plant assets. For example, inventory items may be sold for use in the operations of an affiliated company. In this case, any gross profit on the sale will be realized for consolidated statement purposes as the purchasing affiliate depreciates the property.

Assume that Premier Electronics Company sells a computer that it manufactures at a cost of $150,000 to Service Valley Corporation, its 100%-owned subsidiary, for $200,000. The computer has a five-year expected useful life, and straight-line depreciation is used. Premier's separate income statement includes $200,000 intercompany sales, but Service Valley's cost of sales does *not* include intercompany purchases, because the purchase price is reflected in its plant assets, and the $50,000 gross profit is reflected in its equipment account. Working paper entries to consolidate the financial statements of Premier and Service Valley in the year of sale are:

Sales (–R, –SE)	200,000	
Cost of sales (–E, +SE)		150,000
Equipment (–A)		50,000
To eliminate intercompany sales and to reduce cost of sales		
and equipment for the cost and gross profit, respectively.		
Accumulated depreciation (+A)	10,000	
Depreciation expense (–E, +SE)		10,000
To eliminate depreciation on the gross profit from the sale ($50,000 ÷ 5 years).		

Recognition of the remaining $40,000 unrealized profit will occur as Service Valley depreciates the computer over its remaining four-year useful life. Assuming that Premier adjusts its Investment in Service Valley account for the unrealized profit on the sale under the equity method, the working paper entry for the second year will be:

Investment in Service Valley (+A)	40,000	
Accumulated depreciation—equipment (+A)	20,000	
Equipment (–A)		50,000
Depreciation expense (–E, +SE)		10,000
To reduce equipment to its cost basis to the consolidated entity, to eliminate the effects		
of the intercompany sale from depreciation expense and accumulated depreciation,		
and to establish reciprocity between beginning-of-the-period equity and investment		
amounts.		

Working paper entries for the remaining three years of the computer's useful life will include the same debit and credit items, but the accumulated depreciation debit will increase by $10,000 in each subsequent year to a maximum of $50,000, and the debits to Investment in Service Valley will decrease by $10,000 in each subsequent year as the gross profit is realized. The credit amounts are the same in each year.

SUMMARY

The effects of intercompany gains and losses on plant assets must be eliminated from consolidated financial statements until the consolidated entity realizes the gains and losses through use or through sale of the assets. Realization through use results from the depreciation recorded by the purchasing affiliate. Although all unrealized profit must be eliminated from the consolidated statements, we adjust consolidated net income for all unrealized gains and losses in the case of downstream sales. For upstream sales, however, we allocate the total amount of unrealized gains and losses between consolidated net income and noncontrolling interest expense. One-line consolidation procedures for parent-company financial statements must be compatible with consolidation procedures in order to maintain the equality of parent-company income under the equity method and consolidated net income (see Exhibit 6-5).

EXHIBIT 6-5

Summary
Illustration—
Unrealized Profit
from Plant Assets

Assumptions

1. Parent Company's income, excluding income from Subsidiary, is $100,000.
2. 90%-owned Subsidiary reported net income of $50,000.
3. An intercompany sale of land resulted in a gain of $5,000.
4. The land is still held within the consolidated entity.

	Downstream	Upstream
	Assume that P sells to S	Assume that S sells to P
P's Net Income—Equity Method		
P's separate income	$100,000	$100,000
P's share of S's reported net income	45,000	45,000
Deduct: Unrealized gain from land		
($5,000 × 100%)	(5,000)	
($5,000 × 90%)		(4,500)
	$140,000	$140,500
Consolidated Net Income		
P's separate income plus S's net income	$150,000	$150,000
Less: Unrealized gain on land	(5,000)	(5,000)
Total realized income	145,000	145,000
Less: Noncontrolling interest expense		
($50,000 × 10%)	(5,000)	
(50,000 − $5,000) × 10%		(4,500)
Consolidated net income	$140,000	$140,500

Note that P's net income and consolidated net income are the same as if the intercompany transaction had never taken place. In the downstream example, P's separate income would have been $95,000 ($100,000 − $5,000 gain) without the intercompany transaction, and S's reported income would have remained at $50,000. P's separate income of $95,000 plus P's $45,000 income from S ($50,000 × 90%) equals $140,000.

In the upstream example, P's separate income would have been unchanged at $100,000 in the absence of the intercompany transaction, but S's reported income would have been only $45,000 ($50,000 − $5,000 gain). P's separate income of $100,000 plus P's $40,500 income from S ($45,000 × 90%) equals $140,500. Although helpful in understanding the nature of accounting procedures, these assumptions concerning what the incomes would have been without the intercompany transactions lack economic realism because they ignore the productive use of the land.

QUESTIONS

1. What is the objective of eliminating the effects of intercompany sales of plant assets in the preparation of consolidated financial statements?

2. In accounting for unrealized profits and losses from intercompany sales of plant assets, does it make any difference if the parent company is the purchaser or the seller? Would your answer be different if the subsidiary were 100% owned?

3. When are unrealized gains and losses from intercompany sales of land realized from the viewpoint of the selling affiliate?

4. How is the computation of noncontrolling interest expense affected by downstream sales of land? By upstream sales of land?

5. Consolidation working paper entries are made to eliminate 100% of the unrealized profit from the land account in downstream sales of land. Is 100% also eliminated for upstream sales of land?

6. How are unrealized gains and losses from intercompany transactions involving depreciable assets eventually realized?

7. Describe the computation of noncontrolling interest expense in the year of an upstream sale of depreciable plant assets.

8. How does a parent company eliminate the effects of unrealized gains on intercompany sales of plant assets under the equity method?

9. What is the effect of intercompany sales of plant assets on parent-company and consolidated net income in years subsequent to the year of sale?

10. Explain the sequence of working paper adjustments and eliminations when unrealized gains and losses on plant assets are involved. Is your answer affected by whether the intercompany transaction occurred in the current year or in prior years?

E 6-1

General questions Use the following information in answering questions 1 and 2:

Parent Company sells land with a book value of $5,000 to Subsidiary Company for $6,000 in 2006. Subsidiary Company holds the land during 2007. Subsidiary Company sells the land for $8,000 to an outside entity in 2008.

1. In 2006 the unrealized gain:

   a *To be eliminated is affected by the noncontrolling interest percentage*

   b *Is initially included in the subsidiary's accounts and must be eliminated from Parent Company's income from Subsidiary Company under the equity method*

   c *Is eliminated from consolidated net income by a working paper entry that includes a credit to the land account for $1,000*

   d *Is eliminated from consolidated net income by a working paper entry that includes a credit to the land account for $6,000*

2. Which of the following statements is true?

   a *Under the equity method, Parent Company's Investment in Subsidiary account will be $1,000 less than its underlying equity in Subsidiary throughout 2007.*

   b *No working paper adjustments for the land are required to 2007 if Parent Company has applied the equity method correctly.*

   c *A working paper entry debiting gain on sale of land and crediting land will be required each year until the land is sold outside the consolidated entity.*

   d *In 2008, the year of Subsidiary's sale to an outside entity, the working paper adjustment for the land will include a debit to gain on sale of land for $2,000.*

Use the following information in answering questions 3 and 4:

Perry Corporation sold machinery to its 80%-owned subsidiary, Samuel Corporation, for $100,000 on December 31, 2006. The cost of the machinery to Perry was $80,000, the book value at the time of sale was $60,000, and the machinery had a remaining useful life of five years.

3. How will the intercompany sale affect Perry's income from Samuel and Perry's net income for 2006?

	Perry's Income from Samuel	Perry's Net Income
a	No effect	No effect
b	Increased	No effect
c	Decreased	No effect
d	No effect	Decreased

4. How will the consolidated assets and consolidated net income for 2006 be affected by the intercompany sale?

	Consolidated Net Assets	Consolidated Net Income
a	No effect	Decreased
b	Decreased	Decreased
c	Increased	No effect
d	No effect	No effect

E 6-2

Discuss effect of intercompany sale of land Samit Corporation is a 90%-owned subsidiary of Parsen Corporation, acquired by Parsen in 2006. During 2009 Parsen sells land to Samit for $50,000 for which it paid $25,000. Samit owns this land at December 31, 2009.

REQUIRED

1. How and in what amount will the sale of land affect Parsen's income from Samit and net income for 2009 and the balance of Parsen's Investment in Samit account on December 31, 2009?

2. How will the consolidated financial statements of Parsen Corporation and Subsidiary for 2009 be affected by the intercompany sale of land?

3. If Samit still owns the land at December 31, 2010, how will Parsen's income from Samit and net income for 2010 be affected and what will be the effect on Parsen's Investment in Samit account on December 31, 2010?

4. If Samit sells the land during 2011 for $50,000, how will Parsen's income from Samit and total consolidated income for 2011 be affected?

E 6-3

Computations for downstream and upstream sales of land Silverman Corporation is a 90%-owned subsidiary of Pruitt Corporation, acquired several years ago at book value equal to fair value. For 2006 and 2007, Pruitt and Silverman report the following:

	2006	2007
Pruitt's separate income	$300,000	$400,000
Silverman's net income	80,000	60,000

The only intercompany transaction between Pruitt and Silverman during 2006 and 2007 was the January 1, 2006, sale of land. The land had a book value of $20,000 and was sold intercompany for $30,000, its appraised value at the time of sale.

1. Assume that the land was sold by Pruitt to Silverman and that Silverman still owns the land at December 31, 2007.
   a *Calculate consolidated net income for 2006 and 2007.*
   b *Calculate noncontrolling interest for 2006 and 2007.*

2. Assume that the land was sold by Silverman to Pruitt and Pruitt still holds the land at December 31, 2007.
   a *Calculate consolidated net income for 2006 and 2007.*
   b *Calculate noncontrolling interest expense for 2006 and 2007.*

E 6-4

Journal entries and consolidated income statement (downstream sale of building)
Salmark is a 90%-owned subsidiary of Pigwich Corporation, acquired at book value several years ago. Comparative separate-company income statements for these affiliated corporations for 2006 are as follows:

	Pigwich Corporation	Salmark Corporation
Sales	$1,500,000	$700,000
Income from Salmark	108,000	—
Gain on building	30,000	—
Income credits	1,638,000	700,000
Cost of sales	1,000,000	400,000
Operating expenses	300,000	150,000
Income debits	1,300,000	550,000
Net income	$ 338,000	$150,000

On January 5, 2006, Pigwich sold a building with a 10-year remaining useful life to Salmark at a gain of $30,000. Salmark paid dividends of $100,000 during 2006.

REQUIRED

1. Reconstruct the journal entries made by Pigwich during 2006 to account for its investment in Salmark. Explanations of the journal entries are required.

2. Prepare a consolidated income statement for Pigwich Corporation and Subsidiary for 2006.

E 6-5

[AICPA adapted] General questions

1. On January 1, 2006, the Jonas Company sold equipment to its wholly owned subsidiary, Neptune Company, for $1,800,000. The equipment cost Jonas $2,000,000. Accumulated depreciation at the time of sale was $500,000. Jonas was depreciating the equipment on the straight-line method over 20 years with no salvage value, a procedure that Neptune continued. On the consolidated balance sheet at December 31, 2006 the cost and accumulated depreciation, respectively, should be:
   a *$1,500,000 and $600,000*
   b *$1,800,000 and $100,000*
   c *$1,800,000 and $500,000*
   d *$2,000,000 and $600,000*

2. In the preparation of consolidated financial statements, intercompany items for which eliminations will not be made are:
   a *Purchases and sales where the parent employs the equity method*
   b *Receivables and payables where the parent employs the cost method*
   c *Dividends received and paid where the parent employs the equity method*
   d *Dividends receivable and payable where the parent employs the equity method*

3. Dunn Corporation owns 100% of Grey Corporation's common stock. On January 2, 2006, Dunn sold to Grey for $40,000 machinery with a carrying amount of $30,000. Grey is depreciating the acquired machinery over a five-

year life by the straight-line method. The net adjustments to compute 2006 and 2007 consolidated income before income tax would be an increase (decrease) of:

	2006	2007
a	$ (8,000)	$2,000
b	$ (8,000)	0
c	$(10,000)	$2,000
d	$(10,000)	0

[handwritten notes in right margin:] 2006 elim gain (10,000) adj depree 2,000 ← only this (8,000) 2007

4. Port Company owns 100% of Salem Company. On January 1, 2006, Port sold Salem delivery equipment at a gain. Port had owned the equipment for two years and used a five-year straight-line depreciation rate with no residual value. Salem is using a three-year straight-line depreciation rate with no residual value for the equipment. In the consolidated income statement, Salem's recorded depreciation expense on the equipment for 2006 will be decreased by:

a   *20% of the gain on sale*
b   *33.33% of the gain on sale*
c   *50% of the gain on sale*
d   *100% of the gain on sale*

E 6-6
General problems

1. Schoenfeld Corporation is an 80%-owned subsidiary of Poindexter Corporation. In 2006, Schoenfeld sold land that cost $15,000 to Poindexter for $25,000. Poindexter held the land for eight years before reselling it in 2014 to Elroy Company, an unrelated entity, for $55,000. The consolidated income statement for Poindexter and its subsidiary, Schoenfeld, will show a gain on the sale of land of:

a   *$40,000*
b   *$32,000*
c   *$30,000*
d   *$24,000*

2. On January 3, 2008, Pella Corporation sells equipment with a book value of $90,000 to its 100%-owned subsidiary, Satterman Corporation, for $120,000. The equipment has a remaining useful life of three years with no salvage at the time of transfer. Satterman uses the straight-line method of depreciation. As a result of this intercompany transaction, Pella's Investment in Satterman account balance at December 31, 2008, will be:

a   *$20,000 greater than its underlying equity interest*
b   *$20,000 less than its underlying equity interest*
c   *$30,000 less than its underlying equity interest*
d   *$10,000 greater than its underlying equity interest*

3. Pentex Corporation sells equipment with a book value of $80,000 to Shirley Company, its 75%-owned subsidiary, for $100,000 on January 1, 2008. Shirley determines that the remaining useful life of the equipment is four years and that straight-line depreciation is appropriate. The December 31, 2008, *separate*-company financial statements of Pentex and Shirley show equipment—net of $500,000 and $300,000, respectively. Consolidated equipment—net will be:

a   *$800,000*
b   *$785,000*
c   *$780,000*
d   *$650,000*

4. Parolari Corporation sold equipment with a remaining three-year useful life and a book value of $14,500 to its 80%-owned subsidiary, Sarafin Corporation, for $16,000 on January 2, 2006. A consolidated working paper entry on December 31, 2006, to eliminate the unrealized profits from the intercompany sale of equipment will include:

a   *A debit to gain on sale of equipment for $1,000*
b   *A debit to gain on sale of equipment for $1,500*
c   *A credit to depreciation expense for $1,500*
d   *A debit to machinery for $1,500*

5. A subsidiary sells equipment with a four-year remaining useful life to its parent at a $12,000 gain on January 1, 2006. The effect of this intercompany transaction on the parent company's investment income from its subsidiary for 2006 will be:

a   *An increase of $12,000 if the subsidiary is 100% owned*
b   *An increase of $9,000 if the subsidiary is 100% owned*
c   *A decrease of $9,000 if the subsidiary is 100% owned*
d   *A decrease of $3,600 if the subsidiary is 60% owned*

6. On January 1, 2008, Sartin Corporation, a 60%-owned subsidiary of Pollyparts Company, sells a building with a book value of $300,000 to its parent for $350,000. At the time of sale, the building has an estimated remaining life of 10 years with no salvage value. Pollyparts uses straight-line depreciation. If Sartin reports net income of $1,000,000 for 2008, noncontrolling interest expense will be:

   a $450,000

   b $400,000

   c $382,000

   d $355,000

E 6-7

Consolidated income statement (sale of asset sold upstream 2 years earlier) A summary of the separate income of Pod Corporation and the net income of its 75%-owned subsidiary, Seiver Corporation, for 2006 is as follows:

7590

	Pod	Seiver
Sales	$500,000	$300,000
Gain on sale of machinery	10,000	
Cost of goods sold	(200,000)	(130,000)
Depreciation expense	(50,000)	(30,000)
Other expenses	(80,000)	(40,000)
Separate income (excludes investment income)	$180,000	$100,000

Seiver Corporation sold machinery with a book value of $40,000 to Pod Corporation for $65,000 on January 2, 2004. At the time of the intercompany sale, the machinery had a remaining useful life of five years. Pod uses straight-line depreciation. Pod used the machinery until December 28, 2006, when it was sold to another entity for $36,000.

REQUIRED: Prepare a consolidated income statement for Pod Corporation and Subsidiary for 2006.

E 6-8

Investment income from 40% investee (upstream and downstream sales) Pepper Corporation owns 40% of the outstanding voting stock of Salt Corporation, acquired for $100,000 on July 1, 2006, when Salt's common stockholders' equity was $200,000. The excess of investment cost over book value acquired was due to valuable patents owned by Salt that were expected to give Salt a competitive advantage until July 1, 2011.

Salt's net income for 2006 was $40,000 (for the entire year), and for 2007, Salt's net income was $60,000. Pepper's December 31, 2006 and 2007, inventories included unrealized profit on goods acquired from Salt in the amounts of $4,000 and $6,000, respectively. At December 31, 2006, Pepper sold land to Salt at a gain of $2,000. This land is still owned by Salt at December 31, 2007.

REQUIRED

1. Compute Pepper's investment income from Salt for 2006 on the basis of a one-line consolidation.

2. Compute Pepper's investment income from Salt for 2007 on the basis of a one-line consolidation.

E 6-9

Upstream sale of equipment, noncontrolling interest Plain Corporation has an 80% interest in Simple Corporation, its only subsidiary. The 80% interest was acquired on July 1, 2006, for $400,000, at which time Simple's equity consisted of $300,000 capital stock and $100,000 retained earnings. The excess of cost over book value was allocated to buildings with a 20-year remaining useful life.

On December 31, 2008, Simple sold equipment with a remaining useful life of four years to Plain at a gain of $20,000. Plain Corporation had separate income for 2008 of $500,000 and for 2009 of $600,000.

Income and retained earnings data for Simple Corporation for 2008 and 2009 are as follows:

	2008	2009
Retained earnings January 1	$150,000	$200,000
Add: Net income	100,000	110,000
Deduct: Dividends	−50,000	−60,000
Retained earnings December 31	$200,000	$250,000

REQUIRED

1. Compute Plain Corporation's income from Simple, net income, and consolidated net income for each of the years 2008 and 2009.

2. Compute the correct balances of Plain Corporation's investment in Simple at December 31, 2008 and 2009, assuming no changes in Simple's outstanding stock since Plain acquired its interest.

E 6-10

Inventory items of parent capitalized by subsidiary Ped Industries manufactures heavy equipment used in construction and excavation. On January 3, 2006, Ped sold a piece of equipment from its inventory that cost $180,000 to its 60%-owned subsidiary, Spano Corporation, at Ped's standard price of twice its cost. Spano is depreciating the equipment over six years using straight-line depreciation and no salvage value.

REQUIRED

1. Determine the net amount at which this equipment will be included in the consolidated balance sheets for Ped Industries and Subsidiary at December 31, 2006 and 2007.

2. Ped accounts for its investment in Spano as a one-line consolidation. Prepare the consolidation working paper entries related to this intercompany sale that are necessary to consolidate the financial statements of Ped and Spano at December 31, 2006 and 2007.

E 6-11

Consolidated net income (negative goodwill, upstream and downstream sales) Income data from the records of Pasco Corporation and Slocum Corporation, Pasco's 80%-owned subsidiary, for 2006 through 2009 follow (in thousands):

	2006	2007	2008	2009
Pasco's separate income	$200	$150	$40	$120
Slocum's net income	60	70	80	90

Pasco acquired its interest in Slocum on January 1, 2006, at a price of $40,000 *less* than book value. The $40,000 was assigned to a reduction of plant assets with a remaining useful life of 10 years.

On July 1, 2006, Slocum sold land that cost $25,000 to Pasco for $30,000. This land was resold by Pasco for $35,000 in 2009.

Pasco sold machinery to Slocum for $100,000 on January 2, 2007. This machinery had a book value of $75,000 at the time of sale and is being depreciated by Slocum at the rate of $20,000 per year.

Pasco's December 31, 2008, inventory included $8,000 unrealized profit on merchandise acquired from Slocum during 2008. This merchandise was sold by Pasco during 2009.

REQUIRED: Prepare a schedule to calculate the consolidated net income of Pasco Corporation and Subsidiary for each of the years 2006, 2007, 2008, and 2009.

PROBLEMS

P 6-1

Consolidated income statement (incomplete equity method, downstream sales)

The separate income statements of Pearl Corporation and its 90%-owned subsidiary, Sear Corporation, for 2006 are summarized as follows (in thousands):

	Pearl	Sear
Sales	$1,000	$600
Income from Sear	90	—
Gain on equipment	40	—
Cost of sales	(600)	(400)
Other expenses	(200)	(100)
Net income	$ 330	$100

Investigation reveals that the effects of certain intercompany transactions are not included in Pearl's income from Sear. Information about those intercompany transactions follows:

1. Inventories—Sales of inventory items from Pearl to Sear are summarized as follows:

	2005	2006
Intercompany sales	$100,000	$150,000
Cost of intercompany sales	60,000	90,000
Percentage unsold at year-end	50%	40%

2. Plant assets—Pearl sold equipment with a book value of $60,000 to Sear for $100,000 on January 1, 2006. Sear is depreciating the equipment on a straight-line basis (no scrap) over a four-year period.

REQUIRED

1. Determine the correct amount of Pearl's income from Sear for 2006.

2. Prepare a consolidated income statement for Pearl Corporation and Subsidiary for 2006.

P 6-2

Consolidated working paper (downstream sales, intercompany receivable/payable)
Sim Corporation, a 90%-owned subsidiary of Pal Corporation, was acquired on January 1, 2007, at a price of $40,000 in excess of underlying book value. The excess was allocated $20,000 to buildings with a five-year remaining useful life and $20,000 to goodwill. Separate company financial statements for Pal and Sim for 2008 are as follows (amounts in thousands):

	Pal	Sim
Combined Income and Retained Earnings Statement for the Year Ended December 31, 2008		
Sales	$300	$100
Income from Sim	27	—
Gain on sale of equipment	9	—
Cost of sales	(140)	(50)
Operating expenses	(60)	(10)
Net income	136	40
Add: Beginning retained earnings	148	70
Less: Dividends	(60)	(20)
Retained earnings, December 31, 2008	$224	$ 90
Balance Sheet at December 31, 2008		
Cash	$100	$ 17
Accounts receivable	90	50
Dividends receivable	9	—
Inventories	20	8
Land	40	15
Buildings—net	135	50
Equipment—net	165	60
Investment in Sim	145	—
Total assets	$704	$200
Accounts payable	$ 98	$ 30
Dividends payable	15	10
Other liabilities	67	20
Capital stock	300	50
Retained earnings	224	90
Total equities	$704	$200

ADDITIONAL INFORMATION

1. Pal sold inventory items to Sim during 2007 and 2008 as follows (in thousands):

	2007	2008
Sales	$30	$20
Cost of sales to Pal	15	10
Unrealized profit at December 31	5	4

2. Pal sold land that cost $7,000 to Sim for $10,000 during 2007. The land is still owned by Sim.

3. In January 2008, Pal sold equipment with a book value of $21,000 to Sim for $30,000. The equipment is being depreciated by Sim over a three-year period using the straight-line method.

4. On December 30, 2008, Sim remitted $2,000 to Pal for merchandise purchases. The remittance was not recorded by Pal until January 5, 2009, and it is not reflected in Pal's financial statements at December 31, 2008.

REQUIRED: Prepare consolidation working papers for Pal Corporation and Subsidiary for the year ended December 31, 2008.

P 6-3

Consolidated working paper (downstream sales, intercompany receivable/payable)

Pall Corporation acquired a 90% interest in Stor Corporation on January 1, 2006, for $236,000, at which time Stor's capital stock and retained earnings were $150,000 and $90,000, respectively. The $20,000 cost/book value differential is goodwill, which will not be amortized. Financial statements for Pall and Stor for 2007 are as follows (in thousands):

	Pall	Stor
Combined Income and Retained Earnings Statement for the Year Ended December 31, 2007		
Sales	$ 450	$190
Income from Stor	40	—
Gain on land	5	—
Cost of sales	(200)	(100)
Operating expenses	(113)	(40)
Net income	182	50
Add: Retained earnings January 1	202	120
Less: Dividends	(150)	(20)
Retained earnings, December 31, 2007	$ 234	$150
Balance Sheet at December 31, 2007		
Cash	$ 167	$ 14
Accounts receivable	180	100
Dividends receivable	18	—
Inventories	60	36
Land	100	30
Buildings—net	280	80
Machinery—net	330	140
Investment in Stor	269	—
	$1,404	$400
Accounts payable	$ 200	$ 50
Dividends payable	30	20
Other liabilities	140	30
Capital stock	800	150
Retained earnings	234	150
	$1,404	$400

ADDITIONAL INFORMATION

1. Pall sold inventory items to Stor for $60,000 during 2006 and $72,000 during 2007. Stor's inventories at December 31, 2006 and 2007, included unrealized profits of $10,000 and $12,000, respectively.

2. On July 1, 2006, Pall Corporation sold machinery with a book value of $28,000 to Stor for $35,000. The machinery had a useful life of 3.5 years at the time of intercompany sale, and straight-line depreciation is used.

3. During 2007, Pall sold land with a book value of $15,000 to Stor for $20,000.

4. Pall's accounts receivable on December 31, 2007, includes $10,000 due from Stor Corporation.

5. Pall uses the equity method of accounting for its 90% interest in Stor.

REQUIRED: Prepare consolidation working papers for Pall Corporation and Subsidiary for the year ended December 31, 2007.

P 6-4

Working papers in year of acquisition (equity method, downstream sales) Parch Corporation acquired a 90% interest in Sarg Corporation's outstanding voting common stock on January 1, 2006, for $630,000 cash. The stockholders' equity of Sarg on this date consisted of $500,000 capital stock and $200,000 retained earnings.

The separate financial statements of Parch and Sarg Corporations at and for the year ended December 31, 2006, are summarized as follows (in thousands):

90%

	Parch	Sarg
Combined Income and Retained Earnings Statement for the Year Ended December 31, 2006		
Sales	$ 700	$ 500
Income from Sarg	70 ✓	—
Gain on land	—	10
Gain on equipment	20	—
Cost of sales	(300)	(300)
Depreciation expense	(90)	(35)
Other expenses	(200)	(65)
Net income	200	110
Beginning retained earnings	600	200
Dividends	(100)	(50)
Retained earnings December 31, 2006	$ 700	$ 260
Balance Sheet at December 31, 2006		
Cash	$ 35	$ 30
Accounts receivable—net	90	110
Inventories	100	80
Other current items	70	40
Land	50	70
Buildings—net	200	150
Equipment—net	500	400
Investment in Sarg	655 ✓	—
	$1,700	$ 880
Accounts payable	$ 160	$ 50
Other liabilities	340	70
Capital stock, $10 par	500	500
Retained earnings	700	260
	$1,700	$ 880

During 2006, Parch made sales of $50,000 to Sarg at a gross profit of $15,000. One-third of these sales were inventoried by Sarg at year-end. Sarg owed Parch $10,000 on open account at December 31, 2006.

Sarg sold land that cost $20,000 to Parch for $30,000 on July 1, 2006. Parch still owns the land. On January 1, 2006, Parch sold equipment with a book value of $20,000 and a remaining useful life of four years to Sarg for $40,000. Sarg uses straight-line depreciation and assumes no salvage value on this equipment.

REQUIRED: Prepare consolidation working papers for Parch Corporation and Subsidiary for the year ended December 31, 2006.

P 6-5

Working papers (downstream sales) Sim Corporation, a 90%-owned subsidiary of Pal Corporation, was acquired on January 1, 2007, at a price $40,000 in excess of underlying book value. The excess was allocated $20,000 to buildings with a 5-year remaining useful life and $20,000 to patents with a 10-year amortization period. Separate-company financial statements for Pal and Sim for 2008 are as follows (in thousands):

	Pal	Sim
Combined Income and Retained Earnings Statement for the Year Ended December 31, 2008		
Sales	$300	$100
Income from Sim	25	—

	Pal	Sim
Gain on sale of equipment	9	—
Cost of sales	(140)	(50)
Operating expenses	(60)	(10)
Net income	134	40
Add: Beginning retained earnings	146	70
Less: Dividends	(60)	(20)
Retained earnings, December 31, 2008	$220	$ 90
Balance Sheet at December 31, 2008		
Cash	$100	$ 17
Accounts receivable	90	50
Dividends receivable	9	—
Inventories	20	8
Land	40	15
Buildings—net	135	50
Equipment—net	165	60
Investment in Sim	141	—
Total assets	$700	$200
Accounts payable	$ 98	$ 30
Dividends payable	15	10
Other liabilities	67	20
Capital stock	300	50
Retained earnings	220	90
Total equities	$700	$200

ADDITIONAL INFORMATION

1. Pal sold inventory items to Sim during 2007 and 2008 as follows:

	2007	2008
Sales	$30,000	$20,000
Cost of sales to Pal	15,000	10,000
Unrealized profit at December 3	5,000	4,000

2. Pal sold land that cost $7,000 to Sim for $10,000 during 2007. The land is still owned by Sim.

3. In January 2008, Pal sold equipment with a book value of $21,000 to Sim for $30,000. The equipment is being depreciated by Sim over a three-year period using the straight-line method.

4. On December 30, 2008, Sim remitted $2,000 to Pal for merchandise purchases. The remittance was not recorded by Pal until January 5, 2009, and it is not reflected in Pal's financial statements at December 31, 2008.

REQUIRED: Prepare consolidation working papers for Pal Corporation and Subsidiary for the year ended December 31, 2008.

P 6-6

Working papers (downstream sales, two years) Pall Corporation acquired a 90% interest in Stor Corporation on January 1, 2006, for $236,000, at which time Stor's capital stock and retained earnings were $150,000 and $90,000, respectively. The $20,000 cost/book value differential is assigned to a patent with a 10-year amortization period. Financial statements for Pall and Stor for 2007 are as follows (in thousands):

	Pall	Stor
Combined Income and Retained Earnings Statement for the Year Ended December 31, 2007		
Sales	$ 450	$190
Income from Stor	38	—
Gain on land	5	—
Cost of sales	(200)	(100)
Operating expenses	(113)	(40)
Net income	180	50
Add: Retained earnings January 1	200	120

(continued)

	Pal	Sim
Less: Dividends	(150)	(20)
Retained earnings, December 31, 2007	$ 230	$150
Balance Sheet at December 31, 2007		
Cash	$ 167	$ 14
Accounts receivable	180	100
Dividends receivable	18	—
Inventories	60	36
Land	100	30
Buildings—net	280	80
Machinery—net	330	140
Investment in Stor	265	—
	$1,400	$400
Accounts payable	$ 200	$ 50
Dividends payable	30	20
Other liabilities	140	30
Capital stock	800	150
Retained earnings	230	150
	$1,400	$400

ADDITIONAL INFORMATION

1. Pall sold inventory items to Stor for $60,000 during 2006 and $72,000 during 2007, Stor's inventories at December 31, 2006 and 2007, included unrealized profits of $10,000 and $12,000, respectively.

2. On July 1, 2006, Pall Corporation sold machinery with a book value of $28,000 to Stor for $35,000. The machinery had a useful life of 3.5 years at the time of intercompany sale, and straight-line depreciation is used.

3. During 2007, Pall sold land with a book value of $15,000 to Stor for $20,000.

4. Pall's accounts receivable on December 31, 2007, includes $10,000 due from Stor Corporation.

5. Pall uses the equity method of accounting for its 90% interest in Stor.

REQUIRED: Prepare consolidation working papers for Pall Corporation and Subsidiary for the year ended December 31, 2007.

P 6-7

Working papers (cost/book value differential, downstream and upstream sales)

Financial statements for Pill Corporation and Sank Corporation for 2006 are summarized as follows (in thousands):

	Pill	Sank
Combined Income and Retained Earnings Statement for the Year Ended December 31, 2006		
Sales	$210	$130
Income from Sank	31.9	—
Gain on sale of land	—	10
Depreciation expense	(40)	(30)
Other expenses	(110)	(60)
Net income	91.9	50
Add: Beginning retained earnings	140.4	50
Deduct: Dividends	(30)	—
Retained earnings December 31, 2006	$202.3	$100
Balance Sheet at December 31, 2006		
Current assets	$200	$170
Plant assets	550	350
Accumulated depreciation	(120)	(70)
Investment in Sank	322.3	—
Total assets	$952.3	$450
Current liabilities	$150	$ 50
Capital stock	600	300
Retained earnings	202.3	100
Total equities	$952.3	$450

ADDITIONAL INFORMATION

1. Pill acquired an 80% interest in Sank on January 2, 2004, for $290,000, when Sank's stockholders' equity consisted of $300,000 capital stock and no retained earnings. The excess of investment cost over book value of the net assets acquired related 50% to undervalued inventories (subsequently sold in 2004) and 50% to a patent with a 10-year amortization period.

2. Sank sold equipment to Pill for $25,000 on January 1, 2005, at which time the equipment had a book value of $10,000 and a five-year remaining useful life (included in plant assets in the financial statements).

3. During 2006, Sank sold land to Pill at a profit of $10,000 (included in plant assets in the financial statement).

4. Pill uses the equity method in accounting for its investment in Sank.

REQUIRED: Prepare consolidation working papers for Pill Corporation and Subsidiary for the year ended December 31, 2006.

P 6-8

Working papers (downstream and upstream sales) Port Corporation acquired all the outstanding stock of Skip Corporation on April 1, 2006, for $15,000,000, when Skip's stockholders' equity consisted of $5,000,000 capital stock and $2,000,000 retained earnings. The purchase price reflected a $500,000 undervaluation of Skip's inventory on this date (sold in 2006) and a $3,500,000 undervaluation of Skip's buildings (remaining useful life seven years from April 1, 2006). Goodwill from the acquisition is not amortized.

During 2007, Skip sold land that cost $1,000,000 to Port for $1,500,000. Port resold the land for $2,200,000 during 2010.

Port sells inventory items to Skip on a regular basis. Information relevant to such sales is as follows (in thousands):

	Sales to Skip	Cost to Port	Percentage Unsold by Skip at Year End	Percentage Unpaid by Skip at Year End
2006	$ 500	$300	0%	0%
2007	1,000	600	30	50
2008	1,200	720	18	30
2009	1,000	600	25	20
2010	1,500	900	20	20

Skip sold equipment with a book value of $800,000 to Port on January 3, 2008, for $1,600,000. This equipment had a remaining useful life of four years at the time of sale.

Port uses the equity method of accounting for its investment in Skip. The financial statements for Port and Skip Corporations are summarized as follows (in thousands):

	Port	Skip
Combined Income and Retained Earnings Statement for the Year Ended December 31, 2010		
Sales	$26,000	$11,000
Gain on land	700	—
Gain on equipment	—	800
Income from Skip	1,380	—
Cost of sales	(15,000)	(5,000)
Depreciation expense	(3,700)	(2,000)
Other expenses	(4,280)	(2,800)
Net income	5,100	2,000
Add: Beginning retained earnings	12,375	4,000
Deduct: Dividends	(3,000)	(1,000)
Retained earnings December 31, 2010	$14,475	$ 5,000
Balance Sheet at December 31, 2010		
Cash	$ 1,170	$ 500
Accounts receivable—net	2,000	1,500
Inventories	5,000	2,000
Land	4,000	1,000
Buildings—net	15,000	4,000

(continued)

	Port	Skip
Equipment—net	10,000	4,000
Investment in Skip	14,405	—
Total assets	$51,575	$13,000
Accounts payable	$ 4,100	$ 1,000
Other liabilities	7,000	2,000
Capital stock	26,000	5,000
Retained earnings	14,475	5,000
Total equities	$51,575	$13,000

REQUIRED: Prepare consolidation working papers for Port Corporation and Subsidiary for the year ended December 31, 2010.

P 6-9

Working papers (incomplete equity method, upstream sale) Pic Corporation acquired an 80% interest in Sic Company on January 1, 2006, for $136,000. Sic's capital stock and retained earnings on that date were $100,000 and $70,000, respectively.

At the beginning of 2006, Sic sold a machine to Pic for $10,000. The machine had cost Sic $7,000, had depreciated $2,000 while being used by Sic, and had a remaining useful life of five years from the date of sale.

Trial balances of the two companies on December 31, 2006 and 2007, are as follows (in thousands):

	2006		2007	
	Pic	Sic	Pic	Sic
Debits				
Cash and equivalents	$ 50	$ 30	$ 63	$ 30
Other current assets	130	70	140	80
Plant and equipment	400	200	440	245
Investment in Sic	160	—	192	—
Cost of sales	250	130	260	140
Depreciation expense	50	25	50	25
Other expenses	60	20	55	30
	$1,100	$475	$1,200	$550
Credits				
Accumulated depreciation	$ 150	$ 50	$ 200	$ 75
Liabilities	100	50	48	40
Capital stock	300	100	300	100
Retained earnings	126	70	190	100
Sales	400	200	430	235
Gain on plant asset	—	5	—	—
Income from Sic	24	—	32	—
	$1,100	$475	$1,200	$550

REQUIRED: Prepare consolidation working papers for Pic Corporation and Subsidiary for the year ended December 31, 2006, and the year ended December 31, 2007.

P 6-10

Working papers (upstream sales current and previous years) Park Corporation acquired an 80% interest in Spin Corporation on January 1, 2006, for $108,000 cash, when Spin's capital stock was $100,000 and retained earnings were $10,000. The difference between investment cost and book value acquired is attributed to a patent being amortized over a 10-year period.

Separate-company financial statements for Park and Spin Corporation on December 31, 2009, are summarized as follows (in thousands):

	Park	Spin
Combined Income and Retained Earnings Statement for the Year Ended December 31, 2009		
Sales	$650	$120
Income from Spin	42 ✓	—

	Park	Spin
Cost of sales	(390)	(40)
Other expenses	(170)	(30)
Net income	132	50
Add: Beginning retained earnings	95.6	20
Deduct: Dividends	(70)	(20)
Retained earnings December 31, 2009	$157.6	$ 50
Balance Sheet at December 31, 2009		
Cash	$ 58	$ 20
Accounts receivable	40	20
Inventories	60	35
Plant assets	290	205
Accumulated depreciation	(70)	(100)
Investment in Spin	121.6 ✓	—
Total assets	$499.6	$180
Accounts payable	$ 42	$ 30
Capital stock	300	100
Retained earnings	157.6	50
Total equities	$499.6	$180

Handwritten margin note:

NCIE =
50,000 Net Inc
+ 2,000 2008 Inventory Profit
− 1,000 2009 Inventory Profit
+ 4,000 Piecemeal Recog
55,000
× 20%
11,000

ADDITIONAL INFORMATION

1. Spin's sales include intercompany sales of $8,000, and Park's December 31, 2009, inventory includes $1,000 profit on goods acquired from Spin. Park's December 31, 2008, inventory contained $2,000 profit on goods acquired from Spin.

2. Park owes Spin $4,000 on account.

3. On January 1, 2008, Spin sold plant assets to Park for $60,000. These assets had a book value of $40,000 on that date and are being depreciated by Park over a five-year period.

4. Park uses the equity method to account for its investment in Spin.

REQUIRED: Prepare consolidation working papers for Park Corporation and Subsidiary for 2009.

P 6-11

Consolidation working papers (upstream sales) Financial statements for Pill

Corporation and Sank Corporation for 2006 are summarized as follows (in thousands):

	Pill	Sank
Combined Income and Retained Earnings Statement for the Year Ended December 31, 2006		
Sales	$210	$130
Income from Sank	34.4	—
Gain on sale of land	—	10
Depreciation expense	(40)	(30)
Other expenses	(110)	(60)
Net income	94.4	50
Add: Beginning retained earnings	145.4	50
Deduct: Dividends	(30)	—
Retained earnings December 31, 2006	$209.8	$100
Balance Sheet at December 31, 2006		
Current assets	$200	$170
Plant assets	550	350
Accumulated depreciation	(120)	(70)
Investment in Sank	329.8	—
Total assets	$959.8	$450
Current liabilities	$150	$ 50
Capital stock	600	300
Retained earnings	209.8	100
Total equities	$959.8	$450

ADDITIONAL INFORMATION

1. Pill acquired an 80% interest in Sank on January 2, 2004, for $290,000, when Sank's stockholders' equity consisted of $300,000 capital stock and no retained earnings. The excess of investment cost over book value of the net assets acquired related 50% to undervalued inventories (subsequently sold in 2004) and 50% to goodwill (which will not be amortized).

2. Sank sold equipment to Pill for $25,000 on January 1, 2005, at which time the equipment had a book value of $10,000 and a five-year remaining useful life (included in plant assets in the financial statements).

3. During 2006, Sank sold land to Pill at a profit of $10,000 (included in plant assets in the financial statements).

4. Pill uses the equity method in accounting for its investment in Sank.

REQUIRED: Prepare consolidation working papers for Pill Corporation and Subsidiary for the year ended December 31, 2006.

P 6-12

Analyze provided separate company and consolidated statements Separate company and consolidated financial statements for Pape Corporation and its only subsidiary, Sach Corporation, for 2007 are summarized here. Pape acquired its interest in Sach on January 1, 2006, at a price in excess of book value, which was due to an unrecorded patent.

Pape Corporation and Subsidiary Separate Company and Consolidated Financial Statements at and for the Year Ended December 31, 2007 (in thousands)

	Pape	Sach	Consolidated
Income Statement			
Sales	$ 500	$300	$ 716
Income from Sach	17	—	—
Gain on equipment	20	—	—
Cost of sales	(200)	(150)	(275)
Depreciation expense	(60)	(40)	(95)
Other expenses	(77)	(60)	(141)
Noncontrolling interest expense	—	—	(5)
Net income	$ 200	$ 50	$ 200
Retained Earnings			
Retained earnings	$ 250	$120	$ 250
Net income	200	50	200
Dividends	(100)	(30)	(100)
Retained earnings	$ 350	$140	$ 350
Balance Sheet			
Cash	$ 17.5	$ 35	$ 52.5
Accounts receivable—net	50	30	70
Dividends receivable	13.5	—	—
Inventories	90	60	136
Other current assets	70	40	110
Land	50	20	70
Buildings—net	100	50	150
Equipment—net	300	265	550
Investment in Sach	309	—	—
Patents	—	—	32
Total assets	$1,000	$500	$1,170.5
Accounts payable	$ 60	$ 50	$ 100
Dividends payable	—	15	1.5
Other liabilities	90	95	185
Capital stock, $10 par	500	200	500
Retained earnings	350	140	350
Noncontrolling interest December 31, 2007	—	—	34
Total equities	$1,000	$500	$1,170.5

REQUIRED: Answer the following questions about the financial statements of Pape and Sach.

1. What is Pape Corporation's percentage interest in Sach Corporation? Provide a computation to explain your answer.

2. Does Pape use a one-line consolidation in accounting for its investment in Sach? Explain your answer.

3. Were there intercompany sales between Pape and Sach in 2007? If so, show computations.

4. Are there unrealized inventory profits on December 31, 2007? If so, show computations.

5. Provide computations to explain the difference between the combined separate-company cost of sales and consolidated cost of sales.

6. Explain the difference between combined separate-company and the consolidated "equipment—net" line item by reconstructing the working paper entry(s) that was (were) apparently made.

7. Are there intercompany receivables and payables? If so, identify them and state their amounts.

8. Beginning with the noncontrolling interest at January 1, 2007, provide calculations of the $34,000 non-controlling interest at December 31, 2007.

9. What was the amount of patents at December 31, 2006? Show computations.

10. Provide computations to explain the $309,000 Investment in Sach account balance on December 31, 2007.

INTERNET ASSIGNMENT

Chapter 5 mentioned that some companies, such as **SBC Communications**, provide consolidating statements of income, providing another source of information about intercompany transactions. SBC also provides condensed consolidating balance sheets. Obtain the SBC 2003 annual report from the company's Web site. What information do you find indicating the amount of deferred profit on intercompany asset transfers during 2003?

7 CHAPTER

INTERCOMPANY PROFIT TRANSACTIONS—BONDS

LEARNING OBJECTIVES

1 Differentiate between intercompany receivables and payables, and assets or liabilities of the consolidated reporting entity.

2 Defer unrealized profits and later recognize realized profits on bond transfers between parent and subsidiary companies.

3 Demonstrate how a consolidated reporting entity constructively retires debt.

4 Adjust calculation of noncontrolling interest amounts in the presence of intercompany profits on debt transfers.

5 Electronic supplement: Account for bond transactions by both investors and issuers.

6 Electronic supplement: Understand differences in consolidation techniques for debt transfers when the parent company uses either an incomplete equity method or the cost method.

Companies frequently hold the debt instruments of affiliates and justify such intercompany borrowing and lending activity on the basis of convenience, efficiency, and flexibility. Even though each affiliate is a separate legal entity, the parent company is in a position to negotiate all loans between affiliated companies, and a decision to borrow from or loan directly to affiliates is really only a decision to transfer funds among affiliates. Direct loans among affiliates produce reciprocal receivable and payable accounts for both principal and interest, as well as reciprocal income and expense accounts. Companies eliminate these reciprocal accounts in preparing consolidated financial statements because the intercompany receivables and payables do not reflect assets or obligations of the consolidated entity.

Special problems of accounting for intercompany bonds and notes arise when one company purchases the debt instruments of an affiliate from outside entities. Such purchases constitute a retirement of debt from the viewpoint of the consolidated entity, even though the debt remains outstanding from the viewpoint of the debtor corporation as a separate legal entity. That is, the issuing affiliate (debtor corporation) accounts for its debt obligations as if they were held by unaffiliated entities, and the purchasing affiliate accounts for its investment in the affiliate's obligations as if they were the obligations of unaffiliated entities. Consolidated statements, however, show the financial position and results of operations as if the issuing corporation had purchased and retired its own debt.

Prior experience teaching this material indicates that students often have difficulty with this chapter due to a lack of familiarity with the basics of accounting for bond transactions. You may want to review the bond accounting information included in the Electronic supplement to Chapter 7 (on the Advanced Accounting Web site) before continuing with this chapter.

INTERCOMPANY BOND TRANSACTIONS

LEARNING OBJECTIVE 1

At the time a company issues bonds, its bond liability will reflect the current market rate of interest. However, subsequent changes in the market rate of interest will create a disparity between the book value and the market value of that liability. If the market rate of interest increases, the market value of the liability will be less than book value and the issuing company will have *realized* a gain as a result. The gain is *not recognized* on the issuing company's books under generally accepted accounting principles. Similarly, a decline in the market rate of interest gives rise to a *realized* loss that is *not recognized*. These realized but unrecognized gains and losses are disclosed in the financial statements or footnotes in accordance with *FASB Statement No. 107,* "Disclosure About Fair Value of Financial Instruments."

A firm can recognize realized but unrecognized gains or losses on outstanding bonds by retiring the outstanding bonds. The parent company, which controls all debt retirement and other decisions for the consolidated entity, has the following options:

1. The *issuing company* (parent or subsidiary) can use its available resources to purchase and *retire its own bonds.*

2. The *issuing company* (parent or subsidiary) can borrow money from unaffiliated entities at the market rate of interest and use the proceeds to *retire its own bonds.* (This option constitutes refunding.)

3. The *issuing company* can borrow money from an affiliated company and use the proceeds to *retire its own bonds.*

4. An *affiliated company* (parent or subsidiary) can purchase the bonds of the issuing company, in which case the bonds are *constructively retired.*

The first three options result in an **actual retirement** of the bonds. The issuing company recognizes the previously unrecognized gain or loss in these three situations and includes it appropriately in measuring consolidated net income. The fourth option results in a **constructive retirement**. This means that the bonds are retired for consolidated statement purposes because the bond investment and the bonds payable items of the parent and the subsidiary are reciprocals that must be eliminated in the consolidation process. The difference between the book value of the bond liability and the purchase price of the bond investment is a gain or loss for consolidated statement purposes. It is also a gain or loss for parent-company accounting under the equity method (one-line consolidation). The gain or loss is not recognized on the books of the issuing company, whose bonds are held as an investment by the purchasing affiliate.

Although the constructive retirement is different in form, the substance of the debt extinguishment is the same as for the other three options from the viewpoint of the consolidated entity. Also, the effect of a constructive retirement on consolidated statements is the same as for an actual retirement. The gain or loss is a gain or loss of the issuing company that has been realized by changes in the market rate of interest after the bonds were issued, and it is recognized for consolidated statement purposes when the bonds are repurchased and held within the consolidated entity.

Early extinguishment of debt is the most common type of extraordinary gain or loss reported in published financial statements. The American Institute of Certified Public Accountants' (AICPA) *Accounting Trends & Techniques 2003* reports that 42 extraordinary items were disclosed by sample firms in 2002 annual reports. Of these, 40 were due to debt extinguishment.

For example, **Lockheed Martin Corporation** issued a press release on December 19, 2000, announcing a repurchase of $1.9 billion in outstanding debt obligations, expected to result in an after-tax loss of $95 million. A July 26, 2001, press release by **Chesapeake Energy Corporation** revealed a $46 million after-tax extraordinary loss on early extinguishment of debt in the quarter ended June 30, 2001. In its 2002 annual report (Note 11), **Sprint Corporation** reported an extraordinary gain of $3 million (after tax) from early debt extinguishment.

Perhaps early debt extinguishment is not so extraordinary after all. In fact, the FASB changed the rules in April 2002, issuing *FASB Statement No. 145*. For fiscal years beginning after May 15, 2002, a firm may classify debt extinguishment as extraordinary only if the transaction meets the "unusual and infrequent" criteria of *APB Opinion No. 30*. Most future debt extinguishment will require classification as ordinary gains or losses.

CONSTRUCTIVE GAINS AND LOSSES ON INTERCOMPANY BONDS

If the price paid by one affiliate to acquire the debt of another is greater than the book value of the liability (par value plus unamortized premium or less unamortized discount and issuance costs), a constructive loss on the retirement of debt occurs. Alternatively, if the price paid is less than the book value of the debt, a constructive gain results. The gain or loss is referred to as *constructive* because it is a gain or loss that is realized and recognized from the viewpoint of the consolidated entity, but it is not recorded on the separate books of the affiliated companies at the time of purchase.

Constructive gains and losses on bonds are (1) realized gains and losses from the consolidated viewpoint (2) that arise when a company purchases the bonds of an affiliate (3) from other entities (4) at a price other than the book value of the bonds. No gains or losses result from the purchase of an affiliate's bonds at book value or from direct lending and borrowing between affiliated companies.

Some accounting theorists argue that constructive gains and losses on intercompany bond transactions should be allocated between the purchasing and issuing affiliates according to the par value of the bonds. For example, if Parent Company pays $99,000 for $100,000 par of Subsidiary

Company's outstanding bonds with $2,000 unamortized premium, they would allocate the $3,000 constructive gain ($102,000 less $99,000) $1,000 to Parent and $2,000 to Subsidiary. This is known as the **par value theory**.

The alternative to the par value theory is the **agency theory**, under which the affiliate that purchases the intercompany bonds acts as agent for the issuing company, under directions from Parent Company management. Agency theory assigns the $3,000 constructive gain to Subsidiary Company (the issuing company), and the consolidated statement effect is the same as if Subsidiary Company had purchased its own bonds for $99,000. Although not supported by a separate theory, constructive gains and losses are sometimes assigned 100% to the parent company on the basis of expediency. The accounting is less complicated.

Changes in market interest rates generate gains and losses for the issuing company, so accounting procedures should assign such gains and losses to the issuing affiliate, irrespective of the form of the transaction (direct retirement by the issuing company or purchase by an affiliate). Failure to assign the full amount of a constructive gain or loss to the issuing affiliate results in recognizing form over substance in debt retirement transactions. The substance of a transaction should be considered over its form (incidentally, this is what consolidation is all about); therefore, the agency theory is conceptually superior, and, accordingly, we assign constructive gains and losses to the issuing affiliate in this book.

Most corporate long-term debt is in the form of outstanding bonds, so the analysis in this chapter relates to bonds even though it also applies to other types of debt instruments. Straight-line rather than effective interest amortization of premiums and discounts is used in the illustrations throughout the chapter to make the illustrations easier to follow and to help students learn the concepts involved without the added complexity of effective interest computations. It should be understood that the *effective interest method is generally superior* to the straight-line method.[1] This discussion of intercompany bond transactions among affiliated companies also applies to companies accounted for under the equity method.

The first illustration in this section assumes that the subsidiary purchases parent-company bonds (the parent company is the issuer) and assigns the constructive gain or loss to the parent company. In the second illustration, the parent company purchases bonds issued by the subsidiary, and we assign the constructive gain or loss to the subsidiary.

Acquisition of Parent-Company Bonds

LEARNING OBJECTIVE **2**

Sugar Corporation is an 80%-owned affiliate of Peach Corporation, and Peach sells $1,000,000 par of 10%, 10-year bonds at par value to the public on January 2, 2006. One year later, on December 31, 2006, Sugar purchases $100,000 of these outstanding bonds for $104,500 through the bond market. The purchase by Sugar results in the constructive retirement of $100,000 of Peach bonds and a constructive loss of $4,500 ($104,500 paid to retire bonds with a book value of $100,000).

Peach adjusts its investment income and investment accounts at December 31, 2006, to record the constructive loss under the equity method of accounting. The entry on Peach's books is:

Income from Sugar (−R, −SE)	4,500	
Investment in Sugar (−A)		4,500
To adjust income from Sugar for the constructive loss on bonds.		

Without this entry, the income of Peach on an equity basis would not equal consolidated net income.

We charge the $4,500 constructive loss against Peach's share of Sugar's reported income because Peach is the bond issuer. Agency theory assigns the full amount of any constructive gain or loss on bonds to the issuing affiliate. The parent company is the issuing affiliate, so the analysis is similar to one for a downstream sale, and we charge the full amount to Peach and to consolidated net income.

The $4,500 constructive loss appears in the consolidated income statement of Peach Corporation and Subsidiary for 2006, and the 10% bond issue is reported at $900,000 in the consolidated balance sheet at December 31, 2006. The following working paper adjustment accomplishes this:

---

[1] *APB Opinion No. 21,* "Interest on Receivables and Payables," which generally requires the effective interest method of amortization, does not apply to "transactions between parent and subsidiary companies and between subsidiaries of a common parent" (paragraph 3f).

Loss on constructive retirement of bonds (Lo, −SE)	**4,500**	
10% Bonds payable (−L)	**100,000**	
Investment in bonds (−A)		**104,500**
To enter loss and eliminate reciprocal bond investment and liability amounts.		

Acquisition of Subsidiary Bonds

Assume that Sugar sold $1,000,000 par of 10%, 10-year bonds to the public on January 2, 2006, and that Peach acquires $100,000 par of these bonds for $104,500 on December 31, 2006, in the bond market. The purchase by Peach results in a constructive retirement of $100,000 par of Sugar bonds and a constructive loss of $4,500 to the consolidated entity. We charge only 80% of the constructive loss to majority stockholders because the purchase of subsidiary bonds is equivalent to an upstream sale, in which the intercompany transactions affect noncontrolling interest expense.

In accounting for its investment in Sugar under the equity method, Peach recognizes 80% of the constructive loss with the following entry:

Income from Sugar (−R, −SE)	3,600	
Investment in Sugar (−A)		3,600

The consolidation working paper adjustment in the year of the intercompany bond purchase is the same as that illustrated for the intercompany purchase of Peach bonds. However, the $3,600 decrease in consolidated net income (to equate it with the one-line consolidation effect) consists of the $4,500 constructive loss less the $900 noncontrolling interest share of the loss, which reduces noncontrolling interest expense and thereby increases consolidated net income.

To summarize, when the parent company is the issuing affiliate, no allocation of gains and losses from intercompany bond transactions is necessary. When the subsidiary is the issuing affiliate, intercompany gains and losses on bonds must be allocated between consolidated net income and noncontrolling interest expense in the consolidated income statement. In a one-line consolidation, the parent company recognizes only its proportionate share of the constructive gain or loss on bonds issued by a subsidiary.

PARENT-COMPANY BONDS PURCHASED BY SUBSIDIARY

A constructive retirement of parent-company bonds occurs when an affiliate purchases the outstanding bonds of the parent. The purchasing subsidiary records the amount paid as an investment in bonds. This is the only entry made by either the purchasing or the issuing affiliate at the time of the intercompany purchase. The separate accounts of the affiliated companies do *not* record any gain or loss that results from the constructive retirement. The difference between the bond liability and bond investment accounts on the books of the parent and subsidiary companies reflects the constructive gain or loss.

To illustrate, assume that Sue is a 70%-owned subsidiary of Pam, acquired at its $5,600,000 book value on December 31, 2006, when Sue had capital stock of $5,000,000 and retained earnings of $3,000,000.

Pam has $10,000,000 par of 10% bonds outstanding with a $100,000 unamortized premium on January 1, 2008, at which time Sue Company purchases $1,000,000 par of these bonds for $950,000 from an investment broker. This purchase results in a constructive retirement of 10% of Pam's bonds and a $60,000 constructive gain, computed as follows:

Book value of bonds purchased	$1,010,000
[10% × ($10,000,000 par + $100,000 premium)]	
Purchase price	950,000
Constructive gain on bond retirement	$ 60,000

The only entry Sue makes when purchasing the Pam bonds is:

Investment in Pam bonds (+A)	950,000	
Cash (−A)		950,000
To record acquisition of Pam bonds at 95.		

Equity Method

If we prepare consolidated financial statements immediately after the constructive retirement, the working paper entry to eliminate the intercompany bond investment and liability balances includes the $60,000 gain as follows:

January 1, 2008		
10% bonds payable (−L)	1,010,000	
Investment in Pam bonds (+A)		950,000
Gain on retirement of bonds (Ga, +SE)		60,000

As a result of this working paper entry, the consolidated income statement reflects the gain and eliminates the investment in Pam bonds, and the consolidated balance sheet shows the bond liability to holders outside the consolidated entity at $9,090,000 ($9,000,000 par plus $90,000 unamortized premium).

During 2008, Pam amortizes the bond premium on its separate books and Sue amortizes the discount on its bond investment. Assuming that interest is paid on January 1 and July 1, that the bonds mature on January 1, 2013 (five years after purchase), and that straight-line amortization is used, Pam amortizes 20% of the bond premium and Sue amortizes 20% of the discount as follows:

PAM'S BOOKS

July 1		
Interest expense (E, −SE)	500,000	
Cash (−A)		500,000
($10,000,000 par × 10% × 1/2 year)		
December 31		
Interest expense (E, −SE)	500,000	
Interest payable (+L)		500,000
($10,000,000 par × 10% × 1/2 year)		
December 31		
Bonds payable (−L)	20,000	
Interest expense (−E, +SE)		20,000
($100,000 premium ÷ 5 years)		

SUE'S BOOKS

July 1		
Cash (+A)	50,000	
Interest income (R, +SE)		50,000
($1,000,000 par × 10% × 1/2 year)		
December 31		
Interest receivable (+A)	50,000	
Interest income (R, +SE)		50,000
($1,000,000 par × 10% × 1/2 year)		
December 31		
Investment in Pam bonds (+A)	10,000	
Interest income (R, +SE)		10,000
($50,000 discount ÷ 5 years)		

At December 31, 2008, after posting the forgoing entries, the ledgers of Pam and Sue show the following balances:

Pam's Books
10% Bonds payable (including $80,000 unamortized premium) $10,080,000
Interest expense   980,000

Sue's Books
Investment in Pam bonds $ 960,000
Interest income $ 110,000

The difference between the bond investment ($960,000) and 10% of Pam's bond liability ($1,008,000) is now $48,000 rather than $60,000. The reason is that there has been a piecemeal realization and recognition of the constructive gain on the separate books of Pam and Sue. This piecemeal recognition occurred during 2008 as Pam amortized the $2,000 premium and Sue amortized the $10,000 discount on bonds that were constructively retired on January 1, 2008. This difference is reflected in interest expense and interest income accounts relating to the constructively retired bonds. That is, interest income of $110,000 less 10% of $980,000 interest expense equals $12,000, or 20% of the original constructive gain. The working paper entries to eliminate reciprocal bond accounts at December 31, 2008, are:

a	**10% Bonds payable (–L)**	**1,008,000**	
	Investment in Pam bonds (–A)		**960,000**
	Gain on retirement of bonds (Ga, +SE)		**48,000**
b	**Interest income (–R, –SE)**	**110,000**	
	Interest expense (–E, +SE)		**98,000**
	Gain on retirement of bonds (Ga, +SE)		**12,000**
c	**Interest payable (–L)**	**50,000**	
	Interest receivable (–A)		**50,000**

Because 2008 is the year in which the bonds are constructively retired, the combined gain that is entered by these working paper entries is $60,000, the original gain. If the working paper entries were combined, the gain would appear as a single amount. Note that the amount of piecemeal recognition of a constructive gain or loss is always the difference between the intercompany interest expense and interest income amounts that are eliminated. The fact that the piecemeal recognition was 20% of the $60,000 gain is the result of straight-line amortization, a relationship that would not hold under the effective interest method.

The first two columns of the consolidation working papers in Exhibit 7-1 include separate-company financial statements for Pam and Sue. Except for the Investment in Sue and the Income from Sue accounts, the amounts shown reflect all previous assumptions and computations.

We compute Pam's investment income of $202,000 as follows:

70% of Sue's reported income of $220,000	$154,000
Add: Constructive gain on bonds	60,000
	214,000
Less: Piecemeal recognition of constructive gain	
($60,000 ÷ 5 years)	12,000
Income from Sue	$202,000

Separate entries on the books of Pam to record the investment income from Sue under a one-line consolidation are as follows:

Investment in Sue (+A)	154,000	
Income from Sue (R, +SE)		154,000

To record investment income from Sue ($220,000 × 70%).

Investment in Sue (+A)	60,000	
Income from Sue (R, +SE)		60,000

To adjust income from Sue for 100% of the $60,000 constructive gain on bonds.

(continued)

EXHIBIT 7-1

Parent-Company Bonds Held by Subsidiary

PAM CORPORATION AND SUBSIDIARY CONSOLIDATION WORKING PAPERS FOR THE YEAR ENDED DECEMBER 31, 2008 (IN THOUSANDS)

	Pam	70% Sue	Adjustments and Eliminations Debits	Adjustments and Eliminations Credits	Consolidated Statements
Income Statement					
Sales	$ 4,000	$ 2,000			$ 6,000
Income from Sue	202		c 202		
Gain on retirement of bonds				a 48 b 12	60
Interest income		110	b 110		
Expenses including cost of sales	(1,910)	(1,890)			(3,800)
Interest expense	(980)			b 98	(882)
Noncontrolling interest expense ($220 × 30%)			d 66		(66)
Net income	**$ 1,312**	**$ 220**			**$ 1,312**
Retained Earnings					
Retained earnings—Pam	$ 4,900				$ 4,900
Retained earnings—Sue		$ 4,000	e 4,000		
Add: Net income	1,312	220			1,312
Retained earnings— December 31	**$ 6,212**	**$ 4,220**			**$ 6,212**
Balance Sheet					
Other assets	$39,880	$19,100			$58,980
Interest receivable		50		f 50	
Investment in Sue	6,502			c 202 e 6,300	
Investment in Pam bonds		960		a 960	
	$46,382	$20,110			$58,980
Other liabilities	$ 9,590	$10,890			$20,480
Interest payable	500		f 50		450
10% Bond payable	10,080		a 1,008		9,072
Common stock	20,000	5,000	e 5,000		20,000
Retained earnings	6,212	4,220			6,212
	$46,382	$20,110			
Noncontrolling interest				d 66 e 2,700	2,766
					$58,980

Income from Sue (−R, −SE)	12,000
Investment in Sue (−A)	12,000

To adjust income from Sue for the piecemeal recognition of the
constructive gain on bonds that occurred during 2008. (Either $60,000
gain ÷ 5 years or $110,000 interest income −$98,000 interest expense.)

We add the $60,000 constructive gain to Pam's share of the reported income of Sue because it is realized from the consolidated viewpoint. We recognize this constructive gain on the separate books of the affiliated companies as they continue to account for the $1,000,000 par of bonds constructively retired on January 1, 2008.

Pam's investment income for 2008 increases by $48,000 from the constructive retirement of the bonds ($60,000 constructive gain less $12,000 piecemeal recognition of the gain). In the years 2009, 2010, 2011, and 2012, Pam's investment income will be reduced $12,000 each year as the constructive gain is recognized on the separate books of Pam and Sue. In other words, in addition to recording its share of the reported income of Sue in each of these four years, Pam makes the following entry to adjust its income from Sue for the piecemeal recognition of the constructive gain:

Income from Sue (−R, −SE)	12,000
Investment in Sue (−A)	12,000

At January 1, 2013, the maturity date of the bonds, the full amount of the constructive gain will have been recognized, and Pam's Investment in Sue account will equal 70% of the equity of Sue.

The following working paper entries consolidate the financial statements of Pam Corporation and Subsidiary for 2008 (see Exhibit 7-1):

a	10% Bonds payable (−L)	1,008,000	
	Gain on retirement of bonds (Ga, +SE)		48,000
	Investment in Pam bonds (−A)		960,000
	To enter gain and eliminate reciprocal bond investment and bond liability amounts, including unamortized premium.		
b	Interest income (−R, −SE)	110,000	
	Interest expense (−E, +SE)		98,000
	Gain on retirement of bonds (Ga, +SE)		12,000
	To eliminate reciprocal interest income and interest expense amounts.		
c	Income from Sue (−R, −SE)	202,000	
	Investment in Sue (−A)		202,000
	To establish reciprocity.		
d	Noncontrolling interest expense (E, −SE)	66,000	
	Noncontrolling interest (+L)		66,000
	To enter noncontrolling interest share of subsidiary income.		
e	Retained earnings—Sue (−SE)	4,000,000	
	Common stock—Sue (−SE)	5,000,000	
	Investment in Sue (−A)		6,300,000
	Noncontrolling interest January 1, 2008 (+L)		2,700,000
	To eliminate reciprocal investment and equity accounts and set up beginning noncontrolling interest.		
f	Interest payable (−L)	50,000	
	Interest receivable (−A)		50,000
	To eliminate reciprocal interest payable and interest receivable amounts.		

The first working paper entry eliminates 10% of Pam's bond liability and Sue's bond investment and also enters $48,000 of the gain on retirement of bonds. This $48,000 is that part of the $60,000 constructive gain not recognized on the separate books of Pam and Sue as of December 31, 2008.

Entry b eliminates reciprocal interest expense and interest income. The difference between the interest expense and interest income amounts represents that part of the constructive gain recognized on the separate books of Pam and Sue through amortization in 2008. This amount is $12,000 and, when credited to the gain on retirement of bonds, it brings the gain up to the original $60,000. As mentioned earlier, if entries a and b had been combined, we would enter the constructive gain in the working papers as one amount.

Working paper entry c eliminates investment income and adjusts the Investment in Sue account to its beginning-of-the-period balance. Entry d eliminates the noncontrolling interest share of subsidiary net income. Entry e eliminates Pam's investment in Sue and the equity accounts of Sue and establishes the beginning-of-the-period noncontrolling interest.

Entry f of the consolidation working papers eliminates reciprocal interest payable and interest receivable amounts on the intercompany bonds. This results in showing interest payable in the consolidated balance sheet at $450,000, the nominal interest payable for one-half year on the $9,000,000 par of bonds held outside of the consolidated entity. Note that noncontrolling interest computations in Exhibit 7-1 are not affected by the intercompany bond holdings. This is because Pam issued the bonds, and the full amount of the constructive gain is assigned to the issuing company.

Effect on Consolidated Statements in Subsequent Years

In subsequent years until the actual retirement of the intercompany bonds, Pam and Sue continue to account for the bonds on their separate books—reporting interest expense (Pam) of $98,000 and interest income (Sue) of $110,000. The $12,000 difference is recognized on Pam's separate books as an adjustment of investment income. Consolidated financial statements for 2009 through 2012 eliminate all balances related to the intercompany bonds. Exhibit 7-2 shows the year-end balances related to the intercompany bonds on the separate books of Pam and Sue.

A single adjusting and eliminating entry in the consolidation working papers for 2009 could be used for items relating to the intercompany bonds:

Interest income (−R, −SE)	110,000	
Interest payable (−L)	50,000	
10% Bonds payable (−L)	1,006,000	
Interest expense (−E, +SE)		98,000
Interest receivable (−A)		50,000
Investment in Pam bonds (−A)		970,000
Investment in Sue (−A)		48,000

EXHIBIT 7-2

Year-End Account Balances Relating to Intercompany Bonds

Pam's Books (in thousands)

	December 31,			
	2009	2010	2011	2012
Interest expense	$ 980	$ 980	$ 980	$ 980
Interest payable	500	500	500	500
Bonds payable	10,060	10,040	10,020	10,000

Sue's Books (in thousands)

	December 31,			
	2009	2010	2011	2012
Interest income	$ 110	$ 110	$ 110	$ 110
Interest receivable	50	50	50	50
Investment in Pam bonds	970	980	990	1,000

This entry eliminates reciprocal interest income and interest expense amounts, reciprocal interest receivable and payable amounts, and reciprocal bond investment and bond liability amounts. We credit the remaining difference of $48,000 to the Investment in Sue account to establish reciprocity between Pam's investment in Sue and the equity accounts of Sue at the beginning of 2009. This is necessary because Pam increased its investment account in 2008 when it adjusted its investment income account for the constructive gain. In other words, Pam's Investment in Sue account exceeded its underlying book value in Sue by $48,000 at December 31, 2008. The 2009 working paper entry to adjust the Investment in Sue account establishes reciprocity with the equity accounts of Sue and is entered in the consolidation working papers before eliminating reciprocal investment and equity amounts.

Similar working paper adjustments are necessary in 2010, 2011, and 2012. For example, the consolidation working paper credit to the Investment in Sue account will be $36,000 in 2010, $24,000 in 2011, and $12,000 in 2012.

SUBSIDIARY BONDS PURCHASED BY PARENT

The illustration in this section is similar to that for Pam and Sue, except that the subsidiary is the issuing affiliate and the constructive retirement of bonds results in a loss to the consolidated entity.

Pro Corporation owns 90% of the voting common stock of Sky Corporation. Pro purchased its interest in Sky a number of years ago at its book value of $9,225,000. Sky's capital stock was $10,000,000 and its retained earnings were $250,000 on the acquisition date.

At December 31, 2006, Sky had $10,000,000 par of 10% bonds outstanding with an unamortized discount of $300,000. The bonds pay interest on January 1 and July 1 of each year, and they mature in five years on January 1, 2012.

On January 2, 2007, Pro Corporation purchases 50% of Sky's outstanding bonds for $5,150,000 cash. This transaction is a constructive retirement and results in a loss of $300,000 from the viewpoint of the consolidated entity. The consolidated entity retires a liability of $4,850,000 (50% of the $9,700,000 book value of the bonds) at a cost of $5,150,000. We assign the loss to Sky Corporation under the theory that the parent-company management acts as agent for Sky, the issuing company, in all intercompany bond transactions.

During 2007, Sky records interest expense on the bonds of $1,060,000 [($10,000,000 par × 10%) + $60,000 discount amortization]. Of this interest expense, $530,000 relates to the intercompany bonds. Pro records interest income from its investment in bonds during 2007 of $470,000 [($5,000,000 par × 10%) − $30,000 premium amortization]. The $60,000 difference between the interest expense and the interest income on the intercompany bonds reflects recognition of one-fifth of the constructive loss during 2007. At December 31, 2007, the books of Pro and Sky have not recognized $240,000 of the constructive loss through premium amortization (Pro's books) and discount amortization (Sky's books).

Equity Method

Sky reports net income of $750,000 for 2007, and Pro computes its $459,000 income from Sky as follows:

90% of Sky's $750,000 reported income	$675,000
Deduct: $300,000 constructive loss × 90%	(270,000)
Add: $60,000 recognition of constructive loss × 90%	54,000
Investment income from Sky	$459,000

The journal entries that Pro makes to account for its investment in Sky during 2007 are as follows:

December 31, 2007

Investment in Sky (+A)	675,000	
Income from Sky (R, +SE)		675,000
To record 90% of Sky's reported income for 2007.		

(continued)

December 31, 2007

Income from Sky (−R, −SE)	270,000	
Investment in Sky (−A)		270,000

    To adjust investment income from Sky for 90% of

        the loss on the constructive retirement of Sky's bonds.

    (This entry could be made on January 1, 2007.)

December 31, 2007

Investment in Sky (+A)	54,000	
Income from Sky (R, +SE)		54,000

    To adjust investment income from Sky for 90% of the

        $60,000 piecemeal recognition of the constructive loss on

        Sky bonds during 2007.

In future years until the bonds mature, Pro computes income from Sky by adding $54,000 annually to its share of the reported income of Sky.

Pro Corporation's Investment in Sky account at December 31, 2007, has a balance of $10,584,000. This balance equals the underlying book value of Pro's investment in Sky at January 1, 2007, plus $459,000 investment income from Sky for 2007:

Investment in Sky January 1, 2007 ($11,250,000 × 90%)	$10,125,000
Add: Income from Sky	459,000
Investment in Sky December 31, 2007	$10,584,000

Exhibit 7-3 presents consolidated financial statement working papers for Pro Corporation and Subsidiary. The constructive loss of $300,000 on the intercompany bonds appears in the consolidated income statement for 2007. Because $5,000,000 par of Sky bonds have been constructively retired, the consolidated balance sheet reports bonds payable of $4,880,000 ($5,000,000 par less the unamortized discount of $120,000) related to the bonds held outside of the consolidated entity.

EFFECT OF CONSTRUCTIVE LOSS ON NONCONTROLLING INTEREST EXPENSE AND CONSOLIDATED NET INCOME Noncontrolling interest expense for 2007 is $51,000 [($750,000 − $300,000 + $60,000) × 10%]. We assign the constructive loss to Sky. We charge the noncontrolling interest for 10% of the $300,000 constructive loss and credit it for 10% of the $60,000 piecemeal recognition of the constructive loss during 2007. Accordingly, noncontrolling interest expense for 2007 is 10% of Sky's $510,000 realized income, and not 10% of Sky's $750,000 reported net income.

The constructive loss reduces consolidated net income for 2007 by $216,000. We reflect this reduction in the consolidated income statement through the inclusion of the $300,000 loss on the constructive retirement of the bonds, elimination of interest income of $470,000 and interest expense of $530,000, and reduction of noncontrolling interest expense by $24,000 (from $75,000 based on reported net income of Sky to $51,000 noncontrolling interest expense for the year). An analysis of the effect follows:

Consolidated Net Income–2007

Decreased by:	
Constructive loss	$300,000
Elimination of interest income	470,000
Total decreases	$770,000
Increased by:	
Elimination of interest expense	$530,000
Reduction of noncontrolling interest expense ($75,000 − $51,000)	24,000
Total increases	$554,000
Effect on consolidated net income for 2007	$216,000

The reduction of noncontrolling interest expense is similar to the reduction of other expenses. A decrease in noncontrolling interest expense increases consolidated net income, and vice versa.

CONSOLIDATION WORKING PAPER ENTRIES The entries shown in the consolidation working papers of Exhibit 7-3 are similar to those in the Pam–Sue illustration in Exhibit 7-1 except for the amounts

EXHIBIT 7-3

Subsidiary Bonds
Held by Parent

PRO CORPORATION AND SUBSIDIARY CONSOLIDATION WORKING PAPERS FOR THE YEAR ENDED DECEMBER 31, 2007 (IN THOUSANDS)

	Pro	90% Sky	Adjustments and Eliminations Debits	Credits	Consolidated Statements
Income Statement Sales	$25,750	$14,250			$40,000
Income from Sky	459		c 459		
Interest income	470		b 470		
Expenses including cost of sales	(21,679)	(12,440)			(34,119)
Interest expense		(1,060)		b 530	(530)
Loss on retirement of bonds			a 240 b 60		(300)
Noncontrolling interest expense			c 51		(51)
Net income	**$ 5,000**	**$ 750**			**$ 5,000**
Retained Earnings Retained earnings—Pro	$13,000				$13,000
Retained earnings—Sky		$ 1,250	d 1,250		
Add: Net income	**5,000**	**750**			**5,000**
Retained earnings— December 31	**$18,000**	**$ 2,000**			**$18,000**
Balance Sheet Other assets	$34,046	$25,000			$59,046
Interest receivable	250			e 250	
Investment in Sky	10,584			c 459 d 10,125	
Investment in Sky bonds	5,120			a 5,120	
	$50,000	$25,000			$59,046
Other liabilities	$12,000	$ 2,740			$14,740
Interest payable		500	e 250		250
10% Bonds payable		9,760	a 4,880		4,880
Capital stock	20,000	10,000	d 10,000		20,000
Retained earnings	**18,000**	**2,000**			**18,000**
	$50,000	$25,000			
Noncontrolling interest				c 51 d 1,125	1,176
					$59,046

and the shift to a constructive loss situation. As in the previous illustration, working paper entries a and b are separated for illustrative purposes, but they could be combined into a single entry as follows:

Loss on retirement of bonds (Lo, –SE)	**300,000**	
Interest income (–R, –SE)	**470,000**	
10% Bonds payable (–L)	**4,880,000**	
Investment in Sky bonds (–A)		**5,120,000**
Interest expense (–E, +SE)		**530,000**

Effect on Consolidated Statements in Subsequent Years

The loss on the retirement of bonds only appears in the consolidated income statement in the year in which we constructively retire the bonds. In subsequent years, we allocate the unrecognized portion of the constructive loss between the investment account (the majority interest) and noncontrolling interest. For example, the combined working paper entry to eliminate the bond investment and bonds payable and the interest income and interest expense amounts in 2008 would be as follows:

Investment in Sky (+A)	**216,000**	
Noncontrolling interest (–L)	**24,000**	
Interest income (–R, –SE)	**470,000**	
10% Bonds payable (–L)	**5,000,000**	
Investment in Sky bonds (–A)		**5,180,000**
Interest expense (–E, +SE)		**530,000**

The assignment of the constructive loss to Sky dictates allocation of the unrecognized loss between the investment in Sky ($216,000) and noncontrolling interest ($24,000). The loss is a subsidiary loss, so noncontrolling interest must share in the loss. In computing noncontrolling interest for 2008, we add 10% of the $60,000 constructive loss recognized in 2008 to the noncontrolling interest share of income reported by Sky. We require this adjustment of noncontrolling interest expense each year through 2011. By December 31, 2011, the bond investment will decrease to $5,000,000 through premium amortization, and the intercompany bond liability will increase to $5,000,000 through discount amortization.

The intercompany bond holdings increase consolidated net income by $54,000 each year for 2008 through 2011. Under the equity method of accounting, Pro's income from Sky and net income also increase by $54,000 in each of the years. Computations of the consolidated net income effect for the years 2008 through 2011 follow:

Consolidated Net Income—2008 Through 2011

Increased by:	
Elimination of interest expense	<u>$530,000</u>
Decreased by:	
Elimination of interest income	$470,000
Increase in noncontrolling interest expense ($60,000 piecemeal recognition × 10%)	<u>6,000</u>
Total decreases	<u>$476,000</u>
Annual effect on consolidated net income	<u>$ 54,000</u>

Exhibit 7-4 summarizes the intercompany bond account balances that appear on the separate books of Pro and Sky at year-end 2008 through 2011. The exhibit also summarizes the required working paper adjustments to consolidate the financial statements of Pro and Sky for years subsequent to the year of intercompany purchase of Sky bonds. Because the Investment in Sky account is involved, we make the working paper entries shown in Exhibit 7-4 before eliminating reciprocal investment and subsidiary equity amounts.

The working paper entries shown in Exhibit 7-4 eliminate those amounts that would have been eliminated from the separate statements of Pro and Sky if the bonds had in fact been retired in 2007. The objective is to produce the consolidated financial statements as if Sky had purchased and retired its own bonds.

EXHIBIT 7-4

Subsidiary Bonds
Held by Parent—
Years Subsequent to
Year of Intercompany
Purchase

SUMMARY OF INTERCOMPANY BOND ACCOUNT BALANCES ON SEPARATE BOOKS

December 31,	2008	2009	2010	2011
Pro's Books (in thousands)				
Investment in Sky bonds	$5,090	$5,060	$5,030	$ 5,000
Interest income	470	470	470	470
Interest receivable	250	250	250	250
Sky's Books (in thousands)				
10% Bonds payable	$9,820	$9,880	$9,940	$10,000
Interest expense	1,060	1,060	1,060	1,060
Interest payable	500	500	500	500

SUMMARY OF CONSOLIDATION WORKING PAPER ADJUSTMENTS

December 31,	2008	2009	2010	2011
Debits				
Investment in Sky (90%)*	$ 216	$ 162	$ 108	$ 54
Noncontrolling interest (10%)*	24	18	12	6
Interest income	470	470	470	470
10% Bonds payable†	4,910	4,940	4,970	5,000
Interest payable	250	250	250	250
Credits				
Investment in Sky bonds	5,090	5,060	5,030	5,000
Interest expense†	530	530	530	530
Interest receivable	250	250	250	250

*The unrecognized portion of the constructive loss at the beginning of the year is charged 90% to the Investment in Sky account and 10% to noncontrolling interest.
†Elimination of 50% of Sky's bonds (including 50% of the unamortized discount on the bonds) and 50% of the current interest expense on the bonds.

SUMMARY

Transactions in which one corporation acquires the outstanding bonds of an affiliated company result in constructive gains and losses except when an affiliate purchases bonds at book value. The consolidated entity realizes constructive gains and losses when an affiliate purchases another affiliate's bonds. The constructive gains and losses should be reflected in the income of the parent company and consolidated net income in the year of purchase.

Gains and losses on parent-company bonds are similar to unrealized gains and losses on downstream sales and do not require allocation between noncontrolling and majority interests. However, constructive gains and losses on bonds in which a subsidiary is the issuing entity should be allocated between noncontrolling interest and consolidated net income. Constructive gains or losses on intercompany bonds are recognized on the books of the purchasing and issuing corporations as they amortize differences between the book value and par value of bonds.

A summary illustration comparing the effects of constructive gains and losses from intercompany bond transactions on parent-company and consolidated net incomes is presented in Exhibit 7-5.

QUESTIONS

1. What reciprocal accounts arise when one company borrows from an affiliated company?

2. Do direct lending and borrowing transactions between affiliated companies give rise to unrealized gains or losses? To unrecognized gains or losses?

EXHIBIT 7-5

Summary
Illustration—
Constructive Gains
and Losses on
Intercompany Bonds

Assumptions

1 Parent Company's income, excluding income from Subsidiary, was $100,000 for 2006.
2 90%-owned Subsidiary reported net income of $50,000 for 2006.
3 $100,000 of 10% bonds payable are outstanding with $6,000 unamortized premium as of January 1, 2006.
4 $50,000 par of the bonds were purchased for $51,500 on January 2, 2006.
5 The bonds mature on January 1, 2009.

	S Acquires P's Bonds (similar to downstream)	P Acquires S's Bonds (similar to upstream)
P's Net Income—Equity Method		
P's separate income	$100,000	$100,000
P's share of S's reported net income	45,000	45,000
Add: Constructive gain on bonds		
($53,000 − $51,500) × 100%	1,500	
($53,000 − $51,500) × 90%		1,350
Deduct: Piecemeal recognition of constructive gain		
($1,500 gain ÷ 3 years) × 100%	(500)	
($1,500 gain ÷ 3 years) × 90%		(450)
P's net income	$146,000	$145,900
Consolidated Net Income		
P's separate income plus S's net income	$150,000	$150,000
Add: Constructive gain on bonds	1,500	1,500
Eliminate: Interest expense (increase)	4,000	4,000
Interest income (decrease)	(4,500)	(4,500)
Total realized income	151,000	151,000
Less: Noncontrolling interest expense		
($50,000 × 10%)	(5,000)	
($50,000 + $1,500 − $500) × 10%		(5,100)
Consolidated net income	$146,000	$145,900

P's net income and consolidated net income of $146,000 when S acquires P's bonds are the same as if the bonds had actually been retired by P at the end of 2006. In that case, P's separate income would have been $101,000 ($100,000 plus $1,000 constructive gain), and S's net income would have been unchanged. P's $101,000 plus P's $45,000 share of S's reported net income equals $146,000. An assumption of retirement at year-end is necessary because the interest expense of P and the interest income of S are both realized and recognized during 2006. The amount of the gain is $1,000 ($1,500 less $500 realized and recognized during the current year).

P's net income and consolidated net income of $145,900 when P acquires S's bonds are the same as if the bonds had actually been retired by S at the end of 2006. In that case, P's separate income would have been unchanged at $100,000, and S's reported net income would have been $51,000 ($50,000 plus $1,000 constructive gain). P's $100,000 separate income plus P's $45,900 share of S's reported income ($51,000 × 90%) equals $145,900. Again, the assumption of retirement at year-end is necessary because the interest income of P and the interest expense of S are realized and recognized during the current year.

3. What are constructive gains and losses? Describe a transaction involving a constructive gain.

4. A company has a $1,000,000 bond issue outstanding with unamortized premium of $10,000 and unamortized issuance cost of $5,300. What is the book value of its liability? If an affiliated company purchases half the bonds in the market at 98, what is the gain or loss? Is the gain or loss actual or constructive?

5. Compare a constructive gain on intercompany bonds with an unrealized gain on the intercompany sale of land.

6. Describe the process by which constructive gains on intercompany bonds are realized and recognized on the books of the separate affiliated companies. Does recognition of a constructive gain in consolidated financial statements precede or succeed recognition on the books of the affiliated companies?

7. If a subsidiary purchases parent-company bonds at a price in excess of their recorded book value, is the gain or loss attributed to the parent company or the subsidiary? Explain.

8. The following information related to intercompany bond holdings was taken from the adjusted trial balances of a parent company and its 90%-owned subsidiary four years before the bond issue matured:

	Parent	Subsidiary
Investment in S bonds, $50,000 par	$49,000	
Interest receivable	2,500	
Interest expense		$ 9,000
10% Bonds payable, $100,000 par		100,000
Bond premium		4,000
Interest income	5,250	
Interest payable		5,000

Construct the consolidation working paper entries necessary to eliminate reciprocal balances (a) assuming that the parent acquired its intercompany bond investment at the beginning of the current year, and (b) assuming that the parent company acquired its intercompany bond investment two years prior to the date of the adjusted trial balance.

9. Prepare a journal entry (or entries) to account for the parent-company investment income for the current year if the reported income of its 80%-owned subsidiary is $50,000 and the consolidated entity has a $4,000 constructive gain from the subsidiary's acquisition of parent-company bonds.

10. Calculate the parent company's income from its 75%-owned subsidiary if the reported net income of the subsidiary for the period is $100,000 and the consolidated entity has a constructive loss of $8,000 from the parent's acquisition of subsidiary bonds.

11. If a parent company reports interest expense of $4,300 with respect to bonds held intercompany and the subsidiary reports interest income of $4,500 for the same bonds, (a) Was there a constructive gain or loss on the bonds? (b) Is the gain or loss attributed to the parent company or the subsidiary? and (c) What does the $200 difference between interest income and interest expense represent?

12. How are intercompany receivables and payables of equity investees reported in parent-company and consolidated financial statements?

EXERCISES

E 7-1
General questions

1. Which of the following is not a characteristic of a constructive retirement of bonds from an intercompany bond transaction?
   a Bonds are retired for consolidated statement purposes only.
   b The reciprocal intercompany bond investment and bond liability amounts are eliminated in the consolidation process.
   c Any gain or loss from the intercompany bond transaction is recognized on the books of the issuing affiliate.
   d For consolidated statement purposes, the gain or loss on the constructive retirement of bonds is the difference between the book value of the bond liability and the purchase price of the bond investment.

2. When bonds are purchased in the market by an affiliate, the book value of the intercompany bond liability is:
   a The par value of the bonds less unamortized issuance costs and less unamortized discount or plus unamortized premium
   b The par value of the bonds less issuance costs, less unamortized discount or plus unamortized premiums, and less the costs incurred to purchase the bond investment
   c The par value of the bonds
   d The par value of the bonds less the discount or plus the premium at the time of issuance

3. Constructive gains and losses:
   a Arise when one company purchases the bonds of an affiliate or lends money directly to the affiliate to repurchase its own bonds
   b Are realized gains and losses from the viewpoint of the issuing affiliate
   c Are always assigned to the parent company because its management makes the decisions for intercompany transactions
   d Are realized and recognized from the viewpoint of the consolidated entity

4. Straight-line interest amortization of bond premiums and discounts is used as an expedient in this book. However, the effective interest rate method is generally required under GAAP. When using the effective interest rate method:
   a The amount of the piecemeal recognition of a constructive gain or loss is the difference between the intercompany interest expense and interest income that is eliminated
   b The piecemeal recognition of a constructive gain or loss is recorded in the separate accounts of the affiliated companies

c No piecemeal recognition of the constructive gain or loss is required for consolidated statement purposes

d The issuing and the purchasing affiliates do not amortize the discounts and premiums on their separate books because the bonds are retired

E 7-2

General problems Showalter Corporation is a 70%-owned subsidiary of Pavone Corporation. On January 1, 2006, Showalter purchased $600,000 par of Pavone's $900,000 outstanding bonds for $602,000 in the bond market. Pavone's bonds have an 8% interest rate, pay interest on January 1 and July 1, and mature on January 1, 2010. There was $48,000 unamortized premium on the bond issue on January 1, 2006. Assume straight-line amortization.

1. The constructive gain or loss that should appear in the consolidated income statement of Pavone Corporation and Subsidiary for 2006 is:

   a $30,000 gain

   b $46,000 gain

   c $2,000 loss

   d $30,000 loss

   Par 600,000
   Premium 32,000
   Purchase 602,000
   ―――――
   30,000 Loss

2. Interest expense that should appear in the 2006 consolidated income statement for Pavone's bond issue is:

   a $28,000

   b $24,000

   c $20,800

   d $20,000

   Unretired bonds

   48,000/4 × (1/3)

   300,000 × 8% = 24,000 − 4,000 prem amort = 20,000 int exp

E 7-3

Constructive gain on purchase of parent company bonds Palmer Corporation's long-term debt on January 1, 2006, consists of $400,000 par value of 10% bonds payable due on January 1, 2010, with unamortized discount of $8,000. On January 2, 2006, Scott Corporation, Palmer's 90%-owned subsidiary, purchased $80,000 par of Palmer's 10% bonds for $76,000. Interest payment dates are January 1 and July 1, and straight-line amortization is used.

1. On the consolidated income statement of Palmer Corporation and Subsidiary for 2006, a gain or loss should be reported in the amount of:

   a $5,600

   b $4,000

   c $2,400 — *Gain*

   d $2,000

   Par   80,000
   20% Disc −1,600
   ―――――
   BV = 78,400 − Purchase Price 76,000 = Gain 2,400

2. Bonds payable of Palmer less unamortized discount appears in the consolidated balance sheet at December 31, 2006, in the amount of:

   a $392,000

   b $394,000

   c $320,000

   d $315,200

	1-1-06	*12-31-06*
Par	*320,000*	*320,000*
80% Disc	*−6,400*	*−4,800*
	313,600	*315,200*

3. The amount of the constructive gain or loss that is unrecognized on the separate books of Palmer and Scott at December 31, 2006, is:

   a $2,400

   b $2,200

   c $1,800

   d 0

   Constructive gain $2400 / 4 yrs × 3 yrs = $1,800

4. Interest expense on Palmer bonds appears in the consolidated income statement for 2006 at:

   a $42,000

   b $40,000

   c $33,600

   d $32,000

   Par 320,000 × 10% = 32,000
   80% Disc (8,000) / 4 yrs = 1,600
   ―――――
   33,600

5. Consolidated net income for 2007 will be affected by the intercompany bond transactions as follows:

   a *Increased by 100% of the constructive gain from 2006*

   b *Decreased by 25% of the constructive gain from 2006*

   c *Increased by 25% of the constructive loss from 2006*

   d *Decreased by (25% × 90%) of the constructive loss from 2006*

E 7-4

Subsidiary purchases parent company bonds Paul Corporation acquired an 80% interest in Sally Corporation on January 1, 2006, for $400,000 in excess of book value and fair value. Paul does not amortize goodwill.

On January 1, 2009, Paul had $1,000,000 par, 8% bonds outstanding with $40,000 unamortized discount. On this date, Sally purchased $400,000 par of Paul's bonds at par. The bonds mature on January 1, 2013, and pay interest on January 1 and July 1.

Paul's separate income, not including investment income, for 2009 is $800,000, and Sally's reported net income is $500,000.

REQUIRED: Determine the following:

1. Consolidated net income for Paul Corporation and Subsidiary for 2009

2. Noncontrolling interest expense for 2009

E 7-5

Consolidated income statement (constructive gain on purchase of parent's bonds)

Comparative income statements for Prim Corporation and its 100%-owned subsidiary, Saddie Corporation, for the year ended December 31, 2014, are summarized as follows:

	Prim	Saddie
Sales	$1,000,000	$500,000
Income from Saddie	226,000	—
Bond interest income (includes discount amortization)	—	22,000
Cost of sales	(670,000)	(200,000)
Operating expenses	(150,000)	(100,000)
Bond interest expense	(50,000)	—
Net income	$ 356,000	$222,000

Prim purchased its interest in Saddie at book value on January 1, 2006. On January 1, 2007, Prim sold $500,000 par of 10%, 10-year bonds to the public at par value, and on January 1, 2014, Saddie purchased $200,000 par of the bonds at 97. Both companies use straight-line amortization. There are no other intercompany transactions between the affiliated companies.

REQUIRED: Prepare a consolidated income statement for Prim Corporation and Subsidiary for the year ended December 31, 2014.

E 7-6

Parent purchases subsidiary bonds

Platt Corporation owns a 70% interest in Smedley Corporation acquired several years ago at book value equal to fair value. On January 1, 2006, Smedley had outstanding $1,000,000 of 9% bonds with a book value of $990,000. On this date, Platt purchased $500,000 of Smedley's 9% bonds for $503,000. The bonds are due on January 1, 2010, and pay interest on January 1 and July 1.

REQUIRED

1. Determine the gain or loss on the constructive retirement of Smedley bonds.

2. Smedley reports net income of $14,000 for 2006. Determine Platt's income from Smedley.

E 7-7

Constructive gain purchase of subsidiary's bonds

Comparative balance sheets of Pitt Corporation and Slick Corporation at December 31, 2006, follow:

	Pitt	Slick
Assets		
Accounts receivable—net	$ 1,024,300	$ 300,000
Interest receivable	10,000	—
Inventories	3,000,000	500,000
Other current assets	98,500	200,000
Plant assets—net	3,840,000	2,500,000
Investment in Slick stock	1,830,800	—
Investment in Slick bonds	196,400	—
Total assets	$10,000,000	$3,500,000

	Pitt	Slick
Liabilities and Stockholders' Equity		
Accounts payable	$ 400,000	$ 139,000
Interest payable	—	50,000
10% Bonds payable	—	1,036,000
Capital stock	8,000,000	2,000,000
Retained earnings	1,600,000	275,000
Total equities	$10,000,000	$3,500,000

Pitt acquired 80% of Slick's capital stock for $1,660,000 on January 1, 2004, when Slick's capital stock was $2,000,000 and its retained earnings was $75,000.

On January 1, 2006, Pitt acquired $200,000 par of Slick 10% bonds in the bond market for $195,500, on which date the unamortized premium for bonds payable on Slick's books was $45,000. The bonds pay interest on January 1 and July 1 and mature on January 1, 2011. (Assume straight-line amortization.)

1. The gain or loss on the constructive retirement of $200,000 of Slick bonds on January 1, 2006, is reported in the 2006 consolidated income statement in the amount of:
   a $13,500
   b $11,500
   c $10,500
   d $7,000

2. The portion of the constructive gain or loss on Slick bonds that remains unrecognized on the separate books of Pitt and Slick at December 31, 2006, is:
   a $12,000
   b $10,800
   c $10,500
   d $9,200

3. Consolidated bonds payable at December 31, 2006, should be reported at:
   a $1,036,000
   b $1,000,000
   c $828,800
   d $800,000

E 7-8

Midyear purchase of parent's bonds The consolidated balance sheet of Partie Corporation and Saydo Corporation (its 80%-owned subsidiary) at December 31, 2006, includes the following items related to an 8%, $1,000,000 outstanding bond issue:

Current Liabilities	
Bond interest payable (6 months' interest due January 1, 2007)	$ 40,000
Long-Term Liabilities	
8% bonds payable (maturity date January 1, 2011, net of $30,000 unamortized discount)	$970,000

Partie Corporation is the issuing corporation, and straight-line amortization is applicable. Saydo purchases $600,000 par of the outstanding bonds of Partie on July 1, 2007, for $574,800.

REQUIRED

1. Calculate the following:
   a. The gain or loss on constructive retirement of the bonds
   b. The consolidated bond interest expense for 2007
   c. The consolidated bond liability at December 31, 2007

2. How would the amounts determined in part 1 be different if Partie had purchased Saydo's bonds?

E 7-9

Different assumptions for purchase of parent's bonds and subsidiary's bonds The balance sheets of Picker Company and Skidden Corporation, an 80%-owned subsidiary of Picker, at December 31, 2006, are as follows (in thousands):

8o/o

12/31/06	Picker	Skidden
Assets		
Cash	$ 2,440	$2,500
Accounts receivable—net	3,000	300
Other current assets	8,000	1,200
Plant assets—net	15,000	5,500
Investment in Skidden	6,560	—
Total assets	$35,000	$9,500
Liabilities and Stockholders' Equity		
Accounts payable	$ 750	$ 230
Interest payable	250	50
10% Bonds payable (due January 1, 2012)	4,900	1,020
Capital stock	25,000	7,000
Retained earnings	4,100	1,200
Total liabilities and stockholders' equity	$35,000	$9,500

The book value of Picker's bonds reflects a $100,000 unamortized discount. The book value of Skidden's bonds reflects a $20,000 unamortized premium.

REQUIRED

1. Assume that Skidden purchases $2,000,000 par of Picker's bonds for $1,900,000 on January 2, 2007, and that semiannual interest is paid on July 1 and January 1. Determine the amounts at which the following items should appear in the consolidated financial statements of Picker and Skidden at and for the year ended December 31, 2007.
   a. Gain or loss on bond retirement
   b. Interest payable
   c. Bonds payable ~~at par value~~
   d. Investment in Picker bonds

2. Disregard 1 above and assume that Picker purchases $1,000,000 par of Skidden's bonds for $1,030,000 on January 2, 2007, and that semiannual interest on the bonds is paid on July 1 and January 1. Determine the amounts at which the following items will appear in the consolidated financial statements of Picker and Skidden at and for the year ended December 31, 2007.
   a. Gain or loss on bond retirement
   b. Interest expense (assume straight-line amortization)
   c. Interest receivable
   d. Bonds payable at book value

E 7-10

Constructive retirement of parent's bonds Perdue Corporation has $2,000,000 of 12% bonds outstanding on December 31, 2006, with unamortized premium of $60,000. These bonds pay interest semiannually on July 1 and January 1 and mature on January 1, 2012.

On January 1, 2007, Shelly Corporation, an 80%-owned subsidiary of Perdue, purchases $500,000 par of Perdue's outstanding bonds in the market for $490,000.

ADDITIONAL INFORMATION

1. Perdue and Shelly use the straight-line method of amortization.

2. The financial statements are consolidated.

3. Perdue's bonds are the only outstanding bonds of the affiliated companies.

4. Shelly's net income for 2007 is $200,000 and for 2008, $300,000.

REQUIRED

1. Compute the constructive gain or loss that will appear in the consolidated income statement for 2007.

2. Prepare a consolidation entry (entries) for 2007 to eliminate the effect of the intercompany bondholdings.

3. Compute the amounts that will appear in the consolidated income statement for 2008 for the following:
   a. Constructive gain or loss
   b. Minority interest
   c. Bond interest expense
   d. Bond interest income

4. Compute the amounts that will appear in the consolidated balance sheet at December 31, 2008, for the following:
   a. Investment in Perdue bonds
   b. Book value of bonds payable
   c. Bond interest receivable
   d. Bond interest payable

E 7-11

Consolidated income statement (constructive retirement of all subsidiary bonds)

Comparative income statements for Parrish Corporation and its 80%-owned subsidiary, Sandwood Corporation, for the year ended December 31, 2007, are summarized as follows:

	Parrish	**Sandwood**
Sales	$1,200,000	$600,000
Income from Sandwood	260,800	—
Bond interest income (includes discount amortization)	91,000	—
Cost of sales	(750,000)	(200,000)
Operating expenses	(200,000)	(200,000)
Bond interest expense	$ —	(60,000)
Net income	$ 601,800	$140,000

Parrish purchased its 80% interest in Sandwood at book value on January 1, 2006, when Sandwood's assets and liabilities were equal to their fair values.

On January 1, 2007, Parrish paid $783,000 to purchase all of Sandwood's $1,000,000, 6% outstanding bonds. The bonds were issued at par on January 1, 2005, pay interest semiannually on June 30 and December 31, and mature on December 31, 2013.

REQUIRED: Prepare a consolidated income statement for Parrish Corporation and Subsidiary for the year ended December 31, 2007.

E 7-12

Computations and entries (parent purchases subsidiary bonds)
Public Corporation, which owns an 80% interest in Spede Corporation, purchases $100,000 of Spede Corporation 8% bonds at 106 on July 1, 2006. The bonds pay interest on January 1 and July 1 and mature on July 1, 2009. Public uses the equity method of accounting for its investment in Spede. Selected data from the December 31, 2006, trial balances of the two companies are as follows:

	Public	**Spede**
Interest receivable	$ 4,000	$ —
Investment in Spede 8% bonds	105,000	—
Interest payable	—	40,000
8% Bonds payable	—	$985,000
Interest income	3,000	—
Interest expense	—	86,000
Gain or loss on intercompany bonds		

REQUIRED

1. Determine the amounts for each of the forgoing items that will appear in the consolidated financial statements on or for the year ended December 31, 2006.

2. Prepare in general journal form the working paper adjustments and eliminations related to the forgoing bonds that are required to consolidate the financial statements of Public and Spede Corporations for the year ended December 31, 2006.

3. Prepare in general journal form the working paper adjustments and eliminations related to the bonds that are required to consolidate the financial statements of Public and Spede Corporations for the year ended December 31, 2007.

E 7-13

Computations and entries (constructive gain on purchase of parent bonds)
Pappy Corporation acquired an 80% interest in Sonny Corporation at book value equal to fair value on January 1, 2007, at which time Sonny's capital stock and retained earnings were $100,000 and $40,000, respectively. On January 1, 2008, Sonny purchased $50,000 par of Pappy's 8%, $100,000 par bonds for $48,800 three years before maturity. Interest payment dates are January 1 and July 1. During 2008, Sonny reports interest income of $4,400 in connection with the bonds, and Pappy reports interest expense of $8,000.

ADDITIONAL INFORMATION

1. Pappy's separate income for 2008 is $200,000.
2. Sonny's net income for 2008 is $50,000.
3. Pappy accounts for its investment by the equity method.
4. Straight-line amortization is applicable.

REQUIRED

1. Determine the gain or loss on the bonds.
2. Prepare the journal entries for Sonny to account for its bond investment during 2008.
3. Prepare the journal entries for Pappy to account for its bonds payable during 2008.
4. Prepare the journal entry for Pappy to account for its 80% investment in Sonny for 2008.
5. Calculate noncontrolling interest expense and consolidated net income for 2008.

PROBLEMS

P 7-1

Computations and entries (constructive retirement of parent's bonds) Partial adjusted trial balances for Pongo Corporation and its 90%-owned subsidiary, Song Corporation, for the year ended December 31, 2006, are as follows:

	Pongo Corporation Debit (Credit)	Song Corporation Debit (Credit)
Interest receivable	$ —	$ 1,000
Investment in Pongo bonds	—	52,700
Interest payable	(2,000)	—
8% Bonds payable, due April 1, 2009	(98,200)	—
Interest income	—	(2,100)
Interest expense	8,800	—

Song Corporation acquired $50,000 par of Pongo bonds on April 1, 2006, for $53,600. The bonds pay interest on April 1 and October 1 and mature on April 1, 2009.

REQUIRED

1. Compute the gain or loss on the bonds that will appear in the 2006 consolidated income statement.
2. Determine the amounts of interest income and interest expense that will appear in the 2006 consolidated income statement.
3. Determine the amounts of interest receivable and interest payable that will appear in the December 31, 2006, consolidated balance sheet.
4. Prepare in general journal form the consolidation working paper entries needed to eliminate the effects of the intercompany bonds for 2006.

P 7-2

Four-year income schedule (several intercompany transactions) Intercompany transactions between Pewter Corporation and Steel Corporation, its 80%-owned subsidiary, from January 2006, when Pewter acquired its controlling interest, to December 31, 2009, are summarized as follows:

2006	Pewter sold inventory items that cost $60,000 to Steel for $80,000. Steel sold $60,000 of these inventory items in 2006 and $20,000 of them in 2007. $20 profit
2007	Pewter sold inventory items that cost $30,000 to Steel for $40,000. All of these items were sold by Steel during 2008.
2008	Steel sold land with a book value of $40,000 to Pewter at its fair market value of $55,000. This land is to be used as a future plant site by Pewter.

2008   Pewter sold equipment with a four-year remaining useful life to Steel on January 1 for $80,000. This equipment had a book value of $50,000 at the time of sale and was still in use by Steel at December 31, 2009.

2009   Steel purchased $100,000 par of Pewter's 10% bonds in the bond market for $106,000 on January 1, 2009. These bonds had a book value of $98,000 when acquired by Steel and mature on January 1, 2013.

The separate income of Pewter (does not include income from Steel) and the reported net income of Steel for 2006 through 2009 were:

	2006	2007	2008	2009
Separate income of Pewter	$500,000	$375,000	$460,000	$510,000
Net income of Steel	100,000	120,000	110,000	120,000

REQUIRED: Compute Pewter's net income (and consolidated net income) for each of the years 2006 through 2009. A schedule with columns for 2006, 2007, 2008, and 2009 is suggested as the most efficient approach for solution of this problem. (Use straight-line depreciation and amortization and take a full year's depreciation on the equipment sold to Steel in 2008).

P 7-3

Working papers (constructive retirement of bonds, intercompany sales)

Financial statements for Placid Corporation and its 75%-owned subsidiary, Storm Corporation, for 2006 are summarized as follows (in thousands):

	Placid	Storm
Combined Income and Retained Earnings Statement for the Year Ended December 31, 2006		
Sales	$1,260	$1,000
Gain on land	20	—
Gain on building	40	—
Income from Storm	104	—
Cost of goods sold	(700)	(600)
Depreciation expense	(152)	(80)
Interest expense	(40)	—
Other expenses	(92)	(120)
Net income	440	200
Add: Retained earnings, January 1	300	200
Deduct: Dividends	(320)	(160)
Retained earnings, December 31	$ 420	$ 240
Balance Sheet at December 31, 2006		
Cash	$ 54	$ 162
Bond interest receivable	—	10
Other receivables—net	80	60
Inventories	160	100
Land	180	140
Buildings—net	300	360
Equipment—net	280	180
Investment in Storm	686	—
Investment in Placid Bonds	—	188
Total assets	$1,740	$1,200
Accounts payable	$100	$160
Bond interest payable	20	—
10% Bonds payable	400	—
Common stock	800	800
Retained earnings	420	240
Total equities	$1,740	$1,200

Placid acquired its interest in Storm at book value during 2003, when the fair values of Storm's assets and liabilities were equal to their recorded book values.

ADDITIONAL INFORMATION

1. Placid uses the equity method of accounting for its investment in Storm.

2. Intercompany sales of merchandise totaled $100,000 during 2006. All intercompany balances have been paid except for $20,000 in transit from Storm to Placid at December 31, 2006.

3. Unrealized profits in Storm's inventory of merchandise purchased from Placid were $24,000 on December 31, 2005, and $30,000 on December 31, 2006.

4. Storm sold equipment with a six-year remaining life to Placid on January 3, 2004, at a gain of $48,000. Placid still uses the equipment in its operations.

5. Placid sold land to Storm on July 1, 2006, at a gain of $20,000.

6. Placid sold a building to Storm on July 1, 2006, at a gain of $40,000. The building has a 10-year remaining life and is still used by Storm.

7. Storm purchased $200,000 par value of Placid's 10% bonds in the open market for $188,000 plus $10,000 accrued interest on December 31, 2006. Interest is paid semiannually on January 1 and July 1. The bonds mature on December 31, 2011.

REQUIRED: Prepare consolidation working papers for Placid Corporation and Subsidiary for the year ended December 31, 2006.

P 7-4

Computations separate and consolidated statements given Peter Corporation acquired an 80% interest in Sher Corporation on January 1, 2006, for $320,000, at which time Sher had capital stock of $200,000 outstanding and retained earnings of $100,000. The price paid by Peter reflected a $100,000 undervaluation of Sher's plant and equipment. This equipment had a remaining useful life of eight years when Peter acquired its interest.

Separate-company and consolidated financial statements for Peter Corporation and its subsidiary, Sher Corporation, for the year ended December 31, 2008, are as follows:

	Peter	Sher	Consolidated
Combined Income and Retained Earnings Statement for the Year Ended December 31, 2008			
Sales	$ 180,000	$100,000	$230,000
Income from Sher	20,000	—	—
Interest income	—	8,000	—
Cost of goods sold	(110,000)	(60,000)	(110,000)
Operating expenses	(30,000)	(18,000)	(58,000)
Interest expense	(18,000)	—	(9,000)
Loss	—	—	(3,000)
Noncontrolling interest	—	—	(8,000)
Net income	42,000	30,000	42,000
Add: Beginning retained earnings	294,000	135,000	294,000
Deduct: Dividends	(20,000)	(15,000)	(20,000)
Ending retained earnings	$ 316,000	$150,000	$316,000
Balance Sheet at December 31, 2008			
Cash	$ 60,000	$ 26,000	$ 86,000
Accounts receivable	120,000	$ 60,000	165,000
Inventories	100,000	50,000	140,000
Plant and equipment	500,000	200,000	780,000
Accumulated depreciation	(100,000)	(50,000)	(180,000)
Investment in Sher stock	320,000	—	—
Investment in Peter bonds	—	104,000	—
Total assets	$1,000,000	$390,000	$991,000
Accounts payable	$ 80,000	$ 40,000	$105,000
10% Bonds payable	204,000	—	102,000
Common stock	400,000	200,000	400,000
Retained earnings	316,000	150,000	316,000
Noncontrolling interest	—	—	68,000
Total equities	$1,000,000	$390,000	$991,000

Sher sells merchandise to Peter but never purchases from Peter. On January 1, 2008, Sher purchased $100,000 par of 10% Peter Corporation bonds for $106,000. These bonds mature on December 31, 2010, and Sher expects to hold the bonds until maturity. Both Sher and Peter use straight-line amortization.

REQUIRED: Show computations for each of the following items:

1. The $3,000 loss in the consolidated income statement
2. The $230,000 consolidated sales
3. Consolidated cost of goods sold of $110,000
4. Intercompany profit in beginning inventories
5. Intercompany profit in ending inventories
6. Consolidated accounts receivable of $165,000
7. Noncontrolling interest expense of $8,000
8. Noncontrolling interest at December 31, 2008
9. Investment in Sher stock at December 31, 2007
10. Investment income account of $20,000 (Peter's books)

P 7-5

[AICPA adapted] Computations (constructive retirement of subsidiary bonds)

Selected amounts from the separate unconsolidated financial statements of Poe Corporation and its 90%-owned subsidiary, Shaw Company, at December 31, 2006, are as follows. 90%

	Poe	**Shaw**
Selected Income Statement Amounts		
Sales	$710,000	$530,000
Cost of goods sold	490,000	370,000
Gain on sale of equipment	—	21,000
Earnings from investment in subsidiary (90% Inc)	61,000	—
Interest expense	—	16,000
Depreciation	25,000	20,000
Selected Balance Sheet Amounts		
Cash	$ 50,000	$ 15,000
Inventories	229,000	150,000
Equipment	440,000	360,000
Accumulated depreciation	(200,000)	(120,000)
Investment in Shaw	189,000	—
Investment in bonds	91,000	—
Bonds payable	—	(200,000)
Common stock	(100,000)	(10,000)
Additional paid-in capital	(250,000)	(40,000)
Retained earnings	(402,000)	(140,000)
Selected Statement of Retained Earnings Amounts		
Beginning balance December 31, 2005	$272,000	$100,000
Net income	210,000	70,000
Dividends paid	80,000	30,000

ADDITIONAL INFORMATION

1. On January 2, 2006, Poe purchased 90% of Shaw Company's 100,000 outstanding common stock for cash of $155,000. On that date, Shaw's stockholders' equity equaled $150,000 and the fair values of Shaw's assets and liabilities equaled their carrying amounts. Poe has accounted for the acquisition as a purchase. The difference between fair value and book value was due to a previously unrecorded patent. Poe's policy is to amortize intangibles over 10 years.

2. On September 4, 2006, Shaw paid cash dividends of $30,000.

3. On December 31, 2006, Poe recorded its equity in Shaw's earnings.

4. On January 3, 2006, Shaw sold equipment with an original cost of $30,000 and a carrying value of $15,000 to Poe for $36,000. The equipment had a remaining life of three years and was depreciated using the straight-line method by both companies.

5. During 2006, Shaw sold merchandise to Poe for $60,000, which included a profit of $20,000. At December 31, 2006, half of this merchandise remained in Poe's inventory.

6. On December 31, 2006, Poe paid $91,000 to purchase half of the outstanding bonds issued by Shaw. The bonds mature on December 31, 2012, and were originally issued at par. These bonds pay interest annually on December 31 of each year, and the interest was paid to the prior investor immediately before Poe's purchase of the bonds.

REQUIRED: Determine the amounts at which the following items will appear in the consolidated financial statements of Poe Corporation and Subsidiary for the year ended December 31, 2006.

1. Cash

2. Equipment less accumulated depreciation

3. Investment in Shaw

4. Bonds payable (net of unamortized discount)

5. Common stock

6. Beginning retained earnings

7. Dividends paid

8. Gain on retirement of bonds

9. Cost of goods sold

10. Interest expense

11. Depreciation expense

P 7-6

Working papers (constructive retirement of bonds, intercompany sales)

Financial statements for Paar Corporation and its 75%-owned subsidiary, Sahl Corporation, for 2007 are summarized as follows (in thousands).

	Paar	Sahl
Combined Income and Retained Earnings Statement		
for the Year Ended December 31, 2007		
Sales	$630	$500
Gain on plant	30	—
Income from Sahl	52	—
Cost of goods sold	(350)	(300)
Depreciation expense	(76)	(40)
Interest expense	(20)	—
Other expenses	(46)	(60)
Net income	220	100
Add: Beginning retained earnings	150	100
Deduct: Dividends	(160)	(80)
Retained earnings December 31	$210	$120
Balance Sheet at December 31, 2007		
Cash	$ 27	$ 81
Bond interest receivable	—	5
Other receivables—net	40	30
Inventories	80	50
Land	90	70
Buildings—net	150	180
Equipment—net	140	90
Investment in Sahl	343	—
Investment in Paar bonds	—	94
Total assets	$870	$600
Accounts payable	$ 50	$ 80
Bond interest payable	10	—
10% Bonds payable	200	—
Common stock	400	400
Retained earnings	210	120
Total equities	$870	$600

75%

Paar Corporation acquired its interest in Sahl at book value during 2004, when the fair values of Sahl's assets and liabilities were equal to their recorded book values.

ADDITIONAL INFORMATION

1. Paar uses the equity method in accounting for its investment in Sahl.

2. Intercompany sales of merchandise between the two affiliated companies totaled $50,000 during 2007. All intercompany balances have been paid except for $10,000 in transit from Sahl to Paar at December 31, 2007.

3. Unrealized profits in Sahl's inventories of merchandise acquired from Paar were $12,000 at December 31, 2006, and $15,000 at December 31, 2007. *downstream*

4. Sahl sold equipment with a six-year remaining useful life to Paar on January 2, 2005, at a gain of $24,000. The equipment is still in use by Paar. *2005 - 2006 - 2007 = 3 yrs × $4 = $12,000 recognized ← upstream!*

5. Paar sold a plant to Sahl on July 1, 2007. The land was sold at a gain of $10,000 and the building, which *downstream* had a remaining useful life of 10 years, at a gain of $20,000.

6. Sahl purchased $100,000 par of Paar 10% bonds in the open market for $94,000 plus $5,000 accrued interest on December 31, 2007. Interest is paid semiannually on January 1 and July 1, and the bonds mature on January 1, 2012.

REQUIRED: Prepare consolidation working papers for Paar Corporation and Subsidiary for the year ended December 31, 2007.

INTERNET ASSIGNMENT

Use an Internet search engine such as *Lycos, Google, Yahoo,* or any other you are familiar with to locate two examples of gains or losses on extinguishment of debts. Briefly summarize the financial statement presentation of the gains or losses and any supplemental disclosures provided by the firms.

SELECTED READINGS

Accounting Principles Board Opinion No. 30. "Reporting the Results of Operations." New York: American Institute of Certified Public Accountants, 1973.

Statement of Financial Accounting Standards No. 145: "Rescission of FASB Statements No. 4, 44, and 64, Amendment of FASB Statement No. 13, and Technical Corrections." Stamford, CT: Financial Accounting Standards Board, 2002.

8 CHAPTER

CONSOLIDATIONS-CHANGES IN OWNERSHIP INTERESTS

LEARNING OBJECTIVES

1 Prepare consolidated statements when parent company's ownership percentage increases or decreases during the reporting period.

2 Apply consolidation procedures to interim (midyear) acquisitions.

3 Record subsidiary/investee stock issuances and treasury stock transactions.

4 Electronic supplement: Understand how to account for an interim pooling of interests.

This chapter considers several topics related to changes in parent-company/investor ownership interests. These topics include parent/investor accounting and consolidation procedures for interim acquisitions of stock, piecemeal acquisitions of a controlling interest, sales of ownership interests, and changes in ownership interests through investee stock issuances and treasury stock transactions.

•••

ACQUISITIONS DURING AN ACCOUNTING PERIOD

LEARNING OBJECTIVE 1

Previous chapters in this book have illustrated consolidations for subsidiary acquisitions at the beginning of an accounting period. When the parent acquires a subsidiary during an accounting period, some consolidation adjustments have to be made in order to account for the income of the subsidiary that was earned prior to its acquisition and included in the purchase price. Such income is referred to as **preacquisition earnings** to distinguish it from income of the consolidated entity. Similarly, **preacquisition dividends** are dividends paid on stock before its acquisition that require additional consolidation adjustments.

Such interim acquisitions are common transactions. For example, in Note 3 (pp. 78–79) in its 2003 annual report, *Disney* reports that:

> On October 24, 2001, the Company acquired Fox Family Worldwide, Inc. (FFW) for $5.2 billion, which was funded with $2.9 billion of new long-term borrowings plus the assumption of $2.3 billion of FFW long-term debt. Upon the closing of the acquisition, the Company changed FFW's name to ABC Family Worldwide, Inc. (ABC Family). … The Company's consolidated results of operations have incorporated ABC Family's activity on a consolidated basis from October 24, 2001, the date of acquisition.

Note 3 to *PepsiCo, Inc.*, and Subsidiaries' 2000 annual report discloses the following:

> During 1998, we completed the acquisitions of Tropicana Products, Inc. from The Seagram Company Ltd. for $3.3 billion in cash and The Smith's Snackfoods Company in Australia from United Biscuits Holdings plc for $270 million in cash. The results of operations of acquisitions are generally included in the consolidated financial statements from their respective dates of acquisition. (p. 32)

Preacquisition Earnings

Conceptually we eliminate preacquisition earnings (or *purchased income*) from consolidated income by either of two methods. We could exclude the sales and expenses of the subsidiary prior to acquisition from consolidated sales and expenses. Or we could include the sales and expenses of the subsidiary in the consolidated income statement for the full year and deduct preacquisition income as a separate item.

Assume, for example, that Patter Corporation purchases a 90% interest in Sissy Company on April 1, 2006, for $213,750. Sissy's income, dividends, and stockholders' equity for 2006 are as follows:

	January 1 to April 1	April 1 to December 31	January 1 to December 31
Income			
Sales	$ 25,000	$ 75,000	$100,000
Cost of sales and expenses	12,500	37,500	50,000
Net income	$ 12,500	$ 37,500	$ 50,000
Dividends	$ 10,000	$ 15,000	$ 25,000
	January 1	**April 1**	**December 31**
Stockholders' Equity			
Capital stock	$200,000	$200,000	$200,000
Retained earnings	35,000	37,500	60,000
Stockholders' equity	$235,000	$237,500	$260,000

Sissy's income from January 1 to April 1, 2006, is $12,500 ($25,000 sales − $12,500 expenses), and Sissy's equity at April 1 is $237,500. Therefore, the book value acquired by Patter ($237,500 × 90% interest) is equal to the $213,750 purchase price of Sissy stock.

In recording income from its investment in Sissy at year-end, Patter makes the following entry:

Investment in Sissy (+A)	33,750	
Income from Sissy (R, +SE)		33,750

To record income from the last three quarters
of 2006 ($37,500 × 90%).

Recording investment income on an equity basis increases Patter's income by $33,750, so the effect on consolidated net income must also be $33,750. Conceptually, the consolidated income statement is affected as follows:

Sales (last three quarters of 2006)	$75,000
Expenses (last three quarters of 2006)	(37,500)
Noncontrolling interest expense (last three quarters of 2006)	(3,750)
Effect on consolidated net income	$33,750

This solution poses two practical problems. First, the income of the 10% noncontrolling interest for 2006 is $5,000 for the full year, even though it is only $3,750 for the last nine months. Second, by consolidating sales and expenses for only nine months of the year, the consolidated income statement does not provide a basis for projecting future annual sales and expenses for the consolidated entity.

In considering these problems, the Committee on Accounting Procedure of the AICPA in *ARB No. 51* (paragraph 11) expressed the opinion that the most meaningful consolidated income statement presentation results from including the sales and expenses in the consolidated income statement for the full year and deducting preacquisition income as a separate item. The committee recommended consolidating subsidiary accounts in the following manner:

Sales (full year)	$100,000
Expenses (full year)	(50,000)
Preacquisition income	(11,250)
Noncontrolling interest expense	(5,000)
Effect on consolidated net income	$ 33,750

Preacquisition Dividends

We eliminate dividends paid on stock prior to its acquisition (preacquisition dividends) in the consolidation process because they are not a part of the equity acquired. Sissy paid $25,000 dividends during 2006, but it paid $10,000 of this amount before the acquisition by Patter. Accordingly, Patter makes the following entry to account for dividends actually received.

Cash (+A)	13,500
Investment in Sissy (−A)	13,500
To record dividends received ($15,000 × 90%).	

We eliminate the preacquisition dividends relating to the 90% interest acquired by Patter in the consolidation process along with the preacquisition earnings. We include these eliminations in the working paper entry that eliminates reciprocal investment in subsidiary and subsidiary equity balances in order to compensate for the fact that subsidiary equity balances are eliminated as of the beginning of the period and the investment balance is eliminated as of the date of acquisition within the period. Sissy's allocations of income and dividends are as follows:

	Majority Interest (Patter and Consolidated)	Noncontrolling Interest (10%)	Preacquisition Eliminations	Total
Sissy's net income	$33,750	$5,000	$11,250	$50,000
Sissy's dividends	13,500	2,500	9,000	25,000

Consolidation

Exhibit 8-1 illustrates consolidation procedures for midyear acquisitions for Patter and Subsidiary. The $234,000 Investment in Sissy balance in Patter's balance sheet consists of the $213,750 cost plus $33,750 income less $13,500 dividends received. Although other amounts in the separate statements of Patter and Sissy are introduced for the first time in the consolidation working papers, they are entirely compatible with the previous assumptions and data for Patter and Sissy Corporations.

Working paper entry a eliminates the income from Sissy and dividends received from Sissy and returns the Investment in Sissy account to its $213,750 balance at acquisition on April 1, 2006.

a	Income from Sissy (−R, −SE)	33,750	
	Dividends—Sissy (+SE)		13,500
	Investment in Sissy (−A)		20,250
	To eliminate investment income and the dividends received from Sissy and to adjust the investment in Sissy to its cost on April 1, 2006.		

This entry does not reflect new procedures, but we must be careful to eliminate only dividends actually received (90% × $15,000) rather than multiplying the ownership percentage times dividends paid by the subsidiary for the year.

The second working paper entry in Exhibit 8-1 reflects new working paper procedures because it contains items from preacquisition earnings and dividends. We journalize it as follows:

b	Preacquisition income (E, −SE)	11,250	
	Capital stock—Sissy (−SE)	200,000	
	Retained earnings—Sissy (−SE)	35,000	
	Dividends—Sissy (+SE)		9,000
	Investment in Sissy (−A)		213,750
	Noncontrolling interest—beginning (+L)		23,500
	To eliminate reciprocal investment and equity balances, to record preacquisition income and beginning noncontrolling interest, and to eliminate preacquisition dividends.		
c	Noncontrolling interest expense (E, −SE)	5,000	
	Dividends (+SE)		2,500
	Noncontrolling interest (+L)		2,500
	To enter noncontrolling interest share of subsidiary income and dividends.		

LEARNING OBJECTIVE **2**

EXHIBIT 8-1

Preacquisition
Income and
Dividends in
Consolidation
Working Papers

PATTER CORPORATION AND SUBSIDIARY CONSOLIDATION WORKING PAPERS FOR THE YEAR ENDED DECEMBER 31, 2006

	Patter	90% Sissy	Adjustments and Eliminations Debits	Credits	Consolidated Statements
Income Statement Sales	$300,000	$100,000			$400,000
Income from Sissy	33,750		a 33,750		
Expenses including cost of sales	(200,000)	(50,000)			(250,000)
Noncontrolling interest expense ($50,000 × 10%)			c 5,000		(5,000)
Preacquisition income			b 11,250		(11,250)
Net income	**$133,750**	**$ 50,000**			**$133,750**
Retained Earnings Retained earnings—Patter	$266,250				$266,250
Retained earnings—Sissy		$ 35,000	b 35,000		
Net income	133,750	50,000			133,750
Dividends	(100,000)	(25,000)		a 13,500 b 9,000 c 2,500	(100,000)
Retained earnings— December 31	**$300,000**	**$ 60,000**			**$300,000**
Balance Sheet Other assets	$566,000	$260,000			$826,000
Investment in Sissy	234,000			a 20,250 b 213,750	
	$800,000	$260,000			$826,000
Capital stock	$500,000	$200,000	b 200,000		$500,000
Retained earnings	300,000	60,000			300,000
	$800,000	$260,000			
Noncontrolling interest				b 23,500 c 2,500	26,000
					$826,000

In examining entry b, note that preacquisition income less preacquisition dividends of $2,250 equals the $213,750 investment cost on April 1, 2006, less 90% of Sissy's equity on January 1, 2006. Also note that beginning noncontrolling interest is 10% of Sissy's January 1, 2006, equity. In case of *increases* in ownership interests during a period, we compute noncontrolling interest for the noncontrolling shares outstanding at year-end.

We introduce preacquisition income in the working papers through a working paper entry. Subsequently, we deduct it in measuring consolidated net income. The classification of preacquisition income in a consolidated income statement parallels the classification of noncontrolling interest expense. Midyear acquisitions do not affect consolidation working papers in subsequent accounting periods.

Sissy's 10% ending noncontrolling interest is held outside of the consolidated entity for the entire year, so the noncontrolling interest computation is simply 10% of Sissy's equity at the beginning of the year plus 10% of Sissy's net income for the year less 10% of the dividends declared by Sissy during the year.

PIECEMEAL ACQUISITIONS

A corporation may acquire an interest in another corporation in a series of separate stock purchases over a period of time. For example, *USX Corporation's* Note 28 to its 2000 annual report discloses that:

> On February 7, 2001, Marathon acquired 87% of the outstanding common stock of Pennaco Energy, Inc., a natural gas producer. Marathon plans to acquire the remaining Pennaco shares through a merger.

These **piecemeal acquisitions** pose no new problems of analysis if the parent accounts for its investment on an equity basis. However, they do increase the details of computing investment income and consolidated net income. This section discusses these details and illustrates accounting for them.

Poca Corporation acquires a 90% interest in Sark Corporation in a series of separate stock purchases between July 1, 2006, and October 1, 2008. Data concerning the acquisitions and interests acquired are as follows (in thousands):

Year	Date	Interest Acquired	Investment Cost	Equity January 1	Income for Year	Equity at Acquisition	Equity December 31
2006	July 1	20%	$30	$100	$50	$125	$150
2007	April 1	40	74	150	40	160	190
2008	October 1	30	81	190	40	220	230

The net assets of Sark Corporation are stated at their fair values, and the excess of investment cost over book value acquired in each case is due to goodwill. Accordingly, we compute the initial goodwill from each of the three acquisitions (in thousands):

Year	Investment Cost	Book Value and Fair Value Acquired	Goodwill
2006	$30	($125 × 20%) = $25	$ 5
2007	74	($160 × 40%) = $64	10
2008	81	($220 × 30%) = $66	15

Poca acquired the interests within each accounting period, so the consolidated income statements show preacquisition income in the years 2007 and 2008. Goodwill is not amortized.

At December 31, 2008, Poca's Investment in Sark account balance is $237,000, consisting of $185,000 total cost, plus income of $52,000 (Poca's share of Sark's net income) during the period 2006 through 2008. For purposes of computing gain or loss on subsequent sales, Poca should keep a record for each of the investments. The following schedule is an example of such a record:

	20% Interest	30% Interest	30% Interest	Total
Investment cost	$30	$ 74	$81	$185
Investment income				
2006	5	—	—	5
2007	8	12	—	20
2008	8	16	3	27
	$51	$102	$84	$237

When we consolidate the financial statements of Poca and Sark in 2007 and 2008, preacquisition income will appear in the consolidated income statements. Except for the preacquisition income item, no unusual consolidating procedures result from piecemeal acquisitions. Exhibit 8-2 shows consolidation working papers for Poca Corporation and Subsidiary for 2008. Additional data, compatible with previous information for the Poca-Sark example, is provided for illustrative purposes.

EXHIBIT 8-2

Piecemeal
Acquisition of a
Controlling Interest

POCA CORPORATION AND SUBSIDIARY CONSOLIDATION WORKING PAPERS FOR THE YEAR ENDED DECEMBER 31, 2008

	Poca	90% Sark	Adjustments and Eliminations Debits	Credits	Consolidated Statements
Income Statement Sales	$274,875	$150,000			$424,875
Income from Sark	27,000		a 27,000		
Expenses including cost of sales	(220,000)	(110,000)			(330,000)
Noncontrolling interest expense ($40,000 × 10%)			c 4,000		(4,000)
Preacquisition income			b 9,000		(9,000)
Net income	**$ 81,875**	**$ 40,000**			**$ 81,875**
Retained Earnings Retained earnings—Poca	$221,500				$221,500
Retained earnings—Sark		$ 90,000	b 90,000		
Net income	81,875	40,000			81,875
Retained earnings— December 31	**$303,375**	**$130,000**			**$303,375**
Balance Sheet Other assets	$466,375	$300,000			$766,375
Investment in Sark	237,000			a 27,000 b 210,000	
Goodwill			b 30,000		30,000
	$703,375	$300,000			$796,375
Liabilities	$100,000	$ 70,000			$170,000
Capital stock	300,000	100,000	b 100,000		300,000
Retained earnings	303,375	130,000			303,375
	$703,375	$300,000			
Noncontrolling interest				b 19,000 c 4,000	23,000
					$796,375

The working paper entries are reproduced here for convenient reference:

a **Income from Sark** (−R, −SE)	**27,000**	
Investment in Sark (−A)		**27,000**
To eliminate investment income and return investment account to its beginning-of-the-period balance plus the $81,000 new investment.		

b Preacquisition income (E, –SE)	9,000	
Retained earnings—Sark (–SE)	90,000	
Capital stock—Sark (–SE)	100,000	
Goodwill (+A)	30,000	
Investment in Sark (–A)		210,000
Noncontrolling interest January 1 (+L)		19,000
To eliminate investment in Sark and Sark's equity		
balances and to enter preacquisition income, goodwill,		
and beginning-of-the-period noncontrolling interest.		
c Noncontrolling interest expense (E, –SE)	4,000	
Noncontrolling interest (+L)		4,000
To record noncontrolling interest in Sark's net income.		

Preacquisition income of $9,000 relates to the 30% interest acquired on October 1, 2008 ($40,000 Sark's income × 30% interest × 3/4 year). We compute the noncontrolling interest expense for 2008 on the basis of the 10% minority ownership at December 31, 2008. Goodwill of $30,000 as shown in the consolidated balance sheet of Exhibit 8-2 is equal to the initial unamortized amount. Except for these three items, the consolidation working paper procedures are equivalent to those used in previous chapters.

SALE OF OWNERSHIP INTERESTS

When a parent company/investor sells an ownership interest, we compute the gain or loss on the sale as the difference between the proceeds from the sale and the book value of the investment interest sold. The book value of the investment should, of course, reflect the equity method of accounting when the investor is able to exercise significant influence over the investee corporation. If a parent company acquires its interest in several different purchases, the shares sold must be identified with particular acquisitions. This is usually done on the basis of specific identification or the first-in, first-out flow assumption.

Both Coke and Pepsi regularly sell (and repurchase) ownership interests in their affiliated bottling companies. PepsiCo, Inc., and Subsidiaries' 1999 annual report includes a $1 billion gain on bottling transactions in calculating its $2.05 billion net income for the year. Note 2 provides additional detail:

Investments in Unconsolidated Affiliates

In 1998, our Board of Directors approved a plan for the separation from PepsiCo of certain wholly-owned bottling businesses located in the United States, Canada, Spain, Greece and Russia, referred to as The Pepsi Bottling Group (PBG). On April 6, 1999, PBG completed the sale of 100 million shares of its common stock at $23 per share through an initial public offering, with PepsiCo retaining a direct noncontrolling interest of 35.5%. During the first quarter, we received $5.5 billion of debt proceeds obtained by PBG primarily as settlement of pre-existing intercompany amounts due to us. We recognized a pre-tax gain of $1.0 billion ($476 million after-tax, or $0.32 per share) in the second quarter.

Similarly, although much smaller in amount, the income statement from the 2000 annual report of the **Coca-Cola Company** and Subsidiaries reveals a $27 million gain on stock issued by its equity investees in 1998. Note 1 discloses the following:

Issuances of Stock by Equity Investees

When one of our equity investees issues additional shares to third parties, our percentage ownership interest in the investee decreases. In the event the issuance price per share is more or less than our average carrying amount per share, we recognize a noncash gain or loss on the issuance. This noncash gain or loss, net of any deferred taxes, is generally recognized in our net income in the period the change of ownership interest occurs. (p. 51)

The following information illustrates sale of ownership interests, both at the beginning of the period and during the period. Sergio Corporation is a 90%-owned subsidiary of Pablo Corporation. Pablo's Investment in Sergio account at January 1, 2007, has a balance of $288,000, consisting of its underlying equity in Sergio plus $18,000 unamortized goodwill. Sergio's stockholders' equity at January 1, 2007, consists of $200,000 capital stock and $100,000 retained earnings. During 2007, Sergio reports income of $36,000, earned proportionately throughout the year, and it pays dividends of $20,000 on July 1.

Sale of an Interest at the Beginning of the Period

If Pablo Corporation sells a 10% interest in Sergio (one-ninth of its holdings) on January 1, 2007, for $40,000, we record an $8,000 gain on sale on Pablo's books and reduce the Investment in Sergio account by $32,000 ($288,000 ÷ 9). The $8,000 gain is a gain for consolidated statement purposes as well as for Pablo as a separate entity. The sale of the 10% interest reduces Pablo's ownership percentage in Sergio to 80% and increases the noncontrolling interest to 20%. It also reduces Pablo's goodwill by one-ninth of the total, or $2,000.

During 2007, Pablo accounts for its 80% interest under the equity method of accounting and records income of $28,800 ($36,000 net income of Sergio × 80%) and a reduction in its investment account for dividends received. At December 31, 2007, Pablo's Investment in Sergio account has a balance of $268,800, computed as follows:

Investment balance January 1, 2007	$288,000
Less: Book value of interest sold	32,000
	256,000
Add: Income less dividends ($28,800 − $16,000)	12,800
Investment balance December 31, 2007	$268,800

The investment balance at year-end consists of Pablo's underlying equity in Sergio of $252,800 ($316,000 × 80%) plus $16,000 goodwill on the 80% interest still owned. Consolidation working papers for Pablo Corporation and Subsidiary as shown in Exhibit 8-3 illustrate the effect of a decrease in an ownership interest on working paper procedures.

The sale of the interest was at the beginning of the period, so the effect of the sale on consolidation procedures for 2007 is minimal. The working paper entries from Exhibit 8-3 are in general journal form.

a	Income from Sergio (−R, −SE)	28,800	
	Dividends—Sergio (+SE)		16,000
	Investment in Sergio (−A)		12,800
	To eliminate income and dividends from Sergio and return the investment account to its beginning-of-the-period balance after the sale of the 10% interest.		
b	Capital stock—Sergio (−SE)	200,000	
	Retained earnings—Sergio (−SE)	100,000	
	Goodwill (+A)	16,000	
	Investment in Sergio (−A)		256,000
	Noncontrolling interest (20%) (+L)		60,000
	To eliminate reciprocal investment and equity balances, and to record unamortized goodwill and beginning noncontrolling interest.		
c	Noncontrolling interest expense (E, −SE)	7,200	
	Dividends (+SE)		4,000
	Noncontrolling interest (+L)		3,200
	To enter noncontrolling interest share of subsidiary income and dividends.		

PABLO CORPORATION AND SUBSIDIARY CONSOLIDATION WORKING PAPERS FOR THE YEAR ENDED DECEMBER 31, 2007

EXHIBIT 8-3

Sale of a 10% Interest at the Beginning of the Period

	Pablo	80% Sergio	Adjustments and Eliminations Debits	Credits	Consolidated Statements
Income Statement Sales	$600,000	$136,000			$ 736,000
Income from Sergio	28,800		a 28,800		
Gain on sale	8,000				8,000
Expenses including cost of sales	(508,800)	(100,000)			(608,800)
Noncontrolling interest expense ($36,000 × 20%)			c 7,200		(7,200)
Net income	**$128,000**	**$ 36,000**			**$ 128,000**
Retained Earnings Retained earnings—Pablo	$210,000				$ 210,000
Retained earnings—Sergio		$100,000	b 100,000		
Net income	**128,000**	**36,000**			**128,000**
Dividends	(80,000)	(20,000)		a 16,000 c 4,000	(80,000)
Retained earnings— December 31	**$258,000**	**$116,000**			**$ 258,000**
Balance Sheet Other assets	$639,200	$350,000			$989,200
Investment in Sergio	268,800			a 12,800 b 256,000	
Goodwill			b 16,000		16,000
	$908,000	$350,000			$1,005,200
Liabilities	$150,000	$ 34,000			$ 184,000
Capital stock	500,000	200,000	b 200,000		500,000
Retained earnings	**258,000**	**116,000**			**258,000**
	$908,000	$350,000			
Noncontrolling interest				b 60,000 c 3,200	63,200
					$1,005,200

Working paper entry a reduces the investment in Sergio to its $256,000 beginning-of-the-period balance after sale of the 10% interest, and entry b enters goodwill and noncontrolling interest based on amounts immediately after the 10% interest was sold. The last entry records the noncontrolling interest share of income and dividends. Pablo's income statement includes the $8,000 gain on sale, which we carry directly to the consolidated income statement without adjustment.

Sale of an Interest During an Accounting Period

If Pablo Corporation sells the 10% interest in Sergio Corporation on April 1, 2007, for $40,000, the sale may be recorded as of April 1, 2007, or, as an expedient, as of January 1, 2007. Assuming that Pablo records the sale as of January 1, 2007, Pablo records the $8,000 gain on sale the same as in the beginning-of-the-year sale situation and makes the same one-line consolidation entries as those illustrated in the earlier example. Consistency with the one-line consolidation requires that we prepare the consolidated financial statements using the same beginning-of-the-period sale assumption. That is, we compute noncontrolling interest expense for a 20% noncontrolling interest outstanding throughout 2007, and we base beginning and ending noncontrolling interest amounts on a 20% noncontrolling interest. This alternative beginning-of-the-period sale assumption does not affect parent-company or consolidated net income because any difference in the gain or loss on sale is exactly offset by differences in computing the income from subsidiary under a one-line consolidation and in computing noncontrolling interest amounts in the consolidated financial statements.[1]

If the sale is recorded as of April 1, 2007, the gain on sale will be $7,100, computed as:

Selling price of 10% interest		$40,000
Less: Book value of the interest sold:		
Investment balance January 1	$288,000	
Equity in income		
$36,000 × 1/4 year × 90%	8,100	
	296,100	
Portion of investment sold	× 1/9	32,900
Gain		$ 7,100

Journal entries on Pablo's books during 2007 to account for the 10% interest sold and its investment in Sergio are as follows:

April 1, 2007

Investment in Sergio (+A)	8,100	
Income from Sergio (R, +SE)		8,100

   To record income for first quarter 2007 ($8,100 equity in income).

Cash (+A)	40,000	
Investment in Sergio (−A)		32,900
Gain on sale of investment (Ga, +SE)		7,100

   To record sale of a 10% interest in Sergio. (See earlier computations.)

July 1, 2007

Cash (+A)	16,000	
Investment in Sergio (−A)		16,000

   To record dividends received ($20,000 × 80%).

December 31, 2007

Investment in Sergio (+A)	21,600	
Income from Sergio (R, +SE)		21,600

   To record income for last three quarters of 2007.

The income from Sergio for 2007 is $29,700, consisting of $8,100 the first quarter and $21,600 the last three quarters of the year. At year-end, the Investment in Sergio account has the same $268,800 balance as in the beginning-of-the-period sale illustration, but the balance involves different amounts:

---

[1] If recorded as of the beginning of the period, we must consider dividends actually received on the interest sold prior to sale in calculating the gain or loss on sale and adjust consolidation procedures accordingly.

Investment balance January 1	$288,000
Less: Book value of interest sold	32,900
	255,100
Add: Income less dividends	13,700
Investment balance December 31	$268,800

The investment balance at year-end is the same as before because Pablo holds the same owner-ship interest as under the beginning-of-the-year sale assumption. Further, Pablo has received the same cash inflow from the investment ($40,000 proceeds from the sale and $16,000 dividends) and therefore should report the same income. We explain the income effects under the different assumptions as follows:

	Sale at or Assumed at Beginning of Period	Sale Within the Accounting Period
Gain on sale of investment	$ 8,000	$ 7,100
Income from Sergio	20,800	21,700
Total income effect	$28,800	$28,800

The total income effect on Pablo's net income is the same, so the effect on the consolidated financial statements also must be the same. Consolidation working papers for a sale within an accounting period are illustrated in Exhibit 8-4.

We journalize working paper entries to consolidate the financial statements of Pablo and Sergio as follows:

a	**Income from Sergio (–R, –SE)**	**29,700**	
	Dividends—Sergio (+SE)		**16,000**
	Investment in Sergio (–A)		**13,700**
b	**Capital stock—Sergio (–SE)**	**200,000**	
	Retained earnings—Sergio (–SE)	**100,000**	
	Goodwill (+A)	**16,000**	
	Investment in Sergio (–A)		**255,100**
	Noncontrolling interest January 1 (+L)		**30,000**
	Noncontrolling interest April 1 (+L)		**30,900**
c	**Noncontrolling interest expense (E, –SE)**	**7,200**	
	Dividends (+SE)		**4,000**
	Noncontrolling interest (+L)		**2,300**
	To enter noncontrolling interest share of subsidiary income and dividends.		

NONCONTROLLING INTEREST COMPUTATIONS We separate the noncontrolling interest amounts entered in entry b for illustrative purposes, but they do not have to be separated. We based one part of the non-controlling interest calculation on the 10% noncontrolling interest at the beginning of the period ($300,000 equity of Sergio at January 1 × 10%), and the other part reflects the book value of the 10% increase in noncontrolling interest from the April 1 sale ($309,000 equity of Sergio on April 1 × 10%). Note that we also need a dual calculation for noncontrolling interest expense $6,300 [($36,000 × 10%) + ($36,000 × 10% × 3/4 year)] for midyear sale situations. The investment in Sergio decreased when the interest was sold on April 1; therefore, the $255,100 credit in working paper entry b reflects the $288,000 beginning investment balance less the $32,900 book value of the investment interest sold on April 1.

Except for the items discussed, the working papers in Exhibits 8-3 and 8-4 are comparable, and the resulting consolidated financial statements are equivalent in all material respects. Because of the additional complexity involved when recording a sale as of the actual sale date, it is more effi-cient to use the beginning-of-the-period sale assumption. Use of a beginning-of-the-period assumption is also practical because current earnings information usually is not available during an accounting period.

EXHIBIT 8-4

Sale of a 10%
Interest Within an
Accounting Period

PABLO CORPORATION AND SUBSIDIARY CONSOLIDATION WORKING PAPERS FOR THE YEAR ENDED DECEMBER 31, 2007

	Pablo	80% Sergio	Adjustments and Eliminations Debits	Credits	Consolidated Statements
Income Statement					
Sales	$600,000	$136,000			$ 736,000
Income from Sergio	29,700		a 29,700		
Gain on sale	7,100				7,100
Expenses including cost of sales	(508,800)	(100,000)			(608,800)
Noncontrolling interest expense*			c 6,300		(6,300)
Net income	**$128,000**	**$ 36,000**			**$ 128,000**
Retained Earnings					
Retained earnings—Pablo	$210,000				$ 210,000
Retained earnings—Sergio		$100,000	b 100,000		
Net income	**128,000**	**36,000**			**128,000**
Dividends	(80,000)	(20,000)		a 16,000 c 4,000	(80,000)
Retained earnings— December 31	**$258,000**	**$116,000**			**$ 258,000**
Balance Sheet					
Other assets	$639,200	$350,000			$ 989,200
Investment in Sergio	268,800			a 13,700 b 255,100	
Goodwill			b 16,000		16,000
	$908,000	**$350,000**			**$1,005,200**
Liabilities	$150,000	$ 34,000			$ 184,000
Capital stock	500,000	200,000	b 200,000		500,000
Retained earnings	**258,000**	**116,000**			**258,000**
	$908,000	**$350,000**			
Noncontrolling interest January 1 April 1 December 31				b 30,000 b 30,900 c 2,300	63,200
					$1,005,200

*Noncontrolling interest expense = ($36,000 × 10% × 1 year) + ($36,000 × 10% × 3/4 year)

CHANGES IN OWNERSHIP INTERESTS FROM SUBSIDIARY STOCK TRANSACTIONS

Subsidiary stock issuances provide a means of expanding the operations of a subsidiary through external financing. Both the expansion and the financing decisions are, of course, controlled by the parent company. Parent-company management may decide to construct a new plant for the subsidiary and to finance the construction by selling additional subsidiary stock to the parent.

Subsidiary operations may also be expanded through the issuance of subsidiary stock to the public. The Pepsi Bottling Group initial public offering (IPO) mentioned earlier in the chapter provides one example. A parent may even issue shares of one subsidiary to acquire another. The following note appeared in the 2000 annual report of **USX Corporation** (p. U-11):

> *In August 1998, Marathon Oil Company (Marathon) acquired Tarragon Oil and Gas Limited (Tarragon), a Canadian oil and gas exploration and production company. Securityholders of Tarragon received, at their election, Cdn$14.25 for each Tarragon share, or the economic equivalent in Exchangeable Shares of an indirect Canadian subsidiary of Marathon, which are exchangeable solely on a one-for-one basis into Marathon Stock.*

In the case of a partially owned subsidiary, noncontrolling stockholders may exercise their preemptive rights to subscribe to additional stock issuances in proportion to their holdings.

Subsidiary operations may be curtailed if the parent-company management decides to have the subsidiary reacquire its own shares.

A parent company/investor's ownership in a subsidiary/investee may change as a result of subsidiary sales of additional shares or through subsidiary purchases of its own shares. The effect of such activities on the parent company/investor depends on the price at which additional shares are sold or treasury stock is purchased and on whether the parent company is directly involved in transactions with the subsidiary. In accounting for an equity investment under a one-line consolidation, *APB Opinion No. 18* stipulates that "a transaction of an investee of a capital nature that affects the investor's share of stockholders' equity of the investee should be accounted for as if the investee were a consolidated subsidiary."[2]

Sale of Additional Shares by a Subsidiary

Assume that Purdy Corporation owns an 80% interest in Stroh Corporation and that Purdy's investment in Stroh is $180,000 on January 1, 2007, equal to 80% of Stroh's $200,000 stockholders' equity plus $20,000 of goodwill. Stroh's equity on this date consists of:

Capital stock, $10 par	$100,000
Additional paid-in capital	60,000
Retained earnings	40,000
Total stockholders' equity	$200,000

SUBSIDIARY SELLS SHARES TO PARENT If Stroh sells an additional 2,000 shares of stock to Purdy *at book value of $20 per share* on January 2, 2007, Purdy's investment in Stroh will increase by $40,000 to $220,000, and its interest in Stroh will increase from 80% (8,000 ÷ 10,000 shares) to 83 1/3% (10,000 ÷ 12,000 shares). The amount paid for the 2,000 additional shares is equal to book value, so Purdy's investment in Stroh still reflects the $20,000 goodwill:

	January 1 Before Sale	January 2 After Sale
Stroh's stockholders' equity	$200,000	$240,000
Purdy's interest	80%	83 1/3%
Purdy's equity in Stroh	160,000	200,000
Goodwill	20,000	20,000
Investment in Stroh balance	$180,000	$220,000

If Stroh sells the 2,000 shares to Purdy *at $35 per share*, Purdy's investment in Stroh will increase to $250,000 ($180,000 + $70,000 additional investment), and its ownership interest will increase from 80% to 83 1/3%. Now Purdy's investment in Stroh reflects a $25,000 excess of investment balance over underlying book value. The additional $5,000 excess is the result of Purdy's $70,000 payment to increase its equity in Stroh by $65,000, which we analyze as follows:

---

[2] *APB Opinion No. 18*, "The Equity Method of Accounting for Investments in Common Stock," paragraph 19e.

Price paid by Purdy (2,000 shares × $35)		$70,000
Book value acquired:		
Underlying book value after purchase		
($200,000 + $70,000) × 83 1/3%	$225,000	
Underlying book value before purchase		
($200,000 × 80%)	160,000	
Book value acquired		65,000
Excess cost over book value acquired		$ 5,000

We assign the $5,000 excess to identifiable assets or goodwill as appropriate and amortize over the remaining life of undervalued assets. Purdy should not amortize the $20,000 goodwill.

Now assume that Stroh sells the 2,000 shares to Purdy at *$15 per share* (or $5 per share below book value). Purdy's ownership interest increases from 80% to 83 1/3% as before, and its investment in Stroh increases by $30,000 to $210,000. As a result of paying less than book value for the shares, however, book value acquired exceeds investment cost:

Price paid by Purdy (2,000 shares × $15)		$30,000
Book value acquired:		
Underlying book value after purchase		
($200,000 + $30,000) × 83 1/3%	$191,667	
Underlying book value before purchase		
($200,000 × 80%)	160,000	
Book value acquired		31,667
Excess book value acquired over cost		$ 1,667

Conceptually, the $1,667 excess book value acquired over cost should be assigned to reduce overvalued identifiable net assets. The practical solution, however, is to charge the excess book value to any goodwill from investments in the same company's stock. In this example, reduce goodwill from $20,000 to $18,333.

SUBSIDIARY SELLS SHARES TO OUTSIDE ENTITIES Assume that Stroh sells the 2,000 additional shares to other entities (noncontrolling stockholders). Purdy's ownership interest declines from 80% (8,000 ÷ 10,000 shares) to 66 2/3% (8,000 ÷ 12,000 shares), regardless of the selling price of the shares. But the effect on Purdy's Investment in Stroh account depends on the selling price of the shares. The effect of the sale on Purdy's underlying book value in Stroh under each of three issuance assumptions ($20, $35, and $15 per share) is:

	January 2, 2007, After Sale		
	Sale at $20	**Sale at $35**	**Sale at $15**
Stroh's stockholders' equity	$240,000	$270,000	$230,000
Interest owned	66 2/3%	66 2/3%	66 2/3%
Purdy's equity in Stroh after issuance	160,000	180,000	153,333
Purdy's equity in Stroh before issuance	160,000	160,000	160,000
Increase (decrease) in Purdy's equity in Stroh	0	$ 20,000	$ (6,667)

Sale to outside entities at $20 per share does not affect Purdy's equity in Stroh because the selling price equals book value. If Stroh sells the stock at $35 per share (above book value), Purdy's equity in Stroh will increase by $20,000, and if Stroh sells at $15 per share (below book value), Purdy's equity in Stroh will decrease by $6,667.

Two methods of accounting for the effect of the decreased ownership percentage on the parent company's books are (1) to adjust the additional paid-in capital and the parent's investment account balances for the change in underlying equity and (2) to treat the decrease in ownership as a sale and recognize gain or loss for the difference between the book value of the investment interest sold and the parent's share of the proceeds from the subsidiary's stock issuance.

The first approach is supported by *APB Opinion No. 9*, which excludes adjustments from transactions in a company's own stock from the determination of net income "under all circumstances."[3] From the viewpoint of the consolidated entity, the issuance of subsidiary shares to the public is a

---

[3] *APB Opinion No. 9*, "Reporting the Results of Operations," paragraph 28.

transaction in a company's own shares. Entries to record the changes in underlying equity on Purdy's books under this first method are:

Sale at $20 per Share (Book Value)

None

Sale at $35 per Share (Above Book Value)

Investment in Stroh (+A)	20,000	
Additional paid-in capital (+SE)		20,000

Sale at $15 per Share (Below Book Value)

Additional paid-in capital[4] (−SE)	6,667	
Investment in Stroh (−A)		6,667

Under this method, we do not adjust unamortized cost/book value differentials for the decreased ownership percentage.

Traditionally, the method just illustrated was the only one accepted by the accounting profession and the SEC. In 1980, however, the AICPA released an issues paper, "Accounting in Consolidation for Issuances of a Subsidiary's Stock," in which it recommended the recognition of gains or losses on subsidiary stock sales. Then, in 1983, the SEC issued *Staff Accounting Bulletin (SAB) 51*, which allows SEC companies to follow the recommendations of the issues paper for previously unissued shares, provided that the subsidiary shares are sold in a public offering and are not part of a broader reorganization that will involve other capital transactions.

Subsequently, in 1989, the SEC, in *SAB 84*, affirmed that a parent company can record a gain in the consolidated income statement on its subsidiary's sale of stock to the public if the per-share offering price is greater than the carrying value of the subsidiary on the parent company's books. However, *SAB 84* restricts recognition of gain when there are concerns about realization of the gain. *SAB 84* prohibits gain recognition on subsidiary stock sales to the public if the registrant plans to repurchase the shares, if the subsidiary is a newly formed nonoperating entity or a research and development company, or if the subsidiary is a company whose continued existence is in question.

The argument in favor of gain or loss recognition is that there is no substantive difference between subsidiary stock sales that reduce a parent's investment and direct sales of stock by the parent. The FASB has not acted on the matter, so neither the issues paper nor *SAB 51* constitutes a generally accepted accounting principle at this time. Also, although *SAB 51* is permissive and not mandatory, it may help establish preferability for a firm that changes its accounting policy to recognize gains on subsidiary stock sales.

Under the second method of gain or loss recognition, we assume that Purdy has sold 16 2/3% of its interest in Stroh [(80% − 66 2/3%) ÷ 80%] in exchange for 66 2/3% of the proceeds from the subsidiary sale of stock. Thus, the entries on Purdy's books under the three selling-price assumptions are:

Sale at $20 per Share (Book Value)

Loss on sale (Lo, −SE)	3,333	
Investment in Stroh (−A)		3,333

Computation: ($40,000 × 66 2/3%) − ($180,000 × 16 2/3%)

Sale at $35 per Share (Above Book Value)

Investment in Stroh (+A)	16,667	
Gain on sale (Ga, +SE)		16,667

Computation: ($70,000 × 66 2/3%) − ($180,000 × 16 2/3%)

Sale at $15 per Share (Below Book Value)

Loss on sale (Lo, −SE)	10,000	
Investment in Stroh (−A)		10,000

Computation: ($30,000 × 66 2/3%) − ($180,000 × 16 2/3%)

---

[4] This debit is to retained earnings when the parent company's additional paid-in capital is insufficient to stand the charge.

The different gain or loss amounts under this method and the amounts of adjustment to additional paid-in capital under the first method lie solely in the $3,333 goodwill [$20,000 × (80% − 66 2/3%) ÷ 80%] applicable to the reduction in ownership percentage. We only consider goodwill related to the interest assumed to be sold when recognizing a gain or loss, and in the absence of unamortized cost/book value differences, the amounts are identical.

SUMMARY OF SUBSIDIARY STOCK SALES CONCEPTS Sales of stock by a subsidiary to its parent do not result in gain or loss recognition or adjustments to additional paid-in capital, but they do result in cost/book value differentials equal to the parent company's share of the difference in the subsidiary's stockholders' equity immediately before and immediately after the sale of stock.

GAAP considers sales of stock by a subsidiary to outside parties as capital transactions and requires adjustment of the parent's investment and additional paid-in capital accounts except when the shares are sold at book value. The amount of adjustment is the difference between the underlying book value of the interest held immediately before and after the additional shares are issued to outsiders. The SEC permits recognition of gains or losses on subsidiary stock sales to the public—with certain restrictions. We determine such gain or loss by comparing the parent's share of proceeds from the stock issue with the book value of the investment interest assumed to be sold. Alternatively, we can determine the gain or loss by adjusting the change in the parent's underlying book value in the subsidiary for any unamortized cost/book value differentials related to the interest assumed to be sold.

If a parent company and outside investors purchase shares of a subsidiary in relation to existing stock ownership (ratably), no adjustments to additional paid-in capital will be necessary, regardless of whether the stock is sold at book value, below book value, or above book value. Similarly, no excess or deficiency of investment cost over book value for the parent company can result from this situation. This is true because the increased investment is necessarily equal to the parent's increase (or decrease) in underlying book value from the ratable purchase of additional shares.

Treasury Stock Transactions by a Subsidiary

The acquisition of treasury stock by a subsidiary decreases subsidiary equity and subsidiary shares outstanding. If the subsidiary acquires treasury stock from noncontrolling shareholders at book value, no change in the parent's share of subsidiary equity results even though the parent's percentage ownership increases. Purchase of its own shares from noncontrolling stockholders at an amount above or below book value decreases or increases the parent's share of subsidiary book value and at the same time increases the parent's ownership percentage. This latter situation requires an entry on the parent company's books to adjust the investment in subsidiary balance and to charge or credit additional paid-in capital for the difference in the parent's share of subsidiary book value before and after the treasury stock transaction.

Assume that Shelly Company is an 80% subsidiary of Pointer Corporation and that Shelly has 10,000 shares of common stock outstanding at December 31, 2007. On January 1, 2008, Shelly purchases 400 shares of its own stock from noncontrolling stockholders. Exhibit 8-5 summarizes the effect of this treasury stock acquisition on Pointer's share of Shelly's book value under three different assumptions regarding the purchase price of the treasury shares.

Pointer's equity in Shelly Company before the purchase of the 400 shares of treasury stock by Shelly was $160,000, and its ownership interest was 80%, as shown in the first column of Exhibit 8-5. The purchase of the 400 treasury shares by Shelly increases Pointer's ownership percentage to 83 1/3% (or 8,000 of 9,600 outstanding shares), regardless of the price paid by Shelly to reacquire the shares. If Shelly purchases the 400 shares at their $20-per-share book value, Pointer's share of Shelly's equity remains at $160,000, as shown in the second column of Exhibit 8-5, even though its interest increases to 83 1/3%. This requires no adjustment.

If Shelly purchases the 400 shares of treasury stock at $30 per share, Pointer's equity decreases by $3,333 to $156,667, as shown in column 3 of Exhibit 8-5. Pointer records the decrease with the following entry:

Additional paid-in capital (−SE)	3,333	
Investment in Shelly (−A)		3,333

To record an investment decrease from Shelly's purchase of treasury stock in excess of book value.

EQUITY OF SHELLY COMPANY				
	Column 1: Before Purchase of Treasury Stock	Column 2: After Purchase of 400 Shares at $20	Column 3: After Purchase of 400 Shares at $30	Column 4: After Purchase of 400 Shares at $15
Capital stock, $10 par	$100,000	$100,000	$100,000	$100,000
Retained earnings	100,000	100,000	100,000	100,000
	200,000	200,000	200,000	200,000
Less: Treasury stock (cost)	—	8,000	12,000	6,000
Total equity	$200,000	$192,000	$188,000	$194,000
Pointer's interest	4/5*	5/6†	5/6†	5/6†
Pointer's share of Shelly's book value	$160,000	$160,000	$156,667	$161,667

*8,000 out of 10,000 outstanding shares.
†8,000 out of 9,600 outstanding shares.

EXHIBIT 8-5

**Purchase of Treasury
Stock by Subsidiary**

This entry reduces Pointer's investment in Shelly to its share of the underlying book value in Shelly and also reduces additional paid-in capital. Treasury stock transactions are of a capital nature, so they do not affect gain or loss.

The third situation illustrated in Exhibit 8-5 (column 4) assumes that Shelly purchases 400 shares of treasury stock at $15 per share ($5 per share below book value). As a result of Shelly's acquisition of its own shares, Pointer's share of Shelly's equity increases from $160,000 to $161,667. This increase of $1,667 requires the following adjustment on Pointer's books:

Investment in Shelly (+A)	1,667	
Additional paid-in capital (+SE)		1,667
To record an investment increase from Shelly's purchase of treasury shares below book value.		

Current GAAP supports the parent-company adjustments illustrated here for changes resulting from subsidiary treasury stock transactions. GAAP prohibits the recognition of gain or loss from treasury stock transactions but, at the same time, requires the equity method of accounting with elimination of any differences between the investment and its underlying book value over a maximum period of 40 years. The parent bases accounting from subsidiary treasury stock transactions on the book value of the net assets. During the time treasury shares are held, the book value of net assets would change due to the subsidiary's operations. If the treasury shares are eventually resold, the parent would account for this change on the basis of the book value of the assets at the time of sale. It should be understood, however, that *frequent and insignificant treasury stock transactions by a subsidiary tend to be offsetting with respect to purchases and sales and do not require the adjustments illustrated.*

STOCK DIVIDENDS AND STOCK SPLITS BY A SUBSIDIARY

Stock dividends and splits by substantially owned subsidiaries are not common unless the noncontrolling interest actively trades in the security markets. This is because the management of the parent company controls such actions and there is ordinarily no advantage to the consolidated entity or the parent company from increasing the number of subsidiary shares outstanding through stock splits or stock dividends. Even if a subsidiary splits its stock or issues a stock dividend, the effect of such actions on consolidation procedures is minimal.

A stock split by a subsidiary increases the number of shares outstanding, but it does not affect either the net assets of the subsidiary or the individual equity accounts. Also, parent-company and noncontrolling interest ownership percentages are unaffected by subsidiary stock splits; accordingly, parent-company accounting and consolidation procedures are unaffected.

These same observations apply to stock dividends by subsidiaries except that the individual subsidiary equity accounts are changed in the case of stock dividends. This change occurs because retained earnings equal to par or stated value or to the market price of the additional shares issued is transferred to paid-in capital.[5] Although the capitalization of retained earnings does not affect parent-company accounting for its subsidiaries, it does change the amounts of capital stock, additional paid-in capital, and retained earnings to be eliminated in the consolidation process.

Pictor Corporation owns 80% of the outstanding stock of Sorry Company acquired on January 1, 2006, for $160,000. Sorry's stockholders' equity on that date was as follows:

Capital stock, $10 par	$100,000
Additional paid-in capital	20,000
Retained earnings	80,000
Total stockholders' equity	$200,000

During 2006, Sorry had net income of $30,000 and paid cash dividends of $10,000. Pictor increased its investment in Sorry for its investment income of $24,000 ($30,000 × 80%) and decreased it for dividends received of $8,000 ($10,000 × 80%). Thus, Pictor's Investment in Sorry account at December 31, 2006, was $176,000.

On the basis of the information given, the consolidation working papers for Pictor Corporation and Subsidiary for 2006 would include the following adjustments and eliminations:

Income from Sorry (–R, –SE)	**24,000**	
Dividends (+SE)		**8,000**
Investment in Sorry (–A)		**16,000**
Capital stock—Sorry (–SE)	**100,000**	
Additional paid-in capital—Sorry (–SE)	**20,000**	
Retained earnings—Sorry (–SE)	**80,000**	
Investment in Sorry (–A)		**160,000**
Noncontrolling interest—beginning (+L)		**40,000**

If Sorry had also declared and issued a 10% stock dividend on December 31, 2006, when its stock was selling at $40 per share, Sorry Corporation would record the stock dividend as follows:

Stock dividend on common (–SE)	40,000	
Capital stock, $10 par (+SE)		10,000
Additional paid-in capital (+SE)		30,000

This stock dividend does not affect Pictor's accounting for its investment in Sorry, but it does affect the consolidation working papers, because Sorry's capital stock has increased to $110,000 ($100,000 + $10,000) and its additional paid-in capital has increased to $50,000 ($20,000 + $30,000). Consolidation working paper adjustment and elimination entries for 2006 would be as follows:

Income from Sorry (–R, –SE)	**24,000**	
Dividends (+SE)		**8,000**
Investment in Sorry (–A)		**16,000**
Capital stock—Sorry (–SE)	**110,000**	
Additional paid-in capital—Sorry (–SE)	**50,000**	
Retained earnings—Sorry (–SE)	**80,000**	
Investment in Sorry (–A)		**160,000**
Noncontrolling interest—beginning (+L)		**40,000**
Stock dividend on common (+SE)		**40,000**

---

[5] See *ARB No. 43*, Chapter 7, paragraphs 10 through 14, for accounting procedures relating to stock dividends.

We eliminate the $40,000 stock dividend account along with the reciprocal investment and equity balances because it is really an offset to $10,000 of the capital stock and $30,000 of the additional paid-in capital amounts. In 2007 and subsequent years, the retained earnings account will reflect the $40,000 decrease from the stock dividend, and no further complications will result.

SUMMARY

When a parent company purchases a subsidiary during an accounting period, we deduct the preacquisition earnings relating to the interest acquired in computing consolidated net income. We also eliminate preacquisition dividends on an interest acquired during an accounting period in the consolidation process.

The acquisition of a controlling interest in another company through a series of separate stock purchases over a period of time increases the detail involved in accounting for the total investment under the equity method. It also complicates the preparation of consolidated financial statements because the investment cost/book value differential has to be related to each acquisition on the basis of the total interest held.

When a parent company/investor sells an ownership interest in a subsidiary/investee corporation, the gain or loss on sale is equal to the difference between the selling price and the book value of the investment interest sold. However, if the investment is not accounted for on an equity basis, it has to be adjusted to an equity basis before computing the gain or loss on sale. The sale of an interest in a subsidiary during an accounting period increases the noncontrolling interest and necessitates some changes in the computation of noncontrolling interest expense.

The sale of additional shares by a subsidiary changes the parent's percentage ownership in the subsidiary unless the shares are sold to the parent company and noncontrolling shareholders in proportion to their holdings. The direct sale of additional shares to the parent company increases the parent's interest and decreases the noncontrolling shareholders' interest. The issuance of additional shares to noncontrolling stockholders or outside entities by the subsidiary decreases the parent's percentage interest and increases the noncontrolling shareholders' interests. Similar changes in majority and noncontrolling ownership interests result from a subsidiary's treasury stock transactions. Such changes require special care in accounting for a parent company's investment under the equity method and in preparing consolidated financial statements.

Parent-company accounting and consolidation procedures are not affected by subsidiary stock splits. However, subsidiary stock dividends may lead to changes in the consolidation working papers.

QUESTIONS

1. Explain the terms *preacquisition earnings* and *preacquisition dividends*.

2. How are preacquisition earnings accounted for by a parent company under the equity method? How are they accounted for in the consolidated income statement?

3. Assume that an 80% investor of Sub Company acquires an additional 10% interest in Sub halfway through the current fiscal period. Explain the effect of the 10% acquisition by the parent company on noncontrolling interest expense for the period and on total noncontrolling interest at the end of the current period.

4. Isn't preacquisition income really noncontrolling interest expense? If so, why separate preacquisition income and noncontrolling interest expense in the consolidated income statement?

5. How is the gain or loss determined for the sale of part of an investment interest that is accounted for as a one-line consolidation? Is the amount of gain or loss affected by the accounting method used by the investor?

6. When a parent company sells a part of its interest in a subsidiary during an accounting period, is the income applicable to the interest sold up to the time of sale included in consolidated net income and parent-company income under the equity method? Explain.

7. Assume that a subsidiary has 10,000 shares of stock outstanding, of which 8,000 shares are owned by the parent company. What equity method adjustment will be necessary on the parent-company books if the subsidiary sells 2,000 additional shares of its own stock to outside interests at book value? At an amount in excess of book value?

8. Assume that a subsidiary has 10,000 shares of stock outstanding, of which 8,000 shares are owned by the parent company. If the parent company purchases an additional 2,000 shares of stock directly from the subsidiary at book value, how should the parent company record its additional investment? Would your answer have been different if the purchase of the 2,000 shares had been made above book value? Explain.

9. How do the treasury stock transactions of a subsidiary affect the parent company's accounting for its investment under the equity method?

10. Can gains or losses to a parent company (investor) result from a subsidiary's (investee's) treasury stock transactions? Explain.

11. Do common stock dividends and stock splits by a subsidiary affect the amounts that appear in the consolidated financial statements? Explain, indicating the items, if any, that would be affected.

EXERCISES

E 8-1

Allocate income and dividends to majority, noncontrolling, and preacquisition interests

Pie Corporation increases its ownership interest in its subsidiary, Sweet Corporation, from 70% on January 1, 2006, to 90% at July 1, 2006. Sweet's net income for 2006 is $100,000, and it declares $30,000 dividends on March 1 and $30,000 on September 1.

REQUIRED: Show the allocation of Sweet's net income and dividends among majority interests, noncontrolling interests, and preacquisition interests.

E 8-2

Piecemeal acquisition of majority interest with preacquisition income and dividends

On January 1, 2009, Pinnacle Industries purchased a 40% interest in Superstore Corporation for $800,000, when Superstore's stockholders' equity consisted of $1,000,000 capital stock and $1,000,000 retained earnings. On September 1, 2009, Pinnacle purchased an additional 20% interest in Superstore for $420,000. Both purchases were made at book value equal to fair value.

Superstore had income for 2009 of $240,000, earned evenly throughout the year, and it paid dividends of $60,000 in April and $60,000 in October.

REQUIRED: Compute the following:

1. Pinnacle's income from Superstore for 2009

2. Preacquisition income that will appear on the consolidated income statement of Pinnacle and Subsidiary for 2009

3. Noncontrolling interest expense for 2009

E 8-3

Journal entries (sale of an interest–beginning of year assumption)
Peat Corporation owns 100% (300,000 shares) of the outstanding shares of Swamp Corporation's common stock on January 1, 2006. Its Investment in Swamp account on this date is $4,400,000, equal to Swamp's $4,000,000 stockholders' equity plus $400,000 goodwill. During 2006, Swamp reports net income of $600,000 and pays no dividends.

On April 1, 2006, Peat sells a 15% interest (45,000 shares) in Swamp for $750,000, thereby reducing its holdings to 85%.

REQUIRED: Prepare the journal entries needed for Peat to account for its investment in Swamp for 2006, using a beginning-of-the-period sales assumption.

E 8-4

Sale of equity interest–beginning of year or actual sale date assumption
The balance of Pauley Corporation's investment in Savage Company account at December 31, 2005, was $436,000, consisting of 80% of Savage's $500,000 stockholders' equity on that date and $36,000 goodwill.

On May 1, 2006, Pauley sold a 20% interest in Savage (one-fourth of its holdings) for $130,000. During 2006, Savage had net income of $150,000, and on July 1, 2006, Savage declared dividends of $80,000.

REQUIRED

1. Determine the gain or loss on sale of the 20% interest.

2. Calculate Pauley's income from Savage for 2006.

3. Determine the balance of Pauley's Investment in Savage account at December 31, 2006.

E 8-5

Computations and working paper entries (midyear purchase of a subsidiary) Phrog

Corporation paid $1,290,000 cash for 70% of the common stock of Stork Corporation on June 1, 2009. The assets and liabilities of Stork were fairly valued, and any cost/book value differential is goodwill. Data related to the stockholders' equity of Stork are as follows:

Stockholders' Equity December 31, 2008

Common stock, $10 par	$1,000,000
Retained earnings	480,000
Total stockholders' equity	$1,480,000

Income amd Dividends—2009

Net income (earned evenly throughout the year)	$ 240,000
Dividends (declared and paid in equal	
amounts in January, April, July, and October)	120,000

REQUIRED

1. Determine the following:

   a. Goodwill from the investment in Stork

   b. Phrog's income from Stork for 2009

   c. The Investment in Stork account balance at December 31, 2009

2. Prepare the working paper entries needed to consolidate the financial statements of Phrog and Stork Corporations for 2009.

E 8-6

Additional stock issued by subsidiary directly to parent The stockholders' equities of Petal

Corporation and its 80%-owned subsidiary, Sower Corporation, on December 31, 2006, are as follows (in thousands):

	Petal	**Sower**
Common stock, $10 par	$10,000	$6,000
Retained earnings	4,000	3,000
Total stockholders' equity	$14,000	$9,000

Petal's Investment in Sower account balance on December 31, 2006, is equal to its underlying book value. On January 2, 2007, Sower issued $60,000 previously unissued common shares directly to Petal at $25 per share.

REQUIRED

1. Calculate the balance of Petal's Investment in Sower account on January 2, 2007, after the new investment is recorded.

2. Determine the goodwill, if any, from Petal's purchase of the 60,000 new shares.

E 8-7

Additional stock issued by subsidiary under different assumptions The stockholders' equities of

Pod Corporation and its 80%-owned subsidiary, Sod Corporation, on December 31, 2006, appear as follows (in thousands):

	Pod	**Sod**
Common stock, $10 par	$5,000	$2,200
Retained earnings	2,000	1,000
Total	$7,000	$3,200

Pod's Investment in Sod account on this date is equal to its underlying book value. On January 1, 2007, Sod issues 30,000 previously unissued common shares for $20 per share.

REQUIRED

1. If Pod purchases the 30,000 shares directly from Sod, what is Pod's percentage ownership in Sod after the new shares are acquired?

2. If Sod sells the 30,000 previously unissued common shares to the public, what is Pod's percentage ownership in Sod after the new issuance?

3. If Sod sells the 30,000 shares to the public, prepare the journal entry on Pod's books to account for the effect of the issuance on its Investment in Sod account assuming that *no* gain or loss is recognized.

4. If Sod sells the 30,000 shares to the public, prepare the journal entry on Pod's books to account for the effect of the issuance on its Investment in Sod account assuming that a gain or loss is recognized.

E 8-8

Subsidiary issues additional stock under different assumptions Primetime Corporation owns two-thirds (600,000 shares) of the outstanding $1 par common stock of Satellite Equipment Company on January 1, 2006. In order to raise cash to finance an expansion program, Satellite issues an additional 100,000 shares of its common stock for $5 per share on January 3, 2006. Satellite's stockholders' equity before and after the new stock issuance is as follows (in thousands):

	Before Issuance	**After Issuance**
Common stock, $1 par	$ 900	$1,000
Additional paid-in capital	600	1,000
Retained earnings	600	600
Total stockholders' equity	$2,100	$2,600

REQUIRED

1. Assume that Primetime purchases all 100,000 shares of common stock directly from Satellite.
   a. What is Primetime's percentage ownership interest in Satellite after the purchase?
   b. Calculate goodwill from Primetime's acquisition of the 100,000 shares of Satellite.

2. Assume that the 100,000 shares of common stock are sold to Ivanhoe Company, one of Satellite's non-controlling stockholders.
   a. What is Primetime's percentage ownership interest in Satellite after the new shares are sold to Ivanhoe?
   b. Calculate the change in underlying book value of Primetime's investment in Satellite after the sale to Ivanhoe.
   c. Prepare the journal entry on Primetime's books to recognize the increase or decrease in underlying book value computed in b above assuming that gain or loss is *not* recognized.

E 8-9

Midyear piecemeal acquisition with goodwill The stockholder's equity of Sum Corporation at December 31, 2005, 2006, and 2007, is as follows (in thousands):

	December 31,		
	2005	**2006**	**2007**
Capital stock, $10 par	$200	$200	$200
Retained earnings	80	160	220
	$280	$360	$420

Sum reported income of $80,000 in 2006 and paid no dividends. In 2007, Sum reported net income of $80,000 and declared dividends of $10,000 on May 1 and $10,000 on November 1. Income was earned evenly in both years.

Plum Corporation acquired 4,000 shares of Sum common stock on April 1, 2006, for $64,000 cash and another 8,000 shares on July 1, 2007, for $166,000. Any cost/book value differential is goodwill.

REQUIRED: Determine the following:

1. Plum's income from Sum for 2006 and 2007

2. Noncontrolling interest at December 31, 2007

3. Preacquisition income in 2007

4. Balance of the Investment in Sum account at December 31, 2007

E 8-10

Computations for sale of an interest Piccolo Corporation acquired a 90% interest in Sandridge Mines on July 1, 2007, for $675,000. The stockholders' equity of Sandridge Mines at December 31, 2006, was as follows (in thousands):

Capital stock	$500
Retained earnings	200
Total	$700

During 2007 and 2008, Sandridge Mines reported income and declared dividends in the following amounts:

	2007	**2008**
Net income	$100,000	$80,000
Dividends (December)	50,000	30,000

On July 1, 2008, Piccolo Corporation sold a 10% interest (or one-ninth of its investment) in Sandridge Mines for $85,000.

REQUIRED

1. Determine Piccolo's investment income for 2007 and 2008, and its investment balance on December 31, 2007 and 2008.

2. Determine noncontrolling interest expense for 2007 and 2008, and the total of noncontrolling interest on December 31, 2007 and 2008.

E 8-11

Changes in subsidiary's outstanding shares Panda Corporation purchased a 75% interest in Sanyo Corporation in the open market on January 1, 2007, for $700,000. A summary of Sanyo's stockholders' equity on December 31, 2006 and 2007, is as follows (in thousands):

	December 31	
	2006	**2007**
Capital stock, $10 par	$400	$ 400
Additional paid-in capital	300	300
Retained earnings	100	300
Total stockholders' equity	$800	$1,000

On January 1, 2008, Sanyo sold an additional 10,000 shares of its own $10 par stock for $30 per share. Panda does not amortize any excess or deficiency of investment cost over book value acquired.

REQUIRED: Compute the following:

1. The underlying book value of the interest in Sanyo held by Panda on December 31, 2007.

2. Panda's percentage ownership interest in Sanyo on January 3, 2008, assuming that Panda purchased the 10,000 additional shares directly from Sanyo.

3. Panda's investment in Sanyo on January 3, 2008, assuming that Panda purchased the additional shares directly from Sanyo.

4. Panda's percentage ownership interest in Sanyo on January 3, 2008, assuming that Sanyo sold the 10,000 additional shares to investors outside the consolidated entity.

5. Panda's investment in Sanyo on January 3, 2008, assuming that Sanyo sold the 10,000 additional shares to investors outside the consolidated entity and no gain or loss is recognized.

E 8-12

Journal entries when subsidiary issues additional shares directly to parent Puckett Corporation's Investment in Saton Company account had a balance of $475,000 at December 31, 2006. This balance consisted of goodwill of $35,000 and 80% of Saton's $550,000 stockholders' equity.

On January 2, 2007, Saton increased its outstanding shares from 10,000 to 12,000 shares by selling 2,000 additional shares directly to Puckett at $70 per share. Saton's net income for 2007 was $90,000, and in December 2007 it paid $60,000 dividends.

REQUIRED: Prepare all journal entries other than closing entries to account for Puckett's investment in Saton during 2007. Any difference between investment cost and book value acquired is assumed to be goodwill.

E 8-13

Computations and entries (subsidiary issues additional shares to outside entities)
Patrick Corporation paid $1,800,000 for 90,000 shares of Striper Corporation's 100,000 outstanding shares on January 1, 2006, when Striper's stockholders' equity consisted of $1,000,000 of $10 par common stock and $500,000 retained earnings. The excess cost over book value acquired was assigned to goodwill. On January 2, 2008, Striper sold an additional 20,000 shares to the public for $600,000, and its stockholders' equity before and after issuance of the additional 20,000 shares was as follows (in thousands):

	January 1, 2008 (Before Issuance)	January 2, 2008 (After Issuance)
$10 par common stock	$1,000	$1,200
Additional paid-in capital	—	400
Retained earnings	800	800
Total stockholders' equity	$1,800	$2,400

REQUIRED

1. Determine Patrick's Investment in Striper account balance on January 1, 2008.

2. Prepare the entry on Patrick's books to account for its decreased ownership interest if gain or loss is not recognized.

3. Prepare the entry on Patrick's books to account for its decreased ownership interest if gain or loss is recognized.

PROBLEMS

P 8-1

Midyear acquisition and purchase of additional shares A summary of the changes in the stockholders' equity of Spindle Corporation from January 1, 2006, to December 31, 2007, appears as follows (in thousands):

	Capital Stock $10 Par	Additional Paid-in Capital	Retained Earnings	Total Equity
Balance January 1, 2006	$500	—	$ 50	$550
Dividends, December 2006	—	—	(50)	(50)
Income, 2006	—	—	100	100
Balance December 31, 2006	$500	—	$100	$600
Sale of stock January 1, 2007	100	$ 62	—	162
Dividends, December 2007	—	—	(60)	(60)
Income, 2007	—	—	150	150
Balance December 31, 2007	$600	$ 62	$190	$852

Paper Corporation purchases 40,000 shares of Spindle Corporation's outstanding stock on July 1, 2006, in the open market for $620,000 and an additional 10,000 shares directly from Spindle for $162,000 on January 1, 2007. Any excess of investment cost over book value acquired is due to goodwill.

REQUIRED

1. Determine the balance of Paper's Investment in Spindle account on December 31, 2006.

2. Compute Paper's investment income from Spindle for 2007.

3. Determine the balance of Paper's Investment in Spindle account on December 31, 2007.

P 8-2

Computations and entries (subsidiary issues additional shares to public) Prince Corporation purchased 960,000 shares of Smithtown Corporation's common stock (an 80% interest) for $21,200,000 on January 1, 2006. The $2,000,000 excess of investment cost over book value acquired was allocated to goodwill.

On January 1, 2008, Smithtown sold 400,000 previously unissued shares of common stock to the public for $30 per share. Smithtown's stockholders' equity on January 1, 2006, when Prince acquired its interest, and on January 1, 2008, immediately before and after the issuance of additional shares, was as follows (in thousands):

	January 1, 2006	January 1, 2008 Before Issuance	January 1, 2008 After Issuance
Common stock, $10 par	$12,000	$12,000	$16,000
Other paid-in capital	4,000	4,000	12,000
Retained earnings	8,000	10,000	10,000
Total	$24,000	$26,000	$38,000

REQUIRED

1. Calculate the balance of Prince's Investment in Smithtown account on January 1, 2008, before the additional stock issuance.

2. Determine Prince's percentage interest in Smithtown on January 1, 2008, immediately after the additional stock issuance.

3. Prepare a journal entry on Prince's books to adjust for the additional share issuance on January 1, 2008, if gain or loss is not recognized.

4. Prepare a journal entry on Prince's books to adjust for the additional share issuance on January 1, 2008, if the issuance is treated as a sale and gain or loss is recognized (as permitted by the SEC).

P 8-3

Journal entries for sale of an interest Patterson Corporation owned a 90% interest in Shawnee Corporation, and during 2005 the following changes occurred in Shawnee's equity and Patterson's investment in Shawnee (in thousands):

	Shawnee's Stockholders' Equity	Goodwill	Investment in Shawnee (90%)
Balance, January 1, 2005	$1,000	$49.5	$949.5
Income—2005	250		225
Dividends—2005	(150)		(135)
Balance, December 31, 2005	$1,100	$49.5	$1,039.5

During 2006, Shawnee Corporation's net income was $280,000, and it declared $40,000 dividends each quarter of the year.

Patterson reduced its interest in Shawnee to 80% on July 1, 2006, by selling Shawnee shares for $120,000.

REQUIRED

1. Prepare the journal entry on Patterson's books to record the sale of Shawnee shares as of the actual date of sale.

2. Prepare the journal entry on Patterson's books to record the sale of Shawnee shares as of January 1, 2006.

3. Prepare a schedule to reconcile the answers to parts 1 and 2.

P 8-4

Reduction of interest owned under three options Panama Corporation owns 300,000 of 360,000 outstanding shares of Shenandoah Corporation, and its $8,700,000 Investment in Shenandoah account balance on December 31, 2006, is equal to the underlying equity interest in Shenandoah. A summary of Shenandoah's stockholders' equity at December 31, 2006, is as follows (in thousands):

Common stock, $10 par, 500,000 shares authorized, 400,000 shares issued, of which 40,000 are treasury shares	$ 4,000
Additional paid-in capital	2,500
Retained earnings	5,500
	12,000
Less: Treasury shares at cost	1,560
Total stockholder's equity	$10,440

Because of a cash shortage, Panama has decided to reduce its ownership interest in Shenandoah from a 5/6 interest to a 3/4 interest and is considering the following options:

Option 1. Sell 30,000 of the 300,000 shares held in Shenandoah.
Option 2. Instruct Shenandoah to issue 40,000 shares of previously unissued stock.
Option 3. Instruct Shenandoah to reissue the 40,000 shares of treasury stock.

Assume that the shares can be sold at the current market price of $50 per share under each of the three options and that any tax consequences can be ignored. Panama's stockholders' equity at December 31, 2006, consists of $10,000,000 par value of common stock, $3,000,000 additional paid-in capital, and $7,000,000 retained earnings.

REQUIRED: Compare the consolidated stockholders' equity on January 1, 2007, under each of the three options. (*Hint:* Prepare journal entries on Panama's books as an initial step to your solution.)

P 8-5

Subsidiary issues additional shares Pallo Products Company purchased 9,000 shares of Sala Corporation's $50 par common stock at $90 per share on January 1, 2006, when Sala had capital stock of $500,000 and retained earnings of $300,000. During 2006, Sala Corporation had net income of $50,000 but declared no dividends.

On January 1, 2007, Sala Corporation sold an additional 5,000 shares of stock at $100 per share. Sala's net income for 2007 was $70,000, and no dividends were declared.

REQUIRED: Determine each of the following:

1. The balance of Pallo Products Company's Investment in Sala account on December 31, 2006

2. The goodwill (or negative goodwill) that should appear in the consolidated balance sheet at December 31, 2007, assuming that Pallo Products Company purchased the 5,000 shares issued on January 1, 2007

3. Additional paid-in capital from consolidation at December 31, 2007, assuming that Sala sold the 5,000 shares issued on January 1, 2007, to outside entities

4. Noncontrolling interest at December 31, 2007, assuming that Sala sold the 5,000 shares issued on January 1, 2007, to outsiders

P 8-6

Midyear purchase of additional interest, preacquisition income Post Corporation purchased a 70% interest in Stake Corporation on January 2, 2006, for $94,000, when Stake had capital stock of $100,000 and retained earnings of $20,000. On June 30, 2007, Post purchased an additional 20% interest for $38,000.

Comparative financial statements for Post and Stake Corporations at and for the year ended December 31, 2007, are assumed as follows (in thousands):

	Post	Stake
Combined Income and Retained Earnings Statement		
for the Year Ended December 31, 2007		
Sales	$400	$200
Income from Stake	24	—
Cost of sales	(250)	(150)
Expenses	(50)	(20)
Net income	124	30
Add: Beginning retained earnings	200	50
Less: Dividends, December 1, 2007	(64)	(10)
Retained earnings, December 31, 2007	$260	$ 70
Balance Sheet at December 31, 2007		
Other assets	$432	$200
Investment in Stake	168	—
Total assets	$600	$200
Liabilities	$ 40	$ 30
Common stock	300	100
Retained earnings	260	70
Total equities	$600	$200

REQUIRED

1. Prepare a schedule explaining the $168,000 balance in Post's Investment in Stake account at December 31, 2007.

2. Compute the amount of goodwill that should appear in the December 31, 2007, consolidated balance sheet.

3. Prepare a schedule showing computations of the amount of consolidated net income for 2007.

4. Compute consolidated retained earnings on December 31, 2007.

5. Compute noncontrolling interest on December 31, 2007.

P 8-7

Consolidated income statement (midyear purchase of additional interest)

Comparative separate-company and consolidated balance sheets for Percy Corporation and its 70%-owned subsidiary, Sawyer Corporation, at year-end 2006 were as follows (in thousands):

	Percy	Sawyer	Consolidated
Cash	$ 100	$ 70	$ 170
Inventories	800	100	900
Other current assets	500	130	630
Plant assets—net	3,500	800	4,300
Investment in Sawyer	600	—	—
Goodwill	—	—	40
Total assets	$5,500	$1,100	$6,040
Current liabilities	$ 500	$ 300	$ 800
Capital stock, $10 par	3,000	500	3,000
Other paid-in capital	1,000	100	1,000
Retained earnings	1,000	200	1,000
Noncontrolling interest	—	—	240
Total equities	$5,500	$1,100	$6,040

Sawyer's net income for 2007 was $150,000, and its dividends for the year were $80,000 ($40,000 on March 1, and $40,000 on September 1). On April 1, 2007, Percy increased its interest in Sawyer to 80% by purchasing 5,000 shares in the market at $19 per share.

Percy's goodwill from its 70% interest is not amortized.

Separate incomes of Percy and Sawyer for 2007 are computed as follows:

	Percy	Sawyer
Sales	$2,000	$1,200
Cost of sales	(1,200)	(700)
Gross profit	800	500
Depreciation expense	(400)	(300)
Other expenses	(100)	(50)
Separate incomes	$ 300	$ 150

REQUIRED

1. Prepare a consolidated income statement for Percy Corporation and Subsidiary for the year ended December 31, 2007.

2. Prepare a schedule to show how Sawyer's net income and dividends for 2007 are allocated among non-controlling interests, majority interests, and other interests.

P 8-8

Working papers (midyear acquisition of 80% interest, downstream inventory sales)

Pop Corporation acquired an 80% interest in Sat Corporation on October 1, 2006, for $82,400, equal to 80% of the underlying equity of Sat on that date plus $16,000 goodwill. Financial statements for Pop and Sat Corporations for 2006 are as follows (in thousands):

	Pop	Sat
Combined Income and Retained Earnings Statement for the Year Ended December 31, 2006		
Sales	$112	$ 50
Income from Sat	3.8	—
Cost of sales	(60)	(20)
Operating expenses	(25.1)	(6)
Net income	30.7	24
Retained earnings January 1	30	20
Dividends	(20)	(10)
Retained earnings December 31	$ 40.7	$ 34
Balance Sheet at December 31, 2006		
Cash	$ 5.1	$ 7
Accounts receivable	10.4	17
Note receivable	5	10
Inventories	30	16
Plant assets—net	88	60
Investment in Sat	82.2	—
Total assets	$220.7	$110
Accounts payable	$ 15	$ 16
Notes payable	25	10
Capital stock	140	50
Retained earnings	40.7	34
Total equities	$220.7	$110

ADDITIONAL INFORMATION

1. In November 2006, Pop sold inventory items to Sat for $12,000 at a gross profit of $3,000. One-third of these items remained in Sat's inventory at December 31, 2006, and $6,000 remained unpaid.

2. Sat's dividends were declared in equal amounts on March 15 and November 15, and its income was earned in proportionate amounts throughout each quarter of the year.

3. Pop applies the equity method of accounting such that its net income is equal to consolidated net income.

REQUIRED: Prepare working papers to consolidate the financial statements of Pop Corporation and Subsidiary for the year ended December 31, 2006.

P 8-9

Working papers (noncontrolling interest, preacquisition income, downstream sale of equipment, upstream sale of land, subsidiary holds parent's bonds)

Pal Corporation paid $175,000 for a 70% interest in Sid Corporation's outstanding stock on April 1, 2006. Sid's stockholders' equity on January 1, 2006, consisted of $200,000 capital stock and $50,000 retained earnings.

Accounts and balances taken from the financial statements for Pal and Sid at and for the year ended December 31, 2006, are as follows (in thousands):

	Pal	Sid
Combined Income and Retained Earnings Statement for the Year Ended December 31, 2006		
Sales	$287.1	$150
Income from Sid	12.3	—
Gain	12	2
Interest income	—	5.85
Expenses (includes cost of goods sold)	(200)	(117.85)
Interest expense	(11.4)	—
Net income	100	40
Add: Beginning retained earnings	250	50
Less: Dividends	(50)	(20)
Retained earnings December 31	$300	$ 70

Balance Sheet at December 31, 2006

Cash	$ 17	$ 4
Interest receivable	—	6
Inventories	140	60
Other current assets	110	20
Plant assets—net	502.7	107.3
Investment in Sid common	180.3	—
Investment in Pal bonds	—	102.7
Total assets	$950	$300
Interest payable	$ 6	$ —
Other current liabilities	38.6	30
12% bonds payable	105.4	—
Common stock	500	200
Retained earnings	300	70
Total equities	$950	$300

ADDITIONAL INFORMATION

1. Sid Corporation paid $102,850 for all of Pal's outstanding bonds on July 1, 2006. These bonds were issued on January 1, 2006, bear interest at 12%, have interest payment dates of July 1 and January 1, and mature 10 years from the date of issue. The $6,000 premium on the issue is being amortized under the straight-line method.

2. Other current liabilities of Sid Corporation on December 31, 2006, include $10,000 dividends declared on December 15 and unpaid at year-end. Sid also declared $10,000 dividends on March 15, 2006.

3. Pal Corporation sold equipment to Sid on July 1, 2006, for $30,000. This equipment was purchased by Pal on July 1, 2003, for $36,000 and is being depreciated over a six-year period under the straight-line method (no scrap).

4. Sid sold land that cost $8,000 to Pal for $10,000 on October 15, 2006. Pal still owns the land.

5. Pal uses the equity method of accounting for its 70% interest in Sid.

REQUIRED: Prepare consolidation working papers for Pal Corporation and Subsidiary for the year ended December 31, 2006.

P 8-10

Working papers (midyear purchase of 10% interest, downstream sales) Poco Corporation acquired a 70% interest in Sam Corporation on January 1, 2006, for $450,000 cash. The stockholders' equity of Sam when Poco acquired its 70% interest consisted of $300,000 capital stock and $200,000 retained earnings. On July 1, 2007, Poco acquired an additional 10% interest in Sam for $77,500 to bring its interest in Sam to 80%. The financial statements of Poco and Sam Corporations at and for the year ended December 31, 2007, are as follows (in thousands):

	Poco	Sam
Combined Income and Retained Earnings Statement		
for the Year Ended December 31, 2007		
Sales	$ 900	$500
Income from Sam	38	—
Gain on machinery	40	—
Cost of sales	(400)	(300)
Depreciation expense	(90)	(60)
Other expenses	(160)	(40)
Net income	328	100
Add: Beginning retained earnings	155	250
Less: Dividends	(200)	(50)
Retained earnings December 31	$ 283	$300

Balance Sheet at December 31, 2007

Cash	$ 20	$ 80
Accounts receivable	90	30
Dividends receivable	20	—
Inventories	90	70
Other current items	20	80
Land	50	40
Buildings—net	60	105
Machinery—net	100	320
Investment in Sam	550	—
Total assets	$1,000	$725
Accounts payable	$ 177	$ 40
Dividends payable	100	25
Other liabilities	140	60
Capital stock, $10 par	300	300
Retained earnings	283	300
Total equities	$1,000	$725

ADDITIONAL INFORMATION

1. The cost/book value differential from Poco's two purchases of interests in Sam was allocated to goodwill.

2. Poco Corporation sold inventory items to Sam during 2006 for $60,000, at a gross profit of $10,000. During 2007, Poco's sales to Sam were $48,000, at a gross profit of $8,000. Half of the 2006 intercompany sales were inventoried by Sam at year-end 2006, and three-fourths of the 2007 sales remained unsold by Sam at year-end 2007. Sam owes Poco $25,000 from 2007 purchases.

3. At year-end 2006, Sam purchased land from Poco for $20,000. The cost of this land to Poco was $12,000.

4. Poco sold machinery with a book value of $40,000 to Sam for $80,000 on July 8, 2007. The machinery had a five-year useful life at that time. Sam uses straight-line depreciation without considering salvage value on the machinery.

5. Poco uses a one-line consolidation in accounting for Sam. Both Poco and Sam Corporations declared their dividends for 2007 in equal amounts in June and December.

REQUIRED: Prepare working papers to consolidate the financial statements of Poco Corporation and Subsidiary for the year ended December 31, 2007.

P 8-11

Working papers (midyear acquisition, preacquisition income and dividends, upstream sale of inventory, downstream sale of inventory item used by subsidiary as plant asset) Pak Corporation acquired an 85% interest in Sly Corporation on August 1, 2006, for $522,750, equal to 85% of the underlying equity of Sly on that date.

In August 2006, Sly sold inventory items to Pak for $60,000 at a gross profit of $15,000. One-third of these items remained in Pak's inventory at December 31, 2006.

On September 30, 2006, Pak sold an inventory item (equipment) to Sly for $50,000 at a gross profit to Pak of $10,000. When this equipment was placed in service by Sly, it had a five-year remaining useful life and no expected scrap value.

Sly's dividends were declared in equal amounts on June 15 and December 15, and its income was earned in relatively equal amounts throughout each quarter of the year. Pak applies the equity method of accounting, such that its net income is equal to consolidated net income. Financial statements for Pak and Sly are summarized as follows (in thousands):

	Pak	Sly
Combined Income and Retained Earnings Statement for the Year Ended December 31, 2006		
Sales	$ 910	$400
Income from Sly	7.5	—
Cost of sales	(500)	(250)
Operating expenses	(200.0)	(90)
Net income	217.5	60
Add: Beginning retained earnings	192.5	100
Deduct: Dividends	(100)	(40)
Retained earnings December 31	$ 310	$120

Balance Sheet at December 31, 2006

Cash	$ 33.75	$ 10
Dividends receivable	17	—
Accounts receivable—net	120	70
Inventories	300	150
Plant assets—net	880	500
Investment in Sly—85%	513.25	—
Total assets	$1,864	$730
Accounts payable	$ 154	$ 90
Dividends payable	—	20
Capital stock	1,400	500
Retained earnings	310	120
Total equities	$1,864	$730

REQUIRED: Prepare-consolidation working papers for Pak Corporation and Subsidiary for the year ended December 31, 2006.

P 8-12

Working papers with preacquisition income and dividends (incomplete equity method, downstream inventory sales, upstream sale of machinery)

Separate-company financial statements for Pin Corporation and its 90%-owned subsidiary, Sit Corporation, for the year ended December 31, 2008, are summarized as follows (in thousands):

	Pin	Sit
Combined Income and Retained Earnings Statement for the Year Ended December 31, 2008		
Sales	$1,265	$ 600
Income from Sit	85	—
Cost of goods sold	(800)	(300)
Depreciation expense	(180)	(70)
Other expenses	(120)	(120)
Loss on plant assets	—	(10)
Net income	250	100
Add: Beginning retained earnings	300	150
Deduct: Dividends	(150)	(50)
Retained earnings December 31	$ 400	$ 200
Balance Sheet at December 31, 2008		
Cash	$ 220	$ 160
Receivables	200	160
Inventory	170	140
Plant and equipment	1,417.5	720
Accumulated depreciation	(272.5)	(180)
Investment in Sit	765	—
Total assets	$2,500	$1,000
Current liabilities	$ 300	$ 100
Other liabilities	300	200
Capital stock	1,500	500
Retained earnings	400	200
Total equities	$2,500	$1,000

ADDITIONAL INFORMATION

1. Pin acquired an 80% interest in Sit's common stock on January 5, 2005, for $600,000 and an additional 10% interest on July 1, 2008, for $82,500. These two acquisitions were made in the open market at regularly quoted exchange prices.

2. Sit's capital stock and retained earnings on January 1, 2005, were $500,000 and $100,000, respectively.

3. Any difference between investment cost and book value acquired relates to specifically identifiable intangible assets and is amortized over a 10-year period.

4. Sit paid dividends of $25,000 on April 1 and October 1 of 2008.

5. Pin sold $50,000 merchandise to Sit during 2008. The gross profit of $10,000 on this merchandise is included in Sit's December 31, 2008, inventory. Sit owed Pin $20,000 from intercompany purchases at December 31, 2008.

6. The amount of intercompany profit in Sit's beginning inventory on goods acquired from Pin amounted to $5,000.

7. Sit sold machinery with a book value of $40,000 to Pin for $30,000 on July 2, 2008. At the time of sale, the machinery had a remaining useful life of five years and was being depreciated by Pin on a straight-line basis.

REQUIRED: Prepare the consolidation working papers for Pin and Subsidiary for the year ended December 31, 2008.

P 8-13

[AICPA adapted] Working papers (incomplete equity method, unrealized profits and errors) Presented here are the condensed financial statements (unconsolidated) of Pops Company and its subsidiary, Sink Company, for the year ended December 31, 2006 (in thousands):

	Pops	Sink
Combined Income and Retained Earnings Statement for the Year Ended December 31, 2006		
Sales	$4,000	$1,700
Cost of sales	(2,982)	(1,015)
Operating expenses	(400)	(377.2)
Dividend income	75	—
Subsidiary income	232	—
Interest expense	—	(7.8)
Net income	925	300
Add: Retained earnings January 1	2,100	640
Deduct: Dividends	(170)	(100)
Retained earnings December 31	$2,855	$ 840
Balance Sheet at December 31, 2006		
Cash	$ 486	$ 249.6
Accounts receivable	235	185
Inventories	475	355
Machinery and equipment	2,231	530
Investment in Sink stock	954	—
Investment in Sink bonds	58	—
Total assets	$4,439	$1,319.6
Accounts payable	$ 384	$ 62
Bonds payable	—	117.6
Common stock	1,200	250
Contributed capital	—	50
Retained earnings	2,855	840
Total liabilities and owners' equity	$4,439	$1,319.6

ADDITIONAL INFORMATION

1. On January 3, 2004, Pops acquired from John Roth, the sole stockholder of Sink Company, both a patent valued at $40,000 and 80% of the outstanding stock of Sink for $440,000 cash. The net book value of Sink's stock on the date of acquisition was $500,000, and the book values of the individual assets and liabilities were equal to their fair market values. Pops charged the entire $440,000 to the account "Investment in Sink Company." The patent, for which no amortization has been charged, had a remaining legal life of four years as of January 3, 2004.

2. On July 1, 2006, Pops reduced its investment in Sink to 75% of Sink's outstanding common stock by selling shares for $70,000 to an unaffiliated company at a profit of $16,000. Pops recorded the proceeds as a credit to its investment account.

3. For the six months ended June 30, 2006, Sink had net income of $140,000. Pops recorded 80% of this amount on its books of account prior to the time of sale.

4. During 2005, Sink sold merchandise to Pops for $130,000, which was at a markup of 30% over Sink's cost. On January 1, 2006, $52,000 of this merchandise remained in Pop's inventory. This merchandise was subsequently sold by Pops in February 2006 at a profit of $8,000.

5. In November 2006, Pops sold merchandise to Sink for the first time. Pop's cost for this merchandise was $80,000, and the sale was made at 120% of cost. Sink's inventory at December 31, 2006, contained merchandise that was purchased from Pops at a cost to Sink of $24,000.

6. On December 31, 2006, there was a $45,000 payment in transit from Sink Company to Pops Company. Accounts receivable and accounts payable include intercompany receivables and payables. In December 2006, Sink declared and paid cash dividends of $100,000 to its stockholders.

7. On December 31, 2006, Pops purchased 50% of the outstanding bonds issued by Sink for $58,000. The bonds mature on December 31, 2010, and were originally issued at a discount. It is the intention of the management of Pops to hold these bonds until their maturity.

REQUIRED: Prepare consolidated financial statement working papers for Pops Company and Subsidiary for the year ended December 31, 2006.

P 8-14

Consolidated statement of cash flows–indirect method (sale of an interest)

Comparative consolidated financial statements for Poff Corporation and its subsidiary, Sato Corporation, at and for the years ended December 31, 2007 and 2006 follow.

Poff Corporation and Subsidiary Comparative Consolidated Financial Statements at and for the Years Ended December 31, 2007 and 2006

	Year 2007	Year 2006	Year's Change 2007–2006
Income Statement			
Sales	$3,050,000	$2,850,000	$ 200,000
Gain on 10% interest	5,700		5,700
Cost of sales	(1,750,700)	(1,690,000)	(60,700)
Depreciation expense	(528,000)	(508,000)	(20,000)
Other expenses	(455,000)	(392,000)	(63,000)
Noncontrolling interest expense	(22,000)	(10,000)	(12,000)
Net income	$ 300,000	$ 250,000	$ 50,000
Retained Earnings			
Retained earnings—beginning	$1,000,000	$ 950,000	$ 50,000
Net income	300,000	250,000	50,000
Dividends	(200,000)	(200,000)	0
Retained earnings—ending	$1,100,000	$1,000,000	$ 100,000
Balance Sheet			
Cash	$ 46,500	$ 50,500	$ (4,000)
Accounts receivable—net	87,500	90,000	(2,500)
Inventories	377,500	247,500	130,000
Prepaid expenses	68,000	88,000	(20,000)
Equipment	2,970,000	2,880,000	90,000
Accumulated depreciation	(1,542,000)	(1,044,000)	(498,000)
Land and buildings	960,000	960,000	0
Accumulated depreciation	$ (300,000)	(272,000)	(28,000)
Total assets	$2,667,500	$3,000,000	$(332,500)
Accounts payable	$ 140,000	$ 343,500	$(203,500)
Dividends payable	52,500	52,500	0
Long-term notes payable	245,000	545,000	(300,000)
Capital stock, $10 par	1,000,000	1,000,000	0
Retained earnings	1,100,000	1,000,000	100,000
Noncontrolling interest	130,000	59,000	71,000
Total equities	$2,667,500	$3,000,000	$(332,500)

REQUIRED: Prepare a consolidated statement of cash flows for Poff Corporation and Subsidiary for the year ended December 31, 2007. The changes in equipment are due to a $100,000 equipment acquisition, current depreciation, and the sale of one-ninth of the cost/book value differential allocated to equipment ($10,000) and related accumulated depreciation ($2,000). This reduction in the unamortized cost/book value differential results from selling a 10% interest in Sato for $72,700 and thereby reducing its interest from 90% to 80%. Sato's net income and dividends for 2007 were $110,000 and $50,000, respectively. Use the indirect method.

INTERNET ASSIGNMENT

Visit the Web site of *Corning Incorporated* and Subsidiary Companies and obtain a copy of the 2003 annual report. Prepare a brief summary of Corning's acquisition activities (see Note 20) during 2002 and 2003.

   a How many acquisitions were interim acquisitions?

   b How many acquisitions were recorded using purchase method accounting?

   c Were acquisitions completed by exchanging shares or through cash payments?

SELECTED READINGS

AICPA Accounting Standards Executive Committee. "Accounting in Consolidation for Issuance of a Subsidiary Stock." Issues Paper. New York: American Institute of Certified Public Accountants, 1980.

AICPA Committee on Accounting Procedure. *Accounting Research Bulletin No. 43*. "Restatement and Revision of Accounting Research Bulletins." New York: American Institute of Certified Public Accountants, 1953.

Committee on Accounting Procedure. *Accounting Research Bulletin No. 51*. "Consolidated Financial Statements." New York: American Institute of Certified Public Accountants, 1959.

Financial Accounting Standards Board. "Consolidated Financial Statements: Policy and Procedures." Financial Accounting Series. Exposure Draft. Norwalk, CT: Financial Accounting Standards Board, 1995.

Statement of Financial Accounting Standards No. 141. "Business Combinations." Stamford, CT: Financial Accounting Standards Board, 2001.

Statement of Financial Accounting Standards No. 142. "Goodwill and Other Intangible Assets." Stamford, CT: Financial Accounting Standards Board, 2001.

9 CHAPTER

INDIRECT AND MUTUAL HOLDINGS

The previous chapters of this book presented stock ownership situations in which an investor or parent company directly owned some or all of the voting stock of an investee. The equity method of accounting is appropriate in those situations and equally appropriate when an investor indirectly owns 20% or more of an investee's voting stock. Consolidation is appropriate when one corporation, directly or indirectly, owns a majority of the outstanding voting stock of another corporation.[1]

This chapter discusses parent-company accounting and consolidation procedures for indirect ownership situations under the heading of "Indirect Holdings." The chapter also considers additional complexities that arise when affiliated corporations hold the voting stock of each other. Affiliation structures of this type are covered under the heading of "Mutual Holdings." Discussion of **mutual holding** relationships logically follows the coverage of indirect holdings because such relationships constitute a special type of indirect holdings—the type in which affiliates indirectly own themselves.

Although consolidation procedures for indirectly held and mutually held affiliates are more complex than for directly held affiliates, the basic consolidation objectives remain the same. Most of the problems require measuring the separate realized income of the separate entities and allocating it between majority and noncontrolling interests.

■ ■ ■

LEARNING OBJECTIVES

1 Prepare consolidated statements when the parent company controls through indirect holdings.

2 Apply consolidation procedures of indirect holdings to the special case of mutual holdings.

3 Electronic supplement: Learn how to modify accounting for indirect and mutual holdings when the parent company uses the cost method to account for its investments.

AFFILIATION STRUCTURES

Chapter 8 noted *PepsiCo's* creation of *Pepsi Bottling Group* (PBG). Note 8 to PepsiCo's 2003 annual report (p. 73) offers additional insight on the ownership status of PBG, as well as *PepsiAmericas*, another major bottling affiliate:

> In addition to approximately 41% of PBG's outstanding common stock that we own at year-end 2003, we own 100% of PBG's class B common stock and approximately 7% of the equity of Bottling Group, LLC, PBG's principal operating subsidiary. This gives us economic ownership of approximately 45% of PBG's combined operations. ... At year-end 2003, we owned approximately 40% of PepsiAmericas.

---

[1] *APB Opinion No. 18*, "The Equity Method of Accounting for Investments in Common Stock," paragraphs 3c and 17.

Note 8 also indicates that PepsiCo's consolidated financial statements reflect net revenue from related-party transactions with these bottling affiliates totaling $3.699 billion during 2003.

The 2003 annual report of **SBC Communications** summarizes some of its investments in affiliated companies as follows:

Note 6. Equity Method Investments

We account for our 60% economic interest in Cingular under the equity method of accounting in our consolidated financial statements since we share control equally (i.e., 50/50) with our 40% economic partner in the joint venture. We have equal voting rights and representation on the board of directors that controls Cingular. ... As of December 31, 2003, our investments in equity affiliates included an 8.0% interest in Telmex, Mexico's national telecommunications company; a 7.6% interest in America Movil, primarily a wireless provider in Mexico, with telecommunications investments in the U.S. and Latin America; a 41.6% interest in TDC, the national communications provider in Denmark; a 16.9% interest in Belgacom, the national communications provider in Belgium; and an 18% interest in Telkom, a telecommunications company of South Africa. TDC also holds a 15.9% interest in Belgacom, bringing our effective interest to 23.5%.

The potential complexity of corporate affiliation structures is limited only by one's imagination. Even so, the general types of affiliation structures are not difficult to identify. Exhibit 9-1 illustrates the more basic types of affiliation structures.

Although Exhibit 9-1 illustrates affiliation structures for parent and subsidiary corporations, the diagrams also apply to investor and investee corporations associated through the direct or indirect ownership of 20% or more of the voting stock of an investee corporation. **Direct holdings** result from direct investments in the voting stock of one or more investees. **Indirect holdings** are investments that enable the investor to control or significantly influence the decisions of an investee not directly owned through an investee that is directly owned. Exhibit 9-1 illustrates two types of indirect ownership structures—the **father-son-grandson relationship** and the **connecting affiliates relationship**.

In the father-son-grandson diagram, the parent directly owns an 80% interest in Subsidiary A and indirectly owns a 56% interest ($80\% \times 70\%$) in Subsidiary B. Noncontrolling shareholders own the other 44% of B—the 30% held directly by noncontrolling holders of B stock plus 14% held by the 20% noncontrolling holders of A stock ($20\% \times 70\%$). The parent company indirectly holds 56% of Subsidiary B stock, so consolidation of Subsidiary B is clearly appropriate. It is not the direct and indirect ownership of the parent company, however, that determines whether an affiliate should be consolidated. The decision to consolidate is based on whether a majority of the stock of an affiliate is held within the affiliation structure, thus giving the parent an ability to control the operations of the affiliate.

If Subsidiary A in the father-son-grandson diagram of Exhibit 9-1 had owned 60% of the stock of Subsidiary B, the parent's indirect ownership in Subsidiary B would have been 48% ($80\% \times 60\%$), and the noncontrolling shareholders' interest would have been 52% [$40\% + (20\% \times 60\%)$]. Consolidation of Subsidiary B would still be appropriate, because 60% of B's stock would be held within the affiliation structure.

In the illustration of connecting affiliates, the parent holds 20% of Subsidiary B stock directly and 32% ($80\% \times 40\%$) indirectly, for a total direct and indirect ownership of 52%. The other 48% of Subsidiary B is held 40% by B's noncontrolling shareholders and 8% ($20\% \times 40\%$) indirectly by A's noncontrolling shareholders.

In the first affiliation diagram for mutual holdings, the parent owns 80% of the stock of Subsidiary A, and Subsidiary A owns 10% of the stock of the parent. Thus, 10% of the parent's stock is held within the affiliation structure and 90% is outstanding. In diagram b for mutual holdings, the parent is not a party to the mutual holding relationship, but Subsidiary A owns 40% of Subsidiary B, and Subsidiary B owns 20% of Subsidiary A. The complexity involved in this latter case requires the use of simultaneous equations or other appropriate mathematical procedures to allocate incomes and equities among the affiliated corporations.

EXHIBIT 9-1

Affiliation Structures

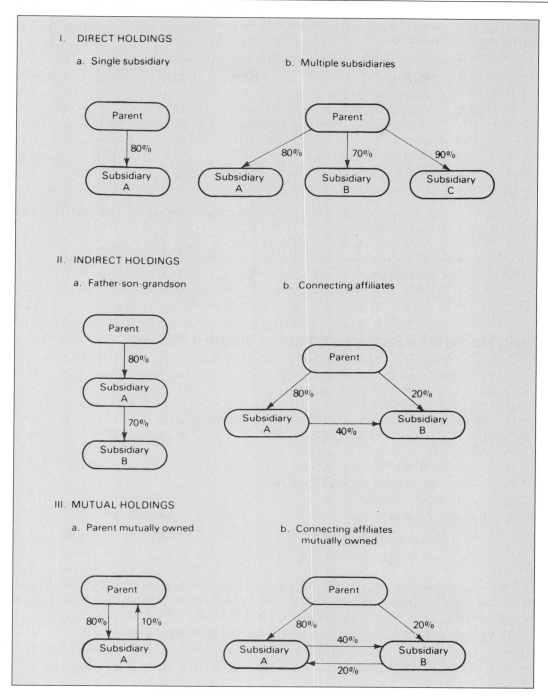

INDIRECT HOLDINGS—FATHER-SON-GRANDSON STRUCTURE

The major problems encountered in connection with indirect control situations involve the determination of earnings and equities of the affiliated companies on an equity basis. Once we adjust the income and equity accounts of the affiliated companies to an equity basis, the consolidation procedures are the same for indirect as for direct ownership situations. The mechanics involved in the consolidation process may be cumbersome, however, because of the additional detail required to consolidate the operations of multiple entities.

Assume that Poe Corporation acquires 80% of the stock of Shaw Corporation on January 1, 2006, and that Shaw acquires 70% of the stock of Turk Corporation on January 1, 2007. Both Poe's investment in Shaw and Shaw's investment in Turk are made at book value. Trial balances for the three corporations on January 1, 2007, immediately after Shaw acquires its 70% interest in Turk, are as follows (in thousands):

	Poe	Shaw	Turk
Other assets	$400	$195	$190
Investment in Shaw (80%)	200	—	—
Investment in Turk (70%)	—	105	—
	$600	$300	$190
Liabilities	$100	$ 50	$ 40
Capital stock	400	200	100
Retained earnings	100	50	50
	$600	$300	$190

Separate earnings of the three corporations (that is, earnings excluding investment income) and dividends for 2007 are (in thousands):

	Poe	Shaw	Turk
Separate earnings	$100	$50	$40
Dividends	60	30	20

Equity Method of Accounting for Father-Son-Grandson Affiliates

In accounting for investment income for 2007 on an equity basis, Shaw determines its investment income from Turk before Poe determines its investment income from Shaw. Shaw accounts for its investment in Turk for 2007 with the following entries:

SHAW'S BOOKS

Cash (+A)	14,000	
Investment in Turk (−A)		14,000
To record dividends received from Turk ($20,000 × 70%).		
Investment in Turk (+A)	28,000	
Income from Turk (R, +SE)		28,000
To record income from Turk ($40,000 × 70%).		

Shaw's net income for 2007 is $78,000 ($50,000 separate income plus $28,000 income from Turk), and its Investment in Turk account balance at December 31, 2007, is $119,000 ($105,000 beginning balance, plus $28,000 income, less $14,000 dividends).

Poe's entries to account for its investment in Shaw for 2007 are as follows:

POE'S BOOKS

Cash (+A)	24,000	
Investment in Shaw (−A)		24,000
To record dividends received from Shaw ($30,000 × 80%).		
Investment in Shaw (+A)	62,400	
Income from Shaw (R, +SE)		62,400
To record income from Shaw ($78,000 × 80%).		

Poe's net income for 2007 is $162,400 ($100,000 separate income plus $62,400 income from Shaw), and its Investment in Shaw account balance at December 31, 2007, is $238,400 ($200,000 beginning balance, plus $62,400 income, less $24,000 dividends). Consolidated net income for Poe Corporation and Subsidiaries for 2007 is $162,400, equal to Poe's net income on an equity basis.

Computational Approaches for Consolidated Net Income

We can determine Poe's income and consolidated net income independently by alternative methods. Computation in terms of the definition of consolidated net income is:

Poe's separate earnings	$100,000
Add: Poe's share of Shaw's separate earnings ($50,000 × 80%)	40,000
Add: Poe's share of Turk's separate earnings ($40,000 × 80% × 70%)	22,400
Poe's net income and consolidated net income	$162,400

We compute parent and consolidated net income in terms of the consolidated income statement presentation by deducting noncontrolling interest expense from combined separate earnings:

Combined separate earnings:		
Poe	$100,000	
Shaw	50,000	
Turk	40,000	$190,000
Less: Noncontrolling interest expenses:		
Direct noncontrolling interest in Turk's income ($40,000 × 30%)	$ 12,000	
Indirect noncontrolling interest in Turk's income ($40,000 × 70% × 20%)	5,600	
Direct noncontrolling interest in Shaw's income ($50,000 × 20%)	10,000	27,600
Poe's net income and consolidated net income		$162,400

Still another computational approach uses a schedule such as the following:

	Poe	**Shaw**	**Turk**
Separate earnings	$100,000	$50,000	$40,000
Allocate Turk's income to Shaw: ($40,000 × 70%)	—	+28,000	−28,000
Allocate Shaw's income to Poe ($78,000 × 80%)	+62,400	−62,400	—
Consolidated net income	$162,400		
Minority interest expense		$15,600	$12,000

Schedules are often helpful in making allocations for complex affiliation structures. This is particularly true when there are intercompany profits and when the equity method of accounting is not used or is applied incorrectly. The schedule illustrated here shows parent-company and consolidated net income, as well as noncontrolling interest expense. It also shows Shaw's investment income from Turk ($28,000) and Poe's investment income from Shaw ($62,400).

Consolidation Working Papers—Equity Method

Exhibit 9-2 illustrates consolidation working papers for Poe Corporation and Subsidiaries for the year 2007. The working papers show that no new consolidation procedures have been introduced. Consolidation working paper entries a and b eliminate investment income, dividends, and investment and equity balances for Shaw's investment in Turk. Entries c and d eliminate investment income, dividends, and investment and equity balances for Poe's investment in Shaw. Entry e records noncontrolling interests in the earnings and dividends of Turk and Shaw.

e	Noncontrolling interest expense—Shaw (E, −SE)	15,600	
	Noncontrolling interest expense—Turk (E, −SE)	12,000	
	Dividends (+SE)		12,000
	Noncontrolling interest—Shaw (+L)		9,600
	Noncontrolling interest—Turk (+L)		6,000
	To enter noncontrolling interest shares of subsidiary income and dividends.		

EXHIBIT 9-2

Indirect Holdings—
Father-Son-
Grandson Type
(Equity Method)

POE CORPORATION AND SUBSIDIARIES CONSOLIDATION WORKING PAPERS FOR THE YEAR ENDED DECEMBER 31, 2007 (IN THOUSANDS)

	Poe	80% Shaw	70% Turk	Adjustments and Eliminations Debits	Adjustments and Eliminations Credits	Consolidated Statements
Income Statement Sales	$200	$140	$100			$440
Income from Shaw	62.4			c 62.4		
Income from Turk		28		a 28		
Expenses including cost of sales	(100)	(90)	(60)			(250)
Noncontrolling interest expense—Shaw				e 15.6		(15.6)
Noncontrolling interest expense—Turk				e 12		(12)
Net income	**$162.4**	**$ 78**	**$ 40**			**$162.4**
Retained Earnings Retained earnings—Poe	$100					$100
Retained earnings—Shaw		$ 50		d 50		
Retained earnings—Turk			$ 50	b 50		
Dividends	(60)	(30)	(20)		a 14 c 24 e 12	(60)
Net income	162.4	78	40			162.4
Retained earnings— December 31	**$202.4**	**$ 98**	**$ 70**			**$202.4**
Balance Sheet Other assets	$461.6	$231	$200			$892.6
Investment in Shaw	238.4				c 38.4 d 200	
Investment in Turk		119			a 14 b 105	
	$700	$350	$200			$892.6
Liabilities	$ 97.6	$ 52	$ 30			$179.6
Capital stock—Poe	400					400
Capital stock—Shaw		200		d 200		
Capital stock—Turk			100	b 100		
Retained earnings	202.4	98	70			202.4
	$700	$350	$200			
Noncontrolling interest in Turk, January 1 Noncontrolling interest in Shaw, January 1 Total noncontrolling interests, December 31					b 45 d 50 e 9.6 e 6	110.6
						$892.6

Turk's $45,000 beginning noncontrolling interest is simply the 30% direct noncontrolling interest percentage times Turk's $150,000 equity at the beginning of 2007. Noncontrolling interest expense of Turk is 30% of Turk's $40,000 reported income. Similarly, the $50,000 beginning noncontrolling interest in Shaw is 20% of Shaw's $250,000 equity at January 1, 2007, and the $15,600 noncontrolling interest expense of Shaw is 20% of Shaw's reported net income. Consolidated net income and consolidated retained earnings of $162,400 and $202,400, respectively, are equal to Poe's net income and retained earnings.

INDIRECT HOLDINGS—CONNECTING AFFILIATES STRUCTURE

Pet Corporation owns a 70% interest in Sal Corporation and a 60% interest in Ty Corporation. In addition, Sal Corporation owns a 20% interest in Ty. We diagram the affiliation structure of Pet Corporation and Subsidiaries as follows:

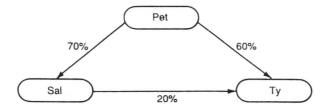

The following table summarizes data relevant to the investments of Pet and Sal.

	Pet's Investment in Sal (70%) Acquired January 1, 2007	Pet's Investment in Ty (60%) Acquired January 1, 2006	Sal's Investment in Ty (20%) Acquired January 1, 2003
Cost	$178,000	$100,000	$20,000
Less: Book value acquired	(168,000)	(90,000)	(20,000)
Goodwill	$ 10,000	$ 10,000	—
Investment Balance December 31, 2007			
Cost	$178,000	$100,000	$20,000
Add: Share of investees' pre-2007 income less dividends	7,000	18,000	16,000
Balance December 31, 2007	$185,000	$118,000	$36,000

During 2008, Pet, Sal, and Ty had earnings from their own operations of $70,000, $35,000, and $20,000 and declared dividends of $40,000, $20,000, and $10,000, respectively. Pet's separate earnings of $70,000 included an unrealized gain of $10,000 from the sale of land to Sal during 2008. Sal's separate earnings of $35,000 included unrealized profit of $5,000 on inventory items sold to Pet for $15,000 during 2008 that remained in Pet's December 31, 2008, inventory. A schedule for the computation of consolidated net income and noncontrolling interest expense for the Pet-Sal-Ty affiliation for 2008 is shown in Exhibit 9-3.

	Pet	Sal	Ty
Separate earnings	$ 70,000	$ 35,000	$20,000
Deduct: Unrealized profit	−10,000	−5,000	—
Separate realized earnings	60,000	30,000	20,000
Allocate Ty's income:			
20% to Sal	—	+4,000	−4,000
60% to Pet	+12,000	—	−12,000
Allocate Sal's income:			
70% to Pet	+23,800	−23,800	—
Pet's net income and consolidated net income	$ 95,800		
Noncontrolling interest expense		$ 10,200	$ 4,000

EXHIBIT 9-3

Income Allocation Schedule

Equity Method of Accounting for Connecting Affiliates

Before allocating the separate earnings of Sal and Ty to Pet, we eliminate any unrealized profits included in such earnings. Exhibit 9-3 shows the allocation of Ty's income as 20% to Sal and 60% to Pet. This allocation must precede the allocation of Sal's income to Pet because Sal's income includes $4,000 investment income from Ty.

In accounting for its investment in Ty for 2008, Sal makes the following entries:

Cash (+A)	2,000	
Investment in Ty (−A)		2,000
To record dividends received from Ty ($10,000 × 20%).		
Investment in Ty (+A)	4,000	
Income from Ty (R, +SE)		4,000
To record income from Ty ($20,000 × 20%).		

Sal's Investment in Ty account at December 31, 2008, has a balance of $38,000—the $36,000 balance at December 31, 2007, plus $4,000 investment income, less $2,000 dividends. We do not reduce Sal's income from Ty for the $5,000 unrealized profit on inventory items sold to Pet because Ty is not a party in the intercompany sale. Sal's $39,000 net income includes $5,000 unrealized profit, which we eliminate when allocating Sal's realized income to Pet and Sal's noncontrolling stockholders.

Pet makes the following entries in accounting for its investments during 2008.

Investment in Ty

Cash (+A)	6,000	
Investment in Ty (−A)		6,000
To record dividends received from Ty ($10,000 × 60%).		
Investment in Ty (+A)	12,000	
Income from Ty (R, +SE)		12,000
To record income from Ty.		

Investment in Sal

Cash (+A)	14,000	
Investment in Sal (−A)		14,000
To record dividends received from Sal ($20,000 × 70%).		
Investment in Sal (+A)	13,800	
Income from Sal (R, +SE)		13,800

To record income from Sal computed as follows:

70% of Sal's reported income of $39,000	$27,300
Less: 70% of Sal's unrealized inventory profit of $5,000	−3,500
Less: 100% of unrealized gain on land	−10,000
	$13,800

Pet's investment accounts at December 31, 2008, show the following balances:

	Investment in Sal (70%)	Investment in Ty (60%)
Balance December 31, 2007	$185,000	$118,000
Add: Investment income	13,800	12,000
Deduct: Dividends	−14,000	−6,000
Balance December 31, 2008	$184,800	$124,000

Consolidation Working Papers—Equity Method

Exhibit 9-4 presents consolidated statement working papers for Pet Corporation and Subsidiaries for 2008.

The adjustment and elimination entries are reproduced in journal form for convenient reference.

PET CORPORATION AND SUBSIDIARIES CONSOLIDATION WORKING PAPERS FOR THE YEAR ENDED DECEMBER 31, 2008 (IN THOUSANDS)

EXHIBIT 9-4

Connecting Affiliates with Intercompany Profits

	Pet	Sal	Ty	Adjustments and Eliminations Debits	Credits	Consolidated Statements
Income Statement Sales	$200	$150	$100	a 15		$435
Income from Sal	13.8			g 13.8		
Income from Ty	12	4		d 16		
Gain on land	10			c 10		
Cost of sales	(100)	(80)	(50)	b 5	a 15	(220)
Other expenses	(40)	(35)	(30)			(105)
Noncontrolling interest expense—Sal [($39 − $5) × 30%]				i 10.2		(10.2)
Noncontrolling interest expense—Ty ($20 × 20%)				f 4		(4)
Net income	**$ 95.8**	**$ 39**	**$ 20**			**$ 95.8**
Retained Earnings Retained earnings—Pet	$223					$223
Retained earnings—Sal		$ 50		h 50		
Retained earnings—Ty			$ 80	e 80		
Dividends	(40)	(20)	(10)		d 8 / f 2 / g 14 / i 6	(40)
Net income	95.8	39	20			95.8
Retained earnings—December 31	$278.8	$ 69	$ 90			$278.8
Balance Sheet Other assets	$ 46.2	$ 22	$ 85			$153.2
Inventories	50	40	15		b 5	100
Plant assets—net	400	200	100		c 10	690
Investment in Sal (70%)	184.8			g .2	h 185	
Investment in Ty (60%)	124				d 6 / e 118	
Investment in Ty (20%)		38			d 2 / e 36	
Goodwill				e 10 / h 10		20
	$805	$300	$200			$963.2
Liabilities	$126.2	$ 31	$ 10			$167.2

(continued)

EXHIBIT 9-4

Connecting Affiliates
with Intercompany
Profits (continued)

PET CORPORATION AND SUBSIDIARIES CONSOLIDATION WORKING PAPERS FOR THE YEAR ENDED DECEMBER 31, 2008 (IN THOUSANDS)

	Pet	Sal	Ty	Adjustments and Eliminations Debits	Adjustments and Eliminations Credits	Consolidated Statements
Capital stock—Pet	400					400
Capital stock—Sal		200		h 200		
Capital stock—Ty			100	e 100		
Retained earnings	278.8	69	90			278.8
	$805	$300	$200			

Noncontrolling interest:
  Noncontrolling interest in Ty, January 1
  Noncontrolling interest in Sal, January 1
					e 36
					h 75
					f 2
					i 4.2
						117.2

						$963.2

a Sales (–R, –SE)   15,000
        Cost of sales (–E, +SE)   15,000
     To eliminate reciprocal sales and cost of sales.

b Cost of sales (E, –SE)   5,000
        Inventory (–A)   5,000
     To eliminate unrealized intercompany profit from inventory
         at December 31, 2008.

c Gain on land (–Ga, –SE)   10,000
        Plant assets—net (–A)   10,000
     To eliminate unrealized profit from intercompany sale of land.

d Income from Ty (–R, –SE)   16,000
        Dividends (Ty's) (+SE)   8,000
        Investment in Ty (60%) (–A)   6,000
        Investment in Ty (20%) (–A)   2,000
     To eliminate income from Ty and dividends from Ty and
         to adjust the Investment in Ty accounts.

e Retained earnings—Ty, January 1, 2008 (–SE)   80,000
   Goodwill (+A)   10,000
   Capital stock—Ty (–SE)   100,000
        Investment in Ty (60%) (–A)   118,000
        Investment in Ty (20%) (–A)   36,000
        Noncontrolling interests—Ty (+L)   36,000
     To eliminate reciprocal investment and equity amounts of
         Ty and to establish goodwill and noncontrolling interest
         at January 1, 2008.

f Noncontrolling interest expense—Ty (E, –SE)   4,000
        Dividends (+SE)   2,000
        Noncontrolling interest—Ty (+L)   2,000
     To enter noncontrolling interest share of subsidiary income and dividends.

g	Income from Sal (−R, −SE)	13,800	
	Investment in Sal (+A)	200	
	Dividends (Sal's) (+SE)		14,000
	To eliminate income from Sal and dividends from Sal and to adjust the Investment in Sal account.		
h	Retained earnings—Sal, January 1, 2008 (−SE)	50,000	
	Goodwill (+A)	10,000	
	Capital stock—Sal (−SE)	200,000	
	Investment in Sal (−A)		185,000
	Noncontrolling interest—Sal (+L)		75,000
	To eliminate reciprocal investment and equity amounts in Sal and to establish goodwill and noncontrolling interest at January 1, 2008.		
i	Noncontrolling interest expense—Sal (E, −SE)	10,200	
	Dividends (+SE)		6,000
	Noncontrolling interest—Sal (+L)		4,200
	To enter noncontrolling interest share of subsidiary income and dividends.		

A check on the $117,200 noncontrolling interest at December 31, 2008, as shown in Exhibit 9-4 may be helpful at this point. We can confirm the noncontrolling interest as follows:

	Noncontrolling Interest in Sal (30%)	Noncontrolling Interest in Ty (20%)	Total Noncontrolling Interest
Book value at December 31, 2008:			
Sal ($269,000 × 30%)	$80,700	—	$ 80,700
Ty ($190,000 × 20%)	—	$38,000	38,000
Less: Unrealized profit of Sal			
($5,000 × 30%)	(1,500)	—	(1,500)
Noncontrolling interest December 31, 2008	$79,200	$38,000	$117,200

Except for the deduction of 30% of the $5,000 unrealized inventory profit on Sal's upstream sale to Pet, the noncontrolling interest is stated at its underlying book value at December 31, 2008.

MUTUAL HOLDINGS—PARENT STOCK HELD BY SUBSIDIARY

When affiliated companies hold ownership interests in each other, a mutual holding situation exists. Parent-company stock held by the subsidiary is not outstanding from the consolidated viewpoint and should not be reported as outstanding stock in a consolidated balance sheet.[2]

For example, if Pace Corporation owns a 90% interest in Salt Corporation and Salt owns a 10% interest in Pace, the 10% interest held by Salt is not outstanding for consolidation purposes, and neither is the 90% interest in Salt held by Pace. Consolidation practice requires the exclusion of both the 10% and the 90% interests from consolidated financial statements, and the question is not whether the 10% interest in Pace should be excluded, but rather how we should eliminate it in the consolidation process. The elimination procedures depend on the method used in accounting for the investment.

There are two generally accepted methods of accounting for parent-company stock held by a subsidiary—the treasury stock approach and the conventional approach. The **treasury stock approach** considers parent-company stock held by a subsidiary to be treasury stock of the consolidated entity. Accordingly, we maintain the investment account on the books of the subsidiary on a cost basis and deduct it at cost from stockholders' equity in the consolidated balance sheet. The **conventional approach** is to account for the subsidiary investment in parent-company stock on an equity basis and to eliminate the subsidiary investment account against the parent-company equity

---

[2]*ARB No. 51*, "Consolidated Financial Statements," paragraph 13.

accounts in the usual manner. Although both approaches are acceptable, they do not result in equivalent consolidated financial statements. In particular, the consolidated retained earnings and noncontrolling interest amounts usually differ under the two methods.

Treasury Stock Approach

Assume that Pace Corporation acquired a 90% interest in Salt Corporation on January 1, 2006, for $270,000, when Salt's capital stock was $200,000 and its retained earnings $100,000. In addition, Salt Corporation purchased a 10% interest in Pace Corporation on January 5, 2006, for $70,000, when Pace's capital stock was $500,000 and its retained earnings $200,000. Trial balances for Pace and Salt on December 31, 2006, before either company recorded its investment income, were as follows (in thousands):

	Pace	Salt
Debits		
Other assets	$480	$260
Investment in Salt (90%)	270	—
Investment in Pace (10%)	—	70
Expenses including cost of goods sold	70	50
	$820	$380
Credits		
Capital stock, $10 par	$500	$200
Retained earnings	200	100
Sales	120	80
	$820	$380

CONSOLIDATION IN YEAR OF ACQUISITION If we use the treasury stock approach, Salt Corporation has no investment income for 2006, and Pace's share of Salt's $30,000 income ($80,000 sales − $50,000 expenses) is $27,000 ($30,000 × 90%). Exhibit 9-5 shows consolidation working papers for Pace Corporation and Subsidiary for 2006. In examining the working papers, notice that Salt's investment in Pace is reclassified as treasury stock and deducted from stockholders' equity in the consolidated balance sheet.

CONSOLIDATION IN SUBSEQUENT YEARS During 2007 the separate earnings and dividends of Pace and Salt Corporations are as follows:

	Pace	Salt
Separate earnings	$60,000	$40,000
Dividends	30,000	20,000

Under the treasury stock approach, Salt records dividend income of $3,000 from Pace (10% of Pace Corporation's $30,000 dividends) and reports its net income for 2007 under the cost method in the amount of $43,000.

Pace Corporation accounts for its investment in Salt under the equity method as follows:

Cash (+A)	18,000	
Investment in Salt (−A)		18,000
To record 90% of $20,000 dividends paid by Salt.		
Investment in Salt (+A)	38,700	
Income from Salt (R, +SE)		38,700
To record 90% of Salt's $43,000 income for 2007.		
Income from Salt (−R, −SE)	3,000	
Dividends (+SE)		3,000

To eliminate intercompany dividends of $3,000 (10% of Pace's $30,000 dividends paid to Salt) and to adjust investment income for Pace's dividends that are included in Salt's income.

Thus, Pace records investment income from Salt of $35,700 ($38,700 − $3,000) and an investment account increase of $20,700 during 2007 ($38,700 − $18,000). The increase of $20,700 in Pace's Investment in Salt account is equal to 90% of Salt's $40,000 separate earnings, plus 90% of the

PACE CORPORATION AND SUBSIDIARY CONSOLIDATION WORKING PAPERS FOR THE YEAR ENDED DECEMBER 31, 2006 (IN THOUSANDS)						
	Pace	90% Salt	**Adjustments and Elimination**		Consolidated Statements	
			Debits	Credits		
Income Statement Sales	$120	$ 80			$200	
Investment income	27		a 27			
Expenses including cost of sales	(70)	(50)			(120)	
Noncontrolling interest expense			d 3		(3)	
Net income	**$ 77**	**$ 30**			**$ 77**	
Retained Earnings Retained earnings—Pace	$200				$200	
Retained earnings—Salt		$100	b 100			
Net income	**77**	**30**			**77**	
Retained earnings— December 31	**$277**	**$130**			**$277**	
Balance Sheet Other assets	$480	$260			$740	
Investment in Salt (90%)	297			a 27 b 270		
Investment in Pace (10%)		70		c 70		
	$777	**$330**			**$740**	
Capital stock—Pace	$500				$500	
Capital stock—Salt		$200	b 200			
Retained earnings	**277**	**130**			**277**	
	$777	**$330**				
Treasury stock			c 70		(70)	
Noncontrolling interest				b 30 d 3	33	
					$740	

EXHIBIT 9-5

Parent Stock Held by Subsidiary—Treasury Stock Approach (Year of Acquisition)

$3,000 dividends paid to Salt that accrued to the benefit of Pace, less 90% of Salt's $20,000 dividends. Pace Corporation's investment income from Salt consists of 90% of Salt's $40,000 separate earnings, less $300 (the part of the $3,000 dividends from Pace that accrues to the benefit of Salt Corporation's noncontrolling stockholders).

Exhibit 9-6 shows consolidation working papers for Pace and Subsidiary for 2007. We compute the $317,700 balance in Pace's Investment in Salt account as follows:

Investment in Salt (90%) December 31, 2007	$297,000
Add: 90% of Salt's reported income	38,700
Deduct: 90% of Salt's dividends	(18,000)
Investment in Salt (90%) December 31, 2007	$317,700

EXHIBIT 9-6

Parent Stock Held by Subsidiary—Treasury Stock Approach (Year After Acquisition)

PACE CORPORATION AND SUBSIDIARY CONSOLIDATION WORKING PAPERS FOR THE YEAR ENDED DECEMBER 31, 2007 (IN THOUSANDS)

	Pace	90% Salt	Adjustments and Eliminations Debits	Credits	Consolidated Statements
Income Statement Sales	$140	$100			$240
Income from Salt	35.7		a 35.7		
Dividend income		3	a 3		
Expenses including cost of sales	(80)	(60)			(140)
Noncontrolling interest expense			d 4.3		(4.3)
Net income	**$ 95.7**	**$ 43**			**$ 95.7**
Retained Earnings Retained earnings—Pace	$277				$277
Retained earnings—Salt		$130	b 130		
Dividends	(27)	(20)		a 18 d 2	(27)
Net income	95.7	43			95.7
Retained earnings— December 31	**$345.7**	**$153**			**$345.7**
Balance Sheet Other assets	$528	$283			$811
Investment in Salt (90%)	317.7			a 20.7 b 297	
Investment in Pace (10%)		70		c 70	
	$845.7	$353			$811
Capital stock—Pace	$500				$500
Capital stock—Salt		$200	b 200		
Retained earnings	345.7	153			345.7
	$845.7	$353			
Treasury stock			c 70		(70)
Noncontrolling interest				b 33 d 2.3	35.3
					$811

Pace's investment in Salt was acquired at book value, so we can also compute the Investment in Salt account balance as 90% of Salt's equity at December 31, 2007 ($353,000 × 90% = $317,700).

Entry a in the consolidation working papers shown in Exhibit 9-6 is affected by the $3,000 dividend adjustment under the equity method and is reproduced for convenient reference:

a	Income from Salt (−R, −SE)	35,700	
	Dividend income (−R, −SE)	3,000	
	Dividends (+SE)		18,000
	Investment in Salt (−A)		20,700

This entry is unusual because we eliminate both Pace Corporation's investment income from Salt and Salt's dividend income from Pace in the process of adjusting the Investment in Salt account to its $297,000 beginning-of-the-period balance. The other working paper adjustments are similar to those in Exhibit 9-5.

Although Pace Corporation paid dividends of $30,000 during 2007, only $27,000 was paid to outside stockholders. Thus, Pace's retained earnings statement and the consolidated retained earnings statement show $27,000 dividends rather than $30,000. The consolidated balance sheet shows a $70,000 equity deduction for the cost of Salt's investment in Pace. This amount is the same as was shown in the working papers in Exhibit 9-5.

Conventional Approach

The consolidated balance sheets in Exhibits 9-5 and 9-6 for the treasury stock approach consolidated 100% of Pace Corporation's capital stock and retained earnings and deducted the cost of Salt's 10% investment in Pace from the consolidated stockholders' equity. Under the conventional approach, we consider parent-company stock held by a subsidiary as constructively retired, and the capital stock and retained earnings applicable to the interest held by the subsidiary do not appear in the consolidated financial statements.

We consider Salt's acquisition of Pace stock under the conventional procedure a constructive retirement of 10% of Pace's capital stock. A consolidated balance sheet for Pace and Subsidiary at the time of acquisition shows capital stock and retained earnings applicable to the 90% of Pace Corporation's equity held outside of the consolidated entity as follows (in thousands):

January 1, 2006

	Pace	Consolidated
Capital stock	$500	$450
Retained earnings	200	180
Total stockholders' equity	$700	$630

Accountants generally agree that the consolidated balance sheet should show the capital stock and retained earnings applicable to majority stockholders outside the consolidated entity. However, this treatment raises a question concerning the applicability of the equity method of accounting to mutual holdings involving parent-company stock. Specifically, is the equity method of accounting applicable to affiliation structures that involve investments in the parent company? If so, the parent company's (investor's) "net income for the period and its stockholders' equity at the end of the period are the same regardless of whether an investment in a subsidiary is accounted for under the equity method or the subsidiary is consolidated."[3]

In spite of some reservations that have been expressed about the applicability of the equity method to mutually held parent-company stock, the position taken in this book is that the equity method applies and is, in fact, required by *APB Opinion No. 18*. Paragraph 19e of that opinion states that "a transaction of an investee of a capital nature that affects the investor's share of stockholders' equity of the investee should be accounted for as if the investee were a consolidated subsidiary." In accounting for Pace's investment in Salt, we apply this requirement as follows:

January 1, 2006

Investment in Salt (90%) (+A)	270,000	
Cash (−A)		270,000
To record acquisition of a 90% interest in Salt at book value.		*(continued)*

---

[3] *APB Opinion No. 18*, paragraph 19.

January 5, 2006

Capital stock, $10 par (−SE)	50,000	
Retained earnings (−SE)	20,000	
Investment in Salt (−A)		70,000

To record the constructive retirement of 10% of Pace's outstanding
stock as a result of Salt's purchase of Pace stock.

These entries reduce parent-company capital stock and retained earnings to reflect amounts applicable to majority stockholders outside the consolidated entity. We base the reduction of the Investment in Salt account on the theory that parent-company stock purchased by a subsidiary is, in effect, returned to the parent company and constructively retired.

By recording the constructive retirement of the parent-company stock on parent-company books, parent-company equity reflects the equity of stockholders outside the consolidated entity. These are the shareholders for which the consolidated statements are intended. In addition, recording the constructive retirement as indicated establishes consistency between capital stock and retained earnings for the parent's outside stockholders (90%) and parent-company net income, dividends, and earnings per share, which also relate to the 90% outside stockholders of the parent. Financial statement notes should explain the details of the constructive retirement.

ALLOCATION OF MUTUAL INCOME When we use the conventional method of accounting for mutually held stock, the income of the parent on an equity basis cannot be determined until the income of the subsidiary has been determined on an equity basis, and vice versa. This is because the incomes are mutually related. The solution to the problem of determining parent and subsidiary incomes lies in the use of some mathematical procedure, the most common procedure being the use of simultaneous equations and substitution. We accomplish the allocation of income to the affiliated entities and to outside stockholders in two steps. First, we compute the incomes of Pace and Salt on a consolidated basis, which includes the mutual income held by the affiliates. Next, we multiply these amounts by the percentage ownership held within the affiliated group and the noncontrolling interest percentage to determine consolidated net income on an equity basis and noncontrolling interest expense.

In the first step, we determine the incomes of Pace and Salt on a consolidated basis for 2006 mathematically as follows:

P = the income of Pace on a consolidated basis (includes mutual income)

S = the income of Salt on a consolidated basis (includes mutual income)

Then,

P = Pace's separate earnings of $50,000 + 90% S

S = Salt's separate earnings of $30,000 + 10% P

By substitution,

$P = \$50,000 + 0.9(\$30,000 + 0.1P)$

$P = \$50,000 + \$27,000 + 0.09P$

$P = \underline{\$84,615}$

$S = \$30,000 + (\$84,615 \times 0.1)$

$S = \underline{\$38,462}$

These are not final solutions because some of the income (mutual income) has been double-counted. The combined separate earnings of Pace and Salt are only $80,000 ($50,000 + $30,000), but P plus S equals $123,077 ($84,615 + $38,462). In the next step, we determine Pace's net income on an equity basis by multiplying the value determined for P in the equation by the 90% interest outstanding, and we determine noncontrolling interest expense by multiplying the value determined for S by the noncontrolling interest percentage. In other words, *Pace's net income on an equity basis is 90% of $84,615, or $76,154, and the noncontrolling interest expense is 10% of*

$38,462, or $3,846. Pace's net income (and consolidated net income) of $76,154, plus noncontrolling interest expense of $3,846, is equal to the $80,000 separate earnings of Pace and Salt.

ACCOUNTING FOR MUTUAL INCOME UNDER THE EQUITY METHOD Pace Corporation records its investment income for 2006 on an equity basis as follows:

Investment in Salt (+A)	26,154	
Income from Salt (R, +SE)		26,154
To record income from Salt.		

The $26,154 income from Salt equals 90% of Salt's $38,462 income on a consolidated basis, less 10% of Pace's $84,615 income on a consolidated basis [($38,462 × 90%) − ($84,615 × 10%)]. This represents Pace's 90% interest in Salt's income less Salt's 10% interest in Pace's income. An alternative calculation that gives the same result deducts Pace's separate earnings from its net income ($76,154 − $50,000).

Assume that Salt Corporation accounts for its investment in Pace on a cost basis because its interest in Pace is only 10%. Pace did not declare dividends during 2006, so Salt would have no investment income for the year, and its investment account would remain at the $70,000 original cost of the 10% interest.

CONSOLIDATION UNDER THE EQUITY METHOD Exhibit 9-7 presents consolidation working papers for Pace Corporation and Subsidiary under the conventional procedure for 2006. The working papers show the investment in Salt (90%) at $226,154 (the $270,000 initial investment, plus $26,154 investment income, less the $70,000 reduction for the constructive retirement of Pace's stock). Entry a in the working papers eliminates the $70,000 investment in Pace (Salt's books) and increases Pace's Investment in Salt account to $296,154. This entry reflects the constructive retirement of Pace stock that was charged to Pace's Investment in Salt account. Entry b eliminates investment income of $26,154 and reduces the investment account to its $270,000 cost at January 5, 2006. Entry c eliminates the reciprocal investment in Salt and equity of Salt amounts and establishes the noncontrolling interest in Salt at $30,000 (10% of $300,000) at the beginning of 2006.

In examining the working papers in Exhibit 9-7, observe that the net income, capital stock, and retained earnings in the separate statements of Pace Corporation are equal to consolidated net income, capital stock, and retained earnings. This equality would not have existed without the entry to record the constructive retirement of stock on Pace Corporation's books.

CONSOLIDATION IN SUBSEQUENT YEARS The separate earnings and dividends of Pace and Salt for 2007 are as follows:

	Pace	Salt
Separate earnings	$60,000	$40,000
Dividends	30,000	20,000

Application of the conventional method of accounting requires the following mathematical computations for Pace and Salt for 2007:

P = Pace's income on a consolidated basis (includes mutual income)

S = Salt's income on a consolidated basis (includes mutual income)

Basic equations:

$$P = \$60,000 + 0.9S$$
$$S = \$40,000 + 01.P$$

Substitution:

$$P = \$60,000 + 0.9(\$40,000 + 0.1P)$$
$$0.91P = \$96,000$$
$$P = \underline{\$105,495}$$

EXHIBIT 9-7

Parent Stock Held by
Subsidiary—
Conventional
Approach (Year of
Acquisition)

PACE CORPORATION AND SUBSIDIARY CONSOLIDATION WORKING PAPERS FOR THE YEAR ENDED DECEMBER 31, 2006

	Pace	90% Salt	Adjustments and Eliminations		Consolidated Statements
			Debits	Credits	
Income Statement Sales	$120,000	$ 80,000			$200,000
Investment income	26,154		b 26,154		
Expenses including cost of sales	(70,000)	(50,000)			(120,000)
Noncontrolling interest expense			d 3,846		(3,846)
Net income	**$ 76,154**	**$ 30,000**			**$ 76,154**
Retained Earnings Retained earnings—Pace	$180,000				$180,000
Retained earnings—Salt		$100,000	c 100,000		
Net income	76,154	30,000			76,154
Retained earnings— December 31	**$256,154**	**$130,000**			**$256,154**
Balance Sheet Other assets	$480,000	$260,000			$740,000
Investment in Salt (90%)	226,154		a 70,000	b 26,154 c 270,000	
Investment in Pace (10%)		70,000		a 70,000	
	$756,154	$330,000			$740,000
Capital stock—Pace	$450,000				$450,000
Capital stock—Salt		$200,000	c 200,000		
Retained earnings	256,154	130,000			256,154
	$706,154	$330,000			
Noncontrolling interest				c 30,000 d 3,846	33,846
					$740,000

$$S = \$40,000 + 0.1(\$105,495)$$

$$S = \underline{\$50,549}$$

These computed amounts for *P* and *S* include mutual income that we must then eliminate. We use these amounts to determine consolidated net income and noncontrolling interest expense as follows:

Pace's net income (and consolidated net income) ($105,495 × 90% outside ownership)	$ 94,945
Noncontrolling interest expense ($50,549 × 10%)	5,055
Total separate earnings of Pace and Salt	$100,000

If Salt accounts for its investment in Pace under the cost method, it will record dividend income from Pace of $3,000 for 2007 (10% of Pace's dividends). Alternatively, Salt will record income from Pace of $10,550 ($105,495 × 10%) if it uses the equity method.

Pace accounts for its investment in Salt on an equity basis as follows:

Cash (+A)	18,000	
Investment in Salt (−A)		18,000
To record 90% of Salt's $20,000 dividend for 2007		

Investment in Salt (+A)	34,945	
Income from Salt (R, +SE)		34,945

To record investment income computed as follows: $94,945 Pace's net income less $60,000 Pace's separate earnings = $34,945. An alternative computation: 90% of Salt's income on a consolidated basis ($50,549 × 90%), less 10% of Pace's income on a consolidated basis ($105,495 × 10%) = $34,945.

Investment in Salt (+A)	3,000	
Dividends (+SE)		3,000

To eliminate parent-company dividends paid to Salt and to adjust the Investment in Salt account.

Pace's Investment in Salt account at December 31, 2007, will have a balance of $246,099 under the equity method. This balance is computed as follows:

Investment in Salt, December 31, 2006	$226,154
Add: Investment income	34,945
Add: Dividends paid to Salt	3,000
Deduct: Dividends received from Salt	−18,000
Investment in Salt, December 31, 2007	$246,099

Exhibit 9-8 presents consolidation working papers for Pace Corporation and Subsidiary for 2007. We assume that Salt accounts for its investment in Pace under the cost method. The equity method of accounting has been applied by Pace. Therefore, parent-company net income of $94,945 is equal to consolidated net income. Parent-company capital stock and retained earnings amounts also equal their corresponding consolidated statement amounts. The working paper adjustments in Exhibit 9-8 are procedurally equivalent to those shown earlier in the chapter.

CONVERSION TO EQUITY METHOD ON SEPARATE COMPANY BOOKS It is helpful at this point to consider the computations that would be necessary to correct consolidated retained earnings and noncontrolling interest if the equity method of accounting had not been used by Pace. First, it would be necessary to determine the separate net asset increases of the mutually held companies. We compute these increases for Pace and Salt from January 1, 2006, to December 31, 2007, as follows:

	Pace	**Salt**	**Total**
Separate earnings—2006	$50,000	$30,000	$ 80,000
Separate earnings—2007	+60,000	+40,000	+100,000
Less: Dividends declared	−30,000	−20,000	−50,000
Add: Dividends received from affiliates	+18,000	+3,000	+21,000
Increase in net assets	$98,000	$53,000	$151,000

Once we determine the separate net asset increases, the simultaneous equations used earlier for determining income allocations allocate the separate net asset increases to consolidated retained earnings and to noncontrolling interest. The computations for Pace and Salt are:

P = increase in net assets of Pace on a consolidated basis since acquisition by Salt

S = increase in net assets of Salt on a consolidated basis since acquisition by Pace

EXHIBIT 9-8

Parent Stock Held by Subsidiary— Conventional Approach (Year After Acquisition)

PACE CORPORATION AND SUBSIDIARY CONSOLIDATION WORKING PAPERS FOR THE YEAR ENDED DECEMBER 31, 2007 (IN THOUSANDS)

	Pace	90% Salt	Adjustments and Eliminations Debits	Credits	Consolidated Statements
Income Statement Sales	$140,000	$100,000			$240,000
Income from Salt	34,945		b 34,945		
Dividend income		3,000	b 3,000		
Expenses including cost of sales	(80,000)	(60,000)			(140,000)
Noncontrolling interest expense			d 5,055		(5,055)
Net income	**$ 94,945**	**$ 43,000**			**$ 94,945**
Retained Earnings Retained earnings—Pace	$256,154				$256,154
Retained earnings—Salt		$130,000	c 130,000		
Dividends	(27,000)	(20,000)		b 18,000 d 2,000	(27,000)
Net income	94,945	43,000			94,945
Retained earnings— December 31	**$324,099**	**$153,000**			**$324,099**
Balance Sheet Other assets	$528,000	$283,000			$811,000
Investment in Salt (90%)	246,099		a 70,000	b 19,945 c 296,154	
Investment in Pace (10%)		70,000		a 70,000	
	$774,099	$353,000			$811,000
Capital stock—Pace	$450,000				$450,000
Capital stock—Salt		$200,000	c 200,000		
Retained earnings	324,099	153,000			324,099
	$774,099	$353,000			
Noncontrolling interest				c 33,846 d 3,055	36,901
					$811,000

Basic equations:

$$P = \$98,000 + 0.9S$$
$$S = \$53,000 + 0.1P$$

By substitution,

$$P = \$98,000 + 0.9(\$53,000 + 0.1P)$$
$$P = \$98,000 + \$47,700 + 0.09P$$
$$0.91P = \$145,700$$

$$P = \underline{\$160{,}110}$$
$$S = \$\ 53{,}000 + (0.1 \times \$160{,}110)$$
$$S = \underline{\$\ 69{,}011}$$

These computations (which still include mutual amounts) could be used to allocate the $151,000 net asset increase to consolidated retained earnings and noncontrolling interest as follows:

Pace's retained earnings increase (or increase in consolidated retained earnings) = $160,110 × 90%	$144,099
Noncontrolling interest's retained earnings increase = $69,011 × 10%	6,901
Total net asset increase	$151,000

At acquisition, Pace's retained earnings were $200,000, and they were adjusted downward to $180,000 for the constructive retirement of 10% of Pace's stock. Thus, we compute the correct amount of consolidated retained earnings at December 31, 2007, as $180,000 + $144,099, or $324,099. This computation provides a convenient check on the $324,099 retained earnings shown in the consolidated balance sheet in Exhibit 9-8.

Noncontrolling interest in Salt Corporation at January 1, 2006, was $30,000 ($300,000 equity × 10%). We compute the noncontrolling interest at December 31, 2007, as $30,000 + $6,901, or $36,901. This computation confirms the $36,901 noncontrolling interest that appears in the consolidation working papers of Exhibit 9-8.

SUBSIDIARY STOCK MUTUALLY HELD

Parent-company stock held within an affiliation structure is not outstanding and is not reported as outstanding stock either in the parent-company statements under the equity method of accounting or in consolidated financial statements. Two generally accepted approaches for eliminating the effect of mutually held parent-company stock—the treasury stock approach and the conventional approach—were explained and illustrated in the previous section of this chapter. In this section, *the mutually held stock involves subsidiaries holding the stock of each other, and the treasury stock approach is not applicable.*

Consider the following diagram of the affiliation structure of Poly, Seth, and Uno. Poly owns an 80% interest in Seth directly. Seth has a 70% interest in Uno, and Uno has a 10% interest in Seth. There is a 10% noncontrolling interest in Seth and a 30% noncontrolling interest in Uno.

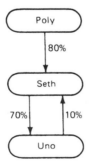

The acquisitions of Poly, Seth, and Uno were as follows:

1. Poly acquired its 80% interest in Seth Corporation on January 2, 2006, for $260,000, when the stockholders' equity of Seth consisted of capital stock of $200,000 and retained earnings of $100,000 ($20,000 goodwill).

2. Seth acquired its 70% interest in Uno Corporation for $115,000 on January 3, 2007, when the stockholders' equity of Uno consisted of $100,000 capital stock and $50,000 retained earnings ($10,000 goodwill).

3. Uno acquired its 10% interest in Seth for $40,000 on December 31, 2007, when the stockholders' equity of Seth consisted of $200,000 capital stock and $200,000 retained earnings (no goodwill).

Accounting Prior to Mutual Holding Relationship

Assume that the recorded net assets from the investments described were equal to their fair values at the time of acquisition and that we allocated any excess of investment over net assets acquired to goodwill. After-closing trial balances for Poly, Seth, and Uno at December 31, 2007, are as follows (in thousands):

	Poly	Seth	Uno
Cash	$ 64	$ 39	$ 20
Other current assets	200	85	80
Plant and equipment—net	500	240	110
Investment in Seth (80%)	340	—	—
Investment in Uno (70%)	—	136	—
Investment in Seth (10%)	—	—	40
	$1,104	$500	$250
Liabilities	$ 200	$100	$ 70
Capital stock	500	200	100
Retained earnings	404	200	80
	$1,104	$500	$250

We compute the balance in Poly's Investment in Seth account at December 31, 2007, as $340,000.

Cost	$260,000
Add: 80% of Seth's $40,000 income less dividends—2006	32,000
80% of Seth's $60,000 income less dividends—2007	48,000
	$340,000

The balance of Uno's 10% Investment in Seth account at December 31, 2007, is equal to the $40,000 cost of the investment on that date. Assume that Uno accounts for this 10% investment in Seth on a cost basis, even though the equity method might be used because absolute control lies with the parent company.

We compute Seth's $136,000 investment in Uno at December 31, 2007, as follows:

Investment in Uno January 3, 2007—cost	$115,000
Add: 70% of Uno's $30,000 income less dividends—2007	21,000
	$136,000

Accounting for Mutually Held Subsidiaries

During 2008, the three affiliated companies had income from their separate operations and dividends as follows (in thousands):

	Poly	Seth	Uno	Total
Income from separate operations	$112	$51	$40	$203
Dividends declared	50	30	20	100

We allocate the total separate incomes of the three companies under the conventional approach.

INCOME ALLOCATION COMPUTATIONS Income allocation computations for the affiliated companies follow:

$$P = \text{separate income of Poly} + 0.8S$$
$$S = \text{separate income of Seth} + 0.7U$$
$$U = \text{separate income of Uno} + 0.1S$$
$$P = \$112,000 + 0.8S$$
$$S = \$51,000 + 0.7U$$
$$U = \$40,000 + 0.1S$$

Solve for S (amounts are rounded to nearest $1):

$$S = \$\ 51{,}000 + 0.7(\$40{,}000 + 0.1S) = \$79{,}000 + 0.07S$$
$$0.93S = \$\ 79{,}000$$
$$S = \underline{\$\ 84{,}946}$$

$$U = \$\ 40{,}000 + 0.1(\$84{,}946)$$
$$U = \underline{\$\ 48{,}495}$$

$$P = \$112{,}000 + 0.8(\$84{,}946)$$
$$P = \underline{\$179{,}957}$$

We allocate total income for the affiliated group to:

Consolidated net income (equal to Poly's net income)	$179,957
Noncontrolling interest in Seth's income ($84,946 × 10%)	8,495
Noncontrolling interest in Uno's income ($48,495 × 30%)	14,548
Total separate income	$203,000

COMPUTATIONS OF INVESTMENT ACCOUNT BALANCES A summary of the investment account balances at December 31, 2008, is as follows:

	Poly (Equity Method)	Seth (Equity Method)	Uno (Cost Method)*
Investment balances December 31, 2007	$340,000	$136,000	$40,000
Add: Investment income			
Poly ($84,946 × 0.8)	67,957	—	—
Seth ($48,495 × 0.7)	—	33,946	—
Deduct: Dividends received:			
Poly ($30,000 × 0.8)	(24,000)	—	—
Seth ($20,000 × 0.7)	—	(14,000)	—
Investment balance December 31, 2008	$383,957	$155,946	$40,000

*$3,000 dividend income and dividends received amounts for Uno's 10% investment in Seth do not affect the investment account because Uno uses the cost method.

CONSOLIDATION WORKING PAPERS—EQUITY METHOD Exhibit 9-9 reflects the investment incomes and balances in the consolidation working papers. We show separate-company financial statements of Poly, Seth, and Uno in the first three columns of the consolidation working papers. Consolidation working paper entries a, b, and c eliminate investment income (including dividend income of Uno) and intercompany dividend balances, and adjust the investment accounts to their beginning-of-the-period balances. Working paper entry d eliminates reciprocal equity and investment balances for Uno, records the $10,000 beginning-of-the-period goodwill from Seth's investment in Uno, and establishes the $54,000 beginning noncontrolling interest in Uno (computed as $180,000 × 30%). Entry e eliminates reciprocal equity and investment balances for Seth (both Poly's 80% and Uno's 10%), records the $20,000 beginning-of-the-period goodwill from Poly's investment in Seth, and establishes the $40,000 beginning noncontrolling interest in Seth (computed as $400,000 × 10%). Although there are two Investment in Seth accounts and therefore two elimination entries could have been made, *it is convenient to prepare one entry for each entity* (Seth in this case) *rather than for each investment account.*

Poly accounts for its investment in Seth as a one-line consolidation, so consolidated net income of $179,957 for 2008 and consolidated retained earnings of $529,957 at December 31, 2008, equal the corresponding amounts in the separate financial statements of Poly. We determine noncontrolling interest expense by equation, as demonstrated earlier.

EXHIBIT 9-9

Consolidation
Involving Mutually
Held Subsidiary
Stock

POLY CORPORATION AND SUBSIDIARIES CONSOLIDATION WORKING PAPERS FOR THE YEAR ENDED DECEMBER 31, 2008

	Poly	Seth	Uno	Adjustments and Eliminations Debits	Credits	Consolidated Statements
Income Statement Sales	$412,000	$161,000	$100,000			$ 673,000
Income from Seth (80%)	67,957			c 67,957		
Income from Uno (70%)		33,946		b 33,946		
Dividend income (10%)			3,000	a 3,000		
Cost of sales	(220,000)	(70,000)	(40,000)			(330,000)
Expenses	(80,000)	(40,000)	(20,000)			(140,000)
Noncontrolling interest expense—Seth				f 8,495		(8,495)
Noncontrolling interest expense—Uno				g 14,548		(14,548)
Net income	**$179,957**	**$ 84,946**	**$ 43,000**			**$ 179,957**
Retained Earnings Retained earnings—Poly	$404,000					$ 404,000
Retained earnings—Seth		$200,000		e 200,000		
Retained earnings—Uno			$ 80,000	d 80,000		
Dividends	(50,000)	(30,000)	(20,000)		a 3,000	
					b 14,000	
					c 24,000	
					f 3,000	
					g 6,000	(50,000)
Net income	179,957	84,946	43,000			179,957
Retained earnings— December 31	**$533,957**	**$254,946**	**$103,000**			**$ 533,957**
Balance Sheet Cash	$ 60,000	$ 30,000	$ 43,000			$ 133,000
Other current assets	250,000	80,000	70,000			400,000
Plant assets—net	550,000	300,000	130,000			980,000
Investment in Seth (80%)	383,957				c 43,957 e 340,000	
Investment in Uno (70%)		155,946			b 19,946 d 136,000	

(continued)

POLY CORPORATION AND SUBSIDIARIES CONSOLIDATION WORKING PAPERS FOR THE YEAR ENDED DECEMBER 31, 2007

	Poly	Seth	Uno	Adjustments and Eliminations Debits	Adjustments and Eliminations Credits	Consolidated Statements
Investment in Seth (10%)			40,000		e 40,000	
Goodwill—Poly				e 20,000		20,000
Goodwill—Seth				d 10,000		10,000
	$1,243,957	$565,946	$283,000			$1,543,000
Liabilities	$ 210,000	$111,000	$ 80,000			$ 401,000
Capital stock—Poly	500,000					500,000
Capital stock—Seth		200,000		e 200,000		
Capital stock—Uno			100,000	d 100,000		
Retained earnings	**533,957**	**254,946**	**103,000**			**533,957**
	$1,243,957	$565,946	$283,000			

Noncontrolling interest:
  Noncontrolling interest in Uno, January 1
  Noncontrolling interest in Seth, January 1
					d 54,000
					e 40,000
					f 5,495
					g 8,548
						108,043

						$1,543,000

SUMMARY

One corporation may control another corporation through direct or indirect ownership of its voting stock. Indirect holdings give the investor an ability to control or significantly influence the operations of the investee not directly owned through an investee that is directly owned. The major problem encountered in consolidating the financial statements of companies in indirect control situations lies in allocating income and equities among majority and noncontrolling stockholders. Several computational approaches are available for such allocations, but the schedule approach is probably the best overall approach because of its simplicity and because it provides a step-by-step reference of all allocations made.

When affiliated companies hold the stock of each other, the stock is not outstanding from the viewpoint of the consolidated entity. We eliminate the effect of mutually held parent-company stock from consolidated financial statements by either the treasury stock approach or the conventional approach. The treasury stock approach deducts the investment in parent-company stock on a cost basis from consolidated stockholders' equity. Under the conventional approach, we treat the investment in parent-company stock as constructively retired by adjusting the parent's investment in subsidiary and the parent's equity accounts to reflect a one-line consolidation. Then we eliminate the subsidiary's investment in parent account against the parent's investment in subsidiary account.

We account for mutual investments by subsidiaries in the stock of each other under the conventional method of eliminating reciprocal investment and equity balances. The treasury stock approach is not applicable to such mutually held investments because only parent-company stock and retained earnings appear in the consolidated financial statements. Under the conventional method, we use simultaneous equations to allocate income and equities among mutually held companies.

QUESTIONS

(Questions 1 through 8 relate to indirect holdings. Questions 9 through 16 relate to mutual holdings.)

1. What is an indirect holding of the stock of an affiliated company?

2. P owns a 60% interest in S, and S owns a 40% interest in T. Should T be consolidated? If not, how should T be included in the consolidated statements of P Company and Subsidiaries?

3. Prepare diagrams of two types of affiliation structures involving indirect ownership. Compute the direct and indirect ownership held by majority and noncontrolling stockholders for each of your diagrams.

4. Distinguish between indirect holding affiliation structures and mutual holding affiliation structures.

5. Parent Company owns 70% of the voting stock of Subsidiary A, and Subsidiary A owns 70% of the stock of Subsidiary B. Is the inside ownership of Subsidiary B more than 50%? Should Subsidiary B be included in the consolidated statements of Parent and Subsidiaries? Explain.

6. Pat Corporation owns 80% of the stock of Sam Corporation, and Sam Corporation owns 70% of the stock of Stan Corporation. Separate earnings of Pat, Sam, and Stan are $100,000, $80,000, and $50,000, respectively. Compute consolidated net income and noncontrolling interest expense under two different approaches.

7. In using the schedule approach for allocating income of subsidiaries to majority and noncontrolling stockholders in an indirect holding affiliation structure, why is it necessary to begin with the lowest subsidiary in the affiliation tier?

8. P owns 80% of S1, and S1 owns 70% of S2. Separate incomes of P, S1, and S2 are $20,000, $10,000, and $5,000, respectively, for 2006. During 2006, S1 sold land to P at a gain of $1,000. Compute S1's income on an equity basis. Discuss why you did or did not adjust S1's investment in S2's account for the unrealized gain.

9. If a parent company owns 80% of the voting stock of a subsidiary, and the subsidiary in turn owns 20% of the stock of the parent, what kind of affiliation structure is involved? Explain.

10. How is the treasury stock approach applied to the elimination of mutually held stock?

11. Are the treasury stock and conventional approaches equally applicable to all mutual holdings? Explain.

12. Under the treasury stock approach, a mutually held subsidiary accounts for its investment in the parent company on a cost basis. Are dividends received by the subsidiary from the parent company included in investment income of the parent under the equity method of accounting?

13. Describe the concept of a constructive retirement of parent-company stock. Should the parent company adjust its equity accounts when its stock is constructively retired?

14. P's separate earnings are $50,000, and S's separate earnings are $20,000. P owns an 80% interest in S, and S owns a 10% interest in P. What is the amount of consolidated net income?

15. How do consolidation procedures for mutual holdings involving the father-son-grandson type of affiliation structure differ from those for mutually held parent-company stock?

16. If all companies in an affiliation structure account for their investments on an equity basis, how can noncontrolling interests be determined without the use of simultaneous equations?

EXERCISES

(Exercises 9-1 through 9-8 relate to indirect holdings. Exercises 9-9 through 9-14 relate to mutual holdings.)

E 9-1

Calculate consolidated net income On January 1, 2006, Pent Corporation purchased a 60% interest in Sal Corporation at book value (equal to fair value). At the time of Pent's acquisition, Sal owned a 60% interest in Terp Corporation (acquired at book value equal to fair value) and a 15% interest in Wint Company. The four companies had the following separate incomes and dividends for 2006 (separate income does not include investment income or dividend income):

	Separate Income	Dividends
Pent Corporation	$800,000	$300,000
Sal Corporation	500,000	200,000
Terp Corporation	200,000	100,000
Wint Company	300,000	100,000

REQUIRED: Determine consolidated net income and noncontrolling interest expense for Pent Corporation and Subsidiaries.

E 9-2

Allocate investment income and loss Pumba Corporation owns 60% of Simba Corporation and 80% of Timon Corporation. Timon owns 20% of Simba Corporation. Separate income and loss data (not including investment income) for the three affiliates for 2006 are as follows:

Pumba $400,000 separate income
Simba $150,000 separate income
Timon   ($200,000) separate loss

There are no cost/book value differentials or unrealized profits to consider in measuring 2006 income.

REQUIRED: Calculate consolidated net income for Pumba Corporation and Subsidiaries for 2006.

E 9-3

Prepare an income allocation schedule (includes unrealized profit on land) The affiliation structure for Place Corporation and its affiliates is as follows:

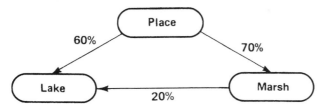

During 2006 the separate incomes of these affiliated companies were as follows:

Place	$200,000
Lake	$ 80,000
Marsh	$ 70,000

Lake's income includes $20,000 unrealized profit on land sold to Marsh during 2006.

REQUIRED: Prepare a schedule that shows the allocation of income among the affiliated companies and also shows consolidated net income and noncontrolling interest expense for 2006.

E 9-4

Determine equation to compute income from subsidiary, noncontrolling interest income, and consolidated net income The affiliation structure for Paine Corporation and its subsidiaries is as follows:

Separate incomes of Paine, Seron, and Trane Corporations for 2006 are $360,000, $160,000, and $100,000, respectively.

1. The equation for determining Paine's income from Seron on a one-line consolidation basis for 2006 is:
   a $160,000 × 70%
   b ($160,000 × 70%) + ($100,000 × 80%)
   c ($160,000 × 70%) + ($100,000 × 56%)
   d 70% × ($160,000 + $100,000)

2. Noncontrolling interest expense for Paine Corporation and Subsidiaries for 2006 is determined as follows:
   a $30% × $160,000
   b (30% × $160,000) + (20% × $100,000)
   c (30% × $160,000) + (24% × $100,000)
   d (30% × $160,000) + (44% × $100,000)

3. Consolidated net income can be determined by the following equation:
   a $620,000 − ($160,000 × 30%)
   b $620,000 − ($160,000 × 30%) − ($100,000 × 20%)
   c $620,000 − ($160,000 × 30%) − ($100,000 × 20%) − ($100,000 × 30% × 90%)
   d $620,000 − ($160,000 × 30%) − ($100,000 × 44%)

E 9-5

Prepare affiliation diagram and income allocation schedule Pal Corporation owns 80% each of the voting common stock of Sal and Tall Corporations. Sal owns 60% of the voting common stock of Ulti Corporation and 10% of the voting stock of Tall Corporation. Tall owns 70% of the voting stock of Val Corporation and 10% of the voting stock of Ulti.

The affiliated companies had separate incomes during 2006 as follows:

Pal Corporation	$50,000
Sal Corporation	$30,000
Tall Corporation	$35,000
Ulti Corporation	($20,000) loss
Val Corporation	$40,000

The only intercompany profits included in the separate incomes of the affiliated companies consisted of $5,000 on merchandise that Pal acquired from Tall and which remained in Pal's December 31, 2006, inventory.

REQUIRED

1. Prepare a diagram of the affiliation structure.

2. Compute consolidated net income and noncontrolling interest expense for Pal Corporation and Subsidiaries.

E 9-6

Calculate consolidated net income and noncontrolling interest income
Pete Corporation owns 90% of the stock of Mike Corporation and 70% of the stock of Nina Corporation. Mike owns 70% of the stock of Ople Corporation and 10% of the stock of Nina Corporation. Nina Corporation owns 20% of the stock of Ople Corporation.

Separate incomes for these corporations for the year ended December 31, 2006, are as follows:

Pete	$65,000
Mike	$18,000
Nina	$28,000
Ople	$ 9,000

During 2006, Mike sold land to Nina at a profit of $4,000. Ople sold inventory items to Pete at a profit of $8,000, half of which remains in Pete's inventory. Pete purchased for $15,000 Nina's bonds, which had a book value of $17,000 on December 31, 2006.

REQUIRED: Calculate consolidated net income and noncontrolling interest expense for 2006.

E 9-7

No intercompany profits
The affiliation structure for a group of interrelated companies is diagrammed as follows:

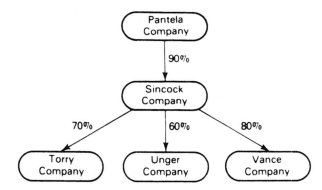

The investments in these companies were acquired at book value in 2003, and there are no unrealized or constructive profits or losses.

Separate incomes and dividends for the companies for 2006 are:

	Separate Income	
	(Loss)	**Dividends**
Pantela	$620,000	$200,000
Sincock	175,000	100,000
Torry	200,000	80,000
Unger	(50,000)	—
Vance	120,000	60,000

1. The noncontrolling interest in Torry Company's net income for 2006 is:

   a **$60,000**

   b **$74,000**

   c **$126,000**

   d **$140,000**

2. The income of the noncontrolling stockholders of Vance Company for 2006 is:

a *$24,000*

b *$48,000*

c *$55,200*

d *$72,000*

3. The total noncontrolling interest expense that should be shown in the consolidated income statement of Pantela Company and Subsidiaries for 2006 is:

a *$122,100*

b *$105,100*

c *$102,100*

d *$38,100*

4. Consolidated net income for Pantela Company and Subsidiaries for 2006 is:

a *$962,900*

b *$940,900*

c *$620,000*

d *$342,900*

5. Pantela Company's Investment in Sincock account should reflect a net increase for 2006 in the amount of:

a *$381,000*

b *$342,900*

c *$312,900*

d *$252,900*

E 9-8

Correcting net income for unrealized profits Pasko Corporation owns an 80% interest in Savoy Corporation and a 70% interest in Trent Corporation. Trent owns a 10% interest in Savoy. These investment interests were acquired at book value.

The net incomes of the affiliated companies for 2006 were as follows:

Pasko	$240,000
Savoy	$ 80,000
Trent	$ 40,000

On December 31, 2006, Pasko's inventory included $10,000 of unrealized profits on merchandise purchased from Savoy during 2006, and Savoy's land account reflected $15,000 unrealized profit on land purchased from Trent during 2006. These unrealized profits have not been eliminated from the net income amounts shown. Except for adjustments related to unrealized profits, the net income amounts were determined on a correct equity basis.

1. The separate incomes of Pasko, Savoy, and Trent for 2006 were:

a *$240,000, $80,000, and $32,000, respectively*

b *$148,000, $80,000, and $32,000, respectively*

c *$148,000, $72,000, and $40,000, respectively*

d *$240,000, $72,000, and $40,000, respectively*

2. The separate realized incomes of Pasko, Savoy, and Trent for 2006 were:

a *$138,000, $80,000, and $25,000, respectively*

b *$138,000, $70,000, and $25,000, respectively*

c *$123,000, $80,000, and $17,000, respectively*

d *$148,000, $70,000, and $17,000, respectively*

3. Consolidated net income for Pasko Corporation and Subsidiaries for 2006 was:

a *$220,800*

b *$215,900*

c *$214,400*

d *$212,400*

4. Noncontrolling interest expense that should be shown in the consolidated income statement for Pasko Corporation and Subsidiaries for 2006 is:

a *$23,600*

b *$21,200*

c *$19,100*

d *$14,200*

E 9-9

Calculate consolidated net income (conventional method, no complications) Pant Corporation owns an 80% interest in Solo Company, acquired at book value, and Solo owns a 30% interest in Pant, acquired at book value. Separate incomes (not including investment income) of the two affiliates for 2006 are:

Pant	$3,000,000
Solo	$1,500,000

REQUIRED: Construct a diagram of the affiliation structure. Compute consolidated net income for Pant Corporation and Subsidiary for 2006 using the conventional (equation) approach.

E 9-10

Prepare an affiliation diagram and make computations (subsidiary stock mutually held, no unrealized profits) Intercompany investment percentages and 2006 separate earnings for three affiliated companies are as follows:

	Percentage Interest in Smedley	Percentage Interest in Tweed	Separate Earnings
Packard Corporation	70%	—	$200,000
Smedley Corporation	—	80%	120,000
Tweed Corporation	10%	—	80,000

REQUIRED

1. Construct a diagram of the affiliation structure.

2. Compute consolidated net income and noncontrolling interest expense for Packard Corporation and Subsidiaries for 2006.

E 9-11

[AICPA adapted] Mutually held parent-company stock Akron, Inc., owns 80% of the capital stock of Benson Company and 70% of the capital stock of Cashin, Inc. Benson Company owns 15% of the capital stock of Cashin, Inc. Cashin, in turn, owns 25% of the capital stock of Akron. These ownership interrelationships are illustrated in the following diagram:

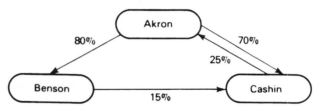

Income before adjusting for interests in intercompany income for each corporation follows:

Akron, Inc.	$190,000
Benson Company	$170,000
Cashin, Inc.	$230,000

The following notations relate to the questions below:

A = Akron's consolidated income—its separate income plus its share of the consolidated incomes of Benson and Cashin

B = Benson's consolidated income—its separate income plus its share of the consolidated income of Cashin

C = Cashin's consolidated income—its separate income plus its share of the consolidated income of Akron

1. The equation, in a set of simultaneous equations, that computes A is:
   a $A = 0.75(190,000 + 0.8B + 0.7C)$
   b $A = 190,000 + 0.8B + 0.7C$
   c $A = 0.75(190,000) + 0.8(170,000) + 0.7(230,000)$
   d $A = 0.75(190,000) + 0.8B + 0.7C$

2. The equation, in a set of simultaneous equations, that computes B is:
   a $B = 170,000 + 0.15C - 0.75A$
   b $B = 170,000 + 0.15C$
   c $B = 0.2(170,000) + 0.15(230,000)$
   d $B = 0.2(170,000) + 0.15C$

3. Cashin's noncontrolling interest in total consolidated income is:
   a $0.15(230,000)$
   b $230,000 + 0.25A$
   c $0.15(230,000) + 0.25A$
   d $0.15C$

4. Benson's noncontrolling interest in total consolidated income is:
  a $34,316
  b $25,500
  c $45,755
  d $30,675

E 9-12

Mutually held parent-company stock Petty Corporation owns 90% of Soma Corporation's common stock, acquired at book value equal to fair value, and Soma Corporation owns 15% of Petty Corporation, acquired at book value. Separate incomes and dividends of these affiliated companies for 2006 are as follows:

	Separate Incomes	Dividends
Petty Corporation	$100,000	$50,000
Soma Corporation	60,000	30,000

1. If the treasury stock approach is used, Petty's income and consolidated net income for 2006 will be computed:
  a $100,000 + (90% × $60,000)$
  b $100,000 + (90% × $67,500)$
  c $100,000 + (90% × $67,500) − (90% × $30,000)$
  d ($100,000 + $60,000) − (10% × $67,500)$

2. If the conventional approach is used, Petty's income on a consolidated basis is denoted $P = \$100,000 + 0.9S$, and Soma's income on a consolidated basis is denoted $S = \$60,000 + 0.15P$. Given these equations, consolidated net income is equal to:
  a P
  b $0.85P$
  c $P - 0.1S$
  d $P + S - 0.15S$

E 9-13

Calculate consolidated net income (subsidiary stock mutually held, with unrealized profits) The affiliation structure of Pusan Corporation and Subsidiaries is diagrammed as follows:

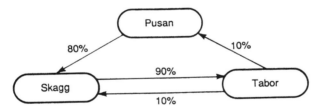

Each of the corporations uses the cost method of accounting for its investments. Separate earnings and dividends paid for 2006 are as follows:

	Separate Earnings	Dividends
Pusan	$50,000	$20,000
Skagg	42,000	10,000
Tabor	20,000	—

Skagg sells merchandise to Pusan on which there is unrealized profit in Pusan's beginning inventory of $3,000 and in the ending inventory of $5,000.

REQUIRED: Compute consolidated net income and noncontrolling interest expense for Pusan Corporation and Subsidiaries for the year ended December 31, 2006.

E 9-14

Computations (treasury stock and conventional) Pumel Corporation acquired a 70% interest in Scat Corporation for $240,000 on January 2, 2005, when Scat's equity consisted of $200,000 capital stock and $50,000 retained earnings. The excess is a patent amortized over a 10-year period. Pumel accounted for its investment in Scat during 2005 as follows:

Investment cost January 2, 2005	$240,000
Income from Scat [($40,000 × 70%) − $6,500]	21,500
Dividends from Scat ($20,000 × 70%)	(14,000)
Investment balance December 31, 2005	$247,500

On January 3, 2006, Scat acquired a 10% interest in Pumel at its $60,000 book value. No intercompany profit transactions have occurred between these companies. Their separate incomes and dividends for 2006 were as follows:

	Pumel	Scat
Separate income 2006	$120,000	$50,000
Dividends	60,000	30,000

REQUIRED

1. Determine the balance of Pumel's Investment in Scat account on December 31, 2006, if the treasury stock approach is used for Scat's investment in Pumel.

2. Compute consolidated net income and noncontrolling interest expense if the conventional approach is used for Scat's investment in Pumel. Also determine the amount of Pumel's income from Scat and the balance in Pumel's Investment in Scat account at December 31, 2006.

PROBLEMS

(Problems 9-1 through 9-3 relate to indirect holdings. Problems 9-4 through 9-7 relate to mutual holdings.)

P 9-1

Schedule for allocating income (unrealized profits and goodwill) The affiliation structure for Pida Corporation and its subsidiaries is diagrammed as follows:

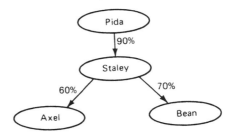

The separate incomes and dividends for the affiliated companies for 2008 are (in thousands):

	Pida	Staley	Axel	Bean
Separate income (loss)	$500	$300	$150	$(20)
Dividends	200	140	50	—

ADDITIONAL INFORMATION

1. Axel sold land to Staley during 2008 at a $20,000 gain. The land is still held by Staley.

2. Staley is amortizing a previously unrecorded patent of Axel at the rate of $14,000 per year.

3. Pida is amortizing a previously unrecorded patent acquired from Staley with a book value of $360,000 over its remaining nine-year life.

REQUIRED: Prepare a schedule to compute consolidated net income and noncontrolling interest expense for each subsidiary for 2008.

P 9-2

Prepare journal entries, computations, and a financial position summary (unrealized profits) A summary of the assets and equities of Posey Corporation and its 80%-owned subsidiary, Seaton Corporation, at December 31, 2006, is given as follows (in thousands):

	Posey	Seaton
Assets	$ 800	$350
Investment in Seaton (80%)	200	—
Total assets	$1,000	$350

Liabilities	$ 150	$100
Capital stock	600	200
Retained earnings	250	50
Total equities	$1,000	$350

On January 2, 2007, Seaton acquired a 70% interest in Thayer Corporation for $150,000. Thayer's net assets of $200,000 were recorded at their fair values on this date. The equity of Thayer on December 31, 2006, consisted of $150,000 capital stock and $50,000 retained earnings.

Data concerning the operations of the three affiliated corporations for 2007 are as follows (in thousands):

	Separate Earnings	Dividends	Unrealized Profit Included in Separate Earnings
Posey	$150	$50	$10
Seaton	50	30	—
Thayer	30	10	5

Posey Corporation's $10,000 unrealized profit resulted from the sale of land to Thayer. Thayer's unrealized profit is from sales of merchandise items to Seaton and is included in Seaton's inventory at December 31, 2007.

REQUIRED

1. Prepare all journal entries required on the books of Posey and Seaton to account for their investments for 2007 on an equity basis. There was no goodwill, but the acquisition included a previously unrecorded patent which is to be amortized over a 10-year period.

2. Compute the net income of Posey, the net income of Seaton, and total noncontrolling interest expense for 2007.

3. Prepare a schedule showing the assets and equities of Posey, Seaton, and Thayer on December 31, 2007, assuming liabilities of $150,000, $100,000, and $50,000 for Posey, Seaton, and Thayer, respectively.

P 9-3

Financial statement working papers (goodwill and unrealized profits) Comparative financial statements for Pony Corporation and its subsidiaries, Star and Teel Corporations, at and for the year ended December 31, 2009, are summarized as follows (in thousands):

	Pony	Star	Teel
Income and Retained Earnings Statement for the Year Ended December 31, 2009			
Sales	$500	$300	$100
Income from Star	72	—	—
Income from Teel	12.5	10	—
Cost of sales	(240)	(150)	(60)
Other expenses	(160)	(70)	(15)
Net income	184.5	90	25
Add: Beginning retained earnings	115.5	160	45
Deduct: Dividends	(80)	(40)	(10)
Ending retained earnings	$220	$210	$ 60
Balance Sheet at December 31, 2009			
Cash	$ 67	$ 36	$ 10
Accounts receivable—net	70	50	20
Inventories	110	75	35
Plant and equipment—net	140	425	115
Investment in Star (80%)	508	—	—
Investment in Teel (50%)	95	—	—
Investment in Teel (40%)	—	74	—
Total assets	$990	$660	$180
Accounts payable	$ 70	$ 40	$ 15
Other liabilities	100	10	5
Capital stock	600	400	100
Retained earnings	220	210	60
Total equities	$990	$660	$180

ADDITIONAL INFORMATION

1. Pony acquired its 80% interest in Star Corporation for $420,000 on January 2, 2007, when Star had capital stock of $400,000 and retained earnings of $100,000. The excess of cost over book value acquired relates to equipment that had a remaining useful life of four years from January 1, 2007.

2. Pony acquired its 50% interest in Teel Corporation for $75,000 on July 1, 2007, when Teel's equity consisted of $100,000 capital stock and $20,000 retained earnings. Star acquired its 40% interest in Teel on December 31, 2008, for $68,000, when Teel's capital stock was $100,000 and its retained earnings were $45,000. The difference between investment costs and book value acquired is due to previously unrecorded intangible assets, amortized over 10 years.

3. Although Pony and Star use the equity method in accounting for their investments, they do not apply the method to intercompany profits or to differences between investment cost and book value acquired.

4. At December 31, 2008, the inventory of Star included inventory items acquired from Pony at a profit of $8,000. This merchandise was sold during 2009.

5. Teel sold merchandise that had cost $30,000 to Star for $50,000 during 2009. All of this merchandise is held by Star at December 31, 2009. Star owes Teel $10,000 on this merchandise.

REQUIRED: Prepare consolidation working papers for Pony Corporation and Subsidiaries for the year ended December 31, 2009.

P 9-4

Diagram and computations for mutually held subsidiaries A schedule of intercompany investment interests and separate earnings for Parish Corporation, Swift Corporation, and Tolbert Corporation is presented as follows:

	Percentage Interest in Swift	Percentage Interest in Tolbert	Separate Earnings Current Year
Parish Corporation	80%	50%	$200,000
Swift Corporation	—	20	100,000
Tolbert Corporation	10	—	50,000

REQUIRED

1. Prepare a diagram of the affiliation structure of Parish Corporation and Subsidiaries.

2. Compute consolidated net income and noncontrolling interest expense assuming no investment differences or unrealized profits.

3. Compute consolidated net income and noncontrolling interest expense assuming $10,000 unrealized inventory profits on Tolbert's sales to Swift and a $20,000 gain on Parish's sale of land to Swift.

P 9-5

Financial statement working papers (treasury stock approach) Prill Corporation acquired a 90% interest in Skill Corporation for $355,000 cash on January 2, 2004, when Skill had capital stock of $200,000 and retained earnings of $150,000. Skill purchased its 10% interest in Prill in 2005 for $80,000. The excess of Prill's investment cost over book value acquired is due to a patent, which is being amortized over eight years.

Comparative financial statements for Prill and Skill at and for the year ended December 31, 2008, are summarized as follows (in thousands):

	Prill	Skill
Combined Income and Retained Earnings Statement for the Year Ended December 31, 2008		
Sales	$400	$100
Investment income	27	—
Dividend income	—	10
Cost of goods sold	(200)	(50)
Expenses	(50)	(30)
Net income	177	30
Add: Beginning retained earnings	300	200
Deduct: Dividends	(100)	(20)
Retained earnings December 31	$377	$210

Balance Sheet at December 31, 2008

Other assets	$491	$420
Investment in Skill (90%)	409	—
Investment in Prill (10%)	—	80
Total assets	$900	$500
Liabilities	$123	$ 90
Capital stock	400	200
Retained earnings	377	210
Total equities	$900	$500

REQUIRED: Prepare consolidation working papers for Prill Corporation and Subsidiary using the treasury stock approach for the mutual holding.

P 9-6

Consolidation working papers second year (conventional approach)

Paroll Corporation acquired an 80% interest in Scimp Corporation for $180,000 cash on January 1, 2006, when Scimp had capital stock of $50,000 and retained earnings of $150,000. The excess of investment cost over book value acquired is due to a patent, which is being amortized over five years. Scimp purchased its 20% interest in Paroll at book value on January 2, 2006, for $100,000.

Comparative financial statements for Paroll and Scimp at and for the year ended December 31, 2007, are summarized as follows:

	Paroll	Scimp
Combined Income and Retained Earnings Statement		
for the Year Ended December 31, 2007		
Sales	$140,000	$100,000
Income from Scimp	28,000	—
Dividend income	—	4,000
Gain on sale of land	—	3,000
Expenses	(80,000)	(60,000)
Net income	88,000	47,000
Add: Beginning retained earnings	405,710	180,000
Deduct: Dividends	(16,000)	(20,000)
Retained earnings December 31	$477,710	$207,000
Balance Sheet at December 31, 2007		
Other assets	$448,000	$157,000
Investment in Scimp (80%)	109,710	—
Investment in Paroll (20%)	—	100,000
Total assets	$557,710	$257,000
Capital stock	$ 80,000	$ 50,000
Retained earnings	477,710	207,000
Total equities	$557,710	$257,000

ADDITIONAL INFORMATION

1. Paroll's separate earnings and dividends for 2007 were $60,000 and $20,000, respectively. Scimp's separate earnings and dividends in 2007 were $40,000 and $20,000, respectively.

2. Scimp sold land to an outside interest for $7,000 on January 3, 2007, that it purchased from Paroll on January 3, 2006, for $4,000. The land had originally cost Paroll $2,000.

REQUIRED: Prepare consolidation working paper entries and the consolidated working papers for Paroll Corporation and Subsidiary using the conventional approach for the mutual holding.

P 9-7

Computations and entries (parent-company stock mutually held)

Pan Corporation (Panco) purchased an 80% interest in Stoker Corporation (Stoco) for $170,000 on January 1, 2006, when Stoco's equity was $200,000. The excess of cost over book value is due to a patent that is being amortized over a 10-year period.

At December 31, 2007, the balance of Panco's Investment in Stoco account is $208,000, and the stockholders' equity of the two corporations is as follows:

	Panco	Stoco
Capital stock	$600,000	$150,000
Retained earnings	200,000	100,000
Total	$800,000	$250,000

On January 2, 2008, Stoco acquires a 10% interest in Panco for $80,000. Separate earnings and dividends for 2008 are:

	Panco	Stoco
Separate earnings	$100,000	$40,000
Dividends	50,000	20,000

REQUIRED

1. Compute consolidated net income and noncontrolling interest expense for 2008 using the conventional approach.

2. Prepare journal entries to account for Panco's investment in Stoco for 2008 under the equity method (conventional approach).

3. Prepare journal entries on Stoco's books to account for its investment in Panco under the equity method (conventional approach).

4. Compute Panco's and Stoco's net incomes for 2008.

5. Determine the balances of Panco's and Stoco's investment accounts on December 31, 2008.

6. Determine the total stockholders' equity of Panco and Stoco on December 31, 2008.

7. Compute the noncontrolling interest in Stoco on December 31, 2008.

8. Prepare the adjustment and elimination entries that are needed to consolidate the financial statements of Panco and Stoco for the year ended December 31, 2008.

9. Prepare the adjustment and elimination entries that are needed to consolidate the balance sheets of Panco and Stoco on December 31, 2008.

INTERNET ASSIGNMENT

Pepsi-Cola and *Frito-Lay* Corporations merged in 1965 to form PepsiCo, Inc. Among PepsiCo's more recent merger and acquisition activity are deals with *Tropicana Products* and *Quaker Oats*. Visit the Web site of PepsiCo (www.pepsico.com) and review the corporate history file. Prepare a list of 10 well-known companies now controlled by PepsiCo in grandfather-father-son-type indirect holdings.

SELECTED READINGS

AICPA Committee on Accounting Procedure. *Accounting Research Bulletin No. 51.* "Consolidated Financial Statements." New York: American Institute of Certified Public Accountants, 1959.

CHILDS, WILLIAM HERBERT. *Consolidated Financial Statements: Principles and Procedures.* Ithaca, NY: Cornell University Press, 1949 (especially see Chapter 8, "Indirect and Reciprocal Relationships").

MINCH, ROLAND A., and ENRICO PETRI. "Reporting Income for Reciprocal Parent–Subsidiary Stockholdings." *CPA Journal* (July 1975), pp. 36–40.

MOONITZ, MAURICE. "Mutual Stockholdings in Consolidated Statements." *Journal of Accountancy* (October 1939), pp. 277–35.

PETRI, ENRICO, and ROLAND A. MINCH. "The Treasury Stock Method and Conventional Method in Reciprocal Stockholdings—An Amalgamation." *Accounting Review* (April 1974), pp. 330–341.

WEIL, ROMAN L. "Reciprocal or Mutual Holdings: Allocating Earnings and Selecting the Accounting Method." *Accounting Review* (October 1973), pp. 749–58.

10 CHAPTER

SUBSIDIARY PREFERRED STOCK, CONSOLIDATED EARNINGS PER SHARE, AND CONSOLIDATED INCOME TAXATION

This chapter covers three miscellaneous topics relating to consolidation: consolidation of a subsidiary with preferred stock in its capital structure, consolidated earnings per share, and accounting for income taxes of consolidated entities. These topics tend to be detailed and technical, and the illustrations often use simplifying assumptions to minimize details and emphasize significant concepts and relationships. An intermediate accounting background in all three areas is assumed.

•••

SUBSIDIARIES WITH PREFERRED STOCK OUTSTANDING

Many modern corporations have complex capital structures, including various categories of preferred stock issued by the parent company, a subsidiary company, or both. For example, in its 2003 annual report, the **Dow Chemical Company** reports $1 billion in "Preferred Securities of Subsidiary." Note P to the consolidated financial statements provides some additional detail (in millions):

> *In July 1999, Tornado Finance V.O.F., a consolidated foreign subsidiary of the Company, issued $500 of preferred securities in the form of preferred partnership units.*
>
> *In September 2001, Hobbes Capital S.A., a consolidated foreign subsidiary of the Company, issued $500 of preferred securities in the form of equity certificates.*

Note 10 to the **Merck & Co., Inc.**, 2003 annual report provides disclosure on preferred stock issued by subsidiary companies. It reads in part:

> *In 2000, a wholly owned subsidiary of the Company issued $1.5 billion par value variable rate preferred units. ...*
>
> *In connection with the 1998 restructuring of AMI (see Note 4), the Company assumed a $2.4 billion par value preferred stock obligation with a dividend rate of 5% per annum, which is carried by KBI and included in Minority interests.*

The 2000 annual report of **Ford Motor Company** discloses an issue of subsidiary preferred shares in Note 1.

LEARNING OBJECTIVES

1 Modify consolidation procedures for subsidiary companies with preferred stock in their capital structure.

2 Calculate basic and diluted earnings per share for a consolidated reporting entity.

3 Understand the complexities of accounting for income taxes by consolidated entities.

4 Electronic supplement: Account for branch operations.

Company-Obligated Mandatorily Redeemable Preferred Securities of a Subsidiary Trust

During 1995, Ford Motor Company Capital Trust 1 (the "Trust") issued $632 million of its 9% Trust Originated Preferred Securities (the "Preferred Securities") in a one-for-one exchange for 25,273,537 shares of the Company's outstanding Series B Depositary Shares (the "Depositary Shares"). Concurrent with the exchange and the related purchase by Ford of the Trust's Common Securities (the "Common Securities"), the Company issued to the Trust $651 million aggregate principal amount of its 9% Junior Subordinated Debentures due December 2025 (the "Debentures"). The sole assets of the Trust are and will be the Debentures. The Debentures are redeemable, in whole or in part, at the Company's option on or after December 1, 2002, at a redemption price of $25 per Debenture plus accrued and unpaid interest. If the Company redeems the Debentures, or upon maturity of the Debentures, the Trust is required to redeem the Preferred Securities and Common Securities at $25 per share plus accrued and unpaid distributions.

Ford guarantees to pay in full to the holders of the Preferred Securities all distributions and other payments on the Preferred Securities to the extent not paid by the Trust only if and to the extent that Ford has made a payment of interest or principal on the Debentures. This guarantee, when taken together with Ford's obligations under the Debentures and the indenture related thereto and its obligations under the Declaration of Trust of the Trust, including its obligations to pay certain costs and expenses of the Trust, constitutes a full and unconditional guarantee by Ford of the Trust's obligations under the Preferred Securities.

The existence of preferred stock in the capital structure of a subsidiary corporation complicates the consolidation process, but the basic procedures do not change. Parent-company/investor accounting under the equity method is also affected when an investee company has preferred stock outstanding. The complications stem from the need to consider the contractual rights of preferred stockholders in allocating the investee company's equity and income between preferred and common stock components.

Most preferred stock issues are cumulative, nonparticipating, and nonvoting. In addition, preferred stock issues usually have preference rights in liquidation and frequently are callable at prices in excess of the par or liquidating values. We allocate net income of an investee corporation with preferred stock outstanding first to preferred stockholders based on the preferred stock contract and then the remainder to common stockholders. Similarly, we first allocate the stockholders' equity of an investee to preferred stockholders based on the preferred stock contract, and then we allocate the remainder to common stockholders.

When preferred stock has a call or redemption price, we use this amount in allocating the investee's equity to preferred stockholders. In the absence of a redemption provision, we base the equity allocated to preferred stock on par value of the stock plus any liquidation premium. In addition, we must include any dividends in arrears on cumulative preferred stock in the equity allocated to preferred stockholders. For nonparticipating preferred stock, we assign income to preferred stockholders on the basis of the preference rate or amount. If the preferred stock is cumulative and nonparticipating, the current year's income assigned to the preferred stockholders is the current year's dividend requirement, irrespective of whether the directors declare only current-year dividends, current-year dividends plus prior-year arrearages, or no dividends at all. We assign income to noncumulative, nonparticipating preferred stock only if dividends are declared and only in the amount declared.

Subsidiary with Preferred Stock Not Held by Parent

Assume that Poe Corporation purchases 90% of Sol Corporation's outstanding common stock for $395,500 on January 1, 2007, and that Sol Corporation's stockholders' equity on December 31, 2006, was as follows:

$10 preferred stock, $100 par, cumulative, nonparticipating, callable at $105 per share	$100,000
Common stock, $10 par	200,000
Other paid-in capital	40,000
Retained earnings	160,000
Total stockholders' equity	$500,000

There were no preferred dividends in arrears as of January 1, 2007. During 2007, Sol reported net income of $50,000 and paid dividends of $30,000 ($20,000 on common stock and $10,000 on preferred stock). Sol's assets and liabilities were stated at their fair values when Poe acquired its interest, so any excess of investment cost over book value acquired is goodwill.

In comparing the price paid for the 90% interest in Sol with the book value of the interest acquired, we separate Sol's December 31, 2006, equity into its preferred and common stock components:

Stockholders' equity of Sol	$500,000
Less: Preferred stockholders' equity (1,000 shares × $105 per share call price)	105,000
Common stockholders' equity	$395,000

We compare the price paid for 90% of the common equity of Sol with the book value (and fair value) acquired to determine goodwill:

Price paid for 90% common stock interest	$395,500
Less: Book value and fair value acquired ($395,000 × 90%)	355,500
Goodwill	$ 40,000

Sol's $50,000 net income for 2007 is allocated $10,000 to preferred stock (1,000 shares × $10 per share) and $40,000 to common stock. The entries to account for Poe's investment in Sol for 2007 are:

January 1, 2007

Investment in Sol common (+A)	395,500	
Cash (−A)		395,500

To record acquisition of 90% of Sol's common stock.

During 2007

Cash (+A)	18,000	
Investment in Sol common (−A)		18,000

To reduce Investment in Sol for dividends received ($20,000 × 90%).

December 31, 2007

Investment in Sol common (+A)	36,000	
Income from Sol (R, +SE)		36,000

To record equity in Sol's income.

In consolidating the financial statements of Poe and Sol for 2007 (see Exhibit 10-1), we assign Sol's $520,000 stockholders' equity at December 31, 2007, to preferred and common stock components as follows:

Total stockholders' equity	$520,000
Less: Preferred stockholders' equity (1,000 shares × $105 call price per share)	105,000
Common stockholders' equity	$415,000

EXHIBIT 10-1

Preferred and
Common Stock
in the Affiliation
Structure

POE CORPORATION AND SUBSIDIARY CONSOLIDATION WORKING PAPERS FOR THE YEAR ENDED DECEMBER 31, 2007 (IN THOUSANDS)

	Poe	90% Sol	Adjustments and Eliminations Debits	Adjustments and Eliminations Credits	Consolidated Statements
Income Statement Sales	$ 618	$300			$ 918
Income from Sol (common)	36		b 36		
Expenses including cost of sales	(450)	(250)			(700)
Noncontrolling interest expense (common) ($40 × 10%)			d 4		(4)
Noncontrolling interest expense (preferred) ($10 × 100%)			e 10		(10)
Net income	**$ 204**	**$ 50**			**$ 204**
Retained Earnings Retained earnings—Poe	$ 300				$ 300
Retained earnings—Sol		$160	a 5 c 155		
Dividends (common)	(100)	(20)		b 18 d 2	(100)
Dividends (preferred)		(10)		e 10	
Net income	204	50			204
Retained earnings— December 31	**$ 404**	**$180**			**$ 404**
Balance Sheet Other assets	$1,290.5	$600			$1,890.5
Investment in Sol (common)	413.5			b 18 c 395.5	
Goodwill			c 40		40
	$1,704	$600			$1,930.5
Liabilities	$ 200	$ 80			$ 280
Preferred stock—Sol		100	a 100		
Common stock	1,000	200	c 200		1,000
Other paid-in capital	100	40	c 40		100
Retained earnings	**404**	**180**			**404**
	$1,704	$600			
Noncontrolling interest: Preferred, January 1 Common, January 1				a 105 c 39.5 d 2	146.5
					$1,930.5

NONCONTROLLING INTEREST IN PREFERRED STOCK The *noncontrolling interest* in Sol at December 31, 2007, consists of 100% of the preferred stockholders' equity and 10% of the common stockholders' equity, or $146,500 [($105,000 × 100%) + ($415,000 × 10%)]. Similarly, *noncontrolling interest expense* for 2007 consists of 100% of the income to preferred stockholders and 10% of the income to common stockholders, or $14,000 [($10,000 × 100%) + ($40,000 × 10%)]. This information is reflected in the consolidation working papers for Poe Corporation and Subsidiary in Exhibit 10-1.

Except for working paper entry a, the working paper entries are the same as those encountered in earlier chapters. Entry a is reproduced in journal form as follows:

a	**Preferred stock—Sol (–SE)**	**100,000**	
	Retained earnings—Sol (–SE)	**5,000**	
	Noncontrolling interest—preferred (+L)		**105,000**

Entry a reclassifies the preferred stockholders' equity as a noncontrolling interest. The $105,000 preferred equity at the beginning of the period exceeded the $100,000 par value, so we debit the $5,000 excess to Sol's retained earnings. We make this charge to Sol's retained earnings because the preferred stockholders have a maximum claim on Sol's retained earnings for the $5,000 call premium.

The consolidated income statement of Exhibit 10-1 shows separate deductions for noncontrolling interest expense applicable to preferred ($10,000) and common stock ($4,000). This division is helpful in preparing working papers, but a consolidated income statement prepared from the working papers would ordinarily show noncontrolling interest expense as one amount. Also, Exhibit 10-1 shows total noncontrolling interest in Sol at December 31, 2007, on one line of the consolidated balance sheet in the single amount of $146,500. Although the consolidation working papers contain the information to separate this amount into preferred and common components, the separation is ordinarily not used for basic financial reporting, because we eliminate all individual subsidiary equity accounts in the consolidation process.[1] Consolidated financial statements are intended primarily for the stockholders and creditors of the parent company, and we do not expect that the noncontrolling stockholders could benefit significantly from the information contained in them.

Subsidiary Preferred Stock Acquired by Parent

A parent company's purchase of the outstanding preferred stock of a subsidiary results in a retirement of the stock purchased from the viewpoint of the consolidated entity. The stock is retired for consolidated statement purposes because its book value no longer appears as a noncontrolling interest in the consolidated balance sheet. However, the retirement is really a constructive retirement because we report the investment in preferred (parent's books) and the preferred stock equity (subsidiary's books) as outstanding in the separate financial statements of the parent and subsidiary companies.

We report the constructive retirement of a subsidiary's preferred stock through purchase by the parent company as an actual retirement in the consolidated financial statements. That is, we eliminate the equity related to the preferred stock held by the parent and the investment in preferred stock, and we charge or credit any difference to the additional paid-in capital that would otherwise be reported in the consolidated balance sheet.[2] Parent-company stockholders' equity in a one-line consolidation is equal to consolidated stockholders' equity, so comparable accounting requires that the parent company adjust its investment in subsidiary preferred stock to its book value at acquisition and charge or credit its additional paid-in capital for the difference between the price paid for the investment and its underlying book value. We account for the investment in preferred stock on the basis of its book value, not on the basis of the cost or equity method.

---

[1] Noncontrolling interest in a subsidiary's preferred stock is sometimes reported as outstanding stock of the consolidated entity with notation of the name of the issuing corporation. This reporting practice is usually confined to regulated companies.

[2] The parent-company retained earnings are reduced when additional paid-in capital is insufficient to absorb an excess of purchase price over book.

CONSTRUCTIVE RETIREMENT OF SUBSIDIARY PREFERRED STOCK Sol Corporation experiences a net loss of $40,000 in 2008 and pays no dividends. Its stockholders' equity decreases from $520,000 at December 31, 2007 (see Exhibit 10-1) to $480,000 at December 31, 2008. Poe's 90% investment in Sol decreases from $413,500 at year-end 2007 to $365,500 at year-end 2008. We compute the $48,000 decrease in Poe's Investment in Sol common account as follows:

Net loss of Sol	$40,000
Add: Income to preferred[3] (1,000 shares × $10)	10,000
Loss to common	50,000
Poe's ownership interest	90%
Loss from Sol for 2008	$45,000

We can verify the $368,500 investment in Sol common at December 31, 2008, as follows:

Stockholders' equity of Sol, December 31, 2008	$480,000
Less: Preferred stockholders' equity [1,000 shares × ($105 per share call price + $10 per share dividend arrearage)]	115,000
Common stockholders' equity, December 31, 2008	365,000
Poe's ownership interest	90%
Share of Sol's common stockholders' equity	328,500
Add: Unamortized goodwill	40,000
Investment in Sol common, December 31, 2008	$368,500

On January 1, 2009, Poe responded to the depressed price of Sol's preferred stock and purchased 800 shares (an 80% interest) at $100 per share. The $80,000 price paid is less than the $92,000 book value of the stock that is constructively retired ($115,000 × 80%), so Poe records the investment in Sol preferred as follows:

Investment in Sol preferred (+A)	80,000	
Cash (−A)		80,000

To record purchase of 80% of Sol's preferred stock.

Investment in Sol preferred (+A)	12,000	
Other paid-in capital (+SE)		12,000

To adjust other paid-in capital to reflect the constructive retirement.

Sol reports net income of $20,000 for 2009, but it again passes dividends for the year. Poe accounts for its investments during 2009 as follows:

Investment in Sol preferred (+A)	8,000	
Income from Sol preferred (R, +SE)		8,000

To record 80% of the $10,000 increase in Sol's preferred dividend arrearage.

Investment in Sol common (+A)	9,000	
Income from Sol common (R, +SE)		9,000

To record equity in Sol's income to common
[($20,000 net income − $10,000
preferred income) × 90%].

A summary of Sol's preferred and common stockholders' equity and Poe's investment-account balances at the end of 2009 follows:

---

[3] A deduction of cumulative preferred dividends in computing income to common stockholders is required by *APB Opinion No. 18,* paragraph 19k, regardless of whether such dividends are declared.

Sol's Stockholders' Equity, December 31, 2009		
Total stockholders' equity ($480,000 on January 1, 2009		
plus $20,000 net income for 2009)		$500,000
Less: Preferred stockholders' equity [1,000 shares × ($105		
call price + $20 dividends in arrears)]		125,000
Common stockholders' equity		$375,000
Poe's Investment Accounts, December 31, 2009		
Investment in Sol preferred ($125,000 preferred		
equity × 80% owned)		$100,000
Investment in Sol common ($375,000 common equity ×		
90% owned + $40,000 unamortized goodwill)		$377,500

This information for 2009 is reflected in consolidation working papers for Poe and Sol Corporations in Exhibit 10-2.

The working paper entries for 2009 are similar to those in Exhibit 10-1 for 2007, except for items related to the investment in Sol's preferred stock. Procedures to eliminate the preferred equity and investment accounts parallel those for common stock. First, we eliminate Poe's income from Sol preferred against the investment in Sol preferred. This working paper entry (entry a) reduces the Investment in Sol preferred account to its $92,000 adjusted balance at January 1, 2009. Next, we eliminate the investment in Sol preferred and the preferred equity of Sol as of January 1, 2009, in working paper entry b. This entry also enters the preferred noncontrolling interest as of the beginning of the year. Entries a and b in journal form follow:

a Income from Sol preferred (–R, –SE)	8,000	
Investment in Sol preferred (–A)		8,000
b Preferred stock—Sol (–SE)	100,000	
Retained earnings—Sol (–SE)	15,000	
Investment in Sol preferred (–A)		92,000
Noncontrolling interest in Sol preferred (+L)		23,000

The remaining entries (c through f) are the same as those for consolidations involving common stock only.

The working papers in Exhibit 10-2 show Poe Corporation's income equal to consolidated net income and its stockholders' equity equal to consolidated stockholders' equity. These equalities result from parent-company entries to adjust the preferred stock investment account to its underlying equity at acquisition and to accrue dividend arrearages on cumulative preferred stock.

PREFERRED STOCK INVESTMENT MAINTAINED ON COST BASIS If the constructive retirement were *not* recorded by Poe at the time of purchase, the Investment in Sol preferred account would remain at its $80,000 cost throughout 2009, and we would recognize no preferred income. In this case, the consolidation working paper entry to eliminate the preferred investment and equity amounts would be:

Retained earnings—Sol (–SE)	15,000	
Preferred stock—Sol (–SE)	100,000	
Investment in Sol preferred (–A)		80,000
Noncontrolling interest in Sol preferred (+L)		23,000
Other paid-in capital—Poe (+SE)		12,000
To eliminate reciprocal preferred equity and investment amounts, establish		
noncontrolling interest at the beginning of the period (20% × $115,000 beginning		
book value of preferred), and adjust Poe's other paid-in capital account for		
the difference between the purchase price and underlying book value of the		
preferred stock.		

EXHIBIT 10-2

Parent Company
Holds Subsidiary's
Common and
Preferred Stock

**POE CORPORATION AND SUBSIDIARY CONSOLIDATION WORKING PAPERS
FOR THE YEAR ENDED DECEMBER 31, 2009 (IN THOUSANDS)**

	Poe	90% Sol	Adjustments and Eliminations Debits	Credits	Consolidated Statements
Income Statement Sales	$ 690	$280			$ 970
Income from Sol (common)	9		c 9		
Income from Sol (preferred)	8		a 8		
Expenses including cost of sales	(583)	(260)			(843)
Noncontrolling interest expense (common) ($10 × 10%)			e 1		(1)
Noncontrolling interest expense (preferred) ($10 × 20%)			f 2		(2)
Net income	$ 124	$ 20			$ 124
Retained Earnings Retained earnings—Poe	$ 458				$ 458
Retained earnings—Sol		$140	b 15 d 125		
Dividends (common)	(70)	—			(70)
Net income	124	20			124
Retained earnings— December 31	$ 512	$160			$ 512
Balance Sheet Other assets	$1,334.5	$600			$1,934.5
Investment in Sol (common)	377.5			c 9 d 368.5	
Investment in Sol (preferred)	100			a 8 b 92	
Goodwill (common)			d 40		40
	$1,812	$600			$1,974.5
Liabilities	$ 188	$100			$ 288
Preferred stock—Sol		100	b 100		
Common stock	1,000	200	d 200		1,000
Other paid-in capital	112	40	d 40		112
Retained earnings	512	160			512
	$1,812	$600			
Noncontrolling interest: Preferred, January 1 Common, January 1				b 23 d 36.5 e 1 f 2	62.5
					$1,974.5

Comparison of Cost Method and Constructive Retirement The consolidated financial statements will be the same whether the investment in preferred stock remains at its original cost or is adjusted to book value in the parent company's books. However, by adjusting the parent company's additional paid-in capital for the constructive retirement of subsidiary preferred stock, we avoid further paid-in capital adjustments in the consolidation process. Under the cost method, we need a working paper entry to adjust additional paid-in capital each time we consolidate parent-company and subsidiary statements.

PARENT-COMPANY AND CONSOLIDATED EARNINGS PER SHARE

LEARNING OBJECTIVE 2

GAAP requires that all firms calculate and report basic and diluted (where applicable) earnings per share (EPS). Consolidated entities disclose EPS on a consolidated basis. For example, the consolidated statement of income included in the 2003 annual report of **Hershey Foods Corporation** reports:

Earnings per share—Basic	
Income before cumulative effect of accounting change	$3.54
Cumulative effect of accounting change, net of $.04 tax benefit	.06
Net income	$3.48
Earnings per share—Diluted	
Income before cumulative effect of accounting change	$3.52
Cumulative effect of accounting change, net of $.04 tax benefit	.06
Net income	$3.46

Note 16 to the statements is titled "Capital Stock and Net Income per Share," and it describes the calculations in detail (pp. A-52–54).

Similarly, the **PepsiCo** 2003 annual report discloses basic earnings per common share of $2.07 and earnings per common share assuming dilution of $2.05. Both amounts appear on the face of the income statement, and Pepsi reports these amounts on a consolidated basis.

A parent company's net income and EPS under the equity method are equal to consolidated net income and consolidated EPS. However, the computational differences in determining parent-company and consolidated net income (that is, one-line consolidation versus consolidation) do not extend to EPS calculations. Parent-company and consolidated EPS calculations are identical. EPS procedures for equity investors who are able to exercise significant influence over their investees are the same as those for parent-company investors. Although parent-company and subsidiary relationships are addressed in this section, the discussion and illustrations apply equally to investments accounted for under the equity method.[4]

Parent-company procedures for computing EPS depend on the subsidiary's capital structure. When the subsidiary (or equity investee) has *no* potentially dilutive securities, the procedures applied in computing consolidated EPS are the same as for separate entities. When the subsidiary does have potentially dilutive securities outstanding, however, the potential dilution has to be considered in computing the parent company's diluted EPS.

We compute basic EPS the same way for a consolidated entity as for separate entities (assuming the equity method is used). The nature of the adjustment to parent-company EPS calculations depends on whether the subsidiary's potentially dilutive securities are convertible into subsidiary or parent-company common stock. If convertible into subsidiary common stock, we reflect the potential dilution in subsidiary EPS computations, which are then used in determining parent-company (and consolidated) EPS. If the dilutive securities of the subsidiary are convertible into parent-company stock, we treat them as parent-company dilutive securities and include them directly in computing the parent-company EPS.[5] In this latter case, we do not need (or use) subsidiary EPS computations in parent-company EPS computations.

---

[4] The provisions of *FASB Statement No. 128*, "Earnings per Share," that apply to subsidiaries also apply to investments accounted for by the equity method. See *APB Opinion No. 18*, "The Equity Method of Accounting for Investments in Common Stock," footnote 8, as amended by *FASB Statement No. 128*.

[5] *FASB Statement No. 128*, paragraphs 62–63.

EXHIBIT 10-3

Parent-Company and Consolidated Diluted EPS Calculations

	Subsidiary Does Not Have Potentially Dilutive Securities Outstanding	Subsidiary Has Potentially Dilutive Securities Convertible into Subsidiary Common Stock	Subsidiary Has Potentially Dilutive Securities Convertible into Parent-Company Common Stock
Numerator in Dollars ($)			
Income to parent's common stockholders	$$$	$$$	$$$
Add: Adjustments for parent's dilutive securities	+$	+$	+$
Add: Adjustments for subsidiary's potentially dilutive securities convertible into parent-company stock	NA	NA	+$
Replacement calculation (must result in a net decrease)			
Deduct: Parent's equity in subsidiary's realized income	NA	−$	NA
Add: Parent's equity in subsidiary's diluted earnings	NA	+$	NA
Parent's diluted earnings = a	$$$	$$$	$$$
Denominator in Shares (Y)			
Parent's common shares outstanding	YYY	YYY	YYY
Add: Shares represented by parent's potentially dilutive securities	+Y	+Y	+Y
Add: Shares represented by subsidiary's potentially dilutive securities convertible into parent-company common shares	NA	NA	+Y
Parent's common shares and common share equivalents = b	YYY	YYY	YYY
Parent-Company and Consolidated Diluted EPS	a/b	a/b	a/b

NA—Not applicable.

General formats for EPS calculations in these situations are summarized in Exhibit 10-3 for diluted EPS. The first column of Exhibit 10-3 shows parent-company computations for diluted EPS when the subsidiary has no potentially dilutive securities. In this case, the EPS computations are the same as those for unrelated entities, and no adjustments are necessary for subsidiary income included in parent-company income, provided that the parent-company applies the equity method correctly.

Dilutive Securities of Subsidiary Convertible into Subsidiary Shares

The second column of Exhibit 10-3 summarizes parent-company EPS computations when subsidiary potentially dilutive securities are convertible into subsidiary common shares. We adjust diluted earnings of the parent company (the numerators of the EPS calculations) by excluding the parent's **equity in subsidiary realized income** and replacing that equity with the parent's share of diluted earnings of the subsidiary.

Equity in subsidiary realized income is the parent's percentage interest in reported income of the subsidiary adjusted for the effects of intercompany profits from upstream sales and constructive gains or losses of the subsidiary. This adjustment to remove the potential dilution from the parent's diluted earnings is based on separate EPS computations for the subsidiary. We make these computations of subsidiary EPS only for the purpose of calculating the parent's EPS, and they are not necessarily the same as those prepared by the subsidiary for its own external reporting.

Note that "parent's equity in subsidiary's realized income" in column 2 of Exhibit 10-3 differs from "parent's income from subsidiary," which includes amortization of valuation differentials and the income effects of all intercompany transactions. The parent company's investment valuation differentials, unrealized profits from downstream sales, and constructive gains and losses assigned to the parent do not affect the equity of the subsidiary's security holders; therefore, we exclude these items from the replacement calculation. In other words, the replacement calculation includes only the parent's equity in subsidiary realized income.

We use the subsidiary's diluted EPS in determining diluted earnings of the parent company (see column 2 of Exhibit 10-3), so EPS computations for the subsidiary (based on subsidiary realized income) are made as a first step in computing the parent company's EPS. In computing the subsidiary's diluted earnings, we eliminate unrealized profits of the subsidiary and include constructive gains and losses of the subsidiary. We reflect the resulting EPS calculations of the subsidiary in the parent-company EPS calculation by replacing the "parent's equity in subsidiary's realized income" with the "parent's equity in subsidiary's diluted earnings." We determine the parent company's equity in the subsidiary's diluted earnings by multiplying the subsidiary shares owned by the parent by the subsidiary's diluted EPS. This replacement allocates the subsidiary's realized income for EPS purposes to holders of the subsidiary's common stock and potentially dilutive securities, rather than only to the subsidiary's common stockholders.

Diluted Securities of Subsidiary Convertible into Parent-Company Shares

Parent-company common shares (the denominators of EPS computations) are identical in columns 1 and 2 of Exhibit 10-3 but increase in column 3 for subsidiary securities that are convertible into parent-company common stock. This adjustment in column 3 is necessary when the subsidiary's potentially dilutive securities are potentially dilutive securities of the parent company rather than of the subsidiary. When potentially dilutive securities of a subsidiary are convertible into parent common stock, income attributable to these securities under the if-converted method must be added back in calculating the parent's diluted earnings. Thus, column 3 of Exhibit 10-3 includes the item "adjustment for subsidiary's dilutive securities convertible into parent common stock," which is not applicable when the subsidiary does not have potentially dilutive securities (column 1) or when such securities are convertible into subsidiary common stock (column 2).

SUBSIDIARY WITH CONVERTIBLE PREFERRED STOCK

Plant Corporation purchases 90% of Seed Corporation's outstanding voting common stock for $328,000 on January 1, 2006. On this date, the stockholders' equity of the two corporations consists of the following (in thousands):

	Plant	**Seed**
Common stock, $5 par, 200,000 shares issued and outstanding	$1,000	
Common stock, $10 par, 20,000 shares outstanding		$200
10% cumulative, convertible preferred stock, $100 par, 1,000 shares outstanding		100
Retained earnings	500	120
Total stockholders' equity	$1,500	$420

During 2006, Seed reports $50,000 net income and pays $25,000 dividends, $10,000 to preferred and $15,000 to common. Plant's net income for 2006 is $186,000, determined as follows:

Income from Plant's operations	$150,000
Income from Seed [($50,000 net income − $10,000 preferred income) × 90%]	36,000
Plant's net income	$186,000

Subsidiary Preferred Stock Convertible into Subsidiary Common Stock

Assume that Seed's preferred stock is convertible into 12,000 shares of Seed's common stock and that neither Plant nor Seed has other potentially dilutive securities outstanding. Seed's diluted EPS is $1.5625 [$50,000 earnings ÷ (20,000 common shares + 12,000 share dilution)], and Plant's diluted EPS is $0.89, computed as follows:

Net income of Plant (equal to income to common)	$186,000
Replacement of Plant's equity in Seed's realized income ($40,000 × 90%)	(36,000)
with Plant's equity in Seed's diluted earnings (18,000 shares of Seed × Seed's $1.5625 diluted EPS)	28,125
Plant's diluted earnings = a	$178,125
Plant's outstanding shares = b	200,000
Plant's diluted EPS = a ÷ b	$ 0.89

The $7,875 potential dilution reflected in Plant's diluted earnings results from replacing Plant's equity in Seed's realized income with Plant's equity in Seed's diluted earnings per share. Note that Plant's equity in Seed's realized income is $36,000, which is the same as Plant's income from Seed.

Subsidiary Preferred Stock Convertible into Parent-Company Common Stock

Assume that Seed's preferred stock is convertible into 24,000 shares of Plant's common stock and that neither Plant nor Seed has other potentially dilutive securities outstanding. Seed's diluted EPS (not used in Plant's EPS computations) is $2 per share ($40,000 income to common ÷ 20,000 common shares outstanding) because the preferred stock is not a dilutive security of Seed Corporation. Plant's diluted EPS is computed as follows:

Net income of Plant (equal to income to common)	$186,000
Add: Income to preferred stockholders of Seed assumed to be converted	10,000
Plant's diluted earnings = a	$196,000
Plant's outstanding shares	200,000
Add: Seed's preferred shares assumed converted	24,000
Plant's common shares and common stock equivalents = b	224,000
Plant's diluted EPS = a ÷ b	$ 0.88

Preferred income is added to Plant's net income because we allocated no income to the preferred stock assumed to be converted.

SUBSIDIARY WITH OPTIONS AND CONVERTIBLE BONDS

Paddy Corporation has $1,500,000 income from its own operations for 2006 and $300,000 income from Syd Corporation, its 80%-owned subsidiary. The $300,000 income from Syd consists of 80% of Syd's $450,000 net income for 2006, less 80% of a $50,000 unrealized gain on land purchased from Syd, less $20,000 amortization of the excess of investment cost over the book value acquired in Syd. The $20,000 excess was assigned to a previously unrecognized patent. Outstanding securities of the two corporations throughout 2006 are:

Paddy: Common stock, 1,000,000 shares

Syd: Common stock, 400,000 shares

Options to purchase 60,000 shares of stock at $10 per share (average market price is $15 per share)

7% convertible bonds, $1,000,000 par outstanding, convertible into 80,000 shares of common stock

	Syd's Diluted EPS
Syd's income to common stockholders	$450,000
Less: Unrealized profit on sale of land	(50,000)
Add: Net-of-tax interest expense assuming subsidiary bonds converted into subsidiary shares ($1,000,000 × 7% × 66% assumed net-of-tax effect)	46,200
Subsidiary adjusted earnings = a	$446,200
Syd's common shares outstanding	400,000
Incremental shares assuming exercise of options [60,000 shares − ($600,000 proceeds from exercise of options ÷ $15 market price)]	20,000
Additional shares assuming bonds converted into subsidiary shares	80,000
Syd's adjusted shares = b	500,000
Syd's EPS = a ÷ b	$ 0.89

EXHIBIT 10-4

Subsidiary's EPS Computations

Options and Bonds Convertible into Subsidiary Common Stock

Assume that the options and bonds are convertible into Syd's common stock. Exhibit 10-4 shows computations for Syd's diluted EPS. Under the treasury stock approach for options and warrants, the effect of options on EPS is dilutive when the average market price of the common shares to which the options apply exceeds the exercise price. If holders of Syd's options had exercised their rights to acquire 60,000 shares of Syd's common stock at $10 per share, Syd would have received $600,000 cash. Under the treasury stock approach, we assume Syd uses this cash to reacquire 40,000 shares of its own stock ($600,000 ÷ $15 average market price). This assumed exercise and repurchase of treasury shares increases Syd's outstanding common stock for EPS computations by 20,000 shares.

The convertible bonds must also be included in Syd's diluted EPS computations. Under the if-converted method, we include $46,200 net-of-tax interest in Syd's diluted earnings and include the 80,000 shares issuable upon conversion in calculating Syd's diluted common shares.

We use Syd's $0.89 diluted EPS in the EPS computations for Paddy Corporation. Exhibit 10-5 shows computations for Paddy's diluted EPS.

In the computation of Paddy's diluted earnings, we replace Paddy's equity in Syd's realized income ($320,000) with Paddy's share of Syd's diluted earnings ($284,800). This replacement decreases Paddy's diluted earnings by $35,200. This dilution results from allocating Syd's $400,000 realized income plus $46,200 net-of-tax interest effect from the convertible bonds to holders of Syd's common shares, options, and convertible bonds, rather than just to Syd's common stockholders.

	Paddy's Diluted EPS
Paddy's income to common stockholders	$1,800,000
Replacement of Paddy's $320,000 equity in Syd's realized income [($450,000 − $50,000 unrealized profit) × 80%] with Paddy's $284,800 equity in Syd's diluted EPS (320,000 shares × Syd's $0.89 diluted EPS)	(320,000)
	284,800
Paddy's adjusted earnings = a	$1,764,800
Paddy's outstanding common shares = b	1,000,000
Paddy's EPS = a ÷ b	$ 1.76

EXHIBIT 10-5

Parent's EPS Computations— Dilution Relates to Subsidiary Shares

	Paddy's Diluted EPS
Paddy's income to common stockholders	$1,800,000
Add: Net-of-tax interest assuming subsidiary bonds converted into parent's common stock ($1,000,000 × 7% × 66% net-of-tax effect)	46,200
Parent's adjusted earnings = a	$1,846,200
Paddy's outstanding shares	1,000,000
Incremental shares assuming options converted into parent's shares [60,000 shares − ($600,000 proceeds from exercise of options ÷ $15 market price)]	20,000
Additional shares assuming subsidiary bonds are converted into parent shares	80,000
Parent's adjusted shares = b	1,100,000
Parent's EPS = a ÷ b	$ 1.68

Options and Bonds Convertible into Parent's Common Stock

Exhibit 10-6 presents computations for Paddy's diluted EPS under the assumptions that Syd Corporation's options are convertible into 60,000 shares of Paddy Corporation's common stock and that Syd Corporation's bonds are convertible into 80,000 shares of Paddy Corporation's common stock. Under these assumptions, we do not need Syd's diluted EPS in determining Paddy's EPS because we only use subsidiary EPS computations for replacement computations when subsidiary dilutive securities are convertible into subsidiary shares. The subsidiary dilutive securities are convertible into parent-company shares in this example, so we only need parent-company EPS computations.

LEARNING
OBJECTIVE 3

ACCOUNTING FOR INCOME TAXES OF CONSOLIDATED ENTITIES

This section of the chapter on accounting for income taxes of consolidated entities begins with a discussion of which companies may file consolidated tax returns, the advantages and disadvantages of filing consolidated tax returns, and the status of accounting pronouncements on income taxes. Temporary differences in consolidated and separate tax returns are discussed, and income tax allocation procedures are illustrated for a parent company and subsidiary that file separate tax returns. Next, four cases compare consolidation procedures when a parent company and subsidiary file separate tax returns with those necessary when filing a consolidated tax return. A final section looks at the tax basis of assets and liabilities acquired in a purchase business combination.

Some consolidated entities prepare consolidated income tax returns and pay taxes on consolidated taxable income. Others prepare income tax returns for each affiliate and pay taxes on the taxable income included in those separate returns. The right of a consolidated entity to file a consolidated income tax return is contingent upon classification as an *affiliated group* under Sections 1501 through 1505 of the U.S. Internal Revenue Code (USIRC). An affiliated group exists when a common parent corporation owns at least 80% of the voting power of all classes of stock and 80% or more of the total value of all outstanding stock of each of the includable corporations. The common parent must meet the 80% requirements directly for at least one includable corporation (USIRC 1504[a]).

A consolidated entity that is an affiliated group may elect to file consolidated income tax returns. All other consolidated entities *must* file separate income tax returns for each affiliated company.

Note 1 to **Home Depot's** 2000 consolidated financial statements discusses its filing status as follows:

> The company and its eligible subsidiaries file a consolidated U.S. federal income tax return. Non-U.S. subsidiaries, which are consolidated for financial reporting, are not eligible to be included in consolidated U.S. federal income tax returns, and separate provisions for income tax have been determined for these entities. The Company intends to reinvest the unremitted earnings of its non-U.S. subsidiaries and postpone their remittance indefinitely. Accordingly, no provision for U.S. income taxes for non-U.S. subsidiaries was required for any year presented.

Advantages of Filing Consolidated Tax Returns

The primary advantages of filing a consolidated return are as follows:

1. Losses of one affiliate are offset against income of other members of the affiliated group. However, loss carryforwards at the time of acquisition of an acquired affiliate can be offset only against taxable income of the affiliate.

2. Intercorporate dividends are excluded from taxable income.

3. Intercompany profits are deferred from income until realized (but unrealized losses are also deferred until realized).

Exclusion of intercorporate dividends is not a unique advantage of filing a consolidated tax return, because a consolidated entity that is classified as an affiliated group is allowed a 100% exclusion on dividends received from members of the same group even if it elects not to file consolidated tax returns. In addition, corporate taxpayers can deduct 80% of the dividends received from domestic corporations that are 20% to 80% owned and can deduct 70% of the dividends received from domestic corporations that are less than 20% owned.

Disadvantages of Filing Consolidated Tax Returns

Consolidated entities that file consolidated tax returns lose some of the flexibility of entities that file separate returns. For example, each subsidiary included in a consolidated tax return must use the parent's taxable year. Different years can be used when filing separate returns. The election to file a consolidated return commits an entity to consolidated returns year after year. It is difficult to get permission to stop filing consolidated returns. Also, deconsolidated corporations cannot rejoin the affiliated group for five years.

INCOME TAX ALLOCATION

FASB Statement No. 109, "Accounting for Income Taxes," is the primary source of GAAP for accounting for income taxes.[6] The objectives of accounting for income taxes under *Statement No. 109* are to recognize the amount of taxes payable or refundable for the current year and to recognize deferred tax liabilities and assets for the future tax consequences of events that have been recognized in the financial statements or tax returns.

Events that have future tax consequences are designated *temporary differences* to separate them from events that do not have tax consequences, such as interest on municipal obligations. The tax consequences of temporary differences must be considered in the measurement of income for a period. Some accounting/income tax differences are the same, regardless of whether the affiliates file separate-entity or consolidated income tax returns, whereas others depend on the kind of return filed. For example, unrealized and constructive gains and losses from intercompany transactions are temporary differences when filing separate returns because the individual entities are taxed on the income included in their separate returns. However, these items are *not* temporary differences when filing consolidated returns because adjustments to defer intercompany profits until realized are reflected in both the consolidation working papers and the consolidated tax return.

Dividends received from members of an affiliated group are excluded from taxation regardless of whether affiliates file separate or consolidated returns, but dividends received from affiliates that are not members of an affiliated group are taxed currently, subject to the 80% dividends-received deduction.

Temporary Differences from Undistributed Earnings of Subsidiaries and Equity Investees

Accounting requirements under the equity method of accounting are generally the same for investments of 20% to 50% of the voting stock of an investee as for subsidiary investments. Investors pay income taxes currently on dividends received (distributed income) from equity investees and subsidiaries that are not members of an affiliated group, and GAAP requires investors to provide for deferred income taxes on their shares of undistributed income of their investees. That is, a temporary difference results when an investor's equity in its investees' income exceeds dividends received.

---

[6]The one notable exception was *APB Opinion No. 23,* "Accounting for Income Taxes—Special Areas."

Under *APB Opinion No. 23,* the parent company/investor could avoid the general presumption that all undistributed earnings will be transferred to the parent company by showing that undistributed earnings of the subsidiary had been invested indefinitely. *Statement No. 109* amends *APB Opinion No. 23* to remove the exception and require the parent company/investor to treat the undistributed income of their domestic subsidiaries as temporary differences unless the tax law provides a means by which the investment can be recovered tax free. *Statement No. 109* continues the *Opinion 23* exception for undistributed earnings of foreign subsidiaries and foreign joint ventures and undistributed earnings of domestic subsidiaries that arose before its effective date.

In accounting for the *tax effect* of a temporary difference relating to income from equity investees, we do not use the one-line consolidation concept because we include investment income in the investor's income *before* income taxes—in other words, on a pretax basis. If undistributed earnings of an investee is the only temporary difference, a parent company or equity investor provides for income taxes on its share of undistributed income by debiting income tax expense and crediting deferred income taxes. The temporary difference related to undistributed earnings is, of course, only one of several possible differences that interact to produce the combined tax impact.

Accounting for Distributed and Undistributed Income

Assume that Parson Corporation owns a 30% interest in Seaton Corporation, a domestic corporation. Seaton reports $600,000 net income for the current year and pays dividends of $200,000. An income tax rate of 34% applies. (The 34% tax rate is the *only* enacted tax rate applicable throughout this illustration.) We analyze Parson's share of Seaton's distributed and undistributed income as follows:

Share of distributed earnings (dividends) ($200,000 × 30%)	$ 60,000
Share of undistributed earnings (retained earnings increase) ($400,000 × 30%)	120,000
Equity in Seaton's earnings ($600,000 × 30%)	$180,000

Parson is taxed currently on 20% of the $60,000 dividends received because Seaton is a domestic corporation that qualifies for the 80% dividends-received deduction. The income tax expense equals income tax liability for this part of Parson's income from Seaton. The current tax liability is $4,080 ($60,000 dividends received × 20% taxable × 34% tax rate).

No income tax is due currently on Parson's share of Seaton's undistributed earnings, but accounting standards require that we recognize income taxes attributable to that temporary difference as if the earnings had been remitted as dividends during the current period. Assuming that undistributed earnings is the only temporary difference, Parson makes the following entry to provide for income taxes on its share of Seaton's undistributed earnings:

December 31, 2003

Income tax expense (E, −SE)	8,160	
Deferred income taxes (+L)		8,160

    To provide for taxes on undistributed earnings of

    Seaton ($120,000 × 20% taxable × 34% rate).

The same procedures for income taxes on undistributed earnings apply to parent-company investors, but not to dividends received from members of an affiliated group because we exclude 100% of those dividends from taxable income of the group.

Unrealized Gains and Losses from Intercompany Transactions

Unrealized and constructive gains and losses from intercompany transactions create temporary differences that may affect deferred tax calculations when filing separate income tax returns. (This is *not* true when filing consolidated tax returns.) In the case of an unrealized gain, the selling entity includes the gain in its separate tax return and pays the tax due on the transaction. We eliminate the unrealized gain in the consolidation process, so we defer the income taxes related to the gain. Similarly, an unrealized loss may reduce deferred tax expense or add to a deferred tax asset.

We include the tax effects of temporary differences from unrealized gains and losses on intercompany transactions in measuring the income tax expense of the selling affiliate. Under this approach, the consolidated income tax expense is equal to the combined income tax expense of the consolidated entities, and we eliminate intercompany profit items on a gross basis. Similarly, this approach permits the parent company/investor to eliminate intercompany profits on a gross, rather than a net-of-tax, basis. (When eliminating intercompany profits on a net-of-tax basis by the parent company/investor, we need a consolidation working paper entry to convert the combined income tax expense of the affiliated companies into consolidated income tax expense and to adjust the deferred tax asset or liability amounts to a consolidated basis.)

Assume that Petit Corporation sells merchandise that cost $100,000 to Sellman Corporation, its 75%-owned subsidiary, for $200,000, and that Sellman still holds 70% of this merchandise at year-end. A 34% tax rate is applicable, and Petit pays $34,000 income tax on the transaction during the current year. Sellman is a 75%-owned subsidiary, so we must file separate tax returns. (Again, assume that the intercompany transaction is the only temporary difference and that the 34% tax rate is the only enacted rate.) Relevant consolidation and one-line consolidation entries are as follows:

Consolidation Working Paper Entries—Year of Sale		
Sales (–R, –SE)	200,000	
Cost of sales (–E, +SE)		200,000
To eliminate intercompany sales and purchases		
Cost of sales (E, –SE)	70,000	
Inventory (–A)		70,000
To eliminate unrealized profit on intercompany merchandise **remaining in inventory ($200,000 – $100,000) × 70%.**		

Petit's One-Line Consolidation Entry—Year of Sale

Income from Sellman (–R, –SE)	70,000	
Investment in Sellman (–A)		70,000
To eliminate unrealized profit on sales to Sellman		
($70,000 unrealized profit × 100%).		

If Sellman sells the merchandise in the next period, the consolidation and one-line consolidation entries in that year will be:

Consolidation Working Paper Entry—Year of Realization		
Investment in Sellman (+A)	70,000	
Cost of sales (–E, +SE)		70,000
To recognize previously deferred profit on inventory and to adjust **Petit's beginning Investment in Sellman account to reflect realization.**		

Petit's One-Line Consolidation Entry—Year of Realization

Investment in Sellman (+A)	70,000	
Income from Sellman (R, +SE)		70,000
To reinstate previously deferred profit on intercompany sales.		

If the sale had been upstream from Sellman to Petit, the $34,000 tax on the intercompany profit would have been paid by Sellman, but Sellman would show $23,800 ($70,000 × 34%) of that amount as a deferred tax asset, rather than as income tax expense for the year. The consolidation working paper entry to eliminate the intercompany profit in the year of sale would be for $70,000, the same amount as in the downstream example. Noncontrolling interest expense in the year of sale would decrease by $17,500 (25% × $70,000 unrealized gain), and the amount of the one-line consolidation entry to eliminate the effect of the unrealized profit on Petit's books would be for $52,500 (75% × $70,000), rather than $70,000 as in the downstream example.

SEPARATE-COMPANY TAX RETURNS WITH INTERCOMPANY GAIN

This section provides an extended illustration of income tax allocation for a parent company and its subsidiary that file separate income tax returns. Paco Corporation paid $375,000 cash for a 75% interest in Step Corporation on January 1, 2006, when Step's equity consisted of $300,000 capital stock and $200,000 retained earnings. At the time Paco acquired its interest in Step, Paco had a deferred income tax liability of $10,200, consisting of $30,000 tax/book depreciation differences that reverse in equal ($7,500) amounts over the years 2007 through 2010.

On January 8, 2006, Paco sold equipment to Step at a gain of $20,000. Step is depreciating the equipment on a straight-line basis over five years. Comparative income and retained earnings data for 2006 are as follows:

	Paco	Step
Sales	$380,000	$300,000
Gain on equipment sale	20,000	—
Income from Step	23,600	—
Cost of sales	(200,000)	(180,000)
Operating expenses	(100,000)	(40,000)
Income tax expense	(31,253)	(27,200)
Net income	92,347	52,800
Add: Beginning retained earnings	357,653	200,000
Deduct: Dividends (December)	(50,000)	(28,000)
Retained earnings December 31	$400,000	$224,800

Statement No. 109 requires Paco to provide for income taxes on its share of Step's $24,800 undistributed earnings ($52,800 net income less $28,000 dividends). The 80% dividends-received deduction is applicable to dividends received from Step. We assume a flat 34% income tax rate for Paco and Step. Paco's deferred tax computation on the undistributed earnings is therefore $1,265 [($24,800 × 75% owned × 20% taxable) = $3,720 × 34% tax rate].

One-Line Consolidation

Paco makes the following journal entries to account for its investment in Step during 2006:

January 1
Investment in Step (+A)	375,000	
Cash (−A)		375,000

To record purchase of a 75% interest in Step.

December 2006
Cash (+A)	21,000	
Investment in Step (−A)		21,000

To record dividends received from Step ($28,000 × 75%).

December 31, 2006
Investment in Step (+A)	23,600	
Income from Step (R, +SE)		23,600

To record income from Step computed as follows:

Paco's share of Step's net income ($52,800 × 75%)	$ 39,600
Less: Unrealized profit on sale of equipment	(20,000)
Add: Piecemeal recognition of gain ($20,000 ÷ 5 years)	4,000
Income from Step	$ 23,600

Note that in computing its investment income from Step, Paco takes up its share of Step's income on which taxes have been paid by Step.

At December 31, 2006, Paco's Investment in Step account has a balance of $377,600 ($375,000 beginning balance + $23,600 income from Step − $21,000 dividends), and Paco's share of Step's equity is $393,600 ($524,800 × 75%). The $16,000 difference ($377,600 − $393,600) is the $16,000 unrealized profit from the downstream sale of equipment.

Income Tax Expense Based on Separate Returns

Step's $27,200 income tax expense is simply 34% of Step's $80,000 pretax accounting income, but Paco's income tax expense of $31,253 requires further analysis. In accordance with the provisions of *FASB Statement No. 109*, we calculate Paco's income tax expense as follows:

Tax on Paco's operating income [($380,000 sales –	
$200,000 cost of sales – $100,000 operating expenses) × 34%]	$27,200
Tax on gain from sale of equipment ($20,000 × 34%)	6,800
Tax on dividends received [($21,000 × 20% taxable) × 34%]	1,428
Income taxes currently payable	35,428
Less: Decrease in deferred income taxes [($16,000 unrealized	
gain on equipment at year-end – $3,720 taxable share of	
Step's undistributed earnings) × 34%]	(4,175)
Income tax expense	$31,253

Exhibit 10-7 provides a schedule to support the computation of Paco's income tax expense. Only one tax rate (34%) is applicable, so the schedule approach is not necessary, but it may be helpful. The calculation for future dividends in the schedule is ($52,800 net income – $28,000 dividends) × 75% owned × 20% taxable portion.

Paco's interest in Step is only 75%, so it must file separate tax returns and pay income taxes on the $20,000 intercompany gain on the equipment sold to Step. Paco also pays income taxes on dividends received from Step, less an 80% dividends-received deduction. The multiplication of dividends received and undistributed income by 20% in calculating Paco's income tax expense effectively takes the 80% dividends-received deduction into account without calculating the amount of the deduction and subtracting it from distributed (dividends) or undistributed earnings.

Step's $27,200 income tax expense is equal to the tax liability indicated on its separate return because it has no temporary differences. Paco's income tax expense of $31,253 consists of $35,428 currently payable, less a $4,175 decrease in deferred income taxes for the year. The balance of Paco's deferred income taxes at December 31 is $6,025 ($10,200 beginning balance – $4,175 decrease for the year). Step and Paco record their income tax expenses as follows:

Step's Books—December 31, 2006

Income tax expense (E, –SE)	27,200	
Income taxes currently payable (+L)		27,200
To accrue income taxes for 2006.		

Paco's Books—December 31

Income tax expense (E, –SE)	31,253	
Deferred income taxes (–L)	4,175	
Income taxes currently payable (+L)		35,428
To accrue income taxes for 2006.		

Temporary Difference	2006	2007	2008	2009	2010	Future Years
Depreciation		$7,500	$7,500	$7,500	$7,500	
Gain on equipment	$20,000					
Piecemeal recognition	(4,000)	(4,000)	(4,000)	(4,000)	(4,000)	
Future dividends	(3,720)	—	—	—	—	$3,720
Taxable in future years		3,500	3,500	3,500	3,500	3,720
Enacted tax rate		34%	34%	34%	34%	34%
Deferred tax liability		$1,190	$1,190	$1,190	$1,190	$1,265

EXHIBIT 10-7

Schedule of Deferred Income Tax Liability at December 31, 2006

Consolidation Working Papers

Exhibit 10-8 presents consolidation working papers for Paco Corporation and Subsidiary. The working paper entries are the same as those encountered in earlier chapters except for the inclusion of income tax considerations. Observe that Paco's income tax expense plus Step's income tax expense equal the $58,453 consolidated income tax expense.

Paco paid income taxes on the $20,000 gain on the intercompany sale of equipment. We do not recognize this gain for consolidated statement purposes, so a temporary difference exists for which we require income tax allocation procedures.

Working Paper Entry for 2007

The working paper entry for 2007 to eliminate the effect of the unrealized profit from the intercompany sale of equipment is as follows:

Investment in Step (+A)	16,000	
Accumulated depreciation (+A)	8,000	
Equipment (−A)		20,000
Depreciation expense (−E, +SE)		4,000
To eliminate unrealized profit from downstream sale of equipment.		

The income tax expense in 2007 will be equal to the income tax currently payable, adjusted for the change in the deferred tax asset or liability that occurs in 2007.

EFFECT OF CONSOLIDATED AND SEPARATE-COMPANY TAX RETURNS ON CONSOLIDATED PROCEDURES

This section compares consolidation procedures for a parent company and its subsidiary when separate-company and consolidated tax returns are filed. Under the provisions of *FASB Statement No. 109*, the income tax expense and the income from subsidiary are the same in both cases. When firms file consolidated tax returns, we allocate the tax liability among the parent company and its subsidiaries.

Allocation of Consolidated Income Tax to Affiliates

A subsidiary that is part of a group filing a consolidated tax return is required to disclose its current and deferred income tax expense amounts and any tax-related balances due to or from affiliates in its separate financial statements. Although GAAP provides no single method of allocating consolidated income tax expense among affiliates, firms must disclose the method used.

Four methods currently used in the allocation of consolidated income taxes to affiliates are as follows:[7]

- **Separate return method.** Each subsidiary computes income taxes as if it were filing a separate return.
- **Agreement method.** Tax expense is allocated by agreement between parent and subsidiaries.
- **With-or-without method.** The income tax provision is computed for the group with and without the pretax income of the subsidiary. The subsidiary's income tax expense is the difference.
- **Percentage allocation method.** Consolidated income tax expense is allocated to a subsidiary on the basis of its pretax income as a percentage of consolidated pretax income.

The percentage allocation method is used for the illustrations in this book.

---

[7] Terry E. Allison and Paula Bevels Thomas, "Unchartered Territory: Subsidiary Financial Reporting," *Journal of Accountancy* (October 1989), p. 80.

PACO CORPORATION AND SUBSIDIARY CONSOLIDATION WORKING PAPERS FOR THE YEAR ENDED DECEMBER 31, 2007			Adjustments and Eliminations		
	Paco	90% Step	Debits	Credits	Consolidated Statements
Income Statement Sales	$380,000	$300,000			$680,000
Gain on equipment	20,000		a 20,000		
Income from Step	23,600		c 23,600		
Cost of sales	(200,000)	(180,000)			(380,000)
Operating expense	(100,000)	(40,000)		b 4,000	(136,000)
Income tax expense	(31,253)	(27,200)			(58,453)
Noncontrolling interest expense			e 13,200		(13,200)
Net income	**$ 92,347**	**$ 52,800**			**$ 92,347**
Retained Earnings Retained earnings—Paco	$357,653				$357,653
Retained earnings—Step		$200,000	d 200,000		
Dividends	(50,000)	(28,000)		c 21,000 e 7,000	(50,000)
Net income	92,347	52,800			92,347
Retained earnings— December 31	**$400,000**	**$224,800**			**$400,000**
Balance Sheet Other assets	$362,400	$432,000			$794,400
Equipment	120,000	200,000		a 20,000	300,000
Accumulated depreciation	(60,000)	(50,000)	b 4,000		(106,000)
Investment in Step	377,600			c 2,600 d 375,000	
	$800,000	**$582,000**			**$988,400**
Deferred tax liability	$ 6,025				$ 6,025
Income tax liability	35,428	$ 27,200			62,628
Other liabilities	58,547	30,000			88,547
Capital stock	300,000	300,000	d 300,000		300,000
Retained earnings	400,000	224,800			400,000
	$800,000	**$582,000**			
Noncontrolling interest				d 125,000 e 6,200	131,200
					$988,400

EXHIBIT 10-8

Parent and Subsidiary Companies File Separate Tax Returns

Background Information for Consolidated and Separate Tax Return Illustrations

The following illustrations for Pool Corporation and its 90%-owned subsidiary, Sal Corporation, compare consolidation procedures used when filing consolidated tax returns with consolidation procedures necessary when filing separate-company tax returns. The income tax effects of intercompany profits from both upstream and downstream inventory sales are also illustrated.

On January 1, 2006, Pool acquired 90% of the outstanding voting stock of Sal for $435,000, when Sal had $300,000 capital stock and $100,000 retained earnings. The $75,000 excess is due to a previously unrecorded patent with a 15-year amortization period. The amortization is deductible for tax purposes. Additional information follows:

1. A flat 34% enacted income tax rate applies to all years.

2. Pool and Sal are an affiliated group entitled to the 100% dividend exclusion.

3. Sal pays dividends of $20,000 during 2006.

4. Intercompany sales are $40,000, of which $10,000 represents unrealized profits at year-end 2006.

5. Pretax operating incomes for the two affiliates are:

	Pool	Sal
Sales	$900,000	$500,000
Cost of sales	(500,000)	(350,000)
Expenses	(250,000)	(100,000)
Pretax operating income	$150,000	$ 50,000

Cases 1 and 2 illustrate a temporary difference for unrealized profits from downstream sales that originates in the current year and reverses in the succeeding year. Subsequently, Cases 3 and 4 repeat illustrations 1 and 2 using an upstream-sale assumption as the only temporary difference.

CASE 1: CONSOLIDATED TAX RETURN WITH DOWNSTREAM SALES

Assume that a consolidated tax return is filed and that the intercompany sales are downstream. The consolidated income tax return includes the $200,000 combined operating income (Pool's $150,000 operating income plus Sal's $50,000 operating income) less $10,000 unrealized profit and the $5,000 patent amortization. The consolidated income tax expense will be $62,900 ($185,000 × 34%). The $62,900 income tax expense is equal to the $62,900 consolidated income tax liability because we eliminate the unrealized profits in the consolidation working papers and in the consolidated income tax return. In addition, no tax is assessed on the $18,000 dividends that Pool receives from Sal.

We allocate the $62,900 consolidated income tax liability to Pool and Sal based on the amounts of their income included in the $185,000 consolidated taxable income. The intercompany sales are downstream in this case, so the allocation is:

$$\text{Pool} = \frac{\$150,000 - \$10,000 - \$5,000}{\$185,000} \times \$62,900 = \$45,900$$

$$\text{Sal} = \frac{\$50,000}{\$185,000} \times \$62,900 = \$17,000$$

Pool and Sal record the 2006 income tax expense amounts determined in this allocation as follows:

Pool's Books—December 31

Income tax expense (E, −SE)	45,900	
Income taxes currently payable (+L)		45,900
To record share of the consolidated income tax liability.		

Sal's Books—December 31

Income tax expense (E, −SE)	17,000	
Income taxes currently payable (+L)		17,000
To record share of the consolidated income tax liability.		

After entering this tax allocation, Sal's net income will be $33,000 ($50,000 − $17,000 income tax), and Pool records income from Sal as follows:

December 31

Investment in Sal (+A)	14,700	
Income from Sal (R, +SE)		14,700

To record investment income from Sal computed as follows:

Share of Sal's net income ($33,000 × 90%)	$29,700
Less: Patent amortization	(5,000)
Less: Unrealized profit in inventory	(10,000)
Income from Sal	$14,700

We deduct the full amount of the unrealized inventory profit because the sale is downstream and no tax is assessed on unrealized profits when filing consolidated income tax returns. Exhibit 10-9 presents consolidation working papers for Pool and Subsidiary.

Relating working paper entries, presented in general journal form, are:

a	**Sales (−R, −SE)**	**40,000**	
	Cost of goods sold (−E, +SE)		**40,000**
	To eliminate intercompany sales and purchases.		
b	**Cost of goods sold (E, −SE)**	**10,000**	
	Inventory (−A)		**10,000**
	To eliminate intercompany profits from downstream sale.		
c	**Income from Sal (−R, −SE)**	**14,700**	
	Investment in Sal (+A)	**3,300**	
	Dividends (+SE)		**18,000**
	To eliminate investment income and dividends and adjust the Investment in Sal account to its beginning-of-the-period balance.		
d	**Capital stock—Sal (−SE)**	**300,000**	
	Retained earnings—Sal (−SE)	**100,000**	
	Patents (+A)	**75,000**	
	Investment in Sal (−A)		**435,000**
	Noncontrolling interest—beginning (+L)		**40,000**
	To eliminate reciprocal beginning-of-the-period investment and equity amounts, establish beginning-of-the-period patents and noncontrolling interest.		
e	**Expenses (E, −SE)**	**5,000**	
	Patents (−A)		**5,000**
	To enter current amortization of patents.		
f	**Noncontrolling interest expense (E, −SE)**	**3,300**	
	Dividends (+SE)		**2,000**
	Noncontrolling interest (+L)		**1,300**
	To enter noncontrolling interest shares of subsidiary income and dividends.		

EXHIBIT 10-9

Consolidated Tax
Return—Unrealized
Profit from
Downstream Sales

POOL CORPORATION AND SUBSIDIARY CONSOLIDATION WORKING PAPERS FOR THE YEAR ENDED DECEMBER 31, 2006 (IN THOUSANDS)

	Pool	Sal	Adjustments and Eliminations Debits	Credits	Consolidated Statements
Income Statement Sales	$900	$500	a 40		$1,360
Income from Sal	14.7		c 14.7		
Cost of goods sold	(500)	(350)	b 10	a 40	(820)
Expenses (excluding income taxes)	(250)	(100)	e 5		(355)
Income tax expense	(45.9)	(17)			(62.9)
Noncontrolling interest expense			f 3.3		(3.3)
Net income	**$118.8**	**$ 33**			**$ 118.8**
Retained Earnings Retained earnings—Pool	$352.9				$ 352.9
Retained earnings—Sal		$100	d 100		
Dividends	(80)	(20)		c 18 f 2	(80)
Net income	**118.8**	**33**			**118.8**
Retained earnings— December 31	**$391.7**	**$113**			**$ 391.7**
Balance Sheet Inventory	$183.3	$ 80		b 10	$ 253.3
Other assets	375	520			895
Investment in Sal	431.7		c 3.3	d 435	
Patents			d 75	e 5	70
	$990	$600			$1,218.3
Income tax payable	$ 45.9	$ 17			$ 62.9
Other liabilities	152.4	170			322.4
Capital stock	400	300	d 300		400
Retained earnings	**391.7**	**113**			**391.7**
	$990	$600			
Noncontrolling interest				d 40 f 1.3	41.3
					$1,218.3

CASE 2: SEPARATE TAX RETURNS WITH DOWNSTREAM SALES

Assume that the intercompany sales are downstream (from Pool to Sal) and that they file separate income tax returns. Sal has an income tax liability of $17,000 and reports net income of $33,000. Pool records income from Sal of $14,700, computed as follows:

Share of Sal's net income ($33,000 × 90%)	$29,700
Less: Patent amortization ($75,000 ÷ 15 years)	(5,000)
Less: Unrealized profit	(10,000)
Income from Sal	$14,700

Pool's income tax currently payable is 34% of its $150,000 operating income, less $5,000 patent amortization, or $49,300. Pool's income tax expense is $45,900, computed as follows:

Income tax currently payable	$49,300
Less: Increase in deferred tax asset from temporary difference ($10,000 unrealized profit × 34% tax rate)	(3,400)
Income tax expense	$45,900

Exhibit 10-10 reflects these observations in the consolidation working papers.

Income taxes currently payable that will appear in the consolidated balance sheet are $66,300 ($49,300 for Pool plus $17,000 for Sal). The difference between the consolidated income tax expense ($62,900) and income taxes currently payable ($66,300) is the $3,400 deferred income tax asset for the $10,000 unrealized profit. The $62,900 income tax expense appearing in the consolidated income statement can be computed independently as follows:

Consolidated income before income taxes and noncontrolling interest expense ($1,360,000 sales − $820,000 cost of goods sold − $355,000 expenses)	$185,000
Tax rate	34%
Income tax expense	$ 62,900

Compare Exhibits 10-9 and 10-10. Income tax expense and income from subsidiary are the same whether we file separate tax returns or consolidated tax returns. However, there is a difference in income tax currently payable and in the deferred income tax liability.

When filing a consolidated tax return, income tax expense is equal to income tax currently payable because no tax is assessed on the unrealized intercompany profit. Consolidated income tax expense is the same whether we file separate-company or consolidated income tax returns. However, with separate tax returns, Pool's income tax expense consists of $49,300 income tax currently payable, less the $3,400 deferred tax asset related to the $10,000 temporary difference.

CASE 3: CONSOLIDATED TAX RETURN WITH UPSTREAM SALES

Now assume that the intercompany sales are upstream (from Sal to Pool). If we file a consolidated return, the consolidated income tax expenses will be $62,900, the same as in the downstream example, but the allocation to Pool and Sal changes because we exclude $10,000 of Sal's $50,000 pretax income from consolidated taxable income. The allocation is:

$$\text{Pool} = \frac{\$150,000 - \$5,000}{\$185,000} \times \$62,900 = \$49,300$$

$$\text{Sal} = \frac{\$50,000 - \$10,000}{\$185,000} \times \$62,900 = \$13,600$$

(continued)

POOL CORPORATION AND SUBSIDIARY CONSOLIDATION WORKING PAPERS FOR THE YEAR ENDED DECEMBER 31, 2006 (IN THOUSANDS)

	Pool	Sal	Adjustments and Eliminations Debits	Adjustments and Eliminations Credits	Consolidated Statements
Income Statement Sales	$900	$500	a 40		$1,360
Income from Sal	14.7		c 14.7		
Cost of goods sold	(500)	(350)	b 10	a 40	(820)
Expenses (excluding income taxes)	(250)	(100)	e 5		(355)
Income tax expense	(45.9)	(17)			(62.9)
Noncontrolling interest expense			f 3.3		(3.3)
Net income	**$118.8**	**$ 33**			**$ 118.8**
Retained Earnings Retained earnings—Pool	$352.9				$ 352.9
Retained earnings—Sal		$100	d 100		
Dividends	(80)	(20)		c 18 f 2	(80)
Net income	118.8	33			118.8
Retained earnings— December 31	**$391.7**	**$113**			**$ 391.7**
Balance Sheet Inventory	$183.3	$ 80		b 10	$ 253.3
Deferred tax asset	3.4				3.4
Other assets	375	520			895
Investment in Sal	431.7		c 3.3	d 435	
Patents			d 75	e 5	70
	$993.4	$600			$1,221.7
Income tax payable	$ 49.3	$ 17			$ 66.3
Other liabilities	152.4	170			322.4
Capital stock	400	300	d 300		400
Retained earnings	391.7	113			391.7
	$993.4	$600			
Noncontrolling interest				d 40 f 1.3	41.3
					$1,221.7

We record these amounts in the separate-company books as follows:

Pool's Books—December 31

Income tax expense (E, −SE)	49,300	
Income taxes currently payable (+L)		49,300
To record share of consolidated income taxes.		

Sal's Books—December 31

Income tax expense (E, −SE)	13,600	
Income taxes currently payable (+L)		13,600
To record share of consolidated income taxes.		

Sal's net income is $36,400 ($50,000 pretax income less $13,600 income tax expense), and Pool determines income from Sal as follows:

Share of Sal's net income ($36,400 × 90%)	$32,760
Less: Patent amortization ($75,000 ÷ 15 years)	(5,000)
Less: Unrealized profit from upstream sales	
($10,000 × 90%)	(9,000)
Income from Sal	$18,760

Consolidation working papers to illustrate the effect of this upstream-sales example appear in Exhibit 10-11. We compute noncontrolling interest expense of $2,640 as 10% of Sal's realized income of $26,400 ($36,400 net income − $10,000 unrealized profit). The consolidated income tax expense of $62,900 is the same as in the downstream-sale example, but consolidated net income is $660 greater because we attribute the $10,000 unrealized gain and the related $3,400 tax allocation effect to subsidiary operations. Thus, noncontrolling interest expense is $660 less than in the downstream-sale examples, and consolidated net income is $660 more ($119,460 instead of $118,800 in Exhibits 10-9 and 10-10). The noncontrolling interest expense computation in Exhibit 10-11 eliminates 100% of the $10,000 unrealized profit because no tax is paid on unrealized profits when filing consolidated returns.

CASE 4: SEPARATE TAX RETURNS WITH UPSTREAM SALES

Assume that the intercompany sales are upstream (from Sal to Pool) and that they file separate income tax returns. Sal's income tax currently payable, as determined from its separate income tax return, is $17,000, because income taxes are assessed on Sal's $50,000 pretax income, which includes the $10,000 unrealized profit. However, Sal's income tax expense is only $13,600, computed as follows:

Income tax currently payable	$17,000
Less: Increase in deferred tax asset from	
temporary difference ($10,000 unrealized	
profit × 34% tax rate)	(3,400)
Income tax expense	$13,600

Sal's net income is $36,400, as in Case 3, and Pool records its income from Sal at $18,760, determined as follows:

Pool's share of Sal's net income ($36,400 × 90%)	$32,760
Less: Patent amortization ($75,000 ÷ 15 years)	(5,000)
Less: Unrealized profit from upstream sales	
($10,000 × 90% owned)	(9,000)
Pool's income from Sal	$18,760

Exhibit 10-12 shows working papers when separate returns are filed and unrealized inventory profit results from upstream sales.

POOL CORPORATION AND SUBSIDIARY CONSOLIDATION WORKING PAPERS FOR THE YEAR ENDED DECEMBER 31, 2006 (IN THOUSANDS)

	Pool	90% Sal	Adjustments and Eliminations Debits	Adjustments and Eliminations Credits	Consolidated Statements
Income Statement Sales	$900	$500	a 40		$1,360
Income from Sal	18.76		c 18.76		
Cost of goods sold	(500)	(350)	b 10	a 40	(820)
Expenses (excluding income taxes)	(250)	(100)	e 5		(355)
Income tax expense	(49.3)	(13.6)			(62.9)
Noncontrolling interest expense			f 2.64		(2.64)
Net income	**$119.46**	**$ 36.4**			**$ 119.46**
Retained Earnings Retained earnings—Pool	$352.9				$ 352.9
Retained earnings—Sal		$100	d 100		
Dividends	(80)	(20)		c 18 f 2	(80)
Net income	**119.46**	**36.4**			**119.46**
Retained earnings— December 31	**$392.36**	**$116.4**			**$ 392.36**
Balance Sheet Inventory	$183.3	$ 80		b 10	$ 253.3
Other assets	375	520			895
Investment in Sal	435.76			c .76 d 435	
Patents			d 75	e 5	70
	$994.06	$600			$1,218.3
Income tax payable	$ 49.3	$ 13.6			$ 62.9
Other liabilities	152.4	170			322.4
Capital stock	400	300	d 300		400
Retained earnings	**392.36**	**116.4**			**392.36**
	$994.06	$600			
Noncontrolling interest				d 40 f .64	40.64
					$1,218.3

POOL CORPORATION AND SUBSIDIARY CONSOLIDATION WORKING PAPERS FOR THE YEAR ENDED DECEMBER 31, 2006 (IN THOUSANDS)

EXHIBIT 10-12

Separate Tax Returns—Unrealized Profit from Upstream Sales

	Pool	Sal	Adjustments and Eliminations Debits	Adjustments and Eliminations Credits	Consolidated Statements
Income Statement					
Sales	$900	$500	a 40		$1,360
Income from Sal	18.76		c 18.76		
Cost of goods sold	(500)	(350)	b 10	a 40	(820)
Expenses (excluding income taxes)	(250)	(100)	e 5		(355)
Income tax expense	(49.3)	(13.6)			(62.9)
Noncontrolling interest expense			f 2.64		(2.64)
Net income	**$119.46**	**$ 36.4**			**$ 119.46**
Retained Earnings					
Retained earnings—Pool	$352.9				$ 352.9
Retained earnings—Sal		$100	d 100		
Dividends	(80)	(20)		c 18, f 2	(80)
Net income	**119.46**	**36.4**			**119.46**
Retained earnings— December 31	**$392.36**	**$116.4**			**$ 392.36**
Balance Sheet					
Inventory	$183.3	$ 80		b 10	$ 253.3
Deferred tax asset		3.4			3.4
Other assets	375	520			895
Investment in Sal	435.76			c .76, d 435	
Patents			d 75	e 5	70
	$994.06	$603.4			$1,221.7
Income tax payable	$ 49.3	$ 17			$ 66.3
Other liabilities	152.4	170			322.4
Capital stock	400	300	d 300		400
Retained earnings	**392.36**	**116.4**			**392.36**
	$994.06	$603.4			
Noncontrolling interest				d 40, f .64	40.64
					$1,221.7

In comparing Exhibits 10-11 and 10-12, note that the income tax expense and the income from the subsidiary are the same whether we file separate or consolidated tax returns. There is, however, a difference in income tax currently payable and in the deferred income tax liability. When filing separate tax returns, the consolidated income tax expense consists of the following:

	Pool	Sal	Consolidated
Income taxes currently payable	$49,300	$17,000	$66,300
Deferred income tax asset	—	(3,400)	(3,400)
Income tax expense	$49,300	$13,600	$62,900

Thus, the consolidated income statement will show income tax expense of $62,900, and the consolidated balance sheet will show a current liability for income tax currently payable of $66,300 and a current asset for the $3,400 deferred income tax asset.

BUSINESS COMBINATIONS

For income tax purposes, the term *reorganization* refers to certain corporate restructurings or combinations that are tax free under Internal Revenue code Section 368. Reorganization transactions include mergers, recapitalizations, and divisions of corporations. Failure to meet any of the required conditions specified in the code may disqualify a reorganization so that the transaction loses its tax-free status. Although the code describes seven types of transactions (Type A through Type G) as reorganizations, only three are discussed here.

- **Merger or consolidation.** A merger occurs when one corporation acquires another corporation, primarily for the acquiring company's stock (but some other consideration may be given), and the acquired corporation is dissolved. Its assets and liabilities are taken over by the acquiring corporation. A consolidation occurs when two or more companies combine to form a new corporation and the original corporations are dissolved.[8]
- **Acquiring another corporation's stock.** If a corporation exchanges any of its voting stock *(and no other consideration is given)* for stock of another corporation and it controls the second corporation immediately after the exchange, the transaction is a reorganization. Control means ownership of at least 80% of the voting stock and at least 80% of all other classes of stock.
- **Acquiring another corporation's assets.** If a corporation exchanges any of its voting stock (and generally nothing else) for substantially all of another corporation's property, the transaction is a reorganization. The assumption of liabilities does not disqualify this transaction as a tax-free reorganization.

These summaries are brief and nontechnical. The point is, the qualifications under the tax code for an exchange of shares to be a tax-free reorganization are *not identical* to the qualifications under accounting principles for the former pooling of interests business combination. Purchase business combinations may be either taxable or tax free, and structuring a transaction to meet the goals of both buyer and seller is an important part of the negotiating process for any business combination.

As you would expect, firms often structure combinations to be tax free. Here are a few recent examples. A September 3, 2001, press release issued by **Hewlett-Packard (HP)** (obtained from HP's Web site) described terms of its proposed merger with **Compaq Computer Corporation:**

> *Under terms of the agreement, unanimously approved by both Boards of Directors, Compaq shareowners will receive 0.6325 of a newly issued HP share for each share of Compaq, giving the merger a current value of approximately $25 billion. HP shareowners will own approximately 64% and Compaq shareowners 36% of the merged company. The transaction, which is expected to be tax-free to shareowners of both companies for U.S. federal income tax purposes, will be accounted for as a purchase.*

---

[8] The accounting concepts of mergers and consolidations were discussed in Chapter 1.

In its 2000 annual report, PepsiCo described its proposed merger with the **Quaker Oats Company:**

> *On December 4, 2000, we announced a merger agreement with The Quaker Oats Company (Quaker). Under the terms of this agreement, Quaker shareholders will receive 2.3 shares of PepsiCo capital stock subject to a maximum value of $105 for each Quaker share. ... Based on the closing price of our stock of $42.375 per share on December 1, 2000, the proposed tax-free transaction is valued at $97.4625 per Quaker share. ... The merger is expected to close in the first half of 2001 and is expected to be accounted for as a "pooling of interests." (p. 42)*

In a taxable business combination, we revalue the assets and liabilities of the acquired corporation to reflect the fair value acquired. The seller recognizes gain or loss equal to the fair value of the consideration received, less the tax bases of the assets or stock sold. In a tax-free reorganization, the tax bases of the assets and liabilities are carried forward with no revaluation.

The Revenue Recognition Act of 1993 allows a tax deduction for amortization of goodwill (which is no longer amortized under *FASB Statement No. 142*) and other intangible assets (called Section 197 intangible assets). This deduction is only allowed when taxes have been paid (gain or loss recognized) by the seller on the purchase transaction.[9] All Section 197 intangible assets are amortized for tax purposes over a 15-year period, regardless of their useful lives.

Purchase Business Combinations

FASB Statement No. 109 requires that firms recognize a deferred tax liability or deferred tax asset for the difference between the book values (tax bases) and the assigned values of the assets and liabilities (except goodwill, negative goodwill, and leveraged leases) acquired in a purchase business combination.[10] In other words, we record the assets and liabilities acquired at their gross fair values and record a deferred tax asset or liability for the related tax effect in a tax-free reorganization.

A difference between book value and tax value only occurs when the assets are not written up to fair value for tax purposes as they are for book purposes. When the assets are written up for tax purposes, the only differences between written-up book value and tax basis should have already been accounted for in the purchased company's separate books as a deferred tax asset or liability (due to an original difference between book and tax value at the point of purchase).

The tax-free business combination of Platt and Shad is used to illustrate the computation of a deferred tax liability for the book value/fair value differentials and for the determination of goodwill. On January 1, 2006, Platt Corporation paid $400,000 for 60% of the outstanding voting stock of Shad Corporation, when Shad's stockholders' equity consisted of $300,000 capital stock and $200,000 retained earnings. Book values were equal to fair values of Shad's assets and liabilities, except for a building and land. The building had a book value of $80,000, a fair value of $120,000, and a remaining useful life of eight years. The land had a book value of $50,000 and a fair value of $150,000. Any goodwill is not amortized. The tax rate applicable to both companies is 34%, and an 80% dividends deduction applies.

We allocate the $100,000 excess of cost over book value acquired [$400,000 cost − ($500,000 book value of net assets × 60% interest)] as follows:

	Book Value	Pretax Fair Value	Difference	Platt's 60% Interest × the Difference
Building	$80,000	$120,000	$ 40,000	$ 24,000
Land	50,000	150,000	100,000	60,000
Revaluation of assets (gross amount)				84,000
Less: Deferred tax on revaluation ($84,000 × 34%)				(28,560)
Net differential from revaluation of assets				55,440
Goodwill				44,560
Excess cost over book value acquired				$100,000

---

[9] The company's liabilities may or may not be assumed in the transaction.

[10] Under *APB Opinion No. 11,* the amounts assigned to the assets and liabilities in a purchase business combination were net-of-tax amounts.

The $24,000 assigned to the building and the $8,160 related deferred tax ($24,000 × 34%) will be written off over the building's remaining eight-year useful life at the annual amounts of $3,000 and $1,020, respectively. Thus, consolidated net income will be decreased by $1,980 each year on an after-tax basis. The $60,000 revaluation of the land and the $20,400 deferred tax on the revalued land will remain on the books until the land is sold to outside entities.

FASB Statement No. 109 elected to not assign a deferred tax liability to the goodwill account (when the goodwill is not deductible), due to the difficulty in the simultaneous calculation of the residual account, goodwill, and a deferred tax assignment to this residual account. The FASB also decided that not much incremental information would be added by this calculation.

Equity Method of Accounting for Purchase Business Combinations

During 2006, Shad has net income of $100,000 and pays dividends of $40,000. Platt makes the following entries on its separate books to account for its investment in Shad.

Investment in Shad (+A)	400,000	
Cash (−A)		400,000

To record purchase of a 60% interest in Shad Corporation.

Cash (+A)	24,000	
Investment in Shad (−A)		24,000

To record receipt of dividends from Shad ($40,000 × 60%).

Note that Platt must also provide for income taxes on its share of the $60,000 undistributed earnings of Shad ($36,000 × 20% taxable × 34% tax rate = $2,448 deferred taxes).

Investment in Shad (+A)	58,020	
Income from Shad (R, +SE)		58,020

To record income from Shad and the related amortization of deferred tax liability on the building computed as follows:

Share of Shad's income ($100,000 × 60%)	60,000
Less: Depreciation on excess allocated to building	(3,000)
Add: Amortization of deferred taxes on building	1,020
Income from Shad	$58,020

The stockholders' equity of Shad at December 31, 2006, consists of $300,000 capital stock and $260,000 retained earnings. The balance of Platt's Investment in Shad account is $434,020. An analysis of the investment account balance shows the following:

	January 1, 2006	**2006 Change**	**December 31, 2006**
Book value of investment	$300,000	$ 36,000	$336,000
Unamortized excess:			
Building	24,000	(3,000)	21,000
Land	60,000		60,000
Deferred income taxes	(28,560)	1,020	(27,540)
Goodwill	44,560		44,560
Investment balance	$400,000	$ 34,020	$434,020

Working Paper Entries

When Platt prepares consolidation working papers at December 31, 2006, the Investment in Shad account will have a balance of $434,020 ($400,000 original investment + $58,020 income from Shad − $24,000 dividends). The working paper entries in general journal form follow.

a	Income from Shad (–R, –SE)	58,020	
	Dividends (+SE)		24,000
	Investment in Shad (–A)		34,020

To eliminate income and dividends from Shad and adjust the Investment in Shad account to its beginning-of-the-period balance.

b	Capital stock—Shad (–SE)	300,000	
	Retained earnings—Shad (–SE)	200,000	
	Building (+A)	24,000	
	Land (+A)	60,000	
	Goodwill (+A)	44,560	
	Investment in Shad (–A)		400,000
	Deferred taxes on revaluation (+L)		28,560
	Noncontrolling interest—beginning (+L)		200,000

To eliminate reciprocal investment and equity balances, establish beginning noncontrolling interest, enter beginning-of-the-period cost/book value differentials, and enter deferred taxes on revaluation.

c	Depreciation expense (E, –SE)	3,000	
	Accumulated depreciation—building (–A)		3,000

To record depreciation on excess allocated to building.

d	Deferred income taxes on revaluation (–L)	1,020	
	Income tax expense (–E, +SE)		1,020

To record amortization of deferred taxes.

e	Noncontrolling interest expense (E, –SE)	40,000	
	Dividends (+SE)		16,000
	Noncontrolling interest (+L)		24,000

To enter noncontrolling interest shares of subsidiary income and dividends.

FINANCIAL STATEMENT DISCLOSURES FOR INCOME TAXES

GAAP divides deferred tax assets or liabilities into two categories, a current amount and a noncurrent amount, for balance sheet presentation. *FASB Statement No. 109* classifies deferred tax liabilities and assets as current or noncurrent based on the classification of the related asset or liability for financial reporting. If the deferred item is not related to an asset or liability for financial reporting, its classification depends on the reversal date of the temporary difference. In addition, the significant components of income tax expense or benefit are disclosed in the financial statements or notes to the financial statements.

GAAP also requires disclosures for income tax expense and benefits allocated to continuing operations, discontinued operations, extraordinary items, cumulative-effect-type items, and prior-period adjustments.

Hershey Foods Corporation's 2000 annual report provides a good example of required disclosures for income taxes. Note 9 offers a detailed description of its income tax calculations for the year. The note is reproduced, in part, in Exhibit 10-13.

EXHIBIT 10-13

Hershey Foods
Corporation Income
Tax Footnote

9. Income Taxes

The provision for income taxes was as follows:

For the years ended December 31,	2000	1999	1998
In thousands of dollars Current:			
Federal	$212,858	$256,054	$119,706
State	12,184	15,998	10,498
Foreign	3,454	3,848	3,673
Current provision for income taxes	228,496	275,900	133,877
Deferred:			
Federal	(28,108)	(23,271)	73,422
State	11,986	16,280	10,568
Foreign	(278)	(1,345)	(1,749)
Deferred income tax (benefit) provision	(16,400)	(8,336)	82,241
Total provision for income taxes	$212,096	$267,564	$216,118

Deferred taxes reflect temporary differences between tax reporting and financial statement reporting in the recognition of revenue and expense. The tax effects of the significant temporary differences which comprised the deferred tax assets and liabilities were as follows:

December 31,	2000	1999
In thousands of dollars		
Deferred tax assets:		
Post-retirement benefit obligations	$ 84,103	$ 84,305
Accrued expenses and other reserves	109,116	103,232
Accrued trade promotion reserves	33,987	34,708
Other	16,159	16,513
Total deferred tax assets	$243,365	238,758
Deferred tax liabilities:		
Depreciation	256,769	289,369
Inventory	24,025	7,304
Other	186,934	187,827
Total deferred tax liabilities	467,728	484,500
Net deferred tax liabilities	$224,363	$245,742
Included in:		
Current deferred tax assets, net	$ 76,136	$ 80,303
Non-current deferred tax liabilities, net	300,499	326,045
Net deferred tax liabilities	$224,363	$245,742

The following table reconciles the federal statutory income tax rate with the corporation's effective income tax rate:

For the years ended December 31,	2000	1999	1998
Federal statutory income tax rate	35.0%	35.0%	35.0%
Increase (reduction) resulting from:			
State income taxes, net of federal income tax benefits	3.5	2.3	3.0
Non-deductible acquisition costs	0.8	0.6	0.9
Utilization of capital loss carryforwards	—	(.9)	—
Other, net	(.5)	(.2)	(.1)
Effective income tax rate	38.8%	36.8%	38.8%

SUMMARY

When the capital structure of a subsidiary or equity investee includes outstanding preferred stock, we allocate the investee's equity and income to the preferred stockholders based on the preferred contract and then allocate to common stockholders. If the subsidiary's preferred stock is not held by the parent company, we include the preferred income and equity in noncontrolling interest. The viewpoint of the consolidated entity considers any of the subsidiary's preferred stock held by the parent as retired for consolidated statement purposes.

Consolidated and parent-company earnings per share computations are identical, and the procedures used in computing parent-company earnings per share also apply to investor accounting under the equity method. Parent-company (investor) relationships do not affect EPS computations unless the subsidiary (investee) has outstanding potentially dilutive securities. When a subsidiary has potentially dilutive securities outstanding, the computational adjustments for EPS differ according to whether the subsidiary's potentially dilutive securities are convertible into subsidiary common stock or parent-company common stock.

A consolidated entity classified as an affiliated group may elect to file consolidated tax returns. All other consolidated entities file separate income tax returns. In determining taxable income, consolidated entities that are members of an affiliated group can exclude all dividends received from group members. Affiliated groups that elect to file consolidated tax returns avoid paying taxes on unrealized profits and can offset losses of one group member against income of other group members.

Investors with equity investees and subsidiaries that are not members of an affiliated group pay income taxes currently on a portion of dividends received and provide for deferred income taxes on their share of undistributed income of their investees.

Unrealized and constructive gains and losses from intercompany transactions create temporary differences that may affect deferred tax calculations when filing separate-company tax returns.

A purchase business combination for accounting purposes may be a taxable combination or tax-free reorganization under the Internal Revenue Code.

In a purchase business combination, we allocate the cost/book value differential to the assets and liabilities acquired at gross fair values and record a deferred tax asset or deferred tax liability for the related tax effect.

QUESTIONS

1. Arom Corporation has 100,000 outstanding shares of no par common stock and 5,000 outstanding shares of $100 par, cumulative, 10% preferred stock. Arom Corporation's net income for the current year is $300,000, and its stockholders' equity at the end of the current year is as follows:

10% cumulative preferred stock, $100 par	$ 500,000
Common stock, $10 par	1,000,000
Additional paid-in capital	600,000
Retained earnings	400,000
Total stockholders' equity	$2,500,000

Flora Corporation owns 60% of the outstanding common stock of Arom, acquired at book value several years ago. Compute Flora's investment income for the current year and the balance of its Investment in Arom account at the end of the current year.

2. Refer to the information in question 1. Assume that Arom pays two years' preferred dividend requirements during the current year. Would this affect your computation of Flora's investment income for the current year? If so, recompute Flora's investment income.

3. How should preferred stock of a subsidiary be shown in a consolidated balance sheet in each case?
   a. If it is held 100% by the parent company
   b. If it is held 50% by the parent company and 50% by outside interests
   c. If it is held 100% by outside interests

4. Describe the computation of noncontrolling interest expense for an 80%-owned subsidiary with both preferred and common stock outstanding.

5. How does consolidated earnings per share differ from parent-company earnings per share?

6. Do investments in nonconsolidated subsidiaries and 20%- to 50%-owned investees affect the nature of the investor company's EPS calculations?

7. Under what conditions will the procedures used in computing a parent company's EPS be the same as those for a company without equity investments?

8. It may be necessary to compute the earnings per share for subsidiaries and equity investees before parent-company (and consolidated) earnings per share can be determined. When are the subsidiary EPS computations used in calculating parent-company earnings per share?

9. Potentially dilutive securities of a subsidiary may be converted into parent-company common stock or subsidiary common stock. Describe how these situations affect the parent company's EPS procedures.

10. In computing diluted earnings for a parent company, it may be necessary to replace the parent's equity in subsidiary realized income with the parent company's equity in the subsidiary's diluted earnings. Does this replacement calculation involve unrealized profits that are included in the parent company's income from subsidiary?

11. Are consolidated income tax returns required for all consolidated entities? Discuss.

12. Can a consolidated entity that is classified as an "affiliated group" under the IRS code elect to file separate tax returns for each affiliate?

13. What are the primary advantages of filing a consolidated tax return?

14. Some or all of the dividends received by a corporation from domestic affiliated companies may be excluded from federal income taxation. When are all of the dividends excluded?

15. Describe the nature of the tax effect of temporary differences that arise from use of the equity method of accounting.

16. Does a parent company/investor provide for income taxes on the undistributed earnings of a subsidiary by adjusting investment and investment income accounts? Explain.

17. When do unrealized and constructive gains and losses create temporary differences for a consolidated entity?

EXERCISES

E 10-1
[AICPA adapted] Preferred stock and income tax

1. [Preferred stock] Moss Corporation owns 20% of Dubro Corporation's preferred stock and 80% of its common stock. Dubro's stock outstanding on December 31, 2006, is as follows:

10% cumulative preferred stock	$100,000
Common stock	700,000

Dubro reported net income of $60,000 for the year ended December 31, 2006. What amount should Moss record as equity in earnings of Dubro for the year ended December 31, 2006?

a $42,000

b $48,000

c $48,400

d $50,000

2. [Tax] Taft Corporation uses the equity method to account for its 25% investment in Flame, Inc. During 2006, Taft received dividends of $30,000 from Flame and recorded $180,000 as its equity in the earnings of Flame. Additional information follows:

■ The dividends received from Flame are eligible for the 80% dividends-received deduction.

■ There are no other temporary differences.

■ Enacted income tax rates are 30% for 2006 and thereafter.

In its December 31, 2006, balance sheet, what amount should Taft report for deferred income tax liability?

a $9,000

b $10,800

c $45,000

d $54,000

3. [Tax] In 2006, Portal Corporation received $100,000 in dividends from Sal Corporation, its 80%-owned subsidiary. What net amount of dividend income should Portal include in its 2006 consolidated tax return?

a $100,000

b $80,000

c $70,000

d 0

4. [Tax] Potter Corporation and Sly Corporation filed consolidated tax returns. In January 2006, Potter sold land, with a basis of $60,000 and a fair value of $75,000, to Sly for $100,000. Sly sold the land in December 2007 for $125,000. In its 2007 and 2006 tax returns, what amount of gain should be reported for these transactions in the consolidated return?

	2007	2006
a	$25,000	$40,000
b	$50,000	0
c	$50,000	$25,000
d	$65,000	0

E 10-2

[Preferred stock] Subsidiary preferred stock with dividends in arrears The stockholders'
equity of Star Corporation at December 31, 2006, was as follows (in thousands):

10% cumulative preferred stock, $100 par, callable at $105, 10,000 shares issued and outstanding, with one year's dividends in arrears	$1,000
Common stock, $10 par, 100,000 shares issued and outstanding	1,000
Additional paid-in capital	2,000
Retained earnings	4,000
Total stockholders' equity	$8,000

On January 1, 2007, Portland Corporation purchased 90% of Star Corporation's common stock at $90 per share. Star's assets and liabilities were recorded at their fair values when Portland acquired its 90% interest. Any cost/book value differential is to be amortized over a 10-year period. During 2007, Star reported net income of $1,200,000 and paid dividends of $600,000.

REQUIRED: Calculate the following:

1. The cost/book value differential from Portland's investment in Star

2. Portland's income from Star for 2007

3. The balance of Portland's investment in Star at December 31, 2007

4. Total noncontrolling interest in Star on December 31, 2007

E 10-3

[Preferred stock] Goodwill and investment income - subsidiary preferred stock The
stockholders' equity of Sommerfeld Corporation at December 31, 2005, was as follows (in thousands):

12% preferred stock, cumulative, nonparticipating, $100 par, callable at $105	$ 600
Common stock, $10 par	1,000
Other paid-in capital	140
Retained earnings	760
Total stockholders' equity	$2,500

Parnell Corporation purchased 80% of Sommerfeld's common stock on January 2, 2006, for $1,536,000. During 2006, Sommerfeld reported a $100,000 net loss and paid no dividends. During 2007, Sommerfeld reported $500,000 net income and declared dividends of $344,000.

REQUIRED

1. Compute the cost/book value differential from Parnell's investment in Sommerfeld.

2. Determine Parnell's income (loss) from Sommerfeld for 2006.

3. Determine Parnell's income (loss) from Sommerfeld for 2007.

4. Compute the balance of Parnell's Investment in Sommerfeld account on December 31, 2007.

E 10-4

[Preferred stock] Investment cost and net income - subsidiary preferred stock Penzance
Corporation owns 80% of Sandalwood Corporation's common stock, having acquired the interest at book value on December 31, 2006. During 2007, Penzance's separate income is $3,000,000 and Sandalwood's net income is $500,000. Penzance and Sandalwood declare dividends in 2007 of $1,000,000 and $300,000, respectively.
The stockholders' equity of Sandalwood at December 31, 2006 and 2007, consists of the following (in thousands):

	December 31, 2006	December 31, 2007
12% cumulative preferred stock, $100 par, callable at $105 per share	$1,000	$1,000
Common stock, $10 par	2,000	2,000
Other paid-in capital	300	300
Retained earnings	700	900
Total stockholders' equity	$4,000	$4,200

REQUIRED

1. Determine the cost of Penzance's investment in Sandalwood on December 31, 2006, if Sandalwood has one year's preferred dividends in arrears on that date.

2. Calculate Penzance's net income (and consolidated net income) and noncontrolling interest expense for 2007.

3. Calculate the underlying book value of Penzance's investment in Sandalwood on December 31, 2007.

E 10-5

[Preferred stock] Journal entries - parent owns both common and preferred stock of subsidiary The stockholders' equity of Shoshone Corporation on December 31, 2006, was as follows (in thousands):

15% preferred stock, $100 par, cumulative, nonparticipating, with one year's dividends in arrears	$1,000
Common stock, $10 par	2,000
Other paid-in capital	200
Retained earnings	300
Total stockholders' equity	$3,500

Pimlico Corporation acquired 50% of Shoshone's preferred stock for $600,000 and 80% of its common stock for $2,000,000 on January 1, 2007. Shoshone reported net income of $400,000 and paid dividends of $300,000 in 2007.

REQUIRED

1. Prepare the journal entries (two entries) to record Pimlico's 50% investment in Shoshone preferred stock.

2. Calculate the excess cost/book value differential from Pimlico's 80% investment in Shoshone common.

3. Compute Pimlico's income from Shoshone—preferred for 2007.

4. Compute Pimlico's income from Shoshone—common for 2007 (assume a 10-year amortization period for the cost/book value differential).

5. Calculate the noncontrolling interest in Shoshone that will appear in the consolidated balance sheet of Pimlico Corporation and Subsidiary on December 31, 2007.

E 10-6

[Preferred stock] Cost/book value differentials for preferred and common stock Perry Corporation purchased 60% of Sketch Corporation's outstanding preferred stock for $6,500,000 and 70% of its outstanding common stock for $35,000,000 on January 1, 2007. Sketch's stockholders' equity on December 31, 2006, consisted of the following (in thousands):

10% cumulative, $100 par, preferred stock, callable at $105 (100,000 shares issued and outstanding with one year's dividends in arrears)	$10,000
Common stock, $10 par	30,000
Other paid-in capital	5,000
Retained earnings	15,000
Total stockholders' equity	$60,000

REQUIRED

1. Determine the cost/book value differentials from Perry's investments in Sketch.

2. Without bias on your part, assume that the cost/book value differential applicable to the preferred investment is a negative $400,000. Describe the accounting treatment of the preferred cost/book value differential if the preferred investment is treated as a constructive retirement for consolidation purposes.

E 10-7

[EPS] General questions

1. A parent company and its 100%-owned subsidiary have only common stock outstanding (10,000 shares for the parent and 3,000 shares for the subsidiary), and neither company has issued other potentially dilutive securities. The equation to compute consolidated EPS for the parent company and its subsidiary is:

 a *(Net income of parent + net income of subsidiary) ÷ 13,000 shares*
 b *(Net income of parent + net income of subsidiary) ÷ 10,000 shares*
 c *Net income of parent ÷ 13,000 shares*
 d *Net income of parent ÷ 10,000 shares*

2. A parent company has a 90% interest in a subsidiary that has no potentially dilutive securities outstanding. In computing consolidated EPS:

  a **Subsidiary common shares are added to parent-company common shares and common share equivalents**

  b **Subsidiary EPS and parent-company EPS amounts are combined**

  c **Subsidiary EPS computations are not needed**

  d **Subsidiary EPS computations are used in computing basic earnings**

3. In computing a parent company's diluted EPS, it may be necessary to subtract the parent's equity in subsidiary realized income and replace it with the parent's equity in subsidiary diluted earnings. The subtraction in this replacement computation is affected by:

  a **Constructive gain from purchase of parent-company bonds**

  b **Current amortization from investment in the subsidiary**

  c **Unrealized profits from downstream sales**

  d **Unrealized profits from upstream sales**

E 10-8

[EPS] Consolidated EPS with goodwill, noncontrolling interest, and warrants Palor Corporation's net income for 2009 is $316,000, including $160,000 income from Solaid Corporation, its 80%-owned subsidiary. The income from Solaid consists of $176,000 equity in income less $16,000 patent amortization. Palor has 300,000 shares of $10 par common stock outstanding, and Solaid has 50,000 shares of $10 par common stock outstanding throughout 2009. In addition, Solaid has 10,000 outstanding warrants to acquire 10,000 shares of Solaid common stock at $10 per share. The average market price of Solaid's common stock was $20 per share during 2009.

1. For purposes of calculating Palor Corporation's (and consolidated) diluted earnings per share, Solaid's diluted earnings are:

  a *$220,000*

  b *$200,000*

  c *$176,000*

  d *$160,000*

2. For purposes of calculating Palor Corporation's (and consolidated) diluted earnings per share, Solaid's outstanding common shares and common share equivalents are:

  a *60,000 shares*

  b *56,000 shares*

  c *55,000 shares*

  d *50,000 shares*

3. For purposes of calculating Palor Corporation's (and consolidated) earnings per share, assume that Solaid's diluted EPS is $4 per share. Palor Corporation's (and consolidated) diluted earnings will be:

  a *$316,000*

  b *$300,000*

  c *$156,000*

  d *$140,000*

4. If Solaid's diluted earnings for 2009 are $4 per share, Palor Corporation's (and consolidated) diluted earnings per share will be:

  a *$1.64*

  b *$1.59*

  c *$1.04*

  d *$1.00*

E 10-9

[EPS] Consolidated basic and diluted EPS The following information is available regarding Putman Corporation and its 80%-owned subsidiary, Sheridan Corporation, at and for the year ended December 31, 2006:

	Putman	Sheridan
Outstanding common stock	8,000 shares	5,000 shares
Warrants to purchase 1,000 shares of Sheridan common stock at $9 per share (average market price is $15)		1,000 warrants
Net income	$20,000	$18,000
Income from Sheridan ($14,400 − $2,400 amortization of excess cost over book value acquired)	$12,000	

REQUIRED: Determine consolidated earnings per share (both basic and diluted).

E 10-10

[EPS] Consolidated EPS with unrealized profit from upstream sale
The income statements of Prince Corporation and its 80%-owned subsidiary, Stanley Corporation, for 2006 are as follows:

	Prince	Stanley
Sales	$1,270,000	$ 740,000
Income from Stanley (see note)	13,920	—
Cost of sales	(700,000)	(470,000)
Expenses	(462,000)	(230,000)
Income before taxes	121,920	40,000
Provision for income taxes	(41,453)	(13,600)
Net income	$ 80,467	$ 26,400

Note: Income from Stanley is computed as [($26,400 reported income × 80%) – $2,000 patent amortization – $5,200 unrealized profit in Stanley's inventory.

Prince had 10,000 shares of common stock and 1,200 shares of $100 par, 10% cumulative preferred stock outstanding throughout 2006. Stanley had 20,000 shares of common stock and warrants to purchase 5,000 shares of Stanley common stock at $24 outstanding throughout 2006. The average market price of Stanley common stock was $30 per share.

REQUIRED: Compute Prince's (and consolidated) basic and diluted EPS.

E 10-11

[EPS] Subsidiary EPS and consolidated EPS with goodwill and warrants
Poway Corporation owns an 80% interest in Scony Corporation. Poway does not have common stock equivalents or other potentially dilutive securities outstanding, so it calculated its EPS for 2007 as follows:

$$\frac{\$1,000 \text{ separate incoming} + \$480,000 \text{ income from Scony}}{1,000,000 \text{ outstanding common shares of Poway}} = \$1.48$$

An examination of Poway's income from Scony shows that it is determined correctly as 80% of Scony's $630,000 net income less $24,000 patent amortization. Poway's EPS computation is in error, however, because it fails to consider outstanding warrants of Scony that permit their holders to acquire 10,000 shares of Scony common stock at $24 per share and increase Scony's outstanding common stock to 60,000 shares. The average price of Scony common stock during 2007 was $40.

REQUIRED

1. Compute Scony Corporation's diluted EPS for use in the determination of consolidated EPS.

2. Compute consolidated EPS for 2007 (both basic and diluted).

E 10-12

[Tax] General questions

1. Income taxes are currently due on intercompany profits when:
   a *Profits originate from upstream sales*
   b *Separate-company tax returns are filed*
   c *Consolidated tax returns are filed*
   d *Affiliates are accounted for as consolidated subsidiaries*

2. The right of a consolidated entity to file a consolidated income tax return is contingent upon:
   a *Ownership by a common parent of all the voting stock of group members*
   b *Ownership by a common parent of 90% of the voting stock of group members*
   c *Classification as an affiliated group*
   d *Direct or indirect ownership of a majority of the outstanding stock of all group members*

3. When affiliates are classified as an affiliated group for tax purposes, the group:
   a *Excludes unrealized profits from intercompany transactions from taxable income*
   b *Must file a consolidated income tax return*
   c *May file separate income tax returns*
   d *Pays lower income taxes*

4. Deferred income taxes are provided for unrealized profits from intercompany transactions when:

  a A consolidated tax return is filed

  b Separate-company tax returns are filed

  c The unrealized profits are from upstream sales

  d The consolidated entity is an affiliated group

E 10-13

[Tax] Asset allocation in business combination, tax effect from equity investees

1. When Petty Corporation acquired its 100% interest in Simon Corporation in a tax-free reorganization, Simon's equipment had a fair value of $6,000,000 and a book value and tax basis of $4,000,000. If Petty's effective tax rate is 34%, how much of the purchase price should be allocated to equipment and to deferred income taxes?

  a $4,000,000 and 0, respectively

  b $5,320,000 and $680,000, respectively

  c $6,600,000 and $680,000, respectively

  d $6,000,000 and $2,040,000, respectively

2. Carl Corporation, whose effective income tax rate is 34%, received $200,000 dividends from its 30%-owned domestic equity investee during the current year and recorded $500,000 equity in the investee's income. Carl's income tax expense for the year should include taxes on the investment of:

  a $13,600

  b $20,400

  c $34,000

  d $68,000

3. During 2006, Palmer Corporation reported $60,000 investment income from Springer Corporation, its 30%-owned investee, and it received $30,000 dividends from Springer. Palmer's effective income tax rate is 34%, and it is entitled to an 80% dividends-received deduction on dividends received from Springer. On the basis of this information, Palmer should:

  a Report investment income from Springer of $57,960

  b Increase its investment in Springer for 2006 in the amount of $27,960

  c Credit its deferred income taxes in the net amount of $2,040 for 2006

  d Debit its deferred income taxes in the net amount of $2,040 for 2006

4. Polines Corporation owns 35% of the voting stock of Sissy Corporation, a domestic corporation. During 2006, Sissy reports net income of $100,000 and pays dividends of $50,000. Poline's effective income tax rate is 34%. What amounts should Polines record as income taxes currently payable and as deferred income taxes from its investment in Sissy?

  a $17,000 and 0, respectively

  b $5,950 and $5,950, respectively

  c $3,400 and $3,400, respectively

  d $1,190 and $1,190, respectively

5. Pint Corporation and its 100%-owned domestic subsidiary, Star Corporation, are classified as an affiliated group for tax purposes. During the current year, Star pays $80,000 in cash dividends. Assuming a 34% income tax rate, how much income tax expense on this dividend should be reported in the consolidated income statement of Pint Corporation and Subsidiary?

  a $0

  b $27,200

  c $5,440

  d $2,720

E 10-14

[Tax] Compare separate and consolidated tax filings

The pretax accounting incomes of Pruit Corporation and its 100%-owned subsidiary, Solo Company, for 2006 are as follows (in thousands):

	Pruit	Solo
Sales	$1,000	$500
Gain on land	200	—
Total revenue	1,200	500
Cost of sales	500	300
Gross profit	700	200
Operating expenses	400	100
Pretax accounting income	$ 300	$100

The only intercompany transaction during 2006 was a gain on land sold to Solo. Assume a 34% flat income tax rate.

REQUIRED

1. What amount should be shown on the consolidated income statement as income tax expense if separate-company tax returns are filed?

2. Compute the consolidated income tax expense if a consolidated tax return is filed.

3. What will be the income taxes currently payable if separate income tax returns are filed? If a consolidated return is filed?

E 10-15

[Tax] Consolidated income statement (downstream gain on sale of equipment) Paxton Corporation and its 70%-owned subsidiary, Sutter Corporation, have pretax operating incomes for 2008 as follows (in thousands):

	Paxton	Sutter
Sales	$8,000	$4,000
Gain on equipment	200	—
Cost of sales	(5,000)	(2,000)
Paxton Sutter		
Other expenses	(1,800)	(1,200)
Pretax income	$1,400	$ 800

Paxton received $280,000 dividends from Sutter during 2008. A previously unrecorded patent from Paxton's investment in Sutter is being amortized at a rate of $50,000 per year (the same time horizon is used for both book and tax purposes).

On January 1, 2008, Paxton sold equipment to Sutter at a $200,000 gain. Sutter is depreciating the equipment at a rate of 20% per year. A flat 34% tax rate is applicable to both companies.

REQUIRED: Prepare a consolidated income statement for Paxton Corporation and Subsidiary for 2008. (Assume no deferred tax balance on January 1, 2008.)

E 10-16

[Tax] Journal entries for unrealized profit with separate and consolidated tax returns
Sullivan Corporation is a 100%-owned subsidiary of Peddicord Corporation. During the current year, Peddicord sold merchandise that cost $50,000 to Sullivan for $100,000. A 34% income tax rate is applicable, and 80% of the merchandise remains unsold by Sullivan at year-end.

REQUIRED

1. Prepare comparative one-line consolidation entries relating to the unrealized profit when separate and consolidated income tax returns are filed.

2. Prepare comparative consolidation working paper entries in general journal form relating to the intercompany sales transaction and the related income tax effect when separate and consolidated income tax returns are filed.

E 10-17

[Tax] Journal entries for unrealized profit from upstream sale and separate tax returns
Sweeney Corporation, an 80%-owned subsidiary of Pioneer Corporation, sold equipment with a book value of $150,000 to Pioneer for $250,000 at December 31, 2006. Separate income tax returns are filed, and a 34% income tax rate is applicable to both Pioneer and Sweeney.

REQUIRED

1. Prepare a one-line consolidation entry for Pioneer to eliminate the effect of the intercompany transaction.

2. Prepare working paper entries in general journal form to eliminate the unrealized profit.

3. Assume that the reported net income of Sweeney is $800,000 and that the sale of equipment is the only intercompany transaction between Pioneer and Sweeney. What is the noncontrolling interest's share of total consolidated income?

P 10-1

[Preferred stock] Investment in common stock (subsidiary preferred stock)

Parrella Corporation paid $3,100,000 for 180,000 shares of Stanley Corporation's outstanding voting common stock on January 1, 2006, when the stockholders' equity of Stanley consisted of (in thousands):

10% cumulative, preferred stock, $100 par. Liquidation preference is $105 per share, and 10,000 shares are issued and outstanding with one year's dividends in arrears	$1,000
Common stock, $10 par, 200,000 shares issued and outstanding	2,000
Other paid-in capital	500
Retained earnings	650
Total stockholders' equity	$4,150

During 2006, Stanley reported net income of $500,000 and declared dividends of $400,000. Any cost/book value differential is due to an undervalued building to be depreciated over a 40-year period.

REQUIRED: Calculate the following:

1. The undervaluation of the building from Parrella's investment in Stanley
2. Parrella's income from Stanley for 2006
3. Noncontrolling interest expense for 2006
4. Noncontrolling interest in Stanley at December 31, 2006
5. Parrella's Investment in Stanley account balance at December 31, 2006

P 10-2

[Preferred stock] Consolidation entries - investments in preferred and common stock - midyear purchases
Pulsen Corporation acquired 80% of Starky Corporation's preferred stock for $175,000 and 90% of Starky's common stock for $650,000 on July 1, 2007. Starky's stockholders' equity on December 31, 2007, was as follows (in thousands):

Stockholders' Equity	
9% preferred stock, cumulative, nonparticipating, $100 par, call price $105	$200
Common stock, $10 par	500
Paid-in capital in excess of par	40
Retained earnings	160
Total stockholders' equity	$900

Starky Corporation had net income of $24,000 in 2006 and $46,000 in 2007, but it declared no dividends in either year. Assume that preferred dividends accrue ratably throughout each year and that Starky's net assets were fairly valued on July 1, 2007.

REQUIRED

1. Determine the account balances of Pulsen Corporation's investments in Starky's preferred and common stocks at December 31, 2007, on the basis of a one-line consolidation.
2. Prepare working paper entries to consolidate the balance sheets of Pulsen and Starky at December 31, 2007.

P 10-3

[Preferred stock] Consolidation working papers (subsidiary preferred stock, equity method, midyear purchase)

Financial statements for Pat and Sal Corporations for 2006 are summarized as follows (in thousands):

	Pat	Sal
Combined Income and Retained Earnings Statements for the Year Ended December 31, 2006		
Sales	$1,233	$700
Income from Sal	68	—
Cost of sales	(610)	(400)
Other expenses	(390)	(210)
Net income	301	90
Add: Retained earnings January 1	501	200
Less: Dividends	(200)	(50)
Retained earnings December 31	$ 602	$240
Balance Sheet at December 31, 2006		
Cash	$ 181	$ 50
Other current assets	200	300
Plant assets—net	900	600
Investment in Sal	721	—
Total assets	$2,002	$950
Current liabilities	$ 200	$ 60
$10 preferred stock	—	100
Common stock	1,200	500
Other paid-in capital	—	50
Retained earnings	602	240
Total equities	$2,002	$950

Pat owns 90,000 shares of Sal's outstanding voting common stock at December 31, 2006. These shares were acquired in two lots as follows:

	Date	Shares	Purchase Price
Lot 1	January 1, 2005	70,000	$500,000
Lot 2	April 1, 2006	20,000	152,000

The stockholders' equity of Sal at year-end 2004, 2005, and 2006 was as follows (in thousands):

	December 31,		
	2004	2005	2006
$10 preferred stock, $100 par, cumulative with no dividends in arrears	$100	$100	$100
Common stock, $5 par	500	500	500
Other paid-in capital	50	50	50
Retained earnings	150	200	240
Total stockholders' equity	$800	$850	$890

Sal's net income for 2006 is $90,000, earned proportionately throughout the year, and its quarterly dividends of $12,500 are declared on March 15, June 15, September 15, and December 15. There are no intercompany receivables or payables at December 31, 2006, and there have been no intercompany transactions other than dividends.

REQUIRED: Prepare consolidation working papers for Pat Corporation and Subsidiary for 2006.

P 10-4

[Preferred stock] Consolidation working papers (subsidiary preferred stock, downstream inventory sales, upstream sale of land, subsidiary bonds)

Pari Corporation acquired an 80% interest in Sak Corporation common stock for $240,000 on January 1, 2005, when Sak's stockholders' equity consisted of $200,000 common stock, $100,000 preferred stock, and $25,000 retained earnings. The excess was allocated to goodwill.

Intercompany sales of inventory items from Pari to Sak were $50,000 in 2005 and $60,000 in 2006. The cost of these items to Pari was 60% of the selling price to Sak, and Sak inventoried

$30,000 of the intercompany sales items at December 31, 2005, and $40,000 at December 31, 2006. Intercompany receivables and payables from these sales were $10,000 at December 31, 2005, and $5,000 at December 31, 2006.

Sak sold land that cost $10,000 to Pari for $20,000 during 2005. During 2006, Pari resold the land outside the consolidated entity for $30,000.

On July 1, 2006, Pari purchased all of Sak's bonds payable in the open market for $91,000. These bonds were issued at par, have interest payment dates of June 30 and December 31, and mature on June 30, 2009.

Sak declared and paid dividends of $10,000 on its cumulative preferred stock and $10,000 on its common stock in each of the years 2005 and 2006.

Financial statements for Pari and Sak Corporations at and for the year ended December 31, 2006, are summarized as follows (in thousands):

	Pari	Sak
Combined Income and Retained Earnings Statement for the Year Ended December 31, 2006		
Sales	$ 900	$ 300
Gain on land	10	—
Interest income	6.5	—
Income from Sak	50	—
Cost of sales	(600)	(140)
Operating expenses	(208.5)	(90)
Interest expense	—	(10)
Net income	158	60
Add: Beginning retained earnings	132	50
Deduct: Dividends	(100)	(20)
Retained earnings December 31	$ 190	$ 90
Balance Sheet at December 31, 2006		
Cash	$ 5.5	$ 15
Accounts receivable	26	20
Inventories	80	60
Other current assets	100	5
Land	160	30
Plant and equipment—net	268	420
Investment in Sak—bonds	92.5	—
Investment in Sak—stock	282	—
Total assets	$1,014	$ 550
Accounts payable	$ 24	$ 15
10% bonds payable	—	100
Other liabilities	100	45
10% preferred stock	—	100
Common stock	700	200
Retained earnings	190	90
Total equities	$1,014	$ 550

REQUIRED:
Prepare consolidation working papers for Pari Corporation and Subsidiary for the year ended December 31, 2006.

P 10-5

[EPS] Computing EPS with convertible debentures
Palace Corporation has $108,000 income from its own operations for 2006, and $42,000 income from Skinner Corporation, its 70%-owned subsidiary. Skinner's net income of $60,000 consists of $66,000 operating income less $6,000 net-of-tax interest on its outstanding 10% convertible debenture bonds. Throughout 2006, Palace has 100,000 shares of common stock outstanding, and Skinner has 50,000 outstanding common shares.

REQUIRED

1. Compute Palace's diluted earnings per share for 2006, assuming that Skinner's convertible bonds are convertible into 10,000 shares of Skinner's common stock.

2. Compute Palace's diluted earnings per share for 2006, assuming that Skinner's convertible bonds are convertible into 10,000 shares of Palace's common stock.

P 10-6

[EPS] Compute basic and diluted EPS (options; preferred stock) Pensacola

Corporation owns an 80% interest in Sheridan Company. Throughout 2008, Pensacola had 20,000 shares of common stock outstanding. Sheridan had the following securities outstanding:

- 10,000 shares of common stock
- Options to purchase 2,000 shares of Sheridan common at $15 per share
- 1,000 shares of 10%, $100 par, convertible, preferred stock that are convertible into 3,000 shares of Sheridan common stock

Income data for the affiliated companies for 2008 are as follows:

	Pensacola	Sheridan
Separate incomes	$120,000	$55,000
Income from Sheridan [($45,000 income to common × 80%) − $6,000 patent amortization]	30,000	
	$150,000	$ 55,000

REQUIRED: Compute basic and diluted earnings per share for Pensacola Corporation and Subsidiary for 2008, assuming average market prices for Sheridan common stock of $30 per share.

P 10-7

[EPS] Convertible preferred stock and amortization of excess Protein Corporation

owns 80% of Starch Corporation's outstanding common stock. The 80% interest was acquired in 2006 at $40,000 in excess of book value due to undervalued equipment with an eight-year remaining useful life. Outstanding securities of the two companies throughout 2007 and at December 31, 2007, are:

	Protein	Starch
Common stock, $5 par	20,000 shares	—
Common stock, $10 par		6,000 shares
14% cumulative, convertible, preferred stock, $100 par	—	1,000 shares

Starch Corporation's net income is $50,000 for 2007, and Protein's net income consists of $70,000 separate income and $23,800 income from Starch.

REQUIRED

1. Compute consolidated basic and diluted earnings per share, assuming that the preferred stock is convertible into 4,000 shares of Starch Corporation's common stock.

2. Compute consolidated basic and diluted earnings per share, assuming that the preferred stock is convertible into 5,000 shares of Protein's common stock.

P 10-8

[EPS] Compute consolidated EPS; subsidiary diluted Premble Company owns 40,000

of 50,000 outstanding shares of Smithfield Company, and during 2006, it recognizes income from Smithfield as follows:

Share of Smithfield's net income ($500,000 × 80%)	$400,000
Patent amortization	(50,000)
Unrealized profit—downstream sales	(40,000)
Unrealized profit—upstream sales ($60,000 × 80%)	(48,000)
Income from Smithfield	$ 262,000

Premble's net income (and consolidated net income) for 2006 is $1,262,000, consisting of separate income from Premble of $1,000,000 and $262,000 income from Smithfield. Premble has 100,000 shares of common stock outstanding, but it does not have common stock equivalents or other potentially dilutive securities.

Smithfield has $100,000 par of 10% convertible bonds outstanding that are convertible into 10,000 shares of Smithfield common stock. The net-of-tax interest on the bonds is $6,400, and Smithfield's diluted earnings per share for purposes of computing consolidated earnings per share are determined as follows:

Net income	$500,000
Add: Net-of-tax interest on convertible bonds	6,400
Less: Unrealized profit on upstream sales	(60,000)
a Diluted earnings	$446,400
Common shares outstanding	50,000
Shares issuable upon conversion of bonds	10,000
b Common shares and equivalents	60,000
Diluted earnings per share (a ÷ b)	$ 7.44

REQUIRED: Compute Premble Company's and consolidated diluted earnings per share for 2006.

P 10-9

[EPS] Computations (subsidiary preferred stock and warrants) Pike Corporation's

net income for 2006 consists of the following:

Separate income		$320,000
Income from Sim Corporation:		
80% of Sim's income to common	$160,000	
Less: Patent amortization	(4,000)	
Less: Unrealized profits on equipment sold to Sim	(10,000)	
Less: 80% of unrealized profit on land purchased from Sim	(16,000)	130,000
Net income for 2006		$450,000

ADDITIONAL INFORMATION

1. Pike has 100,000 shares of common stock, and Sim has 50,000 shares of common and 10,000 shares of $10 cumulative, convertible, preferred stock outstanding throughout 2006. The preferred stock is convertible into 30,000 shares of Sim stock.

2. Sim has warrants outstanding that permit their holders to purchase 10,000 shares of Sim Corporation common stock at $15 per share (average market price $20).

3. Sim's reported net income for 2006 is $300,000, allocated $100,000 to preferred stockholders and $200,000 to common stockholders.

4. Pike owned 40,000 shares of Sim common stock throughout 2006.

REQUIRED: Compute Pike Corporation's (and consolidated) basic and diluted EPS.

P 10-10

[Tax] Comparative income statements (consolidated and separate tax returns)

Pactor Corporation and its 100%-owned subsidiary, Shram Corporation, are members of an affiliated group with pretax accounting incomes as follows (in thousands):

	Pactor	Shram
Sales	$1,200	$700
Gain on sale of land	50	—
Cost of sales	(600)	(300)
Operating expenses	(350)	(250)
Pretax accounting income	$ 300	$150

The gain reported by Pactor relates to land sold to Shram during the current year. A flat 34% income tax rate is applicable.

REQUIRED: Prepare income statements for Pactor Corporation assuming (a) that separate income tax returns are filed and (b) that a consolidated income tax return is filed. (*Note:* Pactor applies the equity method as a one-line consolidation.)

P 10-11

[Tax] Computations and income statement (upstream sales)

Panama Corporation paid $590,000 cash for a 70% interest in Silky Corporation's outstanding common stock on January 2, 2006, when the equity of Silky consisted of $500,000 common stock and $300,000 retained earnings. The excess cost over book value acquired is due to an undervalued building with a 15-year depreciation period.

In December 2006, Silky sold inventory items to Panama at a gross profit of $50,000 (selling price $120,000 and cost $70,000), and all these items were included in Panama's inventory at December 31, 2006.

Silky paid dividends of $50,000 in 2006, and an 80% dividends-received deduction is applicable. A flat 34% income tax rate is applicable to both companies.

Separate pretax incomes of Panama and Silky for 2006 are as follows:

	Panama	Silky
Sales	$4,000,000	$1,000,000
Cost of sales	(2,000,000)	(550,000)
Operating expenses	(1,500,000)	(250,000)
Pretax income	$ 500,000	$ 200,000

REQUIRED:

1. Determine income tax currently payable and income tax expense for Panama and Silky for 2006.

2. Calculate Panama's income from Silky for 2006.

3. Prepare a consolidated income statement for Panama and Silky for 2006.

P 10-12

[Tax] Consolidated income statement (downstream sales)

Taxable incomes for Pulaski Corporation and Stewart Corporation, its 70%-owned subsidiary, for 2006 are as follows (in thousands):

	Pulaski	Stewart
Sales	$500	$300
Dividends received from Stewart	28	—
Total revenue	528	300
Cost of sales	250	120
Operating expenses	78	80
Total deductions	328	200
Taxable income	$200	$100

ADDITIONAL INFORMATION

1. Pulaski acquired its interest in Stewart at book value on December 31, 2005.

2. Stewart paid dividends of $40,000 in 2006.

3. Pulaski sold $90,000 in merchandise to Stewart during 2006, and there was $10,000 in unrealized profit from the sales at year end.

4. A flat 34% income tax rate is applicable.

5. Pulaski is eligible for the 80% dividends-received deduction.

REQUIRED Prepare consolidation income statement working papers for Pulaski Corporation and Subsidiary for 2006.

P 10-13

[Tax] Reconstruct working paper (separate and consolidated income statements) Pen Corporation acquired a 90% interest in Soo Corporation in a taxable transaction on January 1, 2006, for $900,000, when Soo had $500,000 capital stock and $400,000 retained earnings. The $90,000 excess cost over book value is due to a patent with a 15-year remaining life. Pen and Soo are an affiliated group for tax purposes.

During 2006, Pen sold land to Soo at a $20,000 profit. Soo still holds the land. Soo paid dividends of $50,000. A flat 34% tax rate applies to Pen and Soo. Income statements for Pen and Soo Corporations, and a consolidated income statement for Pen Corporation and Subsidiary, are summarized as follows:

	Pen	Soo	Consolidated
Sales	$800,000	$200,000	$1,000,000
Gain on sale of land	20,000	—	—
Income from Soo	36,430	—	—
Cost of sales	(400,000)	(75,000)	(475,000)
Other expenses	(150,000)	(30,000)	(180,000)
Income tax expense	(85,000)	(32,300)	(117,300)
Noncontrolling interest expense	—	—	(6,270)
Net income	$221,430	$ 62,700	$ 221,430

REQUIRED: Reconstruct all the working paper entries needed to consolidate the financial statements of Pen Corporation and Subsidiary for 2006.

P 10-14

[Tax] Allocate cost/book value differentials in a taxable purchase combination

Parson Corporation acquired all the stock of Studio Corporation on January 1, 2006, for $280,000 cash, when the book values and fair values of Studio's assets and liabilities were as follows (in thousands):

	Book Values (Tax Bases)	Fair Values
Current assets	$100	$100
Land	20	60
Buildings—net	80	110
Equipment—net	60	70
Assets	$260	$340
Liabilities	$ 90	$ 90
Capital stock	150	
Retained earnings	20	
Equities	$260	

Studio's buildings have a remaining life of 10 years, and the equipment has a useful life of 2 years from the date of the business combination. Any goodwill is not amortized. During 2006, Studio had income of $50,000 and paid dividends of $20,000. Parson and Studio are subject to a 35% tax rate.

REQUIRED

1. Prepare a schedule to allocate the excess cost over book value to Studio's assets, liabilities, deferred taxes, and goodwill at January 1, 2006, assuming the purchase was a taxable transaction.

2. Prepare a schedule to allocate the excess cost over book value to Studio's assets, liabilities, deferred taxes, and goodwill at January 1, 2006, assuming the purchase was a tax-free reorganization.

3. Compute Parson's income from Studio for 2006 under both options.

P 10-15

[Tax] Consolidated income statement (separate income tax returns with inter-company sale of equipment) The pretax operating incomes of Pommer Corporation and Sooner Corporation, its 70%-owned subsidiary, for 2008 are as follows (in thousands):

	Pommer	Sooner
Sales	$8,000	$4,000
Gain on equipment	500	—
Cost of sales	(5,000)	(2,000)
Other expenses	(2,100)	(1,200)
Pretax income (excluding Pommer's income from Sooner)	$1,400	$ 800

ADDITIONAL INFORMATION

1. Pommer received $280,000 dividends from Sooner during 2008.
2. Goodwill from Pommer's investment in Sooner is not amortized.
3. Pommer sold equipment to Sooner at a gain of $500,000 on January 1, 2008. Sooner is depreciating the equipment at a rate of 20% per year.
4. A flat 34% tax rate is applicable.
5. Pommer provides for income taxes on undistributed income from Sooner.

REQUIRED

1. Determine the separate income tax expenses for Pommer and Sooner.
2. Determine Pommer's income from Sooner on an equity basis.
3. Prepare a consolidated income statement for Pommer Corporation and Subsidiary for the year ended December 31, 2008.

P 10-16

[Tax] Computations (separate tax returns with goodwill, downstream inventory sales, and upstream land sale) On January 3, 2007, Phoenix Corporation purchased a 90% interest in Selica Corporation at a price $120,000 in excess of book value and fair value. The excess is goodwill. During 2007, Phoenix sold inventory items to Selica for $100,000, and $15,000 in profit from the sale remained unrealized at year-end. Selica sold land to Phoenix during the year at a gain of $30,000.

ADDITIONAL INFORMATION

1. The companies are an affiliated group for tax purposes.
2. Selica declared and paid dividends of $100,000 in 2007.
3. Phoenix and Selica file separate income tax returns, and a 34% tax rate is applicable to both companies.
4. Phoenix uses a correct equity method in accounting for its investment in Selica.
5. Pretax accounting incomes, excluding Phoenix's income from Selica, are as follows (in thousands):

	Phoenix	Selica
Sales	$3,815	$2,000
Gain on land	—	30
Cost of sales	(2,200)	(1,200)
Other expenses	(1,000)	(400)
Pretax accounting income	$ 615	$ 430

REQUIRED: Calculate the following:

1. Selica's net income
2. Phoenix's income from Selica
3. Phoenix's net income

INTERNET ASSIGNMENT

Obtain a copy of the 2003 annual report of ***General Motors Corporation*** (GM) from the company's Web site. Prepare a brief summary of information you find related to the major topics covered in this chapter.

    a. Is there any disclosure of preferred stock or subsidiary preferred stock transactions?

    b. What amounts does GM report for earnings per share? Summarize GM's earnings per share calculations.

    c. Summarize GM's reconciliation of its effective tax rate with the federal statutory rate for 2003 only.

SELECTED READINGS

Accounting Principles Board Opinion No. 18. "The Equity Method of Accounting for Investments in Common Stock." New York: American Institute of Certified Public Accountants, 1971.

ALLISON, TERRY E., and PAULA THOMAS. "Uncharted Territory: Subsidiary Financial Reporting." *Journal of Accountancy* (October 1989), pp. 76–84.

COUGHLAN, JOHN W. "ESOs and EPS." *Accounting Horizons* (March 1997), pp. 25–38.

DILLEY, STEVEN C., and James C. Young. "A Pragmatic Approach to Amortization of Intangibles." *The CPA Journal* (December 1994), pp. 46–55.

ENGLEBRECHT, TED D., GOVIND IYER, and STEVEN C. COLBURN. "Type F Reorganizations and the Impact of the *Jobco Manufacturing Company* Decision." *The CPA Journal* (February 1994), pp. 28–32.

Financial Accounting Standards Board, EITF Issue No. 93–7. *Uncertainties Related to Income Taxes in a Purchase Business Combination.* Norwalk, CT: Financial Accounting Standards Board, 1993.

FULLER, DAVID N. "Amortizing Intangibles—A Break-Even Analysis." *Journal of Accountancy* (June 1994), pp. 31–34.

GREGORY, GEORGE J., THOMAS R. PETREE, and RANDALL J. VITRAY. "*FASB 109:* Planning for Implementation and Beyond." *Journal of Accountancy* (December 1992), pp. 44–50.

MANDEL, GARY B. "The Ability to Reconsolidate After Disaffiliation." *The CPA Journal* (January 1993), pp. 61–62.

Statement of Financial Accounting Standards No. 109. "Accounting for Income Taxes." Norwalk, CT: Financial Accounting Standards Board, 1992.

Statement of Financial Accounting Standards No. 128. "Earnings per Share." Norwalk, CT: Financial Accounting Standards Board, 1997.

Statement of Financial Accounting Standards No. 141. "Business Combinations." Stamford, CT: Financial Accounting Standards Board, 2001.

Statement of Financial Accounting Standards No. 142. "Goodwill and Other Intangible Assets." Stamford, CT: Financial Accounting Standards Board, 2001.

WILLENS, ROBERT. "Amortization of Intangibles: Is a Mergers and Acquisitions Boom Imminent?" *The CPA Journal* (November 1993), pp. 46–47 and 91–94.

11 CHAPTER

CONSOLIDATION THEORIES, PUSH-DOWN ACCOUNTING, AND CORPORATE JOINT VENTURES

Previous chapters of this book have described practices used in the preparation of consolidated financial statements and have explained the rationale for those practices. The concepts and procedures discussed in earlier chapters reflect the **contemporary theory** of consolidated statements. Contemporary theory has evolved from accounting practice, and it does *not* reflect an inter-consistent approach to the preparation of consolidated financial statements. Instead, contemporary theory reflects parts of both parent-company theory (proprietary theory) and entity theory.[1]

Parent-company theory assumes that consolidated financial statements are an extension of parent-company statements and should be prepared from the viewpoint of parent-company stockholders. Under parent-company theory, we prepare consolidated statements for the benefit of the stockholders of the parent company, and we do not expect that noncontrolling stockholders can benefit significantly from the statements. Consolidated net income under parent-company theory is a measurement of income to the parent-company stockholders.

Certain problems and inconsistencies in accounting procedures under parent-company theory arise in the case of less-than-100%-owned subsidiaries. For example, the noncontrolling interest is a liability from the viewpoint of parent-company stockholders, and published statements frequently report the noncontrolling interest in the liability section of the consolidated balance sheet. Similarly, noncontrolling interest expense is an expense from the viewpoint of majority stockholders. However, shareholder interests, whether majority or noncontrolling, are not liabilities under any of the accepted concepts of a liability, and income to shareholders does not meet the requirements for expense recognition.[2] The problem lies in the majority shareholder viewpoint.

Entity theory represents an alternative view of consolidation. It was developed by Professor Maurice Moonitz and published by the American Accounting Association in 1944 under the title *The Entity Theory of Consolidated Statements*. The focal point of entity theory is that the consolidated statements reflect the viewpoint of the total business entity, under which all resources controlled by the entity are valued consistently. Under entity theory, the income of noncontrolling interests is a distribution of the total income of the consolidated entity, and the interests of noncontrolling stockholders are a part of consolidated stockholders' equity.

LEARNING OBJECTIVES

1 Compare and contrast the elements of consolidation approaches under contemporary theory, parent-company theory, and entity theory.

2 Adjust subsidiary assets and liabilities to fair values using push-down accounting.

3 Account for corporate and unincorporated joint ventures.

4 Identify variable interest entities.

5 Consolidate a variable interest entity.

6 Electronic supplement: Prepare consolidated financial statements under a current cost accounting system.

---

[1] Parent-company theory is sometimes referred to as the *conventional theory* [for example, see Eldon S. Hendriksen, *Accounting Theory*, 4th ed. (Homewood, IL: Richard D. Irwin, 1982), p. 469]. As viewed here, however, the differences between parent-company and contemporary theory are sufficiently important to merit separate identification.

[2] Hendriksen points out that probably the strongest justification for including noncontrolling interest with the liabilities or between the liabilities and capital is the fact that "the creditors of the parent have only a secondary claim against the assets of a subsidiary, on the same level as the claim of the minority interest." See *Accounting Theory*, p. 472.

Entity theory requires that the income and equity of a subsidiary be determined for all stockholders, so that the total amounts can be allocated between majority and noncontrolling shareholders in a consistent manner. Entity theory accomplishes this by imputing a total value for the subsidiary on the basis of the price paid by the parent company for its majority interest. We assign the excess of total value of the subsidiary over the book value of subsidiary net assets 100% to identifiable assets and to goodwill. In this manner, entity theory consolidates subsidiary assets (including goodwill) and liabilities at their fair values, which are applicable to both noncontrolling and majority interests.

■■■

COMPARISON OF CONSOLIDATION THEORIES

Exhibit 11-1 compares the basic differences between parent-company theory, entity theory, and contemporary theory. Parent-company theory adopts the viewpoint of parent-company stockholders, and entity theory focuses on the total consolidated entity. By contrast, contemporary theory identifies the primary users of consolidated financial statements as the stockholders and creditors of the parent company, but it assumes the objective of reporting financial position and results of operations of a single business entity. Thus, the viewpoint of contemporary theory, as reflected in *ARB No. 51*, appears to be a compromise between the parent-company and entity theories.

Income Reporting

Consolidated net income is a measurement of income to parent-company stockholders under both the parent-company and contemporary theories. Entity theory, however, requires a computation of income to all equity holders, which we label "total consolidated net income." Entity theory then assigns total consolidated net income to noncontrolling and majority stockholders, with appropriate disclosure on the face of the income statement. Consolidated net income under existing practice reflects parent-company theory. This is evidenced by the practice of reporting noncontrolling interest expense as an expense and the equity of noncontrolling stockholders as a liability. However, the preferred accounting practices under contemporary theory show noncontrolling interest expense as a separate deduction in the determination of consolidated net income, and they report the equity of noncontrolling shareholders as a single amount within the consolidated stockholders' equity classification.

In its deliberations on consolidations, the Financial Accounting Standards Board tentatively decided that a noncontrolling interest in a subsidiary should be labeled and displayed as a separate component of equity in the consolidated balance sheet. Further, income attributable to the noncontrolling interest is not an expense or a loss, but it is a deduction from consolidated net income in computing income attributable to the controlling interest. The consolidated income statement should disclose both the portion of consolidated net income attributable to the controlling interest and the portion attributable to noncontrolling interests.[3] As of this writing, the FASB has not issued a final decision on this issue.

Asset Valuation

Perhaps the greatest difference between parent-company theory and entity theory lies in the valuation of subsidiary net assets. Parent-company theory initially consolidates subsidiary assets at their book values, plus the parent company's share of any excess fair value over book values. In other words, we revalue subsidiary assets only to the extent of the net assets (including goodwill) acquired by the parent company. We consolidate the noncontrolling interest in subsidiary net assets at book value. Although this approach reflects the cost principle from the viewpoint of the parent company, it leads to inconsistent treatment of majority and noncontrolling interests in the consolidated financial statements and to a balance sheet valuation that reflects neither historical cost nor fair value.

---

[3] Financial Accounting Standards Board, *Financial Accounting Series No. 145-A*, "Status Report No. 260," January 6, 1995, p. 6.

EXHIBIT 11-1

COMPARISON OF CONSOLIDATION THEORIES

	Parent-Company Theory	Entity Theory	Contemporary Theory
Basic purposes and users of consolidated financial statements	Consolidated statements are an extension of parent-company statements, prepared for the benefit and from the viewpoint of the stockholders of the parent company.	Consolidated statements are prepared from the viewpoint of the total consolidated entity, intended for all parties having an interest in the entity.	Consolidated statements present the financial position and results of operations of a single business enterprise but are prepared primarily for the benefit of the stockholders and creditors of the parent company. (*ARB No. 51*, paras. 2 and 7)
Consolidated net income	Consolidated net income is income to the stockholders of the parent company.	Total consolidated net income is income to all equity holders of the consolidated entity.	Consolidated net income is income to the stockholders of the parent company.
Noncontrolling interest expense	Noncontrolling interest expense is an expense from the viewpoint of the parent-company stockholders, measured on the basis of the subsidiary as a separate legal entity.	Noncontrolling interest expense is an allocation of total consolidated net income to noncontrolling stockholders.	Noncontrolling interest expense is a deduction in determining consolidated net income, but not a true expense. Instead, it is an allocation of realized income of the entity between majority and noncontrolling interests.
Equity of noncontrolling interests	Equity of noncontrolling stockholders is a liability from the viewpoint of the parent-company stockholders, measured based on the subsidiary's legal equity.	Equity of noncontrolling stockholders is a part of consolidated stockholders' equity, equivalent to the presentation accorded the equity of majority stockholders.	Equity of noncontrolling stockholders is a part of consolidated stockholders' equity, presented as a single amount because it is not expected that noncontrolling interests will benefit from the disclosure.
Consolidation of subsidiary net assets	Parent's share of subsidiary net assets is consolidated on the basis of the price paid by the parent for its interest. The noncontrolling interest's share is consolidated at book value.	All net assets of a subsidiary are consolidated at their fair values imputed on the basis of the price paid by the parent for its interest. Thus, majority and noncontrolling interests in net assets are valued consistently.	Subsidiary net assets are consolidated at book value plus the excess of the parent company's investment cost over the book value of the interest acquired.
Unrealized gains and losses	100% elimination from consolidated net income for downstream sales and elimination of the parent company's share for upstream sales.	100% elimination in determining total consolidated net income with allocation between majority and noncontrolling interests for upstream sales.	100% elimination from revenue and expense accounts with allocation between majority and noncontrolling interests for upstream sales. (*ARB No. 51*, paras. 7 and 13)
Constructive gains and losses on debt retirement	100% recognition in consolidated net income on retirement of parent-company debt, and recognition of the parent company's share for retirement of subsidiary debt.	100% recognition in total consolidated net income with allocation between majority and noncontrolling interests for retirement of subsidiary debt.	100% recognition in revenue and expense accounts with allocation between majority and noncontrolling interests for retirement of subsidiary debt.

Entity theory consolidates subsidiary assets and liabilities at their fair values, and it accounts for the majority and noncontrolling interests in those net assets consistently. However, this consistent treatment is obtained through the questionable practice of imputing a total subsidiary valuation on the basis of the price paid by the parent company for its majority interest. Conceptually, this valuation approach has considerable appeal when the parent acquires essentially all of the subsidiary's stock for cash. It has much less appeal when the parent acquires a slim majority of subsidiary outstanding stock for noncash assets or through an exchange of shares. An investor may be willing to pay a premium for the rights to *control* an investee (an investment of more than 50%), but not willing to purchase the remaining stock at the inflated price.

Additional problems with the imputed total valuation of a subsidiary under entity theory develop after the parent company acquires its interest. *Once the parent is able to exercise absolute control over the subsidiary, the shares held by noncontrolling stockholders do not represent equity ownership in the usual sense.* Typically, the stock of a subsidiary will be "delisted" after a business combination, leaving the parent company as the only viable purchaser for noncontrolling shares. In this case, noncontrolling shareholders are at the mercy of the parent company. A noncontrolling share does not have the same equity characteristics as a majority share.

Contemporary theory conforms to the practices of parent-company theory in the consolidation of subsidiary assets and liabilities. Although a conceptual superiority for entity theory in this area is frequently granted, there are practical disadvantages. The price paid by the parent company for its majority interest is not currently considered a valid basis for valuation of noncontrolling interests. Even the current practice of measuring the equity of noncontrolling shareholders at book value is criticized because it tends to overstate the value of the noncontrolling interest (primarily due to the restricted marketability of noncontrolling shares).

Unrealized Gains and Losses

A difference between the parent-company and entity theories of consolidation also exists in the treatment of unrealized gains and losses from intercompany transactions (see Exhibit 11-1). Although there is general agreement that 100% of all unrealized gains and losses from downstream sales should be eliminated, we accord gains and losses arising from upstream sales different treatment under parent-company and entity theories. Under parent-company theory, we eliminate unrealized gains and losses from upstream sales to the extent of the parent company's ownership percentage in the subsidiary. The portion of unrealized gains and losses not eliminated relates to the noncontrolling interest and, from the parent-company viewpoint, is considered to be realized by noncontrolling shareholders.

We eliminate unrealized gains and losses in determining total consolidated net income under entity theory. In the case of upstream sales, however, we allocate the eliminated amounts between income to noncontrolling and majority stockholders according to their respective ownership percentages.

The elimination of unrealized gains and losses under contemporary theory follows the pattern and consistency of entity theory. *ARB No. 51*, paragraph 13, requires all unrealized gains and losses to be eliminated, but "the elimination of the intercompany profit or loss may be allocated proportionately between the majority and minority interests." Presumably, the assignment of the full amount of unrealized gains and losses to majority interests would also be acceptable under *ARB No. 51*. This latter approach was not used in earlier chapters of this book because of its inherent inconsistency for consolidation purposes and because its use seems incompatible with requirements for the equity method of accounting. If unrealized gains and losses from upstream sales are not allocated between majority and noncontrolling interests, the parent company's income and equity will not equal consolidated net income and equity unless the same inconsistency is applied under the equity method.

Constructive Gains and Losses

The pattern of accounting for constructive gains and losses from intercompany debt acquisitions under the three theories parallels the pattern of accounting for unrealized gains and losses (see Exhibit 11-1). Gains and losses on the constructive retirement of debt under contemporary theory are accounted for in the same manner as under entity theory.

FASB accounting standards specify many of the requirements of the contemporary theory of consolidation. As noted earlier in the chapter, these requirements do not constitute an interconsistent theory of consolidated financial statements; instead they contain elements of both parent-company theory and entity theory. Although the contemporary theory of consolidation lacks internal consistency, the theory does adhere reasonably well to other components of accounting theory, such as the cost principle and the basic elements of financial statements.

The Economic Unit Concept—Purchased Goodwill

Chapter 3 introduced an accounting procedure for business combinations that reports a subsidiary's identifiable assets and liabilities, other than goodwill, at their fair values. Only the goodwill actually purchased by the parent company is recorded. This method, titled the "economic unit concept—purchased goodwill," is described in the FASB discussion memorandum "An Analysis of Issues Related to Consolidation Policy and Procedures." Supporters for this method argue that it is inappropriate to consolidate the controlling interest's portion of the subsidiary's assets and liabilities at fair value and the noncontrolling interest's portion at book value. Under this method, the subsidiary's identifiable assets and liabilities are consistently valued at their fair value in the consolidation process at the date of the business combination.

The desire for consistency does not extend to goodwill, however. Supporters of this approach recognize that the parent company may be willing to pay a substantial premium for control of another company, and the control premium may have little to do with the fair value of the subsidiary. Thus, we compute no implied value of goodwill and only report the goodwill actually paid for in the consolidated statements. (See Chapter 3 for an illustration.)

In October 1995, the FASB issued an exposure draft, "Consolidated Financial Statements: Policy and Procedures," that would have required accounting for the acquisition of a subsidiary using the economic unit concept—purchased goodwill method. However, the exposure draft was not adopted as a FASB statement. Since then, the board has decided that purchased goodwill meets the definition of an asset and should be measured as the difference between the fair value of the purchase consideration and the fair value of the net assets acquired. This view is expressed in *FASB Statement No. 141* and is consistent with the superseded *APB Opinion No. 16* requirements. The board, in *FASB Statement No. 142*, also requires that goodwill be reviewed periodically for impairment. If an FASB standard based on entity theory or the economic unit concept—purchased goodwill method is issued, it will become part of the contemporary theory. Contemporary theory continues to evolve with changes in accounting standards.

ILLUSTRATION—CONSOLIDATION UNDER PARENT-COMPANY AND ENTITY THEORIES

Differences between the various consolidation theories may be more comprehensible when shown in numerical examples. The following section relates to the purchase business combination of Pedrich and Sandy Corporations on January 1, 2006. Assume that Pedrich Corporation acquires a 90% interest in Sandy Corporation for $198,000 cash on January 1, 2006. Comparative balance sheets of the two companies immediately before the acquisition are as follows (in thousands):

	Pedrich		*Sandy*	
	Book Value	**Fair Value**	**Book Value**	**Fair Value**
Cash	$220	$220	$ 5	$ 5
Accounts receivable—net	80	80	30	35
Inventory	90	100	40	50
Other current assets	20	20	10	10
Plant assets—net	220	300	60	80
Total assets	$630	$720	$145	$180
Liabilities	$ 80	$ 80	$ 25	$ 25
Capital stock, $10 par	400		100	
Retained earnings	150		20	
Total equities	$630		$145	

The $198,000 purchase price for the 90% interest implies a $220,000 total value for Sandy's Corporation's net assets ($198,000 ÷ 90%). Under entity theory, we revalue all subsidiary assets and liabilities and reflect these values in the consolidated statements on the basis of the $220,000 implied total valuation. Under parent-company theory, we do not reflect the total implied value in the consolidated financial statements; therefore, only 90% of the subsidiary's net assets are revalued. Although *the different theories do not affect parent-company accounting under the equity method*, they do result in different amounts for consolidated assets, liabilities, and noncontrolling interests.

ENTITY THEORY In the Pedrich–Sandy example, entity theory assigns the $100,000 excess of implied value over the $120,000 book value of Sandy's net assets to identifiable net assets and goodwill as follows (in thousands):

	Fair Value		Book Value		Excess Fair Value
Accounts receivable—net	$35	–	$30	=	$ 5
Inventories	50	–	40	=	10
Plant assets—net	80	–	60	=	20
Goodwill (remainder)	—		—		65
Total implied value over book value					$100

PARENT-COMPANY THEORY The amounts assigned to identifiable net assets and goodwill in accordance with parent-company theory (and contemporary theory) would be 90% of the foregoing amounts:

Accounts receivable—net	$ 5,000 × 90% = $ 4,500
Inventories	10,000 × 90% = 9,000
Plant assets—net	20,000 × 90% = 18,000
Goodwill	65,000 × 90% = 58,500
Total purchase price over book value acquired	$90,000

GOODWILL Goodwill under the two theories can be determined independently. Under entity theory, the $65,000 goodwill is equal to the total implied value of Sandy's net assets over the fair value of Sandy's net assets ($220,000 − $155,000). Under parent-company theory, the $58,500 goodwill is equal to the investment cost less 90% of the fair value of Sandy's identifiable net assets ($198,000 − $139,500). Entity theory reflects the $10,000 additional amount assigned to identifiable assets and goodwill ($100,000 − $90,000) in the noncontrolling interest classification in a consolidated balance sheet.[4]

Consolidation at Acquisition

Exhibit 11-2 compares consolidated balance sheet working papers for Pedrich Corporation and Subsidiary under parent-company and entity theories. In examining the working papers, recall that contemporary theory is the same as parent-company theory in matters relating to the initial consolidation of subsidiary assets and liabilities.

The comparative working papers in Exhibit 11-2 begin with separate balance sheets of the affiliated companies and use established procedures for consolidating the separate balance sheets. Although the working papers could be modified under parent-company theory to reflect the noncontrolling interest among the liabilities, this modification does not seem necessary. Such classification differences can be reflected in the consolidated statements without changing working paper procedures.

Parent-company theory allocates 90% of the excess of fair value over book value of identifiable net assets to identifiable assets and liabilities, and it allocates the $58,500 excess of investment cost over fair value acquired to goodwill. Noncontrolling interest of $12,000 for parent-company theory is equal to 10% of the $120,000 book value of Sandy's net assets at the time of acquisition.

Entity theory assigns the full excess of fair value over book value to identifiable net assets, and it enters the excess of implied value over fair value as goodwill. The $22,000 noncontrolling interest is 10% of the implied value of Sandy's net assets.

Consolidated assets under parent-company theory consist of the book value of combined assets plus 90% of the excess of fair value of Sandy's assets over their book value. Under entity theory, consolidated assets consist of the book value of Pedrich's assets plus the fair value of Sandy's assets. Although entity theory consolidates all assets of Sandy at their fair values, total consolidated assets do not reflect fair values under either theory because we never revalue the assets of the parent company at the time of a business combination.

---

[4] Under the economic unit concept—purchased goodwill approach, Sandy's identifiable assets and liabilities at acquisition would be reported at their fair values (as in entity theory), but only purchased goodwill ($58,500, as in parent-company theory) would be reported.

PEDRICH CORPORATION AND SUBSIDIARY CONSOLIDATED BALANCE SHEET WORKING PAPERS AT JANUARY 1, 2006 (IN THOUSANDS)

EXHIBIT 11-2

Balance Sheet
Working Paper
Comparisons

	Pedrich	90% Sandy	Adjustments and Eliminations		Consolidated
Parent-Company Theory					
Assets					
Cash	$ 22	$ 5			$ 27
Accounts receivable—net	80	30	b 4.5		114.5
Inventories	90	40	b 9		139
Other current assets	20	10			30
Plant assets—net	220	60	b 18		298
Investment in Sandy	198			a 198	
Goodwill			b 58.5		58.5
Unamortized excess			a 90	b 90	
Total assets	$630	$145			$667
Liabilities and Equity					
Liabilities	$ 80	$ 25			$105
Capital stock	400	100	a 100		400
Retained earnings	150	20	a 20		150
Noncontrolling interest				a 12	12
Total equities	$630	$145			$667
Entity Theory					
Assets					
Cash	$ 22	$ 5			$ 27
Accounts receivable—net	80	30	b 5		115
Inventories	90	40	b 10		140
Other current assets	20	10			30
Plant assets—net	220	60	b 20		300
Investment in Sandy	198			a 198	
Goodwill			b 65		65
Unamortized excess			a 100	b 100	
Total assets	$630	$145			$677
Liabilities and Equity					
Liabilities	$ 80	$ 25			$105
Capital stock	400	100	a 100		400
Retained earnings	150	20	a 20		150
Noncontrolling interest				a 22	22
Total equities	$630	$145			$677

Consolidation After Acquisition

Differences between parent-company theory and entity theory can be explained further by examining the operations of Pedrich Corporation and Sandy Corporation for 2006. The following assumptions are made:

1. Sandy's net income and dividends for 2006 are $35,000 and $10,000, respectively.

2. The excess of fair value over book value of Sandy's accounts receivable and inventories at January 1, 2006, is realized during 2006.

3. Sandy's plant assets are being depreciated at a 5% annual rate, and goodwill from consolidation is not amortized.

EQUITY METHOD Under these assumptions, Pedrich records $17,100 investment income from Sandy for 2006, computed under the equity method as follows:

Share of Sandy's net income ($35,000 × 90%)	$31,500
Less: Realization of excess allocated to receivables	
($5,000 × 90%)	(4,500)
Realization of excess allocated to inventories	
($10,000 × 90%)	(9,000)
Depreciation on excess allocated to plant assets	
($20,000 × 90%) ÷ 20 years	(900)
Income from Sandy for 2006	$17,100

Pedrich's Investment in Sandy account under the equity method has a balance of $206,100 at December 31, 2006. This investment balance consists of the $198,000 investment cost, plus $17,100 investment income for 2006, less $9,000 dividends received from Sandy during 2006. Accounting under the equity method is not affected by the viewpoint adopted for consolidating the financial statements of affiliated companies; therefore, *the separate statements of Pedrich and Sandy will be the same at December 31, 2006, regardless of the theory adopted.*

CONSOLIDATION PROCEDURES Consolidated net income under parent-company theory is the same as the income allocated to parent-company stockholders under entity theory. Therefore, the differences between the parent-company and entity theories lie solely in the manner of consolidating parent and subsidiary financial statements and in reporting the financial position and results of operations in the consolidated financial statements. Consolidation working papers for Pedrich Corporation and Subsidiary under parent-company theory in Exhibit 11-3 and under entity theory in Exhibit 11-4 reflect these differences. Again, the working paper procedures have not been modified to reflect differences in financial statement classification. Exhibits 11-5 and 11-6 illustrate differences in financial statement presentation for Pedrich Corporation and Subsidiary and show financial statements prepared from the working papers.

In comparing the consolidation working papers under parent-company theory in Exhibit 11-3 with those under entity theory in Exhibit 11-4, note that the working paper adjustment and elimination entries have the same debit and credit items, but the amounts differ for all working paper entries other than entry a. Accounting for the subsidiary investment under the equity method is the same for both consolidation theories, so the entry to eliminate investment income and intercompany dividends and to adjust the investment account to its beginning-of-the-period balance (entry a) is exactly the same under parent-company theory as under entity theory.

The remaining adjustment and elimination entries in Exhibit 11-3 under parent-company theory are the same as under the contemporary theory used in earlier chapters. Entry b eliminates reciprocal subsidiary equity amounts, establishes beginning noncontrolling interest at book value ($120,000 × 10%), and enters the unamortized excess. Entry c then allocates the excess of investment cost over book value acquired: $9,000 to cost of sales (for undervalued inventory items realized during 2006), $4,500 to operating expense (for undervalued receivables realized during 2006), $18,000 to plant assets (for undervalued plant assets at the beginning of 2006), and $58,500 to goodwill. Entries d and e reflect current depreciation on the excess allocated to plant assets ($18,000 × 5%) and the noncontrolling interest in subsidiary income and dividends, respectively. Noncontrolling interest expense of $3,500 is simply 10% of Sandy's $35,000 reported net income.

EXHIBIT 11-3

Parent-Company Theory

PEDRICH CORPORATION AND SUBSIDIARY CONSOLIDATION WORKING PAPERS FOR THE YEAR ENDED DECEMBER 31, 2006 (IN THOUSANDS)

	Pedrich	90% Sandy	Adjustments and Eliminations Debits	Credits	Consolidated Statements
Income Statement Sales	$600	$200			$800
Income from Sandy	17.1		a 17.1		
Cost of sales	(300)	(120)	c 9		(429)
Operating expenses	(211.25)	(45)	c 4.5 d .9		(261.65)
Noncontrolling interest expense ($35 × 10%)			e 3.5		(3.5)
Net income	**$105.85**	**$ 35**			**$105.85**
Retained Earnings Retained earnings	$150	$ 20	b 20		$150
Dividends	(80)	(10)		a 9 e 1	(80)
Net income	**105.85**	**35**			**105.85**
Retained earnings— December 31	**$175.85**	**$ 45**			**$175.85**
Balance Sheet Cash	$ 29.75	$ 13			$ 42.75
Accounts receivable—net	90	32			122
Inventories	100	48			148
Other current assets	30	17			47
Plant assets—net	200	57	c 18	d .9	274.1
Investment in Sandy	206.1			a 8.1 b 198	
Goodwill			c 58.5		58.5
Unamortized excess			b 90	c 90	
	$655.85	**$167**			**$692.35**
Liabilities	$ 80	$ 22			$102
Capital stock	400	100	b 100		400
Retained earnings	**175.85**	**45**			**175.85**
	$655.85	**$167**			
Noncontrolling interest				b 12 e 2.5	14.5
					$692.35

EXHIBIT 11-4

Entity Theory

PEDRICH CORPORATION AND SUBSIDIARY CONSOLIDATION WORKING PAPERS FOR THE YEAR ENDED DECEMBER 31, 2006 (IN THOUSANDS)

	Pedrich	90% Sandy	Adjustments and Eliminations Debits	Credits	Consolidated Statements
Income Statement Sales	$600	$200			$800
Income from Sandy	17.1		a 17.1		
Cost of sales	(300)	(120)	c 10		(430)
Operating expenses	(211.25)	(45)	c 5 d 1		(262.25)
Noncontrolling interest expense*			e 1.9		(1.9)
Net income	**$105.85**	**$ 35**			**$105.85**
Retained Earnings Retained earnings	$150	$ 20	b 20		$150
Dividends	(80)	(10)		a 9 e 1	(80)
Net income	105.85	35			105.85
Retained earnings— December 31	**$175.85**	**$ 45**			**$175.85**
Balance Sheet Cash	$ 29.75	$ 13			$ 42.75
Accounts receivable—net	90	32			122
Inventories	100	48			148
Other current assets	30	17			47
Plant assets—net	200	57	c 20	d 1	276
Investment in Sandy	206.1			a 8.1 b 198	
Goodwill			c 65		65
Unamortized excess			b 100	c 100	
	$655.85	$167			$700.75
Liabilities	$ 80	$ 22			$102
Capital stock	400	100	b 100		400
Retained earnings	175.85	45			175.85
	$655.85	$167			
Noncontrolling interest				b 22 e .9	22.9
					$700.75

*Noncontrolling interest expense: ($35 − $16) × 10%

**PEDRICH CORPORATION AND SUBSIDIARY
CONSOLIDATED INCOME STATEMENTS
FOR THE YEAR ENDED DECEMBER 31, 2006
(IN THOUSANDS)**

Parent-Company Theory

Sales		$800.00
Less: Cost of sales	$429.00	
Operating expenses	261.65	
Noncontrolling interest expense	3.50	
Total expenses		694.15
Consolidated net income		$105.85

Entity Theory

Sales		$800.00
Less: Cost of sales	$430.00	
Operating expenses	262.25	
Total expenses		692.25
Total consolidated net income		$107.75
Distributions: to noncontrolling stockholders	$ 1.90	
to majority stockholders	$105.85	

Contemporary Theory

Sales		$800.00
Less: Cost of sales	$429.00	
Operating expenses	261.65	
Total expenses		690.65
Total consolidated net income		109.35
Less: Noncontrolling interest expense		3.50
Consolidated net income		$105.85

EXHIBIT 11-5

Consolidated Income
Statements Under
Alternative Theories

**PEDRICH CORPORATION AND SUBSIDIARY
CONSOLIDATED BALANCE SHEETS
AT DECEMBER 31, 2006
(IN THOUSANDS)**

	Parent-Company Theory	Entity Theory	Contemporary Theory
Assets			
Cash	$ 42.75	$ 42.75	$ 42.75
Accounts receivable—net	122.00	122.00	122.00
Inventories	148.00	148.00	148.00
Other current assets	47.00	47.00	47.00
Total current assets	359.75	359.75	359.75
Plant assets—net	274.10	276.00	274.10
Goodwill	58.50	65.00	58.50
Total noncurrent assets	332.60	341.00	332.60
Total assets	$692.35	$700.75	$692.35
Liabilities and Equity			
Liabilities	$102.00	$102.00	$102.00
Noncontrolling interest	14.50	—	
Total liabilities	116.50	102.00	102.00
Capital stock	400.00	400.00	400.00
Retained earnings	175.85	175.85	175.85
Noncontrolling interest	—	22.90	14.50
Total stockholders' equity	575.85	598.75	590.35
Total equities	$692.35	$700.75	$692.35

EXHIBIT 11-6

Consolidated
Balance Sheets
Under Alternative
Theories

Entries b, c, d, and e in Exhibit 11-4 under entity theory have the same objective as those for the same items under parent-company theory, except for amounts that relate to the noncontrolling interest. Beginning noncontrolling interest under entity theory is $22,000, equal to 10% of the $220,000 implied total value of Sandy Corporation at January 1, 2006. Beginning noncontrolling interest under entity theory is $10,000 greater than beginning noncontrolling interest of $12,000 under parent-company theory. The additional $10,000 relates to the allocation of 100% of the excess fair value over book value of Sandy's net assets at acquisition under entity theory. In other words, working paper entry b under entity theory is equivalent to entry b under parent-company theory, plus the additional $10,000 unamortized excess applicable to noncontrolling interest.

b Unamortized excess (+A)	100,000	
Capital stock (−SE)	100,000	
Retained earnings January 1, 2006 (−SE)	20,000	
Investment in Sandy (−A)		198,000
Noncontrolling interest January 1, 2006 (+L)		22,000
To eliminate reciprocal investment and equity balances, establish beginning noncontrolling interest, and enter the unamortized excess amount.		

Entry c under entity theory is equivalent to entry c under parent-company theory, plus the additional excess fair value over book value amounts.

c Cost of sales (E, −SE)	10,000	
Operating expenses (E, −SE)	5,000	
Plant assets (+A)	20,000	
Goodwill (+A)	65,000	
Unamortized excess (−A)		100,000
To allocate unamortized excess to identifiable assets and goodwill.		

Working paper entry d for depreciation on the excess allocated to plant assets is $1,000 under entity theory, compared with $900 under parent-company theory. The $100 difference is simply the 5% depreciation rate applied to the additional $2,000 allocated to plant assets under entity theory.

Noncontrolling interest expense under entity theory is $1,900, consisting of 10% of Sandy's $35,000 income, less 10% of the $16,000 amortization on the $100,000 implied value/book value differential. Alternatively, noncontrolling interest expense can be computed as follows:

Share of Sandy's reported income ($35,000 × 10%)	$3,500
Less: Operating expenses for realization of excess allocated to receivables ($5,000 × 10%)	(500)
Cost of sales for realization of excess allocated to inventory ($10,000 × 10%)	(1,000)
Depreciation on excess allocated to plant assets ($20,000 ÷ 20 years × 10%)	(100)
Noncontrolling interest expense	$1,900

COMPARISON OF CONSOLIDATED INCOME STATEMENTS The additional expenses that are deducted in determining total consolidated net income under entity theory can be summarized as follows:

	Parent-Company Theory	Entity Theory
Operating expenses (for receivables)	$ 4,500	$ 5,000
Cost of sales (for inventory)	9,000	10,000
Operating expenses (for depreciation)	900	1,000
	$14,400	$16,000

The $1,600 additional expenses ($16,000 − $14,400) under entity theory are exactly offset by the lower noncontrolling interest ($3,500 − $1,900). Thus, income to the parent-company stockholders is the same under the two theories, even though there are differences in the amounts reported and in the way the amounts are disclosed in the consolidated income statements. These differences are shown in Exhibit 11-5, which compares consolidated income statements for Pedrich Corporation and Subsidiary under parent-company theory, entity theory, and contemporary theory.

Consolidated net income under parent-company theory is the same as under contemporary theory. The reporting of income under entity theory shows a final amount for "total consolidated net income" of $107,750 and distribution of that income to noncontrolling and parent-company stockholders. Although the amounts shown for Pedrich Corporation and Subsidiary are identical under parent-company and contemporary theories, this equivalence would not have existed if there had been unrealized profits from upstream sales or constructive gains or losses from intercompany purchases of subsidiary debt. Consolidation procedures for these items are the same under contemporary theory as under entity theory.

The reporting formats under the three consolidation theories vary somewhat, but it may be helpful to note the following relationships:

1. If a subsidiary investment is made at book value and the book values of individual assets and liabilities are equal to their fair values, the income statement amounts should be the same under entity theory as under contemporary theory.

2. In the absence of intercompany transactions, the income statement amounts should be the same under parent-company theory as under contemporary theory.

3. In the absence of noncontrolling interests, the income statement amounts should be the same under all three theories.

COMPARISON OF CONSOLIDATED BALANCE SHEETS Comparative balance sheets for Pedrich Corporation and Subsidiary at December 31, 2006, are illustrated in Exhibit 11-6 under each of the three theories. The amount of total assets is the same under parent-company and contemporary theories but is greater under entity theory. The difference in total assets is $8,400 ($700,750 − $692,350), and it consists of the unamortized excess of implied value over book value of Sandy's net assets. This difference relates to goodwill of $6,500 ($65,000 − $58,500) and plant assets of $1,900 ($276,000 − $274,100).

Total liabilities and equity are the same under parent-company theory and contemporary theory, but liabilities are $14,500 greater under parent-company theory because noncontrolling interest is classified as a liability. Stockholders' equity is $14,500 greater under contemporary theory because noncontrolling interest is classified as a part of stockholders' equity.

The difference between total liabilities and equity under the entity and contemporary theories lies solely in the $8,400 ($22,900 − $14,500) greater noncontrolling interest under entity theory. As in the case of the income generalizations, balance sheet amounts under the parent-company and contemporary theories will be the same in the absence of intercompany transactions, and they will be the same under entity and contemporary theories in the absence of a difference between investment cost and book value acquired. In the absence of noncontrolling interests, all balance sheet amounts should be identical under the three theories.

OTHER VIEWS OF NONCONTROLLING INTEREST Some accountants believe that noncontrolling interest should not appear as a separate line item in consolidated financial statements. One suggestion for eliminating noncontrolling interest from consolidated statements is to report total consolidated income as the bottom line in the consolidated income statements, with separate *footnote disclosure* of majority and noncontrolling interests in the income. Consistent treatment in the consolidated balance sheet would require total consolidated equity to be reported as a single line item, with separate footnote disclosure of the equity of majority and noncontrolling interests.

Another suggestion for excluding reference to noncontrolling interest in consolidated financial statements is to consolidate only the majority-owned portion of the revenues, expenses, assets, and liabilities of less-than-100%-owned subsidiaries. Proportional consolidation is discussed later in this chapter under accounting for corporate joint ventures.

PUSH-DOWN ACCOUNTING AND OTHER BASIS CONSIDERATIONS

Under the contemporary, entity, and parent-company theories discussed in the first section of this chapter, we allocated cost/book value differentials to the individual identifiable assets and liabilities and goodwill by working paper entries in the process of consolidating the financial statements of the parent and subsidiary. The books of the subsidiary were not affected by the price paid by the parent for its ownership interest.

In certain situations, the SEC requires that the fair values of the acquired subsidiary's assets and liabilities, which represent the parent company's cost basis under the provisions of *APB Opinion No. 16*, be recorded in the separate financial statements of the purchased subsidiary. In other words, the values are "pushed down" to the subsidiary's statements.[5] The SEC requires the use of push-down accounting for SEC filings when a subsidiary is substantially wholly owned (usually 97%) with no substantial publicly held debt or preferred stock outstanding.

The SEC's argument is that when the parent controls the form of ownership of an entity, the basis of accounting for purchased assets and liabilities should be the same regardless of whether the entity continues to exist or is merged into the parent's operations. However, when a subsidiary has outstanding public debt or preferred stock, or when a significant noncontrolling interest exists, the parent company may not be able to control the form of ownership. The SEC encourages push-down accounting in these circumstances, but it does not require it.

The AICPA issues paper "Push-Down Accounting" (October 30, 1979) describes **push-down accounting** as

> *The establishment of a new accounting and reporting basis for an entity in its separate financial statements, based on a purchase transaction in the voting stock of the entity that results in a substantial change of ownership of the outstanding voting stock of the entity.*

When we do not use push-down accounting in an acquisition, we allocate the purchase price to identifiable net assets and goodwill in the consolidation working papers. The consolidated financial statements reflect the purchase allocation. The consolidation process is simplified if the subsidiary records the allocation in its financial statements under push-down accounting.

Push-down accounting is controversial only in the separate-company statements of the subsidiary that are issued to noncontrolling interests, creditors, and other interested parties. Critics of push-down accounting argue that the purchase transaction between the parent company/investor and the subsidiary's old stockholders does not justify a new accounting basis for the subsidiary's assets and liabilities under historical cost principles. The subsidiary is not a party to the transaction—it receives no new funds; it sells no assets. Proponents counter that the price paid by the new owners provides the most relevant basis for measuring the subsidiary's assets, liabilities, and results of operations.

Push-down accounting is not consistently applied among the supporters of the concept, although, in practice, a subsidiary's assets are usually revalued on a proportional basis. What percentage of ownership constitutes a significant noncontrolling interest that would preclude the use of push-down accounting? Should the allocation be done on a proportional basis if less than a 100% change in ownership has occurred?[6] These are questions in need of authoritative answers.

In the illustration that follows, the Pedrich–Sandy example is extended using both a proportional allocation for the purchase of a 90% interest in Sandy (a parent-company-theory approach) and a 100% allocation, in which we impute the entity's market value as a whole from the purchase price of the 90% interest (an entity-theory approach).

---

[5] *SEC Staff Accounting Bulletin, No. 54*, 1983. For further clarification of the SEC's position, see *Staff Accounting Bulletin, No. 73*, 1987.

[6] Colley and Volkan argue that once an entity controls another entity through stock ownership of more than 50%, the noncontrolling stockholders are not owners in the usual sense. There is only one owner, the parent, and the noncontrolling holders are "investors." They contend that this argument supports the use of push-down accounting for all majority-owned subsidiaries and, further, that it supports a total revaluation approach (in other words, imputing values for 100% of the subsidiary's net assets). See J. Ron Colley and Ara G. Volkan, "Business Combinations: Goodwill and Push-Down Accounting," *The CPA Journal* (August 1988), p. 74.

Push-Down Procedures in Year of Acquisition

Recall that Pedrich acquired its 90% interest for $198,000 cash on January 1, 2006. If we use push-down accounting and revalue only 90% of Sandy's identifiable net assets (parent-company theory), we allocate the $90,000 cost/book value differential as follows (in thousands):

	Book Value	Push-Down Adjustment	Book Value After Push Down
Cash	$ 5	—	$ 5
Accounts receivable—net	30	$ 4.5	34.5
Inventory	40	9	49
Other current assets	10	—	10
Plant assets—net	60	18	78
Goodwill	—	58.5	58.5
	$145	$ 90	$235
Liabilities	$ 25	—	$ 25
Capital stock	100	—	100
Retained earnings	20	$ (20)	—
Push-down capital	—	110	110
	$145	$ 90	$235

We record the push-down adjustment on Sandy's separate books as follows:

Accounts receivable (+A)	4,500	
Inventory (+A)	9,000	
Plant assets (+A)	18,000	
Goodwill (+A)	58,500	
Retained earnings (−SE)	20,000	
Push-down capital (+SE)		110,000

If we impute a total value of $220,000 from the purchase price of the 90% interest in Sandy under entity theory ($198,000 cost ÷ 90%), we push down the $100,000 excess on Sandy's books as follows (in thousands):

	Book Value	Push-Down Adjustment	Book Value After Push Down
Cash	$ 5	—	$ 5
Accounts receivable—net	30	$ 5	35
Inventory	40	10	50
Other current assets	10	—	10
Plant assets—net	60	20	80
Goodwill	—	65	65
	$145	$100	$245
Liabilities	$ 25	—	$ 25
Capital stock	100	—	100
Retained earnings	20	$ (20)	—
Push-down capital	—	120	120
	$145	$100	$245

The entry to record the 100% push-down adjustment on Sandy's separate books is:

Accounts receivable (+A)	5,000	
Inventory (+A)	10,000	
Plant assets (+A)	20,000	
Goodwill (+A)	65,000	
Retained earnings (−SE)	20,000	
Push-down capital (+SE)		120,000

Observe that we transfer the balance of Sandy's Retained Earnings account to push-down capital regardless of whether the push down is for 90% or 100% of the fair value/book value differential. This treatment is basic to push-down accounting, which requires a new accounting and reporting basis for the acquired entity. Push-down capital is an additional paid-in capital account. It includes the revaluation of subsidiary identifiable net assets and goodwill, based on the price paid to acquire the subsidiary, and the subsidiary's Retained Earnings account balance, which we eliminate under the new entity concept of push-down accounting.

Exhibit 11-7 presents consolidated balance sheet working papers to illustrate the effect of the push-down adjustments. The balance sheet worksheet at the top of the exhibit reflects the 90% push-down adjustment that is compatible with parent-company theory, and the worksheet at the bottom reflects the 100% push-down adjustment that is compatible with entity theory. Including the push-down adjustments in Sandy's separate balance sheets greatly simplifies the consolidation procedures. The simplification results from not having to allocate unamortized cost/book value differentials in the working papers under push-down accounting. The consolidated balance sheet amounts, however, are identical in Exhibit 11-7 under push-down accounting and in Exhibit 11-2, where we maintain the subsidiary balance sheets on an original-cost basis.

Push-Down Procedures in Year After Acquisition

Exhibits 11-8 and 11-9 illustrate consolidated financial statement working papers for Pedrich and Sandy Corporations under push-down accounting procedures for the year ended December 31, 2006. Exhibit 11-8 reflects the 90% push-down adjustment of parent-company theory, and Exhibit 11-9 reflects the 100% push-down adjustment under entity theory. Both exhibits greatly simplify the consolidation procedures in relation to the comparable working papers for Pedrich and Sandy shown in Exhibits 11-3 and 11-4. As in the case of consolidated balance sheets, however, the amounts shown in the consolidated financial statements are identical.

In the consolidation working paper of Exhibit 11-9 (entity theory), the noncontrolling interest expense of $1,900 is equal to 10% of Sandy's $19,000 net income as measured under push-down accounting procedures. Similarly, the $22,900 noncontrolling interest at December 31, 2006, is equal to 10% of Sandy's $229,000 stockholders' equity on that date. We determine these noncontrolling interest items under standard consolidation procedures. By contrast, in Exhibit 11-8 (parent-company theory), the $3,500 noncontrolling interest expense for 2006 and the $14,500 noncontrolling interest at December 31, 2006, do not have a direct reference to the $20,600 net income of Sandy or the $220,600 stockholders' equity of Sandy, as shown in Sandy's separate income statement and balance sheet under 90% push-down accounting. This is a problem that arises in the use of push-down accounting for a less-than-100%-owned subsidiary, where only the parent's percentage interest is pushed down on the subsidiary's books. In this case, separate cost-based records must be maintained by the subsidiary. The noncontrolling interest amount in Exhibit 11-8 can be determined directly from Sandy's separate cost-based statements as shown in Exhibit 11-3. Noncontrolling shareholders are not expected to get meaningful information from consolidated financial statements; therefore, the 100% push-down approach under entity theory may be preferable, especially when the affiliated group has multiple partially owned subsidiaries.

Leveraged Buyouts

In a **leveraged buyout** (LBO), an investor group (often including company management, an investment banker, and financial institutions) acquires a company (Company A) from the public shareholders in a transaction financed with very little equity and very large amounts of debt. Usually, the investor group raises the money for the buyout by investing perhaps 10% of their own money and borrowing the rest. A holding company may be formed to acquire the shares of Company A.

Usually debt raised by the investor group to finance the LBO is partially secured by Company A's own assets and is serviced with funds generated by Company A's operations and/or the sale of its assets. Because the loans are secured by Company A's assets, banks loaning money to the investor group often require that the debt appear on Company A's financial statements.

If the previous owners were paid a high premium for their stock, which is often the case, and book values, rather than fair values, of the assets and liabilities are carried forward to the balance sheet of the new company (the acquired Company A), the debt incurred in the LBO may cause the new company's financial condition to look worse than it is. The popularity of LBOs is one reason many accountants support a change to push-down accounting for acquisitions, including LBOs, that would allow the assets of the acquired firm to be written up on its financial statements to reflect the purchase price.

PEDRICH CORPORATION AND SUBSIDIARY CONSOLIDATED BALANCE SHEET WORKING PAPERS AT JANUARY 1, 2006 (IN THOUSANDS)

	Pedrich	90% Sandy	Adjustments and Eliminations		Consolidated
Parent-Company Theory					
Assets					
Cash	$ 22	$ 5			$ 27
Accounts receivable—net	80	34.5			114.5
Inventories	90	49			139
Other current assets	20	10			30
Plant assets—net	220	78			298
Investment in Sandy	198			a 198	
Goodwill		58.5			58.5
Total assets	$630	$235			$667
Liabilities and Equity					
Liabilities	$ 80	$ 25			$105
Capital stock	400	100	a 100		400
Retained earnings	150	0			150
Push-down capital—Sandy		110	a 110		
Noncontrolling interest				a 12	12
Total equities	$630	$235			$667
Entity Theory					
Assets					
Cash	$ 22	$ 5			$ 27
Accounts receivable—net	80	35			115
Inventories	90	50			140
Other current assets	20	10			30
Plant assets—net	220	80			300
Investment in Sandy	198			a 198	
Goodwill		65			65
Total assets	$630	$245			$677
Liabilities and Equity					
Liabilities	$ 80	$ 25			$105
Capital stock	400	100	a 100		400
Retained earnings	150	0			150
Push-down capital—Sandy		120	a 120		
Noncontrolling interest				a 22	22
Total equities	$630	$245			$677

EXHIBIT 11-8

Push-Down
Accounting—Parent-
Company Theory

PEDRICH CORPORATION AND SUBSIDIARY CONSOLIDATION WORKING PAPERS FOR THE YEAR ENDED DECEMBER 31, 2006 (IN THOUSANDS)

	Pedrich	90% Sandy	Adjustments and Eliminations Debits	Adjustments and Eliminations Credits	Consolidated Statements
Income Statement Sales	$600	$200			$800
Income from Sandy	17.1		a 17.1		
Cost of sales	(300)	(129)			(429)
Operating expenses	(211.25)	(50.4)			(261.65)
Noncontrolling interest expense ($35 × 10%)			c 3.5		(3.5)
Net income	**$105.85**	**$ 20.6**			**$105.85**
Retained Earnings Retained earnings	$150	$ 0			$150
Dividends	(80)	(10)		a 9 c 1	(80)
Net income	105.85	20.6			105.85
Retained earnings— December 31	**$175.85**	**$ 10.6**			**$175.85**
Balance Sheet Cash	$ 29.75	$ 13			$ 42.75
Accounts receivable—net	90	32			122
Inventories	100	48			148
Other current assets	30	17			47
Plant assets—net	200	74.1			274.1
Investment in Sandy	206.1			a 8.1 b 198	
Goodwill		58.5			58.5
	$655.85	$242.6			$692.35
Liabilities	$ 80	$ 22			$102
Capital stock	400	100	b 100		400
Retained earnings	175.85	10.6			175.85
Push-down capital—Sandy		110	b 110		
	$655.85	$242.6			
Noncontrolling interest				b 12 c 2.5	14.5
					$692.35

PEDRICH CORPORATION AND SUBSIDIARY CONSOLIDATION WORKING PAPERS FOR THE YEAR ENDED DECEMBER 31, 2006 (IN THOUSANDS)						EXHIBIT 11-9

PEDRICH CORPORATION AND SUBSIDIARY CONSOLIDATION WORKING PAPERS FOR THE YEAR ENDED DECEMBER 31, 2006 (IN THOUSANDS)

EXHIBIT 11-9

Push-Down Accounting—Entity Theory

	Pedrich	90% Sandy	Adjustments and Eliminations Debits	Adjustments and Eliminations Credits	Consolidated Statements
Income Statement Sales	$600	$200			$800
Income from Sandy	17.1		a 17.1		
Cost of sales	(300)	(130)			(430)
Operating expenses	(211.25)	(51)			(262.25)
Noncontrolling interest expense*			c 1.9		(1.9)
Net income	**$105.85**	**$ 19**			**$105.85**
Retained Earnings Retained earnings	$150	$ 0			$150
Dividends	(80)	(10)		a 9 c 1	(80)
Net income	105.85	19			105.85
Retained earnings— December 31	**$175.85**	**$ 9**			**$175.85**
Balance Sheet Cash	$ 29.75	$ 13			$ 42.75
Accounts receivable—net	90	32			122
Inventories	100	48			148
Other current assets	30	17			47
Plant assets—net	200	76			276
Investment in Sandy	206.1			a 8.1 b 198	
Goodwill		65			65
	$655.85	$251			$700.75
Liabilities	$ 80	$ 22			$102
Capital stock	400	100	b 100		400
Retained earnings	175.85	9			175.85
Push-down capital—Sandy		120	b 120		
	$655.85	$251			
Noncontrolling interest				b 22 c .9	22.9
					$700.75

*Noncontrolling interest expense ($35 − $16 amortization) = ($19 × 10%)

Both the late 1980s and 1990s witnessed significant LBO activities in U.S. markets. ***Kohlberg, Kravis, Roberts and Company*** (KKR) has been a major acquirer, buying out ***Beatrice Foods*** for $6.25 billion and ***Safeway Stores*** for $4.24 billion, both in 1986, and taking over ***RJR Nabisco*** in 1989 at a cost of $24.72 billion. In 1986, ***Macy Acquisitions Corporation*** was formed to effect an LBO of ***R. H. Macy & Company***, the department store chain, for $3.50 billion.

In 1997, ***Bain Capital*** acquired ***Sealey Corporation***. In 1998, ***Clayton, Dubilier, & Rice*** purchased ***North American Van Lines***, and KKR combined with existing management in a buyout of ***Halley Performance Products***.

In 2000, ***Smithfield Foods*** bid to acquire rival food processor ***IBP***, and ***Silver Lake Partners*** completed an LBO of ***Seagate***, the disk-drive maker, which was subsequently merged into ***Veritas Software*** in a deal valued at $2.1 billion. An April 10, 2001, press release by ***New Dresser*** revealed that a consortium of ***First Reserve Corporation***, ***Odyssey Investment Partners***, and members of Dresser management completed an LBO of Dresser from the ***Halliburton Company*** for $1.3 billion. LBO activity declined in the latter half of 2001, attributed by *The Wall Street Journal* to a lack of loans and bonds needed to fund such deals.[7]

For several years, the SEC and the FASB's Emerging Issues Task Force (EITF) wrestled with the question of whether fair values or book values (predecessor basis) should be carried forward in LBOs. Answers were finally provided in May 1989 in *EITF Issue No. 88-16*, "Basis in Leveraged Buyout Transactions." The structure of a buyout influences the accounting basis. For example, a holding company may be used to acquire the net assets of Company A, a holding company may be used to acquire the equity of Company A, or an investor group may acquire Company A without using a holding company.

The EITF consensus applied to LBOs in which a holding company is used to acquire all the equity of an operating company in a highly leveraged acquisition. The EITF sets forth tests for determining whether the LBO results in a change of the controlling interest. If there has been a change in control, a change in accounting basis is generally appropriate.

The consensus provides complex rules based on the residual interest of each continuing shareholder for determining the accounting basis for the assets and liabilities carried forward to the books of the new entity. The final valuation on the subsidiary's books may be pre-LBO book values, fair values, or something in between, for example, 95% fair value and 5% book (predecessor) value.

Criticism of the consensus generally centers on its complexity, but it also challenges it on conceptual grounds. In particular, critics do not like the resulting accounting basis if it reflects part fair value and part book value. The EITF argues that the method puts substance ahead of form—the new entity has new controlling stockholders and is similar to a purchase business combination.

Another Accounting Basis Solution

Corporations have tried to structure business combinations in ways to avoid goodwill. A corporation acquires a controlling interest in another company (the target), and, in the same transaction, the target issues additional shares to the parent in exchange for the parent's interest in a subsidiary. In substance, the parent company sells its subsidiary to the target as part of the price of acquiring the target. The argument is that this is a combination of enterprises under common control. Therefore, the combination would not be a purchase and the transaction would be accounted for using historical costs. The FASB's EITF addressed these combinations in *EITF Issue No. 90-13*, "Accounting for Simultaneous Common Control Mergers," and concluded that:

- The parent should account for the transfer of the subsidiary to the target as a purchase of the target under *APB Opinion No. 16*. This would now be in accordance with *FASB Statement No. 141*. Obtaining control of the target and the transfer of the subsidiary to the target cannot be separated and should be treated as one transaction.
- The parent should account for the transaction as a partial sale of the subsidiary (to the noncontrolling stockholders of the target) and a partial acquisition of the target. The parent should recognize gain or loss on the portion of the subsidiary sold.

---

[7] Scannell, K., "Leveraged-Buyout Activity Tumbles as Banks Are Reluctant to Lend Money," *The Wall Street Journal*, July 2, 2001.

■ The parent should step up the target's assets and liabilities to the extent acquired by the parent and the subsidiary's assets and liabilities to the extent the ownership interest in the subsidiary was sold.

This structure for business combinations did not avoid purchase accounting and the resulting goodwill. The pressure to search for ways to avoid recording goodwill diminished in 1993 because goodwill became tax deductible. The fact that goodwill will no longer be amortized (i.e., reducing reported earnings) under *FASB Statement No. 142* eliminates the need to structure business combinations to avoid recording goodwill. (It will be interesting to see if goodwill amortization remains tax deductible in the future, since it is no longer amortized for financial reporting purposes.)

JOINT VENTURES

A *joint venture* is a form of partnership that originated with the maritime trading expeditions of the Greeks and Romans. The objective was to combine management participants and capital contributors in undertakings limited to the completion of specific trading projects. Nowadays the joint venture takes many different forms, such as partnership and corporate, domestic and foreign, and temporary as well as relatively permanent.

A common type of joint venture of the temporary type is the formation of syndicates of investment bankers to purchase securities from an issuing corporation and market them to the public. The joint venture enables several participants to share in the risks and rewards of undertakings that would be too large or too risky for a single venturer. It also enables them to combine technology, markets, and human resources to enhance the profit potential of all participants. Other areas in which joint ventures are common are land sales, oil exploration and drilling, and major construction projects.

New areas and uses for the joint venture form of business organization continue to emerge. For example, by mid-1994 in the telecommunications area nearly all major companies were seeking joint venture partners to gain size and capital. The purposes of the proposed joint ventures were to amass capital in order to bid in the multibillion-dollar auction for personal communications services licenses and to build nationwide wireless telephone networks. One perceived advantage of these joint venture alliances is avoidance of expensive acquisition prices.[8]

Joint ventures by U.S. firms are common. An old and well-known example is ***Dow Corning Corporation***, a corporate joint venture of the ***Dow Chemical Company*** and ***Corning Incorporated***. Note 2 to ***PepsiCo's*** 2000 annual report discloses typical joint venture activity. The note reads in part:

> *On July 10, 1999, we formed a business venture with PepCom Industries, Inc., a Pepsi-Cola franchisee, combining bottling businesses in parts of North Carolina and New York. On October 15, 1999, we formed a business venture with Pohlad Companies, a Pepsi-Cola franchisee, combining bottling businesses in Puerto Rico and parts of the southeastern and midwestern United States. Pohlad Companies contributed its interests in Dakota Beverage Company, Delta Beverage Group, Inc. (Delta) and Pepsi-Cola Puerto Rico Bottling Company (PPR). We contributed our interests in Delta and PPR as well as 2.2 million shares of PepsiCo.*

Note C to the 2003 annual report of ***Raytheon Company*** references a recent joint venture. The note reads in part:

> *In 2002, the Company formed a joint venture with Flight Options, Inc., whereby the Company contributed its Flight Travel Air fractional ownership business and loaned the new entity $20 million. In June 2003, the Company participated in a financial recapitalization of Flight Options LLC (FO) and exchanged certain FO debt for equity. As a result of this recapitalization, the Company now owns approximately 66 percent of FO and is consolidating FO's results in its financial statements.*

The joint venture allows for a spreading of risk between or among the venturers, making this business form appealing in the oil and gas and chemical industries, and for international investing. The limited liability enjoyed by shareholders makes the corporate form of joint venture especially appealing.

---

[8]*Mergers & Acquisitions* (September/October 1994), p. 7.

Joint ventures are also common in the pharmaceuticals industry. Note 4 to the 2003 annual report of **Merck & Company** devotes nearly two full pages to descriptions of its primary joint venture activities. Here are a few excerpts from that note:

> *In 1982, Merck entered into an agreement with Astra AB (Astra) to develop and market Astra's products under a royalty-bearing license...*
>
> *In 1989, Merck formed a joint venture with Johnson & Johnson to develop and market a broad range of nonprescription medicines for U.S. consumers.*
>
> *In 1994, Merck and Pasteur Merieux Connaught (now Aventis Pasteur) established an equally-owned joint venture to market vaccines in Europe and to collaborate in the development of combination vaccines for distribution in Europe. ...*
>
> *In 1997, Merck and Rhone-Poulenc (now Aventis) combined their animal health and poultry genetics businesses to form Merial Limited (Merial), a fully integrated animal health company, which is a stand-alone joint venture, equally owned by each party. ...*
>
> *In 2000, the Company and Schering-Plough Corporation (Schering-Plough) entered into agreements to create separate equally-owned partnerships to develop and market in the United States new prescription medicines in the cholesterol-management and respiratory therapeutic areas. ...*
>
> *Investments in affiliates accounted for using the equity method, including the above joint ventures, totaled $2.2 billion at December 31, 2003 and 2002, respectively. These amounts are reported in Other assets. Dividends and distributions received from these affiliates were $553.4 million in 2003, $488.6 million in 2002, and $572.2 million in 2001.*

Nature of Joint Ventures

A **joint venture** is a business entity that is owned, operated, and jointly controlled by a small group of investors (**venturers**) for the conduct of a specific business undertaking that provides mutual benefit for each of the venturers. It is common for each venturer to be active in the management of the venture and to participate in important decisions that typically require the consent of each venturer irrespective of ownership interest. Ownership percentages vary widely, and unequal ownership interests in a specific venture are commonplace.

Organizational Structures of Joint Ventures

Joint ventures may be organized as corporations, partnerships, or undivided interests. These forms are defined in the AICPA's statement of position, "Accounting for Investment in Real Estate Ventures" *(SOP 78-9)*, as follows:

> **Corporate joint venture.** A corporation owned and operated by a small group of venturers to accomplish a mutually beneficial venture or project.
>
> **General partnership.** An association in which each partner has unlimited liability.
>
> **Limited partnership.** An association in which one or more general partners have unlimited liability and one or more partners have limited liability. A limited partnership is usually managed by the general partner or partners, subject to limitations, if any, imposed by the partnership agreement.
>
> **Undivided interest.** An ownership arrangement in which two or more parties jointly own property, and title is held individually to the extent of each party's interest.

Financial reporting requirements for the investors in ventures differ according to the organizational structures.

Accounting for Corporate Joint Ventures

Investors who can participate in the overall management of a *corporate joint venture* should report their investments as equity investments (one-line consolidations) under the provisions of *APB Opinion No. 18*. The approach for establishing significant influence in corporate joint ventures is quite different from that for most common stock investments because *each venturer* usually has to consent to *each significant venture decision*, thus establishing an ability to exercise significant influence regardless of ownership interest. Even so, when a venturer cannot exercise significant influence over its joint venture for whatever reason we account for its investment in the venture by the *cost method*.

An investment in the common stock of a corporate joint venture that exceeds 50% of the venture's outstanding shares is a *subsidiary investment*, for which parent–subsidiary accounting and reporting requirements apply. A corporate joint venture that is more than 50% owned by another entity is not considered a joint venture for purposes of applying the provisions of *APB Opinion No. 18*, even though it continues to be described as a joint venture in financial releases.

Opinion No. 18, paragraph 2d, describes corporate joint ventures as follows:

> *"Corporate joint venture" refers to a corporation owned and operated by a small group of businesses (the "joint venturers") as a separate and specific business or project for the mutual benefit of the members of the group. A government may also be a member of the group. The purpose of a corporate joint venture frequently is to share risks and rewards in developing a new market, product or technology; to combine complementary technological knowledge; or to pool resources in developing production or other facilities. A corporate joint venture also usually provides an arrangement under which each joint venturer may participate, directly or indirectly, in the overall management of the joint venture. Joint venturers thus have an interest or relationship other than as passive investors. An entity which is a subsidiary of one of the "joint venturers" is not a corporate joint venture. The ownership of a corporate joint venture seldom changes, and its stock is usually not traded publicly. A minority public ownership, however, does not preclude a corporation from being a corporate joint venture.*

Note that a subsidiary (more than 50% owned) of a joint venturer is *not* a corporate joint venture under *APB Opinion No. 18*. Instead, we would consolidate it under the provisions of *FASB No. 94*, "Consolidation of All Majority-Owned Subsidiaries."

Opinion No. 18 concludes that investors in the common stock of corporate joint ventures should account for their investments by the equity method in consolidated financial statements. The equity method best enables the investors to reflect the underlying nature of the venture.[9]

Investments in the common stock of joint venturers, or other investments accounted for by the equity method, may be material in relation to the financial position or results of operations of the joint venture investor. If so, it may be necessary for the investor to provide summarized information about the assets, liabilities, and results of operations of its investees in its own financial statements. The required disclosures should be presented *individually* for investments in joint ventures that are material in relation to the financial position or results of operations of the investor. Alternatively, the required disclosures can be *grouped* for investments that are material as a group but are not material individually.

Accounting for Unincorporated Joint Ventures

Accounting Interpretation No. 2 of APB Opinion No. 18 addresses the applicability of *Opinion No. 18* to investments in partnerships and undivided interests in joint ventures. Although the provisions of *Opinion No. 18* apply only to investments in common stock, and therefore do not cover unincorporated ventures, *Interpretation No. 2* explains that many of the provisions of *Opinion No. 18* are appropriate in accounting for investments in unincorporated entities.

For example, partnership profits and losses accrued by investor-partners are generally reflected in the partners' financial statements. Elimination of intercompany profit in accounting for a partnership interest also seems appropriate, as does providing for deferred income tax liabilities on profits accrued by partner-investors. An example of this type of joint venture is the creation of a defense business partnership between **Harsco Corporation** and **FMC Corporation** in 1994. The new partnership was named **United Defense**, **L.P.**, and was formed by combining Harsco's BMY-Combat Systems Division with FMC's Defense Systems Group. The following Harsco partial financial statement note described the joint venture as follows:

> *The consolidated financial statements include the accounts of Harsco Corporation and its majority-owned subsidiaries ("Company"). Investments in United Defense, L.P., a 40% owned partnership and other unconsolidated entities are accounted for on the equity method. The income of unconsolidated entities is on a pre-tax basis for United Defense, L.P. as it is a partnership, and net of taxes for all other unconsolidated entities.*[10]

---

[9] *APB Opinion No. 18*, "The Equity Method of Accounting for Investments in Common Stock," paragraph 16.

[10] Harsco Corporation 1997 10-K, page 34.

In the Harsco example, Harsco's ownership interest in the partnership was only 40%, and Harsco accounted for its interest under the equity method. In contrast, **Southdown** owned a 75% partnership interest in **Kosmos Cement Company**; the other 25% interest was owned by **Lone Star Cement**. Southdown included the following partial financial statement note in its annual report:

> *Kosmos Cement Company (Kosmos Cement) is a partnership which includes a cement plant located in Kosmosdale, Kentucky, and a cement plant located near Pittsburgh, Pennsylvania, along with related terminals and facilities. The partnership is 25% owned by Lone Star Industries, Inc. (Lone Star) and operated and 75% owned by the Company [Southdown]. The Company's Consolidated Balance Sheet includes 100% of the assets and liabilities of Kosmos Cement. Lone Star's 25% interest in Kosmos Cement and earnings therefrom have been reflected as "Minority interest in consolidated joint venture" and "Minority interest in earnings of consolidated joint venture" on the Company's Consolidated Balance Sheet and Statement of Consolidated Earnings, respectively.*[11]

The previous discussion of the applicability of *Opinion No. 18* to partnerships also applies to undivided interests in joint ventures, where the investor-venturer owns an undivided interest in each asset and is proportionately liable for its share of each liability. However, the provisions of *Opinion No. 18* do not apply in some industries that have specialized industry practices. For example, the established industry practice in oil and gas ventures is for the investor-venturer to account for its pro rata share of the assets, liabilities, revenues, and expenses of a joint venture in its own financial statements. This reporting procedure is referred to as **pro rata** or **proportionate consolidation**. **Marathon Oil Corporation** includes a note in its summary of principal accounting policies that "Investments in unincorporated oil and gas joint ventures and undivided interests in certain pipelines, gas processing plants and liquefied natural gas (LNG) tankers are consolidated on a pro rata basis."[12]

Alternatively, *SOP 78-9* recommends against proportionate consolidation for undivided interests in real estate ventures subject to joint control by the investors. A venture is subject to joint control if decisions regarding the financing, development, or sale of property require the approval of two or more owner-venturers. Subsequently, a 1979 AICPA issues paper titled "Joint Venture Accounting" recommended that a joint venture that is not subject to joint control because its liabilities are several rather than joint should be required to use the proportionate consolidation method.

One-Line Consolidation and Proportionate Consolidation

To illustrate the reporting alternatives for unincorporated joint ventures, assume that Price Corporation has a 50% undivided interest in Shield Company, a merchandising joint venture. Comparative financial statements under the two assumptions (accounting under the equity method and proportionate consolidation) appear in Exhibit 11-10. Column 1 presents a summary of Price's income statement and balance sheet, assuming that it uses the equity method of accounting for its investment in Shield, an unconsolidated joint venture company. Shield's income statement and balance sheet are summarized in column 2. In column 3, Price has consolidated its share (50%) of Shield's assets, liabilities, revenues, and expenses (from column 2)—in other words, a proportionate consolidation.

Note that we eliminate Shield's $1,000,000 venture capital in its entirety against the $500,000 Investment in Shield balance, and against half of Shield's asset, liability, revenue, and expense account balances in the proportionate consolidation.

The Accounting Standards Executive Committee of the AICPA is reviewing certain inconsistencies in reporting unincorporated joint ventures that have arisen from the lack of authoritative guidance. Likewise, the Emerging Issues Task Force of the FASB is currently reviewing joint venture accounting.

---

[11] Southdown, Inc., 1996 annual report, p. 47.

[12] Marathon Oil Corporation annual report for the fiscal year ended December 31, 2003, p. F-8.

(All amounts in thousands)	Equity Method—Price Corporation	Shield Unincorporated	Proportionate Consolidation—Price and Shield
Income Statement			
Revenues			
Sales	$2,000	$ 500	$2,250
Income from Shield	100	—	—
Total revenue	2,100	500	2,250
Expenses			
Cost of sales	1,200	200	1,300
Other expenses	400	100	450
Total expenses	1,600	300	1,750
Net income	$ 500	$ 200	$ 500
Balance Sheet			
Cash	$ 200	$ 50	$ 225
Accounts receivable	300	150	375
Inventory	400	300	550
Plant assets	800	800	1,200
Investment in Shield	500	—	—
Total assets	$2,200	$1,300	$2,350
Accounts payable	$ 400	$ 200	$ 500
Other liabilities	500	100	550
Capital stock	1,000	—	1,000
Retained earnings	300	—	300
Venture capital	—	1,000	—
Total equities	$2,200	$1,300	$2,350

EXHIBIT 11-10

The Equity Method and Proportionate Consolidation Compared

ACCOUNTING FOR VARIABLE INTEREST ENTITIES

LEARNING OBJECTIVE **4**

Companies create special-purpose entities for a variety of valid business reasons. For example, companies separately account for employee benefit plans (pension funds or other postretirement-benefit plans) and do not include such plan accounting as a part of the consolidated financial statements. *FASB Statements No. 87, 106*, and *112* set accounting and disclosure rules for these plans. Transfers of financial assets are common in the banking industry, and special-purpose entities deemed qualifying entities are excluded from consolidation under *FASB Statement No. 140, Accounting for Transfers and Servicing of Financial Assets and Extinguishments of Liabilities.* Similarly, life insurance companies are permitted to exclude certain accounts from consolidation.

These special-purpose entities are afforded off-balance-sheet treatment under GAAP. Companies record transactions with these entities, but they do not include the entities in the consolidated financial statements. For example, payments to a pension fund are recorded by the sponsoring company, but the assets and liabilities of the fund are not included in consolidated balance sheet asset and liability totals.

However, ***Enron Corporation*** provides an example in which exclusion of special-purpose entities from the consolidated financial statements gave investors a distorted picture of the company's financial health and business risks. The SEC has alleged financial reporting fraud against Enron in that many of the entities were created primarily to mislead investors, rather than to serve a legitimate business purpose. We will leave discussion of the alleged Enron fraud to other texts and courses on auditing, business law, and business ethics. Our goal here is to provide an introduction to accounting considerations for these special-purpose entities.

In December 2003, the FASB issued *FASB Interpretation No. 46(R), Consolidation of Variable Interest Entities: An Interpretation of ARB No. 51* (a revision of FASB *Interpretation No. 46* issued earlier in the year) (*FIN 46(R)*) to address perceived abuses in accounting for special-purpose entities. The FASB coined the term **"variable interest entities"** (VIEs) to define those special-purpose entities that will require consolidation. There are a few major issues and concepts to cover. First, does an entity meet the conditions for inclusion in consolidated financial statements? Second, if consolidation is required, how should consolidated amounts be determined? Rules for consolidation come from *ARB No. 51*, but that standard relies on voting control or percentage ownership of voting shares to decide both of the issues just noted. The interpretation under *FIN 46(R)* attempts to identify those entities in which financial control exists because of contractual and financial arrangements other than ownership of voting interests. Recall your early childhood. Your parents did not legally "own" you, but they clearly had financial control over your activities. *FIN 46(R)* extends the concept of *ARB No. 51* to include companies in which the equity investors cannot provide financing for the entity's business risks and activities without additional financial support.

FIN 46(R) does not apply just to Enron. Many companies will be required to consolidate variable interest entities under the new interpretation, even ***Disney***. Notes 2 and 4 to Disney's 2003 annual report indicated that the company would likely apply *FIN 46* and would consolidate certain significant investments beginning in the first quarter of 2004. Here are a few excerpts from the 2003 annual report.

> *The Company has equity interests in certain entities, including* Euro Disney S.C.A. *(Euro Disney) and* Hongkong International Theme Parks Limited *(Hong Kong Disneyland), which are currently not consolidated, but under current rules are accounted for under the equity or cost method of accounting. ... While we continue to evaluate the total impact of FIN 46, based on the current exposure draft, the Company anticipates that it will likely be required to consolidate Euro Disney and Hong Kong Disneyland in the first quarter of fiscal 2004. (Note 2, p. 75)*

Note 4, page 81, provides a pro forma income statement and balance sheet assuming consolidation of Euro Disney and Hong Kong Disneyland as of September 30, 2003. A few items are notable. Consolidated net income is unaffected by the additional consolidations. Total assets increase from $49,988 million to $53,347 million, primarily due to the reported increase in fixed assets upon consolidation. Perhaps more importantly for investors evaluating the business and financial risks of Disney, total current liabilities increase from $8,669 million to $11,272 million in the pro forma balance sheet.

Identifying Variable Interest Entities

Under *FIN 46(R)*, a variable interest entity must be consolidated. What is a variable interest? What is a variable interest entity? *FIN 46(R)* is a very complex document. Our goal here is to provide an understanding of the concepts embodied in *FIN 46(R)*, not to cover all of the details.

Paragraph 2c of *FIN 46(R)* states "Variable interests in a variable interest entity are contractual, ownership, or other pecuniary interests in an entity that change with changes in the fair value of the entity's net assets exclusive of variable interests." For example an at-risk equity investment is a variable interest.

The interpretation looks at all forms of business entities to identify VIEs. Therefore, a VIE might be another corporation, partnership, limited liability company, or trust-type arrangement. A potential VIE must be a separate entity, not a subset, branch, or division of another entity. Certain entities, such as pension plans, are specifically excluded, as they are covered by other FASB or SEC reporting standards. Paragraph 5 of *FIN 46(R)* defines VIEs requiring consolidation. Paragraph 5 spans two full pages, but the first sentence of paragraph 5a provides a good feel for the concept and intent of the FASB in writing the interpretation: "The total equity investment at risk is not sufficient to permit the entity to finance its activities without additional subordinated financial support provided by any parties, including equity holders." For example, a company may own only a minimal voting equity interest in an entity, but be contractually required to provide additional financial support in the event of future operating losses.

According to paragraph 6, "The investments or other interests that will absorb portions of a variable interest entity's expected losses or receive portions of the entity's expected residual returns are called variable interests."

Paragraph 8 provides:

> *A variable interest entity's expected losses are the expected negative variability in the fair value of its net assets exclusive of variable interests. A variable interest entity's expected residual returns are the expected positive variability in the fair value of its net assets exclusive of variable interests. Expected variability in the fair value of net assets includes expected variability resulting from operating results of the entity.*

The FASB offers a general guideline of an equity investment at risk of less than 10% of total assets to be indicative of an entity unable to finance operations without additional subordinated financial support. The FASB also describes situations in which an even greater equity interest may be insufficient to indicate financial independence.

Having identified VIEs, entities that will require consolidation, the FASB turns its attention to who will be required to consolidate the VIE. The FASB uses the term **primary beneficiary** to indicate the company that will include the VIE in consolidated statements. Paragraph 14 provides guidance on identifying the primary beneficiary.

> *An enterprise shall consolidate a variable interest entity if that enterprise has a variable interest (or combination of variable interests) that will absorb a majority of the entity's expected losses, receive a majority of the entity's expected residual returns, or both. ... If one enterprise will absorb a majority of a variable interest entity's expected losses and another will receive a majority of that entity's expected residual returns, the enterprise absorbing a majority of the losses shall consolidate the variable interest entity.*

All enterprises holding a significant interest in a VIE are required to make disclosures under *FIN 46(R)*. The primary beneficiary must disclose:

a. The nature, purpose, size, and activities of the VIE

b. The carrying amount and classification of consolidated assets that are collateral for the VIE's obligations

c. Lack of recourse if creditors (or beneficial interest holders) of a consolidated VIE have no recourse to the general credit of the primary beneficiary (Paragraph 23)

Other enterprises, not the primary beneficiary, must disclose:

a. The nature of the involvement with the VIE and when that involvement began

b. The nature, purpose, size, and activities of the VIE

c. The enterprise's maximum exposure to loss as a result of its involvement with the VIE (Paragraph 24)

Here is a simple example. Ten independent companies—Melanie, Troy, Matthew, Emily, Megan, Danielle, Ryan, Corrine, Tricia, and Lisa Corporations—decide to pool their financial resources for a new business venture investing in offshore oil leases, GetRichQuick Corporation. There is no intent to publicly trade shares of the new company. If the concept is successful, GetRichQuick will provide the investors with enormous future returns, but the venture is not without risk. Each investor contributes $1 million and each receives 10% of the voting common stock of GetRichQuick. Additionally, each investor will have one member on the board of directors of the new company. Under the business plan, GetRichQuick will borrow an additional $20 million to help finance acquisition of leasing rights and subsequent exploration, research, and development. Corrine Corporation agrees to assume 75% of losses if the venture is unsuccessful. Corrine believes that the risk is minimal, but offshore oil leasing could produce significant environmental liabilities, well beyond the initial $10 million equity capitalization. In exchange for Corrine's generous offer to absorb a majority of the downside risks, the investors agree that Corrine will receive a 28% share of all future profits. The remaining nine investors will each receive an 8% profit share.

How should the investors account for their investments in GetRichQuick? At first glance, it appears that all 10 investors would apply the cost method of accounting under current GAAP. No company holds a significant influence or controlling voting interest in the new venture. Assume that the investors correctly determine that GetRichQuick is a VIE under *FIN 46(R)*. One of the investors will be required to consolidate the new venture. Corrine's contractual agreement would make Corrine the primary beneficiary. Corrine will be required to consolidate GetRichQuick. The remaining nine investors will not be consolidating; however, because GetRichQuick has been identified as a VIE, they will be required to make *FIN 46(R)* disclosures.

Consolidation of a Variable Interest Entity

We now consider the second issue: how the consolidation should be effected. Recall that *FIN 46(R)* is an interpretation of existing guidance for consolidation. Therefore, the rules essentially follow those for any other consolidation. The primary beneficiary will measure and consolidate based on the fair values of assets, liabilities, and noncontrolling interest at the date it becomes the primary beneficiary. If the primary beneficiary has transferred assets to the VIE, these should be transferred at the same amounts at which they were carried on the primary beneficiary's books (i.e., no gain or loss is recorded on the transfer). Thus, the primary beneficiary treats the initial valuation consistent with an application of *FASB Statement No. 141*. There are two exceptions: (1) Goodwill may be recorded only if the VIE is a business under *FIN 46(R)*. (2) Otherwise, any excess of the consideration paid over fair value of the net assets is treated as an extraordinary loss. Appendix C, paragraph 3 defines a business:

> *A business is a self-sustaining, integrated set of activities and assets conducted and managed for providing a return to investors. A business consists of (a) inputs, (b) processes applied to those inputs, and c) resulting outputs that are used to generate revenues. For a set of activities and assets to be a business, it must contain all of the inputs and processes necessary for it to conduct normal operations, which include the ability to sustain a revenue stream by providing its outputs to customers.*

After the initial measurement of fair values and consolidation, the primary beneficiary will follow normal consolidation principles in subsequent accounting for the VIE. So the primary beneficiary will use voting interests to allocate future performance among the controlling and noncontrolling interests. All intercompany transactions and account balances must be eliminated. Income or expense due to fees between the primary beneficiary and the VIE must be eliminated against the net income of the VIE. None of these fees should be allocated to any noncontrolling interests.

Estimating the fair value of VIE assets will pose challenges for many firms. Often VIEs invest in unique assets for which fair market values cannot be found from simply looking up a current trading value on a stock exchange. Firms will need to estimate expected future cash flows associated with VIE operations as a means of estimating fair values. (Appendix A of *FIN 46(R)* provides an example.)

SUMMARY

This chapter covers several different theories related to consolidating the financial statements of a parent company and its subsidiaries. It also examines "new basis accounting" for assets and liabilities in a subsidiary's separate financial statements under push-down accounting and illustrates accounting for corporate joint ventures.

We identify the concepts and procedures underlying current consolidation practices (i.e., current U.S. GAAP) as the contemporary theory of consolidation to distinguish current practices from accounting practices under parent-company and entity theories. The basic differences among the three theories are compared in a matrix in Exhibit 11-1. Nearly all of the differences disappear when subsidiaries are wholly owned.

Under push-down accounting, we record the cost/book value differentials determined in a purchase business combination in the separate books of the subsidiary. Push-down accounting is ordinarily required by the SEC for purchase business combinations in which all or substantially all of the ownership interests in the acquired company change hands. Some acquisitions can be structured to avoid push-down accounting.

A joint venture is a business entity that is owned, operated, and jointly controlled by a small group of investors for their mutual benefit. The joint venture investors are usually active in the management of the venture, and each venturer usually has the ability to exercise significant influence over the joint venture investee. Investors account for their investments in corporate joint ventures as one-line consolidations under the equity method. Similarly, investors account for investments in unincorporated joint ventures (partnerships and undivided interests) as one-line consolidations or proportionate consolidations, depending on the special accounting practices of the industries in which they operate.

Companies also create entities or relationships with other firms for a variety of special business purposes. Often these entities are structured such that an investor has effective economic control, even though the investor lacks voting control through a significant equity ownership interest. The FASB recognizes these situations and requires that the primary beneficiary investor consolidate these variable interest entities.

QUESTIONS

1. Compare the contemporary, parent-company, and entity theories of consolidated financial statements.
2. Which, if any, of the consolidation theories would be changed by FASB pronouncements? (For example, assume that a new FASB statement requires noncontrolling interest expense to be computed as the non-controlling interest share of subsidiary dividends declared.)
3. Under the entity theory of consolidation, a total valuation of the subsidiary is imputed on the basis of the price paid by the parent company for its controlling interest. Do you see any practical or conceptual problems with this approach to valuation?
4. Assume that Pabst Corporation acquires 60% of the voting common stock of Seller Corporation for $6,000,000 and that a consolidated balance sheet is prepared immediately after the business combination. Would total consolidated assets be equal to their fair values if the parent-company theory were applied? If the entity theory were applied?
5. Why might the current practice of valuing the equity of noncontrolling shareholders at book value overstate the value of the noncontrolling interest?
6. Cite the conditions under which consolidated net income under parent-company theory would equal income to majority stockholders under entity theory.
7. If investment income from a subsidiary is measured under the equity method and the statements are consolidated under the entity theory, will consolidated net income be equal to parent-company net income?
8. Why are the income statement amounts under entity theory and contemporary theory the same if the subsidiary investment is made at book value? (Do not consider the different income statement presentations of majority and noncontrolling interests in responding to this question.)
9. Does contemporary practice correspond to parent-company or entity theory in matters related to unrealized and constructive gains and losses on intercompany transactions?
10. To what extent does push-down accounting facilitate the consolidation process?
11. What is a joint venture and how are joint ventures organized?
12. What accounting and reporting methods are used by investor-venturers in accounting for their joint venture investments?

EXERCISES

E 11-1

Parent-company and entity theories

1. The classification of noncontrolling interest expense as an expense and noncontrolling interest as a liability is preferred under:
   a *Parent-company theory*
   b *Entity theory*
   c *Contemporary theory*
   d *None of the above*

2. Contemporary theory is most similar to parent-company theory in matters relating to:
   a *Goodwill computations*
   b *Noncontrolling interest computations*
   c *Intercompany profit eliminations*
   d *Consolidated financial statement presentations*

3. Contemporary theory is most similar to entity theory in matters relating to:
   a *Goodwill computations*
   b *Noncontrolling interest computations*
   c *Intercompany profit eliminations*
   d *Consolidated financial statement presentations*

4. When "consolidated income allocated to majority stockholders" under entity theory is compared to "consolidated net income" under contemporary theory, one would expect consolidated net income under contemporary theory to be:
   a *Equal to consolidated income allocated to majority stockholders under entity theory*
   b *Greater than consolidated income allocated to majority stockholders under entity theory*
   c *Less than consolidated income allocated to majority stockholders under entity theory*
   d *Greater or less depending on the relationship of investment cost to book value acquired*

5. Consolidated financial statement amounts and classifications should be identical under the contemporary, entity, and parent-company theories of consolidation if:

   a **All subsidiaries are acquired at book value**

   b **Only 100%-owned subsidiaries are consolidated**

   c **There are no intercompany transactions**

   d **All subsidiaries are acquired at book value and there are no intercompany transactions**

6. When the fair values of an acquired subsidiary's assets and liabilities are recorded in the subsidiary's accounts (push-down accounting), the subsidiary's retained earnings will be:

   a **Adjusted for the difference between the push-down capital and goodwill from the acquisition**

   b **Credited for the amount of the push-down capital**

   c **Transferred in its entirety to push-down capital**

   d **Credited for the difference between the total imputed value of the entity and the purchase price of the interest acquired**

7. The most consistent statement of assets in consolidated financial statements would result from applying:

   a **Contemporary theory**

   b **Parent-company theory**

   c **Entity theory**

   d **A current cost system of accounting**

E 11-2

Joint ventures

1. A joint venture would not be organized as a(an):

   a **Corporation**

   b **Proprietorship**

   c **Partnership**

   d **Undivided interest**

2. Corporate joint ventures should be accounted for by the equity method, provided that the joint venturer:

   a **Cannot exercise significant influence over the joint venture**

   b **Can participate in the overall management of the venture**

   c **Owns more than 50% of the joint venture**

   d **All of the above**

3. An investor in a corporate joint venture would be least likely to:

   a **Be active in the management of the venture**

   b **Have an ability to exercise significant influence**

   c **Consent to each significant venture decision**

   d **Hold title to a pro rata share of joint venture assets**

4. Investors account for their investments in corporate joint ventures under the equity method if their individual ownership percentages are at least:

   a **10%**

   b **20%**

   c **50%**

   d **None of the above**

5. Farver, Greta, and Higgs Corporations own 60%, 25%, and 15%, respectively, of the common stock of Produce Corporation, a corporate joint venture that they organized for wholesaling fruits and vegetables. Which of the corporations should report their joint venture interests under the equity method?

   a **Farver, Greta, and Higgs**

   b **Farver and Greta**

   c **Greta and Higgs**

   d **Farver and Higgs**

E 11-3

Parent-company and entity theories

1. Peterson Company pays $720,000 for an 80% interest in Smith Corporation on December 31, 2006, when Smith's net assets at book value and fair value are $800,000. Under entity theory, the noncontrolling interest at acquisition is:

   a **$144,000**

   b **$160,000**

   c **$180,000**

   d **$200,000**

2. Seattle Corporation sold inventory items to its parent company, Portland Corporation, during 2006, and at December 31, 2006, Portland's inventory included items acquired from Seattle at a gross profit of $50,000. If Seattle is an 80%-owned subsidiary of Portland, the amount of unrealized inventory profits to be eliminated in preparing the consolidated income statements of Portland and Subsidiary for 2006 is $40,000 under:

a Parent-company theory

b Contemporary theory

c Entity theory

d The equity method of accounting

3. A parent company that applies the entity theory of consolidation in preparing its consolidated financial statements computed income from its 90%-owned subsidiary under the equity method of accounting as follows:

Equity in subsidiary income ($200,000 × 90%)	$180,000
Patent amortization ($70,000 ÷ 10 years × 90%)	(6,300)
Income from subsidiary	$173,700

Given the foregoing information, noncontrolling interest expense is:

a $20,000

b $19,300

c $18,000

d $17,300

Use the following information in answering questions 4 and 5:

Piedmont Corporation acquired an 80% interest in Swan Corporation on January 1, 2006, when Swan's total stockholders' equity was $840,000. The book values and fair values of Swan's assets and liabilities were equal on this date.

At December 31, 2006, the consolidated balance sheet of Piedmont and Subsidiary shows unamortized patents from consolidation of $54,000, with a note that the patents are being amortized over a 10-year period.

4. If the entity theory of consolidation was used, the purchase price of the 80% interest in Swan must have been:

a $720,000

b $732,000

c $747,000

d $900,000

5. If the contemporary theory of consolidation was used, the purchase price of the 80% interest in Swan must have been:

a $720,000

b $732,000

c $747,000

d $900,000

E 11-4

Computations (parent-company and entity theories) Balance sheet information of Pond and Staff Corporations at December 31, 2006, is summarized as follows (in thousands):

	Pond Book Value	Staff Book Value	Staff Fair Value
Current assets	$ 520	$ 50	$ 90
Plant assets—net	480	250	360
	$1,000	$300	$450
Current liabilities	$ 80	$ 40	$ 50
Capital stock	800	200	
Retained earnings	120	60	
	$1,000	$300	

On January 2, 2006, Pond purchases 80% of Staff's outstanding shares for $500,000 cash.

REQUIRED

1. Determine goodwill from the business combination under (a) parent-company theory and (b) entity theory.

2. Determine noncontrolling interest at January 2, 2006, under (a) parent-company theory and (b) entity theory.

3. Determine the amount of total assets that would appear on a consolidated balance sheet prepared at January 2, 2006, under (a) parent-company theory and (b) entity theory.

E 11-5

Computations under parent-company and entity theories (cost/book value differentials) On January 1, 2006, Perry Corporation pays $300,000 for an 80% interest in Shelly Company, when Shelly's net assets have a book value of $275,000 and a fair value of $350,000. The $75,000 excess fair value is due to undervalued equipment with a five-year remaining useful life. Any goodwill is not written off.

Separate incomes of Perry and Shelly for 2006 are $500,000 and $50,000, respectively.

REQUIRED

1. Calculate consolidated net income and noncontrolling interest expense under (a) parent-company theory and (b) entity theory.

2. Determine goodwill at December 31, 2006, under (a) parent-company theory and (b) entity theory.

E 11-6

Computations under parent-company, entity, and contemporary theories (midyear acquisition) Stahl Corporation's recorded assets and liabilities are equal to their fair values on July 1, 2006, when Polak Corporation purchases 72,000 shares of Stahl common stock for $1,800,000. Identifiable net assets of Stahl on this date are $1,710,000, and Stahl's stockholders' equity consists of $800,000 of $10 par common stock and $910,000 retained earnings.

Stahl has net income for 2006 of $80,000 earned evenly throughout the year and declares no dividends.

REQUIRED

1. Determine the total value of Stahl's net assets at July 1, 2006, under entity theory.

2. Determine goodwill that would appear in a consolidated balance sheet of Polak Corporation and Subsidiary at July 1, 2006, under (a) entity theory, (b) parent-company theory, and (c) contemporary theory.

3. Determine Polak's investment income from Stahl on an equity basis for 2006.

4. Determine noncontrolling interest in Stahl that will be reported in the consolidated balance sheet at December 31, 2006, under entity theory.

E 11-7

Computations under parent-company and entity theories (upstream sales) Palumbo Company acquired an 80% interest in Seal Corporation at book value equal to fair value on January 1, 2006. During the year, Seal sold $100,000 inventory items to Palumbo, and at December 31, 2006, unrealized profits amounted to $30,000. Separate incomes of Palumbo and Seal for 2006 were $500,000 and $300,000, respectively.

REQUIRED

1. Determine consolidated net income for Palumbo Company and Subsidiary under the parent-company theory of consolidation.

2. Determine total consolidated income for Palumbo Company and Subsidiary, income to majority stockholders, and income to noncontrolling stockholders under the entity theory of consolidation.

E 11-8

Compute consolidated net income under three theories (upstream and downstream sales) Palid Corporation acquired an 80% interest in Stark Corporation at book value a number of years ago.

Separate incomes of Palid and Stark for 2006 were $120,000 and $60,000, respectively. The only transactions between Palid and Stark during 2006 were as follows:

1. Palid sold inventory items to Stark for $60,000. These items cost Palid $30,000, and half the items were inventoried at $30,000 by Stark at December 31, 2006.

2. Stark sold land that cost $70,000 to Palid for $96,000 during 2006. The land was held by Palid at December 31, 2006.

3. Stark paid $24,000 dividends to Palid during 2006.

REQUIRED: Compute consolidated net income for Palid Corporation and Subsidiary for 2006 under:

1. Contemporary theory

2. Parent-company theory

3. Entity theory

E 11-9

Journal entries for push-down accounting On January 1, 2006, Pioneer Corporation acquired a 90% interest in Security Corporation for $2,520,000. The book values and fair values of Security's assets and equities on this date are as follows (in thousands):

	Book Value	Fair Value
Cash	$ 200	$ 200
Accounts receivable—net	300	300
Inventories	500	600
Land	300	800
Buildings—net	700	1,000
Equipment—net	800	600
	$2,800	$3,500
Accounts payable	$ 550	$ 550
Other liabilities	450	550
Capital stock	1,000	
Retained earnings	800	
	$2,800	

REQUIRED

1. Prepare the journal entries on Security Corporation's books to push down the values reflected in the purchase price under *parent-company theory*.

2. Prepare the journal entries on Security Corporation's books to push down the values reflected in the purchase price under *entity theory*.

E 11-10

Determine investment income for corporate joint venturers Sun-Belt Land Development Corporation is a corporate joint venture that is jointly controlled and operated by five investor-venturers, four with 15% interests each and one with a 40% interest. Each of the five venturers is active in venture management. Land sales and other important venture decisions require the consent of each venturer. All venturers paid $15 per share for their investments on January 1, 2006, and no changes in ownership interests have occurred since that time. During 2007, Sun-Belt reported net income of $500,000 and paid dividends of $100,000. The stockholders' equity of Sun-Belt at December 31, 2007, is as follows (in thousands):

Sun-Belt Land Development Corporation
Stockholders' Equity at December 31, 2007

Common stock $10 par, 500,000 shares authorized, issued, and outstanding	$5,000
Additional paid-in capital	2,500
Total paid-in capital	7,500
Retained earnings	1,000
Total stockholders' equity	$8,500

REQUIRED: Determine the investment income for 2007 and the investment account balance at December 31, 2007, for the 40% venturer and for one of the 15% venturers.

E 11-11

Accounting for a VIE beyond the initial measurement date Martin Corporation is the primary beneficiary in a VIE, even though Martin owns only 10% of the outstanding voting shares. In the year following the initial consolidation, the VIE earns net income of $500,000. Included in income is a fee paid by Martin for $40,000. What amount of noncontrolling expense will appear in the consolidated income statement?

E 11-12

VIE reporting and disclosure requirements Paxel, Inc., holds an interest in Polo Corporation. Paxel has determined that Polo qualifies as a VIE and that Paxel's contractual position makes Paxel the primary beneficiary. Darden Corporation also holds a significant financial interest in Polo. What are the financial reporting and disclosure requirements for both Paxel and Darden?

E 11-13

Determining the primary beneficiary in a VIE Jennifer Corporation and Laura Company participate in a business classified as a VIE. Under terms of their contractual arrangement, Jennifer and Laura share equally in expected residual returns of the VIE. However, expected losses are allocated 70% to Laura and 30% to Jennifer. Which of the investors is the primary beneficiary in this VIE?

P 11-1

Consolidated balance sheets (parent-company and entity theories) The adjusted trial balances of Picody Corporation and its 80%-owned subsidiary, Scone Corporation, at December 31, 2007, are as follows (in thousands):

	Picody	Scone
Cash	$ 32	$ 20
Receivables—net	120	180
Inventories	300	150
Plant assets—net	1,200	750
Investment in Scone	752	—
Cost of sales	1,300	600
Depreciation	225	75
Other expenses	271	175
Dividends	200	50
	$4,400	$2,000
Accounts payable	$ 204	$ 100
Other liabilities	300	200
Capital stock	1,000	500
Retained earnings	800	200
Sales	2,000	1,000
Income from Scone	96	
	$4,400	$2,000

Picody acquired its interest in Scone for $640,000 on January 1, 2006, when Scone's stockholders' equity consisted of $500,000 capital stock and $100,000 retained earnings. The excess cost was due to a $100,000 undervaluation of plant assets with a 5-year remaining useful life and to previously unrecorded patents with a 10-year amortization period. Picody uses a one-line consolidation in accounting for its investment in Scone.

REQUIRED: Prepare comparative consolidated balance sheets at December 31, 2007, for Picody Corporation and Subsidiary under (a) parent-company theory and (b) entity theory.

P 11-2

Consolidated balance sheet and income statement under entity theory Pisces Corporation acquires an 80% interest in Scorpio Company on January 3, 2006, for $160,000. On this date Scorpio's stockholders' equity consists of $100,000 capital stock and $70,000 retained earnings. The cost/book value differential is assigned to undervalued equipment with a 6-year remaining life. Immediately after acquisition, Scorpio sells equipment with a 10-year remaining useful life to Pisces at a gain of $5,000.

Adjusted trial balances of Pisces and Scorpio at December 31, 2006, are as follows (in thousands):

	Pisces	Scorpio
Current assets	$ 151.6	$ 90
Plant and equipment	400	200
Investment in Scorpio	168.4	—
Cost of sales	250	130
Depreciation	50	25
Other expenses	60	20
Dividends	50	10
	$1,130	$475
Accumulated depreciation	$ 150	$ 50
Liabilities	100	50
Capital stock	300	100
Retained earnings	163.6	70
Sales	400	200
Gain on plant assets	—	5
Income from Scorpio	16.4	—
	$1,130	$475

REQUIRED

1. Prepare a consolidated income statement for 2006 using entity theory.

2. Prepare a consolidated balance sheet at December 31, 2006, using entity theory.

P 11-3

Computations (parent-company and entity theories) Palace Corporation paid $595,000 cash for 70% of the outstanding voting stock of Sign Corporation on January 2, 2006, when Sign's stockholders' equity consisted of $500,000 of $10 par common stock and $250,000 retained earnings. The book values of Sign's assets and liabilities were equal to their fair values on this date.

During 2006, Palace Corporation had separate income of $300,000 and paid dividends of $150,000. Sign's net income for 2006 was $90,000 and its dividends were $50,000. At December 31, 2006, the stockholders' equities of Palace and Sign were as follows (in thousands):

	Palace	Sign
Common stock ($10 par)	$1,400	$500
Retained earnings	450	290
Total stockholders' equity	$1,850	$790

There were no intercompany transactions between Palace Corporation and Sign Corporation during 2006. Palace uses the equity method of accounting for its investment in Sign.

REQUIRED

1. Assume that Palace Corporation uses parent-company theory for preparing consolidated financial statements for 2006. Determine the following amounts:

a Palace Corporation's income from Sign for 2006
b Goodwill that will appear in the consolidated balance sheet at December 31, 2006
c Consolidated net income for 2006
d Noncontrolling interest expense for 2006
e Noncontrolling interest at December 31, 2006

2. Assume that Palace Corporation uses entity theory for preparing consolidated financial statements for 2006. Determine the following amounts:

a Palace Corporation's income from Sign for 2006
b Goodwill that will appear in the consolidated balance sheet at December 31, 2006
c Total consolidated income for 2006
d Noncontrolling interest expense for 2006
e Noncontrolling interest at December 31, 2006

P 11-4

Comparative consolidated statements under alternative theories At December 31, 2006, when the fair values of Smedley Corporation's net assets were equal to their book values of $240,000, Pierre Corporation acquired an 80% interest in Smedley Corporation for $224,000. One year later at December 31, 2007, the comparative adjusted trial balances of the two corporations appear as follows (in thousands):

	Pierre Corporation	Smedley Corporation
Cash	$ 40	$ 70
Accounts receivable	90	30
Inventory	160	40
Land	200	80
Buildings	900	200
Investment in Smedley	240	—
Cost of sales	375	200
Expenses	150	50
Dividends	120	30
Total debits	$2,275	$700

(continued)

Accumulated depreciation	$ 200	$ 60
Accounts payable	175	100
Capital stock	800	200
Retained earnings	360	40
Sales	700	300
Income from Smedley	40	—
Total credits	$2,275	$700

ADDITIONAL INFORMATION: During 2007, Smedley Corporation sold inventory items costing $15,000 to Pierre for $23,000. Half of these inventory items remain unsold at December 31, 2007.

REQUIRED: Prepare comparative consolidated financial statements for Pierre Corporation and Subsidiary at and for the year ended December 31, 2007, under

1. Contemporary theory

2. Parent-company theory

3. Entity theory

P 11-5

Comparative balance sheets under contemporary and entity theories
Balance sheets for Packard Corporation and its 80%-owned subsidiary, Studs Building Supply Company, at December 31, 2007, are summarized as follows (in thousands):

	Packard	Studs
Assets		
Cash	$ 50	$ 20
Receivables—net	75	35
Inventories	110	30
Plant assets—net	215	85
Investment in Studs Building Supply	144	—
Total assets	$594	$170
Liabilities and Stockholders' Equity		
Accounts payable	$ 80	$ 15
Other liabilities	20	5
Total liabilities	100	20
Capital stock	300	100
Retained earnings	194	50
Stockholders' equity	494	150
Total equities	$594	$170

ADDITIONAL INFORMATION

1. Packard Corporation paid $128,000 for its 80% interest in Studs on January 1, 2006, when Studs had capital stock of $100,000 and retained earnings of $10,000.

2. At December 31, 2007, Packard's inventory included items on which Studs had recorded gross profit of $20,000.

REQUIRED: Prepare comparative consolidated balance sheets for Packard Corporation and Subsidiary at December 31, 2007, under the contemporary and entity theories of consolidation.

P 11-6

[AICPA adapted] Separate and consolidated financial statements—entity theory
The individual and consolidated balance sheets and income statements of X and Y Companies for the current year are presented in the accompanying table.

ADDITIONAL INFORMATION

1. X Company purchased its interest in Y Company several years ago.

2. X Company sells products to Y Company for further processing and also sells to firms outside the affiliated entity. The inventories of Y Company include an intercompany profit at both the beginning and the end of the year.

3. At the beginning of the current year, Y Company purchased bonds of X Company having a maturity value of $100,000. These bonds are being held as available-for-sale securities and are, correspondingly, carried at fair value. No change in fair value has occurred over the course of the year. Y Company has agreed to offer X Company the option of reacquiring the bonds at Y's cost before deciding to dispose of them on the open market.

X and Y Companies' Individual and Consolidated
Balance Sheets as of the End of the Current Year (in thousands)

	X Company	Y Company	Consolidated
Assets			
Cash and receivables	$ 35	$108	$ 97.4
Inventories	40	90	122
Plant (net)	460	140	600
Patents	—	—	30
Investment in Y	245	—	—
X bonds owned	—	103	—
Total assets	$780	$441	$849.4
Liabilities and Equity			
Current payables	$ 70	$ 23	$ 53
Dividends payable	10	8	12.4
Mortgage bonds (5%)	200	50	150
Capital stock	300	200	300
Retained earnings	200	160	217
Noncontrolling interest	—	—	117
Total liabilities and equity	$780	$441	$849.4

Individual and Consolidated Income Statements for the Current Year

	X Company	Y Company	Consolidated
Sales	$600	$400	$760
Cost of sales	(360)	(280)	(403)
Gross profit	240	120	357
Operating expenses	(130)	(54)	(189)
Operating profit	110	66	168
Interest revenue	1.8	5	1.8
Dividend revenue	11.2	—	—
	123	71	169.8
Interest expense	(10)	(3)	(8)
Provision for income tax	(56)	(34)	(90)
Nonrecurring loss	—	—	(3)
Noncontrolling share	—	—	(8.7)
Net income	$ 57	$ 34	$ 60.1
Dividends	(20)	(16)	(24.8)
Transfer to retained earnings	$ 37	$ 18	$ 35.3

REQUIRED: Answer the following questions on the basis of the preceding information.

1. Does X Company carry its investment in Y Company on the cost or the equity basis? Explain the basis of your answer.

2. If Y Company's common stock has a stated value of $100 per share, how many shares does X Company own? How did you determine this?

3. When X acquired its interest in Y Company, the assets and liabilities of Y Company were recorded at their fair values. The $30,000 patents represents unamortized patents at the end of the current year. The unrecorded patents were $50,000 under entity theory, and the amortization is over a 10-year period. What was the amount of Y's retained earnings at the date that X Company acquired its interest in Y Company?

4. What is the nature of the nonrecurring loss appearing on the consolidated income statement? Reproduce the consolidating entry from which this figure originated and explain.

5. What is the amount of intercompany sales during the current year by X Company to Y Company?

6. Are there any intercompany debts other than the intercompany bondholdings? Identify any such debts, and state which company is the debtor and which is the creditor in each case. Explain your reasoning.

7. What is the explanation for the difference between the consolidated cost of goods sold and the combined cost of goods sold of the two affiliated companies? Prepare a schedule reconciling combined and consolidated cost of goods sold, showing the amount of intercompany profit in the beginning and ending inventories of Y Company and demonstrating how you determined the amount of intercompany profit. (*Hint:* A well-organized and labeled T-account for cost of goods sold will be an acceptable approach.)

8. Show how the $8,700 noncontrolling interest in total consolidated net income was determined.

9. Show how the total noncontrolling interest on the balance sheet ($117,000) was determined.

10. Beginning with the $200,000 balance in X Company's retained earnings at the end of the current year, prepare a schedule in which you derive the $217,000 balance of consolidated retained earnings at the end of the current year.

P 11-7

Journal entry to record push down, subsidiary balance sheet, and investment income
Played Corporation paid $480,000 cash for a 100% interest in Splash Corporation on January 1, 2007, when Splash's stockholders' equity consisted of $200,000 capital stock and $80,000 retained earnings. Splash's balance sheet on December 31, 2006, is summarized as follows (in thousands):

	Book Value	Fair Value
Cash	$ 30	$ 30
Accounts receivable—net	70	70
Inventories	60	80
Land	50	75
Buildings—net	100	190
Equipment—net	90	75
Total assets	$400	$520
Accounts payable	$ 40	$ 40
Other liabilities	70	60
Capital stock	200	
Retained earnings	90	
Total equities	$400	

Played uses the equity method to account for its interest in Splash. The amortization periods for the fair value/book value differentials at the time of acquisition were as follows:

$20,000	Undervalued inventories (sold in 2007)
25,000	Undervalued land
50,000	Undervalued buildings (10-year useful life remaining)
(15,000)	Overvalued equipment (5-year useful life remaining)
10,000	Other liabilities (2 years before maturity)
20,000	Goodwill

REQUIRED

1. Prepare a journal entry on Splash's books to push down the values reflected in the purchase price.

2. Prepare a balance sheet for Splash Corporation on January 1, 2007.

3. Splash's net income for 2007 under the new push-down accounting system is $90,000. What is Played's income from Splash for 2007?

P 11-8

Journal entries and calculations for push-down accounting
Parker Corporation paid $3,000,000 for an 80% interest in Sanue Corporation on January 1, 2006, when the book values and fair values of Sanue's assets and liabilities were as follows (in thousands):

	Book Value	Fair Value
Cash	$ 300	$ 300
Accounts receivable—net	600	600
Inventories	800	2,400
Land	200	200
Buildings—net	600	600
Equipment—net	1,000	500
	$3,500	$4,600
Accounts payable	$ 500	$ 500
Long-term debt	1,000	1,000
Capital stock, $1 par	800	
Retained earnings	1,200	
	$3,500	

REQUIRED

1. Prepare a journal entry on Sanue's books to push down 80% of the values reflected in the purchase price (the parent-company-theory approach).
2. Prepare a journal entry on Sanue's books to push down 100% of the values reflected in the purchase price (the entity-theory approach).
3. Calculate the noncontrolling interest in Sanue on January 1, 2006, under parent-company theory.
4. Calculate the noncontrolling interest in Sanue on January 1, 2006, under entity theory.

P 11-9

Journal entries and comparative balance sheets at acquisition for push down

Power Corporation paid $180,000 cash for a 90% interest in Swing Corporation on January 1, 2007, when Swing's stockholders' equity consisted of $100,000 capital stock and $20,000 retained earnings. Swing Corporation's balance sheets at book value and fair value on December 31, 2006, are as follows (in thousands):

	Book Value	Fair Value
Cash	$ 20	$ 20
Accounts receivable—net	50	50
Inventories	40	30
Land	15	15
Buildings—net	30	50
Equipment—net	70	100
Total assets	$225	$265
Accounts payable	$ 45	$ 45
Other liabilities	60	60
Capital stock	100	
Retained earnings	20	
Total equities	$225	

ADDITIONAL INFORMATION

1. The amortization periods for the fair value/book value differentials at the time of acquisition are as follows:

Overvalued inventories (sold in 2004)	$10,000
Undervalued buildings (10-year useful lives)	20,000
Undervalued equipment (5-year useful lives)	30,000
Goodwill	Remainder

2. Power uses the equity method to account for its interest in Swing.

REQUIRED

1. Prepare a journal entry on Swing Corporation's books to push down the values reflected in the purchase price under parent-company theory.
2. Prepare a journal entry on Swing Corporation's books to push down the values reflected in the purchase price under entity theory.
3. Prepare comparative balance sheets for Swing Corporation on January 1, 2007, under the approaches of (1) and (2).

P 11-10

Consolidation working papers one year after combination under push-down accounting (both 90%- and 100%-ownership assumptions) Use the information and assumptions from Problem P 11-9 for this problem. The accompanying financial statements are for Power and Swing Corporations, one year after the business combination. Note that Swing's statements are presented first under contemporary theory with no push-down accounting, then under 90% push-down accounting, and finally, under 100% push-down accounting.

Swing mailed a check to Power on December 31, 2007, to settle an account payable of $8,000. Power received the check in 2008. The $8,000 amount is included in Power's December 31, 2007, accounts receivable.

Power Corporation and Swing Corporation Comparative
Financial Statements With and Without Push-Down Accounting
at and for the Year Ended December 31, 2007 (in thousands)

	Basic Accounting Power	Basic Accounting Swing	Push Down 90% Swing	Push Down 100% Swing
Income Statement				
Sales	$310.8	$110	$110	$ 110
Income from Swing	37.8	—	—	—
Cost of sales	(140)	(42)	(33)	(32)
Depreciation expense	(29)	(17)	(24.2)	(25)
Other operating expenses	(45)	(11)	(11)	(11)
Net income	$134.6	$ 40	$ 41.8	$ 42
Retained Earnings				
Retained earnings—beginning	$147	$ 20	$ —	$ —
Add: Net income	134.6	40	41.8	42
Deduct: Dividends	(60)	(10)	(10)	(10)
Retained earnings—ending	$221.6	$ 50	$ 31.8	$ 32
Balance Sheet				
Cash	$ 63.8	$ 27	$ 27	$ 27
Accounts receivable	90	40	40	40
Dividends receivable	9	—	—	—
Inventories	20	35	35	35
Land	40	15	15	15
Buildings—net	140	27	43.2	45
Equipment—net	165	56	77.6	80
Investment in Swing	208.8	—	—	—
Goodwill	—	—	36	40
Total assets	$736.6	$200	$273.8	$ 282
Accounts payable	$125	$ 20	$ 20	$ 20
Dividends payable	15	10	10	10
Other liabilities	75	20	20	20
Capital stock	300	100	100	100
Push-down capital	—	—	92	100
Retained earnings	221.6	50	31.8	32
Total equities	$736.6	$200	$273.8	$ 282

REQUIRED: Prepare consolidation working papers for Power Corporation and Subsidiary for the year ended December 31, 2007, under (a) 90% push-down accounting and (b) 100% push-down accounting.

P 11-11

Working papers for proportionate consolidation (joint venture) Pepper Corporation owns a 40% interest in Jerry Company, a joint venture that is organized as an undivided interest. In its separate financial statements, Pepper accounts for Jerry under the equity method, but for reporting purposes, the proportionate consolidation method is used.

Separate financial statements of Pepper and Jerry at and for the year ended December 31, 2006, are summarized as follows (in thousands):

	Pepper Corporation	Jerry Company
Combined Income and Retained Earnings Statements for the Year Ended December 31, 2006		
Sales	$ 800	$300
Income from Jerry	20	—
Cost of sales	(400)	(150)
Depreciation expense	(100)	(40)
Other expenses	(120)	(60)
Net income	200	50
Beginning retained earnings	300	—
Beginning venture equity	—	250
Dividends	(100)	—
Retained earnings/venture equity	$ 400	$300
Balance Sheets at December 31, 2006		
Cash	$ 100	$ 50
Receivables—net	130	30
Inventories	110	40
Land	140	60
Buildings—net	200	100
Equipment—net	300	180
Investment in Jerry	120	—
Total assets	$1,100	$460
Accounts payable	$ 120	$100
Other liabilities	80	60
Common stock, $10 par	500	—
Retained earnings	400	—
Venture equity	—	300
Total equities	$1,100	$460

REQUIRED: Prepare working papers for a proportionate consolidation of the financial statements of Pepper Corporation and Jerry Company at and for the year ended December 31, 2006.

INTERNET ASSIGNMENT

Visit the Web site of **Corning Incorporated** and obtain a copy of Corning's 2003 annual report. Prepare a brief summary of information you find in Note 10 regarding Corning's joint venture activities.

SELECTED READINGS

Accounting Interpretation No. 2 of APB Opinion No. 18. "Investments in Partnerships and Ventures." New York: American Institute of Certified Public Accountants, November 1971.

Accounting Standards Executive Committee of the American Institute of Certified Public Accountants. Issues Paper. *Joint Venture Accounting.* New York: American Institute of Certified Public Accountants, 1979.

AICPA Committee on Accounting Procedure. *Accounting Research Bulletin No. 51.* "Consolidated Financial Statements." New York: American Institute of Certified Public Accountants, 1959.

American Accounting Association's Financial Accounting Standards Committee. "Comment Letter to the FASB Discussion Memorandum 'New Basis of Accounting.' " *Accounting Horizons* (March 1994), pp. 119–121.

American Accounting Association's Financial Accounting Standards Committee. "Response to the FASB Discussion Memorandum 'Consolidation Policy and Procedures.' " *Accounting Horizons* (June 1994), pp. 120–125.

BIERMAN, HAROLD, JR. "Proportionate Consolidation and Financial Analysis." *Accounting Horizons* (December 1992), pp. 5–17.

COLLEY, J. RON, and ARA G. VOLKAN. "Accounting for Goodwill." *Accounting Horizons* (March 1988), pp. 35–41.

COLLEY, J. RON, and ARA G. VOLKAN. "Business Combinations: Goodwill and Push-Down Accounting." *The CPA Journal* (August 1988), pp. 74–76.

CUNNINGHAM, MICHAEL E. "Push-Down Accounting: Pros and Cons." *Journal of Accountancy* (June 1984), pp. 72–77.

Emerging Issues Task Force. *EITF Issue No. 88–16.* "Basis in Leveraged Buyout Transactions." Stamford, CT: Financial Accounting Standards Board, 1989.

Financial Accounting Standards Board. *An Analysis of Issues Related to Consolidation Policy and Procedures.* Financial Accounting Series, No. 107-A. Discussion Memorandum. Norwalk, CT: Financial Accounting Standards Board, 1991.

Financial Accounting Standards Board. *Consolidation of Variable Interest Entities: An Interpretation of ARB No. 51.* Financial Accounting Series No. 240-A, FASB Interpretation No. 46(R). Norwalk, CT: Financial Accounting Standards Board, January 2003, revised December 2003.

Financial Accounting Standards Board. *EITF Issue No. 90-13.* Norwalk, CT: Financial Accounting Standards Board, 1990.

HENDRIKSEN, ELDON S. *Accounting Theory*, 4th Ed. Homewood, Ill.: Irwin, 1982.

HOLLEY, CHARLES L., EDWARD C. SPEDE, and MICHAEL C. CHESTER, JR. "The Push-Down Accounting Controversy," *Management Accounting* (January 1987), pp. 39–42.

International Accounting Standards Committee. *International Accounting Standards No. 31.* "Financial Reporting of Interests in Joint Ventures." London: IASC, reformatted 1994.

MOONITZ, MAURICE. *The Entity Theory of Consolidated Statements.* American Accounting Association Monograph No. 4. Sarasota, FL: American Accounting Association, 1944.

MORTENSEN, ROGER. "Accounting for Business Combinations in the Global Economy: Purchase, Pooling, or _____?" *Journal of Accounting Education*, Vol. 12, No. 1 (1994), pp. 81–87.

NURNBERG, HUGO, and JAN SWEENEY. "The Effect of Fair Values and Historical Costs on Accounting for Business Combinations." *Issues in Accounting Education* (Fall 1989), pp. 375–395.

PACTER, PAUL. "Revising GAAP for Consolidations: Join the Debate." *The CPA Journal* (July 1992), pp. 38–47.

Statement of Financial Accounting Standards No. 33. "Financial Reporting and Changing Prices." Stamford, CT: Financial Accounting Standards Board, 1979.

Statement of Financial Accounting Standards No. 141. "Business Combinations." Stamford, CT: Financial Accounting Standards Board, 2001.

Statement of Financial Accounting Standards No. 142. "Goodwill and Other Intangible Assets." Stamford, CT: Financial Accounting Standards Board, 2001.

Statement of Position 78-9. "Accounting for Investment in Real Estate Ventures." New York: American Institute of Certified Public Accountants, Accounting Standards Division, 1978.

THOMAS, PAULA B., and J. LARRY HAGLER. "Push-Down Accounting: A Descriptive Assessment." *Accounting Horizons* (September 1988), pp. 26–31.

WYATT, ARTHUR R. "A Critical Study of Accounting for Business Combinations." *Accounting Research Study No. 5.* New York: American Institute of Certified Public Accountants, 1963 (especially see pp. 81–86 on the fair-value pooling concept).

12 CHAPTER

FOREIGN CURRENCY CONCEPTS AND TRANSACTIONS

F oreign business activity by U.S. corporations has expanded rapidly over time. In 2003, exports of U.S. goods and services were $1.020 trillion and imports of foreign goods and services totaled $1.517 trillion.[1]

Just four years earlier, in 1999, exports were $956 billion and imports were $1.221 trillion.

The effect of international branch and subsidiary operations on U.S. companies' operating results is sizeable. Almost 68% of the **Coca-Cola Company's** operating revenues and 80% of its operating income came from operations outside of North America in 2003. Also in 2003, 33% of **Apple's** net sales came from Europe and Japan, and 15% of **Starbucks'** revenues and 19% of **Wal-Mart's** were earned outside the United States. During 2004, nearly 61% of **Nike's** revenues came from non-U.S. sources.

This chapter discusses foreign currency concepts and foreign currency transaction accounting. It also introduces derivative accounting, which will aid you in understanding foreign currency hedge contract accounting. Chapter 13 discusses foreign currency financial statement translation.

●●●

FOREIGN EXCHANGE CONCEPTS AND DEFINITIONS

Currencies provide a standard of value, a medium of exchange, and a unit of measure for economic transactions. Currencies of different countries perform the first two functions with varying degrees of efficiency, but essentially all currencies provide a unit of measure for the economic activities and resources of their respective countries.

For transactions to be included in financial records, they must be measured in a currency. Typically, the currency that a transaction is recorded in and the currency needed to settle the transaction are the same. For example, a Chicago pizza shop buys all of its produce and other inputs and pays all of its employees and other bills using U.S. dollars. The pizza shop collects dollars from its customers. If a receivable or payable arises, it will require receiving or spending dollars for settlement. A receivable or payable is **denominated** in a currency when it must be paid in that currency. A receivable or payable is **measured** in a currency when it is recorded in the financial records in that currency. In this example, the pizza shop's receivables and payables are denominated and measured in the same currency, the U.S. dollar.

---

[1] U.S. Department of Commerce, Bureau of Economic Analysis. *U.S. International Trade in Goods and Services Report.* December 14, 2004.

In the case of transactions between business entities of different countries, the amounts receivable and payable are ordinarily denominated in the local currency of either the buying entity or the selling entity.[2] For example, if a U.S. firm sells merchandise to a British firm, the transaction amount will be denominated (or paid) in either U.S. dollars or British pounds, even though the U.S. firm will measure and record its account receivable and sales in U.S. dollars and the British firm will measure and record its purchase and account payable in British pounds, regardless of the currency in which the transaction is denominated.

If the transaction is denominated in British pounds, the U.S. firm has to determine how many U.S. dollars the transaction represents in order to record it. If the transaction is denominated in U.S. dollars, the British firm has to determine how many British pounds the transaction represents. To measure transactions in their own currencies, businesses around the world rely on exchange rates negotiated on a continuous basis in world currency markets. Exchange rates are essentially prices for currencies expressed in units of other currencies.

Direct and Indirect Quotation of Exchange Rates

An **exchange rate** is the ratio between a unit of one currency and the amount of another currency for which that unit can be exchanged at a particular time. The exchange rate can be computed directly or indirectly. Assume that $1.60 can be exchanged for one British pound (£1).

Direct quotation (U.S. dollar per one foreign currency unit):

$$\frac{\$1.60}{1} = \$1.60$$

Indirect quotation (the number of foreign currency units per U.S. dollar):

$$\frac{1}{\$1.60} = £0.625$$

The first approach is a *direct quotation* (from a U.S. viewpoint) because the rate is expressed in U.S. dollars: $1.60 is equivalent to one British pound (one unit of the foreign currency). The second approach is an *indirect quotation* (from a U.S. viewpoint) because the rate is expressed in British pounds (the foreign currency): £0.625 is equivalent to one U.S. dollar. The Foreign Exchange section of *The Wall Street Journal* shows both direct (U.S. dollar equivalent) and indirect (currency per U.S. dollar) exchange rates on a daily basis.

Floating, Fixed, and Multiple Exchange Rates

Exchange rates may be fixed by a governmental unit or may be allowed to fluctuate (float) with changes in the currency markets. **Official,** or **fixed, exchange rates** are set by a government and do not change as a result of changes in world currency markets. **Free,** or **floating, exchange rates** are those that reflect fluctuating market prices for a currency based on supply and demand and other factors in the world currency markets.

FLOATING EXCHANGE RATES Theoretically, a currency's value should reflect its buying power in world markets. For example, an increase in a country's inflation rate indicates that its currency's purchasing power is decreasing. The currency's value should fall in relation to other currencies. The technical term for this movement in currency value is **weakening.** A currency falls, or *weakens,* relative to another currency if it takes more of the weakening currency to purchase one unit of the other currency.

A large trade surplus (when the amount of exports exceeds imports) usually results in an increased demand for a country's currency because many of those export sales must be paid in the exporting country's currency. The exporting country's currency becomes more valuable relative to the importing countries' currencies, or it **strengthens.** A currency strengthens relative to another currency if it takes fewer units of the strengthening currency to purchase one unit of the other currency.

---

[2] Sometimes the amounts are denominated in the currency of a third country whose currency is relatively more stable than the currency of either the buyer or the seller.

A large trade deficit (when the amount of imports exceeds exports) should lead to a decrease, or weakening, of the currency's value. Although inflation and net trade position (trade surplus or trade deficit) are common causes of changes in floating exchange rates, other factors have occasionally been more influential. Interest rate differences across countries influence supply and demand for a country's currency because many investors buy securities in the international securities markets. Speculative trading to take advantage of currency movements also affects exchange rates.

To reduce its trade deficit, the U.S. government has occasionally asked other countries (Taiwan and South Korea, for example) to let their currencies strengthen against the U.S. dollar. A decline in value of the dollar in relation to other major currencies should increase the price of foreign products in the United States and lead to a reduction of imports to the United States. Similarly, U.S. goods can be sold in international markets for fewer foreign currency units when the dollar weakens against those currencies. Even so, a weakening U.S. dollar has often done little to abate U.S. consumers' demand for imported products, and changes in the exchange rates may have little effect on the trade deficit. Other factors that may affect a country's trade balance include interest rates and tax rates.[3]

A mathematical example of strengthening and weakening of a currency relative to another currency follows. Initially, assume that one British pound can be purchased for $1.50.

If the dollar weakens relative to the pound, each pound is more expensive in dollar terms. If the dollar weakens by 10%, each pound will now cost $1.65. If the quote is indirect, initially $1 can be purchased for 0.6667 pounds. If the dollar weakens by 10%, it takes fewer pounds to buy $1, so now $1 can be purchased for 0.6061 pounds.

If the dollar strengthens relative to the pound, each pound is less expensive in dollar terms. If the dollar strengthens by 10%, each pound will now cost $1.35. If the quote is indirect, $1 can now be purchased for 0.7407 pounds.

FIXED AND MULTIPLE EXCHANGE RATES When exchange rates are fixed, the issuing government is able to set (fix) different rates for different kinds of transactions. For example, it may set a preferential rate for imports (or certain kinds of imports) and penalty rates for exports (or certain kinds of exports) in order to promote the economic objectives of the country. Such rates are referred to as **multiple exchange rates.**

Spot, Current, and Historical Exchange Rates

The exchange rates that are used in accounting for foreign operations and transactions (other than forward contracts) are spot rates, current exchange rates, and historical exchange rates.[4] Spot rate is a *market* term; current and historical rates are *accounting* terms. These are defined as follows:

> **Spot rate.** The exchange rate for immediate delivery of currencies exchanged
>
> **Current rate.** The rate at which one unit of currency can be exchanged for another currency at the balance sheet date or the transaction date
>
> **Historical rate.** The rate in effect at the date a specific transaction or event occurred

Spot, current, and historical rates may be either fixed or floating rates, depending on the particular currency involved. Spot rates for foreign transactions between the United States and a country with fixed exchange rates will normally change in that foreign country only as a result of governmental action (except for transactions in the black market in the foreign country's currency). For example, the Argentine government can control the exchange rate in Buenos Aires, but not in New York. Spot rates for foreign transactions with a country that has floating exchange rates may change daily, or several times in a single day, depending on factors that influence the currency markets. However, only one spot rate exists for a given transaction.

The foreign currency transaction's current rate is the spot rate in effect for immediate settlement of the amounts denominated in foreign currency at the transaction date or at the balance sheet date. Historical rates are the spot rates that were in effect on the date that a particular event or transaction occurred.

---

[3] Domestic savings in the United States have not been sufficient to finance the country's deficit, and the United States has had to bid up interest rates in the world capital markets.

[4] *A forward exchange contract* is an agreement to exchange different currencies at a specified future date and at a specified rate.

Foreign Exchange Quotations

Major U.S. banks facilitate international trade by maintaining departments that provide bank transfer services between U.S. and non-U.S. companies, as well as currency exchange services.

Selected interbank transaction exchange rates on January 4, 2005, were:[5]

	Direct U.S. $ Equivalent	Currency per U.S. $ Indirect	
Britain (pound)	$1.8814	0.5315	pounds
Canada (dollars)	$0.8178	1.2228	Canadian dollars
Euro	$1.3269	0.7536	euros
Japan (yen)	$0.009556	104.65	yen
Mexico (peso)	$0.0878	11.3921	pesos

A payment of $1,881,400 to a U.S. banker at 4 P.M. EST on January 4, 2005, would have entitled a U.S. corporation to purchase British goods selling for £1,000,000 or to settle an account payable denominated at £1,000,000. Similarly, a U.S. company could have purchased merchandise selling for 10,000,000 Canadian dollars for $8,178,000 at that time.

The U.S. bankers that provide foreign exchange services are, of course, paid for their services. The payment is the difference between the amount that they receive from U.S. corporations and the amount they pay out for the foreign currencies, or vice versa. For example, a bank that trades foreign currency may offer to sell British pounds for $1.88 or to buy them for $1.86 when the quoted rate for British pounds is $1.87. Thus, a firm can buy 1,000,000 pounds for $1,880,000 or sell 1,000,000 pounds for $1,860,000, and the bank realizes a $10,000 gain in either case.

FOREIGN CURRENCY TRANSACTIONS OTHER THAN FORWARD CONTRACTS

Transactions within a country that are measured and recorded in the currency of that country are **local transactions.** The transactions of a British subsidiary would be recorded in British pounds, and its financial statements would be stated in British pounds. However, its financial statements must be converted into U.S. dollars before consolidation with a U.S. parent company. Translation of foreign currency financial statements is covered in Chapter 13.

This discussion of foreign currency transactions assumes the point of view of a U.S. firm whose functional currency is the U.S. dollar (which is also its local currency). An entity's *functional currency* is the currency of its primary economic environment. Normally, the predominant currency received or expended to complete transactions is the functional currency. Chapter 13 contains a more extensive discussion of the functional currency concept. **Foreign transactions** are transactions between countries or between enterprises in different countries. **Foreign currency transactions** are transactions whose terms are stated (denominated) in a currency other than an entity's functional currency. Thus, a foreign transaction may or may not be a foreign currency transaction.

The most common types of foreign transactions are imports and exports of goods and services. Import and export transactions are foreign transactions, but they are not foreign currency transactions unless their terms are denominated in a foreign currency—that is, a currency other than the entity's functional currency. An export sale by a U.S. company to a Canadian company is a foreign currency transaction from the viewpoint of the U.S. company only if the invoice is denominated (fixed) in Canadian dollars. Translation is required if the transaction is denominated in a foreign currency, but not if it is denominated in the entity's functional currency.

FASB Requirements

The provisions of *FASB Statement No. 52*, "Foreign Currency Translation" (December 1981), apply only to foreign currency transactions and to foreign currency financial statements. *Statement No. 52* (paragraph 16, as amended by *FASB statement No. 133*) stipulates the following requirements for foreign currency transactions other than derivatives:

1. At the date the transaction is recognized, each asset, liability, revenue, expense, gain, or loss arising from the transaction shall be measured and recorded in the functional currency of the recording entity by use of the exchange rate in effect at that date.

---

[5] *Source: The Wall Street Journal,* January 5, 2005, p. C11.

2. At each balance sheet date, recorded balances that are denominated in a currency other than the functional currency of the recording entity shall be adjusted to reflect the current exchange rate.

TRANSLATION AT THE SPOT RATE The first requirement for recording foreign currency transactions is that they must be translated into U.S. dollars at the spot rate in effect at the *transaction date*. Each asset, liability, revenue, and expense account arising from the transaction is translated into dollars before it is recorded. The unit of measurement is changed from the foreign currency to the U.S. dollar.

Assume that a U.S. corporation imports inventory from a Canadian firm when the spot rate for Canadian dollars is $0.7000. The invoice calls for payment of 10,000 Canadian dollars in 30 days. (*Note:* The $ sign used for the spot rate indicates direct quotation—the U.S. dollar equivalent of one unit of foreign currency.)

The U.S. importer records the transaction as follows:

Inventory (+A)	$7,000	
Accounts payable (fc) (+L)		$7,000
(Translation 10,000 Canadian dollars × $0.7000 spot rate.)		

Except for the foreign currency (fc) notation, the entry is recorded in the usual manner. The notation is used here to indicate that the account payable is denominated in foreign currency. The inventory is measured in U.S. dollars, and no subsequent adjustment is made to the inventory account for foreign currency rate fluctuations.

If the account payable is paid when the spot rate is $0.6900, the payment is recorded as follows:

Accounts payable (fc) (−L)	$7,000	
Exchange gain (+G, +SE)		$ 100
Cash (−A)		6,900
(Cash required equals 10,000 Canadian		
dollars × the $0.6900 spot rate.)		

The $100 exchange gain results because a liability measured at $7,000 is settled for $6,900. This gain reflects a change in the exchange rate between the initial transaction date and the date of payment. If the exchange rate had changed to $0.7200, a $200 exchange loss would have resulted.

Exhibit 12-1 illustrates the accounting differences that arise when foreign transactions are denominated in an entity's functional currency (U.S. dollars) as opposed to a foreign currency. In examining the exhibit, keep in mind that a transaction must be denominated in a foreign currency to be a foreign currency transaction. When the billing for a U.S. company's sale or purchase is denominated in U.S. dollars, no translation is required.

The potential for exchange gains and losses arises only when the receivable or payable is billed in the foreign currency. However, no gain or loss on translation is recorded at the initial recording.

BALANCE SHEET DATE ADJUSTMENTS Gains and losses on foreign currency transactions cannot be deferred until foreign currency is converted into U.S. dollars or until related receivables are collected or payables are settled. Instead, these amounts are adjusted to reflect current exchange rates at the balance sheet date, and any exchange gains or losses that result from the adjustments are included in current-year income.

Purchases Denominated in Foreign Currency

American Trading Company, a U.S. corporation, purchased merchandise from Paris Company on December 1, 2006, for 10,000 euros, when the spot rate for euros was $0.6600. American Trading closed its books at December 31, 2006, when the spot rate for euros was $0.6550, and it settled the account on January 30, 2007, when the spot rate was $0.6650. These transactions and events are recorded by American Trading as follows:

December 1, 2006		
Inventory (+A)	$6,600	
Accounts payable (fc) (+L)		$6,600
To record purchase of merchandise from		
Paris Company (10,000 euros × $0.6600 rate).		

EXHIBIT 12-1

Comparison of
Purchase and Sale
Transactions
Denominated in U.S.
Dollars versus
British Pounds

SALES TRANSACTION

Assumption: U.S. Foods sells merchandise to London Industries Ltd. for $16,500, or £10,000 when the exchange rate is $1.65, and receives payment when the exchange rate is $1.64.

IF BILLING IS IN U.S. DOLLARS

(Date of sale)

Accounts receivable (+A)	$16,500	
Sales (+R, +SE)		$16,500
To record sale to London Industries; invoice is $16,500.		

(Date of receipt)

Cash (+A)	$16,500	
Accounts receivable (–A)		$16,500
To record collection in full from London Industries.		

IF BILLING IS IN BRITISH POUNDS

Accounts receivable (fc) (+A)	$16,500	
Sales (+R, +OE)		$16,500
To record sale to London Industries; billing is for £10,000 (£10,000 × $1.65 = $16,500).		
Cash (fc) (+A)	$16,400	
Exchange loss (+Lo, –SE)	100	
Accounts receivable (fc) (–A)		$16,500
To record collection in full from London Industries (£10,000 × $1.64 = $16,400).		

PURCHASE TRANSACTION

Assumption: U.S. Foods purchases merchandise from London Industries Ltd. for $8,250, or £5,000 pounds when the exchange rate is $1.65, and pays the account when the exchange rate is $1.67.

IF BILLING IS IN U.S. DOLLARS

(Date of purchase)

Inventory (+A)	$8,250	
Accounts payable (+L)		$8,250
To record purchase from London Industries; billing is $8,250.		

(Date of payment)

Accounts payable (–L)	$8,250	
Cash (–A)		$8,250
To record payment in full to London Industries.		

IF BILLING IS IN BRITISH POUNDS

Inventory (+A)	$8,250	
Accounts payable (fc) (+L)		$8,250
To record purchase from London Industries; billing is for £5,000 (£5,000 × $1.65 = $8,250).		
Accounts payable (fc) (–L)	$8,250	
Exchange loss (+Lo, –SE)	100	
Cash (–A)		$8,350
To record payment in full to London Industries (£5,000 × $1.67 = $8,350).		

December 31, 2006

Accounts payable (fc) (–L)	$ 50	
Exchange gain (+G, +SE)		$ 50

To adjust accounts payable to exchange rate at year-end
[10,000 euros × ($0.6550 – $0.6600)].

January 30, 2007

Accounts payable (fc) (–L)	$6,550	
Exchange loss (+Lo, –SE)	100	
Cash (–A)		$6,650

To record payments in full to Paris Company
(10,000 euros × $0.6650 spot rate).

Date	Spot Rate	Inventory	Accounts Payable (10,000 Euros)	Gain (Loss)
12/1/06 (initial transaction date)	$0.6600	$6,600	$6,600	—
12/31/06 (financial statement date)	$0.6550	$6,600	$6,550	$ 50
1/30/07 (settled accounts payable by purchasing and distributing euros)	$0.6650	$6,600	$6,650	($100)
Overall				($ 50)

The example shows that on December 1, 2006, American Trading Company incurred a liability of $6,600 denominated in euros. On December 31, 2006, the liability was adjusted to reflect the current exchange rate, and a $50 exchange gain was included in American Trading Company's 2006 income statement. The exchange gain is the product of multiplying 10,000 euros by the change in the spot rate for euros between December 1 and December 31, 2006. By January 30, 2007, when the liability was settled, the spot rate for euros had increased to $0.6650, and American Trading recorded a $100 exchange loss. The actual total exchange loss is only $50 [10,000 euros × ($0.6650 – $0.6600)], but this loss is reported as a $50 exchange gain in 2006 and a $100 exchange loss in 2007.

In summary, foreign currency–denominated purchases must be measured in dollars at the purchase date using the foreign currency spot rate on that date.

If a balance sheet date occurs before the liability is paid, the accounts payable must be remeasured to reflect the spot rate at the financial statement date. A gain results if the dollar strengthens, because more euros can be purchased by one dollar than when the liability was first recorded. A loss results if the dollar weakens, because fewer euros can be purchased by one dollar than when the liability was first recorded.

When the liability is paid, a gain (when the liability is smaller since the last financial statement date) or loss (when the liability is larger than at the last financial statement date) is recorded because the liability is paid at the spot rate on the payment date. Typically, companies arrange with banks to handle the conversion. The bank charges the company's bank account in dollars (including a transaction fee) and transfers foreign currency to the payee's account.

Sales Denominated in Foreign Currency

On December 16, 2006, American Trading Company sold merchandise to Rome Company for 20,000 euros, when the spot rate for euros was $0.6625. American Trading closed its books on December 31, when the spot rate was $0.6550, collected the account on January 15, 2007, when the spot rate was $0.6700, and held the cash until January 20, when it converted the euros into U.S. dollars at the $0.6725 spot rate in effect on that date. American Trading records the transactions as follows:

December 15, 2006

Accounts receivable (fc) (+A)	$13,250	
Sales (+R, +SE)		$13,250

To record sales to Rome

(20,000 euros × $0.6625 spot rate).

December 31, 2006

Exchange loss (+Lo, −SE)	$ 150	
Accounts receivable (−A)		$ 150

To adjust accounts receivable at year-end

[20,000 euros × ($0.6550 − $0.6625)].

January 15, 2007

Cash (fc) (+A)	$13,400	
Accounts receivable (fc) (−A)		$13,100
Exchange gain (+G, +SE)		300

To record collection in full from Rome (20,000

euros × $0.6700) and recognize exchange gain

for 2007 [20,000 euros × ($0.6700 − $0.6550)].

January 20, 2007

Cash (+A)	$13,450	
Exchange gain (+G, +SE)		$ 50
Cash (fc) (−A)		13,400

To convert 20,000 euros into U.S. dollars

(20,000 euros × $0.6725).

Date	Spot Rate	Accounts Receivable 20,000 Euros	Sales	Gain (Loss)
12/15/06 (initial transaction date)	$0.6625	$13,250	$13,250	—
12/31/06* (financial statement date)	$0.6550	$13,100	Unchanged	($150)
1/15/07 (collection of accounts receivable in euros)	$0.6700	$13,400	Unchanged	$300
1/20/07 (conversion of euros to dollars)	$0.6725	$13,450	Unchanged	$ 50
Overall				$200

*Sales is closed at year-end into retained earnings. The term "unchanged" here means that no further adjustment of the sales amount is necessary because the sales amount was "locked-in" when the accounts receivable and related sales were first recorded.

In summary, foreign currency–denominated sales must be measured in dollars at the purchase date using the foreign currency spot rate on that date.

If a financial statement date occurs before the receivable is paid, the accounts receivable must be remeasured to reflect the spot rate at the financial statement date. A gain results when the dollar has weakened because the foreign currency to be received is worth more dollars than when initially recorded. A loss results when the dollar has strengthened because the foreign currency to be received is worth less in dollars than when it was originally recorded.

When the receivable is paid, a gain or loss is recorded because the receivable will be paid at the spot rate on the payment date. If a company holds foreign currency for a period of time for speculative purposes after a receivable is paid instead of converting it into dollars, gains and losses continue to be reported at each financial statement date until the foreign currency is converted into dollars.

Summary of Direct Rate Changes ($ per Currency Unit) on the Carrying Value of Foreign Currency–Denominated Accounts Receivable and Accounts Payable

Spot Rate Change	Effect on the Dollar Relative to the Foreign Currency	Impact on Foreign Currency–Denominated Account	
Increases	Dollar weaker	Accounts receivable	Increases—Gain
Increases	Dollar weaker	Accounts payable	Decreases—Gain *Inc* *Loss*
Decreases	Dollar stronger	Accounts receivable	Decreases—Loss
Decreases	Dollar stronger	Accounts payable	Increases—Loss *Dec* *Gain*

FASB STATEMENT NO. 133: ACCOUNTING FOR DERIVATIVE INSTRUMENTS AND HEDGING ACTIVITIES

The FASB began to formally consider accounting for derivative instruments and hedges when it added the broad topic of accounting for financial instruments to its agenda in 1986. Financial accounting and reporting standards needed to address newly created financial instruments. The FASB also needed to develop a set of broad, forward-thinking standards that would be able to properly report the impact on financial position of rapidly advancing innovations in financial instruments.

Since then, the FASB has issued many statements addressing aspects of accounting for financial instruments, including the following:

- *FASB Statement No. 105,* "Disclosure of Information About Financial Instruments with Off-Balance Sheet Risk and Financial Instruments with Concentrated Credit Risk" (March 1990)
- *FASB Statement No. 107,* "Disclosures About Fair Value of Financial Instruments" (December 1991), which superseded and amended *Statement No. 105*
- *FASB Statement No. 115,* "Accounting for Certain Investments in Debt and Equity Securities" (May 1993)
- *FASB Statement No. 119,* "Disclosure About Derivative Financial Instruments and Fair Value of Financial Instruments" (October 1994), which *Statement No. 133* supersedes

Many deliberations, public comments, field studies, and revisions occurred between the initial deliberations regarding derivative instruments and hedging activities in January 1992 and June 1998, when the final version of *FASB Statement No. 133,* "Accounting for Derivative Instruments and Hedging Activities," was issued.

Corporations have many implementation question about a standard addressing as complex a topic as derivative instrument accounting. To address these concerns, the FASB formed the Derivatives Implementation Group (DIG) in 1998, which assists the FASB by advising them on how to resolve practical issues that arise when *Statement 133* is applied. The DIG functions in a similar way to the Emerging Issues Task Force (EITF) except that the DIG does not formally vote on issues to reach a consensus. Instead, the resolution from the group's deliberations is presented to the FASB for clearance. The DIG members include high-level executives from companies such as **Time Warner, Inc., General Electric,** and **J. P. Morgan Chase, Inc.,** and partners from international accounting firms.

More than 150 issues have been forwarded to the FASB, and many of them have been cleared by the FASB. Once cleared, guidance is included in the FASB staff implementation guide (Q&A).

Two major standards have amended parts of *Statement No. 133:*

> In June 2000, *FAS 138*, "Accounting for Certain Derivative Instruments and Hedges," was issued. This standard addressed concerns about the accounting for foreign currency derivatives. This topic is discussed later in the chapter.
>
> In April 2003, *FAS 149*, "Amendment of *Statement 133* on Derivative Instruments and Hedging Activities," was issued. This standard clarified the accounting and reporting for derivative instruments, including some types of derivative instruments embedded in other contracts. The latter topic is beyond the scope of our discussion.

This chapter's discussion of *FASB Statement No. 133*, and its amendments defines derivatives and hedge accounting and provides examples of derivatives and accounting for them.

Definitions

Derivative is the name given to a broad range of financial securities. Their common characteristic is that the derivative contract's value to the investor is directly related to fluctuations in price, rate, or some other variable that *underlies* it. Derivative contracts can be used to limit businesses' exposure to price or rate fluctuations. One party to the contract, in effect, bets that the underlying price or rate will move in the opposite direction to what the other party is expecting. The party trying to control its economic rate or price change risk is engaging in a derivative, or *hedge contract*. As illustrated in this chapter, contract structures vary, and the accounting for such contracts also varies.

Interest rates, commodity prices, foreign currency exchange rates, and stock prices are the most common types of price and rate risks that companies hedge. For example, although most of **Starbucks'** business is conducted in U.S. dollars, some activities transacted outside of the United States are denominated in other currencies, primarily the British pound, the euro, the Japanese yen, and the Canadian dollar. Because Starbucks forecasts future revenue to be transacted in these currencies, it enters into forward contracts to hedge the foreign exchange rate risk related to a portion of this anticipated international revenue.[6] By entering into these types of agreements, Starbucks locks in exchange rates, dampening the cash flow and income effects of future fluctuations in exchange rates on its operations.

In 2000, the amusement park chain, **Six Flags, Inc.**, entered into interest rate swap agreements. These agreements, in effect, convert a $600,000,000 term loan from a variable-rate agreement to a fixed-rate agreement. Interest rate swap agreements are usually negotiated with financial institutions. Like Starbucks, Six Flags is reducing the variability of its future cash flow streams and income by entering into this type of agreement.

AMR, parent company of **American Airlines**, hedges aircraft fuel prices, anticipated foreign currency–dominated operating revenues and expenses, and interest rates.

Companies enter into derivative contracts to reduce the vulnerability of their cash flows and earnings to fluctuations in the prices of goods and commodities that they purchase or sell. Typical forms of derivative instruments are option contracts, forward contracts, and futures contracts.

Hedge Structures

Most hedges are accomplished by using one of three types of derivatives: forward contracts, futures contracts, or options.

Forward contracts are negotiated contracts between two parties for the delivery or purchase of a commodity or foreign currency at a pre-agreed price, quantity, and delivery date. The agreement may require actual physical delivery of the good or may allow a net settlement.

Net settlement allows the payment of money so that the parties are in the same economic condition as they would have been if delivery had occurred. For example, in the case of American Trading, assume a bank agreed to deliver 20,000 euros on January 15, 2007, for $0.6600 per euro. American Trading agreed to accept delivery and pay $0.6600.

Under a net settlement agreement, instead of receiving 20,000 euros, American Trading would go into the market and buy 20,000 euros at the prevailing spot price on January 15, 2007, and pay $0.6700 per euro, or $13,400. Because the contract locked in a price of $0.6600, the bank would pay American Trading $200 [($0.6700 − $0.6600) × 20,000] to settle the obligation. American

---

[6] *Source:* Starbucks fiscal 2003 annual report.

Trading and the bank are in the same position economically as they would have been if an actual exchange of foreign currency had occurred between them.

Futures contracts and forward contracts have essentially the same characteristics, except futures differ from forward contracts in ways that allow them to be traded easily in markets.[7]

Futures contracts are very standardized. A futures exchange, not the trading parties, determines the contract termination date, the exact quality and quantity of the goods to be delivered, and the delivery location.

The exchange guarantees the performance of both clearing firms engaged in the trade, who in turn guarantee the performance of the traders whom they represent.

To get out of a futures position, one can simply purchase or sell an identical contract in the opposite direction. The exchange will then cancel the two positions, so the net position is zero. One need not take delivery of the commodity.

At the end of each day, the gain or loss on the futures position is computed. The clearing house representing the losing position for the day pays the exchange for the loss. The exchange then pays the winning position the gain for the day. In essence, the markets use a daily mark-to-market approach through these cash payments.

The cost of contracting in a futures market is generally lower than using a forward contract. In addition, the exchange and clearing houses guarantee performance. One must be careful about the possibility of nonperformance with forward contracts. However, forward contracts have their benefits also. Because the forward contract is a tailored contract, the exact quality of the goods to be delivered can be defined. Although this clearly is not crucial with currencies, it might be with respect to commodities such as oil, copper, and silver.

Forward-contract delivery quantities, prices, product quality, and delivery dates can all be negotiated. Under a futures contract, the quantities, delivery dates, and product quality of each contract are defined by the exchange. The futures price is a market-determined amount.

For example, perhaps the only silver futures contracts available are for 25,000 troy ounces to be delivered on January 6, 2006. If we wish to hedge a future purchase of 110,000 troy ounces of silver, either we underhedge by 10,000 troy ounces or we overhedge by 15,000 troy ounces. Either way, some of the hedge will be ineffective. In a forward contract, the exact amount can be negotiated. In a similar fashion, the delivery date can be negotiated.

Under futures and forward contracts, both parties are committed to perform based on some event in the future.

Options are another commonly used hedging instrument structure. Only one side of the option contract is required to perform at the behest of the other. The other party to the option has the ability but not the obligation to perform.

Companies purchase options to manage risk—quite frequently, price risk. For example, a company may purchase an option to purchase a commodity, say fuel, at a specified price. Assume that the option cost $1,000 and that the company can exercise its option to purchase 100,000 gallons of fuel at $1 per gallon. If the market fuel price is $1.10 at the time the company needs the fuel, then the company will exercise the option and purchase the fuel at the lower price. The total cost of the fuel is $1,000 + ($1 × 100,000), or $101,000. On the other hand, if the market fuel price is $0.90 per gallon, the company will allow the option to expire because it is cheaper to purchase the fuel at the market price. The company still incurs an expense of $1,000 related to the fuel option contract.

Hedge Accounting

Statement No. 133's objective is to account for derivative instruments used to hedge risks so that the financial statements reflect their effectiveness in reducing the company's exposure to risk. For the financial statements to reflect the derivative contract's effectiveness, both changes in the hedged item's fair value and the hedging instrument's fair value resulting from the underlying change must be recorded in the same period. The investor can then clearly assess the effectiveness of the strategy. The term *hedge accounting* refers to accounting designed to record changes in the value of the hedged item and the hedging instrument in the same accounting period.

---

[7] *Derivatives: A Comprehensive Resource for Options, Futures, Interest Rate Swaps and Mortgage Securities*, pp. 150–151. Arditti, Fred D., Harvard Business School Press, Boston MA, 1996.

Statement No. 133 establishes three defining characteristics for a derivative:

1. It has one or more underlyings (defined earlier) and one or more notional amounts or payment provisions or both.
2. It requires no initial net investment or an initial net investment that is smaller than what would be required for other types of contracts that would be expected to have a similar response to changes in market factors.
3. Its terms require or permit net settlement, it can readily be settled net by a means outside the contract, or it provides for delivery of an asset that puts the recipient in a position not substantially different from net settlement. (Par. 249).

The specific requirements of *Statement No. 133* are based on four fundamental or guiding decisions:

■ Derivative instruments represent rights or obligations that meet the definitions of assets or liabilities and should be reported in the financial statements. At year-end, the derivative contract value is recorded on the books as an asset or liability.

■ Fair value is the most relevant measure for financial instruments and the only relevant measure for derivative instruments. Derivative instruments should be measured at fair value, and adjustments to the carrying amounts of the hedged items should reflect changes in their fair value (that is, gains or losses) that are attributable to the risk being hedged and that arise while the hedge is in effect.

■ Only items that are assets or liabilities should be reported as such in financial statements.

■ Special accounting for items designated as being hedged should be provided only for qualifying items. One aspect of qualification should be an assessment of the expectation of effective offsetting changes in fair values or cash flows during the term of the hedge for the risk being hedged. (Par. 217)

For hedged items and the derivative instruments designated to hedge them to qualify for hedge accounting, the following criteria must be met:

At the inception of the hedge, formal documentation must be prepared of:

● The relationship between the hedged item and the derivative instrument
● The risk-management objective and the strategy that the company is achieving through this hedging relationship, including identification of:

>The hedging instrument
>The hedged item
>The nature of the risk being hedged
>For fair value hedges, how the hedging instrument's effectiveness in offsetting the exposure to changes in the hedged item's fair value will be assessed
>For cash flow hedges, how the hedging instrument's effectiveness in hedging the hedged transaction's variability in cash flows attributable to the hedged risk will be assessed

In order to qualify for hedge accounting, management must demonstrate that the derivative is considered highly effective in mitigating an identified risk.

Hedge Effectiveness

Once a type of risk is identified that qualifies for hedge accounting, the effectiveness of the hedge to offset gains or losses in the item being hedged must be assessed. This assessment is done when the hedge is first entered into and during the hedge's existence.

In order for a hedge to qualify for hedge accounting, the derivative instrument must be considered highly effective in offsetting gains or losses in the item being hedged. Statistical or other numerical tests to assess hedge effectiveness are required by Section 2 of Appendix A of *SFAS No. 133*, unless a specific exception exists. Companies must choose a methodology to be applied to assess hedge effectiveness. Two common approaches are critical term analysis and statistical analysis.

Critical term analysis involves examining the nature of the underlying variable, the notional amount of the derivative and the item being hedged, the delivery date for the derivative, and the settlement date for the item being hedged. If the critical terms of the derivative and the hedged item are identical, then an effective hedge is assumed. For example, in the American Trading hedging example:

	Accounts Payable Terms	Forward Contract Terms
Amount	10,000 euros	10,000 euros
Dates	January 30, 2007	January 30, 2007
Underlying variable	euros	
Hedge		euros

This situation would be considered a highly effective hedge because the critical terms match exactly. Hedge accounting could be used for this situation.

If the critical terms don't match, a statistical approach can be used. For example, AMR enters into jet fuel, heating oil, and crude oil swap and option contracts to hedge the effect of jet-fuel price fluctuations on its operations. If AMR only used jet-fuel hedges, it might be able to use only critical term analysis to assess hedge effectiveness. But it uses heating oil and crude oil swaps and options also. Although we could assume that the prices of heating oil and crude oil might move in the same direction as jet fuel, the economics behind these prices are not exactly the same so we cannot conclude that their changes will be 100% correlated. A statistical approach such as correlation analysis or regression analysis can be used to show the relationship of jet-fuel prices to heating oil and crude oil prices over time. *SFAS No. 133* does not define a specific benchmark correlation coefficient or an adjusted R^2, however, correlations of between 80% and 125% are considered to reflect highly effective hedges.

In addition to an initial assessment of a hedge's effectiveness, an ongoing assessment must occur to ensure that the hedge continues to be highly effective. Statistical methods again can be used to gauge ongoing effectiveness. AMR has used a regression model to determine the correlation of percentage changes in the prices of West Texas Intermediate (WTI) crude oil and New York Mercantile Exchange (NYMEX) heating oil to the percentage change in jet fuel prices over 12 to 25 months to assess if its hedges continue to be highly effective.[8]

Another commonly used method used to assess ongoing hedge effectiveness is called the *cumulative dollar-offset method.* This method compares the cumulative changes in the derivative's cash flow or fair value to cumulative changes in the hedged item's fair value. A ratio is computed by dividing the cumulative change in the derivative value by the cumulative change in the hedged item's fair value. Again, no benchmark ratio has been officially mandated, but a ratio in the range of 80% to 125% is generally considered to indicate a highly effective hedge.

If a derivative does not qualify as a highly effective hedge, then the derivative is marked to market at the end of each year regardless of when the gain or loss on the item that management is attempting to hedge is recognized. No offsetting changes in the fair value of the item being hedged are recorded until they are realized.

Types of Hedge Accounting

One of three approaches must be used to account for the derivative and related hedged item that has qualified as a highly effective hedge:

LEARNING OBJECTIVES 7, 8

Fair Value Hedge Accounting— The item being hedged is an existing asset or liability position or firm purchase or sale commitment. In this case, both the item being hedged and the derivative are marked to fair value at the end of the quarter or year-end on the books. The gain or loss on these items is reflected immediately in earnings. The risk being hedged is the variability in the fair value of the asset or liability.

Cash Flow Hedge Accounting— The derivative hedges the exposure to the variability in expected future cash flows associated with a risk. The exposure may be related to a recognized asset or liability (such as a variable-rate financial instrument) or to a forecasted transaction such as a forecasted purchase or sale. The derivative is marked to fair value at year-end and is recorded as an asset or liability. The effective portion of the related gain or loss's recognition is deferred until the forecasted transaction affects income. The gain or loss is included as a component of accumulated other comprehensive income (AOCI) in the balance sheet's stockholders equity section.

Hedge of Net Investment in a Foreign Subsidiary— This will be discussed in Chapter 13.

Statement No. 138, an amendment to *SFAS No. 133,* allows the use of cash flow hedge accounting for certain types of hedges of existing foreign currency–denominated receivables or payables. We will discuss this accounting later.

---

[8] *Source:* AMR 2003 annual report.

ACCOUNTING FOR HEDGE CONTRACTS: ILLUSTRATIONS OF CASH FLOW AND FAIR VALUE HEDGE ACCOUNTING USING INTEREST RATE SWAPS

We will use interest rate swaps to illustrate the differences in accounting for derivatives as fair value and cash flow hedges.

Cash Flow Hedge Accounting

We will assume that on January 1, 2006, Jacobs Company borrows $200,000 from State Bank. The three-year loan with interest paid annually is a variable-rate loan. The initial interest rate is set at 9% for year 1. The subsequent years' interest-rate formula is the London Interbank Offer Rate (LIBOR) + 2%, determined at the end of each year for the next year. The LIBOR rate at December 31, 2006, is used to set the loan interest rate for 2007. The LIBOR rate at December 31, 2007, is used to set the loan interest rate for 2008.

Because Jacobs does not wish to assume the risk that the interest rate could increase and therefore the cash paid for interest could increase, Jacobs decides to hedge this risk.

On January 1, 2006, Jacobs enters into a **pay-fixed, receive-variable interest rate swap** with Watson for the latter two payments. Jacobs agrees to pay a set rate of 9% to Watson and will in return receive LIBOR + 2%. The hedge will be settled net. The notional amount is $200,000. Jacobs or Watson will pay the other the difference between the variable rate and the 9% fixed rate depending on which is higher. For example, if the LIBOR rate is 4% on December 31, 2006, then Watson will receive $6,000 on December 31, 2007. LIBOR + 2% is 6%. Jacobs has agreed to pay 9%, so Watson benefits from the lower interest rate and receives the difference multiplied by $200,000. Jacobs will still end up paying 9% in total— 3% to Watson and 6% to State Bank.

If the LIBOR rate on December 31, 2007, is 8%, then Jacobs will receive $2,000 from Watson. LIBOR + 2% is 10%. Jacobs will again end up paying 9% net. It will pay 10% to State Bank and then receive 1% from Watson. As you can see, this hedge eliminates the cash flow variability related to this debt.

To determine the fair value of the interest rate swap to be recorded on Jacobs's books at December 31, 2006, Jacobs must make some assumptions about what the future LIBOR interest rates will be and, therefore, what its future cash receipts and future cash payments related to the hedge will be.

Assume that the LIBOR rate on December 31, 2006, is 6.5%. This means that Jacobs's interest payment on December 31, 2007, to State Bank will be 8.5% × $200,000, or $17,000. Jacobs has agreed to pay 9% to Watson. This means that, at this point in time, Jacobs knows it will pay $1,000 to Watson in one year. In order to measure the fair value of the swap arrangement, Jacobs will make an assumption about the payment that will be made on December 31, 2008. Assuming that a flat interest rate curve is expected, Jacobs will assume that the interest rate for 2008 will not change from the current rate, so it will expect to pay $1,000 at December 31, 2008, as well.

The interest rate swap fair-value computation at December 31, 2006 is:
Present value at December 31, 2006, of payment to be made to Watson on December 31, 2007:

$$\$1,000/(1.085) = \$922$$

Present value at December 31, 2006, of estimated payment to be paid to Watson on December 31, 2008:

$$\$1,000/(1.085)^2 = \$848$$

The total estimated value of the interest rate swap at December 31, 2006, is:

$$\$922 + \$848 = \$1,770$$

Because Jacobs anticipates paying this amount, the interest rate swap is recorded as a liability.

Assume that at December 31, 2007, the LIBOR rate is 7.25%. Watson will now be required to pay Jacobs under the interest-rate-swap arrangement on December 31, 2008. Watson will pay $200,000 × (0.0925 − 0.0900) = $500. However, this payment will be received by Jacobs in one year. The fair value of the interest-rate-swap asset at December 31, 2007, is $500 ÷ (1.0925) = $458.

Because this hedge is designed to reduce the variability in the cash flows related to the debt, Jacobs designates it as a **cash flow hedge**. This hedge is also expected to be effective because its terms match the terms of the underlying debt interest payments it is hedging. The notional amount of both is $200,000, the term length matches exactly, and initially the fair value of the hedge is zero (the fixed rate of 9% equals the LIBOR +2% at the inception of the hedge).

CASH FLOW HEDGE ACCOUNTING ENTRIES Jacobs's journal entries to account for the debt, the interest, and the derivative under cash flow hedge accounting follow.

January 1, 2006

Cash (+A)	$200,000	
Loan payable (+L)		$200,000

To record receipt of loan proceeds on Jacobs's books.

December 31, 2006

Interest expense (+E, −SE)	$ 18,000	
Cash (−A)		$ 18,000

To record the payment of interest to State Bank.

Other comprehensive income (−SE)	$ 1,770	
Interest rate swap (+L)		$ 1,770

To record the fair value of the interest rate swap.

December 31, 2007

Interest expense (+E, −SE)	$ 17,000	
Cash (−A)		$ 17,000

To record interest payment to State Bank, $200,000 × 0.085 = $17,000; the variable interest rate was determined as of January 1, 2007, as LIBOR + 2%.

Interest expense (+E, −SE)	$ 1,000	
Cash (−A)		$ 1,000

To record payment to Watson of interest-rate-swap settlement.

Interest rate swap (−L)	$ 1,770	
Interest rate swap (+A)	458	
Other comprehensive income (+SE)		$ 2,228

To adjust the interest rate swap to fair value at December 31, 2007; the other comprehensive income account now has a balance of $458 credit.

December 31, 2008

Interest expense (+E, −SE)	$ 18,500	
Cash (−A)		$ 18,500

To record interest payment to State Bank, $200,000 × 0.0925 = $17,000; the variable interest rate was determined as of January 1, 2008, as LIBOR + 2%.

Cash (+A)	$ 500	
Interest expense (−E, +SE)		$ 500

To record receipt of interest-rate-swap settlement from Watson.

Other comprehensive income (−SE)	$ 458	
Interest rate swap (−A)		$ 458

To adjust the interest rate swap to fair value at December 31, 2008, which is zero; notice that the other comprehensive income account is also zero.

Loan payable (−L)	$200,000	
Cash (−A)		$200,000

To record payment of loan agreement.

Fair Value Hedge Accounting

We will now assume that instead of initially borrowing $200,000 from State Bank using a variable-rate note, Jacobs borrows $200,000 for three years at a fixed rate of 9% on January 1, 2006. As a result, Jacobs enters into a pay-fixed, receive-variable swap with Watson. The notional amount is again $200,000, and the variable-rate formula is LIBOR + 2%. Assume that the LIBOR rate is 7% on January 1, 2006.

Jacobs designates this as a **fair value hedge**. This is a fair value hedge because the fair value of the fixed-rate loan fluctuates as a result of the changes in the market rate of interest. The hedge is designed to offset these changes in value.

In this case, both the loan and the interest rate swap will be marked to fair value at each year-end. Recording debt at fair value at year-end is a departure from the GAAP you learned in intermediate accounting. Normally, a bond or loan is recorded initially at its fair value. In subsequent years, the interest expense is based on the market interest rate in effect at the initial borrowing date for the entire bond or loan's existence. Therefore, although amortization of a discount or premium may affect the loan's carrying value, the resulting carrying value is the present value of the cash flows using the original market rate, not the market rate in effect at each year-end.

In this case, the debt carrying value will be adjusted throughout its life for changes in the market interest rate.

FAIR VALUE HEDGE ACCOUNTING ENTRIES

January 1, 2006

Cash (+A)	$200,000	
Loan payable (+L)		$200,000

To record the receipt of a loan from State Bank.

December 31, 2006

Interest expense (+E, −SE)	$ 18,000	
Cash (−A)		$ 18,000

To record fixed rate interest payment to State Bank.

Interest rate swap (+A)	$ 1,770	
Loan payable (+L)		$ 1,770

To mark both the swap and the loan to market to reflect the market rate of interest on the swap agreement at December 31, 2006, 8.5%. Because the market rate is below the fixed interest rate of 9%, the loan's fair value has increased. This is similar to a bond being sold at a premium.

December 31, 2007

Interest expense (+E, −SE)	$ 18,000	
Cash (−A)		$ 18,000

To record fixed rate interest payment to State Bank.

Cash (+A)	$ 1,000	
Interest expense (−E, +SE)		$ 1,000

To record net settlement from Watson; the variable rate is 8.5%, so Watson owes Jacobs $0.005 \times \$200,000 = \$1,000$.

Loan payable (−L)	$ 2,228	
Interest rate swap (−A)		$ 1,770
Interest rate swap (+L)		458

To mark both the swap and the loan to market; the carrying value of the loan is now $200,000 − $458 = $199,542, a discount. Remember that the variable rate, LIBOR + 2%, on December 31, 2008, is 9.25%.

December 31, 2008

Interest Expense (+E, −SE)	$ 18,000	
Cash (−A)		$ 18,000

To record fixed-rate interest payment to State Bank.

Interest expense (+E, −SE)	$ 500	
Cash (−A)		$ 500
Interest rate swap (−L)	$ 458	
Loan payable (+L)		$ 458

To mark the swap and the loan to market;
   the carrying value of the loan is now $200,000,
   which will now be paid.

Loan payable (−L)	$200,000	
Cash (−L)		$200,000

To record payment of the loan.

The following table summarizes the fair value hedge transactions.

Date	Interest Rate Swap Balance Sheet Debit—Asset; Credit—Liability	Loan Payable Balance Sheet	Interest Expense
1/1/06		$200,000	
12/31/06	$1,770 debit	$201,770	$18,000
12/31/07	$ 458 credit	$199,542	$17,000
12/31/08			$18,500

Notice that the fluctuation in the fair value of the loan is reflected in the liability. The company's strategy to hedge this risk is also reflected because the combination of the interest-rate-swap asset value and the loan balance value at December 31, 2006, and December 31, 2007, is $200,000.

Additional Cash Flow Hedge Examples

OPTION CONTRACTS Under *Statement No. 133,* the fuel option contract discussed previously is a cash flow hedge because it is designed to limit the company's exposure to price changes in forecasted purchases of fuel. Because the purchase of the fuel will occur in the future and the company purchases the option contract now, it initially records the option contract price as an asset. Assume that the company signs the contract on January 15, 2006, the contract costs $1,000, the option price on that date is $1 per gallon and the option expires on May 31, 2006. Further assume that the option is a European one, in which the company can elect to exercise it only on the expiration date.[9] The company records the option as follows:

January 15, 2006

Fuel contract option (+A)	1,000	
Cash (−A)		1,000

The company prepares its quarterly report on March 31, 2006. Assume the market price of fuel on March 31, 2006, is $1.25. If the company could exercise the option on this date, it would save $0.25 per gallon on the fuel, or $25,000 in total. The estimate of the option payment is $25,000 if it could be paid on March 31, 2006. But the actual payment will occur on May 31, 2006, two months later. The fair value of the option at March 31 needs to be estimated by computing the present value of the option payment. If we assume that the appropriate discount rate is 6% per year, or 0.5% per month, then we can compute the present value.

$$\$25,000 \div (1.005)^2 = \$24,752$$

---

[9] An American option can be exercised during the contract period, not just at the end.

The fuel contract option account already has a debit balance of $1,000, so the required adjustment is $23,752 to that account.

The estimate of the value of the option to the company on March 31 is $24,752. The company needs to record an adjusting entry on March 31 because the option must be recorded at fair value according to *Statement No. 133*.

The purpose of the option contract is to control the cost that the company will pay when purchasing the fuel, so the increase in the option's value should be recorded in income in the same period that the fuel is used. The gain is deferred by including it as a component of other comprehensive income in the stockholders' equity section of the balance sheet. The gain bypasses that quarter's income statement. The entry is as follows:

March 31, 2006

Fuel contract option (+A)	23,752	
Other comprehensive income—		
unrealized holding gain on		
fuel option contract (+SE)		23,752

On May 31, 2006, we assume that the fuel price is $1.30 per gallon. The fuel's market value is $130,000. The writer of the fuel price option must pay the company $0.30 per gallon, or $30,000. An additional gain of $5,248 occurs as a result of the contract. The company makes the following entries:

May 31, 2006

Fuel inventory (+A)	130,000	
Cash (−A)		130,000
Cash (+A)	30,000	
Fuel contract option (−A)		24,752
Other comprehensive income (+SE)		5,248

Notice that the gain on the contract is still not recognized, because the fuel remains in inventory. Once the fuel is used, the gain on the contract will be recognized as a reduction in cost of goods sold, so the net impact on cost of goods sold is $100,000, not $130,000.

Assume that the fuel inventory is used on June 15, 2006. The entry is as follows:

June 15, 2006

Cost of goods sold (+E, −SE)	130,000	
Fuel inventory (−A)		130,000
Other comprehensive income (−SE)	30,000	
Cost of goods sold (−E, +SE)		30,000

LEARNING OBJECTIVES **7, 9**

FUTURES CONTRACTS—CASH FLOW HEDGE OF FORECASTED TRANSACTION Companies can also hedge forecasted transactions using futures contracts. Here is an illustration. On December 1, 2006, a utility enters into a futures contract to purchase 100,000 barrels of heating oil for delivery on January 31, 2007, at $1.4007 per gallon. Heating oil is traded on the NYMEX exchange. Each contract is for 1,000 barrels (42,000 gallons). The utility must enter into 100 contracts. The exchange requires a margin of $100 per contract to be paid up front.

The utility enters into this contract so that it will have a supply of oil for delivery to customers in February and so it can lock in the $1.4007-per-gallon price. This is a forecasted purchase and therefore is accounted for as a cash flow hedge. The entries are:

December 1, 2006

Futures contract (+A)	$10,000	
Cash (−A)		$10,000

At year-end, the company must mark the futures contract to market. Unlike the interest-rate-swap contracts, which are not traded and which require an estimate of their fair value, the futures contract has a market value at December 31, 2006. Assume that the NYMEX reported that the heating oil futures contract for delivery on January 31, 2007, is $1.4050 per gallon. This price already is adjusted for the time value of money because the market would have adjusted for it in the pricing. We can now write the contracts to market.

December 31, 2006

Futures contract (+A)	$18,060	
Accumulated other comprehensive income (+SE)		$18,060

On January 31, 2007, the spot and futures rate are the same, $1.3995 per gallon. The company settles the futures contract and buys 100,000 barrels of oil on the open market for delivery during the first week in February. The entry to mark the contract to market is:

January 31, 2007

Other comprehensive income (−SE)	$23,100	
Futures contract (−A)		$23,100

[100 contracts × 42,000 gallons per contract × ($1.3995 − $1.4050) = $23,100 — Accumulated Other Comprehensive Income account]

The balance in the Futures Contract account is $4,960 debit ($10,000 margin + $18,060 December 31 adjustment − $23,100 January 31, 2007, adjustment). The company lost $5,040 on the contract. The entries to settle the Futures Contract and record the oil purchase are:

Cash (+A)	$ 4,960	
Futures contract (−A)		$ 4,960
Heating oil inventory (+A)	$5,877,900	
Cash (−A)		$5,877,900

Assume that the company sells the oil for $2.00 per gallon to its customers during the first week in February: The impact of the gain or loss on the futures contract on earnings is deferred until the hedged transaction actually affects income: The entries at the date of sale are:

Cash (+A)	$8,400,000	
Sales (+R, +SE)		$8,400,000
Cost of goods sold (+E, −SE)	$5,877,900	
Inventory (−A)		$5,877,900
Cost of goods sold (+E, −SE)	$ 5,040	
Other comprehensive income (+SE)		$ 5,040

The total cost of goods sold is $5,882,940 ($5,877,900 + $5,040), which is equal to 42,000 × 100 contracts × $1.4007 (the contract rate).

Additional Fair Value Hedge Examples

LEARNING OBJECTIVES **8, 9**

A fair value hedge is a derivative contract that attempts to reduce the price risk of an existing asset or firm purchase commitment. Fair value hedge accounting is used when a highly effective hedge is used to reduce the price risk of an existing asset or liability or a firm sale or purchase commitment contract. Both the item being hedged and the hedge contract are marked to market on an ongoing basis, and the gains and losses are recognized in income immediately. Even though firm sale and purchase commitments are usually not included on the balance sheet until they are executed, *SFAS No. 133* requires the recognition of them on the balance sheet if they are the object of a hedging contract.

Assume that on January 1, 2006, a company agrees to take delivery of 100,000 liters of scotch whiskey from a manufacturer in six months—on June 30, 2006—at $15 per liter, the price of scotch on January 1. In order to take advantage of changes in the market rate of whiskey over time, the company also enters into a pay variable/receive fixed forward contract with a speculator. The company has in essence unlocked the fixed element of the firm purchase commitment.

If the market price is $14 in six months, the company will receive $1 per liter, or $100,000, from the speculator. The company will pay $14 per liter out of its own pocket, and $1 per liter comes from the speculator. If the market price is $17 per liter, the company must pay the speculator $2 per liter and then pay the whiskey supplier $15 per liter. In each case, the whiskey costs the company the market rate.

Notice that the company has a *firm purchase commitment* with the whiskey distiller that is non-cancelable, and it has also entered into a forward contract with the speculator. This transaction qualifies as a fair value hedge because it is aimed at controlling the cost of an existing commitment, not a forecasted transaction.

As discussed earlier, a forward contract is negotiated between the parties, not through an exchange. This allows considerable flexibility in defining the quality, quantity, and delivery schedule.

On January 1, 2006, no entry would be required for either the firm purchase commitment or the forward exchange contract.

On March 31, 2006, assume that the market price of scotch whiskey is $13 per liter. The company has experienced an unrealized gain of $200,000 on the forward contract [($15 − $13) × 100,000]. It has also experienced an unrealized loss on the purchase commitment because the market price of the whiskey is now below the fixed contract price. The change in the firm-purchase-commitment fair value and the offsetting change in the forward contract value are recorded immediately in income at present value, assuming a 0.5% per month interest rate:

March 31, 2006

Forward contract (+A)	197,030	
Unrealized gain on forward contract (+G, +SE)		197,030
To record the change in the fair value of the forward contract.		
Unrealized loss on firm purchase commitment (+Lo, −SE)	197,030	
Firm purchase commitment (+L)		197,030
To record the change in the firm purchase commitment.		

At June 30, 2006, both contracts are settled when the market price of whiskey is $14.50. The entries are as follows:

January 30, 2006

Cash (+A)	50,000	
Unrealized loss on forward contract (+Lo, −SE)	147,030	
Forward contract (−A)		197,030
Firm purchase commitment (−L)	197,030	
Whiskey inventory (+A)	1,450,000	
Cash (−A)		1,500,000
Unrealized gain on firm purchase commitment (+G, +SE)		147,030

FOREIGN CURRENCY DERIVATIVES AND HEDGING ACTIVITIES

Foreign Currency–Denominated Receivables And Payables

Previously, we discussed the accounting for foreign currency–denominated receivables and payables. Companies frequently hedge their exposure to foreign currency exchange risk for existing foreign currency–denominated assets and liabilities and anticipated foreign currency–denominated transactions. In this section, we will focus on hedge accounting when foreign currency transactions are involved. The accounting for such foreign currency hedges is a bit different than for the derivatives discussed already.

Statement 52 requires marking to fair value (the current spot rate) foreign currency–denominated receivables and payables at year-end. The resulting gain or loss is recognized immediately in income. Under *Statements 133* and *138*, a company may be able to choose to account for hedges of such receivables and payables using either a fair value hedge model or a cash flow hedge model. The contract-term requirements for selecting a cash flow hedge model are stringent, as we will discuss later.

The forward premium or discount is the difference between the contracted forward rate and the spot rate prevailing when the contract is entered into. This premium or discount is amortized into income over the life of the contract if the hedge is designated a cash flow hedge. The effective interest method is appropriate.

CASH FLOW HEDGES For a forward contract to qualify for cash flow hedge accounting, the contract must have the following characteristics:

1. Cash flow hedges can be used in recognized foreign currency–denominated asset and liability situations if the variability of the cash flows is completely eliminated by the hedge. This requirement is generally met if the settlement date, currency type, and currency amounts match the expected payment dates and amounts of the foreign currency–denominated receivable or payable. If any of these critical terms don't match between the hedged item and the hedging instrument, then the contract is designated a fair value hedge with current earnings recognition of changes in the value of the hedging derivative and the hedged item. (This will be illustrated later.)

2. According to paragraph 28 of *Statement 138*, the transaction gain or loss arising from the remeasurement of the foreign currency–denominated asset or liability is offset by a related amount reclassified from other comprehensive income to earnings each period. Thus, the foreign currency–denominated asset or liability is marked to fair value at year-end, and the gain or loss is recognized in income. The cash flow hedge is also marked to fair value at year-end. Like other cash flow hedges, the gain or loss is included in other comprehensive income. At year-end, a portion of the gain or loss included in other comprehensive income is then recognized in income to offset the gain or loss on the foreign currency–denominated asset or liability.

3. Finally, the premium or discount related to the hedge is amortized to income using an effective interest rate.

Example of Accounting for a Cash Flow Hedge of an Existing Foreign Currency–Denominated Accounts Receivable

Assume that Winkler Corporation, a U.S. firm, sold hospital equipment to Howard Ltd. of Britain on November 2, 2006, for 100,000 British pounds, payable in 90 days, on January 30, 2007. In addition, on November 2, Winkler enters into a 90-day forward contract with Ross Company to hedge its exposed net accounts receivable position. We will assume that the forward contract allows for net settlement. Assume that a reasonable incremental interest rate is 12%. Selected exchange rates of pounds are:

	November 2, 2006	December 31, 2006	January 30, 2006
Spot rate	$1.650	$1.660	$1.665
90-day forward rate	$1.638		
30-day forward rate		$1.655	

$1200 LOSS [handwritten]

The entry on November 2, 2006, to record the sale is:

①
Accounts receivable (fc) (+A)	$165,000	
Sales (+R, +SE)		$165,000

    To record the sale of equipment to Howard Company,
    £100,000 × $1.6500, the spot rate at 11/2/06.

Because Winkler entered into a forward contract that is to be settled net, no entry is necessary at the date that contract is entered into. Recall that if this were a futures or option contract, an entry would be necessary because some cash would have been paid by Winkler at the inception of these types of contracts.

    Both the foreign currency–denominated accounts receivable and the forward contract must be marked to fair value at year-end, December 31, 2006.

ACCOUNTS RECEIVABLE ADJUSTMENT

②
Accounts Receivable (fc) (+A)	$1,000	
Exchange gain (+G, +SE)		$1,000

    To adjust accounts receivable to spot rate at year-end [£100,000 × ($1.660 − $1.650)].

FORWARD CONTRACT ADJUSTMENT Winkler's 90-day forward contract expires on January 30, 2007, with Winkler set to receive $1.638 per pound. At December 31, 2006, a 30-day forward contract rate is $1.655. Based on the change in the forward rate, the estimated loss on the forward contract is £100,000 × ($1.655 − $1.638) = $1,700. However, this is the estimated loss to be realized in one month. To estimate the fair value of the forward contract on December 31, 2006, we must compute the present value of this amount.

③
Exchange Loss	1,000	
AOCI		1,000
[handwritten]

Date	Forward Contract Rate	Forward Contract Rate at This Date	Difference	× 100,000	Factor	Present Value at Date Below
December 31	1.638	1.655	0.017	1,700	1.01[1]	1,683

The approximate fair value of the forward contract is $1,683. The December 31, 2006, entry is:

Other comprehensive income (−OCI, −SE)	$1,683	
Forward contract (+L)		$1,683

DISCOUNT OR PREMIUM AMORTIZATION This situation qualifies for cash flow hedge accounting because the forward contract completely eliminates the variability in cash flows related to the pound-denominated accounts receivable. Winkler has locked in a rate of $1.638. However, this is not a costless transaction. The spot rate on November 2, 2006 was $1.650. The company knows it will receive $1,200 less than the initial $165,000. This cost must be recognized in income over time. *Statement 133* requires that an effective rate method be used to amortize the discount or premium. In this case, because the asset's ultimate amount to be received is less than the initial amount recorded, this is a discount. The formula to solve for the implicit interest rate is:

$$\text{Hedged asset or liability fair value at the hedge date} \times (1 + r)^n = \text{Hedge contract cash flow}$$

Here the hedged accounts receivable fair value at November 2, 2006, is $165,000, the hedge contract cash flow is £100,000 × $1.638 = $163,800, and $n = 3$ because the contract will expire in 90 days, or three months. We will solve for r, the monthly implicit interest rate.

$$\$165,000(1 + r)^3 = \$163,800$$
$$(1 + r)^3 = 0.99273$$
$$\sqrt[3]{(1 + r)^3} = \sqrt[3]{(0.99273)}$$
$$(1 + r) = 0.9975699$$
$$r = 0.0024301, \text{ or } 0.24301\% \text{ per month}$$

Here is the amortization table for this discount amortization:

	Discount Amortization: Balance × 0.0024301	Balance
		165,000
November 30	401	164,599
December 31	400	164,199
January 30	399	163,800
Total discount amortization	1,200	

The journal entry at December 31, 2006, to record November and December amortization is:

Exchange loss (+Lo, −SE)	$801	
Other comprehensive income (+SE)		$801

On January 30, 2007, four journal entries must be made.

ACCOUNTS RECEIVABLE FAIR VALUE ADJUSTMENT AND SETTLEMENT Assume that the spot rate at January 30, 2007, is $1.665 and that Winkler collects the £100,000 accounts receivable and immediately converts it into dollars.

Cash (+A)	$166,500	
Accounts receivable (−A)		$166,000
Exchange gain (+G, +SE)		$ 500

FORWARD CONTRACT FAIR VALUE ADJUSTMENT AND NET SETTLEMENT Winkler must pay Ross $166,500 − $163,800 = $2,700, because the spot rate on the date the contract expires is $1.665 and the forward contract rate is $1.638. We will first record the forward contract gain or loss from December 31 to January 30 and then record the net settlement payment to Ross.

Other comprehensive income (−SE)	$1,017	
Forward contract (+L)		$1,017

The contract loss is $2,700 (forward contract value at settlement date) − $1,683 (December 31, 2006, forward contract fair value estimate) = $1,017.

Next we must record a loss to offset the exchange gain recorded related to the receivable.

Exchange gain (loss) (−G, −SE)	$ 500	
Other comprehensive income (+SE)		$ 500
Forward contract (−L)	$2,700	
Cash (−A)		$2,700

DISCOUNT OR PREMIUM AMORTIZATION ENTRY From the previous table, $399 of the discount must be amortized for the period December 31, 2006, to January 30, 2007.

Exchange loss (+Lo, −SE)	$399	
Other comprehensive income (+SE)		$399

Let's summarize what has happened to the accounts involved in this cash-flow-hedge situation.

Accounts Receivable (Asset)

November 2, 2006—initial sale date	+ $165,000
December 31, 2006—adjusted to spot rate	+ 1,000
Balance on December 31, 2006	$166,000
(spot rate $1.66 × £100,000)	
January 30, 2007—adjusted to spot rate	+ 500
Balance on January 30, 2007, before settlement	$166,500

Forward Contract

November 2, 2006—initial contract date	No entry—net settlement
December 31, 2006—adjusted to fair value estimate	+1,683—liability
Balance on December 31, 2006	$1,683 credit—liability

Other Comprehensive Income

November 2, 2006	No entry
December 31, 2006—adjust forward contract to fair value estimate	$1,683 debit
Offset gain on hedged item—accounts receivable	1,000 credit
Discount amortization for November and December	801 credit
Balance on December 31, 2006	$ 118 credit
January 30, 2007—adjust forward contract to fair value estimate	$1,017 debit
Offset gain on hedged item—accounts receivable	500—credit
Discount amortization for January	399—debit credit
Balance on January 30, 2007	$ 0

Income Effect

December 31, 2006	
Gain on hedged item	$1,000
Offsetting amount from OCI due to forward contract and cash-flow-hedge accounting	−1,000
Discount amortization—exchange loss	− 801
Net exchange loss at December 31, 2006	−$ 801
January 30, 2006	
Gain on hedged item	$ 500
Offsetting amount from OCI due to forward contract and cash -flow-hedge accounting	−500
Discount amortization-exchange loss	−399
Net exchange loss at January 30, 2006	−$399

What has this accounting accomplished? Notice that the company knew on November 2, 2006, that it was going to lose $1,200 related to the foreign currency–denominated accounts receivable and the related hedging contract. The accounting above reflects management's purpose in entering into this contract because the effect of changes in the exchange rate on the receivable value are exactly off-set by reclassifying an offsetting amount from other comprehensive income. The actual cost of the cash flow hedge to the company, $1,200, is rationally and systematically amortized to income. Finally, both the item being hedged and the hedge contract are valued at fair value at year-end.

Also notice something else. Recall that the amortized value of the hedged item on December 31, 2006, from the discount amortization table above is $164,199. How is this number reflected on the balance sheet at December 31?

Accounts receivable—at fair value	$166,000 debit
Forward contract—at estimated fair value	1,683 credit
Less: other comprehensive income	118 credit
Net balance sheet effect of the cash flow hedge	$164,199 debit

As illustrated previously, a company may incur losses (and garner gains) when the foreign exchange rate of foreign currency–denominated receivables or payables fluctuates between the date that the receivable (payable) is recorded and when it is ultimately received and converted into dollars (or dollars are used to buy the foreign currency used to settle the payable).

Fair Value Hedge Accounting: Foreign Currency–Denominated Receivable Example

ILLUSTRATION: HEDGE AGAINST EXPOSED NET ASSET (ACCOUNTS RECEIVABLE) POSITIONS U.S. Oil Company sells oil to Monato Company of Japan for 15,000,000 yen on December 1, 2006. The billing date for the sale is December 1, 2006, and payment is due in 60 days, on January 30, 2007. Concurrent with the sale, U.S. Oil enters into a forward contract to deliver 15,000,000 yen to its exchange broker in 60 days. Exchange rates for Japanese yen are as follows:

	December 1, 2006	December 31, 2006	January 30, 2007
Spot rate	**$0.007500**	**$0.007498**	**$0.007497**
30-day futures rate	$0.007490	**$0.007489**	$0.007488
60-day futures rate	**$0.007490**	$0.007488	$0.007486

The bold rates are the relevant rates for accounting purposes. The forward contract is carried at market value, which is the forward rate. Journal entries on the books of U.S. Oil are as follows:

December 1, 2006

Accounts receivable (fc) (+A)	$112,500	
Sales (+R, +SE)		$112,500
To record sales to Monato Company (15,000,000 yen × $0.007500 spot rate).		
Contract receivable (+A)	$112,350	
Contract payable (fc) (+L)		$112,350
To record forward contract to deliver 15,000,000 yen in 60 days. Receivable: 15,000,000 yen × $0.007490 forward rate.		

At the time that the forward contract is entered into, the company can compute its total gain or loss on the hedged item and the hedge contract. Fluctuations in exchange rates subsequent to this will not affect the magnitude of this gain or loss. The net gain or loss is the difference between the contracted forward rate and the spot rate on the date the contract is entered into:

$$(\$0.007490 - \$0.00750) \times 15,000,000 = -\$0.00001 \times 15,000,000 = -\$150$$

The company will lose $150, because it has contracted to receive $0.00001 less than the spot rate at the time the contract was entered into.

At December 31, 2006, the accounts receivable from the sale is adjusted to reflect the current exchange rate, and a $30 exchange loss is recorded. Calculating the exchange gain on the forward contract is a bit more complex. On the surface, the gain would appear to be the initial forward rate of $0.007490 × 15,000,000 less the current forward rate of $0.007489 × 15,000,000 ($112,350 − $112,335), which is $15. However, the FASB has elected to discount this amount from the contract termination date to the financial statement date. If we assume that 12% is a reasonable discount rate, this would be a discount of $0.15. The present value of $15 to be received one month is computed as $15 ÷ (1.01)^1 = $14.85.

December 31, 2006

Exchange loss (+Lo, −SE)	$ 30	
Accounts receivable (fc) (−A)		$ 30

To adjust accounts receivable to year-end spot exchange rate
[15,000,000 yen × ($0.007500 − $0.007498) = $30].

Contract payable (fc) (−L)	$14.85	
Exchange gain (+G, +SE)		$14.85

To adjust contract payable to exchange broker to
the year-end forward exchange rate. Payable:
15,000,000 yen × ($0.007490 − $0.007489).

The exchange gain or loss on the hedged underlying asset is not the same as the exchange gain or loss on the forward contract because the underlying asset is carried at the spot rate and the forward contract is carried at the forward rate.

Over the contract period, the forward rate will approach the spot rate, exactly equaling it on the settlement date. In this example, the net change in the relative value was $15.15 ($30 loss − $14.85 gain) for 2007 and $134.85 ($15 loss + $119.85 loss) for 2008.

January 30, 2007

Cash (fc) (+A)	$ 112,455	
Exchange loss (−Lo, −SE)	15	
Accounts receivable (fc) (−A)		$112,470

To record collection of receivable from
Monato Company. Cash: 15,000,000 yen × $0.007497.

Contract payable (fc)	$112,335.15	
Exchange loss (−Lo, −SE)	119.85	
Cash (fc) (−A)		$112,455

To record delivery of 15,000,000 yen from Monato to
foreign exchange broker in settlement of liability.

Cash (+A)	$ 112,350	
Contract receivable (−A)		$112,350

To record receipt of cash from exchange broker.

In the final analysis, U.S. Oil Company makes a sale in the amount of $112,500. It takes a $150 charge on the transaction in order to avoid the risks of foreign currency price fluctuations, and it collects $112,350 in final settlement of the sale transaction. The $150 is charged to income over the term of the forward contract.

HEDGE AGAINST EXPOSED NET LIABILITY POSITION Accounting procedures for hedging an exposed net liability position are comparable to those illustrated for U.S. Oil Company except that the objective is to hedge a liability denominated in foreign currency, rather than a receivable. Normally, the forward rate for buying foreign currency for future receipt is greater than the spot rate. For example, a forward contract to acquire 10,000 British pounds for receipt in 60 days might have a forward rate of $1.675 when the spot rate is $1.66. The forward contract is recorded as follows:

Contract receivable (fc) (+A)	$16,750	
Contract payable (+L)		$16,750

The contract hedges any effect of changes in the exchange rate so that the net cost over the life of the contract will be the $150 differential between the spot and forward rates.

RESULT OF HEDGING Forward rates are ordinarily set so that a cost is incurred related to the hedge. Occasionally, the rates for futures contracts result in hedges that increase income.

In summary, a forward contract is recorded at the forward rate, while the underlying asset or liability is recorded at the spot rate (and adjusted to these respective rates and values at the financial statement date). Over the life of the contract, the initial difference between the spot and the forward rates is the cost of hedging the exchange rate risk. Because the gains and losses on both the hedge and the underlying asset or liability are recorded in current earnings, the net cost reported in the income statement is the change in the relative values of the spot and forward rates.

If a firm enters a forward contract for foreign currency units in excess of the foreign currency units reflected in its exposed net asset or net liability position (a speculation in the currency), the difference ends up as a gain or loss. This is due to the difference in the change in the value of the derivative and the change in the value of the underlying item hedged both being reported in the income statement.

Fair Value Hedge of an Identifiable Foreign Currency Commitment

A **foreign currency commitment** is a contract or agreement denominated in foreign currency that will result in a foreign currency transaction at a later date. For example, a U.S. firm may contract to buy equipment from a Canadian firm at a future date with the invoice price denominated in Canadian dollars. The U.S. firm has an exposure to exchange rate changes because the future price in U.S. dollars may increase or decrease before the transaction is consummated.

An identifiable foreign currency commitment differs from an exposed asset or liability position because the commitment does not meet the accounting tests for recording the related asset or liability in the accounts. The risk of the exposure still may be avoided by hedging. This situation is special because the underlying transaction being hedged is not recorded as an asset or liability. Therefore, some method must be established to record the change in the value of the underlying unrecorded commitment in order to record the derivative instrument as a hedge of the commitment. Once this mechanism has been created, both the change in the derivative instrument and the underlying commitment are recorded—in effect, offsetting each other. Because a forward contract that is a hedge of a firm commitment is based on the forward rate, not the spot rate, any gain or loss on the derivative and underlying contract is based on the forward rate.

The forward contract accounting begins when the forward contract is designated as a hedge of a foreign currency commitment.

ILLUSTRATION: HEDGE OF AN IDENTIFIABLE FOREIGN CURRENCY PURCHASE COMMITMENT On October 2, 2006, American Stores Corporation contracts with Canadian Distillers for delivery of 1,000 cases of bourbon at a price of 60,000 Canadian dollars, when the spot rate for Canadian dollars is $0.70. The bourbon is to be delivered in March and payment made in Canadian dollars on March 31, 2007. In order to hedge this future commitment, American Stores purchases 60,000 Canadian dollars for delivery in 180 days at a forward exchange rate of $0.725. Applicable forward rates on December 31, 2006, and March 31, 2007 (because the maturity is March 31, this rate is also the spot rate) are $0.71 and $0.68, respectively.

Assume that the derivative instrument (the forward contract) is designated as a hedge of this identifiable foreign currency commitment. The purchase of the forward contract on October 2, 2006, is recorded as follows:

October 2, 2006		
Contract receivable (fc) (+A)	$43,500	
Contract payable (+L)		$43,500
To record purchase of 60,000 Canadian dollars for		
delivery in 180 days at a forward rate of $0.725.		

By December 31, 2006, the forward exchange rate for Canadian dollars decreases to $0.71, and American Stores adjusts its receivable to reflect the 60,000 Canadian dollars at the 90-day forward exchange rate. This adjustment creates a $900 exchange loss on the futures contract as follows:

December 31, 2006		
Exchange loss (+Lo, −SE)	$900	
Contract receivable (fc) (−A)		$900
To record exchange loss: 60,000		
Canadian dollars × ($0.725 − $0.71).		

However, this loss is offset by the increase in the value of the underlying firm commitment:

December 31, 2006

Change in value of firm commitment in Canadian dollars (fc) (+A)	$ 900	
Exchange gain (+G, +SE)		$ 900

To record exchange gain: 60,000 Canadian dollars × ($0.725 − $0.71). (Payment in Canadian dollars will cost fewer US$.)

Journal entries on March 31, 2007, to account for the foreign currency transaction and related forward contract are as follows:

March 31, 2007

1. | | | |
   |---|---|---|
   | Contract payable (−L) | $43,500 | |
   | Cash (−A) | | $43,500 |

   To record settlement of forward contract with the exchange broker (denominated in U.S. dollars).

2. | | | |
   |---|---|---|
   | Cash (fc) (+A) | $40,800 | |
   | Exchange loss (+Lo, −SE) | 1,800 | |
   | Contract receivable (fc) (−A) | | $42,600 |

   To record receipt of 60,000 Canadian dollars from the exchange broker when the exchange rate is $0.68.

3. | | | |
   |---|---|---|
   | Change in value of firm commitment in Canadian dollars (+A) | $ 1,800 | |
   | Exchange gain (+G, +SE) | | $ 1,800 |

   To record the change in the value of the underlying firm commitment.

4. | | | |
   |---|---|---|
   | Purchases (+A) | $43,500 | |
   | Change in value of firm commitment in Canadian dollars (−A) | | $ 2,700 |
   | Accounts payable (fc) (+L) | | 40,800 |

   To record receipt of 1,000 cases of bourbon at a cost of 60,000 Canadian dollars × forward exchange rate of $0.725.

5. | | | |
   |---|---|---|
   | Accounts payable (fc) (−L) | $40,800 | |
   | Cash (fc) (−A) | | $40,800 |

   To record payment of 60,000 Canadian dollars to Canadian Distillers.

Entry 1 records payment to the exchange broker for the 60,000 Canadian dollars at the contracted forward rate of $0.725. The second entry reflects collection of the 60,000 Canadian dollars from the broker and records an additional exchange loss on the further decline of the exchange rate from the forward rate of $0.71 at December 31, 2006, to the $0.68 spot rate (this is also the forward rate for the date of settlement) at March 31, 2007. The third entry records the gain on the change in the dollar cost of the firm commitment to buy the bourbon since December 31, 2006. The fourth entry on March 31 records receipt of the 1,000 cases of bourbon from Canadian Distillers and records the liability payable in Canadian dollars. It also incorporates the change in the firm commitment in the inventory value. In entry 5, Canadian Distillers is paid the 60,000 Canadian dollars in final settlement of the account payable.

HEDGE OF AN IDENTIFIABLE FOREIGN CURRENCY SALES COMMITMENT Accounting procedures for hedging an identifiable foreign currency sales commitment are comparable to those illustrated for hedging a purchase commitment, except that the sales, rather than the purchases, account is adjusted for any deferred exchange gains or losses.

Cash Flow Hedge of an Anticipated Foreign Currency Transaction

Winkler Corporation, a U.S. corporation, anticipates a contract based on December 2, 2006, discussions to sell heavy equipment to Smith Ltd. of Scotland for 500,000 British pounds. The equipment is anticipated to be delivered to Winkler and the amount paid to Smith on March 1, 2007, but nothing has been signed.

In order to hedge its anticipated commitment, Winkler enters into a forward contract with Seaser Company to buy 500,000 British pounds for delivery on March 1. The contract is to be settled net. Assume that this qualifies as an effective hedge under *Statement No. 133* and should be accounted for as a cash flow hedge of an anticipated foreign currency commitment.

On December 2, 2006, the spot rate is $1.7000 and the 90-day forward rate is $1.6800 (for delivery on March 1, 2007). Because this is an anticipated commitment, there is no hedged item on the balance sheet that will be marked to fair value until the actual sale occurs, which will be in three months. However, the company has engaged in this forward contract. The contract must be recorded at estimated fair value at year-end. However because this is considered a cash flow hedge of an anticipated foreign currency commitment, the resulting gain or loss is deferred until the item being hedged actually affects income. But the discount or premium related to the forward contract must be amortized to income over time.

FORWARD CONTRACT ADJUSTMENT AT DECEMBER 31, 2006 Assume that the 60-day forward rate at December 31, 2006, is $1.6900. We estimate the fair value of this forward contract as follows assuming a 12% annual incremental borrowing rate.

Date	Forward Contract Rate	Forward Contract Rate at This Date	Difference	× 500,000	Factor	Present Value at Date Below
December 31	1.68	1.69	0.01	5,000	1.01^2	4,901

The journal entry is:

Forward contract (+A)	$4,901	
Other comprehensive income (+SE)		$4,901

FORWARD DISCOUNT ADJUSTMENT The original forward discount was $1.70 − $1.68 = 0.02 × 500,000 = $10,000. Recall from our discussion of cash flow hedges of existing foreign currency-denominated receivables and payables that the discount or premium resulting from the hedge must be amortized to income over the life of the contract. If the spot rate and forward rate on December 1, 2006 had been the same, there would be no discount or premium to amortize. Winkler would have just recorded the forward contract fair value at year-end as illustrated above. Income would not have been affected. However, in this case, the spot and forward rates were different, resulting in a discount which must be amortized to income over the contract's life. A discount arises when the contracted forward rate is lower than the spot rate at that date. A premium arises when the contracted forward rate is higher than the spot rate at the contract date. We again solve for the monthly implicit rate to be used to amortize the $10,000 discount. The rate is .3937% or .003937. The amortization table is presented below:

	Discount amortization	Balance
		850000
December 31	3346	846654
January 31	3333	843320
February 28	3320	840000
Total discount amortization	10000	

The journal entry to record the discount amortization and related gain at December 31 is:

Other comprehensive income (−SE)	3,347	
Exchange gain (+G, +SE)		3,347

There are four journal entries on March 1.

FORWARD CONTRACT ADJUSTMENT AND EQUIPMENT PURCHASE Assume that the spot rate on March 1 is $1.72. The forward contract value on this date is ($1.72 − $1.68) × 500,000 = $20,000. The balance on

December 31, 2006, was $4,901 debit, so we must increase the forward contract to its fair value by increasing the account by $15,099. Winkler will receive $20,000 from Seaser because the spot rate is higher than the forward contract rate.

Forward contract (+A)	15,099	
AOCI (+SE)		15,099
Equipment	860,000	
Cash		860,000
(1.72 × 500,000)		
Cash	20,000	
Forward contract		20,000

Discount Amortization Entry We must record the amortization of the discount for January and February. From the amortization table above, the amortization for those two months is $3,333 + $3,320 = $6,653.

Other comprehensive income (−SE)	6,653	
Exchange gain (+G, +SE)		6,653

This table presents a summary of account balances:

Forward contract

December 2, 2006—no entry required	$ 0
December 31, 2006	+ 4,901 debit
Balance on December 31, 2006	$ 4,901 debit—asset
Fair value adjustment at March 1, 2007	+15,099 debit
Balance before settlement on March 1, 2007	$20,000 debit—asset

Other Comprehensive Income

December 31, 2006, adjustment of forward contract to fair value	$ 4,901 credit
December 31, 2006, amortization of discount	3,347 debit
Balance on December 31, 2006	$ 1,554 credit
March 1, 2007, adjustment of forward contract to fair value	$15,099 credit
March 1, 2007, amortization of discount	$ 6,653 debit
Balance on March 1, 2007	$10,000 credit

Income

December 31, 2006—exchange gain resulting from amortizing discount	$3,347
March 1, 2007—exchange gain resulting from amortizing discount	$6,653

On March 1, 2007, the equipment is recorded at $860,000. As the equipment is depreciated, the $10,000 balance in the other comprehensive income account will be amortized to reduce depreciation expense.

Speculation

Exchange gains or losses on derivative instruments that speculate in foreign currency price movements are included in income in the periods in which the forward exchange rates change. Forward or future exchange rates for 30-, 90-, and 180-day delivery are quoted on a daily basis for the leading world currencies. A foreign currency derivative that is a speculation is valued at forward rates throughout the life of the contract (which is the fair value of the contract at that point in time). The basic accounting is illustrated in the following example.

On November 2, 2006, U.S. International enters into a 90-day forward contract (future) to purchase 10,000 euros when the current quotation for 90-day futures in euros is $0.5400. The spot rate for euros on November 2 is $0.5440. Exchange rates at December 31, 2006, and January 30, 2007, are as follows:

	December 31, 2006	January 30, 2007
30-day futures	$0.5450	$0.5480
Spot rate	0.5500	0.5530

Journal entries on the books of U.S. International to account for the speculation are as follows:

November 2, 2006

Contract receivable (fc) (+A)	$5,400	
Contract payable (+L)		$5,400

To record contract for 10,000 euros × $0.5400 exchange
rate for 90-day futures.

December 31, 2006

Contract receivable (fc) (+A)	$50	
Exchange gain (+G, +SE)		$50

To adjust receivable from exchange broker and recognize
exchange gain (10,000 euros × $0.5450 forward exchange
rate for 30-day futures − $5,400 per books).

January 30, 2007

Cash (fc) (+A)	$5,530	
Exchange gain (+G, +SE)		$ 80
Contract receivable (fc) (−A)		$5,450

To record receipt of 10,000 euros. The current spot
rate for euros is $0.5530.

Contract payable (−L)	$5,400	
Cash (−A)		$5,400

To record payment of the liability to the exchange
broker denominated in dollars.

The entry on November 2 records U.S. International's right to receive 10,000 euros from the exchange broker in 90 days. It also records U.S. International's liability to pay $5,400 to the exchange broker in 90 days. Both the receivable and the liability are recorded at $5,400 (10,000 euros × $0.5400 forward rate), but only the receivable is denominated in euros and is subject to exchange rate fluctuations.

At December 31, 2006, the forward contract has 30 days until maturity. Under the provisions of *Statement No. 133,* the receivable denominated in euros is adjusted to reflect the exchange rate of $0.5450 for 30-day futures on December 31, 2006. This is the fair value of the contract. The amount of the adjustment is included in U.S. International's income for 2006.

On January 30, 2007, U.S. International receives 10,000 euros with a current value of $5,530 (10,000 euros × $0.5530 spot rate). The translated value of the foreign currency received is $80 more than the recorded amount of the receivable, so an additional exchange gain results. U.S. International also settles its liability with the exchange broker on January 30.

A speculation involving the sale of foreign currency for future delivery is accounted for in a similar fashion, except that the receivable is fixed in U.S. dollars and the liability is denominated in the foreign currency.

Forward Contracts Summarized

The accounting required for a forward contract depends primarily on management's intent when entering into the transaction. Exhibit 12-2 summarizes the four types of forward contracts and the purpose, required accounting, and effect on income of each.

Footnote-Disclosure Requirements

Disclosure requirements focus upon how its derivatives fit into a company's overall risk-management objectives and strategy. The company should be specific about the types of risks being hedged and how they are being hedged. In addition, the company should describe initially how it determines hedge effectiveness and how it assesses continuing hedge effectiveness.

The disclosures related to fair value hedges include reporting the net gain or loss included in earnings during the period and where in the financial statements the gain or loss is reported. This gain or

EXHIBIT 12-2

SUMMARY OF FORWARD CONTRACTS

Classification	Purpose	Recognition	Expected Effect of Hedge and Related Item
Speculation	To speculate in exchange rate changes	Exchange gains and losses are recognized currently, based on forward exchange rate changes.	Income effect equals exchange gains and losses recognized.
Hedge of a net asset or liability position	To offset exposure to existing net asset or liability position	Exchange gains and losses are recognized currently, but they are offset by related gains or losses on net asset or liability position.	Income effect equals the amortization of premium or discount. (Gains and losses offset.)
Hedge of an identifiable commitment	To offset exposure to a future purchase or sale and thereby lock in the price of an existing contract in U.S. dollars	Exchange gains and losses are recognized currently, but they are offset by related gains or losses in the firm commitment.	Income effect equals the difference in the change in value of the hedge instrument versus the firm commitment.
Hedge of an anticipated transaction	To offset exposure of possible future purchase or sale	Exchange gains or losses on the hedge are counted in other comprehensive income until the underlying transaction is complete.	No immediate income effect. Adjusts underlying transaction.
Hedge of a net investment in a foreign entity (see Chapter 13)	To offset exposure to an existing net investment in a foreign entity	Exchange gains and losses are recognized as other comprehensive income and will offset translation adjustments recorded on the net investment.	Income effect equals the change in the future value of the hedge versus the value of the net investment.

loss is separated into the portion that represents the hedge's ineffectiveness and the portion of the gain or loss on the hedge instrument that was not included in the assessment of hedge effectiveness.

Cash flow hedging instrument disclosures include reporting the amount of any hedge ineffectiveness gain or loss and any gain or loss from the derivative excluded from the assessment of hedge effectiveness. In addition, location of these gains and losses in the financial statements should be disclosed.

The disclosures for cash flow hedges also include a description of the situations in which the gain or loss included in accumulated other comprehensive income is reclassified to income. An estimate of the amount of reclassification to occur within the next 12 months should also be reported.

Because cash flow hedge accounting can be used for forecasted transactions, the company should report the maximum length of time that the entity is hedging its exposure to these forecasted transactions. This disclosure excludes transactions hedges of variable interest on existing financial instruments.

Finally, the company should report the amount of gains and losses that could be reclassified to income if the cash flow hedges were discontinued because the original forecasted transactions did not occur.

Please attempt the Internet Assignment at the end of the chapter to examine an actual disclosure.

International Accounting Standards

LEARNING OBJECTIVE 11

Three international accounting standards address issues related to accounting for foreign currency transactions and hedge accounting.

International Accounting Standard No. 21, "The Effects of Changes in Foreign Exchange Rates," (revised in December 2003, originally issued in July 1983 as "Accounting for the Effects of Changes in Foreign Exchange Rates") addresses how to include foreign currency transactions and foreign operations in the financial statements. In addition, translation of foreign currency financial statements into the presentation currency is prescribed. Like *U.S. Financial Accounting Statement*

No. 52, the choice of which exchange rate to use and how to report the effects of changes in exchange rates in the financial statements is discussed.

Like *Statement No. 52*, *IAS 21* requires that transactions be recorded initially at the rate of exchange at the date of the transaction. At each subsequent balance sheet date, foreign currency monetary amounts (such as foreign currency–denominated accounts receivables and payables) should be marked to the spot rate at the balance sheet date. Again like *Statement No. 52*, gains and losses from differences between the initial amount recorded and the year-end value for these monetary assets and liabilities are included in current year income.

International Accounting Standard No. 32, "Financial Instruments: Disclosure and Presentation," (revised in December 2003, originally issued in June 1995) and *International Accounting Standard No. 39*, "Financial Instruments: Recognition and Measurement," (a significant revision in December 2003, but also revised in March 2004; originally issued in December 1998) are companion statements. *IAS No. 32's* major points include clarifying when a financial instrument issued by a company should be classified as a liability or as equity and requiring a wide range of disclosures regarding financial instruments, including their fair values. In addition, the statement defines and provides examples of many terms, such as financial assets, financial liability, equity instrument, and fair values.

IAS No. 39 addresses many of the same issues as *U.S. Financial Accounting Statements No. 133* and *138*, including defining and providing examples of derivatives as well as hedge accounting. In fact, the conditions that must be present to use hedge accounting, such as formally designating and documenting the corporation's risk-management objective and strategy for undertaking the hedge, as well as the need to assess hedge effectiveness initially and during the hedge's existence, are almost identical to *Statement No. 133*. For example, the 80% to 125% range mentioned in *Statement 133* is also mentioned in *IAS 39* to assess effectiveness.

The definitions of fair value hedges and cash flow hedges and the general accounting are very similar. However, one difference between IAS and U.S. GAAP is how firm sale or purchase commitments are accounted for. Under U.S. GAAP, such firm sale or purchase commitments are accounted for as fair value hedges, but under *IAS 39* they can be accounted for as either fair value hedges or cash flow hedges. Despite some differences, U.S. GAAP and IAS standards relating to derivatives are converging.

SUMMARY

International accounting is concerned with accounting for foreign currency transactions and operations. An entity's functional currency is the currency of the primary environment in which the entity operates. Foreign currency transactions are denominated in a currency other than an entity's functional currency.

Foreign currency transactions (other than forward contracts) are measured and recorded in U.S. dollars at the spot rate in effect at the transaction date. A change in the exchange rate between the date of the transaction and the settlement date results in an exchange gain or loss that is reflected in income for the period. At the balance sheet date, any remaining balances that are denominated in a currency other than the functional currency are adjusted to reflect the current exchange rate, and the gain or loss is charged to income.

Corporations use forward exchange contracts to avoid the risks of exchange rate changes and to speculate on foreign currency exchange price movements. *Statement No. 133* prescribes different provisions for forward contracts (and other derivatives), depending on their nature and purposes.

QUESTIONS

1. Distinguish between *measurement* and *denomination* in a particular currency.

2. Assume that one euro can be exchanged for 1.20 U.S. dollars. What is the exchange rate if the exchange rate is quoted directly? Indirectly?

3. What is the difference between official and floating foreign exchange rates? Does the United States have floating exchange rates?

4. What is a spot rate with respect to foreign currency transactions? Could a spot rate ever be a historical rate? Could a spot rate ever be a fixed exchange rate? Discuss.

5. Assume that a U.S. corporation imports electronic equipment from Japan in a transaction denominated in U.S. dollars. Is this transaction a foreign currency transaction? A foreign transaction? Explain the difference between these two concepts and their application here.

6. How are assets and liabilities denominated in foreign currency measured and recorded at the transaction date? At the balance sheet date?

7. Criticize the following statement: "Exchange losses arise from foreign import activities, and exchange gains arise from foreign export activities."

8. When are exchange gains and losses reflected in a business's financial statements?

9. A U.S. corporation imported merchandise from a British company for £1,000 when the spot rate was $1.45. It issued financial statements when the current rate was $1.47, and it paid for the merchandise when the spot rate was $1.46. What amount of exchange gain or loss will be included in the U.S. corporation's income statements in the period of purchase and in the period of settlement?

10. Define the term *derivative* and provide examples of risks that derivative contracts are designed to reduce.

11. Explain the objective of hedge accounting and how this objective should improve the transparency of financial statements.

12. Explain the differences between options, forward contracts, and futures contracts and the potential benefits and potential costs of each type of contract.

13. Hedge effectiveness must be documented before a particular hedge qualifies for hedge accounting. Describe the most common approaches used to determine hedge effectiveness and when they are appropriate. In each of the approaches, when would a particular hedge *not* be considered effective?

14. A hedged firm purchase or sale commitment typically qualifies for fair value hedge accounting if the hedge is documented to be effective. Compare the accounting for both the derivative and the firm purchase or sale commitment under each of these circumstances: (a) the hedge relationship is deemed to be effective and (b) the hedge relationship is *not* deemed to be effective.

15. Interest rate swaps were used in the chapter to highlight the differences between fair value and cash flow hedge accounting. Explain what type of risk is being hedged when a *pay-fixed, receive-variable swap* is used to hedge an existing fixed-rate loan.

16. Interest rate swaps were used in the chapter to highlight the differences between fair value and cash flow hedge accounting. Explain what type of risk is being hedged when a *receive-fixed, pay-variable swap* is used to hedge an existing variable-rate loan.

17. Explain the circumstances under which fair value hedge accounting should be used and when cash flow hedge accounting should be used.

18. *Statement No. 138* allows companies to account for certain hedges of existing foreign currency–denominated receivables and payables as cash flow hedges. Under *Statement No. 133*, hedges of existing assets and liabilities must be accounted for as fair value hedges. Explain the circumstances that must be present for a hedge of an existing foreign currency–denominated receivable or payable to be accounted for as a cash flow hedge and how the accounting differs from cash flow hedge accounting in more-general situations.

19. Briefly describe how derivatives are accounted for according to the International Accounting Standards Board. Is the accounting similar to U.S. GAAP? How is it different?

20. Describe how to account for a forward contract that is intended as a hedge of an identifiable foreign currency commitment.

EXERCISES

E 12-1
Quotation conventions, measurement versus denomination

LEARNING OBJECTIVES 1, 2, 3

1. If $1.5625 can be exchanged for 1 British pound, the direct and indirect exchange rate quotations are:
   a *$1.5625 and 1 British pound, respectively*
   b *$1.5625 and 0.64 British pounds, respectively*
   c *$1.00 and 1.5625 British pounds, respectively*
   d *$1.00 and 0.64 British pounds, respectively*

2. A U.S. firm purchases merchandise from a Canadian firm with payment due in 60 days and denominated in Canadian dollars. The U.S. firm will report an exchange gain or loss on settlement if the transaction is:
   a *Recorded in U.S. dollars*
   b *Measured in U.S. dollars*
   c *Not hedged through a forward contract*
   d *Settled after an exchange rate change has occurred*

3. Exchange gains and losses on accounts receivable and payable that are denominated in a foreign currency are:
  a Accumulated and reported upon settlement
  b Deferred and treated as transaction price adjustments
  c Reported as equity adjustments from translation
  d Recognized in the periods in which exchange rates change

E 12-2

Accounting for foreign currency–denominated purchases Zimmer Corporation, a U.S. firm, purchased merchandise from Taisho Company of Japan on November 1, 2006, for 10,000,000 yen, payable on December 1, 2006. The spot rate for yen on November 1 was $0.0075, and on December 1 the spot rate was $0.0076.

REQUIRED

1. Did the dollar weaken or strengthen against the yen between November 1 and December 1, 2006? Explain.

2. On November 1, 2006, at what amount did Zimmer record the account payable to Taisho?

3. On December 1, 2006, Zimmer paid the 10,000,000 yen to Taisho. Prepare the journal entry to record settlement of the account on Zimmer's books.

4. If Zimmer had chosen to hedge its exposed net liability position on November 1, would it have entered a forward contract to purchase yen for future receipt or to sell yen for future delivery? Explain.

E 12-3

Accounting for foreign currency–denominated purchases settled in subsequent year
On December 16, 2006, Aviator Corporation, a U.S. firm, purchased merchandise from Wing Company for 30,000 euros to be paid on January 15, 2007. Relevant exchange rates for euros are as follows:

December 16, 2006	$1.20
December 31, 2006	$1.25
January 15, 2007	$1.24

REQUIRED: Prepare all journal entries on Aviator Corporation's books to account for the purchase on December 16, adjustment of the books on December 31, and payment of the account payable on January 15.

E 12-4

Accounting for foreign currency–denominated sales settled in subsequent year On November 16, 2006, Wick Corporation of the United States sold inventory items to Candle Ltd. of Canada for 90,000 Canadian dollars, to be paid on February 14, 2007. Exchange rates for Canadian dollars on selected dates are as follows:

November 16, 2006	$0.80
December 31, 2006	$0.84
February 14, 2007	$0.83

REQUIRED: Determine the exchange gain or loss on the sale to Candle Ltd. to be included in Wick's income statement for the years 2006 and 2007.

E 12-5

Accounting for foreign currency–denominated sales Door Corporation, a U.S. company, sold inventory items to Royal Cabinets Ltd. of Great Britain for £200,000 on May 1, 2006, when the spot rate was 0.6000 pounds. The invoice was paid by Royal on May 30, 2006, when the spot rate was 0.6050 pounds.

REQUIRED: Prepare Door's journal entries for the sale to Royal on May 1 and receipt of the £200,000 on May 30.

E 12-6

[AICPA adapted] Various foreign currency–denominated transactions

1. On September 1, 2006, Bain Corporation received an order for equipment from a foreign customer for 300,000 euros, when the U.S. dollar equivalent was $400,000. Bain shipped the equipment on October 15, 2006, and billed the customer for 300,000 euros when the U.S. dollar equivalent was $420,000. Bain received the customer's remittance in full on November 16, 2006, and sold the 300,000 euros for $415,000. In its income statement for the year ended December 31, 2006, what should Bain report as a foreign exchange gain?

2. On September 22, 2006, Yumi Corporation purchased merchandise from an unaffiliated foreign company for 10,000 euros. On that date, the spot rate was $1.20. Yumi paid the bill in full on March 20, 2007, when the spot rate was $1.30. The spot rate was $1.24 on December 31, 2006. What amount should Yumi report as a foreign currency transaction loss in its income statement for the year ended December 31, 2006?

3. On July 1, 2006, Clark Company borrowed 1,680,000 pesos from a foreign lender, by signing an interest-bearing note due on July 1, 2007, which is denominated in pesos. The U.S. dollar equivalent of the note principal was as follows:

July 1, 2006 (date borrowed)	$210,000
December 31, 2006 (Clark's year-end)	240,000
July 1, 2007 (date paid)	280,000

In its income statement for 2007, what amount should Clark include as a foreign exchange gain or loss?

4. On July 1, 2006, Stone Company lent $120,000 to a foreign supplier, by accepting an interest-bearing note due on July 1, 2007. The note is denominated in the currency of the borrower and was equivalent to 840,000 pesos on the loan date. The note principal was appropriately included at $140,000 in the receivables section of Stone's December 31, 2006, balance sheet. The note principal was repaid to Stone on the July 1, 2007, due date, when the exchange rate was 8 pesos to $1. In its income statement for the year ended December 31, 2007, what amount should Stone include as a foreign currency transaction gain or loss?

E 12-7

Various foreign currency–denominated transactions settled in subsequent year Monroe Corporation imports merchandise from some Canadian companies and exports its own products to other Canadian companies. The *unadjusted* accounts denominated in Canadian dollars at December 31, 2006, are as follows:

Account receivable from the sale of merchandise on December 16 to Carver Corporation. Billing is for 150,000 Canadian dollars and due January 15, 2007	$103,500
Account payable to Forest Corporation for merchandise received December 2 and payable on January 30, 2007. Billing is for 275,000 Canadian dollars.	$195,250

Exchange rates on selected dates are as follows:

December 31, 2006	$0.68
January 15, 2006	$0.675
January 30, 2007	$0.685

REQUIRED

1. Determine the net exchange gain or loss from the two transactions that will be included in Monroe's income statement for 2006.

2. Determine the exchange gain or loss from settlement of the two transactions that will be included in Monroe's 2007 income statement.

E 12-8

Various foreign currency–denominated transactions settled in subsequent year

American TV Corporation had two foreign currency transactions during December 2006, as follows:

December 12	Purchased electronic parts from Toko Company of Japan at an invoice price of 50,000,000 yen when the spot rate for yen was $0.00750. Payment is due on January 11, 2007.
December 15	Sold television sets to British Products Ltd. for 40,000 pounds when the spot rate for British pounds was $1.65. The invoice is denominated in pounds and is due on January 14, 2007.

REQUIRED

1. Prepare journal entries to record the foregoing transactions.

2. Prepare journal entries to adjust the accounts of American TV Corporation at December 31, 2006, if the current exchange rates are $0.00760 and $1.60 for Japanese yen and British pounds, respectively.

3. Prepare journal entries to record payments to Toko Company on January 11, 2007, when the spot rate for Japanese yen is $0.00765, and to record receipt from British Products Ltd. on January 14, 2007, when the spot rate for British pounds is $1.63.

LEARNING OBJECTIVES **7, 8**

E 12-9

Hedge of an anticipated purchase On December 1, 2006, Jolly Rice Company enters into a 90-day forward contract with a rice speculator to purchase 500 tons of rice at $1,000 per ton. Jolly Rice enters into this contract in order to hedge an anticipated rice purchase. The contract is to be settled net. The spot price of rice at December 1, 2006, is $950.

On December 31, 2006, the forward rate is $980 per ton. The spot and forward rates when the contract is settled are $1,005. Assume that Jolly purchases 500 tons of rice on the date of the forward contract's expiration. Assume that this contract has been documented to be an effective hedge. Also assume an appropriate interest rate is 6%.

1. Prepare the required journal entries to account for this hedge situation and the subsequent rice purchase on:
   a **December 1, 2006**
   b **December 31, 2006**
   c **The settlement date**

2. Assume that the rice is subsequently sold by Jolly on June 1, 2007, for $1,200 per ton. What journal entries will Jolly make on that date?

LEARNING OBJECTIVES **7, 8**

E 12-10

Hedge of a firm purchase commitment Refer to E12-9 and assume that Jolly enters into the forward contract to hedge a firm purchase commitment. Repeat parts 1 and 2 under this assumption.

LEARNING OBJECTIVES **9, 10**

E 12-11

Cash flow hedge—foreign currency–denominated payable Hayes Corporation, a U.S. importer, purchased merchandise from Cavilier Company for 100,000 pesos on March 1, 2006, when the spot rate for pesos was $0.1630. The account payable denominated in pesos was not due until May 30, 2006, so Hayes immediately entered into a 90-day forward contract to hedge the transaction against exchange rate changes. The contract was made at a forward exchange rate of $0.1650. Hayes settled the forward contract and the account payable on May 30, when the spot rate for pesos was $0.1600.

REQUIRED: Prepare the journal entries needed for Hayes to account for the purchase and forward contract on March 1, 2006, and the subsequent settlements on May 30, 2006. Assume that this is properly designated as a cash flow hedge.

LEARNING OBJECTIVES **9, 10**

E 12-12

Cash flow hedge—foreign currency–denominated payable Target Corporation purchases merchandise from Sun Corporation for 10,000,000 yen. The merchandise is received on December 1, 2006, with payment due in 60 days on January 30, 2007. Also on December 1, 2006, Target enters into a 60-day forward contract with the exchange broker to purchase the necessary 10,000,000 yen for delivery on January 30, 2007, to hedge the Sun transaction. Exchange rates for yen on selected dates are as follows:

	12/1/06	12/31/06	1/30/07
Spot rate	$0.00055	$0.00056	$0.00057
30-day forward	0.00056	0.00057	0.00057
60-day forward	0.00057	0.00058	0.00058

REQUIRED: ASSUME A 6% INTEREST RATE.

1. What is the net exchange gain or loss from this transaction and hedge that will be reported on Target's 2006 income statement? Assume that this is properly designated as a cash flow hedge.
2. What effect will the transaction and hedge have on Target's income for 2007?

LEARNING OBJECTIVES **7, 8, 9, 10**

E 12-13

[AICPA adapted] Various foreign currency hedge situations On December 12, 2006, Cardinal Company entered into three forward exchange contracts, each to purchase 100,000 Canadian dollars in 90 days. Assume a 12% interest rate. The relevant exchange rates are as follows:

	Spot Rate	Forward Rate (for March 12, 2007)
December 12, 2006	$0.88	$0.90
December 31, 2006	0.98	0.93

1. Cardinal entered into the first forward contract to hedge a purchase of inventory in November 2006, payable in March 2007. At December 31, 2006, what amount of foreign currency transaction gain should Cardinal include in income from this forward contract? Explain.

2. Cardinal entered into the second forward contract to hedge a commitment to purchase equipment being manufactured to Cardinal's specifications. At December 31, 2006, what amount of net gain or loss on foreign currency transactions should Cardinal include in income from this forward contract? Explain.

3. Cardinal entered into a third forward contract for speculation. At December 31, 2006, what amount of foreign currency transaction gain should Cardinal include in income from this forward contract? Explain.

E 12-14

Firm purchase commitment, foreign currency hedge On April 1, 2006, Windsor Ltd. of Canada ordered customized fittings from Ace Foundry, a U.S. firm, to be delivered on May 31, 2006, at a price of 50,000 Canadian dollars. The spot rate for Canadian dollars on April 1, 2006, was $0.71. Also on April 1, in order to fix the sale price of the fittings at $35,250, Ace entered into a 60-day forward contract with the exchange broker to hedge the Windsor contract. This derivative met the conditions set forth in *FASB Statement No. 133* for a hedge of a foreign currency commitment. Exchange rates for Canadian dollars are as follows:

LEARNING OBJECTIVES **8, 9, 10**

	April 1	May 31
Spot rate	$0.710	$0.725
60-day forward rate	0.705	0.715

REQUIRED: Prepare all journal entries on Ace Foundry's books to account for the commitment and related events on April 1 and May 31, 2006.

E 12-15

Firm purchase commitment, foreign currency hedge On November 2, 2006, Import Bazaar, a U.S. retailer, ordered merchandise from Matsushita Company of Japan. The merchandise is to be delivered to Import Bazaar on January 30, 2007, at a price of 1,000,000 yen. Also on November 2, Import Bazaar hedged the foreign currency commitment with Matsushita by contracting with its exchange broker to buy 1,000,000 yen for delivery on January 30, 2007. Exchange rates for yen are:

LEARNING OBJECTIVES **8, 9, 10**

	11/2/06	12/31/06	1/30/07
Spot rate	$0.0075	$0.0076	$0.0078
30-day forward rate	0.0076	0.0078	0.0079
90-day forward rate	0.0078	0.0079	0.0080

REQUIRED

1. Prepare the entry (or entries) on Import Bazaar's books on November 2, 2006.
2. Prepare the adjusting entry on December 31, 2006.

E 12-16

Accounting for speculative hedges Martin Corporation, a U.S. import–export firm, enters into a forward contract on October 2, 2006, to speculate in euros. The contract requires Martin to deliver 1,000,000 euros to the exchange broker on March 31, 2007. Quoted exchange rates for euros are as follows:

LEARNING OBJECTIVE **12**

	10/2/06	12/31/06	3/31/07
Spot rate	$0.6590	$0.6500	$0.6550
30-day forward rate	0.6580	0.6450	0.6500
90-day forward rate	0.6560	0.6410	0.6460
180-day forward rate	0.6530	0.6360	0.6400

REQUIRED: Prepare the journal entries on Martin's books to account for the speculation throughout the life of the contract.

PROBLEMS

P 12-1

Accounting for foreign currency–denominated receivables and payables— multiple years The accounts of Lincoln International, a U.S. corporation, show $81,300 accounts receivable and $38,900 accounts payable at December 31, 2006, before adjusting entries are made. An analysis of the balances reveals the following:

LEARNING OBJECTIVES **1, 3**

Accounts Receivable

Receivable denominated in U.S. dollars	$28,500
Receivable denominated in 20,000 Swedish krona	11,800
Receivable denominated in 25,000 British pounds	41,000
Total	$81,300

Accounts Payable

Payable denominated in U.S. dollars	$ 6,850
Payable denominated in 10,000 Canadian dollars	7,600
Payable denominated in 15,000 British pounds	24,450
Total	$38,900

Current exchange rates for Swedish krona, British pounds, and Canadian dollars at December 31, 2006, are $0.66, $1.65, and $0.70, respectively.

REQUIRED

1. Determine the net exchange gain or loss that should be reflected in Lincoln's income statement for 2006 from year-end exchange adjustments.

2. Determine the amounts at which the accounts receivable and accounts payable should be included in Lincoln's December 31, 2006, balance sheet.

3. Prepare journal entries to record collection of the receivables in 2007 when the spot rates for Swedish krona and British pounds are $0.67 and $1.63, respectively.

4. Prepare journal entries to record settlement of accounts payable in 2007 when the spot rates for Canadian dollars and British pounds are $0.71 and $1.62, respectively.

LEARNING OBJECTIVES 1, 3

P 12-2

Foreign currency–denominated receivables and payables—multiple years

Shelton Corporation of New York is an international dealer in jewelry and engages in numerous import and export activities. Shelton's receivables and payables in foreign currency units before year-end adjustments on December 31, 2006, are summarized as follows:

Foreign Currency	Currency Units	Rate on Date of Transaction	Per Books in U.S. Dollars	Current Rate on 12/31/06
Accounts Receivable Denominated in Foreign Currency				
British pounds	100,000	$1.6500	$165,000	$1.6600
Euros	250,000	0.6600	165,000	0.6700
Swedish krona	160,000	0.6600	105,600	0.6400
Japanese yen	2,000,000	0.0075	15,000	0.0076
			$450,600	
Accounts Payable Denominated in Foreign Currency				
Canadian dollars	150,000	$0.7000	$105,000	$0.6900
Mexican pesos	220,000	0.1300	28,600	0.1350
Japanese yen	4,500,000	0.0074	33,300	0.0076
			$166,900	

REQUIRED

1. Determine the amount at which the receivables and payables should be reported in Shelton's December 31, 2006, balance sheet.

2. Calculate individual gains and losses on each of the receivables and payables and the net exchange gain that should appear in Shelton's 2006 income statement.

3. Assume that Shelton wants to hedge its exposure to amounts denominated in euros. Should it buy or sell euros for future delivery? In what amount or amounts?

LEARNING OBJECTIVES 3, 5, 6, 7, 9

P 12-3

Cash flow hedges, interest rate swap
On January 1, 2006, Campion Company borrows $400,000 from Veneta Bank. The five-year term note is a variable-rate one in which the 2006 interest rate is determined to be 8%, the LIBOR rate at January 1, 2006 + 2%. Subsequent years' interest rates are determined in a similar manner, with the rate set for a particular year equal to the beginning-of-the-year LIBOR rate + 2%. Interest payments are due on December 31 each year and are computed assuming annual compounding.

Also on January 1, 2006, Campion decides to enter into a pay-fixed, receive-variable interest rate swap arrangement with Graham, Inc. Campion will pay 8%.

Assume that the LIBOR rate on December 31, 2006, is 5%.

1. Why is this considered a cash flow hedge instead of a fair value hedge?

2. Do you think that this hedge would be considered effective and therefore would qualify for hedge accounting?

3. Assuming that this hedge relationship qualifies for hedge accounting:

   a. Determine the estimated fair value of the hedge at December 31, 2006, Recall that the hedge contract is in effect for the 2007, 2008, 2009, and 2010 interest payments.

   b. Prepare the entry at December 31, 2006, to account for this cash flow hedge as well as the December 31, 2006, interest payment.

4. Assuming that the LIBOR rate is 5.5% on December 31, 2007, prepare all the necessary entries to account for the interest rate swap at December 31, 2007, including the 2007 interest payment.

P 12-4

Fair value hedge, interest rate swap Refer to problem 12-3 and assume that instead of initially signing a variable-rate loan Campion receives a fixed rate of 8% on the loan on January 1, 2006. Instead of entering into a pay-fixed, receive-variable interest rate swap with Graham, Campion enters into a pay-variable, receive-fixed interest rate swap. The variable portion of the swap formula is LIBOR rate + 2%, determined at the end of the year to set the rate for the following year. The first year that the swap will be in effect is for interest payments in 2007.

LEARNING OBJECTIVES **4, 5, 6, 8**

Assume that the LIBOR rate on December 31, 2006, is 7%.

1. Why is this considered a fair value hedge instead of a cash flow hedge?

2. Do you think that this hedge would be considered effective and therefore would qualify for hedge accounting?

3. Assuming that this hedge relationship qualifies for hedge accounting:

   a. Determine the estimated fair value of the hedge at December 31, 2006. Recall that the hedge contract is in effect for the 2007, 2008, 2009, and 2010 interest payments.

   b. Prepare the entry at December 31, 2006, to account for this fair value hedge as well as the December 31, 2006, interest payment.

4. Assuming that the LIBOR rate is 6.5% on December 31, 2007, prepare all the necessary entries to account for the interest rate swap at December 31, 2007, including the 2007 interest payment.

P 12-5

Cash flow hedge, futures contract Northwest Gas Works, a consumer gas provider, estimates a rather cold winter. As a result it decides to enter into a futures contract on the NYMEX for natural gas on November 2, 2006. The trading unit is 10,000 million British thermal units (MMBtu). The three-month futures contract rate is $7.00 per MMBtu, so each contract will cost Northwest Gas Works $70,000. In addition, the exchange requires a $5,000 deposit on each contract. Northwest enters into 20 such contracts.

LEARNING OBJECTIVES **4, 5, 6, 7, 9**

REQUIRED

1. Why is this futures contract likely to be considered an effective hedge and therefore qualified for hedge accounting?

2. Why would this transaction be accounted for as a cash flow hedge?

3. Assume that the December 31, 2006, futures contract rate is $6.75 for delivery on February 2, 2007, and the spot rate on February 2, 2007, is $6.85. Assume that Northwest Gas Works sells all of the gas on February 3, 2007, for $8.00 per MMBtu. Prepare all the necessary journal entries from November 2, 2006, through February 3, 2007, to account for this hedge situation.

P 12-6

Fair value hedge, option Instrument Works makes sophisticated medical equipment. A key component of the equipment is Grade A silver. On May 1, 2006, Instrument Works enters into a firm purchase agreement to buy 1,200,000 troy ounces (equal to 100,000 pounds) of Grade A silver from Silver Refiners, Inc., for delivery on February 1, 2007, at the market price on that date. To hedge against volatility in price, Instrument Works also enters into an option contract with Currency Traders to put 1,200,000 troy ounces on February 1, 2007, for $10 per troy ounce, the market price on May 1, 2006. If the market price of silver is below $10 per troy ounce on May 1, then Instrument

LEARNING OBJECTIVES **4, 5, 6, 8, 9**

Works will let the option expire. If it is above $10 per troy ounce, then it will exercise the option. The option is to be settled net. Commodity Traders will pay Instrument Works the difference between the market price and the exercise price. The option costs Instrument Works $1,000 initially. Assume that a 6% annual incremental borrowing rate is reasonable.

1. Why would you expect this situation to qualify for hedge accounting?

2. Why should this hedge be accounted for as a fair value hedge instead of as a cash flow hedge?

3. What entries should be made on May 1, 2006, to account for the firm commitment and the option?

4. Assume that the market price for Grade A silver is $12 per troy ounce on December 31, 2006. What are the required entries?

5. Assume that the market price of Grade A silver is $11.50 per troy ounce on February 1, 2007, when Instrument Works receives the silver from Silver Refiners. Prepare the appropriate journal entries on February 1, 2007.

LEARNING OBJECTIVES 7, 9, 10

P 12-7

Foreign currency hedge, existing receivable On April 1, 2006, Baylor Corporation delivers merchandise to Rameau Corporation for 200,000 pesos when the spot rate for pesos is 6.0496 pesos. The receivable from Rameau is due May 30. Also on April 1, Baylor hedges its foreign currency asset and enters into a 60-day forward contract to sell 200,000 pesos at a forward rate of 6.019 pesos. The spot rate on May 30 was 5.992 pesos.

REQUIRED

1. Prepare journal entries to record the receivable from the sales transaction and the forward contract on April 1.

2. Prepare journal entries to record collection of the receivable and settlement of the forward contract on May 30.

LEARNING OBJECTIVES 8, 10

P 12-8

Foreign currency hedge, firm purchase commitment On October 2, 2006, Flex-American Corporation, a U.S. company, entered into a forward contract to purchase 50,000 euros for delivery in 180 days at a forward rate of $0.6350. The forward contract is a derivative instrument hedging an identifiable foreign currency commitment as defined in *FASB Statement No. 133*. The spot rate for euros on this date was $0.6250. Spot rates and forward rates for euros on December 31, 2006, and March 31, 2007, are as follows:

	December 31, 2006	March 31, 2007
Spot rate	$0.6390	$0.6560
Forward rates		
30-day futures	0.6410	0.6575
90-day futures	0.6420	0.6615
180-day futures	0.6450	0.6680

REQUIRED: Prepare journal entries to:

1. Record the forward contract on October 2, 2006

2. Adjust the accounts at December 31, 2006

3. Account for settlement of the forward contract and record and adjust the related cash purchase on March 31, 2007.

LEARNING OBJECTIVES 7, 9, 10

P 12-9

Foreign currency hedge, anticipated sale Bateman Industries, a U.S. corporation, anticipates a contract based on December 2, 2006, discussions to sell heavy equipment to Ramsay Ltd. of Scotland for 500,000 British pounds. The equipment is likely to be delivered and the amount collected on March 1, 2007.

In order to hedge its anticipated commitment, Bateman entered into a forward contract on December 2 to sell 500,000 British pounds for delivery on March 1. The forward contract meets all the conditions of *FASB Statement No. 133* for a cash flow hedge of an anticipated foreign currency commitment. A 6% interest rate is appropriate.

Exchange rates for British pounds on selected dates are as follows:

British pounds	12/2/06	12/31/06	3/1/07
Spot rate	$1.7000	$1.705	$1.7100
Forward rate for March 1, 2007, delivery	1.6800	1.6900	1.7100

REQUIRED: Prepare the necessary journal entries on Bateman's books to account for:

1. The forward contract on December 2, 2006.

2. Year-end adjustments relating to the forward contract on December 31, 2006.

3. The delivery of the equipment and settlement of all accounts with Ramsay Ltd. and the exchange broker on March 1, 2007.

P 12-10

Foreign currency hedge, existing payable Marlington Corporation, a U.S. firm, purchased equipment for 400,000 British pounds from Thacker Company Ltd. on December 16, 2006. The terms were n/30, payable in British pounds.

LEARNING OBJECTIVES **7, 9, 10**

On December 16, 2006, Marlington also entered into a 30-day forward contract to hedge the account payable to Thacker. Exchange rates for British pounds on selected dates are as follows:

	12/16/06	12/31/06	1/15/07
Spot rate	$1.67	$1.65	$1.64
Forward rate for 1/15/07	1.68	1.66	1.64

REQUIRED

1. Assuming this situation qualities as a cash flow hedge, prepare journal entries on December 16, 2006, to record Marlington's purchase and the forward contract. A 6% interest rate is appropriate.

2. Prepare year-end journal entries for Marlington as needed on December 31, 2006.

3. Prepare journal entries for Marlington's settlement of its accounts payable and the forward contract on January 15, 2007.

OneKey

INTERNET ASSIGNMENT

Go to *Xerox Corporation's* Web site and access their 2003 annual report. Answer the following questions regarding Xerox's derivative and foreign currency transactions.

1. Which categories of derivative transactions does Xerox engage in (cash flow hedges, fair value hedges, speculative hedges)? Describe the types of commodities that Xerox hedges. How do derivative transactions fit into Xerox's overall business strategy?

2. What was the 2003 income statement effect of each category? Give the total dollar amount as well as the effect as a percentage of revenues and income before tax. Have these transactions materially affected the profitability of Xerox? Explain your answer.

3. Where does Xerox disclose the financial statement impact of the cash flow hedges it enters into? Do you consider these to have a material impact on its financial position? Explain.

SELECTED READINGS

Finnerty, JOHN D., and DWIGHT GRANT. "Alternative Approaches to Testing Hedge Effectiveness Under SFAS No. 133." *Accounting Horizons* (June 2002), pp. 95–108.

International Accounting Standard No. 21. "The Effects of Changes in Foreign Exchange Rates." London, UK: International Accounting Standards Board, 2003.

International Accounting Standard No. 32. "Financial Instruments Disclosure and Presentation." London, UK: International Accounting Standards Board, 2003.

International Accounting Standard No. 39, "Financial Instruments: Recognition and Measurement." London, UK: International Accounting Standards Board, 2004.

SOO, BILLY S., and LISA GILBERT SOO. "Accounting for the Multinational Firm: Is the Translation Process Valued by the Stock Market?" *The Accounting Review* (October 1994), pp. 617–637.

Statement of Financial Accounting Standards No. 52. "Foreign Currency Translation." Stamford, CT: Financial Accounting Standards Board, 1981.

Statement of Financial Accounting Standards No. 133. "Accounting for Derivative Instruments and Hedging Activities." Norwalk, CT: Financial Accounting Standards Board, 1998.

Statement of Financial Accounting Standards No. 138. "Accounting for Certain Derivative Instruments and Certain Hedging Activities—An Amendment of FASB Statement No. 133." Norwalk, CT: Financial Accounting Standards Board, 2000.

Statement of Financial Accounting Standards No. 149. "Amendment of Statement 133 on Derivatives and Hedging Activities." Norwalk, CT: Financial Accounting Standards Board, 2003.

STEWARD, JOHN E. "The Challenges of Hedge Accounting." *Journal of Accountancy* (November 1989), pp. 48–56.

TROMBLEY, MARK A. *Accounting for Derivatives and Hedging.* Boston, MA: McGraw-Hill Irwin, 2003.

FOREIGN CURRENCY FINANCIAL STATEMENTS

If a foreign subsidiary does not keep its records in its parent's currency, then the foreign subsidiary's financial statements must be *translated* or *remeasured* into its parent's currency prior to consolidation of the financial statements. U.S. multinational corporations apply the provisions of *FASB Statement No. 52*, "Foreign Currency Translation," to convert the financial statements of their foreign subsidiaries and branches into U.S. dollars. This chapter covers the mechanics of preparing translated and remeasured financial statements as required by *FASB Statement No. 52*.

OBJECTIVES OF TRANSLATION AND THE FUNCTIONAL CURRENCY CONCEPT

The objectives of translation are to (a) provide "information that is generally compatible with the expected economic effects of a rate change on an enterprise's cash flows and equity" and (b) reflect "in consolidated statements the financial results and relationships of the individual consolidated entities as measured in their *functional currencies* in conformity with U.S. generally accepted accounting principles" (*FASB Statement No. 52*, paragraph 4). To decipher these objectives, one must first understand the functional currency concept.

Functional Currency Concept

LEARNING OBJECTIVE 1

An entity's **functional currency** is the currency of the primary economic environment in which it operates. Normally, a foreign entity's functional currency is the currency it receives from its customers and spends to pay its liabilities. Other factors are also considered in defining its functional currency:

1. If *sales prices* of the foreign entity's products are determined by local competition or local government regulation, rather than by short-run exchange rate changes or worldwide markets, then the foreign entity's local currency may be the functional currency.

2. A *sales market* that is primarily in the parent company's country, or sales contracts that are normally denominated in the parent's currency, may indicate that the parent's currency is the functional currency.

3. *Expenses* such as labor and materials that are primarily local costs provide some evidence that the foreign entity's local currency is the functional currency.

4. If *financing* is denominated primarily in the foreign entity's local currency and funds generated by its operations are sufficient to service existing and expected debt, then the foreign entity's local currency is likely to be the functional currency.

5. A high volume of *intercompany transactions and arrangements* indicates that the parent's currency may be the functional currency.

In the final analysis, the functional currency is based on management's judgment, including weighing the preceding factors.

Several definitions from *Statement No. 52* are related to the functional currency concept. A **foreign currency** is a currency other than the entity's functional currency. If the functional currency of a German subsidiary is the euro, the U.S. dollar is a foreign currency of the German subsidiary. If the functional currency of the German subsidiary is the U.S. dollar, the euro is a foreign currency to the German subsidiary.

The **local currency** is the currency of the country to which reference is made. Thus, the Canadian dollar is the local currency of a Canadian subsidiary of a U.S. firm. The subsidiary's books and financial statements will be prepared in the local currency in nearly all cases involving foreign currency financial statements, regardless of the determination of the functional currency.

The **reporting currency** is the currency in which the consolidated financial statements are prepared. The reporting currency for the consolidated statements of a U.S. firm with foreign subsidiaries is the U.S. dollar. **Foreign currency statements** are statements prepared in a currency that is *not* the reporting currency (the U.S. dollar) of the U.S. parent-investor.

Statement No. 52 permits two different methods for converting the foreign subsidiary's financial statements into U.S. dollars, based on the foreign entity's functional currency. If the functional currency is the U.S. dollar, the foreign financial statements are remeasured into U.S. dollars using the **temporal method**. If the functional currency is the local currency of the foreign entity, the foreign financial statements are translated into U.S. dollars using the **current rate method**. A company should select the method that best reflects the nature of its foreign operations.

The designation of a functional currency for a foreign subsidiary is the criterion for choosing which method of foreign currency translation to use—the current rate method or the temporal method. Consolidated financial statement amounts, including net income, differ depending on which of these methods is used.

Recall that the purpose of translation or remeasurement of a foreign subsidiary's financial statements is to convert them to the parent's currency so that consolidation can occur. As a result, one must view the ultimate purpose behind the functional currency choice as being the generation of consolidated financial statements that will reflect the company's underlying economic condition.

Choosing the parent's currency as the functional currency means one should use the temporal method. Selecting this functional currency implies that the resulting consolidated financial statements will reflect the transactions engaged in by the subsidiary as if the parent had engaged in those transactions directly. For example, a company may choose to set up a sales subsidiary in a foreign country for legal or cultural convenience. The parent ships all of the goods to the subsidiary, which sells the goods in the foreign country. The subsidiary then remits the proceeds to the parent. If the foreign currency is remitted to the parent, the parent will report a foreign exchange gain or loss when the currency is converted to dollars. If the subsidiary remits the money to the parent, the final result is the same as if the parent had directly engaged in transactions in the foreign country. The method used to translate the subsidiary's financial statements should result in consolidated financial statements that reflect this underlying similarity. The temporal method is designed to accomplish this. The gain or loss on remeasurement is included in current year consolidated income because the transactions of the subsidiary are assumed to have immediate or almost immediate cash implications for the parent.

In contrast, if the foreign subsidiary functions as a freestanding enterprise that engages in manufacturing and/or providing services within the foreign country, pays for most of its costs in the local currency, receives proceeds from sales and services in the local currency, and rolls these amounts back into the subsidiary operations, economically the subsidiary does not function as a channel for the parent's operations. The functional currency in this case is the subsidiary's local currency, and the current rate method would be used to translate the financial statements.

Presumably, the parent receives most of its cash flow from the subsidiary in the form of dividends. As a result, the impact of exchange rate changes on parent cash flows is limited to the parent's net investment in the subsidiary when distributed. If the parent were to liquidate its entire investment, it would be subject to realized exchange rate gains and losses that would make their way into the income statement. The current rate method measures the effect of exchange rate changes on this net investment. Typically, liquidation is not imminent, so under the current rate method, the effect of changes in the net investment due to exchange rate fluctuations is not included on the income statement, but as part of stockholders' equity, under accumulated other comprehensive income.[1]

APPLICATION OF THE FUNCTIONAL CURRENCY CONCEPT

LEARNING OBJECTIVE **2**

A foreign subsidiary's foreign currency statements must be in conformity with U.S. generally accepted accounting principles before translation into U.S. dollars. Adjustments to the recorded amounts to convert them to U.S. GAAP are required before translation is performed. All account balances on the balance sheet date denominated in a foreign currency (from the foreign entity's point of view) are adjusted to reflect current exchange rates. For example a French subsidiary must adjust a British-pound-denominated receivable to reflect the pound-to-euro exchange rate on the financial statement date. (This is similar to the year-end adjustments illustrated in Chapter 12 for U.S. firms with account balances denominated in a foreign currency.)

Under the objectives of the functional currency concept, a foreign entity's assets, liabilities, and operations must be measured in its functional currency. Subsequently, the foreign entity's balance sheet and income statement are consolidated with those of the parent company in the reporting enterprise's currency.

The accounting procedures required to convert a foreign entity's financial statements into the currency of the parent depend on the foreign subsidiary's functional currency. Because the foreign entity's books are maintained in its local currency, which may be its functional currency or a currency different from the functional currency, the combining or consolidating may require translation, remeasurement, or both.

TRANSLATION When the foreign entity's books are maintained in its functional currency, the statements are *translated* into the reporting entity's currency. **Translation** involves expressing functional currency measurements in the reporting currency.

A basic provision of *Statement No. 52* is that all elements of financial statements, except for stockholders' equity accounts, are translated using a current exchange rate. This is referred to as the *current rate method*. The functional currency is not the parent's; therefore, no direct impact on the reporting entity's cash flows from exchange rate changes is expected. The effects of exchange rate changes are reported as stockholders' equity adjustments in other comprehensive income. The equity adjustments from translation are accumulated in this account until sale or liquidation of the foreign entity investment, at which time they are reported as adjustments of the gain or loss on sale.

REMEASUREMENT When the foreign entity's books are not maintained in its functional currency, the foreign currency financial statements must be **remeasured** into the functional currency. If the foreign currency financial statements are remeasured into a U.S. dollar functional currency, no translation is necessary because the reporting currency of the parent-investor is the U.S. dollar.

The objective of remeasurement is to produce the same financial statements as if the books had been maintained in the functional currency. To accomplish this objective, both historical and current exchange rates are used in the remeasurement process. Under this method (the *temporal method*), monetary assets and liabilities are remeasured at current exchange rates, and other assets and equities are remeasured at historical rates. **Monetary assets and liabilities** are those in which the amounts to be received or paid are fixed in particular currency units. Examples of monetary assets and liabilities are cash, accounts receivable and accounts payable. The remeasurement produces exchange rate adjustments that are included in income because a direct impact on the enterprise's cash flows is expected.

Translation and Remeasurement of Foreign Currency Financial Statements

Patriot Corporation, a U.S. company, has a wholly owned subsidiary, Regal Corporation, that operates in England. The translation/remeasurement possibilities for the accounts of Regal are as follows:

---

[1] For a numerical example of this concept, see L. Revsine, "The Rationale Underlying the Functional Currency Choice," *Accounting Review* (July 1984), pp. 505–514.

	Functional Currency	Currency of Accounting Records	Required Procedures for Consolidating or Combining
Case 1	British pounds	British pounds	Translation
Case 2	U.S. dollar	British pounds	Remeasurement
Case 3	Euro	British pounds	Remeasurement and translation

Under Case 1, Regal Corporation keeps its books in its local currency, pounds (£), which is also the functional currency, and no remeasurement is needed. The accounts require translation into U.S. dollars (the currency of the reporting enterprise). *FASB Statement No. 52* requires translation using the current rate method. The current exchange rate at the balance sheet date is used to translate all assets and liabilities. Theoretically, the exchange rates in effect at each transaction date should be used to translate all revenues, expenses, gains, and losses. As a practical matter, revenues and expenses are generally translated at appropriate weighted average exchange rates for the period. The adjustments from translation are reported in other comprehensive income, as required by *FASB Statement No. 130,* "Reporting Comprehensive Income."

In Case 2, Regal's books are maintained in pounds, but the functional currency is the U.S. dollar. Under *Statement No. 52,* the accounts of Regal are remeasured into the functional currency, the dollar. In this case, no translation is needed because the dollar is also the ultimate reporting currency. The objective of remeasurement is to obtain the results that would have been produced if Regal's books of record had been maintained in the functional currency. Thus, remeasurement requires the use of historical exchange rates for some items and current rates for others and recognition in income of exchange gains and losses from measurement of all monetary assets and liabilities not denominated in the functional currency (the U.S. dollar in this case).

In Case 3, Regal's books are maintained in pounds although the functional currency is the euro. (This situation could arise if the subsidiary is a holding company for operations in France.) The consolidation requires a remeasurement of all assets, liabilities, revenues, expenses, gains, and losses into euros (the functional currency) and recognition in income of exchange gains and losses from remeasurement of the monetary assets and liabilities not denominated in euros. After the remeasurement is completed and Regal's financial statements are stated in euros, the statements are translated into U.S. dollars using the current rate method. This translation from the functional currency to the currency of the reporting entity will create translation adjustments, but such adjustments are not recognized in current income. Instead, they are reported in other comprehensive income, in stockholders' equity.

Exhibit 13-1 summarizes the exchange rates to be used for remeasurement and translation. Once the functional currency has been determined, it should be "used consistently unless significant changes in economic facts and circumstances" indicate that the functional currency has changed. A change in functional currency is not considered a change in an accounting principle (*FASB Statement No. 52,* paragraph 45).

Intercompany Foreign Currency Transactions

Intercompany transactions are foreign currency transactions if they produce receivable or payable balances denominated in a currency other than the entity's (parent's or subsidiary's) functional currency. Such intercompany foreign currency transactions result in exchange gains and losses that generally are included in income. An exception exists when these transactions produce intercompany balances of a long-term investment nature, when settlement is not expected in the foreseeable future. In these cases the translation adjustments are reported in other comprehensive income as an equity adjustment from translation.

An intercompany transaction requires analysis to see if it is a foreign currency transaction for one, both, or neither of the affiliates. To illustrate, assume that a U.S. parent company borrows $1,600,000 (£1,000,000) from its British subsidiary. The following analysis shows that either the parent or the subsidiary will have a foreign currency transaction if the subsidiary's local currency (the pound) is its functional currency.

EXHIBIT 13-1

Summary of Exchange Rates Used for Remeasurement and Translation

	Remeasurement to Functional Currency	Translation to Currency of Reporting Entity
Assets		
Cash, demand deposits, and time deposits	Current	Current
Marketable securities carried at cost		
Equity securities	Historical	Current
Debt securities	Historical	Current
Accounts and notes receivable and related unearned discounts	Current	Current
Accounts for uncollectible accounts and notes	Current	Current
Inventories		
Carried at cost	Historical	Current
Carried at lower of cost or market	*	Current
Prepaid insurance, advertising, and rent	Historical	Current
Refundable deposits	Current	Current
Property, plant, and equipment	Historical	Current
Accumulated depreciation on property, plant, and equipment	Historical	Current
Cash surrender value of life insurance	Current	Current
Deferred income tax assets	Current	Current
Patents, trademarks, licenses, and formulas	Historical	Current
Goodwill	Historical	Current
Other intangible assets	Historical	Current
Liabilities		
Accounts and notes payable and overdrafts	Current	Current
Accrued expenses	Current	Current
Deferred income tax liabilities	Current	Current
Deferred income	Historical	Current
Other deferred credits	Historical	Current
Bonds payable and other long-term debt	Current	Current
Stockholders' Equity		
Common stock	Historical	Historical[†]
Preferred stock carried at issuance price	Historical	Historical[†]
Other paid-in capital	Historical	Historical[‡]
Retained earnings	Not remeasured	Not translated
Income Statement Items Related to Nonmonetary Items[‡]		
Cost of goods sold	Historical	Current
Depreciation on property, plant, and equipment	Historical	Current
Amortization of intangible items (patents, etc.)	Historical	Current
Amortization of deferred income taxes	Current	Current
Amortization of deferred charges and credits	Historical	Current

[*]When the books are not maintained in the functional currency and the lower-of-cost-or-market rule is applied to inventories, inventories at cost are remeasured using historical rates. Then the historical cost in the functional currency is compared to market in the functional currency.

[†]Translation at historical rates is necessary for elimination of reciprocal parent investment and subsidiary equity accounts. It should be noted that conversion of all asset, liability, and equity accounts at current exchange rates would obviate the "equity adjustment from translation" component.

[‡]Income statement items related to monetary items are translated or remeasured at weighted average exchange rates to approximate the exchange rates in existence at the time of the related transactions. Intercompany dividends are converted at the rate in effect at the time of payment under both the remeasurement and translation approaches. Translation of income statement items at current rates is implemented by using weighted average exchange rates.

	Currency in Which Loan Is Denominated	Functional Currency of Subsidiary	*Foreign Currency Transaction of*	
			Subsidiary?	Parent?
Case 1	British pound	British pound	No	Yes
Case 2	British pound	U.S. dollar	Yes	Yes
Case 3	U.S. dollar	British pound	Yes	No
Case 4	U.S. dollar	U.S. dollar	No	No

When the U.S. dollar is the functional currency of the subsidiary, either both affiliates have foreign currency transactions, which offset each other (Case 2), or the intercompany transaction is not a foreign currency transaction (Case 4). Only the cases in which the subsidiary's functional currency is its local currency (Cases 1 and 3) have the potential to affect consolidated income. In these cases, translation adjustments will be reported as equity adjustments from translation on the balance sheet if the loan is of a long-term investment nature; otherwise, they will be reported as exchange gains and losses on the income statement.

Foreign Entities Operating in Highly Inflationary Economies

In a highly inflationary economy, the local currency rapidly loses value, resulting in the escalation of goods and services' prices. Generally, the currency is weakening against other currencies as well. The lack of a stable measuring unit presents special problems for converting foreign currency statements into U.S. dollars.

For example, assume that at the end of year 1, $1 can be exchanged for 50 local currency units (LCU), a $0.02 exchange rate, but at the end of year 2, $1 can be exchanged for 200 LCU, a $0.005 exchange rate. An equity investment of 9,000,000 LCU at the end of year 1 is translated at $180,000 using the current exchange rate, but one year later the same investment of 9,000,000 LCU is translated at $45,000 using the current exchange rate. Under the current rate method, translation gains and losses are accumulated and reported in other comprehensive income. They are not recognized in income until the investment is sold.

The FASB recognized that the current rate method of translation would pose a problem for foreign entities operating in countries with high rates of inflation. Price-level-adjusted financial statements are not basic financial statements under GAAP, so the FASB prescribed a practical alternative. Recall that inflation is a major determinant of exchange rates. In order to reflect the impact of hyperinflation in the consolidated financial statements, the reporting currency (the U.S. dollar) is used to remeasure the financial statements of foreign entities in highly inflationary economies. Exchange gains and losses from remeasuring the financial statements of the foreign entity are recognized in the income for the period, thus reflecting the impact of hyperinflation on the consolidated entity.

Statement No. 52 defines a "highly inflationary economy" as one with a cumulative three-year inflation rate of approximately 100% or more. Consider a foreign country with inflation data for a three-year period as follows:

	Index	Change in Index	Annual Rate of Inflation
January 1, 2006	120		
January 1, 2007	150	30	30 ÷ 120 (or 25%)
January 1, 2008	210	60	60 ÷ 150 (or 40%)
January 1, 2009	250	40	40 ÷ 210 (or 19%)

The three-year inflation rate is 108.3% [(250 − 120) ÷ 120], *not* 84% (25 + 40 + 19). The three-year inflation rate in this example exceeds 100%, so the usual criteria for identifying the functional currency are ignored and the U.S. dollar (the functional currency of the reporting entity) is the functional currency for purposes of preparing consolidated financial statements.

The 1993 annual report of *Kimberly-Clark Corporation* included the following financial statement note:

> *Effective December 31, 1992, the Mexican economy was determined to no longer be hyperinflationary. As a result, the Mexican peso is considered to be the functional currency of the Corporation's operations in Mexico. In conjunction with this change, $25.3 million of deferred income taxes was charged to unrealized currency translation adjustments in 1992.*[2]

---

[2] *Kimberly-Clark annual report 1993*, p. 36.

Because of the increase in inflation in Mexico in subsequent years, the 1997 annual report of Kimberly-Clark Corporation included the following financial statement notes indicating the change in the functional currency of the Mexican subsidiary (KCM) to the U.S. dollar:

> *Prior to 1997 Mexico's economy was deemed to be non-hyperinflationary and because KCM has financed a portion of its operations in U.S. dollar obligations, KCM experienced foreign currency losses on these obligations as the value of the peso declined. Beginning in 1997, the Mexican economy was determined to be hyperinflationary because the country's cumulative inflation rate for the last three years had exceeded 100 percent. For accounting purposes, the functional currency of KCM became the U.S. dollar rather than the Mexican peso. Accordingly, changes in the value of the peso no longer result in foreign currency gains or losses attributable to the U.S. dollar obligations. However, changes in the value of the peso have resulted in gains or losses attributable to peso-denominated monetary assets held by KCM.*
>
> *The income statements and balance sheets of operations in hyperinflationary economies, i.e. Brazil, Mexico (effective January 1, 1997) and Venezuela, are translated into U.S. dollars using both current and historical rates of exchange. For balance sheet accounts translated at current exchange rates, such as cash and accounts receivable, the differences from historical exchange rates are reflected in income.*[3]

Business Combinations

A foreign entity's assets and liabilities are translated into U.S. dollars using the current exchange rate in effect on the date of the business combination.

LEARNING OBJECTIVE **4**

The identifiable assets and liabilities of the foreign operations are adjusted to their local currency fair values and are translated at the exchange rate in effect on the date of the purchase business combination. Any difference between investment cost and translated net assets acquired is accounted for as goodwill or as an excess of net assets acquired over cost, as required by *FASB Statement No. 140*.

COST/BOOK VALUE DIFFERENTIAL When the foreign entity's books are maintained in the functional currency, the excess of cost over book value acquired is assigned to assets, liabilities, and goodwill in local currency units and subsequently is *translated* at current exchange rates under the current rate method.

For example, assume that a 10,000 British-pound excess is allocated to equipment that has a five-year estimated life on January 1, 2006, when the exchange rate is $1.50. If the average exchange rate for 2006 is $1.45 and the year-end exchange rate is $1.40, depreciation on the excess for 2006 will be $2,900 (£2,000 × $1.45) and the undepreciated balance at December 31 will be $11,200 (£8,000 × $1.40). The unrealized translation loss of $900 [$15,000 − ($2,900 + $11,200)] will be recorded in comprehensive income as an equity adjustment from translation.

When the foreign entity's books are not maintained in the functional currency, *remeasurement* is required and the excess allocated to equipment is amortized at the historical exchange rate in effect at the time of the business combination. Thus, the depreciation expense would be $3,000 (£2,000 × $1.50), and the undepreciated balance would be $12,000 (£8,000 × $1.50).

NONCONTROLLING INTEREST The computation of the amount of a noncontrolling interest in a foreign subsidiary must be based on the translated or remeasured financial statements of the subsidiary. Similarly, the financial statements of a foreign investee must be translated or remeasured before the equity method of accounting is applied.

ILLUSTRATION: TRANSLATION UNDER *STATEMENT NO. 52*

Background Information

Pat Corporation, a U.S. firm, paid $525,000 cash to acquire all the stock of the British firm Star Company when the book value of Star's net assets was equal to fair value. This purchase business

---

[3] *Kimberly-Clark annual report 1997*, pp. 51–52.

combination was consummated on December 31, 2006, when the exchange rate for British pounds was $1.50. Star's assets and equities at acquisition on December 31, 2006, were as follows:

	British Pounds	Exchange Rate	U.S. Dollars
Assets			
Cash	£140,000	$1.50	$210,000
Accounts receivable	40,000	1.50	60,000
Inventories (cost)	120,000	1.50	180,000
Plant assets	100,000	1.50	150,000
Less: Accumulated depreciation	(20,000)	1.50	(30,000)
Total assets	£380,000		$570,000
Equities			
Accounts payable	£ 30,000	$1.50	$ 45,000
Bonds payable	100,000	1.50	150,000
Capital stock	200,000	1.50	300,000
Retained earnings	50,000	1.50	75,000
Total equities	£380,000		$570,000

During 2007, the British pound weakened against the U.S. dollar, resulting in a year-end current exchange rate of $1.40. Average exchange rates for 2007 were $1.45. Star paid £30,000 dividends on December 1, 2007, when the exchange rate was $1.42 (U.S.) per British pound.

Intercompany Transaction

The only intercompany transaction between the firms was an $84,000 (£56,000) non-interest-bearing advance by Star to Pat that was made on January 4, 2007, when the exchange rate was still $1.50. The advance is denominated in U.S. dollars. Under the assumption that Star's functional currency is determined to be the British pound, the advance to Pat is a foreign currency transaction from Star's perspective but not to Pat because it is denominated in dollars.

Star adjusts its Advance to Pat account at year-end 2007 to reflect the $1.40 current exchange rate. Star records an exchange gain because there is no evidence that the advance is of a long-term investment nature. The entry on Star's books is as follows:

Advance to Pat (+A)	£4,000	
Exchange gain (+NI, +SE)		£4,000

To adjust receivable denominated in dollars
[($84,000 ÷ $1.40) − £56,000 per books].

Star's adjusted trial balance at December 31, 2007, reflects the advance to Pat, £60,000, and the exchange gain, £4,000.

LEARNING OBJECTIVES 5, 6

Translating the Foreign Subsidiary's Adjusted Trial Balance

Pat translates Star's adjusted trial balance at December 31, 2007, into U.S. dollars before it accounts for its investment under the equity method and consolidates its financial statements with those of Star. The translation of Star's accounts into U.S. dollars is shown in Exhibit 13-2, which illustrates translation working paper procedures.

The *current rate method* is required for foreign subsidiaries whose functional currency is not the parent's reporting currency, here the U.S. dollar. All assets and liabilities are translated at the balance sheet dates' exchange rates. All income statement items are translated at accounting-period average exchange rates. Average rates are applied to approximate the current exchange rates in effect when the revenue and expense transactions occurred during the period. The exchange rates in effect when dividends are paid [declared] are used to translate the foreign subsidiary's dividends.

The subsidiary's stockholders' equity accounts are not translated at current exchange rates. Capital stock and other paid-in capital accounts are translated at the exchange rate in effect when the subsidiary was acquired. The retained earnings ending balance is not translated after acquisition. The retained earnings account balance consists of retained earnings at acquisition, plus

STAR COMPANY LTD. TRANSLATION WORKSHEET FOR 2007 (BRITISH POUNDS FUNCTIONAL CURRENCY)	Trial Balance	Translation Rate	Trial Balance
Debits			
Cash	£110,000	$1.40	$ 154,000
Accounts receivable	80,000	1.40	112,000
Inventories (FIFO)	120,000	1.40	168,000
Plant assets	100,000	1.40	140,000
Advance to Pat	60,000	1.40	84,000
Cost of sales	270,000	1.45	391,500
Depreciation	10,000	1.45	14,500
Wages and salaries	120,000	1.45	174,000
Other expenses	60,000	1.45	87,000
Dividends	30,000	1.42	42,600
Accumulated other comprehensive income			28,600
	£960,000		$1,396,200
Credits			
Accumulated depreciation	£ 30,000	$1.40	$ 42,000
Accounts payable	36,000	1.40	50,400
Bonds payable	100,000	1.40	140,000
Capital stock	200,000	1.50	300,000
Retained earnings	50,000	Computed	75,000
Sales	540,000	1.45	783,000
Exchange gain (advance)	4,000	1.45	5,800
	£960,000		$1,396,200

income, less dividends after acquisition, all in translated dollar amounts. In years subsequent to the year of acquisition, translated beginning retained earnings of one period is simply the prior year's ending translated retained earnings from the financial statements.

After all financial statement items have been translated into dollars, the trial balance debits and credits are totaled and the amount needed to balance debits and credits is entered as an equity adjustment from translation and is included in other comprehensive income. For example, the $28,600 equity adjustment on translation in Exhibit 13-2 is measured by subtracting the $1,367,600 debits from the $1,396,200 credits in the U.S. dollar column. The resulting subsidiary reporting currency financial statements are illustrated in Exhibit 13-3 for Star Company.

Equity Method of Accounting

Pat records the investment in Star at its $525,000 cost on December 31, 2006, and subsequently uses the equity method to account for its foreign subsidiary. Star's translated financial statements are used by Pat when applying the equity method. The entry to record receipt of the £30,000, or $42,600, dividend from Star on December 1, 2007, follows:

Cash (+A)	$42,600	
Investment in Star (−A)		$42,600

Pat received this dividend when the exchange rate was $1.42, so the dividends paid by Star also have to be translated into dollars at the current exchange rate in effect when the dividends were paid, $1.42 (see Exhibit 13-2).

Pat recognizes its equity in Star's income from 2007 in an entry that also recognizes Star's unrecognized loss on translation. The entry for 2007 is as follows:

Investment in Star (+A)	$93,200	
Other comprehensive income: equity adjustment on translation (−OCI, −SE)	28,600	
Income from Star (+NI, +SE)		$121,800

EXHIBIT 13-3

Translated Financial
Statements—British
Pounds Functional
Currency

STAR COMPANY LTD.
INCOME AND RETAINED EARNINGS STATEMENTS
FOR THE YEAR ENDED DECEMBER 31, 2007
(IN U.S. DOLLARS)

Sales		$783,000
Less costs and expenses		
Cost of sales	$391,500	
Depreciation	14,500	
Wages and salaries	174,000	
Other expenses	87,000	
Total costs and expenses		667,000
Operating income		116,000
Exchange gain		5,800
Net income		121,800
Retained earnings January 1		75,000
		196,800
Less: Dividends		42,600
Retained earnings December 31, 2007		$154,200

STAR COMPANY LTD. BALANCE SHEET
AT DECEMBER 31, 2007
(IN U.S. DOLLARS)

Assets	
Cash	$154,000
Accounts receivable	112,000
Inventories	168,000
Plant assets	140,000
Less: Accumulated depreciation	(42,000)
Advance to Pat	84,000
	$616,000
Equities	
Accounts payable	$ 50,400
Bonds payable	140,000
Capital stock	300,000
Retained earnings	154,200
Accumulated other comprehensive income	(28,600)
	$616,000

This entry recognizes 100% of Star's 2007 net income in dollars, as investment income, and it also includes the $28,600 loss from translation on Pat's books in other comprehensive income. The reported income of $121,800 less the $28,600 loss on translation equals the $93,200 investment increase from Star's operations.

ILLUSTRATION OF AMORTIZATION WHEN EXCESS OF COST OVER BOOK VALUE IS ALLOCATED TO IDENTIFIABLE ASSETS AND LIABILITIES: PATENT AMORTIZATION Pat paid $525,000 for its investment in Star. However, Star's book value and the fair value of its recorded net assets acquired were equal to $375,000. The $150,000 excess of cost over net asset book value is all allocable to a patent that has no book value on Star's books because it was internally developed with negligible legal costs. Under the current rate method, the patent-related calculations are based on local currency units (British pounds), rather than U.S. dollar amounts. The first step to calculate patent amortization for Pat's investment in Star is to convert the $150,000 allocated to the patent at acquisition into its pound equivalent. Because the exchange rate at December 31, 2006, the acquisition date, is $1.50, the pound equivalent of $150,000 is £100,000.

The 2007 amortization of the excess on Pat's books is £100,000 ÷ 10 years × $1.45 average exchange rate for 2007, or $14,500. Patent amortization for 2007 is recorded on Pat's books as follows:

Income from Star (−NI, −SE)	$14,500
Other comprehensive income:	
Equity adjustment from translation (−OCI, −SE)	9,500
Investment in Star	$24,000

The equity adjustment on translation of a patent that appears in the entry is the result of changes in exchange rates during 2007, and the $24,000 credit to the investment in Star reflects the decrease in unamortized patent during the year, $150,000 − (£90,000 × $1.40). These relationships are summarized as follows:

	In Pounds	Exchange Rate	In Dollars
Beginning patent	£100,000	$1.50	$150,000
Less: Amortization	10,000	1.45	14,500
	90,000		135,500
Equity adjustment	—		9,500
Ending patent	£ 90,000	1.40	$126,000

Alternatively, the $9,500 equity adjustment can be computed as follows:

£10,000 amortization × ($1.50 − $1.45) exchange rate decline to midyear	$ 500
£90,000 unamortized patent × ($1.50 − $1.40) exchange rate decline for the year	9,000
Equity adjustment	$9,500

Notice that this equity adjustment is *only* recorded on Pat's books because the patent is not recorded on Star's books.

Similar adjustments are required when an excess of cost over book value is allocated to other identifiable assets and liabilities and the current rate method is used.

INVESTMENT IN FOREIGN SUBSIDIARY At this point, it may be helpful to summarize the changes in Pat's Investment in Star account during 2007:

Investment cost December 31, 2006	$525,000
Less: Dividends received 2007	(42,600)
Add: Equity in Star's net income	121,800
Less: Unrealized loss on translation	(28,600)
Less: Patent amortization	(14,500)
Less: Unrealized translation loss on patent	(9,500)
Investment balance December 31, 2007	$551,600

Consolidation

Exihibit 13-4 contains the financial statement consolidation worksheet for Pat Corporation and Star Company for the year ended December 31, 2007. Pat reports income from Star of $107,300. This is its share of Star's reported income ($121,800) less the amortization of the unrecorded patent, $14,500. The Investment in Star account balance of $551,600 agrees with the reconciliation presented above. Pat also has a $38,100 equity adjustment balance that equals Star's equity adjustment of $28,600, recorded by Pat when it applied the equity method to account for its investment in Star and also included in Star's translated financial statements. The remaining $9,500 equity adjustment is related to the unrecorded patent, which was only recorded by Pat.

The procedures to consolidate a foreign subsidiary are basically the same as the procedures needed to consolidate a domestic subsidiary. The sequence of working paper entries is the same also. Working paper entry a in Exhibit 13-4 is as follows:

a	Income from Star (−NI, −SE)	$107,300	
	Dividends (−D, +SE)		$42,600
	Investment in Star (−A)		64,700

Entry b eliminates reciprocal equity and investment balances at beginning-of-the-period amount and enters the beginning-of-the-period patent balance.

EXHIBIT 13-4

Working Papers
Under the British
Pound Functional
Currency
Assumption

PAT CORPORATION AND SUBSIDIARY CONSOLIDATION WORKING PAPERS
TRANSLATION—FUNCTIONAL CURRENCY BRITISH POUND
FOR THE YEAR ENDED DECEMBER 31, 2007

	Pat	Star	Adjustments and Eliminations		Consolidated Statements
Income Statement Sales	$1,218,300	$ 783,000			$2,001,300
Income from Star	107,300		a 107,300		
Cost of sales	(600,000)	(391,500)			(991,500)
Depreciation	(40,000)	(14,500)			(54,500)
Wages and salaries	(300,000)	(174,000)			(474,000)
Other expenses	(150,000)	(87,000)	d 14,500		(251,500)
Exchange gain		5,800			5,800
Net income	**$ 235,600**	**$ 121,800**			**$ 235,600**
Retained Earnings Retained earnings—Pat	$ 245,500				$ 245,500
Retained earnings—Star		$ 75,000	b 75,000		
Net income	235,600	121,800			235,600
Dividends	(100,000)	(42,600)		a 42,600	(100,000)
Retained earnings— December 31, 2007	**$ 381,100**	**$ 154,200**			**$ 381,100**
Balance Sheet Cash	$ 317,600	$ 154,000			$ 471,600
Accounts receivable	150,000	112,000			262,000
Inventories	300,000	168,000			468,000
Plant assets	400,000	140,000			540,000
Accumulated depreciation	(100,000)	(42,000)			(142,000)
Advance to Pat		84,000		e 84,000	
Investment in Star	551,600		c 38,100	a 64,700 b 525,000 c 9,500	
Patent			b 150,000	c 9,500 d 14,500	126,000
	$1,619,200	$ 616,000			$1,725,600
Accounts payable	$ 142,200	$ 50,400			$ 192,600
Advance from Star	84,000		e 84,000		
Bonds payable	250,000	140,000			390,000
Capital stock	800,000	300,000	b 300,000		800,000
Retained earnings	381,100	154,200			381,100
Accumulated other comprehensive income	(38,100)	(28,600)		c 28,600	(38,100)
	$1,619,200	$ 616,000			$1,725,600

Entry c adjusts the Investment in Star account for unrealized translation losses, eliminates the unrealized translation loss for the patent, and eliminates Star's remaining stockholders' equity account—the equity adjustment from translation account.

b Retained earnings—Star (–SE)	$ 75,000	
Capital stock—Star (–SE)	300,000	
Patent (+A)	150,000	
Investment in Star (–A)		$525,000
c Investment in Star (+A)	$ 38,100	
Patent (–A)		$ 9,500
Other comprehensive income: equity adjustment		
from translation—Star (+SE)		28,600

Working paper entry d in Exhibit 13-4 enters the current patent-amortization expense (£10,000 × $1.45 average exchange rate) and reduces the patent to $126,000, the unamortized amount at year-end (£90,000 × $1.40 exchange rate).

The final working paper entry eliminates the reciprocal balances of advance to Pat and advance from Star.

Under the current rate method, the change in the accumulated other comprehensive income account from the beginning to the end of the year represents the change in the dollar amount of the investment in the net assets of the company during the year due to exchange rate changes. The balance in the accumulated other comprehensive income account that represents the amount needed to balance the subsidiary's translated worksheet is the beginning AOCI plus the change in that account resulting from exchange rate changes during the year.

To gain a better understanding of what the change in the accumulated other comprehensive income account balance represents, the change is computed directly for Star:

Star's beginning accumulated other comprehensive income-translation Loss	$ 0
Increase in AOCI—translation loss	$28,600
Ending AOCI—translation loss	$28,600

The impact of exchange rate changes on the book value of Star's net assets is shown here:

		Change in Exchange Rate	
Book value of beginning net assets	£250,000	–0.10 ($1.40 – $1.50)	($25,000)
Net income	£ 84,000	–0.05 ($1.40 – $1.45)	(4,200)
–Dividends	£–30,000	–0.02 ($1.40 – $1.42)	+600
Effect of exchange rate changes on net assets			($28,600)

On a consolidated basis, the change in the AOCI account is a loss of $38,100; the $9,500 loss in excess of the $28,600 computed here is due to changes in the value of the unamortized patent account during the year. The patent is not recorded on Star's books, but here it is a part of the Investment in Star account according to Pat's books.

The computation of the change in the AOCI provides insight into the nature of the loss and why it is included in other comprehensive income instead of being reflected immediately in income. Because the functional currency of the subsidiary is the local currency, the parent will realize a loss due to exchange rate changes when the earnings of the subsidiary are distributed to the parent or when the parent liquidates its investment in the company. The latter occurrence is not an immediate probability, so the gain or loss on translation is not included in current income but is reflected directly in the stockholders' equity section and in the statement of comprehensive income.

ILLUSTRATION: REMEASUREMENT UNDER *STATEMENT NO. 52*

When the functional currency of a foreign entity is the U.S. dollar, the foreign entity's accounts are *remeasured* into its U.S. dollar functional currency, and the net exchange gains or losses that result from the remeasurement are recognized in current income. The objective of remeasurement is to produce the same results as if the books had been maintained in the U.S. dollar (see *FASB Statement No. 52*, paragraph 47).

To enable you to compare the remeasurement (temporal method) and translation (current rate method) procedures, remeasurement procedures are applied to the Pat–Star example, assuming that Star's functional currency is the U.S. dollar and its books of record are maintained in British pounds.

Star's assets, liabilities, and stockholders' equity at acquisition on December 31, 2006, are all remeasured using the $1.50 exchange rate in effect on that date. The remeasurement at acquisition is exactly the same as translation at acquisition. The $525,000 investment cost to Pat over the $375,000 net assets acquired in Star results in $150,000 assigned to the patent. Unlike translation, under remeasurement procedures, the patent's value is not adjusted for subsequent changes in exchange rates. As a result, annual patent amortization over the 10-year period is $15,000.

The £56,000 ($84,000) advance to Pat is not a foreign currency transaction of either Pat or Star because the advance is denominated in dollars and the functional currency of both Pat and Star is the U.S. dollar. As a result, Star does not adjust its advance to Pat to reflect the £60,000 equivalent and does not report a £4,000 exchange gain. Instead, the £56,000 advance to Pat is remeasured at its $84,000 reciprocal amount on Pat's books. Exhibit 13-5 is a remeasurement worksheet for Star Company for 2007. Except for the advance to Pat and the resulting $5,800 exchange gain under translation, Star's December 31, 2007, trial balance in British pounds is the same as the one shown under the British-pound functional currency assumption in Exhibit 13-2.

Except for the intercompany advance, all of Star's monetary items are remeasured at current exchange rates. These monetary items include cash, accounts receivable, accounts payable, and bonds payable. The remeasurement produces the same amounts as translation under the current

---

EXHIBIT 13-5

Remeasurement of Foreign Subsidiary Accounts into U.S. Dollars

STAR COMPANY LTD. REMEASUREMENT WORKSHEET FOR 2007 (U.S. DOLLAR FUNCTIONAL CURRENCY)

	Trial Balance in British Pounds		Exchange Rate	Trial Balance in U.S. Dollars
Debits				
Cash	£110,000	C	$1.40	$ 154,000
Accounts receivable	80,000	C	1.40	112,000
Inventories (FIFO)	120,000	H	1.42	170,400
Plant assets	100,000	H	1.50	150,000
Advance to Pat	56,000*	R		84,000
Cost of sales	270,000	H		401,100
Depreciation	10,000	H	1.50	15,000
Wages and salaries	120,000	A†	1.45	174,000
Other expenses	60,000	A†	1.45	87,000
Dividends	30,000	R		42,600
Exchange loss				3,300
	£956,000			$1,393,400
Credits				
Accumulated depreciation	£ 30,000	H	$1.50	45,000
Accounts payable	36,000	C	1.40	50,400
Bonds payable	100,000	C	1.40	140,000
Capital stock	200,000	H	1.50	300,000
Retained earnings	50,000	Computed		75,000
Sales	540,000	A	1.45	783,000
	£956,000			$1,393,400

A, average exchange rate; C, current exchange rate; H, historical exchange rate; R, reciprocal of U.S. dollar amounts.
*A translation gain might need to be reported under British GAAP to the British government. However, no gain or loss is reported under U.S. GAAP, and the reciprocal rate is used.
†Assumed to be paid in cash during 2007.

rate method. The advance to Pat and the dividends paid are translated at the dollar amounts that Pat recorded on its own books.

The cost of sales and inventory remeasurements shown in the worksheet assume first-in, first-out procedures and acquisition of the ending inventory items on December 1, 2007, when the exchange rate was $1.42. Historical exchange rates are used in the computations as follows:

	Pounds	Exchange Rate	Dollars
Inventory December 31, 2006	£120,000	$1.50 H	$180,000
Purchases 2007	270,000	1.45 A	391,500
	390,000		571,500
Inventory December 31, 2007	120,000	1.42 H	170,400
Cost of sales	£270,000		$401,100

Special procedures are required when inventories are priced under the lower-of-cost-or-market rule. These procedures are explained in Appendix A at the end of this chapter.

All of Star's plant assets were owned by Star when it became a subsidiary of Pat. Therefore, the plant assets, as well as the related depreciation expense and accumulated depreciation, are remeasured at the $1.50 exchange rate in effect at December 31, 2006. If Star had acquired additional plant assets during 2007, the additions and related depreciation would be remeasured at the exchange rates in effect when the additional assets were acquired.

Under *Statement No. 52*, expenses are remeasured at average rates during the period if they relate to monetary items (cash, receivables, and payables), and at historical exchange rates if they relate to nonmonetary items (such as plant assets, deferred charges, or intangibles). The wages and salaries and other expense items in Exhibit 13-5 are remeasured at average exchange rates, assuming they are related to monetary items. When a single expense account includes amounts related to both monetary and nonmonetary items, the remeasurement involves more computations than application of a single average rate. The same reasoning applies to the remeasurement of sales, even though it would be rather unusual for sales to relate to nonmonetary items.

Capital stock and other paid-in capital items are remeasured at historical exchange rates. No difference exists between the amounts that result from remeasurement and translation for these items. As explained earlier, the retained earnings balance is computed but not remeasured or translated. (Ending retained earnings is equal to beginning retained earnings plus remeasured income less remeasured dividends.)

After all items in the remeasurement worksheet, other than the exchange loss, are remeasured into the U.S. dollar functional currency, the trial balance debits and credits are totaled and the difference between debits and credits is determined. If the credits are greater, the difference is entered in the remeasurement working papers as the exchange loss for the period. Thus, the $3,300 exchange loss in Exhibit 13-5 is computed by subtracting $1,390,100 debits, excluding the exchange loss, from $1,393,400 total credits.

Exchange gains and losses on remeasurement are recognized in income currently under the provisions of *Statement No. 52*. Exchange gains and losses on remeasurement and those arising from foreign currency transactions are combined for external reporting purposes. Separate disclosure of transaction and remeasurement gains and losses is provided in financial statement notes.

The Equity Method and Consolidation

LEARNING OBJECTIVES **7, 8**

All remeasurement gains and losses are recognized in current income. The entries on Pat's books to account for its investment in Star are as follows:

Investment in Star (+A)	$525,000	
Cash (−A)		$525,000
To record acquisition on December 31, 2006.		
Cash (+A)	$ 42,600	
Investment in Star (−A)		$ 42,600
To record dividends received on December 1, 2007.		
Investment in Star (+A)	$ 87,600	
Income from Star (+NI, +SE)		$ 87,600
To record investment income for 2007 equal to Star's		
$102,600 net income less $15,000 patent amortization.		

Pat's Investment in Star account at December 31, 2007, has a balance of $570,000 and is equal to Star's $435,000 net assets on that date plus $135,000 unamortized patent. These amounts are shown in the consolidation working papers of Exhibit 13-6.

The consolidation worksheet entries under remeasurement are listed here in journal entry form:

a	Income from Star (−NI, −SE)	$87.600	
	Dividends (−D, +SE)		$42,600
	Investment in Star (−A)		45,000
b	Capital stock—Star (−SE)	300,000	
	Retained earnings—Star (−SE)	75,000	
	Patent (+A)	150,000	
	Investment in Star (−A)		525,000
c	Other expenses (+E, −SE)	15,000	
	Patent (−A)		15,000
d	Advance from Star (−L)	84,000	
	Advance to Pat (−A)		84,000

Consolidation of a foreign subsidiary with a U.S. dollar functional currency is essentially the same as for a domestic subsidiary, once the foreign entity's financial statements have been remeasured in U.S. dollars. Although the remeasurement process is more complex than translation, the consolidation process is less complex because remeasurement does not produce unrealized translation gains and losses or equity adjustments from translation.

In a manner similar to the translation proof illustrated earlier, the gain or loss on remeasurement can also be computed directly. However, as one might expect given the complexity of the remeasurement procedure, the proof is more complicated than under the current rate method. All monetary assets and liabilities are remeasured using the year-end current exchange rate, whereas all non-monetary assets and liabilities are remeasured using the historical exchange rate.

As previously disclosed, Star's December 31, 2006, net monetary assets in pounds were cash, 140,000; accounts receivable, 40,000; accounts payable, 30,000; and bonds payable, 100,000. Thus a beginning net monetary asset (monetary assets − monetary liabilities) exists equal to 180,000 pounds − 130,000 pounds, or 50,000 pounds.

		Change in Exchange rate	
Beginning net monetary asset position	£ 50,000	$1.40 − $1.50	($5,000)
Sales (increases cash or accounts receivable during the year)	£540,000	$1.40 − $1.45	(27,000)
Purchases (decreases cash or accounts receivable or increases accounts payable)	£270,000	$1.40 − $1.45	13,500
Wages and salaries (assumed to be in cash)	£120,000	$1.40 − $1.45	6,000
Other expenses (assumed to be in cash)	£ 60,000	$1.40 − $1.45	3,000
Advance to Pat	£ 56,000	$1.40 − $1.50	(5,600)
Dividends	£ 30,000	$1.40 − $1.42	(600)
Total exchange loss			$(3,300)

The exchange loss results from the effect of exchange rate changes on the monetary position of the firm during the year.

EXHIBIT 13-6						

Working Papers Under the U.S. Dollar Functional Currency Assumption

PAT CORPORATION AND SUBSIDIARY CONSOLIDATION WORKING PAPERS
REMEASUREMENT—FUNCTIONAL CURRENCY U.S. DOLLAR
FOR THE YEAR ENDED DECEMBER 31, 2007

	Pat	Star	Adjustments and Eliminations		Consolidated Statements
Income Statement Sales	$1,218,300	$783,000			$2,001,300
Income from Star	87,600		a 87,600		
Cost of sales	(600,000)	(401,100)			(1,001,100)
Depreciation	(40,000)	(15,000)			(55,000)
Wages and salaries	(300,000)	(174,000)			(474,000)
Other expenses	(150,000)	(87,000)	c 15,000		(252,000)
Exchange loss		(3,300)			(3,300)
Net income	**$ 215,900**	**$102,600**			**$ 215,900**
Retained Earnings Retained earnings—Pat	$ 245,500				$ 245,500
Retained earnings—Star		$ 75,000	b 75,000		
Net income	**215,900**	**102,600**			**215,900**
Dividends	(100,000)	(42,600)		a 42,600	(100,000)
Retained earnings— December 31, 2007	**$ 361,400**	**$135,000**			**$ 361,400**
Balance Sheet Cash	$ 317,600	$154,000			$ 471,600
Accounts receivable	150,000	112,000			262,000
Inventories	300,000	170,400			470,400
Plant assets	400,000	150,000			550,000
Accumulated depreciation	(100,000)	(45,000)			(145,000)
Advance to Pat		84,000		d 84,000	
Investment in Star	570,000			a 45,000 b 525,000	
Patent			b 150,000	c 15,000	135,000
Total assets	$1,637,600	$625,400			$1,744,000
Accounts payable	$ 142,200	$ 50,400			$ 192,600
Advance from Star	84,000		d 84,000		
Bonds payable	250,000	140,000			390,000
Capital stock	800,000	300,000	b 300,000		800,000
Retained earnings	**361,400**	**135,000**			**361,400**
Total equities	$1,637,600	$625,400			$1,744,000

EXHIBIT 13-7

Comparative
Consolidated
Financial Statements

PAT CORPORATION AND BRITISH SUBSIDIARY CONSOLIDATED INCOME AND RETAINED EARNINGS STATEMENTS FOR THE YEAR ENDED DECEMBER 31, 2007

	Translation (Current Rate Method)	Remeasurement (Temporal Method)
Sales	$2,001,300	$2,001,300
Less: Costs and expenses		
Cost of sales	991,500	1,001,100
Wages and salaries	474,000	474,000
Other expenses	237,000	237,000
Depreciation	54,500	55,000
Patent amortization	14,500	15,000
Total costs and expenses	1,771,500	1,782,100
Operating income	229,800	219,200
Exchange gain (loss)	5,800	(3,300)
Net income	235,600	215,900
Retained earnings January 1, 2007	245,500	245,500
	481,100	461,400
Less: Dividends	100,000	100,000
Retained earnings December 31, 2007	$ 381,100	$ 361,400

PAT CORPORATION AND BRITISH SUBSIDIARY CONSOLIDATED BALANCE SHEETS AT DECEMBER 31, 2007

	Translation (Current Rate Method)	Remeasurement (Temporal Method)
Assets		
Cash	$ 471,600	$ 471,600
Accounts receivable	262,000	262,000
Inventories	468,000	470,400
Plant assets	540,000	550,000
Less: Accumulated depreciation	(142,000)	(145,000)
Patent	126,000	135,000
Total assets	$1,725,600	$1,744,000
Liabilities		
Accounts payable	$ 192,600	$ 192,600
Bonds payable	390,000	390,000
Total liabilities	582,600	582,600
Stockholders' Equity		
Capital stock	800,000	800,000
Retained earnings	381,100	361,400
Other comprehensive income: equity adjustment on translation	(38,100)	
Total stockholders' equity	1,143,000	1,161,400
Total liabilities and stockholders' equity	$1,725,600	$1,744,000

Translation and Remeasurement Differences in Consolidated Statements

The consolidated financial statements of Pat Corporation and Subsidiary under the translation (current rate) and remeasurement (temporal) procedures are presented in comparative form in Exhibit 13-7.

DISCLOSURE FOR CHANGES IN TRANSLATION ADJUSTMENTS The Pat–Star illustration involves consolidation in the year of acquisition, so the impact of translation and remeasurement differences is relatively small. For many firms it can be substantial, however. Kimberly-Clark's translation adjustment—a loss—increased from $656.8 million in 1996 to $953.2 million in 1997. *IBM*'s translation adjustment—also a loss—increased from $113 million to $888 million in the same time period.

HEDGING A NET INVESTMENT IN A FOREIGN ENTITY

LEARNING OBJECTIVE 9

U.S. firms with foreign investees may enter into forward exchange contracts or other foreign currency transactions to offset the effects of foreign currency fluctuations on their net investments in the foreign investee. Gains and losses that arise from foreign currency transactions designated as, and effective as, economic hedges of a net investment in a foreign entity are recorded as translation adjustments of stockholders' equity.

Classification as a **translation adjustment** means that these transaction gains and losses are included in comprehensive income (*FASB Statement No. 130*) and are excluded from the determination of net income. This treatment is necessary because translation of the financial statements of a foreign subsidiary *with a functional currency other than the U.S. dollar* also produces translation adjustments, which are included in comprehensive income, rather than charges or credits to net income. Thus, the adjustment from hedging a net investment in a foreign entity offsets the adjustment from translating the foreign investees' financial statements into U.S. dollars.

Procedures to hedge a net investment in a foreign entity are not applicable to investees with a U.S. dollar functional currency. Hedges of these investments are accounted for as speculations. Gains and losses from remeasuring foreign-investee financial statements into U.S. dollars are included in net income for the period if the U.S. dollar is the investee's functional currency. Therefore, the gains and losses resulting from the hedge of the net investment must be included in net income for the period. This means that the gain or loss on the hedge will offset the recognized gain or loss from the remeasurement.

Illustration

To illustrate the hedge of a net investment of a foreign entity, assume that Pinehurst Corporation, a U.S. company, has a 100% equity investment in a British company, Bennett Ltd., acquired at book value equal to fair value. Bennett's functional currency is the British pound. An investee's assets and liabilities hedge each other, so only the net assets are exposed to the risk of exchange rate fluctuations.

To hedge the foreign currency exposure, the translation adjustment from the hedging transaction must move in a direction opposite to the translation adjustment from the net assets of the investee. Thus, Pinehurst borrows British pounds to hedge the equity investment. Any translation losses on the equity investment will be fully or partially offset by the translation gains on the loan, and vice versa.

The balance in Pinehurst's Investment in Bennett account at December 31, 2006, is $1,280,000, 100% of Bennett's £800,000 times a $1.60 year-end current exchange rate. On this date, Pinehurst has no translation adjustment balance relative to its investment in Bennett. In order to hedge its net investment in Bennett, Pinehurst borrows £800,000 for one year at 12% interest on January 1, 2007, at a spot rate of $1.60. The loan is denominated in pounds, with principal and interest payable on January 1, 2008. Pinehurst records its loan as follows:

January 1, 2007

Cash (+A)	$1,280,000	
Loan payable (fc) (+L)		$1,280,000

    To record loan denominated in British pounds
      (£800,000 × $1.60 spot rate).

On November 1, 2007, Bennett declares and pays a £40,000 dividend. Pinehurst records receipt of the dividend at the $1.75 spot rate on this date.

November 1, 2007

Cash (+A)	$70,000	
Investment in Bennett (−A)		$70,000

    To record receipt of dividends from Bennett
      (£40,000 × $1.75 spot rate).

For 2007, Bennett reports net income of £160,000. The weighted average exchange rate for translation of Bennett's revenue and expense items for the year is $1.70, and the current exchange rate at December 31, 2007, is $1.80. These changes in Bennett's net assets are included in the following summary:

	British Pounds		U.S. Dollars
Net assets on January 1, 2007	£800,000	× $1.60	$1,280,000
Add: Net income for 2007	160,000	× $1.70	272,000
Less: Dividends	(40,000)	× $1.75	(70,000)
Equity adjustment—change			174,000
Net assets on December 31, 2007	£920,000	× $1.80	$1,656,000

Pinehurst makes the following entry at December 31, 2007, to record its share of Bennett's income:

December 31, 2007

Investment in Bennett (+A)	$446,000	
Income from Bennett (+ Other Income, +SE)		$ 272,000
Other comprehensive income (+OCI, +SE)		174,000

To record 100% share of Bennett's income (£160,000
× $1.70 weighted average exchange rate)
and to record 100% share of translation
adjustment.

Also, Pinehurst adjusts the loan payable and the equity investment to the current rate at December 31, 2007, and accrues interest on the loan:

Other comprehensive income (−OCI, −SE)	$ 160,000	
Loan payable (fc)		$ 160,000

To adjust loan payable denominated in British pounds
to the current rate at year-end [£800,000 × ($1.80 − $1.60)].

Interest expense (+E, −SE)	$ 163,200	
Exchange loss (+Lo, −SE)	9,600	
Interest payable (+L)		$ 172,800

To record interest expense (at weighted average
exchange rates) and accrue interest payable
denominated in pounds at the year-end current
rate as follows:

Interest payable (£800,000 × 12% interest × 1 year × $1.80 current exchange rate)	$ 172,800
Less: Interest expense (£800,000 × 12% interest × 1 year × 1.70 weighted average exchange rate)	163,200
Exchange loss	$ 9,600

On January 1, 2008, Pinehurst pays the loan and interest at the $1.80 spot rate as follows:

January 1, 2008

Interest payable (fc) (+L)	$ 172,800	
Loan payable (fc) (−L)	1,440,000	
Cash (−A)		$1,612,800

To record payment of loan and interest denominated
in British pounds when the spot rate is $1.80.

As a result of the hedging operation, the changes in Pinehurst's investment in Bennett that were due to changing exchange rates were partially offset by its loan in British pounds. The equity adjustment from translation balance that appears in the stockholders' equity section of Pinehurst's December 31, 2007, balance sheet is a $14,000 credit ($174,000 credit from the equity investment from translation, less $160,000 debit from adjustment of the loan denominated in British pounds).

Limit on Gain or Loss from Translation Adjustment

The gain or loss on an after-tax basis from the hedging operations that can be considered a translation adjustment is limited in amount to the *current* translation adjustment from the equity investment (see paragraph 129 of *Statement No. 52*).

SUMMARY

Before the results of foreign operations can be included in the financial statements of U.S. corporations, they have to be converted into U.S. dollars using procedures specified in *FASB Statement No. 52* that are based on the foreign entity's functional currency.

If the U.S. dollar is determined to be the functional currency, the foreign entity's financial statements are remeasured into U.S. dollar financial statements using the temporal method, and the resulting exchange gain or loss is included in consolidated net income for the period.

If the functional currency is determined to be the local currency of the foreign entity, the financial statements of that entity must be translated into U.S. dollars using the current rate method. The effects of the exchange rate changes from translation are accumulated in an equity adjustment from translation account and are reported in other comprehensive income.

Foreign currency financial statements of subsidiaries operating in highly inflationary economies are remeasured as if the functional currency were the U.S. dollar.

Intercompany transactions between affiliated companies will result in a foreign currency transaction for either the parent or the subsidiary if the subsidiary's local currency is its functional currency. Alternatively, if the subsidiary's functional currency is the U.S. dollar, the intercompany transaction will be a foreign currency transaction to both affiliates or to neither affiliate.

On the date of a business combination, assets and liabilities are translated into U.S. dollars using current exchange rates.

QUESTIONS

1. Define the functional currency concept and briefly describe how a foreign entity's functional currency is determined. Why is this definition critical from a financial reporting perspective?

2. How does *Statement No. 52* define a highly inflationary economy? If the economy is deemed to be highly inflationary, which method for converting the financial statements to the reporting currency is used? How does the use of this method improve the economic representational faithfulness of the financial statements?

3. At the date of acquisition of a foreign subsidiary, what procedure is used to allocate the investment purchase price?

4. Describe what the current rate method is and under what circumstances it should be used.

5. Describe what the temporal method is and under what circumstances it should be used.

6. If the current rate method is used, the gain or loss on translation is included under other comprehensive income. Explain why this makes sense economically.

7. If the temporal method is used, the gain or loss on remeasurement is included in net income each year. Explain why this makes sense economically.

8. Under what circumstances would a foreign entity's financials statements need to be both remeasured and translated? Would this process have an effect on both the income statement and other comprehensive income? Explain.

9. If a company's sales were very seasonal—for example, a holiday-tree grower—would it be appropriate to use the annual average exchange rate to translate and remeasure sales and other expenses? Why or why not?

10. In the current-rate-method example in the chapter, the parent's other comprehensive income adjustment related to its investment in the subsidiary was larger than the other comprehensive income adjustment on the subsidiary's translated financial statements. Why?

11. Under the current rate method, all the expenses are translated using some form of current-period exchange rate. Under the temporal method, some expenses such as salaries and utilities are translated using current rates but others, such as cost of goods sold and depreciation expense, use historical rates. Why are different rates used between the two methods? After all, they are all expenses.

12. How does the choice of functional currency affect how the gain or loss on a hedge of a net investment in a foreign subsidiary is reported in the financial statements?

13. **Appendix A**—Noncontrolling interest—How are the noncontrolling interest balance and the noncontrolling interest-expense balance computations affected if the current rate method is used? If the temporal method is used?

14. **Appendix B**—Cash flow statement—How is the effect of exchange rate changes in cash reported in a consolidated statement of cash flows?

15. **Appendix C**—Discuss the possible accounting problems that can arise in remeasuring inventory items that were accounted for under the lower-of-cost-or-market pricing procedure in the foreign entity's financial statements.

EXERCISES

E 13-1
Translation/remeasurement differences

1. A German subsidiary of a U.S. firm has the British pound as its functional currency. Under the provisions of *FASB Statement No. 52*, the U.S. dollar from the subsidiary's viewpoint would be:
   a Its local currency
   b Its recording currency
   c A foreign currency
   d None of the above

2. Which of the following foreign subsidiary accounts will be converted into the same number of U.S. dollars, regardless of whether translation or remeasurement is used?
   a Accounts receivable
   b Inventories
   c Machinery
   d Prepaid insurance

3. Which one of the following items from the financial statements of a foreign subsidiary would be *translated* into dollars using the historical exchange rate?
   a Accounts payable
   b Amortization of bond premium
   c Common stock
   d Inventories

4. Average exchange rates are used to *translate* certain items from foreign income statements into U.S. dollars. Such averages are used to:
   a Approximate the effects of using the current exchange rates in effect on the transaction dates
   b Avoid using different exchange rates for some revenue and expense accounts
   c Eliminate large and temporary fluctuations in exchange rates that may reverse in the near future
   d Smooth out large exchange gains and losses

5. Palace Corporation made a long-term, dollar-denominated loan of $600,000 to its British subsidiary on January 1, 2006, when the exchange rate for British pounds was $1.73. If the subsidiary's functional currency is its local currency, this transaction is a foreign currency transaction of:
   a The parent company but not the subsidiary
   b The subsidiary company but not the parent
   c Both the subsidiary and the parent
   d Neither the subsidiary nor the parent

6. Sumtora Corporation is a 100%-owned subsidiary of a U.S. corporation. The country in which Sumtora is located has been determined to have a highly inflationary economy. Given this information, the functional currency of Sumtora is:
   a Its local currency
   b The U.S. dollar
   c Its recording currency
   d None of the above

7. An exchange gain on a long-term loan of a U.S. parent company to its British subsidiary whose functional currency is the British pound is:
   a *Recognized in consolidated income currently*
   b *Deferred until the loan is settled*
   c *Treated as an equity adjustment from translation*
   d *Treated as an equity adjustment from remeasurement*

8. A U.S. firm has a $10,000,000 investment in a foreign subsidiary, and the U.S. dollar is weakening against the currency of the country in which the foreign entity is located. On the basis of this information, one would expect the consolidated financial statements to show:
   a *Translation gains*
   b *Translation losses*
   c *Stockholders' equity increase from equity adjustments*
   d *Stockholders' equity decrease from equity adjustments*

9. Which one of the following would *not* give rise to changes in a parent company's equity adjustment from translation account?
   a *Remeasurement of a foreign subsidiary's statements*
   b *Hedge of a net investment in a foreign subsidiary*
   c *Long-term intercompany loans to its foreign subsidiary*
   d *Translation of a foreign subsidiary's statements*

E 13-2
[AICPA adapted]   Translation/remeasurement differences

1. When consolidated financial statements for a U.S. parent and its foreign subsidiary are prepared, the account balances expressed in foreign currency must be converted into the currency of the reporting entity. One objective of the translation process is to provide information that:
   a *Reflects current exchange rates*
   b *Reflects current monetary equivalents*
   c *Is compatible with the economic effects of rate changes on the firm's cash flows*
   d *Reflects each translated account at its unexpired historical cost*

2. A company is translating account balances from another currency into dollars for its December 31, 2006, statement of financial position and its calendar year 2006 earnings statement and statement of cash flows. The average exchange rate for 2006 should be used to translate:
   a *Cash at December 31, 2006*
   b *Land purchased in 2006*
   c *Retained earnings at January 1, 2006*
   d *Sales for 2006*

3. A subsidiary's functional currency is the local currency, which has not experienced significant inflation. The appropriate exchange rate for translating the depreciation on plant assets in the income statement of the foreign subsidiary is the:
   a *Exit rate*
   b *Historical exchange rate*
   c *Weighted average exchange rate over the economic life of each plant asset*
   d *Weighted average exchange rate for the current year*

4. The year-end balance of accounts receivable on the books of a foreign subsidiary should be translated by the parent company for consolidation purposes at the:
   a *Historical rate*
   b *Current rate*
   c *Negotiated rate*
   d *Spot rate*

5. When remeasuring foreign currency financial statements into the functional currency, which of the following items would be *remeasured* using historical exchange rates?
   a *Inventories carried at cost*
   b *Marketable equity securities reported at market values*
   c *Bonds payable*
   d *Accrued liabilities*

E 13-3
Acquisition date effects On January 1, 2006, Paily Company, a U.S. firm, purchases all the outstanding capital stock of Standt Ltd., a British firm, for $990,000, when the exchange rate for British pounds is $1.65. The book values of Standt's assets and liabilities are equal to fair values on this date, except for land that has a fair value of £200,000 and equipment with a fair value of £100,000.

Summarized balance sheet information for Paily in U.S. dollars and for Standt in pounds just before the business combination is as follows:

	Paily	Standt
Current assets	$3,000,000	£100,000
Land	800,000	100,000
Buildings—net	1,200,000	250,000
Equipment—net	1,000,000	50,000
	$6,000,000	£500,000
Current liabilities	$ 600,000	£ 50,000
Notes payable	1,000,000	150,000
Capital stock	3,000,000	200,000
Retained earnings	1,400,000	100,000
	$6,000,000	£500,000

REQUIRED: Prepare a consolidated balance sheet for Paily Corporation and Subsidiary at January 1, 2006, immediately after the business combination.

LEARNING OBJECTIVES 5, 6

E 13-4

Inventory remeasurement effect Stadt Corporation of the Netherlands is a 100%-owned subsidiary of Port Corporation, a U.S. firm, and its functional currency is the U.S. dollar. Stadt's books of record are maintained in euros and its inventory is carried at cost.

The current exchange rate for euros at December 31, 2006, is $0.60.
The historical cost of the inventory is 10,000 euros.
The historical exchange rate is $0.53.

REQUIRED: Determine the amount at which the inventory will be carried on (a) the foreign currency statements and (b) the remeasured statements.

LEARNING OBJECTIVES 4, 7

E 13-5

Acquisition—excess allocation and amortization effect On January 1, 2006, Panama Corporation acquired all the stock of Simenon Company of Belgium for $1,200,000, when Simenon had 20,000,000 euros (Eu) capital stock and Eu 15,000,000 retained earnings. Simenon's net assets were fairly valued on this date and any cost/book value differential is due to a patent with a 10-year amortization period. Simenon's functional currency is the euro. The exchange rates for euros for 2006 were as follows:

January 1, 2006	$.080
Average for 2006	$.082
December 31, 2006	$.085

REQUIRED

1. Calculate the patent value from the business combination on January 1, 2006.

2. Determine patent amortization in U.S. dollars for 2006.

3. Prepare a journal entry on Panama's books to record the patent amortization for 2006.

LEARNING OBJECTIVES 4, 7

E 13-6

Acquisition—excess allocation and amortization effect Psalter Company acquired all the stock of Stanford Ltd. of Britain on January 1, 2006, for $163,800, when Stanford had capital stock of £60,000 and retained earnings of £30,000. Stanford's assets and liabilities were fairly valued, except for equipment with a three-year life that was undervalued by £6,000. Any remaining excess is due to a patent with a useful life of 10 years.

Stanford's functional currency is the pound. Exchange rates for British pounds are as follows:

January 1, 2006	$1.66
Average for the year 2006	1.65
December 31, 2006	1.64

REQUIRED

1. Determine the unrealized translation gain or loss at December 31, 2006, related to the cost/book value differential assigned to equipment.

2. Determine the unrealized translation gain or loss at December 31, 2006, related to the patent.

E 13-7

Acquisition—excess allocation Packer Corporation of the United States purchased all the outstanding stock of Swiss Products Company of Switzerland for $1,350,000 cash on January 1, 2006. The book values of Swiss's assets and liabilities were equal to fair values on this date except for land, which was valued at 1,000,000 euros. Summarized balance sheet information in euros at January 1, 2006, is as follows:

LEARNING OBJECTIVES **4, 7**

Current assets	Eu	800,000	Current liabilities	Eu	400,000
Land		600,000	Bonds payable		500,000
Buildings—net		400,000	Capital stock		1,000,000
Equipment—net		500,000	Retained earnings		400,000
	Eu	2,300,000		Eu	2,300,000

The functional currency of Swiss Products Company is the euro. Exchange rates for euros for 2006 are as follows:

Spot rate January 1, 2006	$0.75
Average rate 2006	0.76
Current rate December 31, 2006	0.77

REQUIRED: Determine the unrealized translation gain or loss at December 31, 2006, relating to the excess allocated to the undervalued land.

E 13-8

[AICPA adapted] Acquisition excess allocation effects, specific account translation and remeasurement

LEARNING OBJECTIVES **4, 5, 7**

1. Fay Corporation had a realized foreign exchange loss of $15,000 for the year ended December 31, 2006, and must also determine whether the following items will require year-end adjustment.

    Fay had an $8,000 equity adjustment resulting from the translation of the accounts of its wholly owned foreign subsidiary for the year ended December 31, 2006.

    Fay had an account payable to an unrelated foreign supplier payable in the supplier's local currency. The U.S. dollar equivalent of the payable was $64,000 on the October 31, 2006, invoice date, and it was $60,000 on December 31, 2006. The invoice is payable on January 30, 2007.

    In Fay's 2006 consolidated income statement, what amount should be included as foreign exchange loss?

    a **$11,000**
    b **$15,000**
    c **$19,000**
    d **$23,000**

    [handwritten: Exch Loss 15,000 / A/P Adj -4,000 / total Loss 11,000]

2. On January 1, 2006, the Ben Company formed a foreign subsidiary. On February 15, 2006, Ben's subsidiary purchased 100,000 local currency units (LCU) of inventory; 25,000 LCU of the original inventory made up the entire inventory on December 31, 2006. The subsidiary's functional currency is the U.S. dollar. The exchange rates were 2.2 LCU to $1 from January 1, 2006, to June 30, 2006, and 2 LCU to $1 from July 1, 2006, to December 31, 2006. The December 31, 2006, inventory balance for Ben's foreign subsidiary should be remeasured into U.S. dollars in the amount of:

    a **$10,500**
    b **$11,364**
    c **$11,905**
    d **$12,500**

    [handwritten: 25,000 LCU @ 2/15/06 / 2.2 LCU @ 2/15/06 / = 11,364]

3. The Dease Company owns a foreign subsidiary with 3,600,000 local currency units of property, plant, and equipment before accumulated depreciation at December 31, 2008. Of this amount, 2,400,000 LCU were acquired in 2006, when the rate of exchange was 1.6 LCU to $1, and 1,200,000 LCU were acquired in 2007, when the rate of exchange was 1.8 LCU to $1.

    The rate of exchange in effect at December 31, 2008, was 2 LCU to $1. The weighted average of exchange rates in effect during 2008 was 1.92 LCU to $1. The subsidiary's functional currency is the U.S. dollar.

    Assuming that the property, plant, and equipment are depreciated using the straight-line method over a 10-year period with no salvage value, how much depreciation expense relating to the foreign subsidiary's property, plant, and equipment should be charged in Dease's income statement for 2008?

    a **$180,000**
    b **$187,500**
    c **$200,000**
    d **$216,667**

    [handwritten: 2,400,000 LCU 2006 / 1.6 = 1,500,000 / 1,200,000 LCU 2007 / 1.8 = 666,667 / 2,166,667 ÷ 10 = 216,667]

4. The Clark Company owns a foreign subsidiary that had net income for the year ended December 31, 2006, of 4,800,000 local currency units, which was appropriately translated into $800,000.

    On October 15, 2006, when the rate of exchange was 5.7 LCU to $1, the foreign subsidiary paid a dividend to Clark of 2,400,000 LCU. The dividend represented the net income of the foreign subsidiary for the six months ended June 30, 2006, during which time the weighted average exchange rate was 5.8 LCU to $1.

The rate of exchange in effect at December 31, 2006, was 5.9 LCU to $1. What rate of exchange should be used to translate the dividend for the December 31, 2006, financial statements?

a 5.7 LCU to $1 *— on dividend paid date*

b 5.8 LCU to $1

c 5.9 LCU to $1

d 6.0 LCU to $1

5. The Jem Company used the current rate method when translating foreign currency amounts at December 31, 2006. At that time, Jem had foreign subsidiaries with 1,500,000 local currency units in long-term receivables and 2,400,000 LCU in long-term debt. The rate of exchange in effect when the specific transactions occurred involving those foreign currency amounts was 2 LCU to $1. The rate of exchange in effect at December 31, 2006, was 1.5 LCU to $1. The translation of these foreign currency amounts into U.S. dollars would result in long-term receivables and long-term debt, respectively, of:

a $750,000 and $1,200,000

b $750,000 and $1,600,000

c $1,000,000 and $1,200,000

d $1,000,000 and $1,600,000

LT Rec 1,500,000 / 1.5 = 1,000,000

LT Debt 2,400,000 / 1.5 = 1,600,000

6. Certain balance sheet accounts of a foreign subsidiary of Rowan at December 31, 2006, have been translated into U.S. dollars as follows:

	Translated at	
	Current Rates	**Historical Rates**
Note receivable, long-term	$240,000	$200,000
Prepaid rent	85,000	80,000
Patent	150,000	170,000
	$475,000	$450,000

The subsidiary's functional currency is the currency of the country in which it is located. What total amount should be included in Rowan's December 31, 2006, consolidated balance sheet for the three accounts?

a $450,000

b $455,000

c $475,000

d $495,000

7. Inflation data of a foreign country for three years are as follows:

	Index	**Change in Index**	**Annual Rate of Inflation**
January 1, 2006	150	—	
January 1, 2007	200	50	$50 \div 150 = 33\%$
January 1, 2008	250	50	$50 \div 200 = 25\%$
January 1, 2009	330	80	$80 \div 250 = 32\%$

The cumulative three-year inflation rate is:

a 45%

b 90%

c 120%

d 180%

$(330 - 150) / 150 = 120\%$

LEARNING OBJECTIVE 10

E 13-9

Appendix A Noncontrolling interest effect Use the following information in answering questions 1 and 2.

Bradstreet Corporation has a 70% interest in Kasan Corporation of Switzerland, acquired in 2006 at a price equal to book value and fair value of Kasan's net assets. Kasan's functional currency is the euro, and changes in Kasan's U.S.-dollar translated stockholders' equity for 2009 are summarized as follows:

	Balance 1/1/09	**Change 2009**	**Balance 12/31/09**
Capital stock	$10,000,000	None	$10,000,000
Other paid-in capital	8,000,000	None	8,000,000
Retained earnings	4,000,000	$1,500,000	5,500,000
Equity adjustment from translation	(2,000,000)	500,000	(1,500,000)
Total	$20,000,000	$2,000,000	$22,000,000

1. Kasan's U.S. dollar net income for 2009 is $1,500,000, and Bradstreet accounts for its investment in Kasan as a one-line consolidation. Bradstreet's income from Kasan for 2009 is:

    a $2,000,000
    b $1,500,000
    c $1,400,000
    d $1,050,000

2. The change in Bradstreet's Investment in Kasan account for 2009 is:
    a $2,000,000
    b $1,500,000
    c $1,400,000
    d $1,050,000

Use the following information in answering questions 3 and 4.

    Martin Corporation loaned its 90%-owned Colombian subsidiary 10,000,000 pesos denominated as $19,000 on July 1, 2006, when the exchange rate for Colombian pesos was $0.0019. The subsidiary's functional currency is its local currency, and the 2006 average and year-end exchange rates are $0.0018 and $0.0016, respectively.

3. If the loan is short-term, the subsidiary's separate financial statements denominated in pesos at and for the year ended December 31, 2006, should reflect:
    a **An exchange gain of 555,556 pesos**
    b **An exchange loss of 1,875,000 pesos**
    c **An equity adjustment of 1,875,000 pesos**
    d **None of the above**

4. If the loan is long-term, the consolidated financial statements of Martin Corporation and Subsidiary at and for the year ended December 31, 2006, should reflect:
    a **An exchange gain of $889**
    b **An exchange loss of $3,000**
    c **An equity adjustment of $2,700**
    d **None of the above**

E 13-10

Appendix A Noncontrolling interest effect Pender Corporation owns an 80% interest in Shinhan Ltd. of South Korea, purchased several years ago at book value equal to fair value. The functional currency of Shinhan is the U.S. dollar.

    Shinhan uses the FIFO inventory method. Data in won relating to Shinhan's cost of sales and inventory are as follows:

Inventory January 1, 2006	9,000,000 won
Inventory December 31, 2006	5,000,000 won
Purchases 2006	86,000,000 won

    The rate of exchange for the won on November 30, 2006, when the ending inventory items were acquired, was $0.00135. Other exchange rates for 2006 are as follows:

Exchange rate January 1, 2006	$0.0012
Exchange rate December 31, 2006	0.0014
Average exchange rate for 2006	0.0013

REQUIRED: Determine the cost-of-sales and ending-inventory amounts in U.S. dollars that will appear in Shinhan's remeasured financial statements.

LEARNING OBJECTIVE **10**

PROBLEMS

AW

P 13-1

Parent accounting under the equity method Parkway Corporation purchased a ~~100~~ 40% interest in Scorpio Company of Germany for $1,080,000 on January 1, 2006. The excess cost over book value is due to a patent with a 10-year amortization period. A summary of Scorpio's net assets at December 31, 2005, and at December 31, 2006, after translation into U.S. dollars, is as follows:

LEARNING OBJECTIVES **4, 7**

	Capital Stock	Retained Earnings	Equity Adjustment	Net Assets
December 31, 2005	$2,000,000	$400,000		$2,400,000
Net income		310,000		310,000
Dividends		(192,000)		(192,000)
Translation adjustment			$212,000	212,000
December 31, 2006	$2,000,000	$518,000	$212,000	$2,730,000

Exchange rates for euros were $0.60 on January 1, 2006; $0.62 average for 2006; $0.64 when dividends were declared; and $0.65 at December 31, 2006. Scorpio had net assets of Eu 4,000,000 at January 1, 2006; net income of Eu 500,000 for 2006; and dividends of Eu 300,000. It ended the year with net assets of Eu 4,200,000. Scorpio's functional currency is the euro.

REQUIRED

1. Calculate Parkway's income from Scorpio for 2006.

2. Determine the balance of Parkway's Investment in Scorpio account at December 31, 2006.

3. Develop a proof of your calculation of the Investment in Scorpio account balance at December 31, 2006.

P 13-2

Parent accounting under the equity method Placid Corporation purchased a 100% interest in Sorrier Company, a foreign company, on January 1, 2006, for $342,000, when Sorrier's stockholders' equity consisted of 3,000,000 LCU capital stock and 1,000,000 LCU retained earnings. Sorrier's functional currency is its local currency unit. The exchange rate at this time was $0.15 per LCU. Any excess allocated to patents is to be amortized over 10 years.

A summary of changes in the stockholders' equity of Sorrier during 2006 (including relevant exchange rates) is as follows:

	LCUs	Exchange Rate	U.S. Dollars
Stockholders' equity January 1, 2006	4,000,000	$0.15 C	$600,000
Net income	800,000	0.14 A	112,000
Dividends	(400,000)	0.14 C	(56,000)
Equity adjustment			(84,000)
Stockholders' equity December 31, 2006	4,400,000	0.13 C	$572,000

REQUIRED: Determine the following:

1. Excess patent from Placid's Investment in Sorrier on January 1, 2006

2. Excess patent amortization for 2006

3. Unamortized excess patent at December 31, 2006

4. Equity adjustment from patents for 2006

5. Income from Sorrier for 2006

6. Investment in Sorrier balance at December 31, 2006

P 13-3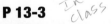

Translation worksheet, parent accounting Pylon Corporation acquired all the outstanding capital stock of Sooth Company of London on January 1, 2006, for $800,000, when the exchange rate for British pounds was $1.60 and Sooth's stockholders' equity consisted of £400,000 capital stock and £100,000 retained earnings. Sooth's functional currency is the British pound. Balance sheet accounts for Sooth at January 1, 2006, in British pounds and U.S. dollars are summarized as follows:

	British Pounds	Exchange Rate	U.S. Dollars
Cash	£ 50,000	$1.60	$ 80,000
Accounts receivable—net	60,000	1.60	96,000
Inventories	40,000	1.60	64,000
Equipment	750,000	1.60	1,200,000
	£900,000		$1,440,000
Accumulated depreciation	£250,000	$1.60	$ 400,000
Accounts payable	150,000	1.60	240,000
Capital stock	400,000	1.60	640,000
Retained earnings	100,000	1.60	160,000
	£900,000		$1,440,000

Exchange rates for 2006 are as follows:

Current exchange rate January 1, 2006	$1.60
Average exchange rate for 2006	1.63
Rate for cash dividends	1.62
Current exchange rate December 31, 2006	1.65

Sooth's adjusted trial balance in British pounds at December 31, 2006, is as follows:

Debits

Cash	£	20,000 ✳ 1.65
Accounts receivable—net		70,000
Inventories		50,000
Equipment		800,000
Cost of sales		350,000
Depreciation expense		80,000
Operating expenses		100,000
Dividends		30,000
		£1,500,000

Credits

Accumulated depreciation	£	330,000
Accounts payable		70,000
Capital stock		400,000
Retained earnings		100,000
Sales		600,000
		£1,500,000

REQUIRED

1. Prepare a translation worksheet to convert Sooth's December 31, 2006, adjusted trial balance into U.S. dollars.

2. Prepare journal entries on Pylon's books to account for the investment in Sooth for 2006.

3. Directly compute the translation gain or loss.

P 13-4

Translation worksheet, parent accounting Peter Corporation acquired 100% of the common stock of Schultz Corporation for $3,200,000 on January 2, 2006, when the stockholders' equity of Schultz consisted of 5,000,000 euros capital stock and 2,000,000 euros retained earnings. The spot rate for euros on this date was $0.50. Any cost/book value difference attributable to a patent is to be amortized over a 10-year period, and Schultz's functional currency is the euro.

LEARNING OBJECTIVES **4, 5, 6, 7**

Accounts from Schultz's adjusted trial balance in euros at December 31, 2006, are as follows:

Debits

Cash	Eu	1,000,000
Accounts receivable		2,000,000
Inventories		4,000,000
Equipment		8,000,000
Cost of sales		4,000,000
Depreciation expense		800,000
Operating expenses		2,700,000
Dividends		500,000
	Eu	23,000,000

Credits

Accumulated depreciation—equipment	Eu	2,400,000
Accounts payable		3,600,000
Capital stock		5,000,000
Retained earnings January 1		2,000,000
Sales		10,000,000
	Eu	23,000,000

Relevant exchange rates in U.S. dollars for euros are as follows:

Current exchange rate December 31, 2006	$0.60
Average exchange rate 2006	0.55
Exchange rate applicable to dividends	0.54

REQUIRED

1. Prepare a translation worksheet for Schultz at December 31, 2006.

2. Calculate Peter's income from Schultz for 2006 on the basis of a one-line consolidation.

3. Determine the correct balance of Peter's investment in Schultz at December 31, 2006.

P 13-5

Remeasurement worksheet Pardi Corporation of Chicago acquired all the outstanding capital stock of Sari Company of London on January 1, 2006, for $1,200,000. The exchange rate for British pounds was $1.60 and Sari's stockholders' equity was £800,000, consisting of £500,000 capital stock and £300,000 retained earnings. The functional currency of Sari is the U.S. dollar.

Exchange rates for British pounds for 2006 are as follows:

Current rate December 31, 2005	$1.60
Current rate December 31, 2006	1.70
Average exchange rate for 2006	1.65
Exchange rate for dividends	1.64

Sari's cost of goods sold consists of £200,000 inventory on hand at January 1, 2006, and purchases of £600,000 less £150,000 inventory on hand at December 31, 2006, that was acquired at an exchange rate of $1.68.

All of Sari's plant assets were on hand when Pardi acquired Sari, and Sari's other expenses were paid in cash or relate to accounts payable.

Sari's adjusted trial balance at December 31, 2006, in British pounds is as follows:

Debits	
Cash	£ 50,000
Accounts receivable	200,000
Short-term note receivable	50,000
Inventories	150,000
Land	300,000
Buildings—net	400,000
Equipment—net	500,000
Cost of sales	650,000
Depreciation expense	200,000
Other expenses	400,000
Dividends	100,000
	£3,000,000

Credits	
Accounts payable	£ 180,000
Bonds payable—10%	500,000
Bond interest payable	20,000
Capital stock	500,000
Retained earnings	300,000
Sales	1,500,000
	£3,000,000

REQUIRED: Prepare a remeasurement worksheet to restate Sari's adjusted trial balance at December 31, 2006, into U.S. dollars.

P 13-6

Remeasurement worksheet Philip Corporation, a U.S. firm, acquired 100% of Stuart Corporation's outstanding stock at book value on January 1, 2006, for $112,000. Stuart is a New Zealand company, and its functional currency is the U.S. dollar. The exchange rate for New Zealand dollars (NZ$) was $0.70 when Philip acquired its interest. Stuart's stockholders' equity on January 1, 2006, consisted of NZ$150,000 capital stock and NZ$10,000 retained earnings. The adjusted trial balance for Stuart at December 31, 2006, is as follows:

Debits	
Cash	NZ$ 15,000
Accounts receivable—net	60,000
Inventories	30,000
Prepaid expenses	10,000
Land	45,000
Equipment	60,000
Cost of sales	120,000
Depreciation expense	12,000
Other operating expenses	28,000
Dividends	20,000
	NZ$400,000
Credits	
Accumulated depreciation	NZ$ 22,000
Accounts payable	18,000
Capital stock	150,000
Retained earnings	10,000
Sales	200,000
	NZ$400,000

ADDITIONAL INFORMATION

1. Prepaid expenses (supplies) of NZ$18,000 were on hand when Philip acquired Stuart. Other operating expenses include NZ$8,000 of these supplies that were used in 2006. The remaining NZ$10,000 of supplies is on hand at year-end.

2. The NZ$120,000 cost of sales consists of NZ$50,000 inventory on hand at January 1, 2006, and NZ$100,000 in purchases during the year, less NZ$30,000 ending inventory that was acquired when the exchange rate was $0.66.

3. The NZ$60,000 of equipment consists of NZ$50,000 included in the business combination and NZ$10,000 purchased during 2006, when the exchange rate was $0.68. A depreciation rate of 20% is applicable to all equipment for 2006.

4. Exchange rates for 2006 are summarized as follows:

Current exchange rate January 1, 2006	$0.70
Exchange rate when new equipment was acquired	0.68
Average exchange rate for 2006	0.67
Exchange rate for December 31, 2006, inventory	0.66
Exchange rate for dividends	0.66
Current exchange rate December 31, 2006	0.65

REQUIRED: Prepare a worksheet to remeasure the adjusted trial balance of Stuart Corporation into U.S. dollars at December 31, 2006.

P 13-7

Translation worksheet, parent accounting Pella Corporation, a U.S. firm, paid $308,000 for all the common stock of Sapir Company of Israel on January 1, 2006, when the exchange rate for shekels was $0.35. Sapir's equity on this date consisted of 500,000 shekels common stock and 300,000 shekels retained earnings. The $28,000 (80,000 shekels) excess is attributable to a patent with a 10-year amortization period. Sapir's functional currency is the shekel.

LEARNING OBJECTIVES **4, 5, 6, 7**

Sapir's adjusted trial balance at December 31, 2006, in shekels is as follows:

Debits	**Shekels**	*Credits*	**Shekels**
Cash	40,000	Accounts payable	120,000
Receivables—net	50,000	Other liabilities	60,000
Inventories	150,000	Advance from Pella	140,000
Land	160,000	Common stock	500,000
Equipment—net	300,000	Retained earnings 1/1	300,000
Buildings—net	500,000	Sales	600,000
Expenses	400,000		
Exchange loss (advance)	20,000		
Dividends	100,000		
	1,720,000		1,720,000

On January 2, 2006, Pella advanced $42,000 (120,000 shekels) to Sapir. This advance was short-term, denominated in U.S. dollars, and made when the exchange rate for shekels was $0.35. In June 2006, Sapir paid a 100,000-shekel dividend when the exchange rate was $0.33. The average and year-end exchange rates for shekels are $0.32 and $0.30, respectively.

REQUIRED

1. Prepare a worksheet to translate Sapir's adjusted trial balance at December 31, 2006, into U.S. dollars.

2. Prepare the necessary journal entries for Pella to account for its investment in Sapir Company for 2006.

LEARNING
OBJECTIVES **6, 8**

P 13-8

Parent accounting and consolidation under translation PWA Corporation paid

$1,710,000 for 100% of the stock of SAA Corporation on January 1, 2006, when the stockholders' equity of SAA consisted of 5,000,000 LCU capital stock and 3,000,000 LCU retained earnings. SAA's functional currency is the local currency unit, and any cost/book value differential is attributable to a patent with a 10-year amortization period.

On July 1, 2006, PWA advanced $333,000 (1,800,000 LCU) to SAA when the exchange rate was $0.185. The advance is short-term and denominated in U.S. dollars.

Relevant exchange rates for LCUs for 2006 are as follows:

Rate at acquisition on January 1	$0.190
Rate applicable to the advance on July 1	0.185
Rate applicable to dividends on September 1	0.185
Average rate for the year	0.185
Current rate at December 31	0.180

A translation worksheet for SAA's adjusted trial balance at December 31, 2006, is as follows:

	LCUs	Exchange Rate	U.S. Dollars
Debits			
Cash	550,000	$0.180 C	$ 99,000
Accounts receivable—net	500,000	0.180 C	90,000
Inventories	1,500,000	0.180 C	270,000
Land	1,600,000	0.180 C	288,000
Equipment—net	3,000,000	0.180 C	540,000
Buildings—net	5,000,000	0.180 C	900,000
Expenses	4,000,000	0.185 A	740,000
Exchange loss (advance)	50,000	0.185 A	9,250
Dividends	1,000,000	0.185 R	185,000
Equity adjustment from translation			84,750
	17,200,000		$3,206,000
Credits			
Accounts payable	750,000	$0.180 C	$ 135,000
Other liabilities	600,000	0.180 C	108,000
Advance from PWA (short-term)	1,850,000	0.180 C	333,000
Capital stock	5,000,000	0.190 H	950,000
Retained earnings January 1	3,000,000	0.190 H	570,000
Sales	6,000,000	0.185 A	1,110,000
	17,200,000		$3,206,000

Financial statements for PWA and SAA at and for the year ended December 31, 2006, are summarized as follows:

	PWA	SAA
Combined Income and Retained Earnings Statement for the Year Ended December 31, 2006		
Sales	$ 569,500	$1,110,000
Income from SAA	342,250	—
Expenses	(400,000)	(740,000)
Exchange loss	—	(9,250)
Net income	511,750	360,750
Add: Beginning retained earnings	856,500	570,000
Less: Dividends	(300,000)	(185,000)
Retained earnings December 31	$1,068,250	$ 745,750

Balance Sheet at December 31, 2006

Cash	$ 90,720	$ 99,000
Accounts receivable—net	128,500	90,000
Advance to SAA	333,000	—
Inventories	120,000	270,000
Land	100,000	288,000
Equipment—net	600,000	540,000
Buildings—net	300,000	900,000
Investment in SAA	1,773,000	—
	$3,445,220	$2,187,000
Accounts payable	$ 162,720	$ 135,000
Advance from PWA	—	333,000
Other liabilities	308,500	108,000
Common stock	2,000,000	950,000
Retained earnings	1,068,250	745,750
Equity adjustment from translation	(94,250)	(84,750)
	$3,445,220	$2,187,000

REQUIRED

1. Prepare journal entries on PWA's books to account for its investment in SAA for 2006.

2. Prepare consolidation working papers for PWA Corporation and Subsidiary for the year ended December 31, 2006.

P 13-9

Translation worksheet, parent accounting, consolidation San Corporation is a 100%-owned foreign subsidiary of Par Corporation, acquired by Par on January 1, 2006, at book value equal to fair value, when the exchange rate for LCUs of San's home country was $0.24. Sans functional currency is the LCU. Par made a 200,000 LCU loan to San on May 1, 2006, when the exchange rate for LCUs was $0.23. The loan is short-term and is denominated at $46,000. Adjusted trial balances of the affiliated companies at year-end 2006 are as follows:

	Par in U.S. Dollars	San in LCU
Debits		
Cash	$ 25,100	150,000
Accounts receivable	90,000	180,000
Short-term loan to San	46,000	—
Inventories	110,000	230,000
Land	150,000	250,000
Buildings	300,000	600,000
Equipment	220,000	800,000
Investment in San (100%)	230,000	—
Cost of sales	400,000	200,000
Depreciation expense	81,000	100,000
Other expenses	200,000	120,000
Exchange loss	—	30,000
Dividends	100,000	100,000
Equity adjustment	44,000	—
	$1,996,100	2,760,000
Credits		
Accumulated depreciation—buildings	$ 120,000	300,000
Accumulated depreciation—equipment	60,000	400,000
Accounts payable	241,100	130,000
Short-term loan from Par	—	230,000
Capital stock	500,000	800,000
Retained earnings January 1	220,000	200,000
Sales	800,000	700,000
Income from San	55,000	—
	$1,996,100	2,760,000

San paid dividends in September, when the exchange rate was $0.21. The exchange rate for LCUs was $0.20 at December 31, 2006, and the average exchange rate for 2006 was $0.22.

REQUIRED

1. Prepare a worksheet to translate San's adjusted trial balance into U.S. dollars at December 31, 2006.

2. Prepare the necessary journal entries for Par to account for its investment in San for 2006 under the equity method.

3. Prepare consolidation working papers for Par Corporation and Subsidiary for the year ended December 31, 2006.

LEARNING OBJECTIVES **4, 5, 6, 7, 10**

P 13-10

Appendix A Translation worksheet, parent accounting—noncontrolling interest

Pence Corporation, based in San Francisco, purchased 90% of Sevin Company's outstanding capital stock on January 1, 2006, for $768,000. Sevin is a British company, and the exchange rate for British pounds was $1.60 when Pence acquired its interest. Sevin's stockholders' equity on January 1, 2006, consisted of £400,000 capital stock and £100,000 retained earnings. Sevin's functional currency is the British pound, and its comparative adjusted trial balances in pounds at December 31, 2006 and 2007, are as follows:

Sevin Company Adjusted Trial Balances in British Pounds at December 31

	2006	2007
Debits		
Cash	£ 30,000	£ 50,000
Accounts receivable	60,000	90,000
Inventories	80,000	150,000
Equipment	900,000	1,000,000
Cost of sales	300,000	360,000
Depreciation expense	100,000	110,000
Operating expenses	80,000	90,000
Dividends	50,000	50,000
	£1,600,000	£1,900,000
Credits		
Accumulated depreciation—equipment	£ 200,000	£ 310,000
Accounts payable	200,000	220,000
Advance from Pence	20,000	20,000
Capital stock	400,000	400,000
Retained earnings	100,000	250,000
Sales	680,000	700,000
	£1,600,000	£1,900,000

COST/BOOK VALUE DIFFERENTIAL: The cost/book value differential from the investment in Sevin is due to a patent with a 10-year amortization period. The original patent is $48,000 [$768,000 − (£500,000 × $1.60 exchange rate × 90%)].

ADVANCE TO PENCE: On January 2, 2006, Pence made a $30,000 (£20,000) short-term advance to Sevin. The advance is non-interest-bearing and is denominated in pounds.

SUMMARY OF EXCHANGE RATES

	2006	2007
Current exchange rate January 1	$1.60	$1.70
Average exchange rate	1.65	1.75
Exchange rate on the date of the advance	1.60	
Exchange rate for dividends	1.68	1.78
Current exchange rate December 31	1.70	1.80

REQUIRED

1. Prepare translation worksheets for Sevin Company for the years ended December 31, 2006 and 2007.

2. Calculate Pence's income from Sevin for 2006 and 2007.

3. Determine the Investment in Sevin balance at year-end 2006 and 2007.

P 13-11

Appendix A Remeasurement worksheet with noncontrolling interest

LEARNING OBJECTIVES **4, 5, 6, 7, 10**

Paragon Corporation, a U.S. company, acquired a 90% interest in Freeman Corporation, an Australian company, on July 1, 2002, when the exchange rate for Australian dollars (A$) was $0.70. Paragon acquired its interest in Freeman at book value equal to fair value. Freeman's functional currency is the U.S. dollar. Relevant exchange rates for Australian dollars are as follows:

Current rate December 31, 2006	$0.80
Current rate December 31, 2005	0.75
Average rate 2006	0.78

Freeman's adjusted trial balance in Australian dollars at December 31, 2006, included the following accounts and amounts.

Debits	
Cash	A$ 50,000
Accounts receivable	85,000
Inventories (at FIFO cost)	170,000
Land	200,000
Buildings	700,000 —Bldgs
Equipment	230,000
Cost of sales	800,000
Depreciation expense—building	50,000
Depreciation expense—equipment	30,000
Other operating expenses	320,000
Dividends	200,000
Total debits	A$2,835,000
Credits	
Allowance for bad debts	A$ 5,000
Accumulated depreciation—buildings	200,000
Accumulated depreciation—equipment	80,000
Accounts payable	150,000
Advance from Paragon	300,000
Capital stock	400,000
Retained earnings	200,000
Sales	1,500,000
Total credits	A$2,835,000

INFORMATION RELEVANT TO SELECTED BALANCE SHEET ITEMS

1. Freeman's inventories at December 31, 2006, are A$170,000, acquired during the last quarter of 2006, when the exchange rate was $0.79. Inventories at December 31, 2005, were A$250,000, acquired during the last quarter of 2005 when the exchange rate was $0.74.

2. The land (A$200,000) and buildings (A$700,000) have been held since the subsidiary was acquired on July 1, 2002.

3. The equipment on hand since July 1, 2002, is A$170,000, less accumulated depreciation of A$70,000, for a net amount of A$100,000. The rest of the equipment was acquired on December 31, 2005, for A$60,000 and has accumulated depreciation of A$10,000, for a book value of A$50,000.

4. There have been no changes in Freeman's capital stock since Paragon purchased its 90% interest on July 1, 2002. Freeman's December 31, 2007, retained earnings in the remeasured balance sheet was $144,000.

5. Other operating expenses (other than A$2,000 bad debt expense) were incurred proportionately throughout 2006.

6. Reciprocal amounts include the following:

   a *Dividends*. Paragon credited its Investment in Freeman account for $135,000 for dividends received from Freeman.

   b *Advance*. The advance is denominated in Australian dollars. It is reported by Paragon at December 31, 2006, as an "advance to Freeman" $240,000, and it is not of a long-term nature.

REQUIRED

1. Remeasure Freeman's trial balance into U.S. dollars.

2. Prepare income and retained earnings statements and a balance sheet for Freeman in U.S. dollars.

P 13-12

Appendix A Parent accounting, noncontrolling interest Pilot Corporation, a U.S. firm, purchased 80% of the outstanding stock of Saussure Corporation of Sweden on January 1, 2006, for $2,255,000, when the exchange rate for Swedish Kronas was $0.55. Fair values were equal to book values of Saussure's assets and liabilities on this date, and its stockholders' equity consisted of KR 3,000,000 capital stock and KR 2,000,000 retained earnings. Any excess cost over book value is attributable to patents from the purchase and is amortized over a 10-year period.

The current exchange rate for kronas at December 31, 2006, is $0.65, and the average for the year is $0.60. The exchange rate on November 1, 2006, when dividends were declared, was $0.63. Saussure's functional currency is its local currency. A translation worksheet for 2006 is as follows:

	Kronas	Exchange Rate	U.S. Dollars
Cash	1,000,000	$0.65	$ 650,000
Accounts receivable	1,500,000	0.65	975,000
Inventories (FIFO)	1,800,000	0.65	1,170,000
Land	1,000,000	0.65	650,000
Building	1,800,000	0.65	1,170,000
Equipment	2,000,000	0.65	1,300,000
Cost of sales	3,000,000	0.60	1,800,000
Depreciation—building	200,000	0.60	120,000
Depreciation—equipment	200,000	0.60	120,000
Expenses	1,000,000	0.60	600,000
Dividends	400,000	0.63	252,000
	13,900,000		$8,807,000
Accumulated depreciation—building	900,000	$0.65	$ 585,000
Accumulated depreciation—equipment	1,100,000	0.65	715,000
Accounts payable	900,000	0.65	585,000
Bonds payable	1,000,000	0.65	650,000
Capital stock	3,000,000	0.55	1,650,000
Retained earnings	2,000,000		1,100,000
Sales	5,000,000	0.60	3,000,000
Equity adjustment from translation			522,000
	13,900,000		$8,807,000

REQUIRED

1. Determine the balance of Pilot's Investment in Saussure account at December 31, 2006.

2. Compute the patent and equity adjustment from translation that will appear in the consolidated balance sheet of Pilot Corporation and Subsidiary at December 31, 2006.

P 13-13

Appendix A Parent accounting, noncontrolling interest Pic Corporation of the United States purchased 80% of the outstanding capital stock of Sol Company, a foreign company, for $75,000 on January 1, 2006. At that time, Sol's stockholders' equity consisted of capital stock of 500,000 LCU and retained earnings of 100,000 LCU. The exchange rate for LCUs on January 1, 2006, is $0.15. Any cost/book value differential from the investment in Sol is attributable to a patent with a 10-year amortization period. Pic's management determines that Sol's functional currency is the LCU.

Relevant exchange rates for the LCU are summarized as follows:

	2006	2007
Current exchange rate January 1	$0.150	$0.160
Average exchange for the year	0.155	0.165
Exchange rate for dividends	0.158	0.168
Current exchange rate December 31	0.160	0.170

Sol's translated adjusted trial balances for 2006 and 2007 are as follows:

	LCUs	Rate	US$	LCUs	Rate	US$
Debits						
Cash	40,000	$0.160	$ 6,400	60,000	$0.170	$ 10,200
Accounts receivable	70,000	0.160	11,200	100,000	0.170	17,000
Inventories	60,000	0.160	9,600	130,000	0.170	22,100
Equipment	300,000	0.160	48,000	400,000	0.170	68,000
Building	600,000	0.160	96,000	600,000	0.170	102,000
Cost of sales	250,000	0.155	38,750	310,000	0.165	51,150
Depreciation expenses	100,000	0.155	15,500	110,000	0.165	18,150
Operating expenses	130,000	0.155	20,150	140,000	0.165	23,100
Dividends	50,000	0.158	7,900	50,000	0.168	8,400
	1,600,000		$253,500	1,900,000		$320,100
Credits						
Accumulated depreciation— equipment	150,000	0.160	$ 24,000	230,000	$0.170	$ 39,100
Accumulated depreciation— building	50,000	0.160	8,000	80,000	0.170	13,600
Accounts payable	120,000	0.160	19,200	140,000	0.170	23,800
Capital stock	500,000	0.150	75,000	500,000	0.150	75,000
Retained earnings	100,000	0.150	15,000	250,000		38,100
Sales	680,000	0.155	105,400	700,000	0.165	115,500
Equity adjustment			6,900			15,000
	1,600,000		$253,500	1,900,000		$320,100

REQUIRED: Determine the following.

1. Patent from the investment in Sol that will appear on the December 31, 2006 and 2007, consolidated balance sheets for Pic Corporation and Subsidiary.

2. The equity adjustment from translation that will appear on the December 31, 2006 and 2007, consolidated balance sheets for Pic Corporation and Subsidiary.

3. Noncontrolling interest that will appear on the December 31, 2006 and 2007, consolidated balance sheets for Pic Corporation and Subsidiary.

P 13-14

Appendix B Consolidation, statement of cash flows, noncontrolling interest
Perry Corporation, based in New York, acquired 75% of the outstanding shares of Smithe Corporation, a foreign company, on January 1, 2006, for $1,421,000, when the exchange rate for local currency units of Smithe's home country was $1.40. At that date, Smithe's stockholders' equity was 1,300,000 LCU, consisting of 1,000,000 LCU capital stock and 300,000 LCU retained earnings. Any cost/book value differential from the investment in Smithe is assigned to a patent with a 10-year amortization period. The functional currency of Smithe is its local currency unit. On January 2, 2006, Smithe made a 40,000 LCU long-term non-interest-bearing advance to Perry, when the exchange rate was still $1.40. The advance is denominated in LCUs. The adjusted trial balances of Smithe in LCUs at December 31, 2006 and 2007, are as follows:

LEARNING OBJECTIVES **10, 11**

Smithe Company Adjusted Trial Balances at December 31

	2006 in LCUs	Exchange Rate	2006 in Dollars	2007 in LCUs	Exchange Rate	2007 in Dollars
Debits						
Cash	70,000	$1.45	101,500	80,000	$1.50	120,000
Accounts receivable	60,000	1.45	87,000	180,000	1.50	270,000
Inventories	150,000	1.45	217,500	200,000	1.50	300,000
Advance to Perry	40,000	1.45	58,000	40,000	1.50	60,000
Equipment	1,500,000	1.45	2,175,000	1,500,000	1.50	2,250,000
Cost of sales	600,000	1.43	858,000	700,000	1.48	1,036,000
Depreciation expense	150,000	1.43	214,500	150,000	1.48	222,000
Operating expenses	180,000	1.43	257,400	200,000	1.48	296,000
Dividends	50,000	1.42	71,000	50,000	1.47	73,500
	2,800,000		$4,039,900	3,100,000		$4,627,500
Credits						
Accumulated depreciation	300,000	$1.45	435,000	450,000	$1.50	675,000
Accounts payable	200,000	1.45	290,000	130,000	1.50	195,000
Capital stock	1,000,000	1.40	1,400,000	1,000,000	1.40	1,400,000
Retained earnings	300,000	1.40	420,000	320,000		449,100
Sales	1,000,000	1.43	1,430,000	1,200,000	1.48	1,776,000
Equity adjustment	—		64,900	—		132,400
	2,800,000		$4,039,900	3,100,000		$4,627,500

Relevant exchange rates for local currency units for 2006 and 2007 are summarized as follows:

	2006	2007
Current exchange rate January 1	$1.40	$1.45
Average exchange rate for year	1.43	1.48
Spot rate for dividends	1.42	1.47
Current exchange rate December 31	1.45	1.50

Financial statements for Perry Corporation for the two years ended December 31, 2006, and 2007, are summarized as follows:

Perry Corporation

	2006	2007
Combined Income and Retained Earnings Statement for the Year Ended December 31		
Sales	$2,000,000	$2,100,000
Income from Smithe	69,355	160,580
Cost of sales	(900,000)	(900,000)
Depreciation expense	(200,000)	(250,000)
Operating expenses	(669,355)	(710,580)
Net income	300,000	400,000
Add: Retained earnings January 1	450,000	500,000
Deduct: Dividends	(250,000)	(250,000)
Retained earnings December 31	$ 500,000	$ 650,000
Balance Sheet at December 31		
Cash	$ 112,300	$ 59,500
Accounts receivable	150,000	195,000
Inventories	250,000	200,000
Equipment—net	2,000,000	2,100,000
Investment in Smithe	1,487,700	1,645,500
	$4,000,000	$4,200,000
Accounts payable	$ 393,405	$ 391,060
Advance from Smithe	58,000	60,000
Capital stock	3,000,000	3,000,000
Retained earnings	500,000	650,000
Equity adjustment	48,595	98,940
	$4,000,000	$4,200,000

REQUIRED

1. Prepare consolidation working papers for Perry Corporation and Subsidiary for the years ended December 31, 2006, and December 31, 2007.

2. Prepare a consolidated statement of cash flows for the year ended December 31, 2007.

P 13-15

Appendix B Consolidation, financial statement preparation, noncontrolling interest

Progress Corporation, a U.S. company based in New York, acquired 90% of the outstanding voting shares of Scheele Corporation, a foreign company, on January 1, 2006, for $2,070,000. The functional currency of Scheele is its local currency unit. The exchange rate for LCUs at the time of the business combination was $0.45. Also on January 1, 2006, Progress made a $450,000 (1,000,000 LCU) short-term advance to Scheele. Adjusted trial balances of Progress and Scheele Corporations at December 31, 2006 and 2007, are as follows:

Adjusted Trial Balances at December 31

| | Progress Corporation | | Scheele Corporation | |
	2006 in Dollars	2007 in Dollars	2006 in LCUs	2007 in LCUs
Cash	$ 406,200	$ 183,800	100,000	600,000
Accounts receivable	1,200,000	1,400,000	400,000	1,000,000
Advance to Scheele	450,000	450,000		
Inventories	1,100,000	1,950,000	500,000	1,500,000
Investment in Scheele	2,196,000	2,426,250		
Equipment	2,500,000	3,000,000	9,000,000	9,000,000
Equity adjustment	247,800	389,950		
Cost of sales	4,300,000	4,800,000	3,000,000	3,600,000
Depreciation expense	600,000	700,000	900,000	900,000
Operating expenses	2,000,000	2,200,000	975,000	1,325,000
Exchange loss			125,000	75,000
	$15,000,000	$17,500,000	15,000,000	18,000,000
Accumulated depreciation	$ 1,200,000	$ 1,900,000	1,800,000	2,700,000
Accounts payable	1,700,000	1,500,000	1,075,000	1,100,000
Advance from Progress			1,125,000	1,200,000
Capital stock	3,000,000	3,000,000	4,000,000	4,000,000
Retained earnings	1,200,000	2,200,000	1,000,000	2,000,000
Income from Scheele	373,800	372,400		
Sales	7,526,200	8,527,600	6,000,000	7,000,000
	$15,000,000	$17,500,000	15,000,000	18,000,000

ADDITIONAL INFORMATION

1. The cost/book value difference is due to a patent with 10-year amortization.

2. The advance to Scheele is a non-interest-bearing loan denominated in U.S. dollars and adjusted on Scheele's books for exchange losses.

3. Current exchange rates are $0.40 at December 31, 2006, and $0.375 at December 31, 2007. Average exchange rates are $0.42 for 2006 and $0.38 for 2007.

REQUIRED: Develop comparative consolidated financial statements for Progress Corporation and Subsidiary at and for the years ended December 31, 2006 and 2007. An income statement, a retained earnings statement, and a balance sheet are required for 2006 and 2007; and a statement of cash flows is required for 2007.

INTERNET ASSIGNMENT

Go to *Ford Motor Company*'s Web site and access its 2003 annual report. Answer the following questions:

1. What are the functional currencies of Ford's subsidiaries?

2. How much and where did Ford report the gain or loss on remeasurement of its subsidiaries' financial statements? From what currencies were the subsidiaries' financial statements remeasured into dollars? How material are these gains or losses with respect to Ford's overall profitability? In examining the comparative financial statements, do these gains and losses appear to change dramatically over time? Does this appear to affect the volatility (and apparent riskiness) of Ford's cash flow stream?

3. How much and where did Ford report the gain or loss on translation of its subsidiaries' financial statements? From what currencies were the subsidiaries' financial statements translated into dollars? How material are these cumulative gains or losses to Ford's overall financial position? Do these cumulative gains or losses appear to fluctuate over time, and what impact would this have on the apparent riskiness of Ford's cash flow stream?

4. Does Ford enter into any cash flow hedges in an attempt to hedge its net investment in these subsidiaries? How are these reported in Ford's financial statements? What is Ford's reasoning for entering into such investments?

Appendix A: Illustration: Translation with Noncontrolling Interest

The Pat and Star illustration provided an introduction to translation and consolidation procedures for foreign subsidiaries, but it omitted some important aspects of accounting for foreign subsidiaries. For example, intercompany profits, noncontrolling interests, long-term intercompany advances, and funds flow were not covered in that illustration. The following illustration provides an extended translation and consolidation example that includes noncontrolling interests, intercompany profits, and long-term intercompany advances. The statement of cash flows is illustrated in Appendix B of this chapter.

Background Information

Pacific Corporation acquired a 90% interest in Sea Corporation, a foreign company, for $232,500 on January 1, 2006. The exchange rate on that date was $0.15 per LCU, and Sea's stockholders' equity consisted of 1,000,000 LCU capital stock and 500,000 LCU retained earnings. Pacific designated Sea's functional currency to be the subsidiary's local currency unit.

COST/BOOK VALUE DIFFERENTIAL The excess cost over book value from Pacific's investment in Sea Corporation is a patent with a 10-year amortization period. Computations are as follows:

Investment in Sea	$232,500
Book value acquired	
(1,500,000 LCU × $0.15 exchange rate × 90%)	202,500
Patent in dollars	$ 30,000
Patent in LCUs ($30,000 ÷ $0.15) = 200,000 LCU	

EXCHANGE RATES Relevant exchange rates for 2006 are as follows:

Current exchange rate January 1, 2006	$0.150
Average exchange rate for 2006	0.160
Exchange rate for dividends	0.160
Current exchange rate December 31, 2006	0.170

Translation and Consolidation in the Year of Acquisition

Exhibit 13-8 presents a translation worksheet based on Sea Corporation's adjusted trial balance in LCUs at December 31, 2006. The translation is based on the background information provided, and the procedures are comparable to those illustrated earlier in the chapter.

In interpreting Sea's U.S.-dollar financial statements, one must consider the existence of the 10% noncontrolling interest. For example, compare Sea's stockholders' equity at the beginning and end of 2006:

EXHIBIT 13-8

Translation
Worksheet—2006

SEA CORPORATION TRANSLATION WORKSHEET AT AND FOR THE YEAR ENDED DECEMBER 31, 2006

	LCUs	Exchange Rate	U.S. Dollars
Cash	10,000	$0.170	$ 1,700
Accounts receivable	40,000	0.170	6,800
Inventories	150,000	0.170	25,500
Land	250,000	0.170	42,500
Buildings	700,000	0.170	119,000
Equipment	1,000,000	0.170	170,000
Cost of sales	700,000	0.160	112,000
Depreciation expense	200,000	0.160	32,000
Operating expenses	150,000	0.160	24,000
Dividends	100,000	0.160	16,000
	3,300,000		$549,500
Accumulated depreciation—buildings	100,000	$0.170	$ 17,000
Accumulated depreciation—equipment	300,000	0.170	51,000
Accounts payable	200,000	0.170	34,000
Capital stock	1,000,000	0.150	150,000
Retained earnings	500,000	0.150	75,000
Sales	1,200,000	0.160	192,000
Equity adjustment on translation			30,500
	3,300,000		$549,500

	January 1	December 31
Capital stock	$150,000	$150,000
Retained earnings	75,000	83,000
Equity adjustment	—	30,500
Stockholders' equity	$225,000	$263,500

The $8,000 increase in Sea's retained earnings comes from Sea's $24,000 net income less $16,000 dividends for 2006. Sea's stockholders' equity increased by the $30,500 equity adjustment, for a total stockholders' equity increase of $38,500. Sea's stockholders' equity at December 31, 2006, can be allocated between majority and noncontrolling interests as follows:

	90% to Pacific	10% to Noncontrolling Interests	Total
Stockholders' equity January 1	$202,500	$22,500	$225,000
Net income	21,600	2,400	24,000
Dividends	(14,400)	(1,600)	(16,000)
Equity adjustment	27,450	3,050	30,500
Stockholders' equity December 31	$237,150	$26,350	$263,500

Pacific's underlying equity in Sea Corporation is $237,150 at December 31, 2006, and its investment in Sea account should equal the underlying equity plus $30,600 unamortized patent (200,000 LCU × 90% unamortized × $0.170 exchange rate) or $267,750.

ONE-LINE CONSOLIDATION IN YEAR OF ACQUISITION Pacific Corporation makes the following one-line consolidation entries in accounting for its investment in Sea for 2006:

Cash $14,400
    Investment in Sea $14,400
      To record dividends ($16,000 × 90%).

Investment in Sea $49,650
    Other comprehensive income: translation adjustment $31,250
    Income from Sea   18,400
      To record income from Sea ($24,000 reported income × 90% − $3,200
        patent amortization [(200,000 LCU × $0.16 average rate)
        ÷ 10 years)] equals $18,400.

The $31,250 increase in other comprehensive income on the parent's books has two components and is computed as follows:

Equity adjustment from translation (from the subsidiary's translation worksheet) multiplied by the parent's ownership percentage is $30,500 × .90 = $27,450.

Equity adjustment related to the change in the patent translated dollar amount from the beginning to the end of the year:

Beginning patent 200,000 LCU × .15	$30,000
Less: Current period amortization	3,200
	$26,800
Current period equity adjustment to adjust Patent to ending exchange rate	3,800
Ending patent 180,000 LCU × .17	$30,600

These two pieces added together equal the credit to other comprehensive income of $31,250 in the journal entry above.

The Investment in Sea account at December 31, 2006, has a balance of $267,750. This balance consists of the $232,500 cost on January 1 plus $49,650 (the total of the equity adjustment and income share for 2006), less $14,400 dividends received. Alternatively, the balance of the investment account can be checked by adding $30,600 unamortized patent value at December 31, 2006 (180,000 LCU patent × $0.17 current exchange rate) to 90% of Sea's $263,500 stockholders' equity on that date. Remember that the equity adjustment from translation account in the subsidiary's U.S.-dollar financial statements is a stockholders' equity account. This account may have a positive (credit) balance or negative (debit) balance, depending on the direction of exchange rate movements.

CONSOLIDATION IN YEAR OF ACQUISITION Working papers to consolidate the financial statements of Pacific Corporation and its subsidiary at and for the year ended December 31, 2006, are presented in Exhibit 13-9.

In examining the consolidation worksheet, observe that the consolidated equity adjustment from translation is equal to Pacific Corporation's equity adjustment. That equity adjustment consists of 90% of Sea's $30,500 equity adjustment plus the $3,800 equity adjustment from the patent. Under a one-line consolidation, the parent-company equity adjustment balance is equal to the consolidated equity adjustment balance.

Entry a eliminates income and dividends from Sea and returns the investment account to its beginning balance plus the $31,250 equity adjustment.

a	Income from Sea (–SE)	$ 18,400	
	Dividends (+SE)		$14,400
	Investment in Sea (–A)		4,000

Although working paper entry a is relatively unaffected by the existence of the noncontrolling interest, entry b is subject to some complications that require explanation. Entry b is reproduced in general journal form for convenient reference.

b	Capital stock—Sea (–SE)	$150,000	
	Retained earnings—Sea (beginning) (–SE)	75,000	
	Equity adjustment—Sea (–SE)	30,500	
	Patent (+A)	33,800	
	Investment in Sea (–A)		$263,750
	Noncontrolling interest (beginning) (–L)		25,550

The $33,800 patent amount in entry b is equal to beginning-of-the-period patent of $30,000 plus the $3,800 equity adjustment from the patent for 2006. The $263,750 Investment in Sea amount in entry b is equal to the $232,500 beginning-of-the-period amount (cost) plus Pacific's $31,250 equity adjustment from translation. Finally, the $25,550 beginning noncontrolling interest amount is equal to Sea Corporation's $225,000 stockholders' equity at the beginning of the period plus Sea's $30,500 equity adjustment from translation times 10%.

EXHIBIT 13-9

Consolidation Working Papers—2006

PACIFIC CORPORATION AND SUBSIDIARY
CONSOLIDATION WORKSHEET FOR THE YEAR ENDED DECEMBER 31, 2006

	Pacific	90% Sea	Adjustments and Eliminations Debit	Adjustments and Eliminations Credit	Consolidated Statements
Income Statement Sales	$ 600,000	$192,000			$ 792,000
Income from Sea	18,400		a 18,400		0
Cost of sales	(300,000)	(112,000)			(412,000)
Depreciation	(120,000)	(32,000)			(152,000)
Operating expense	(68,400)	(24,000)	c 3,200		(95,600)
Noncontrolling interest expense			d 2,400		(2,400)
Net income	$ 130,000	$ 24,000			$ 130,000
Retained earnings Retained earnings	$ 120,000	75,000	b 75,000		$ 120,000
Net income	130,000	24,000			130,000
Dividends	(50,000)	(16,000)		a 14,400 d 1,600	(50,000)
Retained earnings—December 31, 2006	$ 200,000	$ 83,000			$ 200,000
Balance Sheet Cash	$ 12,250	$ 1,700			$ 13,950
Accounts receivable	40,000	6,800			46,800
Inventories	80,000	25,500			105,500
Land	50,000	42,500			92,500
Buildings—net	150,000	102,000			252,000
Equipment—net	400,000	119,000			519,000
Investment in Sea	267,750			a 4,000 b 263,750	
Patent			b 33,800	c 3,200	30,600
Total assets	$1,000,000	$297,500			$1,060,350
Accounts payable	68,750	34,000			102,750
Capital stock	700,000	150,000	b 150,000		700,000
Retained earnings	200,000	83,000			200,000
Accumulated other comprehensive income—equity adjustment	31,250	30,500	b 30,500		31,250
Noncontrolling interest, January 1				b 25,550	
Noncontrolling interest, December 31				d 800	26,350
Total equities	$1,000,000	$297,500			$1,060,350

EXHIBIT 13-10

Translation Worksheets—2007

TRANSLATION WORKSHEETS FOR SEA CORPORATION

	December 31, 2006			December 31, 2007		
	LCUs	Exchange Rate	U.S. Dollars	LCUs	Exchange Rate	U.S. Dollars
Cash	10,000	$0.170	$ 1,700	15,000	$0.190	$ 2,850
Accounts receivable	40,000	0.170	6,800	25,000	0.190	4,750
Inventories	150,000	0.170	25,500	80,000	0.190	15,200
Inventories				120,000	0.175	21,000
Advance to Pacific				300,000	0.190	57,000
Land	250,000	0.170	42,500	250,000	0.190	47,500
Buildings	700,000	0.170	119,000	700,000	0.190	133,000
Equipment	1,000,000	0.170	170,000	1,000,000	0.190	190,000
Equipment (new)				200,000	0.190	38,000
Cost of sales	700,000	0.160	112,000	480,000	0.180	86,400
Cost of sales				360,000	0.175	63,000
Depreciation expense	200,000	0.160	32,000	200,000	0.180	36,000
Operating expenses	150,000	0.160	24,000	170,000	0.180	30,600
Dividends	100,000	0.160	16,000	100,000	0.180	18,000
	3,300,000		$549,500	4,000,000		$743,300
Accumulated depreciation—buildings	100,000	$0.170	$ 17,000	150,000	$0.190	$ 28,500
Accumulated depreciation—equipment	300,000	0.170	51,000	450,000	0.190	85,500
Accounts payable	200,000	0.170	34,000	250,000	0.190	47,500
Notes payable				200,000	0.190	38,000
Capital stock	1,000,000	0.150	150,000	1,000,000	0.150	150,000
Retained earnings	500,000	0.150	75,000	550,000		83,000
Sales	1,200,000	0.160	192,000	1,385,000	0.180	249,300
Interest income				15,000	0.180	2,700
Equity adjustment			30,500			58,800
	3,300,000		$549,500	4,000,000		$743,300

To generalize, in the working paper entry to eliminate reciprocal investment and stockholders' equity balances and enter beginning-of-the-period unamortized cost/book value differentials and noncontrolling interest, the amounts entered are the usual beginning-of-the-period amounts adjusted for end-of-the-period equity adjustments from translation. Translation adjustments under the current rate method do not enter into the computations of noncontrolling interest income and consolidated net income, so the complications are limited to balance sheet items.

Entry c provides for the current year's patent amortization at the average exchange rate [(200,000 LCU × $0.160) ÷ 10 years]:

c	Operating expenses (+E, −SE)	$ 3,200	
	Patent (−A)		$ 3,200
d	Noncontrolling interest expense	$ 2,400	
	Dividends		$ 1,600
	Noncontrolling interest		$ 800

Translation and Consolidation in Year After Acquisition

Pacific Corporation held its 90% interest in Sea Corporation throughout 2007, and the only stockholders' equity changes of the two affiliated entities resulted from income, dividends, and equity adjustments from translation. Exhibit 13-10 presents a translation worksheet based on Sea's adjusted trial balance in LCUs at December 31, 2007. Other information related to 2007 is summarized in the paragraphs that follow.

Exchange Rates Relevant exchange rates for 2007 (and those from 2006 for convenient reference) are as follows:

	2006	2007
Current exchange rate January 1	$0.150	$0.170
Exchange rate for intercompany sales	—	0.175
Average exchange rate	0.160	0.180
Exchange rate for advance	—	0.180
Exchange rate for dividends	0.160	0.180
Current exchange rate December 31	0.170	0.190

ADVANCE FROM SUBSIDIARY Sea Corporation made a 300,000 LCU advance to Pacific on July 1, 2007. This advance is long-term, denominated in LCUs, and bears interest at 10% per year. Pacific Corporation recorded the advance at $54,000 on July 1 but adjusted the advance to $57,000 to reflect current exchange rates at December 31, 2007. The related debit of $3,000 was to Pacific's comprehensive income: equity adjustment account, as required by *FASB Statement No. 52* for translation adjustments from long-term intercompany balances and *Statement No. 130* dealing with comprehensive income.

PLANT ASSET ACQUISITIONS Neither Pacific Corporation nor Sea Corporation had plant disposals during 2006 or 2007, but both companies had acquisitions during 2007. Pacific purchased buildings for $80,000 and equipment for $150,000. Sea purchased equipment for 200,000 LCU at December 31, 2007, issuing a note payable for the purchase price, which is denominated in LCUs. A summary of plant asset changes for Pacific Corporation and Sea Corporation for 2007 is as follows:

	Land		Buildings—Net		Equipment—Net	
2007	**Pacific**	**Sea**	**Pacific**	**Sea**	**Pacific**	**Sea**
Balance January 1	$50,000	$42,500	$150,000	$102,000	$400,000	$119,000
Acquisitions	0	0	80,000	0	150,000	38,000
Depreciation	0	0	(50,000)	(9,000)	(100,000)	(27,000)
Exchange adjustment	0	5,000	0	11,500	0	12,500
Balance December 31	$50,000	$47,500	$180,000	$104,500	$450,000	$142,500

INTERCOMPANY SALES Pacific Corporation sold inventory items that cost $70,000 to Sea Corporation for $84,000, denominated in dollars, during 2007, when the exchange rate for LCUs was $0.175. Sea measured its purchases and accounts payable at 480,000 LCU ($84,000 ÷ $0.175), sold 360,000 LCU of the merchandise during 2007 and included 120,000 LCU in its inventory at December 31, 2007.

TRANSLATION The translation worksheet presented in Exhibit 13-10 repeats the 2006 translation data and shows the translation for 2007. The difference between the $58,800 translation adjustment at year-end 2007 and the $30,500 translation adjustment at year-end 2006 is $28,300, the increase in the equity adjustment from translation for 2007. This increase is allocated 90% to Pacific and 10% to noncontrolling interest.

ONE-LINE CONSOLIDATION IN YEAR AFTER ACQUISITION Pacific Corporation makes the following one-line consolidation entries in accounting for its investment in Sea for 2007:

Cash (+A)	$16,200	
Investment in Sea (−A)		$16,200
To record dividends received ($18,000 × 90%).		

Investment in Sea (+A)	$54,170	
Comprehensive income: equity adjustment from		
translation (+OCI, +SE)		$28,870
Income from Sea (+SE)		25,300

To record income from Sea [($36,000 × 90%) − $3,600 patent amortization − $3,500 unrealized inventory profit] and equity adjustment [($28,300 × 90%) + $3,400 from patent].

In addition, Pacific makes the following entry to adjust its Advance from Sea account at year-end:

Comprehensive income: equity adjustment (−OCI, −SE)	$ 3,000	
Advance from Sea (+L)		$3,000

To adjust the advance from $54,000 to $57,000 to recognize a $0.01 exchange rate change on the 300,000 LCU liability to Sea.

The balance of Pacific Corporation's Investment in Sea account at December 31, 2007, is $305,720, equal to 90% of Sea Corporation's $309,800 stockholders' equity on that date, plus $30,400 unamortized patent, less $3,500 unrealized inventory profit. Alternatively, the $305,720 Investment in Sea account balance is equal to its $267,750 beginning balance, less $16,200 dividends received, plus $25,300 income from Sea, plus $28,870 equity adjustment from translation.

Consolidation in Year After Acquisition

Exhibit 13-11 presents consolidation working papers for Pacific Corporation and Subsidiary. These working papers are complicated by the existence of intercompany transactions and reciprocal items, but no new consolidation procedures are introduced.

Working paper entries a and b of Exhibit 13-11 eliminate intercompany profits from Pacific Corporation's sales to Sea Corporation.

a Sales (−R, −SE)	$84,000	
Cost of sales (−E, +SE)		$84,000
b Cost of sales (+E, −SE)	$ 3,500	
Inventories (−A)		$ 3,500

Entry a eliminates the $84,000 transfer price from sales and cost of sales, and entry b defers recognition of the $3,500 unrealized profit in Sea's ending inventory. The intercompany sales in dollars are analyzed as follows:

	Transfer Price		Cost 5/6	Intercompany Profit 1/6
	In LCUs	**In Dollars**		
Sold by Sea 75%	360,000	$63,000	$52,500	$10,500
Inventoried by Sea 25%	120,000	21,000	17,500	3,500
Total	480,000	$84,000	$70,000	$14,000

The translation worksheet in Exhibit 13-10 shows translation of the 120,000 LCU inventory and 360,000 LCU cost of sales at the $0.175 historical exchange rate at the time of transfer. These items are separated from other inventory and cost of sales items, which are translated at current and average exchange rates, respectively. Paragraph 25 of *FASB Statement No. 52* provides that

> the elimination of intercompany profits that are attributable to sales or other transfers
> between entities that are consolidated, combined, or accounted for by the equity method
> in the enterprise's financial statements shall be based on the exchange rates at the dates
> of the sales or transfers. The use of reasonable approximations or averages is permitted.

When the inventory and cost of sales accounts are translated at historical exchange rates, the inventory profit elimination for a foreign subsidiary is the same as for a domestic subsidiary, and no complications arise in the working papers.

Entry c eliminates income and dividends and returns the investment account to its beginning-of-the-period balance of $267,750 plus the $28,870 equity adjustment for 2007.

c Income from Sea (−SE)	$ 25,300	
Dividends (+SE)		$ 16,200
Investment in Sea (−A)		9,100

Working paper entry d from Exhibit 13-11 is relatively complex and is reproduced in general journal form for convenient reference and analysis as follows:

d Capital stock—Sea (−SE)	$150,000	
Retained earnings—Sea (beginning) (−SE)	83,000	
Equity adjustment—Sea (−SE)	58,800	
Patent (+A)	34,000	
Investment in Sea (−A)		$296,620
Noncontrolling interest (beginning) (+L)		29,180

EXHIBIT 13-11

Consolidation Working Papers—2007

PACIFIC CORPORATION AND SUBSIDIARY CONSOLIDATION WORKSHEET
FOR THE YEAR ENDED DECEMBER 31, 2007

	Pacific	90% Sea	Adjustments and Eliminations Debit	Credit	Consolidated Statements
Income Statement Sales	$ 700,000	$249,300	a 84,000		$ 865,300
Income from Sea	25,300		c 25,300		
Interest income		2,700	f 2,700		
Cost of sales	(400,000)	(149,400)	b 3,500	a 84,000	(468,900)
Depreciation	(150,000)	(36,000)			(186,000)
Operating expense	(72,600)	(30,600)	e 3,600		(106,800)
Interest expense	(2,700)			f 2,700	
Noncontrolling interest expense			i 3,600		(3,600)
Net income	**$ 100,000**	**$36,000**			**$ 100,000**
Retained earnings Retained earnings	$ 200,000	83,000	d 83,000		$ 200,000
Net income	**100,000**	**36,000**			**100,000**
Dividends	(50,000)	(18,000)		c 16,200 i 1,800	(50,000)
Retained Earnings—December 31, 2007	**$ 250,000**	**$101,000**			**$ 250,000**
Balance Sheet Cash	$ 4,280	$ 2,850			$ 7,130
Accounts receivable	30,000	4,750		h 9,500	25,250
Inventories	100,000	36,200		b 3,500	132,700
Advance to Pacific		57,000		g 57,000	
Land	50,000	47,500			97,500
Buildings—net	180,000	104,500			284,500
Equipment—net	450,000	142,500			592,500
Investment in Sea	305,720			c 9,100 d 296,620	
Patent			d 34,000	e 3,600	30,400
Total assets	$1,120,000	$395,300			$1,169,980
Accounts payable	55,880	47,500	h 9,500		93,880
Advance from Sea	57,000		g 57,000		
Note payable		38,000			38,000
Capital stock	700,000	150,000	d 150,000		700,000

(continued)

EXHIBIT 13-11

Consolidation Working Papers—2007 *(Continued)*

PACIFIC CORPORATION AND SUBSIDIARY CONSOLIDATION WORKSHEET
FOR THE YEAR ENDED DECEMBER 31, 2007

	Pacific	90% Sea	Adjustments and Eliminations Debit	Adjustments and Eliminations Credit	Consolidated Statements
Retained Earnings	**250,000**	**101,000**			**250,000**
Accumulated other comprehensive income—equity adjustment*	57,120	58,800	d 58,800		57,120
Noncontrolling interest, January 1				d 29,180	
Noncontrolling interest, December 31				i 1,800	30,980
Total equities	$1,120,000	$395,300			$1,169,980

*Pacific's equity adjustment (90% × $58,800 equity adjustment) + $7,200 patent adjustment − $3,000 advance adjustment.

The $34,000 debit to patent is equal to the $30,600 beginning-of-the-period unamortized patent plus $3,400 equity adjustment to patent for the period. For convenience, the $34,000 patent amount may be calculated as patent amortization for the period (20,000 LCU × $0.18) plus unamortized patent at year-end (160,000 LCU × $0.19).

The $29,180 noncontrolling interest at January 1, 2007, is 10% of Sea Corporation's capital stock and retained earnings at January 1, 2007, plus $58,800 equity adjustment at December 31, 2007, or 10% × ($150,000 + $83,000 + $58,800). The change in Sea's equity adjustment for the period is reflected in the beginning noncontrolling interest amount because neither noncontrolling interest income nor dividends reflect translation adjustments. The $30,980 noncontrolling interest at December 31, 2007, can be confirmed by comparing it with 10% of Sea's $309,800 stockholders' equity at year-end 2007.

Entry e enters the current year's amortization (200,000 LCU × $0.18 average exchange rate), and entry f eliminates interest on the intercompany advance.

e	**Operating expenses (+E, −SE)**	**$3,600**	
	Patent (−A)		**$3,600**
f	**Interest income (−R, −SE)**	**$2,700**	
	Interest expense (−E, +SE)		**$2,700**

Working paper entry g debits advance from Sea for $57,000 and credits advance to Pacific for $57,000. The elimination of these reciprocal items requires no change in working paper procedures even though both amounts reflect a $3,000 increase because the 300,000 LCU ($54,000) advance was made on July 1, 2007. The $3,000 increase in Sea's advance to Pacific is reflected in the $58,800 equity adjustment in Sea Corporation's U.S.-dollar financial statements, and the $3,000 increase in Pacific's advance from Sea is recorded by Pacific as a direct debit to its equity adjustment account.

Pacific Corporation's $57,120 equity adjustment from translation at December 31, 2007, is equal to the consolidated equity adjustment from translation on that date. The amount is calculated as follows:

	2007	2006
PACIFIC CORPORATION AND SUBSIDIARY		
COMPARATIVE CONSOLIDATED FINANCIAL STATEMENTS		
FOR THE YEARS ENDED DECEMBER 31, 2007 AND 2006		
Income Statement		
Sales	$ 865,300	$ 792,000
Cost of sales	(468,900)	(412,000)
Depreciation expense	(186,000)	(152,000)
Operating expense	(106,800)	(95,600)
Noncontrolling income	(3,600)	(2,400)
Net income	100,000	130,000
Other comprehensive income:		
Foreign currency translation adjustment	25,870	31,250
Comprehensive income	$ 125,870	$ 161,250
Retained Earnings		
Retained earnings January 1	$ 200,000	$ 120,000
Net income	100,000	130,000
Dividends	(50,000)	(50,000)
Retained earnings December 31	$ 250,000	$ 200,000
Balance Sheet		
Cash	$ 7,130	$ 13,950
Accounts receivable	25,250	46,800
Inventories	132,700	105,500
Land	97,500	92,500
Buildings—net	284,500	252,000
Equipment—net	592,500	519,000
Patent	30,400	30,600
Total assets	$1,169,980	$1,060,350
Accounts payable	$ 93,880	$ 102,750
Note payable	38,000	0
Capital stock	700,000	700,000
Retained earnings	250,000	200,000
Accumulated other comprehensive income: equity adjustment	57,120	31,250
Noncontrolling interest	30,980	26,350
Total equities	$1,169,980	$1,060,350

EXHIBIT 13-12

Comparative
Financial Statements

Sea's $58,800 equity adjustment at December 31, 2007, × 90%	$52,920
Equity adjustment from patent—2006	3,800
Equity adjustment from patent—2007	3,400
Equity adjustment from advance—2007	(3,000)
Pacific's equity adjustment December 31, 2007	$57,120

Exhibit 13-12 presents comparative consolidated financial statements for Pacific Corporation and Subsidiary for 2007 and 2006. This information provides a convenient summary and comparison of the consolidated financial statement amounts.

Appendix B: Statement of Cash Flows

LEARNING
OBJECTIVE 11

The consolidated statement of cash flows (SCF) for a U.S. parent company and a foreign subsidiary is complicated by the existence of translation adjustments. Individual translation adjustments for the assets and liabilities have to be determined so that their effects can be eliminated in determining the cash flows for a period.

Illustration of a Consolidated Statement of Cash Flows for a Foreign Subsidiary and a U.S. Parent Company

Pac Corporation is a U.S. Company that purchased all the outstanding shares of Soy Corporation for $40,500 on January 1, 2006. Soy is a foreign corporation and its functional currency is its local currency, the LCU. The stockholders' equity of Soy on January 1, 2006, consisted of 2,000,000 LCU capital stock and 200,000 LCU retained earnings. The exchange rate for LCUs on January 1, 2006, was $0.018.

Cost/Book Value Differential The excess cost over the book value of Pac's investment in Soy is a patent with a five-year amortization period. Patent value from Pac's investment in Soy is computed as follows:

Investment in Soy	$40,500
Book value and fair value acquired (2,200,000 LCU stockholders' equity × $0.018 exchange rate)	39,600
Patent in U.S. dollars	$ 900
Patent in LCUs ($900 ÷ $0.018)	50,000 LCU

Exchange Rates for 2006 and 2007 Exchange rates for the two years are as follows:

	2006	2007
Current exchange rate January 1	$0.018	$0.020
Average exchange rate for year	0.019	0.021
Exchange rate for dividends	0.020	0.022
Current exchange rate December 31	0.020	0.022

Patent Computations for 2006 Patent amortization is computed as the patent value in LCUs divided by the amortization period times the average exchange rate for the period:

$$50,000 \text{ LCU} \div 5 \text{ years} \times \$0.019 \text{ average exchange rate} = \underline{\$190}$$

The unamortized patent under the current rate method is computed as the end-of-the-period balance of the patent in LCUs times the December 31, 2006, exchange rate:

$$(50,000 \text{ LCU} - 10,000 \text{ LCU amortization}) \times \$0.020 = \underline{\$800}$$

The equity adjustment from translation of the patent for 2006 is computed as follows:

Beginning patent balance	$900
Less: Patent amortization for 2006	(190)
Less: Ending unamortized patent	(800)
Equity adjustment from patent	$ (90)

Patent Computations for 2007 Patent amortization is computed as follows:

$$50,000 \text{ LCU} \div 5 \text{ years} \times \$0.021 \text{ average exchange rate} = \underline{\$210}$$

The unamortized patent at December 31, 2007, is:

$$30,000 \text{ LCU} \times \$0.022 \text{ current rate} = \underline{\$660}$$

The equity adjustment for the translation of the patent for 2007 is computed as follows:

Beginning patent balance	$800
Less: Patent amortization for 2007	(210)
Less: Unamortized patent at December 31, 2007	(660)
Equity adjustment from patent	$ (70)

Translation Worksheets Translation worksheets of Soy Corporation for 2006 and 2007 are presented in Exhibit 13-13.

EXHIBIT 13-13

Translation Worksheets for 2006 and 2007

TRANSLATION WORKSHEETS FOR SOY COMPANY

	For 2006			For 2007		
	LCUs	Exchange Rate	U.S. Dollars	LCUs	Exchange Rate	U.S. Dollars
Cash	590,000	$0.020	$11,800	800,000	$0.022	$17,600
Accounts receivable—net	310,000	0.020	6,200	350,000	0.022	7,700
Inventories	600,000	0.020	12,000	650,000	0.022	14,300
Plant assets—net	900,000	0.020	18,000	800,000	0.022	17,600
Cost of sales	300,000	0.019	5,700	350,000	0.021	7,350
Depreciation expense	100,000	0.019	1,900	100,000	0.021	2,100
Operating expenses	200,000	0.019	3,800	250,000	0.021	5,250
Dividends	200,000	0.020	4,000	200,000	0.022	4,400
Equity adjustment			0			0
	3,200,000		$63,400	3,500,000		$76,300
Accounts payable	100,000	$0.020	$ 2,000	200,000	$0.022	$ 4,400
Capital stock	2,000,000	0.018	36,000	2,000,000	0.018	36,000
Retained earnings	200,000	0.018	3,600	300,000	*	5,300
Sales	900,000	0.019	17,100	1,000,000	0.021	21,000
Equity adjustment year-end 2006			4,700			4,700
Equity adjustment increase 2007						4,900
	3,200,000		$63,400	3,500,000		$76,300

*Measured.

INVESTMENT IN SOY ACCOUNT BALANCE Soy reports income of $5,700 in 2006 ($17,100 sales – $5,700 cost of sales – $1,900 depreciation expense – $3,800 operating expenses) and income of $6,300 in 2007 ($21,000 sales – $7,350 cost of sales – $2,100 depreciation expense – $5,250 operating expenses). The Investment in Soy account for 2006 and 2007 is analyzed as follows:

Investment cost January 1, 2006		$40,500
Add: Income from Soy 2006:		
Equity in reported income	$5,700	
Less: Patent amortization	(190)	5,510
Less: 2006 dividends		(4,000)
		42,010
Equity adjustment from translation and from patent ($4,700 + $90)		4,790
Investment in Soy balance December 31, 2006		46,800
Add: Income from Soy for 2007:		
Equity in reported income	$6,300	
Less: Patent amortization	(210)	6,090
Less: 2007 dividends		(4,400)
		48,490
Equity adjustment from translation and from patent ($4,900 + $70)		4,970
Investment in Soy balance December 31, 2007		$53,460

CONSOLIDATION WORKING PAPERS Consolidation working papers for Pac Company and Subsidiary for 2006 and 2007 are presented in Exhibits 13-14 and 13-15, respectively. Pac's separate financial statements are introduced in the first column of the working papers, and Soy's financial statements are prepared from the worksheets in Exhibit 13-13.

EXHIBIT 13-14

Consolidation
Working Papers—
2006

PAC CORPORATION AND SUBSIDIARY
CONSOLIDATION WORKING PAPERS
FOR THE YEAR ENDED DECEMBER 31, 2006

	Pac	Soy	Adjustments and Eliminations		Consolidated Statements
Income Statement Sales	$ 57,000	$17,100			$ 74,100
Income from Soy	5,510		a 5,510		
Cost of sales	(18,000)	(5,700)			(23,700)
Depreciation expense	(12,000)	(1,900)			(13,900)
Other operating expenses	(10,000)	(3,800)			(13,800)
Patent amortization			c 190		(190)
Net income	**$ 22,510**	**$ 5,700**			**$ 22,510**
Retained Earnings Retained earnings—Pac	$ 85,000				$ 85,000
Retained earnings—Soy		$ 3,600	b 3,600		
Net income	**22,510**	**5,700**			**22,510**
Dividends	(20,000)	(4,000)		a 4,000	(20,000)
Retained earnings— December 31, 2006	**$ 87,510**	**$ 5,300**			**$ 87,510**
Balance Sheet Cash	$ 49,000	$11,800			$ 60,800
Accounts receivable	55,100	6,200			61,300
Inventories	67,800	12,000			79,800
Plant assets—net	100,000	18,000			118,000
Investment in Soy	46,800			a 1,510 b 45,290	
Patent			b 990	c 190	800
Total assets	$318,700	$48,000			$320,700
Accounts payable	$ 26,400	$ 2,000			$ 28,400
Capital stock	200,000	36,000	b 36,000		200,000
Retained earnings	**87,510**	**5,300**			**87,510**
Accumulated other comprehensive income: equity adjustment from translation	4,790	4,700	b 4,700		4,790
Total equities	$318,700	$48,000			$320,700

EXHIBIT 13-15

Consolidation
Working Papers—
2007

PAC CORPORATION AND SUBSIDIARY
CONSOLIDATION WORKING PAPERS
FOR THE YEAR ENDED DECEMBER 31, 2007

	Pac	Soy	Adjustments and Eliminations				Consolidated Statements
Income Statement							
Sales	$ 57,000	$21,000					$ 78,000
Income from Soy	6,090		a	6,090			
Cost of sales	(18,000)	(7,350)					(25,350)
Depreciation expense	(12,000)	(2,100)					(14,100)
Other operating expenses	(10,000)	(5,250)					(15,250)
Patent amortization			c	210			(210)
Net income	**$ 23,090**	**$ 6,300**					**$ 23,090**
Retained Earnings							
Retained earnings—Pac	$ 87,510						$ 87,510
Retained earnings—Soy		$ 5,300	b	5,300			
Net income	**23,090**	**6,300**					**23,090**
Dividends	(20,000)	(4,400)			a	4,400	(20,000)
Retained earnings— December 31, 2007	**$ 90,600**	**$ 7,200**					**$ 90,600**
Balance Sheet							
Cash	$ 60,000	$17,600					$ 77,600
Accounts receivable	55,100	7,700					62,800
Inventories	49,800	14,300					64,100
Plant assets—net	108,000	17,600					125,600
Investment in Soy	53,460				a	1,690	
					b	51,770	
Patent			b	870	c	210	660
Total assets	$326,360	$57,200					$330,760
Accounts payable	$ 26,000	$ 4,400					$ 30,400
Capital stock	200,000	36,000	b	36,000			200,000
Retained earnings	**90,600**	**7,200**					**90,600**
Accumulated other comprehensive income: equity adjustment from translation	9,760	9,600	b	9,600			9,760
Total equities	$326,360	$57,200					$330,760

EXHIBIT 13-16

Comparative
Financial Statements
and Year's Change

PAC CORPORATION AND SUBSIDIARY
COMPARATIVE CONSOLIDATED FINANCIAL STATEMENTS
FOR THE YEARS ENDED DECEMBER 31, 2007 AND 2006

	2007	2006	Year's Change 2007–2006
Income Statement			
Sales	$ 78,000	$ 74,100	$ 3,900
Cost of sales	(25,350)	(23,700)	(1,650)
Depreciation expense	(14,100)	(13,900)	(200)
Other expenses	(15,250)	(13,800)	(1,450)
Patent amortization	(210)	(190)	(20)
Net income	$ 23,090	$ 22,510	$ 580
Retained Earnings			
Retained earnings January 1	$ 87,510	$ 85,000	$ 2,510
Net income	23,090	22,510	580
Dividends	(20,000)	(20,000)	
Retained earnings December 31	$ 90,600	$ 87,510	$ 3,090
Balance Sheet			
Cash	$ 77,600	$ 60,800	$16,800
Accounts receivable—net	62,800	61,300	1,500
Inventories	64,100	79,800	(15,700)
Plant assets—net	125,600	118,000	7,600
Patent	660	800	(140)
Total assets	$330,760	$320,700	$10,060
Accounts payable	$ 30,400	$ 28,400	$ 2,000
Capital stock	200,000	200,000	
Retained earnings	90,600	87,510	3,090
Other comprehensive income:			
equity adjustment	9,760	4,790	4,970
Total equities	$330,760	$320,700	$10,060

Exhibit 13-16 is developed from the consolidated financial statements column of the working papers. It shows the year's changes from 2006 to 2007. This information is used in preparing the consolidated statement of cash flows.

As a first step in preparing the SCF, a reconciliation of the individual asset and liability translation adjustments for the year is needed, along with the change in the parent-company (and consolidated) translation adjustment.

TRANSLATION ADJUSTMENTS Individual translation adjustments for cash and other balance sheet items are not needed in preparing the consolidation working papers, but they are needed in preparing the consolidated SCF. Because income statement items are translated at average exchange rates under the current rate method, and assets and liabilities are translated at current exchange rates at the balance sheet date, each individual translation adjustment is ordinarily equal to the beginning balance of the account times the exchange rate change from beginning to midpoint in the year, plus the ending balance of the account times the exchange rate change from midpoint in the year to year-end. For example, the dollar translation adjustment of accounts receivable for 2006 is determined as follows:

	Account Balance	×	Exchange Rate Change	=	Translation Adjustment
January 1, 2007	310,000 LCU		($0.021 avg. − $0.020 beg.)		$310
December 31, 2007	350,000 LCU		($0.022 end − $0.021 avg.)		350
Translation adjustment of accounts receivable					$660

EXHIBIT 13-17

Individual Translation Adjustments

PAC CORPORATION AND SUBSIDIARY
INDIVIDUAL ASSET AND LIABILITY TRANSLATION
ADJUSTMENTS AND RECONCILIATION
AT AND FOR THE YEAR ENDED DECEMBER 31, 2007

	1/1/07 Balance in LCUs A	Rate Change 1st Half B	$ Change 1st Half of 2007 C	12/31/07 Balance in LCUs D	Rate Change 2nd Half E	$ Change 2nd Half of 2007 F	Consolidated Translation Changes C + F
Cash	590,000	$0.001	$ 590	800,000	$0.001	$ 800	$1,390
Cash from dividends				200,000	0.001	200	200
Accounts receivable	310,000	0.001	310	350,000	0.001	350	660
Inventories	600,000	0.001	600	650,000	0.001	650	1,250
Plant assets—net	900,000	0.001	900	800,000	0.001	800	1,700
Patent	40,000	0.001	40	30,000	0.001	30	70
			2,440			2,830	5,270
Accounts payable	100,000	0.001	100	200,000	0.001	200	(300)
Effect of translation changes on consolidated net assets							$4,970

Note: An adjustment of cash is needed for 2007 dividends because the dividend rate of $0.022 is not equal to the average exchange rate for the year.

The translation adjustments for most other asset and liability items can be determined by using the procedure illustrated in Exhibit 13-17. In this example, the exchange rate change for the first half of 2007 is $0.001 ($0.021 average exchange rate less $0.020 beginning-of-the-period exchange rate), and the exchange rate change for the second half of 2007 is also $0.001 ($0.022 end-of-the-period exchange rate less $0.021 average exchange rate).

An exception to the usual procedure for determining the translation adjustments for balance sheet items occurs when actual cash flows differ from cash flows expected under the assumption that all cash receipts and cash disbursements are made at average exchange rates for the year. For example, when historical exchange rates are used for intercompany purchase transactions, those rates must be used in determining the translation adjustments, rather than average rates. A translation adjustment of cash is also needed for dividends, except when they are translated at average exchange rates. The calculation of individual translation adjustments for plant asset items requires special analysis for all acquisitions and disposals during a period.

The translation effect on consolidated net assets for a period is necessarily equal to the effect on consolidated stockholders' equity for that period.

CONSOLIDATED SCF WORKSHEET Exhibit 13-18 presents a worksheet for the consolidated SCF using the indirect format. The Year's Change column in that exhibit reflects consolidated balance sheet changes for Pac Corporation and Subsidiary between December 31, 2006 and 2007. This information was presented earlier in Exhibit 13-16. A second column in the SCF worksheet shows the translation adjustments to individual balance sheet items as illustrated in Exhibit 13-17 and discussed in the preceding paragraph. The third column subtracts column 2 from column 1 to obtain the year's changes without translation adjustments. This information is pivotal in preparing a statement of cash flows for a consolidated entity with foreign subsidiaries. Once the translation effects are eliminated from the year's change information, preparation of the consolidated SCF is essentially the same as for a consolidated entity with only domestic subsidiaries.

EXHIBIT 13-18

Worksheet for Consolidated Statement of Cash Flows

**PAC CORPORATION AND SUBSIDIARY CONSOLIDATED
STATEMENT OF CASH FLOWS WORKSHEET
FOR THE YEAR ENDED DECEMBER 31, 2007**

	Year's Change 2007–2006	Translation Adjustments	Year's Change Less Translation Adjustments	Cash Flows from Operating Activities	Cash Flows from Investing Activities	Cash Flows from Financing Activities
Balance Sheet						
Cash	$ 16,800	$1,590*	$ 15,210			
Accounts receivable	1,500	660	840	$ (840)		
Inventories	(15,700)	1,250	(16,950)	16,950		
Plant assets—net	7,600	1,700	5,900	14,100	$(20,000)	
Patent	(140)	70	(210)	210		
Total assets	$ 10,060	$5,270	$ 4,790			
Accounts payable	$ 2,000	$ 300	$ 1,700	1,700		
Capital stock	0	0	0			
Retained earnings	3,090	0	3,090	23,090		$(20,000)
Equity adjustment	4,970	4,970				
Total equities	$ 10,060	$5,270	$ 4,790			
				$55,210	$(20,000)	$(20,000)

*Presented in the SCF immediately below cash flows from financing activities.

Items in the Year's Change Less Translation Adjustments column of Exhibit 13-18 are analyzed and carried to the Cash Flows from Operating Activities, Cash Flows from Investing Activities, or Cash Flows from Financing Activities columns, as appropriate. Information for consolidated net income, noncontrolling interest income, dividends, and depreciation is obtained from the consolidated income and retained earnings statements. Other information relating to plant asset purchases, patent amortization, and noncontrolling interest dividends is found in the consolidated working papers for 2006 and in the background information for the illustration.

The consolidated SCF of Pac Corporation and Subsidiary for 2007 is presented in Exhibit 13-19. This statement is developed directly from the completed worksheet in Exhibit 13-18. The $1,590 translation adjustment of cash is shown as a separate line item immediately below the "cash flows from financing activities" section of the SCF.

Summary

Before a consolidated statement of cash flows for a parent company and its foreign subsidiary can be prepared, the effects of individual translation adjustments for assets and liabilities must be identified. These adjustments are combined and reported as a separate line item under the heading "effect of exchange rate changes on cash."

LEARNING OBJECTIVE 12

Appendix C: Lower-of-Cost-or-Market Rule to Remeasure Inventories

Nonmonetary assets carried at cost are remeasured at historical rates and those carried at market are remeasured at current rates when the foreign entity's books of record are not maintained in the functional currency. Special care must be exercised in applying the lower-of-cost-or-market rule to inventories in remeasured statements because remeasured amounts are affected both by changes in exchange rates and by changes in replacement costs.

EXHIBIT 13-19

Consolidated
Statement of Cash
Flows

PAC CORPORATION AND SUBSIDIARY
CONSOLIDATED STATEMENT OF CASH FLOWS
FOR THE YEAR ENDED DECEMBER 31, 2007

Cash Flows from Operating Activities		
Consolidated net income		$23,090
Noncash expenses, revenues, losses, and gains		
included in income:		
Depreciation	$ 14,100	
Patent amortization	210	
Increase in accounts receivable	(840)	
Increase in accounts payable	1,700	
Decrease in inventories	16,950	32,120
Net cash flows from operating activities		55,210
Cash Flows from Investing Activities		
Purchase of equipment	$(20,000)	
Net cash used in investing activities		(20,000)
Cash Flows from Financing Activities		
Dividends to Pac's stockholders	$(20,000)	
Net cash used in financing activities		(20,000)
Effect of exchange rate changes on cash		1,590
Net increase in cash		16,800
Cash and cash equivalents at beginning of year		60,800
Cash and cash equivalents at end of year		$77,600

Write-downs to market may be appropriate for both foreign currency statements and remeasured statements, for foreign currency statements but not remeasured statements, or for remeasured statements but not foreign currency statements. These three possibilities are illustrated as follows:

	Foreign Currency Units	Exchange Rate	U.S. Dollars
Case A: Inventory carried at market in both foreign currency statements and remeasured statements			
Cost	1,000	$1.80 H	$1,800
Replacement cost	**950**	1.85 C	**1,758**
Case B: Inventory carried at market in foreign currency statements, but cost in remeasured statements			
Cost	1,000	$1.80 H	**$1,800**
Replacement cost	**950**	1.92 C	1,824
Case C: Inventory carried at cost in foreign currency statements, but market in remeasured statements			
Cost	950	$1.92 H	$1,824
Replacement cost	1,000	1.80 C	**1,800**

As noted earlier, the H and C designations represent historical rates and current rates, respectively. In each of the three cases, it is assumed that replacement cost falls between the ceiling and the floor as required by *ARB No. 43*, Chapter 4. The write-downs to market in cases A and C are the result of applying the lower-of-cost-or-market rule in remeasurement statements and are reflected in cost of sales.

SELECTED READINGS

DeMoville, Wig, and Roben Hatami. "Nonowner Equity Transactions—A Review." *The CPA Journal* (June 1990), p. 50.

Houston, Carol. "Translation Exposure Hedging Post *SFAS No. 52.*" *Journal of International Financial Management and Accounting*, Vol. 2, nos. 2 and 3 (1990), pp. 145–169.

Huefner, Ronald J., J. Edward Ketz, and James A. Largay III. "Foreign Currency Translation and the Cash Flow Statement." *Accounting Horizons*, Vol. 3, no. 2. (June 1989), pp. 66–76.

Revsine, Lawrence. "The Rationale Underlying the Functional Currency Choice." *Accounting Review* (July 1984) pp. 505–514.

Statement of Financial Accounting Standards No. 52. "Foreign Currency Translation." Stamford, CT: Financial Accounting Standards Board, 1981.

14 CHAPTER

SEGMENT AND INTERIM FINANCIAL REPORTING

Consolidated financial statements enable investors to assess management's overall effectiveness in managing company resources by providing useful information for computing overall measures of profitability, liquidity, and efficiency. To help investors evaluate a company's business segments' performance, supplemental footnote disclosures are required. The first part of this chapter discusses business segment reporting.

Financial accounting courses typically focus on reporting company performance for a year—the annual report. Many companies are also required to issue financial reports covering shorter periods of time during the year, most notably on a quarterly basis. The second part of this chapter focuses on reporting guidelines for such interim reports.

...

SEGMENT REPORTING UNDER *FASB STATEMENT NO. 131*

FASB Statement No. 131, "Disclosures About Segments of an Enterprise and Related Information" (1997) applies to public business enterprises, which are defined as enterprises that have issued debt or equity securities that are traded in a public market, that are required to file financial statements with the SEC, or that provide financial statements for the purpose of issuing securities in a public market. Enterprises must report segment information in the same way that management organizes the enterprise into units for internal decision-making and performance-evaluation purposes. The standard refers to this approach as the *management approach* to segmentation.

If internal reporting and evaluation are geographically based, segment reporting should be geographically based; if internal reporting and evaluation are product-line or industry based, segment reporting should be similarly based.

For example, *Intel Corporation's* 2003 reported segments are Intel Architecture Business, Intel Communications Group, Wireless Communications and Computing Group, and other. The Architecture operating segment's products include microprocessors and related chipsets and motherboards. The Communications Group's products include wired Ethernet, wireless connectivity, and network processing components. The Wireless Communications and Computing Group's products include flash memory, application processors, and cellular baseband chipsets for cellular handsets and handheld devices. These segments also must be how Intel organizes its financial reporting inside the company.

In contrast to Intel, *Nike Corporation's* 2004 geographic operating segments are the United States; Europe, Middle East, and Africa; Asia Pacific; and the Americas. The operating segments reflect the internal focus of Nike decision making, which appears to be geographic.

LEARNING OBJECTIVES

1 Understand how the management approach is used to identify potentially reportable operating segments.

2 Apply the threshold tests to identify reportable operating segments: the revenue test, the asset test, and the operating-profit test.

3 Apply the 75% external-revenue test to determine if additional segments must be reported.

4 Understand the types of information that may be disclosed for segments and the reasons that the levels of disclosure may vary across companies.

5 Understand what segment disclosures are reconciled to the consolidated amounts.

6 Know the types of enterprisewide disclosures related to products and services, geographic areas of operation, and major customers that are required to be disclosed.

7 Understand the similarities and differences in the reporting of operations in an interim versus an annual reporting period.

8 Compute interim-period income tax expense.

513

Identifying Reportable Segments

Management-approach-based segments are called **operating segments**. *Statement No. 131* characterizes an operating segment as a component of an enterprise (1) that engages in business activities from which it may earn revenues and incur expenses, including intersegment revenues and expenses; (2) whose operating results are regularly reviewed by the enterprise's chief operating decision maker; and (3) for which discrete financial information is available.

Some parts of an enterprise are not included in operating segments. Pension and other postretirement benefit plans are not operating segments. Likewise, corporate headquarters or functional departments that do not earn revenues are not operating segments. Intel reports that in addition to its reported operating segments, it also has sales and marketing, manufacturing, finance, and administrative groups. The costs of these groups are allocated to the operating segments.

AGGREGATION CRITERIA An enterprise may combine similar operating segments if aggregation is consistent with the objectives of *Statement No. 131* and the segments have similar economic characteristics. The segments also must be similar in each of the following areas: (1) the nature of the products and services, (2) the nature of the production processes, (3) the type or class of customer for their products and services, (4) the distribution method for products and services, and (5) if applicable, the nature of the regulatory environment (public utilities, for example).

QUANTITATIVE THRESHOLDS Operating segments are reportable if they meet materiality thresholds. A segment is considered material and separately reportable if one of the following three criteria is met.

1. Its reported revenue, including intersegment revenues, is 10% or more of the combined revenue of all operating segments.
2. The absolute value of its reported profit or loss is 10% or more of the greater of (a) the combined reported profit of all operating segments that reported a profit or (b) the absolute value of the combined reported loss of all operating segments that reported a loss.
3. Its assets are 10% or more of the combined assets of all operating segments.

Once reportable segments are identified, all other operating segments are combined with other business activities in an "all other" category for reporting purposes.

RECONSIDERATION OF REPORTABLE SEGMENTS Reported segments must include 75% of all external revenue. External revenue excludes intersegment revenue. If reportable segments do not meet this criterion, additional segments must be identified as reportable, even if they do not meet the quantitative thresholds. Two or more of the smaller segments that were not reportable on their own may be aggregated to form a reportable operating segment *only if* they meet a majority of the aggregation criteria.

Statement No. 131 does not specify the number of segments that must be reported. However, too many segments would be considered overly detailed and therefore counterproductive. Although no firm limit was established, the FASB encourages enterprises that identify more than 10 reportable segments to consider additional aggregation of their segments.

Illustration of the Tests for Reportable Operating Segments

Acme Corporation has four operating segments. The chief operating decision maker evaluates the company operating results segmented by industry. We apply the three materiality tests to determine which of Acme's operating segments are reportable segments.

REVENUE TEST We apply the revenue test by comparing each operating segment's revenue (revenue to external customers plus intersegment revenue) with 10% of the combined revenue (both internal and external) of all operating segments. Acme's revenue test is as follows:

Segment	Operating Segment Revenue	Intersegment Revenue	Total Segment Revenue		Test Value (10% × $1,500,000)	Reportable Segment Under Revenue Test?
Transportation	$ 360,000	$ 0	$ 360,000	≥	$150,000	Yes
Oil refining	405,000	480,000	885,000	≥	150,000	Yes
Insurance	95,000	20,000	115,000	≤	150,000	No
Finance	140,000	0	140,000	≤	150,000	No
Total	$1,000,000	$500,000	$1,500,000			

The revenue test value is $150,000 because the total revenue for all operating segments is $1,500,000. The transportation ($360,000) and oil refining ($885,000) segments are reportable segments under the revenue test because each of these segments' total revenue exceeds $150,000. The insurance and finance segments are not reportable segments under this criterion.

ASSET TEST The asset test involves comparing the total amount of each operating segment's assets with 10% of the total assets of all operating segments. A segment's assets are defined as those assets included in the measure of the segment's assets that are reviewed by the chief operating decision maker. General corporate assets may be included or excluded in the asset measurement, depending on the way management has organized the assets for operating decision-making purposes.

Assume that all assets of Acme Corporation are assigned to operating segments except those maintained for general corporate purposes.

Segment	Operating Segment's Identifiable Assets		Test Value (10% × $3,000,000)	Reportable Segment Under Asset Test?
Transportation	$ 700,000	≥	$300,000	Yes
Oil refining	950,000	≥	300,000	Yes
Insurance	180,000	≤	300,000	No
Finance	1,170,000	≥	300,000	Yes
Total	$3,000,000			

The finance segment is added to the reportable-segment list because its identifiable assets exceed the $300,000 threshold.

OPERATING PROFIT TEST No uniform definition of operating profit is required in applying this test. An operating segment's operating profit or loss depends on the revenues and expenses that management includes in the measurement reviewed by the chief operating decision maker.

In applying the operating-profit test, the absolute amount of each segment's operating profit or loss is compared with 10% of the greater of the combined operating profits of all profitable operating segments or the combined operating losses of all unprofitable operating segments. Acme's test is as follows:

Segment	Operating Segment's Operating Profit	Operating Segment's Operating Loss		Test Value (10% × $270,000)	Reportable Segment Under Operating Profit Test?
Transportation		$(100,000)	≥	$27,000	Yes
Oil refining	$200,000		≥	27,000	Yes
Insurance	20,000		≤	27,000	No
Finance	50,000		≥	27,000	Yes
Total	$270,000	$(100,000)			

After the $27,000 test value is determined, the test is applied to the absolute amounts of operating profit or loss for each segment. The transportation, oil refining, and finance segments are reportable segments under the 10% operating-profit test.

REEVALUATION OF REPORTABLE SEGMENTS The insurance segment failed to meet any of the 10% tests for a reportable segment. The reportable segments are thus transportation, oil refining, and finance. In the revenue test, the test value is based on 10% of the total external and intersegment revenue. If intersegment revenue is very large, some segments that make up a large percentage of consolidated (or external) revenue may not qualify for reporting under the revenue test. If these segments do not qualify for reporting under either of the other two tests, then investors will not be provided with potentially relevant information. *Statement No. 131* requires that total external revenue from the reportable operating segments equal at least 75% of total consolidated revenue.

In the Acme example, the test value is $750,000 ($1,000,000 × 75%). The external revenue of the transportation, oil refining, and finance operating segments of $905,000 is greater than 75% of consolidated revenue, and thus no additional segments need to be reported. If the 75% test is not met, additional operating segments are added until the 75% criterion is met.

If the insurance segment had been a reportable segment in the previous period and Acme's management considered it still to be significant, Acme would report the insurance segment separately as a reportable operating segment, even though it failed all of the 10% tests for this period.

Segment Disclosures

The basis of organization used by the chief operating decision maker to determine operating segments (for example, products and services, geographic areas, regulatory environments, or some combination of these factors) must be disclosed, as well as any aggregation of operating segments used in arriving at these reportable segments. Each reportable segment's types of products and services are disclosed. Required disclosures are made for each year for which financial statements are presented.

PROFIT/LOSS AND ASSET INFORMATION A measure of *profit or loss* and *total assets* is reported for each reportable operating segment. In addition, *Statement No. 131* (paragraph 27) requires the following information for each reportable segment "if the specified amounts are included in the measure of segment profit or loss reviewed by the chief operating decision maker":

1. Amount of revenue from external customers
2. Amount of revenue from other operating segments of the same enterprise
3. Interest revenue
4. Interest expense (If a segment's revenues are primarily interest and the chief operating decision maker relies on net interest revenue to evaluate performance, the segment may report interest revenue net of interest expense.)
5. Depreciation, depletion, and amortization expense
6. Unusual items (as described in *APB Opinion No. 31*, paragraph 26)
7. Equity in the net income of investees accounted for by the equity method
8. Income tax expense or benefit
9. Extraordinary items
10. Significant noncash items other than depreciation, depletion, and amortization expense

Other disclosures about assets are required if the specified amounts are included for review by the chief operating decision maker. These include the amount of investment in equity investees, the total expenditures for additions to long-lived assets other than financial instruments and certain other items, and deferred tax assets.

MEASUREMENT The amounts reported in segment information disclosures depend on the amounts reported to the chief operating decision maker. If allocations of revenues, expenses, gains, or losses are made to operating segments in determining the profit or loss measures used by the chief operating decision maker, the allocations are also a part of the reported segment data. If assets are allocated to segments in internal reports, assets are allocated to segments for external reporting.

The enterprise also reports the accounting basis of intersegment transactions (cost or market, for example). Any differences between segment profit or loss and assets measurements and the consolidated amounts that are not apparent from the required reconciliation (described below) are disclosed. Changes in measurement methods from prior periods are also disclosed.

RECONCILIATION REQUIREMENTS In addition to the information provided for each segment, a reconciliation between the segment data and consolidated information must be provided for the following items:

1. The total of the reportable segments' revenues and the reported consolidated revenues
2. The total reportable segments' profit or loss and consolidated income before taxes (However, if items like taxes and extraordinary items are included in segment profit or loss, segment profit or loss can be reconciled to consolidated income after these items are included.)
3. The total reportable segments' assets to consolidated assets
4. The total reportable segments' amounts for every other significant item of information disclosed, with their corresponding consolidated amounts.

Enterprisewide Disclosures

LEARNING OBJECTIVE **6**

Enterprises also report limited information about products and services, geographic areas of operation, and major customers, regardless of the operating segmentation used. This additional information is only required if it is not provided as part of the reportable operating-segment information.

PRODUCTS AND SERVICES Enterprises disclose either revenues from each product or service or group of similar products or services or the fact that it is impractical to provide this information.

GEOGRAPHIC INFORMATION If practicable, enterprises disclose geographic information, including revenues from external customers attributed to the enterprise's home country and revenues attributed to all foreign countries in total. If revenue from one country is material (generally considered 10%), it is disclosed separately. Similarly, enterprises disclose long-lived assets by country of domicile and by all other foreign countries in total. Plus, they make separate disclosures for any individual country where the assets are material.

MAJOR CUSTOMERS Enterprises are required to disclose the existence of major customers. The fact that a single customer accounts for 10% or more of the enterprise's revenue must be disclosed, as well as the amount of revenue from each such customer and the segments reporting the revenue. Disclosure of the identity of the customer is not required. In calculating the 10% rule, a group of entities under common control count as a single customer. However, federal, state, and local governments count as different entities. In its 2003 annual report, for example, *Intel* reported that one customer accounted for 19% of the company's revenue in 2003 and 16% in 2002. Another accounted for 15% of its revenue in both 2003 and 2002. The majority of these sales to these customers were Intel Architecture Business products.

Exhibit 14-1 presents segment disclosures *Archer Daniels Midland Company* included in its 2003 annual report. The disclosures are required for each year for which a complete set of financial statements is presented.

EXHIBIT 14-1

ARCHER DANIELS MIDLAND 2003 SEGMENTAL DISCLOSURES (FOOTNOTE NO. 13)

	2003	2002	2001
(In thousands)			
Sales to external customers			
Oilseeds Processing	$ 9,773,379	$ 8,155,530	$ 7,778,440
Corn Processing	2,550,108	1,939,100	2,117,098
Wheat Processing	1,589,116	1,360,895	1,308,692
Agricultural Services	13,441,193	8,280,078	5,644,237
Other	3,354,237	2,876,291	2,634,744
Total	$30,708,033	$22,611,894	$19,483,211
Intersegment sales			
Oilseeds Processing	$ 123,243	$ 123,794	$ 136,276
Corn Processing	337,375	177,520	172,369
Wheat Processing	39,229	25,895	26,160
Agricultural Services	1,425,883	1,694,831	1,525,030
Other	103,770	98,124	105,731
Total	$ 2,029,500	$ 2,120,164	$ 1,965,566
Net sales			
Oilseeds Processing	$ 9,896,622	$ 8,279,324	$ 7,914,716
Corn Processing	2,887,483	2,116,620	2,289,467
Wheat Processing	1,628,345	1,386,790	1,334,852
Agricultural Services	14,867,076	9,974,909	7,169,267
Other	3,458,007	2,974,415	2,740,475
Intersegment elimination	(2,029,500)	(2,120,164)	(1,965,566)
Total	$30,708,033	$22,611,894	$19,483,211
Interest expense			
Oilseeds Processing	$ 35,433	$ 44,360	$ 75,588
Corn Processing	11,282	10,266	21,039
Wheat Processing	7,239	8,831	12,984
Agricultural Services	50,024	35,944	44,214
Other	58,362	62,460	78,753
Total	$ 162,340	$ 161,861	$ 232,578

(continued)

EXHIBIT 14-1

(continued)

ARCHER DANIELS MIDLAND 2003 SEGMENTAL DISCLOSURES (FOOTNOTE NO. 13)

	2003	2002	2001
Depreciation and amortization			
Oilseeds Processing	$ 153,519	$ 154,526	$ 155,736
Corn Processing	163,953	120,478	124,071
Wheat Processing	41,913	41,356	45,452
Agricultural Services	77,516	71,788	71,445
Other	184,496	163,320	153,263
Total	$ 621,397	$ 551,468	$ 549,967
Equity in earnings (losses) of affiliates			
Oilseeds Processing	$ 51,411	$ 17,974	$ 13,883
Corn Processing	15,531	17,204	8,854
Wheat Processing	(1,399)	2,219	305
Agricultural Services	953	29,036	11,797
Other	(10,358)	(25,659)	70,070
Total	$ 56,138	$ 40,774	$ 104,909
Operating profit			
Oilseeds Processing	$ 337,089	$ 387,960	$ 260,116
Corn Processing	326,380	214,875	242,211
Wheat Processing	59,222	78,800	71,519
Agricultural Services	92,124	169,593	119,548
Other	195,097	188,592	210,005
Total operating profit	1,009,912	1,039,820	903,399
Corporate	(378,939)	(320,883)	(381,500)
Income before income taxes	$ 630,973	$ 718,937	$ 521,899
Investments in and advances to affiliates			
Oilseeds Processing	$ 300,241	$ 219,757	$ 219,117
Corn Processing	67,414	155,408	139,555
Wheat Processing	13,759	16,422	16,027
Agricultural Services	157,085	39,660	253,740
Other	954,406	971,963	1,301,444
Total	$ 1,492,905	$ 1,403,210	$ 1,929,883
Identifiable assets			
Oilseeds Processing	$ 4,071,567	$ 3,439,449	$ 3,166,280
Corn Processing	2,129,682	1,362,012	1,425,622
Wheat Processing	767,703	774,817	752,649
Agricultural Services	2,384,590	2,507,722	1,946,320
Other	5,904,833	4,923,006	5,208,809
Corporate	1,924,504	2,372,329	1,840,251
Total	$17,182,879	$15,379,335	$14,339,931
Gross additions to property, plant, and equipment			
Oilseeds Processing	$ 191,843	$ 75,077	$ 109,402
Corn Processing	509,668	152,690	75,116
Wheat Processing	291,471	11,194	29,145
Agricultural Services	50,486	111,043	61,824
Other	99,466	235,936	26,594
Total	$ 1,142,934	$ 585,940	$ 302,081

Geographic Information: The following geographic-area data include net sales and other operating income attributed to the countries based on the location of the subsidiary making the sale and long-lived assets based on physical location.

	2003	2002	2001
(In millions)			
Net sales and other operating income:			
United States	$16,140	$14,695	$13,114
Germany	4,519	2,481	1,381
Other foreign	10,049	5,436	4,988
	$30,708	$22,612	$19,483
Long-lived assets			
United States	$ 4,408	$ 3,838	$ 3,987
Foreign	1,442	1,188	1,052
	$ 5,850	$ 5,026	$ 5,039

Segment Disclosure

Archer Daniels Midland Company (ADM) reports four business segments: Oilseeds Processing, Corn Processing, Wheat Processing, and Agricultural Services. The segments are organized by the nature of the products and services offered. This company also has sizable intersegment sales. According to the disclosure, about $2,030 million out of total sales of about $32,740 million were intersegment. These amounts are eliminated in consolidation but included in the segment disclosure.

ADM reports the following information for each of its segments:

Sales to external customers

Intersegment sales

A reconciliation of segment sales to consolidated sales, which is included under the caption Net Sales

Interest expense

Depreciation and amortization

Equity in earnings (losses) of affiliates

Operating profit, which is again reconciled to consolidated operating profit

Investments in and advances to affiliates

Identifiable assets

Gross additions to property, plant, and equipment

The chief operating decision maker evaluates these segments on many of the dimensions listed on page 516. It appears that income taxes, unusual items, extraordinary items, and interest revenue are not allocated to the individual segments when internal financial statements are prepared for review by the chief operating decision maker. In contrast to ADM, Intel reports only net revenue and operating income or loss for its segments. As we can observe from these two companies, considerable variety exists in the type of information reviewed by the chief operating decision maker when evaluating segments.

In the text of the segment-disclosure footnote, ADM describes how operating profit is determined for each segment (net sales less identifiable operating expenses). Interest expense is allocated to each segment based on working capital usage. ADM also reports that general corporate expenses, investment income, unallocated interest expense, marketable securities transactions, and the FIFO-to-LIFO inventory adjustments are included in the Corporate category under operating profit.

Segment Disclosures for Interim Reports

Statement No. 131 requires limited segment information to be included in interim reports. These requirements are covered in the next section of this chapter.

INTERIM FINANCIAL REPORTING

Interim financial reports provide information about a firm's operations for less than a full year. They are commonly issued on a quarterly basis and typically include cumulative, year-to-date information, as well as comparative information for corresponding periods of the prior year. Before 1973, little uniformity existed in the content of interim financial reports issued to shareholders. This situation and the increasing importance of quarterly reports to investors led to the issuance of *APB Opinion No. 28*, "Interim Financial Reporting," in May 1973.

The guidelines for interim reporting are particularly applicable to publicly traded companies that are required to prepare quarterly reports according to SEC and New York Stock Exchange requirements. Even so, *Opinion No. 28* guidelines apply whenever publicly traded companies issue interim financial information to their security holders (*APB Opinion No. 28*, paragraph 7).

Nature of Interim Reports

Interim financial reports provide more timely, but less complete, information than annual financial reports. Interim reports reflect a trade-off between timeliness and reliability because estimates must replace many of the extensive reviews of receivables, payables, inventory, and the related income effects that support the measurements presented in annual financial reports, which have to meet audit requirements. The minimum-disclosure requirements of *Opinion No. 28* do not constitute fair presentations of financial position and results of operations in conformity with GAAP. Therefore, interim financial statements are usually labeled *unaudited*.

Under *APB Opinion No. 28*, each interim period is considered an integral part of each annual period, rather than a basic accounting period unto itself. Generally, interim-period results should be based on the accounting principles and practices used in the latest annual financial statements. Some modifications may be needed, however, to relate the interim-period to annual-period results in a meaningful manner. For example, interim statements may modify the procedures used in annual statements for product costs and other expenses, as discussed below.

Product Costs

GROSS PROFIT METHOD The gross profit method of estimating inventory and cost of goods sold was discussed in your intermediate accounting course. As you may recall, this method is not acceptable for annual financial statement purposes. However, a company can use the gross profit method for interim reporting purposes when it does not use the perpetual inventory method and it is too costly to perform an inventory count to price out the inventory. Obviously, the gross profit method must yield a reasonable estimate of the inventory and cost of goods sold in order to be used.

LIFO INVENTORIES One reason companies use the LIFO method is to reduce taxable income, and therefore taxes paid, when prices are rising. The IRS requires the LIFO method's use for financial reporting purposes if it is used for tax purposes. To avoid paying taxes previously avoided, companies attempt to avoid LIFO layer liquidation that results in lower cost of goods sold, higher net income, and a higher tax bill.

LIFO inventory layers may be liquidated during an interim period but could be expected to be replaced by year-end. Cost of sales can include the replacement cost of the liquidated LIFO layer if the reduction is determined to be temporary. For example, a firm experiencing a temporary 100-unit LIFO inventory liquidation would expense the current cost of the 100 units, rather than the historical LIFO cost. The amount of current cost in excess of the historical cost is shown as a current liability on the interim balance sheet.

INVENTORY MARKET DECLINES Permanent inventory market declines are recognized in the interim period unless they are considered temporary (i.e., no loss is expected for the fiscal year as a whole).

STANDARD COST SYSTEM Planned variances under a standard cost system that are expected to be absorbed by year-end are usually deferred at the interim date.

Expenses Other Than Product Costs

ANNUAL EXPENSES IN INTERIM REPORTS Annual expenses are allocated to the interim periods expected to be benefited. Major annual repair allowances are an example of this kind of allocation. Expenses arising in an interim period are not deferred unless they would be deferred at year-end. For example, property taxes accrued or deferred for annual purposes are also accrued or deferred for interim periods.

ADVERTISING COSTS Advertising costs are expensed in the interim period in which they are incurred unless the benefits clearly apply to subsequent interim periods.

INCOME TAXES Income taxes for interim reporting are divided into (1) those applicable to income from continuing operations before income taxes, excluding unusual or infrequently occurring items, and (2) those applicable to significant, unusual, or infrequently occurring items, discontinued items, and extraordinary items.[1]

Income tax expense for an interim period is based on an estimated effective annual tax rate that is applied to taxable income from continuing operations, excluding unusual and infrequently occurring items. The year-to-date tax expense, less the tax expense recognized in earlier interim periods, is the tax expense for the current interim period. The tax effects of unusual and infrequently occurring items are calculated separately and added to the tax expense of the interim period in which these items are reported. Gains and losses on discontinued operations and extraordinary items are reported on a net-of-tax basis, as in annual reports.

---

[1] See *FASB Interpretation No. 18*, "An Interpretation of *APB Opinion No. 28*," 1977.

Computation of the Estimated Annual Effective Tax Rate

The following illustration shows how Small Corporation estimates its annual effective tax rate for the purpose of preparing quarterly financial reports. Small Corporation bases its estimate on the following *assumed* tax-rate schedule for corporations for the current year:

If Taxable Income Is:		The Tax Is:			
Over	But Not Over	Pay	+	Excess	Of the Amount Over
0	$ 50,000			15%	0
$ 50,000	75,000	$ 7,500	+	25	$ 50,000
75,000	100,000	13,750	+	34	75,000
100,000	335,000	22,250	+	39	100,000
335,000	—			34	0

Small Corporation estimates quarterly income for the calendar year 2006 as follows:

Quarter	Estimated Income		Rate	Estimated Tax
First	$ 20,000	×	15%	$ 3,000
Second	30,000	×	15	4,500
Third	25,000	×	25	6,250
Fourth	25,000	×	34	8,500
Totals	$100,000			$22,250

The estimated quarterly income and income tax estimates assume that Small anticipates no accounting changes, discontinued operations, or extraordinary items for the year. Thus, the estimated annual effective tax rate is 22.25%, equal to the estimated tax divided by the estimated income ($22,250 ÷ $100,000 = 22.25%). Income tax for the first quarter is $20,000 × 22.25%, or $4,450. This computation reflects the *integral theory*, such that each interim period is an essential part of an annual period, and not the *discrete theory* that each interim period is a basic, independent accounting period. The integral theory is required by *APB Opinion No. 28*. If no changes in the estimates occur during the year, the income by quarter would be calculated as follows:

	First Quarter	Second Quarter	Third Quarter	Fourth Quarter	Fiscal
Income year-to-date	$20,000	$50,000	$75,000	$100,000	$100,000
Quarterly period income	$20,000	$30,000	$25,000	$ 25,000	$100,000
Tax expense (22.25%)	(4,450)	(6,675)	(5,563)	(5,563)	(22,250)
Net income	$15,550	$23,325	$19,438	$ 19,438	$ 77,750

The estimated annual effective tax rate is applied to year-to-date income, and prior-quarter income taxes are deducted to compute the current quarterly income tax expense. For example, the third-quarter tax expense is calculated as follows: ($75,000 × 22.25%) − ($4,450 + $6,675) = $5,563. This procedure provides for revision of the estimated annual effective tax rate to reflect changes in estimated income levels during the year. For example, if the $100,000 estimated income for the year had included $5,000 dividend income subject to an 80% dividend-received deduction, the annual effective tax rate would have been 20.89%. The calculation entails a $1,360 deduction for the tax savings on the dividends-received deduction: $5,000 × 80% × 34% tax rate = $1,360. The estimated annual effective tax rate would have been calculated as follows: ($22,250 − $1,360) ÷ $100,000 = 20.89%.

GUIDELINES FOR PREPARING INTERIM STATEMENTS

The APB summarized the financial information to be disclosed in interim reports in the *APB Opinion No. 28* guidelines. At a minimum, publicly traded companies should report:

    a Sales or gross revenues
    b Provision for income taxes
    c Extraordinary items net of income taxes
    d Cumulative-effect-type changes in accounting principles
    e Net income

1. Basic and diluted earnings per share
2. Seasonal revenue, costs, or expenses
3. Significant changes in estimates of income tax expense
4. Disposal of a segment of a business, extraordinary items, and unusual or infrequently occurring items
5. Contingent items
6. Changes in accounting principles and estimates
7. Significant changes in financial position

In addition, when an enterprise reports interim data on a regular basis, information should also be reported for the current year-to-date, or the last 12 months to date, with comparable information for the preceding year (*APB Opinion No. 18*, paragraph 30). If fourth-quarter reports are not issued, material disposals of business segments, extraordinary items, unusual and infrequently occurring items, and accounting changes for the quarter should be disclosed in notes to the annual report.[2]

Exhibit 14-2 shows a quarterly report for Sample Corporation and Subsidiaries for the three months ended September 30, 2007. In addition to the 2007 quarterly data, the Sample report gives the quarterly data for the previous year and year-to-date information for 2006 and 2007.

SEGMENT DISCLOSURES IN INTERIM REPORTS *Statement No. 131* (paragraph 33) provides specific guidelines on what segment disclosures are to be included in interim reports. The interim reports must include the following information about each reportable segment: (1) revenue from external customers, (2) intersegment revenues, (3) a measure of segment profit or loss, (4) total assets for which there has been a material change since the amount disclosed in the last annual report, (5) a description of any differences in the basis of segmentation or measurement of segment profit or loss since the last annual report, and (6) a reconciliation between segment and total profits, just as in the annual report.

EXHIBIT 14-2

Quarterly Report

SAMPLE CORPORATION AND SUBSIDIARIES CONDENSED CONSOLIDATED STATEMENTS OF INCOME (UNAUDITED) DATA IN THOUSANDS EXCEPT PER-SHARE AMOUNTS

	Three Months Ended September 30		Nine Months Ended September 30	
	2007	2006	2007	2006
Revenues	$2,469	$2,165	$6,725	$6,025
Cost and Expenses				
Cost of sales	1,624	1,409	4,412	3,936
Other operating expenses	691	613	1,969	1,763
Interest expense	26	29	76	77
	2,341	2,051	6,457	5,776
Income from continuing operations before income taxes	128	114	268	249
Income taxes	48	44	100	95
Income from continuing operations	80	70	168	154
Loss on discontinued operations*				34
Net income	$ 80	$ 70	$ 168	$ 120
Earnings per Common Share				
Continuing operations	$ 1.24	$ 1.08	$ 2.60	$ 2.38
Discontinued operations				(0.53)
Net earnings per common share	$ 1.24	$ 1.08	$ 2.60	$ 1.85
Cash Dividends per Common Share	$ 0.52	$ 0.50	$ 1.56	$ 1.50

*Earnings were negatively affected in the first six months of 2006 by discontinued furniture operations.

[2] *FASB Statement No. 3*, paragraph 14.

In addition to a brief description of the products produced by each segment, **Kimberly-Clark** reported the following disclosure in footnote 9 of its September 30, 2004, quarterly financial statement:

The following schedule presents information concerning Kimberly-Clark's consolidated operations by business segment:

(Millions of Dollars)	Three Months Ended September 30		Nine Months Ended September 30	
	2004	2003	2004	2003
Net Sales:				
Personal Care	$1,494.1	$1,432.1	$ 4,465.5	$ 4,244.5
Consumer Tissue	1,323.4	1,278.1	3,925.3	3,689.6
Business-to-Business	1,098.1	970.9	3,211.8	2,826.1
Intersegment sales	(49.3)	(39.5)	(161.5)	(114.3)
Consolidated	$3,866.3	$3,641.6	$11,441.1	$10,645.9
Operating Profit (reconciled to income before income taxes):				
Personal Care	$ 292.0	$ 308.3	$ 941.7	$ 904.4
Consumer Tissue	191.6	161.9	571.8	531.5
Business-to-Business	187.6	179.4	548.9	505.2
Other income (expense)—net	(8.5)	(21.3)	(37.5)	(77.5)
Unallocated items—net	(32.1)	(24.3)	(101.3)	(73.4)
Total operating profit	630.6	604.0	1,923.6	1,790.2
Nonoperating expense	(26.4)	—	(116.6)	—
Interest income	4.7	4.8	12.7	13.9
Interest expense	(41.1)	(40.6)	(120.5)	(128.2)
Income before income taxes	$ 567.8	$ 568.2	$ 1,699.2	$ 1,675.9

Note: Unallocated items—net, consists of expenses not associated with the business segments.

SEC Interim Financial Disclosures

The SEC requires that quarterly reports be prepared for the company's stockholders and for filing with the SEC. These reports are to be prepared using GAAP and are filed on Form 10-Q within 45 days after the end of a quarter. Fourth-quarter reports are not required, but SEC Rule 14a-3 requires inclusion of selected quarterly data in the annual report to shareholders. Quarterly reports are not audited, so the CPA's report states that a *review*, rather than an audit, has been performed.

A company's Form 10-Q report to the SEC includes additional information beyond the minimum reporting requirements under *APB Opinion No. 28*, as amended by *FASB Statement No. 3, FASB Statement No. 131*, and *FASB Interpretation No. 18*. SEC quarterly and annual reporting requirements are similar. For example, Part I of Form 10-Q contains the following summary contents:

Part 1—Financial Information
    Item 1—Consolidated Balance Sheet
        Consolidated Statement of Income
        Consolidated Statement of Cash Flows
        Notes to Consolidated Financial Statements
    Item 2—Management's Discussion of Financial Condition and Results of Operations

Companies present comparative consolidated balance sheets as of the end of the current quarter and at the prior year-end. They present the comparative consolidated income statements for the current quarter and the same quarter of the prior year. Companies also present the current year-to-date and the prior year-to-date results. Comparative consolidated statements of cash flows are presented for the current year-to-date and the prior year-to-date activity.

The information required in Form 10-Q beyond that required by *APB Opinion No. 28* is available from the company to its shareholders upon request. However, many companies include essentially all the information from Form 10-Q in their regular quarterly reports. Exhibit 14-3 illustrates this extended disclosure for Kimberly-Clark Corporation. In addition to the statements in the quarterly report that are reprinted in the exhibit, the company's report includes notes to the consolidated financial statements, a review of the financial information, a letter to shareholders from the company's chairman, and additional corporate information.

EXHIBIT 14-3

Quarterly Report of
the Kimberly-Clark
Corporation

KIMBERLY-CLARK CORPORATION AND SUBSIDIARIES CONSOLIDATED INCOME STATEMENT (UNAUDITED)

(Millions of Dollars Except Per-Share Amounts)	Three Months Ended September 30		Nine Months Ended September 30	
	2004	2003	2004	2003
Net sales	$3,866.3	$ 3,641.6	$11,441.1	$10,645.9
Cost of products sold	2,601.8	2,426.7	7,604.3	7,020.2
Gross profit	1,264.5	1,214.9	3,836.8	3,625.7
Marketing, research, and general expenses	625.4	589.6	1,875.7	1,758.0
Other (income) expense, net	8.5	21.3	37.5	77.5
Operating profit	630.6	604.0	1,923.6	1,790.2
Nonoperating expense	(26.4)	—	(116.6)	—
Interest income	4.7	4.8	12.7	13.9
Interest expense	(41.1)	(40.6)	(120.5)	(128.2)
Income before income taxes	567.8	568.2	1,699.2	1,675.9
Provision for income taxes	139.0	157.8	382.5	480.2
Income before equity interests	428.8	410.4	1,316.7	1,195.7
Share of net income of equity companies	31.3	21.9	92.1	78.2
Minority owners' share of subsidiaries' net income	(18.8)	(12.6)	(53.9)	(39.2)
Net income	$ 441.3	$ 419.7	$ 1,354.9	$ 1,234.7
Per-Share Basis:				
Net income				
Basic	$ .90	$ .83	$ 2.72	$ 2.43
Diluted	$ .89	$ .83	$ 2.70	$ 2.42
Cash dividends declared	$ .40	$ .34	$ 1.20	$ 1.02

KIMBERLY-CLARK CORPORATION AND SUBSIDIARIES CONDENSED CONSOLIDATED BALANCE SHEET (UNAUDITED)— THIRD QUARTER 2004 QUARTERLY REPORT

(Millions of Dollars)	September 30, 2004	December 31, 2003
Assets		
Current assets		
Cash and cash equivalents	$ 315.5	$ 290.6
Accounts receivable	1,958.1	1,955.1
Inventories	1,675.1	1,563.4
Other current assets	598.9	629.0
Total current assets	4,547.6	4,438.1
Property	15,438.7	15,179.5
Less accumulated depreciation	7,309.2	6,916.1
Net property	8,129.5	8,263.4
Investments in equity companies	456.5	427.7
Goodwill	2,623.8	2,649.1
Other assets	959.8	1,001.6
	$16,717.2	$16,779.9
Liabilities and Stockholders' Equity		
Current liabilities		
Debt payable within one year	$ 990.9	$ 864.3
Accounts payable	1,137.9	1,141.4
Accrued expenses	1,394.1	1,374.7
Other current liabilities	542.7	538.3
Total current liabilities	4,065.6	3,918.7

(continued)

EXHIBIT 14-3

Quarterly Report of the Kimberly-Clark Corporation
(continued)

KIMBERLY-CLARK CORPORATION AND SUBSIDIARIES CONDENSED CONSOLIDATED BALANCE SHEET (UNAUDITED)— THIRD QUARTER 2004 QUARTERLY REPORT

	September 30	December 31
(Millions of Dollars)	2004	2003
Liabilities and Stockholders' Equity (cont.)		
Long-term debt	2,363.5	2,733.7
Noncurrent employee benefit and other obligations	1,655.5	1,614.4
Deferred income taxes	987.0	880.6
Minority owners' interests in subsidiaries	326.0	298.3
Preferred securities of subsidiary	714.5	567.9
Stockholders' equity	6,605.1	6,766.3
	$16,717.2	$16,779.9

KIMBERLY-CLARK CORPORATION AND SUBSIDIARIES CONDENSED CONSOLIDATED CASH FLOW STATEMENT (UNAUDITED)

	Nine Months Ended September 30	
(Millions of Dollars)	2004	2003
Operations		
Net income	$1,354.9	$1,234.7
Depreciation and amortization	616.2	561.2
Changes in operating working capital	(51.4)	108.7
Deferred income tax provision	118.5	34.0
Equity companies' earnings in excess of dividends paid	(44.2)	(27.5)
Postretirement benefits	23.3	(7.6)
Other	80.6	115.6
Cash provided by operations	2,097.9	2,019.1
Investing		
Capital spending	(328.7)	(653.2)
Acquisitions of businesses, net of cash acquired	—	(258.3)
Proceeds from sales of investments	26.1	20.7
Net increase in time deposits	(12.0)	(205.4)
Investments in marketable securities	(7.4)	(10.8)
Other	10.2	(14.3)
Cash used for investing	(311.8)	(1,121.3)
Financing		
Cash dividends paid	(571.9)	(500.0)
Net decrease in short-term debt	(205.7)	(261.2)
Proceeds from issuance of long-term debt	33.6	522.7
Repayments of long-term debt	(184.7)	(479.3)
Proceeds from preferred securities of subsidiary	125.0	—
Proceeds from exercise of stock options	256.1	20.3
Acquisitions of common stock for the treasury	(1,197.3)	(357.9)
Other	(12.1)	(44.2)
Cash used for financing	(1,757.0)	(1,099.6)
Effect of exchange-rate changes on cash and cash equivalents	(4.2)	12.3
Increase (decrease) in cash and cash equivalents	24.9	(189.5)
Cash and cash equivalents, beginning of year	290.6	494.5
Cash and cash equivalents, end of period	$ 315.5	$ 305.0

International Focus

International Accounting Standard No. 14, "Segment Reporting," was adopted in August 1997 and became effective on July 1, 1998. Like *Statement 131*, *IAS 14* adopts a management approach in defining reportable segments. Unlike *Statement 131*, however, if the operating segment used by management is not along the lines of product/services or geographic area, then further disaggregation is required.

IAS 14 has the same threshold tests as *Statement 131*: the 10% revenue test, the 10% asset test, and the 10% profit or loss test. In addition, the 75% consolidated-revenue test is also applied to determine if additional segments must be disclosed.

The accounting policies used to determine consolidated financial statements must also be used in segment accounting. A standardized measure of the segment operating results is required, which is basically operating profit before interest, taxes, and head-office administrative expense. In addition, assets, liabilities, capital additions, depreciation, and equity method income are among the other required segmental disclosures.

IAS 14 segment reporting is much more standardized across companies than *Statement 131* because *Statement 131* requires that the definition of operating result reviewed by the chief operating decision maker be reported.

SUMMARY

FASB Statement No. 131 requires disclosures about operating segments. The operating segments of a public business enterprise are determined by the structure of the enterprise's internal organization. This method of identifying segments is called the management approach. Aggregation criteria and materiality tests determine which operating segments are reportable.

Disclosures required for each reportable operating segment include a description of the types of products and services sold, a profit or loss measure used internally to evaluate the segment, and total assets. Other disclosures on revenues, expenses, gains, losses, and assets may be made if these amounts are included in the profit or loss and segment-assets measures reviewed by the chief operating decision maker. Reportable segment data are reconciled with the enterprise's consolidated amounts. Limited segment information is also disclosed in quarterly reports.

Statement No. 131 also requires disclosures on an enterprisewide basis. A company must disclose information about its products and services, geographic areas, and major customers unless the information is included as part of the segment disclosures.

Segment information is important for effective analysis of financial statements because the opportunities for expansion and capital requirements differ by industry and geographic area.

Interim financial report disclosures are defined in *APB Opinion No. 28*, as amended by *FASB Statements No. 3* and *131* and *FASB Interpretation No. 18*. Interim financial reports provide timely information. However, much of the information is based on estimates, and the reports are unaudited.

Each interim period is considered an integral part of the annual period. As a result, interim-period information is based on the accounting principles used in the last annual report. However, some modifications at the interim reporting date may be necessary so that the interim-period results complement the annual results of operations.

QUESTIONS

1. What is an operating segment?

2. What is a reportable segment according to *FASB Statement No. 131*? What criteria are used in determining what operating segments are also reportable segments?

3. How are the segments that are not reportable segments handled in the required disclosures of *FASB Statement No. 131*?

4. Revenue information for Mahoney Corporation is as follows:

Consolidated revenue (from the income statement)	$400,000
Intersegment sales and transfers	80,000
Combined revenues of all industry segments	$480,000

Does the 10% revenue test for a reportable segment apply to 10% of the $400,000 or 10% of the $480,000?

5. Describe the 10% operating-profit test for determining reportable segments.

6. Describe the 10% asset test for determining reportable segments.

7. Describe the 10% revenue test for determining reportable segments.

8. Assume an enterprise has 10 operating segments. Five operating segments qualify as reportable segments by passing one of the 10% tests. However, their combined revenues from sales to unaffiliated customers total only 70% of the combined unaffiliated revenues from all operating segments. Should the remaining five operating segments be aggregated and shown as an "other segments" category? Explain.

9. What disclosures are required for the reportable segments and all remaining segments in the aggregate?

10. When is an enterprise required to include information in its financial statements about its foreign and domestic operations?

11. Must a major customer be identified by name?

12. Do the requirements of *FASB Statement No. 131* apply to financial statements for interim periods? If so, how?

13. Explain how a company estimates its annual effective tax rate for interim reporting purposes.

14. What is the difference between the internal theory and the discrete theory with respect to interim financial reporting?

15. Describe the minimum financial information to be disclosed in interim reports under the provisions of *APB Opinion No. 28*.

EXERCISES

E 14-1
Segment disclosures

LEARNING OBJECTIVES **4, 6**

1. The disclosure requirements for an operating segment do *not* include:
- a **Unusual items**
- b **Income tax expense or benefit**
- c **Extraordinary items**
- d **Cost of goods or services sold**

2. A reconciliation between the numbers disclosed in operating segments and consolidated numbers need *not* be provided for:
- a **Cost of goods sold**
- b **Profit or loss**
- c **Net assets**
- d **Revenues**

3. Each reportable segment is required to disclose the following information except for:
- a **Extraordinary items**
- b **Depreciation, depletion, and amortization**
- c **Capital expenditures**
- d **Gross profit or loss**

4. An enterprise is required to disclose information about its major customers if 10% or more of its revenue is derived from any single customer. This disclosure must include:
- a **The products or services generating the revenue from such sales**
- b **The operating segment or segments making such sales and the total revenue from the customer**
- c **The name of the customer to whom the sales were made**
- d **The dollar amounts of revenue and any profit or loss on the sales**

5. Which of the following is not a criterion for aggregating two or more operating segments?

   a The segments should have similar products or services.

   b The segments should have similar production processes.

   c The distribution of products should be similar.

   d The segments should have similar amounts of revenue.

6. Required segment disclosures in interim-period statements do not include:

   a A measure of segment profit or loss

   b Net interest revenue

   c A description of a change in segmentation from the last annual report

   d Intersegment revenue

 LEARNING OBJECTIVES **2, 3, 4**

E 14-2

Apply threshold tests; disclosure Visclosky Corporation operates entirely in the United States but in different industries. It segments the business based on industry. Total sales of the segments, including intersegment sales, are as follows:

Concrete and stone products	$200,000
Construction	500,000
Lumber and wood products	900,000
Building materials	500,000
Other	50,000

Further analysis reveals sales from one segment to another as follows:

Lumber and wood products	$400,000
Building materials	200,000

REQUIRED

1. Determine which segments are reportable segments under both the 10% and the 75% revenue tests.
2. Prepare a schedule suitable for disclosing revenue by industry segment for external reporting.
3. Prepare a reconciliation of segment revenue with corporate revenue.

LEARNING OBJECTIVE **2**

E 14-3

Apply threshold tests Superior Corporation's internal divisions are based on industry. The revenues, operating profits, and assets of the operating segments of Superior are presented in thousands of dollars as follows:

	Sales to Nonaffiliates	Inter-segment Sales	Total Sales	Operating Profit (Loss)	Assets
Food service industry	$300,000	$40,000	$340,000	$ 40,000	$200,000
Copper mine	80,000	—	80,000	(10,000)	60,000
Information systems	20,000	15,000	35,000	5,000	40,000
Chemical industry	130,000	20,000	150,000	30,500	217,000
Agricultural products	48,000	—	48,000	(15,500)	50,000
Pharmaceutical products	20,000	—	20,000	8,000	18,000
Foreign operations	15,000	—	15,000	5,000	20,000
Corporate assets*					33,000
	$613,000	$75,000	$688,000	$ 63,000	$638,000

*Corporate assets include equity investees of $10,000 and general assets of $23,000.

REQUIRED: Determine the reportable segments of Superior Corporation.

 LEARNING OBJECTIVES **4, 5**

E 14-4

Segment and enterprisewide disclosures The sales in thousands of dollars of the segments of Worldwide Corporation (Worldwide is organized on a geographic basis) for 2006 are as follows:

	Unaffiliated Sales	Intersegment Sales	Total
United States	$50,000	$15,000	$ 65,000
Canada	18,000	8,000	26,000
Europe	10,000	1,000	11,000
Latin America	7,000	3,000	10,000
Japan	3,000	—	3,000
Korea	1,000	—	1,000
	$89,000	$27,000	$116,000

The $89,000 sales to unaffiliated customers is the amount of revenue reported in Worldwide's consolidated income statement.

REQUIRED: Illustrate the disclosure of Worldwide's domestic and foreign revenue in a form acceptable for external reporting, including reconciliation with consolidated revenue.

E 14-5

Apply threshold tests

LEARNING OBJECTIVE **2**

1. Correy Corporation and its divisions are engaged solely in manufacturing operations. The following data (consistent with prior years' data) pertain to the industries in which operations were conducted for the year ended December 31, 2006 (in thousands):

Industry	Total Revenue	Operating Profit	Assets at December 31, 2006
A	$10,000	$1,750	$20,000
B	8,000	1,400	17,500
C	6,000	1,200	12,500
D	3,000	550	7,500
E	4,250	675	7,000
F	1,500	225	3,000
	$32,750	$5,800	$67,500

In its segment information for 2006, how many reportable segments does Correy have?
  a *Three*
  b *Four*
  c *Five*
  d *Six*

2. Kaycee Corporation's revenues for the year ended December 31, 2006, are as follows (in thousands):

Consolidated revenue per income statement	$1,200
Intersegment sales	180
Intersegment transfers	60
Combined revenues of all segments	$1,440

Kaycee has a reportable segment if that segment's revenues exceed:
  a *$6*
  b *$24*
  c *$120*
  d *$144*

3. The following information pertains to Aria Corporation and its divisions for the year ended December 31, 2006 (in thousands):

Sales to unaffiliated customers	$2,000
Intersegment sales of products similar to those sold to unaffiliated customers	600
Interest earned on loans to other industry segments	40

The intersegment interest is not reported by the divisions on internal reports reviewed by the chief operating officer. Aria and all of its divisions are engaged solely in manufacturing operations. Aria has a reportable segment if that segment's revenue exceeds:
  a *$264*
  b *$260*
  c *$204*
  d *$200*

4. The following information pertains to revenue earned by Timm Company's operating segments for the year ended December 31, 2006:

Segment	Sales to Unaffiliated Customers	Intersegment Sales	Total Revenues
Alo	$ 5,000	$ 3,000	$ 8,000
Bix	8,000	4,000	12,000
Cee	4,000	—	4,000
Dil	43,000	16,000	59,000
Combined	60,000	23,000	83,000
Elimination	—	(23,000)	(23,000)
Consolidated	$60,000	—	$60,000

In conformity with the revenue test, Timm's reportable segments were:

a **Only Dil**

b **Bix and Dil**

c **Alo, Bix, and Dil**

d **Alo, Bix, Cee, and Dil**

Use the following information in answering questions 5 and 6: Grum Corporation, a publicly owned corporation, is subject to the requirements for segment reporting. In its income statement for the year ended December 31, 2006, Grum reported revenues of $50,000,000, operating expenses of $47,000,000, and net payroll costs of $15,000,000. Grum's combined identifiable assets of all industry segments at December 31, 2006, were $40,000,000.

5. In its 2006 financial statements, Grum should disclose major customer data if sales to any single customer amount to at least:

a **$300,000**

b **$1,500,000**

c **$4,000,000**

d **$5,000,000**

6. In its 2006 financial statements, if Grum is organized on an industry basis, it should disclose foreign operations data on a specific country if revenues from that country's operations are at least:

a **$5,000,000**

b **$4,700,000**

c **$4,000,000**

d **$1,500,000**

7. Selected data for a segment of a business enterprise are to be separately reported in accordance with *FASB Statement No. 131* when the revenues of the segment exceed 10% of the:

a **Combined net income of all segments reporting profits**

b **Total revenues obtained in transactions with outsiders**

c **Total revenues of all the enterprise's operating segments**

d **Total combined revenues for all segments reporting profits**

8. In financial reporting of segment data, which of the following items is used in determining a segment's operating income?

a **Income tax expense**

b **Sales to other segments**

c **General corporate expense**

d **Gain or loss on discontinued operations**

LEARNING OBJECTIVE 2

E 14-6

Apply threshold tests A summary of the segment operations of the Johnson-Miller Corporation for the year ended December 31, 2006, follows:

	United States	Canada	Germany	Japan	Mexico	Other Foreign	Consolidated
Sales to unaffiliated customers	$ 70,000	$12,000	$ 6,000	$ 7,000	$3,000	$2,000	$100,000
Interarea transfers	20,000	—	—	$ 6,000	—	—	—
Total revenue	$ 90,000	$12,000	$ 6,000	$13,000	$3,000	$2,000	$100,000
Operating profits	$ 16,000	$ 2,000	$ 3,000	$ 2,000	$1,000	$1,000	$ 25,000
Segment assets	$100,000	$15,000	$17,000	$18,000	$4,000	$3,000	$200,000

1. For which of the following geographic areas will separate disclosures be required if only the 10% revenue test is considered?

a **United States, Canada, and Japan**

b **United States and Canada**

c **United States and Japan**

d **United States, Canada, Germany, and Japan**

2. For which of the following geographic areas will separate disclosures be required if only the 10% asset test is considered?

    a *United States*

    b *United States and Canada*

    c *United States, Japan, and Germany*

    d *United States, Canada, Germany, and Japan*

3. For which of the following geographic areas will separate disclosures be required if *all* relevant tests are considered?

    a *United States, Canada, Germany, and Japan*

    b *United States, Germany, and Japan*

    c *United States, Canada, and Japan*

    d *United States and Canada*

E 14-7

Interim accounting for various situations; tax

1. Interim reporting under *APB Opinion No. 28* guidelines refers to financial reporting:

    a *On a monthly basis*

    b *On a quarterly basis*

    c *On a regular basis*

    d *For periods less than a year*

2. A liquidation of LIFO inventories for interim reporting purposes may create a problem in measuring cost of sales. Accordingly, cost of sales in interim periods should:

    a *Be determined using the gross profit method*

    b *Include the income effect of the LIFO liquidation*

    c *Include the expected cost of replacing the liquidated LIFO base*

    d *None of the above*

3. Baker Company's effective annual income tax rates for the first two quarters of 2006 are 34% and 30% for the first and second quarter, respectively. Assume that Baker's pretax income is $120,000 for the first quarter and $90,000 for the second quarter. Income tax expense for the second quarter is computed:

    a *$90,000 × 30%*

    b *($12,000 + $90,000) × 30%*

    c *($12,000 × 34%) + ($90,000 × 30%)*

    d *($210,000 × 30%) − ($120,000 × 34%)*

4. Assume corporate tax rates of 15% on the first $50,000 of taxable income, 25% on taxable income between $50,000 and $75,000, 34% on taxable income between $75,000 and $100,000, and 39% on taxable income between $100,000 and $335,000. If a corporation estimates its pretax income at $20,000 for the first quarter, $25,000 for the second quarter, $30,000 for the third quarter, and $35,000 for the fourth quarter, its estimated annual effective tax rate is:

    a *23.77%*

    b *25%*

    c *24.67%*

    d *34%*

E 14-8

Interim tax The estimated and actual pretax incomes of Endicott Corporation by quarter for 2006 were as follows:

	1st Quarter	2nd Quarter	3rd Quarter	4th Quarter
Estimated pretax income	$30,000	$30,000	$40,000	$50,000
Actual pretax income	30,000	40,000	40,000	40,000

Endicott calculated its estimated annual effective income tax rate to be 27.8333%, based on estimated pretax income and existing income tax rates.

REQUIRED: Prepare a schedule to calculate Endicott Corporation's net income by quarter.

LEARNING OBJECTIVES 7, 8

E 14-9
Interim accounting for various situations; tax

1. An inventory loss from a market price decline occurred in the first quarter, and the decline was not expected to reverse during the fiscal year. However, in the third quarter, the inventory's market price recovery exceeded the market decline that occurred in the first quarter. For interim financial reporting, the dollar amount of net inventory should:

   a *Decrease in the first quarter by the amount of the market price decline and increase in the third quarter by the amount of the decrease in the first quarter*

   b *Decrease in the first quarter by the amount of the market price decline and increase in the third quarter by the amount of the market price recovery*

   c *Decrease in the first quarter by the amount of the market price decline and not be affected in the third quarter*

   d *Not be affected in either the first quarter or the third quarter*

2. Farr Corporation had the following transactions during the quarter ended March 31, 2006:

Loss on early extinguishment of debt	$ 70,000
Payment of fire insurance premium for calendar year 2006	100,000

   What amount should be included in Farr's income statement for the quarter ended March 31, 2006?

	Extraordinary Loss	Insurance Expense
a	$70,000	$100,000
b	$70,000	$ 25,000
c	$17,500	$ 25,000
d	0	$100,000

3. An inventory loss from a permanent market decline of $360,000 occurred in May 2006. Cox Company appropriately recorded this loss in May 2006, after its March 31, 2006, quarterly report was issued. What amount of inventory loss should be reported in Cox's quarterly income statement for the three months ended June 30, 2006?

   a *0*

   b *$90,000*

   c *$180,000*

   d *$360,000*

4. On July 1, 2006, Dolan Corporation incurred an extraordinary loss of $300,000, net of income tax saving. Dolan's operating income for the full year ending December 31, 2006, is expected to be $500,000. In Dolan's income statement for the quarter ended September 30, 2006, how much of this extraordinary loss should be disclosed?

   a *$300,000*

   b *$150,000*

   c *$75,000*

   d *0*

5. In January 2006, Pine Company paid property taxes of $80,000 covering the calendar year 2006. Also in January 2006, Pine estimated that its year-end bonuses to executives would amount to $320,000 for 2006. What is the total amount of expense relating to these two items that should be reflected in Pine's quarterly income statement for the three months ended June 30, 2006?

   a *$100,000*

   b *$80,000*

   c *$20,000*

   d *0*

LEARNING OBJECTIVES 7, 8

E 14-10
Interim accounting for various situations; tax
Trapper Manufacturing Company records sales of $1,000,000 and cost of sales of $550,000 during the first quarter of 2006. Trapper uses the LIFO inventory method, and its inventories are computed as follows:

Beginning LIFO inventory at January 1	10,000 units at $5	$50,000
Ending LIFO inventory at March 31	6,000 units at $5	$30,000

Before year-end, Trapper expects to replace the 4,000 units liquidated in the first quarter. The current cost of the inventory units is $8 each.

REQUIRED: At what amount will Trapper report cost of sales in its first-quarter interim report?

P 14-1

Apply threshold tests The following information has been accumulated for use in preparing segment disclosures for Ledbetter Corporation (in thousands):

	Sales to Unaffiliated Customers	Sales to Affiliated Customers	Total Sales
Apparel	$164	—	$ 164
Construction	112	—	112
Furniture	208	$ 6	214
Lumber and wood products	175	90	265
Paper	90	—	90
Textiles	50	170	220
Tobacco	93	—	93
Total	$892	$266	$1,158

REQUIRED

1. Determine Ledbetter's reportable segments under the 10% revenue test.

2. Are additional reportable segments required under the 75% revenue test?

3. Prepare a schedule to disclose revenue by operating segment for external reporting. Assume that the paper and tobacco segments, both sold in grocery stores, share similar operating characteristics on four of the five aggregation criteria.

P 14-2

Apply threshold tests The following data for 2006 relate to Hawkeye Industries, a worldwide conglomerate:

Segments	Sales to Unaffiliated Customers	Intersegment Sales	Operating Profit (Loss)	Assets
Food	$300,000	$ 50,000	$45,000	$310,000
Chemical	110,000	40,000	23,000	150,000
Textiles	65,000	5,000	(8,000)	60,000
Furniture	48,000	—	9,000	40,000
Beverage	62,000	10,000	18,000	60,000
Oil	15,000	—	(2,000)	25,000
Segment	600,000	105,000	85,000	645,000
Corporate	—	—	(7,000)	15,000
Consolidated	$600,000	0	$78,000	$660,000

REQUIRED: Answer the following questions relating to Hawkeye's required segment disclosures and show computations.

1. Which segments are reportable segments under (a) the revenue test, (b) the operating-profit test, and (c) the asset test?

2. Do additional reportable segments have to be identified?

P 14-3

Apply threshold tests; disclosure Daton-Paulo Corporation's home country is the United States, but it also has operations in Canada, Mexico, Brazil, and South Africa and reports internally on a geographic basis. Information relevant to Daton-Paulo's operating-segment disclosure requirement for the year ended December 31, 2006, is presented in summary form as follows:

	United States	Canada	Mexico	Brazil	South Africa	Consolidated
Sales to unaffiliated customers	$120,000	$13,000	$20,000	$22,000	$15,000	$190,000
Intersegment transfers	29,000	11,000	—	—	10,000	—
Total revenue	$149,000	$24,000	$20,000	$22,000	$25,000	$190,000
Operating profit	$ 24,000	$ 6,000	$ 8,000	$ 5,000	$ 7,000	$ 50,000
Identifiable assets	$150,000	$30,000	$19,000	$20,000	$31,000	$305,000

REQUIRED

1. Prepare schedules to show which of Daton-Paulo's operating segments require separate disclosure under (a) the 10% revenue test, (b) the 10% asset test, and (c) the 10% profit test.

2. Which of Daton-Paulo's operating segments meet at least one of the tests for segment reporting?

3. Prepare a schedule to disclose Daton-Paulo's segment operations from the information given.

LEARNING OBJECTIVES **2, 3, 4, 5**

P 14-4

Apply threshold tests; segment and enterprisewide disclosure

Mid-America Corporation has five major operating segments and operates in both domestic and foreign markets. Mid-America is organized internally on an industry basis. Information about its revenue from operating segments and foreign operations for 2006 is as follows (in thousands):

Sales to Unaffiliated Customers

	Domestic	Foreign	Total
Foods	$ 150	$ 30	$ 180
Soft drinks	650	250	900
Distilled spirits	500	50	550
Cosmetics	200	—	200
Packaging	110	—	110
Other (four minor segments)	240	—	240
	$1,850	$330	$2,180

Sales to Affiliated Customers

	Domestic	Foreign	Total
Foods	$ 30	—	$ 30
Soft drinks	160	—	160
Distilled spirits	—	$20	20
Cosmetics	—	—	—
Packaging	10	—	10
Other (four minor segments)			
	$200	$20	$220

A Japanese subsidiary of Mid-America operates exclusively in the soft drink market. All other foreign operations are carried out through Canadian subsidiaries, none of which are included in the soft drink business.

Only the soft drink and distilled spirits segments are reportable segments under the asset and operating-profit tests for segments.

REQUIRED

1. Determine which industry segments are reportable segments under the revenue test for segment reporting. Assume no further aggregation is possible. Would the possible aggregation of smaller segments change your response?

2. Prepare a schedule suitable for disclosing Mid-America's revenue by segment for 2006, assuming no further aggregation is possible.

3. Prepare a schedule suitable for disclosing Mid-America's revenue by geographic area for 2006.

LEARNING OBJECTIVES **2, 3, 4**

P 14-5

Apply threshold tests; disclosure

Selected information, which is reported to the chief operating officer, for the five segments of Random Choice Company for the year ended December 31, 2006, is as follows:

	Food	Tobacco	Lumber	Textiles	Furniture	General Corporate	Consolidated
Revenue Data							
Sales to unaffiliated customers	$12,000	$10,000	$7,000	$18,000	$7,000		$ 54,000
Sales to affiliated customers	5,000	7,000		8,000			
Income from equity investees				3,000		$ 6,000	9,000
Total revenue	$17,000	$17,000	$7,000	$29,000	$7,000	$ 6,000	$ 63,000
Expense Data							
Cost of sales	$10,000	$ 9,000	$4,000	$16,000	$4,000		$ 23,000
Depreciation expense	1,000	2,000	2,500	3,000	500		9,000
Other operating expenses	2,000	2,000	1,000	2,000	1,000		8,000
Interest expense	2,000			2,000		$ 3,000	7,000
Income taxes	1,000	2,000	(250)	3,000	750	1,500	8,000
Net income	$ 1,000	$ 2,000	$(250)	$ 3,000	$ 750	$ 1,500	$ 8,000
Asset Data							
Segment assets	$18,000	$19,000	$6,000	$22,000	$7,000		$ 72,000
Investment in affiliates				20,000		$40,000	60,000
General corporate assets						4,000	4,000
Intersegment advances	1,000	2,000					
Total assets	$19,000	$21,000	$6,000	$42,000	$7,000	$44,000	$136,000

The lumber segment has not been a reportable segment in prior years and is not expected to be a reportable segment in future years.

REQUIRED

1. Prepare schedules to show which of the segments are reportable segments under:

   a   The 10% revenue test
   b   The 10% operating-profit test
   c   The 10% asset test

2. Which of the segments meet at least one of the tests for reportable segments?

3. Must additional reportable segments be identified?

4. Prepare a schedule for appropriate disclosure of the above segmented data in the financial report of Random Choice Company for the year ended December 31, 2006.

P 14-6

LEARNING OBJECTIVES 2, 3, 4

Apply threshold tests; disclosure The consolidated income statement of Truetest Company for 2006 is as follows (in thousands):

Truetest Consolidated Income Statement for the Year Ended December 31, 2006

Sales	$360
Interest income	10
Income from equity investee	30
Total revenue	400
Cost of sales	$180
General expenses	40
Selling expenses	50
Interest expense	10
Noncontrolling interest expense	15
Income taxes	45
Total expenses	340
Income before extraordinary loss	$ 60
Extraordinary loss (net of income taxes)	10
Consolidated net income	$ 50

Truetest's operations are conducted through three domestic operating segments with sales, expenses, and assets as follows (in thousands):

	Chemical	Food	Drug	Corporate
Sales (including intersegment sales)	$160	$140	$120	
Cost of sales (including intersegment cost of sales)	80	70	60	
General expenses	15	10	10	$ 5
Selling expenses	20	15	15	
Interest expense (unaffiliated)	5		5	
Identifiable assets	200	180	150	200
Investment in equity investee				300

The $10,000 interest income is not related to any industry segment. Consolidated total assets are $1,000,000. The chemical and food segments had intersegment sales of $35,000 and $25,000, respectively.

REQUIRED: Prepare a schedule of required disclosures for Truetest's industry segments in a form acceptable for reporting purposes.

LEARNING OBJECTIVES 2, 3, 4

P 14-7

Apply threshold tests; disclosure The information that follows is for Colby Company at and for the year ended December 31, 2006. Colby's operating segments are cost centers currently used for internal planning and control purposes. Amounts shown in the Total Consolidated column are amounts prepared under GAAP for external reporting. (Data are in thousands of dollars.)

	Food Industry	Packing Industry	Textile Industry	Foreign Operations	All Other Industries	Corporate	Total Consolidated
Income Statement							
Sales to unaffiliated customers	$950	$500	$300	$250	$400		$2,400
Income from equity investees							100
Cost of sales to unaffiliated customers	(600)	(350)	(175)	(125)	(250)		(1,500)
Operating expense	(200)	(75)	(150)	(75)	(75)	$ (25)	(600)
Interest expense							(20)
Income taxes							(150)
Noncontrolling interest expense							(30)
Income (loss)	$150	$ 75	$ (25)	$ 50	$ 75	$ (25)	$ 200
Assets							
Current assets	$300	$100	$ 75	$100	$225	$ 25	$ 825
Plant assets—net	400	400	250	100	175	25	1,350
Advances	50		25			50	
Equity investments						1,000	1,000
Total assets	$750	$500	$350	$200	$400	$1,100	$3,175
Intersegment Transfers							
Sales*	$ 60	$ 60	$ 30	$ 50			
Purchases*	$100	$ 25		$ 75			

*Amounts have been eliminated from the income data given.

REQUIRED

1. Prepare a schedule to determine which of Colby's operating segments are reportable segments under (a) the 10% revenue test, (b) the 10% operating-profit test, and (c) the 10% asset test.

2. Prepare a schedule to show how Colby's segment information would be disclosed under the provisions of *FASB Statement No. 131.*

P 14-8

Interim reporting—tax Trotter Corporation is subject to income tax rates of 20% on its first $50,000 pretax income and 34% on amounts in excess of $50,000. Quarterly pretax accounting income for the calendar year is estimated by Trotter to be as follows:

Quarter	Estimated Pretax Income
First	$ 20,000
Second	30,000
Third	60,000
Fourth	50,000
Total	$160,000

No changes in accounting principles, discontinued items, unusual or infrequently occurring items, or extraordinary items are anticipated for the year. The fourth quarter's pretax income is, however, expected to include $20,000 in dividends from domestic corporations, for which an 80% dividend-received deduction is available.

REQUIRED

1. Calculate the estimated annual effective tax rate for Trotter Corporation for 2006.

2. Prepare a schedule showing Trotter's estimated net income for each quarter and the calendar year 2006.

INTERNET ASSIGNMENT

Go to *H. J. Heinz's* Web site and obtain a copy of its most recent annual report.

a What are Heinz's business segments? Are Heinz's operating segments based on product/ industry or geographical groupings?

b Examine the segment-disclosure totals for revenues, profits, and assets. Do they agree with the totals reported in the consolidated financial statements?

c How significant is intersegment revenue? From this analysis, is Heinz primarily horizontally or vertically integrated or a conglomerate?

d What geographical area provides most of Heinz's revenues? Would you consider Heinz a multinational corporation? Why or why not?

e Qualitatively, do you consider Heinz's segmental reporting to be adequate? What additional information or details would you like to see disclosed regarding its segments?

SELECTED READINGS

Accounting Principles Board Opinion No. 28. "Interim Financial Reporting." New York: American Institute of Certified Public Accountants, 1973.

FASB Interpretation No. 18. "An Interpretation of *APB Opinion No. 28.*" Stamford, CT: Financial Accounting Standards, Board, 1977.

HERRMANN, DON, and WAYNE B. THOMAS. "An Analysis of Segment Disclosures Under *SFAS No. 131* and *SFAS No. 14.*" *Accounting Horizons* (September 2000), pp. 287–302.

International Accounting Standard No. 14. "Segment Reporting." London, UK: International Accounting Standards Board, 1997.

International Accounting Standard No. 34. "Interim Financial Reporting." London, UK: International Accounting Standards Board, 1998.

SALTER, STEPHEN B., et al. "Reporting Financial Information by Segment: A Comment of the American Accounting Association on the IASC Draft Statement of Principles." *Accounting Horizons* (March 1996), pp. 118–123.

Statement of Financial Accounting Standards No. 3. "Reporting Accounting Changes in Interim Financial Statements." Stamford, CT: Financial Accounting Standards Board, 1974.

Statement of Financial Accounting Standards No. 131. "Disclosures About Segments of an Enterprise and Related Information." Stamford, CT: Financial Accounting Standards Board, 1997.

PARTNERSHIPS—FORMATION, OPERATIONS, AND CHANGES IN OWNERSHIP INTERESTS

This chapter and Chapter 16 focus on accounting for partnership entities. This chapter describes general matters involving the partnership form of business organization, including partnership formation, accounting for partnership operations, and accounting for changes in ownership interests. The limited partnership, a special kind of partnership frequently used in professional partnerships such as CPA firms, is described at the end of this chapter. Chapter 16 covers the dissolution and liquidation of partnerships.

Although accounting for partnerships differs from that of other types of business organizations, asset, liability, and income accounting usually follow GAAP comparable to other entities. The analysis and recording of transactions not affecting ownership interests are ordinarily the same for partnerships, proprietorships, and corporations.

...

NATURE OF PARTNERSHIPS

Partnerships allow business ventures' required investment and risk to be shared. Partners also can contribute their expertise to the ventures. Partnerships are found in many areas of business, including service industries; retail trade; wholesale and manufacturing operations; and the professions, particularly the legal, medical, and public accounting professions.

Partnerships are governed by state statutes. In 1914, the National Conference of Commissioners on Uniform State Laws developed the Uniform Partnership Act, which was eventually adopted, with some variations, by all states except Louisiana. In 1992, the Revised Uniform Partnership Act (RUPA) was promulgated by the national conference and has been adopted, with revision, by several states. California, for example, adopted RUPA to govern all partnerships formed after December 31, 1996. The original Uniform Partnership Act still provides legal guidance for general partnerships in most states, and its provisions generally apply to the formation, operation, and dissolution of partnerships in the United States. References made to the act in Chapters 15 and 16 refer to the original Uniform Partnership Act, which can be found on this book's Web site. Remember, however, that each state has its own variation of partnership law.

Partnership Characteristics

Partnership is defined in Section 6 of the Uniform Partnership Act as "an association of two or more persons to carry on as co-owners a business for profit." One legal feature of a partnership is its **limited life**. Under the act, the legal life of a partnership terminates with the admission of a new partner, the

LEARNING OBJECTIVES

1 Comprehend the legal characteristics of partnerships.

2 Understand initial investment valuation and record keeping.

3 Grasp the diverse nature of profit and loss sharing agreements and their computation.

4 Value a new partner's investment in an existing partnership.

5 Value a partner's share upon retirement or death.

6 Understand limited liability partnership characteristics.

withdrawal or death of a partner, voluntary dissolution by the partners, or involuntary dissolution such as through bankruptcy proceedings. The termination of the legal partnership association does not necessarily terminate the partnership as a separate business and accounting entity. Partnership business operations frequently continue to run smoothly when partners are admitted or withdraw.

Under the legal concept of **mutual agency**, each partner is an agent for all partnership activities, with the power to bind all other partners by his or her actions on behalf of the partnership. The implications of mutual agency are particularly significant when considered in conjunction with the **unlimited liability** feature of partnerships. Each partner is liable for all partnership debts and, in case of insolvency, may be required to use personal assets to pay partnership debts authorized by any partner.

Articles of Partnership

A partnership may be formed by a simple oral agreement among two or more people to operate a business for profit. Even though oral agreements may be legal and binding, written **partnership agreements** are a sound business practice. Such agreements should specify:

1. The types of products and services to be provided and other details of the business's operations
2. Each partner's rights and responsibilities in conducting the business
3. Each partner's initial investment, including the value assigned to noncash asset investments
4. Additional investment conditions
5. Asset drawing provisions
6. Profit and loss sharing formulas
7. Procedures for dissolving the partnership

When no specific agreement for dividing profits and losses exists, all partners share equally, irrespective of investments made or time devoted to the business (Section 18 of the act).

Partnership Financial Reporting

The accounting reports of partnerships are designed to meet the needs of three user groups—the partners, the partnership creditors, and the Internal Revenue Service (IRS). Partners need accounting information for planning and controlling partnership assets and activities and for making personal investment decisions with respect to their partnership investments. In the absence of an agreement to the contrary, every partner has access to the partnership books at all times (Section 19 of the act). Credit grantors such as banks and other financial institutions frequently require financial reports in support of loan applications and other credit matters relating to partnerships.

Although partnerships do not pay federal income taxes, partnerships are required to submit financial information returns to the IRS. This allows the IRS to verify that each partner pays income taxes on his or her share of partnership income. Partnerships are not required to prepare annual reports for public inspection.

INITIAL INVESTMENTS IN A PARTNERSHIP

All property brought into the partnership or acquired by the partnership is partnership property (Section 8[1] of the act). Initial investments in a partnership are recorded in capital accounts maintained for each partner. If Ashley and Becker each invest $20,000 cash in a new partnership, they record the investments as follows:

Cash (+A)	20,000	
Ashley capital (+OE)		20,000
To record Ashley's original investment of cash.		
Cash (+A)	20,000	
Becker capital (+OE)		20,000
To record Becker's original investment of cash.		

Noncash Investments

When property other than cash is invested in a partnership, the noncash property is recorded at the fair value of the property at the time of the investment. Conceptually, the fair value should be determined by independent valuations, but as a practical matter, the fair value of noncash property is determined by agreement of all partners. The amounts involved should be specified in the written partnership agreement.

Assume, for example, that C. Cola and R. Crown enter into a partnership with the following investments:

	C. Cola (Fair Value)	R. Crown (Fair Value)
Cash	—	$ 7,000
Land (cost to C. Cola, $5,000)	$10,000	—
Building (cost to C. Cola, $30,000)	40,000	—
Inventory items (cost to R. Crown, $28,000)	—	35,000
Total	$50,000	$42,000

After Cola and Crown agree to the values assigned to the assets, they record the investments as follows:

Land (+A)	10,000	
Building (+A)	40,000	
C. Cola capital (+OE)		50,000

To record C. Cola's original investment of land and building at fair value.

Cash (+A)	7,000	
Inventory (+A)	35,000	
R. Crown capital (+OE)		42,000

To record R. Crown's original investment of cash and inventory items at fair value.

Partnership investments are recorded at fair value because all property brought into the partnership becomes partnership property, and any gains or losses from use or disposal of such property will be divided in the profit and loss sharing ratios of the partners.

Assume that the investments of C. Cola and R. Crown are recorded at original cost to the individual partners, that the noncash assets are immediately sold at their fair values, and that the partnership is liquidated. C. Cola invests assets with a fair value of $50,000 but receives only $46,000 (half of the $92,000 fair value) in liquidation. Crown invests assets with a fair value of $42,000 and receives $46,000 in liquidation. Exhibit 15-1 shows entries on the partnership books to reflect the accounting under these assumptions.

As Exhibit 15-1 illustrates, recording partners' noncash investments at their fair value ensures that any gains and losses on subsequent disposition of the property through use or through sale will be equitable. Such gains or losses are divided in the profit and loss sharing ratios provided in the partnership agreement.

Bonus or Goodwill on Initial Investments

A valuation problem arises when partners agree on relative capital interests that are not aligned with their investments of identifiable assets. For example, C. Cola and R. Crown could agree to divide initial partnership capital equally, even though C. Cola contributed $50,000 in identifiable assets and R. Crown contributed $42,000. Such an agreement implies that R. Crown is contributing an unidentifiable asset such as individual talent, established clientele, or banking connections to the partnership.

The partnership agreement specifies equal capital interests, so we adjust the capital account balances of C. Cola ($50,000) and R. Crown ($42,000) to meet the conditions of the agreement. Either of two approaches may be used to adjust the capital accounts—the bonus approach or the goodwill approach. Under the **bonus approach** the unidentifiable asset is not recorded on the partnership books and the only journal entry necessary is as follows:

EXHIBIT 15-1

Comparison of Initial
Investment Involving
Noncash Assets

	Investment at Original Cost		Investment at Fair Value	
1. To record C. Cola's investment:				
Land (+A)	5,000		10,000	
Building (+A)	30,000		40,000	
C. Cola capital (+OE)		35,000		50,000
2. To record R. Crown's investment:				
Cash (+A)	7,000		7,000	
Inventory (+A)	28,000		35,000	
R. Crown capital (+OE)		35,000		42,000
3. To record sale of assets at fair value:				
Cash (+A)	85,000		85,000	
Land (−A)		5,000		10,000
Building (−A)		30,000		40,000
Inventory (−A)		28,000		35,000
Gain on sale (+G, +OE)		22,000		none
4. To distribute the gain on sale equally:				
Gain on sale (−G, −OE)	22,000		none	
C. Cola capital (+OE)		11,000		none
R. Crown capital (+OE)		11,000		none
5. To distribute cash in final liquidation of the partnership:				
C. Cola capital (−OE)	46,000		50,000	
R. Crown capital (−OE)	46,000		42,000	
Cash (−A)		92,000		92,000

C. Cola capital (−OE)	4,000	
R. Crown capital (−OE)		4,000

To establish equal capital interests of $46,000 by recording
a $4,000 bonus from C. Cola to R. Crown.

When the **goodwill approach** is used, the unidentifiable asset contributed by Crown is measured on the basis of C. Cola's $50,000 investment for a 50% interest. C. Cola's investment implies total partnership capital of $100,000 ($50,000 ÷ 50%) and goodwill of $8,000 ($100,000 total capital − $92,000 identifiable assets). We record the unidentifiable asset as follows:

Goodwill (+A)	8,000	
R. Crown capital (+OE)		8,000

To establish equal capital interests of $50,000 by recognizing
R. Crown's investment of an $8,000 unidentifiable asset.

Both approaches are equally effective in aligning the capital accounts with the agreement and are equitable in assigning capital interests to individual partners. A decision to use one approach over the other will depend on partner attitudes toward recording the $8,000 unidentifiable asset under the goodwill method and on C. Cola's willingness to receive a $46,000 capital credit for a $50,000 investment under the bonus approach.

ADDITIONAL INVESTMENTS AND WITHDRAWALS

The partnership agreement should establish guidelines for additional investments and withdrawals made after partnership operations have begun. Additional investments are credited to the investing partner's capital account at fair value at the time of the investment. Withdrawals of large and irregular amounts are ordinarily recorded directly in the withdrawing partner's capital account. The entry for such a withdrawal is:

Smith capital (−OE)	20,000	
Cash (−A)		20,000
To record the withdrawal of cash.		

Drawings

Partnership profits are the business rewards of partners, so partners do not have take-home pay as do the employees of the partnership business. Instead, active partners commonly withdraw regular amounts of money on a weekly or monthly basis in anticipation of their share of partnership profits. Such withdrawals are called **drawings**, *drawing allowances*, or sometimes *salary allowances*, and they are usually recorded in the partners' drawing accounts rather than directly in the capital accounts. For example, if Townsend and Lee withdraw $1,000 from the partnership each month, they would record the monthly withdrawals as follows:

Townsend drawing (−OE)	1,000	
Cash (−A)		1,000
To record Townsend's drawing allowance for January.		
Lee drawing (−OE)	1,000	
Cash (−A)		1,000
To record Lee's drawing allowance for January.		

The drawing accounts should be closed to the capital accounts at the end of each accounting period. The final effect of such an entry is the same as if direct charges had been made to the capital accounts. Drawing accounts provide a record of each partner's drawings during an accounting period. This record may be compared with drawings allowed in the partnership agreement in order to establish an accounting control over excessive drawings. (Drawings balances are also a factor in many profit and loss sharing agreements and will be discussed in conjunction with such agreements.)

If Townsend draws $1,000 each month during the year, his drawing account balance at year-end is $12,000, and his drawing account is closed by the following entry:

Townsend capital (−OE)	12,000	
Townsend drawing (+OE)		12,000
To close Townsend's drawing account.		

Regardless of the name given to regular withdrawals by partners, such withdrawals are disinvestments of essentially the same nature as large and irregular withdrawals. Drawing accounts should be closed to capital accounts before a partnership balance sheet is prepared.

Loans and Advances

A partner may make a personal loan to the partnership. This situation is provided for in Section 18c of the act, which specifies that "a partner, who in the aid of the partnership makes any payment or advance beyond the amount of capital which he agreed to contribute, shall be paid interest from the date of the payment or advance." Such loans or advances and related accrued interest are correctly regarded as liabilities of the partnership. Similarly, partnership loans and advances to an individual partner are considered partnership assets. Matters concerning loans and advances to or from partners should be covered in the partnership agreement.

PARTNERSHIP OPERATIONS

The operations of a partnership are similar in most respects to those of other forms of organizations operating in the same line of business. In measuring partnership income for a period, however, the expenses should be scrutinized to make sure that partners' personal expenses are excluded from the partnership's business expenses. If personal expenses of a partner are paid with partnership assets, the payment is charged to the drawing or capital account of that partner. Drawings and salary allowances are closed to the capital accounts of the partners rather than to an income summary account.

EXHIBIT 15-2

Format for a
Statement of
Partners' Capital

**RATCLIFFE AND YANCEY
STATEMENT OF PARTNERS' CAPITAL
FOR THE YEAR ENDED DECEMBER 31, 2006**

	60% Ratcliffe	40% Yancey	Total
Capital balances January 1, 2006	$40,000	$35,000	$75,000
Add: Additional investments	5,000	—	5,000
Deduct: Withdrawals	—	(3,000)	(3,000)
Deduct: Drawings	(6,000)	(9,000)	(15,000)
Net contributed capital	39,000	23,000	62,000
Add: Net income for 2006	20,700	13,800	34,500
Capital balances December 31, 2006	$59,700	$36,800	$96,500

Partnership general-purpose financial statements include an income statement, a balance sheet, a statement of partnership capital, and a statement of cash flows. The statement of partnership capital is unique to the partnership form of organization and is illustrated here.

Assume that Ratcliffe and Yancey are partners sharing profits in a 60:40 ratio, respectively. Data relevant to the partnership's equity accounts for 2006 are:

Partnership net income 2006	$34,500
Ratcliffe capital January 1, 2006	40,000
Ratcliffe additional investment 2006	5,000
Ratcliffe drawing 2006	6,000
Yancey capital January 1, 2006	35,000
Yancey drawing 2006	9,000
Yancey withdrawal 2006	3,000

The statement of partners' capital that appears in Exhibit 15-2 reflects this information. Although other forms of presentation can be used, the format illustrated in Exhibit 15-2 provides a comparison of capital changes before and after the division of partnership net income. An ability to compare beginning capital balances and net contributed capital is helpful to the partners in setting investment and withdrawal policies and in controlling abuses of the established policies.

Closing entries for the Ratcliffe and Yancey partnership at December 31, 2006, are as follows:

December 31, 2006

Revenue and expense summary (−OE)	34,500	
Ratcliffe capital (+OE)		20,700
Yancey capital (+OE)		13,800

To divide net income for the year 60% to Ratcliffe and 40% to Yancey.

December 31, 2006

Ratcliffe capital (−OE)	6,000	
Yancey capital (−OE)	9,000	
Ratcliffe drawing (+OE)		6,000
Yancey drawing (+OE)		9,000

To close partner drawing accounts to capital accounts.

LEARNING
OBJECTIVE 3

PROFIT AND LOSS SHARING AGREEMENTS

Equal division of partnership income is required in the absence of a profit and loss sharing agreement. However, partners generally agree to share profits in a specified ratio, such as the 60:40 division illustrated for the Ratcliffe and Yancey partnership. Profit sharing agreements also apply to the division of losses unless the agreement specifies otherwise.

Although agreements to share profits and losses equally or in specified ratios are common, more-complex profit sharing agreements are also encountered in practice. The time that partners devote to the partnership business and the capital invested in the business by individual partners are frequently considered in determining the profit sharing agreement. If one partner manages the partnership, the partnership agreement may allow that partner a salary allowance equal to the amount he or she could earn in an alternative employment opportunity before remaining profits are allocated. Similarly, if one partner invests significantly more than another in a partnership venture, the agreement may provide an interest allowance on capital investments before remaining profits are divided. As in the case of salary allowances, interest allowances are provisions of the partnership agreement and have no effect on the measurement of partnership income.

Service Considerations in Profit and Loss Sharing Agreements

As mentioned earlier, a partner who devotes time to the partnership business while other partners work elsewhere may receive a salary allowance. Salary allowances are also used to compensate for differences in the fair value of the talents of partners, all of whom devote their time to the partnership. Another variation in profit and loss sharing agreements provides salary allowances to active partners and a bonus to the managing partner to encourage profit maximization. These alternatives are illustrated for the partnership of Bob, Gary, and Pete. Bob is the managing partner, Gary is the sales manager, and Pete works outside the partnership.

Salary Allowances In Profit Sharing Agreements

Assume that the partnership agreement provides that Bob and Gary receive salary allowances of $12,000 each, with the remaining income allocated equally among the three partners. If partnership net income is $60,000 for 2006 and $12,000 for 2007, the income allocations are as shown in Exhibit 15-3. The total 2006 allocation is $24,000 each to Bob and Gary and $12,000 to Pete. The 2007 allocation is $8,000 income to Bob and Gary and a $4,000 loss to Pete. Note that the partnership agreement was followed in 2007 even though the salary allowances of $24,000 exceeded partnership net income of $12,000. The income allocation schedule follows the order of the profit sharing agreement even when the partnership has a loss. Salary allowances simply increase the loss to be divided equally.

Journal entries to distribute partnership income to individual capital accounts for 2006 and 2007 follow.

December 31, 2006

Revenue and expense summary (−OE)	60,000	
Bob capital (+OE)		24,000
Gary capital (+OE)		24,000
Pete capital (+OE)		12,000
Partnership income allocation for 2006.		

(continued)

INCOME ALLOCATION SCHEDULE—2006

		Bob	Gary	Pete	Total
Net income	$60,000				
Salary allowances to					
Bob and Gary	(24,000)	$12,000	$12,000		$24,000
Remainder to divide	36,000				
Divided equally	(36,000)	12,000	12,000	$12,000	36,000
Remainder to divide	0				
Net income allocation		$24,000	$24,000	$12,000	$60,000

INCOME ALLOCATION SCHEDULE—2007

		Bob	Gary	Pete	Total
Net income	$12,000				
Salary allowances to					
Bob and Gary	(24,000)	(12,000)	12,000		$24,000
Remainder to divide	(12,000)				
Divided equally	$12,000	(4,000)	(4,000)	$ (4,000)	(12,000)
Remainder to divide	0				
Net income allocation		$ 8,000	$ 8,000	$ (4,000)	$12,000

EXHIBIT 15-3

Salary Allowances in Profit Sharing Agreements

December 31, 2007

Revenue and expense summary (−OE)	12,000	
Pete capital (−OE)	4,000	
Bob capital (+OE)		8,000
Gary capital (+OE)		8,000
Partnership income allocation for 2007.		

In partnership accounting, partner salary allowances are not expenses in the determination of partnership net income. They are a means of achieving a fair division of income among the partners based on the time and talents devoted to partnership business.

Calculating partnership income after salary allowances is appropriate when comparing the performance of a partnership business with similar businesses operated under the corporate organizational form. Stockholders who devote their time to corporate affairs are employees, and their salaries are deducted in measuring corporate net income. Failure to adjust partnership income for salary allowances may result in inaccurate comparisons of a corporation's performance to a partnership's performance. Other adjustments, such as for corporate income taxes, also need to be made for accurate comparisons.

Calculation of partnership income after salary allowances is also appropriate in assessing the success of a business. The financial success of a partnership business lies in its earning a fair return for the services performed by partners, for capital invested in the business, and for the risks taken. If partnership income is not greater than the combined amounts that active partners could earn by working outside of the partnership, then the business is not a financial success. Income after salary allowances (or imputed salaries) should be sufficient to compensate for capital invested and risks undertaken.

BONUS AND SALARY ALLOWANCES The partnership agreement of Bob, Gary, and Pete provides that Bob receive a bonus of 10% of partnership net income for managing the business; that Bob and Gary receive salary allowances of $10,000 and $8,000, respectively, for services rendered; and that the remaining partnership income be divided equally among the three partners. If partnership net income is $60,000 in 2006 and $12,000 in 2007, the partnership income is allocated as shown in Exhibit 15-4.

EXHIBIT 15-4

Bonus and Salary Allowances in Profit Sharing Agreements

INCOME ALLOCATION SCHEDULE—2006

		Bob	Gary	Pete	Total
Net income	$60,000				
Bonus to Bob	(6,000)	$ 6,000			$ 6,000
Remainder to divide	54,000				
Salary allowances to					
Bob and Gary	(18,000)	10,000	$ 8,000		18,000
Remainder to divide	36,000				
Divided equally	(36,000)	12,000	12,000	$12,000	36,000
Remainder to divide	0				
Net income allocation		$28,000	$20,000	$12,000	$60,000

INCOME ALLOCATION SCHEDULE—2007

		Bob	Gary	Pete	Total
Net income	$12,000				
Bonus to Bob	(1,200)	$ 1,200			$ 1,200
Remainder to divide	10,800				
Salary allowances to					
Bob and Gary	(18,000)	10,000	$ 8,000		18,000
Remainder to divide	(7,200)				
Divide equally	7,200	(2,400)	(2,400)	$ (2,400)	(7,200)
Remainder to divide	0				
Net income allocation		$ 8,800	$ 5,600	$ (2,400)	$12,000

The allocation schedules follow the order of the profit sharing agreement in allocating the bonus first, then the salary allowances, and finally the remainder to individual partners. The bonus is computed on the basis of partnership net income as the concept of "partnership net income" is generally understood in accounting practice (i.e., before salary allowances are deducted).

Partners may, however, require salary allowances to be deducted in determining the base for computing the bonus. If this had been the case here, the bonus illustrated for 2006 would have been $4,200 [($60,000 − $18,000) × 10%] rather than $6,000, and the final net income allocation would have been $26,800, $20,600, and $12,600 for Bob, Gary, and Pete, respectively.

Sometimes the partners may want the bonus, as well as salary allowances, to be deducted in determining the base for the bonus computation. Had this been the case in the Bob, Gary, and Pete partnership agreement, the bonus would have been $3,818, computed as follows:

$$\text{Let } B = \text{bonus}$$
$$B = 0.1 \, (\$60,000 - \$18,000 - B)$$
$$B = \$6,000 - \$1,800 - 0.1B$$
$$1.1B = \$4,200$$
$$\underline{B = \$3,818} \text{ (rounded)}$$

$$\textit{Check: } \$60,000 - \$18,000 - 3,818 = \$38,182 \text{ bonus base}$$
$$\$38,182 \times 10\% = \$3,818 \text{ bonus}$$

The partnership agreement should be precise in specifying the measurement procedures to be used in determining the amount of a bonus.

Capital as a Factor in Profit Sharing Agreements

The capital contributions of partners are frequently considered in profit and loss sharing agreements. If capital is to be considered in the division of partnership income, the profit sharing agreement should be specific with respect to which concept of capital is to be applied. For example, *capital* may refer to beginning capital balances, ending capital balances, or average capital balances. In addition, several interpretations of *average capital balances* are possible, and capital balances may be determined before or after drawing accounts are closed to the partner's capital accounts.

When beginning capital balances are used in allocating partnership income, additional investments during the accounting period may be discouraged because the partners making such investments are not compensated in the division of income until a later period. A similar problem exists when ending capital balances are used. Year-end investments are encouraged by their inclusion in determining each partner's share of income, but no incentive exists for a partner to make any investments before year end. Also, no penalty exists for withdrawals if the amounts withdrawn are reinvested before the period's end. Weighted average capital balances provide the fairest basis for allocating partnership income. A weighted average interpretation of capital should be assumed in the absence of evidence to the contrary.

Typically, the drawing allowances specified in a partnership agreement may be withdrawn without affecting the capital balances used in dividing partnership income. Drawing account balances up to the amounts specified in the agreement would not be deducted in determining the partners' average or year-end capital balances. For purposes of dividing partnership income, drawings in excess of allowable amounts are deducted from the partner's capital accounts in computing average or ending capital balances.

INCOME ALLOCATED IN RELATION TO PARTNERSHIP CAPITAL The partnership of Ace and Snoopy was formed on January 1, 2006, with each partner investing $20,000 cash. Changes in the capital accounts during 2006 are summarized as follows:

	Ace	Snoopy
Capital balances January 1, 2006	$20,000	$20,000
Investment April 1	2,000	—
Withdrawal July 1	—	(5,000)
Investment September 1	3,000	—
Withdrawal October 1	—	(4,000)
Investment December 28	—	8,000
Capital balances December 31, 2006	$25,000	$19,000

The beginning, ending, and average capital amounts for Ace and Snoopy for 2006 are as follows (in thousands):

COMPARISON OF CAPITAL BASES

	Beginning Capital Investment	Ending Capital Investment	Weighted Average Capital Investment
Ace	$20	$25	$22.5
Snoopy	20	19	19.5
Total	$40	$44	$42.0

Exhibit 15-5 shows computations of the weighted average capital investments of Ace and Snoopy. Actual investments are multiplied by the number of months outstanding to get dollar-month investment computations. Total dollar-month investments are divided by 12 to get weighted average annual capital balances.

Let's extend the Ace and Snoopy example by assuming that partnership net income is allocated on the basis of capital balances and that net income for 2006 is $100,000. Allocation of partnership income to Ace and Snoopy under each of the three capital bases is as follows:

Beginning Capital Balances
Ace ($100,000 × 20/40)	$ 50,000.00
Snoopy ($100,000 × 20/40)	50,000.00
Total income	$100,000.00

Ending Capital Balances
Ace ($100,000 × 25/44)	$ 56,818.18
Snoopy ($100,000 × 19/44)	43,181.82
Total income	$100,000.00

Average Capital Balances
Ace ($100,000 × 22.5/42)	$ 53,571.43
Snoopy ($100,000 × 19.5/42)	46,428.57
Total income	$100,000.00

If the partnership agreement of Ace and Snoopy specifies that income is to be divided based on capital balances but fails to specify how capital balances are to be computed, the weighted average computation is used. The $100,000 partnership income for 2006 is allocated $53,571.43 to Ace and $46,428.57 to Snoopy.

INTEREST ALLOWANCES ON PARTNERSHIP CAPITAL An agreement may provide for interest allowances on partnership capital in order to encourage capital investments, as well as salary allowances to

EXHIBIT 15-5		
Computations of Weighted Average Capital Investment		

WEIGHTED AVERAGE CAPITAL CALCULATIONS

	Dollar-Month Investment	
Average Capital Investment of Ace		
$20,000 × 3 months (January 1 to April 1)	$ 60,000	
$22,000 × 5 months (April 1 to September 1)	110,000	
$25,000 × 4 months (September 1 to December 31)	100,000	
12 months	$270,000	
Ace's average capital investment ($270,000 ÷ 12 months)		$22,500
Average Capital Investment of Snoopy		
$20,000 × 6 months (January 1 to July 1)	$120,000	
$15,000 × 3 months (July 1 to October 1)	45,000	
$11,000 × 3 months (October 1 to December 28)	33,000	
12 months	$198,000	
Snoopy's average capital investment ($198,000 ÷ 12 months)		$16,500

recognize time devoted to the business. Remaining profits are then divided equally or in any other ratio specified in the profit sharing agreement.

Consider the following information relating to the capital and drawing accounts of the Russo and Stokes partnership for the calendar year 2006 (amounts in thousands):

	Russo	Stokes
Capital Accounts		
Capital balances January 1, 2006	$186	$114
Additional investments June 1, 2006	24	36
Withdrawal July 1, 2006	—	10
Capital balances December 31, 2006 (before drawings)	$210	$140
Drawing Accounts		
Drawing account balances* December 31, 2006	$ 10	$ 12

*Account titles may be labeled partner salaries rather than partner drawings. In either case, the balances should be closed to partner capital accounts and not to the income summary.

The partnership agreement provides that the partnership income is divided equally after salary allowances of $12,000 per year for each partner and after interest allowances at a 10% annual rate on average capital balances. Exhibit 15-6 shows the income allocations for 2006 under this agreement. Part A assumes that partnership net income for 2006 is $91,000, and Part B assumes a partnership loss for 2006 of $3,000.

The average capital balances for Russo and Stokes are computed as follows (amounts in thousands):

EXHIBIT 15-6

Interest and Salary Allowances in Profit Sharing Agreements

PART A—PARTNERSHIP INCOME ASSUMED TO BE $91,000
INCOME ALLOCATION SCHEDULE

		Russo	Stokes	Total
Net income	$91,000			
Salary allowances	(24,000)	$12,000	$12,000	$24,000
Remainder to divide	67,000			
Interest allowances				
$200,000 × 10%	(20,000)	20,000		20,000
$130,000 × 10%	(13,000)		13,000	13,000
Remainder to divide	34,000			
Divided equally	(34,000)	17,000	17,000	34,000
Remainder to divide	0			
Net income allocation		$49,000	$42,000	$91,000

PART B—PARTNERSHIP LOSS ASSUMED TO BE $3,000
INCOME ALLOCATION SCHEDULE

		Russo	Stokes	Total
Net loss	$ (3,000)			
Salary allowances	(24,000)	$12,000	$12,000	$24,000
Remainder to divide	(27,000)			
Interest allowances				
$200,000 × 10%	(20,000)	20,000		20,000
$130,000 × 10%	(13,000)		13,000	13,000
Remainder to divide	(60,000)			
Divided equally	60,000	(30,000)	(30,000)	(60,000)
Remainder to divide	0			
Net income (loss) allocation		$ 2,000	$ (5,000)	$ (3,000)

	Dollar-Month Investment	
Average Capital Investment of Russo		
$186 × 5 months	$ 930	
$210 × 7 months	1,470	
12 months	$2,400	
Average capital ($2,400 ÷ 12 months)		$200
Average Capital Investment of Stokes		
$114 × 5 months	$ 570	
$150 × 1 month	150	
$140 × 6 months	840	
12 months	$1,560	
Average capital ($1,560 ÷ 12 months)		$130

Exhibit 15-6 shows that all provisions of the profit sharing agreement are used in allocating partnership income, regardless of whether the partnership has net income or net loss. The full amount of salary allowances as provided in the agreement is included in the income division, even though Russo only withdrew $10,000 of the $12,000 allowable amount.

In Part A of Exhibit 15-6, partnership income of $91,000 was divided $49,000 to Russo and $42,000 to Stokes. The division of the $3,000 net loss in Part B was allocated as $2,000 income to Russo and a $5,000 loss to Stokes. In both cases, the partnership agreement provided for a $7,000 income difference between the two partners. The amount of this difference was the same for the income and loss situations because the residual income amount was divided equally. A 60:40 division of income after salary and interest allowances would have resulted in a larger difference in Part A ($13,800). For Part B, Russo's allocation would be a loss of $4,000, and Stokes's income would be $1,000. One must be careful in making generalizations about the effect of various profit sharing provisions on final income allocations.

CHANGES IN PARTNERSHIP INTERESTS

The existing legal partnership entity is dissolved when a new partner is admitted or an existing partner retires or dies. However, dissolution does not necessarily result in the termination of the partnership operations or of the partnership as a separate business and accounting entity. **Partnership dissolution** under the Uniform Partnership Act is simply "the change in the relation of the partners caused by any partner ceasing to be associated in the carrying on as distinguished from the winding up of the business" (Section 29). When a partnership is legally dissolved by admitting a new partner or by the retirement or death of an existing partner, a new partnership agreement is necessary for the continued operation of the partnership business.

A question arises regarding whether the assets of the continuing partnership business should be revalued. Some argue that because legal dissolution terminates the old partnership, all assets transferred to the new partnership should be revalued in the same manner as if the assets had been sold to a corporate entity. Others argue that changes in partnership interests are not unlike changes in the stockholders of a corporation, and that private sales of ownership interests provide no basis for revaluation of the business entity. These alternative views reflect the concepts of the legal and business entities, respectively. Both views have merit, and this text does not emphasize either view. Instead, both views are discussed and illustrated in the following sections on changes in partnership interests. The revaluation approach is generally referred to as the *goodwill procedure,* and the absence of revaluation is referred to as the *bonus procedure.*

Assignment of an Interest to a Third Party

A partnership is not dissolved when a partner assigns his or her interest in the partnership to a third party, because such an assignment does not in itself change the relationship of the partners. Such assignment only entitles the assignee to receive the assigning partner's interest in future partnership profits and in partnership assets in the event of liquidation. The assignee does not become a partner and does not obtain the right to share in management of the partnership (Section 27 of the act). Because the assignee does not become a partner, the only change required on the partnership books is to transfer the capital interest of the assignor partner to the assignee.

We record the assignment by Mark to Conn of his 25% interest in the Pilar-Mark partnership as follows:

Mark capital (–OE)	50,000	
Conn capital (+OE)		50,000

The amount of the capital transfer is equal to the recorded amount of Mark's capital at the time of the assignment, and it is independent of the consideration received by Mark for his 25% interest. If the recorded amount of Mark's capital is $50,000, then the amount of the transfer entry is $50,000, regardless of whether Conn pays Mark $50,000 or some other amount.

Admission of a New Partner

A new partner can be admitted with the consent of all continuing partners in the business. However, the old partnership is dissolved and a new agreement is necessary for the continuing operations of the partnership business. In the absence of a new agreement, all profits and losses in the new partnership are divided equally under the provisions of the act.

A person may become a partner in an existing partnership by purchasing an interest from one or more of the existing partners, with the consent of all continuing partners in the new partnership entity, or by investing money or other resources in the partnership. In either case, the partnership books should be closed to update the capital accounts in anticipation of a new partnership agreement. In the new agreement, the partners can agree upon any capital and profit sharing interests they choose.

PURCHASE OF AN INTEREST FROM EXISTING PARTNERS

LEARNING OBJECTIVE 4

With the consent of all continuing partners, a new partner may be admitted into an existing partnership by purchasing an interest directly from the existing partners. The old partnership is dissolved, its books are closed, and a new partnership agreement governs the continuing business operations.

For example, Alfano and Bailey are partners with capital balances $50,000 each, and they share profits and losses equally. Cobb purchases one-half of Alfano's interest from Alfano for $25,000, and a new partnership of Alfano, Bailey, and Cobb is formed such that Alfano and Cobb each have a 25% interest in the capital and profits of the new partnership. The only entry required to record Alfano's transfer to Cobb is:

Alfano capital (–OE)	25,000	
Cobb capital (+OE)		25,000
To record Cobb's admission into the partnership with the purchase of one-half of Alfano's interest.		

In this case, the capital and income interests are aligned before and after the admission of Cobb, and the net assets of the old partnership were correctly valued on the books. Cobb's payment of $25,000 for a 25% interest in the capital and future income of the partnership implies a total valuation for the partnership of $100,000 ($25,000 ÷ 0.25). The net assets of the old partnership were recorded at $100,000, so no basis for revaluation arises.

Now assume that Alfano and Bailey have capital balances of $50,000 and $40,000, respectively, that they share profits equally, and that they agree to take Cobb into the partnership with a payment of $25,000 directly to Alfano. The partners may agree that half of Alfano's capital balance is to be transferred to Cobb (as in the previous example), that the net assets are not to be revalued, and that future profits will be shared 25%, 50%, and 25% to Alfano, Bailey, and Cobb, respectively. Although it seems equitable, there is no compelling reason for such an agreement, because the capital and income interests were not aligned either before or after the admission of Cobb.

	Old Partnership			New Partnership		
	Capital Investment		**Income Interest**	**Capital Investment**		**Income Interest**
Alfano	$50,000	5/9	50%	$25,000	5/18	25%
Bailey	40,000	4/9	50%	40,000	8/18	50%
Cobb				25,000	5/18	25%
	$90,000			$90,000		

The $25,000 payment of Cobb to Alfano does not provide evidence regarding the correct valuation of partnership net assets, because the payment was for five-eighteenths of the partnership net assets but 25% of future partnership profits. If revaluation is desirable, the asset value should be based on appraisals or evidence other than the amount of Cobb's payment to Alfano.

Revaluation: Goodwill Approach

A third possibility is that Alfano and Bailey have capital balances of $50,000 and $40,000, respectively, that they share profits equally, and that Cobb is admitted to the partnership with a total payment of $50,000 directly to the partners. Cobb is to have a 50% interest in the capital and income of the new partnership. Alfano and Bailey will each have a 25% interest in future income of the partnership.

Several additional questions of fairness arise concerning the valuation of total partnership assets, the capital transfers to Cobb, and the division of the $50,000 payment between Alfano and Bailey. Cobb's $50,000 payment for a 50% interest in both capital and future income implies a $100,000 valuation for total partnership assets. If assets are to be revalued, the revaluation should be recorded prior to Cobb's admission to the partnership. The partnership would record the revaluation as follows:

Goodwill (or identifiable net assets) (+A)	10,000	
Alfano capital (+OE)		5,000
Bailey capital (+OE)		5,000

If the assets are revalued and identifiable asset accounts are adjusted, the amount of the adjustments are amortized or depreciated over the remaining asset lives. Although the revaluation procedure is commonly referred to as the goodwill approach, goodwill should not be recorded until all identifiable assets have been adjusted to their fair values. The approach is comparable to the approach used to record business combinations under the purchase method or the acquisition of operating divisions or groups of assets.

The previous entry recording goodwill of $10,000 gives Alfano and Bailey capital balances of $55,000 and $45,000, respectively. If equal amounts of capital are to be transferred to Cobb, the entry to record Cobb's admission to the partnership is:

Alfano capital (−OE)	25,000	
Bailey capital (−OE)	25,000	
Cobb capital (+OE)		50,000

The capital balances are summarized as follows:

CAPITAL BALANCES

	Before Revaluation	Revaluation	After Revaluation	Capital Transferred	Capital After Transfer	
Alfano	$50,000	$ 5,000	$ 55,000	$ −25,000	$ 30,000	(30%)
Bailey	40,000	5,000	45,000	−25,000	20,000	(20%)
Cobb				50,000	50,000	(50%)
	$90,000	$10,000	$100,000	$ 0	$100,000	

Alternatively, it may be desirable to realign the capital balances of Alfano and Bailey in the new partnership such that each will have a 25% interest in the capital and income of the new partnership. In this case, the partnership would record the admission of Cobb as follows:

Alfano capital (−OE)	30,000	
Bailey capital (−OE)	20,000	
Cobb capital (+OE)		50,000

In this case, the capital changes are as follows:

CAPITAL BALANCES

	Before Revaluation	Revaluation	After Revaluation	Capital Transferred	Capital After Transfer	
Alfano	$50,000	$ 5,000	$ 55,000	$-30,000	$ 25,000	(25%)
Bailey	40,000	5,000	45,000	-20,000	25,000	(25%)
Cobb				50,000	50,000	(50%)
	$90,000	$10,000	$100,000	$ 0	$100,000	

Nonrevaulation: Bonus Approach

If the assets of the new partnership are not to be revalued, but equal amounts of capital are to be transferred to Cobb, the entry to record the transfer is:

Alfano capital (−OE)	22,500	
Bailey capital (−OE)	22,500	
Cobb capital (+OE)		45,000

Equal amounts of capital and equal rights to future income are transferred by Alfano and Bailey to Cobb, so each receiving $25,000 cash from Cobb seems equitable. Each of the old partners receives $2,500 in excess of the amount of book capital transferred ($25,000 received less $22,500 capital transferred). The capital accounts before and after the admission of Cobb are as follows:

CAPITAL BALANCES

	Per Books	Capital Transferred	Capital After Transfer	
Alfano	$50,000	$-22,500	$27,500	(30.6%)
Bailey	40,000	-22,500	17,500	(19.4%)
Cobb		45,000	45,000	(50.0%)
	$90,000	$ 0	$90,000	

Should Alfano and Bailey desire that their recorded capital and income interests in the new partnership be equal (that is 25%), Alfano would receive $30,000 of the amount paid by Cobb, and Bailey would receive $20,000. The entry to record the capital transfer in that case would be:

Alfano capital (−OE)	27,500	
Bailey capital (−OE)	17,500	
Cobb capital (+OE)		45,000

A summary of the capital balances follows:

CAPITAL BALANCES

	Per Books	Capital Transferred	Capital After Transfer	
Alfano	$50,000	$-27,500	$22,500	(25%)
Bailey	40,000	-17,500	22,500	(25%)
Cobb		45,000	45,000	(50%)
	$90,000	$ 0	$90,000	

Although the evidence supporting revaluation is not always convincing, a revaluation based on the price paid by an incoming partner does have the advantage of establishing a capital balance for that partner equal to the amount of his or her investment. For example, Cobb's capital credit was equal to his $50,000 payment to Alfano and Bailey when the assets were revalued. It was only $45,000 when the assets were not revalued. Also, the amounts of capital transfer and cash allocations are easier to determine when assets are revalued because gains and losses relating to the old partnership are formally recorded in the accounts.

INVESTING IN AN EXISTING PARTNERSHIP

A new partner may be admitted into an existing partnership by investing cash or other assets in the business or by bringing clients or individual abilities into the business that will contribute to future profitability. In this case, the old partnership is legally dissolved and the investment of the new partner is recorded under the provisions of the new partnership agreement. As in the case of a purchase of an interest, the net assets of the old partnership may or may not be revalued. However, because new assets are being invested in the business, the basis for revaluation is not necessarily determined by the investment of the new partner. If the amount invested by the new partner implies that the old partnership has unrecorded asset values, a total valuation of the new business based on the investment of the new partner seems appropriate. On the other hand, if the capital interest granted to the new partner is greater than the amount of his or her investment and the identifiable assets of the old partnership are recorded at their fair values, there is an implication that the new partner is bringing goodwill into the business. In this case, the total valuation of the new business is determined by reference to the capital of the old partnership.

The evidence provided by the amount of an investment only relates to the total value of the business. Values for identifiable assets are determined on an individual basis by appraisal or other valuation techniques. The identifiable assets of the old partnership are recorded at their fair values, in the absence of evidence to the contrary. If identifiable assets of a partnership are to be revalued, the revaluation must be based on appraisals or other evidence relating to specific assets.

Partnership Investment at Book Value

Andrew and Boyles have capital balances of $40,000 each and share profits equally. They agree to admit Criner to a one-third interest in capital and profits of a new Andrew, Boyles, and Criner partnership for a $40,000 cash investment. Criner's $40,000 investment is equal to the capital interest that she receives [($80,000 + $40,000) ÷ 3], so the issue of revaluation does not arise. Criner's investment is recorded on the partnership books as follows:

Cash (+A)	40,000	
Criner capital (+OE)		40,000
To record Criner's $40,000 cash investment for a one-third interest in partnership capital and income.		

Partnership Assets Revalued (Goodwill to Old Partners)

Now assume that Andrew and Boyles, who have capital balances of $40,000 each and share profits equally, agree to admit Criner to a one-third interest in the capital and profits of a new partnership for a cash investment of $50,000. Because Criner is willing to invest $50,000 for a one-third interest in the $80,000 recorded assets plus her $50,000 investment ($130,000 assets), the implication is that the old partnership has unrecorded asset values. The amount of unrecorded assets is determined by reference to Criner's investment. By implication, total assets of the new partnership will be $150,000 ($50,000 ÷ 1/3). The value of unrecorded assets must be $20,000, the excess of the $150,000 total value less the $80,000 recorded assets plus the $50,000 new investment. If the assets are revalued, the partnership makes the following entries:

Goodwill (+A)	20,000	
Andrew capital (+OE)		10,000
Boyles capital (+OE)		10,000
To revalue the assets of the old partnership based on the amount of Criner's investment.		
Cash (+A)	50,000	
Criner capital (+OE)		50,000
To record Criner's investment in the partnership for a one-third interest in capital and income.		

The $20,000 recorded as goodwill in the first entry is credited to the old partners in their old profit and loss sharing ratios. Conceptually, the revaluation constitutes a final act of the old partnership, and all further entries are those of the new partnership. The second entry merely records

Criner's $50,000 cash investment and capital credit in equal amounts. A summary of the capital balances before and after the $20,000 revaluation and the investment of Criner is as follows:

CAPITAL BALANCES

	Before Revaluation	Revaluation	After Revaluation	New Investment	Capital After Investment	
Andrew	$40,000	$10,000	$ 50,000		$ 50,000	1/3
Boyles	40,000	10,000	50,000		50,000	1/3
Criner				$50,000	50,000	1/3
	$80,000	$20,000	$100,000	$50,000	$150,000	

Partnership Assets Not Revalued (Bonus to Old Partners)

If the partners decide against revaluation, the only entry required to record Criner's admittance into the partnership is as follows:

Cash (+A)	50,000	
Andrew capital (+OE)		3,333
Boyles capital (+OE)		3,333
Criner capital (+OE)		43,334

To record Criner's investment in the partnership and to allow Andrew and Boyles a bonus due to unrecorded asset values.

In this case, partnership net assets are increased only by the amount of the new investment. The new partner's capital account is credited for her one-third interest in the $130,000 capital of the new partnership, and the difference between the investment and capital credit of the new partner is allocated to the capital accounts of the old partners in relation to the old profit sharing agreement.

This situation is referred to as a *bonus to old partners* because the old partners receive capital credits for a part of the new partner's investment. The goodwill and bonus procedures are comparable in the sense that each partner would receive $50,000 if the business were immediately sold for $150,000. The capital balances before and after the admission of Criner are as follows:

CAPITAL BALANCES

	Per Books	Investment	Capital After Investment	
Andrew	$40,000	$ 3,333	$ 43,333	1/3
Boyles	40,000	3,333	43,333	1/3
Criner		43,334	43,334	1/3
	$80,000	$50,000	$130,000	

Partnership Assets Revalued (Goodwill to New Partner)

Suppose that Andrew and Boyles agreed to admit Criner into the partnership *for a 40% interest* in the capital and profit with an investment of $50,000. In this case, the implication is that Criner is bringing goodwill into the partnership. That is, Andrew and Boyles must be willing to admit Criner to a 40% interest in the $80,000 recorded assets plus her $50,000 investment (40% × $130,000 = $52,000) because they expect Criner's total contribution to exceed her cash investment. Accordingly, the total value of the partnership is determined by reference to the 60% interest retained in the new partnership capital and profits by Andrew and Boyles. Total capital of the new partnership is $133,333 ($80,000 old capital assumed to be fairly valued ÷ 60%), and the partnership records the admission of Criner as follows:

Cash (+A)	50,000	
Goodwill (+A)	3,333	
Criner capital (+OE)		53,333

To admit Criner to a 40% interest in capital and profits.

Total capital of the new partnership is $133,333 ($80,000 old capital + $50,000 new investment + $3,333 goodwill), and Criner has a 40% interest in that new capital. A summary of the capital balances before and after the admittance of Criner is as follows:

CAPITAL BALANCES

	Per Books	Investment Plus Goodwill	Capital After Investment	
Andrew	$40,000		$ 40,000	30%
Boyles	40,000		40,000	30%
Criner		$53,333	53,333	40%
	$80,000	$53,333	$133,333	

Partnership Assets Not Revalued (Bonus to New Partner)

Instead of allocating goodwill to the incoming partner, the bonus procedure can be used. Under this procedure the assets are not revalued, but the capital balances of Andrew and Boyles must be reduced to meet the 40% condition of the agreement. Total assets of the new partnership are $130,000, and Criner's 40% interest is $52,000. The $2,000 difference between Criner's capital credit of $52,000 and her $50,000 investment is considered a bonus to Criner. Partnership assets are not revalued, so the excess $2,000 credited to Criner's account must be charged against the capital accounts of Andrew and Boyles in relation to their old profit and loss sharing ratios. The partnership records Criner's admittance under the bonus procedure as follows:

Cash (+A)	50,000	
Andrew capital (−OE)	1,000	
Boyles capital (−OE)	1,000	
Criner capital (+OE)		52,000

To record Criner's investment of $50,000 for a 40% interest in the partnership and allow her a $2,000 bonus.

The capital accounts of the partnership before and after admitting Criner are as follows:

CAPITAL BALANCES

	Per Books	Investment	Capital After Investment	
Andrew	$40,000	$(1,000)	$ 39,000	30%
Boyles	40,000	(1,000)	39,000	30%
Criner		52,000	52,000	40%
	$80,000	$ 50,000	$130,000	

Basis for Revaluation

The revaluation (goodwill) and nonrevaluation (bonus) procedures are alternative approaches for recording changes in partnership interests through direct investments in an existing partnership. In deciding whether the goodwill or bonus relates to the old partners or the new partner, the investment of the new partner is analyzed in terms of the nonrevaluation/bonus procedure.

Under the nonrevaluation assumption, the capital credit of the new partner is determined by multiplying the new partner's capital interest by the net assets of the old partnership plus the investment. The analysis is as follows:

If investment of new partner = capital credit of new partner ⇒ no bonus (or goodwill)

If investment of new partner > capital credit of new partner ⇒ bonus to old partners (or goodwill to old partners if assets are revalued)

If investment of new partner < capital credit of new partner ⇒ bonus to (or goodwill new partner new partner to new partner if assets are revalued)

The amount of the old partnership capital provides no basis for revaluation of the old partners' capital. Any revaluation relating to the old partners' capital should therefore be based on the investment of the new partner. Similarly, the amount of the new partner's investment provides no basis for revaluation of the new partner's capital. Any revaluation of the new partner's capital should therefore be related to the old partnership capital retained. Application of this scenario prevents the downward adjustment of identifiable net assets of the old partnership, which are assumed to be recorded at amounts equal to their fair values. If the evidence indicates an undervaluation or overvaluation of recorded net assets, adjustments should be made before comparing the new partner's investment and capital credit to identify bonus or goodwill.

A summary of the procedures used in the previous examples to compute the amounts of goodwill and bonus for Criner's investments is as follows:

	$50,000 Investment for a One-Third Interest	$50,000 Investment for a 40% Interest
Nonrevaluation—Bonus		
Criner's investment	$ 50,000	$ 50,000
Criner's capital credit		
$130,000 × 1/3	43,334	
$130,000 × 40%		52,000
Bonus to old partners ($50,000 > $43,334)	$ 6,666	
Bonus to Criner ($50,000 < $52,000)		$ 2,000
Revaluation—Goodwill		
Total capital		
$50,000 ÷ 1/3 (based on Criner's investment)	$150,000	
$80,000 ÷ 60% (based on old partnership capital)		$133,333
Book value of old partnership assets + Criner's investment	130,000	130,000
Goodwill (other identifiable assets) to old partners	$ 20,000	
Goodwill to Criner		$ 3,333

DISSOLUTION OF A CONTINUING PARTNERSHIP THROUGH DEATH OR RETIREMENT

The retirement or death of a partner from a continuing partnership business dissolves the old partnership and requires a settlement with the retiring partner or with the estate of the deceased partner. In the absence of a partnership agreement to the contrary, the settlement is in accordance with Section 42 of the Uniform Partnership Act. This section provides that the retiring partner or the estate of a deceased partner "may have the value of his interest at the date of dissolution ascertained, and shall receive as an ordinary creditor an amount equal to the value of his interest in the dissolved partnership with interest." The valuation is at the date of dissolution, so partnership books are closed as of the date of death or retirement. When a time lag exists between death or retirement and final settlement, the capital balance of the deceased or retiring partner is reclassified as a liability. Any interest (or other return) accruing on the liability up to the date of final settlement is considered an expense of the continuing partnership entity.

If the retiring partner (or the estate of a deceased partner) is paid an amount equal to the final balance of his or her capital account, the only entry necessary is a charge to his or her capital account and a credit to cash for the amount paid. When the settlement with a retiring partner is more or less than the final capital account balance, the revaluation (goodwill) and nonrevaluation (bonus) procedures provide alternate methods of accounting for the settlement.

To illustrate, assume that Anne, Mike, and Justin are partners with profit sharing percentages of 40%, 20%, and 40%, respectively, and that Justin decides to retire. The capital and income interests of the three partners on the date of Justin's retirement are as follows:

	Capital Balances	Percentage of Capital	Profit and Loss Percentage
Anne	$ 70,000	35%	40%
Mike	50,000	25	20
Justin	80,000	40	40
Total capital	$200,000	100%	100%

Excess Payment to Retiring Partner

The partners agree that the business is undervalued on the partnership books and that Justin will be paid $92,000 in final settlement of his partnership interest. The excess payment to Justin can be recorded by three methods: (1) Justin may be granted a bonus, (2) partnership capital may be revalued to the extent of the excess payment to Justin, or (3) partnership capital may be revalued based on the amount implied by the excess payment.

BONUS TO RETIRING PARTNER The partnership would record Justin's withdrawal as follows under the bonus procedure:

Justin capital (−OE)	80,000	
Anne capital (−OE)	8,000	
Mike capital (−OE)	4,000	
Cash (−A)		92,000

Because Anne and Mike granted a $12,000 bonus to Justin, that amount reduces their capital accounts using their 40:20 relative profit sharing ratios.

GOODWILL EQUAL TO EXCESS PAYMENT IS RECORDED A second method of recording Justin's withdrawal is to record the $12,000 excess of cash paid to Justin over his capital account balance as goodwill:

Justin capital (−OE)	80,000	
Goodwill (+A)	12,000	
Cash (−A)		92,000

Under this approach, goodwill is recorded only to the extent paid for by the continuing partnership. This approach only provides a revaluation of Justin's share of partnership assets; it does not provide a revaluation of Anne and Mike's capital interests.

REVALUATION OF TOTAL PARTNERSHIP CAPITAL BASED ON EXCESS PAYMENT A third approach for recording Justin's retirement is to revalue total partnership capital on the basis of the $12,000 excess payment. Under this method, total partnership capital is revalued as follows:

Goodwill (other assets) (+A)	30,000	
Anne capital (+OE)		12,000
Mike capital (+OE)		6,000
Justin capital (+OE)		12,000

The total undervaluation of the partnership is measured by the amount implied by the excess payment. In this case, the $30,000 is computed by dividing the $12,000 excess payment by Justin's 40% profit sharing percentage. The partnership then records Justin's retirement as follows:

Justin capital (−OE)	92,000	
Cash (−A)		92,000

Payment to Retiring Partner Less Than Capital Balance

Suppose that Justin is paid $72,000 in final settlement of his capital interest. In this case, the three partners may have agreed that the business is worth less than its book value.

OVERVALUED ASSETS WRITTEN DOWN A retirement payment to Justin of $8,000 less than his final capital balance implies that existing partnership capital is overvalued by $20,000 [($80,000 − $72,000) ÷ 40%]. If the evidence available supports this implication, the overvalued assets should be identified and reduced to their fair values. The partnership records the revaluation and payment to Justin as follows:

Anne capital (−OE)	8,000	
Mike capital (−OE)	4,000	
Justin capital (−OE)	8,000	
Net assets (−A)		20,000
Justin capital (−OE)	$72,000	
Cash (−A)		72,000

This method of recording Justin's withdrawal is appropriate if the $72,000 paid to Justin is the result of a valuation provided for under the act. However, it would not be appropriate if the $72,000 were determined by prior agreement of the partners without regard to total partnership capital at the time of withdrawal.

BONUS TO CONTINUING PARTNERS If evidence indicates that partnership capital is fairly valued, the partnership would record the retirement of Justin under the bonus procedure as follows:

Justin capital (−OE)	$80,000	
Anne capital (+OE)		5,333
Mike capital (+OE)		2,667
Cash (−A)		72,000

This method of recording provides a bonus to Anne and Mike. The bonus is measured by the excess of Justin's capital balance over the cash paid by the partnership for his 40% interest.

LIMITED PARTNERSHIPS

Under some circumstances, the unlimited liability characteristic of general partnerships may be circumvented by creating a special kind of partnership called a *limited partnership*. The Uniform Limited Partnership Act provides legal guidance for limited partnerships. The limited partnership consists of at least one general partner and one or more limited partners. The general partner is like any partner in a general partnership, and he or she has unlimited liability for partnership debt. The limited partner is basically an investor whose risk is limited to his or her equity investment in the partnership. The limited partner is *excluded* from the management of the business. If he or she takes part in management, he or she loses the limited partner status and becomes a general partner with unlimited liability.

A limited partnership is more difficult to form than a general partnership. The limited partnership agreement *must be written*, signed by the partners, and filed with the appropriate public official in the state where the partnership is created. If the statute is not carefully followed, the courts may find the partnership to be a general partnership rather than a limited partnership.

Joint Ventures

Joint ventures have the characteristics of partnerships, except that the joint venture is usually set up for a specific limited purpose. When the activity is complete, the venture is terminated. For this reason, the agency power of joint ventures is limited. Joint ventures are covered in Chapter 11 of this book.

LEARNING
OBJECTIVE **6**

SUMMARY

Partnership accounting procedures are similar to those for other forms of business organization, except for procedures relating to the measurement of partnership capital interests. Accounting measurements relating to the capital and income interests of partners are based on the partnership agreement or, in the absence of an agreement, on the Uniform Partnership Act, except for partnerships in states that have not adopted the act. The partnership agreement should be in writing and should cover matters relating to the amount and valuation of capital contributions, additional investments with withdrawals, loans to partners, profit sharing arrangements, changes in partnership interests, and various other matters.

QUESTIONS

1. Explain why the noncash investments of partners should be recorded at their fair values.

2. Is there a conceptual difference between partner drawings and withdrawals? A practical difference?

3. In the absence of an agreement for the division of profits, how are they divided under the Uniform Partnership Act? Does your answer also apply to losses? Does it apply if one partner invests three times as much as the other partners?

4. Why do some profit sharing agreements provide for salary and interest allowances?

5. Are partner salary allowances expenses of the partnership?

6. When a profit sharing agreement specifies that profits should be divided using the ratio of capital balances, how should capital balances be computed?

7. Explain how a partner could have a loss from partnership operations for a period even though the partnership had net income.

8. The concept of partnership dissolution has a technical meaning under the provisions of the Uniform Partnership Act. Explain the concept.

9. If a partner sells his or her partnership interest directly to a third party, the partnership may or may not be dissolved. Under what conditions is the partnership dissolved?

10. If a partnership is dissolved with the death or retirement of a partner, how do you explain the fact that some partnerships have been in existence for 50 years or more?

11. How does the purchase of an interest from existing partners differ from acquiring an interest by investment in a partnership?

12. What alternative approaches can be used in recording the admission of a new partner?

13. Why is the goodwill procedure best described as a revaluation procedure?

14. Explain the bonus procedure for recording an investment in a partnership. When is the bonus applicable to old partners, and when is it applicable to new partners?

15. The goodwill procedure was used to record the investment of a new partner in the XYZ Partnership, but immediately thereafter, the entire business was sold for an amount equal to the recorded capital of the partnership. Under what conditions would the amounts received in final liquidation of the partnership have been the same as if the bonus procedure had been used?

16. Bob invests $10,000 cash for a 25% interest in the capital and earnings of the BOP Partnership. Explain how this investment could give rise to (a) recording goodwill, (b) the write-down of the partnership assets, (c) a bonus to old partners, and (d) a bonus to Bob.

EXERCISES

E 15-1

Computing initial partner investments Carson and Lamb establish a partnership to operate a used-furniture business under the name of C&L Furniture. Carson contributes furniture that cost $60,000 and has fair value of $90,000. Lamb contributes $30,000 cash and delivery equipment that cost $40,000 and has a fair value of $30,000. The partners agree to share profits and losses 60% to Carson and 40% to Lamb.

REQUIRED: Calculate the dollar amount of inequity that will result if the initial noncash contributions of the partners are recorded at cost rather than fair market value.

E 15-2

Partnership income allocation—bonus Arnold, Beverly, and Carolyn are partners who share profits and losses 40:40:20, respectively, after Beverly, who manages the partnership, receives a bonus of 10% of income. Partnership income for the year is $506,000.

REQUIRED: Prepare a schedule to allocate partnership income to Arnold, Beverly, and Carolyn.

E 15-3

Partnership income allocation—salary allowance and interest The partnership agreement of Cari, Helen, and Brandie provides that profits are to be divided as follows:

- Brandie receives a salary of $12,000, and Helen receives a salary of $9,000 for time spent in the business.
- All partners receive 10% interest on average capital balances.
- Remaining profits and losses are divided equally among the three partners.

On January 1, 2006, the capital balances were Cari, $100,000; Helen, $80,000; and Brandie, $75,000. Cari invested an additional $20,000 on July 1 and withdrew $20,000 on October 1. Helen and Brandie had drawings of $9,000 each during the year.

REQUIRED: Prepare a schedule to allocate partnership net income of $14,000 for 2006.

E 15-4

Partnership income allocation—salary allowance Melanie and David created a partnership to own and operate a health-food store. The partnership agreement provided that Melanie receive a salary of $10,000 and David a salary of $5,000 to recognize their relative time spent in operating the store. Remaining profits and losses were divided 60:40 to Melanie and David, respectively. Income of $13,000 for 2006, the first year of operations, was allocated $8,800 to Melanie and $4,200 to David.

On January 1, 2007, the partnership agreement was changed to reflect the fact that David could no longer devote any time to the store's operations. The new agreement allows Melanie a salary of $18,000, and the remaining profits and losses are divided equally. In 2007 an error was discovered such that the 2006 reported income was understated by $4,000. The partnership income of $25,000 for 2007 included this $4,000 related to 2006.

REQUIRED: Prepare a schedule to allocate the $25,000 reported 2007 partnership income to Melanie and David.

E 15-5

Partnership income allocation—partnership capital statement On December 31, 2006, the total partnership capital (assets less liabilities) for the Bird, Cage, and Dean partnership is $372,000. Selected information related to the preclosing capital balances as follows:

	Bird Capital	Cage Capital	Dean Capital	Total Capital
Balance January 1	$120,000	$ 90,000	$140,000	$350,000
Investments 2006		20,000	20,000	40,000
Withdrawals 2006	(30,000)		(30,000)	(60,000)
Drawings 2006	(10,000)	(10,000)	(10,000)	(30,000)
	$ 80,000	$100,000	$120,000	$300,000

REQUIRED: Prepare a statement of partnership capital for the Bird, Cage, and Dean partnership at year-end 2006.

E 15-6

Partnership income allocation—assignment of interest to a third party Capital balances and profit and loss sharing ratios of the partners in the BIG Entertainment Galley are as follows:

Batty capital (50%)	$140,000
Iggy capital (30%)	160,000
Grabby capital (20%)	100,000
Total	$400,000

Batty needs money and agrees to assign half of his interest in the partnership to Peters for $90,000 cash. Peters pays $90,000 directly to Batty. Peters does not become a partner.

REQUIRED

1. Prepare a journal entry to record the assignment of half of Batty's interest in the partnership to Peters.

2. What is the total capital of the BIG partnership immediately after the assignment of the interest to Peters?

E 15-7

Recording new partner investment—nonrevaluation case The capital accounts of the Klaxon and Bell partnership on September 30, 2006, were:

Klaxon capital (75% profit percentage)	$140,000
Bell capital (25% profit percentage)	60,000
Total capital	$200,000

On October 1, Ring was admitted to a 40% interest in the partnership when he purchased 40% of each existing partner's capital for $120,000, paid directly to Klaxon and Bell.

REQUIRED: Determine the capital balances of Klaxon, Bell, and Ring after Ring's admission to the partnership if goodwill is *not* recorded.

E 15-8

Recording new partner investment—revaluation case Bowen and Monita are partners in a retail business and divide profits 60% to Bowen and 40% to Monita. Their capital balances at December 31, 2006, are as follows:

Bowen capital	$180,000
Monita capital	180,000
Total capital	$360,000

Partnership assets and liabilities have book values equal to fair values. The partners agree to admit Johnson into the partnership. Johnson purchases a one-third interest in partnership capital and profits directly from Bowen and Monita (one-third of each of their capital accounts) for $150,000.

REQUIRED: Prepare journal entries for the admission of Johnson into the partnership, assuming that partnership assets are revalued.

E 15-9

Recording new partner investment—revaluation and nonrevaluation cases The capital balances and profits and loss sharing percentages for the Sprint, Jog, and Run partnership at December 31, 2006, are as follows:

Sprint capital (30%)	$80,000
Jog capital (50%)	$90,000
Run capital (20%)	$70,000

The partners agree to admit Walk into the partnership on January 1, 2007, for a 20% interest in the capital and income of the business.

REQUIRED

1. Prepare the journal entry or entries to record Walk's admission to the partnership assuming that he invests $50,000 in the partnership for the 20% interest and that partnership capital is *revalued*.

2. Prepare the journal entry or entries to record Walk's admission to the partnership assuming that he invests $70,000 in the partnership for the 20% interest and that partnership capital is *revalued*.

E 15-10

Recording new partner investment—nonrevaluation case Capital balances and profit sharing percentages for the partnership of Manda, Emeril, and Fotenot on January 1, 2006, are as follows:

Manda (36%) 35%	$140,000
Emeril (24%) 25%	100,000
Fotenot (40%)	160,000
	$400,000

On January 3, 2006, the partners agree to admit Boudreaux into the partnership for a 25% interest in capital and earnings for his investment in the partnership of $120,000. Partnership assets are not to be revalued.

REQUIRED

1. Determine the capital balances of the four partners immediately after the admission of Boudreaux.

2. What is the profit and loss sharing ratio for Manda, Emeril, Fotenot, and Boudreaux?

E 15-11

Partner retirement entries Capital balances and profit and loss sharing ratios for the Nixon, Mann, and Peter partnership on December 31, 2006, just before the retirement of Nixon, are as follows:

Nixon capital (30%)	$64,000
Mann capital (30%)	$70,000
Peter capital (40%)	$80,000

On January 2, 2007, Nixon is paid $85,000 cash upon his retirement.

REQUIRED: Prepare the journal entry or entries to record Nixon's retirement assuming that goodwill, as implied by the payment to Nixon, is recorded on the partnership books.

E 15-12

Partner retirement entries—fair value adjustment A balance sheet at December 31, 2006, for the Beck, Dee, and Lynn partnership is summarized as follows:

Assets	$80,000	Liabilities	$20,000
Loan to Dee	10,000	Beck capital (50%)	30,000
	$90,000	Dee capital (40%)	30,000
		Lynn capital (10%)	10,000
			$90,000

Dee is retiring from the partnership. The partners agree that partnership assets, excluding Dee's loan, should be adjusted to their fair value of $100,000 and that Dee should receive $31,000 for her capital balance net of the $10,000 loan. No goodwill is to be recorded.

REQUIRED: Determine the capital balances of Beck and Lynn immediately after Dee's retirement.

E 15-13

Partnership income allocation—salary allowance, bonus, and additional contributions during the year Kathy and Eddie formed the K & E partnership several years ago. Capital account balances on January 1, 2006, were as follows:

Kathy	$496,750
Eddie	$268,250

The partnership agreement provides Kathy with an annual salary of $10,000 plus a bonus of 5% of partnership net income for managing the business. Eddie is provided an annual salary of $15,000 with no bonus. The remainder is shared evenly. Partnership net income for 2006 was $30,000. Eddie and Kathy each invested an additional $5,000 during the year to finance a special purchase. Year-end drawing account balances were $15,000 for Kathy and $10,000 for Eddie.

REQUIRED

1. Prepare an income allocation schedule.
2. Create the journal entries to update the equity accounts at the end of the year.
3. Determine the capital balances as of December 31, 2006.

E 15-14

Partnership retirement—revaluation and bonus approaches The capital account balances and profit and loss sharing ratios of the Byden, Boxer, Danner, and Foust partnership on December 31, 2006, after closing entries are as follows:

Byder (30%)	$ 60,000
Boxer (20%)	50,000
Danner (40%)	50,000
Foust (10%)	40,000
Total capital	$200,000

Boxer is retiring from the partnership, and the partners agree that he will receive a cash payment of $70,000 in final settlement of his interest. The book values of partnership assets and liabilities are equal to fair values, except for a building with a book value of $30,000 and a fair value of $50,000.

REQUIRED

1. Prepare the journal entry or entries to record Boxer's retirement assuming that assets are revalued to the basis implied by the excess payment to Boxer.
2. Prepare the journal entry or entries to record Boxer's retirement assuming that assets and liabilities are revalued only to the extent of the excess payment to Boxer.
3. Prepare the journal entry or entries to record Boxer's retirement assuming the bonus approach is used.

E 15-15

Recording new partner investment and partner retirements—various situations

1. Bill and Ken enter into a partnership agreement in which Bill is to have a 60% interest in capital and profits and Ken is to have a 40% interest in capital and profits. Bill contributes the following:

	Cost	Fair Value
Land	$ 10,000	$20,000
Building	100,000	60,000
Equipment	20,000	15,000

There is a $30,000 mortgage on the building that the partnership agrees to assume. Ken contributes $50,000 cash to the partnership. Bill and Ken agree that Ken's capital account should equal Ken's $50,000 cash contribution and that goodwill should be recorded. Goodwill should be recorded in the amount of:

a *$10,000*

b *$15,000*

c *$16,667*

d *$20,000*

2. Thomas and Mark are partners having capital balances of $50,000 and $60,000, respectively. They admit Jay to a one-third interest in partnership capital and profits for an investment of $65,000. If the goodwill procedure is used in recording Jay's admission to the partnership:

a *Jay's capital will be $58,333*

b *Total capital will be $175,000*

c *Mark's capital will be $70,000*

d *Goodwill will be recorded at $15,000*

3. On December 31, 2006, Tina and Webb, who share profits and losses equally, have capital balances of $170,000 and $200,000, respectively. They agree to admit Zen for a one-third interest in capital and profits for his investment of $200,000. Partnership net assets are not to be revalued. Capital accounts of Tina, Webb, and Zen, respectively, immediately after Zen's admission to the partnership are:

a *$170,000, $200,000, and $200,000*

b *$165,000, $195,000, and $200,000*

c *$175,000, $205,000, and $190,000*

d *$185,000, $215,000, and $200,000*

4. Finney and Rhoads have capital balances of $100,000 and $80,000, respectively, and they share profits equally. The partners agree to accept Chesterfield for a 25% interest in capital and profits for her investment of $90,000. If goodwill is recorded, the capital account balances of Finney and Rhoads immediately after Chesterfield's admittance to the partnership will be:

a *Finney, $100,000; Rhoads, $120,000*

b *Finney, $111,250; Rhoads, $91,250*

c *Finney, $145,000; Rhoads, $125,000*

d *Finney, $120,000; Rhoads, $120,000*

5. The balance sheet of the Fred, Gini, and Peggy partnership on December 31, 2006, together with profit sharing ratios, revealed the following:

Cash	$240,000	Fred capital (30%)	$200,000
Other assets	360,000	Gini capital (30%)	170,000
		Peggy capital (40%)	230,000
	$600,000		$600,000

Gini is retiring from the partnership, and the partners agreed that she should receive $200,000 cash as payment in full for her share of partnership assets. If the goodwill implied by the settlement with Gini is recorded on the partnership books, total partnership assets after Gini's withdrawal should be:

a *$566,667*

b *$500,000*

c *$430,000*

d *$400,000*

LEARNING OBJECTIVES **4, 5**

E 15-16
Recording new partner investment and partner retirements—various situations

1. Shirley purchased an interest in the Tony and Olga partnership by paying Tony $40,000 for half of his capital and half of his 50% profit sharing interest. At the time, Tony's capital balance was $30,000 and Olga's capital balance was $70,000. Shirley should receive a credit to her capital account of:

a *$15,000*

b *$20,000*

c *$25,000*

d *$33,333*

2. Linkous and Quesenberry are partners with capital balances of $50,000 and $70,000, respectively, and they share profits and losses equally. The partners agree to take Duncan into the partnership for a 40% interest in capital and profits, while Linkous and Quesenberry each retain a 30% interest. Duncan pays $60,000 cash directly to Linkous and Quesenberry for his 40% interest, and goodwill implied by Duncan's payment is recognized on the partnership books. If Linkous and Quesenberry transfer equal amounts of capital to Duncan, the capital balances after Duncan's admittance will be:

a *Linkous, $35,000; Quesenberry, $55,000; Duncan, $60,000*

b *Linkous, $45,000; Quesenberry, $45,000; Duncan, $60,000*

   c *Linkous, $36,000; Quesenberry, $36,000; Duncan, $48,000*
   d *Linkous, $26,000; Quesenberry, $46,000; Duncan, $48,000*

Use the following information in answering questions 3 and 4:

    Dr. McCall and Dr. Newby are partners with capital balances of $70,000 and $50,000, respectively, and they share profit and losses equally. Dr. Oakes is admitted to the partnership with a contribution of $50,000 cash for a one-third interest in the partnership capital and in future profits and losses.

3. If the goodwill is recognized in accounting for the admission of Dr. Oakes, what amount of goodwill will be recorded?

   a *$60,000*
   b *$20,000*
   c *$10,000*
   d *$6,667*

4. If no goodwill is recognized, the capital balances of Drs. McCall and Newby immediately after the admission of Dr. Oakes will be:

   a *McCall, $65,000; Newby, $45,000*
   b *McCall, $66,667; Newby, $46,666*
   c *McCall, $67,500; Newby, $47,500*
   d *McCall, $70,000; Newby, $50,000*

5. The December 31, 2006, balance sheet of the Bennett, Carter, and Davis partnership is summarized as follows:

Cash	$100,000	Carter loan	$100,000
Other assets, at cost	500,000	Bennett capital	100,000
		Carter capital	200,000
		Davis capital	200,000
	$600,000		$600,000

The partners share profits and losses as follows: Bennett, 20%; Carter 30%; and Davis, 50%. Carter is retiring from the partnership, and the partners have agreed that "other assets" should be adjusted to their fair value of $600,000 at December 31, 2006. They further agree that Carter will receive $244,000 cash for his partnership interest exclusive of his loan, which is to be paid in full, and that no goodwill implied by Carter's payment will be recorded.
    After Carter's retirement, the capital balances of Bennett and Davis, respectively, will be:

   a *$116,000 and $240,000*
   b *$101,714 and $254,286*
   c *$100,000 and $200,000*
   d *$73,143 and $182,857*

E 15-17

[AICPA adapted] Partnership income allocation and new partner investment—various situations

LEARNING OBJECTIVES 3, 4

1. Cobb, Inc., a partner in TLC Partnership, assigns its partnership interest to Bean, who is not made a partner. After the assignment, Bean asserts the rights to:

   I   Participate in the management of TLC
   II Cobb's share of TLC's partnership profits

Bean is correct as to which of these rights?
   a *I only*
   b *II only*
   c *I and II*
   d *Neither I nor II*

2. When property other than cash is invested in a partnership, at what amount should the noncash property be credited to the contributing partner's capital account?
   a *Fair value at the date of contribution*
   b *Contributing partner's original cost*
   c *Assessed valuation for property tax purposes*
   d *Contributing partner's tax basis*

3. Arthur Plack, a partner in the Brite Partnership, has a 30% participation in partnership profits and losses. Plack's capital account had a net decrease of $60,000 during the calendar year 2006. During 2006, Plack withdrew $130,000 (charged against his capital account) and contributed property valued at $25,000 to the partnership. What was the net income of the Brite Partnership for 2006?
   a *$150,000*
   b *$233,333*
   c *$350,000*
   d *$550,000*

4. Fox, Greg, and Howe are partners with average capital balances during 2006 of $120,000, $60,000, and $40,000, respectively. Partners receive 10% interest on their average capital balances. After deducting salaries of $30,000 to Fox and $20,000 to Howe, the residual profit or loss is divided equally. In 2006 the partnership sustained a $33,000 loss before interest and salaries to partners. By what amount should Fox's capital account change?

   a **$7,000 increase**
   b **$11,000 decrease**
   c **$35,000 decrease**
   d **$42,000 increase**

   (handwritten)
	Fox	Greg	Howe
Int	12,000	6,000	4,000
Sal	30,000		20,000
Loss	⟨35,000⟩	⟨35,000⟩	⟨35,000⟩

5. Beck, an active partner in the Beck and Cris partnership, receives an annual bonus of 25% of partnership net income after deducting the bonus. For the year ended December 31, 2006, partnership net income before the bonus amounted to $300,000. Beck's 2006 bonus should be:

   a **$56,250**
   b **$60,000**
   c **$62,500**
   d **$75,000**

   (handwritten)
   $(300,000 * 25\%) - \frac{1}{4}B = B$
   $75,000 = \frac{5}{4}B$
   $60,000 = B$
   $(NI - Bonus) * 25\% = Bonus$

LEARNING OBJECTIVE 5

E 15-18
[AICPA adapted] Partnership retirement—various situations

1. Partners Allen, Baker, and Coe share profits and losses 50:30:20, respectively. The balance sheet at April 30, 2006, follows:

Assets		Equities	
Cash	$ 40,000	Accounts payable	$100,000
Other assets	360,000	Allen capital	74,000
		Baker capital	130,000
		Coe capital	96,000
	$400,000		$400,000

   The assets and liabilities are recorded and presented at their respective fair values. Jones is to be admitted as a new partner with a 20% capital interest and a 20% share of profits and losses in exchange for a cash contribution. No goodwill or bonus is to be recorded. How much cash should Jones contribute?

   a **$60,000**
   b **$72,000**
   c **$75,000**
   d **$80,000**

   (handwritten) $\frac{\$300,000}{80\%} = 375,000 - 300,000 = 75,000$

2. Elton and Don are partners who share profits and losses in the ratio of 7:3, respectively. On November 5, 2006, their respective capital accounts were as follows:

Elton	$ 70,000	70%
Don	60,000	30%
	$130,000	

   On that date they agreed to admit Kravitz as a partner with a one-third interest in the capital and profits and losses upon his investment of $50,000. The new partnership will begin with a total capital of $180,000. Immediately after Kravitz's admission, what are the capital balances of Elton, Don, and Kravitz, respectively?

   a **$60,000, $60,000, $60,000**
   b **$63,000, $57,000, $60,000**
   c **$63,333, $56,667, $60,000**
   d **$70,000, $60,000, $50,000**

   (handwritten)
	Elton	Don	Kravitz
	70,000	60,000	50,000
	⟨7,000⟩	⟨3,000⟩	10,000
	63,000	57,000	60,000

3. William desires to purchase a one-fourth capital and profit and loss interest in the partnership of Eli, George, and Dick. The three partners agree to sell William one-fourth of their respective capital and profit and loss interests in exchange for a total payment of $40,000. The capital accounts and the respective percentage interests in profits and losses immediately before the sale to William are as follows:

   (handwritten header) Goodwill   Sold
Eli capital (60%) ~15%	$ 80,000	+ 12,000 - 24,000 = 68,000
George capital (30%) - 7.5%	40,000	+ 6,000 - 12,000 = 34,000
Dick capital (10%) ~2.5%	20,000	+ 2,000 - 4,000 = 18,000
	$140,000	20,000 40,000

   All other assets and liabilities are fairly valued, and implied goodwill is to be recorded prior to the acquisition by William. Immediately after William's acquisition, what should be the capital balances of Eli, George, and Dick, respectively?

   a **$60,000, $30,000, $15,000**
   b **$69,000, $34,500, $16,500**
   c **$77,000, $38,500, $19,500**
   d **$92,000, $46,000, $22,000**

4. The capital accounts of the partnership of Newton, Sharman, and Jackson on June 1, 2006, are presented, along with their respective profit and loss ratios:

Newton	$139,200	3/6	1/2
Sharman	208,800	2/6	1/3
Jackson	96,000	1/6	1/6
	$444,000		

On June 1, 2006, Sidney was admitted to the partnership when he purchased, for $132,000, a proportionate interest from Newton and Sharman in the net assets and profits of the partnership. As a result of this transaction, Sidney acquired a one-fifth interest in the net assets and profits of the firm. Assuming that implied goodwill is *not* to be recorded, what is the combined gain realized by Newton and Sharman upon the sale of a portion of their interests in the partnership to Sidney?

a 0
b $43,200
c $62,400
d $82,000

(handwritten: 444,000 × 20% = 88,800 Paid 132,000 43,200)

5. Kern and Pate are partners with capital balances of $60,000 and $20,000, respectively. Profits and losses are divided in the ratio of 60:40. Kern and Pate decided to form a new partnership with Grant, who invested land valued at $15,000 for a 20% capital interest in the new partnership. Grant's capital account should be credited for:

a $12,000
b $15,000
c $16,000
d $19,000

(handwritten: Kern 60,000 Pate 20,000 Grant 15,000 = 95,000 × 20% = 19,000 4,000 Bonus 19,000)

6. James Dixon, a partner in an accounting firm, decided to withdraw from the partnership. Dixon's share of the partnership profits and losses was 20%. Upon withdrawing from the partnership, he was paid $74,000 in final settlement for his partnership interest. The total of the partners' capital accounts *before* recognition of partnership goodwill prior to Dixon's withdrawal was $210,000. After his withdrawal, the remaining partners' capital accounts, excluding their share of goodwill, totaled $160,000. The total agreed-upon goodwill of the firm was:

a $120,000
b $140,000
c $160,000
d $250,000

(handwritten: B/4 goodwill 210,000 after w/d −160,000 Dixon's cap 50,000 Paid $74,000 cap −50,000 Excess 24,000 /20% = 120,000)

7. On June 30, 2006, the balance sheet for the partnership of Williams, Brown, and Lowe, together with their respective profit and loss ratios, is summarized as follows:

Assets, at cost	$300,000	Williams loan	$ 15,000
		Williams capital (20%)	70,000
		Brown capital (20%)	65,000
		Lowe capital (60%)	150,000
			$300,000

Williams has decided to retire from the partnership, and by mutual agreement the assets are to be adjusted to their fair value of $360,000 at June 30, 2006. It is agreed that the partnership will pay Williams $102,000 cash for his partnership interest exclusive of his loan, which is to be repaid in full. Goodwill is to be recorded in this transaction, as implied by the excess payment to Williams. After Williams's retirement, what are the capital account balances of Brown and Lowe, respectively?

a $65,000 and $150,000
b $97,000 and $246,000
c $73,000 and $174,000
d $77,000 and $186,000

(handwritten table:
	Wm	Brown	Lowe
	70,000	65,000	150,000
FV adj	12,000	12,000	36,000
Goodwill	20,000	20,000	60,000
	102,000	97,000	246,000
)

E 15-19

Partnership income allocation—salary allowance and interest

The partnership agreement of Kray, Lamb, and Mann provides for the division of net income as follows:

1. Lamb, who manages the partnership, is to receive a salary of $11,000 per year.

2. Each partner is to be allowed interest at 10% on beginning capital.

3. Remaining profits are to be divided equally.

During 2006, Kray invested an additional $4,000 in the partnership. Lamb withdrew $5,000, and Mann withdrew $4,000. No other investments or withdrawals were made during 2006. On January 1, 2006, the capital balances were Kray, $65,000; Lamb, $75,000; and Mann, $70,000. Total capital at year end was $252,000.

REQUIRED: Prepare a statement of partners' capital for the year ended December 31, 2006.

LEARNING OBJECTIVE 3

E 15-20

Recording new partner investment After operating as partners for several years, Grosby and Hambone decided to sell one-half of each of their partnership interests to Iota for a total of $70,000, paid directly to Grosby and Hambone.

At the time of Iota's admittance to the partnership, Grosby and Hambone had capital balances of $45,000 and $65,000, respectively, and shared profits 45% to Grosby and 55% to Hambone.

REQUIRED

1. Calculate the capital balances of each of the partners immediately after Iota is admitted as a partner.
2. In designing a new partnership agreement, how should profits and losses be divided?
3. If a new partnership agreement is not established, how will profits and losses be divided?

E 15-21

Partnership retirement—various situations The Case, Donley, and Early partnership balance sheet and profit and loss percentages at June 30, 2006, are summarized as follows:

Assets	$500,000	Case capital (30%)	$140,000
		Donley capital (30%)	175,000
		Early capital (40%)	185,000
	$500,000		$500,000

On July 1, 2006, the partners agree that Ms. Case is to retire immediately and receive $161,000 for her partnership interest.

REQUIRED: Prepare journal entries to illustrate *three* possible methods of accounting for the retirement of Ms. Case.

PROBLEMS

P 15-1

Partnership income allocation—statement of partnership capital Ellen, Fargo, and Gary are partners who share profits and losses 20%, 20%, and 60%, respectively, after Ellen and Fargo each receive a $12,000 salary allowance. Capital balances on January 1, 2006, are as follows:

Ellen (20%)	$ 69,000
Fargo (20%)	85,500
Gary (60%)	245,500

During 2006, Gary invested an additional $20,000 in the partnership, and Ellen and Fargo each withdrew $12,000, equal to their salary allowances as provided by the profit and loss sharing agreement. The partnership net assets at December 31, 2006, were $481,000.

REQUIRED: Prepare a statement of partnership capital for the year ended December 31, 2006.

P 15-2

Recording new partner investment—revaluation and nonrevaluation cases The partnership of Mortin and Oscar is being dissolved, and the assets and equities at book value and fair value and the profit and loss sharing ratios at January 1, 2006, are as follows:

	Book Value	Fair Value
Cash	$ 20,000	$ 20,000
Accounts receivable—net	100,000	100,000
Inventories	50,000	200,000
Plant assets—net	100,000	120,000
	$270,000	$440,000
Accounts payable	$ 50,000	$ 50,000
Mortin capital (50%)	120,000	
Oscar capital (50%)	100,000	
	$270,000	

Mortin and Oscar agree to admit Trent into the partnership for a one-third interest. Trent invests $95,000 cash and a building to be used in the business with a book value to Trent of $100,000 and a fair value of $120,000.

REQUIRED

1. Prepare a balance sheet for the Mortin, Oscar, and Trent partnership on January 2, 2006, just after the admission of Trent, assuming that the assets are revalued and goodwill is recognized.

2. Prepare a balance sheet for the Mortin, Oscar, and Trent partnership on January 2, 2006, after the admission of Trent, assuming that the assets are not revalued.

P 15-3

Partnership income allocation Ashe and Barbour are partners with capital balances on January 1, 2006, of $40,000 and $50,000, respectively. The partnership agreement provides that each partner be allowed 10% interest on beginning capital balances; that Ashe receive a salary allowance of $12,000 per year and a 20% bonus of partnership income after interest, salary allowance, and bonus; and that remaining income be divided equally.

REQUIRED: Prepare an income distribution schedule to show how the $105,000 partnership net income for 2006 should be divided.

P 15-4

Partnership income allocation—complex, net loss The partnership agreement of Alex, Carl, and Erika provides that profits are to be divided as follows:

1. Alex is to receive a salary allowance of $10,000 for managing the partnership business.
2. Partners are to receive 10% interest on average capital balances.
3. Remaining profits are to be divided 30%, 30%, and 40% to Alex, Carl, and Erika, respectively.

Alex had a capital balance of $60,000 at January 1, 2006, and had drawings of $8,000 during the year ended December 31, 2006. Carl's capital balance on January 1, 2006, was $90,000, and he invested an additional $30,000 on September 1, 2006. Erika's beginning capital balance was $110,000, and she withdrew $10,000 on July 1 but invested an additional $20,000 on October 1, 2006.

The partnership has a net loss of $12,000 during 2006, and the accountant in charge allocated the net loss as follows: $200 profit to Alex, $4,800 loss to Carl, and $7,400 loss to Erika.

REQUIRED

1. A schedule to show the correct allocation of the partnership net loss for 2006
2. A statement of partnership capital for the year ended December 31, 2006
3. Journal entries to correct the books of the partnership at December 31, 2006, assuming that all closing entries for the year have been recorded.

P 15-5

Partnership income allocation—profit sharing based on beginning, ending, and average capital balances A summary of changes in the capital accounts of the Katie, Lynda, and Molly partnership for 2006, before closing partnership net income to the capital accounts, is as follows:

	Katie Capital	Lynda Capital	Molly Capital	Total Capital
Balance January 1, 2006	$80,000	$80,000	$90,000	$250,000
Investment April 1	20,000			20,000
Withdrawal May 1		(15,000)		(15,000)
Withdrawal July 1	(10,000)			(10,000)
Withdrawal September 1			(30,000)	(30,000)
	$90,000	$65,000	$60,000	$215,000

REQUIRED: Determine the allocation of the 2006 net income to the partners under each of the following sets of independent assumptions:

1. Partnership net income is $60,000, and profit is divided on the basis of average capital balances during the year.
2. Partnership net income is $50,000, Katie gets a bonus of 10% of income for managing the business, and the remaining profits are divided on the basis of beginning capital balances.
3. Partnership net loss is $35,000, Molly receives a $12,000 salary, each partner is allowed 10% interest on beginning capital balances, and the remaining profits are divided equally.

LEARNING OBJECTIVE 3

P 15-6

Partner income allocation—correction of error The partnership of Jones, Keller, and Glade was created on January 2, 2006, with each of the partners contributing cash of $30,000. Reported profits, withdrawals, and additional investments were as follows:

	Reported Net Income	Withdrawals	Additional Investments
2006	$19,000	$4,000 Keller	$5,000 Glade
		5,000 Jones	
2007	22,000	8,000 Glade	5,000 Jones
		3,000 Keller	
2008	29,000	2,000 Glade	6,000 Glade
		4,000 Keller	

The partnership agreement provides that partners are to be allowed 10% interest on the beginning-of-the-year capital balances, that Jones is to receive a $7,000 salary allowance, and that remaining profits are to be divided equally.

After the books were closed on December 31, 2008, it was discovered that depreciation had been understated by $2,000 each year and that the inventory taken at December 31, 2008, was understated by $8,000.

REQUIRED

1. Calculate the balances in the three capital accounts on January 1, 2009.

2. Calculate the balances that should be in the three capital accounts on January 1, 2009.

3. Give the journal entry (one entry) to correct the books on January 1, 2009.

LEARNING OBJECTIVE 4

P 15-7

Recording new partner investment and subsequent balance sheet The partnership of Addie and Bailey is being dissolved, and its assets and equities at book value and fair value just prior to dissolution on January 1, 2006, are as follows:

	Book Value	Fair Value
Assets		
Cash	$ 15,000	$ 15,000
Accounts receivable—net	45,000	40,000
Inventories	50,000	60,000
Plant assets—net	90,000	105,000
	$200,000	$220,000
Equities		
Accounts payable	$ 30,000	$ 30,000
15% note payable	50,000	40,000
Addie capital (60%)	64,000	
Bailey capital (40%)	56,000	
	$200,000	

On January 2, 2006, Addie and Bailey take Cathy into the new partnership of Addie, Bailey, and Cathy for a 40% interest in capital and profits.

REQUIRED

1. Prepare journal entries for the admission of Cathy into the partnership for an investment of $150,000 assuming that assets (including any goodwill) are revalued.

2. Prepare a balance sheet for the Addie, Bailey, and Cathy partnership on January 2, 2006, just after the admission of Cathy.

P 15-8

LEARNING OBJECTIVE **4**

Recording new partner investment—various situations The capital accounts of the Abed, Batak, and Cabel partnership at December 31, 2006, together with profit and loss sharing ratios, are as follows:

Abed (25%)	$ 75,000
Batak (25%)	100,000
Cabel (50%)	125,000

The partners agree to admit Darling into the partnership.

REQUIRED: Prepare the journal entry or entries to admit Darling into the partnership and calculate the partners' capital balances immediately after his admission under each of the following independent assumptions.

1. Cabel sells half of her interest to Darling for $90,000, and the partners agree to admit Darling into the partnership.
2. Darling invests $75,000 cash in the partnership for a 25% interest in the partnership capital and profits, and partnership assets are revalued.
3. Darling invests $80,000 cash in the partnership for a 20% interest in the capital and profits, and partnership assets are revalued.
4. Darling invests $90,000 cash in the partnership for a 30% interest in the capital and profits, and partnership assets are *not* revalued.

P 15-9

LEARNING OBJECTIVE **4**

Recording new partner investment—various situations Three partners, Pat, Mike, and Hay, have capital balances and profit sharing ratios at December 31, 2006, as follows:

Pat	$144,000	profit ratio 2/5
Mike	216,000	profit ratio 1/2
Hay	90,000	profit ratio 1/10

On January 1, 2007, Con invests $85,080 in the business for a one-sixth interest in capital and income.

REQUIRED

1. Prepare journal entries giving *two* alternative solutions for recording Con's admission to the partnership.
2. Prepare journal entries giving *two* alternative solutions for recording Con's admission to the partnership if she purchased a one-sixth interest from each of the partners, rather than paying the $85,080 into the business.

P 15-10

LEARNING OBJECTIVE **4**

Recording new partner investment—various situations The AT Partnership was organized several years ago, and on January 1, 2006, the partners agree to admit Carmen for a 40% interest in capital and earnings. Capital account balances and profit and loss sharing ratios at January 1, 2006, before the admission of Carmen, are as follows:

Aida (50%)	$500,000
Thais (50%)	280,000

REQUIRED: Prepare journal entries to record the admission of Carmen for a 40% interest in the capital and rights to future profits under the following independent assumptions.

1. Carmen pays $450,000 directly to Aida and Thais for 40% of each of their interests, and the bonus procedure is used.
2. Carmen pays $600,000 directly to Aida and Thais for 40% of each of their interests, and goodwill is recorded.
3. Carmen invests $450,000 in the partnership for her 40% interest, and goodwill is recorded.
4. Carmen invests $600,000 in the partnership for her 40% interest, and goodwill is recorded.

P 15-11

Partnership income allocation—multiple years Harry, Iona, and Jerry formed a partnership on January 1, 2006, with each partner contributing $20,000 cash. Although the partnership agreement provided that Jerry receive a salary of $1,000 per month for managing the partnership business, Jerry has never withdrawn any money from the partnership. Harry withdrew $4,000 in each of the years 2006 and 2007, and Iona invested an additional $8,000 in 2006 and withdrew $8,000 during 2007. Due to an oversight, the partnership has not maintained formal accounting records, but the following information as of December 31, 2007, is available:

Cash on hand	$ 28,500
Due from customers	20,000
Merchandise on hand (at cost)	40,000
Delivery equipment—net of depreciation	37,000
Prepaid expenses	4,000
Assets	$129,500
Due to suppliers	$ 14,600
Wages payable	4,400
Note payable	10,000
Interest payable	500
Liabilities	$ 29,500

ADDITIONAL INFORMATION

1. The partners agree that income for 2006 was about half of the total income for the first two years of operations.

2. Although profits were not divided in 2006, the partnership agreement provides that profits, after allowance for Jerry's salary, are to be divided each year on the basis of beginning-of-the-year capital balances.

REQUIRED: Prepare statements of partnership capital for the years ended December 31, 2006, and December 31, 2007.

P 15-12

Partnership income allocation The partnership of Parker and Boone was formed and commenced operations on March 1, 2006, with Parker contributing $30,000 cash and Boone investing cash of $10,000 and equipment with an agreed-upon valuation of $20,000. On July 1, 2006, Boone invested an additional $10,000 in the partnership. Parker made a capital withdrawal of $4,000 on May 2, 2006, but reinvested the $4,000 on October 1, 2006. During 2006, Parker withdrew $800 per month, and Boone, the managing partner, withdrew $1,000 per month. These drawings were charged to salary expense. A preclosing trial balance taken at December 31, 2006, is as follows:

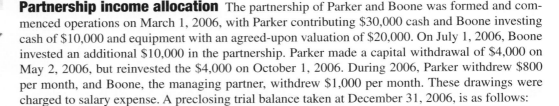

	Debit	Credit
Cash	$ 9,000	
Receivables—net	15,000	
Equipment—net	50,000	
Other assets	19,000	
Liabilities		$ 17,000
Parker capital		30,000
Boone capital		40,000
Service revenue		50,000
Supplies expense	17,000	
Utilities expense	4,000	
Salaries to partners	18,000	
Other miscellaneous expenses	5,000	
Total	$137,000	$137,000

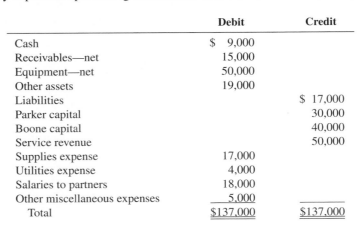

REQUIRED

1. Journalize the entries necessary to close the partnership books assuming that there is no agreement regarding profit distribution.

2. Prepare a statement of partnership capital assuming that the partnership agreement provides for monthly salary allowances of $800 and $1,000 for Parker and Boone, respectively, and for the division of remaining profits in relation to average capital balances.

3. Prepare a profit distribution schedule for the Parker and Boone partnership assuming monthly salary allowances of $800 and $1,000 for Parker and Boone, respectively; interest allowances at a 12% annual rate on average capital balances; and remaining profits divided equally.

P 15-13

Recording new partner investment—complex, nonrevaluation and revaluation cases

A condensed balance sheet for the Peter, Quarry, and Sherel partnership at December 31, 2006, and their profit and loss sharing percentages on that date are as follows:

Condensed Balance Sheet at December 31, 2006

Cash	$ 15,000	Liabilities	$ 50,000
Other assets	185,000	Peter capital (50%)	75,000
Total assets	$200,000	Quarry capital (30%)	50,000
		Sherel capital (20%)	25,000
		Total liabilities and capital	$200,000

On January 1, 2007, the partners decided to bring Tom into the partnership for a one-fourth interest in the capital and profits of the partnership. The following proposals for Tom's admittance into the partnership were considered:

1. Tom would purchase one-half of Peter's capital and right to future profits directly from Peter for $60,000.

2. Tom would purchase one-fourth of each partner's capital and rights to future profits by paying a total of $45,000 directly to the partners.

3. Tom would invest $55,000 cash in the partnership for a 25% interest in capital. Future profits would be divided 37.5%, 22.5%, 15%, and 25% for Peter, Quarry, Sherel, and Tom, respectively.

REQUIRED: Prepare journal entries with supporting computations to show Tom's admittance into the partnership under each of the above proposals assuming that:

1. Partnership net assets are not to be revalued

2. Partnership net assets are to be revalued

P 15-14

Partnership income allocation

Timmy and Lassie have been operating an accounting firm as partners for a number of years, and at the beginning of 2006, their capital balances were $60,000 and $75,000, respectively. During 2006, Timmy invested an additional $10,000 on April 1 and withdrew $6,000 on August 30. Lassie withdrew $12,000 on May 1 and withdrew another $6,000 on November 1. In addition, Timmy and Lassie withdrew their salary allowances of $18,000 and $24,000, respectively. At year-end 2006, total capital of the Timmy and Lassie partnership was $182,000. Timmy and Lassie share income after salary allowances in a 60:40 ratio.

REQUIRED

1. Determine average capital balances for Timmy and Lassie for 2006.

2. Allocate 2006 partnership income to Timmy and Lassie.

INTERNET ASSIGNMENT

Cedar Fair, L.P., is a publicly traded limited partnership that owns and operates six amusement parks, including Cedar Point in Sandusky, Ohio, and Knotts Berry Farm in Buena Park, California. Cedar Fair trades on the New York Stock Exchange, under the ticker symbol "FUN."

1. Go to Cedar Fair's Web site, www.cedarfair.com, and access its most recent annual report. Use the annual report to complete the following questions.

2. a. What is a publicly traded limited partnership?
   b. Instead of common stock, what security represents ownership?
   c. What rights do the partnership security owners have? Are they similar to common stockholders?
   d. Do the owners of trading limited partnerships receive dividends? If not, what types of "dividend"-like distributions do they receive?

3. A partnership needs at least one general partner. In the case of Cedar Fair,
   a. Who (is) are the general partner(s)?
   b. What role does the general partner have in running Cedar Fair?
   c. What is this partner's legal liability for the partnership's liabilities?
   d. What is the percentage of ownership for the general partner?
   e. How is the general partner compensated by the partnership? Does this seems reasonable given the risk and work performed for the partnership?

4. What is the major reason(s) that Cedar Fair was organized as a partnership instead of as a stock corporation?

5. In reviewing the financial statements of Cedar Fair, how are they different from a traditional stock corporation's statements?

SELECTED READINGS

SINKIN, JOSEPH. "Succession Planning/Business Valuation: Price Equals Value Plus Terms." *Journal of Accountancy* (December 2004), pp. 62–67.

Special Report, "Limited Liability CPA Firms: An Attractive Choice." *Journal of Accountancy* (July 1995), pp. 20–21.

WOEHLKE, JAMES A., WILLIAM B. KELLIHER, BRIAN L. SCHORR, and WALTER M. PRIMOFF. "LLCs: The Business Planner's Dream Entity." *The CPA Journal* (June 1995), pp. 16–22.

16 CHAPTER

PARTNERSHIP LIQUIDATION

The dissolution of a partnership is a change in the partners' relationship that terminates the partnership as a legal entity. Chapter 15 discussed partnership agreement termination when the partnership business continues to operate under a new partnership agreement. This chapter covers the situation in which both the partnership agreement is terminated and the business ceases to operate. In this case, the business must be liquidated. The liquidation process includes paying liabilities, selling off assets, and distributing monies to the partners.

■ ■ ■

THE LIQUIDATION PROCESS

LEARNING OBJECTIVE 1

Usually, **partnership liquidation** involves the following:

- Converting noncash assets into cash
- Recognizing gains and losses and liquidating expenses incurred during the liquidation period
- Settling all liabilities
- Distributing cash to the partners according to the final balances in their capital accounts

This general description of the liquidation process assumes the following:

- The partnership is solvent (i.e., partnership assets exceed partnership liabilities).
- All partners have equity in partnership net assets.
- No outstanding loan balances to any partner exist.
- All assets are converted into cash before any cash is distributed to the partners.

As these assumptions are relaxed, the liquidation process becomes more complex. Accordingly, this chapter begins with simple liquidations for solvent partnerships and proceeds to installment liquidations and liquidations of insolvent partnerships.

The rules for distributing assets in the liquidation of a partnership are covered in Section 40 of the Uniform Partnership Act. Section 40b gives the rank order of payment as follows:

I Amounts owed to creditors other than partners
II Amounts owed to partners other than for capital and profits[1]

---

[1] There is a presumption that money advanced to a partnership by a partner is a capital contribution. The partner will need evidence, such as a promissory note, that the money was a loan.

LEARNING OBJECTIVES

1 Understand the legal aspects of partnership liquidation.

2 Apply simple partnership liquidation computations and accounting.

3 Perform safe payment computations.

4 Understand installment liquidations.

5 Learn about cash distribution plans for installment liquidations.

6 Comprehend liquidations when either the partnership or the partners are insolvent.

III   Amounts due to partners with respect to their capital interests
IV   Amounts due to partners in respect of profits

Although the act lists profits as a fourth level of priority, practically, all profits and losses and drawing balances should be closed to the capital accounts before any distributions are made. This chapter assumes that capital accounts are updated before each distribution, so the fourth level is not discussed here.

Simple Partnership Liquidation

A simple partnership liquidation is a conversion of all partnership assets into cash with a single distribution of cash to partners in final settlement of the affairs of the partnership. To illustrate a simple liquidation, assume that the balance sheet of Holmes and Kaiser at December 31, 2006, is as follows (amounts in thousands):

HOLMES AND KAISER
BALANCE SHEET
AT DECEMBER 31, 2006

Assets		Liabilities and Equity	
Cash	$ 10	Accounts payable	$ 40
Accounts receivable—net	30	Loan from Holmes	10
Inventory	30	Holmes capital	25
Plant assets—net	40	Kaiser capital	35
	$110		$110

Holmes and Kaiser share profits and losses 70% and 30%, respectively, and agree to liquidate their partnership as soon as possible after January 1, 2007. We assume here that the assets are sold or settled on January 5, 2007. The inventory items are sold for $25,000, plant assets are sold for $30,000, and $22,000 is collected in final settlement of the accounts receivable.

The balance sheet after these transactions are recorded (see Exhibit 16-1 for the journal entries) is as follows (amounts in thousands):

HOLMES AND KAISER
BALANCE SHEET
JANUARY 5, 2007
(IMMEDIATELY AFTER ASSET SALE AND RECEIVABLE COLLECTION)

Assets		Liabilities and Equity	
Cash	$87	Accounts payable	$40
		Loan from Holmes	10
		Holmes capital	8.9
		Kaiser capital	28.1
	$87		$87

As the final step in the partnership liquidation, the cash is distributed to the creditors and partners as follows:

Order of Payment		
I To creditors for accounts payable	$40,000	
II To Holmes for his loan balance	10,000	
III To Holmes for his capital balance	8,900	
To Kaiser for his capital balance	28,100	
Total distribution	$87,000	

The established profit and loss sharing ratios (in this example, 70% and 30%) are used during the liquidation period unless the partnership agreement specifies a different division of profits and losses during liquidation. In the case of partnership agreements that provide for salary and interest allowances, only the residual profit and loss sharing ratios would be applied during the liquidation period. This is because the gains and losses at liquidation are essentially adjustments of prior profits that would have been shared using the residual profit sharing ratios if they had been recognized prior to dissolution.

Journal Entries to Record the Liquidation		
Cash (+A)	25,000	
Holmes capital (−OE)	3,500	
Kaiser capital (−OE)	1,500	
Inventory (−A)		30,000

To record sale of inventory items and allocation of the $5,000 loss to the partners' capital accounts in their residual profit and loss sharing ratios.

Cash (+A)	30,000	
Holmes capital (−OE)	7,000	
Kaiser capital (−OE)	3,000	
Plant assets—net (−A)		40,000

To record sale of plant assets and allocation of the $10,000 loss to the partners' capital accounts in their residual profit and loss sharing ratios.

Cash (+A)	22,000	
Holmes capital (−OE)	5,600	
Kaiser capital (−OE)	2,400	
Accounts receivable—net (−A)		30,000

To record collection of $22,000 of accounts receivable and to write off the remaining $8,000 receivables as a loss charged to the partners' capital accounts in their residual profit and loss sharing ratios.

Accounts payable (−L)	40,000	
Cash (−A)		40,000

To record payment of nonpartner liabilities.

Loan from Holmes (−L)	10,000	
Cash (−A)		10,000

To pay loan from Holmes.

Holmes capital (−OE)	8,900	
Kaiser capital (−OE)	28,100	
Cash (−A)		37,000

To distribute cash to partners in final liquidation of the partnership.

EXHIBIT 16-1

Simple Liquidation— Holmes and Kaiser Partnership

A liquidating partnership should maintain a summary of transactions and balances during the liquidation stage. This summary of transactions and balances, called a partnership liquidation statement, is presented for the Holmes and Kaiser partnership in Exhibit 16-2.

Debit Capital Balances in a Solvent Partnership

If liquidating partnerships are solvent, sufficient resources exist to pay creditors and distribute some cash to the partners. However, the process of liquidation may result in losses that force the capital accounts of some partners into debit balances. When this happens, those partners with debit balances have an obligation to partners with credit balances, and they can be required to use their personal assets to settle their partnership obligations. If the partners with debit balances are without personal resources, the partners with positive equity absorb losses equal to the debit balances. Such losses are shared in the relative profit and loss sharing ratios of the partners with positive equity balances.

EXHIBIT 16-2

Statement of Partnership Liquidation

HOLMES AND KAISER PARTNERSHIP STATEMENT OF PARTNERSHIP LIQUIDATION FOR THE PERIOD JANUARY 1, 2007, TO JANUARY 31, 2007 (IN THOUSANDS)

	Cash	Noncash Assets	Priority Liabilities	Holmes Loan	Holmes Capital (70%)	Kaiser Capital (30%)
Balances January 1, 2007	$10	$100	$40	$10	$25	$35
Sale of inventory	25	(30)			(3.5)	(1.5)
	35	70	40	10	21.5	33.5
Sale of plant assets	30	(40)			(7)	(3)
	65	30	40	10	14.5	30.5
Collection of receivables	22	(30)			(5.6)	(2.4)
	87	—	40	10	8.9	28.1
Payment of liabilities	(40)		(40)			
	47		—	10	8.9	28.1
Payment of Holmes loan	(10)			(10)		
	37			—	8.9	28.1
Final distribution to partners	(37)				(8.9)	(28.1)
	—				—	—

The partnership of Jay, Jim, and Joe is in the process of liquidation. The partnership accounts have the following balances after all assets have been converted into cash and all liabilities have been paid (amounts in thousands):

	Debit	Credit
Cash	$25	
Jay capital (40%)	3	
Jim capital (40%)		$16
Joe capital (20%)		12
Total	$28	$28

If Jay is personally solvent, he should pay $3,000 into the partnership to eliminate his debit capital account balance. His payment of $3,000 will bring the partnership cash up to $28,000, which can then be distributed to Jim and Joe in final liquidation of the partnership.

If Jay is unable to pay the debit balance, the debit balance represents a $3,000 loss to be absorbed by Jim and Joe according to their relative profit and loss sharing ratios. Jim's share of the loss is $2,000 ($3,000 × 0.4/0.6), and Joe's share is $1,000 ($3,000 × 0.2/0.6). In this case, the $25,000 is distributed $14,000 to Jim and $11,000 to Joe, and the partnership business is terminated.

The Uniform Partnership Act assigns higher payment priority in liquidation to amounts owed to partners other than their capital balances. This priority is usually abandoned and the legal doctrine of *right of offset* is applied when the partner has a debit capital balance. In this situation, the amount owed to the partner offsets up to the debit capital balance amount.

For example, assume that the partnership of Jay, Jim, and Joe had the following account balances (in thousands):

	Debit	Credit
Cash	$25	
Loan from Jay		$ 5
Jay capital (40%)	8	
Jim capital (40%)		16
Joe capital (20%)		12
Total	$33	$33

Under the right of offset rule, the loan from Jay would not be paid even though it has a higher-priority ranking in liquidation than the capital interests of Jim and Joe. Instead, it would be offset against Jay's debit capital balance, leaving Jay with a $3,000 obligation to Jim and Joe. If Jay is personally solvent, he pays $3,000 to the partnership so that Jim and Joe can receive the balances in their capital accounts in final liquidation.

If Jay is personally insolvent, however, the situation is changed considerably. In this case, Jay's personal creditors would have a prior claim on any money paid to Jay because personal creditors have a prior claim on personal assets. If the right of offset is applied by the partnership, $25,000 cash would be paid: $14,000 to Jim and $11,000 to Joe.

If the right of offset is not applied, Jay's personal creditors would be paid the amount of their claims up to $5,000, leaving less than $25,000 for distribution to Jim and Joe. If the entire $5,000 is paid to Jay's creditors, only $20,000 would be distributed to Jim and Joe.

Because of insufficient evidence that the right of offset rule is generally accepted by the courts, it has been recommended that the rule not be applied without agreement from the partners when a partner-creditor is personally insolvent.[2] Upon dissolution and subject to the rights of creditors, partners can agree to different property distributions than provided for under the act.[3]

SAFE PAYMENTS TO PARTNERS

Ordinarily, the process of liquidating a business takes considerable time. Some cash may become available for distribution to partners after all liabilities are paid but before all noncash assets are converted into cash. If the partners decide to distribute available cash before all noncash assets are sold (and before all gains or losses are recognized), the question arises as to how much cash can be safely distributed to the individual partners. **Safe payments** are distributions that can be made to partners with assurance that the amounts distributed will not need to be returned to the partnership at some later date to cover known liabilities or realign partner capital.

The calculation of safe payments is based on the following assumptions: (1) All partners are personally insolvent (that is, partners could not make any payments into the partnership), and (2) all noncash assets represent possible losses (that is, noncash assets should be considered losses for purposes of determining safe payments). In addition, when calculating safe payments, the partnership may withhold specific amounts of cash on hand to cover liquidation expenses, unrecorded liabilities, and general contingencies. The amounts of cash withheld are contingent losses to the partners and are considered losses for purposes of determining safe payments.

Application of a Safe Payments Schedule

Assume that the partnership of Buzz, Maxine, and Nancy is in the process of liquidation and that its account balances are as follows (in thousands):

Debits		**Credits**	
Cash	$ 80	Loan payable to Nancy	$ 20
Loan due from Maxine	10	Buzz capital (50%)	50
Land	20	Maxine capital (30%)	70
Buildings—net	140	Nancy capital (20%)	110
	$250		$250

All liabilities other than to partners have been paid, and the partners expect the sale of the land and buildings to take several months. Therefore, they agree that all cash on hand other than $10,000 to cover expenses and contingencies should be distributed immediately. Given this information, a schedule of safe payments (Exhibit 16-3) is prepared to determine the amount of cash that can be safely distributed to each partner.

The safe payments schedule begins with the equity of each partner shown on the top line. Partner equity is determined by combining the capital and loan balances for each of the partners. Possible losses are allocated to the partners in their profit and loss sharing ratios and are deducted from partner equity balances in the safe payments schedule in the same manner that actual losses would be deducted.

---

[2] Stephen A. Zeff, "Right of Offset vs. Partnership Act in Winding-up Process," *Accounting Review* (January 1957), pp. 68–70.

[3] *Anderson v. Anderson*, 1958, 138 A.2d 880, 215 Md.-483.

EXHIBIT 16-3

Safe Payments
Schedule

BUZZ, MAXINE, AND NANCY PARTNERSHIP
SCHEDULE OF SAFE PAYMENTS (AMOUNTS IN THOUSANDS)

	Possible Losses	Buzz Equity (50%)	Maxine Equity (30%)	Nancy Equity (20%)
Partners' equities (capital ± loan balances)		$50	$60	$130
Possible loss on noncash assets				
Book value of land and buildings	$160	(80)	(48)	(32)
		(30)	12	98
Possible loss on contingencies				
Cash withheld for contingencies	10	(5)	(3)	(2)
		(35)	9	96
Possible loss from Buzz				
Buzz's debit balance allocated				
60:40 to Maxine and Nancy		35	(21)	(14)
		0	(12)	82
Possible loss from Maxine				
Maxine's debit balance assigned				
to Nancy			12	(12)
			0	$ 70

The possible losses shown in Exhibit 16-3 include the $160,000 book value of the land and buildings (the only noncash assets) and the $10,000 cash withheld from distribution. After possible losses are deducted from the equity of each partner for purposes of safe payment calculations, some partners may show negative equity. The negative amounts must be allocated to the partners with positive equity balances using their relative profit and loss sharing ratios. Allocations are continued until none of the partners shows negative equity. At that point, the amount shown for partners with equity balances will be equal to the cash available for distribution. In Exhibit 16-3, the allocations are continued until Nancy's equity shows a $70,000 balance and the equity of Buzz and Maxine is zero. Thus, the $70,000 can be safely distributed to Nancy, but nothing can be safely distributed to either Buzz or Maxine.

Note that the safe payments schedule is used *only* to determine the amount of advance distribution. The safe payments schedule does not affect account balances or the statement of partnership liquidation. Actual cash distributed to Nancy is recorded in the usual fashion, with Nancy's loan balance being reduced to zero before her capital account is charged. The journal entry is as follows (in thousands):

Loan payable to Nancy (−L)	20	
Nancy capital (−OE)	50	
Cash (−A)		70

After this entry is recorded, the account balances of the Buzz, Maxine, and Nancy partnership are as follows (in thousands):

Debits		**Credits**	
Cash	$ 10	Buzz capital (50%)	$ 50
Loan due from Maxine	10	Maxine capital (30%)	70
Land	20	Nancy capital (20%)	60
Buildings—net	140		
	$180		$180

The partnership loan to Maxine can be charged to the capital balance of Maxine at any time, subject to the approval of the partners. Observe that the $10,000 loan to Maxine does not affect the determination of safe payments because the computations are based on the equity rather than the capital balances of the partners. Ordinarily, partnership loans to partners should be charged against partner capital balances at the beginning of the liquidation process.

Advance Distribution Requires Partner Approval

Any distribution to partners before all gains and losses have been realized and recognized requires approval of all partners. Assume that Xavier, Young, and Zebula are partners sharing profits and losses equally and that the partnership is in the process of liquidation with the following account balances after all nonpartner liabilities have been paid (amounts in thousands):

Debits		Credits	
Cash	$30	Xavier loan	$15
Equipment	45	Young capital	30
Xavier capital	10	Zebula capital	40
	$85		$85

If available cash is to be distributed, $10,000 should be paid to Young and $20,000 to Zebula according to the following safe payments computations (in thousands):

	Possible Losses	Xavier Equity	Young Equity	Zebula Equity
Partners' equities		$ 5	$30	$40
Possible loss on noncash asset:				
Equipment	$45	(15)	(15)	(15)
		(10)	15	25
Possible loss on Xavier's debit				
balance shared 50:50		10	(5)	(5)
Safe payments		—	$10	$20

Xavier may object to the immediate distribution of the $30,000 cash to Young and Zebula because his $15,000 loan to the partnership has a higher priority in liquidation than the capital balances of Young and Zebula. The objection simply means that the partners do not agree to the advance distribution of cash, and accordingly, all distributions to partners are delayed until all assets are converted into cash and a final settlement can be made.

INSTALLMENT LIQUIDATIONS

An **installment liquidation** involves the distribution of cash to partners as it becomes available during the liquidation period and before all liquidation gains and losses have been realized. The alternative is a simple liquidation, in which no cash is distributed to partners until all gains and losses on liquidation are realized and reflected in the partners' capital account balances.

General Principles of Installment Liquidation

An orderly liquidation of a solvent partnership may be carried out with distributions of available cash on a regular basis until all noncash assets are converted into cash. Liabilities other than those to the partners must be paid before any distributions are made to the partners.

Once cash is available for distribution to partners, the amounts to be distributed to individual partners can be determined by preparing a schedule of safe payments for each installment distribution. A safe payments schedule will not be necessary, however, when the capital accounts at the start of the liquidation process are in the relative profit and loss sharing ratios of the partners and there are no partner loan or advance balances. In this case, all distributions to partners will be made in the relative profit and loss sharing ratios.

When installment payments to partners are determined using safe payments schedules, the order of distributions will be such that the remaining capital balances (equity balances if there are loans with partners) after each distribution will be ever closer to alignment with the profit and loss sharing ratios of the partners. Once all partners are included in an installment distribution, the remaining capital balances (equities) will be aligned, and further installment payments will be in the profit sharing ratios. Thus, even though the capital accounts (equities) are not aligned at the start of the liquidation process, if all partners are included in the first installment, future installment payments to partners will be in the profit sharing ratios, and additional safe payments schedules are not necessary.

LEARNING OBJECTIVE **4**

Installment Liquidation Illustration

The partnership of Duro, Kemp, and Roth is to be liquidated as soon as possible after December 31, 2006. All cash on hand except for a $20,000 contingency balance is to be distributed at the end of each month until the liquidation is completed. Profits and losses are shared 50%, 30%, and 20% by Duro, Kemp, and Roth, respectively. The partnership balance sheet at December 31, 2006, contains the following (in thousands):

DURO, KEMP, AND ROTH
BALANCE SHEET
AT DECEMBER 31, 2006

Assets		Liabilities and Capital	
Cash	$ 240	Accounts payable	$ 300
Accounts receivable—net	280	Note payable	200
Loan to Roth	40	Loan from Kemp	20
Inventories	400	Duro capital (50%)	340
Land	100	Kemp capital (30%)	340
Equipment—net	300	Roth capital (20%)	200
Goodwill	40		
	$1,400		$1,400

A summary of liquidation events is as follows:

January 2007   The loan to Roth is offset against his capital balance, the goodwill is written off, $200,000 is collected on account, inventory items that cost $160,000 are sold for $200,000, and cash is distributed.

February 2007   Equipment with a book value of $80,000 is sold for $60,000, the remaining inventory items are sold for $180,000, liquidation expenses of $4,000 are paid, a liability of $8,000 is discovered, and cash is distributed.

March 2007   The land is sold for $150,000, liquidation expenses of $5,000 are paid, and cash is distributed.

April 2007   Additional equipment is sold for $150,000, the remaining equipment and receivables are written off, and all cash on hand is distributed in final liquidation of the partnership.

JANUARY LIQUIDATION EVENTS   The events of the Duro, Kemp, and Roth partnership during the month of January 2007 are recorded as follows (in thousands):

Roth capital (−OE)	40	
Loan to Roth (−A)		40
To offset loan against capital.		
Duro capital (−OE)	20	
Kemp capital (−OE)	12	
Roth capital (−OE)	8	
Goodwill (−A)		40
To write off goodwill.		
Cash (+A)	200	
Accounts receivable (−A)		200
To record collection of receivables.		
Cash (+A)	200	
Inventories (−A)		160
Duro capital (+OE)		20
Kemp capital (+OE)		12
Roth capital (+OE)		8
To record sale of inventory items at a gain.		

(continued)

EXHIBIT 16-4

Interim Statement of Partnership Liquidation

DURO, KEMP, AND ROTH
STATEMENT OF PARTNERSHIP LIQUIDATION
FOR THE PERIOD JANUARY 1, 2007, TO FEBRUARY 1, 2007 (AMOUNTS IN THOUSANDS)

	Cash	Noncash Assets	Priority Liabilities	50% Duro Capital	Kemp Loan	30% Kemp Capital	20% Roth Capital
Balances January 1	$240	$1,160	$500	$340	$20	$340	$200
Offset Roth loan		(40)					(40)
Write-off of goodwill		(40)		(20)		(12)	(8)
Collection of receivables	200	(200)					
Sale of inventory items	200	(160)		20		12	8
Predistribution balances January 31	640	720	500	340	20	340	160
January distribution (see Exhibit 16-5)							
Creditors	(500)		(500)				
Kemp	(120)				(20)	(100)	
Balances February 1	20	720	0	340	0	240	160

Accounts payable (–L)	300	
Note payable (–L)	200	
Cash (–A)		500
To record payment of nonpartner liabilities.		
Loan from Kemp (–L)	20	
Kemp capital (–OE)	100	
Cash (–A)		120
To record distribution of cash to Kemp.		

In addition to being recorded in the accounts, each of the foregoing entries should be reflected in a statement of partnership liquidation, such as the one shown in Exhibit 16-4. A liquidation statement is a continuous record that summarizes all transactions and events during the liquidation period, and it will not be complete until the liquidation is finalized. The statement shown in Exhibit 16-4 for January events is really an interim statement. However, interim liquidation statements are probably more important than the final liquidation statement because interim statements show the progress that has been made toward liquidation to date and can provide a basis for current decisions as well as future planning. The completed liquidation statement can do little more than provide interested parties with an ability to check what has been done. The partnership liquidation statement may be an acceptable legal document for partnerships that are liquidated through a bankruptcy court.[4]

In the cash distribution that is made on January 31, 2007 (see Exhibit 16-4), the partnership has $140,000 in cash remaining after all nonpartner debts have been paid. Of this amount, $20,000 is retained by the partnership for contingencies, and $120,000 is available for distribution to the partners. The safe payments schedule that appears in Exhibit 16-5 shows that the full $120,000 should be distributed to Kemp. The partnership has a $20,000 loan payable to Kemp, so the first $20,000 distributed to Kemp is applied to the loan, and the remaining $100,000 is charged to Kemp's capital account.

FEBRUARY LIQUIDATION EVENTS Journal entries to record the February 2007 events of the Duro, Kemp, and Roth liquidation are as follows (in thousands):

---

[4] When a partnership is liquidated under Chapter 7 of the Bankruptcy Act, court approval is required for all distributions.

EXHIBIT 16-5

First Installment—
Safe Payments
Schedule

DURO, KEMP, AND ROTH SCHEDULE OF SAFE PAYMENTS JANUARY 31, 2007

	Possible Losses	50% Duro Capital	30% Kemp Capital and Loan	20% Roth Capital
Partners' equities January 31, 2007 (see statement of liquidation)		$340	$360	$160
Possible loss on noncash assets (see statement of liquidation)	$720	(360)	(216)	(144)
		(20)	144	16
Possible loss on contingencies: cash withheld	20	(10)	(6)	(4)
		(30)	138	12
Possible loss from Duro: debit balance allocated 60:40		30	(18)	(12)
		—	$120	—

Cash (+A)	60	
Duro capital (−OE)	10	
Kemp capital (−OE)	6	
Roth capital (−OE)	4	
Equipment—net (−A)		80

To record sale of equipment at a $20,000 loss.

Cash (+A)	180	
Duro capital (−OE)	30	
Kemp capital (−OE)	18	
Roth capital (−OE)	12	
Inventories (−A)		240

To record sale of remaining inventory items at a $60,000 loss.

Duro capital (−OE)	2	
Kemp capital (−OE)	1.2	
Roth capital (−OE)	.8	
Cash (−A)		4

To record payment of liquidation expenses.

Duro capital (−OE)	4	
Kemp capital (−OE)	2.4	
Roth capital (−OE)	1.6	
Accounts payable (−L)		8

To record identification of an unrecorded liability.

Accounts payable (−L)	8	
Cash (−A)		8

To record payment of accounts payable.

Duro capital (−OE)	84	
Kemp capital (−OE)	86.4	
Roth capital (−OE)	57.6	
Cash (−A)		228

To record distribution of cash to partners.

EXHIBIT 16-6

Interim Statement of Partnership Liquidation

DURO, KEMP, AND ROTH
STATEMENT OF PARTNERSHIP LIQUIDATION
FOR THE PERIOD JANUARY 1, 2007, TO MARCH 1, 2007 (AMOUNTS IN THOUSANDS)

	Cash	Noncash Assets	Priority Liabilities	Duro Capital (50%)	Kemp Loan	Kemp Capital (30%)	Roth Capital (20%)
Balances January 1	$240	$1,160	$500	$340	$20	$340	$200
Offset Roth loan		(40)					(40)
Write-off of goodwill		(40)		(20)		(12)	(8)
Collection of receivables	200	(200)					
Sale of inventory items	200	(160)		20		12	8
Predistribution balances							
January 31	640	720	500	340	20	340	160
January distribution (see Exhibit 16-5)							
Creditors	(500)		(500)				
Kemp	(120)				(20)	(100)	
Balances February 1	20	720	0	340	0	240	160
Equipment sale	60	(80)		(10)		(6)	(4)
Sale of inventory items	180	(240)		(30)		(18)	(12)
Liquidation expenses	(4)			(2)		(1.2)	(.8)
Liability discovered			8	(4)		(2.4)	(1.6)
Predistribution balances							
February 28	256	400	8	294		212.4	141.6
February distribution (see Exhibit 16-7)							
Creditors	(8)		(8)				
Partners	(228)			(84)		(86.4)	(57.6)
Balances March 1	20	400	0	210		126	84

Exhibit 16-6 reflects these entries in a liquidation statement for the period January 1, 2007, to March 1, 2007. Exhibit 16-7 shows computations for the amount of cash distributed to partners on February 28, 2007. All the partners are included in the February 28 distribution, so all future distributions will be in the profit and loss sharing ratios, provided that the liquidation proceeds as planned.

The plan of distribution can be upset by events such as the distribution of noncash assets to specific partners. In the liquidation of a medical practice partnership, for example, doctors might withdraw equipment early in the liquidation process in order to continue their own practices. When noncash assets are distributed to partners, the fair value of such assets should be determined, and any difference between fair value and book value should be recognized as a partnership gain or loss. The distribution of noncash assets to specific partners and the valuation of the property distributed must be approved by all partners.

DURO, KEMP, AND ROTH
SCHEDULE OF SAFE PAYMENTS
FEBRUARY 28, 2007 (AMOUNTS IN THOUSANDS)

	Possible Losses	Duro Capital (50%)	Kemp Capital (30%)	Roth Capital (20%)
Partners' equities February 28, 2007 (see statement of liquidation)		$294	$212.4	$141.6
Possible loss on noncash assets (see statement of liquidation)	$400	(200)	(120)	(80)
		94	92.4	61.6
Possible loss on contingencies: cash withheld	20	(10)	(6)	(4)
		$ 84	$ 86.4	$ 57.6

EXHIBIT 16-7

Second Installment—Safe Payments Schedule

MARCH AND APRIL LIQUIDATION EVENTS By March 2007 the liquidation of the Duro, Kemp, and Roth partnership has progressed to a point at which partner capital balances are in their relative profit and loss sharing ratios. Journal entries for the events of March and April are as follows (in thousands):

Entries for March

Cash (+A)	150	
Duro capital (+OE)		25
Kemp capital (+OE)		15
Roth capital (+OE)		10
Land (−A)		100

    To record sale of land at a $50,000 gain.

Duro capital (−OE)	2.5	
Kemp capital (−OE)	1.5	
Roth capital (−OE)	1	
Cash (−A)		5

    To record payment of liquidation expenses.

Duro capital (−OE)	72.5	
Kemp capital (−OE)	43.5	
Roth capital (−OE)	29	
Cash (−A)		145

    To record the March distribution of cash to partners.

Entries for April

Cash (+A)	150	
Duro capital (−OE)	35	
Kemp capital (−OE)	21	
Roth capital (−OE)	14	
Equipment—net (−A)		220

    To record sale of the remaining equipment at a
      $70,000 loss.

Duro capital (−OE)	40	
Kemp capital (−OE)	24	
Roth capital (−OE)	16	
Accounts receivable (−A)		80

    To record write-off of remaining receivables.

Duro capital (−OE)	85	
Kemp capital (−OE)	51	
Roth capital (−OE)	34	
Cash (−A)		170

    To record distribution of cash to partners in final liquidation.

    Exhibit 16-8 reflects these entries in a complete liquidation statement for the partnership. The complete liquidation statement covers the period January 1 to April 30, 2007. The March and April cash distributions to partners are in the relative profit and loss sharing ratios, so safe payments computations are not necessary. The $145,000 distributed to partners on March 31 is determined by subtracting the $20,000 cash reserve from the $165,000 cash balance immediately before the distribution. All remaining cash is remitted to the partners in the final installment distribution on April 30, 2007.

CASH DISTRIBUTION PLANS

Safe payments schedules are an effective method of computing the amount of safe payments to partners and of preventing excessive payments to any partner. However, the approach is inefficient

EXHIBIT 16-8

Final Statement of Partnership Liquidation

DURO, KEMP, AND ROTH
STATEMENT OF PARTNERSHIP LIQUIDATION
FOR THE PERIOD JANUARY 1, 2007, TO APRIL 30, 2007 (AMOUNTS IN THOUSANDS)

	Cash	Noncash Assets	Priority Liabilities	Duro Capital (50%)	Kemp Loan	Kemp Capital (30%)	Roth Capital (20%)
Balances January 1	$240	$1,160	$500	$340	$20	$340	$200
Offset Roth loan		(40)					(40)
Write-off of goodwill		(40)		(20)		(12)	(8)
Collection of receivables	200	(200)					
Sale of inventory items	200	(160)		20		12	8
Predistribution balances							
January 31	640	720	500	340	20	340	160
January distribution (see Exhibit 16-5)							
Creditors	(500)		(500)				
Kemp	(120)				(20)	(100)	
Balances February 1	20	720	0	340	0	240	160
Equipment sale	60	(80)		(10)		(6)	(4)
Sale of inventory items	180	(240)		(30)		(18)	(12)
Liquidation expenses	(4)			(2)		(1.2)	(.8)
Liability discovered			8	(4)		(2.4)	(1.6)
Predistribution balances							
February 28	256	400	8	294		212.4	141.6
February distribution (see Exhibit 16-7)							
Creditors	(8)		(8)				
Partners	(228)			(84)		(86.4)	(57.6)
Balances March 1	20	400	0	210		126	84
Sale of land	150	(100)		25		15	10
Liquidation expenses	(5)			(2.5)		(1.5)	(1)
Predistribution balances March 31	165	300		232.5		139.5	93
March distribution (50:30:20)	(145)			(72.5)		(43.5)	(29)
Balances April 1	20	300		160		96	64
Sale of equipment	150	(220)		(35)		(21)	(14)
Write-off of receivables		(80)		(40)		(24)	(16)
Predistribution balances April 30	170	0		85		51	34
April distribution (50:30:20)	(170)			(85)		(51)	(34)
Liquidation completed April 30	0			0		0	0

if numerous installment distributions are made to partners, because a safe payments schedule must be prepared for each distribution until the capital balances are aligned with the profit and loss sharing ratios. The safe payments schedule approach is also deficient as a planning device because it does not provide information that will help the partners project when they can expect to be included in cash distributions. These deficiencies of the safe payments approach can be overcome by preparing a cash distribution plan at the start of the liquidation process.

The development of a **cash distribution plan** (also referred to as a *cash predistribution plan*) for the liquidation of a partnership involves ranking the partners in terms of their vulnerability to possible losses, using the vulnerability ranking to prepare a schedule of assumed loss absorption, and developing a cash distribution plan from the assumed-loss-absorption schedule. In illustrating the preparation of a cash distribution plan, the Duro, Kemp, and Roth example is used again.

Vulnerability Ranking

At the inception of the liquidation process, Duro, Kemp, and Roth had capital balances of $340,000, $340,000, and $200,000, respectively, but their equities (capital ± loan balances) were $340,000, $360,000, and $160,000, respectively. In determining their vulnerability to possible losses, the equity of each partner is divided by his or her profit sharing ratio to identify the maximum loss that the partner could absorb without reducing his or her equity below zero. **Vulnerability rankings** for Duro, Kemp, and Roth are determined as follows:

DURO, KEMP, AND ROTH VULNERABILITY RANKING

	Partner's Equity		Profit Sharing Ratio		Loss Absorption Potential	Vulnerability Ranking (1 most vulnerable)
Duro	$340,000	÷	0.5	=	$ 680,000	1
Kemp	360,000	÷	0.3	=	1,200,000	3
Roth	160,000	÷	0.2	=	800,000	2

The vulnerability ranks indicate that Duro is most vulnerable to losses because his equity would be reduced to zero with a total partnership loss on liquidation of $680,000. Kemp, on the other hand, is least vulnerable because his equity is sufficient to absorb his share of liquidation losses up to $1,200,000. This interpretation helps explain why Kemp received all the cash distributed to partners in the first installment distribution in the previous illustration.

Assumed Loss Absorption

A **schedule of assumed loss absorption** is prepared as a second step in developing the cash distribution plan. This schedule starts with the preliquidation equities and charges each partner's equity with its share of the loss that would exactly eliminate the equity of the most vulnerable partner. The next step is to charge each remaining partner's equity with its share of the loss that would exactly eliminate the equity of the next most vulnerable partner. This process is continued until the equities of all but the least vulnerable partner have been reduced to zero. A schedule of assumed loss absorption for the Duro, Kemp, and Roth partnership is as follows (amounts in thousands):

DURO, KEMP, AND ROTH SCHEDULE OF ASSUMED LOSS ABSORPTION

	Duro (50%)	Kemp (30%)	Roth (20%)	Total
Preliquidation equities	$340	$360	$160	$860
Assumed loss to absorb Duro's equity (allocated 50:30:20)	(340)	(204)	(136)	(680)
Balances	—	156	24	180
Assumed loss to absorb Roth's equity (allocated 60:40)		(36)	(24)	(60)
Balances		$120	—	$120

The partnership loss that exactly eliminates Duro's equity is $680,000, an amount computed in preparing the vulnerability ranks. After Duro's equity is reduced to zero in the first step, losses are divided 60% to Kemp and 40% to Roth until Roth's equity is reduced to zero. The additional partnership loss that reduces Roth's equity to zero is $60,000—Roth's $24,000 equity divided by his 40% profit sharing ratio after Duro is eliminated from consideration (in other words, it is assumed that Duro is personally insolvent). After Roth's equity has been reduced to zero, the equity of Kemp, the least vulnerable partner, stands at $120,000.

Cash Distribution Plan

Kemp should receive the first $120,000 distributed to the partners. A cash distribution plan for the Duro, Kemp, and Roth partnership is prepared from the schedule of assumed loss absorption as follows:

DURO, KEMP, AND ROTH CASH DISTRIBUTION PLAN

	Priority Liabilities	Kemp Loan	Duro	Kemp	Roth
First $500,000	100%				
Next $20,000		100%			
Next $100,000				100%	
Next $60,000				60	40%
Remainder			50%	30	20

In developing the cash distribution plan, the first cash available for distribution goes to nonpartner creditors. These consist of the $300,000 accounts payable and the $200,000 note payable of the Duro, Kemp, and Roth partnership at December 31, 2006. The next $20,000 goes to Kemp to settle his loan to the partnership, because partner loans have a higher priority than partner capital balances. The next $100,000 available is distributed to Kemp in consideration of his capital balance. This distribution aligns the capital and profit sharing ratios of Kemp and Roth. The next $60,000 is shared 60% and 40% between Kemp and Roth. This distribution completes the alignment of all capital balances and profit sharing ratios, and the remaining distributions are in accordance with the profit sharing ratios.

Kemp can analyze the cash distribution plan on January 1, 2007, and determine that he will begin to receive cash after $500,000 has been paid to priority creditors. Similarly, Roth and Duro can use the plan to determine their chances of recovering some or all of their partnership equities. For example, if Duro expects $800,000 to be realized from all partnership assets, he can easily compute the amount he would receive [($800,000 − $680,000) × 50% = $60,000].

Cash Distribution Schedule

Further application of the cash distribution plan can be illustrated by assuming that the Duro, Kemp, and Roth partnership is liquidated in two installments, with $550,000 cash being distributed in the first installment and $250,000 in the second and final installment. Under these assumptions, the cash distribution plan would be used in preparing a **cash distribution schedule**, such as the following one. Amounts are in thousands.

DURO, KEMP, AND ROTH CASH DISTRIBUTION SCHEDULE

	Cash Distributed	Priority Liabilities	Kemp Loan	Duro Capital	Kemp Capital	Roth Capital
First Installment						
Priority creditors	$500	$500				
Kemp loan	20		$20			
Kemp capital (remainder)	30				$ 30	
	$550	$500	$20		$ 30	
Second Installment						
Kemp capital	$ 70				$ 70	
Kemp and Roth (60:40)	60				36	$24
Remainder (50:30:20)	120			$60	36	24
	$250			$60	$142	$48

The $550,000 cash distributed in the first installment is allocated $500,000 to nonpartner liabilities and $20,000 to repay the loan from Kemp. The remaining $30,000 is paid to Kemp to reduce the balance of his capital account. In the second installment distribution, as shown in the cash distribution schedule, Kemp receives the first $70,000 in order to align his capital balance with that of Roth. The next $60,000 is allocated to Kemp and Roth in accordance with their 60:40 relative profit and loss sharing ratios, and the final $120,000 is allocated to Duro, Kemp, and Roth in their 50:30:20 relative profit and loss sharing ratios.

The information from the cash distribution schedule is used in the same manner as information from safe payments schedules. The cash payments indicated by the cash distribution schedules are entered in the statement of partnership liquidation and in the partnership records as cash distributions are actually made.

The preparation of a cash distribution plan is more time-consuming than the preparation of a single safe payments schedule. However, as shown here, the cash distribution plan provides a flexible and efficient means of determining safe payments to partners. In addition, the cash distribution plan aids in planning.

INSOLVENT PARTNERS AND PARTNERSHIPS

The order for distributing assets in the liquidation of a partnership was listed earlier in this chapter as:

    I. Amounts owed to creditors other than partners
    II. Amounts owed to partners other than for capital and profits
    III. Amounts due to partners with respect to their capital interests
    IV. Amounts due to partners in respect of profits

This order of distribution is specified in Section 40b of the Uniform Partnership Act. With respect to an insolvent partner, Section 40i of the act gives the following rank order for claims against the separate property of a *bankrupt partner*:

    I. Those owing to separate creditors
    II. Those owing to partnership creditors
    III. Those owing to partners by way of contribution

These priority rankings have important implications for the liquidation of partnerships that are insolvent (partnership assets < partnership liabilities) and for the liquidation of partnerships that are solvent (partnership assets ≥ partnership liabilities) but in which one or more of the individual partners is insolvent (personal assets < personal liabilities). Partnership creditors must first seek recovery of their claims from partnership property, and the creditors of individual partners must first seek recovery of their claims from individual property.

Partnership Solvent—One or More Partners Personally Insolvent

In the liquidation of a solvent partnership, partnership creditors are entitled to recover the full amount of their claims from partnership property. The partnership must be careful not to distribute partnership property to an insolvent partner in excess of his or her capital balance, resulting in a debit balance. This distribution makes the assets personal assets, and his or her personal creditors have a priority claim on the assets over the partnership creditors.

If such a distribution does not occur, personal creditors only have a claim on partnership assets to the extent of the insolvent partner's equity. If an insolvent partner has a credit capital balance and a solvent partner has an equal debit balance (that is, partnership assets = partnership liabilities = 0), the personal creditors of the insolvent partner have a claim against the personal assets of the solvent partner to the extent of the debit capital balance.

Even though the partnership is solvent, individual partners may have debit balances in their capital accounts at the time of dissolution, or they may end up with debit capital balances as a result of losses and expenses incurred during the liquidation process. Such partners are obligated to the partners with equity in the partnership for the amount of such debit balances. However, if a partner with a debit capital balance is personally insolvent (personal assets < personal liabilities), the full amount of that partner's personal assets will go to his or her personal creditors (rank I) under the act, and amounts owing to partners by way of contribution (rank III) will not share in distribution of that partner's personal assets. In some states, however, it is possible under common law or bankruptcy law for the partners to share in the personal assets of an insolvent partner with a debit capital balance.[5]

To illustrate, West, York, and Zeff are partners sharing profits 30%, 30%, and 40%, respectively. West is personally insolvent, with personal assets of $50,000 and personal liabilities of $100,000.

---

[5] A trustee in a partnership case under the Bankruptcy Act of 1978 has a claim against the estate of each general partner who is also a debtor in a bankruptcy case (11 *USC*, paragraph 723c).

The partnership account balances after all partnership liabilities have been paid are as follows (in thousands):

	Case A	**Case B**	**Case C**
Cash	$60 DR	—	—
West capital (30%)	18 CR	$18 CR	$21 DR
York capital (30%)	18 CR	27 DR	9 CR
Zeff capital (40%)	24 CR	9 CR	12 CR

In Case A, West's $18,000 partnership equity should not be paid directly to West because her personal creditors have a prior claim against her $18,000 equity in partnership assets.

In Case B, the personal creditors of West have a claim against the personal assets of York to the extent of the $18,000 that York owes West. Zeff also has a claim against York for $9,000.

In Case C, West's capital account has a debit balance and she is insolvent. Under the provisions of the act, York and Zeff are not allowed to share in West's personal assets. Thus, they must share the $21,000 loss from West using their relative profit sharing ratios of 3:7 and 4:7.

Insolvent Partnership

When a partnership is insolvent, the cash available after all noncash assets have been converted into cash is not enough to pay partnership creditors.[6] Partnership creditors will obtain partial recovery from partnership assets (rank I) and will call upon individual partners to use their personal resources to satisfy remaining claims (rank II).

Although personal creditors have a prior claim (rank I) on personal assets, partnership creditors can seek recovery of their claims from the personal assets of any partner who is personally solvent. Partners are required to contribute the amounts necessary to satisfy partnership liabilities. The Uniform Partnership Act is specific in stating that a partner must contribute his or her share of the payment to satisfy the liabilities, as well as his or her relative share of the liabilities of any partners who are insolvent or who cannot or will not contribute their share of the liabilities (see Section 40b of the act). A partner who pays more than his or her share of partnership liabilities does, of course, have a claim against partners with debit capital balances.

Rose, Faye, and Kate are partners sharing profits equally. Their partnership is in the process of liquidation. After all assets have been converted into cash and all available cash applied to payment of partnership liabilities, the following account balances remain on the partnership books (amounts in thousands):

Liabilities	$90 CR
Rose capital (1/3)	30 DR
Faye capital (1/3)	30 DR
Kate capital (1/3)	30 DR

Provided that all partners have personal resources of at least $30,000, each partner should pay $30,000 into the partnership in full satisfaction of partnership liabilities. However, the creditors may collect the full $90,000 deficiency from any one of the partners. For example, creditors may collect the $90,000 from Rose, in which case the remaining partnership balances would be as follows (in thousands):

Rose capital	$60 CR
Faye capital	30 DR
Kate capital	30 DR

If Faye and Kate can each pay $30,000 into the partnership, the fact that the creditors proceeded against Rose is of no great concern. However, if the creditors proceeded against Rose because Kate is personally insolvent and Faye's net personal assets are only $35,000, the situation is changed considerably. In this case, Rose and Faye share equally the $30,000 loss on Kate's insolvency, after

---

[6] As used in this chapter, an *insolvent partnership* means that partnership liabilities exceed the fair value of partnership assets. Under the Bankruptcy Act of 1978, a partnership is insolvent if partnership liabilities exceed the fair value of partnership assets plus the excess of each general partner's personal assets over personal debts (11 *USC*, paragraph 101[26]B).

which Rose will have a $45,000 credit capital balance and Faye will have a $45,000 debit capital balance. Faye's personal assets are only $35,000, so Rose proceeds to collect the $35,000 from Faye, and the remaining $10,000 debit balance in Faye's capital account is written off as a loss to Rose.

The examples in this section illustrate some of the common problems that can arise in liquidations of partnerships that are insolvent or in which there are insolvent partners.

SUMMARY

The liquidation of a partnership involves converting noncash assets into cash, recognizing gains and losses during the liquidation period, paying liabilities, and distributing cash to partners in final termination of the business entity. A simple liquidation refers to the conversion of all assets into cash before any distributions are made to partners.

A primary financial statement of a liquidating partnership is the statement of partnership liquidation, which summarizes all financial transactions and events during the liquidation period. This statement may also be used as a legal document for liquidations carried out under the jurisdiction of a court.

When partnerships are liquidated through installment distributions to partners, cash is distributed to partners after liabilities have been paid but before all gains and losses on liquidation are recognized in the accounts. To prevent excessive payments to any partner, the amount of cash to be distributed is computed on the basis of two assumptions—that all partners are personally insolvent and that all noncash assets are actual losses. Two approaches exist for computing the amounts that can be safely paid to partners in each installment distribution. A safe payments schedule may be prepared for each installment distribution, or a cash distribution plan may be prepared that can be used throughout the liquidation process.

The Uniform Partnership Act specifies priorities for the distribution of partnership assets in liquidations and for the distribution of the personal assets of insolvent partners. Partnership creditors rank first in recovering their claims from partnership property, and personal creditors rank first in recovering their claims from personal property. Priorities for other claims depend on whether the partnership or the individual partners are insolvent, and each case requires separate analysis.

QUESTIONS

1. How does partnership liquidation differ from partnership dissolution?

2. What is a simple partnership liquidation, and how are distributions to partners computed?

3. The Uniform Partnership Act specifies a priority ranking for distribution of partnership assets in liquidation. What is the ranking?

4. What is the right of offset rule? How does it affect the amount to be distributed to partners in a liquidation?

5. What assumptions are made in determining the amount of distributions (or safe payments) to individual partners prior to the recognition of all gains and losses on liquidation?

6. What are partner equities? Why are partner equities rather than partner capital balances used in the preparation of safe payments schedules?

7. How do safe payments computations affect partnership ledger account balances?

8. What is a statement of partnership liquidation, and how is the statement helpful to partners and other parties involved in partnership liquidation?

9. A partnership in liquidation has satisfied all of its nonpartner liabilities and has cash available for distribution to partners. Under what circumstances would it be permissible to divide available cash in the profit and loss sharing ratios of the partners?

10. What are vulnerability ranks? How are they used in the preparation of cash distribution plans for partnership liquidations?

11. If a partnership is insolvent, how is the amount of cash distributed to individual partners determined?

12. When all partnership assets have been distributed in the liquidation of a partnership, some partners may have debit capital balances and others may have credit capital balances. How are such balances eliminated if the partners with debit balances are personally solvent? If they are personally insolvent?

EXERCISES

E 16-1

Simple liquidation—schedule of cash available The partnership of Folly and Frill is in the process of liquidation. On January 1, 2006, the ledger shows account balances as follows:

LEARNING OBJECTIVE 2

Cash	$10,000	Accounts payable	$15,000
Accounts receivable	25,000	Folly capital	40,000
Lumber inventory	40,000	Frill capital	20,000

On January 10, 2006, the lumber inventory is sold for $25,000, and during January, accounts receivable of $21,000 are collected. No further collections on the receivables are expected. Profits are shared 60% to Folly and 40% to Frill.

REQUIRED: Prepare a schedule showing how the cash available on February 1, 2006, should be distributed.

E 16-2

Liquidation—journal entries After closing entries were made on December 31, 2006, the ledger of Mike, Nancy, and Okey contained the following balances:

LEARNING OBJECTIVE 2

Cash	$39,000	Accounts payable	$ 5,000
Inventory	16,000	Mike capital (40%)	15,000
		Nancy capital (30%)	8,000
		Okey capital (30%)	27,000

Due to unsuccessful operations, the partners decide to liquidate the business. During January some of the inventory is sold for $10,000, and on January 31, 2007, all available cash is distributed. It is not known if the remaining inventory items can be sold.

REQUIRED: Prepare all journal entries necessary to account for the transactions of the partnership during January 2007.

E 16-3

Liquidation—cash distribution computation, safe payments schedule Terry, Vivian, and Walter have decided to liquidate their partnership. Account balances on January 1, 2006, are as follows:

LEARNING OBJECTIVES 2, 3

Cash	$120,000	Accounts payable	$ 40,000
Other assets	120,000	Terry capital (30%)	85,000
	$240,000	Vivian capital (30%)	25,000
		Walter capital (40%)	90,000
			$240,000

The partners agree to keep a $10,000 contingency fund and to distribute available cash immediately.

REQUIRED: Determine the amount of cash that should be paid to each partner.

E 16-4

Liquidation—cash distribution computation, safe payments schedule Jan, Kim, and Lee announce plans to liquidate their partnership immediately. The assets, equities, and profit and loss sharing ratios are summarized as follows.

LEARNING OBJECTIVES 2, 3

Loan to Kim	$ 20,000	Accounts payable	$ 60,000
Other assets	180,000	Jan capital (50%)	59,000
	$200,000	Kim capital (30%)	29,000
		Lee capital (20%)	52,000
			$200,000

The other assets are sold for $120,000, and an overlooked bill for landscaping services of $5,000 is discovered. Kim cannot pay her partnership debt at the present time, but she expects to have the money in a month or two.

REQUIRED: Determine how cash should be distributed to creditors and partners.

E 16-5

Liquidation—capital balance computation correcting an error The profit and loss sharing agreement of the partnership of Anita, Bernice, and Colleen provides that the partners are allowed 10% interest on their average capital balances for the year; Anita is allowed a $15,000 salary; and the remainder is divided 50% to Anita, 30% to Bernice, and 20% to Colleen. The December 31, 2006, after-closing balances are as follows:

Net assets	$100,000	Anita capital	$ 40,000
		Bernice capital	35,000
		Colleen capital	25,000
			$100,000

In January 2007 the partners are preparing to liquidate the business and discover that the year-end inventory was overvalued by $10,000, resulting in an error in calculating the 2006 net income.

REQUIRED: Determine the correct capital balances of Anita, Bernice, and Colleen.

E 16-6

Liquidation—capital balance computation correcting an error The profit and loss sharing agreement of the partnership of Ali, Bart, and Carrie provides a salary allowance for Ali and Carrie of $10,000 each. Partners receive a 10% interest allowance on their average capital balances for the year. The remainder is divided 40% to Ali, 20% to Bart, and 40% to Carrie. The December 31, 2006, after-closing balances are as follows:

Net assets	$150,000	Ali capital	$ 60,000
		Bart capital	25,000
		Carrie capital	65,000
			$150,000

In January 2007 the partners are preparing to liquidate the business and discover that the year-end inventory was erroneously undervalued by $15,000, resulting in an error in calculating the 2006 net income.

REQUIRED: Determine the correct capital balances of Ali, Bart, and Carrie.

E 16-7

Safe payments schedule A condensed balance sheet with profit sharing percentages for the Evers, Freda, and Grace partnership on January 1, 2006, shows the following:

Cash	$100,000	Liabilities	$ 80,000
Other assets	500,000	Evers capital (40%)	100,000
		Freda capital (40%)	250,000
		Grace capital (20%)	170,000
	$600,000		$600,000

On January 2, 2006, the partners decide to liquidate the business, and during January they sell assets with a book value of $300,000 for $170,000.

REQUIRED: Prepare a safe payments schedule to show the amount of cash to be distributed to each partner if all available cash, except for a $10,000 contingency fund, is distributed immediately after the sale.

E 16-8

Safe payments schedule The partnership of Jerry, Joan, and Jill is in the process of liquidation. Its account balances on November 30, 2006, are as follows:

Cash	$ 8,000	Accounts payable	$ 4,000
Inventory	16,000	Due to Joan	4,000
Patent	8,000	Jerry capital	10,800
Receivable from Jerry	3,000	Joan capital	13,200
		Jill capital	3,000

Profits and losses are shared 40:50:10 to Jerry, Joan, and Jill, respectively.

REQUIRED: Prepare a statement of liquidation and a safe payments schedule for immediate distribution of all cash on hand.

E 16-9

Safe payments schedule, statement of partnership liquidation The Larry, Moe, and Curly partnership became insolvent on January 1, 2006, and the partnership is being liquidated as soon as practicable. In this respect the following information for the partners has been marshaled:

	Capital Balances	Personal Assets	Personal Liabilities
Larry	$ 70,000	$80,000	$40,000
Moe	(60,000)	30,000	50,000
Curly	(30,000)	70,000	30,000
Total	$(20,000)		

REQUIRED: Assume that residual profits and losses are shared equally among the three partners. Based on this information, calculate the *maximum* amount that Larry can expect to receive from the partnership liquidation.

E 16-10

Statement of partnership liquidation and final journal entries The partnership of Alice, Betty, and Carle became insolvent during 2006, and the partnership ledger shows the following balances after all partnership assets have been converted into cash and all available cash distributed:

	Debit	Credit
Accounts payable		$ 30,000
Alice capital		20,000
Betty capital	$120,000	
Carle capital		70,000
	$120,000	$120,000

Profit and loss sharing percentages for the three partners are Alice, 30%; Betty, 40%; and Carle, 30%. The personal assets and liabilities of the partners are as follows:

	Alice	Betty ~~Now 80,000~~	Carle
Personal assets	$60,000	~~$110,000~~	$60,000
Personal liabilities	50,000	60,000	40,000

REQUIRED: Prepare a schedule to show the phaseout of the partnership and final closing of the books if the partnership creditors recover $30,000 from Betty.

E 16-11

Statement of partnership liquidation—partner insolvency case After all partnership assets were converted into cash and all available cash distributed to creditors, the ledger of the Daniel, Eric, and Fred partnership showed the following balances:

	Debit	Credit
Accounts payable		$20,000
Daniel capital (40%)		10,000
Eric capital (30%)		60,000
Fred capital (30%)	$90,000	
	$90,000	$90,000

The percentages indicated are residual profit and loss sharing ratios. Personal assets and liabilities of the partners are as follows:

	Daniel	Eric	Fred
Personal assets	$50,000	$50,000	$100,000
Personal liabilities	45,000	40,000	40,000

The partnership creditors proceed against Fred for recovery of their claims, and the partners settle their claims against each other in accordance with the Uniform Partnership Act.

REQUIRED: Prepare a schedule to show the phaseout of the partnership and final closing of the books.

E 16-12

Statement of partnership liquidation—partner insolvency case The partnership of Ace, Ben, Cid, and Don is dissolved on January 5, 2006, and the account balances at June 30, 2006, after all noncash assets are converted into cash, are as follows:

	Debits	Credits
Cash	$200,000	
Cid capital (20%)	170,000	
Don capital (10%)	80,000	
Accounts payable		$400,000
Ace capital (50%)		40,000
Ben capital (20%)		10,000
	$450,000	$450,000

ADDITIONAL INFORMATION

1. The percentages indicated represent the relevant profit and loss sharing ratios.

2. Personal assets and liabilities of the partners at June 30, 2006, are as follows:

	Personal Assets	Personal Liabilities
Ace	$600,000	$300,000
Ben	100,000	150,000
Cid	400,000	300,000
Don	100,000	20,000

3. Ace pays $200,000 into the partnership, and partnership liabilities are paid on July 1, 2006.

4. On July 15, 2006, Cid pays $100,000 into the partnership and Don pays $80,000. No further contributions from either Cid or Don are possible.

5. Losses from the bankruptcy of Cid are divided among the solvent partners on July 15, 2006.

6. Available cash is distributed and the partnership books are closed on July 31, 2006.

REQUIRED: Prepare a liquidation statement for the Ace, Ben, Cid, and Don partnership for the period June 30, 2006, to July 31, 2006.

E 16-13

Safe payments schedule The partnership of Denver, Elsie, Fannie, and George is being liquidated over the first few months of 2006. The trial balance at January 1, 2006, is as follows:

	Debits	Credits
Cash	$200,000	
Accounts receivable	56,000	
Inventory	142,000	
Equipment (net)	300,000	
Land	150,000	
Loan to Denver	20,000	
Accounts payable		$400,000
Denver capital (20%)		170,000
Elsie capital (10%)		80,000
Fannie capital (50%)		140,000
George capital (20%)		78,000
	$868,000	$868,000

ADDITIONAL INFORMATION

1. The partners agree to retain $20,000 cash on hand for contingencies and to distribute the rest of the available cash at the end of each month.

2. In January, half of the receivables were collected. Inventory that cost $75,000 was liquidated for $45,000. The land was sold for $250,000.

REQUIRED: Prepare a schedule of safe payments for the Denver, Elsie, Fannie, and George partnership for January 31, 2006.

E 16-14

Installment liquidation—various situations The assets and equities of the Quen, Reed, and Stac partnership at the end of its fiscal year on October 31, 2006, are as follows:

Assets		Equities	
Cash	$ 15,000	Liabilities	$ 50,000
Receivables—net	20,000	Loan from Stac	10,000
Inventory	40,000	Quen capital (30%)	45,000
Plant assets—net	70,000	Reed capital (50%)	30,000
Loan to Reed	5,000	Stac capital (20%)	15,000
	$150,000		$150,000

The partners decide to liquidate the partnership. They estimate that the noncash assets, other than the loan to Reed, can be converted into $100,000 cash over the two-month period ending December 31, 2006. Cash is to be distributed to the appropriate parties as it becomes available during the liquidation process.

1. The partner most vulnerable to partnership losses on liquidation is:

a Quen
b Reed
c Reed and Quen equally
d Stac

2. If $65,000 is available for the first distribution, it should be paid to:

	Priority Creditors	Quen	Reed	Stac
a	$60,000	$ 5,000	$ 0	$ 0
b	60,000	1,500	2,500	1,000
c	50,000	5,000	0	10,000
d	50,000	12,000	0	3,000

3. If a total amount of $7,500 is available for distribution to partners after all nonpartner liabilities are paid, it should be paid as follows:

	Quen	Reed	Stac
a	$7,500	$ 0	$ 0
b	0	3,750	3,750
c	2,250	3,750	1,500
d	2,500	2,500	2,500

E 16-15

Liquidation—various situations

1. In a partnership liquidation, the final cash distribution to the partners should be made in accordance with the:

a Partner profit and loss sharing ratios
b Balances of partner capital accounts
c Ratio of the capital contributions by partners
d Safe payments computations

2. In accounting for the liquidation of a partnership, cash payments to partners after all nonpartner creditors' claims have been satisfied, but before final cash distribution, should be according to:

a Relative profit and loss sharing ratios
b The final balances in partner capital accounts
c The relative share of gain or loss on liquidation
d Safe payments computations

3. After all noncash assets have been converted into cash in the liquidation of the Maris and DeMarco partnership, the ledger contains the following account balances:

	Debit	Credit
Cash	$34,000	—
Accounts payable	—	$25,000
Loan payable to Maris	—	9,000
Maris capital	8,000	—
DeMarco capital	—	8,000

Available cash should be distributed as follows: $25,000 to accounts payable and:

a $9,000 for loan payable to Maris
b $4,500 each to Maris and DeMarco
c $1,000 to Maris and $8,000 to DeMarco
d $8,000 to Maris and $1,000 to DeMarco

4. The partnership of Gwen, Bill, and Sissy is liquidating and the ledger shows the following:

Cash	$ 80,000
Inventories	100,000
Accounts payable	60,000
Gwen capital (50%)	40,000
Bill capital (25%)	45,000
Sissy capital (25%)	35,000

If all available cash is distributed immediately:

a **Gwen, Bill, and Sissy should get $26,667 each**
b **Gwen, Bill, and Sissy should get $6,667 each**
c **Gwen should get $10,000, and Bill and Sissy should get $5,000 each**
d **Bill should get $15,000, and Sissy $5,000**

5. The following balance sheet summary, together with residual profit sharing ratios, was developed on April 1, 2006, when the Dick, Frank, and Helen partnership began its liquidation:

Cash	$140,000	Liabilities	$ 60,000
Accounts receivable	60,000	Loan from Frank	20,000
Inventories	85,000	Dick capital (20%)	75,000
Plant assets—net	200,000	Frank capital (40%)	200,000
Loan to Dick	25,000	Helen capital (40%)	155,000
	$510,000		$510,000

If available cash except for a $5,000 contingency fund is distributed immediately, Dick, Frank, and Helen, respectively, should receive:

a **0, $80,000, and $15,000**
b **$16,000, $32,000, and $32,000**
c **0, $70,000, and $5,000**
d **0, $72,500, and $7,500**

6. The partnership of Unsel, Vance, and Wayne was dissolved on June 30, 2006, and account balances after noncash assets were converted into cash on September 1, 2006, are:

Cash	$50,000	Accounts payable	$120,000
		Unsel capital (30%)	90,000
		Vance capital (30%)	(60,000)
		Wayne capital (40%)	(100,000)

Personal assets and liabilities of the partners at September 1, 2006, are:

	Personal Assets	Personal Liabilities
Unsel	$ 80,000	$90,000
Vance	100,000	61,000
Wayne	190,000	80,000

If Wayne contributes $70,000 to the partnership to provide cash to pay the creditors, what amount of Unsel's $90,000 partnership equity would appear to be recoverable?

a **$90,000**
b **$81,000**
c **$79,000**
d **None of the above**

LEARNING OBJECTIVES **2, 3, 6**

E 16-16

[AICPA adapted]—Liquidation—various situations, including insolvency Use the following information in answering questions 1, 2, and 3. Q, R, S, and T are partners sharing profits and losses equally. The partnership is insolvent and is to be liquidated. The status of the partnership and each partner is as follows:

	Partnership Capital Balance	Personal Assets (Exclusive of Partnership Interest)	Personal Liabilities (Exclusive of Partnership Interest)
Q	$ 15,000	$100,000	$40,000
R	10,000	30,000	60,000
S	(20,000)	80,000	5,000
T	(30,000)	1,000	28,000
Total	$(25,000)		

Assume that the Uniform Partnership Act applies to these questions.

1. The partnership creditors:
   a   **Must first seek recovery against S because he is personally solvent and he has a negative capital balance**
   b   **Will not be paid in full regardless of how they proceed legally because the partnership assets are less than partnership liabilities**
   c   **Will have to share R's interest in the partnership on a pro rata basis with R's personal creditors**
   d   **Have first claim to partnership assets before any partner's personal creditors have rights to the partnership assets**

2. The partnership creditors may obtain recovery of their claims:
   a   **In the amount of $6,250 from each partner**
   b   **From the personal assets of either Q or R**
   c   **From the personal assets of either S or T**
   d   **From the personal assets of either Q or S for some or all of their claims**

3. If Q pays the full amount owed to partnership creditors from his personal assets, then:
   a   **Q's partnership loss will be increased by $25,000**
   b   **Q's partnership loss will be increased by $12,500**
   c   **Q will have a $40,000 total partnership loss**
   d   **Q's partnership loss will be the same as if S had paid partnership creditors from his personal assets**

4. X, Y, and Z have capital balances of $30,000, $15,000, and $5,000, respectively, in the XYZ Partnership. The general partnership agreement is silent as to the manner in which partnership losses are to be allocated but does provide that partnership profits are to be allocated as follows: 40% to X, 25% to Y, and 35% to Z. The partners have decided to dissolve and liquidate the partnership. After paying all creditors, the amount available for distribution will be $20,000. X, Y, and Z are individually solvent. Under the circumstances, Z will:
   a   **Receive $7,000**
   b   **Receive $12,000**
   c   **Personally have to contribute an additional $5,500**
   d   **Personally have to contribute an additional $5,000**

5. The following condensed balance sheet is presented for the partnership of Smith and Jones, who share profits and losses in the ratio of 60:40, respectively:

Other assets	$450,000	Accounts payable	$120,000
Smith loan	20,000	Smith capital	195,000
	$470,000	Jones capital	155,000
			$470,000

The partners have decided to liquidate the partnership. If the other assets are sold for $385,000, what amount of the available cash should be distributed to Smith?
   a   **$136,000**
   b   **$156,000**
   c   **$159,000**
   d   **$195,000**

PROBLEMS

P 16-1

Cash distribution plan and entries—installment Barney, Betty, and Rubble are partners in a business that is in the process of liquidation. On January 1, 2006, the ledger accounts show the balances indicated:

Cash	$25,000	Barney capital	$72,000
Inventory	72,000	Betty capital	28,000
Supplies	18,000	Rubble capital	15,000

The cash is distributed to partners on January 1, 2006. Inventory and supplies are sold for a lump-sum price of $81,000 on February 9, 2006, and on February 10, 2006, cash on hand is distributed to the partners in final liquidation of the business.

LEARNING OBJECTIVES 2, 3, 4, 5

REQUIRED

1. Prepare the journal entry to distribute available cash on January 1, 2006. Include a safe payments schedule as proper explanation of who should receive cash.

2. Prepare journal entries necessary on February 9, 2006, to record the sale of assets and distribution of the gain or loss to the partners' capital accounts.

3. Prepare the journal entry to distribute cash on February 10, 2006, in final liquidation of the business.

P 16-2

Cash distribution plan The December 31, 2006, balance sheet of the Chan, Dickerson, and Grunther partnership, along with the partners' residual profit and loss sharing ratios, is summarized as follows:

Assets		Equities	
Cash	$ 60,000	Accounts payable	$ 90,000
Receivables	120,000	Loan from Dickerson	50,000
Inventories	150,000	Chan capital (20%)	95,000
Due from Chan	15,000	Dickerson capital (30%)	160,000
Other assets	255,000	Grunther capital (50%)	205,000
	$600,000		$600,000

The partners agree to liquidate their partnership as soon as possible after January 1, 2007, and to distribute all cash as it becomes available.

REQUIRED: Prepare a cash distribution plan to show how cash will be distributed as it becomes available.

P 16-3

Cash distribution plan Fred, Flint, and Wilma announced the liquidation of their partnership beginning on January 1, 2006. Profits and losses are divided 30% to Fred, 20% to Flint, and 50% to Wilma. Balance sheet items are summarized as follows:

Cash	$ 45,000	Accounts payable	$ 20,000
Accounts receivable—net	25,000	Fred capital (30%)	75,000
Inventories	25,000	Flint capital (20%)	30,000
Plant assets—net	80,000	Wilma capital (50%)	60,000
Flint loan	10,000		
	$185,000		$185,000

REQUIRED: Prepare a cash distribution plan as of January 1, 2006, for the Fred, Flint, and Wilma partnership.

P 16-4

Installment liquidation The partnership of Gary, Henry, Illa, and Joseph is preparing to liquidate. Profit and loss sharing ratios are shown in the summarized balance sheet at December 31, 2006, as follows:

Cash	$200,000	Other liabilities	$100,000
Inventories	200,000	Gary loan	100,000
Loan to Henry	20,000	Gary capital (40%)	200,000
Other assets	510,000	Henry capital (30%)	320,000
		Illa capital (20%)	100,000
		Joseph capital (10%)	110,000
	$930,000		$930,000

REQUIRED

1. The partners anticipate an installment liquidation. Prepare a cash distribution plan as of January 1, 2007, that includes a $50,000 contingency fund to help the partners predict when they will be included in cash distributions.

2. During January 2007, the inventories are sold for $100,000, the other liabilities are paid, and $50,000 is set aside for contingencies. The partners agree that loan balances should be closed to capital accounts and that remaining cash (less the contingency fund) should be distributed to partners. How much cash should each partner receive?

P 16-5

Statement of partnership liquidation Eli, Joe, and Ned agree to liquidate their consulting practice as soon as possible after the close of business on July 31, 2006. The trial balance on that date shows the following account balances.

	Debits	Credits
Cash	$13,000	
Accounts receivable	12,000	
Furniture and fixtures	35,000	
Accounts payable		$ 6,000
Loan from Eli		4,000
Eli capital		20,000
Joe capital		15,000
Ned capital		15,000
	$60,000	$60,000

The partners share profits and losses 20%, 30%, and 50% to Eli, Joe, and Ned, respectively, after Ned is allowed a monthly salary of $4,000.

August transactions and events are as follows:

1. The accounts payable are paid.

2. Accounts receivable of $8,000 are collected in full. Ned accepts accounts receivable with a face value and fair value of $3,000 in partial satisfaction of his capital balance. The remaining accounts receivable are written off as uncollectible.

3. Furniture with a book value of $25,000 is sold for $15,000.

4. Furniture with a book value of $4,000 and an agreed-upon fair value of $1,000 is taken by Joe in partial settlement of his capital balance. The remaining furniture and fixtures are donated to Goodwill Industries.

5. Liquidation expenses of $3,000 are paid.

6. Available cash is distributed to partners on August 31.

REQUIRED: Prepare a statement of partnership liquidation for the Eli, Joe, and Ned partnership for August.

P 16-6

Installment liquidation Jones, Smith, and Tandy are partners in a furniture store that began liquidation on January 1, 2006, when the ledger contained the following account balances:

	Debit	Credit
Cash	$ 15,000	
Accounts receivable	20,000	
Inventories	65,000	
Land	50,000	
Buildings	100,000	
Accumulated depreciation—buildings		$ 40,000
Furniture and fixtures	50,000	
Accumulated depreciation—furniture and fixtures		30,000
Accounts payable		80,000
Jones capital (20%)		40,000
Smith capital (30%)		60,000
Tandy capital (50%)		50,000
	$300,000	$300,000

The following transactions and events occurred during the liquidation process:

January — Inventories were sold for $20,000 cash, collections on account totaled $14,000, and half of the amount due to creditors was paid.

February — Land costing $40,000 was sold for $60,000, the remaining land and buildings were sold for 40,000, half of the remaining receivables were collected, and the remainder were uncollectible.

March — The remaining liabilities were paid, and available cash was distributed to the partners in final liquidation.

REQUIRED: Prepare a statement of liquidation for the Jones, Smith, and Tandy partnership.

LEARNING OBJECTIVES 4, 5

P 16-7

Installment liquidation The after-closing trial balance of the Link, Mack, and Nell partnership at December 31, 2006, was as follows:

	Debit	Credit
Cash	$ 47,000	
Receivables—net	25,000	
Loan to Mack	8,000	
Inventories	20,000	
Plant assets—net	50,000	
Accounts payable		$ 55,000
Loan from Link		15,000
Link capital (50%)		40,000
Mack capital (30%)		20,000
Nell capital (20%)		20,000
Total	$150,000	$150,000

ADDITIONAL INFORMATION

1. The partnership is to be liquidated as soon as the assets can be converted into cash. Cash realized on conversion of assets is to be distributed as it becomes available, except that $10,000 is to be held to provide for contingencies during the liquidation period.

2. Profits and losses on liquidation are to be divided in the percentages indicated in the trial balance.

REQUIRED

1. Prepare a cash distribution plan for the Link, Mack, and Nell partnership.

2. If $25,000 cash is realized from the receivables and inventories during January 2007, how should the cash be distributed at the end of January? (Assume that this is the first distribution of cash during the liquidation period.)

LEARNING OBJECTIVES 4, 5

P 16-8

Installment liquidation—safe payments schedule Jason, Kelly, and Becky, who share partnership profits 50%, 30%, and 20%, respectively, decide to liquidate their partnership. They need the cash from the partnership as soon as possible but do not want to sell the assets at fire-sale prices, so they agree to an installment liquidation. A summary balance sheet on January 1, 2006, is as follows:

Cash	$ 16,500	Accounts payable	$ 21,000
Accounts receivable	28,000	Loan from Becky	9,500
Inventory	20,500	Jason capital	69,000
Equipment—net	101,000	Kelly capital	47,000
Loan to Jason	14,000	Becky capital	33,500
	$180,000		$180,000

Cash is distributed to the partners at the end of each month, with $5,000 retained for possible contingencies in the liquidation process.

During January 2006, Jason agreed to offset his capital balance with his loan from the partnership, $25,000 was collected on the accounts receivable, and the balance is determined to be uncollectible. Liquidation expenses of $2,000 were paid.

During February 2006, $18,000 was collected from the sale of inventories and $90,000 collected from the sale of equipment. Additional liabilities of $3,000 were discovered, and $2,000 of liquidation expenses were paid. All cash was then distributed in a final liquidation.

REQUIRED: Prepare a statement of partnership liquidation with supporting safe payments schedules for each cash distribution.

P 16-9

Installment liquidation—safe payments schedules The balance sheet of Roger, Susan, and Tom, who share partnership profits 30%, 30%, and 40%, respectively, included the following balances on January 1, 2006, the date of dissolution:

Cash	$ 20,000	Liabilities	$ 40,100
Other assets	130,000	Roger loan	5,000
Loan to Susan	10,000	Roger capital	9,900
		Susan capital	45,000
		Tom capital	60,000
	$160,000		$160,000

During January 2006, part of the firm's assets are sold for $40,000. In February the remaining assets are sold for $21,000. Assume that available cash is distributed to the proper parties at the end of January and at the end of February.

REQUIRED: Prepare a statement of partnership liquidation with supporting safe payments schedules for each cash distribution. (It will not be possible to determine the actual gains and losses in January.)

P 16-10

Installment liquidation Account balances for the Ral, Tom, and Vic partnership on October 1, 2006, are as follows:

Cash	$ 21,000	Accounts payable	$ 80,000
Accounts receivable	63,000	Note payable	50,000
Inventory	120,000	Ral capital (30%)	43,600
Equipment	150,000	Tom capital (50%)	150,000
Ral loan	15,000	Vic capital (20%)	45,400
	$369,000		$369,000

The partners have decided to liquidate the business. Activities for October and November are as follows.

October

1 Ral is short of funds, and the partners agree to charge her loan to her capital account.

2 $40,000 is collected on the accounts receivable; $4,000 is written off as uncollectible.

3 Half the inventory is sold for $50,000.

4 Equipment with a book value of $55,000 is sold for $60,000.

5 The $50,000 bank note plus $600 accrued interest is paid in full.

6 The accounts payable are paid.

7 Liquidation expenses of $2,000 are paid.

8 Except for a $5,000 contingency fund, all available cash is distributed to partners at the end of October.

November

9 The remaining equipment is sold for $38,000.

10 Vic accepts inventory with a book value of $20,000 and a fair value of $10,000 as payment for part of her capital balance. The rest of the inventory is written off.

11 Accounts receivable of $10,000 are collected. The remaining receivables are written off.

12 Liquidation expenses of $800 are paid.

13 Remaining cash, including the contingency fund, is distributed to the partners.

REQUIRED: Prepare a statement of partnership liquidation for the period October 1 through November 30.

LEARNING OBJECTIVES **2, 3**

P 16-11

Cash distribution plan, safe payments schedule

The balance sheet of the Tucker, Gilliam, and Simpson partnership at December 31, 2006, follows:

Tucker, Gilliam, and Simpson Partnership Balance Sheet at December 31, 2006

Assets		Liabilities	
Cash	$120,000	Accounts payable	$ 65,000
Receivables—net	80,000	Due to Simpson	35,000
Due from Gilliam	10,000	Total liabilities	100,000
Inventories	90,000		
Land	50,000	*Capital*	
Buildings—net	120,000	Tucker capital (20%)	$130,000
Machinery—net	30,000	Gilliam capital (30%)	110,000
		Simpson capital (50%)	160,000
		Total capital	400,000
Total assets	$500,000	Total liabilities and capital	$500,000

On January 1, 2007, the partners agree to dissolve the partnership, distribute available cash immediately except for $10,000 to be held to cover contingencies, and liquidate the other assets as soon as possible. Profit sharing percentages are indicated in the balance sheet.

REQUIRED

1. Prepare a schedule showing the cash distribution on January 1, 2007.

2. Prepare a cash distribution plan to show how all cash could be safely distributed to partners as it becomes available (assume no cash has been distributed).

LEARNING OBJECTIVES **4, 5**

P 16-12

Installment liquidation

The adjusted trial balance of the Jee, Moore, and Olsen partnership at December 31, 2006, is as follows:

Cash	$ 50,000
Accounts receivable—net	100,000
Nonmonetary assets	800,000
Loan to Jee	50,000
Expenses	400,000
Total debits	$1,400,000
Accounts payable	$ 80,000
Loan from Olsen	20,000
Jee capital	300,000
Moore capital	450,000
Olsen capital	350,000
Revenue	200,000
Total credits	$1,400,000

ADDITIONAL INFORMATION

1. Partnership profits are divided 20%, 40%, and 40% to Jee, Moore, and Olsen, respectively, after salary allowances of $25,000 each to Jee and Moore for time devoted to the business.

2. Due to the disastrous results of 2006, the partners agreed to liquidate the business as soon as possible after January 1, 2007, and to distribute available cash on a weekly basis.

3. During the first week in January, $85,500 was collected on the accounts receivable, and cash was distributed on January 8, 2007.

REQUIRED

1. Prepare the journal entries to close the partnership books at December 31, 2006.

2. Develop a cash distribution plan for the partnership as of January 1, 2007.

3. Prepare a cash distribution schedule for the January 8, 2007, distribution of available cash.

P 16-13

Installment liquidation The after-closing trial balances of the Beams, Plank, and Timbers partnership at December 31, 2006, included the following accounts and balances:

LEARNING OBJECTIVES 4, 5

Cash	$120,000
Accounts receivable—net	140,000
Loan to Timbers	20,000
Inventory	200,000
Plant assets—net	200,000
Trademarks	20,000
Total debits	$700,000
Accounts payable	$150,000
Notes payable	100,000
Loan from Plank	10,000
Beams capital (profit sharing ratio, 50%)	170,000
Plank capital (profit sharing ratio, 30%)	170,000
Timbers capital (profit sharing ratio, 20%)	100,000
Total credits	$700,000

The partnership is to be liquidated as soon as possible, and all available cash except for a $10,000 contingency balance is to be distributed at the end of each month prior to the time that all assets are converted into cash.

During January 2007, $100,000 was collected from accounts receivable, inventory items with a book value of $80,000 were sold for $100,000, and available cash was distributed.

During February 2007, Beams received plant assets with a book value of $60,000 and a fair value of $50,000 in partial settlement of her equity in the partnership. Also during February, the remaining inventory items were sold for $60,000, liquidation expenses of $2,000 were paid, and a liability of $8,000 was discovered. Cash was distributed on February 28.

During March 2007, the plant assets were sold for $110,000, the remaining noncash assets were written off, final liquidation expenses of $5,000 were paid, and cash was distributed. The dissolution of the partnership was completed on March 31, 2007.

REQUIRED: Prepare a statement of partnership liquidation for the Beams, Plank, and Timbers partnership for the period January 1 to March 31, 2007.

INTERNET ASSIGNMENT

Many investment clubs are organized as partnerships. Perform an Internet search and find a club organized as a partnership. In reviewing the partnership bylaws, what provisions has the club made for the death or retirement of a partner and the ultimate liquidation of the partnership?

17 CHAPTER

CORPORATE LIQUIDATIONS AND REORGANIZATIONS

This chapter examines accounting and legal matters related to financially distressed corporations.[1] Some corporations are able to recover from financial adversity through internal operating and policy changes, whereas others with more serious financial problems are forced to seek external remedies. These remedies are classified as direct agreements with creditors, reorganizations, and liquidations.

If a company is unable to meet its debt payments on time, direct negotiations with its creditors can result in a debt restructuring agreement or a debt settlement agreement. You probably covered accounting for troubled debt restructuring in an intermediate accounting class. The *Advanced Accounting* Web site includes a review of this subject.

This chapter focuses on bankruptcy that results in either corporate liquidation or reorganization. We first provide an overview of U.S. bankruptcy law. We then discuss the requirements and procedures related to liquidations and reorganizations.

■ ■ ■

LEARNING OBJECTIVES

1 Understand differences among types of bankruptcy filing.

2 Comprehend trustee responsibilities and accounting during liquidation.

3 Understand financial reporting during reorganization.

4 Understand financial reporting after emerging from reorganization, including fresh-start accounting.

BANKRUPTCY REFORM ACT OF 1978

A debtor corporation is considered insolvent when it is unable to pay its debts as they come due, or when its total debts exceed the fair value of its assets. The inability to make payment on time is referred to as **equity insolvency**. Having total debts that exceed the fair value of total assets is referred to as **bankruptcy insolvency**. Debtor corporations that are insolvent in the equity sense may be able to avoid bankruptcy proceedings by negotiating an agreement directly with creditors. Debtor corporations that are insolvent in the bankruptcy sense ordinarily will be reorganized or liquidated under the supervision of a bankruptcy court.

Prior to 1898, state government legislation governed bankruptcy proceedings. The 1898 Bankruptcy Act, a federal law, preempted the state legislation.

The 1898 Bankruptcy Act and its numerous amendments were repealed when Congress enacted Title 11 of the *United States Code*, the Bankruptcy Reform Act of 1978, which reflects the entire bankruptcy law and became effective October 1, 1979. The 1978 act established comprehensive bankruptcy law as well as new bankruptcy judges and new bankruptcy courts. The act has been amended several times since it was enacted, most recently in 1994.

---

[1] Municipalities, railroads, stockbrokers, and commodity brokers are excluded from the discussion in this chapter. Bankruptcies of these entities are covered by special provisions of Title 11 of the *United States Code*.

EXHIBIT 17-1

Types of Bankruptcies

LEARNING OBJECTIVE

Type	Description
Chapter 7: Liquidation	A trustee is appointed to sell off the assets of the individual or company and pay claims to creditors.
Chapter 9: Adjustments of debts of a municipality	Municipalities (not covered here).
Chapter 11: Reorganization	The debtor corporation is expected to be rehabilitated, and the reorganization of the corporation is anticipated. • Either a trustee is appointed or the company performs the duties of a trustee (debtor in possession). • A plan of reorganization is negotiated with creditors, stockholders, employees, and others so that claims are settled and the company can continue to operate during bankruptcy proceedings and emerge from bankruptcy. • Although Chapter 11 also applies to individuals, Chapter 13 bankruptcy is usually easier.
Chapter 12: Farmers	Family farmers with regular income (not covered here).
Chapter 13: Adjustments of debts of an individual with regular income	Exclusively applies to individuals, including sole proprietorships. Unsecured debts less than $250,000 and secured debts less than $750,000 (not covered here).

The bankruptcy law facilitates debt relief to individuals and corporations under various provisions, called chapters. Exhibit 17-1 summarizes the major bankruptcy-code chapters. The purposes of the bankruptcy law are to protect the interests of creditors, to ensure an equitable distribution of assets in settlement of liabilities, and to give debtors a "fresh start." Once the debtor has settled its debts through the bankruptcy process, the debtor can start anew without the constant threat of legal actions and collection agencies.

Chapter 11 reorganizations provide businesses and individuals time to put together a business plan. It is hoped that the plan will ensure the future survival of the corporation once it emerges from bankruptcy proceedings, as well as provide for the settlement of its existing debts. The bankruptcy court and creditors' committees must approve of the plan.

If a corporation cannot produce a plan the court approves, the corporation may be forced into Chapter 7 bankruptcy, or liquidation. Some companies (such as *Montgomery Ward*, *LTV Steel* and *US Airways*) emerge from Chapter 11 bankruptcy and subsequently file for bankruptcy again because their business plan does not work.

Occasionally, corporations may file for bankruptcy protection even though they have sufficient fair value of assets to cover their debts, because they have liquidity problems and cannot meet debt payments as they come due. A few times in history, the bankruptcy court has allowed companies to file for bankruptcy even though they had sufficient liquidity to meet current debts, because they were parties to potentially large lawsuit findings. For example, *Dow Chemical* filed for bankruptcy as a result of silicon-breast-implant lawsuits; in 1985, *AH Robins* filed for bankruptcy as a result of Dalkon Shield IUD lawsuits; and *Johns Manville* filed for bankruptcy in 1982 as result of threatened asbestos lawsuits. Unfortunately in recent years, corporate accounting scandals have emerged as another reason firms file for bankruptcy. Some examples include *Enron*, *Worldcom*, and *Adelphia*.

If an order of relief is issued, the debtor company is protected from further litigation during the time the reorganization plan is being developed. Under court supervision, the creditors and the debtor work out a plan to settle the creditors' claims. The court is the final arbiter in such cases.

Manville filed its first Chapter 11 reorganization plan in 1983 and its second in 1986. On November 28, 1988, it emerged from bankruptcy. Also in 1988, Manville established the Manville Personal Injury and Property Damage Settlement Trusts to pay asbestos claims. In 2001, *Berkshire Hathaway* purchased Johns Manville Corporation in a cash tender offer.

Sometimes companies are acquired by other companies as part of the reorganization plan. For example, *American Home Products* (AHP) acquired AH Robins in 1989. Part of the purchase price included AHP contributing $2.25 billion to establish a trust fund for Dalkon Shield victims.

Montgomery Ward filed for bankruptcy protection in 1997 and was acquired by **General Electric** (GE Capital) in 1999, bringing it out of bankruptcy. Despite an active plan to return the firm to profitability, Montgomery Ward again filed for bankruptcy in 2001, shuttered all of its stores, and set about liquidating its assets.

Other well-known companies have recently filed for bankruptcy protection—for example, **Chiquita Brands** ($1,788 million in liabilities) in January 2001, **Fruit of the Loom** ($1,741 million) in December 1999, **Loews Cineplex** ($1,506 million) in February 2001, **Boston Chicken** ($1,202 million) in October 1998, and **Pacific Gas & Electric, Inc.** (the retail arm of **Pacific Gas & Electric Corporation**) ($25,717 million) in April 2001. Even a large accounting firm has filed for bankruptcy—**Laventhol and Horwath** ($2,000 million) in November 1990. As you can see from these examples, bankruptcy is a tool that companies use to help them in difficult situations.

The jurisdiction of the bankruptcy court covers all cases under Title 11 of the *U.S. Code*. A case begins with the filing of a petition under which a debtor is initially brought into bankruptcy court. Usually, the petition is filed in the U.S. bankruptcy court district where the debtor's principal place of business or principal assets have been located for at least 180 days. Either the debtor corporation or its creditors may file the petition. If the debtor corporation files the petition, the proceeding is termed a **voluntary bankruptcy proceeding**; if creditors file, it is an **involuntary bankruptcy proceeding**. Most bankruptcy filings are voluntary.

A petition commencing a case by or against a corporate debtor may be filed under either Chapter 7 or Chapter 11 of the bankruptcy act. **Chapter 7 of the Bankruptcy Reform Act** covers straight bankruptcy, under which liquidation of the debtor corporation is expected, and **Chapter 11 of the Bankruptcy Reform Act** covers rehabilitation of the debtor and anticipates reorganization of the debtor corporation.[2] The bankruptcy court has the power (subject to various requests and conditions) to dismiss a case, to enter the order for relief (in other words, accept the petition), or to convert a Chapter 11 reorganization case into a Chapter 7 liquidation case or vice versa.

The Office of U.S. Trustee

The Bankruptcy Reform Act created the Office of U.S. Trustee, a branch of the Department of Justice, to be responsible for the administrative duties of bankruptcy cases. U.S. trustees are appointed by the U.S. Attorney General for seven-year terms. The duties of the U.S. trustee are to maintain and supervise a panel of private trustees eligible to serve in Chapter 7 cases, to serve as trustee or interim trustee in some bankruptcy cases (such as in a Chapter 7 case in which a qualified private trustee is not available), to supervise the administration of bankruptcy cases, to monitor appointed creditors' committees, and to preside over creditor meetings.

Duties of the Debtor Corporation

In both Chapter 7 liquidation cases and Chapter 11 reorganization cases, the debtor corporation is required to do the following:

- File a list of creditors, a schedule of assets and liabilities, and a statement of debtor's financial affairs
- Cooperate with the trustee as necessary to enable the trustee to perform his or her duties
- Surrender all property to the trustee, including books, documents, records, and papers relating to the estate in cases involving a trustee
- Appear at hearings of the court as required

Identifying creditors and filing documents may take several months. It is an important task because creditors who have been notified of the bankruptcy proceedings may receive only a percentage of their claims. Those creditors not notified are entitled to the full amount.

---

[2] Not all liquidations result from financial adversity. Voluntary liquidations are often based on the belief that the market value of the company's stock is less than the amount that could be realized by selling the company's assets. This type of liquidation does not involve restructurings or judicial remedies, and established accounting principles are applicable to winding up the company's affairs through liquidating dividends. For a discussion of voluntary liquidations, see Ronald J. Kudle, *Voluntary Corporate Liquidations* (Westport, CT: Quorum Books, Greenwood Press, 1988), or George E. Nogler and Kenneth B. Schwartz, "Financial Reporting and Auditors' Opinions on Voluntary Liquidations," *Accounting Horizons* (September 1989), pp. 12–20.

Duties of the Bankruptcy Judge

The bankruptcy judge settles disputes that occur during the case and approves all payments of debts incurred before the bankruptcy filing, as well as other payments that are considered extraordinary.

LIQUIDATION

The Administrative Office of the U.S. Courts reported that of the 36,785 business bankruptcy filings for the 12 months ended March 31, 2004, 20,502, or about 55%, were filed under Chapter 7 of the bankruptcy act. Chapter 7 liquidations are cheaper and faster than Chapter 11 reorganizations. A Chapter 7 liquidation case begins voluntarily when a debtor corporation files a petition with the bankruptcy court, or involuntarily through filing by three or more entities holding non-contingent, unsecured claims totaling at least $10,000.[3] A single creditor with an unsecured claim of $10,000 or more may also file a petition if there are fewer than 12 unsecured creditors.

The court will grant the order for relief (accept the petition) under Chapter 7 if the creditors prove their claims or if the debtor fails to contest the petition on a timely basis. The order for relief prevents creditors from seeking payment of their claims directly from the debtor. If the creditors fail to prove their alleged claims, the court will dismiss the case. The debtor may respond to the petition by filing for protection from creditors under Chapter 11, under which, instead of being liquidated, it can reorganize.

If an order for relief under Chapter 7 is granted, the U.S. trustee (or the court) appoints an interim trustee to take possession of the debtor corporation's estate until a trustee is elected. (An interim trustee may be appointed at any time after commencement of a case if the court considers it necessary to preserve the property of the estate or prevent losses.)

The election for trustee takes place at a meeting of creditors, and only unsecured creditors with undisputed claims are eligible to vote. A trustee is elected if creditors holding a minimum of 20% of the dollar amount of claims vote for a candidate and one candidate obtains the votes of creditors holding a majority in the dollar amount of claims actually voting. If a trustee is not elected, the interim trustee serves as trustee. The unsecured creditors eligible to vote may also elect a creditors' committee of 3 to 11 members to consult with the trustee and to submit questions regarding the debtor's estate to the court.

Duties of the Trustee in Liquidation Cases

The filing of a case creates an estate. The trustee takes possession of the estate, converts the estate assets into cash, and distributes the proceeds according to the priority of claims, as directed by the bankruptcy court. Other duties of the trustee in a liquidation case are as follows:

- To investigate the financial affairs of the debtor
- To provide information about the debtor's estate and its administration to interested parties
- To examine creditor claims and object to claims that appear improper
- If authorized to operate the debtor's business, to provide periodic reports and summaries of operations, a statement of receipts and disbursements, and other information as the court specifies
- To file final reports on trusteeship as required by the court

Payment of Claims

Claims in a Chapter 7 liquidation case are paid in the order shown in Exhibit 17-2. Claims secured by valid liens are paid to the extent of the proceeds from property pledged as security. If the proceeds are insufficient to satisfy the claims of secured creditors, the amounts not satisfied are classified as unsecured nonpriority claims (or general unsecured claims). Unsecured claims are divided into priority and nonpriority classes for Chapter 7 liquidation cases (see Exhibit 17-2). Unsecured priority claims are paid in full before any distributions are made to unsecured nonpriority claims.

Claims within the unsecured priority claims class are ranked 1 through 6, such that claims in the first rank (administrative expenses) are paid in full before any distribution is made for claims in the

---

[3] An *entity* under Title 11 means a person, estate, trustee, or governmental unit. *Person* means an individual, partnership, or corporation, but not a governmental unit.

EXHIBIT 17-2

Ranking of Claims in Chapter 7 Liquidation Cases

I Secured Claims
Claims secured by valid liens.

II Unsecured Priority Claims

1. Administrative expenses incurred in preserving and liquidating the estate, including trustee's fees and legal and accounting fees.
2. Claims incurred between the date of filing an involuntary petition and the date an interim trustee is appointed.
3. Claims for wages, salaries, and commissions earned within 90 days of filing the petition and not exceeding $4,000 per individual.
4. Claims for contributions to employee benefit plans arising from services rendered within 180 days of filing the petition and limited to $4,000 per employee.
5. Claims of individuals, not to exceed $1,800, arising from the purchase, lease, or rental of property that was not delivered or the purchase of services that were not provided by the debtor.
6. Claims of governmental units for income or gross receipts taxes, property taxes, employment taxes, excise taxes, and customs duties that originated within one to four years before filing (periods vary for different claims). Taxes collected or withheld for which the debtor is liable and penalties related to the foregoing are also included.

III Unsecured Nonpriority Claims

1. Allowed claims that were timely filed.
2. Allowed claims whose proof of claim was filed late.
3. Allowed claims (secured and unsecured) for any fine, penalty, or forfeiture, or for multiple, exemplary, or punitive charges arising to the order for relief or appointment of trustee.
4. Claims for interest on the unsecured priority claims or the unsecured nonpriority claims.

IV Stockholders' Claims
Remaining assets are returned to the debtor corporation or its stockholders.

second rank, and so forth. Within each of the six priority ranks, however, distributions are made on a pro rata basis when available cash is insufficient to pay all claims of that rank. Equivalent procedures apply to cash distributions in the four ranks included within the unsecured nonpriority class. Stockholders under a Chapter 7 liquidation case are included in distributions only when all valid creditor claims have been fully satisfied.

ILLUSTRATION OF A LIQUIDATION CASE

Camden Corporation experienced a large operating loss in 2006 and the first half of 2007. By July 2007 its accounts payable were overdue, and its accounts receivable had been pledged to support a bank loan that was in default. Camden's creditors were unwilling to extend additional credit or to amend the terms of any of their loans, and on August 1, 2007, Camden filed a voluntary petition for relief under Chapter 7 of the bankruptcy act.

Exhibit 17-3 presents a balance sheet prepared at the filing date. Although the balance sheet shows stockholders' equity of $13,000, historical cost valuations are not good indicators of financial condition for a liquidating company.[4] An accounting statement that does provide relevant information for a liquidating company is the *statement of affairs*.

Statement of Affairs

A trustee's duties may include filing a statement of financial affairs with the bankruptcy court. This statement is a legal document prepared for the bankruptcy court. The **statement of affairs** is a financial statement that emphasizes liquidation values and provides relevant information for the trustee in liquidating the debtor corporation. It also provides information that may be useful to creditors and to the bankruptcy court.

A statement of affairs is prepared at a specific date and shows balance sheet information. Assets are measured at expected net realizable values and are classified on the basis of availability for fully secured, partially secured, priority, and unsecured creditors. Liabilities are classified as priority, fully secured, partially secured, and unsecured. Historical cost valuations are included in the statement for reference purposes.

---

[4] Generally accepted accounting principles are based on the assumption that a firm will continue to operate in the foreseeable future. However, this going-concern assumption is inappropriate for firms in serious financial difficulty. When available evidence contradicts the going-concern assumption, independent auditors issue going-concern qualifications (or disclaimers) in their audit reports.

CAMDEN CORPORATION BALANCE SHEET AUGUST 1, 2007

Assets

Current Assets		
Cash	$ 3,000	
Marketable securities (at market)	7,000	
Accounts receivable (net of estimated uncollectible accounts)	25,000	
Inventories	50,000	
Prepaid expenses	4,000	$ 89,000
Long-Term Assets		
Land	$ 15,000	
Building—net	40,000	
Equipment—net	30,000	
Intangible assets	6,000	91,000
Total assets		$180,000

Liabilities and Stockholders' Equity

Current Liabilities		
Accounts payable	$ 65,000	
Wages payable	13,000	
Property taxes payable	2,000	
Note payable—bank	25,000	
Notes payable—suppliers	5,000	
Interest payable	7,000	$117,000
Long-Term Liabilities		
Mortgage payable		50,000
Total liabilities		167,000
Stockholders' Equity		
Capital stock	$200,000	
Retained earnings	(187,000)	
Total stockholders' equity		13,000
Total liabilities and stockholders' equity		$180,000

Exhibit 17-4 presents the statement of affairs for Camden Corporation. Information for the statement is derived from the balance sheet (see Exhibit 17-3) at the filing date and other sources, such as appraisals of the assets' expected liquidation values and contractual agreements with creditors. The mortgage payable, together with $5,000 interest payable, is secured by the land and building. All accounts receivable are pledged as security for the bank loan and $2,000 interest payable.

It is expected that Camden's assets can be converted into cash within three months. The estimated realizable values are as follows:

Cash	$ 3,000
Marketable securities	7,000
Accounts receivable	22,000
Inventories (net of selling expenses)	55,000
Prepaid expenses	—
Land and building	60,000
Equipment	12,000
Intangible assets	—
	$159,000

Assets pledged as security for creditor claims are offset against the estimated claims of secured creditors in the asset section of the statement of affairs. Any excess of the realizable value of assets pledged over related claims is carried to the right-hand column of the statement to indicate the amount available for unsecured creditors. An excess of secured creditor claims over the estimated

CAMDEN CORPORATION STATEMENT OF AFFAIRS ON AUGUST 1, 2007

EXHIBIT 17-4

Statement of Affairs

Assets

Book Value		Estimated Realizable Values Less Secured Creditor Liabilities		Estimated Realizable Value Available for Unsecured Creditors
	Pledged for Fully Secured Creditors			
$ 55,000	Land and buildings—net		$60,000	
	Less: Mortgage payable	$50,000		
	Interest payable	5,000	55,000	$ 5,000
	Pledged for Partially Secured Creditors			
25,000	Accounts receivable		$22,000	
	Less: Note payable to bank	$25,000		
	Interest payable	2,000	27,000	0
	Available for Priority and Unsecured Creditors			
3,000	Cash			3,000
7,000	Marketable securities			7,000
50,000	Inventories			55,000
4,000	Prepaid expenses			0
30,000	Equipment—net			12,000
6,000	Intangible assets			0
	Total available for priority and unsecured creditors			82,000
	Less: Priority liabilities			15,000
	Total available for unsecured creditors			67,000
	Estimated deficiency			8,000
$180,000				$75,000

Liabilities and Stockholders' Equity

Book Value		Secured and Priority Claims	Unsecured Nonpriority Claims
	Priority Liabilities		
$ 13,000	Wages payable	$13,000	
2,000	Property taxes payable	2,000	
		15,000	
	Fully Secured Creditors		
50,000	Mortgage payable	50,000	
5,000	Interest payable	5,000	
		55,000	
	Partially Secured Creditors		
25,000	Note payable—bank	25,000	
2,000	Interest payable	2,000	
		27,000	
	Less: Accounts receivable pledged	22,000	$ 5,000
	Unsecured Creditors		
65,000	Accounts payable		65,000
5,000	Notes payable to suppliers		5,000
	Stockholders' Equity		
200,000	Capital stock		
(187,000)	Retained earnings		
$180,000			$75,000

value of assets pledged as security indicates that these claims are only partially secured. The unsecured portion is shown in the liability section of the statement as an unsecured nonpriority claim. The value of total assets available to pay unsecured creditors is estimated to fall short by $8,000.

Trustee Accounting

A trustee in a Chapter 7 bankruptcy case stewards the assets of the debtor corporation until being released by the bankruptcy court. The bankruptcy act does not cover procedural accounting details such as whether the trustee should create a new set of accounting records to establish accountability for the estate and show the eventual discharge of responsibility, or whether the corporation's existing accounting records should be continued under the direction of the trustee.

The trustee for Camden Corporation creates a new set of accounting records. The assets are recorded on the trustee's books at book values, rather than at expected realizable values, because of the subjectivity involved in estimating realizable amounts at the time of filing. Contra asset accounts are omitted from the trustee's books because they are not meaningful in a liquidation case and because it is desirable to keep the trustee accounts as simple as possible. The following entry could be prepared to open the trustee's books for Camden:

Cash (+A)	3,000	
Marketable securities (+A)	7,000	
Accounts receivable (+A)	25,000	
Inventories (+A)	50,000	
Prepaid expenses (+A)	4,000	
Land (+A)	15,000	
Building (+A)	40,000	
Equipment (+A)	30,000	
Intangible assets (+A)	6,000	
Accounts payable (+L)		65,000
Wages payable (+L)		13,000
Property taxes payable (+L)		2,000
Note payable—bank (+L)		25,000
Notes payable—suppliers (+L)		5,000
Interest payable (+L)		7,000
Mortgage payable (+L)		50,000
Estate equity (+EE)		13,000

To record custody of Camden Corporation in liquidation.

After assuming custody of the estate, the trustee records gains, losses, and liquidation expenses directly in the estate equity account. Any unrecorded assets or liabilities that the trustee discovers are also entered in the estate equity account. To distinguish assets and liabilities included in the initial estate and those acquired or incurred by the trustee, the assets and liabilities recorded after the trustee takes charge of the estate are identified as "new."

Transactions and events during the first month of Camden's trusteeship are described and journal entries to record them in the trustee's books are illustrated as follows:

1. A previously unrecorded utility bill for $500 is received.

Estate equity (−EE)	500	
Utilities payable—discovered (+L)		500

2. Intangible assets are deemed worthless and are written off.

Estate equity (−EE)	6,000	
Intangible assets (−A)		6,000

3. All inventory items are sold for $48,000, of which $18,000 is on account and $30,000 is in cash.

Cash (+A)	30,000	
Accounts receivable—new (+A)	18,000	
Estate equity (−EE)	2,000	
Inventories (−A)		50,000

4. The equipment is sold for $14,200 cash.

Cash (+A)	14,200	
Estate equity (−EE)	15,800	
Equipment (−A)		30,000

5. Wages and property taxes owed on August 1 (priority liabilities) are paid.

Wages payable (−L)	13,000	
Property taxes payable (−L)	2,000	
Cash (−A)		15,000

6. Land and building are sold for $64,000 cash, and the mortgage payable and related interest are paid.

Cash (+A)	64,000	
Land (−A)		15,000
Building (−A)		40,000
Estate equity (+EE)		9,000
Mortgage payable (−L)	50,000	
Interest payable (−L)	5,000	
Cash (−A)		55,000

7. Insurance policies (included in prepaid expenses) are canceled, and a $1,000 cash refund is received.

Cash (+A)	1,000	
Prepaid expenses (−A)		1,000

8. Accounts receivable of $21,000 are collected from the amounts owed to Camden at August 1. The remaining $4,000 is uncollectible.

Cash (+A)	21,000	
Estate equity (−EE)	4,000	
Accounts receivable (−A)		25,000

9. The $21,000 received on account is applied to the bank note payable and related interest.

Interest payable (−L)	2,000	
Note payable—bank (−L)	19,000	
Cash (−A)		21,000

10. Estate administration expenses of $3,000 are paid.

Estate equity (−EE)	3,000	
Cash (−A)		3,000

11. Trustee fees of $2,000 are accrued.

Estate equity (−EE)	2,000	
Trustee's fee payable—new (+L)		2,000

After the transactions and events occurring through August 31 are entered on the trustee's books, financial statements can be prepared as needed to show progress toward liquidation and financial position at that date.

STATEMENT OF CASH RECEIPTS AND DISBURSEMENTS The statement of cash receipts and disbursements is prepared directly from entries in the cash account. It appears in summary form here.

CASH

Balance, August 1, 2007	$ 3,000	Wages and property taxes	$ 15,000
Inventory items sold	30,000	Mortgage and interest	
Equipment sold	14,200	payment	55,000
Land and building sold	64,000	Bank notes and interest	21,000
Insurance refund	1,000	Administrative expenses	3,000
Accounts receivable	21,000	**Balance forward**	**39,200**
	$133,200		$133,200
Balance, August 31, 2007	$ 39,200		

EXHIBIT 17-5

Trustee's Interim
Statement of Cash
Receipts and Cash
Disbursements

CAMDEN CORPORATION IN TRUSTEESHIP
STATEMENT OF CASH RECEIPTS AND DISBURSEMENTS
FROM AUGUST 1 TO AUGUST 31, 2007

Cash balance, August 1, 2007		$ 3,000
Add: Cash receipts		
Sale of inventory items	$30,000	
Sale of equipment	14,200	
Sale of land and building	64,000	
Refund from insurance policy	1,000	
Collection of receivables	21,000	
Total cash receipts		130,200
		133,200
Deduct: Cash disbursements		
Wages payable (priority claim)	$13,000	
Property taxes payable (priority claim)	2,000	
Mortgage payable and interest (fully secured)	55,000	
Bank note payable and interest (for secured portion)	21,000	
Administrative expenses (priority item)	3,000	
Total cash disbursements		94,000
Cash balance, August 31, 2007		$ 39,200

Exhibit 17-5 illustrates the trustee's interim statement of cash receipts and cash disbursements for the period August 1 to August 31, 2007. All disbursements require approval of the court, so the statement should be a useful financial summary.

STATEMENT OF CHANGES IN ESTATE EQUITY The estate equity account in summary form is as follows:

ESTATE EQUITY (DEFICIT)

Utility bill discovered	$ 500	August 1, 2007, balance	$13,000
Intangibles written off	6,000	Land and building gain	9,000
Inventory loss	2,000		
Equipment loss	15,800		
Accounts receivable written off	4,000		
Administrative expenses	3,000		
Trustee's fee	2,000	**Balance forward (deficit)**	**11,300**
	$33,300		$33,300
August 31, 2007	$11,300		

Exhibit 17-6 illustrates the statement of changes in estate equity for Camden Corporation from August 1 to August 31, 2007. Observe that the statement separates gains and losses on asset realization from expenses involved in liquidating the corporation.

BALANCE SHEET A balance sheet is prepared directly from the ledger account balances of the trustee and is presented in Exhibit 17-7. Two key amounts that appear in the balance sheet—cash and estate deficit—are supported by amounts from the statements of cash receipts and disbursements (Exhibit 17-5) and changes in estate equity (Exhibit 17-6). The statements presented in Exhibits 17-5, 17-6, and 17-7 are in a format familiar to accountants, but you will want to compare these financial statements with the traditional statement of realization and liquidation that is presented in Exhibit 17-8.

STATEMENT OF REALIZATION AND LIQUIDATION A **statement of realization and liquidation** is an activity statement that shows progress toward the liquidation of a debtor's estate. It also informs the bankruptcy court and interested creditors of the accomplishments of the trustee. The bankruptcy act does not require such a statement; instead, the act allows the judge in a bankruptcy case to prescribe the form in which information is presented to the court.

Exhibit 17-8 presents a statement of realization and liquidation for Camden Corporation. The statement is presented in its traditional format except for bracketed explanations of the various categories. An examination of Camden's statement of realization and liquidation shows that the

EXHIBIT 17-6

Trustee's Statement of Changes in Estate Equity and Schedule of Net Losses on Asset Liquidation

CAMDEN CORPORATION IN TRUSTEESHIP
STATEMENT OF CHANGES IN ESTATE EQUITY
FROM AUGUST 1 TO AUGUST 31, 2007

Estate equity August 1, 2007		$ 13,000
Less: Net loss on asset liquidation		
(see schedule below)	$18,800	
Liability for utilities discovered	500	
Administrative expenses	3,000	
Trustee's fee	2,000	
Net decrease for the period		(24,300)
Estate deficit August 31, 2007		$ 11,300

SCHEDULE OF NET LOSSES ON ASSET LIQUIDATION

	Book Value August 1	–	Proceeds on Realization	=	Gain (Loss)
Accounts receivable	$25,000		$21,000		$ (4,000)
Inventories	50,000		48,000		(2,000)
Land and building	55,000		64,000		9,000
Equipment	30,000		14,200		(15,800)
Intangible assets	6,000		0		(6,000)
Net loss on liquidation of assets					$(18,800)

statement is complex and that its format is unusual. In addition, the logic of the statement's construction is not immediately apparent. Although a number of alternative formats for the statement have been proposed, many accountants feel that basic financial statements with supporting schedules provide more relevant information about liquidation activity than the statement of realization and liquidation.

Winding Up the Case

During September 2007 the trustee for Camden Corporation collected the $18,000 accounts receivable, sold the marketable securities for $7,300, sold supplies (included in prepaid expenses) for $995, wrote off the remaining prepaid expenses, and distributed cash in final liquidation of the estate. Journal entries to record these transactions and events are as follows:

EXHIBIT 17-7

Trustee's Interim Balance Sheet During the Liquidation Phase

CAMDEN CORPORATION IN TRUSTEESHIP
BALANCE SHEET
ON AUGUST 31, 2007

Assets	
Cash	$39,200
Marketable securities	7,000
Accounts receivable—net	18,000
Prepaid expenses	3,000
Total assets	$67,200
Liabilities and Deficit	
Accounts payable	$65,000
Utilities payable—discovered	500
Trustee's fee payable—new	2,000
Note payable—bank (unsecured portion)	6,000
Notes payable—suppliers	5,000
Total liabilities	78,500
Less: Estate deficit	11,300
Total liabilities less deficit	$67,200

EXHIBIT 17-8

Statement of Realization and Liquidation

CAMDEN CORPORATION IN TRUSTEESHIP
STATEMENT OF REALIZATION AND LIQUIDATION
AUGUST 1, 2007, TO AUGUST 31, 2007

Assets

Assets to Be Realized [Noncash assets at August 1]			*Assets Realized* [Proceeds from sale, disposal, or write-off]		
Marketable securities	$ 7,000		Accounts receivable	$21,000	
Accounts receivable	25,000		Inventories	48,000	
Inventories	50,000		Prepaid expenses	1,000	
Prepaid expenses	4,000		Land and building	64,000	
Land	15,000		Equipment	14,200	
Building	40,000		Intangible assets	none	$148,200
Equipment	30,000				
Intangible assets	6,000	$177,000			
Assets Acquired [New noncash assets received]			*Assets Not Realized* [Noncash assets at August 31]		
Accounts receivable—new		18,000	Marketable securities	$ 7,000	
			Prepaid expenses	3,000	
			Accounts receivable—new	18,000	28,000

Liabilities

Liabilities to Be Liquidated [Liabilities at August 1]			*Liabilities Liquidated* [Amounts paid on liabilities]		
Accounts payable	$65,000		Wages payable	13,000	
Wages payable	$13,000		Property taxes payable	2,000	
Property taxes payable	2,000		Note payable—bank	19,000	
Note payable—bank	25,000		Interest payable	7,000	
Notes payable—suppliers	5,000		Mortgage payable	50,000	91,000
Interest payable	7,000				
Mortgage payable	50,000	167,000	*Liabilities Not Liquidated* [Liabilities at August 31]		
Liabilities Incurred or Discovered [Amounts incurred or discovered but unpaid at August 31]			Accounts payable	$65,000	
			Note payable—bank	6,000	
			Notes payable—suppliers	5,000	
Liability discovered for utilities	$ 500		Liability discovered for utilities	500	
Trustee's fee payable—new	2,000	2,500	Trustee's fee payable—new	2,000	78,500

Income or Loss and Supplemental Items

Supplementary Expenses [Expenses excluding asset losses and write-offs]			*Supplementary Revenues* [Revenues excluding gains on assets or liability settlements]		
Liability discovered for utilities	$ 500		None		
Trustee's fee	2,000		*Net Loss*		24,300
Administrative expenses —new	3,000	5,500			
		$370,000			$370,000

Cash (+A)		18,000	
Accounts receivable—new (−A)			18,000
Collection of receivable in full.			
Cash (+A)		7,300	
Marketable securities (−A)			7,000

(continued)

Estate equity (+EE)		300
Sale of marketable securities for cash.		
Cash (+A)	995	
Estate equity (−EE)	2,005	
Prepaid expenses (−A)		3,000
Sale of supplies and write-off of prepaid expenses.		

Account balances after these entries are entered in the trustee's records are as follows:

	Debit	Credit
Cash	$65,495	
Accounts payable		$65,000
Utilities payable		500
Trustee's fee payable—new		2,000
Note payable—bank (unsecured portion)		6,000
Notes payable—suppliers		5,000
Estate equity	13,005	
	$78,500	$78,500

The trustee's fee is a priority claim, so it is paid in full. The remaining claims of $76,500 (all first-rank unsecured creditors) receive 83¢ on the dollar ($63,495 ÷ $76,500) in final settlement of their claims. Entries to record the cash distributions are as follows:

Trustee's fee payable—new (−L)	2,000	
Cash (−A)		2,000
To record payment of trustee's fee.		
Accounts payable (−L)	53,950	
Utilities payable (−L)	415	
Note payable—bank (−L)	4,980	
Notes payable—suppliers (−L)	4,150	
Cash (−A)		63,495
To record payment of 83¢ on the dollar to the general unsecured creditors.		

A case involving a corporation is closed when the estate is fully administered and the trustee is dismissed. The trustee makes the following entry in closing out the Camden Corporation case:

Accounts payable (−L)	11,050	
Utilities payable (−L)	85	
Note payable—bank (−L)	1,020	
Notes payable—suppliers (−L)	850	
Estate equity (EE)		13,005
To close the trustee's records.		

REORGANIZATION

LEARNING OBJECTIVE 3

Fewer than 30% of business bankruptcy cases filed each year are filed under Chapter 11. For example, for the 12 months ended March 31, 2004, 10,682 Chapter 11 business cases were filed out of 36,785 total business bankruptcy cases (29%). Chapter 11 reorganization cases usually involve very large amounts of money.

A Chapter 11 reorganization case is initiated voluntarily when a debtor corporation files a petition with the bankruptcy court or involuntarily when creditors file a petition. The same $10,000 claim limitations applicable to Chapter 7 filings apply here.

The act of filing commences the case and initiates a hearing before the bankruptcy court. As mentioned earlier, the court may enter an order for relief under Chapter 11, convert the case to a Chapter 7 liquidation, or dismiss the case (for example, the case will be dismissed if the bankruptcy court believes that the filing was an act of bad faith). A U.S. trustee is appointed by the bankruptcy judge to be responsible for the administration of the Chapter 11 case.

Trustee or Debtor in Possession

In a Chapter 11 case, a private trustee may be appointed for cause, but otherwise the debtor corporation is continued in possession of the estate and is referred to as a **debtor in possession**. A trustee may be appointed in cases involving fraud, dishonesty, or gross mismanagement, or if the court rules that appointment of a trustee is in the best interest of creditors, equity holders, and other parties with an interest in the estate. For the most part, bankruptcy judges have been reluctant to appoint private trustees to operate businesses in reorganization cases because company management is usually more qualified to operate and reorganize insolvent companies.[5] However, trustees are occasionally appointed. In 2003, at the behest of a major creditor, a subsidiary of *Boeing*, a trustee was appointed to operate *Hawaiian Airlines*, which filed for bankruptcy on March 21, 2003.

If the court orders the appointment of a private trustee, one is appointed by the U.S. trustee or by the bankruptcy court in non–U.S. trustee districts. Within 30 days of the order to appoint a private trustee, any party in interest in the case may request the election of a disinterested person to serve as trustee, and the U.S. trustee will call a meeting of creditors for that purpose. The option to elect a trustee is an important change provided by the 1994 Bankruptcy Reform Act.

The duties of a trustee or debtor in possession include the following:

- Being accountable for the debtor's property, including operations of the debtor's business
- Filing a list of creditors, schedules of assets and liabilities, and a statement of financial affairs (if not filed by the debtor)
- Furnishing information to the court about the debtor's estate and its administration
- Examining creditor claims and objecting to claims that appear to be improper (normally, only the trustee can object)
- Filing a reorganization plan or reporting why a plan will not be filed
- Filing final reports on the trusteeship as required by the court

Trustees and debtors in possession negotiate with the creditors, stockholders, and others in creating a plan of reorganization that will be approved by the bankruptcy court.

If a debtor in possession is appointed, an examiner will be appointed if loans to outsiders other than for goods and services exceed $5,000,000 or if the court concludes that such appointment is in the interests of the creditors, equity holders, or other parties with an interest in the estate. A primary function of the examiner is to value the debtor's assets and report such valuations to the court.

Committee Representation

Creditors' committees are responsible for protecting the interests of the creditors they represent and preserving the debtor's assets. The committees may review debtor transactions proposed to the court during bankruptcy, such as debtor-in-possession financing and disposal of assets. Committees can bring their objections to the court for consideration. All negotiations between prepetition creditors and the debtor in possession must take place through the creditors' committees.

Unlike in Chapter 7 cases, creditors' committees are not elected in Chapter 11 cases. A creditors' committee is appointed by the U.S. trustee as soon as practicable after the bankruptcy court grants an order for relief under Chapter 11. The creditors' committee (usually seven members) is selected from the largest unsecured creditors. Subsequently, the composition of that committee may be changed and other committees of creditors or equity holders may be appointed. The selection of creditors' committees can be extremely important to the final disposition of a reorganization case. If creditors' committees begin fighting each other, a simple and timely reorganization is nearly impossible.

Governmental units are generally not eligible to serve on creditors' committees. Prior to 1994, the Pension Benefit Guaranty Corporation (PBGC) sat on creditors' committees, but only as a nonvoting member. However, the 1994 Bankruptcy Reform Act gave the PBGC voting rights on creditors' committees.

---

[5] One notable exception was the *Eastern Airlines* bankruptcy case. Eastern is often cited as an example of how badly a reorganization case can turn out for creditors. The bankruptcy judge appointed a private trustee to operate Eastern after company management lost $1.2 billion during the year the company operated under the protection of the bankruptcy court. The bankruptcy judge further noted that Eastern's management had been unable to make reliable forecasts even in the short run (*The Wall Street Journal*, April 20, 1990, p. A3, and June 17, 1993).

Operating Under Chapter 11

Reorganization may take from six months to several years. In the meantime, subject to restrictions of the Bankruptcy Code and the bankruptcy court, the debtor in possession continues operating the business while working out a reorganization plan that is acceptable to all parties concerned. On the day of the bankruptcy filing, the company's existing bank accounts and books are closed and new accounts and books opened.

Usually, the company will arrange a new line of credit with its banks to enable it to continue to operate. This is often referred to as *debtor-in-possession financing*. New financing agreements must be approved by the bankruptcy court.

POSSIBLE BENEFITS OF CHAPTER 11 PROTECTION TO THE DEBTOR IN POSSESSION With the bankruptcy court's approval, the company may be able to reduce its labor costs through layoffs or wage reductions, or by terminating its pension plans. With the bankruptcy court's approval, the company can reject certain executory contracts and unexpired leases. (**Executory contracts** are those that have not been completely performed by both parties, such as purchase commitments.) Any claims for damages resulting from the cancellation of unfavorable contracts are treated as unsecured debt. Interest on unsecured debt stops at the time of filing. This can be a big factor for some companies. Interest of nearly $3 million a day was accruing on *Pennzoil's* $10.3 billion award from *Texaco* until the date of Texaco's Chapter 11 filing.

Creditors subject to the jurisdiction of the bankruptcy court may not commence or continue a lawsuit to take possession of the debtor's property without permission of the bankruptcy court; however, secured creditors may receive payments to protect their interest in collateral that the debtor continues to use in its operations. This is particularly applicable when the debtor continues to use collateralized property subject to depreciation, depletion, or amortization. Payments to the secured creditor may reduce the loan balance as the value of the collateral declines.

Financially distressed companies that find it necessary to restructure or swap debt may have difficulty gaining the necessary support from bondholders without filing for bankruptcy. A debt restructuring plan typically requires approval of 95% of each class of bondholders and a majority of stockholders. However, a debt restructuring under the bankruptcy court requires only two-thirds approval of each class of bondholders.

DISADVANTAGES OF A CHAPTER 11 FILING A Chapter 11 filing creates the obvious disadvantage for the debtor corporation of losing the confidence of its lenders, suppliers, customers, and employees. Beyond this stigma of bankruptcy, there is the additional disadvantage of operating a business in competitive markets when capital expenditures, acquisitions, disposals of assets, borrowing money, and so on, require prior approval of the court. Depending on the circumstances of a particular case, the bankruptcy court may impose so many restrictions on company management that even day-to-day operations of the business become difficult. The company may have to sell off its profitable units to meet creditor demands for emerging from Chapter 11.

The biggest disadvantage to the debtor is the cost of the bankruptcy proceedings.[6] Lawyers and other advisers are hired by the creditors' committees and the stockholders' committees, as well as by the debtor, but they are all paid from the debtor's assets. Expenses of the creditors' committees may also be reimbursed. Soaring fees in bankruptcy cases prompted some judges to cut fees that they considered unreasonable. The 1994 amendments to the bankruptcy act specifically granted the court the authority to award compensation less than the compensation requested when the fees seem unreasonable.

The Plan of Reorganization

Confirmation of a **reorganization plan** that is "fair and equitable" to all interests concerned is the final objective of Chapter 11. Only the debtor corporation may file a plan during the first 120 days after the order for relief is granted. Subsequently, the debtor, the trustee, the creditors' committees, an equity security holders' committee, or other parties in interest may file plans.

---

[6] *Finley Kumble* is a good example of how costly and drawn out bankruptcy cases can be. The company filed for bankruptcy in 1988. During the next six years while in Chapter 11, the trustee collected $60 million in cash for creditors. However, 80% of the money went for operating and administering the bankruptcy case, including $37 million for lawyers, trustees, and accountants. (*The Wall Street Journal*, April 8, 1994, pp. B1 and B5.)

To reduce bankruptcy expenses and reduce the time a debtor must operate under bankruptcy court restrictions, some firms file preapproved reorganization plans with the court at the same time as they file under Chapter 11 (often called a *prepackaged bankruptcy*). In other words, the terms of the debt restructuring have been worked out with creditors, and some or all creditors have agreed to the plan before the bankruptcy filing. In 2001, **Chiquita Brands International** filed for bankruptcy under a prearranged plan. Before filing for bankruptcy, Chiquita negotiated with its bondholders to reduce debt and issue new common stock and debt. The prearrangement with creditors was intended to shorten the time before Chiquita emerged from bankruptcy.

Chapter 11 provisions stipulate that the plan of reorganization must:

- Identify classes of claims (except for the administrative expenses, claims arising after an involuntary filing but before the order for relief or appointment of a trustee, and certain tax claims that are given priority)
- Specify any class of claims that is not impaired (a class of claims is *impaired* unless the plan leaves unaltered the legal rights of each claim in the class)
- Specify any class of claims that is impaired
- Treat all claims within a particular class alike
- Provide adequate means for the plan's execution (such as retention of property by the debtor, merger, modification of a lien, and extension of maturity dates)
- Prohibit the issuance of nonvoting equity securities
- Contain provisions for selection of officers and directors that are consistent with the interests of creditors, equity holders, and public policy

A reorganization plan may provide for sale of the debtor's property and distribution of the proceeds. A debtor corporation may prefer to liquidate under Chapter 11 instead of Chapter 7 because it expects that an orderly sale by company management will raise more money than a liquidating sale by a trustee. Montgomery Ward and **Service Merchandise** are examples of filing for Chapter 11 bankruptcy with the intent to liquidate.

A reorganization plan may be confirmed by the court if it is accepted by each class of creditors and stockholders whose claims or interests will be impaired. Alternatively, the plan may be confirmed even if it is rejected by some impaired classes, a "cramdown," if the bankruptcy judge determines the plan is fair and equitable.

Acceptance of a plan by a class of claims requires approval by at least two-thirds of those claim holders in dollar amount and more than half in number of claims. Classes of claims that are unimpaired are assumed to have accepted the plan, and classes that receive nothing are assumed to have rejected it without the necessity of a vote. In order for the bankruptcy court to confirm a plan, each class of claims must have accepted the plan or not be impaired under it. Within each class, each holder of a claim must either have accepted the plan or must receive (or retain an interest) not less than that holder would receive if the debtor corporation were liquidated.

After the necessary approval has been obtained, the court holds a confirmation hearing to entertain objections to confirmation and to confirm that the plan is "fair and equitable." Confirmation by the court constitutes discharge of the debtor except for claims provided for in the reorganization plan.

The ranking of unsecured creditors in a large reorganization case is seldom simple and is often the result of negotiation rather than rules. Many reorganizations are complicated by professional investors who buy debt claims from the original holders at deep discounts and then push for settlements to turn a quick profit from their investment.

Two years after **R. H. Macy & Company** filed for Chapter 11, **Federated Department Stores** purchased half of Macy's billion-dollar secured creditor claims held by **Prudential Insurance Company of America** for $449.3 million and took an option to buy the rest. This gave Federated the ability to block any takeover attempt by another retailer while it negotiated its own Macy takeover with the eight major creditors' committees.

Shareholders have also become more aggressive in bankruptcies. One reason for the increased shareholder activism is the increase in investors who speculate in the stock of companies in Chapter 11. Another reason is the rise of lawyers and financial advisers who specialize in leading equity committees against creditors and management. When solvent companies seek bankruptcy reorganization (AH Robins and Texaco, for example), shareholders have equity to protect.

FINANCIAL REPORTING DURING REORGANIZATION

The reorganization process can take several years. The corporation must still prepare financial statements and filings for the SEC during this time period and after it emerges from reorganization.

In 1990 the Accounting Standards Executive Committee (AcSEC) of the AICPA issued *Statement of Position (SOP) 90-7*, "Financial Reporting by Entities in Reorganization Under the Bankruptcy Code," to provide guidance for financial reporting by firms during Chapter 11 reorganization and when they emerge from Chapter 11. Accounting practices were diverse prior to this standard because no prescribed accounting for reorganization existed.

The objective of financial statements prepared for a company operating under Chapter 11 is to reflect the financial evolution during the bankruptcy proceedings. Therefore, the financial statements should distinguish the transactions and events directly related to the reorganization from the ongoing operations of the business.

Effects of Chapter 11 Proceedings on the Balance Sheet

Unsecured liabilities (no collateral) and undersecured liabilities incurred before the company entered Chapter 11 proceedings are **prepetition liabilities subject to compromise**. The debtor corporation and creditors' committees negotiate payment of these liabilities, which may result in payment of less than the claimed amount. The total of these liabilities is reported as a separate line item on the balance sheet. The remainder of a company's liabilities is reported in the usual manner. These represent secured prepetition liabilities and postpetition liabilities. Recall that liabilities incurred after entering Chapter 11 must be preapproved by the bankruptcy court.

On its December 31, 2000, balance sheet, debtor in possession *Fruit of the Loom (FOL)* reported liabilities subject to compromise of $540,700,000, which represented 27.1% of its total liabilities at that date.

Prepetition claims discovered after the Chapter 11 filing are included in the balance sheet at the court-allowed amount of the claims, rather than the amount at which they may be settled. Claims that cannot be reasonably estimated should be disclosed in notes to the financial statements under the provisions of *FASB Statement No. 5*, "Accounting for Contingencies."

Effects of Chapter 11 Proceedings on the Income Statement and the Statement of Cash Flows

Professional fees and similar expenses related directly to the Chapter 11 proceedings are expensed as incurred. "Income, expenses, realized gains and losses, and provisions for losses that result from the restructuring of the business should be reported separately in the income statement as *reorganization items*, except for those required to be reported as discontinued operations" (*SOP 90-7*, paragraph 27).

Hawaiian Airlines reported $115,063,000 of reorganization costs for the year ended December 31, 2003. Without these charges, Hawaiian's pretax operating income was $77,478,000. Over $14,000,000 of the reorganization costs were attributable to professional fees.

Interest expense to be reported is the amount that will be paid during the proceedings, or the probable amount to be allowed as a priority, secured, or unsecured claim. Amounts by which reported interest expense differs from contractual interest should be disclosed.

Earnings per share for Chapter 11 companies should be reported as usual. Probable issuance of common stock or common stock equivalents under a reorganization plan should be disclosed.

Cash flow items relating to reorganization are disclosed separately from cash flow items relating to the ongoing operations of the business in the statement of cash flows. *SOP 90-7* recommends the direct method of presenting cash flows.

Supplementary Combined Financial Statements

The AcSEC concluded that consolidated financial statements that include one or more companies operating under Chapter 11 do not provide adequate information about the bankruptcy proceedings. Therefore, *SOP 90-7* requires the presentation of *condensed combined financial statements* for all entities in reorganization proceedings, as supplementary information. Intercompany receivables and payables are disclosed, with receivables written down if necessary. Consolidation may be inappropriate for some subsidiaries in bankruptcy, particularly if a trustee is appointed to operate the company in bankruptcy.

FINANCIAL REPORTING FOR THE EMERGING COMPANY

Ordinarily, a corporate reorganization involves a restructuring of liabilities and capital accounts and a revaluation of assets. Participation of stockholders in the reorganized company depends upon whether they are deemed to have an equitable interest by the bankruptcy court. Many companies cannot emerge from bankruptcy as independent companies, and their reorganization plans include sale of the company. To aid in the plan's execution, the debtor corporation typically amends its charter to provide for the issuance of new securities for cash or in exchange for creditor claims.

The financial condition of companies filing for bankruptcy court protection varies drastically. Occasionally, profitable corporations file for protection under Chapter 11. Settlements under a reorganization plan are influenced by the ability of the interested parties to negotiate and manipulate their relative positions through creditors' and equity holders' committees. Bankruptcy judges also have broad discretionary powers in bankruptcy settlements. A provision of the Bankruptcy Code known as the *doctrine of equitable subordination* allows judges to move unsecured creditors ahead of secured creditors in certain situations in the interest of "fairness."

Reorganization Value

Determining the reorganization value of the entity emerging from bankruptcy is an important part of the reorganization plan. The emerging entity's **reorganization value** approximates fair value of the entity without considering liabilities. Generally, the reorganization value is determined by discounting future cash flows for the reconstituted business, plus the expected proceeds from sale of assets not required in the new business. The discount rates should reflect the business and financial risks involved (*SOP 90-7*, paragraph 9).

The reorganization value determines how much creditors will recover and how much stock of the reorganized company each class of creditors will receive when the company emerges from bankruptcy. For example, in the Macy bankruptcy case, senior creditors were owed $3.1 billion, and public bondholders were owed $1.2 billion. Macy's board of directors debated a $3.5 billion reorganization value under one plan and a $3.8 billion value under another. Senior creditors would receive a smaller stake in the reorganized company under the higher reorganization value, and bondholders would receive almost nothing under the lower value. The unsecured bondholders' committee pushed for a reorganization value of $4 billion, and another plan put forth by Federated Department Stores, a major creditor, was based on a $3.35 billion reorganization value. After months of negotiation, Federated and Macy filed a joint plan that called for the merger of the two companies and a reorganization value of $4.1 billion.

Financial reporting by a company whose reorganization plan has been confirmed by the court is determined by whether the reorganized entity is essentially a new company that qualifies for fresh-start reporting. The SOP provides two conditions that must be met for **fresh-start reporting**:

1. The reorganization value of the emerging entity's assets immediately before the date of confirmation of the reorganization plan must be less than the total of all postpetition liabilities and allowed claims.
2. Holders of existing voting shares immediately before confirmation of the reorganization plan must receive less than 50% of the emerging entity. This loss of control must be substantive and not temporary.

When both of these conditions are met, the emerging entity is in effect a new company and should adopt fresh-start reporting.

Fresh-Start Reporting

Fresh-start reporting results in a new reporting entity with no retained earnings or deficit balance.

ALLOCATING THE REORGANIZATION VALUE TO IDENTIFIABLE ASSETS The reorganization value of the company should be allocated to tangible and identifiable intangible assets according to the purchase method of accounting for transactions as set forth in *SFAS No. 141*, "Business Combinations."[7] Any amount of reorganization value not attributed to the tangible and identifiable intangible assets is reported as an unidentifiable intangible asset, "reorganization value in excess of amounts allocable to identifiable assets."

---

[7] See Chapter 1, "Business Combinations," for a discussion on assigning fair values to specific categories of assets and then allocating the total purchase price, or in this case, the reorganization value, to those assets on the basis of the assigned fair values.

REPORTING LIABILITIES Liabilities, other than deferred income taxes, should be reported at their current value at the confirmation date of the reorganization plan. Deferred taxes are reported as required in *FASB Statement No. 109*, "Accounting for Income Taxes." Benefits realized from prior net operating loss carryforwards are applied first to reduction of the reorganization value in excess of amounts allocable to identifiable assets and to other intangibles until exhausted and, finally, as a reduction of income tax expense.

FINAL STATEMENTS OF OLD ENTITY The final statements of the old entity as of and for the period ending on the date of confirmation of the plan disclose the effects of the adjustments on the individual asset and liability accounts resulting from adopting fresh-start reporting. The statements also show the effect of debt forgiveness. The ending balance sheet of the old entity is the same as the opening balance sheet of the new entity, including a zero retained earnings balance.

DISCLOSURES IN INITIAL FINANCIAL STATEMENTS OF NEW ENTITY Paragraph 39 of *SOP 90-7* lists the following disclosures that are included in notes to the initial financial statements of the new entity:

■ Adjustments to the historical amounts of individual assets and liabilities
■ The amount of debt forgiveness
■ The amount of prior retained earnings or deficit eliminated
■ Significant factors relating to the determination of reorganization value

COMPARATIVE FINANCIAL STATEMENTS The new entity's fresh-start financial statements are not comparable with those prepared by the predecessor company before confirmation of the reorganization plan. If predecessor statements are required by the SEC or another regulatory agency, a clear distinction is made between the fresh-start statements of the new entity and the statements of the predecessor company.

Reporting by Entities That Do Not Qualify for Fresh-Start Reporting

Companies emerging from reorganization that do not meet the criteria for fresh-start reporting report liabilities at present values using appropriate interest rates under *APB Opinion No. 21*, "Interest on Receivables and Payables." Forgiveness of debt should be reported as an extraordinary item. Quasi-reorganization accounting is *not* used for any entities emerging from bankruptcy court protection.

ILLUSTRATION OF A REORGANIZATION CASE

Tiger Corporation files for protection from creditors under Chapter 11 of the bankruptcy act on January 5, 2006. Tiger is a debtor in possession and, at the time of filing, its balance sheet includes the following (amounts in thousands):

Current assets		
Cash	$ 50	
Accounts receivable—net	500	
Inventory	300	
Other current assets	50	$ 900
Plant assets		
Land	$200	
Building—net	500	
Equipment—net	300	
Patent	200	1,200
		$2,100
Current liabilities		
Accounts payable	$600	
Taxes payable	150	
Accrued interest on 15% bonds	90	
Note payable to bank	260	$1,100
15% bonds payable (partially secured		
with land and building)		1,200
Stockholders' deficit		
Capital stock	$500	
Deficit	(700)	(200)
		$2,100

On the filing date Tiger's bank accounts and books are closed, and a new set of books is opened. The company arranges short-term financing with a bank (with the bankruptcy court's approval) in order to continue operations while working out a reorganization plan.

During 2006, no prepetition liabilities are paid and no interest is accrued on the bank note or the bonds payable. The bankruptcy court allows Tiger Corporation to invest $100,000 in new equipment in August 2006. This new equipment has a useful life of five years, and Tiger uses straight-line depreciation calculated to the nearest half-year. The building's depreciation expense is $50,000 per year, and the old equipment's rate is $60,000 per year. Patent amortization is $50,000 per year.

Costs related to the bankruptcy, including all expenses of the creditors' committees and the equity holder committee, are expensed as incurred and paid in cash.

Reclassification of Liabilities Subject to Compromise

At the beginning of 2006, Tiger reclassifies the liabilities subject to compromise into a separate account. The entry to record the reclassification is as follows (in thousands):

Accounts payable (–L)	600	
Taxes payable (–L)	150	
Accrued interest on 15% bonds (–OE)	90	
Note payable to bank (–L)	260	
15% bonds payable (partially secured) (–L)	1,200	
Liabilities subject to compromise (+L)		2,300
To reclassify liabilities subject to compromise.		

The $2,300,000 prepetition claims are included in the December 31, 2006, balance sheet separately. A supplemental schedule shows details of these claims.

DISCLOSING RECLASSIFIED LIABILITIES IN THE FINANCIAL STATEMENTS Exhibit 17-9 presents a combined income and retained earnings statement for 2006, as well as a balance sheet at December 31, 2006.

Although the reclassification of liabilities subject to compromise poses no difficulties in preparing balance sheets and income statements, it does complicate the preparation of the cash flow statement. The year's changes in the account balances that are reclassified must be separated from changes that affect operations and cash flows for the period. Exhibit 17-10 presents the cash flows statement. Only the direct method of presenting the cash flows statement is illustrated because *SOP 90-7* recommends this format.

One item unique to firms in reorganization is professional fees relating to bankruptcy proceedings. Cash paid for these items is classified as cash flows from operating activities, but separate disclosure of operating cash flows *before* and *after* the bankruptcy proceedings is recommended.

Operations Under Chapter 11

During the next six months, Tiger continues to operate under Chapter 11 of the Bankruptcy Code while it works out a reorganization plan, and by June 30, 2007, Tiger has a plan. Balance sheet and income statement amounts reflecting operations for the first six months of 2007 are summarized as follows (in thousands):

COMPARATIVE BALANCE SHEETS 2007

	January 1	June 30	Change
Cash	$ 150	$ 300	$150
Accounts receivable	350	335	(15)
Inventory	370	350	(20)
Other current assets	50	30	(20)
Land	200	200	—
Building—net	450	425	(25)
Equipment—net	330	290	(40)
Patent	150	125	(25)
Assets	$2,050	$2,055	$ 5
Liabilities subject to compromise	$2,300	$2,300	—
Short-term loan	150	75	$(75)
Accounts payable	100	125	25
Wages and salaries	50	55	5
Liabilities	2,600	2,555	(45)
Common stock	500	500	—
Deficit	(1,050)	(1,000)	50
Equities	$2,050	$2,055	$ 5

EXHIBIT 17-9

Balance Sheet and
Income Statement
During Chapter 11
Reorganization

TIGER CORPORATION
INCOME AND RETAINED EARNINGS STATEMENT
FOR THE YEAR 2006

Sales	$ 1,000,000
Cost of sales	(430,000)
Wages and salaries	(250,000)
Depreciation and amortization	(170,000)
Other expenses	(50,000)
Earnings before reorganization items	100,000
Professional fees related to bankruptcy proceedings	(450,000)
Net loss	(350,000)
Beginning deficit	(700,000)
Deficit December 31, 2006	$(1,050,000)

BALANCE SHEET AT DECEMBER 31, 2006

Current assets		
Cash	$ 150,000	
Accounts receivable—net	350,000	
Inventory	370,000	
Other current assets	50,000	$ 920,000
Plant assets		
Land	$ 200,000	
Building—net	450,000	
Equipment—net	330,000	
Patent	150,000	1,130,000
		$2,050,000
Current liabilities		
Short-term borrowings	$ 150,000	
Accounts payable	100,000	
Wages and salaries payable	50,000	300,000
Liabilities subject to compromise*		2,300,000
Stockholders' deficit		
Capital stock	$ 500,000	
Deficit	(1,050,000)	(550,000)
		$2,050,000

*Liabilities subject to compromise:

Partially secured 15% bonds payable plus $90,000 interest, secured by first mortgage on land and building	$1,290,000
Priority tax claim	150,000
Accounts payable and unsecured note to bank	860,000
	$2,300,000

INCOME STATEMENT FOR SIX MONTHS ENDING JUNE 30, 2007

Sales		$ 600
Cost of sales		(200)
Wages and salaries expense		(100)
Depreciation and amortization		
Building	$25	
Old equipment	30	
New equipment	10	
Patent	25	(90)
Other expenses		(30)
Earnings before reorganization items		180
Professional fees related to bankruptcy proceedings		(130)
Net income		50
Beginning deficit		(1,050)
Ending deficit		$(1,000)

EXHIBIT 17-10

Statement of Cash
Flows During
Chapter 11
Reorganization

**TIGER CORPORATION
STATEMENT OF CASH FLOWS
FOR THE YEAR ENDED DECEMBER 31, 2006 (IN THOUSANDS)**

Cash Flows from Operating Activities		
Cash received from customers		$1,150
Cash paid to suppliers		(400)
Cash paid to employees		(200)
Cash paid for other expenses		(50)
Net cash flows provided by operating activities		
before reorganization items		500
Operating cash flows from reorganization		
Professional fees paid for services relating to		
bankruptcy proceedings		(450)
Net cash provided by operating activities		50
Cash Flows from Investing Activities		
Capital expenditures	$(100)	
Net cash used in investing activities		(100)
Cash Flows from Financing Activities		
Net short-term borrowings	$ 150	
Net cash provided by financing activities		150
Net increase in cash		$ 100
Reconciliation of net income to net cash provided		
by operating activities		
Net loss		$ (350)
Adjustments to reconcile net loss to net cash		
provided by operations:		
Depreciation and amortization		170
Increase in postpetition payables (operating activities)		150
Decreases in accounts receivable		150
Increase in inventory		(70)
Cash provided by operating activities		$ 50

The Reorganization Plan

After extensive negotiations among the parties of interest, a reorganization value of $2,200,000 is agreed upon, and a plan of reorganization is filed with the court. The terms of Tiger's proposed reorganization plan include the following:

1. Tiger's 15% bonds payable were secured with the land and building. The bondholders agree to accept $500,000 new common stock, $500,000 senior debt of 12% bonds, and $100,000 cash payable December 31, 2007.

2. The priority tax claims of $150,000 will be paid in cash as soon as the reorganization plan is confirmed by the bankruptcy court.

3. The remaining unsecured, nonpriority, prepetition claims of $950,000 will be settled as follows:
   a Creditors represented by the accounts payable will receive $275,000 subordinated debt and $140,000 common stock.
   b The $90,000 accrued interest on the 15% bonds will be forgiven.
   c The $260,000 note payable to the bank will be exchanged for $120,000 subordinated debt and $60,000 common stock.

4. Equity holders will exchange their stock for $100,000 common stock of the emerging company.

Fresh-Start Reporting

LEARNING OBJECTIVE 4

The reorganization value is compared with the total postpetition liabilities and court-allowed claims at June 30 to determine if fresh-start reporting is appropriate (amounts in thousands):

Postpetition liabilities	$ 255
Allowed claims subject to compromise	2,300
Total liabilities on June 30, 2007	2,555
Less: Reorganization value	(2,200)
Excess liabilities over reorganization value	$ 355

The excess liabilities over reorganization value indicates that the first condition for fresh-start reporting is met. The reorganization plan calls for the old equity holders to retain less than a 50% interest in the emerging company, so the second condition also is met, and fresh-start reporting is appropriate. A summary of the proposed reorganized capital structure is as follows (in thousands):

Postpetition liabilities	$ 255
Taxes payable	150
Current portion of senior debt, due December 31, 2007	100
Senior debt, 12% bonds	500
Subordinated debt	395
Common stock	800
	$2,200

The plan is approved by each class of claims and confirmed by the bankruptcy court on June 30, 2007. Tiger Corporation records the provisions of the reorganization plan and the adoption of fresh-start reporting in the books of the old entity as follows (in thousands):

Accounts payable (prepetition) (−L)	600	
Interest (prepetition) (−L)	90	
Bank note (prepetition) (−L)	260	
15% bonds payable (prepetition) (−L)	1,200	
12% senior debt (+L)		500
12% senior debt—current (+L)		100
Subordinated debt (+L)		395
Common stock (new) (+SE)		700
Gain on debt discharge (+G, +SE)		455

To record settlement of the prepetition claims. (The summary account "prepetition claims subject to compromise" could have been used.)

Common stock (old) (−SE)	500	
Common stock (new) (+SE)		100
Additional paid-in capital (+SE)		400

To record exchange of stock by equity holders.

Tiger's assets that have fair values different from their recorded book values on June 30, 2007, are summarized as follows (in thousands):

	Fair Value	Book Value	Difference
Inventory	$ 375	$ 350	$ 25
Land	300	200	100
Buildings—net	350	425	(75)
Equipment—net	260	290	(30)
Patent	0	125	(125)
	$1,285	$1,390	$(105)

The entries to adjust Tiger's assets for the fair value/book value differences and record the fresh start are as follows (in thousands):

Inventory (+A)	25	
Land (+A)	100	
Loss on asset revaluation (+Lo, −SE)	105	
Buildings—net (−A)		75
Equipment—net (−A)		30
Patent (−A)		125

To adjust Tiger's assets to their fair values.

Reorganization value in excess of identifiable assets (+A)	250	
Gain on debt discharge (−G, −SE)	455	
Additional paid-in capital (−SE)	400	
Loss on asset revaluation (−Lo, +SE)		105
Deficit (+SE)		1,000

To eliminate the deficit and additional paid-in capital and to record the excess reorganization value and the fresh start.

Exhibit 17-11 presents working papers to show the effect of the reorganization plan on Tiger's balance sheet.

EXHIBIT 17-11

Working Papers to Show Confirmation of Reorganization Plan with Fresh-Start Reporting

TIGER CORPORATION COMPARATIVE BALANCE SHEETS AT JUNE 30, 2007 (IN THOUSANDS)

	Preconfirmation Balance Sheet	Adjustments to Record Confirmation of Plan — Debits	Adjustments to Record Confirmation of Plan — Credits	Reorganized Balance Sheet
Assets				
Cash	$ 300			$ 300
Accounts receivable	335			335
Inventory	350	a 25		375
Other current assets	30			30
Land	200	b 100		300
Building	425		c 75	350
Equipment	290		d 30	260
Patent	125		e 125	—
Reorganization excess	—	f 250		250
	$2,055			$2,200
Equities				
Postpetition Claims				
Short-term bank loan	$ 75			$ 75
Accounts payable	125			125

(continued)

EXHIBIT 17-11

Working Papers to Show Confirmation of Reorganization Plan with Fresh-Start Reporting *(continued)*

TIGER CORPORATION COMPARATIVE BALANCE SHEETS AT JUNE 30, 2007 (IN THOUSANDS)

	Preconfirmation Balance Sheet	Adjustments to Record Confirmation of Plan		Reorganized Balance Sheet
		Debits	Credits	
Wages payable	55			55
Prepetition Claims Accounts payable—old	600	h 600		—
Taxes payable	150			150
Interest	90	i 90		—
Bank note	260	j 260		—
15% bonds payable	1,200	g 1,200		—
Stockholders' Equity Capital stock—old	500	k 500		—
Deficit	(1,000)	c 75 d 30 e 125	a 25 b 100 f 250 g 100 h 185 i 90 j 80 k 400	—
New Equities Current portion—bonds	—		g 100	100
12% senior debt	—		g 500	500
Subordinated debt	—		h 275 j 120	395
Common stock—new	—		g 500 h 140 j 60 k 100	800
Retained earnings—new	—			0
	$2,055			$2,200

The first column of the working papers reflects the balance sheet at June 30, 2007, immediately before recognizing the terms of the reorganization plan and establishing fresh-start reporting. Entries a through f in the adjustment columns adjust the identifiable assets to their reorganization value, which approximates fair value. The excess reorganization value over the fair value of identifiable assets is entered. Working paper entries g through k impose the terms of the reorganization plan.

Note that the last column, Reorganized Balance Sheet, is both the final balance sheet of the old entity and the opening balance sheet of the emerging entity. Although the opening balance sheet of the new entity reflects the reorganization values of the assets, *SOP 90-7* provides that the adjustments to historical cost should be disclosed in notes to the initial financial statements. The new Tiger Corporation should also disclose the amount of debt forgiveness, the deficit eliminated, and key factors used in the determination of the reorganization value.

SUMMARY

A debtor corporation that cannot solve its financial problems internally may be able to obtain relief by direct negotiation with creditors. Failing this, the debtor may seek protection from creditors by filing a petition for bankruptcy under Title 11 of the *United States Code*. Either the debtor or the creditors can file a petition. A petition filed under Chapter 11 of the bankruptcy act covers reorganization of the debtor; a Chapter 7 filing covers liquidation of the debtor.

In a Chapter 7 liquidation case, a trustee and creditors' committee are elected by the unsecured creditors. The trustee takes possession of the debtor's estate, converts the assets into cash, and distributes the proceeds according to the priority of claims, as directed by the bankruptcy court.

In a Chapter 11 reorganization case, the U.S. trustee appoints a creditors' committee as soon as practicable after the filing. A trustee may be appointed for cause, but generally the debtor continues in possession. The debtor corporation continues operations while it works out a reorganization plan that is fair and equitable.

The AICPA's *Statement of Position 90-7*, "Financial Reporting by Entities in Reorganization Under the Bankruptcy Code," prescribes financial reporting for companies operating under Chapter 11. Some companies emerging from Chapter 11 are essentially new companies and qualify for fresh-start reporting. Emerging companies that do not meet the criteria for fresh-start reporting account for their liabilities in accordance with *APB Opinion No. 21*, "Interest on Receivables and Payables."

QUESTIONS

1. What is the distinction between *equity insolvency* and *bankruptcy insolvency*?

2. Is a Title 11 case under the Bankruptcy Reform Act of 1978 the same as a Chapter 11 case? Discuss.

3. Bankruptcy proceedings may be designated as *voluntary* or *involuntary*. Distinguish between the two types, including the requirements for the filing of an involuntary petition.

4. Consider the following statement: "A bankrupt company is liquidated under Chapter 7 of the bankruptcy act, but a company that is not bankrupt will be rehabilitated under Chapter 11." Do you agree? Discuss.

5. What are the duties of the U.S. trustee under the Bankruptcy Reform Act of 1978? Do U.S. trustees supervise the administration of all bankruptcy cases?

6. What obligations does a debtor corporation have in a bankruptcy case?

7. Is a trustee appointed in Title 11 cases? In all Chapter 7 cases? Discuss.

8. Do you agree with the following statement? "Trustees and creditors' committees are appointed in Chapter 11 cases and elected in Chapter 7 cases."

9. Describe the duties of a trustee in a liquidation case under the Bankruptcy Reform Act of 1978.

10. Which unsecured claims have priority in a Chapter 7 liquidation case? Discuss in terms of priority ranks.

11. Does the Bankruptcy Reform Act of 1978 establish priorities for holders of unsecured nonpriority claims (that is, general unsecured claims)?

12. What is the purpose of a statement of affairs, and how are assets valued in this statement?

13. Does the bankruptcy act require a trustee to prepare a statement of realization and liquidation for the bankruptcy court?

14. Does filing a case under Chapter 11 of the bankruptcy act mean that the company will not be liquidated? Discuss.

15. What is a debtor-in-possession reorganization case?

16. When can a creditors' committee file a plan of reorganization under a Chapter 11 case?

17. Discuss the requirements for approval of a plan of reorganization.

18. Does acceptance of a plan by two-thirds in amount and more than half in number of claims constitute confirmation of a reorganization plan? Discuss.

19. Describe *prepetition liabilities subject to compromise* on the balance sheet of a company operating under Chapter 11 of the bankruptcy act.

20. The *reorganization value* of a firm emerging from Chapter 11 bankruptcy is used to determine the accounting of the reorganized company. Explain reorganization value as used in the AICPA's *SOP 90-7*, "Financial Reporting by Entities in Reorganization Under the Bankruptcy Code."

21. *SOP 90-7* provides two conditions that must be met for an emerging firm to use fresh-start reporting. What are these two conditions?

22. A firm emerging from Chapter 11 bankruptcy that does not qualify for fresh-start reporting must still report the effect of the reorganization plan on its financial position and results of operations. How is debt forgiveness reported in the reorganized company's financial statements?

EXERCISES

E 17-1

Differences among types of bankruptcy filings and other terminology related to bankruptcy law

LEARNING OBJECTIVES 1, 2

1. *Insolvency* in the bankruptcy sense means:
- a *Book value of assets is greater than liabilities*
- b *Fair value of assets is less than liabilities*
- c *Inability to meet financial obligations as they come due*
- d *Liabilities are greater than book value of assets*

2. Discharge of a debtor corporation's liabilities other than those provided for in the reorganization plan results when:
- a *The plan is accepted by a majority of unsecured creditors*
- b *Each class of claims has accepted the plan or is not impaired under it*
- c *Each holder of a claim has accepted the plan or will receive at least as much as if the company were liquidated*
- d *The court confirms that the plan is fair and equitable*

3. Election of a trustee in a Chapter 7 case requires:
- a *Approval by a majority of creditors*
- b *Approval by a majority of claims represented*
- c *Approval by a majority in dollar amount and at least 20% of claims eligible to vote*
- d *Approval of two-thirds in dollar amount and a majority of holders of all claims*

4. The order of payments for unsecured priority claims in a Chapter 7 bankruptcy case is such that:
- a *Tax claims of governmental units are paid before claims for administrative expenses incurred by the trustee*
- b *Tax claims of governmental units are paid before claims of employees for wages*
- c *Claims of employees for wages are paid before administrative expenses incurred by the trustee*
- d *Claims incurred between the filing of an involuntary petition and appointment of a trustee are paid before claims for contributions to employee benefit plans*

5. A judge in a corporate bankruptcy case may *not*:
- a *Dismiss a case*
- b *Transfer a Chapter 11 case to Chapter 7*
- c *Transfer a Chapter 7 case to Chapter 11*
- d *Transfer a Chapter 7 case to Chapter 5*

6. A debtor's duties under a Chapter 7 bankruptcy case do *not* include:
- a *Filing a schedule of assets and liabilities with the court*
- b *Surrendering the firm's property to the trustee*
- c *Relinquishing stockholders' claims in the estate*
- d *Cooperating with the trustee*

7. A specific duty of a U.S. trustee in a bankruptcy case is to:
- a *Preside over the meetings of creditors' committees*
- b *Convert the estate assets into cash*
- c *Investigate the financial affairs of the debtor*
- d *Operate the debtor's business*

8. A corporation may *not* be a debtor in possession if:
- a *The case is initiated in a voluntary filing*
- b *The case is initiated in an involuntary filing*
- c *Loans other than for goods and services exceed $5,000,000*
- d *The court concludes that appointment of a trustee is in the best interests of creditors*

9. Among other provisions, a Chapter 11 plan for reorganization must:
   a *Rank claims according to their liquidation priorities*
   b *Not impair the claims of secured creditors*
   c *Provide adequate means for the plan's execution*
   d *Treat all claims alike*

10. Which of the following claims *would not* be entitled to a priority in a Chapter 7 bankruptcy proceeding?
   a *Administrative expenses incurred by the trustee*
   b *Salaries payable of $1,500*
   c *Claims of governmental units for taxes*
   d *Claims of creditors for $2,000 interest*

11. Under Chapter 11 of the bankruptcy act:
   a *Only involuntary filings are accepted by the court*
   b *The court is required to appoint a trustee*
   c *A solvent corporation may file a petition for relief from creditors*
   d *Only the debtor corporation can file a reorganization plan*

12. A debtor-in-possession case is:
   a *A voluntary case*
   b *An involuntary case*
   c *A Chapter 7 case*
   d *A Chapter 11 case*

13. The term *insider* is frequently used in relation to preferential transfers under the bankruptcy act. Which of the following is *not* an insider?
   a *An officer of the corporation*
   b *An officer of an affiliated corporation*
   c *The family members of a client corporation's president*
   d *A family member of the corporation's controller*

LEARNING
OBJECTIVE 3

E 17-2

Financial reporting during bankruptcy Use the following information in answering questions 1 and 2:

Hale Company filed for protection from creditors under Chapter 11 of the bankruptcy act on July 1, 2006. Hale had the following liabilities at the time of filing:

10% mortgage bonds payable, secured by a building with a book value and fair value of $100,000	$200,000
Accrued interest on mortgage (January 1–July 1)	10,000
Accounts payable	80,000
Priority tax claims	50,000
	$340,000

1. The December 31, 2006, balance sheet will show prepetition liabilities of:
   a *$340,000 (the claims at filing)*
   b *$240,000 (the original claims less the secured portion of the mortgage bonds)*
   c *$350,000 (the original claims plus six months' interest on the bonds)*
   d *$290,000 (the original claims less the priority tax claims)*

2. Two and a half years after filing the petition for bankruptcy, Hale's management, its creditors, the equity holders, and other parties in interest agree on a reorganization value of $500,000. Which of the following statements is most likely?
   a *The reorganization value approximates the appraised value of the firm as a going concern less the prepetition liabilities.*
   b *The reorganization value approximates the fair value of the assets less the fair value of the prepetition and postpetition liabilities.*
   c *The reorganization value approximates the fair value of the assets less the book value of the postpetition liabilities and the estimated settlement value of the prepetition liabilities.*
   d *The reorganization value approximates the fair value of the entity without considering the liabilities.*

3. Universal Industries, a parent company with five wholly owned operating subsidiaries, is in the process of preparing consolidated financial statements for the year. Two of Universal's subsidiaries are operating as debtors in possession under Chapter 11 of the bankruptcy act. Which of the following statements is correct?
   a *FASB Statement No. 94, "Consolidation of All Majority-Owned Subsidiaries," prohibits Universal Industries from consolidating the financial statements of the two subsidiaries in bankruptcy with those of the other affiliated companies.*
   b *FASB Statement No. 94, "Consolidation of All Majority-Owned Subsidiaries," requires that the financial statements of all five of the subsidiaries be consolidated with those of the parent company.*

c If Universal's consolidated financial statements include the operations of the two subsidiaries in bankruptcy, Statement of Position 90-7 *requires that condensed combined financial statements for all entities in reorganization be presented as supplementary financial statements.*

d If Universal's consolidated financial statements do not *include the operations of the two subsidiaries in bankruptcy, those subsidiaries must be accounted for under the cost method.*

4. When fresh-start reporting is used, the initial financial statement disclosures should not include:

a *Adjustments made in the amounts of individual assets and liabilities*

b *The amount of debt forgiven*

c *The amount of prior retained earnings or deficit eliminated*

d *Current and prior-year EPS amounts*

E 17-3

Financial reporting during bankruptcy—distributions to creditors Rams Corporation holds a $100,000 note receivable from Patriots Supply Company. It has been learned that Patriots Supply filed for Chapter 7 bankruptcy and that the expected recovery of nonsecured claims is 35¢ on the dollar. Patriots' note payable to Rams is secured by inventory items with an estimated recoverable value of $30,000.

REQUIRED: Determine Rams's expected recovery on the note.

E 17-4

Fresh-start reporting requirements Baxter Hardware has been operating under Chapter 11 of the Bankruptcy Code for the past 15 months. On March 31, 2006, just before confirmation of its reorganization plan, Baxter's reorganization value is estimated at $2,000,000. A balance sheet for Baxter prepared on the same date is summarized as follows:

Current assets	$ 750,000
Plant assets	3,000,000
	$3,750,000
Postpetition liabilities	$1,200,000
Prepetition liabilities subject to compromise*	1,500,000
Fully secured debt	900,000
Capital stock	900,000
Deficit	(750,000)
	$3,750,000

*Represents allowed claims. The reorganization plan calls for payment of $150,000 and issuance of $300,000 notes and $375,000 common stock in settlement of the prepetition liabilities.

REQUIRED

1. On the basis of the reorganization value, does Baxter Hardware qualify for fresh-start reporting?

2. What other conditions must be met for fresh-start reporting? Show calculations.

E 17-5

Financial reporting during bankruptcy—distributions to creditors Holiday Corporation is in bankruptcy and is being liquidated by a court-appointed trustee. The financial report that follows was prepared by the trustee just before the final cash distribution:

Assets	
Cash	$100,000

Approved Claims	
Mortgage payable (secured by property that was sold for $50,000)	$ 80,000
Accounts payable, unsecured	50,000
Administrative expenses payable, unsecured	8,000
Salaries payable, unsecured	2,000
Interest payable, unsecured	10,000
Total approved claims	$150,000

The administrative expenses are for trustee fees and other costs of administering the debtor corporation's estate.

REQUIRED: Show how the $100,000 cash will be distributed to holders of each of the claims.

P 17-1

Financial reporting during bankruptcy The balance sheet of Scott Corporation appeared as follows on March 1, 2006, when an interim trustee was appointed by the U.S. trustee to assume control of Scott's estate in a Chapter 7 case.

Assets		Liabilities and Stockholders' Equity	
Cash	$ 4,000	Accounts payable	$ 50,000
Accounts receivable—net	8,000	Note payable—unsecured	40,000
Inventories	36,000	Revenue received in advance	1,000
Land	20,000	Wages payable	3,000
Buildings—net	100,000	Mortgage payable	80,000
Intangible assets	26,000	Capital stock	40,000
		Retained earnings deficit	(20,000)
Assets	$194,000	Liabilities and equity	$194,000

ADDITIONAL INFORMATION

1. Creditors failed to elect a trustee; accordingly, the interim trustee became trustee for the case.

2. The land and buildings are pledged as security for the mortgage payable.

3. In January 2006, Scott received $1,000 from a customer as a payment in advance for merchandise that is no longer marketed.

4. Activities of the trustee during March are summarized as follows:

   a $7,200 is collected on the receivables.
   b Inventories are sold for $19,400.
   c Land and buildings bring a total of $90,000.
   d Nothing is realized from the intangible assets.
   e Administrative expenses of $8,200 are incurred by the trustee.

REQUIRED

1. Prepare a separate set of books for the trustee to assume possession of the estate and convert its assets into cash.

2. Prepare financial statements on March 31 for Scott in trusteeship (balance sheet, cash receipts and disbursements, and changes in estate equity).

3. Prepare journal entries on the trustee's books to distribute available cash to creditors and close the case.

P 17-2

Financial reporting during bankruptcy Justin Corporation filed a petition under Chapter 7 of the bankruptcy act in January 2006. On March 15, 2006, the trustee provided the following information about the corporation's financial affairs.

	Book Values	Estimated Realizable Values
Assets		
Cash	$ 20,000	$ 20,000
Accounts receivable—net	100,000	75,000
Inventories	150,000	70,000
Plant assets—net	250,000	280,000
Total assets	$520,000	
Liabilities		
Liability for priority claims	$ 80,000	
Accounts payable—unsecured	150,000	
Note payable, secured by accounts receivable	100,000	
Mortgage payable, secured by all plant assets	220,000	
Total liabilities	$550,000	

REQUIRED

1. Determine the amount expected to be available for unsecured claims.

2. Determine the expected recovery per dollar of unsecured claims.

3. Estimate the amount of recovery for each class of creditors.

P 17-3

Claims rankings and cash distribution upon liquidation Fabulous Fakes Corporation is being liquidated under Chapter 7 of the bankruptcy act. All assets have been converted into cash, and $374,500 cash is available to pay the following claims:

1. Administrative expenses of preserving and liquidating the debtor corporation's estate	$ 12,500
2. Merchandise creditors	99,000
3. Local government for property taxes	4,000
4. Local bank for unsecured loan (principal is $30,000 and interest is $4,500)	34,500
5. State government for gross receipts taxes	3,000
6. Employees for unpaid wages during the month before filing (includes $5,000 for the company president and less than $4,000 for each of the other employees)	48,000
7. Customers for prepaid merchandise that was not delivered	1,500
8. Holders of the first mortgage on the company's real estate that was sold for $240,000 (includes $220,000 principal and $8,500 interest)	228,500

Assume that all the claims are allowed and that they were timely filed.

REQUIRED

1. Rank the claims according to priority under the bankruptcy act.

2. Show how the available cash will be distributed in final liquidation of the corporation.

P 17-4

Financial reporting during bankruptcy—statement of affairs Hanna Corporation filed a petition under Chapter 7 of the bankruptcy act on June 30, 2006. Data relevant to its financial position as of this date are:

	Book Value	Estimated Net Realizable Values
Cash	$ 2,200	$ 2,200
Accounts receivable—net	15,000	13,500
Inventories	20,000	22,500
Equipment—net	55,000	28,000
Total assets	$92,200	$66,200
Accounts payable	$26,400	
Rent payable	7,600	
Wages payable	12,000	
Note payable plus accrued interest	31,000	
Capital stock	55,000	
Retained earnings (deficit)	(39,800)	
Total liabilities and equity	$92,200	

REQUIRED

1. Prepare a statement of affairs assuming that the note payable and interest are secured by a mortgage on the equipment and that wages are less than $4,000 per employee.

2. Estimate the amount that will be paid to each class of claims if priority liquidation expenses, including trustee fees, are $4,000 and estimated net realizable values are actually realized.

P 17-5

Financial reporting during bankruptcy The unsecured creditors of Dawn Corporation filed a petition under Chapter 7 of the bankruptcy act on July 1, 2006, to force Dawn into bankruptcy. The court order for relief was granted on July 10, at which time an interim trustee was appointed to supervise liquidation of the estate. A listing of assets and liabilities of Dawn Corporation as of July 10, 2006, along with estimated realizable values, is as follows:

	Book Values	Estimated Realizable Values
Assets		
Cash	$ 80,000	$ 80,000
Accounts receivable—net	210,000	160,000
Inventories	200,000	210,000
Equipment—net	150,000	60,000
Land and buildings—net	250,000	140,000
Intangible assets	10,000	—
	$900,000	$650,000
Accounts payable	$400,000	
Note payable	100,000	
Wages payable (from June and July)	24,000	
Taxes payable	76,000	
Mortgage payable $200,000, plus $5,000 unpaid interest to July 10	205,000	
Capital stock	300,000	
Retained earnings deficit	(205,000)	
	$900,000	

ADDITIONAL INFORMATION

1. Accounts receivable are pledged as security for the note payable.

2. No more than $1,000 is owed to any employee.

3. Taxes payable is a priority item.

4. Inventory items include $50,000 acquired on July 5, 2006; the unpaid invoice is included in accounts payable.

5. The mortgage payable and interest are secured by the land and buildings.

6. Trustee fees and other costs of liquidating the estate are expected to be $11,000.

REQUIRED

1. Prepare a statement of affairs for Dawn Corporation on July 10, 2006.

2. Develop a schedule showing how available cash will be distributed to each class of claims assuming (a) the estimated realizable values are actually received and (b) the trustee and other fees of liquidating the estate are $11,000.

P 17-6

Financial reporting during bankruptcy The balance sheet of Everlast Window Corporation at June 30, 2006, contains the following items:

Assets	
Cash	$ 40,000
Accounts receivable—net	70,000
Inventories	50,000
Land	30,000
Building—net	200,000
Machinery—net	60,000
Patent	50,000
	$500,000

(continued)

Equities

Accounts payable	$110,000
Wages payable	60,000
Property taxes payable	10,000
Mortgage payable	150,000
Interest on mortgage payable	15,000
Note payable—unsecured	50,000
Interest payable—unsecured	5,000
Capital stock	200,000
Retained earnings deficit	(100,000)
	$500,000

The company is in financial difficulty, and its stockholders and creditors have requested a statement of affairs for planning purposes. The following information is available:

1. The company estimates that $63,000 is the maximum amount collectible for the accounts receivable.

2. Except for 20% of the inventory items that are damaged and worth only $2,000, the cost of the other items is expected to be recovered in full.

3. The land and building have a combined appraisal value of $170,000 and are subject to the $150,000 mortgage and related accrued interest.

4. The appraised value of the machinery is $20,000.

5. Wages payable and property taxes payable are unsecured priority items that do not exceed any limitations of the bankruptcy act.

REQUIRED

1. Prepare a statement of affairs for Everlast Window Corporation as of June 30, 2006.

2. Compute the estimated settlement per dollar of unsecured liabilities.

P 17-7

Installment liquidation Lowstep Corporation filed for relief under Chapter 11 of the bankruptcy act on January 2, 2006. A summary of Lowstep's assets and equities on this date, and at June 30, 2006, follows. Estimated fair values of Lowstep's assets at June 30 are also shown.

LEARNING OBJECTIVE **4**

	January 2, 2006	June 30, 2006	
		Per Books	Estimated Fair Value
Assets			
Cash	$ 200	$ 6,700	$ 6,700
Trade receivables—net	800	1,000	1,000
Inventories	2,000	1,600	2,000
Prepaid items	500	—	—
Land	1,000	1,000	2,000
Buildings—net	3,000	2,900	1,500
Equipment—net	2,000	1,800	1,800
Patent	4,500	4,000	0
	$14,000	$19,000	$15,000
Equities			
Accounts payable	$ 1,000	$ 3,000	
Wages payable	500	1,000	
Bank note payable (includes $500 interest)	5,000		
Long-term note payable (secured with equipment)	6,000		
Prepetition liabilities allowed		12,500	
Common stock	7,000	7,000	
Deficit	(5,500)	(4,500)	
	$14,000	$19,000	

The parties in interest agree to a reorganization plan on July 1, 2006, and a hearing to confirm that the plan is fair and equitable is scheduled for July 8. Under the reorganization plan, the reorganization value is set at $16,000, and the debt and equity holders will receive value as follows:

	To Receive Cash Consideration	To Receive Noncash Consideration	
Postpetition Claims			
Accounts payable (in full)	$3,000		
Wages payable (in full)	1,000		
Prepetition Claims			
Accounts payable (80%)	800		
Wages payable (80%)	400		
Bank note payable and interest (80%)		$ 2,000	note payable
		2,000	common stock
Long-term note payable (80%)		1,800	note payable
		3,000	common stock
Common stockholders*		2,000	common stock
	$5,200	$10,800	

*Reorganization value over consideration allocated to creditors.

The reorganization plan is confirmed on July 8, 2006, under the new name of Highstep Corporation. There are no asset or liability changes between July 1 and July 8.

REQUIRED

1. Is the reorganization of Lowstep eligible for fresh-start accounting? Show calculations.

2. Prepare journal entries to adjust Lowstep's accounts for the reorganization plan.

3. Prepare a fresh-start balance sheet as of July 8, 2006.

INTERNET EXERCISE

Access *McLeodUSA Inc.'s* 2002 10-K (filed in March 2003) on the SEC Edgar Web site. Using the 10-K, answer the following questions:

1. When and why did McLeodUSA apply for Chapter 11 bankruptcy protection?
2. When did the court approve McLeodUSA's plan of reorganization?
3. What were the terms of the reorganization with respect to its debt and stockholders?
4. Did the company qualify for fresh-start reporting?
5. In reviewing the consolidated financial statements, how do the financial statements differ from what you would typically observe for a non-bankrupt company?
6. How much money did the reorganization cost in litigation, reorganization, and restructuring charges? Was this a material amount relative to income and assets?
7. How much debt was forgiven? Was this a material amount?
8. How was fresh-start reporting presented in the financial statements?
9. Access McLeodUSA's 2003 10-K. How are fiscal year 2003's financial results affected by the reorganization?
10. Overall, do you believe that McLeodUSA's presentation of its bankruptcy process is informative to investors? What additional information would you like to know?

SELECTED READINGS

ALTMAN, EDWARD I. *Corporation Financial Distress.* New York: John Wiley, 1983.

American Accounting Association's Financial Accounting Standards Committee. "Response to the FASB Exposure Draft 'Accounting by Creditors for Impairment of a Loan.'" *Accounting Horizons* (September 1993), pp. 114–117.

ARUTT, DIANE, et al. "Implementation of SFAS No. 114, *Accounting by Creditors for Impairment of a Loan.*" *The CPA Journal* (January 1995), pp. 36–41.

BRADLEY, MICHAEL, and MICHAEL ROSENZWEIG. "The Untenable Case for Chapter 11." *The Yale Law Journal*, vol. 101 (1992), pp. 1043–1095.

FRETT, JEROME. "Bankruptcy: When Is It Good News?" *Journal of Accountancy* (November 1991), pp. 135–138.

HERZ, ROBERT H., and EDWARD J. ABAHOONIE, "Restructuring Business in the 1990s." *Journal of Accountancy* (April 1992), pp. 28–33.

KUDLA, RONALD J. *Voluntary Corporate Liquidations.* Westport, CT: Quorum Books, Greenwood Press, 1988.

NEWTON, GRANT W. *Bankruptcy and Insolvency Accounting: Practice and Procedure.* 2nd ed. New York: John Wiley, 1981.

PARISER, DAVID B. "Financial Reporting Implications of Troubled Debt." *The CPA Journal* (February 1989), pp. 32–40.

ROBBINS, JOHN, AL GOLL, and PAUL ROSENFELD. "Accounting for Companies in Chapter 11 Reorganization." *Journal of Accountancy* (January 1991), pp. 74–80.

Statement of Financial Accounting Standards No. 114. "Accounting by Creditors for Impairment of a Loan." Norwalk, CT: Financial Accounting Standards Board, 1993.

Statement of Financial Accounting Standards No. 118. "Accounting by Creditors for Impairment of a Loan—Income Recognition and Disclosures." Norwalk, CT: Financial Accounting Standards Board, 1994.

Statement of Position 90-7. "Financial Reporting by Entities in Reorganization Under the Bankruptcy Code." Executive Committee of the Accounting Standards Division of the American Institute of Certified Public Accountants, 1990.

18 CHAPTER

AN INTRODUCTION TO ACCOUNTING FOR STATE AND LOCAL GOVERNMENTAL UNITS

Have you ever examined a set of financial statements for the city where you live, or have you wondered how your donation to the Salvation Army is accounted for? The preceding 17 chapters of this book have highlighted issues affecting the accounting and financial reporting practices of commercial business organizations. Other organizations exist whose composition or operations differ to some extent from those of the commercial business organizations with which you have become most familiar as an accounting student. For example, governmental units, not-for-profit organizations, colleges and universities, and some health care entities are deemed different enough to warrant the establishment of accounting standards for their specific use. In fact, generally accepted accounting principles of state and local governments are established by the **Governmental Accounting Standards Board (GASB)** under the auspices of the Financial Accounting Foundation. As you will recall, GAAP for businesses and other nongovernment (essentially, private not-for-profit) organizations are established by the GASB's sister organization, the Financial Accounting Standards Board.

This chapter provides an overview of fund accounting and financial reporting for state and local governmental units under *GASB Statement No. 34.* Chapters 19 and 20 illustrate fund accounting practices for specific funds of a local governmental entity. Chapter 21 provides an introduction to accounting principles and reporting practices for not-for-profit organizations.

■ ■ ■

HISTORICAL DEVELOPMENT OF ACCOUNTING PRINCIPLES FOR STATE AND LOCAL GOVERNMENTAL UNITS

LEARNING OBJECTIVE 1

According to the U.S. Census Bureau's 2002 *Census of Governments,* there are more than 87,000 general and special-purpose governmental entities in the United States. A governmental entity is generally created for the administration of public affairs and has one or more of the following characteristics:[1]

- Popular election of officers or appointment (or approval) of a controlling majority of the members of the organization's governing body by officials of one or more state or local governments
- The potential for unilateral dissolution by a government with the net assets reverting to a government
- The power to enact or enforce a tax

---

[1] *AICPA Audit and Accounting Guide; Audits of State and Local Governments* (*GASB 34* edition), 2003, page 1.

LEARNING OBJECTIVES

1 Learn about the historical development of accounting principles for state and local governmental units.

2 Understand the need for fund accounting and its basic premises.

3 Perform transaction analysis using proprietary and governmental accounting models.

4 Recognize various fund categories, as well as their measurement focus and basis of accounting.

5 Review basic governmental accounting principles.

6 Learn about the contents of a governmental entity's comprehensive annual financial report under GASB 34.

An organization may also be classified as a governmental entity if it possesses the ability to issue debt that is exempt from federal taxation.

With the exception of the federal government, state and local governmental units such as the State of Maine, New York City, and the City of Golden, Colorado, constitute the largest single category of nonprofit organizations in terms of the dollar volume of annual expenditures. Since 1984, the primary source of accounting principles for states, cities, counties, towns, villages, school districts, special districts and authorities, and other local governmental entities has been the statements and interpretations of the GASB. Before 1984, the most important continuous source of accounting principles for state and local governmental units was the Municipal Finance Officers Association (MFOA) and its committees on governmental accounting.[2] The MFOA's National Committee on Governmental Accounting issued *Municipal Accounting and Auditing* in 1951 and *Governmental Accounting, Auditing, and Financial Reporting (GAAFR)* in 1968. These resources constituted the most complete frameworks of accounting principles specific to governmental units, and they provided standards for preparing and evaluating the financial reports of governmental units. In 1974 the AICPA issued its industry audit guide, *Audits of State and Local Governmental Units*, in which it noted that *GAAFR*'s accounting and reporting principles constituted GAAP except when they were modified by the audit guide. The AICPA's endorsement was important to the *GAAFR*'s authority and general acceptance by preparers, auditors, and users of governmental financial statements.

The AICPA's audit guide prompted the 1980 revision of *GAAFR* to update and clarify governmental accounting and financial reporting principles and to incorporate pertinent aspects of the audit guide. The MFOA established a new committee, the National Council on Governmental Accounting (NCGA), to develop the *GAAFR* restatement. As part of this project, the NCGA issued *Governmental Accounting and Financial Reporting Principles, Statement No. 1* (NCGA1) in 1979. The following year, a new *GAAFR* was issued as a comprehensive volume to explain and illustrate the principles of NCGA1. Shortly thereafter, the AICPA issued *Statement of Position 80-2*, which amended *Audits of State and Local Governmental Units* to recognize the principles of NCGA1 as generally accepted accounting principles.

The Governmental Accounting Standards Board

Although the NCGA was successful in developing and documenting governmental accounting principles, it was criticized for its lack of independence (due to its MFOA sponsorship) and slow progress. Thus, in 1984, the Financial Accounting Foundation (which also oversees the FASB) formed the Governmental Accounting Standards Board to establish and improve standards for governmental accounting and financial reporting. Financial Accounting Foundation trustees appoint one full-time chair and six part-time members to serve on the board.

In July 1984, GASB issued *GASB Statement No. 1*, "Authoritative Status of NCGA Pronouncements and AICPA Industry Audit Guide," designating all NCGA statements and interpretations issued and currently in effect as "generally accepted accounting principles" until changed or superseded.

The GASB in 1985 integrated all effective accounting and reporting standards into one publication called *Codification of Governmental Accounting and Financial Reporting Standards*. The *Codification* is revised annually to reflect all current GASB official pronouncements. In 1986, the AICPA council declared that Rule 203 of its Rules of Conduct applies to the GASB's pronouncements. Therefore, those pronouncements constitute GAAP for governments. At this writing, the GASB has issued 46 statements of standards and six interpretations setting forth governmental accounting and reporting requirements. The GASB issues concept statements, technical bulletins, implementation guides, and user guides as well.

GAAP Hierarchy for State and Local Governmental Entities

During the first five years of the GASB's existence, discussions arose about the jurisdiction of the GASB and FASB. In 1990 the Financial Accounting Foundation and constituents of the two boards agreed on a jurisdictional formula. The resulting agreement, which is reflected in the AICPA's 1991

---

[2] The Municipal Finance Officers Association was renamed the Government Finance Officers Association in 1985.

Statement on Auditing Standards No. 69, addressed the potential overlap between the two bodies by identifying the relative authoritative strength of available resources. For state and local governments, in particular, GAAP guidelines include the following, listed in descending order of authority:[3]

1. *GASB statements and interpretations.* This category also includes AICPA and FASB pronouncements made applicable to state and local governments by a GASB statement or interpretation.

2. *GASB technical bulletins.* This category also includes AICPA industry audit and accounting guides and statements of position if specifically made applicable to state and local governments by the AICPA and cleared by the GASB.

3. *Consensus positions* of GASB's Emerging Issues Task Force (EITF) and AICPA practice bulletins if specifically made applicable to state and local governments by the AICPA and cleared by the GASB. (No GASB EITF exists currently.)

4. *Implementation guides* published by the GASB staff and industry practices that are widely recognized and prevalent in state and local government.

5. *Other accounting literature* (including FASB standards not made applicable to governments by a GASB standard).

Thus, when addressing an accounting issue, governmental financial statement preparers should first look to GASB statements and interpretations, followed by GASB technical bulletins, and so on. From a practical standpoint, *SAS 69* requires independent auditors who audit governmental entities to express an opinion about whether the auditee has complied with GASB pronouncements. Bond rating agencies consider the audit opinion when assessing a governmental entity's rating for a municipal bond offering, which provides further incentive for compliance with GASB standards.

OVERVIEW OF BASIC GOVERNMENTAL ACCOUNTING MODELS AND PRINCIPLES

LEARNING OBJECTIVE 2

Governmental accounting and financial reporting differ from corporate accounting and financial reporting. The primary reasons for the differences are that governments lack a profit motive and must focus on demonstrating accountability to the public and governmental authorities. Governments focus on their continuing ability to provide and fund goods and services, rather than on measures of income. In doing so, they must simultaneously utilize two bases of accounting and two measurement focuses. In this section, you will be introduced to some of the unique aspects of governmental accounting. This discussion continues in Chapters 19 and 20 .

State and local governmental units engage in both business-type activities and general governmental activities. **Business-type activities** provide services to users for fees that are intended to recover all, or at least the primary portion, of the costs of providing the services. Some of these activities provide services to the constituency, such as water and sewer services, electric service, golf courses, public docks and wharves, and transit systems. Others provide services to departments or agencies within the government, such as central motor pools, self-insurance activities, and central printing and data processing services.

General governmental activities provide goods and services to citizens without regard to their ability to pay. The level of goods and services provided is mandated by the citizens through their elected officials or is determined by persuasion from a higher level of government. General governmental activities (police and fire protection, road maintenance) are usually financed by taxes or intergovernmental grants and subsidies, and there may be no relationship between the people receiving the services and those paying for them (for example, free immunizations provided to children of low-income families). Limited governmental resources are allocated by establishing fixed dollar budgets and legally restricting the use of resources to various general governmental projects and programs. For example, the City of Portland, Maine, may levy taxes to finance the construction of a new school, the State of Montana may provide monies to finance a drug

---

[3] *Statement on Auditing Standards No. 69.* "The Meaning of *Present Fairly in Conformity with Generally Accepted Accounting Principles* in the Independent Auditor's Report," Auditing Standards Board.

prevention program at local levels, or Orange County, California, may borrow resources to finance a convention center addition. In each of these cases, the resources collected are formally restricted for a specific purpose. Expenditures beyond the allocated limits must be approved by the appropriate governmental bodies.

Because general governmental activities and business-type activities constitute two different models of financing and providing services, governments are said to have a dual nature. Furthermore, the existence of restrictions on most governmental resources is the primary reason for fund accounting, a major feature of governmental accounting that helps governments demonstrate compliance with resource restrictions.

Fund accounting supports the practice of restricting financial resource usage to specific purposes as a means of controlling governmental operations, and it also accommodates the differing accounting bases that general governmental activities and business-type activities use for resource allocation. It is a system that requires multiple accounting entities, called funds, for a single government. Governments use an individual fund to account for a certain business-type activity or a certain subset of general governmental financial resources that are set aside for a certain purpose or purposes. Indeed, not only are funds separate accounting entities, but they also use different accounting models for business-type activities and general governmental activities. Thus, just as governments have a dual nature, they also have dual accounting models.

Fund Definition and Categories

GASB defines a fund as

> ... a fiscal and accounting entity with a self-balancing set of accounts recording cash and other financial resources, together with all related liabilities and residual equities or balances, and changes therein, which are segregated for the purpose of carrying on specific activities or attaining certain objectives in accordance with special regulations, restrictions, or limitations.[4]

Note that because a fund is an accounting entity, each fund has the following:

- Its own accounting equation
- Its own journals, ledgers, and other accounting records needed to account for the effects of external transactions or interfund activities on the net assets/activities accounted for in the fund
- Financial statements that report on the fund itself

Business-type activities are accounted for in a category of funds called **proprietary funds**. General governmental activities are accounted for in **governmental funds**. There are two types of proprietary funds and five types of governmental funds. Fortunately, accounting for each of the two types of proprietary funds is quite similar, and accounting for each of the five types of governmental funds is also quite similar. Thus, once you learn to account for one type of proprietary fund, you will know most of what is needed to account for all other proprietary funds. Likewise, once you can account for one type of governmental fund, you know most of what is needed to account for all governmental funds.

A third category of funds is the **fiduciary** or **trust and agency funds.** Most transactions or interfund activities within funds in this category are accounted for like proprietary activities. Hence, learning how to account for proprietary funds enables one to account for most fiduciary funds as well. The following sections focus on accounting for proprietary funds and governmental funds, and they begin to discuss the various models of accounting.

The Proprietary Fund Accounting Model

The most effective way to understand the nature and working of funds is to understand the basic accounting model or accounting equation. Proprietary funds are explained first because accounting for a proprietary fund is very similar to accounting for a commercial business. In fact, the GASB requires governments to apply a substantial portion of the FASB's standards to proprietary funds.

---

[4] *GASB Codification* Section 1100.102.

The accounting equation for a proprietary fund is the same as that for a business:

Current assets + Noncurrent assets − Current liabilities − Noncurrent liabilities = Net assets

With the exception of the term *net assets*, which is used to represent fund equity, the same accounting equation is used for businesses and proprietary funds. Proprietary funds report revenues and expenses using the accrual basis of accounting, and the measurement focus is on economic resources. Because most proprietary fund transactions are accounted for and reported in the same manner as commercial businesses, your business accounting background is directly applicable to proprietary fund accounting. The transactions and events that are unique to governments or that are accounted for differently from a commercial business enterprise are the focus of much of the discussion of proprietary funds in Chapter 20.

The Governmental Fund Accounting Model

Accounting for general governmental activities (for example, public safety, general administration, and the judicial system) differs from the accounting for business-type activities. Governmental funds, in their purest and simplest form, are essentially working capital entities. The accounting equation for a governmental fund is:

Current assets − Current liabilities = Fund balance

The measurement focus of governmental funds is current financial resources. Although this equation becomes complicated by practical considerations, it is important to continue to think of governmental funds as working capital entities, which focus on current assets and current liabilities, even as you address more-advanced issues. In fact, governmental funds generally record **expenditures** to reflect the use of governmental fund working capital, instead of traditional "expenses." Expenditures normally represent the disbursement of working capital funds during a period, whether or not consumption of resources occurs.

Obviously, the governmental funds are not adequate to account for all the assets and liabilities of general governmental activities. When comparing the proprietary and governmental fund models, note that noncurrent assets (for example, fixed assets) and long-term liabilities are excluded from the governmental fund equation. General governmental activities, however, require significant investments in fixed assets, and governments commonly incur large debt obligations associated with general governmental operations. General governmental fixed assets (that is, all fixed assets except those of specific proprietary or similar fiduciary funds) are referred to as *general fixed assets*. Although governments do not account for and record these fixed assets and their depreciation within the governmental funds or governmental fund statements, they do maintain fixed asset records. The general fixed assets and related depreciation are reflected in governmentwide financial statements, which are discussed later in the chapter.

General governmental long-term liabilities (that is, all governmental long-term liabilities except those of specific proprietary or similar fiduciary funds) are referred to as *general long-term debt*. These long-term liabilities include bonds, notes, warrants, claims and judgments, unfunded pension obligations, and accumulated vacation and sick leave that will be paid with general governmental resources. As in the accounting for general fixed assets, governments do not account for and record long-term liabilities within the governmental funds or governmental fund statements. Again, debt records are maintained, and general long-term debt is reflected in governmentwide financial statements, which are discussed later in the chapter.

Although the governmental fund model has never included noncurrent assets and liabilities, general fixed assets and general long-term debt have been historically reported in governmental-entity financial statements within account groups called the *general fixed asset account group* and the *general long-term debt account group*. GASB Statement No. 34, issued in 1999, eliminated these account groups, but it requires inclusion of these noncurrent items in governmentwide financial statements. Many governmental entities may accomplish the recordkeeping requirements associated with the noncurrent items through maintenance of the account groups; however, in name, they no longer exist.

Applying the Models—Transaction Analysis

To solidify your understanding of the proprietary (or business-type activity) fund accounting model and the governmental fund accounting model, consider the effects of several transactions on each of those models. The various types of governmental and proprietary funds are discussed later.

EXHIBIT 18-1

Transaction Analysis—Only Working Capital Accounts Affected

Proprietary Fund	Business-Type Activity				Governmental Fund	General Governmental Activity			
	No. 1	No. 2	No. 3	No. 4		No. 1	No. 2	No. 3	No. 4
Current assets		+2,500	+30,000		Current assets		+2,500	+30,000	
Noncurrent assets									
Current liabilities	+5,000		+30,000	+900	Current liabilities	+5,000		+30,000	+900
Noncurrent liabilities									
Net assets	−5,000	+2,500		−900	Fund balance	−5,000	+2,500		−900

Some transactions have essentially the same impact on a proprietary fund as they would on a governmental fund. This is true for most events that affect only working capital accounts. Consider the analysis of the following four transactions in Exhibit 18-1.

Transactions

1. Incurred salary cost of $5,000.
2. Charges for services rendered, $2,500, were billed and collected immediately.
3. Borrowed $30,000 on a one-year, 6% note six months before year-end.
4. Year-end accrual of interest on the note.

Note that the analysis is identical except that net increases and decreases in proprietary fund asset and liability accounts affect net assets, whereas net increases and decreases in governmental fund assets and liabilities affect fund balance. We would report transaction 1 as an *expense* of $5,000 in a proprietary fund and as an *expenditure* of $5,000 in a governmental fund. We would report transaction 2 as revenue of $2,500 in each case. Transaction 3 does not affect the operating statement of either a proprietary fund or a governmental fund. We would report transaction 4 as interest expense of $900 in a proprietary fund and as $900 of interest expenditures in a governmental fund.

In many other cases, identical transactions impact proprietary and governmental funds differently. This is particularly true for transactions that relate to long-term liabilities or fixed assets. The full effects of such transactions related to business-type activities are accounted for completely within a proprietary fund. The same transaction involving general governmental activity is handled quite differently, because governmental funds focus on current financial resources and are not equipped to record noncurrent assets and liabilities. Therefore, we make memorandum entries in fixed asset or long-term debt records to accommodate subsequent reporting of these items as appropriate within the financial statements. Consider the analysis of the following four transactions in Exhibit 18-2.

EXHIBIT 18-2

Transaction Analysis—Non–Working Capital Accounts Affected

Proprietary Fund	Business-Type Activity				Governmental Fund	General Governmental Activity			
	No. 5	No. 6	No. 7	No. 8		No. 5	No. 6	No. 7	No. 8
Current assets	+15,000	−2,800	+1,000		Current assets	+15,000	−2,800	+1,000	
Noncurrent assets		+2,800	−1,200 (Book value)	−875					
Current liabilities					Current liabilities				
Noncurrent liabilities	+15,000								
Net assets			−200	−875	Fund balance	+15,000	−2,800	+1,000	

Transactions

5. Borrowed $15,000 by issuing a three-year note.
6. Purchased computer equipment costing $2,800 for cash.
7. Sold a truck for $1,000. It was originally purchased three years ago for $18,000, has an estimated residual value of $1,200, and is fully depreciated.
8. Computed depreciation on the computer equipment for the year, $875.

Notice the dramatic difference in the accounting and reporting of these transactions under the two models. Transactions 5 and 6 do not affect a proprietary fund's net assets. However, both of these transactions do affect working capital. Therefore, the fund balance of a governmental fund is affected by both transactions. We report fund balance increases resulting from issuance of general long-term debt as other financing sources in governmental funds and refer to them as "long-term note proceeds, $15,000." Transaction 6 is reported as expenditures for capital outlay in the governmental fund and is capitalized as computer equipment in the proprietary fund.

Transaction 7 affects the proprietary fund net assets and the fund balance in very different ways. A proprietary fund would report a $200 loss on disposal of fixed assets for transaction 7, whereas a governmental fund would report the $1,000 of "proceeds from the sale of fixed assets" as an other financing source, because it has experienced a cash inflow and carried no fixed assets in its fund balance sheet.

Transaction 8 requires that we report $875 of depreciation expense in the proprietary fund operating statement. However, if the computers are general fixed assets, we do not report depreciation in the governmental fund because depreciation is not a use of working capital, and we do not recognize the fixed asset within the fund.

After you have mastered the transaction analysis for a generic proprietary fund and that for a generic governmental fund, two primary elements remain to establish a good understanding of the basic governmental accounting model. The first is to know and distinguish the specific types of funds. The second is to understand the basis of accounting used for each type of fund. In addition, it is helpful to be able to identify and classify interfund transactions, which are simply transactions between two funds.

Proprietary Fund Types

Governments account for their business-type activities in one of two types of proprietary funds: enterprise funds and internal service funds. Some governments do not have any enterprise or internal service funds; other governments have several of each type. The primary distinction between the two types of proprietary funds is that governmental units use **internal service funds** to account for activities operated and financed on a business-type basis that provide goods or services either solely or almost solely to *internal customers,* that is, other departments or agencies of the government. Governments use **enterprise funds** to account for business-type activities that serve primarily *outside customers,* typically the public. Enterprise fund activities often provide services to internal customers as well, but those customers are not the predominant customers.

Exhibit 18-3 contains the formal definitions of the specific fund types. Common examples of activities accounted for in internal service funds include centralized data processing services, central motor pools and garages, centralized risk financing activities, and central inventory stores. Activities commonly accounted for in enterprise funds include public (government-owned) gas and electric utilities, water and sewer departments, government trash and garbage services, parking garages, civic centers, toll roads, mass transit services, and golf courses.

Notice how the internal service fund definition requires departments or agencies that provide goods or services to other departments or agencies on a cost-reimbursement basis to use these funds for accounting. A cost-reimbursement basis means that the fee charged is intended to cover the costs (expenses) of providing the good or service, rather than to produce net income. Proprietary funds, which provide goods and services to external parties, are more apt to produce net income. As noted earlier, the key distinction between the two types of proprietary funds is whether they primarily serve the public or external entities or they predominantly serve internal departments and agencies.

Governmental Fund Types

Five types of governmental funds are used to account for general governmental activities. Each is a working capital entity that accounts for only a portion of the general governmental working capital. The difference between these funds, then, is the purpose or purposes for which the working capital

EXHIBIT 18-3

**Fund Type
Definitions**

Proprietary Fund Types

■ **Enterprise funds.** Report any activity for which a fee is charged to external users for goods and services. Activities are required to be reported as enterprise funds if any of the following criteria are met: (a) the activity is financed with debt that is secured solely by a pledge of the net revenues from fees and charges of the activity; (b) laws and regulations require that the activity's costs of providing services, including capital costs (such as depreciation or debt service), be recovered with fees and charges, rather than with taxes or similar revenues; or (c) the pricing policies of the activity establish fees and charges designed to recover its costs, including capital costs (such as depreciation or debt service).

■ **Internal service funds.** Report any activity that provides goods or services to other funds, departments, or agencies of the primary government and its component units, or to other governments, on a cost-reimbursement basis. Internal service funds should be used only if the reporting government is the predominant participant in the activity.

Governmental Fund Types

■ **Special revenue funds.** Account for the proceeds of specific revenue sources (other than trusts for individuals, private organizations, or other governments or for major capital projects) that are legally restricted to expenditure for specified purposes.

■ **Permanent funds.** Report resources that are legally restricted to the extent that only earnings, and not principal, may be used for purposes that support the reporting government's programs—that is, for the benefit of the government or its citizenry.

■ **Capital projects funds.** Account for financial resources to be used for the acquisition or construction of major capital facilities (other than those financed by proprietary funds or in trust funds for individuals, private organizations, or other governments).

■ **Debt service funds.** Account for the accumulation of resources for, and the payment of, general long-term debt principal and interest.

■ **General fund.** Accounts for all financial resources except those required to be accounted for in another fund.

Fiduciary Fund Types

■ **Trust and agency funds.** Report assets held in a trustee capacity for others that therefore cannot be used to support the government's own programs. The fiduciary fund category includes (a) pension (and other employee benefit) trust funds, (b) investment trust funds, (c) private-purpose trust funds, and (d) agency funds.

---

accounted for in each of them may or must be used. **Special revenue funds** account for general governmental financial resources restricted for specific purposes. **Permanent funds** report resources whose use is permanently restricted, but whose earnings are expendable for the benefit of the government or its citizens. A **capital projects fund** accounts for resources to be used to construct or acquire a major general governmental fixed asset and the related current liabilities. A **debt service fund** accounts for resources to be used to pay principal, interest, and related charges on general long-term debt. Finally, the **general fund** accounts for working capital available for general use. A government has only one general fund, but it may have any number of each of the other fund types. Recall that each of these governmental funds has the same accounting equation that was discussed and illustrated earlier for a generic governmental fund. The only added complexity is that we must understand which governmental fund is affected in order to account for general governmental activities properly.

Fiduciary (Trust and Agency) Fund Types

As indicated in Exhibit 18-3, trust and agency funds include three types of trust funds as well as agency funds. Note that all fiduciary funds contain resources held for the benefit of parties other than the government itself. **Pension trust funds** account for government pension plans, if the government acts as a trustee. **Investment trust funds** account for the external portion of investment pools reported by the sponsoring government. **Private-purpose trust funds** report all other trust arrangements whose resources provide benefits to parties outside the government.

Agency funds are essentially "receive-hold-remit" or "bill-collect-hold-remit" accountability devices, which account for resources a government is holding as an agent on behalf of parties outside the government. The accounting equation for an agency fund is:

$$\text{Assets} = \text{Liabilities}$$

Every asset received by an agency fund results in a corresponding increase in liabilities or a decrease in another asset. Agency funds have no equity or fund balance and, therefore, have no operations to report. No revenues, expenditures or expenses, or transfers are reported in an agency fund.

Governmental Fund		Accounting Equation		
No.	Fund	Current Assets	Current Liabilities	Fund Balance
1	Capital projects	+3,030,000		+3,030,000
2a	Capital projects	−30,000		−30,000
2b	Debt service	+30,000		+30,000
3	Capital projects	−12,500		−12,500
4	Special revenue	+6,000		+6,000
5	General	−4,500	+500	−5,000
6	General	+7,500	+7,500	

Applying the Model Using Specific Funds

A useful way to solidify your understanding of the funds and the model at this point is to expand your knowledge using transactions. Exhibit 18-4 analyzes the following general governmental transactions.

Transactions

1. Issued general obligation bonds, par value of $3,000,000, at 101 to finance construction of a government office building.
2. Transferred the premium on the bonds to the fund used to account for payment of principal and interest on the bonds.
3. Incurred and paid construction costs of $12,500 on the building.
4. Levied and collected sales taxes restricted to use for economic development, $6,000.
5. Paid general governmental employees' salaries, $4,500. Another $500 of salaries accrued but has not been paid.
6. Borrowed $7,500 on a six-month note to finance general operating costs of the government.

Note that the transaction analysis is the same as for general governmental activities in the previous section on applying the model, except that the exhibit identifies the specific governmental fund affected by each transaction. Transaction 2 illustrates a transfer of resources between funds. The premium amount transferred to the debt service fund will be held for the purpose of debt repayment. The premium amount, which represents an increase to fund balance in the debt service fund, is recognized as an "other financing source—nonreciprocal transfer from the capital projects fund." The premium is termed an "other financing source" to distinguish it from a revenue, and it is non-reciprocal because it will not be repaid to the capital projects fund.

Bases of Accounting

Key aspects of the proprietary fund and governmental fund models are the *basis of accounting* and *measurement focus* used for each. Consistent with having fundamentally different accounting equations and models, governmental and proprietary funds use different bases of accounting in measuring financial position and operating results. The GASB specifies when the accrual and modified accrual bases of accounting are to be used.

In essence, the *accrual basis* refers to recognition of revenues and expenses as in business accounting. It follows an "economic resources" measurement focus, whereby all economic resources, whether current or noncurrent, are reported. We report proprietary funds using the accrual basis of accounting.

The *modified accrual basis* refers to recognition of revenues when resources become available to meet current obligations and recognition of expenditures when incurred. The modified accrual basis of accounting is consistent with a "flow of current financial resources" measurement focus, whereby funds report on current resources and current obligations. In general, we report governmental funds using the modified accrual basis of accounting, which is consistent with the governmental model introduced earlier in the chapter. However, a new financial reporting model, described in the following section, also requires governmentwide financial statements, which present governmental and proprietary funds together on the accrual basis of accounting.

You must understand the differences between the accrual basis of accounting and the modified accrual basis of accounting. We always report proprietary (or business-type) funds on the accrual basis of accounting, whereas we report governmental funds using the modified accrual basis of accounting in the fund statements and the accrual basis of accounting in the governmentwide statements. Chapter 19 focuses on governmental funds and governmental fund financial statements. We record governmental fund transactions using the modified accrual basis of accounting. Later, when we prepare the governmentwide statements, we make adjustments to reflect governmental fund activities under the accrual basis of accounting.[5] Chapter 20 discusses the accounting and financial reporting for proprietary and fiduciary funds in detail.

Revenue Recognition

Governmental revenue sources are varied and include taxes, grant receipts, and collections of user fees and fines. Revenue recognition within governmental entities is determined by the nature of the underlying transaction. *GASB Statement No. 33,* "Accounting and Financial Reporting for Nonexchange Transactions," characterizes revenue transactions as (1) exchange (and exchange-like) transactions or (2) nonexchange transactions. *Exchange transactions* are those "in which each party receives and gives up essentially equal values."[6] *Nonexchange transactions* are those "in which a government gives (or receives) value without directly receiving (or giving) equal value in exchange." Many of the transactions in governmental funds are nonexchange in nature, because general governmental activities often address the needs of the public and are funded by taxpayers who generally do not receive benefits in direct relation to their tax payments.

Exhibit 18-5 provides an overview of the four classifications of nonexchange transactions identified in *GASB Statement No. 33* (derived tax revenues, imposed nonexchange revenues, government-mandated nonexchange transactions, and voluntary nonexchange transactions) and the criteria that must be met prior to revenue and asset recognition. Derived tax revenues include sales and income taxes, because they are assessed based on a value that a taxpayer spends or earns. Imposed nonexchange revenues include property taxes. Although the tax is assessed based on property value, the governmental resources available to the taxpayer (police and fire protection) are not necessarily relative to the amount paid. Government-mandated and voluntary nonexchange transactions, which include grant funds and donations, do not require an equal exchange by the governmental entity.

In general, a transaction should be substantially complete prior to revenue recognition. Recall, however, that the modified accrual basis of accounting used for governmental funds requires that revenues be objectively measurable and "available" in order to be recognized. To be available, the revenues must be "collectible within the current period or soon enough thereafter to pay liabilities of the current period."[7] Recognition of revenues that do not meet these "available" criteria must be *deferred* (recorded as "deferred revenues," a liability) initially. Then revenues are recognized when "available." (Thus, revenues may be recognized later in governmental funds than in proprietary funds.)

The criterion of being collected "soon enough" after the current period to pay liabilities for current expenditures is not defined in the *GASB Codification*. However, with respect to property tax revenue recognition, the *Codification* limits this period to not more than 60 days after the end of the fiscal year. Most government accountants extend this "not more than 60 days" limitation to all other governmental fund revenues as well. Governments are required to disclose their revenue recognition policies in the notes to the financial statements.

The GASB established an exception to the 60-day rule of thumb in *GASB Statement No. 31,* "Accounting and Financial Reporting for Certain Investments and for External Investment Pools." This statement requires most investments to be reported at their fair value. Investment income of each fund of a government, therefore, is increased or decreased by the net change in the fair value of investments. Governments report income as a single line item in the financial statements, with the effect of the change in fair value disclosed in the notes, or they present details in the financial statements as follows:

---

[5] Governments may choose to record governmental fund transactions under the accrual basis of accounting and later adjust balances to the modified accrual basis for presentation in fund financial statements. We choose to present the traditional fund accounting approach to accounting for governmental funds, because it will likely be the option selected by most governmental units using their current accounting systems.

[6] *GASB Statement No. 33.*

[7] *GASB Codification*, Section 1600.106.

EXHIBIT 18-5

Recognition Criteria for Nonexchange Transactions

Class of Revenue	Recognition
Derived Tax Revenues Examples: sales taxes, personal and corporate income taxes, motor fuel taxes, and similar taxes on earnings and consumption	*Assets* Period when underlying exchange has occurred or when resources are received, whichever is first. *Revenues* Period when underlying exchange has occurred. (Report advance receipts as deferred revenues.) When modified accrual accounting is used, resources should be "available."
Imposed Nonexchange Revenues Examples: property taxes, most fines and forfeitures	*Assets* Period when an enforceable legal claim has arisen or when resources are received, whichever is first. *Revenues* Period when resources are required to be used or first period that use is permitted (for example, for property taxes, the period for which levied). When modified accrual accounting is used, resources should be "available."
Government-Mandated Nonexchange Transactions Examples: federal government mandates on state and local governments *Voluntary Nonexchange Transactions* Examples: certain grants and entitlements, most donations	*Assets and Liabilities* Period when all eligibility requirements have been met or (for asset recognition) when resources are received, whichever is first. *Revenues and Expenses or Expenditures* Period when all eligibility requirements have been met. (Report advance receipts or payments for use in the following period as deferred revenues or advances, respectively.) However, when a provider precludes the sale, disbursement, or consumption of resources for a specified number of years, until a specified event has occurred, or permanently (for example, permanent and term endowments), report revenues and expenses or expenditures when the resources are received or paid, respectively, and report resulting net assets, equity, or fund balance as restricted. When modified accrual accounting is used, resources should be "available."

Source: GASB Statement 33, p. 48

Interest income	XXX
Net increase (decrease) in fair value of investments	YYY
Total investment income	ZZZ

A final point is that governmental funds recognize revenues on the net revenue approach. These funds recognize revenues net of allowances for uncollectible accounts, rather than at gross amounts earned or levied. Therefore, whereas a proprietary fund that levied charges on customers of $1,000 but expected $10 to prove uncollectible would report revenues of $1,000 and expenses of $10, a governmental fund in a similar scenario would report only the net realizable value, or $990, as revenues.

Expense and Expenditure Recognition

The expenses of a governmental unit are similar to those of a commercial business enterprise. Expenses essentially reflect the cost of assets or services used by an entity, and they are recognized in the period incurred. Expenditures, unique to government accounting, typically reflect the use of governmental fund working capital. Thus, expenditures normally reflect the cost of goods or services acquired during a period, whether or not consumed, and the maturing of general long-term debt principal. With limited exceptions, governmental funds recognize expenditures in the period that the fund liability is incurred.

Recall that under fund accounting, proprietary funds recognize expenses, whereas governmental funds recognize expenditures, based on the modified accrual basis of accounting. However, *GASB Statement No. 34* requires both proprietary funds and governmental funds to report expenses within the governmentwide statements. In fund statements, governmental funds report expenditures, whereas proprietary funds report expenses. Although this may sound confusing, examples in Chapters 19 and 20 should help clarify the difference between expenses and expenditures, as well as their treatment within the financial statements.

Many operating expenses and expenditures occur simultaneously. For instance, the use of electricity results in an expense and an expenditure in the same amount at the same point in time. The same is true for salaries and wages of government employees. For other items, the timing of expense and expenditure recognition differs dramatically. The purchase of a fixed asset that is to be used by a governmental fund over a 10-year period results in a capital outlay *expenditure* in the year of acquisition and no additional expenditures over the next 9 years. The same purchase within a proprietary fund results in a depreciation *expense* each year over the 10-year period of its use, however. Note that a fixed asset acquired by a governmental fund is treated differently within a set of financial statements. In the fund statements, a governmental fund records an expenditure for the full cost of the asset in the year purchased. In the governmentwide statements, an adjustment is made to capitalize and depreciate the same fixed asset. This occurs because of the unique bases of accounting used in the governmentwide and fund financial statements.

Likewise, the government as a whole sometimes incurs liabilities that do not result in governmental fund liabilities being incurred at the same point in time. This may be true for general government claims and judgments, compensated absences, or pension contributions. For example, proceeds of general long-term debt issuances increase both the fund balance and the current assets of the governmental funds, but the liability is not recorded in the fund statements. In the fund statements, the recipient governmental fund will report the fund balance increase as bond issue proceeds, or a similar title, and show it as an other financing source in the statement of revenues, expenditures, and changes in fund balance (a fund statement). Long-term debt appears as a long-term liability within the governmentwide statement of net assets.

The primary exception to recognizing expenditures when a governmental fund incurs a liability relates to interest and principal expenditures on general long-term debt. Governmental funds record these amounts "when due"; however, although they are never required to be reported before the legal due date, it is permissible to accrue such expenditures if (1) they are due early in the next year and (2) the financial resources for their payment have been provided in the current year.

Interfund Activity

Governments use several funds to account for their activities, and numerous transactions between funds, or interfund transactions, occur annually. Examples include sales of services from an enterprise or internal service fund department to other departments, shifts of general fund resources to capital projects funds to cover part of the cost of a capital project, and interfund loans. *GASB Codification*, Section 1800.102, classifies interfund transactions into several types, each of which is reported differently in the financial statements.

Interfund loans are loans that are made by one fund to another and must be repaid. The receivable and payable resulting from an interfund loan appear in the lender and borrower funds. If prompt payment is not expected, the activity may require reclassification as a transfer. Interfund transfers occur when one fund provides resources to another for legally authorized purposes (an operating transfer) or when one fund helps to establish or enhance another (a residual equity transfer). Transfers are either reciprocal or nonreciprocal, depending on whether or not repayment is expected. Governmental funds record transfers as other financing sources/uses, whereas proprietary funds record transfers in a category following nonoperating revenues/expenses. Interfund services provided and used include sales and purchases between funds at approximate external market value. The seller fund records these activities as revenues, whereas the purchasing fund recognizes an expense or expenditure; however, unpaid amounts should be reported as interfund receivables and payables in the fund financial statements. An interfund reimbursement is necessary when an expenditure applicable to one fund is made by a different fund. Reimbursements are not reported in the financial statements.

The Role of the Budget

Because resource use within governments typically must be authorized by laws or ordinances, the role and impact of the budget is dramatically more significant in governments than in business accounting. In fact, every governmental unit is required to adopt a budget document, which is often considered more significant than the financial reports.[8] Governmental accounting systems are required to provide appropriate budgetary control either formally through the use of budgetary

---

[8] *GASB Codification*, Section 1100.111.

accounts (typical in the general fund, special revenue funds, and other governmental funds) or informally through the maintenance of separate budgetary records and comparisons. In addition, a comparison of actual and budgetary amounts is required to be included in the annual operating statements of all governmental funds for which an annual budget has been adopted. (We will illustrate how budgets are used within fund accounting in Chapter 19.)

A **budget** is a plan of financial operation consisting of an estimate of proposed expenditures for a given period and the proposed means of financing them. Ordinarily, the preparation of a budget is the responsibility of the executive branch of government—the mayor, city manager, governor, and so on. Approval of a budget, however, is a legislative responsibility. A legislative body may approve a proposed budget as submitted by the chief executive, or it may amend the executive budget prior to approval. *When approved by the legislative body, the budget for expenditures becomes a spending ordinance that has the force of law. An approved revenue plan also has the force of law,* because it provides the governmental unit with the power to levy taxes, to sell licenses, to charge for services, and so on, in the amount or at the rate approved.

Appropriations are approved or authorized expenditures. They provide legislative control over the expenditure budget prepared by the executive branch. Such control may be in detail, such as when the legislative body makes appropriations for each item included in the budget. The legislative body, however, may approve expenditures (make appropriations) by category (by department, for example) or in total. Line-item approval provides maximum control over the management by the legislative branch because any change in the budget must be approved by the legislative body. If appropriations are made by department, however, managers could allocate more resources to some items within a department (supplies, for example) and less to others (salaries, for example) without legislative approval of the change.

If an appropriation is allocated to a specific time period, it is termed an **allotment.** In other words, the yearly appropriations may be allotted to months or quarters to prevent expenditure of the appropriation too early in the year. Furthermore, allotments may be necessary for coordinating revenues collected with payments for expenditures (that is, managing cash flows).

A current budget is normally for a one-year period, and it includes the operating budget as well as the capital budget for the current period. A **capital budget,** as used here, represents the current portion of a **capital program** (a plan of capital expenditures to be incurred each year over a fixed period of years).

THE FINANCIAL REPORTING ENTITY

Many governments are closely associated with other entities or governmental units, which may or may not be economically dependent on the government. For example, Genesee County, New York, houses a local community college, and your hometown has probably established a public housing authority to provide low-cost housing to residents. When a government has such relationships, the question arises about how (or if) these entities should be reported in the financial statements of the government. *GASB Statement No. 14,* "The Financial Reporting Entity," explains that the financial reporting entity is made up of the primary government and its component units. Each state government and each general-purpose local government (city, town, county, and so on) is a **primary government**, whereas a special-purpose government (a water district, hospital, or transit authority, for example) is a primary government if it has a separately elected governing body, is legally separate, and is fiscally independent of other state or local governments. **Component units** are legally separate organizations for which the primary government is financially accountable. They can also be other organizations for which the nature and significance of their relationship with the primary government are such that their exclusion would result in the reporting entity's statements being misleading or incomplete.

Some component units are so closely related to the primary government that they should be blended with the primary government for financial reporting purposes. Component units that provide services primarily to the public or to other entities use blending only if a voting majority of the primary-government governing body serves on the component-unit governing board and also constitutes a voting majority of that board (for example, the component unit has substantively the same governing body as the primary government). If this strict criterion is not met, the component unit is discretely presented in the reporting entity's financial statements. Discrete presentation requires the presentation of the component unit's financial data in a column or columns separate from the primary government's financial data in the governmentwide statements. Supporting information for the individual component units should be provided in combining statements that follow the fund financial statements or in condensed financial statements included in the notes to the financial statements of the primary government.

GASB Statement No. 39, "Determining Whether Certain Organizations Are Component Units," provides criteria for deciding whether organizations for which the primary government is not financially accountable but with which it maintains significant relationships should be reported as component units. *Statement 39* primarily refers to organizations that raise and hold economic resources for the direct benefit of a governmental unit.

COMPREHENSIVE ANNUAL FINANCIAL REPORT

All state and local governmental units must report their activities to residents and other interested parties. *GASB Codification,* Section 2200.101, states that "Every governmental entity should prepare and publish, as a matter of public record, a *comprehensive annual financial report* (CAFR) that encompasses all funds of the primary government (including its blended component units). The CAFR should also encompass all discretely presented component units of the reporting entity."

In 1999, the GASB issued *GASB Statement No. 34,* "Basic Financial Statement—and Management's Discussion and Analysis—for State and Local Governments" (*GASB 34*), which instituted major changes to the manner in which governmental entities prepare and present their financial statements. *GASB 34* retains traditional fund accounting and fund financial statements; however, it also introduces *governmentwide financial statements,* which are prepared using accrual accounting for all of a government's activities—both governmental and business-type. Prior to *GASB 34,* each of the basic financial statements (referred to as general-purpose financial statements) was prepared using the appropriate fund basis of accounting. For example, governmental fund statements were prepared on the modified accrual basis of accounting, and proprietary fund statements were prepared on the accrual basis of accounting. The combined balance sheet included columns for each fund type, and governmental funds used modified accrual accounting, whereas proprietary funds followed accrual accounting. Under *GASB 34,* the two bases of accounting no longer appear on the same financial statement. Instead, governmental fund activity is converted to the accrual basis of accounting on the combined of *governmentwide* financial statements.

CAFRs contain three major sections (introductory, financial, and statistical) and are considered an entity's "official annual report." Exhibit 18-6 lists the contents of a *GASB 34* CAFR, which are described in detail here.

Introductory Section of a CAFR

The introductory section of a CAFR includes a table of contents, a letter of transmittal, a list of principal officers, and an organizational chart. It might also include copies of awards that were received for financial reporting. The transmittal letter provides an introduction to the financial report, describes management's responsibility for the statements, and outlines significant developments within the entity during the fiscal year. Prior to GASB 34 implementation, transmittal letters were quite extensive, but *GASB 34* requires an in-depth analysis of the entity's economic condition in a new portion of the CAFR's financial section known as the management's discussion and analysis, which is found in the financial section. Thus, transmittal letters are now relatively brief in comparison.

Financial Section

The financial section includes the management's discussion and analysis, the auditor's report, the governmentwide financial statements, and the fund financial statements.

MANAGEMENT'S DISCUSSION AND ANALYSIS (MD&A) The MD&A is a new requirement under *GASB 34.* Considered *required supplementary information*, the MD&A precedes the financial statements and is comparable to the MD&A of a corporate financial statement. Intended to "provide an objective and easily readable analysis of the government's financial activities based on the currently known facts, decisions, or conditions,"[9] the MD&A should include the following:

1. A brief discussion of the basic financial statements, including the relationships of the statements to each other, and the significant differences in the information they provide. This discussion should include analyses that assist readers in understand-

---

[9] *GASB Statement 34,* paragraph 11.

EXHIBIT 18-6

GASB 34 CAFR
Contents

CAFR CONTENTS REQUIRED UNDER *GASB 34*

Introductory Section
Table of contents
Letter of transmittal
List of principal officers
Organization chart

Financial Section
Management's discussion and analysis
Auditor's report
Basic financial statements
  Governmentwide statements

    Statement of net assets (accrual basis)
    Statement of activities (accrual basis)

  Fund financial statements

    Balance sheet—governmental funds (modified accrual basis)
    Statement of revenues, expenditures, and changes in fund balance—governmental funds
      (modified accrual basis)
    Statement of net assets—proprietary funds (accrual basis)
    Statement of revenues, expenses, and changes in net assets—all proprietary and similar trust fund types
      (accrual basis)
    Statement of cash flows—all proprietary and similar trust fund types (accrual basis)
    Statement of fiduciary net assets—fiduciary funds (accrual basis)
    Statement of changes in fiduciary net assets—fiduciary funds (accrual basis)
Notes to the financial statements
Required supplementary information other than MD&A
Combining statements and individual fund statements and schedules
Statistical Section

ing why measurements and results reported in fund financial statements either reinforce information in governmentwide statements or provide additional information.

2. Condensed financial information derived from governmentwide financial statements comparing the current year to the prior year. At a minimum, governments should present the information needed to support their analysis of financial position and results of operations required in 3. below, including these elements:
   a. Total assets, distinguishing between capital and other assets
   b. Total liabilities, distinguishing between long-term liabilities and other liabilities
   c. Total net assets, distinguishing among amounts invested in capital assets, net of related debt; restricted amounts; and unrestricted amounts
   d. Program revenues, by major source
   e. General revenues, by major source
   f. Total revenues
   g. Program expenses, at a minimum by function
   h. Total expenses
   i. Excess (deficiency) before contributions to term and permanent endowments or permanent fund principal, special and extraordinary items, and transfers
   j. Contributions
   k. Special and extraordinary items
   l. Transfers
   m. Change in net assets
   n. Ending net assets

3. An analysis of the government's overall financial position and results of operations to assist users in assessing whether financial position has improved or deteriorated as a result of the year's operations. The analysis should address both governmental and business-type activities as reported in the governmentwide financial statements and should include *reasons* for significant changes from the prior year, not simply the amounts or percentages of change. In addition, important economic factors,

such as changes in the tax or employment bases, that significantly affected operating results for the year should be discussed.

4. An analysis of balances and transactions of individual funds. The analysis should address the reasons for significant changes in fund balances or fund net assets and whether restrictions, commitments, or other limitations significantly affect the availability of fund resources for future use.

5. An analysis of significant variations between original and final budget amounts and between final budget amounts and actual results for the general fund (or its equivalent). The analysis should include any currently known reasons for those variations that are expected to have a significant effect on future services or liquidity.

6. A description of significant capital asset and long-term debt activity during the year, including a discussion of commitments made for capital expenditures, changes in credit ratings, and debt limitations that may affect the financing of planned facilities or services.

7. A discussion by governments that use the modified approach to report some or all of their infrastructure assets.

8. A description of currently known facts, decisions, or conditions that are expected to have a significant effect on financial position (net assets) or results of operations (revenues, expenses, and other changes in net assets).

A sample MD&A appears in the appendix to *GASB Statement No. 34*.

AUDITOR'S REPORT The auditor's report within the financial section of a CAFR indicates that the financial statements are the responsibility of the government's management. It identifies the financial statements that have been audited and expresses an opinion about whether the financial statements are presented in conformity with generally accepted accounting principles. It should also specify the information included within the CAFR that was unaudited.

GOVERNMENTWIDE FINANCIAL STATEMENTS Governmentwide statements were added to the CAFR by *GASB Statement No. 34*. These statements, which consist of the statement of net assets and the statement of activities, provide consolidated information for the government as a whole and introduce the concept of operational accountability to governmental financial reporting. **Operational accountability** measures the extent of a government's success at meeting operating objectives efficiently and effectively and its ability to meet operating objectives in the future.[10]

The governmentwide statements report governmental activities, business-type activities, and discretely presented component units; however, they do not include fiduciary funds. All data are reported on the accrual basis of accounting. Thus, it may be necessary to convert governmental fund balances to the accrual basis of accounting. Chapter 19 examines this conversion process.

The **statement of net assets** reports the difference between assets and liabilities as *net assets,* preferably in the format of assets less liabilities equal net assets.[11] The statement lists both assets and liabilities in terms of liquidity and categorizes net assets as invested in capital assets, net of related debt, restricted, and unrestricted.[12] The statement of net assets contains columns for governmental activities, business-type activities, totals of the primary government, and component unit totals, if applicable. Columns for reporting entity totals and prior-year comparative data are optional. The governmental activity column aggregates all general governmental assets and liabilities, including fixed assets and general long-term debt, from the general, special revenue, permanent, debt service, and capital projects funds. This column also includes most internal service fund assets and liabilities, because general governmental departments are typically the largest customers of internal service funds. Exhibit 18-7 presents the statement of net assets for the City of Golden, Colorado.

The **statement of activities** presents governmental and proprietary fund revenues and expenses on the same statement using full accrual accounting. The format, which appears quite complex at first glance, can be viewed as two distinct parts. The upper portion focuses on costs of services and reports to taxpayers both the total expenses and the net expenses of the government by functional

---

[10] *GASB Statement No. 34*, page 78.

[11] *GASB Statement No. 34*, page 199.

[12] *GASB Statement No. 46* provides additional guidance regarding restricted net asset classification.

EXHIBIT 18-7

Statement of Net Assets

CITY OF GOLDEN, COLORADO, STATEMENT OF NET ASSETS, DECEMBER 31, 2003

	Governmental Activities	Business-Type Activities	Totals 2003	Totals 2002	Component Unit
Assets					
Cash and investments	$13,079,286	$ 9,692,717	$ 22,772,003	$ 27,413,804	$ 445,871
Property taxes receivable	3,613,000	—	3,613,000	3,334,000	600,000
Accounts receivable	2,521,597	859,898	3,381,495	3,508,726	7,565
Inventory	—	44,459	44.459	12,333	—
Restricted cash and investments	2,880,380	494,119	3,374,499	3,323,119	—
Bond issuance costs					
(net of amortization)	397,762	261,306	659,068	701,120	—
Capital assets					
(net of accumulated depreciation)	43,072,919	82,008,137	125,081,056	109,527,451	1,642,747
Total assets	$65,564,944	$93,360,636	$158,925,580	$147,820,553	$2,696,183
Liabilities					
Accounts payable	$ 1,947,963	$ 2,512,589	$ 4,460,552	$ 3,573,007	$ 2,076
Accrued liabilities	821,787	220,169	1,041,956	1,806,455	87,602
Claims payable	319,525	—	319,525	230,000	—
Deferred property taxes	3,613,000	—	3,613,000	3,334,000	600,000
Deferred revenue	182,785	226,419	409,204	692,805	—
Noncurrent liabilities					
Due within one year	1,022,000	580,000	1,602,000	1,786,254	65,690
Due in more than one year	28,178,199	16,618,844	44,797,043	39,677,691	1,845,677
Total liabilities	36,085,259	20,158,021	56,243,280	51,100,212	2,601,045
Net Assets					
Invested in capital assets, net of related debt	14,962,466	65,070,599	80,033,065	69,258,745	235,973
Restricted for					
Parks & recreation	737,071	—	737,071	771,441	—
Capital projects	6,608,014	—	6,608,014	9,243,347	—
Cemetery perpetual care (nonexpendable)	820,046	—	820,046	771,020	—
Cemetery perpetual care (expendable)	352,927	—	352,927	378,113	—
Emergency reserves	690,000	—	690,000	710,000	—
Unrestricted	5,309,161	8,132,016	13,441,177	15,587,675	(140,835)
Total net assets	$29,479,685	$73,202,615	$102,682,300	$ 96,720,341	$ 95,138

Source: City of Golden, Colorado, comprehensive annual financial report, 2003.

area or program. The lower portion of the statement displays how the net program expenses incurred during the year compared with general revenues. For example, during 2003, $338,644 of expenses may have been incurred for cemetery operations in Golden, while only $255,855 in revenues were recognized in conjunction with the cemetery. Thus, this functional area (the cemetery) was not totally self-financed and had a net expense of $82,789 for the year. The $82,789 net expense is subsidized by general governmental revenues, such as taxes or grant receipts. Note that this does not necessarily reflect negatively on the cemetery or its operations, because a cemetery is a necessary institution that need not be self-supportive. The statement simply informs taxpayers of the governmental functions or activities that are partially supported by taxes.

The complete format of the statement of activities for the City of Golden, Colorado, appears in Exhibit 18-8. In the upper portion of the statement, program revenues are deducted from the expenses incurred for the function to derive the net expenses or revenues and changes in net assets for that function. *Program revenues* are defined as being "directly from the program itself or from parties outside the reporting government's constituency." They are categorized as charges for services, (program-specific) operating grants and contributions, or (program-specific) capital grants and contributions within the statement's columns. For example, revenues from a public utility company or grants for public transportation are program revenues. All revenues other than program revenues are considered *general revenues*. General revenues, which include all taxes (even those restricted to programs), grants and investment income not considered program revenue, contributions to endowments, special and extraordinary items, and transfer, are reported in the lower section. Note that governmental activities and business-type activities are distinguished both in the presentation of functional classifications (the rows) and in the presentation of net expenses or revenues and changes in net assets (the columns).

FUND FINANCIAL STATEMENTS Fund financial statements focus on fiscal accountability rather than operational accountability. **Fiscal accountability** is the responsibility of a government to demonstrate

EXHIBIT 18-8

Statement of
Activities

CITY OF GOLDEN, COLORADO, STATEMENT OF ACTIVITIES FOR THE YEAR ENDED DECEMBER 31, 2003

Functions/Programs	Expenses	Charges for Services	Operating Grants and Contributions	Capital Grants and Contributions
		Program Revenues		
Primary Government				
Governmental activities				
General government	$ 3,576,208	$ 1,047,572	$ 24,000	$ —
Planning & economic development	1,935,502	146,107	—	—
Police	4,887,874	240,650	60,312	—
Fire	1,360,971	345,671	18,637	—
Public works	4,073,730	30,916	460,713	703,629
Parks and recreation	2,047,281	439,884	—	979,866
Interest on long-term debt	1,504,351	—		
Total governmental activities	19,385,917	2,250,800	563,662	1,683,495
Business-type activities				
Water	3,723,526	3,461,268	—	663,048
Wastewater	1,625,174	1,610,462	—	—
Drainage	543,753	752,735	—	915,783
Fossil Trace Golf Course	1,408,707	1,068,406	—	—
Splash Aquatic Park	416,100	285,072	—	—
Community center	1,689,337	1,201,844	—	—
Cemetery operations	338,644	255,855	—	—
Rooney Road Sports Complex	—	—	—	310,420
Total business-type activities	9,745,241	8,635,642	—	1,889,251
Total primary government	$29,131,158	$10,886,442	$563,662	$3,572,746
Component Unit				
Golden Urban Renewal Authority	$ 843,873	$ —	$ —	$ —

General Revenues
Taxes
  Property
  Sales and use
  Other
Grants and contributions not restricted to specific programs
Investment income
Miscellaneous
Gain (loss) on sale of capital assets
Transfers
          Total general revenues and transfers

          Change in net assets

Net assets, beginning

Net assets, ending

Source: City of Golden, Colorado, comprehensive annual financial report, 2003.

compliance with public decisions regarding the use of financial resources.[13] The individual fund statements include the following: balance sheet—governmental funds; statement of revenues, expenditures, and changes in fund balance—governmental funds; statement of net assets—proprietary funds; statement of revenues, expenses, and changes in net assets—all proprietary and similar trust fund types (if applicable); statement of cash flows—all proprietary and similar trust fund types (if applicable); statement of fiduciary net assets—fiduciary funds; and statement of changes in fiduciary net assets—fiduciary funds. Exhibits 18-9 through 18-13 present illustrative statements for the City of Golden, Colorado. (Fiduciary fund statements are shown in Chapter 20.)

EXHIBIT 18-8

(continued)

		Net (Expense) Revenue and Changes in Net Assets		
Governmental Activities	Business-Type Activities	Totals 2003	2002	Component Unit
$ (2,504,636)	$ —	$ (2,504,636)	$ (2,710,603)	$ —
(1,789,395)	—	(1,789,395)	(2,132,175)	—
(4,586,912)	—	(4,586,912)	(4,235,046)	—
(996,663)	—	(996,663)	(837,688)	—
(2,878,472)	—	(2,878,472)	(2,620,540)	—
(627,531)	—	(627,531)	(777,956)	—
(1,504,351)	—	(1,504,351)	(1,305,886)	—
(14,887,960)	—	(14,887,960)	(14,619,894)	—
—	400,790	400,790	(1,076,347)	—
—	(14,712)	(14,712)	240,806	—
—	1,124,765	1,124,765	1,015,825	—
—	(340,301)	(340,301)	—	—
—	(131,028)	(131,028)	5,627,481	—
—	(487,493)	(487,493)	(679,234)	—
—	(82,789)	(82,789)	(88,559)	—
—	310,420	310,420	—	—
—	779,652	779,652	5,039,972	—
(14,887,960)	779,652	(14,108,308)	(9,579,922)	—
—	—	—	—	(843,873)
3,312,869	—	3,312,869	3,315,441	540,594
11,997,723	—	11,997,723	12,370,458	320,355
1,285,525	—	1,285,525	1,299,152	—
386,692	—	386,692	453,532	—
202,552	155,930	358,482	989,516	5,107
548,001	303,098	851,099	1,083,723	1,627
—	1,877,877	1,877,877	2,811,916	—
(17,549,858)	17,549,858	—	—	—
183,504	19,886,763	20,070,267	22,323,738	867,683
(14,704,456)	20,666,415	5,961,959	12,743,816	23,810
44,184,141	52,536,200	96,720,341	83,976,525	71,328
$29,479,685	$73,202,615	$102,682,300	$96,720,341	$95,138

[13] *GASB Statement No. 34*, page 78.

EXHIBIT 18-9

Balance Sheet—Governmental Funds

CITY OF GOLDEN, COLORADO, BALANCE SHEET—GOVERNMENTAL FUNDS, DECEMBER 31, 2003

	General	Sales and Use Tax Capital Improvement	Other Governmental Funds	Total Governmental Funds 2003	Total Governmental Funds 2002
Assets					
Cash and investments	$2,987,811	$3,976,951	$2,346,556	$ 9,311,318	$13,131,054
Property taxes receivable	3,596,000	—	17,000	3,613,000	3,334,000
Accounts and taxes receivable	1,714,989	468,394	12,909	2,196,292	2,293,425
Due from other funds	—	—	—	—	70,476
Due from other governments	142,317	—	154,761	297,078	260,040
Inventory	—	—	—	—	3,030
Restricted cash and investments	—	2,880,380	—	2,880,380	2,829,000
Total assets	$8,441,117	$7,325,725	$2,531,226	$18,298,068	$21,921,025
Liabilities and fund balance					
Liabilities					
Accounts payable	$1,103,820	$ 295,370	$ 352,197	$ 1,751,387	$ 2,192,829
Accrued liabilities	360,433	422,341	—	782,774	1,419,850
Accrued compensated absences	—	—	—	—	60,723
Due to other funds	—	—	—	—	70,476
Deferred property taxes	3,596,000	—	17,000	3,613,000	3,334,000
Deferred revenue	730,322	—	—	730,322	1,168,370
Total liabilities	5,790,575	717,711	369,197	6,877,483	8,246,248
Fund balance					
Reserved for inventory	—	—	—	—	3,030
Reserved for encumbrances	—	—	—	—	13,326
Reserved for Parks & Recreation	—	—	737,071	737,071	771,441
Reserved for capital projects	—	6,608,014	—	6,608,014	9,243,347
Reserved for cemetery perpetual care (nonexpendable)	—	—	820,046	820,046	771,020
Reserved for cemetery perpetual care (expendable)	—	—	352,927	352,927	378,113
Emergency reserves	690,000	—	—	690,000	710,000
Unreserved, reported in					
General fund	1,960,542	—	—	1,960,542	1,626,581
Special revenue funds	—	—	41,038	41,038	36,102
Capital projects funds	—	—	210,947	210,947	121,817
Total fund balance	2,650,542	6,608,014	2,162,029	11,420,585	13,674,777
Total liabilities and fund balance	$8,441,117	$7,325,725	$2,531,226		

Amounts reported for governmental activities in the Statement of Net Assets are different because:		
Capital assets used in governmental activities are not financial resources and therefore are not reported in the funds.	41,354,589	53,262,988
Long-term assets are not available to pay current expenditures, and therefore, are deferred in the funds.	547,537	738,978
Internal service funds are used by management to charge the costs of certain activities to individual funds, such as insurance, fleet and information technology management. The assets and liabilities of the internal service funds are included in governmental activities in the statement of net assets.	4,959,411	4,885,858
Long-term liabilities, including bonds payable ($27,070,000), bond premium ($295,469), capital leases ($1,142,746), compensated absences ($691,984), and bond issuance costs ($397,762) are not due and payable in the current period and therefore are not reported in the funds.	(28,802,437)	(28,378,460)
Net assets of governmental activities	$29,479,685	$44,184,141

Source: City of Golden, Colorado, comprehensive annual financial report, 2003.

EXHIBIT 18-10

Statement of Revenues, Expenditures, and Changes in Fund Balances—Governmental Funds

CITY OF GOLDEN, COLORADO, STATEMENT OF REVENUES, EXPENDITURES, AND CHANGES IN FUND BALANCES—GOVERNMENTAL FUNDS FOR THE YEAR ENDED DECEMBER 31, 2003

	General	Sales and Use Tax Capital Improvement	Other Governmental Funds	Total Governmental Funds 2003	2002
Revenues					
Taxes	$12,522,035	$4,001,801	$ 72,281	$16,596,117	$16,985,051
Licenses and permits	351,047	—	—	351,047	446,619
Intergovernmental	872,534	320,736	1,440,579	2,633,849	1,951,322
Charges for services	1,618,470	—	49,025	1,667,495	1,466,484
Fines and forfeitures	232,258	—	—	232,258	244,486
Investment income	30,306	81,633	34,562	146,501	562,933
Miscellaneous	685,010	25,644	19,614	730,268	664,640
Total revenues	16,311,660	4,429,814	1,616,061	22,357,535	22,321,535
Expenditures					
Current					
General government	3,159,031	—	18,987	3,178,018	3,217,929
Planning & Economic Development	1,939,562	—	—	1,939,562	2,256,132
Police	5,003,546	—	—	5,003,546	4,564,806
Fire	942,258	—	—	942,258	972,402
Public Works	2,657,829	—	—	2,657,829	2,644,389
Parks and Recreation	1,669,129	—	—	1,669,129	1,353,008
Debt service					
Principal	—	927,551	—	927,551	600,000
Interest and other charges	—	1,504,351	—	1,504,351	1,400,186
Capital outlay	—	4,680,145	1,474,538	6,154,683	18,039,507
Total expenditures	15,371,355	7,112,047	1,493,525	23,976,927	35,048,359
Excess (deficiency) of revenues over expenditures	940,305	(2,682,233)	122,536	(1,619,392)	(12,726,824)
Other financing sources (uses)					
Transfers in	50,000	146,900	301,900	498,800	940,000
Transfers (out)	(692,700)	(100,000)	(340,900)	(1,133,600)	(1,600,000)
Total other financing sources (uses)	(642,700)	46,900	(39,000)	(634,800)	(660,000)
Net change in fund balances	297,605	(2,635,333)	83,536	(2,254,192)	(13,386,824)
Fund balances, beginning	2,352,937	9,243,347	2,078,493	13,674,777	27,800,579
Prior-period adjustment	—	—	—	—	(738,978)
Fund balances, ending	$ 2,650,542	$6,608,014	$2,162,029	$11,420,585	$13,674,777

Reconciliation of the Statement of Revenues, Expenditures, and Changes in Fund Balances of Governmental Funds to the Statement of Activities

Net change in fund balances—total governmental funds	$ (2,254,192)
Amounts reported for governmental activities in the statement of activities are different because:	
Payments from long-term assets are revenues in the governmental funds. However, in the statement of activities, these payments reduce the asset.	(191,441)
Governmental funds report capital outlays as expenditures. However, in the statement of activities, the cost of those assets is allocated over their estimated useful lives as depreciation expense. This is the amount by which capital outlays ($5,530,247) exceeded depreciation ($1,873,885) in the current period. In addition, $17,015,058 of governmental capital assets were transferred to enterprise funds during the year.	(13,358,696)
Repayment of bond principal is an expenditure in the governmental funds, but the repayment reduces long-term debt liabilities in the statement of net assets. These include bond payments ($620,000), capital lease payments ($601,254), amortization of bond premium ($32,830) amortization of bond issuance costs ($22,098), and an increase in accrued compensated absences ($205,666).	1,026,320
Internal service funds are used by management to charge the costs of certain activities to funds, such as insurance, fleet and information technology management. The net revenue (expense) of the internal service funds is reported with governmental activities.	73,553
Change in net assets of governmental activities	$(14,704,456)

Source: City of Golden, Colorado, comprehensive annual financial report, 2003.

EXHIBIT 18-11

Statement of Net
Assets—Proprietary
Funds

CITY OF GOLDEN, COLORADO, STATEMENT OF NET ASSETS—PROPRIETARY FUNDS, DECEMBER 31, 2003

	Business-Type Activities—Enterprise Funds		
	Water Fund	Wastewater Fund	Drainage Fund
Assets			
Current assets			
Cash and investments	$ 3,005,899	$5,177,805	$ 443,597
Accounts receivable	452,561	255,336	138,640
Inventory	10,114	—	—
Restricted cash and investments	494,119	—	—
Total current assets	3,962,693	5,433,141	582,237
Other assets			
Bond issuance costs (net of amortization)	195,166	—	66,140
Total other assets	195,166	—	66,140
Capital assets			
Capital assets (net of accumulated depreciation)	40,858,707	3,980,596	10,355,717
Total assets	$45,016,566	$9,413,737	$11,004,094
Liabilities			
Current liabilities			
Accounts payable	$ 1,504,949	$ 237,806	$ 242,585
Accrued liabilities	—	—	—
Accrued interest payable	44,316	—	15,458
Claims payable	—	—	—
Deferred revenue	—	—	—
Bonds payable, current portion	410,000	—	170,000
Total current liabilities	1,959,265	237,806	428,043
Long-term liabilities			
Accrued compensated absences	53,476	22,385	—
Notes payable	6,500,000	—	—
Bonds payable, long-term portion			
(net of unamortized premium)	6,643,844	—	3,475,000
Total long-term liabilities	13,197,320	22,385	3,475,000
Total liabilities	15,156,585	260,191	3,903,043
Net Assets			
Invested in capital assets, net of related debt	27,500,029	3,980,596	6,776,857
Unrestricted	2,359,952	5,172,950	324,194
Total net assets	$29,859,981	$9,153,546	$ 7,101,051

Source: City of Golden, Colorado, comprehensive annual financial report, 2003.

The most significant change that *GASB Statement No. 34* made to fund financial statements was introduction of the concept of a *major fund*. The general fund is always a major fund. Other funds are considered major funds if they meet both of the following criteria:

1. Total assets, liabilities, revenues, or expenditures/expenses (excluding extraordinary items) of that individual governmental or enterprise fund are at least 10% of the *corresponding* total (assets, liabilities, and so forth) for *all* funds of that *category* or *type* (that is, total governmental or total enterprise funds).

2. Total assets, liabilities, revenues, or expenditures/expenses (excluding extraordinary items) of that individual governmental or enterprise fund are at least 5% of the *corresponding* total for all governmental and enterprise funds *combined*.

Using the concept of major fund reporting, the required governmental fund statements will include a separate column for each major governmental fund and a column with aggregated information for all other governmental funds, as well as a total column for all governmental funds. Proprietary fund statements will include a separate column for each major enterprise fund, a col-

EXHIBIT 18-11

(continued)

	Fossil Trace Golf Course Fund	Total Nonmajor Enterprise Funds	Totals		Governmental Activities— Internal Service Funds
			2003	2002	
	$ 34,207	$ 1,031,209	$ 9,692,717	$10,822,502	$3,767,968
	6,845	6,516	859,898	885,030	28,227
	34,345	—	44,459	9,303	—
	—	—	494,119	494,119	—
	75,397	1,037,725	11,091,193	12,210,954	3,796,195
	—	—	261,306	281,260	—
	—	—	261,306	281,260	—
	15,244,006	11,569,111	82,008,137	53,111,654	1,718,330
	$15,319,403	$12,606,836	$93,360,636	$65,603,868	$5,514,525
	$ 88,539	$ 438,710	$ 2,512,589	$ 1,303,882	$ 196,576
	598	36,653	37,251	89,349	17,636
	—	—	59,774	62,610	—
	—	—	—	—	319,525
	36,839	189,580	226,419	263,413	—
	—	—	580,000	565,000	—
	125,976	664,943	3,416,033	2,284,254	533,737
	12,821	34,462	123,144	133,086	21,377
	—	—	6,500,000	—	—
	—	—	10,118,844	10,650,328	—
	12,821	34,462	16,741,988	10,783,414	21,377
	138,797	699,405	20,158,021	13,067,668	555,114
	15,244,006	11,569,111	65,070,599	42,671,705	1,718,330
	(63,400)	338,320	8,132,016	9,864,495	3,241,081
	$15,180,606	$11,907,431	$73,202,615	$52,536,200	$4,959,411

umn with aggregated information for all other enterprise funds, a total column for all enterprise funds, and a column with aggregated information for *all* internal service funds. (The City of Golden has one major governmental fund—Sales and use tax capital improvement—and four major proprietary funds: Water, Wastewater, Drainage, and Fossil Trace Golf Course.) Governmental officials may also present a separate column for any nonmajor fund that they feel is particularly important and therefore should be presented to financial statement users. For both governmental and proprietary fund statements, whenever a nonmajor total column is used, a combining statement must be presented.

Because governmental funds are accounted for using the accrual basis of accounting in the governmentwide statements and using the modified accrual basis of accounting in the fund statements, a reconciliation between the governmentwide statements of net assets and activities and the fund balance sheet and statement of revenues, expenditures, and changes in fund balance is required either on the face of the fund financial statements or in an accompanying schedule. (See Golden's reconciliations at the bottom of Exhibits 18-9 and 18-10.)

The information in the business-type activities column is basically the same as that currently provided by the enterprise fund columns within the fund financial statements.

EXHIBIT 18-12

Statement of
Revenues, Expenses,
and Changes in Fund
Net Assets—
Proprietary Funds

CITY OF GOLDEN, COLORADO, STATEMENT OF REVENUES, EXPENSES, AND CHANGES IN FUND NET ASSETS—PROPRIETARY FUNDS FOR THE YEAR ENDED DECEMBER 31, 2003

	Business-Type Activities—Enterprise Funds		
	Water Fund	Wastewater Fund	Drainage Fund
Operating revenues			
Charges for services	$ 3,461,268	$1,610,462	$ 752,735
Miscellaneous	148,223	92,736	14,071
Total operating revenues	3,609,491	1,703,198	766,806
Operating expenses			
Personnel services	1,514,202	316,726	—
Operating	976,851	1,125,592	220,501
Depreciation and amortization	807,174	182,856	130,749
Claims	—	—	—
Premiums	—	—	—
Total operating expenses	3,298,227	1,625,174	351,250
Operating income (loss)	311,264	78,024	415,556
Nonoperating revenues (expenses)			
Investment income	50,871	84,100	12,010
Interest expense	(425,299)	—	(192,503)
Gain (loss) on sale of capital assets	1,877,877	—	—
Total nonoperating revenues (expenses)	1,503,449	84,100	(180,493)
Income (loss) before transfers and capital contributions	1,814,713	162,124	235,063
Transfers in	—	—	—
Capital contributions	663,048	—	2,422,146
Change in net assets	2,477,761	162,124	2,657,209
Net assets, beginning	27,382,220	8,991,422	4,443,842
Net assets, ending	$29,859,981	$9,153,546	$7,101,051

Source: City of Golden, Colorado, comprehensive annual financial report, 2003.

EXHIBIT 18-12

(continued)

Fossil Trace Golf Course Fund	Total Nonmajor Proprietary Funds	Totals 2003	Totals 2002	Governmental Activities— Internal Service Funds
$ 1,068,406	$ 1,742,771	$ 8,635,642	$ 7,546,115	$3,105,208
5,657	43,191	303,878	448,620	4,693
1,074,063	1,785,962	8,939,520	7,994,735	3,109,901
427,469	1,124,163	3,382,560	2,943,260	505,166
704,761	1,005,977	4,033,682	4,922,647	820,214
276,477	313,941	1,711,197	1,448,300	470,784
—	—	—	—	1,003,707
—	—	—	—	401,702
1,408,707	2,444,081	9,127,439	9,314,207	3,201,573
(334,644)	(658,119)	(187,919)	(1,319,472)	(91,672)
2,055	6,894	155,930	330,555	56,051
—	—	(617,802)	(531,239)	—
4,500	(5,280)	1,877,097	8,588,922	9,174
6,555	1,614	1,415,225	8,388,238	65,225
(328,089)	(656,505)	1,227,306	7,068,766	(26,447)
—	534,800	534,800	610,000	100,000
15,508,695	310,420	18,904,309	7,339,303	—
15,180,606	188,715	20,666,415	15,018,069	73,553
—	11,718,716	52,536,200	37,518,131	4,885,858
$15,180,606	$11,907,431	$73,202,615	$52,536,200	$4,959,411

EXHIBIT 18-13

Statement of Cash Flows—Proprietary Funds

CITY OF GOLDEN, COLORADO, STATEMENT OF CASH FLOWS—PROPRIETARY FUNDS FOR THE YEAR ENDED DECEMBER 31, 2003

	Business-Type Activities—Enterprise Funds		
	Water Fund	Wastewater Fund	Drainage Fund
Cash Flows from Operating Activities			
Cash received from customers/users	$3,619,901	$1,626,346	$ 731,481
Cash paid to suppliers	(2,791)	(1,052,874)	(534,963)
Cash paid to employees	(1,517,992)	(317,106)	—
Cash paid to providers	—	—	—
Cash paid to claimants	—	—	—
Net cash provided by operating activities	2,099,118	256,366	196,518
Cash Flows from Noncapital Financing Activities			
Transfers in	—	—	—
Cash Flows from Capital Financing Activities			
Purchase of capital assets	(11,927,964)	(285,630)	(715,933)
Proceeds from sale of capital assets	2,506,128	—	—
Proceeds from issuance of debt	6,500,000	—	—
Interest paid	(361,239)	—	(193,140)
Principal payments	(400,000)	—	(165,000)
Payments for bond discount	—	—	—
Transfers from other funds	—	—	—
Contributed capital	663,048	—	—
Net cash provided (used) by capital Financing activities	(3,020,027)	(285,630)	(1,074,073)
Cash Flows from Investing Activities			
Purchase/sale of investments, net	3,861,998	5,115,553	1,196,169
Interest received	50,871	84,100	12,010
Net cash provided (used) by investing activities	3,912,869	5,199,653	1,208,179
Net increase (decrease) in cash and cash equivalents	2,991,960	5,170,389	330,624
Cash and cash equivalents, beginning	13,939	7,416	112,973
Cash and cash equivalents, ending	$3,005,899	$5,177,805	$ 443,597
Reconciliation of Operating Income (Loss) to Net Cash Provided by Operating Activities			
Operating income (loss)	$ 311,264	$ 78,024	$ 415,556
Adjustments to reconcile operating income (loss) to net cash provided by operating activities			
Depreciation expense	807,174	182,856	130,749
Amortization expense	64,060	—	4,410
Changes in assets and liabilities			
Accounts receivable	(30,504)	29,478	9,873
Inventory	(811)	—	—
Accounts payable	1,000,754	80,754	(318,872)
Accrued liabilities	(26,694)	(8,036)	—
Claims payable	—	—	—
Deferred revenue	(22,335)	(106,330)	(45,198)
Accrued compensated absences	(3,790)	(380)	—
Total adjustments	1,787,854	178,342	(219,038)
Net cash provided by operating activities	$2,099,118	$ 256,366	$ 196,518
Noncash Transactions			
Capital assets contributed by (to) other funds	$ —	$ —	$2,422,146

Source: City of Golden, Colorado, comprehensive annual financial report, 2003.

EXHIBIT 18-13

(continued)

Fossil Trace Golf Course Fund	Total Nonmajor Proprietary Funds	Totals 2003	Totals 2002	Governmental Activities— Internal Service Funds
$ 1,104,057	$1,720,363	$ 8,802,148	$ 8,029,122	$3,151,905
(650,567)	(958,865)	(3,200,060)	(4,084,277)	(663,502)
(414,050)	(1,162,921)	(3,412,069)	(2,717,349)	(493,789)
—	—	—	—	(461,335)
—	—	—	—	(914,182)
39,440	(401,423)	2,190,019	1,227,496	629,097
—	534,800	534,800	610,000	—
(7,288)	(58,725)	(12,995,540)	(7,620,335)	(554,810)
—	—	2,506,128	8,588,922	76,452
—	—	6,500,000	5,076,838	—
—	—	(554,379)	(518,851)	—
—	—	(565,000)	(2,260,000)	—
—	—	—	—	—
—	500,000	500,000	847,000	100,000
—	—	663,048	838,472	—
(7,288)	441,275	(3,945,743)	4,952,046	(378,358)
—	105,763	10,279,483	(7,047,752)	3,338,480
2,055	6,073	155,109	330,555	56,051
2,055	111,836	10,434,592	(6,717,197)	3,394,531
34,207	686,488	9,213,668	(86,401)	3,645,270
—	344,721	479,049	565,450	122,699
$ 34,207	$1,031,209	$ 9,692,717	$ 479,049	$3,767,969
$ (334,644)	$ (658,119)	$ (187,919)	$(1,319,472)	$ (91,672)
276,477	313,941	1,711,197	1,386,132	470,784
—	—	68,470	62,168	—
(6,845)	23,951	25,953	38,638	42,004
(34,345)	—	(35,156)	(2,240)	120,280
88,539	47,112	898,287	778,884	(23,201)
598	(46,584)	(80,716)	61,726	—
—	—	—	—	89,525
36,839	(89,550)	(226,574)	(4,251)	—
12,821	7,826	16,477	15,046	21,377
374,084	256,696	2,377,938	2,336,103	720,769
$ 39,440	$ (401,423)	$ 2,190,019	$ 1,227,496	$ 629,097
$15,508,695	$ —	$17,930,841	$ 5,777,006	$ —

EXHIBIT 18-14

Budgetary Comparison Statement

CITY OF GOLDEN, COLORADO, BUDGETARY COMPARISON STATEMENT—GENERAL FUND FOR THE YEAR ENDED DECEMBER 31, 2003

	Budgeted Amounts		Actual	Variance with Final Budget Over (Under)	Actual 2002
	Original	Final			
Budgetary fund balance, beginning	$ 2,915,600	$ 3,091,900	$ 2,352,937	$(739,963)	$ 2,438,099
Resources (inflows)					
Taxes	13,104,000	13,104,000	12,522,035	(581,965)	12,768,698
Licenses and permits	357,500	357,500	351,047	(6,453)	446,619
Intergovernmental	797,000	831,300	872,534	41,234	745,243
Charges for services	1,524,100	1,524,100	1,618,470	94,370	1,412,489
Fines and forfeitures	270,000	270,000	232,258	(37,742)	244,486
Investment income	87,000	87,000	30,306	(56,694)	122,862
Miscellaneous	354,000	354,000	685,010	331,010	424,131
Transfers in	50,000	50,000	50,000	—	—
Amounts available for appropriation	$ 19,459,200	$19,669,800	$18,714,597	$(955,203)	$18,602,627
Charges to appropriations (outflows)					
Current					
General government	3,198,900	3,209,600	3,159,031	50,569	3,130,853
Planning & Economic Development	2,172,700	2,207,300	1,939,562	267,738	2,256,132
Police	5,023,900	5,023,900	5,003,546	20,354	4,564,806
Fire	994,100	1,028,400	942,258	86,142	972,402
Public Works	2,977,700	2,977,700	2,657,829	319,871	2,644,389
Parks and Recreation	1,755,500	1,755,500	1,669,129	86,371	1,353,008
Transfers out	692,700	692,700	692,700	—	1,328,100
Total charges to appropriations	16,815,500	16,895,100	16,064,055	831,045	16,249,690
Budgetary fund balance, ending	2,643,700	2,774,700	2,650,542	(124,158)	2,352,937
Total appropriations	$ 19,459,200	$19,669,800	$18,714,597	$(955,203)	$18,602,627

Budget-to-GAAP Reconciliation

Resources (inflows)

Actual amounts (budgetary basis) available for appropriation			$18,714,597		$18,602,627
Differences—budget to GAAP					
The fund balance at the beginning of the year is a budgetary resource but is not a current-year revenue for financial reporting purposes			(2,352,937)		(2,438,099)
Transfers from other funds are inflows of budgetary resources but are not revenues for financial reporting purposes			(50,000)		—
Total revenues as reported on the statement of revenues, expenditures, and changes in fund balances—governmental funds			$16,311,660		$16,164,528

Charges to Appropriations (Outflows)

Actual amount (budgetary basis) of total charges to appropriations			16,064,055		16,249,690
Diferences—budget to GAAP					
Transfers to other fiends are outflows of budgetary resources but are not expenditures for financial reporting purposes			(692,700)		(1,328,100)
Total expenditures as reported on the statement of revenues, expenditures, and changes in fund balances—governmental funds			$15,371,355		$14,921,590

Source: City of Golden, Colorado, comprehensive annual financial report, 2003.

BUDGETARY COMPARISONS Governments must present budgetary comparison information for the general fund and each special revenue fund that has a legally adopted annual budget. The comparison may be presented as a comparison statement within the basic financial statements or as a schedule within CAFR-required supplementary information. The statement or schedule must disclose the budgetary basis of accounting and include columns presenting the original budget, the final appropriated budget, and actual balances (on the budgetary basis) for the fiscal year. Variance columns are optional. Exhibit 18-14 on page 670 presents the budgetary comparison statement for Golden, Colorado.

REQUIRED SUPPLEMENTARY INFORMATION Governments are required to supply supplementary information, including schedule(s) of funding progress of pension plans, schedule(s) of employer contributions to pension plans, budgetary comparison schedules for the general and special revenue funds, and information about infrastructure assets reported using the modified approach (if applicable).

NOTES TO THE FINANCIAL STATEMENTS The basic financial statements also include notes to the financial statements. The *GASB Codification* provides details regarding required CAFR note disclosure.[14] The purpose of the notes is to communicate information essential for fair presentation of the financial statements that is not displayed on the face of the financial statements. Given this, the notes are an integral part of the basic financial statements. The notes should focus on the primary government—specifically, its governmental activities, business-type activities, major funds, and nonmajor funds in the aggregate.

INFRASTRUCTURE The most controversial portion of *GASB Statement No. 34* regards capital assets, particularly infrastructure assets. Prior to the issuance of *GASB 34*, capital assets acquired by governmental funds (general governmental assets) were not capitalized and recorded as assets in governmental funds. They were treated as expenditures in the period of acquisition and also were recorded in a general fixed asset account group. (*GASB Statement No. 34* eliminated account groups.) Infrastructure assets, which are long-lived capital assets that are normally stationary in nature and include roads, bridges, drainage systems, and other public-domain capital assets, were not required to be reported in governmental financial statements. Depreciation was also optional. Under *GASB 34*, general governmental assets, including infrastructure assets, are capitalized and depreciated within the governmentwide statements.

For many governments, the historical costs of infrastructure assets, such as roads and sidewalks, may be somewhat difficult to ascertain. Expenditures may not have been closely traced to infrastructure projects, because financial statement reporting of these assets was not required. Many infrastructure assets, such as sidewalks and streets, were constructed long ago, and costs are not readily available or may have little current economic meaning. Understandably, finance directors and preparers of governmental financial statements strongly opposed *GASB 34*'s infrastructure reporting requirements. To alleviate the difficulty of complying with the new infrastructure requirements, the GASB allowed prospective reporting of general infrastructure assets during a transition period ending in 2005. From now on, governments with total assets in excess of $10 million will be required to retroactively report the estimated historical cost of infrastructure assets acquired or significantly improved or reconstructed in fiscal years ending after June 30, 1980.

GASB 34 also allows adoption of a modified approach for handling infrastructure assets that are part of a network. Under the modified approach, a government must maintain an up-to-date inventory of eligible infrastructure assets, perform condition assessments of the assets a minimum of every three years using a measurement scale, and estimate the annual amount necessary to maintain and preserve the eligible assets at a condition established by the government. If the infrastructure assets are shown to be preserved at the condition level determined by the government, all expenditures for these assets (except for additions and improvements, which should be capitalized) should be expensed in the period incurred, and depreciation will not be necessary.

COMBINING AND INDIVIDUAL FUND STATEMENTS In each of the governmentwide and fund financial statements, column data often include the activity of several individual funds. Combining financial statements aggregate individual fund account balances and produce relevant totals by classification or activity (for example, governmental, business-type, type of program revenue). The combining statement total data correspond to an aggregated column on an associated financial statement. For

---

[14] *GASB Codification* Section 2300.103.

EXHIBIT 18-15

Combining Statement—Internal Service Funds

CITY OF GOLDEN, COLORADO, COMBINING STATEMENT OF NET ASSETS—NONMAJOR ENTERPRISE FUNDS, DECEMBER 31, 2003

	Splash Aquatic Fund	Community Center Fund	Cemetery Operations Fund	Rooney Road Sports Complex Fund	*Total Nonmajor Enterprise Funds*
Assets					
Current assets					
Cash and investments	$ 23,225	$ 387,916	$120,050	$500,018	$ 1,031,209
Accounts receivable	144	2,603	2,948	821	6,516
Total current assets	23,369	390,519	122,998	500,839	1,037,725
Capital assets					
Capital assets (net of accumulated depreciation)	5,580,156	5,294,577	383,958	310,420	11,569,111
Total assets	$5,603,525	$5,685,096	$506,956	$811,259	$12,606,836
Liabilities					
Current liabilities					
Accounts payable	$ 1,855	$ 89,920	$ 36,515	$310,420	$ 438,710
Accrued liabilities	285	22,704	13,664	—	36,653
Deferred revenue	—	—	—	189,580	189,580
Total current liabilities	2,140	112,624	50,179	500,000	664,943
Long-term liabilities					
Accrued compensated absences	1,065	13,611	19,786	—	34,462
Total liabilities	3,205	126,235	69,965	500,000	699,405
Net Assets					
Invested in capital assets	5,580,156	5,294,577	383,958	310,420	11,569,111
Unrestricted	20,164	264,284	53,033	839	338,320
Total net assets	$5,600,320	$5,558,861	$436,991	$311,259	$11,907,431

Source: City of Golden, Colorado, comprehensive annual financial report, 2003.

example, see Exhibit 18-15 for the nonmajor enterprise funds of the City of Golden, Colorado. Individual fund balances are combined to arrive at totals that agree with the appropriate columns on the proprietary fund statement of net assets shown in Exhibit 18-11. The *GASB Codification* requires that comprehensive annual financial reports include combining financial statements; however, combining statements that detail the aggregation of nonmajor funds are optional.

Statistical Section

The final required section of a CAFR contains statistical tables with comparative data from several periods of time. The tables, which focus on social and economic data, financial trends, and the fiscal capacity of the government, include both accounting and nonaccounting information. According to *GASB Codification*, Section 2800, 15 specific tables or schedules should be included in a CAFR, unless they are inapplicable.

As you can well imagine, the CAFR of a large metropolitan government amounts to hundreds of pages of information. Although the preceding discussion has provided a brief description of CAFR contents, each CAFR is unique, especially in terms of its transmittal letter and MD&A presentation. Although it is not required, many governments also publish other information, such as Single Audit reports, with their annual CAFR.

Additional Reporting

In recent years, the GASB has suggested that governments supplement CAFR reporting with nonfinancial information that is deemed important to their citizens. *Service efforts and accomplishment (SEA)* reporting is a form of performance measurement that provides more-complete information about an entity's performance than is found in the CAFR. SEA indicators are concerned with the *results* of services delivered by the government and the assessment of whether an entity is progressing toward stated goals. Governments gather information about the *outputs* and *outcomes* of the services they provide and the relationship between the use of resources of those output and outcomes. SE indicators enable management and citizens to evaluate the manner and effectiveness with which a branch or agency of a political system functions, operates, or behaves in carrying out a given task.

SUMMARY

Accounting principles for state and local governmental units have been developed through the efforts of the Municipal Finance Officers Association and its committees and, more recently, the Governmental Accounting Standards Board. The *GASB Codification of Governmental Accounting and Financial Reporting Standards* provides GAAP for the financial statements of state and local governmental units. Twelve basic accounting principles from *Governmental Accounting and Financial Reporting Principles, Statement No. 1*, which are included in the *GASB Codification*, establish the objectives and underlying support for the accounting and reporting practices of state and local governments.

Governmental entities utilize fund accounting as a means of ensuring and demonstrating compliance with formal budgetary constraints. There are five governmental fund types, which generally follow the modified accrual basis of accounting and maintain a focus on current financial resources, and two proprietary fund types, which follow the accrual basis of accounting and maintain an economic resources measurement focus. Fiduciary fund types are also reported in governmental financial statements.

The formal financial report of a governmental unit is called a comprehensive annual financial report. A CAFR under *GASB Statement No. 34*, a statement that initiated major changes to governmental financial reporting, contains three major sections: introductory, financial, and statistical.

QUESTIONS

1. What organization provides accounting standards for state and local governmental units? What organization or organizations preceded this group?

2. What is the *GAAFR*? Who creates the *GAAFR*?

3. What is the AICPA's role in governmental accounting?

4. Why do governmental entities use fund accounting? How many funds might be used by a single governmental unit? How many fund types?

5. Distinguish between governmental funds, proprietary funds, and fiduciary funds. Which funds are classified as governmental funds?

6. List the five types of governmental funds. What are the primary distinctions among them?

7. What is the accounting equation for a governmental fund?

8. List the two types of proprietary funds. What distinguishes them from each other?

9. What is the accounting equation for a proprietary fund?

10. Why aren't fixed assets recorded in the accounts of a general fund? Where are they recorded?

11. What is the modified accrual basis of accounting? Which funds utilize the modified accrual basis of accounting?

12. What does *measurement focus* mean? What two focuses are used in governmental accounting? Which fund types use each?

13. What types of revenue do governments have? How do nonexchange transactions differ from exchange transactions?

14. How does the accounting treatment of a nine-month note payable differ from the accounting treatment of a five-year note payable within a governmental fund? Why?

15. Are interfund transfers expenditures? Expenses? Explain.

16. What is an appropriation? How can budgetary approval be arranged to give the legislative body maximum control over the budget? How can it be arranged to give the executive maximum flexibility?

17. List the required governmental fund and proprietary fund financial statements under *GASB 34*. On what basis of accounting are these statements prepared?

18. How do nonreciprocal transfers differ from reciprocal transfers?

19. List the authoritative documents available to financial statement preparers and auditors related to governmental accounting and financial reporting. Which is the most authoritative according to *SAS 69*?

20. Distinguish between the various types of interfund activity.

21. How does an expenditure differ from an expense? Identify the funds that report expenditures and those that report expenses.
22. What are the three sections of a CAFR? Briefly identify the contents of each section.
23. How do operational accountability and fiscal accountability differ? In what context are they used?

EXERCISES

E 18-1

Multiple choice

1. Which of the following items has the greatest GAAP authority under *SAS 69*?
   a *GASB implementation guides*
   b *Consensus positions of GASB's Emerging Issues Task Force*
   c *GASB statements and interpretations*
   d *FASB statements and interpretations*
2. The primary emphasis in accounting and reporting for governmental funds is on:
   a *Flow of current financial resources*
   b *Income determination*
   c *Capital transfers*
   d *Transfers relating to proprietary activities*
3. The term *appropriation*, as used in governmental accounting, is
   a *A budget request*
   b *A commitment*
   c *An authorization to spend*
   d *An allotment*
4. Which of the following will not appear in financial statements prepared under *GASB 34?*
   a *Governmentwide statements*
   b *Fund financial statements*
   c *Management's discussion and analysis*
   d *General long-term debt account group*
5. Ketchum County issues general obligation serial bonds to finance construction of a new high school. Which of the following funds are affected by the transaction?
   a *Special revenue fund*
   b *Capital projects fund and general fund*
   c *Capital projects fund, general fund, and debt service fund*
   d *Capital projects fund and debt service fund*

E 18-2

Multiple choice [AICPA adapted]

1. Depreciation expense accounts would likely be found in the
   a *General fund*
   b *Capital projects fund*
   c *Debt service fund*
   d *Enterprise fund*
2. The governmentwide statements of a state government
   a *May not be issued separately from the comprehensive annual financial report*
   b *Are prepared on both the accrual and modified accrual bases of accounting*
   c *Include both governmental and proprietary funds*
   d *Contain more-detailed information regarding the state government's finances than is contained in the comprehensive annual financial report*
3. Under the modified accrual basis of accounting for a governmental unit, revenues should be recognized in the accounting period in which they
   a *Are earned and become measurable*
   b *Are collected*
   c *Become available and measurable*
   d *Become available and earned*
4. Authority granted by a legislative body to make expenditures and to incur obligations is the definition of an
   a *Appropriation*
   b *Allowance*
   c *Encumbrance*
   d *Expenditure*

5. An expense would be reported in which of the following funds?
- a *Special revenue funds*
- b *Capital projects funds*
- c *Enterprise funds*
- d *Permanent funds*

E 18-3
Multiple choice

1. Which of the following is considered an exchange transaction under *GASB 33?*
- a *A city receives a federal grant*
- b *A bus driver collects bus fare from a rider*
- c *Property taxes are collected from a homeowner*
- d *An employer withholds state income tax from employee paychecks*

2. One would not expect to find fixed asset accounts in the
- a *Governmental fund financial statements*
- b *Proprietary fund financial statements*
- c *Governmentwide financial statements*
- d *Financial statements of a governmental entity*

3. The cash received from the sale of vehicles used by the sheriff's office should be recorded in
- a *The general fund*
- b *The general fixed assets account group*
- c *A capital projects fund*
- d *A debt service fund*

4. Which fund follows the modified accrual basis of accounting?
- a *General fund*
- b *Special revenue fund*
- c *Debt service fund*
- d *All of the above*

5. The governmental fund accounting model is as follows:
- a *Assets = Liabilities + Fund Balance*
- b *Current Assets – Current Liabilities = Fund Balance*
- c *Current Assets + Noncurrent Assets – Current Liabilities – Noncurrent Liabilities = Fund Balance*
- d *Current Assets + Noncurrent Assets – Current Liabilities – Noncurrent Liabilities = Net Assets*

E 18-4
Multiple choice

1. Which of the following is not a governmental fund?
- a *Special revenue fund*
- b *Debt service fund*
- c *Trust fund*
- d *General fund*

2. Which of these funds generally follows the accrual basis of accounting?
- a *General fund*
- b *Internal service fund*
- c *Debt service fund*
- d *Special revenue fund*

3. Which of the following funds will report fixed assets in the fund financial statements?
- a *General fund*
- b *Special revenue fund*
- c *Debt service fund*
- d *None of the above*

4. Which of the following funds would not be included in governmental fund financial statements?
- a *Debt service fund*
- b *General fund*
- c *Pension trust fund*
- d *Permanent fund*

5. Which of the following funds would be used to account for an activity that provides goods or services to other funds?
- a *General fund*
- b *Enterprise fund*
- c *Debt service fund*
- d *Internal service fund*

E 18-5
Multiple choice

1. Which of the following are eliminated from the financial statements under *GASB 34?*
   a *General long-term debt account group*
   b *General fixed asset account group*
   c *Both a and b*
   d *None of the above*

2. An expense would be reported in which of the following funds?
   a *General fund*
   b *Internal service fund*
   c *Debt service fund*
   d *Special revenue fund*

3. A component unit
   a *Is financially accountable to the primary government*
   b *Must be discretely presented in a primary government's CAFR*
   c *Is excluded from a primary government's CAFR*
   d *Is a legally separate organization for which the primary government is financially accountable*

4. Budgetary comparison information must be presented for the
   a *Debt service fund*
   b *General fund*
   c *Pension fund*
   d *Permanent trust fund*

5. Required supplementary information includes
   a *Schedule(s) of funding progress of pension plans*
   b *Schedule(s) of employer contributions to pension plans*
   c *Budgetary comparison schedules for the general and special revenue funds*
   d *All of the above*

E 18-6
Identification of fund type Identify each of the fund types described.

1. A fund that is used to report assets held in a trustee capacity for others and that cannot be used to support the government's own programs

2. A fund used to report any activity for which a fee is charged to external users for goods and services

3. A fund used to account for all financial resources except those required to be accounted for in another fund

4. A fund used to account for the accumulation of resources for, and the payment of, general long-term debt principal and interest

5. A fund used to report resources that are legally restricted to the extent that only earnings, and not principal, may be used for purposes that support the reporting government's programs—that is, for the benefit of the government or its citizenry

6. A fund used to account for the proceeds of specific revenue sources (other than trusts for individuals, private organizations, or other governments or for major capital projects) that are legally restricted to expenditures for specified purposes

7. A fund used to report any activity that provides goods or services to other funds, departments, or agencies of the primary government and its component units, or to other governments, on a cost-reimbursement basis

8. A fund used to account for financial resources to be used for the acquisition or construction of major capital facilities (other than those financed by proprietary funds or in trust funds for individuals, private organizations, or other governments)

E 18-7
Transaction analysis—governmental funds Use transaction analysis to determine the effects of each of the following transactions in the general fund.

1. Salaries paid totaled $30,000. Additional salaries incurred, but not paid, totaled $2,500.

2. Levied property taxes of $100,000; $98,000 was collected during the year. The balance is expected to be uncollectible.

3. Borrowed $60,000 by issuing a nine-month note bearing interest at 7%.

4. Repaid the note plus interest when due.

5. Borrowed $600,000 by issuing bonds at par. The bonds mature in 10 years.

6. Purchased equipment costing $25,000 with cash.

7. Sold equipment at the end of its expected useful life. The equipment had no expected residual value when acquired (at a cost of $13,000), but it sold for $1,200.

8. Determined that it is probable that a lawsuit involving a claim against a department will result in a settlement of at least $50,000. However, it is not expected that any payments will be required for two years or more.

E 18-8

Transaction analysis—proprietary funds Repeat Exercise 18-7 under the assumption that the transactions involve a proprietary activity instead of a general governmental activity.

E 18-9

Identification of fund type For each of the following events or transactions, identify the fund or funds that will be affected.

1. The principal, interest, and related charges from a city's general long-term debt bond issue will be handled in a fund established for that purpose.
2. A wealthy citizen donates $10,000,000 for city park maintenance. The principal cannot be spent.
3. A wealthy citizen donates $10,000,000 for city park maintenance. The principal may be spent as needed.
4. A village collects cigarette taxes from vendors. The tax funds must be remitted to the state.
5. The city issued general obligation bonds at par to finance construction of a government office building.

E 18-10

Identification of fund type For each of the following events or transactions, identify the fund or funds that will be affected.

1. The Board of County Commissioners approved the construction of a new town band shell.
2. A central computing center was established to handle the data processing needs of a municipality.
3. A local municipality provides water and sewer services to residents of nearby communities for a fee.
4. A village receives a grant from the state government. The funds are to be used solely for preserving wetlands.
5. Property taxes are levied by a city government.

E 18-11

Identification of fund type For each of the following events or transactions, identify the fund or funds that will be affected.

1. A new city government establishes an employee pension program.
2. A utility department constructs a new building.
3. A truck is purchased for use at the centralized storage center.
4. A new fleet of police cars is purchased.
5. Property taxes are collected by a city government.

E 18-12

Identification of fund type and transaction analysis The City of Sioux Falls entered into a number of transactions for the current fiscal year. Identify the fund or funds affected by each transaction and determine how each transaction will affect the accounting equation of the particular fund.

1. Sioux Falls paid salaries to general government employees, $95,000.
2. Sioux Falls purchased an automobile by issuing a $25,000, 8% note to the vendor. The purchase occurred at midyear, and the note is a one-year note.
3. The city sold general fixed assets with an original cost of $300,000 for $30,000 at the end of their useful life. The use of the resources received is not restricted.
4. In the second fiscal year, the city repaid the principal and interest on the note issued in transaction 2 at the due date of the note.
5. "Profits" of $500,000 from the airport enterprise fund were transferred to the general fund of the city to subsidize general fund operations.
6. Interest income collected on Sioux Falls's general fund investments totaled $70,000 for the year.

E 18-13

Identification of fund type and transaction analysis Perez County entered into a number of transactions for the current fiscal year. Identify the fund or funds affected by each transaction and determine how each transaction will affect the accounting equation of the particular fund.

1. Perez County issued $10 million of general obligation bonds at par to finance construction of a new county office building.
2. The county purchased a truck for a general governmental department. The cost of the truck, $22,000, was paid in cash.
3. The county-owned and -operated electric utility billed residents and businesses $500,000 for electricity sales.

4. The county paid $2 million to High Rise Construction Company during 2008 for work completed during the year.

5. The country paid general governmental employee salaries of $4,500. Another $500 of salaries accrued but has not been paid.

6. The country borrowed $7,500 on a six-month note to finance general operating costs of the government.

INTERNET ASSIGNMENT

1. Visit the GASB's Web site at www.GASB.org. Click on the Publications icon and select Summaries/Status. What is the title of the most recently issued GASB standard? When was it issued? What is its effective date?

2. Visit the GASB's Web site at www.GASB.org. Click on the Links icon and select CAFRs. Choose a CAFR from a city, county, or other local government. Review the CAFR and answer the following questions:

   a. How many governmental funds does the government have? List the name of one special revenue fund.

   b. Does the government have a capital projects fund? For what purpose was it created?

   c. How many enterprise funds does the government have? List the name of one enterprise fund.

   d. How many trust and agency funds does the government have? List the name of one such fund.

3. Locate the Web site for the municipality in which your college or university is located. Is the municipality's financial report available on the Web site?

SELECTED READINGS

AICPA. *Audits of State and Local Governmental Units, Audit and Accounting Guide* (*GASB 34* edition). New York: American Institute of Certified Public Accountants, 2003.

CHASE, BRUCE W., AND ROBERT H. PHILLIPS. "*GASB 34* and Government Financial Condition, An Analytical Toolbox." *Government Finance Review* (April 2004), pp. 26–31.

FREEMAN, ROBERT J., AND CRAIG D. SHOULDERS. *Governmental and Non-Profit Accounting* (7th ed.). New York: Prentice Hall, 2003.

GAUTHIER, STEPHEN. "New Guidance on the Letter of Transmittal." *Government Finance Review* (April 2004), pp. 62–64.

Governmental Accounting Standards Board. *Codification of Governmental Accounting and Financial Reporting Standards*. Norwalk, CT: Governmental Accounting Standards Board, 2004.

Governmental Accounting Standards Board. *Reporting Performance Information: Suggested Criteria for Effective Communication*. Norwalk, CT: Governmental Accounting Standards Board, 2004.

Governmental Accounting Standards Board. *Statement No. 34*, "Basic Financial Statements—and Management's Discussion and Analysis—for State and Local Governments." Norwalk, CT: Governmental Accounting Standards Board, 1999.

Government Finance Officers Association of the United States and Canada. *Governmental Accounting, Auditing, and Financial Reporting*. Chicago: Municipal Finance Officers Association of the United States and Canada, 2005.

National Council on Government Accounting. *Governmental Accounting and Financial Reporting Principles, Statement 1*. Chicago: Municipal Finance Officers Association of the United States and Canada, 1979.

U.S. General Accounting Office. *Government Auditing Standards*. Washington, D.C.: Government Printing Office, 2003.

ACCOUNTING FOR STATE AND LOCAL GOVERNMENTAL UNITS—GOVERNMENTAL FUNDS

LEARNING OBJECTIVES

1 Prepare journal entries for governmental funds.

2 Learn about accounting methods unique to government accounting— budgetary issues, encumbrance accounting, and interfund transactions.

3 Determine the appropriate governmental fund to be used.

4 Prepare governmental fund financial statements.

5 Convert fund financial statements to governmentwide financial statements.

Chapter 18 introduced accounting and financial reporting practices applicable to state and local governments. This chapter continues the discussion of fund accounting by illustrating the proper accounting for governmental funds. It also provides examples of fund statements for governmental funds and outlines the process of converting the modified-accrual-basis financial information in the governmental fund statements into the accrual-basis information presented in the governmentwide statements.

Recall that governmental funds include the general fund as well as special revenue, permanent, capital projects, and debt service funds. Every governmental entity has one general fund and may have zero, one, or many of each of the other four governmental funds. The general governmental activities included within governmental funds are accounted for in the same manner, regardless of specific fund type. This chapter reviews transactions in the general fund and each of the other four governmental funds so that you may recognize the different purpose of each governmental fund.

...

THE GENERAL FUND

The *general fund (GF)* is the entity that a government uses to account for all unrestricted resources except those required to be accounted for in a specific fund. In more descriptive terms, the general fund is the governmental fund used to account for the general operations of government, including the revenue received and the expenditures made in providing public goods and services to citizens. If a general-purpose government has only one fund accounting entity, that fund is a general fund. Recall that the general fund follows the modified accrual basis of accounting.[1]

ACCOUNTING FOR THE GENERAL FUND

LEARNING OBJECTIVES 1, 2

This chapter uses the small town of Grantville to demonstrate accounting for the general fund. The postclosing trial balance of the Town of Grantville general fund at September 30, 2006, shows the following ledger account balances:

---

[1] Governments may choose to record governmental fund transactions under the accrual basis of accounting and later adjust balances to the modified accrual basis for presentation in fund financial statements. This book presents the traditional fund accounting approach to accounting for governmental funds.

Debits

Cash	$310,000
Taxes receivable—delinquent	150,000
Accounts receivable	30,000
Supplies inventory	60,000
Total debits	$550,000

Credits

Allowances for uncollectible taxes—delinquent	$ 10,000
Vouchers payable	140,000
Note payable (short-term)	150,000
Reserve for encumbrances	90,000
Unreserved fund balance	160,000
Total credits	$550,000

Events for the town during the year October 1, 2006, to September 30, 2007, that involve the general fund include recording an approved budget, accounting for revenues from various sources, accounting for expenditures with encumbrance controls, preparing year-end adjusting and closing entries, and preparing the fund financial statements.

The Budget

The Town of Grantville approved the following general fund budget for the fiscal year October 1, 2006, to September 30, 2007.

**TOWN OF GRANTVILLE GENERAL
FUND BUDGET SUMMARY FOR THE YEAR
OCTOBER 1, 2006, TO SEPTEMBER 30, 2007**

Revenue Sources

Taxes	$2,075,000
Licenses and permits	205,000
Intergovernmental revenue	400,000
Charges for services	557,000
Fines and forfeitures	118,000
Investment income	100,000
Miscellaneous revenues	45,000
Total budgeted revenues	$3,500,000

Expenditures

Current services	
General government	$ 477,500
Public safety	897,750
Highways and streets	825,000
Sanitation	525,000
Health and welfare	175,000
Recreation	270,000
Capital outlays	150,000
Total appropriations	$3,320,250

Other Financing Sources (Uses)

Transfers out	115,000
Budgeted increase in fund balance	$ 64,750

The budgeted general fund activity includes revenue from various sources, expenditures, and a category of other sources and uses of working capital funds. Section 1100.110 of the *GASB Codification* addresses classification requirements for revenue and expenditure accounts. As required, the town classifies budgeted general fund revenue items by source (taxes, licenses and permits, and so on). Budgeted expenditures are organized by character class (current services, capital outlays) and by function within each character category (general government, public safety). If desired, the town could further classify expenditures for each of the functions by specific departments or units within the organization (such as police department and fire department). It could also present expenditures in each of the organizational units in terms of the object of expenditure (such as personal services, supplies, and other services and charges). The classification scheme is an important part of operational control over expenditures, because most governmental entities limit expenditures within a functional or object category to the amount of the formal budget approval. Any excess requires administrative approval.

RECORDING THE BUDGET At the beginning of the year, the approved budget of Grantville is recorded. Although many business entities adopt and approve budgets, only governmental entities formally prepare journal entries to record the budget within the accounting records. The town makes the following general journal entry to record the budget in the accounts of the general fund.

General Fund

Estimated revenues	3,500,000	
Appropriations		3,320,250
Estimated other financing uses—transfers out		115,000
Unreserved fund balance		64,750

    To record the budget for the year October 1, 2006, to September 30, 2007.

The entry records total estimated revenues, total appropriations, and estimated other financing uses in the general ledger and credits the budgeted excess to the fund balance account. Some governments require budgeted revenues to exceed appropriations, resulting in a balanced budget.

SUBSIDIARY LEDGERS Although budgets may be approved in terms of broad categories, governments record details of the planned revenues (such as property taxes, sales taxes, and license revenue) and appropriations (such as police supplies, mayor's office expenses, and maintenance of the town hall) in subsidiary revenue and expenditure ledgers. Recording estimated revenues for individual items as debits in the subsidiary revenue ledger and recording actual revenue items as credits allows the outstanding subsidiary account balances during the year to reveal differences between actual and budgeted revenue for each item to date, as well as the final excess or deficiency at year-end. Similarly, recording appropriations as credits and recording actual expenditures or commitments for expenditures (encumbrances) as debits helps a government monitor expenditures. The account balances shown in the individual accounts of the subsidiary expenditure ledger represent unencumbered, unexpended appropriations (or amounts that remain to be spent) for each expenditure item. These subsidiary ledger techniques provide the means of achieving formal budgetary control over the items included in the approved budget. The financial statements or their notes will later report budget compliance for the general and budgeted special revenue funds, as illustrated in Chapter 18.

Transactions and Interfund Activities for the Year

ACCOUNTING FOR PROPERTY TAXES Recall that under the modified accrual basis of accounting, revenues are generally recognized in the period in which they become measurable and available to finance expenditures of the period. Governments recognize property tax revenues, which are considered imposed nonexchange revenues under *GASB Statement No. 33*, when taxpayers are billed for the amount of taxes levied, if the resources collected can be used in that period.

The treasurer of Grantville records the following entry when property tax bills of $2,000,000 are mailed:

General Fund

Taxes receivable—current	2,000,000	
Allowance for uncollectible taxes—current		20,000
Revenue		1,980,000
To record the property tax levy.		

This entry assumes that 1% of property tax levies are not collectible and that the rest of the taxes will be collected either during the current year or within not more than 60 days thereafter. Therefore, it recognizes revenue for 99% of the amount billed. However, governments must record a liability for taxes not collected by year-end or within 60 days thereafter, because they are not "available." Likewise, governments record taxes collected in a period before they become legally available to finance expenditures as deferred taxes (or taxes collected in advance). Governments cannot recognize revenue until the period when it becomes legally available to cover expenditures.

Uncollectible taxes are not expenditures in governmental accounting; instead, they are revenue adjustments. Like accounts receivable, taxes receivable is a control account for individual amounts owed. The current designation for taxes receivable distinguishes current taxes receivable from taxes that are past due. Governments also reclassify any balances remaining in the "taxes receivable—current" and "allowance for uncollectible taxes—current" accounts after the due date for payment as "taxes receivable—delinquent" and "allowance for uncollectible taxes receivable—delinquent." Note that the postclosing trial balance for the Town of Grantville's general fund at September 30, 2006, includes a debit account, "taxes receivable—delinquent," of $150,000 and a credit account, "allowance for uncollectible taxes—delinquent," of $10,000.

The town records collection of current property taxes of $1,760,000 and past-due taxes of $140,000 in the usual manner for receivables as follows:

General Fund

Cash	1,900,000	
Taxes receivable—current		1,760,000
Taxes receivable—delinquent		140,000

To record collection of property taxes.

When specific delinquent property tax bills totaling $10,000 are determined to be uncollectible, the town writes them off with the following entry:

General Fund

Allowance for uncollectible taxes—delinquent	10,000	
Taxes receivable—delinquent		10,000

To record write-off of uncollectible account.

DERIVED TAX REVENUES Derived tax revenues, such as sales and income taxes, require the taxpayer or merchant to determine the tax base. Under *GASB Statement No. 33*, governments recognize derived tax revenues when the underlying exchange (e.g., the sale) has occurred; however, within governmental funds, the resources must also be measurable and available. Thus, the taxing authority should accrue sales taxes collected and held by merchants at the end of the fiscal year if they will be remitted in time to pay liabilities of the current period.[2] The same is true for taxes collected and held by one government agency at year-end for another.

Governments recognize sales tax revenue when tax returns are received from merchants, and the taxes are expected to be remitted to the government by year-end (or within 60 days thereafter). The entry to record $150,000 in sales taxes reported on tax returns, of which three equal payments are required to be remitted by the fifteenth day of October, November, and December, is as follows:

General Fund

Accounts receivable	150,000	
Revenue		100,000
Deferred revenue		50,000

To record sales tax activity.

Because October 15 and November 15 fall within 60 days of the September 30 year-end, two of the payment amounts will be available to meet current obligations and thus should be recognized as income under the modified accrual basis of accounting. The amount scheduled to be received in December is recorded as deferred revenue.

---

[2] Although the 60-day rule applies to property tax revenue collections only, many governments choose to use the same criterion for other revenues. Thus, revenues collected within 60 days of year-end are considered available to meet the liabilities of the current period. *GASB 38* requires governments to disclose the length of time used to define "available" in the financial statement note that summarizes significant accounting principles.

REVENUE FROM OTHER SOURCES Unlike levied or derived taxes, other imposed nonexchange revenues, such as revenues from licenses, permits, fines, and the like, cannot be measured objectively until cash is actually received. Therefore, revenues from these sources are usually recognized when cash is collected. Thus, the town records the collection of fees ($200,000) from business licenses as follows:

General Fund

Cash	200,000	
Revenue		200,000
To record collection of business license fees.		

Other revenues for the 2006–2007 fiscal year are recognized as cash is received. The amount in the following entry includes all revenue items not listed individually:

General Fund

Cash	1,240,000	
Revenue		1,240,000
To summarize other revenue items for the year.		

Although the general ledger ordinarily includes only one revenue account, remember that a government has to record the detailed revenue sources individually in a subsidiary revenue ledger.

RECORDING EXPENDITURES Expenditures are decreases in the net financial resources of a governmental fund, as noted earlier. Under modified accrual accounting, we normally record expenditures when the related fund liability is incurred. Do not confuse this concept with the expense concept, in which proprietary funds recognize expenses when the funds use the related goods or services. Under modified accrual accounting, governmental funds recognize salaries, supplies, utilities, and fixed assets alike as expenditures when they incur the related liabilities.

When salaries ($200,000) are vouchered for payment (that is, a payroll document is prepared and approved), the town records the following general fund entry:

General Fund

Expenditures	200,000	
Vouchers payable		200,000
To record accrual of salaries.		

ACCOUNTING FOR ENCUMBRANCES The law limits expenditures for each period, as measured on a government's budgetary basis, to those for which appropriations have been made. Thus, it is extremely important to keep expenditures within authorized levels. Approving expenditures without considering outstanding purchase orders or unperformed contracts could result in overspending appropriations. For example, assume that total appropriations for the year exceed actual expenditures to date by $4,000 and that an unknowing employee approves an additional equipment purchase for $3,000. If $2,000 worth of supplies are already on order and expenditures are made for both the equipment and the supplies, actual expenditures for the period will exceed appropriations by $1,000. Encumbrance accounting helps prevent this type of situation by maintaining a running total of actual purchases as well as purchase commitments. *Encumbrance* means "commitment," and encumbrance accounting records commitments made for goods on order and for unperformed contracts in order to provide additional control over expenditures.

During the year, the town orders snow-removal equipment expected to cost $150,000. Grantville makes the following encumbrance entry *at the time the purchase order is placed* to recognize a commitment to pay for the equipment when it is received:

General Fund

Encumbrances	150,000	
Reserve for encumbrances		150,000
To record a purchase order for $150,000 of snow-removal		
equipment.		

This information helps prevent overspending because encumbrances can be deducted from unexpended appropriations to determine unencumbered appropriations (that is, maximum additional authorizations):

Appropriations (authorized expenditures)	$ X
Less: Expenditures to date	Y
Unexpended appropriations	X – Y
Less: Encumbrances (commitments for expenditures)	Z
Unencumbered appropriations	$X – Y – Z

The remaining expenditure authority for the budgetary period appears in the amount of unencumbered appropriations.

When the snow-removal equipment is received, Grantville reverses the entry recording the encumbrance:

General Fund

Reserve for encumbrances	150,000	
Encumbrances		150,000

    To reverse the encumbrance entry for snow-removal equipment.

The entry to record the receipt of the equipment is unaffected by the encumbrance entries and reflects the actual amount of the invoice. Assuming that the actual cost of the equipment purchased is $140,000, the town records the expenditure as follows:

General Fund

Expenditures	140,000	
Vouchers payable		140,000

    To record the purchase of snow-removal equipment.

As noted in the transaction analysis in the previous chapter, the acquisition of fixed assets (such as the snow-removal equipment) by a governmental fund decreases net assets (working capital) and the fund balance. Therefore, under the modified accrual basis of accounting, we do not record fixed assets as assets in the general fund, and they will not appear in the fund statements; however, we maintain fixed asset records and include governmental fund fixed assets in the governmentwide statements, which we prepare on the accrual basis of accounting. Thus, fixed assets are one of the reconciling items between the fund financial statements and the governmentwide financial statements.

Note that the amount of the encumbrance was an estimate of the actual cost, which was $10,000 less than the estimate. Like formal budgetary accounting, encumbrance accounting does not affect the recording of actual transactions and events.

If a governmental unit does not spend the full amount of an appropriation during the period covered by an appropriation, a question arises about whether the unexpended portion can be carried over as authorization for expenditures in the succeeding year. Although laws of the governmental unit will cover this matter, a common position is that all appropriations lapse at the end of the year for which they are made, with the exception of committed appropriations (that is, encumbrances outstanding), which can continue to serve as authorizations for items on order or under contract. Because total expenditure and encumbrance amounts are closed to fund balance at year-end, reserve for encumbrance credits remain in the accounting records as reservations of fund balance within the governmental fund statements. Note that the postclosing trial balance for the Town of Grantville includes a credit account, "reserve for encumbrances," of $90,000. This account represents a reservation of fund balance and communicates the amount of committed appropriations carried over to serve as authorization for the actual expenditures as they occur in the succeeding year. One of the first entries made in the year beginning October 1, 2006, would be to reclassify this account to identify it as a carryover from the prior year:

General Fund

Reserve for encumbrances	90,000	
Reserve for encumbrances—prior year		90,000

This entry notes that the $90,000 commitment was approved in the previous year and included in the prior-year budget.

In October 2006, Grantville receives the equipment that was ordered in the previous fiscal year and for which an encumbrance of $90,000 had been recorded. If the actual invoice is $85,000, the entry to record receipt of the equipment is as follows:

General Fund

Expenditures—prior year	85,000	
Vouchers payable		85,000

    To record receipt of equipment ordered during the prior
       year and chargeable against the prior year's reserve for encumbrances.

If the actual invoice had been more than the encumbered amount carried over from the prior year, the difference would have been charged to the current year's expenditures.

SUPPLIES Within governmental funds, a government may treat supply acquisitions as expenditures either when purchased (purchases method) or when used (consumption method), as long as it reports *significant* amounts of inventory in the balance sheet.[3] Although the consumption method is similar to the manner in which commercial businesses record supplies, the purchases method better allows for comparison of expenditures and appropriations. Thus, if a government's annual appropriations include all inventory acquisitions for the period, the government will likely select the purchases method. Under the purchases method, a government with significant inventory balances at year-end will recognize the balances as assets in the fund balance sheet and establish an accompanying reservation of fund balance to reflect the fact that the supply amount is not an available financial asset. This reservation of fund balance is *optional* under the consumption method.

Under the consumption method, which is preferred by the GASB, we record the process of acquiring supplies as follows:

General Fund

Encumbrances	60,000	
Reserve for encumbrances		60,000

    To record the purchase order for operating supplies.

General Fund

Reserve for encumbrances	60,000	
Encumbrances		60,000

    To reverse the encumbrance entry upon receipt of the
       supplies.

General Fund

Supplies inventory	60,000	
Vouchers payable		60,000

    To record receipt of operating supplies.

When an additional $50,000 of supplies is ordered, the entry is:

General Fund

Encumbrances	50,000	
Reserve for encumbrances		50,000

    To record encumbrances for a purchase order for
       supplies.

These supplies have not been received at year-end, September 30, 2007.

---

[3] *GASB Codification*, Section 1600.123.

CAPITAL LEASE Lease agreements of state and local governments fall under the provisions of *FASB Statement No. 13*, "Accounting for Leases," as amended and interpreted by *NCGA Statement No. 5*, "Accounting and Financial Reporting Principles for Lease Agreements of State and Local Governments," and by *GASB No. 13*, "Accounting for Operating Leases with Scheduled Rent Increases." A lease agreement that is financed from general government resources must be accounted for under governmental fund accounting principles. (See *GASB Codification*, Section L20.)

When governments use capital leases to acquire general fixed assets by purchase or construction, the governmental fund acquiring the general fixed asset records an expenditure and other financing source, as if long-term debt had been issued (*GASB Codification*, Section L20.115).

The Town of Grantville enters into a general government capital lease with an initial down payment of $5,000 and a present value of minimum lease payments of $50,000 and records the following entry:

General Fund		
Expenditures	50,000	
Cash		5,000
Other financing sources—capital lease		45,000

At the same time, the town notes a liability (capital lease payable) in the general long-term debt account records for the amount remaining due ($45,000) and adds an asset to the general fixed asset account records at the present value of the minimum lease payments determined by *FASB 13* criteria ($50,000). The asset and liability, as well as associated depreciation, will appear in the governmentwide financial statements; however, only an expenditure and other financing source appear in the governmental fund statements. The town may record future capital lease payments as expenditures of principal and interest in the general fund or transfer resources to the debt service fund, which will recognize the expenditures. The notes to the financial statements disclose minimum lease payments for each of the following five years and in five-year increments thereafter.

INTERFUND TRANSACTIONS During the year, the general fund transfers funds to three other governmental funds. (The transactions are covered from the perspectives of the other funds later in this chapter.) The town transfers a total of $50,000 to establish a special revenue fund balance, $100,000 to help finance a capital project, and $14,250 to the debt service fund to finance general long-term debt payments. (Note that the $50,000 transfer was not appropriated in the general fund budget and therefore will require administrative approval.) A summary entry for these transfers is as follows:

General Fund		
Other financing uses—nonreciprocal transfer to town hall capital project fund (CPF)	100,000	
Other financing uses—reciprocal transfer to special revenue fund (SRF)	50,000	
Other financing uses—nonreciprocal transfer to debt service fund (DSF)	14,250	
Cash		164,250
To record transfers to town hall CPF, the SRF, and the DSF.		

This entry recognizes slight differences between the interfund transfers. *GASB 34* distinguishes between reciprocal and nonreciprocal transfers. **Reciprocal transfers** are loans for which a fund expects repayment, whereas **nonreciprocal transfers** represent flows of assets that do not require repayment. Furthermore, *GASB Statement No. 38*, "Certain Financial Statement Note Disclosures," requires note disclosure of significant transfers that are considered nonroutine or are inconsistent with the activities of the fund making the transfer.[4] The transfers in the previous entry include non-reciprocal transfers to the capital projects and debt service funds and a reciprocal transfer (loan) to a special revenue fund. Each of these transfers is considered routine and consistent with the activities of the general fund.

OTHER TRANSACTIONS FOR THE YEAR The note payable that was outstanding at September 30, 2006, becomes due and is paid:

General Fund		
Note payable	150,000	
Cash		150,000

Here is a summary entry for the remainder of the various expenditures throughout the year:

General Fund		
Expenditures	2,843,500	
Vouchers payable		2,843,500
Summary entry for accrual of salaries, purchase of supplies, and other expenditures.		

General Fund		
Vouchers payable	3,143,000	
Cash		3,143,000
To record payment of vouchers during the year in summary form.		

Year-End Procedures

ADJUSTING ENTRIES If supplies with a historical cost of $90,000 are on hand at the balance sheet date, the town needs to make a $30,000 adjusting entry under the consumption method of accounting for inventory balances ($60,000 beginning balance + $60,000 purchased − $90,000 remaining). (Under the purchases method, the town would adjust supplies inventory and the fund balance reservation for inventory.)

General Fund		
Expenditures	30,000	
Supplies inventory		30,000
To adjust the supplies inventory and supplies expenditures accounts.		

Assume that uncollected taxes on September 30, 2007, are past due. Accordingly, the $240,000 taxes receivable—current and the $20,000 allowance for uncollectible taxes—current are reclassified as delinquent. The entry for this reclassification is as follows:

General Fund		
Taxes receivable—delinquent	240,000	
Allowance for uncollectible taxes—current	20,000	
Taxes receivable—current		240,000
Allowance for uncollectible taxes—delinquent		20,000
To reclassify past-due taxes receivable as delinquent.		

---

[4] *GASB Codification*, Section 2300.120–121.

Grantville's adjusted general fund trial balance at September 30, 2007, includes the following accounts and balances:

Debits	
Cash	$ 187,250
Taxes receivable—delinquent	240,000
Accounts receivable	180,000
Supplies inventory	90,000
Estimated revenues	3,500,000
Expenditures	3,263,500
Expenditures—prior year	85,000
Encumbrances	50,000
Other financing uses	164,250
Total debits	$7,760,000
Credits	
Allowance for uncollectible taxes—delinquent	$ 20,000
Vouchers payable	325,000
Deferred revenue	50,000
Reserve for encumbrances—prior year	90,000
Reserve for encumbrances	50,000
Unreserved fund balance	224,750
Appropriations	3,320,250
Revenues	3,520,000
Estimated other financing uses—transfers out	115,000
Other financing sources	45,000
Total credits	$7,760,000

CLOSING ENTRIES By year-end, the budgetary accounts will have served their purpose and must be closed. The most direct method of closing budgetary accounts is to reverse the original entry used to record the budget. At September 30, 2007, Grantville could close its accounts as follows:

General Fund		
Appropriations	3,320,250	
Estimated other financing uses—transfers out	115,000	
Unreserved fund balance	64,750	
Estimated revenues		3,500,000
To close the budgetary accounts.		

This closing approach emphasizes the fact that formal budgetary accounting does not affect actual revenues, expenditures, or any balance sheet account. When the town makes this entry to close the appropriations, other financing uses, and estimated revenue accounts, the unreserved fund balance account returns to its $160,000 beginning-of-the-year balance.

The town closes actual revenues and expenditures directly to the unreserved fund balance account. Under the assumption that committed appropriations can be carried over to the succeeding fiscal period to serve as authorization for items on order, it can also close any outstanding encumbrances at year-end to the unreserved fund balance account. The adjusted trial balance shows that Grantville had revenue of $3,520,000, expenditures of $3,263,500 for the current year, other financing sources of $45,000, other financing uses of $164,250, and encumbrances outstanding at September 30, 2007, of $50,000. The entry to close these accounts is as follows:

General Fund		
Revenues	3,520,000	
Other financing sources (OFS)	45,000	
Expenditures		3,263,500
Encumbrances		50,000
Other financing uses (OFU)—nonreciprocal transfer		
to town hall CPF		100,000
Other financing uses—reciprocal transfer to SRF		50,000
Other financing uses—nonreciprocal transfer to DSF		14,250
Unreserved fund balance		87,250

To close revenue, expenditures, OFS/OFU, and encumbrances accounts.

This entry reveals that actual revenues and other financing sources exceeded expenditures and other financing uses by $137,250, of which $50,000 is committed for supplies ordered but not yet received. The $50,000 reserve for encumbrances account (that is, the credit related to the $50,000 encumbrances account closed out above) remains intact at year-end as a reservation of fund balance on the balance sheet. The $85,000 expenditure from the prior year's appropriations is a charge against the prior year's reserve for encumbrances account.

General Fund

Reserve for encumbrances—prior year	90,000	
Expenditures—prior year		85,000
Unreserved fund balance		5,000

To close prior-year reserve for encumbrances and related
expenditures and credit the fund balance for the excess.

SPECIAL REVENUE FUNDS

A *special revenue fund (SRF)* is the entity that a government uses to account for the proceeds of specific revenue sources (other than resources for permanent funds, major capital projects, or debt service on general long-term debt) that are restricted by law or administrative action to expenditures for specified purposes. Although a government has only one general fund, it can have many special revenue funds, or none at all. If specific revenue sources are earmarked for education, the government should use a special revenue education fund to account for the earmarked resources. Similarly, if a city receives state or federal funds specifically designated for highway maintenance, the government should create an SRF to account for such fund resources.

Governments account for earmarked revenues in separate special revenue funds to show compliance with legal or administrative requirements. Outside of this need to separate earmarked revenue sources, there is no essential difference between an SRF and a general fund. Indeed, if a special revenue fund is not legally or contractually required, governments have the option of accounting for a special revenue source in the general fund. Both types of funds are governmental funds, use the modified accrual basis for fund statements, and typically integrate their budgets into their accounting systems. Because the accounting requirements for special revenue funds are the same as for a general fund, this chapter illustrates only special revenue fund entries used to record grant proceeds.

GRANTS Governments often receive grants from other governments or private sources. For example, the federal government provides grant funds for public safety at the local level, and private organizations donate grant funds for senior citizen activities. If the grant funds are restricted to a specific purpose other than a capital acquisition, they will usually be accounted for in a special revenue fund. Grant revenues can be recognized when all eligibility requirements set forth in the grant contract have been met, if the funds are available to meet current liabilities. If the grant funds are disbursed to the government prior to the eligibility requirements having been met, they must be accounted for as deferred revenue.

In July 2007, the state awards a highway beautification grant of up to $50,000 to the Town of Grantville for the purchase and placement of trees on the major highway within town jurisdiction. Because the grant funds are not paid to the town until after approved expenditures have been incurred, the general fund "loans" cash to the special revenue fund. (Recall the interfund transfer entry in the general fund.) During July and August, the town incurs $38,000 in approved expenditures and records the following entries in a special revenue fund:

Special Revenue Fund—Highway Beautification

Cash	50,000	
Other financing sources—reciprocal transfer from GF		50,000

To record a transfer of cash from the general fund.

Special Revenue Fund—Highway Beautification

Expenditures	38,000	
Vouchers payable		38,000

To record expenditures related to highway beautification.

Special Revenue Fund—Highway Beautification

Accounts receivable—grant	38,000	
Grant revenue		38,000
To recognize grant revenue related to approved grant expenditures.		

Note that the town recognizes revenue and a receivable equal to the amount of acceptable expenditures, because the state will reimburse Grantville the $38,000 of approved expenditures. This amount is now measurable and should be available to meet current obligations.

In July 2007, the Town of Grantville receives $20,000 from the state to be used for police and fire officer training sessions on the proper installation of child car seats. The town records the following entry:

Special Revenue Fund—Officer Training

Cash	20,000	
Deferred revenue		20,000
To record the receipt of grant funds from the state.		

When expenditures have been incurred for the training sessions in the amount of $18,500, the entry is as follows:

Special Revenue Fund—Officer Training

Expenditures	18,500	
Vouchers payable		18,500
To record expenditures for an officer training program.		

Special Revenue Fund—Officer Training

Deferred revenue	18,500	
Grant revenue		18,500
To recognize grant revenue.		

If additional training will take place in the time span identified in the grant agreement (if any), then the special revenue fund can remain open. If the town has completed all training related to the grant's purpose and will not spend the remaining $1,500, the town will return the money to the state and close the special revenue fund.

At the end of the year, the town will prepare closing entries for special revenue fund revenues and expenditures (including encumbrances, if any), as well as budgetary funds, in the same manner as was illustrated for the general fund earlier in the chapter.

PERMANENT FUNDS

GASB 34 created a new governmental fund category, permanent funds, for nonexpendable resources set aside for support of a government's programs or citizenry. *Permanent funds (PF)* typically account for contributions for which the grantor specifies that a principal amount must be maintained but for which interest accumulation or asset appreciation, or both, are to be used for a specified purpose. (Such resources were previously referred to as nonexpendable trust funds.) In contrast, if funds are expendable (that is, they can be spent), a government accounts for them in a special revenue fund.

In April 2007, the Town of Grantville receives a gift of $500,000 in bonds. The 5% bonds pay interest semiannually in September and March. The contributor wants to ensure that the seal exhibit at the town zoo is maintained for years to come. He instructs that the principal shall be maintained, but all interest income and asset appreciation may be used for the benefit of the seal exhibit. During the year, the town receives an interest installment and incurs $3,000 in approved expenditures. The town makes the following entries in a permanent fund:

Permanent Fund—Seal Exhibit

Investments—bonds	500,000	
Revenues—additions to permanent endowments		500,000
To record the receipt of a permanent endowment.		

Permanent Fund—Seal Exhibit

Cash	12,500	
Revenues—investment income—interest		12,500

To record the receipt of interest ($500,000 × 5% × 1/2 year).

Permanent Fund—Seal Exhibit

Expenditures	3,000	
Cash		3,000

To record allowable expenditures.

The town may reserve the expendable interest in the permanent fund until the funds are used for the seal exhibit, or it may transfer the expendable funds to a special revenue fund (or the general fund); however, the interest must be earmarked for the seal exhibit.

According to *GASB Statement No. 31*, "Accounting and Financial Reporting for Certain Investments and for External Investment Pools," governments should record investments with determinable fair values at fair value. Thus, if the fair value of the bonds, excluding accrued interest, had changed, the town would have made an entry to reflect the fair market value of the bonds. The value of the bonds in this example remained unchanged.

At the end of the year, the town will close the permanent fund's revenues and expenditures (including encumbrances, if any), as well as budgetary funds, in the same manner as was illustrated for the general fund earlier in the chapter.

CAPITAL PROJECTS FUNDS

Governments account for the acquisition of most general fixed assets from expenditures of annual appropriations in the general fund or special revenue funds; however, *major* general fixed assets are not financed through appropriations of these funds. The purpose of *capital projects funds (CPF)* is to account for resources segregated for the acquisition or construction of major capital facilities other than those financed by trust and proprietary funds. Typical sources of financing include the proceeds of bond issues, grants and shared revenues, transfers from other funds, and contributions from property owners.

Capital projects funds are governmental funds that account for working capital to be used for major general governmental capital projects. Capital projects funds use modified accrual accounting and revenue and expenditure accounts. Governments use encumbrance accounting procedures to account for commitments made to contractors and for material and supply orders. Ordinarily, a governmental unit will create a separate CPF to account for each major capital project that has been legally authorized. Once created, a CPF exists for the life of the project. Capital projects funds typically do not use formal budgetary accounting unless numerous capital projects are financed through the same fund or facilities are being constructed with the governmental unit as the primary contractor.

The next section illustrates the accounting and reporting for a CPF during a two-year construction period.

Accounting for a Capital Projects Fund

The Town of Grantville authorizes an addition to the town hall on December 15, 2006, in the amount of $1,000,000. Financing for the project consists of $500,000 from a 6.5% serial bond issue, $400,000 from a federal grant, and $100,000 from the general fund. Transactions and events during the life of the project are as follows:

2006–2007 Fiscal Year

1. The town transfers $100,000 from the general fund to the town hall addition capital projects fund (a CPF created to account for the town hall construction).

2. Planning and architect's fees are paid in the amount of $40,000.

3. The contract is awarded to the lowest bidder for $950,000.

4. The bonds are sold for $502,000 (at a premium of $2,000).

5. The amount of the premium is transferred to the debt service fund.

6. The construction is certified to be 50% complete, and a bill for $475,000 is received from the contractor.

7. Contract payable, less a 10% retained percentage, is paid.

8. The books are closed and financial statements are prepared.

2007–2008 Fiscal Year

9. The amount due from the federal grant is received.

10. Construction is completed and the contractor is paid.

11. Closing entries are recorded.

12. Remaining cash is transferred to the GF.

CREATION OF THE CPF When the town hall addition CPF is created, the town makes a memorandum entry in the CPF noting the $1,000,000 authorization.

> *Capital Projects Fund*
>
> Memorandum—town hall project authorization $1,000,000

INTERFUND TRANSFER (1) Transaction 1 increases CPF current assets and fund balance. As discussed earlier, the town classifies this interfund transaction as a nonreciprocal transfer, because it does not expect it to be repaid. The town reports fund balance increases from transfers as other financing sources, not as revenues, in the fund receiving the transfer. Likewise, it records this transaction, which decreases general fund current assets and fund balance, as an other financing use, not an expenditure. The $100,000 transfer requires an entry in both funds. Recall the interfund transfer entry in the general fund. The corresponding entry in the capital projects fund to receive the $100,000 is as follows:

> *Capital Projects Fund*
>
> | | | |
> |---|---|---|
> | Cash | 100,000 | |
> | Other financing sources—nonreciprocal transfer | | |
> | from general fund | | 100,000 |
> | To record receipt of funds from the GF. | | |

RECORDING EXPENDITURES (2) The town records payments for planning and architect's fees as follows:

> *Capital Projects Fund*
>
> | | | |
> |---|---|---|
> | Expenditures | 40,000 | |
> | Cash | | 40,000 |
> | To record payments for planning and architect's fees. | | |

RECORDING ENCUMBRANCES (3) When the contract is awarded to a contractor, the town makes an encumbrance entry for the full amount of the contract:

> *Capital Projects Fund*
>
> | | | |
> |---|---|---|
> | Encumbrances | 950,000 | |
> | Reserve for encumbrances | | 950,000 |
> | To record encumbrances for the amount of the contract. | | |

ACCOUNTING FOR THE BOND PROCEEDS (4 AND 5) Governments recognize the proceeds of bond issues in the CPF at the time the bonds are sold. The sale of the bonds increases CPF current assets (cash). The bond liability is long-term, so the town does not account for it in the CPF; rather, it includes it in long-term debt records. As in the general fund treatment of the capital lease, this debt will appear on the governmentwide statements; however, within the CPF, the fund balance increases by the amount of the bond proceeds ($502,000). The increase is classified as an other financing source (bond issue proceeds), not as revenue.

The town sold the bonds at a premium. Although the following entry places the full amount of the proceeds in the CPF, the premium is not available to finance the project; however, premiums often are set aside to service the debt. Thus, a second entry transfers the premium to the debt service fund through which the bond liability will be serviced. (The corresponding entry for the debt service fund is illustrated in the next section of this chapter.) Journal entries for the sale of bonds and transfer of the premium are as follows:

Capital Projects Fund

Cash	502,000	
Other financing sources—proceeds from bond issue		502,000
To record sale of bonds.		
Other financing uses—nonreciprocal transfer to debt service fund	2,000	
Cash		2,000
To transfer the premium to the town hall addition debt service fund.		

When bonds sell at a discount, bond proceeds equal the amount received. Governments selling bonds at a discount must reduce the project authorization or transfer additional resources to the CPF.

PROGRESS PAYMENTS AND RETAINED PERCENTAGES (6 AND 7) A construction contract often stipulates that a portion of the contractor's remuneration be withheld until completion of the construction project and final inspection. Note that the fixed asset (construction in progress) is not recorded in the CPF, because it is a governmental fund. The fixed asset does not represent CPF working capital. Instead, the incurrence of the contract payable liability increases CPF liabilities and decreases CPF fund balance. Governments report this fund balance decrease as an expenditure. Accounting entries for the amount owed on partial completion of the contract and the first progress payment on the contract appear as follows:

Capital Projects Fund

Reserve for encumbrances	475,000	
Encumbrances		475,000
To reverse half of the amount encumbered.		
Expenditures	475,000	
Contracts payable		427,500
Contracts payable—retained percentage		47,500
To record expenditures and a 10% retained percentage on the town hall construction.		
Contracts payable	427,500	
Cash		427,500
To record partial payment to the contractor.		

Adjusting and Closing Entries (8)

At the end of the fiscal year, the town closes the CPF books and prepares financial statements. The town hall construction project has not been completed, and the statements for the CPF are interim statements from the standpoint of the project.

INTERGOVERNMENTAL REVENUE The grant from the federal government is intergovernmental revenue. Under modified accrual accounting, a governmental fund recognizes revenue on restricted grants when qualifying costs have been incurred (and other significant conditions, if any, have been met), assuming that the funds are measurable and available.

Because the CPF did not receive the federal grant proceeds for the town hall project at the time the books were closed, the town will prepare an accrual entry, provided that the commitment is firm. Just as previously discussed in the section on special revenue funds, governments recognize revenue if the receivable will be collected and available to meet current obligations. Otherwise, they must credit deferred revenue. Failure to recognize revenue from the grant could make the CPF appear to be in financial difficulty for interim reporting purposes when, in fact, it has progressed as planned.

Capital Projects Fund (Adjusting Entry)

Due from federal government	400,000	
Grant revenue		400,000
To recognize revenue from the federal grant.		

This entry assumes that the federal government has agreed to contribute $400,000 to the project regardless of the total cost. Therefore, because more than $400,000 of costs were incurred in 2007, the town records the full $400,000 as revenue. If the grant had specified that the federal government would pay a percentage of the cost of the project up to $400,000, the town would prorate the amounts in the entry.

CLOSING ENTRY—SEPTEMBER 30, 2007 The town records a closing entry for the CPF as follows:

Capital Projects Fund (Closing Entry)

Grant revenue	400,000	
Other financing sources—nonreciprocal transfer from general fund	100,000	
Other financing sources—proceeds from bond issue	502,000	
Expenditures		515,000
Other financing uses—nonreciprocal transfer to debt service fund		2,000
Encumbrances		475,000
Unreserved fund balance		10,000

To close the books at the end of fiscal year 2007.

UNISSUED BONDS AT AN INTERIM STATEMENT DATE The bonds to finance the town hall capital project have been issued by September 30, 2007, but in some cases there will be authorized but unissued bonds at an interim reporting date. The existence of the unissued bonds would be disclosed only in a statement note. The authorization of the bonds does not represent a CPF asset. Assets are received only upon bond issuance.

Entries for 2007 to 2008

The following entries illustrate the proper accounting treatment for the completion of a capital project; however, they will not be reflected in the October 1, 2006, to September 30, 2007, financial statements at the end of the chapter.

REINSTATEMENT OF ENCUMBRANCES At the start of the 2007–2008 fiscal year, the $475,000 encumbrance that was closed to unreserved fund balance at the end of the prior fiscal year is reinstated in the accounts as follows:

Capital Projects Fund

Encumbrances	475,000	
Unreserved fund balance		475,000

To reinstate the encumbrances.

It is not necessary to denote the encumbrance in the CPF as related to the prior year, because capital projects are budgeted by project rather than on an annual basis.

RECEIPT OF GRANT (9) When the federal grant is received, it is recorded:

Capital Projects Fund

Cash	400,000	
Due from federal government		400,000

To record receipt of the federal grant.

COMPLETION OF THE PROJECT (10) The journal entries to record completion of construction and payment to the contractor are as follows:

Capital Projects Fund

Reserve for encumbrances	475,000	
Encumbrances		475,000

To remove encumbrances when construction is complete.

Expenditures	475,000	
Contracts payable		475,000
To record expenditures on town hall construction.		
Contracts payable	475,000	
Contracts payable—retained percentage	47,500	
Cash		522,500
To record final payment to contractor.		

CLOSING ENTRIES—SEPTEMBER 30, 2008 (11) The town makes an entry to close expenditures:

Capital Projects Fund

Unreserved fund balance	475,000	
Expenditures		475,000
To close the expenditures to fund balance.		

NONRECIPROCAL TRANSFER (12) The town records the transfer of the remaining fund balance to the general fund in final termination of the town hall addition CPF as follows:

Capital Projects Fund

Other financing uses—nonreciprocal transfer to GF	10,000	
Cash		10,000
To record transfer of cash to the general fund.		
Unreserved fund balance	10,000	
Other financing uses—nonreciprocal transfer to GF		10,000
To close town hall addition CPF ledger.		

A corresponding entry is required in the general fund to receive the cash transferred. That entry is as follows:

General Fund

Cash	10,000	
Other financing sources—nonreciprocal transfer from CPF		10,000
To record receipt of cash from town hall addition CPF.		

The $10,000 transfer to the general fund is a nonreciprocal transfer because the fund is being terminated. It should be presented separately as an increase or decrease in fund balance in the financial statements.

SPECIAL ASSESSMENT ACTIVITIES

Governments sometimes finance public improvements that benefit a limited group of property owners through special taxes levied against these residents. These special tax levies are known as *special assessment levies,* or just *special assessments*. The more common types of special assessment projects include street paving, the construction of sidewalks, and the installation of sewer lines. Ordinarily, a special assessment project originates when property owners in an area petition the government to construct the improvements desired. If the project is authorized, the government obtains the financing, makes the improvement, and levies special assessments on the property owners for some or all of the cost incurred. If the project will benefit the general citizenry, the government may pay a portion of the cost.

The property owners may pay the special assessments immediately, in which case the governmental unit is repaid for the resources it uses in constructing the improvement, and the special assessment project is terminated. In many cases, however, the government issues special assessment bonds to pay the construction costs and collects the assessment in installments over the term of the special assessment bond issue. Interest charged on the unpaid balances of special assessment receivables covers the interest on the special assessment bonds. If special assessments are not paid as they come due, the governmental unit has the power to enforce collection through seizure of the real property against which special assessments are levied.

The GASB requires that governments account for capital improvements related to special assessment projects in capital projects funds. If the special assessment involves general obligation debt that will be repaid, in part, from special assessments, or if *the government is obligated in some manner* for debt repayment, the government should report the debt in the governmental activities column of the governmentwide statement of net assets. If, however, *the governmental unit is not obligated in any manner,* it should not report the special assessment obligation in its financial statements.[5] In this case, special assessment receipts can be accounted for in an agency fund, and the related special assessment obligation is only disclosed in notes to the financial statements.

DEBT SERVICE FUNDS

Debt service funds (DSF) are governmental funds that account for the receipt of resources from designated sources (such as taxes or transfers from the general fund) and for the use of these resources to make principal and interest payments on general long-term debt obligations. Ordinarily, governments create a separate DSF to account for servicing each general long-term debt issue. Although debt service funds make interest and principal payments on general long-term debt, they do not record the liability for general long-term debt. You will recall that governments maintain internal records of general long-term debt, which coordinate with the records of debt service. When long-term debt matures, governments record the appropriate expenditures in debt service funds and reduce the liability for the debt in the internal debt records and the appropriate financial statements.

Debt service funds generally follow the modified accrual basis of accounting. *GASB Codification,* Section 1600.122, identifies a major exception for DSF expenditures. Because resources for debt service are often appropriated in other funds and transferred to a DSF, the DSF may recognize principal and interest expenditures on general long-term debt when due (i.e., in the year of payment). This exception is made to avoid showing an expenditure and a liability for debt service in one period and the transfer of resources from the general fund or other sources to pay the liability in the following period.[6]

The operations of debt service funds for serial bond issues differ from those for term bond issues. In the case of a serial bond issue, in which bonds are retired at regular intervals, resources typically are received as needed to service the debt, and no significant balances are carried over from one period to the next. However, debt service funds for term bond issues accumulate resources over time to retire all of the debt at maturity as well as make periodic interest payments. Debt service funds for term bond issues accommodate both sinking fund operations and operations for current debt service. Thus, they are much more complex than those for serial bond issues. Formal budgetary accounting is ordinarily needed for term bond issues but not for serial bond issues. This chapter illustrates only debt service fund operations for serial bond issues.

Accounting for the Debt Service Fund

Assume that the $500,000, 6.5% serial bond issue of the Town of Grantville that was issued for $502,000 on April 3, 2007, has interest payment dates of April 1 and October 1 of each year. Principal amounts of $50,000 are due each year starting on April 1, 2008, and cash for all debt service is to be provided by transfers from the general fund. The town transfers amounts needed for debt service payments from the general fund during the month before the due date. Under these assumptions, the required journal entries for the town hall addition debt service fund for the 2006–2007 and 2007–2008 fiscal years are as follows:

Debt Service Fund—April 3, 2007

Cash	2,000	
Other financing sources—nonreciprocal transfer from town hall CPF		2,000
To record receipt of issue premium from town hall addition CPF.		

---

[5] *GASB Codification,* Section S40.

[6] Accrual is permitted, but not required, if two conditions are met. First, the resources to be used for payment must be available in the DSF by year-end. Second, the payment must be due early (the first few weeks) in the next year.

Debt Service Fund—September 2007

Cash	14,250	
Other financing sources—nonreciprocal transfer from general fund		14,250

To record receipt of resources for the October 1, 2007,
    interest payment from the general fund, less the $2,000
    already accumulated.

($500,000 × 6.5% × 1/2 year) − 2,000 = $14,250.

Debt Service Fund—Adjusting Entry

Expenditures—interest payment	16,250	
Matured interest payable		16,250

To accrue payment of interest due on 6.5% serial bond issue, due October 1.

Debt Service Fund Closing Entries—September 30, 2007

Other financing sources—nonreciprocal transfer from town hall CPF	2,000	
Other financing sources—nonreciprocal transfer from general fund	14,250	
Expenditures – interest payment		16,250

To close the accounts.

The following entries illustrate the proper accounting treatment for debt service transactions; however, they will not be reflected in the October 1, 2006, to September 30, 2007, financial statements at the end of the chapter.

Debt Service Fund—March 2008

Cash	66,250	
Other financing sources—nonreciprocal transfer from general fund		66,250

To record receipt of $16,250 for interest payment plus
    $50,000 for the first serial payment due April 1, 2008.

Debt Service Fund—April 1, 2008

Expenditures—principal payment	50,000	
Expenditures—interest payment	16,250	
Cash		66,250

To record payment of principal and interest on the serial
    bond issue.

Debt Service Fund—September 2008

Cash	14,625	
Other financing sources—nonreciprocal transfer from general fund		14,625

To record receipt of cash from GF for the October 1, 2008,
    interest payment ($450,000 × 6.5% × 1/2 year).

Debt Service Fund—Adjusting Entry

Expenditures—interest payment	14,625	
Matured interest payable		14,625

To accrue payment of interest due.

Debt Service Fund Closing Entries—September 30, 2008

Other financing sources—nonreciprocal transfer from general fund	80,875	
Expenditures—principal payment		50,000
Expenditures—interest payment		30,875
To close the accounts.		

NONRECIPROCAL, ROUTINE TRANSFERS The receipts of cash from the general fund in September 2007, March 2008, and September 2008 are nonreciprocal, routine transfers made in connection with the normal operations of government. Such recurring transfers are not revenues or expenditures of either fund in the transaction. Instead, governments report recurring transfers as "other financing sources (uses)." In this case, the town reports the $2,000 transfer of the bond premium on April 3, 2007, the $14,250 nonreciprocal, routine transfer in September 2007 for the payment of interest; the $66,250 recurring transfer in March 2008 for interest and the first principal payment; and the $14,625 nonreciprocal, routine transfer in September 2008 for interest as other financing sources in the DSF and as other financing uses in the GF or in the CPF.

Note that interest payable was accrued on September 30, 2007 and 2008, for interest payments due on October 1, 2007 and 2008. The interest could be accrued because the amounts payable are due on October 1 and resources are available in the DSF at year-end to cover the interest payments due early in the next fiscal year. Interest could not be accrued at September 30 if the general fund nonreciprocal, routine transfers were made on October 1 to pay interest on October 1.

GOVERNMENTAL FUND FINANCIAL STATEMENTS

As noted in discussing the new *GASB 34* financial reporting model, the required governmental fund financial statements include a statement of net assets or balance sheet and a statement of revenues, expenditures, and changes in fund balance. Exhibits 19-1 and 19-2 present examples of these statements for Grantville's 2006–2007 fiscal year governmental activities. In addition, governments must present budgetary comparison information for the general fund and each special revenue fund that has a legally adopted annual budget. Exhibit 19-3 illustrates one accepted method of presenting this information for the Town of Grantville general fund.

The balance sheet in Exhibit 19-1 contains separate columns for the general fund, the seal exhibit permanent fund, and the town hall capital projects fund. Each of these funds meets the criteria of a *major fund* outlined in Chapter 18. The balance sheet also has a column for the debt service fund, which was not considered a major fund in this example; however, the town's management opted to disclose the fund because they felt it was important to financial statement users. Also, just prior to a totals column, there is a column for other governmental funds, where all nonmajor governmental fund balances are presented in aggregate. The special revenue funds within the chapter example that the town used to account for the highway beautification grant and the state grant for police and fire officer training are included in this column, because they are relatively small in dollar amount and their separate presentation on the face of the balance sheet is not essential. Note that the balance sheet does not include fixed assets or long-term debt. This is consistent with the accounting model and makes governmental fund balance sheets relatively straightforward.

The total fund balance reported on the balance sheet is the same as the ending fund balance reported in the statement of revenues, expenditures, and changes in fund balance in Exhibit 19-2. This governmental fund operating statement has the same columns as the balance sheet and lists revenues, expenditures, and other financing sources (uses) to illustrate changes in fund balance (working capital) for the governmental funds.

Finally, Exhibit 19-3 presents a budgetary comparison schedule for the general fund. This statement, which is required supplementary information for the general fund and for all special revenue funds with legally adopted budgets, includes columns for the original budget, the final budget, actual amounts and variances (optional). It typically includes the same classifications as the GAAP operating statement. Often, however, the amounts reported for revenues, expenditures, and fund balance differ between the two statements. Differences exist when a government uses a non-GAAP basis of accounting for budgeting purposes, as Grantville does because of its use of encumbrance

EXHIBIT 19-1

Balance Sheet—Governmental Funds

TOWN OF GRANTVILLE BALANCE SHEET—GOVERNMENTAL FUNDS SEPTEMBER 30, 2007

	General Fund	Seal Exhibit Permanent Fund	Debt Service Fund	Town Hall Capital Projects Fund	Other Governmental Funds	Total Governmental Funds
Assets						
Cash and cash equivalents	$187,250	$ 9,500	$16,250	$132,500	$ 95,605	$ 441,105
Investments	—	500,000	—	—	11,435	511,435
Receivables						
Taxes receivable—delinquent (net of						
$20,000 estimated uncollectible taxes)	220,000	—	—	—	—	220,000
Accounts receivable	180,000	—	—	—	14,950	194,950
Due from other governments	—	—	—	400,000	53,225	453,225
Supplies inventory	90,000	—	—	—	—	90,000
Total assets	$677,250	$509,500	$ 16,250	$532,500	$175,215	$1,910,715
Liabilities and Fund Balances						
Liabilities						
Vouchers payable	$325,000	—	—	—	$ 58,000	$ 383,000
Matured interest payable	—	—	$ 16,250	—	—	16,250
Contracts payable	—	—	—	$ 47,500	—	47,500
Deferred revenue	50,000	—	—	—	5,000	55,000
Total liabilities	375,000	—	16,250	47,500	63,000	501,750
Fund balances						
Reserved for encumbrances	50,000	—	—	475,000	15,215	540,215
Reserved for debt service	—	—	—	—	—	16,250
Reserved for capital projects	—	—	—	10,000	—	10,000
Reserved for other purposes	—	509,500	—	—	—	509,500
Unreserved	252,250	—	—	—	97,000	349,250
Total fund balance	302,250	509,500	0	485,000	112,215	1,408,965
Total liabilities and fund balance	$677,250	$509,500	$ 16,250	$532,500	$175,215	$1,910,715

accounting. The budget and actual comparison statement must be presented on the budgetary basis of accounting even if it differs from GAAP. The differences between the two statements must be reconciled on the face of the statements, as done here, or in the notes to the financial statements. The reconciliation can explain differences between GAAP-basis and budgetary-basis fund balance amounts or differences between the excess of revenues and other financing sources over expenditures and other financing uses reported in the two statements.

The exhibits do not present budgetary data for the special revenue funds, because it appears that they did not have legally adopted budgets. You can see that the $50,000 transfer of cash from the general fund to the special revenue fund was not originally budgeted. Transfers of $115,000 were originally budgeted for debt service and capital projects only. Note, however, that the town's elected officials must have approved the transfers and amendments to the budget during the year. In fact, each time the actual expenditures or outflows of the general fund exceeded budget, approvals had to be sought and the budget had to be amended. This demonstrates the legal level of control that a governmental entity's budget has over spending. *GASB 34* requires disclosure of the original and final budget information, along with actual figures, in budgetary comparison disclosures. Thus a user of the financial statements can examine the extent of budgetary amendments that were necessary during the financial statement period.

EXHIBIT 19-2

Statement of Revenues, Expenditures, and Changes in Fund Balance

TOWN OF GRANTVILLE GOVERNMENTAL FUNDS STATEMENT OF REVENUES, EXPENDITURES, AND CHANGES IN FUND BALANCE FOR THE FISCAL YEAR ENDED SEPTEMBER 30, 2007

	General Fund	Seal Exhibit Permanent Fund	Debt Service Fund	Town Hall Capital Projects Fund	Other Governmental Funds	Total Governmental Funds
Revenues						
Taxes	$2,080,000	—	—	—	$ 5,250	$2,085,250
Licenses and permits	203,000	—	—	—	—	203,000
Intergovernmental revenues	400,000	—	—	$400,000	61,500	861,500
Charges for services	563,000	—	—	—	—	563,000
Fines and forfeitures	122,000	—	—	—	—	122,000
Addition to permanent endowments	0	$500,000	—	—	—	500,000
Investment income	110,000	12,500	—	—	—	122,500
Miscellaneous revenue	42,000	—	—	—	8,200	50,200
Total revenues	$3,520,000	$512,500	—	$400,000	$ 74,950	$4,507,450
Expenditures						
Current services						
General government	896,000	—	—	—	6,150	902,150
Public safety	927,750	—	—	—	23,500	951,250
Highways and streets	528,750	—	—	—	38,000	566,750
Sanitation	427,000	—	—	—	—	427,000
Health and welfare	175,000	—	—	—	4,200	179,200
Recreation	204,000	3,000	—	—	—	207,000
Capital outlays	190,000	—	—	515,000	—	705,000
Debt service	—	—	$ 16,250	—	—	16,250
Total expenditure	3,348,500	3,000	16,250	515,000	71,850	3,954,600
Excess of revenues over expenditures	171,500	509,500	(16,250)	(115,000)	3,100	552,850
Other Financing Sources (Uses)						
Bond proceeds	—	—	—	502,000	—	502,000
Capital lease	45,000	—	—	—	—	45,000
Transfers in	—	—	16,250	100,000	50,000	166,250
Transfers out	(164,250)	—	—	(2,000)	—	(166,250)
Excess of revenues and other financing sources over expenditures and other financing uses	52,250	509,500	0	485,000	53,100	1,099,850
Fund balance at October 1, 2006	250,000	0	0	0	59,115	309,115
Fund balance at September 30, 2007	$ 302,250	$509,500	$ 0	$485,000	$112,215	$1,408,965

PREPARING THE GOVERNMENTWIDE FINANCIAL STATEMENTS

In addition to the fund financial statements illustrated previously, a government must include governmental fund activities in the governmentwide statements. You may recall, however, that the governmentwide statements are prepared on the accrual basis of accounting, whereas the fund financial statements for the governmental funds are prepared on the modified accrual basis of accounting. Thus, governments must convert governmental fund financial information to the accrual basis of accounting for inclusion in the governmentwide statements of activities and net assets. This conversion, illustrated for the Town of Grantville in Exhibit 19-4, includes the following actions. (The letters in the list correspond with those in the exhibit.)

a Governments must capitalize governmental fund fixed assets, which were recorded as expenditures in the fund statements, at cost in the governmentwide statements. During the year, Grantville purchased $190,000 in equipment. For simplicity, we treat the equipment purchases as the only fixed assets in this example; however,

EXHIBIT 19-3

General Fund
Budgetary
Comparison
Statement

TOWN OF GRANTVILLE BUDGETARY COMPARISON SCHEDULE
GENERAL FUND FOR THE YEAR ENDED SEPTEMBER 30, 2007

	Original Budget	Final Budget	Actual Amounts (Budgetary Basis)	Variance with Final Budget, Positive (Negative)
Revenues				
Taxes	$2,075,000	$2,075,000	$2,080,000	$ 5,000
Licenses and permits	205,000	205,000	203,000	(2,000)
Intergovernmental revenues	400,000	400,000	400,000	—
Charges for services	557,000	557,000	563,000	6,000
Fines and forfeitures	118,000	118,000	122,000	4,000
Investment income	100,000	105,000	110,000	5,000
Miscellaneous revenue	45,000	45,000	42,000	(3,000)
Total revenues	$3,500,000	$3,505,000	$3,520,000	$15,000
Expenditures and Encumbrances				
Current services				
General government	$ 477,500	$ 477,500	$ 475,000	$ 2,500
Public safety	897,750	897,750	892,750	5,000
Highways and streets	825,000	830,000	828,750	1,250
Sanitation	525,000	527,000	527,000	—
Health and welfare	175,000	175,000	175,000	—
Recreation	270,000	275,000	275,000	—
Capital outlays	150,000	150,000	140,000	10,000
Total expenditures and encumbrances	3,320,250	3,332,250	3,313,500*	18,750
Excess of revenues over expenditures and encumbrances	179,750	172,750	206,500	33,750
Other Financing Sources (Uses)				
Capital lease	—	45,000	45,000	—
Transfers out	(115,000)	(164,250)	(164,250)	—
Net change in fund balance	64,750	53,500	87,250	33,750
Budgetary fund balance—beginning	160,000	160,000	160,000	—
Add: Excess prior year encumbrance over actual expenditure	—	—	5,000	5,000
Budgetary fund balance—ending	$ 224,750	$ 213,500	$ 252,250	$38,750
Encumbrances outstanding at September 30, 2007			50,000	
Fund balance—ending			$ 302,250	

*Actual expenditures on a budgetary basis include the $50,000 supplies purchase commitment chargeable against the 2007 appropriations, but exclude the $85,000 expenditure chargeable against the prior year's carryover appropriation.

most governmental entities possess extensive general fixed asset balances, which must be reinstated in total each year as part of the conversion process.

b Grantville must also record depreciation associated with the governmental fixed assets in the governmentwide statements. If the equipment has a 10-year estimated useful life and the town uses straight-line depreciation, depreciation expense and accumulated depreciation amount to $19,000. Until the equipment is retired or sold, this $19,000, as well as annual depreciation expense, will be reinstated as accumulated depreciation in the conversion process.

c Grantville should recognize capital projects fund construction expenditures as "construction in progress" in the governmentwide statements. These expenditures will later be reclassified as "buildings" once construction of the town hall addition is completed.

d Governments must report governmental fund long-term liabilities, where applicable, in the governmentwide statements. Thus, Grantville's capital lease, which was

EXHIBIT 19-4

Conversion Worksheet

	Fund Financial Statement Balances—Governmental Funds		Adjustments/Eliminations		(h) Internal Service Funds	Total Governmental Activities			
	DR	CR	DR	CR		Statement of Activities DR	Statement of Activities CR	Statement of Net Assets DR	Statement of Net Assets CR
Cash and cash equivalents	441,105				0			441,105	
Investments	511,435				0			511,435	
Taxes receivable	220,000				0			220,000	
Accounts receivable	194,950				0			194,950	
Due from other governments	453,225				0			453,225	
Supplies inventory	90,000				0			90,000	
Vouchers payable		383,000			0				383,000
Matured interest payable		16,250			0				16,250
Contracts payable		47,500			0				47,500
Deferred revenue		55,000	(f) 50,000		0				5,000
Fund balance/Net assets, beg.		309,115			0				309,115
Revenues		4,507,450		(f) 50,000	0		4,557,450		
Expenditures	3,954,600		(b) 19,000	(a) 190,000 (c) 515,000	0	3,268,600			
OFS—Bond proceeds		502,000	(e) 502,000		0				
OFS—Capital lease		45,000	(d) 45,000		0				
OFS—Transfers in		166,250	(g) 166,250		0				
OFU—Transfers out	166,250			(g) 166,250	0				
Construction in progress			(c) 515,000		0			515,000	
Equipment			(a) 190,000		0			190,000	
Accumulated depreciation				(b) 19,000	0				19,000

(Continued)

EXHIBIT 19-4

Conversion Worksheet (Continued)

	Fund Financial Statement Balances—Governmental Funds		Adjustments/Eliminations		(h) Internal Service Funds	Total Governmental Activities			
	DR	CR	DR	CR		Statement of Activities DR	Statement of Activities CR	Statement of Net Assets DR	Statement of Net Assets CR
Capital leases payable				(d) 45,000					45,000
Bonds payable				(e) 500,000					500,000
Premium on bonds payable				(e) 2,000					2,000
	6,031,565	6,031,565	1,487,250	1,487,250		3,268,600	4,557,450	2,615,715	1,326,865
Change in net assets						1,288,850			1,288,850
						4,557,450	4,557,450	2,615,715	2,615,715

CR, credit; DR, debit; OFS, other financing source; OFU, other financing use.

recorded as an "other financing source," should be recognized as a long-term liability, "capital lease payable."

e Similar to the capital lease in (d), Grantville recorded bond proceeds as an "other financing source" and must reclassify them as a long-term liability, "bonds payable," on the governmentwide statements.

f Governments must also adjust for instances when revenue recognition differs between the modified accrual and accrual bases of accounting. The sales tax revenue in Grantville's general fund that was deferred because it would not be collected within 60 days of year-end was earned within the fiscal year, so it should be recognized under the accrual basis of accounting. Thus, for Grantville, the $50,000 general fund deferred revenue will be treated as governmentwide revenue.

g Because the governmentwide statement is, in essence, a combined financial statement, it is necessary to eliminate interfund balances within the governmental funds. For Grantville, the $166,250 transfers between funds are eliminated.

h Internal service funds primarily provide goods and services within a governmental entity. Therefore, internal service funds are reported with the governmental activities in the governmentwide statements. In the statement of net assets, internal service fund balance sheet accounts are included in the governmental activity column; however, the statement of activities will include only those internal service fund transactions involving entities other than the primary reporting entity. Thus, internal service fund revenues (and expenditures) resulting from transactions with parties external to the government are added to the statement of activities, and internal governmental transactions are excluded from governmentwide statements.

This chapter did not review the accounting for internal service funds for Grantville, so internal service balances are noted as zero, but the column is included to show how internal service funds would be treated in the conversion worksheet.

Note that the conversion worksheet is an internal, optional document that will never be presented in the financial statements. It is simply helpful for use in preparing the governmentwide statement of net assets and statement of activities, as well as required reconciliations.

STATEMENT OF NET ASSETS We can prepare the governmental activities column of the governmentwide statement of net assets by transferring the converted balance sheet numbers from the conversion worksheet to the statement of net assets. Exhibit 19-5 presents a sample statement of net assets.

GASB 34 requires a reconciliation between the fund and governmentwide financial statements to be presented either at the bottom of the fund financial statements or in an accompanying schedule. We can easily prepare the reconciliation by referencing adjustments on the conversion schedule. An acceptable format for the reconciliation follows:

Total fund balance—governmental funds	$1,408,965
Amounts reported for *governmental activities* in the statement of net assets differ from those in the governmental fund balance sheet because:	
Capital assets (net) used in governmental activities are not financial resources and therefore are not reported in the fund balance sheet	686,000
Revenues reported as deferred on the fund balance sheet using the 60-day criteria are recognized as revenue in the governmentwide statement	50,000
Long-term liabilities (bonds and capital lease payable) are not due and payable in the current period and therefore are not reported in the governmental fund balance sheet	(547,000)
Net assets—governmental funds	$1,597,965

STATEMENT OF ACTIVITIES Governmental activities reported on the governmentwide statement of activities correspond to figures on the conversion worksheet. Exhibit 19-6 presents the statement of activities for the Town of Grantville. You can trace the total expenses of $3,268,600 to the conversion worksheet. Also, the various revenues ($938,200 + $412,500 + $461,500 + $2,745,250) agree with the $4,557,450 on the conversion worksheet.[7]

---

[7] Criteria for classification of the "converted" revenues and expenses into the program and function categories are provided in *GASB Statement No. 34,* paragraphs 38–56.

EXHIBIT 19-5

Governmentwide
Statement of Net
Assets

TOWN OF GRANTVILLE STATEMENT OF NET ASSETS SEPTEMBER 30, 2007

	Governmental Activities	Business-Type Activities	Total
Assets			
Cash and cash equivalents	$ 441,105	$ xxx,xxx	$ x,xxx,xxx
Investments	511,435	xxx,xxx	x,xxx,xxx
Receivables			
Taxes receivable—delinquent (net of $20,000 estimated uncollectible taxes)	220,000	xx,xxx	xxx,xxx
Accounts receivable	194,950	xxx,xxx	xxx,xxx
Due from other governments	453,225	xx,xxx	xxx,xxx
Supplies inventory	90,000	xx,xxx	xxx,xxx
Capital assets, net	686,000	xxx,xxx	x,xxx,xxx
Total assets	$2,596,715	$x,xxx,xxx	$ x,xxx,xxx
Liabilities and Fund Balances			
Liabilities			
Vouchers payable	$ 383,000	$ xxx,xxx	$ xxx,xxx
Matured interest payable	16,250	xx,xxx	xx,xxx
Contracts payable	47,500	xx,xxx	xx,xxx
Deferred revenue	5,000	xx,xxx	xx,xxx
Capital leases payable	45,000	xx,xxx	xxx,xxx
Bonds payable	500,000	xxx,xxx	x,xxx,xxx
Premium on bonds payable	2,000	x,xxx	x,xxx
Total liabilities	998,750	xxx,xxx	x,xxx,xxx
Net assets			
Invested in capital assets, net of related debt	110,000	x,xxx,xxx	x,xxx,xxx
Restricted for debt service	—	—	—
Restricted for capital projects	10,000	—	10,000
Restricted for other purposes	509,500	xx,xxx	xxx,xxx
Unrestricted	968,465	x,xxx,xxx	x,xxx,xxx
Total net assets	$1,597,965	$x,xxx,xxx	$xx,xxx,xxx

GASB 34 also requires a reconciliation between the change in fund balance reported on the fund statement of revenues, expenditures, and changes in fund balance and the change in net assets reported on the statement of activities. This reconciliation may be presented either on the face of the fund financial statements or in an accompanying schedule. Again, the conversion worksheet is helpful. An acceptable format for the reconciliation follows:

Net change in fund balance—total governmental funds	$1,099,850
Amounts reported for *governmental activities* in the statement of net assets differ from those in the governmental fund balance sheet because:	
Governmental funds report capital outlays as expenditures; the assets are capitalized and depreciated in the governmentwide statements	686,000
Revenues in the statement of activities that do not provide current financial resources are not reported as revenues in the funds	50,000
Bond proceeds provide current financial resources in the fund statement, but issuing debt increases long-term liabilities in the statement of net assets	(502,000)
A capital lease is treated as an expenditure in the governmental funds in the year that the lease agreement is entered into; however, it increases long-term liabilities in the statement of net assets	(45,000)
Change in net assets of governmental activities	$1,288,850

Although the two reconciliations between fund financial statements and governmentwide statements will include many of the same items, they will not be identical, and reconciling items will often differ between the two schedules.

EXHIBIT 19-6

Governmentwide Statement of Activities

TOWN OF GRANTVILLE STATEMENT OF ACTIVITIES FOR THE FISCAL YEAR ENDED SEPTEMBER 30, 2007

Functions/Programs	Expenses	Charges for Services	Operating Grants and Contributions	Capital Gains and Contributions	Governmental Activities	Business-Type Activities	Total
Governmental activities							
General government	$ 921,150	$ 138,250	—	$ 405,000	($377,900)	—	$(377,900)
Public safety	951,250	129,650	—	18,500	(803,100)	—	(803,100)
Highways and streets	566,750	23,350	$400,000	38,000	(103,400)	—	(103,400)
Sanitation	427,000	390,750	—	—	(36,250)	—	(36,250)
Health and welfare	179,200	102,200	—	—	(77,000)	—	(77,000)
Recreation	207,000	152,000	12,500	—	(42,500)	—	(42,500)
Debt service	16,250	—	—	—	(16,250)	—	(16,250)
Total governmental activities	3,268,600	938,200	412,500	461,500	(1,456,400)	—	(1,456,400)
Business-type activities							
Utilities	x,xxx,xxx	x,xxx,xxx	—	xxx,xxx	—	xx,xxx	xx,xxx
Parking facilities	xx,xxx	xx,xxx	x,xxx	—	—	x,xxx	x,xxx
Total business-type activities	x,xxx,xxx	x,xxx,xxx	—	—	—	—	xx,xxx
Total government	$x,xxx,xxx	$x,xxx,xxx	$xxx,xxx	$x,xxx,xxx	($1,456,400)	$xx,xxx	$x,xxx,xxx

General Revenues	
Property taxes	$1,980,000
Sales taxes	155,250
Investment Earnings	110,000
Special item—permanent fund contribution	500,000
Total general revenues and special items	2,745,250
Change in net assets	1,288,850
Net assets—beginning	309,115
Net assets—ending	$1,597,965

Governmental funds are used to account for general governmental activities affecting a governmental entity. They generally follow the modified accrual basis for accounting and reporting within the fund financial statements. This chapter included a review of appropriate accounting for the general fund, as well as special revenue, permanent, capital projects, and debt service funds using the governmental fund model introduced in Chapter 18.

Acounting for each of the governmental funds is the same, but the purpose of each fund type differs. The essential difference between a general fund and a special revenue fund lies in the fact that general fund revenues are available to finance the general needs of government, whereas the revenues of special revenue funds are restricted to specific uses. Permanent funds are used to account for nonexpendable resources set aside for support of a government's programs or citizenry. Capital projects funds are used to account for the acquisition of major capital facilities, and debt service funds are used to account for the receipt and use of resources to service general long-term debt obligations.

General and special revenue activities normally are controlled with formal budgetary procedures and accounting practices. Compliance with the budget is demonstrated by presenting budgetary comparison statements comparing actual and budgeted revenues and expenditures. Required fund financial statements for governmental funds include a statement of net assets or balance sheet and a statement of revenues, expenditures, and changes in fund balance. Those governments that record governmental fund transactions in the accounting records on the modified accrual basis of accounting must convert governmental fund statement data into their governmentwide statement counterparts.

QUESTIONS

1. What is the accounting equation for a governmental fund?

2. If property tax bills totaling $200,000 are mailed to taxpayers and a 3% loss on uncollectible taxes is expected, what amount should be recorded as revenue?

3. What are encumbrances, and how does encumbrance accounting help control expenditures?

4. List the required governmental fund financial statements under *GASB 34*. On what basis of accounting are these statements prepared?

5. What is the purpose of capital projects funds? Are all general fixed assets of a governmental unit acquired through capital projects funds? Explain.

6. How are capital projects funds financed, and when would a capital projects fund be terminated?

7. How do the purchases and consumption methods of accounting for inventory differ?

8. Are debt service funds used to account for debt service on all long-term obligations of a governmental unit? If not, which long-term debt obligations are excluded?

9. Describe a transaction that would affect the general fund and the debt service fund at the same time.

10. How do special assessment levies differ from general tax levies?

11. Which funds may be used to account for the activities of a general governmental special assessment construction project with long-term financing? Explain.

12. How are capital leases recorded in governmental funds?

13. Assume that supplies on hand at the beginning of the year amount to $60,000 and that supply purchases during the year are $400,000. Supplies on hand at year-end are $40,000, and the consumption basis of accounting for supplies is used. What adjusting entry for supplies should be made at year-end?

14. What is the role of a subsidiary ledger in a governmental entity?

15. The Village of Lester had appropriations of $250,000 for the current fiscal year. If $175,000 worth of items has been ordered but only $150,000 of the $175,000 has been received, what amount can city officials order prior to year-end? What happens if they have not spent the full $250,000 prior to year-end?

16. Purchase orders totaling $60,000 for supplies are outstanding at June 30, 2007, the close of the fiscal year. The supplies are received on July 18, 2007, at a cost of $59,800. Prepare the journal entries needed in the 2007–2008 fiscal year assuming that committed appropriations can be carried over to the next period.

17. How does a permanent fund differ from a special revenue fund?

18. How can you determine whether or not a governmental fund should be considered major? (Chapter 18)

19. What is included on a budgetary comparison schedule? Is such a schedule required to be included in a CAFR?

20. How is a conversion worksheet used? Why is it necessary?

21. List three items that might appear on the reconciliation between the governmental fund balance sheet and the governmentwide statement of net assets. List three items that might appear on the reconciliation between the governmental fund operating statement and the governmentwide statement of activities.

EXERCISES

E 19-1

Multiple Choice

1. The estimated revenues control account balance of a governmental fund type is eliminated when:
   a   *The budget is recorded*
   b   *The budgetary accounts are closed*
   c   *Appropriations are closed*
   d   *Property taxes are recorded*

2. When equipment is purchased with general fund resources, which of the following accounts should be increased in the general fund?
   a   *Due from general fixed assets account group*
   b   *Expenditures*
   c   *Appropriations*
   d   *No entry should be made in the general fund*

3. A municipality's debt service fund regularly receives cash from the general fund to pay interest and serial payments on the city's outstanding serial bond issue. The transfer of cash from the general fund is:
   a   *Recorded as an expenditure of the general fund and as revenue of the debt service fund*
   b   *A quasi-external transaction that will appear in the operating statements of the respective funds, even though it is not an expenditure or revenue of the governmental unit*
   c   *An operating transfer that will be included as "other financing sources and uses" in the respective funds*
   d   *Paid immediately to outside interests and therefore has no effect on the financial statements of the debt service fund*

4. Encumbrances outstanding at year-end in a state's general fund should be reported as a:
   a   *Liabilities in the general fund*
   b   *Fund balance reserves in the general fund*
   c   *Liabilities in the general long-term debt account group*
   d   *Expenditures in the general fund*

5. Which of the following funds would not be included in governmental fund financial statements?
   a   *Debt service fund*
   b   *General fund*
   c   *Permanent fund*
   d   *Pension trust fund*

E 19-2

Multiple Choice

1. The accounts "estimated revenues" and "appropriations" appear in the trial balance of the general fund. These accounts indicate:
   a   *The use of cash basis accounting*
   b   *The use of accrual basis accounting*
   c   *The formal use of budgetary accounts*
   d   *The informal use of budgetary accounts*

2. When a complete system of encumbrance accounting is used, the authorizations remaining available for expenditures at any interim date will be equal to:
   a   *Appropriations less encumbrances*
   b   *Appropriations less expenditures*
   c   *Appropriations plus encumbrances less expenditures*
   d   *Appropriations less expenditures and encumbrances*

3. Encumbrance accounting is designed to:

 a   Prevent overspending of amounts appropriated

 b   Replace expenditure accounting for governmental organizations

 c   Prevent excessive appropriations

 d   Prevent or reduce waste in governmental spending

4. Reserve for encumbrance accounts in general fund balance sheets at year-end indicate:

 a   The amount of net assets required to complete the transaction(s) in the succeeding period

 b   Noncompliance with GAAP

 c   Cash on hand

 d   Valuation reserves

5. The reserve for encumbrances—past year account typically represents amounts recorded by a governmental unit for:

 a   Anticipated expenditures in the next year

 b   Expenditures for which purchase orders were made in the prior year but for which expenditure and disbursement will be in the current year

 c   Excess expenditures in the prior year that will be offset against the current-year budgeted amounts

 d   Unanticipated expenditures of the prior year that become evident in the current year

E 19-3

Multiple Choice [AICPA adapted]

1. Of the items listed, those most likely to have parallel accounting procedures, account titles, and financial statements are:

 a   Special revenue funds and trust funds

 b   Internal service funds and debt service funds

 c   The general fixed assets account group and the general long-term debt account group

 d   The general fund and special revenue funds

2. The encumbrance account of a governmental unit is debited when:

 a   The budget is recorded

 b   A purchase order is approved

 c   Goods are received

 d   A voucher payable is recorded

3. When the purchases method of accounting for supplies is used, the financial statements of the related fund entity:

 a   Need not show material amounts of supplies on hand as an asset

 b   Must disclose the cost of supplies used during the period

 c   Are substantially the same as they would be under the consumption method

 d   Must disclose a fund balance reserve for material amounts of supplies on hand

4. When the consumption basis of accounting for supplies is used, the financial statements of the related fund entity:

 a   Must show supply purchases as expenditures of the period

 b   Must show a fund balance restriction for material amounts of supplies on hand

 c   Must reflect the fact that perpetual inventory procedures have been used in accounting for supplies

 d   Must show supplies on hand as an asset

5. The following information pertains to Clute City:

2007 governmental fund revenues that became measurable and available in time to be used for payment of 2007 liabilities	$16,000,000
Revenues earned in 2005 and 2006 and included in the $16,000,000 indicated	2,000,000
Sales taxes collected by merchants in 2007 but not required to be remitted to Clute until January 2008	3,000,000

For the year ended December 31, 2007, Clute should recognize fund financial statement revenues of:

 a $14,000,000

 b $16,000,000

 c $17,000,000

 d $19,000,000

E 19-4

Multiple Choice

1. Howard City should use a capital projects fund to account for:

 a   Proceeds of a capital grant to finance a new civic center that will not provide services primarily on a user-charge basis

 b   Construction of sewer lines by the water and sewer utility to be financed by user costs c The accumulation of resources to retire bonds issued to construct the town hall

d Construction of an addition to the airport terminal owned by the Howard City Municipal Airport, an enterprise fund

2. When a capital projects fund is dissolved by paying any remaining assets to another fund, the decrease in fund balance is a (an):

a Expenditure

b Operating transfer

c Residual equity transfer

d Reimbursement

3. Which of the following items would be least likely to appear in the account titles of a capital projects fund?

a Due from federal government (for grant)

b Due from general fund

c Proceeds from bond issue

d Construction in progress

4. Three financial statements may be required to present the results of operations and financial position of a special revenue fund. Which of the following is not one of these required statements?

a Statement of cash flows

b Statement of revenues, expenditures, and changes in fund balance

c Statement of revenues, expenditures, and changes in fund balance—budget and actual

d Balance sheet

5. Assets financed through a capital projects fund should be capitalized in the governmentwide financial statements:

a Only when construction is completed

b On the basis of expenditures to date

c On the basis of expenditures and encumbrances to date

d On the basis of amounts paid to date

E 19-5
Multiple Choice [AICPA adapted]

1. The receipts from a special tax levy to retire and pay interest on general obligation bonds should be recorded in a:

a Debt service fund

b Capital projects fund

c Revolving interests fund

d Special revenue fund

2. Proceeds of general obligation bonds is an account of a governmental unit that typically would be included in the:

a Enterprise fund

b Special revenue fund

c Capital projects fund

d Governmentwide financial statements

3. Assets in general governmental service that had been constructed 10 years before by a capital projects fund were sold. The receipts were accounted for as an other financing source. Entries are necessary in the:

a General fund and capital projects fund

b General fund only

c General fund, capital projects fund, and enterprise fund

d General fund, capital projects fund, and general fixed assets account group

4. Martha County issues general obligation serial bonds at a premium to finance construction of a sheriff's office. Which of the following funds are affected by the transaction?

a Special revenue fund

b Capital projects fund and general fund

c Capital projects fund, general fund, and debt service fund

d Capital projects fund and debt service fund

5. Property taxes are considered:

a Derived tax revenues

b Imposed nonexchange revenues

c Government-mandated nonexchange transactions

d Voluntary nonexchange transactions

E 19-6

Multiple Choice [AICPA adapted]

1. For the budgetary year ending December 31, 2006, Sponge City's general fund expects the following inflows of resources:

Property taxes, licenses, and fees	$9,000,000
Proceeds of debt issue	5,000,000
Interfund transfers for debt service	1,000,000

In the budgetary entry, what amount should Sponge record for estimated revenues?

a **$9,000,000**
b **$10,000,000**
c **$14,000,000**
d **$15,000,000**

2. During its fiscal year ended June 30, 2006, Nomar City issued purchase orders totaling $5,000,000, which were properly charged to encumbrances at that time. Nomar received goods and related invoices at the encumbered amounts totaling $4,500,000 before year-end. The remaining goods of $500,000 were not received until after year-end. Nomar paid $4,200,000 of the invoices received during the year. What amount of Nomar's encumbrances was outstanding at June 30, 2006?

a **0**
b **$300,000**
c **$500,000**
d **$800,000**

3. The following information pertains to property taxes levied by Oval City for the calendar year 2005:

Collections during 2005	$500,000
Expected collections during the first 60 days of 2006	100,000
Expected collections during the balance of 2006	60,000
Expected collections during January 2007	30,000
Estimated to be uncollectible	10,000
Total levy	$700,000

What amount should Oval report for 2005 net property tax revenues?

a **$700,000**
b **$690,000**
c **$600,000**
d **$500,000**

4. The following information pertains to Square City's general fund for 2009:

Appropriations	$6,500,000
Expenditures	5,000,000
Other financing sources	1,500,000
Other financing uses	2,000,000
Revenues	8,000,000

In 2009, Square's total fund balance increased by:

a **$3,000,000**
b **$2,500,000**
c **$1,500,000**
d **$1,000,000**

5. The following information pertains to Amber Township's general fund at December 31, 2007:

Total assets, including $200,000 of cash	$1,000,000
Total liabilities	600,000
Reserved for encumbrances	100,000

Appropriations do not lapse at year-end. At December 31, 2007, what amount should Amber report as unreserved fund balance in its general fund balance sheet?

a **$200,000**
b **$300,000**
c **$400,000**
d **$500,000**

E 19-7

General fund journal entries (property taxes) The following events and transactions relate to the levy and collection of property taxes for Jedville Township.

March 21, 2006—Property tax bills for $2,500,000 are sent to property owners. An estimated 2% of the property tax levies are uncollectible. The taxes are due on May 1.

May 4, 2006—$1,900,000 in taxes have been collected. The remaining receivables are reclassified as delinquent.

May 5 to December 31, 2006—An additional $150,000 of taxes are collected.

November 1, 2006—A $5,000 tax receivable account is determined to be uncollectible and is written off.

January 1, 2007, to February 28, 2007—An additional $87,750 of 2006 taxes are collected.

REQUIRED

1. Prepare summary journal entries for the events and transactions described for the Jedville general fund.

2. How will property taxes be presented in the December 31, 2006, balance sheet?

3. What amount of property tax revenues should be reported for 2006?

E 19-8

Governmental fund closing entries A general ledger trial balance for Any City contained the following balances at June 30, 2007, just before closing entries were made:

Due from other funds	$ 600
Unreserved fund balance	3,000
Estimated revenues	18,000
Revenues	17,380
Appropriations	17,500
Expenditures—current year	16,450
Expenditures—prior year	1,900
Encumbrances	1,000
Nonreciprocal transfer in	3,200
Reserve for encumbrances	1,000
Reserve for encumbrances—prior year	2,000

REQUIRED: Prepare the necessary closing entries.

E 19-9

Preparation of fund balance sheet A general ledger trial balance at June 30, 2006, for Millar City is as follows:

	Debits	Credits
Cash	$ 12,000	—
Taxes receivable	30,000	—
Allowance for uncollectible taxes	—	$ 2,000
Due from other funds	3,000	—
Supplies inventory, June 30, 2006	4,000	—
Estimated revenues	300,000	—
Expenditures	290,000	—
Expenditures—prior year	5,000	—
Encumbrances	6,000	—
Vouchers payable	—	15,000
Due to other funds	—	5,000
Reserve for encumbrances	—	6,000
Reserve for encumbrances—prior year	—	5,000
Reserve for inventory	—	2,000
Unreserved fund balance	—	10,000
Appropriations	—	300,000
Revenues	—	305,000
	$650,000	$650,000

Millar City uses a purchases basis in accounting for supplies.

REQUIRED: Prepare a fund balance sheet as of June 30, 2006.

E 19-10

Preparation of a fund statement of revenues, expenditures, and changes in fund balance The trial balance of the general fund of McGwire City before closing at December 31, 2005, contained the following accounts and balances:

Unreserved fund balance	$ 25,000
Estimated revenues	100,000
Appropriations	95,000
Encumbrances	4,000
Reserve for encumbrances	4,000
Reserve for encumbrances—prior year	5,000
Revenues	101,000
Expenditures	94,000
Expenditures—prior year	4,800
Nonreciprocal transfers out	18,000
Reciprocal transfers in	27,000

REQUIRED: Prepare a statement of revenues, expenditures, and changes in (total) fund balance for McGwire City's general fund in 2005. (Details of revenue and expenditure accounts are omitted to simplify the requirement.)

E 19-11

General fund journal entries Prepare entries in the general fund to record the following transactions and events:

1. Estimated revenues for the fiscal year were $250,000 and appropriations were $248,000.
2. The tax levy for the fiscal year, of which 99% is believed to be collectible, was $200,000.
3. Taxes collected were $150,000.
4. A short-term loan of $15,000 was made to the special revenue fund.
5. Orders for supplies were placed in the amount of $18,000.
6. The items ordered in transaction 5 were received. Actual cost was $18,150, and vouchers for that amount were prepared.
7. Materials were acquired from the stores fund (an internal service fund) in the amount of $800 (without encumbrance).
8. A $5,000 payment (transfer) was made to the debt service fund.
9. A cash payment of $15,000 was made for the purchase of equipment.
10. Licenses were collected in the amount of $3,000.
11. The balance of taxes receivable became delinquent.
12. Delinquent taxes of $30,000 were collected before year-end. The remaining net realizable value of delinquent taxes is expected to be collected uniformly over the first four months of the next fiscal year.

E 19-12

General fund journal entries Prepare the journal entries required to record the following transactions in the general fund of Rochester Township.

1. Borrowed $75,000 by issuing six-month tax anticipation notes.
2. Ordered equipment with an estimated cost of $33,000.
3. Received the equipment along with an invoice for its actual cost, $33,250.
4. Transferred $200,000 of general fund resources to a debt service fund.
5. On January 1, the township levied property taxes of $1,000,000. The township expects to collect all except $100,000 by the end of the fiscal year or within not more than 60 days thereafter. Of the remaining $100,000, half is expected to prove uncollectible.
6. The township received a $100,000 restricted grant for certain library programs from another unit of government. The grant will be accounted for in the general fund.
7. The township incurred $75,000 of expenditures for the programs covered by the library grant.

E 19-13

Governmental fund journal entries For each of the following transactions, note the fund(s) affected, and prepare appropriate journal entries.

1. General obligation bonds with a par value of $750,000 are issued at $769,000 to finance construction of a government office building.

2. A Community Block Development Grant in the amount of $450,000 is awarded for residential services within a city.

3. Upon approval of a new town band shell, the general fund transfers $500,000 to create a new fund.

4. A wealthy citizen donates $10,000,000 for city park maintenance. The principal cannot be spent.

5. Automobiles and vans for general governmental use are purchased for $375,000.

6. General fixed assets with an original cost of $300,000 sold for $30,000 at the end of their useful life.

7. Sold equipment at the end of its expected useful life. The equipment had no expected residual value when acquired (at a cost of $13,000), but it sold for $1,200.

8. The general fund transfers $50,000 for an interest payment on debt. The interest payment is made.

E 19-14

Governmental fund reconciliation to total net assets The postclosing trial balance for the Village of Collins general fund at June 30, 2008, shows the following ledger account balances:

Debits	
Cash	$410,000
Investments	300,000
Tax receivable—delinquent	150,000
Accounts receivable	30,000
Supplies inventory	60,000
Total debits	$950,000

Credits	
Allowances for uncollectible taxes— delinquent	$ 10,000
Vouchers payable	140,000
Deferred revenue	40,000
Note payable (short-term)	150,000
Reserve for encumbrances	90,000
Unreserved fund balance	520,000
Total credits	$950,000

ADDITIONAL INFORMATION

a. The village owns general fixed assets with a historical cost of $100,000 and accumulated depreciation totaling $65,000.

b. General long-term debt recorded in the internal debt records is $100,000. This was recorded as an other financing source in the general fund.

c. A capital lease payable in the amount of $75,000 is noted in the internal debt records. This was recorded as an other financing source in the general fund.

d. Revenues reported as deferred on the fund balance sheet using the 60-day criteria are recognized as revenue in the governmentwide statement.

REQUIRED: Determine the village's general fund net assets that will appear on the governmentwide statement of net assets.

E 19-15

Governmental fund reconciliation to total net assets The following data are available from the City of Boulder's financial records on September 30, 2007:

a. The net change in fund balance—total governmental funds for the city is $1,408,950.

b. The city purchased general fixed assets at a historical cost of $225,000 during the year. No depreciation is recorded in the year of purchase.

c. Grants receivable in the amount of $165,000 are recorded as deferred revenue in the fund statements but would be recognized as revenue under accrual accounting.

d. A capital lease payable in the amount of $75,000 has been recorded as an expenditure in the general fund. The related long-term debt at year-end is $55,000.

e. General long-term debt in the amount of $350,000 has been issued and recorded in the general fund.

REQUIRED: Determine the city's change in net assets of governmental activities that will appear in the governmentwide statements.

PROBLEMS

P 19-1

Preparation of a general fund balance sheet The unadjusted trial balance for the general fund of the City of Orchard Park at December 31, 2008, is as follows:

	Debit	Credit
Accounts receivable	$ 25,000	—
Allowance for bad debts	—	$ 2,000
Allowance for uncollectible taxes	—	30,000
Appropriations	—	900,000
Cash	40,000	—
Due from agency fund	10,000	—
Due to utility fund	—	20,000
Encumbrances	50,000	—
Estimated revenues	910,000	—
Expenditures	858,000	—
Fund balance	—	26,000
Reserve for encumbrances	—	50,000
Revenues	—	910,000
Taxes receivable—delinquent	210,000	—
Taxes received in advance	—	10,000
Vouchers payable	—	155,000
	$2,103,000	$2,103,000

Supplies on hand at December 31, 2008, are $3,000. The $50,000 encumbrance relates to equipment ordered November 28 for the Department of Public Works but not received by year-end.

REQUIRED: Prepare a balance sheet for the general fund of the City of Orchard Park at December 31, 2008.

P 19-2

Preparation of general fund statements The preclosing account balances of the general fund of the City of Batavia on June 30, 2006, were as follows:

Debits
Cash	$ 80,000
Taxes receivable—delinquent	160,000
Supplies inventory	18,000
Estimated revenues	1,000,000
Expenditures	940,000
Nonreciprocal transfers out	10,000
Encumbrances	20,000
	$2,228,000

Credits
Allowance for uncollectible taxes—delinquent	$ 30,000
Vouchers payable	40,000
Notes payable	60,000
Reserve for encumbrances	20,000
Reserve for supplies	18,000
Unreserved fund balance	120,000
Revenues	980,000
Appropriations	960,000
	$2,228,000

The unreserved fund balance at the beginning of the year was $80,000, and there were no carryover encumbrances at the beginning of the fiscal year.

REQUIRED

1. Prepare a statement of revenues, expenditures, and changes in total fund balance for the year ended June 30, 2006.

2. Prepare a general fund balance sheet at June 30, 2006.

LEARNING OBJECTIVES 1, 2, 4, 5

P 19-3

Governmental fund journal entries, budgetary comparison, and reconciling items

The Town of Tyler approved the following general fund budget for the fiscal year July 1, 2006, to June 30, 2007.

TOWN OF TYLER
GENERAL FUND BUDGET SUMMARY
FOR THE YEAR JULY 1, 2006 TO JUNE 30, 2007

Revenue Sources	
Taxes	$250,000
Licenses and permits	20,000
Intergovernmental revenue	40,000
Charges for services	60,000
Fines and forfeits	15,000
Rents and royalties	10,000
Miscellaneous revenues	5,000
Total budgeted revenues	$400,000
Expenditures	
Current services	
General government	$ 45,000
Public safety	140,000
Highways and streets	90,000
Sanitation	55,000
Health and welfare	20,000
Recreation	30,000
Capital outlays	15,000
Total appropriations	$395,000
Budgeted increase in fund balance	$ 5,000

The after-closing trial balance of the Town of Tyler general fund at June 30, 2006, shows the following ledger account balances:

Debits	
Cash	$31,000
Tax receivable—delinquent	15,000
Accounts receivable	3,000
Supplies inventory	6,000
Total debits	$55,000
Credits	
Allowances for uncollectible taxes—delinquent	$ 1,000
Vouchers payable	14,000
Note payable (short-term)	15,000
Reserve for encumbrances	9,000
Unreserved fund balance	16,000
Total credits	$55,000

1. Prepare journal entries to record the budget and each of the following transactions:
   a. *The treasurer of Tyler sends out property tax bills of $200,000; 1% is considered uncollectible.*
   b. *Current property taxes of $176,000 and past-due taxes of $14,000 were collected.*
   c. *A specific property tax bill ($1,000) is determined to be uncollectible.*
   d. *Fees in the amount of $20,000 are collected for hunting licenses.*
   e. *Other revenues in the amount of $200,000 are collected.*
   f. *The payroll for salaries of $20,000 is vouchered for payment.*
   g. *Playground equipment expected to cost $15,000 is ordered.*
   h. *The playground equipment is received and has an actual cost of $14,000.*
   i. *Tyler received equipment that had been ordered in the previous fiscal year. The actual cost was $18,500.*
   j. *Supplies in the amount of $11,000 were ordered. By year-end, only $5,000 worth of these supplies has been received. The consumption method is used.*
   k. *The note payable that was outstanding at June 30, 2006, becomes due and is paid.*
   l. *Various expenditures throughout the year totaled $348,040.*

m. Supplies in the amount of $3,000 are on hand at year-end.

n. Assume that uncollected taxes on June 30, 2006, are past due.

o. Closing entries are made.

2. Prepare a budgetary comparison statement for the Tyler general fund.

3. Identify the transactions above that will be reconciling items between the fund financial statements and the governmentwide financial statements.

P 19-4

Governmental fund conversion worksheet
The post-closing trial balance for the City of Fort Collins governmental funds at June 30, 2008, shows the following ledger account balances:

	DR	CR
Cash and cash equivalents	$ 541,100	
Investments	520,000	
Taxes receivable	520,000	
Accounts receivable	187,500	
Due from other governments	364,970	
Supplies inventory	290,000	
Vouchers payable		$ 379,500
Contracts payable		47,500
Deferred revenue		55,000
Fund balance/Net assets, beg.		912,720
Revenues		3,507,450
Expenditures	3,043,600	
OFS—Bond proceeds		500,000
OFS—Capital lease		65,000
OFS—Transfers in		75,250
OFU—Transfers out	75,250	
	$5,542,420	$5,542,420

ADDITIONAL INFORMATION

a. During the year, Fort Collins purchased $9,000 in equipment, which was not depreciated.

b. Fort Collins also has other fixed assets with a historical cost of $95,000 and accumulated depreciation of $65,000.

c. Fort Collins has capital project fund construction expenditures totaling $20,000.

d. During the year, the city issued a bond at $500,000 par value.

e. During the year, the city entered into a lease agreement. The entire amount should be recognized as general long-term debt.

f. The city's deferred revenue would be treated as revenue under accrual accounting.

g. The transfers in and out were made between governmental funds.

h. The city does not report internal service funds.

REQUIRED: Prepare a conversion worksheet to determine the change in net assets and the net asset balance for the city's governmental funds.

P 19-5

LEARNING OBJECTIVES **1, 2**

Reconstruct general fund journal entries [AICPA adapted]
The following summary of transactions was taken from the accounts of the Oslo School District general fund before the books had been closed for the fiscal year ended June 30, 2005.

	Postclosing Balances June 30, 2004	Preclosing Balances June 30, 2005
Cash	$400,000	$ 700,000
Taxes receivable	150,000	170,000
Estimated uncollectible taxes	(40,000)	(70,000)
Estimated revenues	—	3,000,000
Expenditures	—	2,842,000
Expenditures—prior years	—	—
Encumbrances	—	91,000
	$510,000	$6,733,000

	Postclosing Balances June 30, 2004	Preclosing Balances June 30, 2005
Vouchers payable	$ 80,000	$ 408,000
Due to other funds	210,000	142,000
Reserve for encumbrances	60,000	91,000
Unreserved fund balance	160,000	182,000
Revenues from taxes	—	2,800,000
Miscellaneous revenues	—	130,000
Appropriations	—	2,980,000
	$510,000	$6,733,000

ADDITIONAL INFORMATION

1. The estimated taxes receivable for the year ended June 30, 2005, were $2,870,000, and current-year taxes collected during the year totaled $2,810,000.

2. Estimated uncollectible taxes from the prior year were written off.

3. An analysis of the transactions in the vouchers payable for the year ended June 30, 2005, follows:

	Debit (Credit)
Current expenditures	$(2,700,000)
Expenditures for prior years	(58,000)
Vouchers for payment to other funds	(210,000)
Cash payments during the year	2,640,000
Net change	$ (328,000)

4. During the year the general fund was billed $142,000 for services performed on its behalf by other city funds.

5. On May 2, 2005, commitment documents were issued for the purchase of new textbooks at a cost of $91,000.

REQUIRED: Based on the data presented, reconstruct the original detailed journal entries that were required to record all transactions for the fiscal year ended June 30, 2005, including the recording of the current year's budget. Do not prepare closing entries at June 30, 2005.

LEARNING OBJECTIVES **1, 2**

P 19-6

Journal entries from trial balance [AICPA adapted] The following information was abstracted from the accounts of the general fund of the City of Lahti after the books had been closed for the fiscal year ended June 30, 2008.

	Trial Balance June 30, 2007	Transactions July 1, 2007 to June 30, 2008 Debit	Transactions July 1, 2007 to June 30, 2008 Credit	Postclosing Trial Balance June 30, 2008
Cash	$700,000	$1,820,000	$1,852,000	$668,000
Taxes receivable	40,000	1,870,000	1,828,000	82,000
	$740,000			$750,000
Allowances for uncollectible taxes	$ 8,000	8,000	10,000	$ 10,000
Vouchers payable	132,000	1,852,000	1,840,000	120,000
Fund balance:				
Reserve for encumbrances	—	1,000,000	1,070,000	70,000
Unreserved	600,000	140,000	60,000	
			30,000	550,000
	$740,000			$750,000

ADDITIONAL INFORMATION: The budget for the fiscal year ended June 30, 2008, provided for estimated revenues of $2,000,000 and appropriations of $1,940,000.

REQUIRED: Prepare journal entries to record the budgeted and actual transactions for the fiscal year ended June 30, 2008.

P 19-7

Preparation of a fund statement of revenues, expenditures and changes in fund balance The following information regarding the fiscal year ended December 31, 2005, was drawn from the accounts and records of the Volendam County general fund.

Revenues and Other Asset Inflows	
Taxes	$10,000,000
Licenses and permits	2,000,000
Intergovernmental grants	300,000
Proceeds of short-term note issuances	1,000,000
Collection of interfund advance to other fund	450,000
Receipt of net assets of terminated fund	2,000,000
Expenditures and Other Asset Outflows	
General government expenditures	8,000,000
Public safety expenditures	1,500,000
Judicial system expenditures	1,000,000
Health and welfare expenditures	1,200,000
Equipment purchases	600,000
Payment to debt service fund to cover future debt service on general government bonds	320,000
Unreserved fund balance, January 1, 2005	$ 3,130,000

REQUIRED: Prepare a statement of revenues, expenditures, and changes in fund balance for the Volendam County general fund for the year ended December 31, 2005.

P 19-8

Debt service fund journal entries The Town of Lilehammar has $3,000,000 of 6% bonds outstanding. Interest on the general obligation, general government indebtedness is payable semiannually each March 31 and September 30. December 31 is the fiscal year-end. Record the following transactions in the town's debt service fund.

1. Received a transfer from the general fund to provide financing for the March 31, 2007, interest payment.

2. Paid the interest due on March 31, 2007.

3. Received a transfer from the general fund to provide financing for the September 30, 2007, interest payment and retirement of $1,000,000 of the bonds.

4. Paid the interest on September 31, 2007, and repaid $1,000,000 of the bonds.

5. December 31 is the fiscal year-end. Record any appropriate adjustments.

6. Received a transfer from the general fund to provide financing for the March 31, 2008, interest payment.

7. Paid the interest due on March 31, 2008.

P 19-9

Capital projects fund journal entries The City of Stockholm authorized construction of a $600,000 addition to the municipal building in September 2006. The addition will be financed by $200,000 from the general fund and a $400,000 serial bond issue to be sold in April 2007.

REQUIRED: Prepare journal entries for the capital projects fund and any other fund involved to the extent of requiring journal entries to record the transactions described.

1. On October 1, 2006, the general fund transferred $200,000 to the capital projects fund.

2. On November 1, 2006, a contract for the addition was awarded to Crooked Construction for $580,000.

3. On April 15, 2007, the $400,000, 7% bonds were sold for $401,000 and the premium was transferred to the debt service fund.

4. On May 2, 2007, construction was completed and Crooked Construction submitted a bill for $580,000.

5. On May 12, 2007, the bill to Crooked Construction was paid in full. The CPF was closed, and the remaining cash was transferred to the general fund.

LEARNING OBJECTIVE 4

LEARNING OBJECTIVES 1, 3

LEARNING OBJECTIVES 1, 3

LEARNING OBJECTIVES 1, 3

P 19-10

Journal entries associated with a capital project On June 15, 2007, Malmo City authorizes the issuance of $500,000 par of 6% serial bonds to be issued on July 1, 2007, and to mature in annual serials of $100,000 beginning on July 1, 2008. The proceeds of the bond issue are to be used to finance a new tourist rest area.

During the fiscal year ended June 30, 2008, the following events and transactions occurred:

> July 1, 2007—A contract for construction of the rest area is awarded to Gunnarsson Construction Company for $480,000.
> July 1, 2007—$250,000 par value of 6% serial bonds are sold at a premium of 2%.
> December 20, 2007—A bill is received from Gunnarsson Construction Company for one-third of the contract price.
> January 1, 2008—Gunnarsson Construction Company is paid for work completed to date, less a 10% retained percentage to ensure performance.
> January 1, 2008—Bond interest due is paid with funds transferred from the general fund and from the premium that was made available for interest payments.
> June 30, 2008—A bill is received from Gunnarsson Construction Company for one-third of the contract price.

REQUIRED

1. Prepare journal entries in each of the affected funds to account for the transactions and events described. Identify the fund for each journal entry.

2. Prepare a closing journal entry for the capital projects fund at June 30, 2008.

LEARNING OBJECTIVES 1, 2, 4

P 19-11

Capital projects fund journal entries and balance sheet [AICPA adapted] In a special election held on May 1, 2007, the voters of the City of Cerone approved a $10,000,000 issue of 6% general obligation bonds maturing in 20 years. The proceeds of this sale will be used to help finance the construction of a new civic center. The total cost of the project was estimated at $15,000,000. The remaining $5,000,000 will be financed by a state grant, which has been awarded. A capital projects fund was established to account for this project and was designated the civic center construction fund. The formal project authorization was appropriately recorded in a memorandum entry.

The following transactions occurred during the fiscal year beginning July 1, 2007, and ending June 30, 2008.

1. On July 1 the general fund loaned $500,000 to the civic center construction fund for defraying engineering and other expenses.

2. Preliminary engineering and planning costs of $320,000 were paid to Eminem Engineering Company. There had been no encumbrance for this cost.

3. On December 1 the bonds were sold at 101. The premium on the bonds was transferred to the debt service fund.

4. On March 15 a contract for $12,000,000 was entered into with Candu Construction Company for the major part of the project.

5. Orders were placed for materials estimated to cost $55,000.

6. On April 1 a partial payment of $2,500,000 was received from the state.

7. The materials that were previously ordered were received at a cost of $51,000 and paid.

8. On June 15 a progress billing of $2,000,000 was received from Candu Construction for work done on the project. As per the terms of the contract, the city will withhold 6% of any billing until the project is completed.

9. The general fund was repaid the $500,000 previously loaned.

REQUIRED

1. Prepare journal entries to record the transactions in the civic center construction fund for the period July 1, 2007, through June 30, 2008, and the appropriate closing entries at June 30, 2008.

2. Prepare a balance sheet for the civic center construction fund on June 30, 2008.

P 19-12

Capital projects fund journal entries and financial statements The City of Catalina authorized the construction of a new recreation center at a total cost of $1,000,000 on June 15, 2007. On the same date, the city approved a $1,000,000, 8%, 10-year general obligation serial bond issue to finance the project. During the year July 1, 2007, to June 30, 2008, the following transactions and events occurred relative to the recreation center project.

LEARNING OBJECTIVES 1, 4

1. On July 1, 2007, the city sold $500,000 par of the authorized bonds, with interest payment dates on December 31 and June 30 and the first serial retirement to be made on June 30, 2008. The bonds were sold at 102.

2. On July 5, 2007, a construction contract for the recreation center was let in the amount of $960,000.

3. On December 15, 2007, the contractor's bill for $320,000 was received based on certification that the work was one-third completed.

4. The contractor was paid for one-third of the contract less a 10% retained percentage to ensure performance.

5. On December 30, 2007, the GF transferred $30,000 to the fund responsible for servicing the serial bonds.

6. Interest on the serial bonds was paid on December 31, 2007, with the money transferred from the GF and the CPF.

7. On June 15, 2008, the contractor's bill for $320,000 was received based on certification that the work was two-thirds completed.

8. On June 28, 2008, the GF transferred $90,000 to the fund responsible for servicing the serial bonds: $40,000 for interest and $50,000 for principal.

9. Interest and principal on the serial bonds were paid on June 30, 2008.

10. On June 30, 2008, the city sold the remaining $500,000 par of authorized bonds at par.

REQUIRED:

1. Prepare all journal entries in all the funds necessary to account for the transactions and events given. (If amounts are not known, use XXX.)

2. Prepare financial statements for the CPF for the year ended June 30, 2008.

INTERNET ASSIGNMENT

1. Visit the GASB's Web site at www.GASB.org. Click on the Links icon and select CAFRs. Choose a CAFR from a city, county, or other local government. Review the CAFR and answer the following questions:

   a. How many governmental funds does the government have? List the name of one special revenue fund.

   b. Does the government have a capital projects fund? For what purpose was it created? Is it a major fund?

   c. Does the government use a debt service fund?

   d. Does the government use encumbrance accounting? How can you tell?

   e. If *GASB 34* has been adopted, locate the reconciliations between the fund and governmentwide statements. List two reconciling items.

   f. If *GASB 34* has been adopted, locate the budgetary comparison statement for the general fund. Comment on the extent of the differences between the original and final budgets.

2. Locate the Web site for the municipality in which your college or university is located. List one major event that has occurred recently and will be recorded in the accounting records. What fund or funds will be affected by this event?

3. Locate the Web site for the county in which your college or university is located. Has the county recorded any new debt this year in its governmental funds? How much? How can you tell?

20 CHAPTER

ACCOUNTING FOR STATE AND LOCAL GOVERNMENTAL UNITS—PROPRIETARY AND FIDUCIARY FUNDS

his chapter concludes coverage of state and local governmental accounting practices with a review of accounting and reporting procedures applicable to proprietary funds (internal service funds and enterprise funds) and fiduciary funds (trust funds and agency funds). Recall that the accounting for proprietary funds is similar to that of commercial business organizations, with a few differences. Governments use fiduciary funds to account for resources that are held for the benefit of others.

● ● ●

PROPRIETARY FUNDS

Governmental units use *proprietary funds* to account for business-type activities that provide goods and services to users and that finance those services largely from user charges. The objective of proprietary funds is to maintain capital or to produce income, or both, and full accrual accounting procedures apply. Thus, proprietary funds have revenue and expense, not expenditure, accounts. Within proprietary funds, governments recognize revenues in the accounting period in which they are earned (or in which similar recognition criteria have been met) and become measurable, and they recognize expenses in the period incurred, if measurable. The availability criterion for governmental fund revenue recognition does not apply to proprietary fund and similar trust fund revenue recognition.

Recall that the accounting equation for proprietary funds is:

Current assets + Noncurrent assets − Current liabilities − Noncurrent liabilities = Net assets

The fixed assets of proprietary funds are fund fixed assets and not general fixed assets. Long-term liabilities incurred by a proprietary fund and expected to be serviced from its revenues are fund liabilities, rather than general long-term debt. Lease agreements of proprietary funds are accounted for entirely within the fund under the provisions of *FASB Statement No. 13*, "Accounting for Leases," except for operating leases with scheduled rent increases. When governments report operating leases with scheduled rent increases in proprietary funds and similar trust funds, they recognize rental revenue as it accrues over the lease term.

As noted in Chapter 18, *GASB Statement No. 34* requires the preparation of three fund financial statements for proprietary funds. The required statements are a statement of net assets; a statement of revenues, expenses, and changes in net assets; and a statement of cash flows.

LEARNING OBJECTIVES

1 Review the appropriate accounting and financial reporting for proprietary funds.

2 Introduce the differences between a proprietary fund statement of cash flows and its commercial business counterpart.

3 Prepare journal entries and fund financial statements for fiduciary funds.

4 Learn about GASB guidance for pension fund accounting.

LEARNING
OBJECTIVE 1

Because proprietary funds account for transactions in much the same manner as commercial business organizations, the GASB allows some reference to FASB statements. *GASB Statement No. 20*, "Accounting and Financial Reporting for Proprietary Activities," governs accounting and reporting standards that apply to proprietary activities. Governmental proprietary activities *must apply*:

- All applicable GASB statements *and*
- All FASB and predecessor standards issued before November 30, 1989, that do not conflict with GASB standards.[1]

Governmental proprietary activities *may either apply*:

- All FASB standards issued after November 30, 1989, as long as they do not conflict with GASB standards, *or*
- No FASB standards issued after November 30, 1989, even if they modify or rescind earlier issued FASB statements. (This election does not completely prohibit applying an FASB standard. In essence, they are in the lowest level of the GAAP hierarchy.)

Governments must disclose the option selected in the notes to the financial statements.

The two types of funds within the proprietary fund classification are internal service funds and enterprise funds. The key difference between an internal service fund and an enterprise fund lies in the user group for which the goods and services are intended. Enterprise funds provide goods and services primarily to the general public, whereas internal service funds provide their goods and services primarily to other departments or agencies within the same governmental unit (or, on a limited basis, to other governmental units). Even though the user groups for enterprise and internal service funds differ, the accounting treatment is similar. Under *GASB Statement No. 34*, however, presentation within both the governmentwide and fund financial statements differs for internal service and enterprise funds. This chapter discusses and illustrates these differences.

INTERNAL SERVICE FUNDS

Internal service funds (ISF) are proprietary funds that a government uses to account for governmental activities that provide goods and services to other departments or agencies of the governmental unit, or to other governmental units, on a cost-reimbursement basis. The account classifications used by an ISF are those that would be used in accounting for similar operations of a private business enterprise.

Centralized purchasing, motor pools, printing shops, and self-insurance are examples of internal service fund operations. Each activity offers potential efficiencies through economies of scale, improved services, and better control.

In many cases, governmental units provide the initial financing of an ISF through a contribution of cash or operating facilities, while expecting the ISF to be self-sustaining in future periods. Alternatively, the governmental unit may provide a loan to an ISF to be repaid from future operating flows of the fund. A contribution is classified as a nonreciprocal transfer, which flows through the statement of revenues, expenses, and changes in fund net assets; whereas a loan is recorded as a long-term liability of the ISF in the statement of net assets. A government records short-term interfund loans as due to Fund A and due from Fund B.

Accounting for an Internal Service Fund

The Village of Tara creates a central motor pool fund with a cash contribution of $200,000 from the general fund and a contribution of existing motor vehicles with a book value of $120,000. Because the cash is not expected to be repaid, the village will record the cash contribution as a $200,000 nonreciprocal transfer. The village will also remove the transferred equipment from the records of general fixed assets at its original cost, or at book value if accumulated depreciation has been recorded. In the records of the central motor pool fund, the appropriate journal entry is as follows:

---

[1] November 30, 1989, is the date that the Financial Accounting Foundation reaffirmed that the GASB was responsible for setting standards for state and local governments.

Internal Service Fund

Cash	200,000	
Motor vehicles	120,000	
Nonreciprocal transfer from GF		200,000
Contributed capital from municipality		120,000
To record establishment of the fund.		

The village also records the transfer in the general fund.

General Fund

Other financing use—nonreciprocal transfer to ISF	200,000	
Cash		200,000
To record the transfer of resources to establish an ISF.		

Note that there is no need to reflect the fixed asset contribution in the general fund accounting system; however, we will remove the assets from the internal general fixed asset *records* and record them as internal service fund fixed assets. Because internal service funds are reported as governmental activities on the governmentwide statement of net assets, this interfund activity will not affect the amount of fixed assets reported in the governmental activity column of the governmentwide statement of net assets.

The village obtains a maintenance facility at a cost of $100,000, purchases equipment for $50,000, and acquires operating supplies for $20,000. The village records these cash expenditures, in summary form, as follows:

Internal Service Fund

Building	100,000	
Equipment	50,000	
Supplies on hand	20,000	
Cash		170,000
To record purchase of building, equipment, and supplies.		

During the first year of operation, the central motor pool fund supplies motor pool vehicles to municipal departments and bills these departments at a predetermined rate based on miles driven. The rate is set to cover all costs of operating the motor pool and servicing the vehicles, including the cost of replacing worn-out vehicles. Journal entries to record revenue and expense transactions and year-end entries related to internal service fund transactions are shown next in summary form. Note the similarity to business accounting entries.

When the internal service fund bills user funds, individual funds will record entries at the amount charged:

Internal Service Fund

Due from general fund	100,000	
Due from special revenue fund	30,000	
Service revenue		130,000
To charge user funds for vehicle services.		

General Fund

Expenditures	100,000	
Due to internal service fund		100,000
To record user charges for vehicle services.		

Special Revenue Fund

Expenditures	30,000	
Due to internal service fund		30,000
To record user charges for vehicle services.		

Similarly, collection of the user charges triggers entries in the funds involved:

Internal Service Fund

Cash	100,000	
Due from general fund		100,000
To record collections from user funds.		

General Fund

Due to internal service fund	100,000	
Cash		100,000
To record payment of user charges for vehicle services.		

If revenue is received from external parties, the village will record ISF revenue in the following manner:

Internal Service Fund

Cash	1,000	
Interest revenue		1,000
To record interest revenue.		

Internal service funds record expenses as they are incurred. The predetermined billing rate was designed to cover such expenses:

Internal Service Fund

Salaries expense	40,000	
Utilities expense	18,000	
Insurance expense	16,000	
Cash		74,000
To record payments for expense items.		

Adjusting and closing entries are similar to those noted in a commercial enterprise:

Internal Service Fund—Adjusting Entries

Supplies expense	15,000	
Supplies on hand		15,000
To adjust supplies expense and supplies on hand accounts at year-end.		
Salaries expense	4,000	
Accrued salaries payable		4,000
To accrue salaries.		
Depreciation expense—building	5,000	
Accumulated depreciation—building		5,000
To record depreciation on building ($100,000 ÷ 20 years).		
Depreciation expense—motor vehicles	20,000	
Accumulated depreciation—motor vehicles		20,000
To record depreciation on vehicles (200,000 miles driven × 10 cents per mile).		
Depreciation expense—equipment	10,000	
Accumulated depreciation—equipment		10,000
To record depreciation on equipment ($50,000 ÷ 5 years).		

Internal Service Fund—Closing Entries

Nonreciprocal transfer from GF	200,000	
Net assets		200,000
To close transfer to net assets.		
Contributed capital from municipality	120,000	
Net assets		120,000
To close contributed capital to net assets.		
Service revenue	130,000	
Interest revenue	1,000	
Supplies expense		15,000
Insurance expense		16,000
Salaries expense		44,000
Utilities expense		18,000
Depreciation expense—building		5,000
Depreciation expense—motor vehicles		20,000
Depreciation expense—equipment		10,000
Net assets, unrestricted		3,000
To close revenue and expense accounts to net assets.		

Notice that the internal service fund had revenue in excess of expenses in the amount of $3,000. This slight income figure indicates that the predetermined rate charged to users was appropriate.

Reporting Internal Service Funds in the Financial Statements

Internal service funds are officially designated as proprietary funds; however, their intended purpose is to provide goods and services to governmental and enterprise funds of the governmental entity. Thus, they possess a unique nature, and, under *GASB Statement No. 34*, governments report them in a unique manner. In the fund financial statements, governments include internal service funds with the proprietary funds. Due to their nature, though, they are never considered major funds, and all internal service funds are aggregated into a single column within the proprietary fund statement of net assets, the statement of revenues, expenses, and changes in net assets, and the statement of cash flows. The column containing internal service fund activities is captioned Governmental Activities. Exhibits 20-1, 20-2, and 20-3 use this format for the sample proprietary fund financial statements for the Village of Tara.

Within the governmentwide statements, governments report internal service funds with the governmental activities. The internal service fund balance sheet accounts are included in the governmental activity column of the statement of net assets. However, the statement of activities will include only those internal service fund transactions involving entities other than the primary reporting entity. Thus, governments add external internal service fund revenues (and expenditures) to the statement of activities, while they exclude internal governmental transactions. For example, Tara includes only the $1,000 of ISF interest in the governmental activities totals in the governmentwide statement of activities. This, in essence, eliminates double counting of interfund transactions, much like consolidated entities eliminate intercompany transactions. This process is reviewed later in the chapter.

ENTERPRISE FUNDS

Enterprise funds (EF) are proprietary funds that a government uses to account for activities that are financed and operated similarly to those of private business enterprises. Typically, enterprise funds provide goods and services to the general public on a continuing basis, with the costs being financed primarily through user charges. Governments may use enterprise funds to record any business activities for which a user fee is charged. However, they are required to use an enterprise fund for activities that (1) are financed with debt secured solely by net revenue from fees and charges to external users; (2) operate under laws or regulations requiring that the activity's costs of providing services, including capital costs, be recovered with fees and charges; or (3) have prices established by management to cover the costs (including capital costs) of providing services.[2] As you can imagine, enterprise fund operations are about as diverse as those found in private enterprise. They range from the operation of electric and water utilities, which are intended to produce income, to swimming pool and golf course operations, in which costs are intended to be recovered primarily from user charges, to activities such as mass transit authorities and civic centers, which are often heavily subsidized from general governmental revenues.

The objective of an enterprise fund is to maintain capital or to generate net income, or both; thus, full accrual accounting procedures are applicable. Like internal service funds, enterprise funds are proprietary funds that use revenue and expense accounts and accrual accounting practices similar to those of private business enterprises. Enterprise fund fixed assets and long-term liabilities are fund fixed assets and fund long-term liabilities. Therefore, governments record them in the enterprise fund. Often, the long-term debt obligations are in the form of revenue bonds secured only by enterprise fund operations. If such bonds are also secured by the "full faith and credit" of the governmental unit, the enterprise fund still records the liability in the fund, but the notes to the financial statements will also disclose a contingent liability, indicating the extent of general government responsibility for repayment.

Initial financing of many enterprise funds is typically the same as for an internal service fund. The governmental unit makes a capital contribution (a transfer from the general fund) or provides a long-term interfund loan to the enterprise fund. Future operations are expected to cover all costs, including depreciation on fund fixed assets, so operations can continue indefinitely without further capital contributions.

The following section presents sample entries related to a utility department's operations. Because the accounting for enterprise funds is quite similar to accounting for commercial business enterprises, the discussion and examples are abbreviated.

Accounting for an Enterprise Fund

Utility-type enterprise funds often require customer deposits to assure timely payment for services. The utility normally collects the deposit before service starts and refunds the money after a minimum holding period has elapsed or when service is terminated. Land developers may also be required to make good-faith deposits to finance the cost of extending utility service lines. Governments segregate such assets and report them as restricted assets in the enterprise fund balance sheet. Customer deposits remain in current liabilities until they are applied against unpaid billings or refunded to customers. Entries related to customer deposits are as follows:

Enterprise Fund

Restricted cash	10,000	
Customer deposits		10,000
To record customer deposits collected.		

Enterprise Fund

Customer deposits	3,000	
Restricted cash		3,000
To record customer deposit refunds.		

An enterprise fund records customer billings and receipts as follows:

Enterprise Fund

Accounts receivable	680,000	
Charges for services		680,000
To record customer charges for utility services.		

---

[2] *GASB Statement No. 34*, paragraph 387.

Enterprise Fund

Cash	640,000	
Accounts receivable		640,000

To record collection from customers for utility services.

Enterprise funds often receive intergovernmental grants that are designated for operations (operating grants) or capital asset acquisition (capital grants). For example, the Gator County Waste Management Facility may receive grant funds from the Environmental Protection Agency designated for pollution control. Governments report operating grants as nonoperating revenues in proprietary funds, whereas they recognize capital grants as contributed capital, not as revenues. Under *GASB Statement No. 33*, enterprise funds recognize grant revenues and capital contributions in the period in which qualifying expenses are incurred, assuming any other significant conditions have been met. If funds are received before qualifying expenses are incurred, a deferred revenue is recorded. The entry to record an intergovernmental capital grant once qualified expenses have been made is as follows:

Enterprise Fund

Due from other governments	50,000	
Contributed capital—grant		50,000

To recognize capital grant revenue for qualified expenses.

If a new generator is purchased by issuing a note payable, the enterprise fund entry will be as follows:

Enterprise Fund

Equipment	35,000	
Notes payable		35,000

To record the purchase of equipment.

Using accrual accounting, enterprise funds record other operating expenses as they are incurred:

Enterprise Fund

Salaries expense	150,000	
Repairs and maintenance	78,000	
Supplies expense	132,000	
Utilities	60,000	
Insurance expense	15,000	
Cash		435,000

To record payments for expense items.

Adjusting and closing entries are similar to those recorded in internal service funds:

Enterprise Fund—Adjusting Entries

Salaries expense	17,000	
Accrued salaries payable		17,000
To accrue salaries.		
Interest expense	2,000	
Interest payable		2,000
To accrue interest on note payable.		
Depreciation expense	42,000	
Accumulated depreciation		42,000

To record depreciation for the year.

Enterprise Fund—Closing Entries

Charges for services	680,000	
Salaries expense		167,000
Repairs and maintenance		78,000
Supplies expense		132,000
Depreciation expense		42,000
Interest expense		2,000
Utilities		60,000
Insurance expense		15,000
Net assets, unrestricted		184,000

To close revenue and expense accounts to net assets.

Contributed capital—grant	50,000	
Net assets, restricted		50,000

To close contributed capital to net assets.

PROPRIETARY FUND FINANCIAL STATEMENTS

Required fund financial statements for proprietary funds consist of a statement of net assets; a statement of revenues, expenses, and changes in net assets; and a statement of cash flows. Each of these statements includes a column for each enterprise fund that is considered a major fund, as well as a column totaling all nonmajor enterprise fund activity.[3] As noted earlier, proprietary fund statements report internal service funds with the enterprise funds. The fund financial statements aggregate all internal service funds in a single column. Exhibits 20-1, 20-2, and 20-3 illustrate this format for the sample proprietary fund financial statements for the Village of Tara.

The financial statements of proprietary funds are similar to those of a business enterprise, with a few exceptions. Internal service and enterprise funds do not pay property taxes or income taxes, and thus these items are noticeably absent from the operating statement. The funds may exhibit interfund activity; therefore, governmental entity financial statements may include interfund account titles such as due from general fund (for utility charges or supply acquisitions), advance from general fund (for long-term financing), and transfers.

In addition, proprietary funds do not have capital stock or paid-in capital. In place of stockholders' equity, their statement of net assets (balance sheet) shows a net assets section, such as the following:

Net Assets	
Invested in capital assets, net of related debt	$500,000
Restricted	150,000
Unrestricted	300,000
Total fund equity	$950,000

Net assets *invested in capital (fixed) assets, net of related debt* are equal to the fixed assets of the fund less all fixed-asset-related debt, whether current or long-term. *Restricted net assets* are equal to the difference between (1) assets externally restricted by creditors (perhaps through debt covenants), grantors, donors, or laws and regulations of other governments, or internally by constitutional provisions or enabling legislation and (2) liabilities payable from those restricted assets. The restrictions must be more narrow than the purposes of the fund being reported. *Unrestricted net assets* are equal to the difference between the remaining assets and liabilities of the fund. Restricted net assets must be reclassified as unrestricted when the government satisfies the restriction.

---

[3] Recall from Chapter 18 that a fund is considered a major fund if it meets both of the following criteria: (a) Total assets, liabilities, revenues, or expenditures/expenses (excluding extraordinary items) of that individual governmental or enterprise fund are at least 10% of the *corresponding* total (assets, liabilities, and so forth) for *all* funds of that *category* or *type* (that is, total governmental or total enterprise funds), and (b) total assets, liabilities, revenues, or expenditures/expenses (excluding extraordinary items) of that individual governmental or enterprise fund are at least 5% of the *corresponding total* for all governmental *and* enterprise funds *combined*.

EXHIBIT 20-1

Proprietary Fund
Statement of Net
Assets

VILLAGE OF TARA STATEMENT OF NET ASSETS PROPRIETARY FUNDS
JUNE 30, 2006

	Business-Type Activities—Enterprise Funds				Governmental Activities
	Utilities	Parking Facilities	Other Enterprise Funds	Totals	Internal Service Funds
Assets					
Current assets					
Cash and cash equivalents	$ 614,635	$ 75,000	$ 30,000	$ 719,635	$ 57,000
Receivables, net	235,915	20,000	5,000	260,915	—
Due from other funds	—	—	—	—	30,000
Due from other governments	32,112	—	—	32,112	—
Supplies	61,443	1,000	—	62,443	5,000
Total current assets	944,105	96,000	35,000	1,075,105	92,000
Noncurrent assets					
Restricted cash and cash equivalents	185,000	—	—	185,000	—
Land	45,000	50,000	—	95,000	—
Buildings and equipment	1,000,000	850,000	140,000	1,990,000	150,000
Vehicles	220,000	—	—	220,000	120,000
Less accumulated depreciation	(520,000)	(450,000)	(35,000)	(1,005,000)	(35,000)
Total noncurrent assets	930,000	450,000	105,000	1,485,000	235,000
Total assets	$1,874,105	$546,000	$140,000	$2,560,105	$327,000
Liabilities					
Current liabilities					
Accounts payable	$ 45,000	$ 20,000	$ 3,000	$ 68,000	—
Accrued liabilities	19,000	20,000	5,000	44,000	$ 4,000
Due to other funds	—	—	4,000	4,000	—
Compensated absences	3,000	2,000	—	5,000	—
Bonds and notes payable	20,000	50,000	10,000	80,000	—
Total current liabilities	87,000	92,000	22,000	201,000	4,000
Noncurrent liabilities					
Customer deposits	185,000	—	—	185,000	—
Compensated absences	230,000	65,000	—	295,000	—
Bonds and notes payable	275,000	100,000	90,000	465,000	—
Total noncurrent liabilities	690,000	165,000	90,000	945,000	—
Total liabilities	$ 777,000	$257,000	$112,000	$1,146,000	$ 4,000
Net Assets					
Invested in capital assets, net of related debt	$ 425,000	$150,000	—	$ 575,000	$235,000
Restricted	250,000	—	$ 20,000	270,000	—
Unrestricted	422,105	139,000	8,000	569,105	88,000
Total net assets	$1,097,105	$289,000	$ 28,000	$1,414,105	$323,000

Statement of Cash Flows for Proprietary Funds

The statement of cash flows for proprietary funds also differs slightly from its commercial business counterpart. First of all, *GASB Statement No. 34* makes the direct method mandatory for statement presentation. Also, cash flow classifications have been modified. You may recall that *FASB Statement No. 95* specifies a three-section format for cash flow statements of business enterprises: operating activities, investing activities, and financing activities. *GASB Statement No. 9*, "Reporting Cash Flows of Proprietary and Nonexpendable Trust Funds and Governmental Entities That Use Proprietary Fund Accounting," which establishes standards for cash flow reporting for proprietary funds, separates financing activities into noncapital and capital related. Therefore, a proprietary fund cash flow statement has four separate sections: cash flows from operating activities, cash flows from noncapital financing activities, cash flows from capital and related financing activities, and cash flows from investing activities. The following sections review the content of the

EXHIBIT 20-2

Proprietary Fund
Statement of
Revenues, Expenses,
and Changes in Net
Assets

VILLAGE OF TARA STATEMENT OF REVENUES, EXPENSES, AND CHANGES IN FUND NET ASSETS PROPRIETARY FUNDS FOR THE YEAR ENDED JUNE 30, 2006

	Business-Type Activities—Enterprise Funds				Governmental Activities
	Utilities	Parking Facilities	Other Enterprise Funds	Totals	Internal Service Funds
Operating Revenues					
Charges for services	$ 680,000	$500,000	$40,000	$1,220,000	$130,000
Miscellaneous	—	—	—	—	—
Total operating revenues	680,000	500,000	40,000	1,220,000	130,000
Operating Expenses					
Salaries	167,000	25,000	12,000	204,000	44,000
Contractual services	—	275,000	—	275,000	—
Utilities	60,000	24,000	—	84,000	18,000
Repairs and maintenance	78,000	11,000	—	89,000	—
Insurance expense	15,000	8,000	—	23,000	16,000
Supplies and other expenses	132,000	1,200	3,000	136,200	15,000
Depreciation	42,000	65,000	18,000	125,000	35,000
Total operating expenses	494,000	409,200	33,000	936,200	128,000
Operating income (loss)	186,000	90,800	7,000	283,800	2,000
Nonoperating Revenues (Expenses)					
Interest	—	—	—	—	1,000
Miscellaneous revenue (expense)	—	—	—	—	—
Interest expense	2,000	12,000	5,000	19,000	—
Total nonoperating revenue (expense)	(2,000)	(12,000)	(5,000)	(19,000)	1,000
Income (loss) before contributions and transfers	184,000	78,800	2,000	234,800	3,000
Capital contributions	50,000	—	—	50,000	120,000
Transfers in	—	—	—	—	200,000
Transfers out	—	—	—	—	—
Change in net assets	234,000	78,800	2,000	284,800	323,000
Total net assets—beginning	863,105	210,200	26,000	1,099,305	—
Total net assets—ending	$1,097,105	$289,000	$28,000	$1,414,105	$323,000

four separate sections of the statement of cash flows for proprietary funds and government entities that use proprietary fund accounting.

CASH FLOWS FROM OPERATING ACTIVITIES Cash inflows of the operating activities section include the following:

Receipts from sales of goods or services

Receipts from interfund services provided

Receipts from interfund reimbursements

All other receipts not included in one of the other three sections

Cash outflows of the operating activities section include the following:

Payments for materials used in providing services or manufacturing goods for resale

Principal payments to suppliers of those materials or goods on account or under short-term or long-term notes payable

Payments to suppliers for other goods and services

Payments to employees for salaries

Payments to other governments as grants for operating activities

Payments for taxes and in lieu of taxes

All other cash payments not included in one of the other three sections

VILLAGE OF TARA STATEMENT OF CASH FLOWS PROPRIETARY FUNDS FOR THE YEAR ENDED JUNE 30, 2006

EXHIBIT 20-3

Proprietary Fund
Cash Flow
Statement

	Business-Type Activities—Enterprise Funds				Governmental Activities
	Utilities	Parking Facilities	Other Enterprise Funds	Totals	Internal Service Funds
Cash Flows from Operating Activities					
Cash received from customers	$640,000	$489,000	$32,000	$1,161,000	$100,000
Cash paid to suppliers	(132,000)	(2,000)	(6,000)	(140,000)	(20,000)
Cash paid for salaries	(150,000)	(25,000)	(11,000)	(186,000)	(40,000)
Cash paid for utilities	(60,000)	(24,000)	—	(84,000)	(18,000)
Cash paid for contractual services	—	(275,000)	—	(275,000)	—
Cash paid for insurance	(15,000)	(8,000)	—	(23,000)	(16,000)
Cash paid for repairs and maintenance	(78,000)	(11,000)	—	(89,000)	—
Net cash provided (used) by operating activities	205,000	144,000	15,000	364,000	6,000
Cash Flows from Noncapital Financing Activities					
Cash received from general fund (noncapital loan)	—	—	3,000	3,000	200,000
Net cash provided (used) by noncapital financing activities	—	—	3,000	3,000	200,000
Cash Flows from Capital and Related Financing Activities					
Purchase of building	—	—	—	—	(100,000)
Purchase of equipment	—	(12,000)	(6,000)	(18,000)	(50,000)
Principal paid on capital debt	—	(75,000)	—	(75,000)	—
Interest paid on capital debt	—	(12,000)	—	(12,000)	—
Net cash provided by investing activities	—	(99,000)	(6,000)	(105,000)	(150,000)
Cash Flows from Investing Activities					
Interest and dividends	—	—	—	—	1,000
Net cash provided by investing activities	—	—	—	—	1,000
Net (decrease) increase in unrestricted cash and cash equivalents	205,000	45,000	12,000	262,000	57,000
Balances—beginning	409,635	30,000	18,000	457,635	—
Balances—ending	$614,635	$ 75,000	$30,000	$ 719,635	$ 57,000

CASH FLOWS FROM NONCAPITAL FINANCING ACTIVITIES Items to be considered cash inflows for the noncapital financing activities section include the following:

Proceeds from bonds and notes not clearly issued specifically for the acquisition, construction, or improvement of capital assets

Receipts from grants and subsidies and receipts from other funds (except those restricted for capital purposes or operating activities)

Receipts from property taxes and other taxes collected for the governmental enterprise and not restricted for capital purposes

Cash outflows for this section include the following:

Repayments of amounts borrowed (including interest payments) other than those related to acquiring or constructing capital assets

Amounts paid for grants and subsidies (except those for specific operating activities of the grantor government)

Cash paid to other funds, except for interfund services used

CASH FLOWS FROM CAPITAL (FIXED ASSET) AND RELATED FINANCING ACTIVITIES Capital and related activities include acquiring and disposing of capital assets used in providing goods and services, including borrowing money to finance fixed asset construction or acquisition and repaying it with interest. Cash inflows include amounts from capital grants (i.e., grants for the sole purpose of acquiring, constructing, or improving a fixed asset), contributions, special assessments, insurance proceeds, and so on, as long as they are received specifically to defray the cost of acquiring, constructing, or improving capital assets. Cash received from sale or disposal of fixed assets is included in this section also.

Cash outflows include amounts to acquire, construct, or improve capital assets, and to repay amounts borrowed (including interest), as long as the purpose of the borrowing was directly related to acquiring, constructing, or improving capital assets.

CASH FLOWS FROM INVESTING ACTIVITIES Investing activities include making and collecting loans and acquiring and disposing of investments in debt or equity instruments. Cash inflows include collections of loans and sales of investment securities (other than from cash equivalents) and the receipt of interest and dividends. Cash outflows include making loans and payments to acquire investment securities (other than for cash equivalents).

FIDUCIARY FUNDS

Governmental units use *fiduciary funds* to account for assets held in a trustee or agency capacity on behalf of others external to the governmental entity. Such resources cannot be used for the benefit of the government's own programs. The fiduciary grouping includes trust funds (private-purpose, investment, and pension) and agency funds, which are similar in the sense that the governmental unit acts in a fiduciary capacity for both types of funds. The accounting emphasis for trust and agency funds lies in demonstrating how the government's fiduciary responsibilities have been met. The basic difference between the two fund types is that a trust agreement, which mandates the degree of management involvement and the duration of the trust, typically exists for trust fund resources. Furthermore, agency funds are more temporary in nature.

Accounting for fiduciary funds follows the accrual basis of accounting; however, agency funds do not have revenues or expenses because their operations are of a custodial nature. Governments report fiduciary funds in the fund financial statements on a statement of fiduciary net assets and a statement of changes in fiduciary net assets. Fiduciary funds are not included in the government-wide statements.

AGENCY FUNDS

Agency funds are fiduciary funds used to account for resources that governments hold in a custodial or agency capacity. For example, a local government acts as an agent for the federal government when it withholds income and Social Security taxes, which will later be remitted to other government agencies, from employee payrolls. Also, an agency fund reports the debt service transactions of a special assessment bond issue for which the government is not obligated in any manner in order to reflect the fact that the government's duties are limited to acting as an agent for the assessed property owners and bondholders. Thus, the government acts as an agent for the property owners in collecting special assessments and remitting the amounts collected to bondholders.

Governments utilize agency funds when their agency responsibilities involve numerous transactions, include several different governmental units, or do not arise from normal and recurring operations of any other fund. For example, if a county unit of government serves as a tax collection agency for all towns and cities located within the county, the county will create an agency fund to demonstrate acceptance of responsibility for collecting and remitting taxes for other governmental units. To use an agency fund, however, the governmental entity should only act as a cash conduit, collecting and dispersing cash. If the governmental entity undertakes any administrative duties, such as determining who will receive the cash or monitoring recipient eligibility, it cannot use an agency fund.

The accounting treatment for agency funds is quite simple, as reflected in the following accounting equation:

$$\text{Assets} = \text{Liabilities}$$

There is no fund balance or equity. Assets and liabilities are recognized at the time that the government becomes responsible for the assets.

Accounting for an Agency Fund

Assume that Morris County collects property taxes for its own purposes as well as for the cities of Howard Lake, Brownsville, and Clute, and that total property tax levies for the 2007–2008 fiscal year are as follows:

Morris County	$100,000	50%
Howard Lake	50,000	25
Brownsville	20,000	10
Clute	30,000	15
Total	$200,000	100%

When the tax levies are certified to the county for collection, a tax agency fund records the county's custodial responsibility for collecting the taxes:

Agency Fund

Taxes receivable for local governmental units	200,000	
Liability to Morris County		100,000
Liability to Howard Lake		50,000
Liability to Brownsville		20,000
Liability to Clute		30,000

The county collects $180,000 of the levy for remittance to the respective units of government during the year. The following entry is made to record the collection:

Agency Fund

Cash	180,000	
Taxes receivable for local governmental units		180,000
To record collection of taxes receivable.		

If Morris County charges Howard Lake, Brownsville, and Clute a fee of 1% of taxes collected, the total charges would be $900 ($90,000 collected for these three cities multiplied by 1%), recorded as follows:

Agency Fund

Liability to Howard Lake	450	
Liability to Brownsville	180	
Liability to Clute	270	
Due to general fund (of Morris County)		900
To charge cities a 1% fee for taxes collected for them.		

The following entry reflects the remittance:

Agency Fund

Due to general fund	900	
Liability to Morris County	90,000	
Liability to Howard Lake	44,550	
Liability to Brownsville	17,820	
Liability to Clute	26,730	
Cash		180,000
To record remittance of taxes collected net of 1% fee.		

EXHIBIT 20-4

Statement of
Fiduciary Net Assets

MORRIS COUNTY STATEMENT OF FIDUCIARY NET ASSETS FIDUCIARY FUNDS JUNE 30, 2008

	Tax Collection Agency Fund	School Library Trust Fund
Assets		
Cash and cash equivalents	0	0
Investments	0	$100,000
Taxes receivable	$20,000	0
Interest receivable	0	1,667
Total assets	$20,000	$101,667
Liabilities		
Liability to Morris County	10,000	0
Liability to Howard Lake	5,000	0
Liability to Brownsville	2,000	0
Liability to Clute	3,000	0
Total liabilities	$20,000	$ 0
Net Assets		
Available for distribution to school libraries	0	1,667
Held in trust for endowment	0	100,000
Total net assets	$ 0	$101,667

Financial Statements for the Agency Fund

Morris County includes the tax collection agency fund in the statement of fiduciary net assets shown in Exhibit 20-4. Because agency funds do not have revenues and expenditures, they need not be included in the statement of changes in fiduciary net assets. Agency funds are not included in the governmentwide statements.

TRUST FUNDS

Investment trust funds are fiduciary funds used to account for multigovernment external investment pools sponsored by the governmental entity. For example, a county government may offer to pool the cash available for investment from cities located within its boundaries. Because the cash is not an asset of the county government and cannot be used for its benefit, the resources should be accounted for in a fiduciary fund. Furthermore, if a formal agreement exists and income will be recognized in the fund, it would be appropriate to establish a trust. *GASB Statement No. 31* describes the accounting for investment trust funds. Accounting for investment trust funds is beyond the scope of this chapter, so the following discussion focuses on private-purpose and pension trust funds.

Private-purpose trust funds are fiduciary funds used to account for resources (other than investment pools and employee benefits) that are held for the benefit of parties outside the governmental entity.[4] *Pension trust funds* are fiduciary funds used when a government acts as trustee for defined benefit and defined contribution pension plans of a government or for other employee benefit programs.

Accounting for a Private-Purpose Trust Fund

Assume that on July 2, 2007, Morris County receives a $100,000 contribution from the Hurricane Valley Historical Society. A trust agreement specifying that the income from the contribution must be distributed each May 15 to the three school libraries in Morris County accompanies the contribution. The principal amount is intended to remain intact indefinitely. The county establishes a private-purpose trust fund to account for the contribution and associated activities, because the county itself will not benefit from these resources. The entry is as follows:

---

[4] Recall that permanent funds are used to account for restricted resources that will benefit the government or its citizens.

Trust Fund

Cash	100,000	
Contributions—foundations		100,000
To record a contribution received.		

This principal amount is not expendable and will remain in the trust fund. Expendable income amounts may be either accounted for within the same trust fund or transferred to a separate expendable trust fund.

On September 1, the county invests the contribution in bonds, which yield 5% annually (payable on March 1 and September 1):

Trust Fund

Investments	100,000	
Cash		100,000
To record an investment in bonds.		

On March 1, the county receives the first interest payment:

Trust Fund

Cash	2,500	
Interest income		2,500
To record the collection of interest.		

On May 15, Morris County distributes the interest to local school libraries:

Trust Fund

Distribution to school libraries	2,500	
Cash		2,500
To record the distribution of interest.		

On June 30, the county adjusts and closes its accounts:

Trust Fund—Adjusting Entry

Interest receivable	1,667	
Interest income		1,667
To accrue interest income ($100,000 \times .05 \times 4/12$).		

Trust Fund—Closing Entry

Interest income	4,167	
Contributions—foundations	100,000	
Distribution to school libraries		2,500
Net assets held in trust for school libraries—nonexpendable		100,000
Net assets held in trust for school libraries—expendable		1,667
To close accounts.		

Financial Statements for the Trust Fund

Morris County includes the school library trust fund in the statement of fiduciary net assets (Exhibit 20-4) and the statement of changes in fiduciary net assets (Exhibit 20-5). Trust funds are not included in the governmentwide statements.

Accounting for a Pension Trust Fund

Governments account and report for public employee retirement systems (PERS) through pension trust funds. PERS are not subject to the regulations of ERISA (the federal government's Employee Retirement Income Security Act); consequently, some governmental pension plans are

EXHIBIT 20-5

Statement of
Changes in Fiduciary
Net Assets

MORRIS COUNTY STATEMENT OF CHANGES IN FIDUCIARY NET ASSETS TRUST FUND FOR THE YEAR ENDED JUNE 30, 2008

Additions	
Contributions	
Foundations	$100,000
Total contributions	100,000
Investment earnings	
Interest	4,167
Total investment earnings	4,167
Total additions	104,167
Deductions	
Distributions to school libraries	2,500
Total deductions	2,500
Change in net assets	101,667
Net assets—beginning of the year	0
Net assets—end of the year	$101,667

fully funded, others are partially funded, and still others make all pension payments from current revenue. Pension trust fund accounting and financial reporting requirements are set forth primarily in *GASB Statement No. 25*, "Financial Reporting for Defined Benefit Pension Plans and Note Disclosures for Defined Contribution Plans." *GASB Statement No. 27*, "Accounting for Pensions by State and Local Governmental Employers," provides guidance for financial accounting and reporting for state and local governmental employers' pension expenses, expenditures, assets, and liabilities. FASB pension accounting guidance is never to be applied by governments.

GASB STATEMENT NO. 25 This statement outlines the information that should be reported about each pension plan, whether the plan issues a separate report or is included in the financial reports of the plan sponsor or participating employer. Two financial statements are required for defined benefit pension plans:

- **Statement of plan net assets.** Reports the fair value and composition of plan assets, liabilities, and net assets held in trust for pension benefits
- **Statement of changes in plan assets.** Reports the principal year-to-year changes resulting from contributions, net investment income, benefit payments, and so on

These statements do not indicate the financial soundness of a pension plan. Rather, the statements essentially reflect the current balance of financial resources available to pay pension benefits and the changes in that balance during the year, without any indication of its adequacy.

Two schedules, which must be presented as required supplementary information immediately after the financial statement notes, indicate the adequacy or inadequacy of the plan's net assets. The schedules provide information on the funded status of the plan and the extent to which required employer contributions are being fully funded. The schedules include information for six plan years. The required schedules are as follows:

- **Schedule of funding progress.** Reports actuarial value of assets, actuarial accrued liability, and the relationship between the two over time. *GASB Statement No. 25* establishes parameters for measuring the actuarially determined information.
- **Schedule of employer contributions.** Reports annual required employer contributions and the percentage that is recognized by the plan as contributed.

Disclosures accompanying the schedules should include actuarial methods and significant assumptions used for financial reporting as well as any major factors that affect the user's ability to interpret trends.

GASB Statement No. 25 also provides disclosure requirements for defined contribution plans, including a brief plan description, summary of significant accounting policies, fair value of plan assets (unless reported at fair value), and information about contributions and investment concentrations.

GASB STATEMENT NO. 27 This statement "establishes standards for the measurement, recognition, and display of pension expenditures/expenses and related liabilities, assets, note disclosures, and, if applicable, required supplementary information in the financial reports of state and local governmental employers."[5] Employers in single-employer and agent multiple-employer defined benefit pension plans should measure and disclose their annual pension cost on the accrual basis of accounting, regardless of the amount recognized as pension expenditures/expenses on the modified accrual or accrual basis. The annual pension cost will equal the employer's annual required contributions unless the employer has a net pension obligation for past undercontributions or overcontributions. *GASB Statement No. 27* defines net pension obligation as "the cumulative difference between annual pension cost and the employers' contributions to the plan, including the pension liability or asset at transition, if any." When an employer has a net pension obligation at the beginning of a year, annual pension cost is equal to the annual required contributions plus one year's interest on the net pension obligation plus or minus an adjustment to the annual required contribution to offset the effect of actuarial amortization of past under- or overcontributions.

In fund financial statements, governmental funds should recognize pension expenditures on the modified accrual basis, meaning that expenditures equal actual contributions plus or minus any change in the current portion of the net pension obligation. A long-term liability balance in the net pension obligation is reported as long-term debt within the governmentwide statements. An asset balance (cumulative net contributions greater than cumulative pension cost) is not recognized in the financial statements, but it should be disclosed.

Proprietary and similar trust funds and other entities that use proprietary fund accounting should recognize pension expense on the accrual basis in both governmentwide and fund financial statements. Net pension obligations or assets should be recognized as fund liabilities or assets.

Statement No. 27 requires disclosure of the plan and funding policy, annual pension cost for three years, and, if applicable, (also for three years) components of annual pension cost, change for the year in the net pension obligation, and the year-end balance of the net pension obligation. Disclosure about the plan's funding progress is also required in notes or supplements. Employers that participate in a cost-sharing multiple-employer defined benefit pension plan typically pay the required contribution each year. In this case, the pension expenditure or expense equals the employer's contractually required contributions. Likewise, employers participating in defined contribution plans typically pay the required contribution and should recognize pension expenditures or expenses equal to the employer's required contributions to the plan. In both cases a liability is recognized for unpaid contributions. If this liability is noncurrent, expenditures of governmental funds are reduced by the increase in the long-term liability for unpaid contributions.

Accounting and reporting for pension trust funds is quite complex, and, as noted above, differs by pension fund classification. Thus, pension trust fund accounting is not examined in detail here.

In addition to pensions, many state and local governmental employers provide other postemployment benefits (OPEB) to qualified employees. OPEB includes postemployment healthcare, as well as other forms of postemployment benefits (for example, life insurance) provided separately from a pension plan. *GASB Statement No. 44*, "Financial Reporting for Postemployment Benefit Plans Other Than Pension Plans," and *GASB Statement No. 45*, "Accounting and Financial Reporting by Employers for Postemployment Benefits Other Than Pensions," establish standards for the reporting, measurement, recognition, and display of OPEB expense/expenditures and related liabilities (assets), note disclosures, and, if applicable, required supplementary information (RSI) in the financial reports of state and local governmental employers. The statements are generally consistent with *GASB Statements 25* and *27*, described previously.

PREPARING THE GOVERNMENTWIDE FINANCIAL STATEMENTS

The governmentwide statements include a column for business-type activities. This column includes enterprise fund amounts only. Because the governmentwide statement of activities and statement of net assets report all items using the accrual basis of accounting, conversion between the fund and governmentwide statements is not necessary. Governments can simply transfer enterprise fund figures from the proprietary fund statements to the governmentwide statements, *with one exception.*

---

[5] *GASB Statement No. 27*, Summary.

Governments must either eliminate internal balances or report them as interfund balances in the asset section of the statement of net assets. For example, in the Village of Tara illustration, $4,000 is due to other funds from an enterprise fund. Because the enterprise fund owes this interfund payable to a governmental fund, the village will report the amount as an "internal balance." It appears in the asset section of the statement of net assets as a debit in the governmental activities column (for the governmental fund receivable) and as a credit in the business-type activity column (for the enterprise fund payable). Internal balances account for the only difference between enterprise balances on the fund statements and the governmentwide statements, so no reconciliations are necessary.

Recall that governmentwide statements report internal service funds with governmental activities. When preparing the governmentwide statements, governments add internal service fund assets and liabilities to governmental fund assets and liabilities, as was indicated in the conversion worksheet in Exhibit 19-4; however, note that internal balances among governmental activities are eliminated. For example, in the Village of Tara illustration, Tara will eliminate the $30,000 due to the internal service fund from the special revenue fund in the governmental activities column. Also, Tara will eliminate the $200,000 transfer in from the general fund. Any revenues from external parties, such as the $1,000 interest revenue recognized earlier in the chapter, will be included in governmental totals reported on the statement of activities. However, because the internal service fund benefited the governmental funds only, the operating revenue and expenses for the internal service fund are eliminated by debiting internal service fund net assets and crediting governmental fund expenditures. This adjustment ensures that figures in the governmental activity column are not "grossed up."

REQUIRED PROPRIETARY FUND NOTE DISCLOSURES

Enterprise funds follow the accrual basis of accounting and are therefore able to report long-term debt within their funds. If an enterprise fund issues debt that is backed by its revenue-generating activity (i.e., revenue-backed debt instruments), the government must present certain detailed segment information in the notes to the financial statements.[6] The information helps creditors and financial statement users to determine if the segment that has issued the debt is generating the proceeds to fund the debt. The segment disclosure includes a description of the type of goods and services provided by the segment, as well as condensed statements of net assets; revenues, expenses, and changes in net assets; and cash flows.

SUMMARY

Governmental units use proprietary funds to account for business-type activities and use fiduciary funds to account for assets held in a trustee or agency capacity on behalf of others external to the governmental entity. This chapter reviewed the appropriate accounting and financial reporting for proprietary and fiduciary funds, which generally follow the accrual basis for accounting and reporting.

Accounting for each of the proprietary funds is the same; however, financial statement presentation differs. Within the proprietary fund financial statements, each major enterprise fund appears in a separate column, whereas nonmajor enterprise fund activities are totaled and reported in a single column. A separate column reports the total of all internal service fund balances. Within the governmentwide statements, however, enterprise funds appear in a column labeled Business-Type Activities, whereas internal service funds are included with governmental activities. Governmental financial statements report fiduciary funds in fund statements, but governmentwide statements do not include these funds.

QUESTIONS

1. How are enterprise and internal service funds similar? How are they different?

2. Cite some governmental operations that might be accounted for through an internal service fund.

3. What fund financial statements are needed for an enterprise fund to meet the requirements for fair presentation in accordance with GAAP? Which governmentwide statements include enterprise fund data?

---

[6] *GASB Statement No. 34*, paragraph 122.

4. Which fund financial statements include internal service fund data? Which governmentwide statements include internal service fund data?

5. How does the presentation of an enterprise *major* fund differ from the presentation of an internal service *major* fund?

6. Because proprietary funds are accounted for in much the same manner as commercial business organizations, is it appropriate for FASB pronouncements to be used for their accounting?

7. Why is it important for internal service funds to differentiate between revenues generated by interfund transactions and transactions with external parties?

8. How does a proprietary fund statement of cash flows differ from a commercial enterprise's statement of cash flows?

9. What fund types are included in the fiduciary fund category? Where are they reported in the financial statements?

10. How might an internal service fund be financed initially? How will the financing appear in the fund financial statements?

11. How does a private-purpose trust fund differ from a permanent fund?

12. How many columns (not including total columns) are needed for a governmentwide statement of net assets of a governmental unit with a general fund, two special revenue funds, three internal service funds, four enterprise funds, and a component unit? Explain.

13. Do pension trust fund financial statements indicate whether or not the plan is fully funded? Explain.

14. What is the accounting equation for an agency fund?

15. Under what circumstances will a proprietary fund be required to report segment information?

16. How might the enterprise fund amounts on the proprietary fund statement of net assets differ from the amounts reported as "business-type activities" on the governmentwide statement of net assets?

EXERCISES

E 20-1

Multiple choice

1. Internal service funds are reported:
   a **With governmental funds on the fund financial statements**
   b **With governmental funds on the governmentwide statement of net assets**
   c **With proprietary funds on the governmentwide statement of net assets**
   d **All of the above**

2. Which of the following is not a fiduciary fund?
   a **Agency fund**
   b **Trust fund**
   c **Permanent fund**
   d **All of the above are fiduciary funds**

3. The proprietary fund statement of cash flows includes all of the following sections except:
   a **Cash flows from operating activities**
   b **Cash flows from investing activities**
   c **Cash flows from capital and related financing activities**
   d **Cash flows from noncapital investing activities**

4. The accounting equation for proprietary funds is:
   a **Current assets – Noncurrent assets – All liabilities = Fund balance**
   b **Current assets – Noncurrent assets – All liabilities = Net assets**
   c **Current assets + Noncurrent assets – All liabilities = Net assets**
   d **Assets = Liabilities**

5. The accounting equation for agency funds is:
   a **Current assets – Noncurrent assets – All liabilities = Fund balance**
   b **Current assets – Noncurrent assets – All liabilities = Net assets**
   c **Current assets + Noncurrent assets – All liabilities = Net assets**
   d **Assets = Liabilities**

E 20-2
Multiple choice [AICPA adapted]

1. The billings for transportation services provided to other governmental units are recorded by the internal service fund as:

   a *Interfund exchanges*

   b *Intergovernmental transfers*

   c *Transportation appropriations*

   d *Operating revenues*

2. Which of the following does not affect an internal service fund's net income?

   a *Depreciation expense on its fixed assets*

   b *Operating transfers in*

   c *Operating transfers out*

   d *Residual equity transfers*

3. Customers' security deposits that cannot be spent for normal operating purposes are collected by a governmental unit and accounted for in an enterprise fund. A portion of the amount collected is invested in marketable debt securities and a portion in marketable equity securities. How will each portion be classified in the balance sheet?

	Portion in Marketable Debt Securities	Portion in Marketable Equity Securities
a	Unrestricted asset	Restricted asset
b	Unrestricted asset	Unrestricted asset
c	Restricted asset	Unrestricted asset
d	Restricted asset	Restricted asset

4. Carlton City serves as a collecting agency for the local independent school district and for a local water district. For this purpose, Carlton has created a single agency fund and charges the other entities a fee of 1% of the gross amounts collected. (The service fee is treated as a general fund revenue.) During the latest fiscal year, a gross amount of $268,000 was collected for the independent school district and $80,000 for the water district. As a consequence of the forgoing, Carlton's general fund should:

   a *Recognize receipts of $348,000*

   b *Recognize receipts of $344,520*

   c *Record revenue of $3,480*

   d *Record encumbrances of $344,520*

5. Through an internal service fund, Floyd County operates a centralized data processing center to provide services to Floyd's other departments. In 2009, this internal service fund billed Floyd's parks and recreation fund $75,000 for data processing services. What account should Floyd's internal service fund credit to record this $75,000 billing to the parks and recreation fund?

   a *Operating revenues*

   b *Interfund exchanges*

   c *Intergovernmental transfers*

   d *Data processing department expenses*

E 20-3
Multiple choice

1. Charges for services are a major source of revenue for:

   a *A debt service fund*

   b *A trust fund*

   c *An enterprise fund*

   d *A capital projects fund*

2. A city provides initial financing for its enterprise fund with the stipulation that the amount advanced be returned to the general fund within five years. The general fund expects prompt repayment. In recording the payment to the enterprise fund, the general fund should:

   a *Debit the contribution to enterprise fund account*

   b *Debit the expenditures account*

   c *Debit a reserve for advance to enterprise fund account*

   d *Debit a due from enterprise fund account*

3. If enterprise fund assets are financed through general obligation bonds, rather than revenue bonds, the debt:

   a *Is not an enterprise fund liability*

   b *Must be serviced through a debt service fund*

   c *Is an enterprise fund liability if enterprise fund revenues are intended to service the debt*

   d *Is reported both as a long-term fund liability and a general obligation liability*

4. An internal service fund would most likely be created to provide:

   a *Debt service*

   b *Centralized purchasing*

   c *Perpetual care of cemeteries*

   d *Tax collection and recording services*

5. Enterprise funds should be used in accounting for governmental activities that involve:

   a *Providing goods and services to the public*

   b *Providing goods and services to other departments of the government*

   c *Providing goods and services to the public if a substantial amount of revenue is derived from user charges*

   d *Collection of money from the public*

E 20-4

Multiple choice

1. Fiduciary funds include four different types of funds. Which of the following is *not* one of these types?

   a *Agency funds*

   b *Tax collection funds*

   c *Private-purpose trust funds*

   d *Pension trust funds*

2. Agency funds maintain accounts for:

   a *Liabilities*

   b *Revenues*

   c *Fund balance*

   d *Expenditures*

3. Fiduciary responsibilities:

   a *Must be accounted for in trust and agency funds according to GAAP*

   b *May be accounted for as liabilities of the general fund*

   c *Are infrequently encountered in accounting for governments*

   d *Arise whenever assets are placed in trust for particular purposes*

4. If Hudack County established a separate fund entity to account for state income taxes collected and remitted to the state, the fund would likely be:

   a *An agency fund*

   b *An internal service fund*

   c *An endowment fund*

   d *A trust fund*

5. Each year Broihahn County invests $100,000 from general revenue in marketable securities to provide for the eventual retirement of general obligation term bonds. The investment activity is accounted for in:

   a *A private-purpose trust fund*

   b *A permanent fund*

   c *A debt service fund*

   d *An agency fund*

E 20-5

Multiple choice [AICPA adapted]

1. The following revenues were among those reported by Arvida Township in 2009:

Net rental revenue (after depreciation) from a parking garage owned by Arvida	$ 40,000
Interest earned on investments held for employees' retirement benefits	100,000
Property taxes	6,000,000

What amount of the forgoing revenues should be accounted for in Arvida's governmental-type funds?

   a *$6,140,000*

   b *$6,100,000*

   c *$6,040,000*

   d *$6,000,000*

2. Taylor City issued the following long-term obligations:

Revenue bonds to be repaid from admission fees collected from users of the city swimming pool	$1,000,000
General obligation bonds issued for the city water and sewer fund that will service the debt	$1,800,000

Although these bonds are expected to be paid from enterprise funds, the full faith and credit of the city has been pledged as further assurance that the obligations will be paid. What amount of these bonds should be accounted for in the proprietary funds?

a 0

b $1,000,000

c $1,800,000

d $2,800,000

3. The following proceeds received by Glad City in 2007 are legally restricted to expenditure for specified purposes:

Donation by a benefactor mandated to provide meals for the needy	$300,000
Sales taxes to finance the maintenance of tourist facilities owned by the city	900,000

What amount should be accounted for in Glad's fiduciary funds?

a 0

b $300,000

c $900,000

d $1,200,000

4. In connection with Thurman Township's long-term debt, the following cash accumulations are available to cover payment of principal and interest on:

Bonds for financing of water treatment plant construction	$1,000,000
General long-term obligations	400,000

The amount of these cash accumulations that should be accounted for in Thurman's debt service funds is:

a 0

b $400,000

c $1,000,000

d $1,400,000

Use the following information in answering questions 5 and 6:

On December 31, 2007, Cane City paid a contractor $3,000,000 for the total cost of a new municipal annex built in 2007 on city-owned land. Financing was provided by a $2,000,000 general obligation bond issue sold at face amount on December 31, 2007, with the remaining $1,000,000 transferred from the general fund.

5. What account and amount should be reported in Cane's 2007 financial statements for the general fund?

a *Other financing uses, $1,000,000*

b *Other financing sources, $2,000,000*

c *Expenditures, $3,000,000*

d *Other financing sources, $3,000,000*

6. What accounts and amounts should be reported in Cane's 2007 financial statements for the capital projects fund?

a *Other financing sources, $2,000,000; general long-term debt, $2,000,000*

b *Revenues, $2,000,000; expenditures, $2,000,000*

c *Other financing sources, $3,000,000; expenditures, $3,000,000*

d *Revenue, $3,000,000; expenditures, $3,000,000*

LEARNING OBJECTIVE 3

E 20-6

Agency fund statement of net assets The City of Laramee established a tax agency fund to collect property taxes for the City of Laramee, Bloomer County, and Bloomer School District. Total tax levies of the three governmental units were $200,000 for 2005, of which $60,000 was for the City of Laramee, $40,000 for Bloomer County, and $100,000 for Bloomer School District.

The tax agency fund charges Bloomer County and Bloomer School District a 2% collection fee that it transfers to the general fund of the City of Laramee in order to cover costs incurred for agency fund operations.

During 2005 the tax agency fund collected and remitted $150,000 of the 2005 levies to the various governmental units. The collection fees associated with the $150,000 were remitted to Laramee's general fund before year-end.

REQUIRED: Prepare a statement of fiduciary net assets for the City of Laramee Tax Agency Fund at December 31, 2005.

LEARNING OBJECTIVE 1

E 20-7

Enterprise fund journal entries and reporting Prepare journal entries to record the following grant-related transactions of an enterprise fund activity. Explain how these transactions should be reported in the enterprise fund's financial statements, including the statement of cash flows.

1. Received an operating grant in cash from the state, $3,000,000.

2. Incurred qualifying expenses on the grant program, $1,200,000.

3. Received a federal grant to finance construction of a processing plant, $7,000,000. (The cash was received in advance.)

4. Incurred and paid construction costs on the processing plant, $4,000,000.

E 20-8

Identification of fund type For each of the following events or transactions, identify the fund or funds that will be affected.

1. A governmental unit operates a municipal pool. Costs are intended to be recovered primarily from user charges.

2. A bond offering was issued at par to subsidize the construction of a new convention center.

3. A bond offering was issued at a premium to subsidize the construction of a new convention center.

4. A town receives a donation of cash that must be used for the benefit of a local bird sanctuary.

5. A central computing center was established to handle the data processing needs of a municipality.

6. A local municipality provides water and sewer services to residents of nearby communities for a fee.

7. A village receives a grant from the state government. The funds are to be used solely for preserving wetlands.

8. Property taxes are levied by a city government.

9. A county government serves as a tax collection agency for all towns and cities located within the county.

10. A county government offers to pool the cash available for investment from cities located within its boundaries. A formal agreement exists, and income will be recognized in the fund.

E 20-9

Journal entries—various funds For each of the following events or transactions, prepare the necessary journal entry or entries and identify the fund or funds that will be affected.

1. A governmental unit collects fees totaling $4,500 at the municipal pool. The fees are charged to recover costs of pool operation and maintenance.

2. A county government that serves as a tax collection agency for all towns and cities located within the county collects county sales taxes totaling $125,000 for the month.

3. A $1,000,000 bond offering was issued, with a premium of $50,000, to subsidize the construction of a city visitor center.

4. A town receives a donation of $50,000 in bonds. The bonds should be held indefinitely, but bond income is to be donated to the local zoo. The zoo is not associated with the town.

5. A central printing shop is established with a $150,000 nonreciprocal transfer from the general fund.

6. A $1,000,000 revenue bond offering was issued at par by a fund that provides water and sewer services to residents of nearby communities for a fee. The funds are to be used for facility expansion.

7. A village is awarded a grant of $250,000 from the state government for highway beautification. The general fund provides a $50,000 loan, because grant funds will be disbursed after valid expenditures are documented.

8. Property taxes of $5,000,000 are levied by a city government. One percent is considered uncollectible, and the taxes will be used to fund current obligations.

PROBLEMS

P 20-1

Internal service fund journal entries The City of Thomasville established an internal service fund to provide printing services to all city offices and departments. The following transactions related to the fund took place in 2005:

1. On January 15, 2005, the general fund transferred equipment valued at $550,000 and provided a $500,000 loan to the internal service fund.

2. On February 1, 2005, the internal service fund acquired $200,000 worth of printing equipment and computers. The assets have a five-year life with no salvage, and the city uses straight-line depreciation.

3. Throughout the year, the internal service fund billed various departments $345,000 for service rendered and collected $300,000 of the amount billed.

4. Various expenses for the year were as follows: wages and salaries, $180,000; payroll taxes, $37,800; repayment to the general fund, $50,000; and other operating expenses, $120,000.

REQUIRED: Prepare all necessary journal entries for the printing services internal service fund for the year ended December 31, 2005.

P 20-2

Enterprise fund journal entries and trial balance The following transactions relate to the Fiedler County Utility Plant, a newly established municipal facility financed with debt secured solely by net revenue from fees and charges to external users.

1. The general fund made a $30,000,000 contribution to establish the working capital of the new utility enterprise fund.

2. The utility fund purchased a utility plant for $25,250,000.

3. The utility fund issued a $5,000,000 revenue bond for renovations to the facility.

4. Utility bills of $4,500,000 were mailed to customers.

5. Utility collections totaled $4,400,000.

6. Renovations of $3,500,000 were completed during the year and recorded as building improvements.

7. Salaries of $700,000 were paid to employees.

8. Interest expense of $300,000 related to the revenue bonds was paid during the year, and $100,000 was accrued at year-end.

9. Operating expenses totaling $1,000,000 were paid during the year, and an additional $100,000 of operating expenses were accrued at year-end.

10. Depreciation of $1,050,000 was recorded.

REQUIRED: Prepare all necessary journal entries and an adjusted trial balance for the utility enterprise fund for the year.

P 20-3

Preparation of internal service fund statements Comparative adjusted trial balances for the motor pool of Douwe County at June 30, 2004, and June 30, 2005, are as follows:

	June 30, 2005	June 30, 2004
Cash	$ 37,000	$ 44,000
Due from general fund	—	8,000
Due from electric fund	4,000	3,000
Supplies on hand	14,000	12,000
Autos	99,000	80,000
Supplies used	68,000	60,000
Salaries expense	25,000	20,000
Utilities expense	9,000	8,000
Depreciation expense	16,000	15,000
Operating transfer to general fund	12,000	—
	$284,000	$250,000
Accumulated depreciation—autos	$ 56,000	$ 40,000
Accounts payable	11,000	10,000
Advance from general fund (current)	5,000	5,000
Contribution from general fund	50,000	50,000
Retained earnings	42,000	35,000
Revenue from billings	120,000	110,000
	$284,000	$250,000

REQUIRED: Prepare fund financial statements for the motor pool for the year ended June 30, 2005. (The statement of cash flows is to be included.)

P 20-4

Preparation of trust fund statements On January 1, 2006, J. G. Monee created a student aid trust fund to which he donated a building valued at $400,000 (his cost was $250,000), bonds having a market value of $500,000, and $100,000 cash. The trust agreement stipulated that principal was to be maintained intact and earnings were to be used to support needy students. Consider gains on investments and depreciation as adjustments of earnings rather than of trust fund principal.

Activities for 2006

1. During the year, net rentals of $40,000 were collected for building rental.

2. The bonds were sold for $550,000 on June 30, 2006. Of the proceeds, $30,000 represented interest accrued from January 1 to June 30.

3. Stocks were purchased for $600,000 cash.

4. Depreciation on the building was calculated at $20,000 for the year.

5. Dividends receivable of $60,000 were recorded at December 31, 2006.

REQUIRED: Prepare a statement of fiduciary net assets and a statement of changes in fiduciary net assets for this private-purpose trust fund at December 31, 2006.

P 20-5

Preparation of trust fund statements On July 1, 2007, Duchy County receives a
$500,000 contribution from the local chapter of Homeless No More. A trust agreement specifying that the income from the contribution be distributed each May 15 to the downtown homeless shelter accompanies the contribution. The principal amount is intended to remain intact indefinitely. The following transactions related to the contribution occur during the fiscal year:

1. On September 1, the county invests the contribution in bonds, which yield 5% annually (payable on March 1 and September 1).

2. On March 1, the county receives the first interest payment.

3. On May 15, the county distributes the interest to the homeless shelter.

4. On June 30, the county closes its accounts.

REQUIRED: Prepare a statement of fiduciary net assets and a statement of changes in fiduciary net assets for this private-purpose trust fund at June 30, 2008.

P 20-6

Internal service fund journal entries [AICPA adapted] The City of Meringen operates
a central garage through an internal service fund to provide garage space and repairs for all city-owned and -operated vehicles. The central garage fund was established by a contribution of $200,000 from the general fund on July 1, 2006, when the building was acquired. The postclosing trial balance at June 30, 2008, was as follows:

	Debit	Credit
Cash	$150,000	
Due from general fund	20,000	
Inventory of materials and supplies	80,000	
Land	60,000	
Building	200,000	
Accumulated depreciation—building		$ 10,000
Machinery and equipment	56,000	
Accumulated depreciation—machinery		
and equipment		12,000
Vouchers payable		38,000
Contribution from general fund		200,000
Retained earnings		306,000
	$566,000	$566,000

The following information applies to the fiscal year ended June 30, 2009:

1. Materials and supplies were purchased on account for $74,000.

2. The inventory of materials and supplies at June 30, 2009, was $58,000, which agreed with the physical count taken.

3. Salaries and wages paid to employees totaled $230,000, including related costs.

4. A billing was received from the enterprise fund for utility charges totaling $30,000, and it was paid.

5. Depreciation of the building was recorded in the amount of $5,000. Depreciation of the machinery and equipment totaled $8,000.

6. Billings to other departments for services rendered to them were as follows:

General fund	$262,000
Water and sewer fund	84,000
Special revenue fund	32,000

7. Unpaid interfund receivable balances at June 30, 2009, were as follows:

General fund	$ 6,000
Special revenue fund	16,000

8. Vouchers payable at June 30, 2009, were $14,000.

REQUIRED

1. For the period July 1, 2008, through June 30, 2009, prepare journal entries to record all the transactions in the central garage fund accounts.

2. Prepare closing entries for the central garage fund at June 30, 2009.

P 20-7

Enterprise fund statement of cash flows
Caleb County had a beginning cash balance in its enterprise fund of $714,525. During the year, the following transactions affecting cash flows occurred:

a Acquired equity investments totaling $165,000.
b Receipts from sales of goods or services totaled $3,276,500.
c Payments for materials used in providing services were made in the amount of $2,694,500.
d A capital grant, whose proceeds of $750,000 are restricted for the acquisition of constructing or improving a fixed asset, was awarded. (Cash was received during the year.)
e Payments to employees for salaries amounted to $479,300.
f The fund's allocated portion of property taxes was $217,000.
g Other cash expenses for operations were $819,200.
h Capital assets used in providing goods and services were sold for $522,000. They had a book value of $550,000.
i Long-term debt payments totaled $515,000.

REQUIRED: Prepare a statement of cash flows for the Caleb County enterprise fund.

INTERNET ASSIGNMENT

1. Visit the GASB's Web site at **www.GASB.org**. Click on the Links icon and select CAFRs. Choose a CAFR from a city, county, or other local government. Review the CAFR and answer the following questions:

   a. How many proprietary funds does the government have? List the name of one enterprise fund.
   b. Does the government have an internal service fund? What product or service does it provide?
   c. Does the government have an agency fund? What is its title?
   d. What type of pension fund is reported in the financial statements? Are the required disclosures contained in the CAFR?

2. Locate the Web site for the municipality in which your college or university is located. Does this municipality provide utilities, sewer, or water to its residents? Are these activities accounted for in the appropriate fund?

3. Locate the Web site for your hometown. Does this municipality provide local transit service (i.e., bus, subway, etc.)? If so, how is it funded? Did the government receive any capital or operating grants during the year?

ACCOUNTING FOR NOT-FOR-PROFIT ORGANIZATIONS

This chapter provides an introduction to accounting principles and reporting practices of not-for-profit (NFP) entities, which include voluntary health and welfare organizations, other not-for-profit organizations (such as churches and museums), health care entities, and colleges and universities. Each of these organizational types is important for the resources it controls and for its impact on society.

Although these four NFP organizational types often share a focus on service objectives, their sources of financing and degree of autonomy vary significantly. Also, some of these organizations are governments required to follow the pronouncements of the GASB, whereas others are nongovernmental not-for-profit organizations, whose standards are established by the FASB. This chapter describes not-for-profit organizations, introduces the FASB standards applicable to nongovernmental not-for-profits, and provides detailed examples of journal entries and financial statements for nongovernmental not-for-profit organizations.

THE NATURE OF NOT-FOR-PROFIT ORGANIZATIONS

You can distinguish a not-for-profit entity from a commercial business enterprise by examining underlying characteristics. A not-for-profit entity (1) receives contributions of significant amounts of resources from resource providers who do not expect commensurate or proportionate pecuniary return, (2) operates for purposes other than to provide goods or services at a profit, and (3) does not possess ownership interests like those of business enterprises.[1]

Once designated as such, a not-for-profit organization finds itself in a quite diverse sector of entities whose members are public and private, charitable and self-promoting, and tax-exempt and taxable. Although the term *not-for-profit* conjures up thoughts of the Salvation Army or your local church, NFP entities can fall into one of four categories: voluntary health and welfare organizations (such as the Salvation Army), other not-for-profit organizations (such as churches and museums), health care entities, and colleges and universities. The accounting and financial reporting methods of each type of NFP vary. Thus, not-for-profit entities are first designated as governmental or nongovernmental to determine whether they should follow GASB or FASB standards.

A governmental not-for-profit organization meets the aforementioned not-for-profit criteria and also possesses one of the following characteristics: officers are elected by popular vote or appointment by a state or local government; a government can unilaterally dissolve the entity, with the assets reverting back to the government; or the entity has the power to enact and enforce a tax

LEARNING OBJECTIVES

1 Learn about the four main categories of not-for-profit organizations.

2 Differentiate between governmental and nongovernmental not-for-profit organizations.

3 Introduce FASB not-for-profit accounting principles.

4 Apply not-for-profit accounting principles to voluntary health and welfare organizations.

5 Apply not-for-profit accounting principles to hospitals and other health care organizations.

6 Apply not-for-profit accounting principles to private not-for-profit colleges and universities.

LEARNING OBJECTIVE 1

---

[1] *FASB Statement No. 116*, "Accounting for Contributions Received and Contributions Made," 1993, Appendix D.

levy.[2,3] Unlike *general-purpose governments*, such as the state and local municipalities discussed in Chapters 18 to 20, the GASB defines other legally separate governmental entities as *special-purpose governments*. Governmental not-for-profit organizations are therefore special-purpose governments and are generally required to follow GASB standards; however, their reporting requirements may be reduced. *GASB Statements No. 34* and *35* require special-purpose governments with more than one governmental program or both governmental and business-type activities to present both governmentwide and fund financial statements, as well as the MD&A, notes, and required supplementary information. Special-purpose governments with only one governmental program may combine fund and governmentwide statements, whereas those with only business-type activities should report only the financial statements required for enterprise funds, as well as the MD&A, notes, and required supplementary information. Because accounting and financial reporting under *GASB 34* was covered extensively in previous chapters, the remainder of this chapter is devoted to the accounting and financial reporting required for nongovernmental not-for-profit entities, and mention of governmental not-for-profits is limited.

Nongovernmental not-for-profit organizations are NFP entities that lack the governmental element. All nongovernmental, not-for-profit organizations—whether voluntary health and welfare organizations (VHWOs), health care organizations, colleges and universities, or other—use essentially the same basic guidance, although the nature of their transactions differs. The primary FASB standards that provide guidance for such entities are *FASB Statement No. 116*, "Accounting for Contributions Received and Contributions Made," which establishes accounting standards for contributions, and *Statement No. 117*, "Financial Statements of Not-for-Profit Organizations," which identifies the required statements to be presented by nongovernmental, not-for-profit organizations.

NOT-FOR-PROFIT ACCOUNTING PRINCIPLES

Until 1993, not-for-profit organizations looked primarily to the AICPA for accounting principles and financial reporting guidance. The AICPA published four industry audit guides related to voluntary health and welfare organizations, health care entities, colleges and universities, and other not-for-profit organizations. (This is the reason for the four categories of NFP organizations.) In the early 1990s, the FASB took a more active role in setting NFP standards with its issuance of *Statements No. 116* and *117*. These standards, applicable to all nongovernmental not-for-profit entities, served to standardize accounting and financial reporting in the not-for-profit sector. More recently, the FASB issued *Statements No. 124* and *136*, which are specifically related to not-for-profit organizations.[4] The 2004 *AICPA Audit and Accounting Guide: Not-for-Profit Organizations*, which incorporates three of the prior audit guides (VHWOs, colleges and universities, and "other" NFP organizations), includes FASB NFP standards as well as additional guidance for such organizations.

Financial Statements

FASB Statement No. 117 requires not-for-profit organizations to provide a set of financial statements that includes a statement of financial position, statement of activities, statement of cash flows, and accompanying notes. Voluntary health and welfare organizations must also provide a statement of functional expenses.

Within the financial statements, not-for-profit organizations classify net assets, revenues, expenses, gains, and losses according to three classes of net assets—unrestricted, temporarily restricted, and permanently restricted—based on the existence or absence of donor-imposed restrictions. *FASB Statement No. 116* defines the three classes of net assets as follows:

---

[2] American Institute of Certified Public Accountants, *AICPA Audit and Accounting Guide: Not-for-Profit Organizations*, 2004.

[3] An organization may also be considered a government if it has the ability to issue tax-exempt debt directly; however, if this is the only governmental characteristic that it possesses, the organization can dispute the presumption that it is governmental in nature.

[4] The FASB has issued an exposure draft, titled "Combinations of Not-for-Profit Organizations." The project, which aims to develop guidance on the accounting and reporting for combinations of not-for-profit organizations, is expected to be issued as an FASB standard in 2006.

- **Permanently restricted net assets** are the portion of net assets whose use is limited by donor-imposed stipulations that do not expire and cannot be removed by action of the not-for-profit entity.
- **Temporarily restricted net assets** are the portion of net assets whose use is limited by donor-imposed stipulations that either expire (time restrictions) or can be removed by the organization fulfilling the stipulations (purpose restrictions).
- **Unrestricted net assets** are the portion of net assets that carry no donor-imposed stipulations.

Organizations can report revenues, gains, and losses in each net asset class, but expenses are reported only in the unrestricted net assets class.

STATEMENT OF FINANCIAL POSITION The statement of financial position or balance sheet reports assets, liabilities, and net assets. It reports net assets in total and by the three classes of net assets—unrestricted, temporarily restricted, and permanently restricted. Permanently and temporarily restricted amounts appear on the face of the balance sheet or in notes. Assets received with donor-imposed restrictions that limit their use to long-term purposes should be separated from assets available for current use. Comparative statements from the prior period are not required.

STATEMENT OF ACTIVITIES The statement of activities provides information about the change in amount and nature of net assets and reports how resources are used to provide various programs or services. Not-for-profit organizations account for revenues and expenses using the accrual basis of accounting. *Statement No. 93* requires not-for-profit organizations that issue GAAP-basis financial statements to recognize depreciation expense on long-lived assets. NFP organizations should record depreciation even if the assets are gifts; however, certain works of art and certain historical treasures that meet the definition of "collections" need not be capitalized or depreciated.

The statement of activities focuses on the organization as a whole. It reports the amount of change in net assets, ending with a net asset figure that is the same as net assets in the balance sheet. The statement presents revenues, expenses, gains, and losses by net asset class; thus, there are columns or sections reporting the amount of change in permanently restricted net assets, temporarily restricted net assets, and unrestricted net assets.

Not-for-profit revenues, described in detail later, increase unrestricted net assets unless use of the assets received is limited by donor-imposed restrictions. Gains and losses on investments are increases or decreases in unrestricted net assets unless their use is restricted by explicit donor stipulations or by law. Expenses always decrease unrestricted net assets; thus, they cannot appear in the temporarily restricted or permanently restricted net asset classes. Temporarily restricted or permanently restricted net assets consist of donor-restricted contributions whose restrictions have not yet been met. If restrictions placed on donor-restricted contributions are met in the same reporting period in which the contribution is made, the organization may report the contribution as unrestricted as long as the organization follows a consistent policy. Reclassifications are reported separately.

Generally, NFP organizations report revenues and expenses at gross amounts. Gains and losses from peripheral or incidental transactions or events beyond the control of the organization may be reported at net amounts, and investment income is reported net of related expenses. Further classifications of revenues, expenses, gains, and losses (such as operating or nonoperating, recurring or nonrecurring, and so on) are optional.

NFP organizations report expenses by functional classification—major classes of program services and supporting services—in the statement or notes. *Program services* are the activities that distribute goods and services that fulfill the purpose or mission of the organization to beneficiaries, customers, or members. *Supporting services* are all activities other than program services. Supporting services include the following:

- **Management and general.** Oversight, business management, general record keeping, budgeting, financing, and related administrative activities
- **Fund-raising.** Publicizing and conducting fund-raising campaigns; maintaining donor mailing lists; conducting special fund-raising events; preparing and distributing fund-raising manuals, instructions, and other materials; and other activities to solicit contributions

■ **Membership-development activities.** Soliciting for prospective members and membership dues, membership relations, and so on

STATEMENT OF FUNCTIONAL EXPENSES Voluntary health and welfare organizations must report expenses classified by function and by natural classification (salaries, rent, etc.) in a matrix format as a separate statement. Other not-for-profit organizations are encouraged, but not required, to provide this additional expense information.

STATEMENT OF CASH FLOWS *Statement No. 117* extends the provisions of *FASB Statement No. 95*, "Statement of Cash Flows," to not-for-profit organizations. Not-for-profit organizations use the same classifications and definitions as business enterprises, except that the description of financing activities is expanded to include resources that are donor restricted for long-term purposes. The NFP statement of cash flows reports investing activities of permanent endowments as cash flows of investing activities.

When preparing the statement of cash flows, organizations cannot aggregate cash restricted for long-term purposes with cash available for current uses in the balance sheet. Similarly, they should exclude cash and cash equivalents that are restricted for long-term purposes from cash in the cash flows statement.

Statement No. 117 encourages NFP organizations to use the direct method for presenting cash flows, but it also permits the indirect method. Organizations that select the direct method must provide a schedule to reconcile the change in net assets in the statement of activities to net cash flows from operating activities.

Contributions

For some not-for-profit entities, contributions are a major source of revenue. *Statement No. 116* defines a **contribution** as "an unconditional transfer of cash or other assets to an entity or a settlement or cancellation of its liabilities in a voluntary, nonreciprocal transfer by another entity acting other than as an owner." Examples of other assets include buildings, securities, the use of facilities or services, and unconditional promises to give. *Statement No. 116* describes a *promise to give* as a written or oral agreement to contribute cash or other assets to another entity. The promise should be verifiable by evidence such as pledge cards or tape recordings of oral promises. A promise to give may be conditional or unconditional.

A *conditional promise to give* depends on the occurrence of a specified future and uncertain event to bind the promisor. For example, a church parishioner may pledge to contribute a sum of money if a local government approves a proposed church renovation. Organizations recognize conditional promises to give as contribution revenue and receivables when the conditions are substantially met (in other words, when the conditional promise to give becomes unconditional); however, they account for a conditional gift of cash or other asset that may have to be returned to the donor if the condition is not met as a refundable advance (liability). Disclosures in notes to the financial statements for conditional promises to give include the total amounts promised and a description and amount for each group of promises having similar characteristics.

An *unconditional promise to give* depends only on the passage of time or demand by the promisee for performance. Promises to give are unconditional if the possibility that a condition will not be met is remote. Organizations recognize unconditional promises to give as contribution revenue and receivables in the period in which the promise is received. They report such promises as restricted support (in other words, as contribution revenues in temporarily restricted net assets, based on the time restriction), even if the resources are not restricted for specific purposes, until cash is received and available for expenditure.[5] Not-for-profit entities should disclose both anticipated time frame for receipt (amounts of unconditional promises receivable in less than one year, in one to five years, and in more than five years) and the allowance for uncollectible promises receivable.

Generally, NFP organizations measure restricted and unrestricted contributions at fair value and recognize them as revenues or gains in the period in which they are received. As previously noted, contributions are separated into the three classes of net assets on the statement of activities: those

---

[5] An exception is provided when the donor explicitly stipulates that the contribution is intended to support current-period activities, in which case it is reported as unrestricted support.

that increase unrestricted net assets, those that increase temporarily restricted net assets, and those that increase permanently restricted net assets.

DONOR-IMPOSED RESTRICTIONS OR CONDITIONS A *donor-imposed condition* provides that the donor's money be returned or the donor be released from the promise to give if the condition is not met. *Donor-imposed restrictions* simply limit the use of contributed assets. If it is unclear whether donor stipulations are conditions or restrictions, the organization should presume that the promise is conditional. A donor-imposed restriction expires in the period in which the restriction is satisfied (i.e., when a time restriction is met or a purpose restriction satisfied). If a given contribution is subject to more than one restriction, the restrictions expire in the period in which the last restriction is satisfied.

When a temporary restriction is met (either by the passage of time or by the incurrence of expenses for the restricted purpose), organizations reclassify resources in the temporarily restricted net assets category as unrestricted net assets. On the statement of activities, they report the reclassified amount as net assets released from restrictions. These assets increase unrestricted net assets and decrease temporarily restricted net assets. If donor-imposed restrictions are met in the same period in which the contributions are received, organizations may report the contributions as unrestricted if the following conditions are met: (1) the policy must be disclosed in the notes and followed consistently, and (2) the organization must have the same policy for temporarily restricted investment income whose restrictions are met in the same period as income is recognized.

GIFTS OF LONG-LIVED ASSETS Gifts of long-lived assets may be restricted or unrestricted, depending on the organization's accounting policy or the donor's restriction. If the donor restricts contributed long-lived assets for use over a certain period of time, recipients report the assets as restricted support in temporarily restricted net assets. Later, the recipient organization recognizes depreciation by recording an expense in unrestricted net assets and reclassifying the amount of the depreciation from temporarily restricted to unrestricted net assets.

If the donor contributes the long-lived assets with no restrictions or if the assets are purchased with contributions restricted to the acquisition of long-lived assets, the organization can choose either of two accounting methods, which should be used consistently. The accounting policy must be disclosed in notes to the financial statements. The methods are as follows:

1. The organization may adopt an accounting policy that implies a time restriction that expires over the useful life of the donated asset. As in the case of contributed long-lived assets with an explicit donor-imposed time restriction, the gift is reported as restricted support in temporarily restricted net assets. Depreciation is recorded as an expense in unrestricted net assets, which results in a reclassification for the amount of the depreciation from temporarily restricted to unrestricted net assets. (This also applies to assets purchased with cash that was restricted to the purchase of long-lived assets.)

2. If no policy implying a time restriction exists and there are no donor-imposed restrictions, the gifts are unrestricted support.

INVESTMENTS AND INVESTMENT INCOME Not-for-profit organizations initially record purchased investments at their cost and contributed investments at fair value in the appropriate net asset classification. They recognize investment income as earned and report the income as an increase in unrestricted, temporarily restricted, or permanently restricted net assets, depending on donor-imposed restrictions on the use of the investment income. *FASB Statement No. 124*, "Accounting for Certain Investments Held by Not-for-Profit Organizations," requires organizations to report investments in debt securities at their fair values. Investments in equity securities that have readily determinable fair values also must be reported at fair values. Changes in fair values are reported in the statement of activities. The fair value accounting requirement does not apply to equity investments that are accounted for by the equity method or investments in consolidated subsidiaries.

Transfers That Are Not Contributions

Contributions do not include transfers that are exchange transactions; transfers in which the not-for-profit enterprise is acting as an agent, trustee, or intermediary for the donor; or tax exemptions, tax incentives, and tax abatements.

EXCHANGE TRANSACTIONS Exchange transactions are reciprocal transfers in which both parties give and receive approximately equal value. Sales of products and services are exchange transactions. Exchange transactions are sometimes difficult to distinguish from contributions. Assume that a not-for-profit organization sends calendars (premiums) to potential donors in a fund-raising appeal. The recipients keep the premium whether or not they make a donation. In this case the donations are contributions and the cost of premiums is a fund-raising expense. The same is true if the not-for-profit organization gives the premiums only to donors, but the premiums are nominal in relation to the donations. If donors receive gifts that approximate the value of their donations, however, the transaction is an exchange.

Dues charged to members of not-for-profit entities may have characteristics of both contributions and exchange transactions. The portion of the dues representing contributions will be recognized as revenue when received, but the portion representing an exchange transaction will be recognized as revenue as it is earned. A grant is an exchange transaction if the potential public benefit is secondary to the grantor's potential direct benefit; thus, grants must also be analyzed to determine if they are exchange transactions.

Resources received in exchange transactions are classified as unrestricted revenues and unrestricted net assets even if the resource provider limits use of the resources.

AGENCY TRANSACTIONS An agency transaction is one in which assets are transferred to the not-for-profit organization, but the not-for-profit organization has little or no discretion over the use of those assets, and the assets are passed on to a third party. The resource provider is using the not-for-profit entity as an agent or intermediary to transfer assets to a third-party donee. For example, the United Way often collects contributions for a number of local organizations. *FASB Statement No. 136,* "Transfers of Assets to a Not-for-Profit Organization or Charitable Trust That Raises or Holds Contributions for Others," addresses such transactions. Generally, the receipt of assets in an agency transaction increases the assets and liabilities of the not-for-profit entity, and disbursement of those assets decreases assets and liabilities. No contribution is recorded. The NFP organization reports the cash received and paid as cash flows from operating activities in the statement of cash flows.

GIFTS IN KIND Gifts in kind are noncash contributions, such as clothing, furniture, and services. They are contributions if the not-for-profit entity has discretion over the disposition of the resources. If it has little or no discretion over the disposition, the entity will account for the gifts as agency transactions. Organizations measure gifts in kind that are contributions at fair value, if practicable. When fair value cannot be reasonably determined, NFP entities should not record the gifts as contributions. Instead, they record the items as sales revenue when they are sold. Cost of sales is the cost of getting the inventory ready for sale. *FASB Statement No. 116* limits the recognition of contributed services to those that (1) create or enhance nonfinancial assets of the organization or (2) require specialized skills, are provided by individuals possessing those skills, and would typically need to be purchased if not provided by donation. If contributed services do not meet these criteria, they should not be recognized; however, information about services contributed to the organization's programs and activities should be described in the financial statement notes.

Measurement Principles

Not-for-profit organizations measure contributions at fair value. *Statement No. 116* identifies quoted market prices as the best estimate of fair values for both monetary and nonmonetary assets. Other valuation methods that might be used include quoted market prices for similar assets or independent appraisals. If a reasonable estimate for fair value cannot be made, the contribution should not be recognized.

Recall that not-for-profit organizations record unconditional promises to give when pledges are made. If the fair value of the contributed asset changes significantly between the pledge date and the date the asset is received, the not-for-profit entity accounts for the contribution as follows:

- No additional revenue is recognized if the fair value increases.
- If the fair value decreases, the difference is recognized in the period the decrease occurred and is reported as a change in the net asset class in which the revenue was originally reported or in the class where the net assets are represented.

A not-for-profit entity may record unconditional promises to give that it expects to collect within one year of the financial statement date at their net realizable value (gross amount less an allowance for uncollectible accounts). However, the entity should measure unconditional promises to give that are not expected to be collected within the year at the present value of the amounts expected to be collected (estimated future cash flows). The discount rate to be used in computing the present value should be a risk-free rate of return for a like time period.[6] The discount rate should be determined at the time the receivable is recognized. The discount is amortized using the interest rate method (see *APB Opinion No. 21*, paragraph 15). Amortization of the discount is included in contribution revenue and as an increase in the appropriate net asset class.

Collections

FASB Statement No. 116 encourages capitalization of collections of works of art, historical treasures, and similar items, but it does not require it so long as the following conditions are satisfied:

- They are held for public exhibition, education, or research in furtherance of public service rather than financial gain.
- They are protected, kept encumbered, cared for, and preserved.
- They are subject to an organizational policy that requires proceeds from sales of collection items to be used to acquire other items for collections.[7]

Organizations that choose not to capitalize collections should describe the collections in the notes to the financial statements. Contributed collection items are recognized as revenues or gains if the collection is capitalized.

When collection items are not recognized, the costs of collection items, proceeds from sales, and proceeds from insurance recoveries appear as increases or decreases of the appropriate net asset class on the activities statement, separately from revenues, expenses, gains, and losses.

Fund Accounting

Not-for-profit entities receive resources from contributions, charges for services, grants, appropriations, and so on, and the use of some of these resources is restricted for specific activities or purposes. Fund accounting principles provide a convenient method for segregating the accounting records of resources restricted for specific purposes. Many not-for-profit organizations choose to use fund accounting for internal accounting, although FASB issuances and the AICPA guide do not require fund accounting. Although *FASB Statement No. 117* does allow fund reporting as additional information, fund information is rarely presented in financial statements of nongovernmental, not-for-profit organizations. Therefore, this chapter does not discuss or illustrate fund accounting for nongovernmental organizations.

VOLUNTARY HEALTH AND WELFARE ORGANIZATIONS

Voluntary health and welfare organizations encompass a diverse group of not-for-profit entities that are supported by and provide voluntary services to the public. They may expend their resources to solve basic social problems in the areas of health or welfare either globally, nationally, at the community level, or on an individual basis. Examples include charities such as the March of Dimes or the American Cancer Society, Girl Scouts, Boy Scouts, and Meals on Wheels. VHWOs follow FASB standards, and the 2004 *AICPA Audit and Accounting Guide: Not-for-Profit Organizations* provides additional guidance for accounting and reporting for all nongovernmental voluntary health and welfare organizations.

Accounting for a VHWO

A group of concerned citizens organized a voluntary health and welfare organization called Neighbors Helping Neighbors (NHN) in 2004. The following journal entries provide examples of some typical accounting procedures for this organization.

CONTRIBUTIONS As part of its fund-raising effort in 2005, NHN distributed decals to all residents in the community. The decals cost NHN $145. As a result of the campaign, the organization received unrestricted cash contributions of $4,000 and unconditional promises to give totaling $6,000. Of

---

[6] *AICPA Audit and Accounting Guide: Not-for-Profit Organizations*, paragraph 5.52.

[7] *FASB 116*, Paragraph 11.

this $6,000 contribution receivable, $2,000 is not collectible until 2006. A presumption exists that the $2,000 due in 2006 is restricted for use in 2006. NHN estimates that 10% of the pledges will be uncollectible and makes the following entries in 2005:

Expenses—supporting services—fund-raising	145	
Cash		145
To record payment for decals used in fund-raising.		
Cash	4,000	
Unrestricted support—contributions		4,000
To record cash contributions.		
Contributions receivable	6,000	
Allowance for uncollectible contributions		600
Unrestricted support—contributions		3,600
Temporarily restricted support—contributions		1,800
To record unrestricted promises to give, promises restricted for use in 2006, and estimated uncollectibles.		

NHN collected $3,600 of the contributions receivable due in 2005 and wrote off the remaining $400 as uncollectible:

Cash	3,600	
Allowance for uncollectible contributions	400	
Contributions receivable		4,000
To record collection of contributions receivable.		

NHN collects the full $2,000 due in 2006 during that year. When the receivables are collected, NHN reports any difference between the estimated amount of uncollectibles and the actual amount as a gain or loss in the appropriate net asset class. The implied time restriction is met, so NHN reclassifies $1,800 of temporarily restricted net assets as unrestricted net assets.

Cash	2,000	
Allowance for uncollectible contributions	200	
Contributions receivable		2,000
Unrestricted support—contributions		200

To record collection of receivables and recognize support
    for the difference between the estimated and actual
    allowance for uncollectible amounts.		

Temporarily restricted net assets—reclassifications out	1,800	
Unrestricted net assets—reclassifications in		1,800
To reclassify net assets for which the restriction has been met.		

A donor gives NHN $1,000 that is restricted for a playground project. NHN purchases supplies for the playground project for $900 and reports the expenses as changes in unrestricted net assets. The organization makes an entry to reclassify $900 of temporarily restricted net assets. The reclassification is entered even though unrestricted resources were used to pay for the playground supplies.

Cash	1,000	
Temporarily restricted support—contributions		1,000
To record a gift restricted for a special project.		
Expenses—program services—community service	900	
Cash		900
To record purchase of supplies used in the playground project.		

Temporarily restricted net assets—reclassifications out	900	
Unrestricted net assets—reclassifications in		900
To reclassify net assets restricted for the playground project for which the restriction has been met.		

As shown earlier, a VHWO classifies its expenses as program services or supporting services and reports them on a functional basis under these classifications (for example, community service, recreation programs, fund-raising). Program services relate to the expenses incurred in providing the organization's social service activities. Supporting services consist of administrative expenses and fund-raising costs.

DONATED LONG-LIVED ASSETS NHN has a policy of implying a time restriction on donated fixed assets over the life of each asset. On January 1, 2005, Martin Construction donated a used van to the organization. The fair value of the van is $1,500, and it has a three-year remaining useful life. The van will be used in the organization's community service program.

NHN initially records the donated van as temporarily restricted support. Later, NHN records depreciation expense on the van as a program expense. The amount of depreciation expense is reclassified from temporarily restricted net assets to unrestricted net assets, because all expenses decrease unrestricted net assets.

Equipment	1,500	
Temporarily restricted support—contributions		1,500
To record receipt of donated van.		
Depreciation expense—program services—community service	500	
Accumulated depreciation—equipment		500
To record depreciation.		
Temporarily restricted net assets—reclassifications out	500	
Unrestricted net assets—reclassifications in		500
To record reclassification of net assets for which the temporary restriction is satisfied.		

SPECIAL EVENT FUND-RAISERS A fund-raising event for NHN featured a dinner and dance. Ticket sales for the dinner totaled $950, and expenses of the fund-raiser amounted to $650. VHWOs generally report gross revenues and expenses for special events related to the major ongoing activities of the organization in which attendees receive a benefit. If the special event is incidental to the activities of the organization, the organization may report the proceeds of the special event as gains and net of direct costs.

Cash	950	
Unrestricted gains—special event		950
To record proceeds from a fund-raising event.		
Unrestricted gains—special event	650	
Cash		650
To charge costs of fund-raising event against support from the event.		

GIFTS IN KIND Throughout the summer, NHN receives donations of used housewares and furniture that are then sold at a rummage sale held in August. Fair values for the donated items cannot be reasonably determined, but the cost of storing and moving the items to the rummage sale location is $550. Proceeds from the sale are $6,595. Because the fair value cannot be determined, NHN cannot record the items as contributions.

Cost of goods sold	550	
Cash		550
To pay costs of storing and moving rummage sale items.		

Cash	6,595	
Unrestricted revenues—sales		6,595
To record proceeds from rummage sale.		

Alternatively, if the fair value of donated items can be reasonably determined, the gifts in kind are recorded as contributions. Office-Mate Company donates office supplies with a fair value of $390 to NHN. Office-Mate puts no restrictions on the use of the donated items. The organization records the gift as follows:

Materials and supplies inventory	390	
Unrestricted support—contributions		390
To record receipt of office supplies.		

MEMBERSHIP FEES Memberships give members certain benefits, such as the right to receive the organization's newsletters. Dues from members may represent exchange transactions, contributions, or both, depending on the benefits provided to members. Revenues from exchange transactions are classified as unrestricted and are recognized as revenue as benefits are provided. Dues received when member benefits are negligible are recognized as contributions when received with a credit to "unrestricted support—contributions."

In cases in which the fair value of member benefits is less than the amount of dues, VHWOs divide the transfers between contributions and revenues. An organization may have levels of memberships, but the more-expensive memberships do not entitle the members to additional benefits. The excess payments are classified as contributions. NHN offers regular memberships for $10 and sustaining memberships for $50 and over. All members are entitled to the same newsletter and local discount coupons that are distributed when the dues are received. NHN received 500 regular memberships ($5,000) and 130 sustaining memberships ($6,500), which it records as follows:

Cash	11,500	
Unrestricted revenues—dues		6,300
Unrestricted support—contributions		5,200
To record revenue and support from the sale of memberships.		

DONATED SECURITIES AND INVESTMENT INCOME NHN receives securities (fair value of $5,000) with a stipulation that they permanently endow a park enhancement project. Income earned on the securities is restricted to use for the park enhancement project. Dividend income is $475.

Securities	5,000	
Permanently restricted support—contribution		5,000
To record receipt of securities permanently restricted for a park enhancement project.		

Cash	475	
Temporarily restricted revenue—investment income		475
To record investment income restricted for a park enhancement project.		

SUPPLIES NHN had supplies on hand of $1,600 at January 1, 2005. The organization purchased supplies for $1,500 during the year and received donations of supplies that had a fair value of $2,050 in addition to the $390 already received. At the end of 2005, the inventory on hand was $750. The supplies used were allocated to recreation programs, $2,000; community service programs, $1,400; fund-raising expenses, $600; and general administration, $790.

Materials and supplies inventory	3,550	
Unrestricted support—contributions		2,050
Cash		1,500
To record donated materials and supplies and to record purchase of supplies.		

Expenses—supporting services—management and general	790	
Expenses—program services—recreation programs	2,000	
Expenses—program services—community service	1,400	
Expenses—supporting services—fund-raising	600	
Materials and supplies inventory		4,790
To record allocation of supplies expense.		

DONATED SERVICES AND PAYMENT OF SALARIES An accounting firm donated its services to audit the books of NHN. The audit would have cost the association $1,200 if the services had not been donated. NHN also paid salaries allocated to program services and administration as follows: recreation programs, $6,000; community services, $4,000; and management and general, $2,000.

Expenses—management and general	1,200	
Unrestricted support—donated services		1,200
To record donated services allocated to management and general expenses.		
Expenses—program services—recreation programs	6,000	
Expenses—program services—community service	4,000	
Expenses—supporting services—management and general	2,000	
Cash		12,000
To record salaries allocated to program services and administration.		

DEPRECIATION Equipment owned by NHN is used to travel through the neighborhood and provide park programs. There are no explicit or implicit donor-imposed restrictions on the fixed assets. The organization allocates the $8,000 depreciation expense on the equipment to its programs and general administration as follows:

Depreciation expense—program services— recreation programs	3,000	
Depreciation expense—program services— community service	4,000	
Depreciation expense—supporting services— management and general	1,000	
Accumulated depreciation		8,000
To record depreciation allocated to programs and general administration.		

FIXED ASSET PURCHASE WITH RESTRICTED RESOURCES NHN purchased equipment costing $4,000. The equipment was financed by $3,000 from contributions with donor-imposed restrictions that were accumulated for purchase of the equipment and $1,000 from general resources.

Equipment	4,000	
Cash		4,000
To record payment for the purchase of equipment.		
Temporarily restricted net assets—reclassifications out	3,000	
Unrestricted net assets—reclassifications in		3,000
To record reclassification of temporarily restricted net assets.		

CLOSING ENTRIES NHN's closing entries for 2005 are as follows:

Unrestricted support—contributions	15,240	
Unrestricted revenues—dues	6,300	
Unrestricted support—donated services	1,200	
Unrestricted revenues—sales	6,595	
Unrestricted gains—special event	300	
Unrestricted net assets—reclassifications in	4,400	
Expenses—program services—community service		10,800
Expenses—program services—recreation programs		11,000
Expenses—supporting services—fund-raising		745
Expenses—supporting services—management and general		4,990
Cost of goods sold		550
Unrestricted net assets		5,950
Temporarily restricted support—contributions	4,300	
Temporarily restricted revenue—investment income	475	
Temporarily restricted net assets—reclassifications out		4,400
Temporarily restricted net assets		375
Permanently restricted support—contribution	5,000	
Permanently restricted net assets		5,000

Financial Reporting

Exhibits 21-1 to 21-4 present sample financial statements for NHN. The basic financial statements of nongovernmental voluntary health and welfare organizations include the same statements required for other not-for-profit organizations (a statement of financial position, a statement of

EXHIBIT 21-1 **Balance Sheet for Nongovernmental Voluntary Health and Welfare Organization**	

NEIGHBORS HELPING NEIGHBORS (A VHWO) STATEMENTS OF FINANCIAL POSITION—DECEMBER 31, 2005 AND 2004

	2005	2004
Assets		
Cash and cash equivalents	$22,375	$14,000
Inventories	750	1,600
Contributions receivable (less allowance of $300 in 2005 and $100 in 2004)	2,200	400
Short-term investments	1,000	1,000
Land, buildings, and equipment (less accumulated depreciation of $16,500 in 2005 and $8,000 in 2004)	34,000	37,000
Assets restricted for endowment	10,000	5,000
Total assets	$70,325	$59,000
Liabilities and Net Assets		
Liabilities		
Accounts payable	$ 2,300	$ 2,300
Grants payable	1,550	1,550
Mortgage payable	3,000	3,000
Interest payable	50	50
Total liabilities	6,900	6,900
Net assets		
Unrestricted	24,350	18,400
Temporarily restricted	29,075	28,700
Permanently restricted	10,000	5,000
Total net assets	63,425	52,100
Total liabilities and net assets	$70,325	$59,000

EXHIBIT 21-2

Statement of Activities

NEIGHBORS HELPING NEIGHBORS (A VHWO) STATEMENT OF ACTIVITIES FOR THE YEAR ENDED DECEMBER 31, 2005

Changes in Unrestricted Net Assets			
Revenues and gains			
Contributions		$15,240	
Membership dues		6,300	
Donated services		1,200	
Sales, net		6,045	
Special event	$950		
Less: Direct costs	650	300	
Total unrestricted revenues and gains			$29,085
Net assets released from restrictions			
Satisfaction of program restriction		900	
Expiration of time restriction		3,500	
Total net assets released from restrictions			4,400
Total unrestricted revenues, gains, and			
other support			33,485
Expenses and losses			
Program services			
Community service		10,800	
Recreation programs		11,000	21,800
Supporting services			
Fund-raising		745	
Management and general		4,990	5,735
Total expenses and losses			27,535
Increase in unrestricted net assets			5,950
Changes in Temporarily Restricted Net Assets			
Contributions		4,300	
Income on investments		475	
Net assets released from restrictions		(4,400)	
Increase in temporarily restricted net assets			375
Changes in Permanently Restricted Net Assets			
Contributions			5,000
Increase in net assets			11,325
Net assets at the beginning of the year			52,100
Net assets at the end of the year			$63,425

activities, and a statement of cash flows). The statement of activities reports revenues in the net asset class to which they relate, using the accrual basis of accounting. Revenues with no donor-imposed restrictions increase unrestricted net assets; revenues with donor-imposed restrictions increase temporarily restricted or permanently restricted net assets. Expenses decrease unrestricted net assets only. Note that expenses are classified as either program services or supporting services and are reported on a functional basis under these classifications (for example, community service, recreation programs). The functional basis of reporting expenses results in an informative but highly aggregated form of statement presentation. To overcome the limitations of aggregation, voluntary health and welfare organizations prepare an additional, separate statement of functional expenses, as shown in Exhibit 21-4. This statement reconciles the functional classifications with basic object-of-expense classifications such as salaries, supplies, postage, and awards and grants.

A national VHWO may have financially interrelated local affiliates. Unless the local organizations are independent of the national organization, with separate purposes and separate governing boards, the financial statements of the national and local organizations are combined for reporting in accordance with GAAP.

"OTHER" NOT-FOR-PROFIT ORGANIZATIONS

As noted earlier, not-for-profit classifications include four categories corresponding to four previously published AICPA audit and accounting guides: voluntary health and welfare organizations, health care entities, colleges and universities, and other not-for-profit organizations. The "other"

EXHIBIT 21-3

Statement of Cash
Flows (Indirect
Method)

NEIGHBORS HELPING NEIGHBORS (A VHWO) STATEMENT OF CASH FLOWS—INDIRECT METHOD YEAR ENDED DECEMBER 31, 2005

Cash Flows from Operating Activities		
Change in net assets		$11,325
Adjustments to reconcile change in net assets to cash used by operating activities		
Depreciation	$ 8,500	
Increase in net contributions receivable	(1,800)	
Decrease in inventories	850	
Noncash contribution of securities	(5,000)	2,550
Net cash provided by operating activities		
Cash Flows from Investing Activities		
Cash paid for equipment	(5,500)	
Net cash used for investing activities		(5,500)
Cash Flows from Financing Activities		
Net cash used in financing activities		—
Increase in cash and cash equivalents		8,375
Cash and cash equivalents at beginning of year		14,000
Cash and cash equivalents at end of year		$22,375

category encompasses a variety of organizations, such as cemetery associations, civic organizations, libraries, museums, social organizations, political organizations, and religious organizations. The accounting and financial reporting for each of these entities is quite similar to that for the VHWO illustrated previously, although the statement of functional expenses would be optional. In fact, "other" not-for-profits follow the same FASB standards and fall under the 2004 umbrella *AICPA Audit and Accounting Guide: Not-for-Profit Organizations*, which supersedes and consolidates the AICPA guides for voluntary health and welfare organizations, colleges and universities, and other not-for-profit organizations. Because the accounting for other not-for-profit organizations is similar to the example provided, this book does not provide further illustrations.

NONGOVERNMENTAL NOT-FOR-PROFIT HOSPITALS AND OTHER HEALTH CARE ORGANIZATIONS

Hospitals and other health care providers constitute a significant area of accounting, both in terms of the entities represented and the cost of services provided. Health care providers include clinics, ambulatory care organizations, continuing-care retirement communities, health maintenance organizations, home health agencies, hospitals, government-owned health care entities, and nursing homes that provide health care. Health care entities may be organized as not-for-profit entities, governmental entities, or private business enterprises owned by investors (stockholders, partners, or sole proprietors). General accounting and reporting standards for health care organizations appear in the

EXHIBIT 21-4

Statement of
Functional Expenses

NEIGHBORS HELPING NEIGHBORS (A VHWO) STATEMENT OF FUNCTIONAL EXPENSES FOR THE YEAR ENDED DECEMBER 31, 2005

	Total	Community Service	Recreation Programs	Fund-Raising	Management and General
Salaries	$12,000	$ 4,000	$ 6,000	—	$2,000
Supplies	5,835	2,300	2,000	745	790
Professional fees	1,200	—	—	—	1,200
Depreciation	8,500	4,500	3,000	—	1,000
	$27,535	$10,800	$11,000	$745	$4,990

AICPA Audit and Accounting Guide: Health Care Organizations. The audit guide provides guidance on accounting and reporting for both governmental and nongovernmental health care organizations, even though there are significant differences between the two. Although the FASB and GASB have primary responsibility for setting accounting standards, both have approved the AICPA guide, which provides accounting and reporting requirements that exceed FASB and GASB standards.

The discussion in this chapter generally refers to hospitals as a matter of convenience, but the principles apply to other health care organizations as well. Accounting and reporting for a nongovernmental not-for-profit hospital are based on the same standards and principles as for any other nongovernmental not-for-profit organization. However, there are unique characteristics of a health care entity that warrant specific discussion. First, health care entities have unique revenue sources, such as patient service revenues and premium fees, and their expense classifications are relatively specialized. Also, health care organizations present a statement of financial position, a statement of operations, a statement of changes in net assets, and a statement of cash flows. The health care audit guide requires that the statement of operations, which replaces the statement of activities reported by other not-for-profit organizations, report a performance measurement (such as excess of revenues over expenses or earned income) and the change in unrestricted net assets. These differences are covered in detail here.

Accounting for a Nongovernmental Not-for-Profit Hospital

The following situations review typical activities often unique to a health care entity. The sample journal entries demonstrate how the activities are reflected in the accounting system of a nongovernmental, not-for-profit hospital.

PATIENT SERVICE REVENUE Patient service revenues include room and board, nursing services, and other professional services. Patient revenues are recorded at full established rates when service has been provided. However, because a hospital's objective is to report the amount of revenues that it will ultimately collect, adjustments are made for deductions from revenues, such as the following:

- **Courtesy allowances.** Discounts for doctors and employees
- **Contractual adjustments.** Discounts arranged with third-party payors (Medicare and Blue Cross, for example) that frequently have agreements to reimburse at less-than-established rates

Courtesy allowances and contractual adjustments are not expenses. They are revenue deductions that are subtracted from gross patient service revenues to arrive at the net patient service revenue reported in the statement of operations. In addition, bad debt expense is recorded and allowance accounts are used to reduce net receivables for estimated bad debts. Charity care services—those provided free of charge to patients who qualify under a hospital's charity care policy—are excluded from both gross and net patient service revenues, because they are not expected to generate cash flow.

Community General Hospital is a nongovernmental not-for-profit hospital. Gross charges at established rates for services rendered to patients amounted to $1,300,000 during 2005. The hospital had contractual adjustments with insurers and Medicare of $300,000. Hospital staff and their dependents received courtesy discounts of $9,000. Bad debts are estimated at 2%. Community General records these transactions as follows:

Patient accounts receivable	1,300,000	
Patient service revenues—unrestricted		1,300,000
To record patient service charges at established rates.		
Courtesy discounts	9,000	
Contractual adjustments	300,000	
Patient accounts receivable		309,000
To record courtesy discounts and contractual adjustments.		
Bad debt expense	26,000	
Allowance for uncollectible patient accounts receivable		26,000
To establish an allowance for uncollectible receivables.		

PREMIUM FEES Premium fees, also known as subscriber fees or capitation fees, are revenues from agreements under which a hospital provides any necessary patient services (perhaps from a contractually established list of services) for a specific fee. The fee is usually a specific fee per member per month. Hospitals earn the agreed-upon fee whether the standard charges for services actually rendered are more or less than the amount of the fee—that is, without regard to services actually provided in the period. Therefore, hospitals report premium fees, which constitute a growing portion of revenues in many hospitals, separately from patient service revenues.

Community General Hospital receives premium revenue from capitation agreements totaling $454,000. The revenues are recognized as follows:

Cash	454,000	
Premium revenue—unrestricted		454,000
To record premium revenue from capitation agreements.		

OTHER OPERATING REVENUES The "other operating revenue" classification includes revenue from services to patients other than for health care and revenues from sales and services provided to nonpatients. This classification might include tuition from schools operated by the hospital, rentals of hospital space, charges for preparing and reproducing medical records, room charges for telephone calls and television, and proceeds from cafeterias, gift shops, and snack bars.

Community General Hospital charges patients rent for telephones and televisions in their rooms. Throughout the year, the hospital offers several health care courses, for which it charges tuition. Revenue for television and telephone rental was $72,000 for the year, and the tuition charges for courses were $24,000. The hospital also receives revenue from the gift shop ($85,000) and cafeteria ($135,000). Community General records these other revenues as follows:

Cash (or accounts receivable)	316,000	
Other operating revenue—unrestricted		316,000
To record revenue from rentals, fees charged for courses,		
and gift shop and cafeteria proceeds.		

GIFTS AND BEQUESTS Community General Hospital received unrestricted cash donations of $25,000 and a $250,000 donation for a pediatric care room.

Cash	275,000	
Unrestricted support—nonoperating gains		25,000
Temporarily restricted support		250,000
To record receipt of contributions.		

DONATED ASSETS Community General Hospital received marketable equity securities valued at $500,000 that were donor restricted for the purchase of diagnostic equipment. (Income from the securities is also restricted.) Community General records the donation in a restricted fund until the funds are used to purchase the equipment.

Investments	500,000	
Temporarily restricted support		500,000
To record donation of securities.		

At year-end, Community General determined that the market value of the investment increased by $50,000.

Investments	50,000	
Net realized and unrealized gains on investments—		
temporarily restricted		50,000
To record receipt of dividend income restricted to the		
acquisition of diagnostic equipment.		

Assume that these securities, which now have a book value of $550,000, are sold for $600,000. The hospital uses the proceeds to purchase the diagnostic equipment, which costs $560,000, and records the following entries:

Cash	600,000	
Investments		550,000
Temporarily restricted support—gain on the sale of investments		50,000
To record sale of securities.		
Equipment	560,000	
Cash		560,000
To record purchase of diagnostic equipment.		
Temporarily restricted net assets—reclassifications out	560,000	
Unrestricted net assets—reclassifications in		560,000
To record reclassification of net assets for which the temporary restriction is satisfied.		

OPERATING EXPENSES Hospitals record operating expenses on an accrual basis and normally specify functional categories for nursing services (medical and surgical, intensive care, nurseries, operating rooms), other professional services (laboratories, radiology, anesthesiology, pharmacy), general services (housekeeping, maintenance, laundry), fiscal services (accounting, admissions, credits and collections, data processing), administrative services (personnel, purchasing, insurance, governing board), interest, and depreciation provisions.

The hospital pays salaries and wages allocated to functional categories as follows: nursing services, $355,000; other professional services, $115,000; general services, $170,000; fiscal services, $112,000; and administrative services, $120,000.

Nursing services expense	355,000	
Other professional services	115,000	
General services	170,000	
Fiscal services	112,000	
Administrative services	120,000	
Wages and salaries payable		872,000
To record accrual of payroll.		

The hospital purchases materials and supplies for $130,000. The supplies usage by the major functional categories during the year is as follows: nursing services, $50,000; other professional services, $40,000; general services, $20,000; fiscal services, $5,000; and administrative services, $8,000.

Inventory of materials and supplies	130,000	
Cash (or accounts payable)		130,000
To record purchase of supplies.		
Nursing services expense	50,000	
Other professional services expense	40,000	
General services expense	20,000	
Fiscal services expense	5,000	
Administrative services expense	8,000	
Inventory of materials and supplies		123,000
To record usage of materials and supplies.		

Community General Hospital recognizes depreciation on its equipment ($50,000) and building ($20,000).

Depreciation expense	70,000	
Accumulated depreciation—equipment		50,000
Accumulated depreciation—building		20,000
To record depreciation on major equipment and building.		

Statement of Operations and Other Hospital Financial Statements

Basic statements for nongovernmental not-for-profit health care entities consist of a balance sheet, or statement of financial position, a statement of operations, a statement of changes in net assets, and a statement of cash flows. Exhibits 21-5 to 21-8 illustrate these basic statements for a fictitious

EXHIBIT 21-5

Nongovernmental Not-for-Profit Hospital Statement of Financial Position

CARE HOSPITAL STATEMENT OF FINANCIAL POSITION AT DECEMBER 31, 2006

Current Assets
Cash and cash equivalents		$ 60,000
Investments		540,000
Accounts receivable—patients, less $120,000 estimated uncollectible receivables		1,080,000
Accounts receivable—Medicare		400,000
Receivable from limited-use assets		100,000
Inventories and prepaid items		170,000
Total current assets		2,350,000

Noncurrent Assets
Assets whose use is limited by board for capital improvements		230,000
Property, plant, and equipment:		
Land		650,000
Buildings	$5,000,000	
Fixed equipment	2,000,000	
Movable equipment	1,500,000	
	8,500,000	
Less: Accumulated depreciation	2,800,000	5,700,000
Total property, plant, and equipment		6,350,000
Assets restricted for plant purposes		300,000
Assets restricted for endowment		1,420,000
Total assets		$10,650,000

Current Liabilities
Accounts payable		$ 300,000
Accrued interest		150,000
Accrued salaries		210,000
Payroll taxes payable		140,000
Accrued pension expense		50,000
Current portion of long-term debt		100,000
Total current liabilities		950,000

Long-Term Debt
Notes payable		500,000
Bonds payable (net of current portion)		900,000
Mortgage payable		3,000,000
Total long-term liabilities		4,400,000
Total liabilities		5,350,000

Net Assets
Unrestricted		$ 3,220,000
Temporarily restricted		660,000
Permanently restricted		1,420,000
Total net assets		5,300,000
Total liabilities and net assets		$10,650,000

nongovernmental not-for-profit hospital unrelated to the preceding journal entries. Note that the statement of operations and the statement of changes in net assets taken together present essentially the same information as a statement of activities. Also, in Exhibit 21-6, Care Hospital reports the excess of revenues, gains, and other support over expenses and losses, as well as the increase in unrestricted net assets. The statement of cash flows illustrated in Exhibit 21-8 is prepared using the indirect method.

PRIVATE NOT-FOR-PROFIT COLLEGES AND UNIVERSITIES

The primary objective of a college or university is to provide educational services to its constituents. Like governmental entities, colleges and universities often provide their services on the basis of social desirability and finance them, at least in part, without reference to those receiving the benefits. For example, very bright students may receive a full academic scholarship, or needy students might receive federal subsidies and financial aid to cover the costs of their education. The objectives of college and university accounting are to show the sources from which resources have been received and to demonstrate how those resources have been utilized in meeting educational objectives.

The primary authority over accounting principles for private (nongovernmental) colleges and universities is the Financial Accounting Standards Board. FASB standards have been incorporated into the *AICPA Audit and Accounting Guide: Not-for-Profit Organizations*, which provides accounting and reporting guidance for private colleges and universities as well as voluntary health and welfare organizations and other not-for-profit organizations. In addition to the audit guide, much college and university implementation guidance comes from the *Financial Accounting and Reporting Manual*, an accounting manual prepared by the National Association of College and University Business Officers (NACUBO). The required financial statements of private not-for-profit colleges and universities are the same as those for voluntary health and welfare organizations, except for the statement of functional expenses.

CARE HOSPITAL STATEMENT OF OPERATIONS FOR THE YEAR ENDED DECEMBER 31, 2006		
Unrestricted Revenues, Gains, and Other Support		
Net patient service revenues	$7,740,000	
Other operating revenues	950,000	
Unrestricted donations	150,000	
Unrestricted income from endowments	120,000	
Income from board-designated funds	20,000	
Net assets released from restrictions upon		
satisfaction of program restrictions	50,000	
Total unrestricted revenues, gains, and other support		$9,030,000
Expenses and Losses		
Nursing services	$2,700,000	
Other professional services	1,800,000	
General services	1,500,000	
Fiscal services	500,000	
Administrative services	300,000	
Medical malpractice costs	180,000	
Provision for uncollectible accounts	600,000	
Provision for depreciation	400,000	
Total expenses and losses		7,980,000
Excess (deficiency) of revenues, gains, and other support over expenses and losses		1,050,000
Net assets released from restrictions for plant-asset purposes		20,000
Increase in unrestricted net assets		$1,070,000

EXHIBIT 21-6

Nongovernmental Not-for-Profit Hospital Statement of Operations

EXHIBIT 21-7

Nongovernmental
Not-for-Profit
Hospital Statement
of Changes in Net
Assets

CARE HOSPITAL STATEMENT OF CHANGES IN NET ASSETS FOR THE YEAR ENDED DECEMBER 31, 2006

	Unrestricted	Temporarily Restricted	Permanently Restricted	Total
Balance, January 1, 2006	$2,150,000	$450,000	$1,010,000	$3,610,000
Excess of revenues, gains, and other support over expenses and losses	1,050,000	—	—	1,050,000
Contributions	—	270,000	300,000	570,000
Restricted investment income	—	10,000	110,000	120,000
Net assets released from restrictions	20,000	(70,000)	—	(50,000)
Changes in net assets	1,070,000	210,000	410,000	1,690,000
Balance, December 31, 2006	$3,220,000	$660,000	$1,420,000	$5,300,000

Colleges and universities maintain accounts and reports on an accrual basis; thus, revenues are recognized when earned and expenses are recognized when the related materials or services are received. They report expenses by function, either on the face of the financial statements or in the notes. As with other NFP organizations, private institutions classify net assets and revenues, expenses, gains, and losses based on the existence or absence of donor-imposed restrictions (unrestricted, temporarily restricted, or permanently restricted), in accordance with FASB pronouncements.

EXHIBIT 21-8

Nongovernmental
Not-for-Profit
Hospital Statement
of Cash Flows

CARE HOSPITAL STATEMENT OF CASH FLOWS (INDIRECT METHOD) FOR THE YEAR ENDED DECEMBER 31, 2006

Cash Flows from Operating Activities and Gains and Losses

Change in net assets		$1,690,000
Adjustments to reconcile change in net assets to net cash used by operating activities		
Provision for depreciation	$ 400,000	
Provision for uncollectible accounts	600,000	
Decrease in Medicare accounts receivable	40,000	
Decrease in unearned interest (limited-use assets)	15,000	
Increase in accounts payable and accrued expenses	60,000	
Increase in patient accounts receivable	(195,000)	
Increase in inventories and supplies	(40,000)	880,000
Net cash provided by operating activities and gains and losses		2,570,000

Cash Flows from Investing Activities

Purchase of property, plant, and equipment	(2,280,000)	
Purchase of investments	(300,000)	
Cash invested in limited-use assets	(350,000)	
Net cash used by investing activities		(2,930,000)

Cash Flows from Financing Activities

Proceeds from contributions restricted for investment in endowment	300,000	
Other financing activities		
Proceeds from long-term note payable	500,000	
Repayment of bonds payable	(100,000)	
Repayment of mortgage note payable	(800,000)	
Net cash used by financing activities		(100,000)
Net decrease in cash for 2006		(460,000)
Cash and cash equivalents at beginning of year		520,000
Cash and cash equivalents at end of year		$ 60,000

Accounting for a Private Not-for-Profit College or University

This section presents several journal entries to illustrate the recording of typical events and transactions that would occur in a private not-for-profit college or university.

TUITION AND FEES Private colleges and universities recognize the full amount of tuition and fees (net of refunds) assessed against students for educational purposes as revenue. Tuition waivers for scholarships appear in a contra revenue account, while estimated bad debts are recorded as institutional support expenses.

Student tuition and fees for Cane College total $1,000,000. Student tuition and fees also include $50,000 of tuition reductions provided under a fellowship program that requires no services on the part of the student. The college estimates bad debts at 3% of gross revenue from student tuition and fees, or $30,000. The following entries, recorded in the unrestricted category, reflect these events:

Accounts receivable	1,000,000	
Unrestricted revenues—tuition and fees		1,000,000
To record tuition and fees.		
Tuition reduction: unrestricted—student aid	50,000	
Accounts receivable		50,000
To record tuition reductions.		
Expenses—educational and general—institutional support	30,000	
Allowance for uncollectible accounts		30,000
To record allowance for uncollectible accounts.		

APPROPRIATIONS FROM FEDERAL, STATE, AND LOCAL GOVERNMENTS Appropriations include unrestricted amounts for current operations that are received, or made available, from legislative acts or from a local taxing authority. Institutions may classify restricted appropriations as unrestricted if the governing board can change a restriction without going through a legislative process. Cane College receives appropriations on a per-student basis from the state totaling $700,000. The funds are unrestricted.

Cash	700,000	
Unrestricted revenues—state appropriation		700,000
To record appropriations from the state government.		

STUDENT FINANCIAL AID Universities often receive financial aid funds from third parties that are intended to be used by students to cover educational costs. For example, Cane College receives federal grants through the Pell Grant program in the amount of $150,000 for its students. Cane College plays an agency role by holding the funds until they are disbursed to the students. The funds are not considered revenue for the college.

Cash	150,000	
Grant funds held for students		150,000
To record the receipt of Pell Grant funds.		
Grant funds held for students	150,000	
Cash		150,000
To record the distribution of Pell Grant funds.		

CONTRIBUTIONS Universities record contributions that carry no specifications regarding the time period or purpose of use as unrestricted revenue, whereas they must record contributions that may only be expended after a point in time or for a specific purpose as temporarily restricted. Cane College received contributions totaling $300,000; $225,000 were unrestricted, and $75,000 were for gymnasium renovations. An additional $12,000 was pledged for the gym.

Cash	300,000	
Contributions receivable	12,000	
Unrestricted revenues—contributions		225,000
Temporarily restricted revenues—contributions		87,000
To record contributions received and pledged.		

ENDOWMENTS Universities record contributions of principal that must be held indefinitely but whose income is available for restricted or unrestricted purposes as special contributions termed *endowments*. Endowment principal is permanently restricted, but endowment income may be unrestricted or restricted. At Cane College, an elderly alumnus established a $50,000 endowment for book scholarships for athletes. During the year, investment income on the endowment was $4,000 and book scholarships for Cane athletes totaled $2,500.

Cash	50,000	
Permanently restricted revenues—endowment contribution		50,000
To record receipt of an endowment.		
Cash	4,000	
Temporarily restricted revenues—endowment income		4,000
To record endowment income.		
Expenses: Unrestricted—student aid	2,500	
Cash		2,500
To record payment of scholarships.		
Temporarily restricted net assets—reclassifications out	2,500	
Unrestricted net assets—reclassifications in		2,500
To record reclassification of net assets for which the temporary restriction is satisfied.		

SALES AND SERVICES OF AUXILIARY ENTERPRISES The revenue of auxiliary enterprises includes amounts earned in providing facilities and services to faculty, staff, and students. It includes amounts charged for residence halls, food services, intercollegiate athletics, and college unions, as well as sales and receipts from college stores, barber shops, movie houses, and so on. Colleges and universities classify all revenue and expenses directly related to the operations of auxiliary enterprises as "auxiliary" and report them as unrestricted.

The dining hall at Cane College had sales of $60,800 and purchased $30,000 worth of supplies during May. The supplies used by the auxiliary enterprise during the period amounted to $28,000. Salaries paid to auxiliary employees were $31,000. Summary entries are as follows:

Cash	60,800	
Revenues—auxiliary enterprises		60,800
To record sales and services related to auxiliary enterprises.		
Supplies inventory	30,000	
Cash (or accounts payable)		30,000
To record purchase of supplies.		
Expenses—auxiliary enterprises—supplies	28,000	
Supplies inventory		28,000
To record utilization of supplies related to auxiliary enterprises.		
Expenses—auxiliary enterprises	31,000	
Cash		31,000
To record expenses for salaries of auxiliary enterprises.		

Because colleges and universities use accrual accounting, they recognize an expense when the supplies and materials are used. The purchase of supplies and materials increases an inventory account when the liability is incurred. The supplies inventory, if significant, is included in the financial statements as an asset.

SALES AND SERVICES OF EDUCATIONAL ACTIVITIES The sale of goods and services that are related incidentally to educational activities of the university can generate unrestricted revenue. Often, the goods and services sold are a by-product of training or instruction. An example of this category of revenue is the dairy creamery of Cane College, which has $550 revenue from sales of its products.

Cash	550	
Revenue—educational and general		550

To record sales related to educational activities.

EXPENSES For reporting purposes, colleges and universities classify unrestricted expenses broadly, as either educational and general or as auxiliary enterprises. Expenses are further classified on a functional basis in the statement of activities. Functional classifications include the following:

- **Instruction.** Expenses for the instruction program
- **Research.** Expenses to produce research outcome
- **Public service.** Expenses for activities to provide noninstructional services to external groups
- **Academic support.** Expenses to provide support for instruction, research, and publications (i.e., computing, libraries)
- **Student services.** Amounts expended for admissions and registrar, and amounts expended for students' emotional, social, and physical well-being
- **Institutional support.** Amounts expended for administration and the long-range planning of the university
- **Operation and maintenance of plant.** Expenses of current operating funds for operating and maintaining the physical plant (net of amounts to auxiliary enterprises and university hospitals)
- **Student aid.** Expenses from restricted or unrestricted funds in the form of grants, scholarships, or fellowships to students

Cane College incurred the following expenses in June: instruction, $45,000; research, $22,000; public service, $4,500; academic support, $3,000; student services, $12,000; and institutional support, $3,500.

Expenses—educational and general—instruction	45,000	
Expenses—educational and general—research	22,000	
Expenses—educational and general—public service	4,500	
Expenses—educational and general—academic support	3,000	
Expenses—educational and general—student services	12,000	
Expenses—educational and general—institutional support	3,500	
Cash (or payables)		90,000

To record expenses for June.

PURCHASE OF PLANT ASSETS Recall that property, plant, and equipment acquired by a not-for-profit organization with unrestricted or restricted resources may be recorded at acquisition as unrestricted or temporarily restricted. If temporarily restricted, the assets are reclassified when depreciation is recognized.

Cane College purchases equipment with unrestricted assets in the amount of $35,000. Depreciation expense for the year is $3,500, and the equipment is allocated to each of the functional categories as shown here. The entries for the year are as follows:

Equipment	35,000	
Cash		35,000

To record purchase of equipment with unrestricted funds.

Expenses—educational and general—instruction	500	
Expenses—educational and general—research	100	
Expenses—educational and general—public service	500	
Expenses—educational and general—academic support	1,000	
Expenses—educational and general—student services	1,000	
Expenses—educational and general—institutional support	400	
Accumulated depreciation		3,500

To record depreciation of equipment.

Cane College purchases land adjacent to the campus. The land costs $200,000, and financial resources were previously restricted for the purchase. The entries to record this transaction are as follows:

Land	200,000	
Cash		200,000
To record payment for the purchase of land.		
Temporarily restricted net assets—reclassifications out	200,000	
Unrestricted net assets—reclassifications in		200,000
To record reclassification of temporarily restricted net assets.		

Financial Statements of Private Not-for-Profit Colleges and Universities

The required financial statements of private not-for-profit colleges and universities include a statement of financial position, a statement of activities, and a statement of cash flows. There are several acceptable alternatives for the statement of activities, so long as revenues, expenses, and reclassifications are clearly shown and changes in net assets are presented by classification (unrestricted, temporarily restricted, and permanently restricted). One popular, acceptable alternative to the statement of activities is to present two other statements: a statement of unrestricted revenues, expenses, and other changes in unrestricted net assets; and a statement of changes in net assets. The statement of financial position need not be classified, but assets are generally shown in order of liquidity. The statement of cash flows may be prepared using either the direct or the indirect method.

Exhibits 21-9 to 21-11 illustrate sample statements for a fictitious university. (The statements are for illustrative purposes only. They have no relationship to the preceding sample journal entries for Cane College.)

Internal Accounting and Control—the AICPA Model

Traditionally, colleges and universities used fund accounting practices within their accounting systems. Many adopted a fund structure referred to as the *AICPA model*. Although not-for-profit colleges and universities are now only required to report their resources based on restrictions rather than fund, the fund structure is often used for internal accounting and control. For this reason, the current AICPA NFP guide includes the AICPA fund structure. The structure includes the following fund classifications: current operating, loan, endowment, annuity and life income, plant, and agency.

The *current operating funds* grouping includes resources that are expendable for operating purposes. The current operating funds grouping contains two subgroups—one for unrestricted current funds and the other for restricted current funds.

The *loan funds* group accounts for resources held by colleges and universities under agreements to provide loans to students (and possibly faculty and staff). The *endowment fund* group consists of gifts with specifications about the manner in which the cash or donated item should be maintained and distributed. A separate fund is used for each endowment. *Annuity and life income funds* account for special types of endowment funds whereby the donor or a specified beneficiary receives a return from the gift for a specified period of time. After that time, the remainder of the gift belongs to the educational institution.

The *plant funds* group comprises four subgroups: unexpended plant funds, renewal and replacement funds, retirement of indebtedness funds, and investment in plant accounts. Colleges and universities use the first three funds to account for their financial resources, and the last subgroup (the investment in plant accounts) to account for the physical plant and related long-term debt. Institutions use unexpended plant funds to account for resources held for additions and improvements to the physical plant, whereas they use renewal and replacement funds for resources held for renewal and replacements of the existing plant. Fund assets of a retirement of indebtedness fund consist of liquid resources for current debt service and investments held for future debt retirement,

ALMA MATER UNIVERSITY STATEMENT OF ACTIVITIES FOR THE YEAR ENDED JUNE 30, 2007

Revenues	
Tuition and fees	$1,000,000
State appropriations	1,200,000
Federal grants and contracts	50,000
Private grants and gifts	400,000
Endowment income	75,000
Sales and services of educational departments	60,000
Sales and services of auxiliary enterprises	800,000
Total current revenues	3,585,000
Total net assets released from	
restrictions for operations	370,000
Total revenues and reclassifications	3,955,000
Expenses	
Educational and general	
Instruction	1,640,000
Research	850,000
Public service and extension	100,000
Academic support	50,000
Student services	40,000
Institutional support	90,000
Operation and maintenance	
of plant	80,000
Student aid	150,000
Educational and general expenditures	3,000,000
Auxiliary enterprises	
Expenses	865,000
Total operating expenses	3,865,000
Net increase in unrestricted net assets	90,000
Changes in temporarily restricted net assets:	
Federal grants and contracts	100,000
Private grants and gifts	250,000
Endowment income	20,000
Net assets released from restrictions	(370,000)
Increase in temporarily restricted net assets	0
Changes in permanently restricted net assets:	
Private grants and gifts	100,000
Increase in permanently restricted net assets	100,000
Change in net assets	$ 190,000
Net assets, July 1, 2006	535,000
Net assets, June 30, 2007	$ 725,000

including sinking fund investments. The assets of the investment in plant accounts consist of the physical plant (land, buildings, improvements other than buildings, and equipment, which includes library books).

Agency funds are used to account for assets held by the college or university for individual students and faculty members and for their organizations. As with the agency funds of governmental entities, transactions of college and university agency funds only affect asset and liability accounts and do not result in revenues and expenses.

EXHIBIT 21-10

Private Not-for-Profit College or University Statement of Financial Position

ALMA MATER UNIVERSITY STATEMENT OF FINANCIAL POSITION FOR THE YEAR ENDED JUNE 30, 2007

	2007	2006
Assets		
Cash and cash equivalents	$ 95,000	$ 25,000
Investments	500,000	400,000
Accounts receivable (net of allowances)	70,000	44,500
Accrued interest receivable	5,000	—
Contributions receivable (net of allowances)	20,000	15,000
Loans to students	7,500	5,000
Inventories	12,000	5,000
Property, plant, and equipment (net of accumulated depreciation)	175,500	190,500
Total assets	885,000	685,000
Liabilities		
Accounts payable	90,000	75,000
Students' deposits	25,000	25,000
Bonds payable	45,000	50,000
Total liabilities	160,000	150,000
Net Assets		
Unrestricted	190,000	100,000
Temporarily restricted	35,000	35,000
Permanently restricted	500,000	400,000
Total net assets	725,000	535,000
Total liabilities and net assets	$885,000	$685,000

EXHIBIT 21-11

Private Not-for-Profit College or University Statement of Cash Flows

ALMA MATER UNIVERSITY STAEMENT OF CASH FLOWS—INDIRECT METHOD FOR THE YEAR ENDED JUNE 30, 2007

Cash Flows from Operating Activities		
Change in net assets		$190,000
Adjustments to reconcile change in net assets to cash used by operating activities		
Depreciation	$ 15,000	
Increase in investments	(100,000)	
Increase in net accounts receivable	(25,500)	
Increase in accrued interest receivable	(5,000)	
Increase in net contributions receivable	(5,000)	
Increase in inventories	(7,000)	
Increase in accounts payable	15,000	
Net cash provided by operating activities		(112,500)
Cash Flows from Investing Activities		
Increase in loans to students	(2,500)	
Net cash used for investing activities		(2,500)
Cash Flows from Financing Activities		
Payment of bonds payable	(5,000)	
Net cash used in financing activities		(5,000)
Increase in cash and cash equivalents		70,000
Cash and cash equivalents at beginning of year		25,000
Cash and cash equivalents at end of year		$ 95,000

SUMMARY

Not-for-profit organizations include a diverse group of governmental and private entities. Governmental not-for-profit organizations must follow the GASB standards covered in prior chapters, whereas private not-for-profit organizations look to the FASB and AICPA for guidance. In recent years, the FASB has issued several statements aimed at improving comparability in the financial statements of all nongovernmental not-for-profit entities that issue statements in accordance with GAAP. Thus, nongovernmental voluntary health and welfare organizations, health care entities, and colleges and universities prepare a set of financial statements that present unrestricted net assets, temporarily restricted net assets, permanently restricted net assets, and total net assets, as well as changes in each class of net assets and in total.

Financial statements of nongovernmental not-for-profit entities include the statement of financial position, statement of activities, and statement of cash flows. Voluntary health and welfare organizations also prepare a statement of functional expenses. The financial statements and notes include all information required by GAAP and from which not-for-profit entities are not specifically exempt, as well as information required by applicable specialized accounting and reporting principles and practices. The focus of the financial statements is on the entity as a whole.

QUESTIONS

1. What statements are included in a set of financial statements for nongovernmental not-for-profit entities?
2. How does one determine whether a hospital, college, or voluntary health and welfare organization should be reported in accordance with FASB standards or GASB standards?
3. Explain the difference between a conditional promise to give and an unconditional promise to give.
4. Explain the difference between donor-imposed conditions and donor-imposed restrictions.
5. How are unconditional promises to give with collections due in the next period accounted for?
6. How is the expiration of a time restriction recognized?
7. Are gifts in kind always reported as unrestricted support that increases unrestricted net assets?
8. Expenses of voluntary health and welfare organizations include classifications for program services and supporting services. Explain these classifications.
9. What is the purpose of the statement of functional expenses of voluntary health and welfare organizations?
10. Are contributed services reported in the statement of activities of a nongovernmental voluntary health and welfare organization?
11. Health care entities frequently provide charity care to qualified individuals. How is charity care reported in the financial statements of a hospital?
12. How are net patient service revenues of hospitals measured, and in which hospital financial statement are they reported?
13. What are the major revenue groupings of hospitals? Give an example of a revenue item that would be included in each grouping.
14. Are provisions for bad debts and depreciation of hospitals reported as expenses? Explain.
15. Describe the difference in a set of financial statements for a governmental university and a private not-for-profit university.
16. When is the AICPA college guide model used?
17. Other than FASB standards and the AICPA guide, where can you find guidance on accounting and reporting issues for colleges and universities?
18. Describe the reporting requirements for a governmental not-for-profit entity with both governmental and business-type activities.
19. Identify the functional expense classifications for a university. Provide an example of each.
20. Discuss the two options that not-for-profit organizations have for recording fixed assets.

EXERCISES

E 21-1

Multiple choice

1. Contributions that are restricted by a donor to a nongovernmental not-for-profit organization are reported as a part of:
   a *Permanently restricted net assets*
   b *Temporarily restricted net assets*
   c *Unrestricted net assets*
   d *Either permanently restricted or temporarily restricted net assets, depending on the term of the restriction*

2. Unconditional promises to give are recognized as contribution revenue under *FASB Statement No. 116* when:

   a *The promise is received*

   b *The related receivable is collected*

   c *The time or purpose restriction is satisfied*

   d *The future event that binds the promisor occurs*

3. Which of the following is not a characteristic of a conditional promise to give?

   a *It depends on the occurrence of a specified future and uncertain event to bind the promisor.*

   b *The gift may have to be returned to the donor if the condition is not met.*

   c *It is recognized as contribution revenue when the conditions are substantially met.*

   d *It depends on demand by the promisee for performance.*

4. Contributed long-lived assets that are donor restricted for a certain time period are reported by a nongovernmental not-for-profit entity as:

   a *Unrestricted support in unrestricted net assets*

   b *Restricted support in permanently restricted net assets*

   c *Restricted support in temporarily restricted net assets*

   d *Unrestricted support in temporarily restricted net assets*

5. Long-lived assets are purchased by a nongovernmental not-for-profit entity with cash that was restricted for that purpose. The assets are reported in temporarily restricted net assets. Depreciation expense is reported in unrestricted net assets.

   a *The depreciation expense is incorrectly reported.*

   b *An amount equal to the depreciation is reclassified from temporarily restricted to unrestricted net assets.*

   c *An amount equal to the depreciation is reclassified from unrestricted to temporarily restricted net assets.*

   d *An amount equal to the depreciation is reported as revenues.*

E 21-2

Multiple choice

1. When a temporary restriction on resources of a nongovernmental not-for-profit entity is met by the incurrence of an expense for the restricted purpose:

   a *The expense is reported in the statement of activities as an increase in unrestricted net assets*

   b *Amounts reported in the temporarily restricted net assets are reclassified as unrestricted net assets*

   c *The entry is a debit to expense and a credit to the program services*

   d *The expense is reported in restricted net assets*

2. A nongovernmental not-for-profit entity gives donors a sweatshirt imprinted with its logo when they pay $15 dues. The value of the sweatshirt is approximately $15. This transaction is most likely reported as:

   a *An exchange transaction*

   b *An agency transaction*

   c *A contribution*

   d *A gift in kind*

3. How will a nongovernmental not-for-profit entity record an agency transaction in which it receives resources?

   a *No entry is made in the accounts.*

   b *Debit the asset account and credit contribution revenue.*

   c *Debit the asset account and credit temporarily restricted net assets.*

   d *Debit the asset account and credit a liability account.*

4. Unconditional promises to give that are collectible within one year of the financial statement date:

   a *Should be reported at their gross amount*

   b *Should be reported at the gross amount less an allowance for uncollectible accounts*

   c *Should be reported at the present value of the amounts expected to be collected, using the donor's incremental borrowing rate*

   d *Should not be reported until collected*

5. In preparing the statement of cash flows for a nongovernmental not-for-profit entity, cash contributions that are restricted for long-term purposes are classified as:

   a *Operating activities*

   b *Investing activities*

   c *Financing activities*

   d *None of the above*

E 21-3

Multiple choice

1. Which of the following statements is not required for nongovernmental voluntary health and welfare organizations that issue financial statements in accordance with GAAP?

   a *Balance sheet*

   b *Statement of support, revenues, and expenses, and changes in retained earnings c* *Statement of functional expenses*

    d *Statement of cash flows*

2. Voluntary health and welfare organizations:

    a *Are required to use fund accounting principles to segregate unrestricted and restricted net assets*

    b *May report fund accounting information as additional information, as discussed in* FASB Statement No. 117

    c *Must report by funds if fund accounting principles are used for internal accounting purposes*

    d *Are prohibited from reporting by funds, even if fund accounting is used for internal accounting purposes*

3. Fund-raising costs of voluntary health and welfare organizations are classified as:

    a *Functional expenses*

    b *Program services*

    c *Supporting services*

    d *Management and general expenses*

4. Volunteers collect money and nonperishable food for the Food Pantry, a nongovernmental VHWO, by going house to house once each year for donations. The services of the volunteers should be accounted for as follows:

    a *The fair value of the service is estimated and recorded as contributions that increase unrestricted net assets.*

    b *The fair value of the service is estimated and recorded as contributions that increase either unrestricted net assets or temporarily restricted net assets, depending on donor-imposed restrictions on the resources collected.*

    c *The per diem wage rates of the donors are recorded in unrestricted net assets.*

    d *None of the above*

5. Unconditional promises to give (pledges) of nongovernmental voluntary health and welfare organizations are recognized as revenue and support in the period in which:

    a *The pledges are received*

    b *Cash is received from the pledges*

    c *All restrictions on pledged resources have been removed*

    d *Pledged resources are expended*

E 21-4

Multiple choice

1. A university that is considered a special-purpose government:

    a *Is generally required to follow GASB standards*

    b *Is generally required to follow FASB standards*

    c *Should refer to the* AICPA Audit and Accounting Guide *for governmental colleges and universities*

    d *May choose whether to follow FASB, GASB, or AICPA guidelines*

2. The operations of dormitories and dining halls for colleges and universities are reported as:

    a *Operating income*

    b *Auxiliary operations*

    c *Restricted income*

    d *Specific-purpose income*

3. A university that follows the AICPA college model for internal control may have all of the following funds, *except*:

    a *Property, plant, and equipment*

    b *Loan*

    c *Life income*

    d *Endowment*

4. Required financial statements for a private, nongovernmental not-for-profit college include which of the following?

    a *A statement of cash flows*

    b *A statement of functional expenses*

    c *A statement of changes in fund balances*

    d *A statement of revenues, expenses, and other changes*

5. Grant funds received from the federal government and remitted directly to students provide an example of:

    a *An exchange transaction*

    b *An endowment*

    c *An agency transaction*

    d *A restricted contribution*

E 21-5

Multiple choice

1. Tuition waivers for scholarships are:

    a *Not reflected in the accounting records*

    b *Recorded in a contra revenue account*

    c *Recorded as institutional support expenses*

    d *None of the above*

2. Auxiliary enterprises in a college and university include all of the following, *except*:
   a   *Bookstore*
   b   *Research*
   c   *Cafeteria*
   d   *Dormitories*

3. Under *GASB 35*, a state university (governmental) with only business-type activities may present:
   a   *Fund financial statements*
   b   *Governmentwide financial statements*
   c   *Only the financial statements required of enterprise funds*
   d   *Condensed financial information*

4. Contributions of principal that must be held indefinitely but whose income is available for restricted or unrestricted purposes are termed:
   a   *Bequests*
   b   *Annuities*
   c   *Endowments*
   d   *Support*

5. Scholarships are classified as:
   a   *Academic support*
   b   *Student services*
   c   *Institutional support*
   d   *Student aid*

E 21-6

Multiple choice

1. A principal source of revenue for hospitals is from patient services. Patient services revenue for hospitals is recorded at:
   a   *Amounts actually billed to patients*
   b   *The hospital's full established rates for services provided*
   c   *Amounts actually received from patients*
   d   *Amounts actually billed to patients less discounts granted*

2. Premium fees:
   a   *Are earned whether the standard charges for services actually rendered are more or less than the amount of the fee*
   b   *Are earned only to the extent of services actually provided in the period*
   c   *Must be returned to the subscriber if services are not provided*
   d   *Are initially recorded as deferred revenues*

3. Oliver Hardwick, a roofing contractor, repaired the roof on the Mosely Clinic, a nongovernmental health care entity, at no charge to the clinic. The estimate for the job was $3,000.
   a   *The donated services meet the criteria in* **FASB Statement No.116** *and should be reported in the statement of operations as unrestricted support—donated services.*
   b   *The donated services should be described in notes to the financial statements, but not included in the statement of operations.*
   c   *Only donated services that directly provide health care to patients can be recognized in the financial statements.*
   d   *The donated services are a direct addition to the current fund.*

4. Charity care provided by a not-for-profit hospital:
   a   *Is reported as an operating expense in the statement of operations of unrestricted funds*
   b   *Is reported as a deduction from gross patient service revenues in the statement of operations of unrestricted funds*
   c   *Is excluded from both gross patient service revenue and expense*
   d   *Is reported in the statement of functional expenses*

5. Discounts allowed to third-party payors in hospital accounting are recorded as:
   a   *Charity care*
   b   *Contractual adjustments*
   c   *Courtesy allowances*
   d   *Mandatory discounts*

E 21-7

Multiple choice

1. Hospital room charges for telephone and television rentals should be classified as:
   a   *Patient service revenues*
   b   *Other operating revenues*

   c *Nonoperating gains*

   d *Premium fees*

2. A hospital bills patients at gross rates and provides for courtesy allowances for employees when they settle their accounts at less than gross rates. In accordance with this system, the journal entry to record courtesy allowances would appear as:

   a *Debit—cash; debit—courtesy allowance; credit—accounts receivable*

   b *Debit—courtesy discount; credit—allowance for courtesy discounts*

   c *Debit—cash; debit—patient service revenue; credit—accounts receivable*

   d *Debit—accounts receivable; credit—courtesy allowances; credit—patient service revenue*

3. Unrestricted income from a nongovernmental health care entity's permanent endowment investments should be reported:

   a *In the permanently restricted net assets as unrestricted support—nonoperating gains*

   b *In the statement of operations as unrestricted support—operating gains*

   c *In the statement of operations as unrestricted revenues—investment income*

   d *In the permanently restricted net assets as restricted revenues—investment income*

4. Depreciation and amortization of hospital property and equipment:

   a *Are required for both governmental and nongovernmental hospitals*

   b *Are not recorded in the statement of operations, but accumulated depreciation is disclosed in the statement of financial position*

   c *Are reported in the plant replacement and expansion fund of hospitals that use fund accounting*

   d *Are optional on donated property*

5. A nongovernmental health care entity receives a gift of cash that is specified by the donor to be used for cancer research. The contribution will most likely be reported in:

   a *Unrestricted net assets*

   b *Temporarily restricted net assets*

   c *Permanently restricted net assets*

   d *Either a or b, depending on the mission and activities of the health care entity*

E 21-8

Not-for-profit expense classifications A voluntary health and welfare organization summarizes its expenses by functions, as follows:

Education	$20,400
Fund-raising	11,400
Management and general	5,500
Public health	15,700
Research	12,000

REQUIRED: Determine the expenses for program services and for supporting services.

E 21-9

Journal Entries—various not-for-profit organizations

1. A nongovernmental VHWO receives $20,000 of unconditional promises to give with no donor-imposed restrictions. Of this amount $14,000 is due during the current period and $6,000 is due in the next period. The organization estimates that 3% of the pledges will be uncollectible.

2. A nongovernmental VHWO receives a $200 cash gift that is restricted for use in a project to provide immediate assistance to qualified people with temporary hardships. Money is given to a qualified individual during the same period.

3. The Uptown Restaurant donated restaurant equipment to the Food Kitchen, a nongovernmental VHWO. The equipment had a fair value of $6,000 and a remaining useful life of four years, with no scrap value. No restrictions were imposed on the use of the equipment, either by the Uptown Restaurant or the Food Kitchen.

4. A donor contributed $8,000 to a homeless shelter that was restricted to the purchase of a new truck. The money was invested in a CD that pays 5% interest. Accrued interest on the investment totaled $215 at year-end. The income from the investment was also restricted for the purchase of a truck.

5. Orleans Community College assessed its students $750,000 tuition for the 2007 fall term. The college estimates bad debts will be 1% of the gross assessed tuition. Orleans's scholarship program provides for tuition waivers totaling $65,000. Because of class cancellations, $15,000 is refunded to the students.

6. Your State University received donations of $3 million in 2006 that were restricted to certain research projects on the feasibility of growing tobacco for pharmaceutical uses. The university incurred $1.2 million of expenses on this research in 2006.

REQUIRED: Prepare journal entries to account for these transactions. Include net asset classifications, where applicable.

LEARNING OBJECTIVES **3, 4**

LEARNING OBJECTIVES **3, 4, 6**

P 21-1

Journal Entries—various not-for-profit organizations Three wealthy friends, Tom, Grant, and Tara, each decided to donate $5,000,000 to the not-for-profit organization of their choice. Each donation was made on May 21, 2003. Prepare the entries required for each of the recipient organizations under the following scenarios.

1. Tom chose to contribute to a local voluntary health and welfare organization, and no restrictions were placed on the use of the donated resources.
   a. Prepare the May 21, 2003, entry.
   b. Prepare any entries necessary in 2004 if $2,300,000 of the gift is used to finance operating expenses.

2. Grant contributed to a local private university, and the donation was restricted to research.
   a. Prepare the May 21, 2003, entry.
   b. Prepare any entries necessary in 2004 if $2,300,000 of the gift is used to finance research expenses.

3. Tara gave to the local hospital, and the donation was restricted for construction of a fixed asset.
   a. Prepare the May 21, 2003, entry.
   b. Prepare any entries necessary in 2004 if $2,300,000 of the gift is used to finance construction costs.

P 21-2

Journal Entries—voluntary health and welfare organization At the beginning of 2006, the citizens of North Ptarmigan created Share Shop, a voluntary health and welfare organization. Share receives donations of money, nonperishable groceries, and household items from contributors. The food and household items are distributed free of charge to families on the basis of need. Share allocates expenses 80% to community services and 20% to management and general services, unless otherwise noted.

Share has one paid administrator with a yearly salary of $14,600. An accountant donates accounting services to Share that have a fair value of $900 and are allocated to management and general. Work is also performed by regular volunteers whose services cannot be measured.

A local transit company has provided free warehouse space for the operations of Share Shop. Fair value of rent for the warehouse is $3,000 a year. Utilities of $1,800 are paid by Share for 2006.

During the year, Share purchased supplies for $300. At December 31, 2006, the supplies inventory was insignificant. Expenses incurred in determining which families were eligible for Share's services and other accounting and reporting expenses totaled $6,000.

Donated assets for 2006 included nonperishable groceries with a fair value of $60,000 and household items with a fair value of $40,000. During the year, Share Shop distributed three-fourths of the groceries and half of the household items. No portion of these distributions was allocated to management and general services.

In addition to the donated assets, Share received cash donations of $10,000 and pledges of $20,000. Share estimated that 10% of the pledges would be uncollectible. At year-end 2006, $15,000 of the pledges had been collected. Share estimates that only $1,000 of the remaining pledges will be uncollectible.

The town council of North Ptarmigan made a $25,000 grant to Share Shop that will be paid in January 2007.

REQUIRED: Prepare summary entries for Share Shop for 2006.

P 21-3

Statement of operations—nongovernmental not-for-profit health care organization The following selected items were taken from the accounts of Hometown Memorial Hospital, a not-for-profit hospital, at December 31, 2006:

Debits	
Administrative services	$ 310,000
Contractual allowances	400,000
Depreciation	200,000
Employee discounts	100,000
General services	290,000
Loss on sale of assets	50,000
Nursing services	1,000,000
Other professional services	500,000
Provision for bad debts	150,000
Credits	
Donated medicine	300,000
Income from investment in affiliate	80,000
Patient service revenues	2,500,000
Television rentals to patients	50,000
Unrestricted donations	200,000
Unrestricted income from investments of endowment funds	270,000
Restricted donations for fixed asset purchases	300,000
Restricted donations for specific operating purposes	100,000

REQUIRED: Use the information given to prepare a statement of operations for Hometown Memorial Hospital at December 31, 2006. Assume that $80,000 of expenses were for purposes for which restricted donations were available and that fixed assets costing $97,000 were purchased from donations restricted for their purchase.

P 21-4

Journal entries and statement of activities—nongovernmental not-for-profit college The following information relates to revenues and expenses for a private not-for-profit college:

Tuition and Fees	
Total assessed	$2,000,000
Tuition waivers	120,000
Appropriations	
State	800,000
Local	300,000
Auxiliary Enterprises	
Sales	500,000
Expenses	480,000
Endowment Income	
Restricted to research	70,000
Unrestricted	20,000
Private Gifts and Grants	
Restricted to student scholarships	300,000
Unrestricted	80,000
Expenses	
Instruction	2,100,000
Research	100,000
Student services	120,000
Operation of plant	180,000
Scholarships (does not include tuition waivers)	200,000

REQUIRED: Prepare journal entries and a statement of activities for the college.

LEARNING OBJECTIVES 3, 4

P 21-5

Statement of activities—nongovernmental not-for-profit organization The following information was taken from the accounts and records of the Community Society, a nongovernmental not-for-profit organization. The balances are as of December 31, 2005, unless otherwise stated.

Unrestricted support—contributions	$3,000,000
Unrestricted support—membership dues	400,000
Unrestricted revenues—investment income	83,000
Temporarily restricted gain on sale of investments	5,000
Expenses—education	300,000
Expenses—research	2,300,000
Expenses—fund-raising	223,000
Expenses—management and general	117,000
Restricted support—contributions	438,000
Restricted revenues—investment income	22,500
Permanently restricted support—contributions	37,000
Unrestricted net assets, January 1, 2005	435,000
Temporarily restricted net assets, January 1, 2005	5,000,000
Permanently restricted net assets, January 1, 2005	40,000

The unrestricted support from contributions was all received in cash during the year. Additionally, the society received pledges totaling $425,000. The pledges should be collected during 2006, except for the estimated uncollectible portion of $16,000. The society spent $3,789,000 of restricted resources on construction of a major capital facility during 2005, and $500,000 of research expenses were for research financed from restricted donations.

REQUIRED: Prepare the statement of activities for the Community Society for 2005.

LEARNING OBJECTIVES 3, 6

P 21-6

Journal entries—nongovernmental not-for-profit university Prepare journal entries to record the following transactions in the appropriate funds of a nongovernmental not-for-profit university:

1. Tuition and fees assessed total $6,000,000. Eighty percent is collected by year-end, scholarships are granted for $200,000, and $100,000 is expected to be uncollectible.

2. Revenues collected from sales and services of the university bookstore, an auxiliary enterprise, were $800,000.

3. Salaries and wages were paid, $2,600,000. Of this amount, $170,000 was for employees of the university bookstore.

4. Unrestricted resources were used to service the long-term mortgage on the university's buildings, $1,000,000.

5. Mortgage payments totaled $960,000, of which $600,000 was for interest.

6. Restricted contributions for a specific academic program were received, $440,000.

7. Expenses for the restricted program were incurred and paid, $237,000.

8. Equipment was purchased from resources previously set aside for that purpose, $44,000.

LEARNING OBJECTIVES 3, 4

P 21-7

Journal entries—voluntary health and welfare organization The Good Grubb Food for the Hungry Institute is a nongovernmental not-for-profit organization that provides free meals for the destitute in a large metropolitan area. Record the following transactions in the accounts of Good Grubb.

1. Cash gifts that were received last year, but designated for use in the current year, totaled $20,000.

2. Unrestricted pledges of $65,000 were received. Five percent of pledges typically prove uncollectible. Additional cash contributions during the year totaled $35,000.

3. Donations of food totaled $150,000. The inventory of food on hand decreased by $1,200 during the year.

4. Expenses were incurred as follows: salary of director, $10,000; facility rental, $8,000; purchases of food, $70,000; and supplies, $27,000. Supplies inventory increased by $5,000 during the year.

5. Restricted pledges of $300,000 were received during the year. The pledges are restricted for use in constructing a new kitchen and dining hall.

P 21-8

Journal entries—nongovernmental not-for-profit health care organization The Fort Collins Health Center is a nongovernmental not-for-profit health care organization. During March 2007, the following occurred:

LEARNING OBJECTIVES **3, 5**

1. Gross charges at established rates for services rendered to patients amounted to $102,300. The clinic had contractual adjustments with insurers and Medicare of $30,000. Bad debts are estimated at 2%.

2. The health center receives premium revenue from capitation agreements totaling $54,000.

3. The center also receives revenue from the pharmacy housed in its building.

4. The center paid salaries and wages allocated to functional categories as follows: nursing services, $35,000; other professional services, $11,000; general services, $10,000; fiscal services, $2,000; and administrative services, $20,000.

5. The health center receives a federal grant for $12,000. The money must be used for medical equipment.

6. Supplies costing $13,000 were purchased during the month, and $6,700 in nursing supplies were used.

REQUIRED: Prepare journal entries to account for these transactions. Include net asset classifications, where applicable.

INTERNET ASSIGNMENT

1. Search the Internet for the financial statements of the United Way (**www.national.unitedway.org**) or a charity of your choice.

   a. Print a copy of the financial statements and bring them to class for discussion.

   b. Is the charity a VHWO? How can you tell?

   c. Are net assets properly classified into three categories?

   d. Are expenses classified into function categories on the face of the financial statements or in the notes?

   e. Were any temporarily restricted net assets reclassified as unrestricted? Can you determine the nature of the restrictions that were met?

2. Visit the AICPA's Web site at **www.AICPA.org**. Select Online Publications and then select Archive Issues under *Journal of Accountancy.* Select a year and find an article under Not-for-Profits. Read the article and prepare a one-page summary.

3. Visit NACUBO's Web site at **www.nacubo.org**. Select Accounting and Finance on the top of the screen and select Advisory Reports from the side panel. View the most recent advisory report related to institutions of higher learning, and prepare a one-paragraph summary of its purpose.

4. Visit **Guidestar.com** and obtain the Form 990 for a local not-for-profit organization.

   a. Examine Statement 1 of the 990 to determine gross receipts of the organization.

   b. Examine Statement 2 of the 990. What category contained the majority of the organization's expenses?

   c. From Statement 2, note the salaries of officers.

   d. After examining Statement 2, do you think spending is in line with the organization's mission?

SELECTED READINGS

American Institute of Certified Public Accountants. *AICPA Audit and Accounting Guide: Health Care Organizations.* New York: AICPA, 2004.

American Institute of Certified Public Accountants. *AICPA Audit and Accounting Guide: Not-for-Profit Organizations.* New York: AICPA, 2004.

BENSON, MARTHA L., ALAN S. GLAZER, and HENRY R. JAENICKE. "Coping with NPO Standards—It's Not Difficult." *Journal of Accountancy* (September 1998), pp. 67–74.

BOOKER, QUINTON. "Accounting for Transfers to Non-Profits That Raise or Hold Contributions for Others: An Overview of *SFAS No. 136.*" *National Public Accountant* (Feb/Mar 2001), p. 14.

Financial Accounting and Reporting Manual for Higher Education. Washington, DC: National Association of College and University Business Officers, 2003.

Governmental Accounting Standards Board. *Statement No. 29*, "The Use of Not-for-Profit Accounting Principles by Governmental Entities." Norwalk, CT: Governmental Accounting Standards Board, 1995.

Governmental Accounting Standards Board. *Statement No. 34*, "Basic Financial Statements—and Management's Discussion and Analysis—for State and Local Governments." Norwalk, CT: Governmental Accounting Standards Board, 1999.

Governmental Accounting Standards Board. *Statement No. 35*, "Basic Financial Statements—and Management's Discussion and Analysis—for Public Colleges and Universities." Norwalk, CT: Governmental Accounting Standards Board, 1999.

PELFREY, SANDRA. "*SFAS No. 117* and Its Impact on Not-for-Profit Colleges and Universities." *The CPA Journal* (November 1993), pp. 54–56.

Statement of Financial Accounting Standards No. 93. "Recognition of Depreciation by Not-for-Profit Organizations." Stamford, CT: Financial Accounting Standards Board, 1987.

Statement of Financial Accounting Standards No. 116. "Accounting for Contributions Received and Contributions Made." Norwalk, CT: Financial Accounting Standards Board, 1993.

Statement of Financial Accounting Standards No. 117. "Financial Statements of Not-for-Profit Organizations." Norwalk, CT: Financial Accounting Standards Board, 1993.

Statement of Financial Accounting Standards No. 124. "Accounting for Certain Investments Held by Not-for-Profit Organizations." Norwalk, CT: Financial Accounting Standards Board, 1995.

Statement of Financial Accounting Standards No. 136. "Transfers of Assets to a Not-for-Profit Organization or Charitable Trust That Raises or Holds Contributions for Others." Norwalk, CT: Financial Accounting Standards Board, 1999.

APPENDIX A

SEC INFLUENCE ON ACCOUNTING

Accountants recognize the influence of the Securities and Exchange Commission (SEC) on the development of accounting and reporting principles. Congress gave the SEC authority to establish accounting principles when it passed the Securities Exchange Act of 1934, which created the SEC. Initially, Congress assigned the administration of the Securities Act of 1933 to the Federal Trade Commission. But a year later, the 1934 act created the Securities and Exchange Commission and made it responsible for establishing regulations over accounting and auditing matters for firms under its jurisdiction. Thus, the SEC has the authority to prescribe accounting principles for entities that fall under its jurisdiction.[1]

A combination of inadequate regulation of securities at the federal and state levels, the stock market crash of 1929, and the Great Depression of the 1930s contributed to the enactment of new securities legislation in the early 1930s. Similar circumstances surrounding the collapse of **Enron Corporation, WorldCom**, and others led to passage of the Sarbanes-Oxley Act and related legislation in recent years.

THE 1933 SECURITIES ACT

A primary objective of the Securities Act of 1933 was "to provide full and fair disclosure of the character of securities sold in interstate and foreign commerce and the mails, and to prevent fraud in the sale thereof" (Securities Act of 1933). Another objective of the 1933 act was to protect investors against fraud, deceit, and misrepresentation. There have been many amendments, but these objectives still constitute the primary thrust of the 1933 act.

The Securities Act of 1933 is often called the "truth in securities act." This is because the SEC's objective is to prevent the issuers of securities from disclosing false, incomplete, or otherwise misleading information to prospective buyers of their securities. The SEC emphasizes that its objective is not to pass judgment on the merits of any firm's securities. The SEC imposes severe penalties on firms and individuals that violate its disclosure requirements.

Issuance of Securities in Public Offerings

The Securities Act of 1933 regulates the issuance of specific securities to investors in public offerings. Public offerings of securities must be registered with the SEC and be advertised in a prospectus before being offered for sale to the public.

---

[1] For example, in 1993 the SEC issued *Staff Accounting Bulletin No. 93,* which requires discontinued operations that have not been divested within one year of their measurement dates to be accounted for prospectively as investments held for sale.

EXEMPT SECURITY ISSUES Certain security issuances are exempt from the 1933 act. A partial list of exempt securities includes those issued by governmental units, not-for-profit organizations, firms in bankruptcy and subject to court order, firms in stock splits or in direct sales to existing shareholders (private placements), and firms issuing intrastate securities with sales limited to residents of that state.

ISSUES OF $5,000,000 OR LESS *Regulation A* provides less-restrictive registration procedures for security issuances not exceeding $5,000,000. Regulation A permits firms to use an *offering circular* rather than the prospectus required for full registration.

THE PROSPECTUS The **prospectus** is a part of the registration statement that provides detailed information about the background of the registrant firm, including its development, its business, and its financial statements. An **offering circular** is like a prospectus but has fewer disclosure requirements. A copy of the prospectus must be presented to prospective buyers before the securities are offered for sale. A **preliminary prospectus** (also known as a *red herring prospectus*) is a communication that identifies the nature of the securities to be issued, states that they have not been approved or disapproved by the SEC, and explains how to obtain the prospectus when it becomes available.

THE SECURITIES EXCHANGE ACT OF 1934

The Securities Exchange Act of 1934 created the Securities and Exchange Commission and gave it authority to administer the 1933 act as well as to regulate the trading of securities on national exchanges. Subsequently, the 1934 act was amended to include securities traded in over-the-counter markets, provided that the firms have total assets of more than $10 million and at least 500 stockholders. Firms that want their securities traded on the national exchanges or in over-the-counter markets subject to the net-asset and stockholder limitations, must file **registration statements** with the SEC. Form 10 is the primary form used for registering securities on national stock exchanges or in over-the-counter markets. This registration for trading purposes is required in addition to the registration prepared for new security issuances under the 1933 act.

ADDITIONAL PERIODIC REPORTING REQUIREMENTS Companies covered by the 1934 act also have periodic reporting responsibilities. These include filing 10-K annual reports, 10-Q quarterly reports, and 8-K current "material event" reports with the SEC. The information in these reports is publicly available so that company officers, directors, and major stockholders (insiders) will not be able to use it to gain an unfair advantage over the investing public. In other words, the objective is to provide full disclosure of all material facts about the company and thereby contribute to a more efficient and ethical securities market.

THE SEC AND NATIONAL EXCHANGES In addition to the registration and periodic reporting rules for publicly traded companies, the Securities Exchange Act contains registration and reporting requirements for the national securities exchanges. The SEC has responsibility for monitoring the activities of the national exchanges and ensuring their compliance with applicable legal provisions. The 1934 act also gave the SEC broad enforcement powers over stockbrokers and dealers and over accountants involved in SEC work.

THE SARBANES-OXLEY ACT

The passage of Sarbanes-Oxley and related legislation provides the SEC with even broader powers and an increased budget for enforcement activities. SEC inquiries and enforcement actions against public companies have increased substantially since 2000. Many firms, for example, *Krispy Kreme Doughnuts* in January 2005, have restated earnings as a result of SEC investigations. Such activity is likely to continue.

Among recent SEC pronouncements, one of the most far-reaching is *Staff Accounting Bulletin No. 101, Revenue Recognition in Financial Statements,* which was issued in December 1999. Here the SEC addresses and clarifies revenue recognition issues commonly encountered in the modern and increasingly complex business world. Current common practices of selling bundled products and services and how to separate and recognize the components of revenue in such contracts are some of the SEC's many concerns. *SAB No. 101* represents the SEC's response to a research study on fraudulent reporting practices conducted by the Committee of Sponsoring Organizations (COSO) of the Treadway Commission in March 1999. That report indicated that more than one-half of the reporting frauds reviewed involved overstatement of revenues.

Additional Responsibilities of the SEC

Subsequent to the Securities Exchange Act of 1934, the SEC acquired regulatory and administrative responsibilities under the Public Utilities Holding Company Act of 1935, the Trust Indenture Act of 1939, the Investment Company Act of 1940, the Investment Advisers Act of 1940, the Securities Investor Protection Act of 1970, and the Foreign Corrupt Practices Act of 1977. These acts are listed for identification purposes, but this appendix does not discuss the SEC's responsibility under them.

THE REGISTRATION STATEMENT FOR SECURITY ISSUES

The Securities Act of 1933 requires firms issuing securities to the public to provide full and fair disclosure of all material facts about those securities. The disclosures are provided in a registration statement filed with the SEC at least 20 days before the securities are offered for sale to the public. The SEC may extend the 20-day waiting period if it finds deficient or misleading information in the registration statement. In addition, if a firm files an amendment to the registration statement, the SEC treats the amended statement as a new one for purposes of applying the 20-day rule.

Security Registration

The registration of securities with the SEC is ordinarily a major undertaking for the registrant company. The process includes developing a registration team consisting of financial managers, legal counsel, security underwriters, public accountants, and other professionals as needed. The team plans the registration process in detail, assigns responsibility for each task, coordinates the efforts of all team members, and maintains a viable timetable throughout each phase of the project. Because of its complexity, the coordination of efforts is sometimes referred to as a balancing act.

REGISTERING SECURITIES UNDER THE INTEGRATED DISCLOSURE SYSTEM In 1980 the SEC changed the process of registering securities when it adopted an integrated disclosure system for almost all reports required by the 1933 and 1934 securities acts. The integrated system revised the registration forms and streamlined the process for filing with the SEC. As a result, the registration statement is now completed in accordance with instructions for the particular registration form deemed appropriate for a specific registrant company.

For example, Form S-1 is a general form to be used by firms going public (issuing securities to the public for the first time) and by firms that have been SEC registrants for fewer than three years. It is also a default form to be used unless another form is specified. Forms S-2 and S-3 are forms with fewer disclosure requirements than S-1. They are used primarily for registrations of established firms that have been SEC registrants for more than three years and that meet certain other criteria. Form S-4 is used for registering securities issued in a business combination. Firms issuing securities under Regulation A use Form 1-A. A number of other registration forms are applicable to selected types of security issues and firm situations.

THE INTEGRATED DISCLOSURE SYSTEM

The basic regulations of the Securities and Exchange Commission are found in *Regulation S-X,* which prescribes rules for the form and content of financial statements filed with the SEC, and *Regulation S-K,* which covers the nonfinancial statement disclosures of the registration statements and other periodic filings with the SEC. Before the 1980s, the two regulations sometimes had conflicting requirements, and firms often had difficulty in identifying the appropriate rules and procedures for reporting to the SEC.

From 1933 to 1980 the SEC issued numerous *Accounting Series Releases* (ASRs)—official supplements to AICPA and FASB pronouncements—and *Staff Accounting Bulletins* (SABs)—informal interpretations by the SEC staff on GAAP and S-X provisions. The issuance of these ASRs and SABs often increased the difficulty of complying with SEC regulations because their provisions were sometimes inconsistent with GAAP or other SEC regulations.

Codification of SABs and ASRs

In implementing the integrated disclosure system, the SEC issued *SAB No. 40* to codify *SABs 1 through 38*. This was done to revise the content of the SABs to conform to GAAP, to eliminate duplicate material contained in some SABs, and in some cases to recognize FASB pronouncements as meeting the SEC's requirements. The SEC also codified the relevant accounting-related ASRs into *Financial Reporting Release* (FRR) *No. 1*. Thus, the current series consists of FRRs rather than ASRs.

Objectives of Integrated Disclosure System

The objectives of the integrated disclosure system are to simplify the registration process, to reduce the cost of compliance with SEC regulations, and to improve the quality of information provided to investors and other parties. Under the integrated system, the disclosure included in SEC filings and those distributed to investors via prospectuses, proxy statements, and annual reports are essentially the same.

Standardization of Audited Financial Statements

The integrated disclosure system amended Regulation S-X in order to standardize the financial statement requirements in most SEC filings. For example, Regulation S-X, which prescribes the form and content of financial statements filed with the SEC, was amended in 1992 to conform certain of its accounting and disclosure requirements to those contained in FASB statements, including *FASB Statement No. 109,* "Accounting for Income Taxes" (effective December 15, 1992); *FASB Statement No. 95,* "Statement of Cash Flows" (effective July 15, 1988); *FASB Statement No. 91,* "Accounting for Nonrefundable Fees and Costs Associated with Originating or Acquiring Loans and Initial Direct Costs of Leases" (effective December 15, 1987); and *FASB Statement No. 69,* "Disclosures About Oil and Gas Producing Activities" (effective December 15, 1982). This permits the financial statements included in annual reports to shareholders to be the same as those included in the prospectus, the 10-K, and other reports filed with the SEC.

Note that the SEC's proxy rules govern the content of annual reports to shareholders. Under current rules, the content of the annual report to shareholders is the same as in 10-K filings. **Form 10-K** is the general form for the annual report that registrants file with the SEC. It is required to be filed within 90 days after the end of the registrant company's fiscal year. The 10-K report must be signed by the chief executive officer, the chief financial officer, the chief accounting officer, and a majority of the company's board of directors.

Exhibit A-1 summarizes the 10-K disclosures required by the SEC for public companies. As shown in the exhibit, the SEC divides the disclosures into four groups. This is done to distinguish the information required to be disclosed in annual reports to shareholders from the complete 10-K information package required for filings with the SEC. For example, the information included in Part II of the exhibit is primarily accounting information that is required for annual reports filed with the SEC as well as the annual reports distributed to the company's shareholders. The disclosure requirements summarized in Parts I, III, and IV of the exhibit are only required for SEC filings, but they may be included in annual reports to shareholders.

In implementing its integrated disclosure system, the SEC eliminated a number of differences between reports filed with the SEC and those contained in annual reports to shareholders. This permitted public companies to meet many of the SEC filing requirements by reference to disclosures made in the annual reports to shareholders. That is, companies can include copies of their annual shareholder reports in their 10-K filings and satisfy many SEC disclosure requirements with one report. The SEC encourages the incorporation of information by reference to other reports and does not require that information to be duplicated. This "incorporation by reference" ruling resulted in a substantial increase in the size of corporate annual reports and a corresponding decrease in the size of 10-K reports filed with the SEC.

FORM 8-K Form 8-K is a report that requires registrants to inform the SEC about significant changes that take place regarding firm policies or financial condition. Firms must submit the report within 15 days (5 days in some cases) of the occurrence of the event. Items that might be disclosed in Form 8-K include changes in management, major acquisitions or disposals of assets, lawsuits, bankruptcy filings, and unexpected changes in directors.

SUMMARY OF REQUIRED DISCLOSURES UNDER SEC FORM 10-K

Part I

Item 1: Business (nature and history of the business, industry segments, etc.)
Item 2: Properties (location, description, and use of property, etc.)
Item 3: Legal proceedings (details of pending legal proceedings)
Item 4: Voting by security holders (items submitted to shareholders for voting)

Part II

Item 5: Market for common equity (place traded, shares, dividends, etc.)
Item 6: Selected financial data (five-year trend data for net sales, income from continuing operations including EPS, total assets, long-term debt, cash dividends, etc.)
Item 7: Management's discussion and analysis (discussion of the firm's liquidity, capital resources, operations, financial condition, etc.)
Item 8: Financial statements and supplementary data (requirements include audited balance sheets for two years and audited income statements and statements of cash flows for three years; three-year and five-year summaries are required for selected statement items)
Item 9: Changes in accountants and disagreements on accounting matters (changes in accountants and accounting changes, disagreements, disclosures, etc.)

Part III

Item 10: Directors and executive officers (names, ages, positions, etc.)
Item 11: Executive compensation (names, positions, salaries, stock options, etc.)
Item 12: Security ownership of beneficial owners and management (listing of insider owners of securities)
Item 13: Certain relationships (business relations and transactions with management, etc.)

Part IV

Item 14: Exhibits, financial statement schedules, and 8-K reports (supporting schedules of securities, borrowings, subsidiaries, ratios, etc.)

FORM 10-Q Form 10-Q contains quarterly data prepared in accordance with GAAP and must be filed within 45 days of the end of each of the registrant's first three quarters. Chapter 14 of this text describes and illustrates the SEC requirements for quarterly reports. The SEC Web site (*www.sec.gov*) provides access to details of various SEC forms and filing requirements under the Securities Acts of 1933 and 1934, as well as subsequent legislation. The Web site also provides access to all of the SEC's rules and pronouncements.

SEC DEVELOPMENTS

REGULATION S The SEC issued **Regulation S** in 1990 to clarify the applicability of U.S. securities laws across national boundaries. Generally, the regulation provides that sales of securities outside the United States are not subject to the 1933 Securities Act. The regulation also provides "safe harbor" rules to exempt any U.S. companies that sell securities offshore from SEC registration requirements.

THE EDGAR SYSTEM The Securities and Exchange Commission introduced a massive new computerized system to facilitate the process of filing, reviewing, and disseminating corporate information to the public in 1984. [*www.sec.gov/edaux/searches.htm*] **EDGAR** is an abbreviation for the SEC's system, titled Electronic Data Gathering Analysis and Retrieval System. One of the SEC's goals under the integrated disclosure system is to provide investors, analysts, and other interested parties with instant access to corporate information on file with the SEC.

SMALL BUSINESS Although most SEC registrants are large public companies, the capital needs of small business issuers (under $25 million in both revenue and public float) have been addressed by the SEC, and new financial rules for small business enterprises were adopted in 1992 and 1993. Those rules provide new opportunities for small firms to raise capital to start or expand their businesses. Rule 504 relating to certain tax-exempt private offerings was amended to allow issuers other than development-stage enterprises to raise up to $1,000,000 in any 12-month period without registering under the 1933 Securities Act. Also, safe-harbor rules for information or trends and future events that may affect future operating results have been revised.

SUMMARY

This appendix provides an overview of securities legislation related to financial accounting and reporting. It also explains the function of the Securities and Exchange Commission and its authority to prescribe accounting principles. SEC requirements that are relevant to particular topics are integrated into the chapters throughout this book. For example, Chapters 3 and 11 discuss and illustrate the SEC's requirement to push down the purchase price of a subsidiary to the subsidiary's financial statements. Chapter 8 discusses the SEC's position on recognizing gain on a subsidiary's stock sales, and Chapter 14 traces the history of the SEC's efforts in requiring segment disclosures and SEC requirements for interim reports.

SELECTED READINGS

American Accounting Association's Securities and Exchange Commission Liaison Committee. "Mountaintop Issues: From the Perspective of the SEC." *Accounting Horizons* (March 1995), pp. 79–86.

Committee of Sponsoring Organizations of the Treadway Commission. *Fraudulent Financial Reporting: 1987–1997; An Analysis of U.S. Public Companies.* March 1999 AICPA (New York).

IANNACONI, TERESA E. "The SEC's Expanded Role in Small Business Capital Formation." *Journal of Accountancy* (August 1993), pp. 47–48.

JAYSON, SUSAN. "EDGAR Update: No More Fear of Filing." *Management Accounting* (March 1994), pp. 24–26.

SKOUSEN, K. FRED. *An Introduction to the SEC,* 5th ed. Cincinnati: South-Western Publishing Co., 1991.

U.S. Securities and Exchange Commission. *Staff Accounting Bulletin No. 101—Revenue Recognition in Financial Statements.* Dec. 3, 1999 New York.

ESTATES AND TRUSTS

Accountants frequently refer to estate and trust accounting as **fiduciary accounting** because estate and trust managers operate in a good-faith custodial or stewardship relationship with beneficiaries of the estate or trust property. A *fiduciary* is a person who is held in particular confidence by other people. Fiduciaries may be executors, trustees, administrators, and guardians, depending on the nature of their duties and the demands of custom.

In legal terms, a **fiduciary** is an individual or an entity authorized to take possession of the property of others. Upon taking possession of estate or trust property, the fiduciary (administrator of an estate or trustee of a trust, for example) has an obligation to administer it in the best interest of all beneficiaries. Although similar practices are used in accounting for estates and trusts, there are a number of differences between the two types of entities. These include the manner in which the entities are created, the objectives of their activities, and the time spans of their existence. This appendix discusses these differences and reviews and illustrates accounting practices for estates and trusts.

CREATION OF AN ESTATE

An estate comes into existence at the death of an individual. If the deceased person (**decedent**) had a valid will in force at the time of death, he or she is said to have died **testate**.[1] In the absence of a valid will, the decedent is said to have died **intestate**. The estate consists of the property of the decedent at the time of death. Ordinarily, a probate court appoints a **personal representative** of the decedent to take control of the decedent's property, but some flexibility is provided if a valid will is in force at the time of death. In this case, the personal representative may leave real or tangible personal property under the control of the person presumably entitled to it under the terms of the will.

PROBATE PROCEEDINGS

The personal representative of the deceased (or other interested party) files a petition with the appropriate probate court requesting that an existing will be **probated**, that is, for the will to be validated. The hearing of the probate court to establish validity is called a **testacy proceeding** because it determines whether the deceased died testate or intestate. Under the **Uniform Probate Code** [§ 1-201 (30)], the term *personal representative* includes both executor and administrator, as well as other designations for persons who perform the same functions.

---

[1] People with sizable estates usually have lawyers draw up their wills. The lawyer can provide for the eventual validation of the will and also help with estate planning so that property is distributed according to the client's wishes and taxes are minimized.

Confirmation

A confirmation by a probate court that a will is valid means that the decedent died testate. Ordinarily, this leads to appointment of the personal representative named in the will as **executor** of the will. It also leads to the presumption that estate property will be distributed in accordance with the provisions of the will, in the absence of extenuating circumstances.

A person dies intestate when he or she dies without leaving a will. Failure of the probate court to validate a will submitted for probate also means that the decedent died intestate. In either case, the court appoints an **administrator** to take control of the estate and supervise the distribution of estate assets in accordance with applicable state laws.

Uniform Probate Code

The state laws governing probate and distribution of estate property vary considerably and do not provide a uniform basis for classifying the legal and accounting characteristics of estates. Therefore, this appendix bases its discussion and illustrations on the 1974 edition of the Uniform Probate Code, which was approved by the National Conference of Commissioners on Uniform State Laws. The Uniform Probate Code has been approved by the American Bar Association, even though most states have not adopted it.

ADMINISTRATION OF THE ESTATE

The personal representative (executor or administrator) of the estate is a fiduciary who is expected to observe the standards of care applicable to trustees. Appointment by a probate court gives the executor authority to carry out the written instructions of the decedent, including the settlement and distribution of the estate. The executor is expected to perform this duty as expeditiously and efficiently as possible.

Within 30 days after appointment, the personal representative (executor or administrator) must inform the heirs and devisees of his or her appointment and provide selected information about certain other matters. **Heirs** are the persons entitled to the property of the decedent under the statutes of intestate succession. **Intestate succession** is the order in which estate property is distributed to the surviving spouse, parents, children, and so on, if any estate property is not effectively distributed by will. **Devisees** are those persons designated in a will to receive a *devise* (a testamentary disposition of real or personal property). Under the Uniform Probate Code, "to devise" means to dispose of real or personal property by will. A *specific devise* is the gift of an object, and a *general devise* is a gift of money.

Intestate Succession

Under the Uniform Probate Code, as amended, the entire estate of a person who dies intestate passes to the spouse if (1) the decedent has no living descendants or (2) all surviving descendants are also descendants of the surviving spouse. If there are descendants from a prior marriage or relationship, the surviving spouse receives the first $100,000 (the amount varies by state) and one-half of the remaining intestate estate. The remaining part of the estate not passing to the spouse (or the entire estate if there is no surviving spouse) passes to the descendants as directed in the state code.

Inventory of Estate Property

The executor or administrator of a will is required to prepare and file an inventory of property owned by the deceased within three months of appointment. This inventory must list the property in reasonable detail and show the fair market value on the date of death for each item of property. Any encumbrance on the property (such as a lien or other claim) must also be disclosed for each item. This inventory is filed with the probate court, and additional copies must be provided to interested persons on request. If appraisers are employed to assist in valuing the property, their names and addresses must accompany the property inventory. Subsequent discovery of property omitted from the inventory, or errors in valuing certain items, are corrected by preparing and filing a new or supplementary inventory of the estate property. Personal items of limited value are usually excluded from the inventory.

Exempt Property and Allowances

The Uniform Probate Code entitles the surviving spouse to a **homestead allowance** that is exempt from, and has priority over, all claims against the estate. The amount of the allowance varies, but in some states it is $15,000. In the absence of a surviving spouse, the minor children would share the allowance equally. The surviving spouse also has an entitlement of up to $10,000 (varies by state) in household furniture, automobiles, and personal effects from the estate, depending on whether or not the property has been used to secure a loan. In the absence of a surviving spouse, the minor children share this property jointly.

The surviving spouse and minor children who were dependent on the deceased are also entitled to a reasonable family allowance to be paid out of the estate property during the period in which the estate is being administered. This family allowance is exempt from and has priority over all claims except the homestead allowance.

Claims Against the Estate

Under the Uniform Probate Code, the personal representative publishes a notice in a newspaper of general circulation in the county for three consecutive weeks. The purpose is to announce his or her appointment and to notify creditors to present their claims within four months of the date of first publication of the notice.

Claims against the estate *that arose before death* and were not presented within four months (or three years, if the required notice to creditors was not published) are barred forever against the estate, the personal representative, the heirs, and the devisees [Uniform Probate Code, § 3-801-3].

All claims against the decedent's estate *that arose after death* are barred as claims against the estate, the personal representative, the heirs, and the devisees unless presented as:

1. A claim based on a contract with the personal representative within four months after performance is due and discharged

2. Any other claim within four months after it arises

CLASSIFICATION OF CLAIMS When estate assets are insufficient to pay all claims in full, payments are made as follows [Uniform Probate Code, § 3-805]:

1. Costs and expenses of administration of the estate

2. Reasonable funeral expenses and reasonable and necessary medical and hospital expenses of the last illness of the decedent

3. Debts and taxes with preference under federal or state law

4. All other claims

No preference is given for payment within a given class of claims.

SECURED CLAIMS Payment of secured claims against the estate depends on the amount allowed if the creditor surrenders his or her security. However, if the assets of the estate are encumbered by mortgage, pledge, lien, or other security interest, the personal representative may pay the encumbrance if it appears to be in the best interests of the estate [Uniform Probate Code, § 3-814].

ACCOUNTING FOR THE ESTATE

The executor (personal representative) records the inventory of estate property in a self-balancing set of accounts that show

1. The property for which responsibility has been assumed

2. The manner in which that responsibility is subsequently discharged

The executor does not accept responsibility for obligations of the decedent (testator), so the liabilities of the estate are not recorded until paid.

Estate Principal and Income

The focus of fiduciary accounting lies in distinguishing between principal and income. That focus applies to accounting for both estates and trusts. Estates frequently realize income from various investments between the time that the property inventory is filed by the executor and the time the estate is fully administered. A primary reason for dividing estate principal and income is that the beneficiaries are likely to be different. For example, some devises specified in the will are distributed to the devises from estate principal, but the income may accrue to the residual beneficiaries of the estate. **Residual beneficiaries** are those entitled to the remainder of the estate after all other rightful claims on the estate have been satisfied.

The National Conference of Commissioners on Uniform State Laws approved a Revised Uniform Principal and Income Act in 1978 to provide guidance in distinguishing between estate principal and income. That act provides that expenses incurred in settling a decedent's estate be charged against the principal of the estate. These expenses include debts, funeral expenses, estate taxes, interest and penalties, family allowances, attorney's fees, personal representative's fees, and court costs [Uniform Probate Code, § 5].

Alternatively, income (less expenses) earned after death on assets included in the decedent's estate is distributed to the specific devisee to whom the property was devised. Any remaining income that accrues during the period of estate administration is distributed to the devisees in proportion to their interests in the undivided (residual) assets of the estate.

ESTATE INCOME, GAINS, AND LOSSES In accounting for the decedent's estate, the receipts due but unpaid at the date of death are a part of the estate principal. These include items such as interest, dividends, rents, royalties, and annuities due at the time of death. After death, earnings from income-producing property are estate income, unless the will specifically provides otherwise. That is, amounts earned for the items listed would be classified as income, rather than principal, if they came due during the period of estate administration. In accounting for interest income on bond investments included in the estate inventory, no provision is made for amortization of bond issue premiums and discounts. This is because the bonds (and other securities) are included in the estate inventory at fair market value, and any gains or losses on disposal are adjustments of estate principal.

Depreciation is a related matter that requires interpretation under the Uniform Principal and Income Act [Uniform Probate Code, §§ 13a(2) and c(3)]. The act provides that a reasonable allowance for depreciation be made on depreciable property of the estate, except that no depreciation is to be made on real property used by a beneficiary as a residence or on personal property held by a trustee who is not then making a depreciation allowance.

ILLUSTRATION OF ESTATE ACCOUNTING

On April 1, 2006, Harry Olds entered the hospital with a terminal illness. He died May 1, 2006, at the age of 70. Laura Hunt, Harry's only daughter, was appointed executor of the estate by the probate court, which also confirmed that Harry had died testate. The will provided specific devises at estimated values to be awarded as follows:

Summer home to his daughter, Laura Hunt	$45,000
1973 Datsun 240Z to his grandson, Gary Hunt	8,000
200 shares of FFF stock to his friend, Michael Wallace	5,000
All other personal effects to Harry's widow, Gloria Olds	

The following general devises of cash were also provided:

Laura Hunt, in lieu of fees as executor	$19,000
Sara Tyson, Harry's housekeeper	6,000
First Methodist Church	5,000
Humane Society	10,000
Gloria Olds is to receive the income in excess of expenses during the administration of the estate.	
The residue of the estate is to be placed in trust, with the income used to support Harry's widow during her lifetime. Upon her mother's death, Laura gets the remainder of the estate.	

Laura informed the heirs and devisees of her appointment as executor of Harry's estate on May 19, 2006, and at the same time, placed the required notice to creditors in the newspaper. On June 15, 2006, she filed the estate inventory that appears in Exhibit B-1 with the probate court.

HARRY OLDS, TESTATOR
INVENTORY OF ESTATE ASSETS
AS OF THE DATE OF DEATH ON MAY 1, 2006

Description of Property	Fair Value
Cash in Commercial National Bank	$ 30,000
Cash in savings account at First National Bank	93,000
Certificate of deposit, 8%, 18 months, due August 1 (includes $10,000 accrued interest)	110,000
Certificate of deposit, 9%, one year, due July 1 (includes $7,500 interest)	107,500
Note receivable plus $1,500 accrued interest from George Stein, 10%, due June 1	21,500
Rocky Mountain Power common stock, 1,000 shares	40,000
Southern Natural Gas common stock, 2,000 shares	30,000
Danville City 9%, $50,000 par municipal bonds	58,000
Interest on Danville City bonds, due June 1	1,875
Dividends receivable—utility stocks	1,500
Summer home	45,000
FFF common stock, 200 shares	5,000
1973 Datsun 240Z	8,000
Personal effects*	—
	$551, 375

*The probate court permitted Laura to exclude Harry's personal effects other than specific devises from the inventory.
Submitted by Laura Hunt, executor on June 15, 2006.

Laura subsequently prepared the following entries to record transactions and events during the period of estate administration.[2]

May 19, 2006 Memorandum: Placed a notice in the *Montgomery County News Messenger* that creditors of the estate of Harry Olds should present their claims against the estate within four months.

June 15, 2006 Recorded the inventory of estate assets as of May 1, 2006:

Cash—principal (+A)	30,000	
Savings account (+A)	93,000	
Certificate of deposit, due August 1, 2006 (+A)	100,000	
Certificate of deposit, due July 1, 2006 (+A)	100,000	
Note receivable—George Stein (+A)	20,000	
Rocky Mountain Power common stock (+A)	40,000	
Southern Natural Gas common stock (+A)	30,000	
FFF Company common stock (+A)	5,000	
Danville municipal bonds (+A)	58,000	
Summer home (+A)	45,000	
1973 Datsun 240Z (+A)	8,000	
Interest receivable on CDs (+A)	17,500	
Interest receivable—George Stein (+A)	1,500	
Interest receivable—municipal bonds (+A)	1,875	
Dividends receivable—common stock (+A)	1,500	
Estate principal (+SE)		551,375

June 16, 2006 Cashed dividend checks received May 5 on utility stock:

Cash—principal (+A)	1,500	
Dividends receivable—common stock (−A)		1,500

[2] This appendix treats the estate principal as a stockholders' equity–type account, to be consistent with other topics in the text.

June 18, 2006 Collected interest of $2,250 on Danville City bonds. Interest of $375 was earned after the date of death:

Cash—principal (+A)	1,875	
Cash—income (+A)	375	
Interest receivable—municipal bonds (−A)		1,875
Estate income (R, +SE)		375

June 23, 2006 Funeral expenses of $4,500 were paid:

Funeral expenses (E, −SE)	4,500	
Cash—principal (−A)		4,500

June 24, 2006 Collected the $20,000 George Stein note and $1,650 interest. Interest of $150 was earned after the date of death:

Cash—principal (+A)	21,500	
Cash—income (+A)	150	
Note receivable—George Stein (−A)		20,000
Interest receivable—George Stein (−A)		1,500
Estate income (R, +SE)		150

June 25, 2006 Discovered and cashed a certificate of deposit that matured on April 15 and was excluded from the estate inventory. The proceeds were $10,800:

Cash—principal (+A)	10,800	
Assets subsequently discovered (−A)		10,800

June 28, 2006 Paid hospital and medical bills in excess of amounts paid by Medicare and private health insurance policies:

Hospital and medical expenses (E, −SE)	19,000	
Cash—principal (−A)		19,000

July 1, 2006 Cashed the certificate of deposit that was due on July 1:

Cash—principal (+A)	107,500	
Cash—income (+A)	1,500	
Certificate of deposit (−A)		100,000
Interest receivable on CD (−A)		7,500
Estate income (R, +SE)		1,500

July 12, 2006 Paid cash to general devisees as provided in the will:

Devise—Laura Hunt (E, −SE)	19,000	
Devise—Sara Tyson (E, −SE)	6,000	
Devise—First Methodist Church (E, −SE)	5,000	
Devise—Humane Society (E, −SE)	10,000	
Cash—principal (−A)		40,000

August 1, 2006 Recorded interest from savings account for the quarter ending July 31:

Cash—income (+A)	1,395	
Estate income (R, +SE)		1,395

August 1, 2006 Cashed in the certificate of deposit due August 1:

Cash—principal (+A)	110,000	
Cash—income (+A)	2,000	
Certificate of deposit (−A)		100,000
Interest receivable on CD (−A)		10,000
Estate income (R, +SE)		2,000

August 5, 2006 Received dividend checks on utilities stock:

Cash—income (+A)	1,500	
Estate income (R, +SE)		1,500

August 15, 2006 Paid a $500 mechanics bill on the Datsun 240Z that was incurred on April 10, 2006, and submitted for payment on August 10:

Debts of decedent paid (E, −SE)	500	
Cash—principal (−A)		500

August 15, 2006 Delivered specific devises as provided in the will. Personal effects not included in the estate inventory were left with the widow, Gloria Olds:

Devise—summer home to Laura Hunt (E, −SE)	45,000	
Devise—1973 Datsun 240Z to Gary Hunt (E, −SE)	8,000	
Devise—FFF stock to Michael Wallace (E, −SE)	5,000	
Summer home (−A)		45,000
1973 Datsun 240Z (−A)		8,000
FFF Company common stock (−A)		5,000

August 28, 2006 Payment of attorney fees and court costs:

Attorney fees paid (E, −SE)	4,500	
Court costs paid (E, −SE)	500	
Cash—principal (−A)		5,000

August 31, 2006 Distribution of estate income to Gloria Olds:

Distribution to Gloria Olds (E, −SE)	6,920	
Cash—income (−A)		6,920

Closing Entries

Entries to close the nominal accounts to estate income and estate principal on August 31 are as follows:

Estate principal (−SE)	127,000	
Funeral expenses paid (−E, +SE)		4,500
Hospital and medical expenses paid (−E, +SE)		19,000
Devise—Laura Hunt (−E, +SE)		64,000
Devise—Sara Tyson (−E, +SE)		6,000
Devise—First Methodist Church (−E, +SE)		5,000
Devise—Humane Society (−E, +SE)		10,000
Debts of decedent paid (−E, +SE)		500
Devise to Gary Hunt (−E, +SE)		8,000
Devise to Michael Wallace (−E, +SE)		5,000
Attorney fees paid (−E, +SE)		4,500
Court costs paid (−E, +SE)		500
Estate income (−R, −SE)	6,920	
Distribution to Gloria Olds (−E, +SE)		6,920
Assets subsequently discovered (+A)	10,800	
Estate principal (+SE)		10,800

After these closing entries are made, the remaining account balances are as follows:

Cash—principal	$214,175
Savings account	93,000
Rocky Mountain Power common stock	40,000
Southern Natural Gas common stock	30,000
Danville municipal bonds	58,000
Estate principal	$435,175

August 31, 2006 Laura Hunt transfers estate property to Ed Jones, trustee for Gloria Olds, in accordance with the income trust established by Harry Olds's will:

Estate principal (−SE)	435,175	
Cash—principal (−A)		214,175
Savings account (−A)		93,000
Rocky Mountain Power common stock (−A)		40,000
Southern Natural Gas common stock (−A)		30,000
Danville municipal bonds (−A)		58,000

Charge-Discharge Statement

The **charge-discharge statement** is a document prepared by the personal representative (executor or administrator) to show accountability for estate property received and maintained or disbursed in accordance with the will (or the probate court in intestate cases). A charge-discharge statement shows progress in the administration of the estate and termination of responsibility when the will has been fully administered. Exhibit B-2 shows a final charge-discharge statement by Laura Hunt for her father's estate. The statement consists of two major parts: one for estate principal and one for estate income. The extent of detail is determined by the complexity of the estate, the number of devises, and instructions from the probate court.

Income Taxes on Estate Income

Income on resources held by the estate while it is being settled is taxable, even though the inheritance may not be taxable to the beneficiary. The tax may be paid by the estate or by the beneficiary if estate property has already been distributed to the beneficiary. Estates and trusts file federal income tax returns on Form 1041, U.S. Fiduciary Income Tax Return. The beneficiary's share of income is reported on Schedule K-1 of Form 1041.

For tax purposes, the beneficiary treats each item of income earned on estate property in the same way that it is treated by the estate. For example, if interest is earned on bonds held by the estate, the beneficiary classifies the income as interest. If the estate receives dividends from stock holdings, the beneficiary classifies the income as dividends. The fiduciary of the estate must provide this information to the beneficiary on Schedule K-1.

ACCOUNTING FOR TRUSTS

The will of Harry Olds resulted in the creation of an income trust for Gloria Olds. A trust created pursuant to a will is referred to as a **testamentary trust**. The fiduciary that administers a trust is the **trustee**. A trustee may be a business entity or a natural person. As in the case of estates, guidance in accounting for trusts comes from state laws, the Uniform Trusts Act, the Uniform Probate Code, and the Revised Uniform Principal and Income Act.

The entry made by Ed Jones, the trustee, to open the books for the creation of the Gloria Olds Trust is as follows:

Cash (+A)	214,175	
Savings account (+A)	93,000	
Rocky Mountain Power common stock (+A)	40,000	
Southern Natural Gas common stock (+A)	30,000	
Danville municipal bonds (+A)	58,000	
Trust fund principal (+SE)		435,175

To record receipt of property transferred from Laura Hunt, executor.

A primary concern in accounting for trust entities is distinguishing between principal and income. This is especially true of income trusts such as the one created for Gloria Olds because the principal amount of the trust is to be maintained intact to provide income for Mrs. Olds's care until her death. Separate trust fund principal and trust fund income accounts are used to separate principal and income balances for accounting purposes. The use of separate principal and income cash accounts, however, is of limited value, and the practice is usually not necessary.

ESTATE OF HARRY OLDS
CHARGE-DISCHARGE STATEMENT
FOR THE PERIOD OF ESTATE ADMINISTRATION
MAY 1 TO AUGUST 31, 2006

Estate Principal

I charge myself for:

Assets included in estate inventory	$551,375	
Assets discovered after inventory	10,800	562,175
Total estate principal charge		$562,175

I credit myself for:

Funeral expenses paid	$ 4,500	
Hospital and medical expenses paid	19,000	
Mechanic's bill paid	500	
Attorney fees and court costs	5,000	$ 29,000
Devises paid in cash to:		
Laura Hunt	$ 19,000	
Sara Tyson	6,000	
First Methodist Church	5,000	
Humane Society	10,000	40,000
Devises distributed in kind to:		
Laura Hunt (Summer home)	$ 45,000	
Gary Hunt (Datsun 240Z)	8,000	
Michael Wallace (FFF stock)	5,000	58,000
Transferred to Ed Jones, trustee for Gloria Olds:		
Cash—principal	$214,175	
Savings account	93,000	
Rocky Mountain Power Company stock	40,000	
Southern Natural Gas Company stock	30,000	
Danville municipal bonds	58,000	435,175
Total estate principal discharge		$562,175

Estate Income

I charge myself for:

Estate income received during estate administration		$ 6,920

I credit myself for:

Payment of estate income to Gloria Olds as directed by the will		$ 6,920

Respectfully submitted: Laura Hunt, Estate Executor, August 31, 2006.

SUMMARY

When a person dies without a valid will, he or she dies intestate. The deceased person's estate is distributed under the statutes of intestate succession. When the decedent has a valid will in force, he or she dies testate. The probate court normally names the personal representative named in the will as executor of the estate. The executor is a fiduciary charged with carrying out the provisions of the will, including the settlement and distribution of the estate.

The executor records an inventory of the estate in a self-balancing set of accounts; however, obligations of the decedent are not recorded until paid. The executor must distinguish estate principal and income in accounting for the estate. Guidance for distinguishing estate principal and estate income is found in the Uniform Principal and Income Act. The executor prepares a charge-discharge statement to show accountability for estate property and progress in the administration of the estate. A final charge-discharge statement is prepared when the estate has been fully administered.

SELECTED READINGS

BERNSTEIN, PHYLLIS, J., STEPHEN J. ROJAS, and MURRAY B. SCHWARTZBERG. "A Primer on Trusts." *Journal of Accountancy* (May 1993), pp. 57–61.

HIRA, LABH S. "Revocable Trusts: Appealing, But Beware." *Journal of Accountancy* (October 1991), pp. 91–96.

WILSON, DOUGLAS D. "Providing Guidance to Executors and Trustees." *Journal of Accountancy* 184, No. 4 (October 1997), pp. 37–43.

GLOSSARY

Acquisition: a business combination in which one corporation acquires control over the operations of another entity.

Actual Retirement of Bonds: the repurchase and retirement of bonds by the issuing affiliate.

Additions (Governmental Colleges and Universities): increases to the fund balance of fund groupings other than current unrestricted funds and current restricted funds to the extent that expenditures have not been made.

Administrator: the court-appointed representative who takes control of the estate of a person who died intestate and supervises the estate's distribution.

Affiliate: a subsidiary in a technical sense, although the term is sometimes used to refer to 20%- to 50%-owned equity investees.

Agency Funds (Governmental Accounting): used to account for resources held by the governmental unit as agent for other funds, other governmental units, or individuals.

Agency Theory: a theory of intercompany bondholdings that allocates constructive gains and losses to the issuing affiliate.

Allotments: divisions of the appropriation authority by time period.

Annuity Funds: a college and university fund type to account for resources acquired under the condition that stipulated periodic payments be made to individuals as directed by the donor of the resources.

Appropriations: budget authorizations of expenditures.

Auxiliary Enterprises: a college and university activity encompassing student unions, dormitories, resident halls, and intercollegiate athletics that are intended to be self-sustaining.

Bankruptcy Insolvency: a condition in which an entity has total debts in excess of the fair market value of its assets.

Bonus Approach (Partnerships): the adjustment of partner capital balances as an alternative to revaluing partnership assets or recording goodwill.

Branch Operation: a company outlet that stocks goods, makes sales, maintains accounting records, and functions much like a separate business enterprise.

Budget: a plan of financial operations including proposed expenditures for a period and the means of financing them.

Business Combination: a uniting of previously separate business entities through acquisition by one entity of another entity's net assets or a majority of its outstanding voting common stock, or through an exchange of common stock.

Capital Budget (Governmental Accounting): the current portion of a capital program.

Capital Program (Governmental Accounting): a plan of capital expenditures by year over a fixed period of years.

Capital Projects Funds (Governmental Accounting): used to account for resources to be used for acquisition or construction of major general government capital facilities.

Cash Distribution Plan (Partnerships): a plan developed at the beginning of the liquidation period that shows how cash will be distributed throughout the phase-out period.

Cash Distribution Schedule (Partnerships): a schedule of cash distributions made to creditors and partners in a partnership liquidation.

Chapter 11 of the Bankruptcy Reform Act: Chapter 11 covers rehabilitation of the debtor and anticipates a reorganization of the debtor corporation.

Chapter 7 of the Bankruptcy Reform Act: Chapter 7 covers straight bankruptcy under which the debtor entity is expected to be liquidated.

Charge-Discharge Statement (Estates and Trusts): a document prepared by the executor or administrator of an estate to show accountability for property received and disbursed.

Charity Care: hospital terminology for services provided free of charge to qualifying patients.

Conditional Promise to Give (Not-for-Profit Accounting): a pledge that is dependent upon the occurrence or failure to occur of an uncertain future event.

Conglomeration: the combination of firms in unrelated and diverse product lines and/or service functions.

Connecting Affiliates Relationship: a type of affiliation structure involving indirect or mutual holdings between a parent company and its subsidiaries.

Consolidation: (1) a business combination in which a new corporation is formed to take over two or more business entities that then go out of existence; (2) in a generic sense, it means the same as acquisition or merger; (3) the process of combining parent-company and subsidiary financial statements.

Constructive Retirement of Bonds: the repurchase of bonds of one affiliate by another so that the bonds are held within the parent–subsidiary affiliation and, in effect, retired.

Constructive Retirement of Preferred Stock: the purchase of a subsidiary's preferred stock by the parent company results in a retirement of the preferred stock from the viewpoint of the consolidated entity.

Contemporary Theory: the current theory underlying consolidated financial statements; it reflects certain aspects of both entity and parent-company theory.

Contribution (Not-for-Profit Accounting): a transfer of cash or other assets to an entity or a settlement or cancellation of its liabilities from a voluntary nonreciprocal transfer.

Conventional Approach of Accounting for Mutually Held Common Stock: parent-company stock held by a subsidiary is accounted for as being constructively retired for consolidation purposes.

Conversion to Equity Method Approach: an approach used in the preparation of consolidation working papers when the parent company has used an incomplete equity or cost method in accounting for its subsidiaries: the parent company's accounts are converted to the equity method as the first working paper entry.

Corporate Joint Venture: a joint venture organized under the corporate form of business organization.

Current Funds: a college and university fund grouping to account for resources expendable for operating purposes; includes unrestricted current funds and restricted current funds.

Current Rate: the exchange rate in effect at the balance sheet date or the transaction date.

Current Rate Method: translation of all assets, liabilities, revenues, and expenses at current exchange rates.

Debtor in Possession: a Chapter 11 case in which the debtor corporation keeps control of the business and performs the duties of a trustee.

Debt Service Funds (Governmental Accounting): used to account for the accumulation of resources for payment of principal and interest on general long-term debt.

Decedent: a person that is deceased.

Defeasance of Debt: occurs when the debt is legally satisfied even though the debt is not actually paid (legal defeasance) or when the debtor irrevocably places cash or certain other assets with an escrow agent in a trust for the payment of the debt (in substance defeasance).

Denominated: to denominate in a currency is to fix the amount in units of that currency.

Devisees: those persons designated in a will to receive real or personal property.

Direct Holdings: direct investments in voting stock of one or more investee companies.

Direct Quotation: the expression of an exchange rate in U.S. dollars (U.S. dollar equivalent).

Donor-Imposed Conditions (Not-for-Profit Accounting): the occurrence or failure to occur of an uncertain future event that releases the donor from its obligation.

Donor-Imposed Restrictions (Not-for-Profit Accounting): specifications of how or when the assets promised or received must be used.

Downstream Sale: sales or other intercompany transactions from parent company to subsidiary.

Drawings (Partnerships): regular partner withdrawals as provided in the partnership agreement and closed to partner capital at year-end.

EDGAR System: the SEC's electronic data gathering, analysis, and retrieval system. Forms filed with the SEC can be downloaded from the EDGAR system at http://www.sec.gov/edaux/formlynx.htm by providing the form desired and company name.

Encumbrance Accounting: recording commitments made for goods on order and for unperformed contracts to prevent overspending of amounts appropriated.

Endowment Funds (Not-for-Profit Accounting): used to account for gifts and bequests received from donors under endowment agreements (hospitals); a fund type for colleges and universities to account for resources received from donors or outside agencies with the stipulation that the principal be maintained in perpetuity and income be used as directed.

Endowment Trust Funds (Governmental Accounting): a trust fund in which the principal must remain intact but the earnings may be expended for authorized purposes.

Enterprise Funds (Governmental Accounting): used to account for operations that are financed and operated in a manner similar to private enterprise.

Entitlements (Governmental Accounting): payments to which state and local governmental units are entitled based on an allocation formula.

Entity Theory: a theory under which consolidated financial statements are prepared from the view of the total business entity.

Equity Adjustment on Translation: an exchange gain or loss that is reported as a stockholders' equity adjustment (and in other comprehensive income).

Equity Insolvency: the inability of an entity to pay its debts as they come due.

Equity in Subsidiary Realized Income: the parent company's or noncontrolling interest's share of subsidiary income adjusted for intercompany gains and losses and amortization of cost/book value differentials.

Equity Method: accounting for a common stock investment on an accrual basis; earnings increase the investment and dividends decrease it.

Exchange Rate: the ratio between a unit of one currency and the amount of another currency for which it can be exchanged.

Executor: the court-appointed representative who takes control of the estate of a decedent who died testate and supervises its distribution.

Executory Contracts: contracts that have not been completely performed by the parties to the contract (purchase commitments and leases, for example).

Expendable Funds: those in which resources can be expended to meet the objective of the fund.

Expendable Trust Funds: a trust fund in which the assets can be expended as needed to meet the fund's objectives.

Expenditures: decreases in the net financial resources of a governmental type fund other than those caused by transfers or similar other financing uses.

Fair Value/Cost Method (for Equity Investments): If the stock is not marketable, a common stock investment is accounted for at its original cost. If the stock is marketable, the investment is carried at fair market value with an associated adjunct/contra equity account for the change in value from original cost (assuming an available-for-sale security). In both cases, dividends received are recorded as income from the investment.

Family Allowance: an allowance to a surviving spouse and minor children to be paid out of estate property during the period of estate administration.

Father-Son-Grandson Relationship: a type of affiliation structure involving indirect or mutual holdings between a parent company and its subsidiaries.

Fiduciary: an individual or entity authorized to take possession of the property of others.

Fiduciary Accounting: a term used to describe accounting for estates and trusts whose managers have a custodial or stewardship relationship with the trust or estate beneficiaries.

Fiduciary Funds: a category of funds to account for assets held by the government as trustee or agent; includes expendable, nonexpendable, and pension trust funds and agency funds.

Fixed Exchange Rates: exchange rates set by a government and subject to change only by that government. (Also *official exchange rates.*)

Floating Exchange Rates: exchange rates that are market driven and reflect supply and demand factors, inflation, and so on. (Also *free exchange rates.*)

Foreign Currency: a currency other than the entity's functional currency.

Foreign Currency Commitment: a contract or agreement that will result in a foreign currency transaction at a later date.

Foreign Currency Cash Flow Hedge: a derivative instrument that hedges against the effect of the change in the relative value of two currencies due to the inherent exposure in forecasted transactions denominated in the foreign currency.

Foreign Currency Fair Value Hedge: a derivative instrument that hedges against the effect of the change in the relative value of two currencies due to the inherent exposure of holding an asset, liability, or firm commitment denominated in a foreign currency.

Foreign Currency Statements: the financial statements of a foreign subsidiary or other foreign entity and expressed in its local currency.

Foreign Currency Transactions: transactions whose terms are denominated in a currency other than the entity's functional currency.

Foreign Transactions: transactions between entities in different countries.

Form 8-K: form to disclose significant changes in firm policies, financial condition, etc., to the SEC.

Form 10-K: basic form for the annual report that firms file with the SEC.

Form 10-Q: form for quarterly reports that firms file with the SEC.

Fraudulent Transfer: a transfer of an interest or an obligation incurred by the debtor within one year prior to the date of filing a bankruptcy petition with the intent to defraud creditors.

Free Exchange Rates: exchange rates that are market driven and reflect supply and demand factors, inflation, and so on. (Also *floating exchange rates.*)

Fresh-Start Reporting: accounting under a reorganization plan that meets prescribed conditions and enables the new entity to eliminate its prior deficit and report zero retained earnings.

Functional Currency: the currency of the primary environment in which an entity operates.

Fund: a fiscal and accounting entity with a self-balancing set of accounts that records cash and other assets together with related liabilities and residual balances.

Fund Accounting or Fund Basis: financial systems that are segmented into separate accounting and reporting entities (funds) on the basis of their objectives and restrictions on their operations and resources.

Fund Balance: assets less liabilities of a governmental fund; often is essentially the working capital of a governmental fund.

Fund Equity: an amount equal to assets less liabilities of a fund.

Fund Fixed Assets (Governmental Accounting): fixed assets related to specific proprietary or trust funds and accounted for in those funds.

Fund Long-Term Liabilities (Governmental Accounting): long-term liabilities of proprietary and trust funds are designated fund long-term liabilities and are accounted for in those funds.

General Fixed Assets (Governmental Accounting): all fixed assets not classified as fund fixed assets; general fixed assets are accounted for in the general fixed assets account group.

General Fund (Governmental Accounting): used to account for all financial resources not accounted for in another fund.

General Governmental Activities: in a simple situation, they are essentially taxpayer finance activities made available to all members of a government's constituency without charges for use. These activities commonly include general administration, public safety, education, the judicial system, and so on.

General Long-Term Debt (Governmental Accounting): all unmatured long-term liabilities other than fund long-term liabilities; accounted for in the general long-term debt account group.

General Partnership: an association in which each partner has unlimited liability.

Goodwill Approach (Partnerships): the adjustment of assets and liabilities to fair values and recording goodwill as an alternative to adjusting partner equity balances (also, a partnership revaluation approach).

Governmental Accounting Standards Board (GASB): the standards-setting body for governmental accounting and financial reporting.

Governmental Fund Expenditures: decreases in fund financial resources other than from interfund transfers and other financing uses.

Governmental Fund Revenues: increases in fund financial resources other than from transfers, debt issue proceeds, and interfund reimbursement transactions.

Governmental Funds: a category of funds used to account for most governmental functions that are basically different from private enterprise; they include the general fund, special revenue funds, capital projects funds, and debt service funds.

Grants: contributions from other governmental units to be used for specific purposes.

Hedging Operations: purchase or sale of a foreign currency contract to offset the risks of holding receivables or payables denominated in a foreign currency.

Heirs: the persons entitled to the property of the decedent under the statutes of intestate succession.

Historical Rate: the exchange rate in effect at the time a specific transaction or event occurred.

Homestead Allowance: an allowance to a surviving spouse that has priority over all other claims against the estate.

Horizontal Integration: the combination of firms in the same business lines or markets.

IASC: International Accounting Standards Committee.

Incomplete Application of the Equity Method: accounting for an equity investee without considering amortization of cost-book value differentials or intercompany profits (also called the simple equity method).

Indirect Holdings: investments that enable an investor company to control an investee that is not directly owned through an investee that is directly owned.

Indirect Quotation: the expression of an exchange rate in foreign currency units (foreign currency per U.S. dollar).

Installment Liquidation (Partnerships): distribution of cash as it becomes available during the liquidation period.

Interfund Loans: loans made by one fund to another and that must be repaid.

Intergovernmental Revenue: revenues received from other governmental units.

Interim Financial Reports: unaudited financial reports that are issued for periods of less than a full year and frequently are called quarterly reports.

Internal Service Funds (Governmental Accounting): used to account for financing goods and services provided by one department to other departments on a cost-reimbursement basis.

Intestate: having died without a valid will.

Intestate Succession: the order in which intestate estate property is distributed to the surviving spouse, descendants, parents, and so on.

Investment in Plant Accounts: used by colleges and universities to account for the physical plant, which includes land, buildings, improvements other than buildings, and equipment including library books, and for related debt.

Involuntary Bankruptcy Proceedings: the filing is involuntary if the creditors file the bankruptcy petition.

Joint Venture: a business entity that is owned, operated, and jointly controlled by a small group of investors (venturers) for a specific undertaking; it may be temporary or relatively permanent, and it may be corporate or partnership.

Leveraged Buyout: acquisition of a public-held company directly from its shareholders in a transaction financed primarily by debt.

Liabilities Not Subject to Compromise: the fully secured liabilities incurred before a Chapter 11 bankruptcy filing and all post-petition claims.

Life Income Funds: a college and university fund type to account for resources acquired under the condition that the income be paid to a designated individual until death.

Limited Life: the legal life of partnerships terminates with the admission of a new partner, death or retirement of an old partner, etc.

Limited Partnership: an association in which one or more partners have limited liability and at least one partner has unlimited liability.

Loan Funds: a college and university fund grouping to account for resources available for student and faculty loans.

Local Currency: the currency of the country being referred to.

Local Transactions: transactions within a country that are measured in the currency of that country.

Mandatory Transfers (Colleges and Universities): transfers of resources under binding agreements with outside agencies or donors; a matching gift to a student loan fund, for example.

Measurement Focus (Governmental Accounting): that which is expressed in reporting an entity's financial performance and position.

Merger: a business combination in which one corporation takes over the operations of another entity and that entity goes out of existence; also, a business combination or an acquisition in a generic sense.

Monetary Assets and Liabilities: are assets and liabilities in which the amounts are fixed in currency units. If the value of the currency unit changes, it is still settled with the same number of units.

Monetary–Nonmonetary Method: translation of monetary items at current exchange rates and nonmonetary items at historical rates.

Multiple Exchange Rates: fixed exchange rates with preferential rates set for different kinds of transactions.

Mutual Agency (Partnerships): each partner has the power to bind all other partners, in the absence of notification to the contrary.

Mutual Holdings: two or more affiliated companies that hold stock in each other.

Negative Goodwill: the excess of the fair market value of assets acquired in a purchase business combination over the investment cost.

Noncontrolling Interest: the stockholder interest in a subsidiary not owned by the parent company.

Nonexpendable Funds (Governmental Accounting): funds that have a profit or capital maintenance objective; includes enterprise and internal service funds as well as nonexpendable trust funds.

Nonexpendable Trust Funds: principal is maintained intact but income may or may not be expendable.

Nonmandatory Transfers (Colleges and Universities): funds transferred back to unrestricted current funds or transfers at the discretion of the governing board.

Nonmonetary Items: are items that would change with changes in market price or changes in the value of the currency.

Nonprofit or Not-for-Profit Entities: nonbusiness organizations that have neither individual ownership nor private-profit objectives.

Offering Circular: similar to a prospectus, but with fewer disclosure requirements.

Official Exchange Rates: exchange rates set by a government and subject to change only by that government. (Also *fixed exchange rates.*)

One-Line Consolidation: another name for the equity method of accounting; under the equity method the investor's income and consolidated net income are equal.

Operating Profit Test: a test to determine if an operating segment is a reportable segment of the enterprise.

Operating Segment: a component of an enterprise engaged in providing goods and services to unaffiliated or affiliated customers for a profit.

Operating Transfers (Governmental Accounting): legally authorized shifts of resources from one fund to another that are not revenues, expenditures or expenses, or residual equity transfers.

Parent-Company Theory: a theory under which consolidated financial statements are prepared from the view of parent-company stockholders.

Parent–Subsidiary Relationship: a relationship that gives one corporation the power to control another corporation through its majority common stock ownership.

Partnership: an association of two or more persons to carry on as co-owners in a business for profit.

Partnership Agreement: a contract between partners covering duties of partners, investments, withdrawals, profit sharing, and so on. Without this agreement, these issues are settled by the Uniform Partnership Act.

Partnership Dissolution: the change in the relation of partners when any partner is no longer involved in carrying on the business. The business may continue as an operating business despite the dissolution of the partnership.

Partnership Liquidation: the process of converting assets into cash, settling all liabilities, and distributing any remaining cash to partners.

Par Value Theory: a theory of intercompany bond holdings that allocates constructive gains or losses between the purchasing and issuing affiliates on the basis of the par value of the bonds.

Patient Service Revenue (Hospitals): revenue from board and room, nursing services, and other professional services, and recorded on an accrual basis.

Payments in Lieu of Taxes: payments by one governmental unit to another for revenues lost because governments cannot tax each other. Also, similar payments from a government's enterprise fund to its other tax-supported funds.

Performance Budget: a budget that emphasizes measurable performance of work programs and activities.

Permanently Restricted Net Assets (Not-for-Profit Accounting): the portion of a not-for-profit entity's net assets whose use is limited by donor-imposed stipulations that do not expire and cannot be removed by action of the entity.

Personal Representative: a person named by the probate court to take control of a decedent's estate.

Piecemeal Acquisition: a corporation gains control of a subsidiary through a series of separate stock purchases.

Plant Funds: a college and university fund grouping to account for unexpended plant funds, renewal and replacement funds, retirement of indebtedness funds, and investment in plant funds.

Plant Replacement and Expansion Funds (Hospitals): a hospital fund group to account for donor-restricted resources for plant, property and equipment.

Pledge (Nonprofit Accounting): a written or oral promise to contribute cash or other assets to the organization.

Pooling of Interests Method: a business combination consummated through an exchange of common shares and accounted for on a book value basis.

Postpetition Liabilities: liabilities incurred after a Chapter 11 filing and not associated with prebankruptcy events.

Preacquisition Dividends: dividends paid on an equity investment prior to the date the investment was acquired during the year.

Preacquisition Earnings: income on an equity investment from beginning of the year up to the date the investment was acquired during the year.

Preferences: certain transfers of property of a debtor or certain obligations incurred by a debtor prior to filing a bankruptcy petition.

Preliminary Prospectus: a preliminary communication about securities to be issued that also explains how to get a copy of the prospectus filed with the SEC.

Prepetition Liabilities: liabilities of the debtor corporation at the time of a bankruptcy filing.

Prepetition Liabilities Subject to Compromise: unsecured and undersecured liabilities incurred before a Chapter 11 bankruptcy filing.

Probate: to probate a will is to validate a will.

Program Budget: an expenditure budget of the total cost of programs to be carried out or functions to be performed.

Proportionate or Pro Rata Consolidation: a practice in accounting for joint ventures in which each investor-venturer accounts for its share of assets, equities, revenues, and expenses.

Proprietary Funds (Governmental Accounting): a category of funds to account for operations that are similar to those of private business enterprises; including enterprise funds and internal service funds.

Prospectus: information about an SEC registrant firm that includes its type of business, company background, and financial statements; it is a part of the SEC registration statement.

Purchase Method: a method of accounting for a business combination in which one corporation acquires a controlling interest in another entity; the acquisition is accounted for on a fair value basis.

Pure Endowments: endowments for which the principal is permanently restricted. (*Quasi-endowments* can be changed by the governing board.)

Push-Down Accounting: establishment of a new basis of subsidiary accounting based on the price paid by the parent company.

Quasi-Endowment Funds: a college and university fund type to account for resources designated by the governing board to be invested indefinitely, with income being expended as directed.

Quasi-External Transactions: those that would be revenues and expenses or expenditures for organizations external to the governmental unit.

Registration Statements: statements required to be filed with the SEC for firms that issue securities to the public, and for firms whose shares are traded on national stock exchanges.

Regulation S: a 1990 regulation to clarify the applicability of security laws across national boundaries.

Reimbursements: transactions between two funds of a government that constitute reimbursements of a fund for expenditures or expenses initially made from it that are properly applicable to another fund. Reimbursements are recorded as expenditures or expenses in the reimbursing fund and as reductions of expenditures or expenses in the reimbursed fund.

Remeasurement: the conversion of a foreign entity's financial statements from another currency into its own functional currency.

Renewal and Replacement Funds (Colleges and Universities): used to account for the resources held by colleges and universities for renewal and replacement of the physical plant.

Reorganization Items: income, expenses, realized gains and losses, and provisions for losses that result from restructuring a business under Chapter 11 of the Bankruptcy Act.

Reorganization Plan: a plan for rehabilitation of the debtor corporation in a Chapter 11 case; to be confirmed, the plan must be fair and equitable to all interests concerned.

Reorganization Value: an approximation of the amount a willing buyer would pay for the assets of the corporation at the time of restructuring.

Reportable Operating Segment: an operating segment for which information is required to be reported.

Reporting Currency: the currency in which consolidated financial statements are prepared.

Residual Beneficiaries: those entitled to the remainder of an estate after all other rightful claims have been satisfied.

Residual Equity Transfer (Governmental Accounting): nonrecurring or nonroutine transfers of equity between funds.

Restricted Current Funds (Colleges and Universities): encompasses resources expendable currently but restricted to expenditures for specified operating purposes.

Restricted Funds (Hospitals): a hospital fund grouping that includes specific purpose funds, plant replacement and expansion funds, and endowment funds.

Retirement of Indebtedness Fund: used in college and university accounting for liquid resources held for current debt service, and investments held for future debt retirement.

Safe Payments (Partnerships): distributions that can be made to partners with assurance that the amounts are not excessive.

Salary Allowances (Partnerships): partner salary allowances are drawings authorized in lieu of salaries because partner rewards come from sharing in partnership earnings.

Sales Agency: a business office established to display merchandise and take customer orders, but not to fill orders or grant credit.

Schedule of Assumed Loss Absorption: used in developing the cash distribution plan in a partnership liquidation. Each partner's equity is charged with a loss amount to eliminate the equity of the most vulnerable partner, and so on.

Shared Revenues (Governmental Accounting): specific revenue sources shared with other governmental units; sales taxes and gasoline taxes are examples.

Special Assessments: special tax levies against benefited property owners for improvements that benefit the owner's property.

Special Revenue Funds (Governmental Accounting): used to account for proceeds from specific revenue sources that are legally restricted to specified purposes.

Specific Purpose Funds (Hospitals): a hospital fund group to account for resources restricted by donors for specific operating purposes.

Spot Rate: the exchange rate in effect for immediate delivery of the currencies exchanged.

Statement of Affairs: a financial statement that shows liquidation values of a bankrupt entity and provides estimates of possible recovery for unsecured creditors.

Statement of Functional Expenses (Voluntary Health and Welfare Organizations): a financial statement that shows the costs associated with the program services or other activities of the organization.

Statement of Realization and Liquidation: statement showing progress toward liquidation in a bankruptcy case.

Step-by-Step Acquisitions: acquiring an equity interest in a series of separate stock purchases.

Subsidiary: a corporation in which the controlling stockholders' interest lies with a parent company that controls its decisions and operations.

Substantially All Test: used in determining if 90% of the combining entity's voting common stock is exchanged, required in a pooling of interests.

Temporal Method: translation of items carried at past, current, and future prices in a manner that retains their measurement bases.

Temporarily Restricted Net Assets (Not-for-Profit Accounting): the portion of a not-for-profit entity's net assets whose use is limited by donor-imposed stipulations that either expire or can be removed by fulfilling the stipulations.

Temporary Differences: differences in taxable income and accounting income that originate in one accounting period and reverse in a later period.

Term Endowment Funds: a college and university fund type to account for resources received from donors or outside agencies with the stipulation that the principal may be expended after a period of time or the occurence of some event.

Term Endowments: endowments for which the principal is temporarily restricted.

Testacy Proceeding: a hearing of a probate court to determine if the deceased died testate or intestate (that is, with or without a will).

Testate: having died with a valid will in force.

Testamentary Trust: a trust that is created pursuant to a will.

Translation: expressing functional currency measurements in the reporting currency.

Translation Adjustment (also *Equity Adjustment on Translation*): an exchange gain or loss that is reported as an equity adjustment in other comprehensive income.

Treasury Stock Approach: accounting for parent-company stock held by a subsidiary as treasury stock in consolidated statements.

Troubled Debt Restructuring: occurs when a creditor grants a concession to a debtor because of the debtor's financial difficulties.

Trust and Agency Funds: used to account for assets held in a trustee capacity or as agent for individuals, private organizations, and other governmental units.

Trustee: a lawyer appointed by the U.S. trustee or by the bankruptcy court to assume control of the debtor's estate and coordinate its administration with the court.

Unconditional Promises to Give (Nonprofit Accounting): a pledge without conditions.

Undivided Interest (Joint Ventures): an ownership arrangement in which two or more parties own property and title is held individually to the extent of each party's interest.

Unexpended Plant Funds: used by colleges and universities to account for resources held for additions and improvements to the physical plant.

Uniform Probate Code: a document prepared by the National Conference of Commissioners on Uniform State Laws that provides guidelines for estate and trust administration.

Unlimited Liability: each partner is liable for all partnership debts. Limited partners in a limited partnership, which is allowed in some states, do not have unlimited liability.

Unrestricted Current Funds (Colleges and Universities): encompasses resources received and expended for instruction, research, extension, and public services, as well as auxiliary enterprises.

Unrestricted Funds (Hospitals): used to account for all resources of a hospital not restricted by donors or grantors.

Unrestricted Net Assets (Not-for-Profit Accounting): the portion of net assets of a not-for-profit entity that carries no donor-imposed restrictions.

Upstream Sale: sales or other intercompany transactions from subsidiary to parent company.

U.S. Trustee: an administrative officer of the bankruptcy court; appointed by the attorney general for five-year terms.

Venturers: the owner participants in a joint venture.

Vertical Integration: the combination of firms with operations in different but successive stages of production and/or distribution.

Voidable Preferences: preferences that can be voided by a trustee in a bankruptcy case.

Voluntary Bankruptcy Proceedings: the filing is voluntary if the debtor files the bankruptcy petition.

Voluntary Health and Welfare Organizations: a diverse group of nonprofit entities that is supported by donations and seeks to solve basic social problems of health and welfare.

Vulnerability Ranking (Partnerships): a ranking of partners on the basis of the amount of partnership losses they could absorb without reducing their capital accounts below zero.

Zero-Base Budgeting: making budgetary appropriations without direct reference to prior years' programs or expenditure budgets.

INDEX

A page number preceded by "ES" indicates the Electronic Supplement